THE GUINNESS ENCYCLOPEDIA OF SCIENCE

DR ROBERT M. YOUNGSON

GUINNESS PUBLISHING

First published 1994

© Guinness Publishing Ltd. 1994

Published in Great Britain by
Guinness Publishing Ltd., 33 London Road, Enfield,
Middlesex EN2 6DJ

Colour reproduction by
Bright Arts (HK) Ltd., Hong Kong

Printed and bound in Italy by New
Interlitho Italia SpA, Milan

British Library Cataloguing in
Publication Data:
A catalogue record for this book is
available from the British Library.

ISBN 0-85112-544-1

Project Editor
Christine Winters

Additional Editing
Tina Persaud
Paola Simoneschi

Design
Amanda Sedge
Sarah Silvé

Systems Support
Alex Reid
Kathy Milligan

Picture Research
Image Select

Illustrators
Peter Harper
Pat Gibbon
Robert and Rhoda Burns
Peters and Zabransky
Lesley Alexander
Jon Mitchell
The Maltings Partnership

Art Director
David Roberts

Managing Editor
Stephen Adamson

CONSULTANT EDITORS

Dr Simon Gouldsworthy ....Department of Astrophysics, University of Durham
Michael Kenward OBE ....Science writer and consultant. Formerly Editor of the *New Scientist*
David Sweet...Member of the Institute of Biology

PREFACE

Of the many possible definitions of science, one I particularly like is simply *reliable truth*. By explaining, as clearly as possible, the fundamentals of science, and by describing science in its historical perspective (showing how superstitions have gradually been displaced by fact), I have tried to set before the reader the most important of those reliable truths on which modern society so critically depends. This book is an invitation to people with little or no prior knowledge of science to discover how satisfying and informative it can be to understand scientific principles, to relate them to one another and to life in general, and, in the light of them, to revise old ideas and integrate knowledge into a secure, consistent and trustworthy system.

In attempting to achieve these ambitious aims I have been assisted by a group of remarkable and dedicated people whose contribution I am anxious to acknowledge, and whom I am delighted to have the opportunity to thank. Dr Simon Gouldsworthy read every word of my original text. When, as often, I went completely off the rails, he, firmly but diplomatically, nudged me back on again. For the correction of my scientific jargon, overworked adjectives, general literary infelicity and occasional sheer incomprehensibility, and for the splendid design and layout of the book I am indebted to the dedicated band of editors, designers and illustrators at Guinness Publishing. I am most grateful to Stephen Adamson, Head of Reference, who has overseen the operation and who has exercised his duties steadfastly but with a nice regard to my sensitivities. Tina Persaud, invariably cheerful, efficient and helpful, has elegantly polished many of the rough corners of my prose. Above all, I am more grateful than I can say to my principal editor, Christine Winters, who has laboured devotedly for many months to make this book the model of clarity, readability and attractiveness it so manifestly is. Christine's piercing intelligence and critical eye have led to countless improvements. She has been ruthless in her insistence that every unusual term should be explained and every ambiguity resolved, but has done it all with such consummate tact as to leave me no grounds for complaint. Christine has also been responsible for the selection of the majority of the illustrations and the briefing of the illustrators, but the actual design and layout of the book have been excellently accomplished by Sarah Silvé and Amanda Sedge. I also want to thank the skilled artists whose work has so enhanced the appearance and usefulness of the book. Finally, I am extremely grateful to another distinguished scientist, Michael Kenward, who has carried out a scrupulous final overall check on much of the text to ensure that no inaccuracies have been missed.

It has been a great privilege and satisfaction to work with such a talented group of people. Books of this kind can be produced only as a team effort, and much of the credit for the final quality of the product must go to them.

R. M. Youngson

HOW TO USE THIS BOOK

The Guinness Encyclopedia of Science follows a **thematic approach**, and is arranged in a series of self-contained articles focusing on particular topics of interest. There is also an A-to-Z **Factfinder** section, providing quick access to information on key concepts, technical terms, major figures, and many other topics.

In the thematic section, the pages are colour coded to indicate the chapter to which they belong. Within each article there is a 'See Also' box referring to related spreads within the same section or elsewhere. There are also cross-references within the text itself to guide the reader to pages where further relevant details will be found.

The Factfinder at the back of the book consists of alphabetically arranged entries providing at-a-glance information on a range of matters and issues relating to the world of science. Many of the entries apply to topics that receive some treatment in the main text; such entries tend to be brief, providing basic details such as a concise description of a particular element or mathematical term, together with a page reference to the relevant article in the thematic section as appropriate. The Factfinder also contains numerous entries for items not covered in the main text. In addition, there are entries providing further details on concepts or technical terms to which only brief allusion is made in the thematic section.

The Factfinder is linked with the main thematic section by means of a simple cross-referencing and indexing system. The words in small capital letters refer the user to important related entries within the Factfinder itself.

Contents

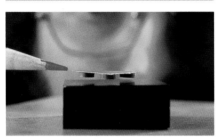

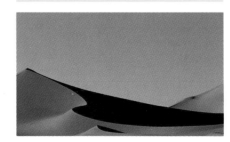
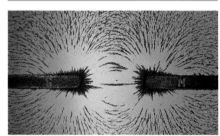
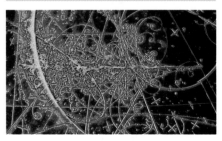

CONTENTS

7. OUR EARTH, OUR COSMOS

The Earth and the Milky Way. (Images)

8. THE CHEMISTRY OF MATTER

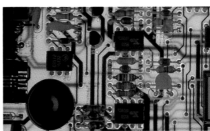

Electronmicrograph of paint layers and rusty bodywork on a car. (Dr Jeremy Burgess, SPL)

9. THE SCIENCE OF LIFE

Bee-imitating wild orchid *Orphrys scolopax*. (Claude Nuridsany and Marie Perennou, SPL)

10. COMPUTING AND ARTIFICIAL INTELLIGENCE

Computer circuit board. (Art Stein, SPL)

FACTFINDER

THE
GUINNESS
ENCYCLOPEDIA
OF
SCIENCE

THE NATURE
OF SCIENCE

What is Science?

The term 'science' comes from the Latin *scientia*, meaning 'knowledge', but this is too wide a definition to be useful. Most people would agree to define science as a systematic study of nature by observation and experiment, leading to the formulation of descriptive generalizations about it. But even the best definitions say little about the real nature of science.

'Science' covers a remarkably wide range of activities. There was a time when it was possible for one person to know almost all that was included within the compass of the subject. But there are no polymaths nowadays; science has long outstripped in sheer size any possibility of comprehension by a single person. All scientists, however, despite their diversity of interest, share one characteristic that helps to distinguish science from many other activities and helps illustrate its nature. Scientists are sceptical.

By their training, scientists take nothing on trust and are, on the whole, inclined to disbelieve new propositions rather than to accept them. Scientists have a strong instinct for detecting the inherently implausible in matters relating to their own disciplines. This is because they are able to extrapolate from established fact so as to see what is likely and what is not. They are suspicious of assertion and of authority.

James Watson (left) and Francis Crick, discoverers of the structure of the DNA molecule, together with a model of the molecule. Major scientific advances do not happen in isolation; Crick and Watson drew on Erwin Chargaff's discoveries about the bases of DNA, and were dependent upon the X-ray crystallography of their contemporaries Maurice Wilkins and Rosalind Franklin at King's College, London. (SPL)

Scientists do not claim that science establishes eternal truths – or even tries to. Scientific generalizations are really descriptions of various aspects of nature which, by virtue of being tested, have acquired a certain – often high – degree of reliability. The emphasis is on the word 'reliable'. There is plenty of knowledge that is far from reliable, that is no more than unsupported assertion, however 'authoritative'. Science has no interest in this kind of information and scientists are opposed to entities that masquerade as science and deal in nondemonstrable knowledge. These they call 'pseudosciences'.

Science as a process of advance

'If I have seen further than other men,' said Isaac Newton – one of the greatest scientific geniuses of all time – 'it is because I have stood on the shoulders of giants.' Histories of science can give the impression that science is dominated by a few people. It is true that there are giants in science's past, but even they have developed the work of others. This is Newton's point, that every new scientific discovery is an extension of what is already known, a development of the work of other scientists. To say this is not to belittle major new discoveries, such as Newton's own concept of gravitational attraction, for each new scientific advance represents a leap into the unknown, but such discoveries are seldom made except by people who have a thorough knowledge and understanding of current science. The story of science is one of constant advance.

How scientific discoveries are made

Few scientists can tell us how a great new idea was generated. Most of them agree, however, that the direct frontal attack on a problem seldom works. Many have found that ideas occur, apparently spontaneously, when the mind is not consciously directed to the problem, often while falling asleep or on waking in the morning. The brain, apparently, doesn't like to be directly pressurized. 'Lateral thinking' seems to be the better approach – if it can be achieved.

It is no coincidence, however, that the great preponderance of major scientific and technological advances are made by people with well-stocked minds. Many of them achieve eminence because of their discoveries, but it is the eminence of mind that is the prior requirement and the discoveries are made because of this. Luck in science comes to the well informed. Another common feature of the nature of discovery is that, in most cases, the scientist concerned has been preoccupied with the problem for weeks or months, constantly mulling it over. Although the frontal attack seems fruitless, this process may allow the scientist to look at the problem in different ways.

The history of science is full of examples of important discoveries that appeared to happen by sheer chance or good luck. These include the laws of planetary motion, X-rays, radioactivity, insulin, vitamin D, the basis of quantum theory, penicillin and antimatter. Such serendipitous happenings must, however, be recognized for what they are by people equipped with the necessary knowledge to do so. Many accidental findings must have been made that have held within them the clue to major scientific developments but have come to nothing because of the absence of someone equipped to appreciate their significance.

Is there a 'scientific method'?

The scepticism that science demands of its practitioners is an aspect of its objectivity. Classically, the 'scientific method' involves making an observation, forming a hypothesis to account for it, designing an experiment to test the hypothesis, performing the experiment, perhaps many times, and then, depending on the result, rejecting, modifying or tentatively accepting the hypothesis. If many experiments support the hypothesis it may be elevated to the status of a 'theory'. The process should not in any way be coloured by the scientist's desiring any particular result.

That is the principle; in the real world scientists work in a wide variety of ways. Some research programmes are conducted in accordance with a fixed policy. Faced with a new and difficult problem, however, many scientists abandon their high ideals and resort to pure empiricism. Rather than allowing themselves to remain apparently idle while searching for a logical hypothesis, they will simply try one thing after another. Scientific advances cannot be made to order, but pressure on scientists to achieve such advances may affect the way a scientist approaches a problem. Surprisingly, very few scientists have had any formal instruction in scientific methodology, and those who have may be little affected by it.

Scientific research

The pursuit of scientific knowledge for its own sake is called *pure research*. Today, pure research is limited almost entirely to the universities, where it is conducted largely by Ph.D candidates. Even they are not entirely free to choose their own line of work but have to undertake a project in basic science approved by the professor or head of the department. This is called *oriented fundamental research*. *Applied research* is not concerned with extending the frontiers of basic science but has a specified and clear aim. Most research done in industry is of this kind and the scientist undertaking it is expected to deliver practical results.

Once a usefully applicable scientific advance has been made it may, in many cases, be handed over to the development staff whose job is to convert a laboratory process into something that can be done on a large scale on a production line. This is technology and is no longer within the province of science.

Science and technology

We live in a scientific age, in that we are surrounded by manufactured objects. Science, however, does not make them, although it does make them possible. Science and technology are often confused, because so much of the range of contemporary technology is based on scientific discovery. The great consumer industries, especially domestic electronics, plastics, artificial fibre textiles, cleaning materials, detergents and pharmaceuticals, as well as automobile engineering and biologically engineered products, are all based on science.

How all these things are made is, however, the province of technology, not of science. But they all became possible because of some fundamental discovery about nature that resulted from scientific investigation. Essentially, science is concerned with why things happen, and technology with how things are made.

The value of science

The list of contributions that science has made to our health, comfort and well-being is endless. Yet, in spite of this many people have an ambivalent attitude towards science and scientists. On the one hand, there is a greater popular interest in, and knowledge of, science than ever before; on the other there is deep suspicion of science and a wide concern that it provides a threat to the future of the planet.

Science is a human activity that can never be repressed, for it is in the nature of human beings to feel curiosity and to seek answers to questions. Scientists seek to reveal truth; it is tyrants and bigots who seek to conceal it. Truth is not always pleasant but it is liberating. Science demolishes myths that enslave people, breaks down walls of ignorance and prejudice. If some of its truths can be misapplied to the destruction of humans, the misapplication is the work of humans, not of science.

Critics of science often seem to imply that humanity should not attempt to wrest the secrets from nature. But if this had been our course from the beginning, our lives would still be what they once were – nasty, brutish and short. Humanity would remain drowning in superstition and fear. If we did not know the true nature of the sun and planets we might, like the Aztecs, feel the need for daily human sacrifice so that the gods would continue to make the sun rise every morning. Without medical science we would be prone to disease and the average lifespan would be stuck at about half its current length in the West.

Science itself, like any form of knowledge, is neutral. Our discoveries about

chemicals has enabled us to make plastics and life-saving drugs, but it has also led to chemical warfare. How we apply the knowledge we have gained is an ethical issue. Moreover, if the applications of science create problems for mankind, it is not through ignorance that we will solve them.

For many people, science provides a continuing framework of interest and comprehension that illuminates and enriches their entire lives. Most people to whom science means so much have had some kind of scientific education. But there are also many whose scientific interests are of a wholly informal kind and, for these, the range of possibilities for study and the accessibility of information are almost unlimited. Few, once so engaged, ever wholly lose interest in science and most have found their sustained interest to be valuable. Scientific awareness has become an almost essential constituent of the contemporary cultivated mind and a feature of the liberally educated. It is by no means incompatible with artistic or literary interests and engagements.

The world's need of science

Many major problems face humanity today. To some, such as overpopulation, science has contributed. To others, such as greed and inhumanity, it has not. These problems, however, will be solved only both if science provides the tools to attack them and world leaders find the will. We will not defeat famine by turning our

backs on science, whether the answer is by producing more food, or by finding ways of producing and distributing it in areas where at present it is not available. Science may have produced the technology which, thoughtlessly applied, has damaged agricultural environments, but science is addressing how to control soil erosion and reverse desertification. Science originally showed how to burn fossil fuels for our benefit, but is now looking at how to conserve them and also how to exploit renewable sources of power.

But the value of science does not only lie in its opening the door to the means of increasing the wealth of humanity and improving its standard of living. Science includes the study of humanity itself, telling us ever more about our own nature. Psychology, which has been one of the growth sciences of recent years, is still only in its infancy. More than all this science satisfies our thirst for knowledge and hence is an activity that is fundamental to the human being. Science can show us the tiniest elements of life that we can never ourselves see, or can take us to the edges of the universe that we can never visit.

Medicine or magic? Without science we would still be at the mercy of superstition. The African medicine man (above right) may well have a valuable cultural and social role, but biochemists are contributing far more today to the health of humanity.

(Zefa/L. Schröter and Zefa)

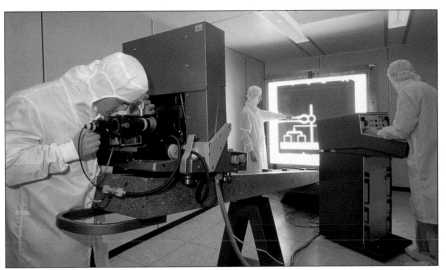

Electronic research laboratory. The distinction between applied research and technology is not always a clear one, and much modern scientific research not only has technological ends but relies enormously on technological input. (Images)

SEE ALSO

● THE RANGE OF THE SCIENCES p. 6
● THE PHILOSOPHY AND METHOD OF SCIENCE p. 12

The Range of the Sciences

QUICK GUIDE TO THE BIOLOGICAL SCIENCES

• **Anatomy** – the science of the structure of animals and plants.

• **Biophysics** – the study of the physical principles of biological phenomena.

• **Botany** – the classification, structure and functioning of plants.

• **Cytology** – the study of cell form and functioning.

• **Ecology** – the relationship of animals and plants to their environment.

• **Embryology** – the study of bodily development from conception to birth.

• **Entomology** – the classification of insects and the study of their structure and functioning.

• **Ethology** – the science of the behaviour of animals in their natural habitat.

• **Genetic engineering** – the techniques for modifying DNA (⇨ p. 202) so as to change the genetic characteristics of living organisms.

• **Genetics** – the science of the inheritance of characteristics.

• **Herpetology** – the classification and study of amphibians and reptiles.

• **Ichthyology** – the classification of fishes and the study of their structure, functioning and behaviour.

• **Microbiology** – the study of the structure and functioning of organisms too small to be seen by the naked eye, especially viruses, bacteria and fungi.

• **Ornithology** – the classification of birds and the study of their structure, functioning and behaviour.

• **Palaeontology** – the science of prehistoric life.

• **Parasitology** – the study of the structure, functioning and behaviour of animal and plant parasites.

• **Physiology** – the science of the functioning of the living body.

• **Protozoology** – the classification of microscopic single-celled organisms and the study of their structure, functioning and behaviour.

• **Taxonomy** – the classification of biological species.

• **Zoology** – the classification of animals generally and the study of their structure, functioning and behaviour.

It is a characteristic of science continuously to open up new areas of knowledge, and new sciences appear regularly as some of these areas blossom into discrete disciplines. Various schemes of classification can be used to show how the different branches are related.

Auguste Comte, 19th-century French philosopher who produced the first significant classification of the sciences. (Popper)

One of the earliest formal attempts to classify the sciences was that of the French philosopher Auguste Comte (1798–1857). He classified the sciences in terms of increasing complexity, starting with mathematics, and progressing through astronomy, physics and chemistry to biology. Comte's main interest was in social problems and it was he who coined the term 'sociology', believing that it would become a science and would head the list in complexity.

One difficulty in classifying the sciences today is to decide whether a subject – however large – is a science in its own right or simply a branch of another science. No one would deny, for instance, that human anatomy is a science in its own right, distinct from the parent science of medicine. But there are, within anatomy, various sub-disciplines such as osteology (the study of bones), myology (the study of muscles), histology (microscopic anatomy), neurology (the study of the nervous system), and so on. This difficulty is perennial and is caused by the endless enlargement of knowledge and the consequent necessity for specialization.

The broadest classification of the sciences divides them into those concerned with living things – the biological sciences – and those concerned with non-living things – the non-biological or physical sciences. Each of these is a huge group that encompasses many different disciplines.

The biological sciences

Until the early part of the 20th century the biological sciences were concerned largely with descriptive and comparative accounts of the almost infinite variety of living plants and animals (morphology), with their origins and evolution (phylogeny), their classification into kingdoms, phyla, classes, orders, families, genera and species (taxonomy) and with the grosser features of their function (physiology). This group of sciences was also concerned with the study of humanity in all its aspects (anthropology). After the turn of the century scientists began increasingly to look into the very nature of life itself and to direct their attention to the microscopic processes

The interrelationship of the sciences. Modern science has produced so many disciplines and sub-disciplines that the relationships between them have become complex and fluid. At the root are the three main branches of science, each drawing upon mathematics. Even this is a new development as it used to be thought that maths was far less relevant to biology than to the other sciences. An example of the divisions of science is provided by the branches of psychology, which can be linked to chemistry and biology through biochemistry, although other equally valid pathways could be traced.

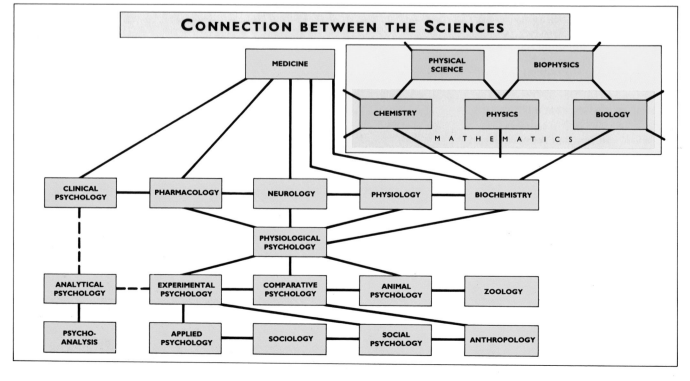

CONNECTION BETWEEN THE SCIENCES

by which the characteristics of living things were determined. It had long been obvious that chemistry had an important, even central, part to play in the functioning of living organisms, and the science of biochemistry – the chemistry of living things – was already well established. Soon it became clear, however, that an understanding of fundamental biological processes could be achieved only by a study of the detailed structure of the molecules from which living things were made. It was, in fact, necessary to look into the ultimate chemical structures of the cells themselves. A whole new science of cell biology quickly developed, which, in turn, was soon subdivided into even more highly specialized branches, such as molecular biology, molecular genetics and biophysics.

At this level of subdivision scientists are working in a region in which there is a considerable overlap between formerly distinct disciplines. For example, people concerned with establishing the structure of biological molecules so as to understand how they function must have a thorough knowledge of chemistry, of the principles by which atoms link together to form molecules and of the three-dimensional shape of these molecules (stereochemistry). They must also know something about the physics of electron microscopy, X-ray crystallography, spectroscopy, chromatography, nuclear magnetic resonance and other equally important modern investigative techniques.

The position of medicine, in the classification of the biological sciences, is anomalous. Some purists even deny that it is entitled to be considered a science. However, while it is true that most medical practitioners would not consider themselves to be scientists, those engaged in fundamental medical research are certainly entitled to do so. Clinical medicine is, or ought to be, an applied science, but at the same time it is an art and should also be an exercise of humane principles. For these reasons, when considering 'medicine' in the context of scientific classification, one must use the term 'medicine' in a restricted sense.

The physical sciences

The main subdivisions of the physical sciences are astronomy, physics, chemistry and the earth sciences. Each has expanded considerably in the 20th century.

Astronomy, like botany and zoology, was formerly concerned largely with identification and location, but has now become a highly investigative discipline because of enormous developments that have been made in both optical and radio astronomy. Astronomers are now preoccupied with such problems as the size of the universe, the chemical constitution of the stars, radiation of all kinds from space, pulsating stars, quasars, novas and supernovas, black holes and the origins of the universe. In the latter study (cosmology) astronomers' work overlaps considerably with that of the theoretical

---

QUICK GUIDE TO THE PHYSICAL SCIENCES

- **Acoustics** – the science of sound production, propagation and reception.
- **Analytical chemistry** – the determination of the chemical composition of materials.
- **Astronomy** – the study of the universe.
- **Astrophysics** – the investigation of observed astronomical phenomena.
- **Atomic physics** – the study of the constituent parts of atoms and the interaction between them.
- **Chemistry** – the science of the composition of material substances.
- **Climatology** – the study of the causes of climatic changes.
- **Computer science** – the physical principles underlying computer function.
- **Cosmology** – the study of the origin, evolution and structure of the universe.
- **Cryogenics** – the science of extreme cold and of the properties of materials at very low temperatures.
- **Crystallography** – the study of the crystalline structure of matter.
- **Dynamics** – the science of the motion of objects and the influence of forces.
- **Electricity** – the science of the effects of the mass movement of electrons in conductors and of their accumulation on non-conductors.
- **Electronics** – the study of the ways in which electrons can be manipulated so as to convey, store, modify and transmit information.
- **Fluid mechanics** – the study of the effects of forces on fluids whether at rest or in motion.
- **Geology** – the science of the physical history of the earth and of its structure.
- **Geophysics** – the application of physics to the study of the earth, its atmosphere and its relation to the solar system.
- **Information science** – the study of the meaning of information and of the modes of its transmission.
- **Inorganic chemistry** – the chemistry of the non-carbon compounds, i.e. those molecules not primarily associated with living things.

- **Magnetism** – the study of the fields and forces produced by the movement of electrons in atoms similarly oriented in large groups (domains).
- **Mechanics** – the science of the effects of forces on bodies and of the resultant movement.
- **Metallurgy** – the science of metals.
- **Meteorology** – the study of the atmosphere and of its movements.
- **Nuclear physics** – the science of the structure and properties of the nucleus of the atom.
- **Optics** – the study of all phenomena, both physical and physiological, connected with light.
- **Organic chemistry** – the chemistry of the carbon compounds.
- **Particle physics** – the science of the elementary particles of which atoms are constituted and of those with independent existence.
- **Pharmacology** – the science of drugs.
- **Physics** – the parent discipline encompassing the studies of heat, light, sound, electricity, magnetism, statics, dynamics, radioactivity and the structural and mechanical properties of materials.
- **Physical chemistry** – the study of the way in which the physical properties of materials depend on their chemical constitution.
- **Plasma physics** – the physics of high-temperature gases composed of atomic nuclei and electrons separated by intense heat.
- **Quantum mechanics** – the physical theory that describes the behaviour of matter and energy on a scale so small that the constituent atoms or subatomic particles can operate as individuals rather than statistically.
- **Relativity** – the mathematical concept that all motion is relative to the observer; that humanity resides in a space-time continuum that is modified by gravity; and that mass and energy are equivalent.
- **Solid-state physics** – the physics of solid materials and especially of the movement of electric charges within them.
- **Thermodynamics** – the science of the transfer of heat and of the relationship of heat and work.

---

physicists and mathematicians; indeed, many cosmologists would probably deny that they are astronomers.

Physics has evolved from a discipline concerned with descriptive accounts of largely mechanical phenomena – such as the motion of solid bodies, fluids and heat, friction, gravitation, optics, electricity and magnetism – to a highly theoretical preoccupation with the basics of the universe: the elementary particles of which all matter is constituted; the fundamental nature of time, space and gravitation, quantum phenomena, superconductivity, the equivalence of matter and energy, and the generation of energy by the splitting (fission) or joining together (fusion) of atomic nuclei.

Among the most important 20th-century extensions of chemistry – the study of the nature and reactions of substances – have been advances in the understanding of the chemical bond, the development of catalysts to accelerate chemical reactions, the extension of the chemistry

of the element silicon, mass spectroscopy, a huge growth in the power of synthesizing new compounds especially large polymers, the production of synthetic enzymes and other new proteins ('designer' proteins), the study of new approaches to chemical synthesis, and the production of spherical carbon compounds (Buckminsterfullerenes or 'Buckyballs').

The earth sciences have extended steadily from a largely descriptive geology to a series of wide investigative studies of the way the continents were formed, the atmosphere with its changes and their effects, the ocean floor, the structure of the crust and centre of the earth, active volcanoes and earthquakes, and of the planet as an ecosystem. One of the most revolutionary concepts of the last fifty years, has been the idea that whole continents move and merge into each other, and the consequent study of plate tectonics is now one of the major branches of the science.

SEE ALSO
● WHAT IS SCIENCE? p. 4

The Development of Science 1: The Ancient World

The human being is insatiably curious and many of the earliest scientific discoveries must have been made simply as a result of the urge to investigate the unknown. The possession of knowledge conferred power, so, from the earliest times, there seems to have been a continuous process of acquisition of new knowledge and strong motives for preserving it in some form of written record.

SEE ALSO

● THE DEVELOPMENT OF SCIENCE 2: THE RENAISSANCE AND AFTER p. 10
● COSMOLOGY: UNDERSTANDING THE UNIVERSE p. 120

All existing evidence suggests that Western science dawned in the areas of the Middle East that are now Iraq and Egypt. The inhabitants of the areas watered by the lower and middle reaches of the Tigris and Euphrates rivers in Sumeria (Mesopotamia) and by the Nile in Egypt enjoyed long periods of comparative economic and political stability.

Pythagoras and the medieval philosopher Boethius (on the left) from a book of 1508. Pythagoras is using an ancient calculating aid, the abacus, while Boethius employs a much faster method, the algorithm, derived from an Arab mathematician, Muhammad ibn-Musa al-Khwarizmi. Arab mathematicians were the true heirs of the Greeks, and enormously influenced medieval European thinkers. (AR)

Because the fertility of the soil was perennially renewed by seasonal flooding, there was less urgency than elsewhere in the western world to ensure food supplies, and some of the inhabitants were able to concern themselves with other matters. City states with social stratification rapidly developed and a ruling and leisured class appeared with time to ponder on nature.

Sumerian and Egyptian science

Documentary evidence of early science is scanty and begins with the Sumerians around 2500 BC. These early records make it clear that the Sumerians, and later the Babylonians, used arithmetic with a positional notation, like ours – later, unfortunately, lost – and were able to perform calculations of area and volume. Geometry was used for practical purposes and they were even aware, from practical experience, that the area of the square on the hypotenuse of a right-angled triangle was equal to the sum of the squares on the other two sides – an important theorem subsequently proved by, and unfailingly attributed to, the Greek mathematician Pythagoras.

Such records as we have of the Sumerians and the Babylonians were made on fragile clay tablets, most of which survived only in a fragmented state. More is known about Egyptian science because, having invented paper (papyrus), they were able to make more extensive records, some of which have survived. The earliest known scientific treatise, the Rhind papyrus, dating from about 1700 BC and named after the Scottish antiquary Alexander Henry Rhind (1833–63) who bought it in a town on the Nile, starts: 'Rules for enquiring into nature, and for knowing all that exists, every mystery, every secret.' This title is sanguine as the work is limited to arithmetic and geometry and is largely concerned with the manipulation of fractions. It contains a table of the analysis of them, 40 arithmetical problems concerning the division of numbers by 10 and problems on areas and volumes. This arithmetic was a reflection of the concerns of the time – the measurement, subdivision and distribution of land and the sharing out of grain among the people.

Other early Egyptian papyri show the extent of the Egyptians' knowledge of medical and other sciences. They knew how to embalm and hence preserve dead bodies. They had anatomical knowledge and surgical and dental skills and understood how to manage fractures. They were advanced in engineering and constructional principles and used set squares, plumb lines and levels and beam balances for weighing. They had an accurate calendar with a year of 365 days and were aware that the solar year was slightly longer than this. Their astronomical knowledge allowed them to align the face of the great pyramid to the north to an accuracy of less than a degree. They calculated π ('pi'), the ratio of the circumference of a circle to its diameter, to a high degree of accuracy (3.1605).

In contrast, because of the absence of documentary evidence we know little of what was happening around that time in Western Europe. There is, however, evidence, in the great Neolithic structures of Stonehenge and elsewhere, of at least the beginnings of a scientific culture in Britain around 1500 BC, but there are no written records. We do not know the purpose of the stone circles and we have no positive reason to suppose that they were used as astronomical or calendric instruments, but the very existence of these large structures speaks of some knowledge of the means of amplifying muscle power by levers, inclined planes and possibly even pulleys.

Greek science

The Greek philosopher and astronomer Thales of Miletus (c. 624–545 BC) is traditionally considered to be the founder of Greek philosophy and science. Thales is said to have visited Egypt, where he learned the Egyptians' empirical rules for surveying and astronomical observation. It is believed to be on the bases of these that he evolved the science of deductive geometry and advanced the science of astronomy. He is famed for having predicted an eclipse of the sun in 585 BC, and he also proposed the first non-theological cosmology.

Anaximander (c. 611–546 BC), who may have been his pupil, noted that the sky revolved around the pole star and deduced that the visible sky was, in fact, half of a sphere with the earth at its centre. He still believed, however, that the earth was a flat disc under which the sun passed at night.

One of the earliest experimental scientists was the Greek Pythagoras of Samos (c. 580–500 BC). He settled in a Greek colony in southern Italy in 530 BC and formed a religious community there. So far as can be derived from the myth and legend surrounding his name, Pythagoras' ideas were a strange confusion on the one hand of mysticism, magic and ritual, and on the other of strict logic and mathematics. He taught the transmigration of souls and forbade his followers to eat meat. He made remarkable discoveries in the physics of musical tones and the temperament of musical scales, and he greatly advanced geometry. He was able to think of number in the abstract, but at the same time he attributed magical significance to number, which he thought was at the root of all being, and when he discovered

Aristotle,
in a Roman
copy of a
Greek bust made in
Aristotle's life or shortly after his death.
Aristotle's system of logic was an important contribution to the history of science. (AKG)

that the square of a number could never be equal to twice the square of another number he concealed the fact as it seemed to run counter to his philosophy.

The 'laughing philosopher' Democritus of Thrace (c. 460–370 BC) is credited by later writers such as Aristotle, Epicurus and the Roman poet Lucretius with the development of the idea that all matter is formed from tiny, indivisible particles or atoms which consist of a common substance but differ in size and shape, and hence in their properties. This remarkably imaginative suggestion anticipated modern atomic theory by over 2000 years. Although Democritus was trying to explain the world on rational grounds, his

Egyptian beam balance from a 10th-century BC papyrus. Also depicted are the god Anubis and Princess Nesitanebtashru; the balance is in the same style as models used up to the present day. (AR)

ideas of atomicity were, of course, purely speculative and not based on any evidence. They were, in fact, dismissed and rejected by later philosophers such as Aristotle.

The great philosophers Socrates and his disciple and historian Plato, who did so much to promote methods of clear thought, did not significantly advance science. This was chiefly because both believed that new knowledge should be derived from pure thought and logic rather than from observation and experiment. Their scientific ideas were fanciful and, for the most part, misleading. Plato's pupil Aristotle of Chalcidice (384–322 BC), however, was a notable collector of contemporary knowledge, unrivalled in scholarship until the Renaissance. His main scientific achievements were in biology and physiology and in the description and classification of animals. In logic he was supreme, evolving a system of formal deduction by syllogism that has helped many thinkers to avoid error, although it has encouraged many others into a hopeless search for certainty and truth. He was also the tutor of Alexander the Great.

Probably the greatest name in Greek science and possibly the first true scientist was Archimedes of Syracuse (287–212 BC). Working sometimes with and sometimes against the Greek tradition, Archimedes applied his mind to the solution of practical problems. He deduced the principle of the lever (⇨ p. 26). He also derived the idea of density (specific gravity) by pure logic, from observing that his body immersed in a bath displaced an equal volume of water, and deducing from this and from the fact that some objects float while others sink that weights and volumes could thus be related. He laid the foundations of the sciences of mechanics and hydrostatics, developed a famous screw system for raising water, worked out the principle of compound pulleys and showed how concave mirrors could concentrate the sun's heat and start fires.

The Arabs

For all their technological and engineering skills the Romans were not great scientific innovators. For a thousand years after the end of the Roman Empire and the loss of classical learning (⇨ box) scientific advance in the Christian countries was at a standstill.

During the 'dark ages', however, there was a great upsurge of Arab culture based, initially, on Greek learning, but later on their own efforts. The 8th and 9th centuries were notable for the development of Arab medicine, and Arab studies in alchemy (an Arab word) led to notable advances in chemistry. Arabic numerals acquired a zero sign and positional notation was reinvented. The mathematician al Khwarizmi (active c. 825) wrote an important treatise on algebra, which also gave us the word. Arab astronomers produced new and better sets of astronomical tables. Under the impetus of such works as an encyclopedia of medicine, mathematics and the natural sciences compiled by Avicenna (Abu-Ali al-Husayn ibn-Sina, 980–1037) Arabic became the language of scholarship and was accorded the prestige formerly given to Greek.

Archimedes' principle of levers, from an English magazine of 1824. A giant in the early history of science, Archimedes realized, amongst his other contributions to our understanding of the world, that the force exerted by a lever was determined by its length (⇨ p. 26). (AR)

THE ALEXANDRIAN LIBRARY

In the early 3rd century BC a great academy of learning was founded in Alexandria in the Nile delta, with departments of astronomy, mathematics, literature and medicine. The library was one of the Seven Wonders of the World and lasted for over 600 years. At its height it contained almost half a million handwritten books in the form of papyrus rolls and, although not the only major library of ancient times, was by far the greatest depository of learning for a long time afterwards. Almost every work on science then existing must have been held in it. All travellers to Alexandria were required to surrender their books for inspection, and if no copies were in the library they were confiscated and cheap copies given to them in their place.

Part of the library was looted and destroyed by the Romans during a civil war in the 3rd century AD. Its final downfall, however, was the work of early Christians on the grounds that it was a pagan institution. To an important extent, the theology of the early centuries of the Christian era disapproved of enquiry into the things of this world and proscribed such 'pagan learning'. Accordingly, Theophilos, Bishop of Alexandria, an antipagan fanatic, ordered the library's destruction about AD 390. This was one of the greatest losses ever suffered by humanity. With the destruction of the great library, the enlivening influence of the Greeks on the minds of men was lost.

The Development of Science 2: The Renaissance and After

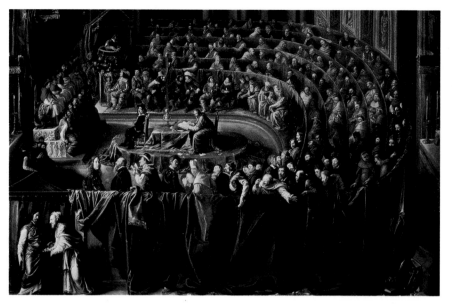

Galileo Galilei before the Inquisition, painting by unknown 17th-century artist. Galileo may not actually have been the first person to design a telescope, but he was certainly the first to put it to effective use. He also made major breakthroughs in the understanding of motion and gravity. He had to recant his championing of the Copernican solar system, on possible pain of death. (AKG)

The Renaissance saw the real beginning of empirical science – science based not on the pronouncements of those who claimed to have knowledge, but on the unequivocal proof of observations that could be made by anyone and on the basis of experimental trials of explanatory suggestions (hypotheses).

Even in the Renaissance authoritarianism – that of the ancient savants such as Plato, Aristotle and Galen, and of the theologians – was hard to set aside, but increasingly, as these men were shown to be wrong, scientists looked to new methods of enquiry proposed by Francis Bacon and others and found them fruitful. Since then enormous advances have been made in science. Thousands of men – and a few women – have made important contributions to scientific knowledge during the last 500 years. All scientists draws on the work of their predecessors (⇨ p. 4), but in a brief survey such as this, only a few key figures – those responsible for the most fundamental advances – can be mentioned.

Leonardo

The great Italian artist, engineer and scientist Leonardo da Vinci (1452–1519) was the very archetype of the Renaissance man and a model for other scientists to follow. Close observation, accurate recording and careful experiment were, for him, the only way to acquire knowledge. Nothing was to be taken on trust. 'Consider', he wrote, 'what trust we can

place in the ancients, who tried to define what the soul and life are – which are beyond proof – while those things which can be clearly known and proved by experience remained for many centuries unknown or falsely understood.' Leonardo was critical of alchemy, believed that the sun did not move, understood how the moon reflected the sun's light, and mastered friction, leverage, inertia, the laws of sound and the propagation of waves in water, hydrodynamics and elementary optics. He knew that perpetual motion machines (⇨ p. 44) were impossible, but he invented many real machines, some practicable, some even now beyond the range of technology. He studied the principles of flight and proposed flapping-wing machines (ornithopters), an early helicopter and a parachute. Moreover, he had a detailed knowledge of anatomy, derived from dissections he carried out himself.

Copernicus

The Polish astronomer Nicholaus Copernicus (1473–1543) was the first man seriously to point out the flaws in the then prevailing belief that the earth was the centre of the universe. In his book *De revolutionibus orbium coelestium* ('On the Revolution of the Celestial Spheres'; 1543) he showed how many facts of nature could be more easily explained on the assumption that the sun was fixed and that the earth and other planets moved in orbits around it. Day and night were to be explained by proposing that the earth rotated on its own axis, while the frame of the universe was a scheme of fixed stars outside our solar system. Gravity applied everywhere. His book was criticized and rejected, and consequently did not gain wide recognition until Galileo's telescope proved his view of the solar system.

Galileo

If one man can be said to have brought the idea of modern physical science to the attention of the world, that man was the Italian astronomer, mathematician

and physicist Galileo Galilei (1564–1642). In 1609 he heard that a Dutch lens-maker had produced a glass that could magnify distant objects. Galileo immediately obtained some of these lenses and made his own telescope. He followed this up with a series of important observations, seeing and describing the mountains of the moon, resolving the Milky Way into millions of separate stars, and showing that there were four satellites revolving in orbit around the planet Jupiter. This demonstration of a miniature model of the Copernican solar system provided strong support for his ideas and seriously alarmed the Church. The notion of a sun-centred system was condemned as contrary to holy scripture, and Galileo, who now accepted the idea (but recanted under threat), was persecuted and briefly detained in prison.

Galileo's most important work, however, was in dynamics – the study of moving bodies. He showed that heavy and light bodies fall at the same rate, that the speed of falling bodies is a function of time (acceleration) and that a moving body continues to move until acted on by some external force. This was to anticipate the great work of Isaac Newton.

Harvey

The English anatomist and physiologist William Harvey (1578–1657) can fairly be described as the father of modern medicine. By an ingenious demonstration on the veins of the arm – an experiment that could be repeated by anyone – he showed conclusively that the blood did not ebb and flow in the vessels, as was then supposed, but was in continuous circulation. By throwing new light on almost

Leonardo da Vinci's design for an ornithopter. Leonardo's acute interest in the workings of nature led him to investigate how humanity could replicate its mechanisms, as in this speculative flapping-wing machine. (IS)

every aspect of body function, this proof had momentous consequences for medical science.

Promulgated in his book *De motu cordis et sanguinis in animalibus* ('On the Motion of the Heart and Blood in Animals'; 1628), the proof also had the effect of arousing interest in the possibilities of an experimental and logical approach to medicine and led to the science of physiology. Many of the ideas of the earlier medical writers, such as the Greeks Hippocrates and Galen, were shown to be wrong, and the thousand-year stranglehold of Galen (AD 129–c. 199) on medicine, with his belief that the health of the body depended upon four 'humours', was broken.

Newton

The English physicist and mathematician Isaac Newton (1642–1727) is widely considered to be the greatest figure in physical science of all time. The poet Alexander Pope well expressed the way he was regarded in his own day:

'Nature and Nature's laws lay hid in Night:
God said, Let Newton be ! and All was Light.'

First, Copernicus had placed the sun at the centre of our planetary system. Next, Galileo had shown that there must be a force that prevented the fast-moving planets from flying away from the sun. Then while idly observing the fall of an apple in an orchard and speculating on the cause of the earth's attraction for it, Newton asked himself whether this attraction might extend as far as the moon. Starting from here he was able to show mathematically that all bodies attracted each other with a force proportional to the product of their masses and inversely proportional to the square of their distance apart (⇨ p. 30). Large spherical bodies like the earth attracted as if all their mass were concentrated at their centres. The attraction was mutual but the mass of most bodies – such as the apple – was so small compared to that of the earth that only the apple was seen to move.

Newton proceeded to prove his ideas mathematically and to show that the planets moved in accordance with demonstrable principles. His book *Philosophiae naturalis principia mathematica* ('Mathematical Principles of Natural Philosophy', generally just called the *Principia*; 1687) has been described as the greatest book in the history of science. It reigned supreme until, in the 20th century, Albert Einstein showed that some of Newton's ideas had to be amended. In the course of his work Newton also invented the mathematical technique of the calculus; he placed the science of light and optics on a firm basis, and established the fundamental laws of motion.

Faraday

The achievements in electricity and electro-magnetism of the English chemist and physicist Michael Faraday (1791–1867) were as great as was his long-term influence on society. Entirely self-taught, he quickly mastered all that was known about electricity and magnetism from the work of William Gilbert, Luigi Galvani, Alessandro Volta, Benjamin Franklin, Charles Coulomb, Karl Gauss and others. Working in the Royal Institution, London, Faraday then proceeded to investigate the idea of electrical polarity, the conduction of electricity in fluids, the idea of anodes and cathodes, the concept of the ion, electrolysis, the heating effect of an electric current, and the magnetic effect of current flow.

His most important work, on electromagnetic induction, led him to invent the electric transformer and the dynamo, thereby providing for the first time sustainable large electric currents. Faraday was no mathematician but his ideas, expressed with great clarity in his meticulous notebooks, were put into mathematical form by Clerk Maxwell (1831–79), and this led to the establishment of the speed of propagation of an electric current (186,000 miles per second) and to the important conclusion that light was an electromagnetic wave.

Darwin

In any roll-call of men who developed great scientific ideas, the English naturalist Charles Darwin (1809–82) must rate somewhere amongst the most important. Produced in a climate where even the existence of the process of evolution was doubted by many naturalists, Darwin's theory of the evolution of species by natural selection was the fruit of 20 years of patient observation. But the germ of his idea came from a reading of a work by the English thinker Robert Malthus (1766–1834) on population. Convinced that species could change and that he had worked out how this happened, Darwin was finally persuaded to publish, in 1859, his great work *The Origin of Species*.

The essence of the idea was that random but inherited individual physical variations could give those possessing them a survival advantage over others in relation to their environment. More of them would therefore survive to be able to breed, and the advantageous characteristic would be passed on and would be possessed by more individuals than before. In the same way, disadvantageous characteristics would tend to die out. At once this idea was seen to be almost self-evident by all the open-minded scientists of the day. Darwin, however, was condemned by the Church for his implied rejection of Biblical truth, and some religious groups still do not accept his theories today.

Einstein

If light were to travel in a medium, as sound travels in air, and if the earth moved through this medium without disturbing it, light moving on the surface of the earth would take less time to travel in

The Copernican solar system from a manuscript of 1660. Copernicus' displacement of the earth from the centre of the universe met enormous opposition, and was only accepted after some time when observation proved his theory to be true. (IS)

the direction of motion of the earth and back again than to and fro at right angles to the movement. It was widely held that light did indeed travel through such a medium ('the ether'), but when the hypothesis was tested by Michelson and Morley in 1887, it was disproved by finding that light travels at the same speed along both axes. This not only suggested that light did not need a medium to travel through, but seemed to contradict the known laws of physics. The problem was solved in 1905 by the German-born physicist Albert Einstein (1879–1955), who claimed that we had no good reason for the assumption that dimensions and time were absolutes. He proposed that the apparent dimensions of an object and the time of its observation are, in fact, relative to the observer, and that light always travels relative to an observer with the same velocity (⇨ p. 38).

Einstein also concluded that the mass of a body increased as its velocity increased and that it was progressively shortened in the direction of motion. At the speed of light the mass would be infinite, so no body could exceed the speed of light. These effects applied to an almost infinitesimally small degree at customary speeds and became apparent only as speeds approached that of light. This theory, the Special Theory of Relativity, was triumphantly vindicated later by astronomical observations and by observations of subatomic particles. The theory also demonstrated the equivalence of mass and energy, expressed in the now-famous equation: $E = mc^2$ (⇨ p. 38) and led to the practical uses of atomic energy.

Einstein's Special Theory was largely formulated by pulling together the ideas of other people, such as Hendrik Antoon Lorentz and George Francis Fitzgerald. His General Theory of Relativity (⇨ p. 38) – his greatest triumph – is a truly original and revolutionary principle worked out by him alone.

SEE ALSO
● MATHEMATICS 2: CALCULUS AND GEOMETRY p. 20
● MECHANICS p. 26
● CIRCULAR MOTION AND GRAVITATION p. 30
● BEYOND NEWTON I: RELATIVITY p. 38
● INDUCTANCE p. 100
● COSMOLOGY: UNDERSTANDING THE UNIVERSE p. 120

The Philosophy and Method of Science

The notion of a 'philosophy of science' as a formal discipline is of comparatively recent origin and has arisen to a large extent because of the ever-growing concern over the increasing influence wielded by science over modern life. But philosophic interest in science goes back to classical times.

Francis Bacon in an 18th-century engraving. Bacon formulated and developed the principle of induction, which has determined the methodology of science from his day to ours. (AR)

The pursuit of science – using the term 'science' in its broadest sense – has, from its origins, been a major source of change in society and will continue to be so. It is not therefore surprising that since the time science began thoughtful people should have been concerned about the nature of scientific enquiry, its aims, methods, reliability and limitations. The moral implications of science have also received close attention and continue to do so, especially in relation to developments in medicine and biotechnology. Throughout the ages, all the major philosophers have concerned themselves, to a greater or lesser degree, with these questions.

Aristotle

The most important figure of early philosophers of science was Aristotle (c. 384–322 BC). For his time he was extraordinarily well informed, particularly so in the branches of science then cultivated. He wrote many treatises on science, including eight books on physics, four books on astronomy, numerous books on biology and a book on mechanical science. Before pronouncing on any matter, it was his habit to enquire in minute detail into existing knowledge on the subject. Aristotle has also been credited as the originator of a philosophical tool, the *syllogism*, which has had considerable bearing on scientific thinking. In a syllogism a proposition is derived by *deduction* from two other propositions – for example, 'My master Plato is a man. All men are mortal. Therefore Plato is mortal.' This method of *deduction* was central to Aristotle's philosophy, and he worked out its laws so carefully and completely that nothing has been added to this day.

Aristotle did not, however, claim that deductive logic was the only way in which knowledge could advance. He firmly believed and constantly taught that the premises on which syllogisms could be based were to be derived from experience and the observation of facts. Collected facts should be classified and brought under particular headings.

Aristotle was concerned to find explanations of phenomena, and he decided that having classified as many facts as possible one should then proceed to form generalizations about these facts so as to provide premises for deductive reasoning. This is essentially an inductive process, and as such is not beyond criticism. However, Aristotle was determined to reduce everything to a form in which deductive reasoning might be applied, but this has proved to be hopelessly impracticable.

Aristotle was also vague about what constituted a 'fact' and failed to make important distinctions between objectively observed data and the ideas or hypotheses associated with them. Also, because of the time in which he lived, many of his ideas of science were severely defective, so his contributions to the body of scientific knowledge were negligible. But it is not as a scientist that Aristotle is important. His influence as a philosopher of science was enormous and persists, to some extent, even to this day. Unfortunately, he was also taken as an authority on scientific matters in which he was wrong, and this misled European thinkers and scientists for many centuries.

John Stuart Mill further developed Bacon's method of induction into a 'law of causality'. (ME)

Francis Bacon

For the last 500 years, the perceived 'standard model' of scientific procedure has been the process of *induction*. This idea, initially proposed by Aristotle, was first formalized by the English philosopher and statesman Francis Bacon, Lord Verulam (1561–1626). In his celebrated works *The Advancement of Learning* (1605) and *Novum organum* (1620) he argued that the deductive logic of Aristotle should be abandoned and suggested that scientists should proceed only by the process of induction, that is, by deriving general laws from the observation of particular cases. The indispensable first step in this was observation and the accumulation of as much reliable information as possible. As he wrote in *Novum organum*: 'Man the servant and interpreter of Nature, can do and understand so much, and only so much, as he has observed in fact or in thought of the course of nature; beyond this he neither knows anything nor can do anything.' This remarkable reversal of the conventional methods of the time was the first positive statement of a philosophy that remains important in science to this day.

Bacon went on to argue that scientists should prepare a 'history' of all the phenomena to be explained which should include both observations and experiment. 'It ought to be composed with great care; the facts accurately related and distinctly arranged; their authenticity diligently examined; those that rest on doubtful evidence ... noted as uncertain.' From these facts, he believed, new conclusions, even new laws of nature, would automatically emerge. Understandably, Bacon was unrealistic in his estimate of the sheer size of the task. He believed that it was possible to form a collection of all the data which were to be the materials of a science prior to the development of the science itself. We now recognize, however, that observations cannot be isolated, as he thought, from the influence of the observer. Different forms and degrees of prior knowledge in different observers, for instance, will inevitably colour and modify the observations in different ways.

Bacon's general principles were strong enough to survive the attack of the sceptical Scottish philosopher David Hume (1711–76), who pointed out that if induction is used to obtain new knowledge it may sometimes lead to wrong results, and that natural laws derived in this way can only be more or less probable, never certain. Arguing from the particular to the general is a notorious source of error and is one of the commonest logical fallacies in everyday conversation. Scientists accept that as a basis for the production of new scientific knowledge it must be used with great care, but this has not meant abandoning Bacon's methods.

In his book *A System of Logic* (1843) the English philosopher John Stuart Mill (1806–73) elevated Baconian induction into a 'law of causality' which he held to be proved by enumerating a large number of instances in which the causes of events can be shown. The most powerful modern proponent of induction, notably in *The Grammar of Science* (1892), was Professor Karl Pearson (1857–1936), the founder of modern statistical theory. In fact, Bacon's ideas on the inductive method and those of his followers carried enormous weight right up to the end of the 19th century. It was not until the dawn of the 20th century that thinkers on science began to pose some searching questions and subjected Bacon's ideas to critical scrutiny. Some philosophers then rejected them outright as a realistic account of how science is, in practice, performed.

The pragmatism of Pasteur

The epitome of the pragmatic approach to science was the great French chemist and microbiologist Louis Pasteur (1822–95). Pasteur's direct, logical handling of problems and his clearly thought-out methods of investigation led to a virtual revolution in the scientific methods of his time.

However, his clear demonstration of the lack of evidence for the widely held belief in the spontaneous generation of living organisms, and his proofs of the cause and methods of prevention of the previously fatal disease rabies, aroused hostile opposition, especially from a medical establishment unable to adapt its thought processes.

Pierce and abduction

Another major figure in the philosophy of science was the American scientist, logician and philosopher Charles Sanders Pierce (1839–1914). Although Pierce won international recognition for his astronomical work and for his measurements of gravitational force, his principal interests were in philosophy and in the logic of science, especially induction. Pierce proposed that there was a logical process, which he called *abduction*, in which hypotheses to explain surprising facts were formed and accepted on probation. He hoped to show that abduction had the same status as deduction and induction and that all three were related, although clearly distinguishable.

Pierce held that the scientific method was but one of a number of ways of establishing beliefs. The essence of belief, he taught, was rooted in our habits of behaviour: we believe something because of our habits of action in relation to it. Using the same principles Pierce tried to explain the idea of probability. Most of his work is very difficult and his full significance as a thinker is only now beginning to be appreciated.

Karl Popper and the hypothetico-deductive system

The 20th century's outstanding commentator on how science is practised is the Austrian-born British thinker Sir Karl Raimund Popper (1902–), especially in his major work on scientific methodology *Die Logik der Forschung* ('The Logic of Scientific Discovery'; 1959).

Popper teaches that the proper way for science to operate is as follows: the scientist must create a hypothesis that predicts a phenomenon that can be tested. If the prediction is shown to be wrong, the hypothesis must be abandoned; if the prediction is right, the scientist is not entitled to claim that he has proved the hypothesis but merely that it provides an adequate basis for further research. His criterion for judging a scientific theory is not its truth but its testability or falsifiability. This, the *hypothetico-inductive* process, is now generally regarded as the way in which the best scientific work should be conducted.

Sir Karl Popper has produced the first major revision of Baconian method since the 18th-century philosopher David Hume pointed out that the process of arguing from the particular to the general can lead to error. (Topham)

THE FALLACY OF INDUCTION

The British navigator and explorer Captain James Cook (1728–79) landed at Botany Bay, Australia, in 1770, thereby opening up a world of new and sometimes strange phenomena to the West. One of the many surprises to be had was the existence there of black swans. Until this time, it had been assumed, using the inductive process, that all swans had to be white, since only white swans had ever been encountered before. This simple example points out the inherent weakness in the inductive argument, in which a general conclusion, rooted in common experience or experimental evidence, is drawn from a set of premises. Even where the premises are undeniably true, and where the conclusion is seen to follow absolutely from them, the inductive process is vulnerable to accusations of illogicality because one crucial factor is ignored – the significance of the unknown. It was exactly this problem that later led the Austrian-born British philosopher Karl Popper (1902–) to postulate the theory of falsifiability, which states that knowledge can be advanced only by continually disproving current theories and replacing them with equally provisional but wider-ranging ones.

Black swan. (Spectrum)

Theory and practice

It may be significant that hardly any of the philosophy of science has been written by scientists themselves. This is a reflection of the fact that few scientists are interested in philosophy or deliberately practise a formal methodology, although some have erroneously thought that they did. Charles Darwin, for example, claimed in his autobiography to have 'without any theory, collected facts on a wholesale scale', but, as the British immunologist and writer on science topics Sir Peter Medawar (1915–87) has pointed out, Darwin's other writings make it clear that he could not resist forming a hypothesis on every subject.

Medawar, a distinguished Nobel Prizewinner, insists that nearly all scientists practise this kind of self-deception. He said in a lecture to the American Philosophical Society, 'Science, broadly considered, is incomparably the most successful enterprise human beings have ever engaged upon; yet the methodology that has presumably made it so, when propounded by learned laymen, is not attended to by scientists, and when propounded by scientists is a misrepresentation of what they do.'

SEE ALSO
- WHAT IS SCIENCE? p. 4.
- THE DEVELOPMENT OF SCIENCE 1: THE ANCIENT WORLD p. 8
- THE DEVELOPMENT OF SCIENCE 2: THE RENAISSANCE AND AFTER p. 10

Scientific Instruments 1: Observation

Scientific research takes many different forms and not all of it involves the use of instruments, nor does it all take place in laboratories. But whether working indoors or out, scientists rely heavily on the use of devices – the instruments of science – to extend the range and accuracy of their senses.

The instruments used by modern scientists can be as large as several kilometres in diameter, such as the particle accelerators used in elementary particle physics, but most of the instruments used in laboratories today are comparatively small and, except to the initiated, appear anonymous. A great many of the processes are now hidden from view in plastic-covered metal boxes with digital read-outs and connections for coaxial cables. Personal computers are, of course, everywhere, often directly connected to the experimental equipment by means of devices known as analogue-to-digital

converters. These turn changing quantities or readings of any kind into strings of numbers in digital form that computers can use, manipulate and display.

Beyond the range of the senses

Much scientific observation can, of course, be done with the unaided senses, but a great deal of scientific work is concerned with observations of things much too small or much too far away to be seen adequately, or at all, with the naked eye. Telescopes of various kinds, both optical and radio are the primary instruments of astronomy, while microscopes, also of various kinds, are extensively used in many branches of scientific work.

Scientific observations often have to be made in inaccessible or dangerous places, such as inside the human body or in areas of high radiation intensity. For such purposes, remote sensing or observing devices, such as fibre-optic viewers or miniature closed-circuit television cameras, have to be used. Another common method is a technique of local detection and transmission of data by radio signals from an inaccessible site, known as telemetry.

Many of the things that scientists observe or measure are not detectable by the senses – chemical changes, small changes in acidity, electrical resistance, levels of various kinds of radiation, magnetic fields, and so on. Such observations require special detecting instruments, many of which measure as well as detect, and many involve transducers (⇨ p. 16), which convert energy from one form into another more usable one. The list of such instruments is a long one: photocells to detect light, strain gauges to detect small movements, spectroscopes to detect changes in light spectra, radiation detectors (Geiger tubes, fogging film and dose rate meters), galvanometers to detect electric charges, pH meters to detect changes in acidity, gas chromatographs to analyse small samples of material, colorimeters to detect changes in colour, microphones to detect sound, radio receivers to tune in and detect radio waves of all frequencies, and many more.

Telescopes

The earliest *optical telescopes* were of the *refracting* type (⇨ p. 78) and consisted of a convex object lens of long focal length at the outer end (the objective) and a convex eyepiece lens of short focal length. The objective forms a small inverted image that is then magnified by the closely applied eyepiece. Such an arrangement produces an inverted but

False-colour scanning electronmicrograph of platinum crystals. The shorter the wavelength of the electrons the higher the resolution of the image, making electron microscopes particularly good at revealing flaws in crystal structure. (SPL)

enlarged image of a distant object. The greater the focal length of the objective and the smaller the focal length of the eyepiece, the greater the magnification.

Hardly any modern optical astronomical telescopes are now of this type as large ones are hard to build. Accurate large concave mirrors can be made and mounted much more easily than large convex lenses, so most modern astronomical telescopes are of *reflecting* design (⇨ p. 78). In these the objective, which lies at the back of the instrument, is a large concave mirror, accurately ground to a parabolic curve so as to have a suitably long focal length. Near the point where the rays from this mirror come to a focus – at the front of the instrument – a small, angled plane mirror or prism is placed which deflects the rays through a right angle so that they come to a focus at a point where the short-focal-length eyepiece can be conveniently sited.

The most conspicuous parts of *radio telescopes* are the reflectors or the antennae. Reflectors take the form of the familiar steerable concave metal dish – analogous to the concave lens of the reflecting optical telescope. These dishes are also parabolic, and they reflect electromagnetic signals within the radio spectrum to a small antenna supported at the focus of the parabola in front of the centre of the dish. In some designs antennae take the form of massive arrays of aerial wires strung across valleys or fields.

Radio telescopes detect the radio waves emitted by many celestial bodies and these can provide important information supplementary to optical observations. The detection by such means of background microwave radiation from all regions of space has provided data of central importance to cosmology (⇨ p. 6).

Microscopes

Microscopes are instruments designed to form magnified images of very small objects illuminated by transmitted or reflected light or other radiation. A simple microscope consists of a single lens of short focal length; a compound microscope has two separated lens systems. No object can be perceived if it is smaller than the wavelength of the medium used to perceive it, and the

The United Kingdom Infrared Telescope. Like most modern astronomical telescopes operating in the visible light range, this is a reflecting telescope, with its main mirror in the blue cell and the secondary mirror held in the four grey vanes at upper centre. An infrared telescope registers light only at the infrared wavelengths, so as it is not affected by visible light it can observe celestial bodies in daylight. (SPL)

shorter the wavelength, relative to the size of the object, the greater the detail revealed. For this reason, the smallest objects that can be usefully seen with an optical microscope are about one millionth of a metre (1 micron) across, and the upper limit of magnification of an optical microscope is about 2,000 times. By using a medium with a shorter wavelength than visible light, such as ultra violet light, these limits can be extended somewhat.

In an *optical microscope*, the object to be examined is usually placed on a transparent slide over a hole in the central platform or 'stage'. A strong light is reflected through the slide and into the objective lens, which is brought very close to the object. In this way an inverted image is formed within the tube of the microscope and this is magnified by the eyepiece lens. The objective lenses, which may be changed, usually have a focal length of only a few millimetres and a magnifying power of upwards of 50 times, while the various eyepieces that may be used have a magnifying power of 10 times or more. The total magnification is the multiple of the two.

Electron microscopes use beams of electrons with a wavelength very much smaller than those of visible light and can magnify a million times more than optical microscopes. Moreover, the wavelength of the associated wave varies with the momentum of the electrons (de Broglie's relation). The greater the momentum the shorter the wavelength and the higher the resolving power of the microscope. So simply by increasing the speed of the electrons used, the resolution of the microscope can be increased. The best modern electron microscopes can work at wavelengths so short that they can resolve arrays of atoms and can, for instance, make out defects in crystal structure.

A stream of electrons is produced by a heated filament at one end of the microscope and these are powerfully attracted by a positive charge, typically of 100,000 volts, though some modern instruments operate at only 1,000 volts. It is the strength of this voltage that determines the speed of the electrons. The equivalent of the lenses of an optical microscope are coils of wire carrying electric currents, which produce electromagnetic fields that focus the electron beam just as glass does light. The image formed by the electron beam is easily made visible by projecting it on to a glass plate coated with phosphors which convert electron impact into visible light, as happens in a normal television tube. The analogy with the light microscope is close; the only fundamental difference between the two systems is in the medium used.

Spectroscopes and spectrometers

Electromagnetic radiation such as light, radio waves, X-rays and gamma rays form part of a continuous spectrum of different wavelengths. Any such radiation can be separated into its constituent wavelengths. Visible light, for instance, will split up into its component colours if a narrow beam is passed through a glass prism. The instruments that are made to separate wavelengths in this way, and allow the results to be seen or detected, are known as *spectroscopes*, and those that measure wavelengths and the amounts of energy in different parts of the spectrum are called *spectrometers*.

Light spectroscopes exploit the fact that the spectrum produced by any light contains characteristic wavelengths that differ according to the source of the light: the excited atoms of any particular element emit light of a wavelength unique to it. These wavelengths appear as bright lines in the spectrum, and because the position of these lines is known, this enables identification of the element. Also, when white light passes through a cooler gas or vapour, as in the sun's chromosphere, the characteristic wavelengths of the elements are absorbed by the gas. This provides dark lines in the spectrum corresponding to these elements (Fraunhofer dark lines). Spectroscopes, which are now commonly automated, are thus able to identify with certainty the heated elements present in a distant body such as a star. They are also widely used in laboratories to analyse chemical substances, by showing the absorption of ultraviolet and infrared light by different compounds.

A diffraction grating is often used in spectroscopes and spectrometers instead of a prism. This is a piece of glass engraved with thousands of fine parallel lines about 0.002 mm apart. The lines are effectively opaque but light can pass through the glass between the lines, where it suffers interference (⊳ p. 80). The device will produce a very sharp spectrum and can be used to measure wavelengths accurately if the distance

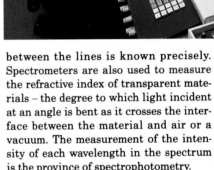

between the lines is known precisely. Spectrometers are also used to measure the refractive index of transparent materials – the degree to which light incident at an angle is bent as it crosses the interface between the material and air or a vacuum. The measurement of the intensity of each wavelength in the spectrum is the province of spectrophotometry.

Scanning transmission electron microscope. Electron microscopes can resolve objects far too small to be seen by optical microscopes. A beam of electrons is generated at the top of the column and travels down through the object. (SPL)

Mass spectrometer being used for protein analysis. As with many scientific instruments, the computer attached to the spectrometer does the work of analysing the data it produces. (SPL)

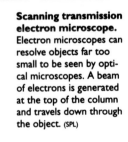

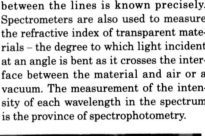

Scientific Instruments 2: Data Collection and Analysis

Modern technology has considerably extended the capabilities of scientists to observe, test and record, far beyond the limitations of the primarily visual observations that they used to rely on.

Triple-beam balance (above right) as used in chemistry laboratories. Although not able to measure with accuracy down to microscopic level, this balance can measure in tenths of a gram (registered on the bottom beam). (SPL)

Whatever his or her subject, much of the work of the scientist is concerned with measuring and recording. For these purposes, the instruments scientists use are often those customarily employed in other non-scientific tasks – clocks, stopwatches, measuring rules, calipers, milliammeters, pressure gauges, speedometers, cameras, tape recorders and so on. Sometimes, however, such general equipment is insufficiently accurate for scientific purposes and more refined versions of the same instruments are needed. Highly accurate measurement of time intervals, for instance, demands atomic clocks with a direct connection between the clock and a rapidly acting sensor of the event under investigation.

Transducers

Devices that convert changing physical events into a form that can be recorded, measured, used or observed in a more convenient or useful way are known as *transducers*. They are used extensively and may take a wide variety of forms.

Almost any accessible physical event – such as a dimensional change, a change in position, a pressure change, a change in temperature, a sound, a change in light intensity or colour, an alteration in electrical current or charge, a change in acidity or in the concentration of any dissolved substance – can be sensitively detected by one of a wide variety of sensing devices and converted, by a suitable transducer, into a form that the scientist can use. In the past, transducers used for scientific purposes usually had an analog output such as the movement of a needle across a scale or a change in the position of the top of a column of mercury in a glass tube. Today many transducers incorporate an analog-to-digital conversion chip so that the output can be read in digital form. This is why many laboratory instruments have a digital read-out.

Transducer technology has made rapid advances in recent years and has given rise to a major industry. The remarkable progress that has been made in miniaturization has led to the increasingly wide application of transducers in many different fields of science, industry and medicine. It is now, for instance, commonplace for transducers on the end of catheters to be introduced into the living human heart to monitor such things as the blood pressure and the oxygen tension in the different chambers. Many sub-miniature transducers are now fabricated directly on to silicon chips as part of integrated circuits, and can give a direct digital output proportional to changes in the physical property being measured.

A problem arises in all forms of scientific observation in that it is impossible to make any measurement without having some effect on what is being measured, and the smaller the quantity being measured the more difficult it is to avoid a significant alteration. If, for instance, a very small electrical current is being measured by connecting a sensitive meter in series with the circuit, some of the energy of the current will be consumed in moving the needle, so the current now flowing in the circuit will be less than it was before the meter was connected. For this reason scientific instruments often have to be carefully designed so that they have the least possible effect on the quantity they are measuring. This sometimes makes them very expensive.

It cannot necessarily be taken for granted that measuring and recording instruments are accurate. To do so might be to acquire defective and misleading data, so it is often necessary to use reliable standards by which the accuracy of the instruments can be checked or by the use of which instruments can be calibrated. In some scientific tasks calibration of instruments may take as long as the experiment itself and scientists can be constantly concerned about the possibility of calibration drift during the course of the experiment. Developments in modern electronics and in sensor and transducer technology have done much to overcome such problems.

Data recording

The recording of data may be done in many ways, but it most commonly takes the form of a plot drawn out by a mechanical pen on a circular or endless strip paper chart, or magnetic recording on tape or disk. Photography is also much used and many scientific machines are fitted with ports to which cameras can be attached and the almost instant polaroid prints taken. Computers are also widely used to record data and these can readily make copies and can represent the data in a variety of forms – as numbers, graphs, bar charts, pie charts or as 'three-dimensional' representations.

Weighing

Scientists often need to quantify material with great accuracy and may have to obtain the weight of an object to within a fraction of a milligram (one thousandth of a gram). For such purposes the familiar laboratory balance with its knife-edge suspension, weight and material pans and draught-excluding glass cover is no longer good enough. Modern laboratory balances are electronically operated, often employing the piezoelectric principle (⇨ p. 70) and usually have a single pan. The read-out of the weight is in digital form, frequently with an automatic print-out on a paper strip. Working at such limits requires the use of meticulous

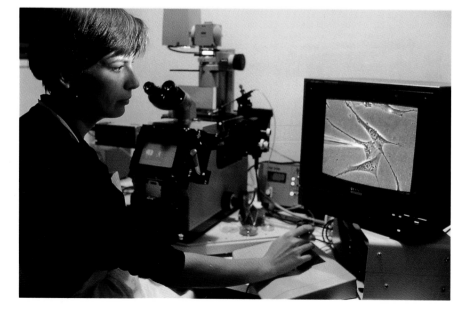

DNA micro-injection using a micropipette, controlled by a joystick in the scientist's right hand. The scientist is using this micromanipulation tool to introduce a corrective gene into a human white blood cell. (SPL)

techniques if the results are to be meaningful, and accordingly experiments have to be particularly carefully designed.

Analysis

A major part of scientific work is concerned with analysis – determining what something is made of – and scientists, especially those in the chemical and biological disciplines, commonly find themselves separating complex materials into their component parts. This can be done in a number of ways.

Centrifuges are laboratory machines used for separating solids suspended in liquids, molecules dissolved in liquids, or liquids that do not mix. They make use of the principle of centrifugal force, familiar to most people from the experience of whirling a weight such as a stone on the end of a piece of string. Centrifuges consist of strong glass tubes inserted into hinged holders set around a central spindle driven by an electric motor. As the spindle rotates the tubes swing outwards into a horizontal position. Very high speeds produce strong centrifugal forces – commonly 1,000 times that of gravity – while ultra-high-speed centrifuges known as ultracentrifuges can achieve forces approaching a million times that of gravity. The principle of the centrifuge can be applied to gases as well as to liquids, and special devices are available that allow continuous separation.

Chromatography is a widely used technique for separating and thus analysing mixtures of compounds, such as proteins, in a solution. If such mixtures are made to flow in a particular direction over a surface such as a piece of paper or a gel, differences in adhesiveness will result in some moving less far than others, and the materials will separate out into bands that can be stained and seen. In *electrophoresis* the substances move under the influence of an electric voltage.

In gas chromatography the compounds in a mixture migrate at different speeds when conveyed by an inert gas along a tube packed with an inert powdered material. The sample material is injected into the flowing gas and forms a vapour. Separation of the component molecules then occurs as the vapour moves down the tube. Different components cause changing electrical resistance in the output gas as the different components pass, and the instrument can easily be calibrated by feeding in samples of known materials.

Chromatography can readily be automated and hundreds of different models of automatic chromatographs have been produced.

Laboratory computer software

'Software' is the generic term for the programs used to instruct the operating systems of computers to perform any of the almost unlimited range of their possible functions. The introduction of the personal computer proved a godsend to scientists who, from the beginning, saw the possibilities and exploited them, and the computer has become of central importance in many different processes in all scientific disciplines. There is now a mountain of software dedicated to specific science projects as well as a great deal used for more general scientific purposes, such as statistical analysis and computation. Software is available for all sorts of purposes such as performing cell analysis, chromatography, chromosome analysis, densitometry, DNA analysis, electrophoresis analysis, equation solving, image analysis, molecular modelling, optical design, DNA restriction mapping, DNA sequencing, speech processing and X-ray diffraction. It is also available to provide the scientists with huge databases of information and expert systems (⇨ p. 218). One especially significant case is the human genome project (⇨ p. 202); as this massive research project has progressed new data on DNA sequencing has been added to a computer database that is accessible to all interested scientists. However, despite the considerable commercial

scientific software that is available, scientists often have to write their own for special requirements.

Many important scientific experiments are performed entirely at the computer and much software exists that has been written solely for the purpose of simulating experiments in real life. Once the software has been properly debugged, such computer modelling of experiments allows them to be performed much more quickly and with many more variables than in real life. The scientist must, however, be sure that the computer model adequately reflects reality.

Low-pressure chromatograph. Chromatography is much used by biologists to separate out complex substances or to isolate particular constituents. In this experiment monoclonal antibodies are being separated from a liquid cell culture. (SPL)

SEE ALSO

● SCIENTIFIC INSTRUMENTS 1: OBSERVATION p. 14
● INFORMATION p. 216
● PROGRAMMING, SOFTWARE AND APPLICATIONS p. 218

Centrifugal auto-analyser from which cholesterol is being unloaded. Centrifuges are used to separate liquids or gases, or substances dissolved or suspended in liquids. (SPL)

Mathematics and Science I: The Language of Scientific Thought

Mathematics is a language, a very concise and efficient one, that is also universal: its symbols have the same meaning all over the world.

The symbols in mathematics serve more than one function. On the one hand they convey information – often a great deal of information – and on the other they indicate that a mathematical operation is being performed. They combine in expressions as words combine in sentences, the most important of which are equations; these are statements of the exact equality between two conditions. Such equations are far more concise than words, as is shown in the famous expression $E = mc^2$. Each symbol has a precise meaning: e is the energy locked up in any quantity of matter, m the mass of the material, c the speed of light, and ^{2} is familiar as meaning 'squared', or multiplied by itself. As two symbols placed adjacent, as in the m and c in this equation, are understood to be multiplied together, the equation says in very brief form that the energy of any material is equal to the material's mass times the speed of light multiplied by itself.

Scientific notation

Scientists commonly have to express very large or very small numbers. A brief and clear way of expressing these numbers is the form known as *scientific*

(or *exponential*) notation. 100 is 10 multiplied by itself (two 10s multiplied together); 1,000 is three tens multiplied together; 10,000 is four tens multiplied together, and so on. But 100 can also be written 10^2 (10 squared); 1,000 can be written 10^3 (10 cubed); 10,000 can be written 10^4 (10 to the power of 4) and so on. The small upper number is called the *index* or *exponent*, and indicates the number of times 10 is to be multiplied by itself – that is, the power to which the number 10 is *raised*. Raising in this way by powers rather than by just adding numbers is called an *exponential* process. Exponential notation is very convenient for very large numbers that would otherwise contain a large number of zeros that had to be carefully counted by the reader. 10^6 is 1 million, and 10^{12} is one million million (12 zeros). A rough estimate of the total number of particles in the universe is 10^{78} – an inconveniently long number to write out in full.

In the real world of science, however, numbers are seldom as nicely rounded as 10, 100, 1,000 and 10,000. Therefore large numbers are expressed by taking a number between 1 and 10, which may contain a decimal fraction – e.g. 2.365 – and multiplying it by a power of 10. For instance, 2.365×10^3 is 23,650.

Numbers below 1 are expressed using a negative index. Thus 0.000000002365 becomes 2.365 × 10 to the power of minus 9 (2.365×10^9). To convert a long number below 1 using an index of 10 the simple rule is to count the number of zeros and also the first number, and the total gives the figure for the index.

Logarithms

The notion of using indices to express a wide range of numbers can be extended to graphs. If equal spaces along one scale of a graph are marked 0, 10, 100, 1,000, 10,000 and so on, or 0, 1, 2, 4, 8, 16, 32, 64 and so on, we have what are called *logarithmic graphs*, based in this case, respectively, on 10 and on 2 (⇨ below). The distance from 1 to 4 on a logarithmic graph based on 2 is the same as the distance from 4 to 16. So adding the first two points after 1 to the next and two points along the axis is equivalent to multiplying 4 by 4. $2^2 \times 2^4$ is 4×16 i.e. 64, which is 2^6. Again, we have simply added the indices. In *logarithms* addition of indices is equivalent to multiplication and subtraction of them is equivalent to division.

The logarithm of a number to a given base is the power to which the base must be raised to equal the number. So, in a base 10 system, the logarithm of 10,000 is 4 (because $10^4 = 10,000$). The logarithm of 64 to the base 2 is 6 (because $2^6 = 64$). Logarithms used to be widely used and were the basis of the slide rule, but now that pocket calculators are universal, log tables and slide rules have become museum items. The idea of bases and logarithms, however, remains important in mathematics, and logarithmic graphs are widely used.

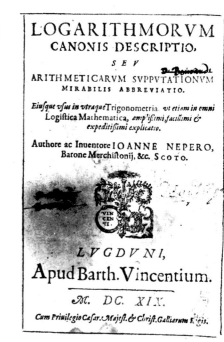

Title page of the first work on logarithms, by the Scottish mathematician John Napier. Napier published his discovery of logarithms in 1614; this edition of the work dates from 1619. (AR)

The idea of a base

Arithmetic took a great step forward when someone thought of representing magnitude by the position of numbers relative to each other. In our familiar decimal system, the magnitude of a number increases ten times with each shift to the left. The number 2,365, for instance, actually means 5 units plus (10 × 6) plus (100 × 3) plus (1,000 × 2). As numbers are usually written, the right-hand column indicates units, the next to the left 10s, the next left 100s, and so on. Numbers expressed in this way can readily be placed one below the other and added or subtracted, so long as one remembers that moves from one column to the next occur when 9 is exceeded. The Romans with their cumbersome non-sequential numbers, such as MCXVIII (1,118), could not do this.

Our normal system is to the base 10, but this is by no means the only possible system. Any number can form the base of a system. With a base of 4 the number 2312 would be equal to 2 units plus (1 × 4) plus (3 × 16) plus (2 × 64) – a total of 182 in decimal notation. A system to the base 4 would not be especially useful, but scientists have found considerable use for systems to other bases, especially the base 2 (binary systems), and, to a lesser extent, the base 8 (octal systems). The binary system is routinely used in computers. Digital computers work with transistors that are switched either on or off (⇨ p. 22). As this system needs only two alternatives, it is much simpler and more reliable than a system based on ten, which would need ten levels of voltage to represent the ten decimal digits. In binary, the number 10111011 is equal

Professor Andrew Wiles. Maths is a universal language governed by precise laws. For 300 years mathematicians were frustrated because experience showed that the last theorem of the French mathematician Pierre de Fermat was correct, but no one had published a proof of it. Professor Wiles excited the mathematical community by cracking this problem in 1993. (SPL)

SYSTÈME INTERNATIONAL (SI) UNITS AND THEIR COMMON EQUIVALENTS

When making calculations scientists are careful to ensure that the units they use come from the same system. The units of measurement used universally for scientific and most technical purposes are SI units – Système international d'unités. SI is the modern form of the metric system, which is based on the metre as a unit of length and the kilogram as a unit of weight, and was first adopted in France in 1799. Other systems of units commonly employed include the British imperial system and the related US customary units.

In the SI system there are several fundamental units which relate to standards of length, mass, time, etc. These may be combined to form derived units, for example the SI units of length and time may be combined to form units of acceleration or velocity.

FUNDAMENTAL UNITS

QUANTITY	UNIT	SYMBOL	EQUIVALENT
Mass	kilogram	kg	pound (0.4536 kg)
Length	metre	m	foot (0.3048 m)
Time	second	s	
Angle	radian	rad	degree (0.017453 rad)
Electric current	ampere	A	
Luminosity	candela	cd	lambert (0.318309 cd/cm^2)
Temperature	kelvin	K	
Amount	mole	mol	

DERIVED UNITS

QUANTITY	UNIT	SYMBOL	EQUIVALENT
Area	square m	m^2	square foot (0.292 m^2)
Volume	cubic m	m^3	litre (0.001 m^3)
Energy	joule	j	calorie (4.1868 j)
Force	newton	N	1 j = 1 Newton metre
Velocity	metre/second	m/s	mile/hour (0.447 m/s)
Acceleration	metre/second^2	m/s^2	feet per second per second
Density	kg/cubic m	kg/m^3	pound/cu ft (16.02 kg/m^3)
Power	watt	W	horsepower (746 W)
Pressure	pascal	Pa	mm of mercury (133.3 Pa)
Voltage	volt	V	watts per amp
Electric charge	coulomb	C	ampère seconds
Capacitance	farad	F	ampère seconds per volt
Magnetic flux	tesla	T	volt seconds
Resistance	ohm	Ω	volts per ampère

important function in the study of the calculus (⇨ p. 20) and is written log e x or ln x. The value of e can be found from the following equation, in which ! means multiply the number by all its integral factors (6! is $1 \times 2 \times 3 \times 4 \times 5 \times 6$, that is 720)

$$e = 1 + \frac{1}{1!} + \frac{1}{2!} + \frac{1}{3!} + \ldots \frac{1}{n!} + \ldots$$

which gives 2.71828 . . ., as we saw with the turkey starting at 1 kg.

Square roots and imaginary numbers

The square root of a number is the number which multiplied by itself gives the original number, and the square of a number is the result of multiplying a number by itself. 100 is the square of 10, and 10 is the square root of 100. 10 is also the cube root of 1,000 and the fourth root of 10,000. By the laws of algebra (and logic), when a negative number is multiplied by a positive number, the result is negative. But when two negative numbers are multiplied the result must always be positive. This is because multiplication is really just repetitive adding and multiplying two negative numbers together is just repetitively subtracting negativity. So there is no number whose square is a minus number. Likewise the idea of the square root of a minus number has no meaning in the real number system.

Nevertheless, an *imaginary number* taken to be equal to the square root of minus 1 has been shown to be so useful in mathematics that it is treated as real, with the symbol *i*. *Complex numbers* are numbers with a real part and an imaginary part, such as 7 + 4*i*. Surprisingly, such numbers can be used just like other numbers, and are especially useful in electrical engineering calculations. Used in this way, *i* is known as an *operator* – a symbol representing a particular mathematical operation to be carried out on a number or group of numbers.

SEE ALSO

● MATHEMATICS AND SCIENCE 3: THE THEORETICAL BASIS OF COMPUTING p. 22
● BEYOND NEWTON 1: RELATIVITY p. 38
● INSIDE A DIGITAL COMPUTER p. 214

Logarithmic graph showing inflation in Bolivia from 1982 to 1989. A scale that goes up in factors of base numbers, usually of 10 as here, is useful for showing dramatic changes where one also wants to see the detail of the points where change is more gradual.

(reading from right to left) to 1 unit plus (2×1) plus (4×0) plus (8×1) plus (16×1) plus (32×1) plus (64×0) plus (128×1), that is 187 in decimal notation.

Another base commonly used in mathematics is symbolized by the letter e. This number is transcendental – its digits go on for ever with no obvious pattern. Normal logarithms are to the base 10, but e also provides a base for logarithms which are called *natural logarithms*. The number e is the value reached in unit time by a unit quantity that continues to grow at a rate equal to itself. To give an example: imagine a young turkey that weighs 1 kg on 1 January and grows at an annual rate equal to its own weight at any moment. When it weighs 1.3 kg its rate of growth will be 1.3 kg per year; when it weighs 1.6 kg its rate of growth

will be 1.6 kg per year, and so on. At the end of the year the turkey will weigh e kg – that is approximately 2.718 kg. In the following year each unit (kg) of e will grow to e kg, so at the end of that year the turkey will weigh e^2 kg, that is 7.387 kg. We chose to start with a turkey of 1 kg. If the unit is still in kilograms, and the turkey starts heavier, say at 3 kg, each kg will grow to e kg by the end of the year, which means that the turkey will weigh 8.154 kg. If the unit were height we could, instead, be measuring a turkey that starts at 50 cm and at 50 cm annual growth rate.

A rate of growth that varies with the current state of the thing growing is common in nature, so e is commonly found in equations concerned with growth. The natural logarithm is an

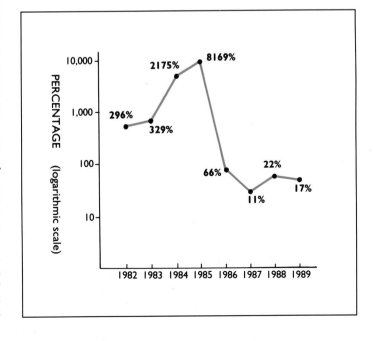

Mathematics and Science 2: Calculus and Geometry

Among the many mathematical tools used by scientists, the most powerful is the differential and integral calculus. Probably the most useful mathematical tool ever developed, the calculus is concerned with the description of changing phenomena. Other mathematical tools are almost as important to science: coordinate geometry, which is concerned with the location of points in space; conic sections, which describe the particular curves formed by points moving under particular constraints; and trigonometry, which greatly simplifies a host of measurements.

The calculus

The area of an irregularly shaped surface cannot be calculated by a simple formula, so one way to do it is to cover the area with very thin rectangular strips of equal width but different height, and then to add together their areas. A similar method enables one to calculate the volumes of regularly and irregularly shaped solids. The sum of the areas or volumes of all the small parts will not give the exact area or volume but approaches it as a 'limit' determined by the size of the 'little bits' chosen. However, by proposing that the 'little bits' of the object should be made very small indeed – infinitesimally so – the calculus provides a way of precisely calculating quantities that formerly could only be roughly estimated.

The calculus has two main branches, *differential calculus* and *integral calculus*. The differential calculus is concerned essentially with the rate of change of one variable with respect to another, i.e. the rate of change of what are known as 'functions'. When we are travelling along a road in a car, the distance travelled is a function of time; the greater the time, the greater the distance. It is also a function of speed; the greater the speed, the greater the distance.

We do not need calculus to solve simple problems such as ascertaining the distance travelled if the time is known and the speed is constant, but if the driver is accelerating gradually and progressively, the calculation of speed over any time period becomes more difficult. If we take a very short distance travelled and divide it by a very short period of time, we get a fairly close approximation to the speed during that period of time. If both the distance and time used are made infinitesimally small, but are still in the appropriate ratio, we get an answer that approaches the exact speed as a limit.

The differential calculus uses the Greek letter delta, Δ, to represent 'a small increment of', so the approximate speed at a point is Δ times the distance (x) divided by Δ times the time (t). As Δ gets smaller and smaller the approximation gets closer and closer to the actual speed at that point. The quantity $\Delta x/t$ is called the derivative of distance with respect to time, or the rate of change of distance with respect to time. In integral calculus the methods of the differential calculus are reversed and one can integrate all the little bits of distance by adding them together to make the total distance. This process is represented mathematically by $\int dx$ (the letter d being substituted for the Greek Δ); the symbol $\int$ is simply an old-fashioned S, which represents 'the sum of'.

Coordinate geometry

The idea of representing the position of a point by a system of coordinates is generally credited to the French

CARTESIAN COORDINATES

P = +3, +3
D = -4, +2
N = -2, -3

mathematician and philosopher René Descartes (1596–1650). Some years earlier than Descartes, the French mathematician Pierre de Fermat (1601–65) had worked out a similar system, but he did not get the credit for the idea as his book, *Introduction to Loci*, was not published until 1679, after his death and 42 years after Descartes had published his idea, in *Géométrie*.

Essentially, coordinate geometry involves drawing two axes, known as Cartesian (i.e. of Descartes) coordinates. A horizonal line, the X axis, is cut by a vertical line, the Y axis. The point of intersection is marked zero and a scale is marked along both axes as positive numbers to the right and upwards and negative numbers to the left and downwards. So any point in the upper right quadrant can be represented by two positive numbers, such as +3 (X axis), +4 (Y axis); any point in the upper left quadrant as a negative and a positive number, such as –2 (X axis), +3 (Y axis); any point in the lower right quadrant as a positive and a negative number, such as +3 (X axis), –2 (Y axis); and any point in the lower left quadrant as two negative numbers, such as –4 (X axis), –2 (Y axis).

By representing points as numbers, coordinate geometry allows position and space to be related to the more numerical branches of mathematics, especially algebra. If, for instance, we take a simple equation such as y=2x, we can now proceed to plot the line of this equation for a series of values of x, such as 1, 2, 3, 4, 5 and 6. With x shown on the horizontal axis the slope of this line is less steep than that of the line for the equation y=x. If we plot the equation y=sin x (⇨ below) for values of y at 10° intervals up to 360°, we get a sine wave (⇨ p. 104), a wave that is found often in different circumstances.

Trigonometry

Elementary trigonometry (from the Greek *trigonon*, a triangle, and *metron*, a measure) can be mastered quickly. It deals with right-angle triangles. The side opposite the right angle of a right-angle

Gottfried Wilhelm von Leibnitz (left) and **Isaac Newton** (right), both credited with the invention of the calculus.
(AR/IS)

triangle is called the hypotenuse, and the side that is opposite the angle of interest – i.e. angle **A** in the diagram below – is called the 'opposite'. The

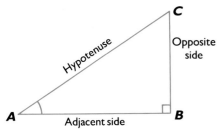

remaining side of the triangle is called the 'adjacent'.

For any right-angle triangle, the number obtained by dividing the length of the opposite over the length of the hypotenuse is constant for any value of the angle of interest and is called the sine of that angle. This number can be obtained by keying a number on a calculator and then pressing the 'sin' key. Similarly, the length of the adjacent side divided by that of the hypotenuse is also a constant for any angle and is called the cosine (cos). The opposite divided by the adjacent is called the tangent (tan).

MEASURING HEIGHTS

To arrive at the height of a structure, in this case a chimney, a surveyor uses a theodolite to measure the angle from the top of the structure (T) to the horizontal, and also the angle between the bottom of the structure (F) and the horizontal. If the structure is vertical the angles where the horizontal meets it are right angles, and he can then apply trigonometry. By measuring the distance from the bottom of the structure to the sight point (S) he can apply the formula sin ø =HF/SF to work out the length HF and the distance SH. The latter figure also enables him to calculate the length HT, and by adding that to FH he gets the total height.

The value of this is that angles can readily be measured using devices such as protractors or theodolites, and once an angle and one side of a right-angle triangle is known the other sides can easily be calculated using the sines, cosines or tangents. The practical uses of trigonometry, include land surveying, which is made much easier by it.

Conic sections

A cone has a circular base and a circular cross section reducing steadily to a point

Throughout the history of science there have been numerous instances of the same discovery being made almost simultaneously by two or more independent scientists. This is often no more than a reflection of the fact that the foremost workers in a particular discipline all tend to be at the 'cutting edge' of knowledge. In fact, the idea of trying to solve problems by considering quantities as consisting of many very small parts had occurred to the ancient Greek mathematicians, especially to Archimedes, who attempted to find the area of a circle by drawing within and around it a series of polygons of increasing numbers of equal sides ('squaring the circle').

The French mathematician Pierre de Fermat (⇨ main text) was also interested in the method of infinitesimal quantities. He developed a method of finding the maxima and minima of tangents to curves and, by a summation process, found formulae for the areas bounded by these curves. Some authorities hold that he was the real inventor of the differential calculus.

The historic controversy, however, concerns the relative claims of Isaac Newton (1642–1727) and Gottfried Wilhelm von Leibnitz (1646–1716). Both men were mathematicians of the first rank; Newton was a scientist, Leibnitz a philosopher. As early as 1666 Newton was using the method of 'fluxions', as he called it, in his calculations when composing his great work *Principia* (⇨ p. 10). He did not, however, publish a work explicitly on the calculus until 1693.

In the meantime Leibnitz had been working out his system and he published it in 1684. Newton's supporters at once alleged that Leibnitz had got the idea from one of Newton's manuscripts which had been shown to him. Leibnitz retaliated by accusing Newton of stealing his ideas and a bitter and unseemly quarrel resulted that delayed development of the subject for almost a hundred years. To this day, the question of who was the true inventor remains unanswered.

(apex). If a second cone is placed vertically above the first with the apexes in contact, some interesting curves can be produced by imagining that the cones are cut by a flat plane at various angles. The conic sections were first worked out by the Greek geometer Apollonius of Perga (c. 247–205 BC), whose book on the subject remained the standard text until the 16th century.

A cut of a cone in a plane parallel to the base simply produces a perfect circle of any size below that of the base. If the plane is tilted and cuts right across one cone above the base, the curve produced is an *ellipse*. So, in this context the circle can be considered as a particular case of

the ellipse. A plane that cuts the cone parallel to one side and through the base produces a curve known as a *parabola*. This is an open curve, the sides of which continue to open out. Finally, the plane may cut both cones, producing a curve in two separate parts, each continuing to open out. This curve is called a *hyperbola*.

For eighteen hundred years the conic sections remained of abstract and aesthetic interest only. Then advances in knowledge by the German astronomer Johannes Kepler (1571–1630) proved that the orbit of the planets around the sun were elliptical with the sun at one focus. Soon afterwards, Newton showed that comets could move in parabolic or hyperbolic paths. It has since been realized that a thrown stone or a fired bullet describes a parabola. Parabolas also appear in the mirrors of reflecting telescopes (⇨ p. 14), and in radio telescopes, whose reflecting dishes or microwave antennae must also be parabolic. Scientists, especially those concerned with the mathematics of electric current flow in conductors and filters, now commonly use a set of functions based on hyperbolas, analogous to the trigonometrical functions sin, cos and tan, and known as sinh, cosh and tanh.

SEE ALSO

● THE DEVELOPMENT OF SCIENCE 2: THE RENAISSANCE AND AFTER p. 10
● MATHEMATICS AND SCIENCE 1: THE LANGUAGE OF SCIENTIFIC THOUGHT p. 18

CONIC SECTION

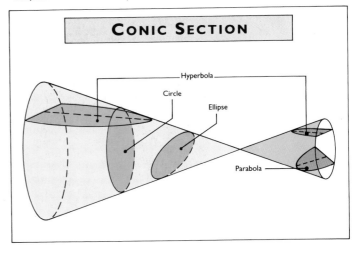

Hyperbola
Circle
Ellipse
Parabola

Mathematics and Science 3: The Theoretical Basis of Computing

Computer software has allowed scientists to leave much of the drudgery of mathematical calculations to the machine. However, in modern science the computer is far more than just a fast calculating machine; it is primarily a device for producing models of scientific hypotheses, which scientists can then test.

In the early days of computing, access to terminals was limited and scientists would have to queue for time on a machine. Instances have been frequently reported of individuals getting up in the middle of the night to take advantage of a free time slot. But today individual scientists have exclusive use of desk machines with many times the computing power of even the largest of the early mainframe machines.

The basic operations of computing are based on mathematical principles, specifically the pioneering work of the English mathematician George Boole.

Boolean algebra

Although the English mathematician George Boole (1815–64) was entirely self-taught and had no university degree, his brilliance was recognized early and he was appointed Professor of Mathematics at Queen's College, Cork, in 1849. There he published many papers on differential equations, algebra and logic. His most important work, however, as is now appreciated, was the development of a system of symbolic logic, which he described in the book *An Investigation of the Laws of Thought on*

George Boole, inventor of the binary algebra which is the basis on which digital computers operate. (ME)

Which are Founded the Mathematical Theories of Logic and Probabilities (normally known just as *An Investigation of the Laws of Thought*; 1854). For the first time, logic was considered mathematically and reduced to a simple algebra. The book showed how logical processes could be represented by unequivocal mathematical symbols which could be put into equations.

Boole's work also aroused new interest in the possibilities of formal logic, which had become a somewhat moribund discipline. Even more importantly, it paved the way for symbolic logic to be used by such men as the German mathematician Gottlob Frege (1848–1925), and the English mathematicians and philosophers Alfred North Whitehead (1861–1947) and Bertrand Russell (1872–1970), in such a way as to put mathematics on a strictly logical basis.

As a simple subset of the more general algebra that Boole developed he envisaged a two-value (binary) algebra using only 1s and 0s. 1 can be taken to represent 'true' and 0 to represent 'false'. This idea has since become of enormous importance as the basis of the operation of digital computers (⇔ pp. 102, 104 and 216). Boolean logic, in which all values are reduced to 'true' or 'false', fits well with the binary system in computers in which information is expressed solely in 1s and zeros. The laws of Boolean algebra are easily implemented by simple electronic computer 'gates' which give 'true' or 'false' outputs (⇔ p. 104). These gates – called AND, OR, XOR, NOT and NAND according to how the output relates to the input – arranged in various ways can perform any logical operation. Countless millions of them are in constant use all over the world, carrying out Boolean algebra at speeds of millions of operations per second.

Computer modelling

Computers can not only perform calculations extremely fast but they can also produce complex images which can readily be modified, and this combination makes them ideal tools for displaying, analysing and graphically plotting scientific data and for carrying out experiments. One of their great advantages is the ease with which they can represent scientific results in three-dimensional graphic form, thus providing an immediate and detailed representation of the real significance of long lists of figures. Another common use is for statistical and probability analysis, which is catered for by a wide variety of powerful statistical programs that enable the scientist to apply strict statistical criteria so as to assess the significance of his or her results.

A more powerful technique, however, for scientists is computer modelling. It has numerous applications and is used by scientists in all disciplines. A computer model need not necessarily be a recognizable representation of reality, although it often is. Moreover, computer modelling need not involve graphics but commonly involves purely numerical 'what if' modelling, although commercial computer-aided design (CAD) programs are commonly used to construct three-dimensional models. Whatever form the model takes, various analytical techniques can be used to study its properties. For example, a chemist, using a computer graphics program that represents atoms much as they are represented in physical models might try to construct a new molecule from various chemical subunits. As it would be informed of the laws of stereochemistry, the computer might refuse to allow certain groups to be put together in the ways he wants but would accept other combinations. This is what is meant by a 'what if' facility, and programs that have it are designed to allow arbitrary changes to be made and the result inspected. In this way, once the software is written, experiments can be performed in much less time than was previously possible.

The mathematical basis of most models of natural phenomena is the differential

Computer-aided design being used by a scientist at General Motors to simulate aerodynamics on a three-dimensional model of a new car. Computer modelling has widespread uses in commercial design. (SPL)

HOW MANY APPLES?

By any method of counting there are twenty-one apples here. In our normal number system, which works to a base of ten, this is shown as 21 – two 10s and one unit. With a numbering system to the base 9 the same number is shown as 23 – two 9s and three units. With a base of 4 it is 111 – one 16, one 4 and one unit. With a base of 2 it is 10101 – one 16, no 8s, one 4, no 2s and one unit. And with a base of 15 it is 16 – one 15 and six units.

equation (⇨ p. 20), which relates quantities and their rate of change. Chemical reactions, for instance, occur at a rate proportional to the concentrations of the reactants, and that relationship can be expressed as a differential equation. The solution of the equation would show the concentration of each reactant as a function of time. To solve large numbers of such equations in a short space of time is child's play for a computer, but would otherwise be so time-consuming as to be impracticable.

Fourier analysis

The French mathematician Jean Baptiste Fourier (1768–1830) was a scientific adviser to Napoleon's army during its invasion of Egypt, and was subsequently appointed prefect of the department of Isère by the grateful Emperor.

Fourier made several important contributions to mathematics and physics and is especially remembered for his mathematical treatment of the diffusion of heat. As a part of this work he devised a method of analysing the waveform of any periodic (repetitive) phenomenon, such as electromagnetic radiation, musical sound, planetary orbits and alternating current. Numbers of both natural and artificial phenomena occur in repetitive cycles and such periodic functions are often of great interest to scientists. A function is any relationship between two factors when the first depends on, or varies with, the second. Thus, the height of a growing boy is a function of time, and the thinness of the atmosphere is a function of altitude. The position of the bob of a swinging pendulum is also a function of time, and if the position is plotted on a graph against time, the graph will take a particular shape known as a sine wave (⇨ p. 104). The purpose of *Fourier analysis* (sometimes called harmonic analysis), first developed by Fourier in 1807, is to represent any periodic function as being made up of a number of simpler functions superimposed on each other. These simpler functions are known as harmonics of the fundamental frequency (number of cycles per second) of the wave, and always occur at a frequency which is a whole-number multiple of the fundamental frequency. The individual components in the series are, in fact, pure sine waves. Fourier had discovered the remarkable fact that any periodic waveform, however complicated, could be analysed into simple individual sine waves of different frequency and magnitude.

The original methods of Fourier analysis were laborious and time-consuming and various mechanical and electrical devices were developed for wave analysis. Today Fourier analysis is done almost exclusively by computers.

FOURIER ANALYSIS

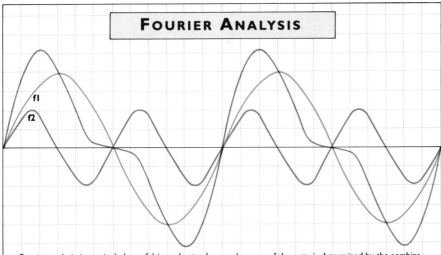

Fourier analysis is particularly useful in understanding sound. Very few sounds are pure, but most consist of several tones working in harmony. This explains the tone colour of sound, why a note on one musical instrument has a different sound from the same note played on a different instrument. Each component tone itself takes the form of a regular wave (a sine wave). When plotted on a graph the wave of the note is determined by the combination of these component waves. At a point where one of these (f1) is two squares above any designated line and the other (f2) is one square above it, the resultant wave will be three notes above the line. If f1 is two above and f2 one below the line, the wave will be one above, and if f1 is three below and f2 one below the wave will be four below.

CHAOS THEORY

Until comparatively recently, nearly all scientists have assumed that dynamic (changing) phenomena could be divided into two classes – those that are susceptible to orderly description and those that are not. Orderly phenomena could be described by the calculus; the others, such as the movement of a leaf in the wind, the changing pattern of clouds, turbulence in streams or in the rising smoke from a cigarette, the patterns of traffic jams or disease epidemics, or the patterns of the brain waves on the electroencephalogram, were so inherently disordered and chaotic that there was no point in trying to find laws to describe them.

In 1903 an interesting observation was made by the French mathematician Jules Henri Poincaré (1854–1912). Poincaré recognized that very tiny differences or inaccuracies in initial conditions can often be multiplied so as to lead to huge differences in the outcome. His work was largely forgotten, however, until the American meteorologist and mathematician Edward N. Lorenz began to use an early computer to try to produce a mathematical model of how the atmosphere behaves. While doing so, Lorenz accidentally came across a mathematical system in which small changes in the initial conditions led to very large differences in the outcome. Unfortunately for his purposes Lorenz found that this phenomenon made long-range weather prediction almost impossible. But this work was noted by scientists in other fields and led to the development of a new branch of mathematics – chaos theory. The best-known analogy of the theory is the 'butterfly effect': the idea that the air perturbation caused by the movement of a butterfly wing in China can cause a storm a month later in New York.

By the 1970s some scientists, mathematicians and others were beginning to investigate the possible principle underlying disorder and instability. Electronic engineers were hoping to account for the sometimes chaotic behaviour of oscillators; chemists were investigating unexpected fluctuations in chemical reactions; physiologists were asking themselves about the significance of patterns of chaos in the action of the heart that could lead to sudden cardiac arrest; ecologists were examining the seemingly random way in which wild-life populations changed; and economists were wondering whether stock-market price fluctuations might be predictable.

The first signs of an underlying pattern in chaos was found by the American physicist Mitchell Feigenbaum. In 1976 he noticed that when an ordered system starts to break down into chaos, it often does so in accordance with a consistent pattern in which the rate of occurrence of some event suddenly doubles over and over again. This is reminiscent of what happens in fractal geometry, in which any part of a figure is a reduced copy of a larger part. Feigenbaum also discovered that at a certain constant number of doublings, the structure cannot be distinguished from the previous level. This numerical constant, called Feigenbaum's number, can be applied to a wide range of chaotic systems, and seemed to suggest that there was, after all, some order underlying chaos.

Fractal geometry in fir trees. The overall structure of a fir tree is repeated in each branch, and then again in each group of needles. Chaos theory has identified the same pattern in apparently chaotic phenomena, where any part of a figure is a smaller copy of a larger part. (Images)

Scientists are divided on the question of whether chaos theory can ever adequately describe seemingly disordered dynamic systems in nature and whether it really is, as some claim, a new mathematical tool as important as calculus and a discipline that can be ranged with relativity and quantum mechanics.

THE
NEWTONIAN
UNIVERSE
AND
BEYOND

Mechanics

Mechanics – probably the oldest of the physical sciences – is the branch of physics concerned with the action of forces on things.

SEE ALSO

● FORCE AND MOTION p. 28
● CIRCULAR MOTION AND
  GRAVITATION p. 30
● WHAT ARE WAVES? pp. 64–7

The commonest effect of a force is to make something move. The branch of mechanics concerned with forces that move things is called *dynamics*. But no force ever acts entirely on its own, so forces are often balanced and the system concerned may be in a state of equilibrium. The branch of mechanics that deals with balanced forces is called *statics*.

Although mechanics is a pure science, it is very widely applied in the real world, especially in the practical world of engineering. This is, however, by no means the limit of its applications. Classical mechanics, as evolved through the ages by countless scientific thinkers, culminating in the unifying genius of Isaac Newton (⇨ p. 10), underlies a wide range of science and technology, from atomic physics to modern cosmology. Although superseded by the more general theories of quantum mechanics and relativity (⇨ pp. 38–41), classical mechanics continues to reign supreme, for almost all practical purposes outside the limits of the extremely fast and the extremely small. However atoms and subatomic particles may behave as individuals, when present en masse they behave statistically and obey the laws of classical mechanics.

Forces and motion

Forces are *vector* quantities – that is, they have both size and direction. As a rule, bodies are acted on by more than one force at a time, and these forces may help or hinder each other in causing movement. But if we want to find out their combined effect, it will not do simply to add them together as one might with a *scalar* (linear) quantity such as mass or time. The direction of action of different forces cannot be ignored in such calculations and various 'tricks' must be employed. One of these is known as the *parallelogram of forces*. If two adjacent sides of a parallelogram are drawn from a certain point, and the length and direction of the two sides are chosen so as to represent the size and direction of two forces acting on that point, the total effect of the two forces on the point will be equal to one force represented by the length and direction of the diagonal of the parallelogram (⇨ illustration). The process can also be done in reverse in order to resolve a single force into two forces acting in different directions.

Force applied to a pivot

When a force is applied to something pivoted or hinged at one end, the body will, if the force is large enough, turn about that hinge. So much is a matter of common observation. The turning effect of the force is called a *moment* or *torque* (⇨ illustration). If the force increases, the torque also increases. More importantly, if the same force is applied at a point on the body further away from the hinge, the torque will also increase. The general rule is that the moment (torque) of a force about a pivot is equal to the strength of the force multiplied by the perpendicular distance from the pivot to the point at which the force is applied. If the force is applied perpendicularly to the body, as in (a), there is no problem. If it is not, as in (b), the relevant distance is the perpendicular distance from the pivot to the line of action of the force.

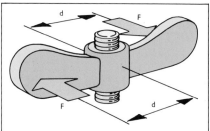

A couple. The total turning force acting on the wing nut is F x (d + d), that is, the force multiplied by the perpendicular distance between the two points of application of the force.

This important idea is, of course, the principle of the lever (⇨ illustration). Human influence over nature was greatly enlarged as soon as it was recognized that the power of the muscles could be multiplied by applying their force to the end of a long lever. The gain is not, however, obtained for nothing. The distance moved by the end of the lever to which the small force is applied is much greater than the distance moved near the pivot, where the magnified force (increased torque) is obtained. So the total energy taken out of the system is the same as the total energy put in. Archimedes was so enthusiastic about this principle that he is said to have announced: 'Give me a long enough lever and I will move the Earth.' When two equal and opposite forces act in parallel on a body, they cause it to rotate or to change its rotation. This is what happens when we unscrew the lid of a coffee jar, for instance. Such forces are called a *couple* (⇨ illustration), and the combined effect of the two – the moment of the couple – is equal to the strength of one force multiplied by the perpendicular distance between the two.

Pulleys and gears

A rope passing over a hanging, grooved pulley exerts a couple on it, but achieves no *mechanical advantage* (this is the number of times the force on the load exceeds the effort applied). It merely converts a downward pull into an upward

---

SCALAR AND VECTOR QUANTITIES

Scalar quantities a + b = c

Identical linear scales

Vector quantities a + b = c

Parallelogram of forces

Torque (right). Torque or moment of a force = force x perpendicular distance = *Fd*.

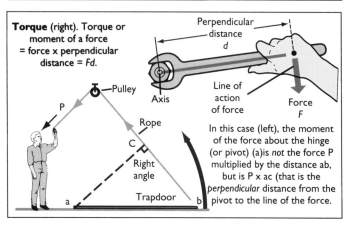

Perpendicular distance *d*

Line of action of force

Force *F*

In this case (left), the moment of the force about the hinge (or pivot) (a) is *not* the force P multiplied by the distance ab, but is P x ac (that is the *perpendicular* distance from the pivot to the line of the force).

FIRST, SECOND AND THIRD-ORDER LEVERS

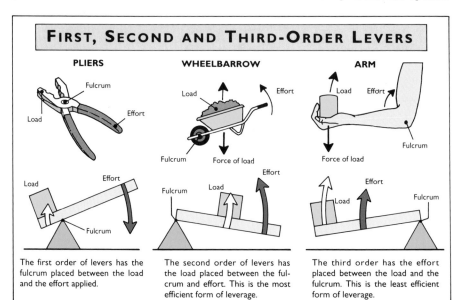

PLIERS

Fulcrum

Load

Load   Effort

WHEELBARROW

Load   Effort

Fulcrum   Force of load

ARM

Load   Effort

Fulcrum

Force of load

Load   Effort

Fulcrum

Fulcrum   Load   Effort

Load   Effort

Load   Fulcrum

The first order of levers has the fulcrum placed between the load and the effort applied.

The second order of levers has the load placed between the fulcrum and effort. This is the most efficient form of leverage.

The third order has the effort placed between the load and the fulcrum. This is the least efficient form of leverage.

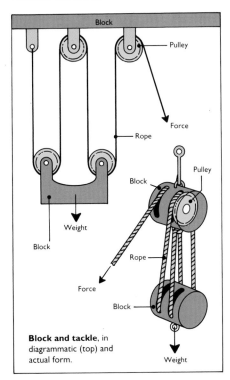

Block and tackle, in diagrammatic (top) and actual form.

pull. But if a second pulley is added alongside the first and a third pulley (plus subsequent ones if needed) is then added below (⇨ illustration) we have a block-and-tackle arrangement that can greatly magnify a force. If the rope passes up and down twice between the upper and lowest pulleys, the mechanical advantage is four to one, and the lifting force exerted by the lower pulley (neglecting frictional losses) will be four times the pulling force applied to the free end of the rope. The length of rope pulled will, however, be four times that of the distance risen by the load, so the input and output energy will be the same.

Flat pulleys driven by flat belts were once widely used to transmit power to factory machinery. If a large pulley drives a small pulley, the smaller one will turn faster than the larger but the torque on the smaller pulley will be decreased in the ratio of their diameters. If, on the other hand, a small pulley drives a large pulley, the speed of rotation of the latter will be less but its torque greater than that of the small pulley. The energy within a system is, as always, conserved – that is, input and output are equal. Exactly the same principle applies to gears. Torque and speed are reciprocally altered in the ratio of the number of teeth in the two gears. A gear wheel with 50 teeth meshed with a gear wheel with 200 will turn four times as fast as its fellow, but will exert only one quarter of the torque.

Forces acting on a pendulum

A simple pendulum might consist of a bob (weight) suspended by a light, flexible string from a fixed point. If the bob is pulled a little to one side and then released, it swings to and fro in the arc of a circle, describing what is called *simple harmonic motion*. When the bob is

SIMPLE HARMONIC MOTION

The graph shows two possible paths for the same pendulum. The height of the curve depends on the extent of the swing of the pendulum. The time period (frequency) depends on the length of the string from which the bob swings and is not affected by the weight of the bob.

released, the force causing it to move towards the mid position is the pull of gravity, which accelerates it down to its lowest position. This force, however, is not the whole of the gravitational pull on the bob, but only that part not balanced by the upward pull of the string. As the bob descends, the unbalanced pull of gravity decreases, and, when the bob reaches the lowest position, gravitational force is totally balanced by the string tension. It is now moving at maximal speed and continues under the influence of inertia (⇨ p. 28). As it rises, it now becomes increasingly pulled back by the mounting unbalanced gravitational force until it is finally stopped. The process then repeats. It can be shown mathematically that the strength of the restoring force (force returning a body to its former position) is proportional to the amount of the displacement in accordance with exactly the same law that governs deformation and recoil, by force, of elastic solids (⇨ below). The time taken for the pendulum to complete one swing is entirely independent of the mass of the bob, and is determined only by the length of the string and the local gravitational field strength.

Deforming forces and Hooke's Law

A force may be applied to an elastic material, such as steel, in such a way as to stretch or compress it without causing a permanent dimensional change (that is, a change in length). Such a force is said to operate within the elastic limits of the material (⇨ illustration). In this context, the scientific terms strain and stress have particular meanings.

Strain is the state of deformation of a material acted on by a force or forces, while stress is the force per unit area acting on the material and tending to cause it to change shape.

Robert Hooke showed that for an elastic material the amount of deformation (the strain) is proportional to the applied distorting force (the stress). The greater the deformation, the greater is the restoring force. This law obviously applies only within strict limits, and the value of the stress at which a material ceases to obey Hooke's law is known as the *limit of proportionality*. We now know that material deformation under applied force can be explained at an atomic level. Elastic strain is due to an actual stretching of the bonds between atoms. The increased separation between any two atoms is, of course, very small indeed, but because so many atoms are involved, the total effect may be considerable. But when the distorting force is removed, the atoms return to their former distance of separation.

Hooke's law can be expressed more succinctly: strain is proportional to stress. Stress divided by strain is a constant for any particular elastic material, and is a measure of its elastic stiffness. This ratio, stress:strain, is called *Young's modulus of elasticity*, after another distinguished English scientist Thomas Young (1773–1829). It is of critical importance in designing structures such as bridges so as to ensure that the elastic limits will not be exceeded under any possible loads.

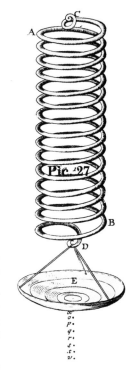

Illustration of a spring from Hooke's studies of the elasticity of materials. From his *De potentia restitutiva* (1678). (AR)

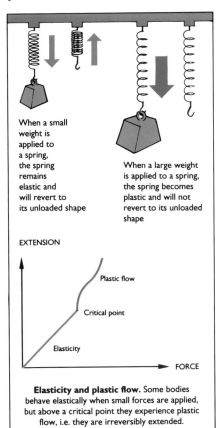

When a small weight is applied to a spring, the spring remains elastic and will revert to its unloaded shape

When a large weight is applied to a spring, the spring becomes plastic and will not revert to its unloaded shape

EXTENSION

Plastic flow

Critical point

Elasticity

FORCE

Elasticity and plastic flow. Some bodies behave elastically when small forces are applied, but above a critical point they experience plastic flow, i.e. they are irreversibly extended.

Force and Motion

Bodily and other movement, speed, acceleration and deceleration are all the products of a variety of forces.

Most of us become aware of some of the fundamental laws of nature only in unusual physical circumstances – such as diving or falling from a height, or enjoying the thrills of the fairground. While much of modern technology is devoted to protecting us from the effects of these laws, it has also made it possible for us to feel the extreme effects of some of them. At the same time that a parachute may be protecting one person from the effects of gravity, a highly advanced aircraft may be exposing another to high *G-forces* (forces experienced on rapid acceleration or deceleration).

Speed and velocity

A body moving in a straight line or along a curve changes its distance with time. The rate of this change is the *speed* of the body, and may be expressed in a unit such as miles per hour or metres per second. When a body moves in a certain

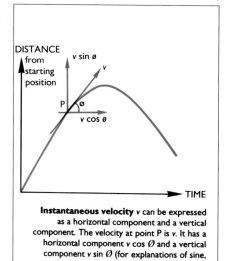

Instantaneous velocity v can be expressed as a horizontal component and a vertical component. The velocity at point P is v. It has a horizontal component v cos Ø and a vertical component v sin Ø (for explanations of sine, cosine and Ø ⇨ pp. 20–1).

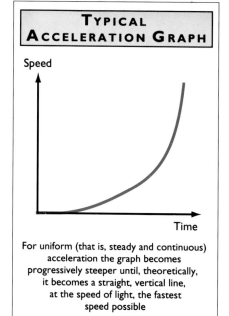

TYPICAL ACCELERATION GRAPH

For uniform (that is, steady and continuous) acceleration the graph becomes progressively steeper until, theoretically, it becomes a straight, vertical line, at the speed of light, the fastest speed possible

direction, stated or implied, it is said to have a *velocity*. A body moving in a circle, for instance, is said to have an angular velocity, which may be expressed in revolutions per second, for instance. Velocities are vector quantities (⇨ p. 26) and cannot be added together arithmetically. They can be calculated as an average, or, for a body in flight, for example, instantaneous velocities can be measured (⇨ illustration). Speed is a scalar quantity and various speeds can be added together or subtracted. Speeds must be expressed relative to something deemed to be static – usually the surface of the Earth. We know that the Earth is moving through space, but because everything on its surface is also moving at the same speed, it can, for most practical purposes, be considered to be still. So long as the speeds we are concerned with are below about 90 per cent of that of light, this system works very well, and speeds can be accurately calculated and added together using simple arithmetic.

Acceleration

Speeds need not be uniform. When they change they do so at a particular rate. This rate is called *acceleration*, whether it increases or decreases (⇨ illustration). A decrease in speed (negative acceleration) is sometimes called *deceleration*. Acceleration is measured in units such as feet, or metres, per second per second, indicating the amount that the speed changes in one second.

As long as we are shielded from such indications of movement as air pressure on the skin or visible clues, we are unaware of uniform motion in a straight line. When we travel at uniform velocity in a train on perfectly smooth rails with the blinds drawn, for example, there is nothing to tell us that we are moving at all. Sometimes the movement of an adjacent train causes the familiar illusion of movement when, in fact, we are stationary relative to the ground.

We are, however, often very much aware of acceleration or of movement in a

curve – which amounts to the same thing (⇨ p. 30).

When a car we are travelling in accelerates, for example, we seem to be pressed back in our seats. Conversely, when the brakes are suddenly applied, we seem to be thrown forwards. These are, in fact, illusions. In the first case it is the seat that is pressed forward against us because the whole car is increasing its speed. In the second, the speed of the car is being suddenly retarded but our bodies continue to move forward at the previous speed, and will continue to do so unless restrained by seat belts. This tendency for a moving body – any moving body – to continue to move at the same speed unless acted on by a retarding or accelerating force is one of the most important ideas in all nature and is encapsulated in the first of Newton's laws of motion.

Newton's laws of motion

Three remarkable generalizations, first clearly expressed in Newton's *Principia mathematica* (1687; ⇨ box), provided a new and reliable basis for the understanding of the physical universe.

Newton's first law: a stationary body remains at rest unless some external force makes it move; a moving body continues at uniform motion and at uniform speed in a straight line unless acted on by an external force.

The essence of this deceptively simple statement is that a moving body will go on moving for ever in a straight line and at a constant speed unless something happens to change the situation. That something can be only an external force. In the real world it is very hard to arrange for such external forces to be entirely absent. Objects are retarded by forces such as friction, air resistance, gravity and magnetic fields. A great deal of technology has been devoted, however,

Parachutists in free fall hurtle towards the ground, acted upon only by the forces of gravity and air resistance. (Images)

to trying to remove or minimize such external forces.

In space it is easier to see Newton's first law in action. There is no appreciable air resistance; friction is negligible; and almost the only force acting on moving bodies, such as the planets or artificial satellites, is the gravitational pull of the Sun and the other planets. It is a matter of common observation that a large force has a greater effect on a particular body than a small force. The snooker ball will roll gently forward after a caressing tap of the cue, and will move like a bullet after a powerful stroke. It is also common experience that the more massive the body we are trying to move, the less is the effect on it of a given force. When a body at rest or in uniform motion is acted on by an unbalanced force it suffers a change of speed – an acceleration. These concepts are generalized in Newton's second law.

Newton's second law: the acceleration caused by a force acting on a body is directly proportional to the size of the force and inversely proportional to the mass of the body.

Both of these factors must be taken into account when determining the effect of a new force. *Inertia* – the tendency for the body's movement not to be changed – is obviously connected with its mass. You can move a half-inch steel ball with one finger; a one-foot diameter cannonball is harder to move.

It is impossible to walk on a perfectly smooth and frictionless surface (⇨ p. 32). The reason for this is that when we walk on normal ground we are, in fact, being pushed along by it. This is because when we push with one foot against the ground, the ground pushes back against the foot with an equal and opposite force. The inertia of the Earth is very large, so its backward movement is negligible. The inertia of the body is, however, much less, so it moves forward. Newton expressed this idea of action and reaction in his third law.

ISAAC NEWTON

The English mathematician and scientist Isaac Newton (1642–1727) was born in the year that Galileo died (⇨ p. 10). He was a solitary and unhappy schoolboy, who seemed more interested in mechanical matters than in his books, and was an undistinguished undergraduate at Cambridge University, from which he took his degree in 1665. The same year, to avoid the plague, he retired to his mother's farm in Lincolnshire. Inspired by recent works by Descartes, Robert Boyle (⇨ p. 50) and Galileo, his mind was now alive with mathematical and scientific speculation.

Aristotle had taught, and most people then believed, that the physical laws for 'heavenly bodies' were different from those on Earth. Pondering on the nature of gravity, Newton was moved to question this dogma when it occurred to him that the same force that attracted a falling apple to the Earth might also attract the Moon and keep it in orbit. Unable, at the time, to prove this quantitatively, he abandoned the idea, but did succeed in calculating that the planets moved in elliptical rather than circular orbits – then an entirely new notion. At about the same time he began to experiment with light, and proved conclusively that white light was a combination of all the spectral colours. In the meantime he developed the mathematical technique now known as the differential calculus (⇨ p. 20), and designed and built an efficient reflecting telescope (⇨ p. 14).

His fame spread, and, at the age of 27, he became Lucasian Professor of Mathematics at Cambridge University (the post to which the English theoretical physicist Stephen Hawking was appointed in 1979). In 1672 Newton became a Fellow of the Royal Society, and, in 1687, published his great work *Philosophiae naturalis principia mathematica* ('Mathematical Principles of Natural Philosophy') – generally considered to be the greatest scientific publication of all time.

The work:

● **Contained the three laws of motion and explained their implications.**

● **Confirmed the principles of planetary movement and explained their irregularities.**

Title page of Newton's *Philosophiae naturalis principia mathematica* (1687). (AR)

● **Distinguished *mass* (a measure of a body's inertia) from *weight* (the force exerted on a body by gravity).**

● **Quantified acceleration.**

● **Showed how gravitation acted and could be calculated.**

● **Demonstrated that gravitation was universal.**

A magnificent piece of unifying scientific generalization, it was one of the key elements that ushered in the Age of Reason.

Newton's third law: when a body exerts a force on another body, the second body exerts an equal force on the first, in the opposite direction. To every action there is an equal and opposite reaction.

The force of the reaction occurs simultaneously with, and is identical in strength to, the action, and varies exactly with it. The implications of this law are wide: it explains the movement of all kinds of vehicles, the bouncing of balls, the throwing of projectiles, and the operation of rockets in space.

People sometimes wonder why two such opposite and equal forces do not simply cancel each other. The reason is that the two forces are not applied to the same body. One is applied to the body, and the equal and opposite force is applied to the thing that is pushing it.

Test pilot in an F-16 fighter plane. Such aircraft are capable of very fast acceleration and deceleration, exposing their pilots to high G-forces (one G is the pull of gravity under ordinary circumstances). Special clothing is available to help avoid the effects of an excessive G-force, which can make the blood rush from the brain, so causing unconsciousness. (IB)

Circular Motion and Gravitation

Movement in a circle is a commonplace of everyday life. Modern society depends on the wheel for all sorts of purposes in addition to transport. Circular movement, or movement in paths that are almost circular, is also a feature of many of the phenomena – ranging from the atomic to the astronomical – studied by scientists.

From the time people first tied strips of hide to stones and whirled them around their heads, they have been familiar with some of the characteristics of movement in a circle. In particular, hunters and warriors were aware that when they let go of such a thong the stone would fly off in what appeared to be a straight line. This useful observation was early followed by the development of the sling as a weapon.

Angular velocity

Movement in a circle is not, however, quite as obvious as it might first appear. A body travelling at uniform speed in a circle – such as a stone whirled on a string – does not have a constant velocity ($\Leftrightarrow$ p. 28). By definition a constant velocity is fixed both in speed and in direction. The whirling stone is said to

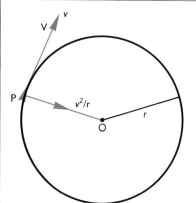

Angular velocity or centripetal acceleration. At point P the body is moving with instantaneous velocity v. The centripetal acceleration along PO is v^2/r^2 (where r is the radius of the circle), and this force prevents the body from moving in a straight line along PV.

have an *angular velocity* as it is constantly changing direction. By Newton's first law of motion, a moving body continues in a straight line unless acted on by an external force. This is what is happening to the stone. If at any time one were to let go of the string, the force that is pulling the stone in from its straight-line path – the pull of the string – would be removed, and the stone would try to continue on its straight path.

Any change of velocity is an acceleration, even if the speed remains constant ($\Leftrightarrow$ p. 28). This, too, is a matter of common experience. If we are travelling in a straight line in a closed car at constant speed on a smooth road, we are hardly aware of any motion. But as soon as the car takes a sharp turn at speed, we are at once aware of the tendency for our bodies to be thrown in the direction away from that of the turn. Velocity is speed in a given direction, so a turn at speed is, therefore, a change of velocity. The reason for the experience is, of course, the principle stated in Newton's first law of motion.

Centripetal and centrifugal forces

Any acceleration (change of velocity) of a body necessarily implies that a force has been, or is being, applied to it. In the case of the whirling stone, the force that causes it to deviate continuously from a straight line is clearly pulling inwards towards the hand at the centre of the circle. Such a force is called a *centripetal force*, from the Latin verb *petere*, meaning 'to seek'. As a rule, we are much less aware of centripetal force than of its equal and opposite (and much more obvious) force, the *centrifugal force* (from the Latin *fugere*, 'to flee'). It is only when the restraining centripetal force is removed – as, for instance, if the string holding the whirling stone were to break – that we become aware of its effect. Physicists are not very happy about the idea of a centrifugal force and prefer to think of it

as an imaginary force envisaged by an observer. They say that a body relieved of centripetal force simply obeys Newton's first law and tries to move off in a straight line.

Newton's second law of motion ($\Leftrightarrow$ p. 28) tells us that the acceleration caused to a body by a force is proportional to the force and inversely proportional to the mass of the body – that is, the greater the mass, the smaller the effect of a given force. So the heavier the stone and the faster it is rotated, the greater will be the centripetal force needed to prevent it from flying off. If the stone is whirled fast enough, the string will break, and the stone, deprived of its centripetal force, will fly off. Similarly, if a rocket is driven round the Earth fast enough, it, too, will fly off, defying gravity and making for outer space. The speed needed to get from the surface of the Earth to a point far outside the effective pull of the Earth's gravitation is known as the *escape velocity*.

When a car goes round a bend at high speed, the centripetal force that prevents it from skidding off the road is provided almost entirely by the friction ($\Leftrightarrow$ p. 32) of the tyres with the surface of the road. This friction is equivalent in effect to the string holding the whirling stone. It is therefore apparent how important to safety is the state of the road surface and the grip of the tyres. If, however, the road is banked so that the vehicle is tilted, the force tending to swing the car off the road can be neutralized. The degree of banking will, however, be appropriate only for one particular speed.

Centripetal force has many applications and provides a number of surprising effects. A bucket of water can be swung

The space shuttle *Columbia* lifting off. It will continue to accelerate until it reaches its *orbital velocity*, at which the force of the Earth's gravitational pull is exactly balanced, so that the shuttle stays in orbit. The minimum acceleration needed to take a spacecraft out of its orbit and further into space is called its *escape velocity*. (Spectrum)

A figure skater will spin much faster if she pulls her arms in towards her body than if she holds them stretched out. This is because the angular momentum (mass x speed x radius of motion) of any system must always amount to the same. The skater's mass obviously remains constant, so, if the radius of her motion decreases, her speed must increase. (Allsport) in a vertical plane; a light aircraft with an open cockpit can 'loop-the-loop' without the pilot falling out, and various fairground novelties, such as the rotor drum, rely on the centripetal force for their entertainment value.

Moment of inertia

When a skater spins on the spot with arms extended and then brings the arms close to the body, the speed of the spin increases dramatically. This demonstrates how the angular velocity of a rotating system depends on the way the mass is distributed. Newton's second law of motion describes how the reluctance of an object to change its velocity (that is, its inertia) depends on its mass. The reluctance of a rotating body to change its angular velocity is called its *moment of inertia*. And the harder it is to change the angular velocity, the greater is its moment of inertia. As might be expected from the analogy of the lever (⇨ p. 26), the further out the mass is placed, the greater is this quantity. Common experience shows that a flywheel with most of its mass in the rim is harder to get moving and harder to stop than a wheel with its mass near the centre.

Newton's concept of gravity

When Newton observed the fall of an apple and recognized that it was attracted by the Earth, he at once began to consider whether the Moon was kept in its orbit around the Earth by the same force – the force of gravitation. The analogy between the Earth–Moon situation and that of the stone whirled round on a string is, in fact, close. In the case of the Moon, as Newton proceeded to demonstrate, gravity is the centripetal force that prevents it from flying off into space at a tangent.

The calculation of the Moon's centripetal acceleration is not particularly difficult as we know the radius of the Moon's orbit and the length of time it takes to complete one orbit – about a month. We also know, from measurements of falling bodies, the acceleration due to gravity at the Earth's surface. If we assume that the gravitational pull falls off uniformly with distance from the Earth's surface, the figure we get for the acceleration at the Moon is far too large to make sense. But if we assume that the force of gravity falls off in proportion to the square of the distance, that is, becomes a quarter for twice the distance, a ninth for three times the distance, a hundredth for ten times the distance, and so on, the answer we get is just right and corresponds to results from our previous calculation.

In his *Principia mathematica* (⇨ p. 28) Newton proceeded to apply the same ideas to the other planets in our solar system, and to show how the planets are kept in orbit around the Sun by the centripetal force of gravitation between them and the Sun. The planets themselves exert a gravitational pull on each other, but, except for the large Jupiter

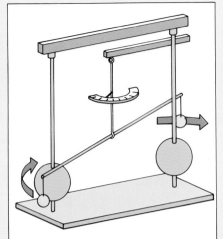
and Saturn, this is small compared with the Sun's attraction. The disturbances in their orbits by mutual attraction are called *perturbations* and are easily calculated.

Generalizing further, Newton made an important statement that has come to be known as the *law of universal gravitation*. It can be stated thus: every particle of matter in the universe attracts every other particle with a force that is directly proportional to the masses multiplied together, and inversely proportional to the square of the distance that separates them.

This is a purely descriptive statement. Newton had nothing to say about the causes of gravitation, but merely stated that a mutual force, called gravitation, existed. Newton found that he also had a problem when considering the Earth's

gravitational field. Since the Earth was so large, from what point did one assume gravitation to act? This difficulty was finally overcome when he showed that the attraction exerted at the surface of a large body was the same as if the whole mass of the body were concentrated at its centre. This greatly simplified the calculations. The force of gravitation, F, between two bodies m1 and m2, separated by a distance d, is given by the equation:

$$F = G \frac{(m1 \times m2)}{d^2}.$$

G is a factor known as the *universal gravitational constant* and is very small. Newton did not know the value of this constant, but it was later calculated by another English scientist, Henry Cavendish (⇨ box).

A fairground carousel. When the wheel spins around, the suspended seats swing outwards and upwards. As the speed increases, the tendency for the chairs to travel off in a straight line also increases. This is opposed by a corresponding increase in the centripetal force, which anchors them to the hub. The chairs are also acted upon by gravity, but, because gravity remains constant, the result of the two forces (tendency to travel in a straight line and the centripetal force) causes the chairs to rise, overcoming the gravitational effect. (TCL)

Friction

Friction is the force that opposes motion between two surfaces when one slides over the other, or, if the frictional force is great enough, tries to slide. The precise nature and cause of friction is not obvious, but it is so important in the practical world that a new science – *tribology* – has arisen to study its nature and consequences and its reduction by lubrication.

Without friction we would be unable to hold anything or to use tools or implements, to walk, to remain seated or lying still on any surface, even to talk or eat. All of these actions require friction so that surfaces brought together can remain, at least for a time, in firm contact. Walking, for instance, is possible only because when we push back against the ground with a foot, the ground exerts a forward-pushing force against the foot (⇨ p. 28). In the absence of friction, neither of these forces could be applied. A person placed on a perfectly horizontal and frictionless surface would be constantly moving about as a result of his or her breathing, in accordance with Newton's third law of motion.

The nature and cause of friction

Microscopic examination of surfaces, however apparently smooth, shows that they are, in fact, marked by bumps and hollows. Although different materials have inherently different surface characteristics, and can be polished to different degrees, even the most conscientious smoothing and polishing cannot reduce the height of these bumps to less than that of about 100 atoms. Because of the bumpiness of surfaces, contact between

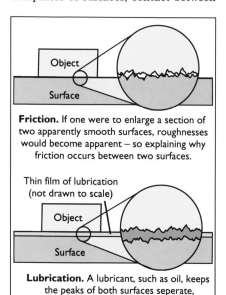

Friction. If one were to enlarge a section of two apparently smooth surfaces, roughnesses would become apparent – so explaining why friction occurs between two surfaces.

Lubrication. A lubricant, such as oil, keeps the peaks of both surfaces seperate, so reducing friction between them.

them is never close and occurs only between the peaks of the bumps. This means that the areas in actual contact may be far smaller than the apparent areas in contact. In the case of surfaces that conduct electricity, such as steel, estimates of the actual areas of contact can be obtained by measuring the differences in electrical conductivity or resistance between areas of solid metal and areas where metals are touching. These tests have shown that the actual contact area may be as little as 1/10,000th of the measured areas.

Because the real areas in contact are so small, the pressure on them is very high, even if the weight applied is not excessive. As a result, the bumps flatten and widen until the contact area is sufficient to support the weight concerned. Such intimate local contact leads to the formation of 'welded' joints, occurring as a result of strong adhesive forces forming between closely applied molecules. Before movement between the surfaces can occur, these 'cold welds' have to be broken.

Clearly, the total friction between two surfaces must depend on the real area in contact rather than the apparent area, and the real area depends on the vertically acting downwards weight applied. Increasing the apparent area of contact has little effect on the real area of contact so long as the vertically acting weight remains the same. So, in practice, the frictional force for any particular material is proportional to the downward force.

Laws of friction

When friction was first scientifically investigated, the true nature of what was going on between the surfaces was unknown and the laws of friction had to be worked out by empirical experiment. This was done by the French physicist Charles Augustinde Coulomb (1736–1806), and the results published in his book *The Theory of Simple Machines* (1779). Coulomb appreciated that sliding between surfaces could occur only if a horizontally acting (*tangential*) force was great enough to overcome the effect of friction. Weight acting vertically downwards and pressing the two surfaces together, while obviously important, could not itself cause movement. Vertically acting force is known as the *normal* force, because in mathematics the term 'normal' means a line perpendicular to a line or surface. So two forces had to be considered, the normal and the tangential.

Coulomb's studies showed, surprisingly, that the friction developed between two sliding surfaces increased and decreased as the downward (normal) pressure increased or decreased, but did not change as the area of the surfaces in contact changed. If he were sliding a brick along a table it was of no consequence, as far as the resistance to movement (as measured on a spring balance) was concerned, whether the brick was resting on its main surface, on its edge or on one end. But if another brick was placed on

LUBRICATION

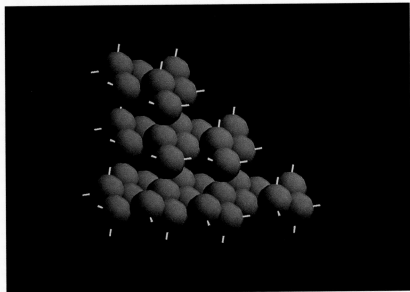

Chemical structure of graphite, an industrial lubricant, represented here in computer graphics. Graphite has a crystalline structure composed of parallel layers of hexagonally arranged carbon atoms (green spheres). Within layers, these carbon atoms are linked by strong covalent bonds. The layers themselves are linked together by weak intermolecular forces known as *van der Waals' forces* (yellow lines), which allow them to slide over one another. (SPL)

The negative results of friction are enormous economic losses and mechanical inefficiency. The use of lubricants to reduce friction and wear has, however, been understood from the earliest times. Even before the invention of the wheel, mud and reeds were used to lubricate the movement of dragged sledges. The wheel axles of the earliest vehicles were lubricated with animal fats, a practice that continued right up to the development of the petroleum oil industry in the 19th century. Since then, the ever greater refinement of lubricants has played a vital part in the development of mechanical engineering.

Effective lubrication can reduce friction to as little as a 200th of the dry level. The interposition of a thin film of lubricant between the surfaces in question can completely separate them and prevent the cold welding (⊳ main text) that causes most of the friction. In order to maintain this film under high loads, the lubricant must be of a certain viscosity. In some cases, liquid lubricants are unsuitable for this. In addition, liquid lubricants may be unable to withstand the high temperatures often involved, for instance, in industry. Both of these problems can be solved by the use of solid lubricants such as graphite and molybdenum disulphide. These are used for lubrication in conditions of high temperatures and/or for surfaces that cannot be readily accessed, making the renewal of a liquid lubricant difficult. They have a crystal lattice structure arranged in layers. Because the atomic bonds are strong inside the layers, but weak between them, the layers are able to slide about on one another. Thus the friction occurs between layers of a material with a very much lower coefficient of friction than that of the main bearing surfaces.

EDWARD GOODRICH ACHESON AND GRAPHITE LUBRICANTS

The American physicist Edward Goodrich Acheson (1856–1931) was a man of humble beginnings and little formal education. In 1880, however, he was able to obtain a position in the laboratories, in New Jersey, of the great inventor Thomas A. Edison. There he showed promise and was soon helping to develop the electric light bulb. Becoming interested in the possibility of producing artificial diamonds in an electric furnace, Acheson left Edison in 1884 and began his own experiments. After seven years of work he developed a method of using an electric carbon arc to heat a mixture of clay and coke in an iron bowl. This resulted in the production of some exceedingly hard, shiny, hexagonal crystals. Thinking that these were crystals of carbon and alumina, he called the new material carborundum. Although he was mistaken as to the nature of the crystals, which were actually silicon carbide, he had discovered a new and valuable abrasive that could be used to make grindstones and other tools of unprecedented durability. He then obtained a patent for this material and, to get cheap electric power to produce it, he moved to Niagara Falls, where he set up the Carborundum Company.

Later, while studying the new material, Acheson discovered that it vaporized at about 7,500°C (13,500°F). leaving behind graphitic carbon. Soon he was producing 'synthetic' graphite in quantity from coke. In 1906, he discovered how to make highly effective lubricants from colloidal graphite substances patented as 'Aquadag' and 'Oildag'. Acheson achieved 69 patents in all and founded several firms to exploit them.

MEASURING FRICTION

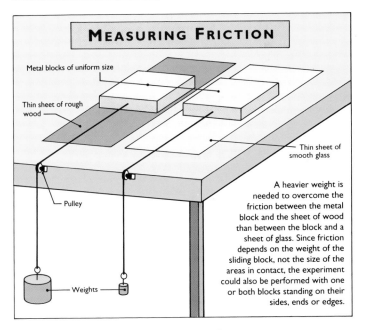

Metal blocks of uniform size

Thin sheet of rough wood

Thin sheet of smooth glass

Pulley

Weights

A heavier weight is needed to overcome the friction between the metal block and the sheet of wood than between the block and a sheet of glass. Since friction depends on the weight of the sliding block, not the size of the areas in contact, the experiment could also be performed with one or both blocks standing on their sides, ends or edges.

top of the first the friction was doubled. The friction was also unchanged whether the movement was slow or rapid. Coulomb put these findings in the terms of a statement that has since been known as *Coulomb's law*.

It states: when two surfaces are in contact and slide relative to one another, the frictional force is proportional to the normal force and is independent of the areas in contact and the speed of sliding.

Coulomb also discovered that the horizontal force needed to start the movement was greater, just before slippage began, than was necessary to maintain sliding after it had started. He had no idea as to why this should be, but today, with the benefit of knowledge of the microscopic structure of surfaces, we can see that all of Coulomb's findings readily make sense.

Comparing friction

If we try to push a heavy block of any particular material along a surface made of the same material we must apply a horizontal force to the block. If the force we apply is insufficient to cause movement it must be being opposed by an equal and opposite force – friction. If we increase the force, measuring it constantly, we eventually reach a point at which the block will move. The force needed to do this is a fixed proportion of the downward weight of the block. The ratio between these two forces – vertical and tangential – is very important. When different materials are tried it is found that, when sliding occurs, each material produces a characteristic ratio between the forces. This ratio – the tangential force divided by the normal force – is called the *coefficient of friction* and is given as a constant value for particular substances and for combinations of substances. For, instance, the coefficient of friction for dry steel on steel is given in some reference texts as 0.15; that is, the horizontal force needed to cause slipping of a block of steel on a steel surface is only about one sixth of the weight of the block. Because surfaces vary so much in smoothness, however, such figures are very approximate. Coulomb's figures for the coefficient of friction of various materials, which were unquestioned for nearly a hundred years, were found, when more rigorously determined by the Institute of Mechanical Engineers in 1879, to be 6–60 times too high.

Fluids

We are accustomed to thinking of fluids as liquids, but to the scientist, a fluid is anything that can flow. So the class of fluids includes gases, molten solids, fine suspensions such as mud, powdered solids, and even some materials normally considered solid, such as glass (a sheet of which will, over time, bulge towards the bottom).

SEE ALSO

- MECHANICS p. 26
- FORCE AND MOTION p. 28
- FRICTION p. 32
- AERODYNAMICS AND HYDRODYNAMICS p. 36
- GAS LAWS p. 50
- THE STRUCTURE OF SOLIDS p. 166

The basic properties of fluids, especially of fluids at rest, are, however, most easily understood by considering liquids. These vary considerably in the weight of a given volume. A pint of mercury, for instance, is very much heavier than a pint of milk. This difference in weight of equal volumes is the difference in their *density* or *specific gravity,* and it has an important bearing on how fluids behave. In particular, it affects the pressure a liquid exerts.

Floating object

Fluid

mg (mass x gravitational force)   Upthrust

Archimedes' principle. Total upward force is equal to the weight of fluid displaced.

Liquid pressure

The dramatic scene of a bursting dam reveals, all too clearly, the enormous pressures that can be exerted by large volumes of restrained water. Anything in contact with a liquid experiences pressure from it. For a body submerged in a liquid, this pressure increases as the body moves deeper and deeper because of the additional weight of liquid pressing on it from above. To compare pressures we must take into account the area over which the force or weight is applied. Pressure is defined as force per unit area, such as a square inch or a square centimetre. The force should be given in

comparable units, so we represent pressure in pounds per square inch or kilograms per square centimetre.

The pressure on a body immersed in a liquid will be affected not only by the depth but also by the density of the liquid. In effect, we are assessing the weight of a column of liquid of height equal to the depth under the surface of the object. This might be a column of cross section 1 cm². This pressure is exerted not only on the top of a submerged body, but all round, and the pressure on the underside will be greater than that on the top because the column length will be greater.

Liquids as levers

The principle of leverage (⇨ p. 26) can be applied using liquids because a liquid will transmit external pressure applied to it to all of its volume (⇨ illustration).

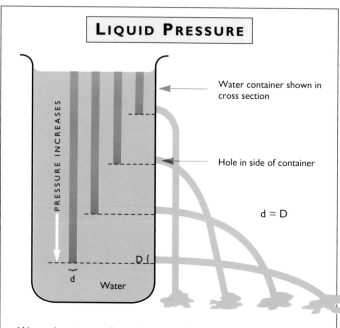

Large movement in narrow cylinder

Brake-operating cylinder

Brake pedal

Pipe containing fluid

Small movement in wide cylinder

Large movement with small force = small movement with large force

Hydraulic brakes: a simple hydraulic system that illustrates the ability of liquids to be used as levers.

This idea is widely used in hydraulic engineering, a discipline in which very high pressures can be conveniently conveyed to any location and applied in any direction by means of liquids. Such methods are used in tipper trucks, cranes, bulldozers, presses and many other applications. Specially reinforced, high-pressure hoses are used to transmit the liquid pressure, and their connections have to be particularly secure.

For practical purposes liquids may be considered to be incompressible (that is, there is no space between the constituent molecules) so there is no loss of efficiency when they are used as levers. In the hydraulic jack a relatively wide cylinder fitted with a *piston* (a sliding metal part of the same size as the cross section of the cylinder) is connected to a much narrower cylinder also fitted with a piston. The whole is then completely filled with a liquid such as oil. If the piston on the narrow side is pressed down, the other piston will rise, but the amount of movement will be different, as in the case of the simple lever. In this case it will depend on the ratio of the cross sections of the two cylinders. If the larger has a cross section ten times that of the smaller, its movement will be only one tenth of that of the other, but the pressure it exerts will be ten times that applied to the piston in the small cylinder.

Measuring pressure in a fluid

A liquid in a column, arranged in the form of a U-tube, can be used to measure pressure. Pressure in a uniform column

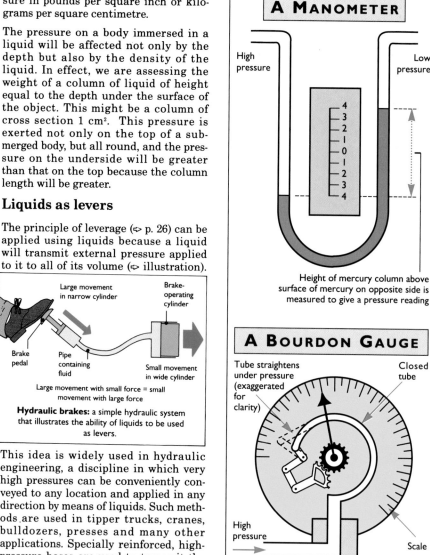

A MANOMETER

High pressure   Low pressure

4 3 2 1 0 1 2 3 4

Height of mercury column above surface of mercury on opposite side is measured to give a pressure reading

A BOURDON GAUGE

Tube straightens under pressure (exaggerated for clarity)

Closed tube

High pressure

Scale

is proportional to the height of the column. For higher pressures, a dense liquid, such as mercury, is used, and the pressure represented in millimetres of mercury (⇨ diagram). This type of pressure gauge is called a *manometer.* Very high pressures, as in the hydraulic parts of tipper trucks, cranes, bulldozers and industrial presses, would, however, simply blow the mercury out of the tube, so, to measure those, different methods are needed. A commonly used instrument is the Bourdon gauge, which consists of a curved tube of flexible metal, sealed at one end and connected to the source of pressure at the other. As the applied pressure rises the tube tends to straighten. This movement acts through a lever to turn a geared rack against a pinion and move a pointer around a calibrated scale (⇨ diagram).

Archimedes' principle

Named after the Greek mathematician who first stated it (⇨ box), Archimedes' principle is the basic law of buoyancy. Any body weighed with a spring balance and then, while still hanging from the

LIQUID PRESSURE

PRESSURE INCREASES

Water container shown in cross section

Hole in side of container

d = D

D

d   Water

Water shooting out from the lowest hole travels furthest because it is under the most pressure. That water squirts through the holes demonstrates the fact that liquid pressure acts in all directions.

A hot-air balloon is able to fly because the air inside it expands on heating, leaving it lighter than the surrounding atmosphere. The greater density of the atmosphere therefore exercises pressure on the balloon, creating an upthrust.
(Spectrum)

balance, immersed in a liquid, will show a reduced reading on the scale. The body appears to be lighter while in the liquid. The reason for this is that, as we have seen, pressure in a liquid increases with depth, so the pressure exerted by the liquid on the bottom of the body is greater than the pressure on the top. This causes an upthrust, which we recognize as buoyancy. Archimedes' experiments showed how to discover this upthrust, and led to his formulation of an important law:

When a body is completely or partially immersed in a fluid, it experiences an apparent loss of weight equal to the weight of the fluid displaced.

Floating bodies are a special, and particularly important, case of this principle. These (such as ships), or bodies suspended completely immersed in a liquid (submarines), or in a gas (balloons), appear to be weightless. In these cases, the upthrust is clearly equal to the weight of the body. As Archimedes showed, the upthrust is equal to the weight of the fluid displaced.

Surface tension

Many insects can walk on water; drops of water on a car form hemispheres; spilled mercury forms small spheres; water dropping slowly from an eye-dropper forms almost perfect spheres; soap bubbles form perfect spheres as do drops of oil suspended in water; a paper clip carefully placed on an undisturbed water surface makes a small depression and will float, although its density is many times that of the water. These are all examples of the phenomenon of surface tension – a force that causes the surface of any liquid to behave as if it were like an elastic skin. The sphere is the shape that offers the smallest surface area for a given volume, so any free, small quantity of liquid tries to adopt a spherical shape to minimize the force of surface tension.

The explanation of surface tension is to be found in the attractive forces between the molecules of the liquid. Deep in the liquid there is a state of equilibrium between attraction and repulsion of the molecules, but in the boundary layer the molecules at the surface are attracted only inwards as there are effectively no

molecules outside the surface to balance this attraction. Different fluids have widely differing surface tensions. In order of increasing surface tension are soap solution, ethyl alcohol, carbon tetrachloride, benzene, olive oil, water and mercury. Water has a surface tension about three times that of soap solution. The surface tension of mercury is about six times that of water.

Liquids and solids in contact

The surface of a fluid in a container is mainly horizontal, but when it is in contact with a solid, such as the walls of the container, it is usually curved. The direction of curvature depends on whether the attraction of the molecules of the container is greater or less than the attractive forces between the molecules of the liquid. If it is greater, as in the case of

SURFACE TENSION

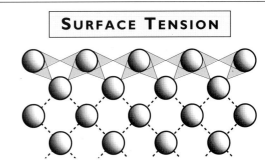

Molecules at the surface of a liquid are attracted inwards. Other molecules experience a balanced attraction in all directions.

The attraction between the water and the glass molecules of the beaker (the adhesive force) is greater than that between the water molecules themselves (the cohesive force). In the case of mercury, the reverse holds true.

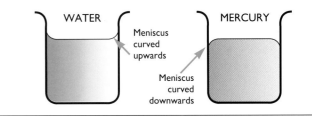

WATER   MERCURY
Meniscus curved upwards
Meniscus curved downwards

water in a glass container, the surface in contact will curve upwards. If less, as in the case of mercury in glass, it will curve downwards. This curvature is known as the *meniscus*. The difference in its direction for water and mercury is explained by the fact that water is a 'wetting' liquid, strongly attracted by the molecules of a solid, while mercury is not.

ARCHIMEDES

One of the best-known anecdotes of science is apocryphal – that of the great Greek mathematician Archimedes (c. 287–212 BC) running naked down the road shouting 'Eureka!' ('I have found it!') after formulating the theory of displacement of water. It is, however, a reflection of the great popular interest, throughout the ages, aroused by this remarkable man. More detail exists about the life of Archimedes than about any other scientist of the time, but, as in the case of any well-known figure, much of this is likely to be anecdotal.

Nine treatises of his, written in Greek, exist, and later references to his work show that there were others written that have since been lost. His surviving writings include part of a work on floating bodies and contains the ideas leading to his principle. Archimedes is thus credited with being the founder of the science of *hydrostatics* (the study of the mechanical properties and behaviour of static fluids). This was by no means his most important contribution to science since Archimedes was by far the greatest mathematician and technician of ancient times. He calculated an accurate value for the ratio of the circumference to the diameter of a circle (π); worked out the formulae for the volume and surface area of a sphere; determined the square roots of several numbers; and calculated the ratio of the volume of a cylinder to that of a sphere fitting into it. He also developed a method of positional notation for numbers, thereby greatly improving the old methods of arithmetic. Although deeply interested in the theoretical aspects of mechanics, Archimedes thought little of his mechanical inventions – the helical screw

for raising water, the military catapults, siege engines and other mechanical weapons of war – since such practical applications were considered unworthy of a philosopher. In 212 or 211 BC Archimedes was killed by a Roman soldier from the forces attacking Syracuse. It seems that anecdote surrounds even his death. It is said that he was working out a problem on a sand surface and had drawn a large diagram when a soldier tried to move him on. Archimedes, more concerned about the solution than about his personal safety, refused and was stabbed to death.

ARCHIMEDES' SCREW

River

An instrument for drawing up liquids, Archimedes' screw consists of a cylinder enclosing a large screw (inclined plane). When the handle is turned, the water, in this case, is carried up the screw to be poured into a collecting vessel.

Aerodynamics and Hydrodynamics

To be able to fly was long a dream of humanity, but became possible only once the principles of aerodynamics were understood. If the medium concerned is water rather than air, these principles become known as hydrodynamics.

SEE ALSO

- MECHANICS p. 26
- FORCE AND MOTION p. 28
- CIRCULAR MOTION AND GRAVITATION p. 30
- FRICTION p. 32
- FLUIDS p. 34

Throughout history, people watching the flight of birds have been inspired to try to emulate them. The earliest known designs of flying machines were those of Leonardo da Vinci (1452–1519; ⇨ p. 8), who proposed both a flapping-wing machine (an *ornithopter*) and a type of helicopter. In 1799 the English engineer Sir George Cayley (1773–1857) drew up a design that contained, in essence, all the elements of a modern aircraft – a fixed wing, a tailpiece with vertical and horizontal control surfaces, and a propulsion system. Cayley employed gliders (suitable engines did not yet exist), and in 1853 constructed the first successful person-carrying glider. The German pioneer Otto Lilienthal (1848–96) carried this work further and recorded over 2,000 flights in the five-year period from 1891 before crashing to his death near Berlin. Many of the pioneers of flying suffered a similar fate, and it was not until 1903 that power flight was finally conquered (⇨ box).

Aerodynamics

Aerodynamics, a branch of fluid mechanics, is the study of gases, such as air in motion, and of the forces that, as a result of such motion, are applied to bodies moving through them. Underlying the subject are Newton's laws of motion (⇨ p. 28), which describe the effects of forces acting on bodies. The Swiss mathematician Daniel Bernoulli (1700–82) applied Newton's laws to the movement of fluids, and investigated the relationship between pressure in a fluid, whether liquid or gas, and its velocity. Bernoulli found that as the speed of a moving fluid increases the pressure in it decreases. Water in a pipe flows faster through narrowed parts and slower through wider parts. But the pressure must be greater in the wider parts in order to accelerate the water moving to the narrowed parts. This principle is known as *Bernoulli's law*.

Principles of fixed-wing flight

The problem of achieving heavier-than-air flight is essentially to find how to apply a force acting vertically upwards that is greater than the force of gravity acting vertically downwards (the weight of the aircraft). At the same time, the vehicle must be capable of forward movement. It is one of the triumphs of invention that the latter (the forward movement) has been made to achieve the former (the upwards-acting force, or lift) in a highly efficient manner.

An aircraft wing is a plate that moves forward through the air with the front (*leading*) edge slightly higher than the rear (*trailing*) edge. Simple experiments will show that even with a flat plate such an arrangement can readily produce lift as a result of air pressing against the underside of the plate. The movement of the air that streams over the top of the plate and in the region just behind it, however, is far from smooth and the resulting turbulence causes severe retardation of the plate. This is called *drag*. In order to minimize drag and improve lift, the section of the wing must be of a particular shape known as an *aerofoil* (⇨ illustration). The shape is such as to promote a much smoother flow of air (streamlining) than over a flat plate, so that drag is reduced or almost eliminated. The shape also means that the airstreams over the top of the wing surface move faster than those over the lower surface. By Bernoulli's law, faster movement means lower pressure; slower movement means higher pressure. Thus there is a pressure difference between the upper surface of the wing (low pressure) and the lower surface (high pressure) and the resulting upthrust pushes the wing upwards.

These principles apply as long as the angle of the wing to the direction of travel (*angle of attack*) remains fairly small. If this angle is unduly increased, as by an injudicious attempt to climb too steeply at too low a speed, there is a considerable rise in turbulence and drag, and a marked reduction in lift and severe slowing. The result may be a stall in which the aircraft ceases to fly and falls steeply. As long as the aircraft is flying at a high enough altitude, however, its nose can be put down and recovery is possible.

The same principles of aerofoil design apply to propeller blades, which produce a powerful forward force by the rapidity of their rotary movement through the air. Because the velocity of any part of a propeller blade depends on how far it is from the centre of the circle that the tip of the blade describes, each blade is suitably twisted so as to maintain an appropriate angle of attack all the way along. Increasing the thickness of the aerofoil section increases the lift but also increases the drag. For this reason heavy load-carrying cargo aircraft will have thicker wings than high-speed military aircraft. The overall shape of the wing also affects the lift. A long, narrow wing (high aspect ratio) produces maximum lift, and is suitable for relatively slow, high-altitude machines and motorless sailplanes. Short, stubby wings (low aspect ratio) are used in fast, highly manoeuvrable machines.

Control

Stability in flight is greatly improved if the wings are set so that the tips are higher in the air than the roots. This upward tilt is called *dihedral* and its effect is slightly to reduce the lift of both wings. This means that if the aircraft rolls to one side so that one wing becomes horizontal, that wing will then experience increased lift so that the roll is automatically corrected.

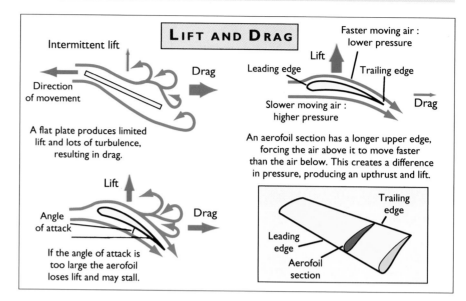

LIFT AND DRAG

Intermittent lift — Drag — Direction of movement

A flat plate produces limited lift and lots of turbulence, resulting in drag.

Lift — Angle of attack — Drag

If the angle of attack is too large the aerofoil loses lift and may stall.

Faster moving air : lower pressure — Lift — Leading edge — Trailing edge — Slower moving air : higher pressure — Drag

An aerofoil section has a longer upper edge, forcing the air above it to move faster than the air below. This creates a difference in pressure, producing an upthrust and lift.

Trailing edge — Leading edge — Aerofoil section

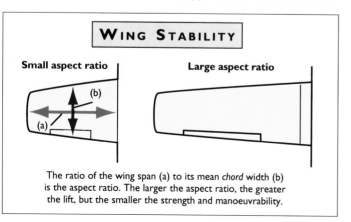

WING STABILITY

Small aspect ratio — Large aspect ratio

The ratio of the wing span (a) to its mean *chord* width (b) is the aspect ratio. The larger the aspect ratio, the greater the lift, but the smaller the strength and manoeuvrability.

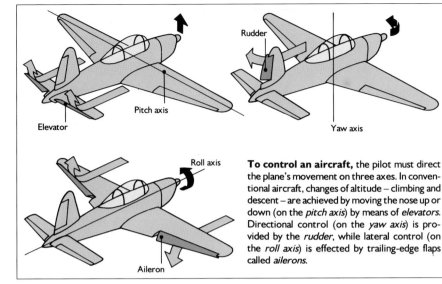

To control an aircraft, the pilot must direct the plane's movement on three axes. In conventional aircraft, changes of altitude – climbing and descent – are achieved by moving the nose up or down (on the *pitch axis*) by means of *elevators*. Directional control (on the *yaw axis*) is provided by the *rudder*, while lateral control (on the *roll axis*) is effected by trailing-edge flaps called *ailerons*.

The Wright Brothers' Flyer III. From a set of 50 cigarette cards on aviation, published in 1910. (IS)

Aircraft control is effected by control surfaces on the wings and tail. The wing *ailerons* (hinged flaps on the wing's trailing edge) move in opposite directions; when the aileron in one wing goes up, that in the other goes down. This causes the aircraft to bank and develop a centripetal force (⇨ p. 30) that leads to a turn. The turning moment is enhanced by the *rudder* (vertical control surface) in the tail. The tail elevators work together, both turning down to increase the tail lift and cause a dive, or turning up to depress the tail and cause a climb.

Hydrodynamics

The term hydrodynamics derives from the Greek *hudor*, 'water', and *dunamikos*, 'strength'. It is the science of the movement of liquids and their relation to solid bodies, and is concerned with such matters as the direction of fluid flow (flow lines and streamlines), the movement of layers of fluid over each other (laminar flow), and the causes and nature of *turbulence* (irregular flow).

The speed limitations of sea-going craft have led many marine engineers to study the possibility of building craft that might travel on or above the surface of the water rather than partially immersed in it. It was soon appreciated that hydrodynamics was based on exactly the same principles as aerodynamics, and that water craft could be designed on these principles. Strictly speaking, a hydrofoil is a specially shaped surface, fitted below the hull of the boat, that provides lift as it is moved through the water just as an aerofoil provides lift as it moves through the air. The term has been extended, however, to refer to the whole craft. As the vehicle gains speed the foil rises and lifts the hull out of the water, thereby greatly reducing the resistance to movement from drag. Hydrofoils are fitted in pairs, and may take one of two basic forms – the surface-piercing foil that raises the craft right out of the water so that the foils move along the surface, and the partially submerged type. One highly efficient design uses surface-piercing, V-section foils at the front and a horizontal, submerged foil at the stern. Most of the weight of the craft is borne by the V foils. As the speed increases the tips of the foils emerge from the water, and, at full speed, the whole weight of the boat is carried by the lowest central portion of the foils. V foils, like the dihedral of aircraft wings, are inherently self-stabilizing.

The Americans Wilbur Wright (1867–1912) and his brother Orville (1871–1948) were largely self-taught mechanics, who, after designing and building printing machinery while still young men, became successful bicycle manufacturers. This venture provided the necessary capital for experiments into aircraft design and manufacture, and in 1900, 1901 and 1902 they built three biplane gliders. Encouraged by their ability to control these machines in flight by 'wing-warping' and the use of elevators and a rudder, they decided to attempt powered flight. First, however, they had to produce an engine light enough for the purpose. They also had the task of designing an efficient propeller, since nothing of the sort existed at that time.

In 1902, at their home in Dayton, Ohio, they designed and constructed a machine they called the 'Flyer', later popularly called 'Kitty Hawk'. This machine was a tailless biplane with a 'pusher' propeller driven by a 12-horse-power petrol engine that they had designed and built. On 17 December 1903 at Kitty Hawk, North Carolina, this aircraft took off, piloted by Orville, and flew straight and level for 12 seconds, travelling about forty yards at a height of a few feet and a speed of about thirty miles per hour. Three longer flights were made the same day, the longest lasting for 59 seconds and covering about two hundred and eighty yards under full control. Unfortunately, the Flyer was then blown over by the wind and damaged.

Flyer II had an improved engine and achieved longer flights, and Flyer III was able to bank and circle, and made flights of more than half an hour's duration. By 1908 Wilbur was demonstrating his aircraft in Europe and had made a flight duration of 2 hours and 20 minutes. Their ideas were quickly adopted by others, and Orville, flying in America, after some difficulty, finally persuaded the military authorities that flying was practicable and won a contract to build machines for the United States Army.

This Hong Kong jetfoil is an advanced form of hydrofoil craft. Its horizontal hydrofoils, attached to the front and back of the boat, are fully immersed during motion. (IB)

Beyond Newton 1:
Relativity

In 1887 an event occurred the consequences of which were to turn the scientific world upside down, and, for the first time, reveal that the great work of Isaac Newton (⬦ p. 28) was seriously incomplete as a description of the fundamental laws of the universe.

Nicolas Roeg's film *Insignificance* (1985), starring Theresa Russell as the Actress (based on Marilyn Monroe) and Michael Emil as the Professor (based on Albert Einstein), contains a remarkable passage in which the Actress explains the theory of relativity, with the aid only of moving model trains and flashlights. Einstein's theory of relativity has held the public's attention like no theory since Newton's. (Kobal)

Nineteenth-century thinkers assumed that waves could travel only through a medium. Water waves were inconceivable without water; and sound waves could not travel in a vacuum because they were waves in air or other material. This seemed axiomatic. But it was by no means clear what the medium was that light travelled through. The Scottish physicist and mathematician James Clerk Maxwell (1831–79) had shown that light was an electromagnetic wave (⬦ pp. 72–5), so it seemed essential to postulate a medium for its transmission. The puzzling thing was that light travelled unimpeded through a vacuum. It was also known to travel almost inconceivable distances from remote stars.

Light and the ether

Scientists were also perplexed about the motion of light relative to other things. Since not only the Earth and the planets, but also the Sun and the other stars were moving, a stationary reference point, or frame, by which such motion could be measured, was badly needed.

The purported medium, although invisible, and as yet undetected, was entitled the *ether* – an appropriate name for such an ethereal entity. It was deemed to pervade all space and matter, and to provide both a medium for light and a fixed frame of reference for movement.

Because the Earth was moving through the ether, light travelling for a known distance in the direction of the Earth's motion and reflected back to its point of origin would take less time to complete its journey than light travelling the same distance and back at right angles to the direction of the Earth's motion. This was simple common sense. On this basis, two physicists, Albert Michelson (1852–1931) and Edward Morley (1838–1923), working in America, decided to prove the existence of the ether by means of a sensitive device called an *interferometer*, set up on a rotating table. This equipment produced interference fringes (⬦ p. 40), and was more than sensitive enough to detect the difference in the time taken by the two beams. To everyone's surprise, the experiment produced completely unexpected results: however often the experiment was done, the time taken was exactly the same for both orientations of the beams of light.

The bewildered scientists tried to account for the result. The most fruitful suggestion was that of the Irish physicist George Francis Fitzgerald (1851–1901), who postulated that all matter (including the interferometer) contracts in the direction of its motion. Fitzgerald's equation was such that at low speeds the contraction was negligible, but at speeds approaching that of light it would be substantial, that is, the increase in mass was logarithmic in proportion to the increase in speed. The Dutch physicist

Hendrick Antoon Lorentz (1853–1928) took the idea further and suggested that, in addition, mass increased in a similar way with motion. Soon there was evidence that this was indeed the case, contradicting Newton's assumption that mass is constant. Experiments with accelerated electrons showed that they actually did increase in mass as they accelerated, and that they did so to an extent accurately described by Fitzgerald's equation.

The special theory of relativity

Albert Einstein, a devoted physics student (⬦ box), was thoroughly familiar with the Michelson–Morley experiment and later developments. He was also aware that Maxwell's equations indicated that the speed of light in a vacuum was a constant – just under 300,000,000 m/s (186,000 mi/s).

His genius, however, was to see that science was not taking relativity far enough. People had always used arbitrary frames of reference, selecting whatever frame was convenient for any particular purpose. But Einstein saw that it was now necessary to abandon altogether the idea that space or time had any absolute existence at all. Also, if the speed of light was a constant in all frames of reference it was necessary to explore the consequences of this fact. The speed of light in a vacuum (light travels more slowly through transparent media, such as glass or water) was the maximum possible speed in the whole universe. Nothing could go faster because a body travelling at this speed would have infinite mass and zero length in the direction of motion (this is the Lorentz–Fitzgerald contraction). Moreover, Michelson and Morley found that,

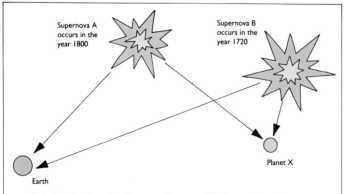

Relative simultaneity. Supernova A occurs 120 light years from Earth (i.e. light takes 120 years to travel from Supernova A to Earth), and Supernova B is 200 light years from Earth. From Earth the two events are observed simultaneously in 1920, even though Supernova B occurred 80 years before Supernova A. In contrast, the two events are not observed simultaneously. Planet X is only 40 light years from Supernova B, but 150 light years from Supernova A. Therefore, on Planet X, Supernova B is observed in 1760, while Supernova A is not seen until 1950.

regardless of how an observer might move relative to the source of a light, the light would be found to move at the same speed.

This has extraordinary implications. If a man sitting in the centre of a long carriage in a moving train turns on a light, the light will be seen by him to reach both ends of the carriage at the same time. But to an observer outside, who is being passed by the train, the light – travelling at a constant speed – will seem to reach the rear wall before it reaches the front wall (⇨ illustration on relative simultaneity). Thus two events (illumination of the two walls), which are simultaneous to the person in the train are not simultaneous to the person outside. One consequence of the constancy of the speed of light is, therefore, that simultaneity is relative.

We measure time by checking the movement of something – that of the Earth round the Sun, the swinging of a pendulum, the vibration of a quartz crystal, the movement of an atom, and so on. And an excellent standard for time is the speed of light. A person carrying a clock that works on the principle of the time taken for light to travel a fixed distance will find it highly accurate. But if that person is moving relative to another observer, the distance the light travels will not appear to the second observer to be the same, and the light, moving at a constant speed, will take a longer or shorter time to traverse the fixed distance. So time, too, is relative. Of course, because simultaneity is also relative the two observers can never see the clock (to read the time) at exactly the same time.

This is not just hypothesis. Experiments with subatomic particles have shown that time extends (*dilates*) with movement, demonstrating that their lifetime is increased if their speed is increased. So we must accept that clocks slow and people live longer when they are moving quickly. At near the speed of light, time almost stands still for the moving object.

Einstein's equations for his special theory of relativity account mathematically for all these strange-seeming phenomena. At the kinds of speeds to which we are accustomed, measurements of speed of two and two add up to four; but at speeds approaching that of light, an addition of the same unit of speed contributes less and less until, at the speed of light, it adds nothing.

Mass and energy

A moving body possesses kinetic energy (⇨ p. 46). The increase in mass with movement is equal to the increase in energy (because movement and energy are identical) divided by c^2 (the speed of light multiplied by itself). Einstein inferred from this that the whole of the resting mass must be equivalent to a quantity of energy E divided by c^2. From this he derived the celebrated equation $E = mc^2$. At a stroke he had abolished the distinction between mass and energy and,

Albert Einstein (1879–1955), the man who was to make the most important advance in pure science since Isaac Newton (⇨ p. 28), had been a poor student. After leaving school without a certificate he managed with great effort to pass the entrance examination to the Federal Polytechnic School in Zurich. Although meant to be studying electrical engineering, he spent his time reading widely in physics instead of attending the prescribed lectures. He did, however, take a reasonable degree, graduating in 1900.

After two years of casual teaching jobs he was fortunate enough to get a junior post in the Swiss Patent Office in Berne, where he remained for the next seven years, preparing summaries of patents. His real interest, however, was in mastering the most advanced theoretical physics of the day, and in making his own contribution to it. In 1905 five of his papers were published in the *German Yearbook of Physics* and he was awarded a PhD. One of these papers was on the photoelectric effect (⇨ p. 60) for which there was then no plausible theory. Einstein explained it on the basis of the quantum theory (⇨ p. 40) that Max Planck (1858–1947) had published five years before, and that had been largely ignored. This paper led to Einstein being awarded the Nobel Prize for physics in 1921.

Another of Einstein's papers explained *Brownian motion* (the random motion of microscopic particles in a fluid). A third paper considered the implications of the Michelson–Morley experiment and put forward the special theory of relativity (⇨ main text).

Recognition came slowly and it was not until 1913 that, at the instigation of Planck, a post was created for him at the Kaiser Wilhelm Physical Institute in Berlin. In 1915 he published his greatest work, the *General Theory of Relativity*. This predicted a red shift in light (that is, light would be displaced towards the red end of the spectrum) in a strong gravitational field, and showed that

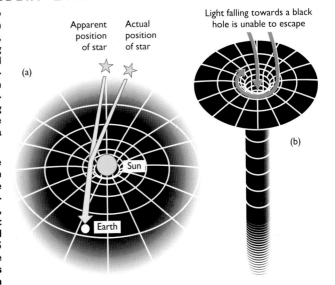

Einstein's general theory of relativity proposed a new view of gravity, arguing that it was a feature of space-time and not a force acting between bodies. The theory proposed that space-time was curved around the bodies in it, and that bodies 'fall', rather than are attracted by gravity, towards one another. This was indeed found to be the case when, during the eclipse of the Sun in 1919, light from a distant star was observed to pass around the Sun from behind (a). The theory also predicted the presence of black holes – bodies of such enormous density that nothing, not even light, can escape a fall towards them. These black holes have a point of infinite density (*singularity*) at their centres, and each pulls space-time into an abyss of infinite depth (b).

light itself would be deflected by gravitation. (Photons [light particles], although massless, do possess momentum and energy.) Both predictions were proved correct by astronomical observations and Einstein became world famous. In 1930 he visited America to lecture at the Californian Institute of Technology and, as Hitler had come to power in Germany, he decided to stay on in the USA, where he accepted an appointment at the Institute for Advanced Studies in Princeton, New Jersey. He remained there for the rest of his life. Heaped with honours, he was unquestionably the best-known and most distinguished scientist of the 20th century, if not of all time.

among other things, had explained the energy given off by radioactive elements. This work led directly to the development of atomic energy and to the arrival of the atomic bomb.

The fourth dimension

The appreciation of the relativity of space and time quickly reduced the strength of the distinction between them and led to an important concept – that of the space–time continuum. In such a continuum, time can readily be considered and treated as a fourth dimension. If, for instance, one makes successive observations of a three-dimensional body at successive moments in time, these might involve different orientations and hence different perceptions of its dimensions, as, for instance, by foreshortening. So a fuller description of the object can be given in terms of a four-dimensional continuum. The mathematical working out of this idea was an important stage in the development by Einstein of his general theory of relativity (⇨ box).

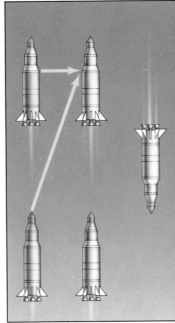

Relative time. Spaceships 1 and 2 are travelling side by side while 3 passes in the opposite direction. When 1 flashes a beam of light to 2, this is seen by 2 to travel in a straight line along the shortest route possible (distance A). This is because 1 and 2 are stationary relative to one another. For spaceship 3, however, the beam of light seems to travel along the longer, diagonal route (distance B). Since the speed of light is constant, the time taken for the light to go from 1 to 2 seems longer for 3 than it does for 1 or 2. This is the phenomenon of *time dilation*; the faster 1 and 2 travel relative to 3, the greater the dilation will seem until, at speeds approaching that of light, the time taken for light to travel distance B (as seen by spaceship 3) will be almost infinite.

Beyond Newton 2: Quantum Theory

Quantum theory describes events on an atomic and subatomic scale. It arises out of the German physicist Max Planck's idea that particles of matter possess certain properties, such as energy, in discrete amounts (*quanta*).

Isaac Newton believed that light was a stream of particles, but in 1807 the English physicist Thomas Young (1773–1829) showed that its nature was 'undulatory' – that of a wave. He did this by examining wave interference (⇨ p. 66). This occurs when waves of any kind – marine, acoustic, electrical, or radio – interact. Two waves of similar wavelength will reinforce each other if they occur together (are *in phase*), or may diminish each other if the peaks of one coincide with the troughs of the other (are *out of phase*). When Thomas Young passed a beam of light through two narrow slits placed close together, he observed the interference pattern thrown on a screen beyond the slits (⇨ illustration). This could be explained only by assuming that light was a wave. The idea that light is indeed a wave has been accepted by science ever since.

Radiation and energy

All bodies in the universe emits electromagnetic radiation with a spectrum of wavelengths whose peak depends on its temperature (⇨ p. 84). A white-hot body like the tungsten filament of an electric light bulb at 3,000°C (5,432°F) emits radiation of a wavelength mainly in the visible part of the spectrum – around 500 millionths of a millimetre; a dull red body emits mainly at a longer wavelength – around a millionth of a millimetre. Colder bodies emit mainly longer waves, from a thousandth of a millimetre up to a few centimetres in length. The longest waves can be picked up by microwave radio receivers.

At the end of the 19th century a serious problem for scientists arose over radiation. Conventional physics implied that the shorter the wavelength the greater the energy radiated. This was because, for a constant speed, c, wavelength and frequency are reciprocal (the larger the former, the smaller the latter, and vice versa), and because energy is proportional to frequency. Unfortunately, according to this theory, the energy radiated in the ultraviolet region and beyond should be enormous and should, contrary to common sense, continue to increase towards infinity as the wavelength becomes ever shorter. This was obviously not the case, as demonstrated by the fact that X-rays, which have very short wavelengths, do not burn us. Also, observation showed that the spectrum of radiation (known as 'black-body' radiation) always shows a definite peak of radiation for a body at a particular temperature (⇨ illustration), rather than a rising scale. So there was clearly something wrong with the theory. This was the problem addressed by Max Planck (1858–1947) in 1900.

The quantum theory

Planck proposed that electromagnetic radiation, including light, is not emitted as a continuous wave, but comes off in tiny bundles of energy called quanta. He further suggested that radiation could be emitted only in bundles greater than a certain minimum size. The relationship of energy to frequency was, he proposed, described by the equation:

$$E = hf.$$

E is the energy, f the frequency, and h is a fixed but very small number, later to become widely known as *Planck's constant* (6.6262×10^{-34} joule seconds). This idea has had momentous consequences. Niels Bohr (1885–1962), inspired by it, suggested that electrons can occupy only certain defined energy levels around the nucleus of the atom (⇨ p. 108). Radiation is emitted when electrons jump from a high energy level to a lower one. At high frequencies (high temperatures) a large amount of energy is needed to emit one quantum of radiation; at lower frequencies there are many more electrons able to emit quanta, but each carries little energy. Statistically applied, this idea elegantly fitted the facts, and accounted for the observed peak of radiation for objects at different temperatures. Planck's theory proved to be one of the most successful in the history of science and formed the basis for the understanding of many other phenomena. He had, however, to wait some years for recognition.

Einstein and the photoelectric effect

Electrons are emitted when light or other forms of electromagnetic radiation fall on certain metals such as selenium or caesium. This is the photoelectric effect. These can be picked up by a nearby positively charged plate so that a small current flows in an external circuit. Such a *photocell* has important technological and scientific applications, as in the reproduction of sound from a film's soundtrack, and the exploitation of solar radiation (⇨ p. 60). When Albert Einstein

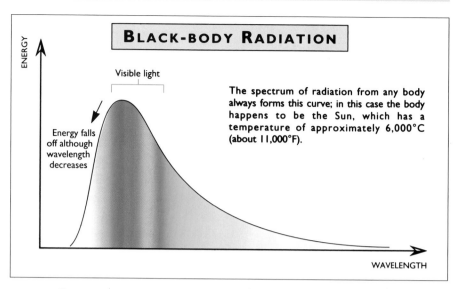

BLACK-BODY RADIATION

ENERGY

Visible light

Energy falls off although wavelength decreases

The spectrum of radiation from any body always forms this curve; in this case the body happens to be the Sun, which has a temperature of approximately 6,000°C (about 11,000°F).

WAVELENGTH

YOUNG'S DOUBLE-SLIT EXPERIMENT

The light and dark interference fringes produced where wavefronts meet and either reinforce one another (*constructive interference*) or cancel one another out (*destructive interference*) can be explained only by assuming that light takes the form of a wave, contary to Newton's theory (and later to the quantum theory) of light, which put forward the particle as the basic constituent of light.

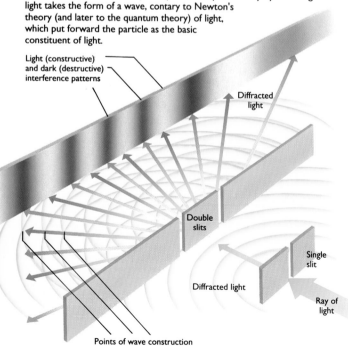

Light (constructive) and dark (destructive) interference patterns

Diffracted light

Double slits

Single slit

Diffracted light

Ray of light

Points of wave construction

was working in the Swiss Patent Office in Berne, the photoelectric effect caught his attention. Having digested Planck's work, he published a paper in 1905 suggesting that this effect could be explained only if Planck was correct in his view that light came in bundles (quanta) with a particular level of energy for a particular wavelength. He went on to suggest that light and other forms of radiation could occur only in quantized bundles of energy. Light quanta were, in effect, a stream of particles. These were later called *photons*.

This paper came to carry enormous scientific weight and led to the award to Einstein of the Nobel Prize for physics in 1921. But it threw the whole logic of radiation physics into confusion. Young and others had proved that light was a wave phenomenon, and now Einstein was suggesting that it was particulate. Ever since, the wave–particle duality of light – there is ample evidence for both – has puzzled scientists and laypeople alike.

De Broglie's electron waves

Matters were even further confounded when the French physicist Louis de Broglie (1892–1987; ⇨ box) suggested that Einstein's ideas of the quantization of light might also be applied to electrons and that these, too, might partake of a wave–particle duality. Einstein's equations, he pointed out, could apply equally well in describing electrons as waves. This, if true, had enormous implications as it suggested the beginnings of a further breakdown in the distinction between matter and energy. In 1927 de Broglie's idea was proved when wave interference in an electron beam was demonstrated by other scientists using a

Mosaic depicting Niels Bohr (1885–1962), the Danish physicist who proposed a model of the atom that linked Max Planck's quantum theory with Ernest Rutherford's idea that atoms consisted of a nucleus surrounded by a field of electrons. Bohr suggested that electrons could occupy only permitted orbits, each associated with certain energy levels, around the nucleus. They could, however, move from one orbit to another, and, in so doing, would release a packet, or *quantum*, of energy. (J.-L. Charmet, SPL)

nickel crystal lattice (Clinton Davisson (1881–1958), US physicist) and a thin gold foil (G. P. Thomson (1892–1975), British physicist) as diffraction gratings, which act in the same way as narrow, closely spaced slits (⇨ p. 66).

De Broglie's equation for the wavelength of matter waves was:

$$\lambda = \frac{h}{p};$$

λ (the Greek letter lambda) is the wavelength; h is Planck's constant; and p is the momentum. Because Planck's constant is so small, everyday matter, with its relatively massive momentum, has a very short wavelength; hence its wavelike nature is imperceptible. Tiny particles such as electrons have a longer wavelength. The wave–particle duality is thus apparent only at an atomic or subatomic level – not at an everyday level. It is closely related to another strange phenomenon – quantum uncertainty.

Heisenberg's uncertainty principle

In 1927 the German theoretical physicist Werner Heisenberg (1901–76) pointed out that the new quantum ideas implied an inherent limitation in the accuracy of observations of matters at an atomic or subatomic level. In classical Newtonian physics it was assumed that both the position and velocity of a body can be determined simultaneously to an arbitrary degree. Heisenberg showed that in the case of very small particles, this is not so. Any attempt to measure the position of a particle accurately results in serious uncertainty as to its velocity, and vice versa. To see something we need to bounce light off it, and if the thing we are trying to observe is of the same general magnitude as a quantum of light, the procedure cannot fail to affect its position or its velocity.

The uncertainty principle is not, however, simply a matter of the practical difficulties of carrying out observations with tools that are too crude for the job. There is plenty of evidence to show that uncertainty is an inherent feature of the nature of particles such as electrons. Our common-sense ideas of position and momentum, like our ideas of the summation of velocities (⇨ p. 38), are derived from observation of the everyday world, but we should not assume that they must apply in subatomic situations as well.

Heisenberg was able to quantify uncertainty and showed that the uncertainty (V) in position (p) multiplied by the uncertainty in momentum (m; momentum is mass × velocity) worked out at roughly equal to Planck's constant (that is, Up × Um = h, h being Planck's constant). Quantum theory and uncertainty, however strange, must now be accepted as facts of nature. Neither of them, applied statistically, has any significant effect on the world of everyday objects, but only in the submicroscopic world. An under-

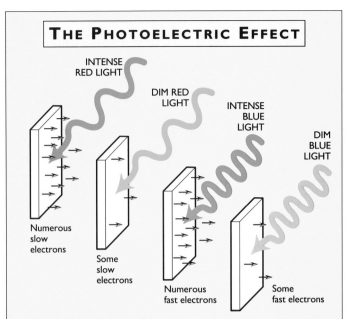

THE PHOTOELECTRIC EFFECT

INTENSE RED LIGHT

DIM RED LIGHT

INTENSE BLUE LIGHT

DIM BLUE LIGHT

Numerous slow electrons

Some slow electrons

Numerous fast electrons

Some fast electrons

During the photoelectric effect, light dislodges electrons from the surface of the metal it falls on. For this to be so, light has to be explained as consisting of photons ('packets' of light), contrary to the classical wave theory. Changing the intensity of the light has an effect on the number of electrons liberated, while changing the frequency of the light increases the energy of the electrons emitted.

standing of them has, however, revolutionized science and has had an enormous impact on all our lives. Among many other things, quantum theory led directly to the development of semiconductors and hence to transistors, integrated circuits, calculators, small computers, quartz watches and the vast field of domestic and industrial electronics (⇨ pp. 102–5). It has led to the development of the laser (⇨ p. 82) with all its numerous applications; and it has given us new insights into the nature of the atom (⇨ chapter 6).

SEE ALSO

● FORCE AND MOTION p. 28
● BEYOND NEWTON 1: RELATIVITY p. 38
● WHAT IS ENERGY? pp. 46–9
● WHAT ARE WAVES? pp. 64–7
● LIGHT pp. 72–5
● THE ELECTROMAGNETIC SPECTRUM AND ITS PROPERTIES p. 84
● THE CLASSICAL THEORY OF THE ATOM p. 108
● THE QUARK THEORY p. 110
● ATOMS AND MOLECULES p. 156

LOUIS DE BROGLIE AND THE WAVES OF MATTER

Prince Louis Victor de Broglie (1892–1987), the 7th Duke of Broglie, was a French aristocrat whose great-great-grandfather had been guillotined in the French Revolution. De Broglie took a history degree at the Sorbonne (University of Paris), but was employed on radio communications at the Eiffel Tower transmitter during World War I and, through this, became interested in science. When, in 1924, de Broglie suggested in his PhD thesis that electrons had wavelike properties, his examiners were astonished. One of them, however, a Professor Langevin, asked for another copy of the thesis, which he sent to Einstein for his opinion. Einstein, impressed, felt that de Broglie's insight was correct and that his ideas were likely to bear fruit. He gave a favourable judgement and de Broglie was awarded his doctorate.

De Broglie's doctoral thesis was published as a paper of over 100 pages in the *Annales de physique* in 1925, and attracted the attention of other scientists who went on experimentally to prove that he was right. He was awarded the Nobel Prize for physics in 1929. By a remarkable irony, one of those who confirmed de Broglie's suggestion was the British physicist G. P. Thomson (⇨ main text), the only son of the great J. J. Thomson (1856–1940) who had discovered the electron in 1897. The father was awarded the Nobel Prize for physics in 1906 for proving that the electron was a particle; his son was given the Prize, also for physics, in 1937 for proving that it was a wave.

ENERGY

History and the Perpetual-motion Machine

The word 'energy' was first used in its modern scientific sense as recently as 1807 by the English physicist Thomas Young (1773–1829). Prior to that, although scientific progress had been made in the field of what we now call energy, few people had a clear idea of what energy actually was. This lack of understanding of the essential meaning of energy led scientists to devise all kinds of impossible energy-related schemes; a favourite was to design a machine that, without external stimulus, was capable of *perpetual motion* (running for ever).

A perpetual-motion machine designed in about 1747 by a Colonel Kranach of Hamburg. Iron balls drive the water wheel, which, in turn, operates the Archimedes' screw (long, cylindrical object). This then raises the balls once more. Kranach insisted that the machine stood in water, which would have hindered its operation by increasing energy losses, but was probably necessary to hide a secret driving mechanism. From *The Gentleman's Magazine*, London (1747). (AR)

The earliest serious consideration of the nature of energy – by the Greek philosopher Aristotle (⇨ p. 8) – was distorted by a prevailing disregard at that time for practical philosophy. Distortion was also encouraged by the preference of Plato, Aristotle's master, for framing elegant but imaginary schemes of nature rather than observing nature from an objective point of view. In Plato's opinion, everything had its proper place in nature, and change was simply a tendency to return to that place or to the *status quo*. Archimedes' practical experience could have brought him to a reasonable understanding of energy, but he was rather ashamed of his

inventions and looked on them as playthings rather than as matters for scientific consideration.

The period towards the end of the Middle Ages was more fertile for science and invention than has often been thought. During this period, the inadequacies of Platonic and Aristotelian physics became apparent when the leading thinkers began to concentrate on the idea of action. Leonardo da Vinci (⇨ p. 10) was one of the most perceptive. He worked out the principle of the lever (⇨ p. 26), appreciated that movement was brought about only by force, and saw that there must be a balance of power on either side of a fulcrum. He also deduced that perpetual-motion machines (⇨ below) were impossible.

Simon Stevinus of Bruges (1548–1620) – who, incidentally, introduced the decimal system to Europe in 1585 – took the matter further. He investigated the principle of single and multiple pulleys (⇨ p. 26), and had a clear enough idea about the nature of energy and work to appreciate that at least some forms of perpetual-motion machine were impossible. Considering the case of an endless chain hung over a triangular support with a long side and a short side, he set himself the task of working out why the chain did not move in the direction of the long side where the weight of chain was greater than on the short side. Stevinus soon realized that the effective weight of chain on one side of the apex of the triangle exactly balanced that on the other side, regardless of which side was longer, because the extra weight on the long side had an additional area of support.

The German philosopher Gottfried Wilhelm Leibnitz (1646–1716) was one of the first to have a clear idea of the notion of work in the modern scientific sense, and he defined it as *vis viva* (Latin, 'living force'). As the steam engine was developed and the industrial revolution began, it became clear that a term was needed to describe the essential quality of anything with a capacity for doing work. Eventually, the existing term, *energy* – which dated back to Aristotle – was adopted by Thomas Young. Not long afterwards, it was to become apparent that this entity might exist in a variety of forms (⇨ pp. 46–9).

The chimera of perpetual-motion

From the dawn of mechanical science people have dreamed of producing machines that would turn for ever, producing endless power, doing useful work and consuming no fuel. The dream persists to this day. Every year, patent offices receive hundreds of applications for patents for some form of perpetual-motion machine. Consideration of these machines and the fallacies inherent in their design provides valuable insight into the nature of energy.

In many cases, the proposed machines used gravity as the source of energy. One of the commonest types was based on falling weights. These could perform work – but only because work has already been done in raising them to a height. The machines tried to overcome this problem by means of devices such as an unbalanced wheel with hinged arms, each with a weight at one end, that would swing out on one side and fold in on the opposite side. The theory was that the weight on the extended arm would exert more downward force than that required to raise the folded arm. A single pair of arms clearly would not promote rotation, so these machines had a large number of articulated arms. However, an analysis of the forces shows that, whatever the position of the arms, the forces on one side add up to exactly the same as those on the other.

Machines of this kind were devised by the 17th-century French architect Vilard de Honnecourt and funded by the Marquis of Worcester (1601–67). Some were so massive and well balanced that, given a good start, they continued to run for a long time in accordance with Newton's first law of motion (⇨ p. 28). All such machines came to a standstill eventually, however, and this happened more quickly if any attempt was made to get them to perform work.

Another class of perpetual-motion machine depends on the belief that the desired result could be achieved if all sources of impediment to free movement – mainly friction – could be removed.

Section through a superconducting cable. The six triangular areas contain bundles of fine superconducting wire (here, a niobium/titanium alloy). These are surrounded by an electrically insulating layer. At extremely low temperatures, cables such as this act virtually as perpetual-motion machines, since they offer no resistance to an electric current, allowing it to run indefinitely. (Manfred Kage, SPL)

This is, in fact, true. Virtual perpetual motion is manifested, for instance, by the movement of the Earth in its orbit around the Sun, in which frictional losses are very small indeed. In the case of a practical machine – such as a well-balanced and massive flywheel – it is possible to reduce friction, including air resistance, to a very low level. Such a machine, once run up to speed by an external source of energy, will go on rotating for a very long time. But there is not much point in a wheel that simply rotates. As soon as any work is done by the wheel it slows, and the more work done by it the more rapidly it slows down.

Modern perpetual motion

The nearest modern scientists have come to achieving perpetual motion is in the development of superconductors (⇨ pp. 88 and 102–5) – materials of such low electrical resistance that once a current is started in a continuous circuit of the material, it will continue to circulate endlessly with negligible losses after the source is removed. Such a current flow produces a magnetic field that can perform work. It can, for instance, levitate an iron body.

There is a snag, however. Superconductors display their remarkable property only at very low temperatures, close to absolute zero (0 K, which is –273°C or –460°F; ⇨ p. 50). Recent developments continue to achieve superconductivity at higher and higher temperatures, but

the highest reached so far is about 125 K (125 degrees above absolute zero). The energy needed to maintain such low temperatures is greater than the energy that can be taken from a superconducting system.

Pseudoperpetual-motion machines

Those dreaming of creating a perpetual motion machine have been encouraged by a number of devices that appear to achieve successful perpetual motion, but that are, in fact, making use of natural sources of energy. For example, changes of atmospheric pressure operating an evacuated bellows of thin, corrugated metal (an *aneroid barometer*) can be made to do work, such as lifting weights or winding up a clock. The energy used in this case is a tiny part of the vast amount that is constantly poured onto the Earth from the Sun. Solar energy can be derived more directly – to heat water or to generate electricity from photocells – and the heat and the electric current so produced can be made to do work (⇨ p. 60).

Even the energy from radioactive material can be made to do work. The distinguished British physicist Lord Rayleigh (1875–1947) designed a radium clock in which the leaves of a sealed gold-leaf electroscope separated and closed perpetually with no apparent source of energy. At the time, even sceptical people were convinced that this was a

EARLY DEVICES

In 1619, the English physician Robert Fludd (1574–1637) put forward an ingenious suggestion for a perpetual-motion system. This consisted of a water wheel driven by a fall of water from a source above the wheel, the source being constantly replenished by the return of the same water by an Archimedes' screw (⇨ p. 34) driven by the wheel. Dr Fludd's assumption – that the falling water would give up more energy than was needed to return the water to the point above the wheel – was unfortunately mistaken.

The Abbé de la Roque devised a water-powered perpetual motion machine in 1686. He reasoned that if a wide glass vessel were made that narrowed to a small-cross-section open tube below, and the tube were bent up and over the side of the vessel, water would continue to flow perpetually out of the narrow tube into the open top. It seemed to him that the weight of the water in the wide section would force water high enough up the narrowed tube to flow continuously. Unfortunately, the Abbé was wrong and trials showed that a balance was quickly struck between the two sides of the system. This had in fact been shown to be so, years before, by Stevinus of Bruges (⇨ main text), who demonstrated experimentally that the pressure exerted by a liquid depends only on its vertical height and not on the shape of the vessel in which it is contained. The actual pressure on the narrow outlet tube is simply that of the vertical column of liquid above it, which has a cross section equal to that of the narrow tube (⇨ p. 34).

With each advance in science and technology, new ideas for achieving perpetual motion appeared. When Michael Faraday (⇨ chapter 5) showed that electricity could be generated from magnetism, and magnetism produced by electricity, schemes were proposed in which an electrical generator (*dynamo*) produced a current that drove a motor that turned the generator. In the end, however, such schemes served only to demonstrate that the limitations to perpetual motion that apply to mechanical force also apply to electromagnetic force.

Robert Fludd (1574–1637), English physician whose experiments making perpetual-motion machines inevitably failed. (AR)

genuine perpetual-motion machine. As the facts of radioactivity became known, however, it became clear that the recurrent charges on the electroscope leaves came from the emission of charged particles from the nuclei of radium atoms – a result of spontaneous nuclear fission, in which matter is converted to energy (⇨ p. 160).

What is Energy? 1

Energy is commonly defined as the capacity for doing work, and the relationship of energy to work is so close that the units of energy are the same as those of work. But energy can exist in many different forms.

Because of the way our bodies are made, we all have experience of the way that effects are produced by mechanical force acting over a distance. For example, exerting muscular force to move or lift an object makes us aware of mechanical force. To move a heavy object we must exert a large force; to perform a delicate action, we exert a small force. When we apply a strong force for a long time, we feel tired and consider, rightly, that we have expended energy.

The energy we use comes from the food we eat and most people are aware that food has to be chemically changed before the energy locked up in it can be released. The usual way to release this kind of stored energy is to burn (*oxidize*) something. Oxidation can occur quickly at high temperatures, as in the combustion of petrol in a car engine; or it can occur more slowly at much lower temperatures, for instance by enzyme action on carbohydrates in the body. But the process is essentially the same – a complex hydrocarbon chemical substance is burnt and reduced to simpler substances with a release of energy.

Potential and kinetic energy

The amount of energy expended when moving an object is calculated by multiplying the force we exert by the distance through which we move the object. If we raise a weight of 1 kg (2.2 lb) 3 m (about 9 ft) off the ground, we expend 3 metre-kilograms of energy and do 3 metre-kilograms of work. We would expend exactly the same amount by raising a weight of 3 kg 1 m off the ground. A crane that raises a 500-kg steel beam a height of 50 m does 25,000 metre-kilograms of work and consumes the same amount of energy. Any weight raised in this way therefore acquires energy, and this form of energy is called potential energy. The 25,000 metre-kilograms of potential energy acquired by the steel beam is a considerable amount, as is readily shown if the cable breaks and the beam falls 50 m. The release of the 25,000 metre-kilograms of energy stored in the raised steel beam can do a great deal of damage, but the essential point is that when the beam has reached the ground all this energy has been released.

As the beam falls its potential energy is converted into another form of energy known as *kinetic energy* – the energy of movement. Another way of thinking of these terms is to see 'potential' energy as energy that has not been used (but could be) and 'kinetic' energy as energy that has been used, or is in the process of being used, and so has done something or made something happen. Both these forms of energy – potential and kinetic – are used at different stages to move things and thus perform work.

Potential energy does not have to be released suddenly, as it would be in the dropping of the beam or the release of a compressed spring in an air rifle. It can be let out gradually, as in the 24-hour fall of the weights in a grandfather clock or the slow relaxation of the springs in a car with efficient shock-absorbers.

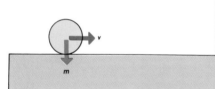

Potential energy. The potential energy of a body is the product of its mass, its height above the ground, and the acceleration due to gravity: $E_p = mgh$.

Kinetic energy. Kinetic energy is equal to half the product of the mass and the square of the velocity: $E_k = \frac{1}{2}mv^2$.

The 'Rocket', a steam-driven locomotive engine (converting heat energy to movement), invented by George Stephenson (1781–1848), British engineer. (AR)

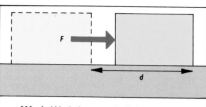

Work. Work done on a body by a constant force is the product of the magnitude of the force and the displacement of the body as a result of the action of the force: $W = Fd$.

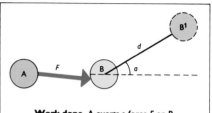

Work done. A exerts a force F on B and as a result B moves to position B^1 with displacement d at angle a to the line of F. Work $W = Fd \cos a$. (For an explanation of cosine ⇨ p. 20.)

Kinetic energy was the first kind of energy to be clearly recognized. It was obvious that a sailing boat would not move if the air was calm but only if the air was in motion, in the form of wind. Similarly, a mill wheel would not move if the stream was dammed and the water motionless. The energy was therefore seen to be not in the air or the water but in the *motion*.

The conversion of kinetic into potential energy and vice versa is happening all the time. If a ball is thrown vertically upwards, it leaves the thrower's hand with a certain amount of kinetic energy. As it rises and slows under the pull of gravity it gradually loses its kinetic energy, but at the same time – because of its altitude – it acquires potential energy. At the point of greatest altitude it has no kinetic energy and maximal potential energy. Then, as it falls, it gains kinetic energy and loses potential energy. When it is caught and smacks into the catcher's hands it possesses almost the same amount of kinetic energy it started with.

This is an example of the law of conservation of energy. In practice, energy is never lost but is simply converted from one form into another. The kinetic energy possessed by the ball when it strikes the catcher's hands is slightly less than the kinetic energy it started with, because some energy has been used overcoming air resistance and, in fact, heating the air. When the ball strikes the hands the kinetic energy ceases but the energy is not lost: it is simply converted to another form – in this case the work of mechanical deformation of the ball, heating the hands and the ball, producing sound, pain, tingling of the fingers, and so on. The idea of conservation of energy is best expressed by saying that the total of all forms of energy in a system is constant.

Energy is neither created nor destroyed, but can readily be converted from one form to another.

Other forms of energy

The relationship of mechanical or kinetic energy to heat is a matter of everyday experience, as any child who has slid down a rope in the school gymnasium will testify. As the child slides, kinetic energy is converted into heat – through friction (⇨ p. 32), which is the resistance to movement between surfaces. This conversion also occurs in the opposite direction, and heat can be transformed into motion. If this were not true, the world as we know it could not exist, because radiant heat from the Sun continuously evaporates billions of tonnes of water from the oceans, carrying it high into the atmosphere to form clouds from which it falls as rain, filling lakes and rivers and ultimately returning to the sea. All these stages perform work.

On a smaller scale, heat from burning petrol or diesel oil causes the gas expansion that moves engine pistons, immediately converting itself into kinetic energy manifested in the movement of the vehicle. The realization in the 18th century that heat could cause movement by turning water into steam led to the first steam engine (⇨ pp. 56–7).

Since heat can be converted into kinetic energy, it is easy to see how it can also be converted into potential energy – simply by raising weights, for instance.

A 5-litre (1-gallon) can of petrol contains a considerable amount of energy – enough to move a tonne-weight of motor car and its passengers for 65 km (40 mi) or more. As long as the cap remains on the can this energy remains potential in form, but since energy of this kind can be released only when a chemical change occurs in the material concerned, it is usually described as *chemical energy*. The chemical energy in petrol is first converted to *thermal* (heat) energy by burning and this, in turn, is then converted to kinetic energy.

Chemical sources of energy such as petroleum-oil products, coal, wood and natural gas are not used only to provide kinetic energy. They can also be burned to heat water, producing steam, which drives turbines coupled to electric generators in a chain of energy conversion that ends with another form of energy – electricity. High concentrations of electrons (⇨ pp. 90–1), whether stored in a charged battery or in a thundercloud, represent a form of potential energy that requires only a conducting path (⇨ p. 90) to manifest itself in other forms.

Electrical energy is readily converted into kinetic or potential mechanical energy, into heat, light, sound, or even muscular contraction. Electricity's ready 'convertibility' is one of its chief advantages as a form of energy. But storage of large quantities of electrical energy is often inconvenient, so it is reconverted when not immediately required into mechanical potential energy – for example, in hydroelectric schemes it is used to pump water to a height from which it can be released later, to drive the turbines again.

When Lord Rayleigh astonished the scientific world with his 'radium clock' (⇨ p. 44) it seemed, at first, that the law of conservation of energy had been broken and that a perpetual-motion machine had in fact been achieved. However, we now know that the movement of the electroscope leaves was caused by energy released by the radioactive radium atoms. The horrific power of this form of energy – nuclear energy – was apparent in 1945, when part of the energy from a kilogram of the uranium isotope U-235 was released over Hiroshima in Japan.

UNITS OF ENERGY AND WORK

The work done by a force is the force multiplied by the distance through which it acts, so a particular quantity of work – or energy – might be represented as so many gram-centimetres, foot-pounds, watt-hours, joules or ergs, depending on the system of units used.

Dyne: the unit of force in the centimetre-gram-second system and the force that imparts an acceleration of 1 cm/s/s on a mass of 1 gram.

Erg: the unit of energy in the centimetre-gram-second system of units. 1 erg of work is done when a force of 1 dyne moves something 1 cm in the direction of its application.

Foot-pound: the unit of energy or work in the foot-pound-second system of units. 1 foot-pound is the energy expended or the work done in raising a weight of 1 lb a distance of 1 ft against gravity.

Joule: the SI (*Système Internationale*) unit of energy, work and heat – all three being equivalent. 1 joule is the work done when a force of 1 newton moves something 1 m in the direction of its application.

Newton: the SI unit of force and is equal to 0.2248 lb – actually the force that produces an acceleration of 1 m/s/s in a mass of 1 kg.

Watt-hour: the unit of energy or work done by 1 watt (1 volt x 1 amp) acting for one hour and equal to 3,600 joules.

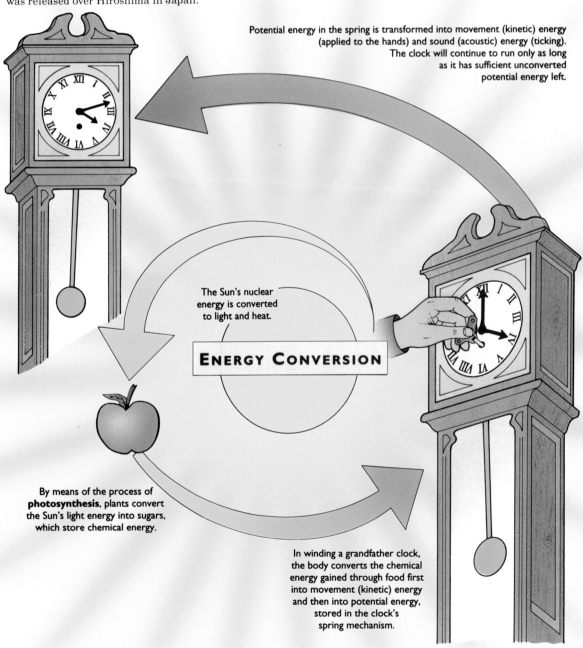

Potential energy in the spring is transformed into movement (kinetic) energy (applied to the hands) and sound (acoustic) energy (ticking). The clock will continue to run only as long as it has sufficient unconverted potential energy left.

The Sun's nuclear energy is converted to light and heat.

ENERGY CONVERSION

By means of the process of **photosynthesis**, plants convert the Sun's light energy into sugars, which store chemical energy.

In winding a grandfather clock, the body converts the chemical energy gained through food first into movement (kinetic) energy and then into potential energy, stored in the clock's spring mechanism.

What is Energy? 2

Every object possesses energy. It may take different forms, even in the same object, and these can be converted into one another. Energy can be quantified in various ways, and it is possible to calculate how the different forms relate to each other in numerical terms. Matter itself is also a form of energy that can be quantified.

A moving body possesses kinetic energy (⇨ p. 46). It can, at the same time, possess potential energy – by virtue of its altitude, heat energy from raised temperature, electrical energy from a surface charge and, as we shall see, nuclear energy in the binding forces that hold together the subatomic particles of which it is made (⇨ chapter 6).

Energy transformation

Few of us are accustomed to expressing energy conversions in numerical terms, but it is not as difficult as it might seem. For instance, work and mechanical potential energy can be expressed in units such as metre-kilograms or foot-pounds (⇨ p. 46). An object's kinetic energy is related to both its mass and its velocity, although not in equal proportions – it is more

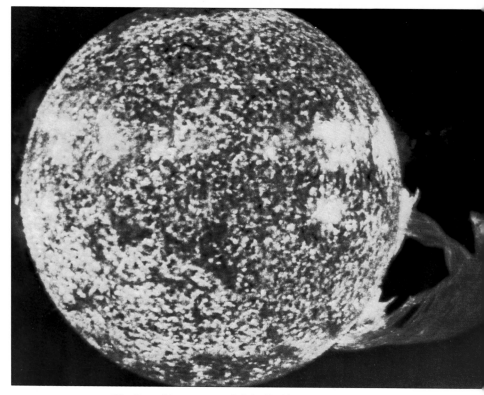

The Sun, ultimate source of all the Earth's energy. (RC)

James Prescott Joule (1818–89), English physicist and brewer who first quantified the mechanical equivalent of heat energy. The SI unit of energy, the joule, is named after him. (ME)

affected by velocity than by mass. Kinetic energy can be calculated by the formula $\frac{1}{2}mv^2$, where m equals mass, and v, velocity.

When an object of mass m is raised to a height h against gravity, it has a potential energy of $m \times h \times g$, i.e. mhg, where g is the acceleration due to gravity (⇨ p. 30). If all the object's kinetic energy is converted into potential energy, then $\frac{1}{2}mv^2 = mhg$. The mass is the same on both sides of the equation and so cancels out. If we then multiply both sides by 2, the $\frac{1}{2}$ is removed, leaving $v^2 = 2hg$. This is the work–energy equation that allows us to calculate, for instance, the height to which an object will rise if we know its initial velocity. In practice, it is rare for all the kinetic energy to be converted, and there are usually losses from such things as air resistance.

Because heat is a form of energy (⇨ pp. 52–7), it is possible to convert a given amount of heat, quantitatively, into mechanical energy. This was first done experimentally by an English physicist, James Prescott Joule (1818–89), who tried various ways of converting movement into heat – such as friction, compressing gases, turning paddle wheels in water, and so on – and compared the energy expended with the heat produced. His trials showed that a particular amount of one form of energy was converted into a particular amount of the other kind, and he was able to calculate the conversion factor. A unit for heat is the amount needed to raise the temperature of a given amount of water by one degree – for instance, the calorie (small c) is the amount of heat needed to raise 1 gram of water by 1°C. Because he had calculated a conversion factor, Joule was

able to express the mechanical equivalent of heat in the same units. His work was so important that he was later honoured when the unit of work and energy in the metre-kilogram-second system of units (⇨ p. 46) was named the joule. 1 calorie is equivalent to 4.18 joules.

Einstein and the equivalence of mass and energy

As we have seen, the kinetic energy of a body moving at 'normal' speeds is calculated by the formula $\frac{1}{2}mv^2$. According to Newton, the increase in energy with speed is solely the result of the increase in speed. However, Albert Einstein (⇨ p. 38) showed that this simple formula, while satisfactory for 'normal' speeds, does not apply at all speeds. This is because the increase in energy is actually due to an increase in mass, and this mass increase depends on the speed in a more complicated way. At normal speeds the increase in mass is negligible, but as speeds approach those of light the mass increase becomes significant, then considerable, then, indeed, overwhelming. Motion does not increase mass. The change in mass is simply one aspect of the increase in kinetic energy occurring when a body is accelerated by energy from outside of itself.

We have never had any practical experience of this, and are inclined to think of mass and energy as two quite separate entities – and to ignore mass when we consider the law of conservation of energy. But if we assume the universal validity of this law – that energy can neither be created nor destroyed, but can readily be changed from one form to another – it follows that energy (in the classical sense) must be convertible into

ENERGY FIXATION, PLANTS AND THE ATMOSPHERE

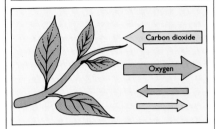

Day: plants absorb more carbon dioxide from the atmosphere by photosynthesis than they give out by respiration. They also give out more oxygen by photosynthesis than they absorb from the atmosphere for respiration.

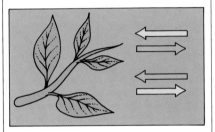

Dawn and dusk: with less light available for photosynthesis, plants give out similar amounts of oxygen and carbon dioxide to those they take in.

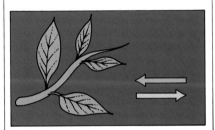

Night: with no light available, photosynthesis ceases. However, respiration continues, with oxygen being absorbed and carbon dioxide being given out.

mass and mass into energy. This is what Einstein proposed to an astonished world in his epoch-making paper in 1905 (⇨ p. 38).

The Fitzgerald expression for the contraction of a moving body (⇨ p. 38) can be expanded into a series consisting of 1 + an endless succession of progressively smaller added fractions. At low speeds, all the terms of the series are such small fractions that they can be ignored. But at higher speeds, they become ever more significant. The Lorentz mass relationship, which involves the Fitzgerald expression, can be rearranged as $m = \frac{1}{2}mv^2/c^2$, where m is the gain in mass with motion. The expression $\frac{1}{2}mv^2$ is the well-known formula for the kinetic energy of a moving body assuming it has its rest mass. If we substitute the term e (energy) for this, we have $m = e/c^2$, and this can easily be rearranged as Einstein's famous expression for the energy equivalent of mass, $e = mc^2$.

Using the centimetre-gram-second system of units, the speed of light is 30,000,000,000 c/s. Therefore c^2 is 900,000,000,000,000,000,000 cm²/sec². In order to find the total energy equivalent of 1 gram of matter, e is equal to 900,000,000,000,000,000,000 gram-cm²/sec². Now 1 gram-cm²/sec² is equal to 1 erg (⇨ p. 46), so this very large number is the number of ergs of energy in 1 gram of matter. To use more familiar terms, we can convert ergs into kilocalories. The result – 21,500,000,000 – is the amount of heat that would raise the temperature of 215,000,000 kg of water by 100°C.

Energy cycles in nature

The Earth is not a closed system as far as energy is concerned. It constantly receives almost immeasurable quantities of energy from the Sun's nuclear fusion reactions by way of radiation of heat and light (solar radiation). At the top of the Earth's atmosphere the quantity of this radiation is equal to 1,370 watts/m². But much of the energy is screened out by the atmosphere so that the intensity at the surface is much less. More of this energy is lost by re-radiation into space than is gained by solar radiation, but the temperature of the Earth is maintained by a continuous heat flow, mainly by convection (⇨ p. 52), from the molten centre of the Earth towards the surface.

Considerable amounts of energy from the Sun are *fixed* (⇨ below) on the surface of the Earth by the activity of plants. Without this vital process animal life would be impossible. The first clue to its existence came in 1779, when the Dutch physician Jan Ingenhousz published the results of experiments examining changes in the activities of green plants when exposed to light. He proved that plants in the dark absorb oxygen and give off carbon dioxide. But when they are exposed to light, the reverse happens and they take up carbon dioxide and give off oxygen.

Light from the Sun is taken up by molecules of a green pigment called chlorophyll. This energy is converted into two high-energy molecules ATP (adenosine triphosphate) and NADPH (nicotinamide adenine dinucleotide phosphate). Energy contained in these molecules is then used to build carbohydrates such as sugars and starches from carbon dioxide and water. In the process water molecules are split into hydrogen and oxygen. The hydrogen is needed for synthesis, but the oxygen is released into the atmosphere to replenish its oxygen supply – which would otherwise be gradually depleted by burning and animal respiration.

The food chain

The food-chain process provides the beginning of a chain on which all animals depend. It also provides the ultimate source of all the hydrocarbon fossil fuels (coal and oil) contained in the Earth's crust.

The food chain is a succession of stages of energy transfer, starting with plants and proceeding to a series of organisms each of which feeds on the one before it in the chain. Its essential feature is the fixation of energy in the form of complex chemical molecules. Carbon dioxide and water are simple molecules. The carbon dioxide molecule contains only one carbon atom and two oxygen atoms; water contains two hydrogen atoms and one oxygen atom. To build these up into simple sugars and more complex carbohydrates and then, higher in the food chain, to synthesize other complex molecules such as fats and proteins, involves the fixation of energy. These complex molecules are the food supply of the next member of the chain.

No energy is created in this process and energy cannot be released and re-fixed without substantial losses. The energy fixed by a consumer will always be less than that fixed by the member before it in the chain. For example, at best efficiency about 50 kg (approximately 100 lb) of grain will produce about 10 kg (20 lb) of weight gain in cattle, but 10 kg of meat will produce only about 1 kg (2 lb) of weight gain in a human being. If humans were to subsist on grain (assuming a small protein supplement, vitamins and minerals) the same 1 kg weight gain would be produced by 5 kg (10 lb) of grain.

SEE ALSO

- WHAT IS ENERGY? pp. 46–9
- GAS LAWS p. 50
- HEAT TRANSFER p. 52
- THERMODYNAMICS p. 54
- HEAT ENGINES p. 56
- SOURCES OF ENERGY pp. 58–61
- WHAT ARE WAVES? pp. 64–7
- SOURCES OF ELECTRICITY pp. 92–5
- THE BIOSPHERE p. 206

ENERGY FLOW IN THE FOOD CHAIN

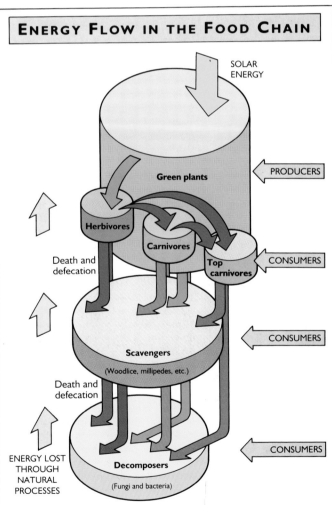

Energy enters the biosphere in the form of solar energy, which is used by the primary producers – predominantly green plants – to fuel the photosynthetic reactions by which atmospheric carbon dioxide is converted into organic sugars. Virtually all other organisms – animals, fungi and most bacteria – are consumers, ultimately relying on the organic matter of plants for their support.

Gas Laws

A gas is best regarded as one of the states of matter – a state in which any kind of matter can exist if the temperature is high enough. Many substances, such as oxygen, nitrogen or carbon dioxide, are in the gaseous state at temperatures at which many other substances, such as iron or diamond, are solid. At temperatures between 0 and 100°C (32 and 212°F) water is usually liquid, but above 100°C it is usually a gas. The behaviour of gases under different conditions of temperature and pressure is the subject of the gas laws.

A gas may be defined in various ways. Most commonly it is seen as a state of matter in which molecules are free to move in any direction, so that the volume of the gas increases indefinitely unless constrained by an enclosure. A gas will always tend to expand to fill the space in which it is contained. Gas is also defined as a fluid (⇨ p. 34) that, unlike liquids and solids, is able to be compressed. Since the state of matter – solid, liquid or gas – depends on the temperature, some definitions of gas include a statement about the critical temperature at which a substance becomes gaseous. If we lived in a world at which 'room' temperature was about 200°C (392°F) we would be accustomed to thinking of water as a gas and would regard liquid water much in the way that we now regard liquid nitrogen.

Robert Boyle (1627–91). Engraving by George Vertue (1684–1756). (AR)

One of the most striking characteristics of gases is their low density compared to that of liquids or solids. Water at about room temperature has a density of 1 gram/cm³, and this provides a useful standard by which the density of other materials can be compared. We use the term *specific gravity* to describe the ratio of the density of a substance to that of water. On this scale, with water as 1, the specific gravity of the most dense liquid, mercury, is over 13.5. On the same scale, the specific gravity of air is about 0.0013 and that of the lightest gas, hydrogen, is 0.00009. All gases are much less dense than any liquids or solids.

Robert Boyle and the relationship of pressure to volume

Robert Boyle (1627–91) was an Irish aristocrat who spent three years at school, at Eton, then studied under a private tutor and, as a teenager, travelled widely in Europe on a circuit of scientific discovery. On his return to England he settled in Oxford to a life of scientific experiment and, with other like-minded companions, founded the Royal Society, to which he was later offered the Presidency.

Many of Boyle's contemporaries followed the Greek belief that advance in knowledge could be achieved only by reason, and that attempting to find things out by experiment was unworthy and demeaning. But Boyle had been influenced by Francis Bacon's important treatises, *Advancement of Learning* (1605) and *Novum organum* (1620), which criticized the deductive processes of Aristotle (⇨ p. 8) and stressed the importance of experiment. Boyle had also been impressed by the methods and successes of Galileo Galilei (1564–1642), which he had studied on his European tour.

In 1662 Boyle showed that gases were compressible – a fact that now seems almost self-evident – and, more importantly, that there was a definite relationship between the pressure applied to a gas and the volume it occupied. He demonstrated this elegantly, using a very tall U-shaped tube that was closed at one end. Air was trapped in the closed end and mercury was poured into the other so that, by its weight, it applied pressure to the air in the tube. By this means he was able to show that if the pressure on the air were doubled, its volume was reduced to half; if the pressure were tripled, the volume reduced to one third; and so on. He also showed that compressed air did not remain compressed when the pressure was released – if the pressure were halved, the volume doubled. This phenomenon reminded Boyle of the behaviour of some coiled metal springs he had observed, and he described it as the 'spring of the air'.

The only way Boyle could account for these findings was to suggest that a gas consisted of large numbers of invisibly small particles separated by empty space. On compression, the particles were

THERMOMETERS

The measurement of temperature is essential for many scientific and practical purposes. Most instruments that measure temperature make use of the fact that liquids expand when heated. If the liquid is contained in a sealed, transparent tube that has been evacuated (emptied of air) and that has a very narrow bore and a bulb at one end, a small rise in temperature can result in a substantial movement of the liquid along the tube. Various liquids, such as mercury or coloured alcohol or pentane, can be used, depending on the temperature range required. Scales are commonly set by calibration against other thermometers, or by immersing the bulb in wet ice for the lower (0°C/32°F) setting and in boiling water for the upper (100°C/212°F) setting.

Other substances that vary with temperature can be used to make thermometers. If strips of two different metals that expand to different degrees for the same rise of temperature are riveted together, changes of temperature will cause the bimetal strip to bend. This can be connected to a pointer moving over a scale. If the junction of two different metals is heated a small current will flow and this can be read on a milliammeter, which can be calibrated in degrees. Such a device – a *thermocouple* – is useful for measuring high temperatures. A *thermistor* is a semiconductor device (⇨ p. 102) that acts sensitively in a similar way at lower temperatures. Specially doped (the addition of known impurities) semiconductors can measure temperatures in the very low range from about 0.2 to 20 Kelvin – a temperature very close to absolute zero.

forced closer together; when the pressure was released, they sprang apart. This was an example of the atomist idea, which was ultimately found to be correct. Later it was proved that Boyle's law applied, in general, to *all* gases. It is now usually stated in the following form:

If the temperature is kept constant, the pressure of a fixed amount of a gas is inversely proportional to its volume.

Boyle also made notable advances in chemistry and published a book, *The Sceptical Chemist* (1661). His example as a skilled experimenter and scientist had a profound effect on those thinkers who followed him, including Isaac Newton (⇨ chapter 2).

Jacques Charles and the relationship of volume and temperature

An important component of Boyle's law is the effect of temperature on gases. This point was appreciated by the French physicist and Sorbonne teacher Jacques Charles (1746–1823), who, in

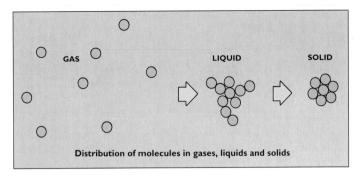

Distribution of molecules in gases, liquids and solids

At different temperatures the volume of this balloon increases or decreases, in accordance with Charles' law. In the beaker on the left, the balloon is anchored in iced water; on the right it is heated from below by a Bunsen burner. (Sinclair Stammers, SPL)

around 1787, succeeded in demonstrating that if the pressure of a gas was kept constant, its volume increased in proportion to a rise in temperature. This applied to all gases. Charles then went further and established a point with profound implications. Working with the centigrade scale and starting at 0° he showed that for each degree rise in temperature, the volume of the gas increased by 1/273 of its volume at 0°. The fact that the change in volume was linear with temperature meant that, assuming the law held good over the whole range of temperature, there was a temperature – specifically –273°C (–523°F) – at which gases would have no volume at all. It seemed that nothing could have a temperature lower than this, and so this temperature was given the name 'absolute zero'.

This concept of *absolute zero* has since been confirmed and we now use a temperature scale, known as the Kelvin scale, in which the lowest point (0 K) is equal to –273.15°C and each degree is exactly equal to 1°C. Charles' law is now usually stated as follows:

The volume of a gas at constant pressure is directly proportional to the absolute (Kelvin) temperature.

Charles did not publish his findings and the principle was worked out independently in 1802 by another scientist, the French chemist Joseph Louis Gay-Lussac (1779–1850), who is often credited with the discovery.

The laws combined

Since the gas laws involve three parameters – volume, pressure and temperature – there is room for another law, implicit in Boyle's and Charles' laws. This is that if the volume is kept constant, the temperature is proportional to

the pressure. This fact is well known to anyone who has used a hand pump to blow up a bicycle tyre and has experienced the remarkable heating effect of compressing the air in the pump. As all three factors are interrelated, they can be expressed as the general law that the product of the pressure and the volume divided by the absolute (Kelvin) temperature is roughly a constant.

Gases are difficult to weigh – because of their very low density and their fluid properties – but it is often important, especially for chemists, to do so. The solution to this difficulty is to measure the volume of a gas, which is easy, and simultaneously check the pressure and temperature. Once these three quantities are known, the weight can be calculated using the gas laws.

Temperature and the kinetic theory of gases

The gas laws have been of enormous value to scientists and engineers. For much of the time since they were first formulated by Boyle, they have been thought to be true in all circumstances, but we now know that this is not so. Accurate measurement of the volumes of different gases under different pressures, made in the 1850s, showed that under constant temperatures, the product of pressure (P) and volume (V) was not actually constant over a wide range of measurements. Under high pressure, P × V starts to rise, and under very high pressures of the order of 1,000 atmospheres, it may double.

Today, scientists think of the gas laws in terms of what is called the kinetic theory of gases. Gas molecules are thought of as highly active and mobile elastic spheres – these constantly strike against the

walls of the object containing the gas and this activity is responsible for the pressure exerted by the gas. It is assumed that the spheres are very small compared to the space between them and that they exert little influence on each other. The rise in pressure with temperature is simply due to the increased activity of the spheres. This theory also accounts for other properties of gases, one of which is their ability to conduct heat and their viscosity (that is, their resistance to flow).

In fact, however, it is wrong to assume that the spheres exert no effect on each other. They are subject to weak forces of mutual attraction, and, although their volume is small compared to the volume of the gas, it is not zero. These facts become significant under extreme conditions and lead to the failure of the simple gas laws to describe the behaviour of gases under all conditions.

SEE ALSO

● FLUIDS p. 34
● AERODYNAMICS AND HYDRODYNAMICS p. 36
● WHAT IS ENERGY? pp. 46–9
● HEAT TRANSFER p. 52
● ATOMS AND MOLECULES p. 156

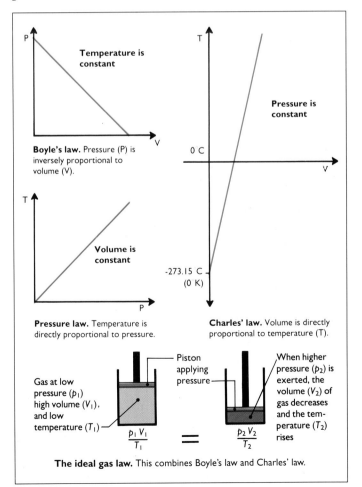

Boyle's law. Pressure (P) is inversely proportional to volume (V).

Pressure law. Temperature is directly proportional to pressure.

Charles' law. Volume is directly proportional to temperature (T).

Gas at low pressure (p_1) high volume (V_1), and low temperature (T_1)

Piston applying pressure

When higher pressure (p_2) is exerted, the volume (V_2) of gas decreases and the temperature (T_2) rises

$$\frac{p_1 V_1}{T_1} = \frac{p_2 V_2}{T_2}$$

The ideal gas law. This combines Boyle's law and Charles' law.

Heat Transfer

Heat and cold are familiar to us all and we may think of them as different entities. But cold is simply the absence of heat, relative to the comfortable temperature range to which we are most accustomed. Heat can pass readily from one body to another and it can do so in several different ways.

In 1791 the Swiss physicist Pierre Prévost (1751–1839), Professor of Physics at the University of Geneva, dispelled the notion held at that time that cold, like heat, could flow from one body to another. It was, he showed, the absence of heat rather than the presence of cold that caused the familiar unpleasant sensation. Prévost went further and suggested that all objects, even very cold ones, give off heat at all times. Even bodies whose temperature was constant were radiating heat, but these were at the same time receiving an equal amount of heat from their surroundings. This was later shown to be correct, but was a remarkable proposition at that time.

Heat as a form of motion

In 1798 the American physicist Count Benjamin Rumford (1753–1814) was impressed by the amount of heat produced when cannon barrels were being bored out. A rough estimate of the heat produced made it clear that the prevailing theory of the nature of heat – that it was a fluid (called *caloric*) contained in the metal and released as the shavings

were separated – was nonsensical. The following year Rumford proved that the weight of a quantity of water did not change when it was frozen solid, providing another blow to the caloric theory. Rumford concluded that the movement of the person boring the cannon was the source of the heat and that, consequently, heat was a form of motion. The same year, in England, the chemist Humphry Davy (1778–1829) showed that two pieces of ice could be melted by rubbing them together.

In 1860 the Scottish mathematician and physicist James Clerk Maxwell (1831–79) decided to study the problem of heat. Maxwell conceived of the molecules of a gas as being perfectly elastic and as moving randomly in all directions and at various speeds, bouncing off each other and off the walls of the container. Maxwell's equations showed that the velocities of the particles followed a familiar statistical pattern – the bell-shaped distribution first described earlier that century by the Belgian statistician Lambert Quetelet. They also indicated that a rise in temperature would increase the average velocity of the molecules, while a drop would decrease it. It was clear that Rumford and Davy were right – and that the idea of heat as a fluid (caloric) could be abandoned.

How heat moves

Heat consists solely of molecular movement and the temperature of a body depends solely on the average velocity of

its molecules. The transfer of heat from a hotter body to a colder one, therefore, involves a reduction in the average velocity of the particles of the first and an increase in the average velocity of those of the second. The natural direction of heat movement is from a hot to a cooler body and, in practice, a significant quantity of heat cannot move spontaneously from a cool to a hot body. This movement of heat can be done only by using special devices (such as refrigerators; ⇨ p. 54) and by expending energy.

The heat content of a body, however, is not simply a matter of its temperature. A small body at a high temperature may have a smaller heat content than a large body at a lower temperature. The material of which a body is made can also determine its capacity to contain heat. So the *quantity* of heat in a body depends not only on the average velocity of its molecules but also on their number and type.

There are three fundamental mechanisms of heat transfer – by the direct transfer of molecular movement by *conduction*, by the process of *convection* or by *electromagnetic radiation*.

Heat conduction

The direct movement of heat through solids, liquids or gases is effected simply by molecular collisions. If one end of a long, thin metal rod is held in a flame, the molecules at that end rapidly reach much higher velocities. Those molecules

Heat travels along this iron bar by means of heat conduction. Its progress along the bar is visible, since light energy is also given off. (Zefa)

Sir Humphry Davy (1778–1829), English chemist, inventor of the Davy lamp and contributor to the understanding of heat transfer, here shown performing an experiment at the Royal Institution, London, in a detail from a James Gillray cartoon (1802). (ME)

James Dewar (1842–1923) was a Scottish chemist, a connoisseur of the arts and a man of wide scientific interests. Although a distinguished chemist, he devoted most of his working life to physics and for forty-six years held two professorial chairs simultaneously, at Cambridge University and at the Royal Institution, London. Dewar made some notable advances in low-temperature physics and became fascinated with the problems of achieving ever lower temperatures. In 1905 he discovered that the absorbency of charcoal increased greatly at low temperatures, and he used this effect to achieve higher levels of vacua than were possible using pumps alone. He managed to liquefy oxygen and then hydrogen, and also showed how helium might be liquefied.

Earlier, Dewar had been troubled by the problem of keeping cold material from warming up. Using his knowledge of the ways in which heat moved and his skills in achieving high vacua, he constructed a double-walled flask and evacuated the space between the walls so as to avoid heat losses by conduction. He then silvered the walls so that radiant heat would be reflected back to the interior and fitted the flask with a stopper of low conductivity that also prevented convection losses. This device was so successful that it soon came into general use and, since heat movement was largely blocked in both directions, it also quickly proved useful as a way of keeping things hot. This vacuum flask can now be found in most homes.

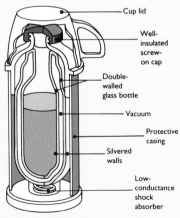

Cup lid

Well-insulated screw-on cap

Double-walled glass bottle

Vacuum

Protective casing

Silvered walls

Low-conductance shock absorber

Vacuum (or thermos) flasks are efficient at keeping their contents at their original temperature (hot or cold). Heat radiation is prevented by the silvering; conduction and convection are blocked by the vacuum.

nearer the centre of the rod come into violent collision with the less energetic molecules there and cause an increase in their velocity. In this way, the surge of excitation passes along the rod towards the colder end. This process continues as long as there is a difference in temperature between the ends.

Heat convection

Convection is the principal mode of heat transfer in liquids and gases and involves the motion of heat-containing quantities of liquid or gas that are free to expand when heated by conduction. Just as a cork released at the bottom of a bucket of water rises to the top because it is less dense than the volume of water it displaces (⇨ p. 34), so an expanded volume of liquid or gas rises if it is enclosed in a volume at lower temperature.

When a restricted volume of lower density liquid or gas rises in this way, its place is immediately taken by cooler liquid or gas from the surrounding area. This, in turn, is heated by the heat source and expands and rises. This cycle of movement continues for as long as there is a temperature difference between the different parts of the whole volume of liquid or gas.

Heat radiation

This method of heat transfer differs fundamentally from the others because it does not depend on the presence of matter. Every body in the universe above a temperature of absolute zero is emitting electromagnetic radiation. The most powerful emitter we know of is the Sun. Electromagnetic radiation is propagated at the speed of light and passes easily though a vacuum. The part of the electromagnetic spectrum (⇨ p. 84) concerned mainly with heat transfer is the wide infrared band lying between the wavelengths for visible light and those for microwaves.

The different parts of the spectrum differ only in wavelength – and consequently frequency (number of cycles per second) – and in intensity. The wavelength depends on the temperature of the source, those at the microwave end being given off by bodies close in temperature to absolute zero. The background radiation of the universe, for instance, peaks at a wavelength corresponding to a temperature of about 3 Kelvin (37°F or 3°C; ⇨ p. 84). Heat radiation has a wavelength ranging from about 1 mm (1,000 micrometres or 0.03937 in) at the cold end to less than one thousandth of a mm (1 micrometre, μm) at the hot end.

The higher the temperature of the emitting body, the shorter, on average, the wavelength – and the higher the frequency – of the emitted radiation. The effects of different frequencies of electromagnetic radiation become apparent when they react with matter. A central-heating radiator in a dark room at a temperature of, say, 323 Kelvin (273 + 50) gives off radiation of a wavelength far too long to be visible, but the incandescent tungsten filament in the light bulb at about 6,000 Kelvin gives off much shorter wavelength radiation that is appreciated as white light.

THE GREENHOUSE EFFECT

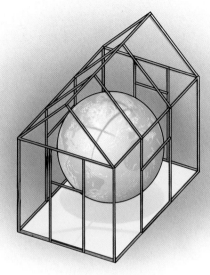

The metaphor of the Earth inside a greenhouse can explain the effect of increasing CO_2 emissions on the planet. Just as the greenhouse glass traps radiant heat from the Sun, warming the plants inside, so higher levels of CO_2 absorb infrared radiation from the Earth's surface (which originated in ultraviolet light from the Sun), thus raising the Earth's surface temperature.

Most of the radiation from the Sun is in the visible and ultraviolet part of the electromagnetic spectrum and in the shorter-wave part of the infrared band – the part that causes a sensation of warmth. The Sun's surface temperature is about 6,000°C (10,832°F), corresponding to visible light. The Earth's surface is at a much lower temperature and radiates in the infrared band only, mainly in the range of 4–100 μm. The Earth's atmosphere contains a large amount of water vapour – which absorbs best at wavelengths between 4–7 μm – and carbon dioxide – which absorbs best at 13–19 μm. This gap of low absorption between 7 and 13 μm allows more than 70 per cent of the Earth's radiation to escape into space. The remainder is absorbed and radiated back to the Earth's surface.

This mechanism of radiation and reabsorption maintains a balance between energy received from the Sun and energy lost into space. The result is that average surface temperatures on Earth stay at a level with which humans can cope safely. However, many scientists contend that the present rate of increase in the production of carbon dioxide – mainly from the burning of fossil fuels – will result in a doubling of atmospheric carbon dioxide levels in only a few decades. Doubled carbon-dioxide levels would increase the amount of heat reradiated back to Earth, which, in turn, would cause a rise in the average surface temperature of around 2°C (3.6°F). As a consequence of making the world warmer, the thermal expansion of the seas would cause a rise in sea level of about 30 cm (12 in). However, a 2°C (3.6°F) rise in average temperature would not be enough to cause the disappearance of the polar ice caps, as some people have feared.

Radiation in the infrared band can convey molecular movement to bodies upon which it falls if these bodies are at a lower temperature than the bodies emitting the radiation. In other words, if a body is to be heated by radiation, the frequency of the radiation emitted by the sending body must be higher – the wavelength shorter – than that of the radiation emitted by the receiving body. Radiant heat passes readily through a transparent material such as glass, can be reflected by mirrors and is absorbed by most materials.

Thermo-dynamics

Thermodynamics is the branch of science concerned with the movement of heat and the interrelationship of heat and work. It is a study with wide implications both in science and in engineering, and it is applied extensively in chemistry, physics, biology and the earth sciences.

There are three branches of thermodynamics: classical thermodynamics deals with systems large enough to ignore the interactions between individual molecules; statistical thermodynamics considers these interactions on the basis of quantum theory (⇨ p. 40); and chemical thermodynamics is concerned with energy transfer during chemical reactions, including many important biochemical processes.

James Watt's improvements to the primitive steam engines of Thomas Savery and Thomas Newcomen (⇨ p. 56) were so considerable that they initiated the Industrial Revolution, which brought about profound changes to the way societies were organized. By the end of the 18th century about 500 of Watt's engines were in use in England and soon almost everyone believed that Watt had actually invented the steam engine. Watt's engines, although the first practical and

Hermann von Helmholtz (1821–94). As a physiologist, mathematician and physicist, one of his many achievements was to help found the theory of conservation of energy, which is encapsulated in the first law of thermodynamics. (AKG)

Watt's steam engine. James Watt (1736–1819), Scottish engineer and inventor, made crucial improvements to the steam engine, allowing industry to take widespread advantage of the power of heat to perform work. (TSM/S&SPL)

useful mechanical prime movers, were in fact seriously inefficient and wasted about 95 per cent of the fuel burnt. Few people at the time concerned themselves with this fact, since wood and coal were cheap and plentiful. One person, at least, however, was not indifferent.

Nicholas Carnot and engine efficiency

The French physicist Nicholas Sadi Carnot (1796–1832), well aware of the enormous industrial importance of the steam engine, began to investigate how much work could actually be obtained from such an engine. His results were published in the book *Reflections on the Motive Power of Fire* (1824). This work was so far ahead of its time, though, that it was ignored both by scientists and by practical engineers. Indeed, it would have been entirely forgotten had not a reference to it in a scientific paper of 1834 brought it – separately – to the attention of Lord Kelvin and Rudolf Clausius (⇨ below). Carnot's ideas as expressed in his book then led them independently to formulate the second law of thermodynamics (⇨ below).

Carnot calculated that, even assuming a machine could work at 100 per cent efficiency, the greatest fraction of the heat energy that could be converted into work was the temperature difference between the hottest and the coldest parts of the engine divided by the temperature of the

coldest part. Kelvin later pointed out that this was true if the temperatures were expressed on a scale starting at absolute zero (0 K).

The implication of Carnot's work was that the way to achieve higher efficiencies would be to increase the difference between the temperatures – to raise the higher and reduce the lower. However, in spite of the importance of the advances he made, Carnot never completely abandoned the caloric theory of heat (⇨ p. 52).

At about the same time, the English physicist James Joule (1818–89) was experimenting with the mechanical equivalent of heat (⇨ p. 48) and reported the results of his work in a notable paper to the Royal Society in London in 1849. By the middle of the 19th century it had become evident that the caloric theory could no longer be squared with the facts and would have to be replaced by ideas that were more consistent with the evidence for the mechanical hypothesis.

The first law of thermodynamics

In the middle of the 19th century, the idea of conservation of energy (⇨ pp. 46–9) appealed to certain scientific thinkers. Among these thinkers was the German polymath Hermann von Helmholtz (1821–94), who had been studying muscle action and its relationship with body heat. In 1847 he developed a full expression of the principle of energy conservation with some telling examples, including many from human physiology. He encountered strong opposition from the 'vitalists', who believed that there were special laws of nature for living organisms and that living systems could not, without impiety, be considered in this way. Because of this resistance he had to publish his work privately. But he was not alone; his opinion was supported by James Joule and by the German physicist Robert Mayer (1814–78), who had proposed the idea of conservation of energy as early as 1842.

The first law of thermodynamics is simply an expression of the law of conservation of energy (⇨ p. 46) and is now usually stated as follows:

The total energy of a thermodynamic system is constant, although energy can be converted from one form to another.

In other words, no process can release more energy than it takes in, nor can it have an efficiency greater than 100 per cent; consequently, a perpetual-motion machine (⇨ p. 44) can never fulfil the claim of its inventor. In practice, processes invariably operate at *less* than 100 per cent efficiency because of the losses in waste heat. These losses are

considerable – the best engines achieve about 65 per cent efficiency, most much less than this. The human body has an efficiency of only about 20 per cent.

Von Helmholtz's ideas were triumphantly extended many years later, in 1894, when the German physiologist Max Rubner (1854–1932) proved that the energy produced by food eaten, digested and assimilated was exactly the same as if it were burned in a flame. This showed that the first law of thermodynamics applied just as rigorously to living organisms as it did to machines, and is reflected in the tables of calories or joules so familiar on the sides of today's food packaging. Rubner's work was also a blow to the increasingly discredited 'vitalist' theories.

Rudolf Clausius and the second law of thermodynamics

In 1850 the German theoretical physicist Rudolf Clausius (1822–88) greatly advanced scientific understanding of heat. He argued that Carnot's theorem could be made consistent with the mechanical theory of heat (⇨ p. 52), provided it was assumed that heat could not pass spontaneously from a cooler to a hotter body. He also reasoned that – even for systems that were theoretically perfect – there were always losses when heat was converted into work, or vice versa. Clausius called this inevitable loss of useful energy an 'increase in entropy' (⇨ box), and defined this increase as the amount of heat transfer divided by the absolute temperature at which the transfer occurs. In making these statements Clausius had discovered one of the fundamental laws of nature that is now known as *the second law of thermodynamics*. This can be expressed in various ways, usually in terms of Clausius's original hypothesis that heat can never pass *spontaneously* from a cool body to a hotter one. This is, of course, a matter of statistical probabilities, but the law is true for all practical purposes.

In a heat engine (⇨ p. 56), of the total heat absorbed at the high-temperature side from the burning of fuel, only a part is converted into work. The remainder is ejected in the exhaust. It is impossible for any engine, even theoretically, to take heat from a source and convert it entirely into work. This is another expression of the second law. Heat pumps and refrigerators operate in the reverse manner from heat engines, taking heat from a low-temperature area and moving it to a higher-temperature area. This is possible only if work is done by an external agency. This, too, is an expression of the second law.

The third law of thermodynamics follows from an understanding of the second law and of entropy (⇨ box). It states that:

The entropy of a substance approaches zero as its temperature approaches absolute zero.

The zeroth law

After the first law of thermodynamics had been stated and universally accepted it became clear that there was another, linked idea that should be the subject of a thermodynamic law. This arose from the common observation that after bodies of different temperatures had been in contact for a time, movement of energy from one to the other stops as their temperatures become equal. The final state is called *thermal equilibrium* and the property they have in common is their temperature. From this was derived the following law:

If two systems are both in thermal equilibrium with a third system they are in thermal equilibrium with each other.

This law is tacitly invoked every time the temperature of anything is measured; one can do this only when the thermometer and the thing whose temperature is being measured are in thermal equilibrium. The new law was perceived as being even more fundamental than the first law and was therefore whimsically entitled the 0th or zeroth law of thermodynamics.

SEE ALSO
- WHAT IS ENERGY? pp. 46–9
- GAS LAWS p. 50
- HEAT TRANSFER p. 52
- HEAT ENGINES p. 56
- SOURCES OF ENERGY pp. 58–61

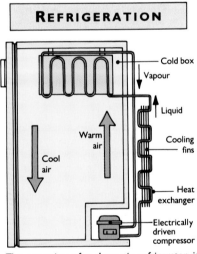

REFRIGERATION

Cold box
Vapour
Liquid
Warm air
Cooling fins
Cool air
Heat exchanger
Electrically driven compressor

The operation of a domestic refrigerator is based on the fact that the working fluid – the *refrigerant* – becomes cooler as it expands and changes from liquid to vapour while circulating through pipes within the cold box. As it does so, it takes in heat from the warmer air within the fridge, so cooling the interior.

The refrigerant – now vapour – is withdrawn by a pump. The pump then compresses the refrigerant, so raising its temperature above that of the room and allowing it to transfer heat through a heat exchanger into the air outside the fridge. Becoming liquid again as it cools, the refrigerant is then ready to pass into the cold box to repeat the cycle.

This system – the *vapour-compression cycle* – is the basis of most domestic and industrial refrigeration. A commonly used refrigerant is the chlorofluorocarbon (CFC) Freon-12. Otherwise inert and ideally suited for refrigeration and other uses, this and other CFCs react with ozone and are responsible for depleting the ozone layer

THE MEANING OF ENTROPY

In 1865 the German theoretical physicist Rudolf Clausius first introduced the term *entropy* to indicate the relationship of the heat content of a system to its absolute temperature (that is, its temperature measured in relation to absolute zero; ⇨ p. 50). As we now usually state it in this context, entropy is an inverse measure of the extent to which the energy of a system is available for conversion to work. The higher the entropy, the smaller the quantity of energy available for conversion. Theoretically, in any closed system – that is, any system that is neither gaining nor losing energy – entropy could remain constant. It can never decrease spontaneously and, in practice, it always increases with time. The statement that entropy increases with time is essentially a statement of the second law of thermodynamics – that heat can never pass spontaneously from a body at a lower temperature to one at a higher temperature.

Entropy is a measure of disorder, randomness or the degree of breakdown – the opposite of organization and synthesis. In biology, an increase in entropy means an increased breakdown of complex systems to their elements. The growth and development of an organism such as a human baby is a temporary decrease in entropy, but this is not a breach of the second law of thermodynamics, because this does not occur without the expenditure of a great deal of energy in converting milk and oxygen into body tissues. In the end, however, the second law will invariably have its way. After death, entropy increases as the body is reduced again to its elements, whether by fire or by bacterial action.

In chemistry, an increase in entropy means the breakdown of complex molecules to simpler substances. When petrol is burned in a car engine, entropy increases as the complex hydrocarbons in petrol are converted to simple carbon dioxide and water with release of energy. Such a reaction will not spontaneously reverse so as to form petrol once again.

The idea of a 'closed system' is entirely theoretical. The only probable closed system is the whole universe, and, in the universe as a whole, entropy is rising steadily and the amount of energy available for work is constantly falling. If the universe is indeed a closed system, increasing entropy will lead, eventually, to a temperature equilibrium in which there are no longer any sources of useful energy to allow motion or support life.

The concept of entropy also provides a unique direction to time – something the other laws of physics fail to do as they work equally well in both directions.

Heat Engines

Heat is energy moving from one system to another or energy contained within a system. Unless heat energy moves from one place to another it is unable to do work. A *heat engine* is any device that makes use of the production and movement of heat to perform work.

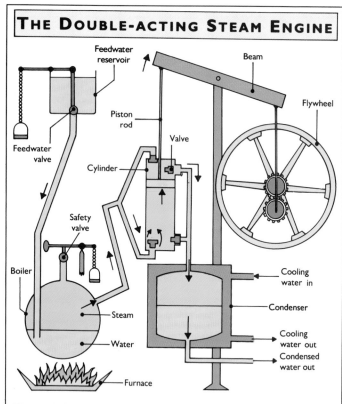

THE DOUBLE-ACTING STEAM ENGINE

The principal components of a typical Watt double-acting steam engine, as built c. 1790. Steam from a boiler was introduced alternately on either side of the piston, so that the engine was 'double-acting' – both the upstroke and the downstroke were powered by steam. After passing through the cylinder, the steam was condensed to water, which was extracted by means of an air pump. As the steam condensed, a partial vacuum was created in the part of the cylinder into which the piston was moving. Thus – although the steam pressure in Watt's engines did not exceed 1½ atmospheres – the relative pressure difference within the cylinder increased the effective power of the engine.

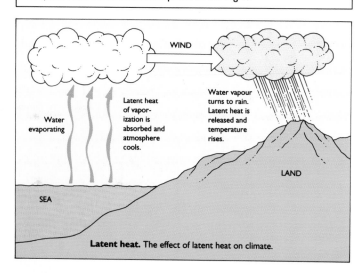

Latent heat. The effect of latent heat on climate.

The gas laws (⬦ p. 50) tell us that a rise in the temperature of a gas causes it to expand – or, if it is prevented from expanding, causes its pressure to increase. This is because the free molecules of the gas become more active, and their average velocity greater. An expanding gas can cause physical objects – such as the lid on a pan of boiling water – to move. Once this fact was appreciated by scientists it was a simple step to the idea of a piston that could be pushed along a cylinder by the expansion of a gas. This is the basis of a large class of heat engines, including conventional steam, petrol and diesel engines. The first of these to be developed was the steam engine.

Latent heat

When a body changes from solid to liquid (melts) or from liquid to gas (evaporates), it absorbs heat; and when it changes from the gas to liquid (condenses) or from liquid to solid (freezes or solidifies), it releases this heat again. When heat is applied to ice at 0°C (32°F), it maintains the same temperature, however much it is heated, until it has turned to liquid water. In so doing it takes up a great deal of heat energy. Similarly, liquid water boiling at 100°C (212°F) maintains the same temperature, however much heat is applied, until it has changed to a gas known as steam. In the process of changing from solid to liquid, or liquid or solid to gas, a great deal of energy is needed to separate the molecules so that they can move about individually as the particles of a liquid or a gas. In both cases the energy is supplied by the heat source and is called *latent heat*. It takes 1 calorie of heat to raise 1 gram of water by 1°C (1.8 °F). But to change 1 gram of water to steam at 100°C (212°F) it takes 550 calories (2,300 joules); the same amount of heat energy is given out when 1 gram of steam turns to water at 100°C. This is why a burn from a steam jet at 100°C is more serious than a burn from water at 100°C because when the gas cools and turns to liquid it can transfer far more heat than when water cools.

The phenomenon of latent heat was first discovered by the Scottish chemist and physicist Joseph Black (1728–99). When Black told his colleague, the engineer James Watt (1736–1819), about his discovery Watt realized that this remarkable fact about heat could be applied to improve the efficiency of existing steam engines. The result was the first practical and reasonably efficient steam engine.

Steam engines

Watt had been repairing a model of a Newcomen engine, which was used to pump water from mines. Thinking about the design while walking one Sunday, he suddenly saw why it was so inefficient and slow, and how it could be improved. In the Newcomen engine, after the piston had been moved along by expanding steam, the cylinder had to be cooled so that the steam condensed and a vacuum was formed that sucked back

the piston. The cylinder was then heated again by the incoming steam. Watt's idea was to have a second chamber, the condenser, into which exhaust steam entered after it had driven down the piston. This chamber could be kept constantly cool and the cylinder left to remain hot. Because the long pause in the cycle for cooling the cylinder was now avoided, the engine ran much more quickly, and because the cylinder did not need to be cooled while the engine was running, heat losses were greatly reduced and efficiency greatly increased.

Watt made many other important improvements, especially that of converting the reciprocal movement of the piston into a rotary movement by means of a crank. The steam engine soon became a great commercial and economic success. It was used to power numerous industrial processes that were being mechanized. The practical steam engine, powered by burning coal, allowed factories to be set up anywhere. Watt's name is immortalized in the unit of power in the metric system – 1 horsepower (550 foot-pounds per second), which is equal to 746 watts. As Carnot subsequently discovered (⬦ p. 56), the efficiency of a heat engine depends on the difference between the highest temperature achieved and that of the cooling water or the exhaust gas. Any heat lost from an engine is heat wasted and not turned into work. In redesigning the Newcomen engine, Watt was unconsciously applying this principle. He was also taking into account the importance of latent heat.

The four-stroke internal combustion engine

The idea of an internal combustion engine that would produce expanding gases by burning material within the cylinder is even older than that of the piston steam engine. Towards the end of the 17th century, the Dutch scientist Christiaan Huygens (1629–95) devised an engine that burned a small amount of gunpowder to raise a piston against gravity. In 1859, when the principles of the steam engine were widely familiar, the French engineer Étienne Lenoir (1822–1900) designed an engine, based on a steam design, that would run on an explosive mixture of gas and air.

At about the same time, the German inventor Nikolas August Otto (1832–91) began his experiments. By 1878, after nearly twenty years of work, he had developed an engine that was, in all important particulars, the same as the petrol engine of today. This was the four-stroke 'silent Otto' gas engine. On the first stroke of the piston an explosive mixture of air and gas was sucked into the cylinder. On the closure of the inlet valve and the return of the piston this mixture was compressed in the cylinder, quickly raising the temperature of the mixture – as the gas laws (⬦ p. 50) would indicate. When the mixture was fully compressed, it was fired (initially by exposing a small pilot flame, but later by an electric spark). This caused a rapid rise in temperature and pressure, and the piston was forced quickly along the cylinder. On the opening of the exhaust valve and the return of the piston, the burnt gases were pushed out into the atmosphere – and the cycle could then start once again. The opening of the inlet and exhaust valves was timed mechanically to the rotation of the crankshaft of the engine. By 1885, Otto's four-stoke engine had proved so successful that it was beginning to rival the steam engine in popularity. Soon afterwards the Otto cycle was used in engines adapted to burn oil or petrol vaporized in a carburettor (a device that mixes air and petrol) such as that developed by Gottlieb Daimler (1834–1900) in 1885.

In 1892 the German engineer Rudolf Diesel (1858–1913) took out a patent for a four-stroke engine, working on the Otto cycle, but using the principle, contained in the gas laws, that an increase in pressure without an increase in volume leads to an increase in temperature. Diesel knew that if a gas were compressed enough its temperature would rise very high – higher, for instance, than the explosive temperature of an air-oil vapour mixture. Diesel's idea was to design an engine in which the difference between the maximum and minimum volume of the closed cylinder (the *compression ratio*) was so great that air in it would, on compression, reach the required temperature. A small, measured quantity of explosive mixture injected into it would ignite spontaneously without the need for a spark. Diesel's design worked very well and was found to operate satisfactorily with all kinds of unrefined oil at an efficiency greater than that of any existing prime mover (a device that converts a natural source of energy into mechanical power).

Turbines

Turbines are machines in which the kinetic energy (⇨ p. 46) of a moving stream of gas or liquid is converted directly into rotary energy. The general idea of the turbine – familiar from the water wheel – was so obvious that by 1880 about 100 patents had been lodged for such engines worked by steam. Many people were attracted by the idea of being able to bypass the cumbersome and slow system of a reciprocating

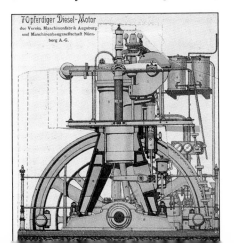

A 70-horsepower diesel motor, named after its inventor, Rudolf Diesel (1858–1913). (AKG)

piston rod and a crank, and convert the energy of expanding steam directly into rotary motion. This was particularly needed to drive electricity-generating dynamos at high speeds. None of the early devices was able to reach a level of efficiency that allowed it to compete with existing engines. In 1884, however, the Irish engineer Sir Charles Parsons (1854–1931) developed a design in which the drop of steam pressure was spread over a number of stages. The high-pressure steam was directed against a circle of small blades arranged around the rotor, causing it to turn. The steam leaving these blades, now at a lower pressure, was then redirected – by a circle of unmoving blades fixed to the casing (the *stator*) – on to another circle of larger blades on the rotor. Several such stages of ever-larger and ever-lower pressure blades were provided. In this way, each stage could have an efficiency of up to 80 per cent. The idea was highly successful and the principle is used to this day. Indeed, many of the largest ships and the majority of the world's electricity generators are still powered in this way.

Gas turbines are rotary engines of a high weight–power ratio, largely based on engines developed by the English engineer Sir Frank Whittle (1907–). In these engines, air is sucked in and compressed by a rotary compressor, and forced into a combustion chamber where fuel is continuously injected and burns at intensely high temperatures. The expanding gases pass back and drive a turbine on the

same shaft as the compressor, then pass out of the rear of the engine. The pressure of the rapidly expanding gases applies a considerable force to the front parts of the inside of the engine, but, because the rear is open, there is no backward force. In this way a powerful forward thrust is generated, making such engines particularly suitable for aircraft (⇨ p. 36). Gas turbine jet engines are used in almost all present-day, large aircraft.

THE FOUR-STROKE ENGINE

In the four-stroke (or Otto) cycle, the piston makes four movements in each power cycle. Most cars have at least four cylinders linked to the same crankshaft, both cylinders and crankshaft being set within a heavy cast-iron cylinder block.

The crankshaft also drives a camshaft, which opens and closes the valves at the top of each cylinder in the correct sequence. The four cylinders fire in turn, usually in the order 1–3–4–2, so that there is a power stroke for every half-revolution of the crankshaft.

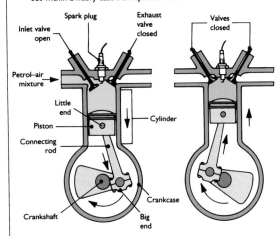

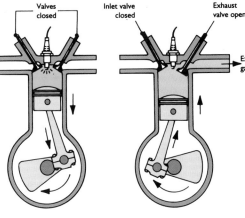

1. The induction stroke. The piston moves down as the crankshaft is turned (by the starter motor, in a car), causing a reduction in pressure inside the cylinder. The partial vacuum thus created draws petrol and air (mixed in the carburettor or by a fuel-injection system) through the open inlet valve into the cylinder.

2. The compression stroke. The fuel–air mixture is compressed as the piston ascends with both valves closed.

3. The power stroke. The mixture is ignited by the spark plug, timed to produce a brief spark at the top of the compression stroke. The piston is driven down as the burning fuel expands.

4. The exhaust stroke. The exhaust valve opens and the piston rises, expelling the burnt mixture from the cylinder to make room for fresh fuel on the next induction stroke.

THE JET ENGINE

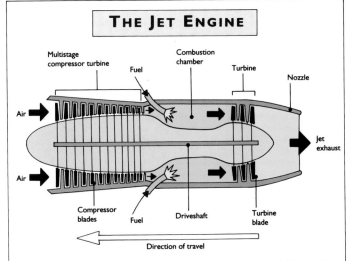

The *turbojet* is the simplest form of gas-turbine (or jet) engine. Forward thrust is created by the rapid expulsion of high-pressure exhaust gases through the nozzle at the rear of the unit. The compressor turbine, initially set in motion by an electric motor, acts like a series of fans to compress air drawn in at the front of the engine. The hot, compressed air passes into the combustion chambers, where it is mixed with fuel (kerosene) and ignited. Once ignited, the temperature within the engine – typically in excess of 450°C (840°F) – is sufficient to keep the fuel-air mixture burning. Before exiting through the tail nozzle, the exhaust gases pass through a second turbine, which itself drives the compressor turbine via the driveshaft.

SEE ALSO

● MECHANICS p. 26
● FORCE AND MOTION p. 28
● AERODYNAMICS AND HYDRODYNAMICS p. 36
● WHAT IS ENERGY? pp. 46–9
● HEAT TRANSFER p. 52
● THERMODYNAMICS p. 54
● SOURCES OF ENERGY pp. 58–61
● SOURCES OF ELECTRICITY pp. 92–5

Sources of Energy 1

Almost all the Earth's energy is derived from the Sun. Plants trap solar radiation as chemical energy by the process of photosynthesis (⇨ p. 48), in which carbon, hydrogen and oxygen from the atmosphere are combined to form sugars. Fossil fuels – such as coal and oil – are derived, either directly or indirectly, from plants.

The primary energy source for humans and other animals is a fuel known as glucose, a simple sugar that is continuously synthesized all over the world by plants, using energy supplied by the Sun. Everything we eat is either glucose or a more complex substance that can be broken down in the body to form glucose. When it is broken down, the energy needed to power all the biochemical reactions of the body – to enable our muscles to contract and our brains to continue to function – is released.

In photosynthesis, the green colouring dye chlorophyll is involved in a complex chain of chemical reactions in which solar energy is used to combine atmospheric carbon, oxygen and hydrogen atoms – derived from molecules of carbon dioxide and water – into simple sugars. These can then be linked together in chains to form more elaborate carbohydrates (polysaccharides) such as starches and celluloses that form the structural elements of plants. In this process a great deal of energy, originally derived from the Sun, is trapped. If vegetable matter is burned immediately, the energy is released in the form of heat, light and sound – and the carbon dioxide and water are returned to the atmosphere.

How energy is generated in the stars

From the time people became aware of the scientific concept of energy, the source of the energy in stars such as our sun became one of the major mysteries. At first, it was assumed that the Sun and other stars were simply huge, burning bodies. But a knowledge of the timescale and the mass of material involved soon showed that this theory would not meet the facts. If the Sun were no more than a vast coal fire, it would have burned out a very long time ago.

The first person to suggest a plausible hypothesis was the American chemist William Draper Harkins (1873–1951), whose interest in the new science of nuclear chemistry led him to predict the existence of the neutron (⇨ pp. 108–17 and 156) and that of a hydrogen atom of greater atomic weight than ordinary hydrogen (*heavy hydrogen*) – both of which predictions were later proved correct. Harkins was intrigued by the fact that the mass of each atomic nucleus differed a little from that of the total of its components. This difference he called the *packing fraction*, and suggested that it represented the energy required to keep the nuclear elements together. Einstein's equations relating mass and energy (⇨ pp. 38–41) led Harkins to suggest that if four hydrogen atoms were fused to form one helium atom, some mass would be lost and would appear as energy. He knew that the Sun contained vast quantities of helium (the name of this element was derived from the Greek word helios, meaning 'sun'). This nuclear reaction – converting hydrogen to helium – was, he suggested, the source of the Sun's energy.

We now know that the helium nucleus consists of two hydrogen nuclei (protons) and two neutrons (⇨ pp. 108–17), but Harkins's general idea was correct. When helium is formed from protons and neutrons considerable fusion energy is liberated and this is the reason the Sun has been able to continue producing such vast quantities of energy for billions of years.

Formation of fossil fuels

Plants die, decompose and become buried. In the period from Devonian times, nearly four hundred million years ago, until about two million years ago, vast forests were buried and covered by geological formations. The resulting deposits of hydrocarbons were turned into coal by the combination of heat and pressure over long periods of time. The first stage was the formation of *peat* – decomposed organic matter with a high water content. When this was covered with heavy sedimentary deposits, the water was pressed out and the material changed to coal. The level and duration of the downward pressure determined the quality of the coal formed – shallow levels led to brown coal (*lignite*), middle levels to *bituminous* coal and deep levels to the hardest and driest coal, *anthracite*.

The world's known coal deposits are enormous. The largest quantities exist in southern Russia, China, Silesia, the German Ruhr, in Britain, Belgium, Holland, Nova Scotia and in North America. The USA has about 30 per cent of the currently known deposits, Russia and China about 20 per cent each and Europe about 13 per cent. At the present rate of extraction, it would take several hundred years for these resources to become seriously depleted. In many areas, however, the best and most readily

---

FUTURE DEMAND

At present there is a large disparity between the more-developed and less-developed countries with regard to the consumption of fossil fuels per head of population. Citizens of the USA and Canada each consume the equivalent of between forty and forty-five barrels of oil annually; in Britain the figure is about twenty. In countries such as India and Nigeria, however, the consumption per head is around the equivalent of two barrels. In future decades, 90 per cent of population growth will be in the less-developed countries – and as this occurs, and these countries industrialize, there will be great pressures for the consumption of fossil fuels, especially oil, to rise.

This combination of dwindling stocks and rising demand poses considerable problems for humanity – that can be solved only by a large reduction in the currently wasteful consumption of fossil fuels, and by a radical reconsideration of the use of solar energy. For instance, great economies are possible in the conversion of chemical energy into other forms such as movement, light and heat, and in the conservation of energy. Science and technology have much to offer in the development of methods of converting solar radiation into other usable forms of energy (⇨ p. 60).

Traffic jams represent our hitherto wasteful use of nonrenewable and polluting energy sources, in this case, crude oil, from which petrol is distilled. By necessity, our reliance on other cleaner and limitless sources, such as solar and hydroelectric power, is on the increase. (Zefa)

WORLD ENERGY SOURCES

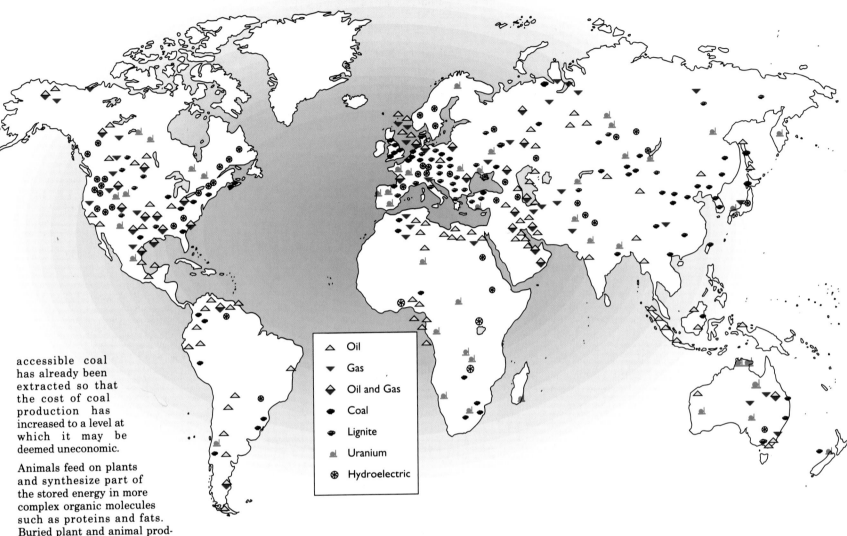

Legend:
- △ Oil
- ▼ Gas
- ◇ Oil and Gas
- ⬣ Coal
- ⬬ Lignite
- Uranium
- ✳ Hydroelectric

accessible coal has already been extracted so that the cost of coal production has increased to a level at which it may be deemed uneconomic.

Animals feed on plants and synthesize part of the stored energy in more complex organic molecules such as proteins and fats. Buried plant and animal products may form petroleum oil and gas deposits instead of coal. The exact processes by which petroleum oils are formed are still not clear, but there is general agreement that the chief source is aquatic organisms, both animal and plant, that have died and settled to become incorporated in sedimentary rock on seabeds. Decomposition by bacterial action is an important preliminary stage, and the higher temperatures found at greater depths also appear to be important. Most petroleum has probably been formed at temperatures of 65–120°C (149–248°F).

Significant deposits of oil and gas occur in pools in the sedimentary rocks. Many of these pools are very large – several kilometres wide and hundreds of metres deep. The way in which these pools of oil and gas form is also uncertain, but it appears likely that the oil first forms within water as tiny globules, which progressively coalesce into ever-larger masses of oil and gas. Being less dense than water and rock, these migrate upwards through permeable rock until adequate spaces are found, from which they displace water. Most deposits remain underground, but some of this

rising petroleum and gas reaches the surface of the Earth. Gas is immediately lost into the atmosphere but the oil may form large surface deposits of heavy oil. The more volatile fractions (such as petrol and naphtha) will then evaporate, leaving oxidized residues in the form of tar (asphalt). Surface deposits of these substances are found, for instance, in the 'tar pools' of California and the 'pitch lake' in Trinidad.

Petroleum is a complex mixture of hydrocarbons with a few other elements such as sulphur, oxygen and nitrogen. Natural gas is 88–95 per cent methane mixed with smaller quantities of other members of the paraffin series – ethane, butane and propane. Unlike the domestic gas previously in use, which was derived from heated coal, natural gas does not contain the poisonous gas carbon monoxide.

Fossil-fuel consumption

For most purposes oil, gas and electricity are more convenient than coal and have replaced it. The enormous increase in human mobility and the development

of the internal combustion engine (⇨ p. 56) have made oil the premier source of energy. In 1920 more than 70 per cent of the fuel used was coal; today the figure is only 25 per cent.

About 40 per cent of the world's fuel consumption is in the form of petroleum products and about 20 per cent is natural gas – a percentage that is expected to rise. Traditional fuels such as wood, peat, dried dung and agricultural waste make up the remainder. The world's stocks of oil and gas are being consumed at a much faster rate than its retrievable coal stocks, although the stocks of coal are much larger.

Electricity is also much more convenient than coal for many domestic and industrial purposes, and, since about 1950, there has been a tremendous rise in the consumption of electricity in developed countries, in parallel with the rise of their services-oriented economies. Much of the coal now being consumed is burnt to drive turbines (⇨ pp. 52–7) for the generation of electricity.

SEE ALSO

- ● WHAT IS ENERGY? pp. 46–9
- ● GAS LAWS p. 50
- ● HEAT TRANSFER p. 52
- ● THERMODYNAMICS p. 54
- ● HEAT ENGINES p. 56
- ● SOURCES OF ENERGY 2 p. 60
- ● SOURCES OF ELECTRICITY pp. 92–5

Sources of Energy 2

At the present rates of consumption the Earth's known stocks of fossil fuels (⇨ p. 58) are likely to be exhausted in only a few hundred years' time.

Fossil fuels, which are built up over millions of years by the fixation of light energy from the Sun by photosynthesis, have been largely squandered, and the rate of usage continues to increase. In addition, the energy derived from burning fossil fuels has been wasted by inefficient methods of use and recovery. As a result, science and technology are investigating the possibilities of renewable natural energy sources and more efficient uses of energy.

Nearly all our energy comes from the Sun (⇨ p. 46). Traditionally, this energy has been exploited by way of fossil fuels whose solar energy was trapped millions of years ago, but today we must look for more immediate ways of tapping into the vast amount of energy that continuously falls on the Earth from the Sun. The energy in solar radiation that strikes the Earth is about 180,000 million million watts (180,000 terawatts). One thousand watts is the power output of an average electric-fire element. Running for one

hour this consumes a unit of electricity and costs only a nominal amount.

Renewable energy sources

Biofuels – mainly wood and agricultural waste – are important in many economies for cooking, heating and lighting, but are hardly used at all in the more industrialized societies. Biomass energy sources, such as trees, can be used to fire power plants or to make alcohol to run internal combustion engines (⇨ p. 56). If the consumed biomass is replaced at the same rate by rapidly growing vegetation, the amount of carbon dioxide produced by its consumption (⇨ p. 52) can be balanced by the carbon dioxide consumed in photosynthesis (⇨ p. 48).

Hydroelectric power is widely exploited wherever natural features and economic conditions make it feasible. Solar evaporation of water from the seas raises millions of tonnes of water to great heights, conferring on it potential and kinetic energy – some of which can be tapped when it falls on mountains, or runs down to the sea in rivers on which dams can be built. Scientists estimate that the potential for an increase in the use of hydroelectric power is about five times the present usage.

Direct solar-energy exploitation

Scientists have known of the photoelectric or photovoltaic effect (⇨ pp. 40 and 90) since the end of the 19th century – and have cherished the dream of economically converting sunlight directly into electricity. Because of the high cost and low efficiency of the devices concerned, however, it is only recently that this dream has shown any probability of becoming a reality. Solar cells are passive semiconductor devices that consume no energy and require no maintenance – other than being kept clean. They absorb photons from sunlight and produce a voltage that causes an electric current to flow. They may be of any size, from less

One of three Luz international solar-energy complexes in the Mohave Desert, California, USA. The three sites cover 1,000 acres and generate 275 megawatts of electricity. Computer-controlled parabolic mirrors track the Sun, focusing its light onto tubes of synthetic oil. This oil is thus superheated to 391°C (736°F), and is used to boil water for steam turbine generators in connected power plants.

(Hank Morgan, SPL)

than a square millimetre to many square metres, and the output is proportional to the area. They are highly portable, which allows them to be sited where the electricity is needed – often in remote and inaccessible regions. Photoelectric generators require comparatively large areas. To supply all the electrical needs of an average house would require a solar cell area of about 10 × 4 m (11 × 4½ yd), assuming an efficiency of 12 per cent. Electricity generated in this way could be used immediately or could be used to charge storage batteries for later use. The output depends on the light intensity as well as on the area of exposed cells. This means that the cost-effectiveness of a project may depend on the location.

The cost of generating photoelectricity has declined sharply in recent years. In 1970 it was about 20,000 per cent more than in the early 1990s. It still costs about five times more than the cost of generation by conventional means, but scientific developments continue to lead to ever-greater efficiencies. A recently developed cell made of layered gallium arsenide and gallium antimonide has achieved an efficiency of 35 per cent, compared with a figure of about 12 per cent for cells currently in use. New economy thin-film cells under development promise to reduce the capital cost of the method to as little as one tenth of present levels.

Photoelectricity is not the only way in which solar energy can be directly tapped. In areas of high solar radiation many effective installations exist in

TIDAL POWER

The tidal power station at La Rance in Brittany, France, opened in 1966, consists of a barrage blocking the 750 m (2460 ft) wide estuary of the River Rance. The tidal waters are channelled through 24 tunnels in the barrage (seen in cross-section below). Each tunnel houses a reversible turbine generator that can operate efficiently both on the flood tide (when the water flow is from sea to basin) and on the ebb tide (from basin to sea). At high tide, the sluices are closed, trapping the water in the tidal basin. The water can then be released to turn the turbines when the tide is low but when demand for power is high. Each of the 24 turbines can generate up to 10 MW – the total output of the plant being sufficient to satisfy the needs of around a million consumers.

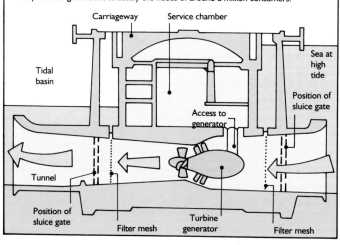

ECONOMIES IN ELECTRICAL CONSUMPTION

Studies of the economies that can be made in industrial and domestic energy expenditure by applying scientific and technological advances have shown that savings of 25–50 per cent are feasible while still achieving the desired effect. Some of the most impressive examples are in the field of more efficient electricity use. In many highly industrialized countries, electric motors consume over half of all electricity generated. Many of these motors, especially those driving fans or pumps, are run continuously at full speed while their output is damped or throttled according to varying requirements. Enormous energy savings can be achieved if the motors are electronically controlled so as to run only as fast as is required at any one time – and the working life of the motors is also increased. Modern electric motor design and the use of new and improved materials in their construction can also increase efficiency and achieve savings that can quickly recoup the capital costs involved.

About a quarter of the electricity consumed in industrialized societies is for lighting. Today, much of this consumption is grossly inefficient because of the

Heat distribution over the surface of a house can be shown by a thermogram, in which white, orange and red show the warmer areas, while green and blue indicate the cooler ones. Here the greatest heat losses are through the single-glazed windows. Although the roof is relatively well insulated, some heat still escapes.
(Agema Infrared Systems, SPL)

use of incandescent-filament light bulbs, which produce far more heat than light. In the USA, for instance, about 5 per cent of generated electricity is wasted in powering cooling equipment needed to dispose of the unwanted heat produced by lighting systems. If the most advanced lighting methods were universally adopted, 80–90 per cent of the electricity used for lighting would be saved. Compact fluorescent bulbs run cold, produce the same light output for only 20 per cent of the electricity consumption, and last more than ten times as long as filament bulbs. Light-intensity sensors can readily adjust the brightness of artificial light to compensate for changing outdoor brightness, and can even turn off lights when there is no one in the room. Room layout, light-coloured walls and high, transparent wall panels can all reduce wastage and produce more comfortable working conditions capable of improving productivity. American estimates, based on such methods, suggest that about 100 billion watts and over $20 billion a year could be saved on lighting alone.

Improvements in the energy efficiency of houses and office buildings also offer great opportunities for economies. Single-layer glass windows, for instance, conduct heat almost as well as metal and readily transmit radiant heat in the infrared region (⇨ p. 52). Two layers, separated by less than 1 cm (½ in) of air, will halve heat losses – and internal coatings can be applied that will reflect heat back into the room without impairing transparency to visible light. Application of the latest technology can reduce heat losses to one tenth and, if there is even a small amount of sunshine, can turn a window into a net gainer of heat.

Effective wall and roof insulation, coupled with sophisticated electronic control of heating and heat loss that takes account of changing external conditions, can reach such a level of efficiency that a domestic hot-water heater is sufficient to maintain room temperatures at the required level, even in severe winters, completely eliminating the need for central heating.

HYDROELECTRIC POWER

In a typical hydroelectric power plant, a river is dammed to create a reservoir that can provide a steady and controllable supply or running water. Water from the reservoir is channelled downstream to the power plant, where it causes a turbine to rotate, which in turn drives an electric generator. The electricity generated is then stepped up by transformers at a substation to the high voltages suitable for transmission.

In areas where there are considerable fluctuations in electricity demand, pumped-storage plants may be installed. The surplus power available at off-peak periods is used to pump water to a separate reservoir. At peak times, the stored water is released to generate extra electrical power.

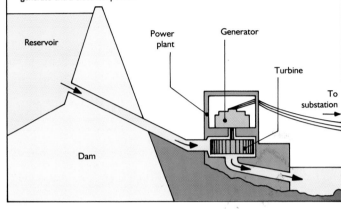

which sunlight is used – either directly or, more efficiently, by way of flat or trough-shaped mirrors – to heat water or oil that can then be used to power an electricity generator. Systems of this kind of up to 300 megawatts (300 million watts) have been built and used successfully in desert regions. Other similar but smaller systems use parabolic mirrors that move and track the Sun so that they continue to focus very-high-temperature beams on a target for many hours each day. A 30-megawatt power plant of this kind is being built in Jordan.

Wind power

Solar radiation energy is converted naturally to mechanical energy when it causes atmospheric disturbances in the form of winds. This source of energy is readily converted to electricity simply by mounting a dynamo on a tower and fitting wind-sail blades to the rotor shaft. The early windmill generators were inefficient and unreliable, but research has led to great improvements and the cost of generating a kilowatt-hour of electricity in this way has now dropped markedly, with further reductions likely.

The Nordfriesland wind park, near Niebull in northern Germany, consists of 50 wind turbines, each producing 250 kilowatts of electricity.
(Martin Bond, SPL)

WAVES

SCIENCE

What are Waves? 1

Russian gymnast producing a transverse wave in a ribbon as part of her floor routine. (Yann Guichaoua, Allsport-Vandystadt)

We are all familiar with waves in water – especially those caused in the seas by wind and lunar attraction – but this is only one specific example of various kinds. In fact, the entire universe is permeated with waves.

Some waves move in an obvious medium, such as water, and can be seen. Some move in solid media but with such a small amplitude that nothing can be seen, although vibration may be felt and sound can be heard. Some move in an invisible medium, such as air, and can only be heard. Once, scientists thought that all waves were forces acting in a medium (⇨ p. 40), but it is now known that the great majority of waves – electromagnetic waves – can move where there is no medium, and are propagated best through the vacuum of empty space.

The one thing that all waves have in common is that they represent a disturbance moving away from its source. If they do move in a medium, that medium does not experience any net movement; although the wavefront continues to move outwards, the particles of the medium do not move in any permanent sense. In fact they do move briefly outwards, but quickly return to their original position, characteristically repeating this to-and-fro vibrational movement at a particular rate about a fixed point. A wave breaking on a beach does not consist of water that has travelled in from a long way out at sea, but of water that has been at the sea's edge all along.

Types of wave

Waves may be either *longitudinal* or *transverse*. In longitudinal waves – for instance, sound – the vibrations occur in the same direction as the propagation of the waves. In transverse waves – for instance, electromagnetic propagation – the vibrations occur at right angles to the direction of wave motion.

To be able to travel, sound waves require a medium, which may be a gas, a liquid or a solid. In air, groups of molecules oscillate forwards and backwards – being alternately compressed together and pulled apart so that the air is made, by turns, more and less dense. The pattern of movement in an electromagnetic wave is like the wave form you see if you fix one end of a long thin rope about 1 m (about 3 ft) from the ground, letting the rope hang a little loose, and then give it a series of regular flips up and down. A succession of waves passes along the rope towards the fixed end – and, although the waves move rapidly along, the rope itself does not move towards the fixed point. Any part of the rope moves only up and down in a direction at right angles to the direction of movement of the waves.

A short-exposure photograph taken of this demonstration would produce an illustration typical of the way in which wave motion is represented graphically (⇨ illustration). This represents what is called a *sine wave* (⇨ pp. 20 and 26), whose waveform is a sine curve, expressed in the equation $y = \sin x$, and is a rather inadequate representation of

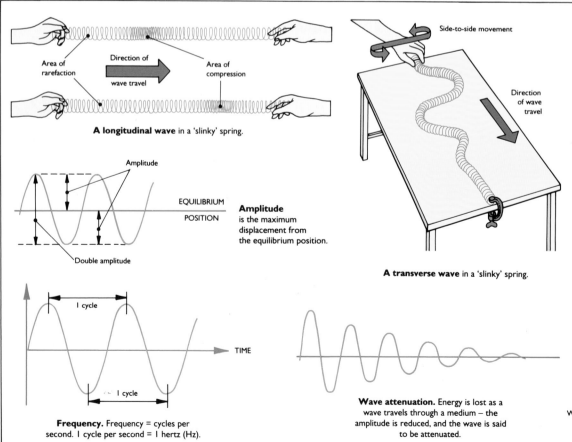

A longitudinal wave in a 'slinky' spring.

Area of rarefaction — Direction of wave travel — Area of compression

Amplitude is the maximum displacement from the equilibrium position.

EQUILIBRIUM POSITION

Double amplitude

Frequency. Frequency = cycles per second. 1 cycle per second = 1 hertz (Hz).

TIME

1 cycle

Side-to-side movement

Direction of wave travel

A transverse wave in a 'slinky' spring.

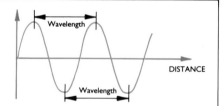

Wavelength. Wavelength is the distance between two successive points along a wave with similar amplitudes.

Wavelength

DISTANCE

Wave attenuation. Energy is lost as a wave travels through a medium – the amplitude is reduced, and the wave is said to be attenuated.

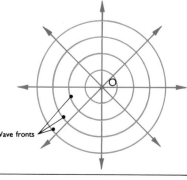

Spherical and plane wavefronts. Wavefronts propagating outwards from point source O will be spherical in a three-dimensional context (such as light waves propagating from the Sun) or circular in a two-dimensional context (such as water waves propagating from a dropped pebble). Once far enough from the source, such wavefronts can for most practical purposes be considered as straight lines – *plane wavefronts* – much in the same way that the curvature of the Earth is not noticeable to someone standing on it.

Wave fronts

the dynamic process that is actually in progress. But it is the easiest way to visualize a wave.

The highest point of the wave is called the *peak* and the lowest point the *trough*. The line that cuts horizontally through the centre of the wave is the *datum line*, from which heights and depths are measured, and represents zero. Anything above the datum line is considered to be positive and anything below it is said to be negative.

Frequency and wavelength

The most important characteristics of a wave are the *wavelength* – the distance from one peak to the next (or from one trough to the next); the *amplitude* – the height of the peak above the datum line; and the *form* of the wave – usually, but not necessarily, a sine wave. For some purposes it is more convenient to consider the number of peaks (and troughs) that occur in a particular time – the *frequency* – rather than the wavelength. As long as the speed of propagation is constant, these two parameters – frequency and wavelength – are reciprocally related. The shorter the wavelength, the higher the frequency; the longer the wavelength, the lower the frequency. A group of waves of limited duration, or 'wave-train', travelling at 1 m/s and producing 100 peaks per second will have a wavelength of 1 cm. In other words, a wave-train of 1 cm wavelength travelling at 1 m/s will have a frequency of 100 cycles per second – that is, 100 peaks and troughs each second. The unit 'cycle per second' is called a *Hertz* (abbreviation Hz) after the German physicist Heinrich Hertz (1857–94), who discovered electromagnetic waves.

All electromagnetic waves travel at the same speed in a vacuum – commonly referred to as the speed of light. But light is just one example of the wide spectrum of electromagnetic waves that includes radio, television, radar, microwaves, heat, visible light, ultraviolet, X-rays and gamma rays

(⇨ p. 84). For all of these it is equally valid to talk of wavelength or frequency. Frequency is usually designated by the Greek letter ν (nu) and wavelength by the Greek letter λ (lambda).

$$\nu \times \lambda = \text{velocity.}$$

The amplitude of a wave – the height of the peak from the datum line – can be considered an indication of *intensity*. The energy of a wave is proportional to the square of the amplitude. The amplitude from the height of one peak vertically downward to the depth of a trough (peak-to-peak amplitude) is called the *double amplitude*.

Given suitable conditions, all wave-trains can be bounced back (reflected; ⇨ box), bent or caused to change direction (refracted; ⇨ box) and diverted into a region in which they would normally be obscured (diffracted; ⇨ box). They are also all subject to constructive or destructive interference (⇨ p. 66).

REFLECTION

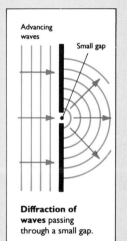 *(see diagrams at top of centre column)*

Reflection of plane waves at a plane surface. The waves are parallel as they approach XY and after they are reflected. AN is the *normal* (the perpendicular) to XY at A. *i* is the angle of incidence of the wave as it meets XY. The angle of reflection is *r*, and *i = r*.

Waves reflected at a curved surface. Waves behave in the same way as light reflected in a concave mirror. S is the principal focus of the surface A.

The size of a reflector must be appropriate for the wavelength of the waves to be reflected. Audible sound waves have frequencies about 16–20,000 Hz and travel at a speed of roughly 300 m/s. This means that low-pitched sounds have wavelengths of around 10 m (32 ft) and can be reflected only by large surfaces such as walls or mountain sides. Ultrasound frequencies, as used in scanners, are much higher than audible frequencies – up to about 10,000,000 Hz – and thus have very short wavelengths that readily reflect off small surfaces.

Radio waves have wavelengths of about 10–10,000 m (32–32,000 ft). Most of these are too long to be reflected by equipment of any practical size. Television, radar and microwave frequencies, however, have shorter wavelengths – down to a few centimetres – and can be reflected by comparatively small surfaces such as parabolic dishes (⇨ pp. 78). Visible light has wavelengths of only thousandths of a millimetre and reflects well off any smooth surface.

When a wave-train strikes a surface the angle at which it strikes the surface is called the *angle of incidence*. If it is reflected, it returns from, or 'bounces off', the surface at an angle (the *angle of reflection*) equal to the angle of incidence. This law of reflection still holds even if the surface is curved, because curved reflecting surfaces are imagined to consist of a large number of very small plane surfaces each set at a tangent to the curve – this assumption enables the way in which curved surfaces reflect waves to be calculated on the same basis as plane surfaces.

DIFFRACTION

When light is passed through a very small pinhole and projected on to a screen it does not, as might be supposed, form a sharp image of the pinhole on the screen. Instead, the image is blurred and is surrounded by a series of concentric light and dark rings lying in the area that ought to be in shadow. Similarly, the edge of the shadow of a very sharp, smooth-edged object is not sharp and smooth but forms a series of alternately bright and dark fringes. The phenomenon that causes these effects is known as *diffraction*.

The first explanations of diffraction were provided in around 1676 by the Dutch astronomer and physicist Christiaan Huygens (1629–95). He suggested that every point on the surface of an expanding sphere of light could be considered as a new source of light and that the light from all these secondary sources interacted. On this basis Huygens could explain reflection and refraction. He assumed that light waves were longitudinal (⇨ main text), as in the case of sound. Later, the French physicist Augustin Fresnel (1788–1827) extended Huygens's idea. The English physicist Thomas Young (1773–1829) had suggested that light was a transverse wave motion, rather than a longitudinal one, and Fresnel realized that if this were so it could, in conjunction with Huygens's idea, explain the light and dark rings produced by diffraction on the basis of interference.

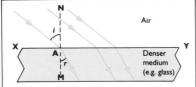 *(diagram: Advancing waves / Small gap)*

Diffraction of waves passing through a small gap.

A calcite crystal demonstrating the phenomenon of *double refraction* – the formation of two refracted rays from one incident ray.
(Paul Silverman, Fundamental Photos, SPL)

Fresnel went further and suggested that transverse light waves could exist in any plane, just as the rope (⇨ main text) might be flipped vertically, horizontally or at any angle in between. This important idea – that light oscillated in an infinite number of planes at right angles to the direction of propagation – explained some other phenomena, notably the double refraction of light passing through crystals of Iceland spar (a variety of calcite). It led on to the concept of the polarization of light and the possibility of confining light to a single plane of polarization – *plane polarization* (⇨ p. 72).

REFRACTION

We are all familiar with the way in which a stick pushed partly under water at an angle appears to be bent at the point of entry. This is an example of the *refraction* of light. The effect is brought about because of the difference between the light reaching our eyes from the part of the stick above the water and the light from the submerged part. The second has passed through a more dense medium (water) than the first, which has passed only through air. The speed of light is maximal when it passes through a vacuum. It is slower when it passes through any other medium and the more dense the medium the more it is slowed.

If a light beam passing from a less to a more dense medium hits the interface between the two media perpendicularly, it continues in a straight line although at

a lower speed. But if it strikes the interface at an angle, it is bent towards a line vertical to the surface when it enters the denser medium. When light moves from one medium to another, its speed changes but its frequency does not. The change in wavelength causes the bending. Refraction applies to all waves.

Refraction of a plane wavefront. MAN is the *normal* (the perpendicular) to XY; *i* is the angle of incidence; *r* is the angle of refraction. The waves are parallel after refraction.

What are Waves? 2

The interaction of waves with each other can have annoying effects, such as when an aircraft passes overhead and interferes with television reception. But it is very useful to scientists in making certain kinds of measurement.

One of the most convincing demonstrations that sound, light, radio waves, X-rays and other forms of radiation all have something in common is the way in which they show similar effects when two or more beams of the same kind of radiation interfere. This is because they are all essentially periodic in nature – involving the continuously repetitive changes or cycles that we call waves.

Interference

Two or more waves of the same kind can combine to produce a wave with new characteristics. *Interference* is most easily appreciated by considering two waves of the same frequency and amplitude. These waves may combine in various ways, the two most striking being combination in phase and combination out of phase.

Combination in phase means that the peaks and troughs of the two waves (⇨ p. 64) occur at exactly the same time. The effect of this is that the amplitude of the combined wave is double that of the separate waves. As a result the energy of the combination is much increased. This is called *constructive interference*.

Out-of-phase combination means that the peaks of one wave coincide with the troughs of the other. The effect of this is actually to cancel out the amplitude and energy of both waves. This is called *destructive interference*. It does not result in any actual loss of energy – that would be contrary to the law of conservation of energy (⇨ p. 28). In the case of light what actually happens is that the light lost at the frequency concerned is gained at other frequencies, by means of constructive interference.

Swirls of colour in a thin film of soap. The colours are seen as a result of the interference between the light reflected from the top and bottom of the film. Their differences result from varying film thicknesses and viewing angles. (Tom Branch, SPL)

It is not always easy for scientists to arrange for two waves to be exactly in or out of phase, but if this is achieved it is possible, for instance, for two identical sounds to produce either an increase in volume or almost complete silence. It is also possible to arrange for two beams of light to be out of phase so as to produce darkness. White light is a continuum of a range of frequencies divided into a number of narrow bands, each associated with a particular colour. When two beams of white light interfere, some of these frequencies interfere destructively and are removed, leaving the light coloured. This can happen, for instance, when light passes through a very thin

film of a transparent material and is the explanation of the display of colours often seen in a thin film of oil on a wet road. In this case, one beam is reflected from the surface of the oil and another from the oil–water interface. The two paths are thus of different length and this can give rise to constructive interference for one colour or another. A similar effect can occur in a soap bubble and

---

Two waves of the same wavelength

→ results in

Constructive interference results in the effect of the waves being combined.

Two waves of the same wavelength but totally out of phase

→ results in →

Destructive interference results in the waves cancelling each other out.

THE INTERFEROMETER

Wave interference produces discernible effects from minute differences – such as the tiny difference in the wavelength of light of different colours. Scientific instruments exploiting this – effectively the magnification of small phenomena – can achieve a remarkable degree of sensitivity and precision. Because of the range of wave phenomena in nature, these instruments can be used for a wide variety of purposes.

Light passing through transparent materials of different optical density undergoes a change in its speed and wavelength. This light will therefore be out of phase with light from the same source that has not passed through the material and interference fringes can be formed. This allows the refractive index (⇨ p. 78) of different materials to be compared and measured in an instrument known as an interference refractometer. Interference can be used to assess the flatness of optical surfaces in the surface interferometer.

In astronomy, many double stars occur so closely together that they cannot be separated using a normal optical telescope. But if two widely spaced mirrors are used to reflect the light from each star to a single point, the two beams will be slightly out of phase and will tend to form interference patterns – depending on the distance apart of the mirrors. These can be cancelled by changing the separation of the mirrors, and, from this

distance and the knowledge of the wavelength of the light, the separation of the stars can be calculated. Perhaps the most celebrated light interferometer in history was that invented by the German-born American physicist Albert Michelson (1852–1931; ⇨ p. 40) to try to check the differences in the speed of light caused by the movement of the Earth – the failed experiment that led Lorentz, Fitzgerald and finally Albert Einstein to momentous conclusions about the nature and speed of light (⇨ pp. 38–41).

Interferometers can be used in many ways to make precise measurements of length, angle or displacement, and were used at the end of the 19th century to establish the standard metre in terms of wavelengths. They can readily measure angles smaller than a one thousandth of a second of arc (less than one three millionth of a degree). Laser interferometers are used to measure short lengths to an astonishing degree of accuracy.

Radio astronomy (⇨ pp. 14 and 122–5), using two or more antennae, makes extensive use of interferometry, working on the same principles as optical interferometry. Acoustic interferometers are used to measure the speed and absorption of sound waves. Interferometers are also used in space for the tracking and guidance of space vehicles.

accounts for the iridescence of mother-of-pearl. The same mechanism causes the fluttering effect sometimes seen on television when the aerial receives a direct signal from the transmitter and also a second signal reflected from a passing aircraft. Because the path lengths are different the two wave-trains can interfere.

Phase differences

Any phase difference can exist between two waves, from fully in phase to fully out of phase. These differences occur because waves from the same source may travel different distances before combining – one might, for instance, be reflected from a mirror. Phase differences depend on the difference in the number of wavelengths in the two paths. If the difference is a whole number, then the waves will combine exactly in phase, with peaks and troughs coinciding – and the two waves constructively interfering. If the difference is half a wavelength, then the combined waves will be exactly out of phase and will cancel. If the difference is some other fraction of a wavelength the two waves will partially cancel one another.

When two waves of slightly different frequency interfere the situation is more complicated. Because each association of peaks is slightly different from the previous one, the two waves 'beat' together to produce new frequencies that are both the sum and the difference of the two original waves. This phenomenon is important in many contexts, including acoustics and electronics.

A standard way to represent phase difference quantitatively is by considering a single cycle of a wave (from datum line to positive peak, to datum line, to negative peak and back to datum line; ⇨ p. 64) as being analogous to the rotation of the radius of a circle. In this scheme, one cycle corresponds to 360°. Waves in phase have 0° phase difference. Waves wholly out of phase have 180° of phase shift. Waves leading other waves or lagging behind them have a phase shift of more or less than 180°. So engineers will talk of one wave as, for instance, lagging another wave by 45°.

It is almost impossible to make sense of the phenomenon of interference except on the basis of the properties of waves. Because of this, any beam that can suffer interference is deemed to have a wavelike nature even if, for other reasons, its nature is thought to be that of a stream of particles. In 1927 the American physicist Clinton Davisson (1881–1958) accidentally showed that two beams of electrons could be made to interfere; scientists regarded it as merely a demonstration of the fact, suggested three years earlier by de Broglie (⇨ p. 40), that electrons could exhibit wave properties.

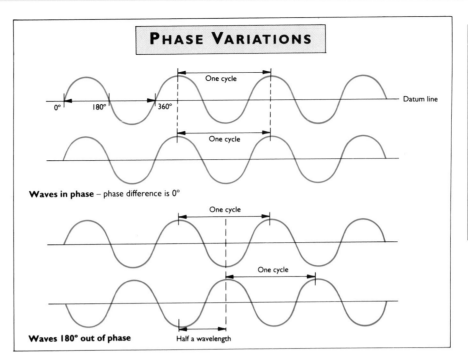

PHASE VARIATIONS

One cycle

0°   180°   360°   Datum line

One cycle

Waves in phase – phase difference is 0°

One cycle

One cycle

Waves 180° out of phase   Half a wavelength

SEE ALSO

● BEYOND NEWTON 2: QUANTUM THEORY p. 40
● WHAT IS ENERGY? pp. 46–9
● WHAT ARE WAVES? 2 p. 66
● ACOUSTICS p. 68
● WAVES OUTSIDE THE AUDIBLE SPECTRUM p. 70
● LIGHT pp. 72–5
● COLOUR p. 76
● REFLECTION AND REFRACTION p. 78
● SPECTRA AND SPECTROSCOPY p. 80
● COHERENT LIGHT – MASERS AND LASERS p. 82
● THE ELECTROMAGNETIC SPECTRUM AND ITS PROPERTIES p. 84

THOMAS YOUNG AND OPTICAL INTERFERENCE

The English physicist Thomas Young (1773–1829) was not fully appreciated in his time, but is now regarded as one of the two or three profoundly important scientists of his day. He was something of a prodigy who was said to have read the Bible twice before the age of four, could speak many languages, played several musical instruments and became a physician as well as a scientist. His lectures at the Royal Institution in London were so far ahead of their time that few understood them, but fortunately they were preserved. It was later found that Young had anticipated several other people in important discoveries. He established the cause of astigmatism, worked out the nature of colour vision, originated the modern concept of energy (⇨ pp. 44–9), investigated and elucidated elasticity and surface tension, investigated the nature of sound, and contributed to the deciphering of the Rosetta stone (a slab inscribed with the same text in Greek, demotic characters and Egyptian hieroglyphics, which provided the key to understanding Egyptian texts).

One of his most important contributions, however, was his work to prove the wave nature of light. In 1803 Young passed a beam of light of a single colour (*monochromatic*) through a very narrow vertical slit, and then through two slits very close together on to a screen. The image on the screen consisted of alternate bright and dark bands. If one of the pair of closely set slits was covered, these bands disappeared. Young saw that this phenomenon could be explained only if light was a wave phenomenon – and was inexplicable if light was a stream of particles as Isaac Newton had believed. Young's work met with considerable hostility but, in the end, had to be accepted. Ironically, in due course Planck and Einstein were to show that *both* Newton and Young were right (⇨ pp. 38–41).

Thomas Young (1773–1829), English physicist who made important contributions to the wave theory of light with experiments on optical interference. (AR)

Acoustics

The term 'acoustics' means more than simply the science of sound. It covers a wide field of engineering and technology and – because physical acoustics is the basis of musical tones and physiological acoustics is the basis of the experience of music – it also incorporates a branch of the arts. An understanding of acoustics is central to the study of hearing and speech production and to certain methods of medical diagnosis.

Acoustics is concerned with all mechanical waves, not only those that can be heard. Although the term suggests hearing, there are important branches of acoustics dealing with both subsonic and ultrasonic (supersonic) waves (⇨ p. 70). These have important properties and implications, and wide applications. But the main ideas about acoustics can best be understood by studying the range of frequencies (⇨ p. 64) to which the human ear is sensitive.

Sound can be propagated through any elastic medium – through air and other gases, through liquids and even through solids. But it cannot be propagated through a vacuum. In this it differs from some other forms of wave propagation that do not require a physical medium (⇨ p. 64).

Propagation in air

In air, sound radiates from a source as a succession of rapidly alternating compressions and decompressions, spreading outwards at a speed of about 700 mph (1,126 km/h) from the source. All sound sources, of whatever kind, are vibrating surfaces that alternately compress and *rarefy* (that is, lessen the density of) the medium. This results in local areas of alternating higher and lower density.

For sounds audible to humans, the frequency of these alternations ranges from about 16 to about 20,000 Hz (cycles per second). Almost everyone can hear low-frequency sound, but the upper limit of people's hearing nearly always reduces with increasing age. The eardrums are thin membranes at the inner end of the outer ear canal; they are lightly loaded and are free to move a little, in or out, under the most minute changes in the pressure of the external air. The rapid fluctuations in the air pressure caused by sources of sound therefore result in a vibratory movement of the eardrums. These vibrations are conveyed to the inner ear, where they stimulate specialized 'hair cells' whose movement causes nerve impulses to be sent to the brain along the acoustic nerves.

ECHOES

Echoes are rebounding waves of energy that reproduce the frequency pattern of the ambient waves, but with some loss of amplitude. Sounds readily suffer interference, which can generate the repetitive sense of 'beats'.

Sympathetic vibration

Just as the eardrum is caused to move in and out by alternating high and low pressure in the air, so any other free surface will vibrate in 'sympathy' with the sound vibrations in the air. Sympathetic vibration can be significant, especially if the sound happens to be of a frequency at which the object concerned can vibrate especially freely – the *resonant frequency*. For instance, if the sustaining (right) pedal of a piano is depressed and a note sung or whistled near the instrument, the appropriate strings will vibrate in sympathy and can be heard sounding on their own afterwards. This fact is important in musical instruments, most of which depend on sympathetic and forced vibration for the quality and volume of the sound they produce.

Pitch, loudness and attack

Audible sounds are characterized by pitch, loudness or volume and attack. The sense of the *pitch* of a sound – whether it resembles a note produced by the keys at the right (high-pitch) or left (low-pitch) end of a piano keyboard – is determined by the frequency (number of cycles per second) of the vibrations. A high frequency causes a high-pitched note; a low frequency a low-pitched note. The *loudness* or *volume* of a note depends on the amplitude of the vibrations – that is, the energy, and hence the extent to which the air is compressed and decompressed. The greater the amplitude, the louder the sound. The ears are exquisitely sensitive to very low-amplitude pressure changes. *Attack* is the term for the suddenness with which a sound starts and builds up. Plucked or percussively struck strings produce notes with a rapid attack. Gently bowed strings have a slow attack. Either can be sustained, or can *decay* (drop in amplitude) quickly or slowly. We tend to recognize sounds as much by their attack and decay as by their inherent quality.

Harmonics

Antinode

Node   Node

IST HARMONIC (FUNDAMENTAL)

Antinode   Antinode

Node

Node   Node

2ND HARMONIC (IST OVERTONE)

Antinode   Antinode   Antinode

Node   Node

Node   Node

3RD HARMONIC (2ND OVERTONE)

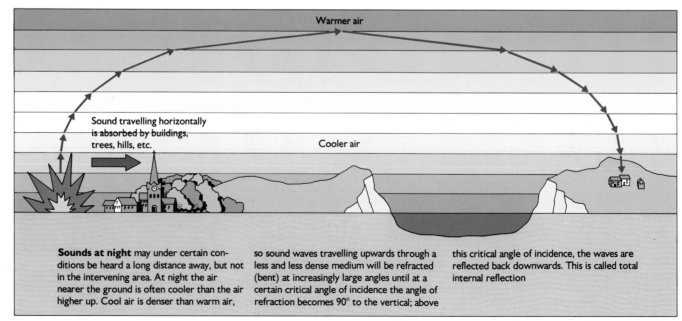

Warmer air

Sound travelling horizontally is absorbed by buildings, trees, hills, etc.

Cooler air

Sounds at night may under certain conditions be heard a long distance away, but not in the intervening area. At night the air nearer the ground is often cooler than the air higher up. Cool air is denser than warm air, so sound waves travelling upwards through a less and less dense medium will be refracted (bent) at increasingly large angles until at a certain critical angle of incidence the angle of refraction becomes 90° to the vertical; above this critical angle of incidence, the waves are reflected back downwards. This is called total internal reflection

CHRISTIAN JOHANN DOPPLER AND THE DOPPLER EFFECT

One of the most important and widely applied principles in acoustic science, the Doppler effect, has been familiar since humans started throwing stones or shooting arrows at each other. When we describe or try to imitate the sound of a missile – or any other speeding object – passing the ear, we instinctively make a sound like 'wheeeeoooooo'. This is no coincidence. An analysis of the frequency peaks of the vowel sounds (the *formant*) shows that, for any voice, the vowel 'e', as in 'steam', has a high peak at 2,400 Hz. The vowel 'oo', as in 'pool' has a high peak at the much lower frequency of only 800 Hz.

It took the genius of the Austrian physicist Christian Johann Doppler (1803–53), however, to analyse and explain the familiar fact that a moving source of sound appears to have a rising pitch if it is approaching the listener and a falling pitch if it is retreating. The effect is especially striking if the speed is high and the emitted sound loud, as in the case of a passing express train or the siren of a passing emergency vehicle.

Doppler reasoned that sound waves coming to the listener from an approaching source would reach the ear at shorter intervals than would be the case it if were stationary, and in 1842 set out a precise mathematical equation for the effect. This incorporated the relationship of the pitch of the sound to the relative motion of the source and the observer. To test his equation, a series of experiments was carried out in Holland using trumpeters on a moving locomotive flat car and musicians with perfect pitch on the ground. The listeners jotted down the notes they heard as the flat car approached and receded, and the results were compared with the actual notes played. Doppler's equation fitted every time.

The Doppler effect has wider applications than simply in acoustics, and its application has been very fruitful in science generally. It can, of course, be applied to *any* wave-train propagated from a moving source. Applied, for instance, to light ($\Rightarrow$ pp. 72–5), it has contributed to the general acceptance of one of the most astonishing propositions of modern times – that the universe is rapidly expanding and must, at one point, have had a beginning ($\Rightarrow$ p. 126).

The Doppler effect. The sound of a moving vehicle gets higher as it approaches an observer and lower as it moves away. The reason for this is that the moving vehicle compresses the soundwaves by constantly moving into them, and extends the waves behind it, as it moves away from them.

Simple and complex sounds

The air vibrations associated with musical sounds can be represented by comparatively simple periodic waveforms, which can be analysed into a fairly small number of different frequencies. A sine wave ($\Rightarrow$ pp. 20, 26 and 64), for instance, produces the simplest and purest of all sounds, featuring only pitch and volume. Few musical sounds are as simple as this, the nearest approach to a sine wave being that produced by a flute played softly. All other sounds contain other frequencies, in addition to the basic frequency (which determines the pitch) and which is called the *fundamental*. Differences in the quality, or tone, of a sound of given pitch – such as the difference between the same note played on an oboe or on a violin, for instance – depend on the presence and amplitude of these other frequencies. These additional and superimposed frequencies are called *harmonics* – these are simple

multiples of the basic frequency and are in phase ($\Rightarrow$ p. 66) with it. In most cases, the amplitude of the harmonics is less than that of the fundamental and, usually, the amplitude of the higher harmonics is less than that of the lower ones. Acoustic physicists can look at a pattern of harmonic amplitude on an analysing oscilloscope and distinguish different musical instruments without hearing any sounds.

No matter how complex the pattern of sounds that is imposed simultaneously on the air – even the sound produced by a large symphony orchestra – the corresponding air vibrations form a single, although often highly complex and varied, waveform. The eardrums move in sympathy with this waveform. Remarkably, the brain is able to analyse the resulting nerve-impulse pattern and reproduce, subjectively, the effect of separate sound sources.

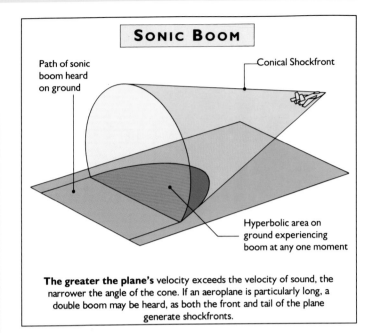

SONIC BOOM

Path of sonic boom heard on ground

Conical Shockfront

Hyperbolic area on ground experiencing boom at any one moment

The greater the plane's velocity exceeds the velocity of sound, the narrower the angle of the cone. If an aeroplane is particularly long, a double boom may be heard, as both the front and tail of the plane generate shockfronts.

However complex they are, musical sounds retain periodic elements and a repetitive pattern can be recognized. 'Noise', on the other hand, is aperiodic – its waveforms are far more complex and contain a wide range of unrelated frequencies. 'White noise' is the sound heard when nearly all the frequencies in the audible spectrum occur together and are of roughly equal amplitude. Noise is often impulsive rather than sustained.

The speed of sound

Speed, in sound waves, has nothing to do with the frequency of the sounds propagated but only with the density and compressibility of the medium through which the waves are passing. The harder it is to compress the medium, the faster the sound travels. The greater the density, the slower the speed. Although the density of air is low it is very easy to compress, so sound travels relatively slowly in air. Solids and liquids, such as metals or water, are more dense, but the difficulty in compressing them is very great, so sound travels much faster through solids and liquids than through air. For the same reasons, because changes in density are proportional to changes in pressure ($\Rightarrow$ p. 50) the speed of sound in air does not vary with changes in atmospheric pressure. It does, however, increase with a rise in temperature and with an increase in humidity. And, of course, if the air is moving in the direction of propagation, this will tend to increase the speed too.

Sonic boom is a shock wave, heard like a clap of thunder. It occurs when an aircraft flies at, or in excess of, the speed of sound. An aircraft moving at very high speed compresses the air in a particular way so that a cone of high pressure (a *Mach* cone) forms, following the aircraft. This cone, which expands steadily, is surrounded by a zone of silence. When its edge strikes the ground a loud bang is heard, that is preceded and followed by silence.

SEE ALSO
● WHAT IS ENERGY? pp. 46–9
● WHAT ARE WAVES? pp. 64–7
● WAVES OUTSIDE THE AUDIBLE SPECTRUM p. 70

Waves Outside the Audible Spectrum

We are inclined to think of sound as something we can hear, but the range of audibility varies considerably, even in humans (⇨ p. 68), and other animals can hear sounds three times the frequency of the upper limits of human hearing. Ultrasonic waves – those above the upper limit of human hearing – have special and valuable properties, and wide applications in science, engineering and medicine.

Ultrasonic waves are of the same type as audible sound vibrations (⇨ p. 68) but have a higher frequency – generally above about 20,000 Hertz (cycles per second). Frequency and wavelength are reciprocal: the higher the frequency, the shorter the wavelength. This short wavelength is one of the facts that makes ultrasonic waves so useful. Audible sound wavelengths are so long that large surfaces are needed to reflect them and cause echoes. Ultrasound, by contrast, can be reflected from small surfaces – and the higher the frequency, the smaller the reflective area needed.

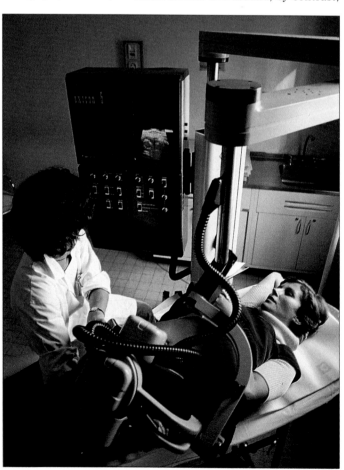

Ultrasound scanner being used to assess the health of this pregnant mother's baby. Such scanning (in contrast to X-rays) is harmless to the fetus and gives a clear image. (François Lehr, Gamma)

Generating ultrasonic waves

The most important method of generating ultrasonic waves uses the principle of piezoelectricity (⇨ box). Initially an alternating current is generated at the required frequency. This is done with an electronic *oscillator* – an amplifying device that feeds its output back into its input. A crystal must be selected or cut so that its natural frequency of resonance (⇨ p. 68) is the same as that of the oscillator, or to a whole-number multiple of the oscillator's frequency. The alternating current is then applied to metal plates attached to either side of the crystal. When the oscillator is switched on, the crystal vibrates at the required frequency and so acts as a source of waves at that frequency. Piezoelectric materials exhibit resonance, and give their greatest output if the frequency of vibration is equal to the speed of sound in the medium concerned divided by twice the thickness of the crystal plate.

Any device that converts signal energy from one physical form to another is called a *transducer*. The piezoelectric transducer converts in both directions. Because it works both ways, the crystal and its electrodes will produce a tiny alternating current if it is exposed to sound waves or to the equivalent vibrations. This property is widely used in microphones, record-player pickups, sonar and ultrasound scanners.

Another important application of piezoelectricity is the use of tiny quartz crystals – which have a very precise natural resonant frequency – to make a highly stable oscillator that will produce alternating currents of a very precise frequency. A high proportion of people in the Western world carry a piezoelectric quartz oscillator on their wrists every day – in quartz wristwatches. Such quartz-controlled oscillators are also essential for the control of many electronic devices – including all modern computers. In addition, quartz oscillators are used to fix the frequency of radio transmitters.

One other important way of generating ultrasonic waves uses the principle of *magnetostriction*. This is very similar to piezoelectricity except that the material undergoing elastic deformation is a ferromagnetic material, such as a nickel or iron rod, and the alternating field is magnetic rather than electric. Such a field is produced by passing the alternating current from the oscillator through a coil of wire wrapped round the iron rod. Iron stretches slightly in the presence of a weak magnetic field and contracts slightly in a strong field – as the English physicist James Joule (1818–89; ⇨ p. 90) discovered in 1846.

Detection and display

The detection of returning echoes can be carried out by the same device that sends out the waves – the transducer. The emitted waves have to be in the form of very short pulses, each containing a number of cycles, but also short enough to have ceased before the echo returns. The electrical signal produced in the transducer by the echo is much smaller than the signal used to energize it, but it can easily be amplified to a level at which it can be shown on a display of some kind, such as a cathode-ray oscilloscope. This might show a blip at the time of the outgoing pulse and a second blip for the echo. If the speed of movement of the spot across the tube is known, the time between the two events can easily be measured. And if the speed in the medium is known, the distance can be calculated.

Properties and uses of ultrasound

Ultrasonic waves pass through matter at about the same speed as audible sound waves (⇨ p. 68). The speed in liquids is greater than in gases and the speed in solids greater still. The properties of reflection, refraction (⇨ p. 64) and *dispersion* (the separation of electromagnetic radiation into different wavelengths) are also displayed by ultrasound. The higher the frequency of the waves, however, the greater the loss of energy in passing through a medium. Sound waves in water at 20,000 Hz, for instance, are reduced to half their intensity in about 50 km (30 mi); ultrasound at 1,000,000 Hz are reduced to half their intensity in only about 20 m (66 ft). For this reason, echo sounding in water usually employs fairly low ultrasound frequencies. The short wavelengths of the higher frequency waves allow them to be focused and concentrated in much the same way as light by using shaped pieces of light (in weight) metal such as titanium.

Ultrasonic body scanning is now one of the best-known applications of ultrasound. Piezoelectric transducers working at tens of megahertz and arranged so as to scan areas of the body serially in a fanlike manner have been in widespread use for many years now. Such scanners are especially favoured in obstetrics because of the dangers of X-rays to the fetus. The resolution of modern scanners is sufficient to enable doctors to determine the sex of fetuses and to allow certain surgical procedures to be performed within the womb. Similar scanners are used for a wide range of medical investigation.

The energy in sound waves is proportional to the square of the frequency. Vibrations of frequencies of millions of cycles per second can be very powerful. If the waves are focused on a small area a great deal of energy can be released there. Ultrasound is routinely used in medicine to fragment bladder and kidney stones and gallstones so that the gravel can be passed naturally. The instruments used for this purpose focus ultrasound pulses through lenses into the body and are called *lithotripters* (from the Latin for 'rock breakers'). Ultrasound beams of higher power can also produce enough heat to destroy diseased tissue including cancers and, as long as the diseased areas can be visualized with a scanner, this can be done without open operation.

Ultrasonic waves are also widely used for nondestructive testing of materials. If a material is unflawed and homogeneous a short pulse of ultrasound passed into it will be reflected only from the front and back surfaces. But if the material is flawed, internally cracked, or has blowholes, these, too, will send back echoes.

In liquids, ultrasonic waves can literally shake dirt away from objects immersed in them. For many purposes, this form of cleaning is more suitable and convenient than other methods. Since bacteria exposed to the ultrasound are literally exploded, it can be extended to provide sterilization. Ultrasound is currently widely used in industry for heating, welding, cutting and emulsifying.

SEE ALSO
● WHAT IS ENERGY? pp. 46–9
● WHAT ARE WAVES? pp. 64–7
● ACOUSTICS p. 68

A LITHOTRIPTER

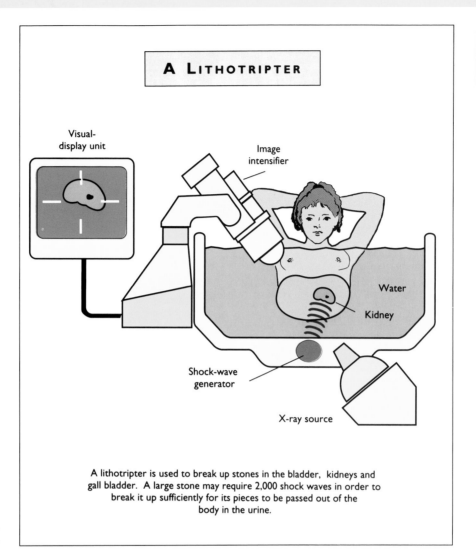

Visual-display unit

Image intensifier

Water

Kidney

Shock-wave generator

X-ray source

A lithotripter is used to break up stones in the bladder, kidneys and gall bladder. A large stone may require 2,000 shock waves in order to break it up sufficiently for its pieces to be passed out of the body in the urine.

PIERRE CURIE AND PIEZOELECTRICITY

The French physicist Pierre Curie (1859–1906) was a slow starter and had his early lessons at home. But he managed to enter the Sorbonne in Paris, where he took degrees in 1875 and 1877, and a year later became an assistant lecturer in the physics laboratory there. In 1880, working with his brother Jacques, he made a notable discovery – that when certain crystals, especially quartz, were squeezed in a certain direction an electric charge was generated that could cause a current to flow in an external circuit. Adopting the Greek word for compression, the brothers called this effect *piezoelectricity*. Soon they made the further important finding that the process could be reversed: when an electric current was applied to the crystal it immediately deformed slightly. And when the current was removed, the crystal returned to its original dimensions. Later, many other substances, including a number of ceramics, were found to exhibit piezoelectricity. These materials could be made to any required shape.

Pierre was at first convinced that he must devote himself exclusively to his scientific work and that marriage would be an unjustified distraction. But in 1894 he met a girl called Marya Sklodovska, fell in love, and married her the next year – thereby initiating probably the most celebrated husband-and-wife scientific collaboration in the history of science. The Curies' work on radioactivity and their discovery of radium led to a Nobel prize in 1903 and a professorship in physics for Pierre at the Sorbonne. Tragically, he was run over by a wagon and killed in 1906. Marie succeeded to his professorship at the Sorbonne.

Marie and Pierre Curie. Although most famous for his work, with Marie, on radioactivity, Pierre Curie also contributed to the discovery of piezoelectricity. Cartoon from *Vanity Fair*, London (1904). (AR)

Light 1

Light – as most of us know it – is a subjective phenomenon, an experience that results when an electromagnetic wave (⇨ p. 84) impinges upon the retina at the back of the eye and prompts a series of neurological and psychological reactions. In the sense of the word used by physicists, light *is* the electromagnetic wave.

Just as cold is no more than the absence of heat (⇨ p. 52), so darkness is no more than the absence of light. Vision is possible only because objects either emit light or are bathed in and reflect it.

The nature of light

Human experience of light occurs at the end of a chain of events that starts when electromagnetic radiation within a very narrow range of wavelengths strikes the specialized cells in the retina, the *rods* and *cones*. Rod cells are colour blind but are remarkably sensitive and will fire off a nerve impulse on receipt of a single photon of light. Cone cells are less sensitive but are colour-responsive (⇨ p. 76). The nerve impulses stimulated in this way pass back along the optic nerves, optic tracts and optic radiations to reach the surface of the brain. Here, a great deal of neurological activity occurs and the result, for reasons that are still completely unknown, is the experience of vision.

This experience is quite unlike the actual nature of light itself, which, in common with all physical phenomena, is explicable only in terms of a number of known properties. Light is a form of energy (⇨ pp. 46–9), an electromagnetic radiation consisting of oscillating (or vibrating) electric and magnetic fields at

THE DUAL NATURE OF LIGHT

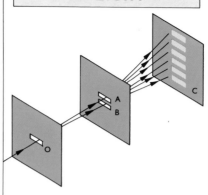

The wave nature of light is demonstrable by means of interference apparatus. The waves passing through slits A and B and reaching the screen C will be either in phase or out of phase and will either reinforce or cancel each other. The result is a series of light and dark bands on the screen. Reinforcement occurs when the path difference is a whole number of wavelengths.

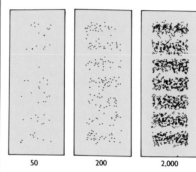

50	200	2,000

The photon nature of light. The results of two-slit interference after the passage of 50, 200 and 2,000 photons have passed through. The characteristic pattern is observed only after many photons have passed. The initial results appear random.

right angles to each other and to the direction of propagation. Visible light is characterized by a specific band of wavelengths, between 0.38 and 0.78 millionths of a metre (380–780 nanometres). Ordinary white light is a mixture of all the wavelengths within this range, but can be separated into what we perceive as its component colours, each having a narrower band of wavelengths. Light is also characterized by intensity, which is perceived as brightness.

Most light waves vibrate in any of the infinite number of planes at right angles to the direction of propagation (⇨ p. 64), but light can be confined to a particular narrow plane, and, in this case, is described as *plane-polarized*. (A *plane* is a two-dimensional flat 'surface' in which a straight line joining any two points will lie entirely on the surface). Light passing through two polarizing filters at right angles to each other will be completely obscured (⇨ p. 74).

Another characteristic of light is its degree of *coherence*. This is the degree to which its waves move in unison – that is,

PLANE POLARIZATION

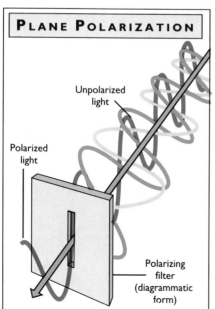

Unpolarized light

Polarized light

Polarizing filter (diagrammatic form)

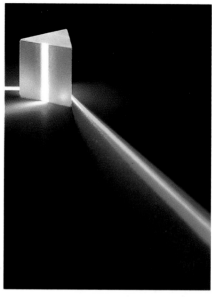

When a beam of white light is passed through a triangular prism it is split into its component colours: red, orange, yellow, green, blue, indigo and violet. Daylight, while being composed of these colours, also contains infrared and ultraviolet light, which are both invisible to the human eye. (David Parker, SPL)

are in phase (⇨ p. 66) with each other. Fully coherent light must therefore be of one colour only and must be polarized to a single plane. This is the principal feature of light from a laser (⇨ p. 82). Light's speed of propagation is the same as that of any other electromagnetic radiation and is a universal constant equal, in a vacuum, to 299,792,458 m/s. The investigation of the speed of light and its putative relation to the movement of the Earth by Michelson and Morley (⇨ p. 38) led to Einstein's special theory of relativity.

Light production

Like any other electromagnetic radiation, light results either from the acceleration of electric charges or directly from nuclear reactions. The commonest way to accelerate charges is to heat the material concerned – and a great deal of light is produced in this way, as in the case of the Sun or an incandescent light-bulb filament heated by electricity. In heating, the electrons of the atoms of the material, each of which carries a negative charge, move to higher energy levels, and as each drops back to its earlier level it emits a photon of light radiation (⇨ chapter 6). Light produced in this way contains a mixture of wavelengths peaking around a point that is proportional to the absolute (Kelvin) temperature of the body (0°C equals 273.15K; ⇨ p. 84). Light is often described in terms of its *colour temperature*. White light has a colour temperature between about 6,000–10,000 Kelvin, yellow light around 3,000 K and red light around 1,500 K.

In a flame, or a fluorescent light tube, the atoms are gaseous. Energy levels depend on the electron structure of the gas concerned, and the wavelengths produced are more restricted. Such sources do not produce a continuous spectrum, but concentrate the light in narrow bands, depending on the gas concerned. Such light is often confined to a single colour. Laser light (⇨ p. 82) is of one colour only – strictly monochromatic – and coherent.

Ultraviolet light

On the short-wavelength (high-frequency) side of the narrow spectrum of visible light is a wide band of light that cannot be seen by the human eye. This is the band of ultraviolet radiation that extends over about four orders of magnitude of wavelength right down to X-rays and gamma rays. The wavelengths range from about 380 nanometres (1 nm equals one thousand-millionth of a metre) to about 0.1 nm. Although ultraviolet light is invisible, it is readily converted to visible light by various pigments or phosphors that can be coated onto fluorescent screens.

Ultraviolet (UV) light is produced in much the same way as visible light and most visible light sources also produce UV. Some artificial sources, such as the mercury-vapour lamp, produce very large quantities of it. UV has marked biological effects and is the cause of sunburning and tanning. It can also cause severe damage to living cells, either killing them, or, sometimes, causing them to become cancerous. The delicate transparent membranes of the eyes are readily affected. Bacteria can be killed by UV, so it is useful for sterilizing accessible surfaces. The shorter the wavelength, the more dangerous the UV.

Brightness

Light intensity is mediated by the amplitude (⇨ p. 64) of the waves and is experienced as brightness. It is measured by comparison with a standard – originally that of a candle made to careful specifications. One simple way of making this comparison is to allow the light to be measured to fall on a sheet of paper with a central oily spot, which immediately becomes apparent because of the increased local transparency. If the standard candle, or a light of equivalent brightness, is now moved backward and forward on the other side of the paper, a distance will be found at which the grease spot disappears.

At this point the illumination is equal on the two sides, and the brightness of the unknown light can be calculated in terms of the distance of the standard light from the paper. Candle power was the unit used to measure intensity of light until replaced by the candela in the SI system.

Today, light intensity is usually measured by a light meter (in photography, an exposure meter) containing a cadmium-sulphide cell whose electrical resistance varies sensitively according to the brightness of the light falling on it. This cell is connected in series (⇨ p. 90) with a small battery and an electric meter whose scale is calibrated in brightness units. The brighter the light, the lower the resistance of the cell – and the greater the current and the deflection of the meter.

⇨ p. 82; ⇨ p. 64; ⇨ p. 90

MEASURING THE SPEED OF LIGHT

The early attempts to measure the speed of light all failed. Galileo Galilei (1564–1642; ⇨ p. 10) tried to measure the speed by flashing a light from one hilltop to another, where an assistant would flash his light as soon as he saw Galileo's. This was tried at different distances, but the crude results obtained did not vary with distance and it was assumed that light travelled at an infinite speed. In 1676, however, the Danish astronomer Ole Roemer (1644–1710) made an important observation that showed that light travelled at a finite speed. Roemer noticed that the time at which one of Jupiter's moons passed around behind the planet was earlier than predicted when the Earth was near to Jupiter, and later when the Earth was further away in its orbit round the Sun. The only way this could be explained was to suppose that the difference was due to the time the light took to travel different distances. Roemer's calculation of the speed was about 227 million m/s, somewhat below the correct figure (⇨ below), but a creditable estimate, nevertheless. Little attention was paid to his work at the time.

Just over fifty years later the English astronomer James Bradley (1693–1762) was able for the first time to show that because of the movement of the Earth, it was necessary to angle his telescope slightly in the direction of the Earth's motion to view a distant star. From this angle Bradley was able to calculate the ratio of the speed of the Earth to the speed of light – and from this establish the speed of light. His figure came even closer to the true one than that of Roemer, but Bradley acknowledged the other's priority.

Here matters rested until around 1849 when the French physicist Armand Fizeau (1819–96) thought of an ingenious method of making more direct measurements of the speed of light. On top of one hill he set up a rotatable disc with a toothed edge, and on another hill, five miles away, he set up a mirror. A light close behind the disc shone between the teeth, passed to the mirror and returned to the observer. As the disc was speeded up the returning light met a tooth and could no longer be seen; but when the disc was rotated faster still the light was able to pass through the next gap. So the light took the same time to travel 10 mi (16 km) as the one tooth took to pass to the next position. From knowledge of the speed of the disc it was easy to calculate the speed of the light. An improvement on this method developed by the French physicist Jean Bernard Foucault (1819–68), using rapidly rotating mirrors, produced a result only fractionally below the modern figure obtained by Michelson using an interferometer. Michelson's figure of 299,798,000 km/h is within a tiny fraction of the figure reached by the best modern methods.

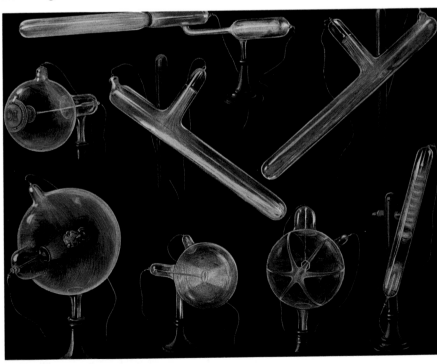

Fluorescent light of various colours given off by a range of substances in vacuum tubes. Sodium is used in modern-day streetlamps to give off yellow light. And neon (which gives off red light) is commonly seen in shop and advertising signs. From Wilhelm M. Meyer, *Die Naturkräfte*, Leipzig (1903). (AR)

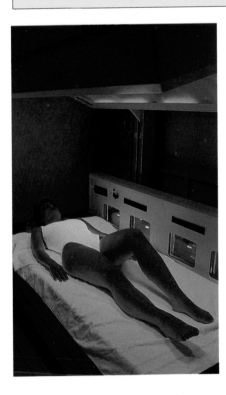

Ultraviolet light, given out by a sun bed, will tan light-coloured skin if exposure to it is moderate. Over-exposure, however, can result in burning and possible long-term damage to the skin's cell structure. (Zefa)

Light 2

Light may seem a familiar phenomenon, but many of its most surprising properties are normally hidden from us.

When light passes directly from an external object to the human eye, we have no difficulty in deciding where the object is situated. But when light rays enter the eye after having been reflected or bent (refracted; ⇨ 78), the position of the object is not always so obvious.

Locating and sizing objects

When an object is in front of a mirror some of the light rays from it strike the mirror, which reflects these rays so that they can be seen by an observer who is also in front of the mirror. If the object is

Stress patterns in the walls of a plastic dish are visible when photographed through polarized light. Plastic models such as this one are used in the stress analysis of real structures in industry. The interference patterns displayed can be used to make calculations about the direction and magnitude of the stresses occurring. Such calculations can then be applied to the real metal component. (Tony Craddock, SPL)

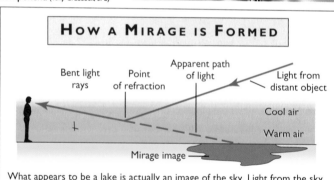

HOW A MIRAGE IS FORMED

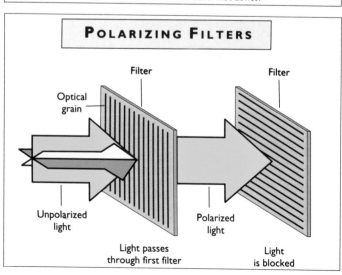

Bent light rays — Point of refraction — Apparent path of light — Light from distant object

Cool air

Warm air

Mirage image

What appears to be a lake is actually an image of the sky. Light from the sky is refracted by warm air near the ground. For this reason, mirages most often occur in deserts and other hot zones.

POLARIZING FILTERS

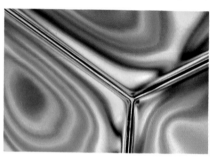

Filter   Filter

Optical grain

Unpolarized light

Polarized light

Light passes through first filter

Light is blocked

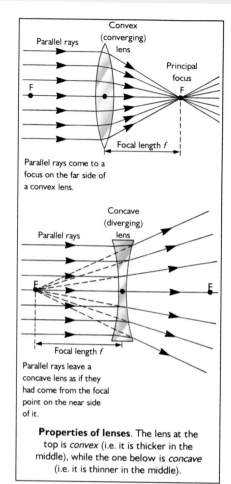

Parallel rays — Convex (converging) lens — Principal focus — F — F — Focal length *f*

Parallel rays come to a focus on the far side of a convex lens.

Parallel rays — Concave (diverging) lens — F — F — Focal length *f*

Parallel rays leave a concave lens as if they had come from the focal point on the near side of it.

Properties of lenses. The lens at the top is *convex* (i.e. it is thicker in the middle), while the one below is *concave* (i.e. it is thinner in the middle).

---

small enough, rays from every point on the side that faces the mirror will enter the observer's eye. The observer will then see the whole object apparently as far *behind* the mirror as it is in front, and this is so whether or not the observer is aware that the light rays have been reflected at the mirror surface.

The brain takes no account of the fact that rays may have been bent before entering the eye. Rays that enter the eye from any direction are assumed to come from an object situated somewhere along the line of these rays – that the surface of a mirror may have been interposed makes no difference. In this case the object has to be seen as if it were behind the mirror.

The principle of seeing things as if they were located on the line of the rays entering the eye applies in a wide range of cases. It is the reason that a stick poked at an angle into water (⇨ p. 64) appears bent, and it is also the cause of mirages and the illusion that the setting Sun grows larger as it approaches the horizon.

When we look at a near object through a convex or convergent lens (a lens that increases the convergence or decreases the divergence of a beam of light), the light rays from points near its periphery are sharply converged as they approach the eye. The brain 'projects' the rays backwards towards the object, but takes no account of the fact that they have been bent and sees them as if they came from much further out – that is, from a much larger object. In the case of the

---

LIQUID-CRYSTAL DISPLAYS

Liquid crystals are organic compounds with long, narrow molecules arranged in a lattice. In an electric field, generated for instance when a voltage is applied to them, liquid crystals line up and rotate the plane of polarized light. This principle can be used in various ways to produce a display. One is to sandwich the thin cell of liquid crystals between two polarizing filters and illuminate them from behind. Liquid-crystal displays (LCDs) are widely used to present changing visible information, for instance in digital wristwatches and in laptop computers – where LCDs allow a thin, flat screen with a very small current consumption to be substituted for the clumsy, heavy and expensive cathode-ray-tube monitor used in conventional desktop computers.

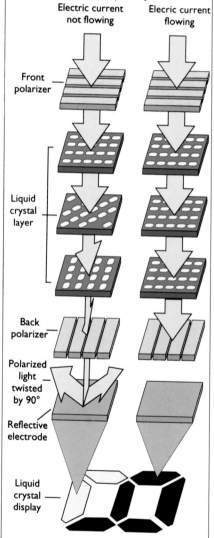

Electric current not flowing   Electric current flowing

Front polarizer

Liquid crystal layer

Back polarizer

Polarized light twisted by 90°

Reflective electrode

Liquid crystal display

The liquid crystal is sandwiched between two polarizing filters, which are positioned at right angles to one another. When an electric current is applied, the crystals become aligned so that the light is plane polarized, and is consequently blocked by the rear polarizer.
The appropriate segment of the display thus turns black. When no current flows, light is rotated through 90° and passes through the rear polarizer to be reflected back.

setting Sun, it is the denser atmosphere near the horizon acting as a converging lens that makes the Sun look larger.

Polarization

Sound waves are *longitudinal* (⇨ p. 64) – the vibrations occur backwards and forwards in the same direction in which the waves are being propagated. Light waves, on the other hand, are *transverse* oscillations of an electromagnetic field – they vibrate at a right angle to the direction of propagation (⇨ p. 84).

A simple experiment using polarizing glass demonstrates that normal light waves vibrate in all the possible planes (⇨ p. 72). *Polaroid* is the trade name for a transparent material widely used to make sunglasses. It consists of millions of tiny crystals of quinine iodosulphate, all accurately oriented and fused into a sheet of transparent plastic. Because of the common orientation of the crystals, this material confines light vibrations to a single plane by allowing only the vibrations in that plane to pass through. When one looks through a sheet of *Polaroid* at a distant scene, brightness is considerably reduced, but rotating the sheet does not change the brightness. If another sheet is placed behind the first and one rotated while the other is held still, however, two positions will be found by the observer in which the scene is almost completely blacked out and

another in which the brightness is at a maximum. The brightest image is seen when the polarization orientations of the two sheets are the same, and the black-out occurs when the polarizations are perpendicular to each other.

If one *Polaroid* sheet is rotated a few degrees at a time, it will be found easy to black out the scene by rotating the other sheet; and this can be done *whatever* the orientation of the first. This shows that light waves occur in any of the possible planes at right angles to its direction. Once light is plane-polarized, a sheet of *Polaroid* acts as a detector of polarization, because rotating it will then show a maximum and a minimum brightness.

Practical applications

In nature, light is often partially plane-polarized. This happens, for instance, when it is reflected from the surface of water (or glass) – in this case, the vibrations of the light waves are parallel to the surface. Reflections in glass such as a shop window can be greatly reduced by looking through and rotating a polarizing filter, such as a sheet of *Polaroid*. Because reflected light is plane-polarized, the uncomfortable glare from such reflections can be greatly reduced by polarizing filters, such as *Polaroid* sunglasses. Photographers also often use polarizing filters on their cameras to

reduce the degradation of their images caused by reflections.

Many substances placed in solution cause the plane of plane-polarized light to rotate. Such substances are said to be optically active. The chemical known as amphetamine, for instance, consists of a mixture of molecules all of the same chemical composition, but some of which have the property of rotating light in a right-handed direction (called *dextrorotary,* or right-rotating) and others of which rotate light to the left (*laevorotary,* or left-rotating). It is a characteristic of light-rotating molecules that the angle through which the light is rotated depends on the concentration of the solution and this fact can be used to measure concentration in some chemicals, notably with sugar solutions.

When glass and various plastics are subjected to twisting (*torsion*) stresses – when they are exposed to uneven heating in manufacture, for instance – they produce strain patterns that can be made visible when light passing through them is viewed through polarizing filters. This property can be made use of to measure or monitor torsion stress in these and other materials. For example, thin layers of a suitable plastic material can be applied to the surface of any object subjected to distortional stress and the strain patterns viewed by reflected light, using an instrument called a *polariscope.*

HOLOGRAPHY

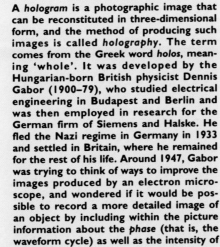

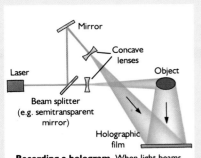

Recording a hologram. When light beams from sources such as lasers overlap they produce interference fringes due to the wave nature of light. A hologram is produced by recording the fringes from the interference of two beams of laser light. The reference beam (RB) falls directly onto the film, while the object beam (OB) is reflected from the object.

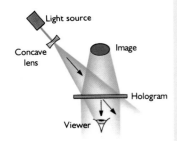

Replaying a hologram. When the hologram is replayed by shining a beam of light onto it, the light is diffracted in such a way that is appears to come from the position of the original object. The image can be viewed from a range of angles and is a true three-dimensional reconstruction of the object.

A *hologram* is a photographic image that can be reconstituted in three-dimensional form, and the method of producing such images is called *holography.* The term comes from the Greek word *holos*, meaning 'whole'. It was developed by the Hungarian-born British physicist Dennis Gabor (1900–79), who studied electrical engineering in Budapest and Berlin and was then employed in research for the German firm of Siemens and Halske. He fled the Nazi regime in Germany in 1933 and settled in Britain, where he remained for the rest of his life. Around 1947, Gabor was trying to think of ways to improve the images produced by an electron microscope, and wondered if it would be possible to record a more detailed image of an object by including within the picture information about the *phase* (that is, the waveform cycle) as well as the intensity of light waves.

He reasoned that this could be done if the object were illuminated by rays coming from a coherent light source (that is, one emitting light of a single, pure frequency with all the waves exactly in phase; ⇨ p. 66) that were at the same time allowed to mix with the light reflected from the object before striking the photographic film.

Waves reflected from different parts of a solid object have different distances to travel – different numbers of wavelengths – before they reach the film. When these were mixed with light direct from the source, the different waves from the object would interfere to different degrees – being potentiated or partially

cancelled as the case might be. In this way, the film would record an image of the object incorporating the interference pattern produced by the interaction of the two sets of rays.

Gabor's idea was right in principle but hard to implement at the time because no light sources were sufficiently coherent. The best he could do was to try to achieve coherence by projecting light from a mercury-vapour lamp through a pinhole. When the laser was invented in 1960 (⇨ p. 82), practical holography became possible and was soon in widespread use, and Dennis Gabor was awarded the Nobel Prize for physics in 1971.

In making a hologram, a beam from a laser is first split into two. One of these, the *reference beam*, is reflected from a mirror and then spread out by a lens so that it approaches the photographic film at an angle. The other, the *object beam*, is treated in a similar way but is used to illuminate the object. Interference takes place between the object and the film when the reference beam meets the light reflected from the object. The film is developed just like any other photograph, and, when the resulting print is viewed by light falling on it at the same angle as the reference beam, a three-dimensional image is seen apparently floating in space. The original holograms had to be viewed in laser light, but recent improvements in the resolution of photographic emulsions allows the recording of so much detail that holograms can be successfully viewed in ordinary white light.

Colour

The study of colour involves three major branches of science – physics, physiology and psychology. A full understanding of colour requires knowledge of a range of specialities: optics and the nature of light, light diffraction, the nature of dyes and pigments, luminescence, the physiological basis of colour perception, the psychology of perception – and even philosophy.

The perception of colour is subjective, and we have no way of knowing for certain whether the experience of other people corresponds with any precision to our own. We know that different people often perceive colours slightly differently, but assume that the general experience is the same. There is in fact no real basis for this assumption. We have no way of knowing, for instance, whether the 'blue' some people experience when they look at the summer sky may not be what others experience when they look at a 'red' rose. There are, however, certain shared assumptions about the characters of particular colours, and most people would agree that a certain shade of, for instance, blue was indeed blue and not red.

Wavelength and colour

In 1666 Isaac Newton (⇨ chapter 2) placed a glass prism in a narrow beam of light coming through a small hole in the blind of a darkened room and observed that light split into its component colours. It can hardly have been the first time that this phenomenon was observed, but it was the first time anyone had appreciated its significance. Newton then went further, and showed that the spectral colours could be recombined, with another identical prism, into white light.

When a prism disperses white light, the different wavelengths of which it is composed are 'spread out'. If an opaque barrier containing a narrow slit is interposed so that the spectrum is focused on it, light of only one colour will pass through the slit. As the barrier is moved across the spectrum, light passing through the slit will change colour in turn to the seven familiar hues – red, orange, yellow, green, blue, indigo and violet.

This does not imply that there are only seven different wavelengths in white light. In fact, a person with a good eye for colour can make out many more colours, and machines for measuring pure colours (*colorimeters*) can distinguish even more. The wavelength of violet light is about 380 nm (1 nanometre is a millionth of a millimetre, or one thousand-millionth of a metre) and that of red is about 780 nm.

Greater difficulties arise when attempts are made to measure or compare colours in the real world. These do not have a single narrow band of wavelengths, but consist of a range of wavelengths. A typical pigment illuminated with white light does not reflect a narrow band of wavelengths, but a range covering the whole of the spectrum with a peak at the wavelength corresponding to its nominal colour. A green pigment, for instance, might reflect 70 per cent of the light at its peak (green) wavelength in the middle of the spectrum, about 40 per cent at blue wavelengths, 30 per cent at yellow wavelengths and 10 per cent at red and violet wavelengths. Other pigments have spectral reflection curves peaking at different wavelengths.

The basic property of colour, as determined by its wavelength, is called *hue*. The width of the band of wavelengths – or, in other words, the purity or amount of white light mixed with it – is called the *saturation*; the smaller the amount of white, the more saturated the colour. And the intensity of the colour – the amplitude of the wave – is called the *brightness*. Hue and saturation, taken together, are called the *chromaticity*.

Luminescent dyes and pigments

The term *luminescence* is used for any light that is not primarily produced by high temperatures. Some substances have the remarkable property of being able to absorb light of a particular wavelength, or range of wavelengths, and to emit light with a different wavelength. This is the basis of the familiar brilliant

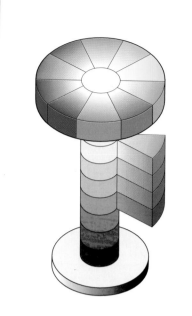

The Munsell colour tree grades colours according to hue, saturation and brightness. Hue is marked by the colour's position on the circumference of the 'tree'. Saturation is shown by its distance from the trunk, and brightness is delineated by its position along the trunk.

effect of certain luminescent or fluorescent surfaces. Some luminescent dyes can absorb ultraviolet light and convert it into visible light of a particular colour. Because ultraviolet is invisible, we are unaware of its intensity – and when it is converted into visible light the effect can be as if the surface were brightly illuminated with a light of the colour that we see.

This property of wavelength conversion (in effect, colour conversion) is widely used in safety devices such as cyclists' warning belts or cats' collars, and as a promotional device by the manufacturers of washing powders and liquids. Some powders are designed deliberately to leave a residue of wavelength-converting material in the fabric so that ultraviolet light is converted to blue. This neutralizes any yellowing left in white material and so justifies the claim of 'whiter than white'.

The perception of colour

Although objects appear coloured, their colour, as we know it, is an illusion. The surface of 'coloured' objects has the property of absorbing some wavelengths and reflecting others. An object that appears red is an object whose surface absorbs all other wavelengths within the visible spectrum more than it does those for red. Thus, it is the peak of 'red' wavelengths that reaches the eye. Colour pigments on surfaces, or in transparent substances through which light can pass, all work in this *subtractive way*, removing some colours from white light and displaying the others. Objects that reflect no light appear black. In the absence of

---

ADDING AND SUBTRACTING COLOURS

Magenta   Cyan

Yellow

Mixing lights of primary colours red, green and blue, produces colour by addition. Any two together produce one of the secondary colours, magenta, yellow or cyan; all three together are seen as white light.

Magenta absorbs green light, reflecting red and blue

Cyan absorbs red light, reflecting blue and green

Yellow absorbs blue light, reflecting red and green

Mixing paints produces colour by subtraction. Yellow, cyan and magenta pigments each absorb only one primary colour from white light. Any two together produce a primary colour; all three together produce black.

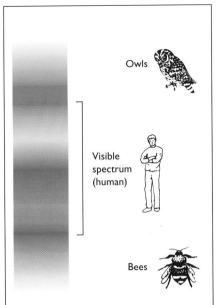

Some species can see light from outside our visible spectrum. Nocturnal animals, such as owls, can see infrared light, which has a wavelength longer than red light. Conversely, some insects (bees for example) can detect ultraviolet light, from, for instance, certain flower markings. Cats and dogs see no colours other than black and white.

light, the concept of the colour of an object is meaningless.

The outer zones of our retinas, with which we see objects in the periphery of our fields of vision, contain mainly rod cells – and these respond to very low light intensities. Towards the centres of them, with which we see objects straight ahead, we have

mostly cone cells. The millions of cones in each retina are of three kinds, thoroughly mixed up together. One kind gives its greatest output when stimulated by yellow–red light, another when triggered by green and the third when exposed to blue–violet light. Any colour can be simulated by additive mixtures of these three primary colours. Assuming the cones are normal, the retina will analyse any colour falling on it and inform the brain of the result. By contrast with the process on surfaces, this is an *additive* mode of colour production.

From a psychological point of view, colour perception is less obvious than it might seem. The mind appears concerned to maintain the constancy of what we regard as the appearance of objects – in spite of differences in the information received from them. We perceive a table-cloth as white whether the light reflected from it and entering our eyes is white light from a nearby window or yellow light from candles. It is for the same reason that we continue to think of a round table as round, even when almost all our perceptions of it are of an oval.

Colour-perception defects

True colour blindness, in the sense of total lack of perception of colour, is almost unknown, but defects in colour perception are common. These occur far more often in males – about 10 per cent of whom are affected – than females. This is because the genes that cause them occur on the X sex chromosome and are recessive; females would have to have *both* X chromosomes affected to show the effect, and would have had to inherit the trait from both parents. Males, though, have only one

HERMANN VON HELMHOLTZ, THE LAST POLYMATH

The idea that colour perception involves retinal elements sensitive to only three primary colours (the trichromatic theory) is usually attributed to the German physiologist, physicist and mathematician Hermann Ludwig Ferdinand von Helmholtz (1821–94). As a 21-year-old medical cadet in the Prussian Army he began investigating the conversion of food into energy, and showed that the work performed (and the heat produced) by the muscles exactly equalled the chemical energy contained in the food (⇨ p. 54). He also showed that body heat was produced almost wholly by muscle contraction. Prior to this, the prevailing theory was that work energy displayed by the body was derived from some mysterious 'vital force', emanating from the soul. Helmholtz later developed this research to prove the fundamentally important principle of the conservation of energy (⇨ pp. 44–7).

Because of his work, Helmholtz was released from his military obligations and became an instructor in anatomy in Berlin and, a year later, in 1848, was appointed Professor of Pathology and Physiology at Königsberg. Subsequently he held chairs of anatomy and physiology at Bonn, of physiology at Heidelberg and of physics at Berlin. His contributions to medicine and science were legion, but he is particularly remembered for his work on vision and hearing. He wrote the definitive textbook on the function of the eye, invented the ophthalmoscope and was the first to explain colour vision.

The list of his other achievements is astonishing: he did original work in neurology and was the first to measure the speed of the nerve impulse; he pioneered thermodynamics (⇨ p. 54) and meteorological physics; he mastered physiological acoustics and wrote the still-standard work on the nature and perception of musical tones; he carried out investigations into electricity and inspired Hertz in his work on radio propagation (⇨ p. 84); he was also a brilliant mathematician and philosopher, producing works on nonEuclidean geometry, empiricist scientific philosophy and epistemology – especially on the metaphysics of perception. A great deal of his research was fruitfully followed up by such scientists as Pavlov (the mental basis of the conditioned reflex), Kelvin (the atom), Kölliker (evolution), Clausius and Boltzmann (thermodynamics), Arrhenius (ionization in liquids) and de Vries (the theory of mutations).

X chromosome, derived from the mother, and so can inherit colour perception defects only from the mother. An affected man, however, cannot pass the trait on to his sons because they receive only a Y chromosome from the father.

Colour perception defects are due to abnormalities in the cones (⇨ above) of the retinas. Normally, the sensitivity of the three types of cones is roughly equal. But in a person with a colour-perception defect, the peaks in the sensitivities of one or more type are flattened. This occurs most commonly in the cones that respond best to red, or in those for red and green. Defective sensitivity to both (red–green perception defect) is the most common kind of all. People suffering from this defect have difficulty in distinguishing reds and greens and may sometimes be almost unable to perceive either of these colours. Defects of blue perception are extremely rare.

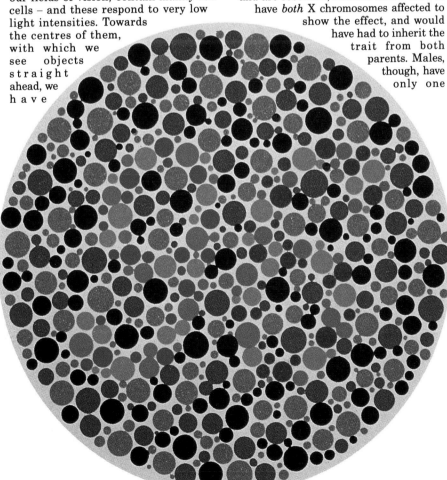

A test for colour blindness. People with normal vision will see the number 96; those with red–green deficiencies will see only a 9 or a 6, depending on the type of deficiency. Red–green colour blindness affects approximately one person in thirty, and is more common in men than women. (Adam Hart-Davis, SPL)

SEE ALSO

- WHAT IS ENERGY? pp. 46–9
- WHAT ARE WAVES? pp. 64–7
- LIGHT pp. 72–5
- REFLECTION AND REFRACTION p. 78
- SPECTRA AND SPECTROSCOPY p. 80
- COHERENT LIGHT – MASERS AND LASERS p. 82
- THE ELECTROMAGNETIC SPECTRUM AND ITS PROPERTIES p. 84

Reflection and Refraction

The reflection and refraction of light are part of our everyday experience. Both also have important scientific applications.

The term reflection comes from the Latin *re-* ('back') and *flectere*, ('to bend'). All kinds of waves (⇨ pp. 64–7) can be bent back by a surface of suitable size and physical structure, but we are more familiar with the reflection of light waves than with that of other waves – partly because we can see the process all around us.

Reflection and mirrors

For almost all practical optical purposes light can be considered as being propagated in rays, or bundles of rays ('pencils'), both of which are perfectly straight lines. Light falling on a surface is partly absorbed, partly reflected and partly transmitted through the surface – the proportions depend on the nature of the material, especially its transparency and apparent colour (⇨ pp. 78–9), and the quality of the surface. Most surfaces are rough, which means that they consist of numerous tiny areas set at different angles to the nominal plane of the

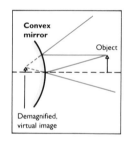

Convex mirror

Object

Demagnified, virtual image

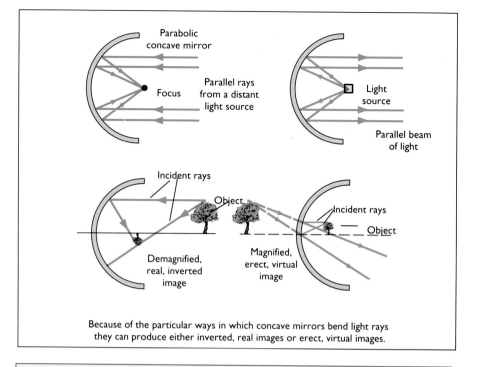

Parabolic concave mirror

Parallel rays from a distant light source

Focus

Light source

Parallel beam of light

Incident rays

Object

Incident rays

Object

Demagnified, real, inverted image

Magnified, erect, virtual image

Because of the particular ways in which concave mirrors bend light rays they can produce either inverted, real images or erect, virtual images.

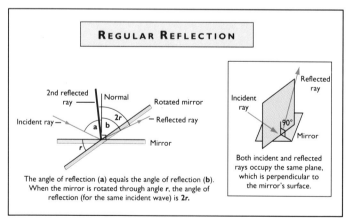

REGULAR REFLECTION

2nd reflected ray

Normal

Rotated mirror

Incident ray

Reflected ray

Mirror

Reflected ray

Incident ray

Mirror

Both incident and reflected rays occupy the same plane, which is perpendicular to the mirror's surface.

The angle of reflection (**a**) equals the angle of reflection (**b**). When the mirror is rotated through angle **r**, the angle of reflection (for the same incident wave) is **2r**.

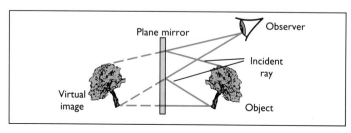

Plane mirror

Observer

Virtual image

Incident ray

Object

TOTAL INTERNAL REFLECTION

When an oblique light ray strikes the interface between two media of different optical density it turns through an angle. As the angle at which the ray meets the interface is made smaller, a point will eventually be reached at which the ray skims the plane of the interface. Any ray striking at a smaller angle than this will be totally reflected back into the medium from which it came. This has some interesting and useful applications. Totally reflecting prisms are used in many optical instruments in place of silvered mirrors – which may tarnish. The same method can also be used to invert an image and to bend rays back through 180°. One common application of these effects is in prismatic binoculars, in which the optics divert the course of the light so that it can follow a longer path, and be magnified more effectively, than the actual length of the binoculars would normally allow.

An increasingly important use of total internal reflection is in fibre optics. Optical fibres (fibres of specially formulated glass) can carry light long distances with little loss, even if the fibres are coiled. One application is in telecommunications: if the light comes from a laser (⇨ p. 82) it can be modulated (modified) to carry millions of different communication channels. In medicine, bundles of fibres are used in endoscopic examinations and have enabled the development of 'keyhole' surgery, allowing doctors to investigate and operate inside the body with a minimum of intrusion. The fibres must bear the same relationship to each other at each end of the bundle, otherwise the image will be destroyed.

Optical fibres can guide light around corners by virtue of the principle of total internal reflection. (Zefa)

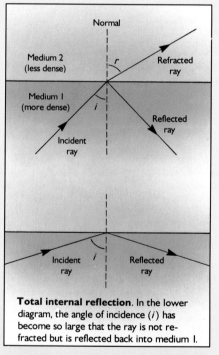

Normal

Medium 2 (less dense)

r

Refracted ray

Medium 1 (more dense)

i

Reflected ray

Incident ray

Incident ray

i

Reflected ray

Total internal reflection. In the lower diagram, the angle of incidence (*i*) has become so large that the ray is not refracted but is reflected back into medium 1.

surface. Because of this, light rays striking a rough surface are reflected from it at many different angles. This is called *diffuse reflection*. A highly polished surface, on the other hand, may be thought of as consisting of numerous tiny areas all set parallel to the plane of the surface. It will reflect light rays in a particular way, known as *regular reflection*.

The laws of regular reflection are simple:

• First, a ray of light striking the surface (the *incident ray*) lies in the same plane (⇨ pp. 72–5) as the resulting reflected ray, and this plane is perpendicular to the surface (⇨ illustration). The reflected ray is never turned out of this plane.

• Second, the reflected ray makes exactly the same angle with the surface as the incident ray.

• Third, when the reflecting surface is rotated through any angle without changing the position of the source of the light, the reflected ray turns through *twice* the angle through which the surface was turned.

The effect of these laws is clear when viewing an image in a flat (*plane*) mirror. Rays diverging from an object strike the mirror and are reflected at the same angle and in the same plane. When these rays enter the eye, the brain has no way of knowing that they have, in fact, been reflected and have not come straight from the object. So they appear to come from an object situated *behind* the mirror (⇨ pp. 72–5). The image of this object that is perceived is called a *virtual image* because the rays of light do not pass through it – as they do through a real image. The rays from the object to the mirror are real rays, but those from the image are not real. They are virtual rays.

Parallel light rays (such as those coming from a very distant light source) can be brought to a focus by a concave mirror (⇨ illustration) and, since optical laws always work in both directions, diverging light from a point source can equally well be converted into a parallel beam. Concave mirrors, which produce these effects, are widely used in car headlights and reflecting telescopes. Strictly, such concave mirrors must be parabolic (⇨ p. 20) rather than spherical to work properly, especially in telescopes. Convex mirrors, on the other hand, cannot form a real image and will turn a parallel beam into divergent rays (⇨ illustration).

Refraction and lenses

The human eye, spectacles, magnifying glasses, cameras, telescopes (monocular and binocular), microscopes, stereoscopes, projectors and medical and engineering endoscopes are all practical applications of light refraction. They depend on the fact that light travels more slowly through some transparent media than through others.

A narrow beam of light falling perpendicularly on the surface of a more dense

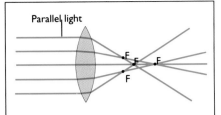

Spherical aberration occurs when a wide beam of light passes through a lens. The angle of incidence varies at the edge of the lens so that rays here come to a focus (F) in a different place from rays passing through the centre of the lens. The effect can be lessened by narrowing the lens, and by using different lenses together, each cancelling out the other's defects.

medium than that in which it is travelling will be slowed but not deflected, but if it strikes the denser medium at an angle, the beam will be bent towards the *normal* (perpendicular). The amount of bending differs with different transparent material and is characterized by what is called the *refractive index* of the material. Light travels fastest in a vacuum and slower in a denser medium. The refractive index of a vaccum could be regarded as 1, therefore the index of a denser medium will be greater than 1. The denser the medium the higher the refraction.

Light striking the side of a glass prism at an angle is bent towards the perpendicular, according to the normal rules of refraction, because glass is denser than air. Emerging from the prism, the ray passes from a dense to a less dense medium so it is bent away from the perpendicular. Because the surfaces of the prism are angled towards each other, however, the combined effect is to alter the overall course of the ray of light (⇨ illustration). This principle applies to lenses, which can also be regarded as having angled surfaces, even though in fact the surfaces also curve. Converging lenses (convex lenses) can be thought of as prisms set base to base, diverging lenses (concave lenses) as prisms set apex to apex.

Lenses are shaped so as to change the *vergence* – the angle of coming together or separating – of light rays. Convex lenses increase convergence, concave lenses increase divergence (⇨ p.74). A converging lens will bring parallel light rays to a focus at a point on the other side, and the distance from the lens to this point is called the *focal length* of the lens. Such a lens can form a real image of an object, for instance one that can be cast on a screen. A diverging lens cannot form a real image and has only a *virtual focus* – in other words, although the image can be seen directly by the eye, it cannot be projected on to a surface.

Single, thin lenses are widely used to compensate for various optical defects in the eye. Thicker lenses can be used in

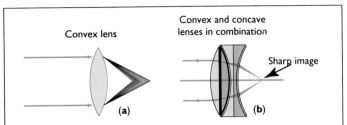

Chromatic aberration occurs because the refractive index of any material varies with wavelength of light. Lenses thus bend blue light (shorter wavelength) more (**a**) than they bend red light (longer wavelength). The effect can be cancelled by using convex and concave lenses (of material of different refractive index) in conjunction (**b**).

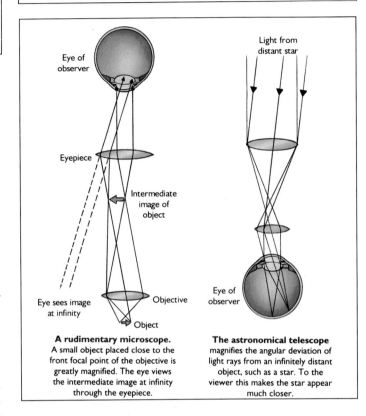

A rudimentary microscope. A small object placed close to the front focal point of the objective is greatly magnified. The eye views the intermediate image at infinity through the eyepiece.

The astronomical telescope magnifies the angular deviation of light rays from an infinitely distant object, such as a star. To the viewer this makes the star appear much closer.

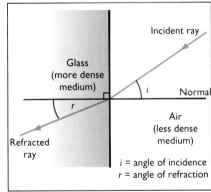

combination with each other to make telescopes, microscopes and other optical devices.

Light of different wavelength is refracted to different degrees, thus displaying the spectrum. This causes a problem for lens designers, who call this phenomenon *chromatic aberration*. This can be cancelled out to a large extent by making compound lenses that combine converging and diverging glasses of different refractive index.

SEE ALSO

● WHAT ARE WAVES? pp. 64–7
● LIGHT. pp. 72–5
● COLOUR p. 76
● SPECTRA AND SPECTROSCOPY p. 80
● COHERENT LIGHT – MASERS AND LASERS p. 82
● THE ELECTROMAGNETIC SPECTRUM AND ITS PROPERTIES p. 84

Spectra and Spectroscopy

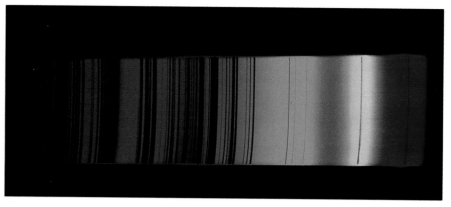

Since the end of the 19th century, spectroscopy has become one of the most important techniques in scientific research. It is an effective method of chemical analysis and an indispensable technique in astronomy.

Spectroscopy is the analysis of the electromagnetic spectrum (⇨ p. 84) – a vast range of frequencies stretching from radio waves tens of thousands of metres long to gamma rays billionths of a millimetre short. Until comparatively recently, this analysis was confined to the narrow band concerned with visible light near the centre of the spectrum.

When light from a luminous source is dispersed by a prism or a *diffraction grating* (an optical device for producing spectra; ⇨ p. 64) and falls on a screen, a coloured spectrum is seen. If the light first passes through a narrow slit, the spectrum is no longer continuous but consists of a number of separate bright lines of different colours (wavelengths; ⇨ p. 76). These are actually images of the slit formed by different degrees of dispersion of the individual wavelengths. In chemical analysis, spectroscopy can be used to analyse the light emitted by luminous gases and vapours at low pressure. A unique colour spectrum is generated by each element. For example, the spectrum for sodium consists of two bright yellow lines close together, while the spectrum for hydrogen has widely separated red, blue-green and violet lines.

The spectroscope used by the German physicist G. R. Kirchhoff (1824–87) to analyse the solar spectrum in the late-19th century. From H. Schellen, *Spectrum Analysis*, London (1872). (AR)

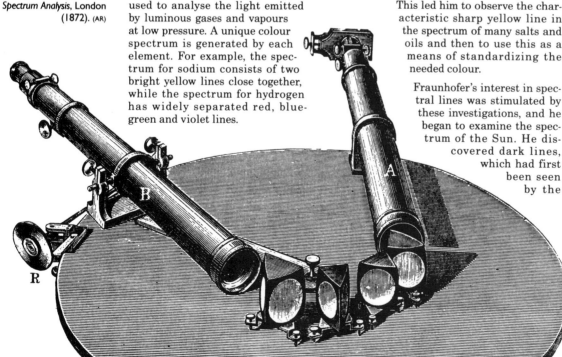

Joseph von Fraunhofer and the dark lines in the spectrum

The German optical worker Joseph von Fraunhofer (1787–1826) was the son of a poor glazier – and was the sole survivor of the family when their tenement building collapsed. At an early age he was apprenticed to a mirror maker and glass polisher. He taught himself about optics and glass and became a skilled maker of optical instruments. At 19 he was employed at the Mechanical-Optical Institute of Herr von Utzschneider at Benediktbeuern.

Fraunhofer was interested in improving the production of quality lenses and began investigating the dispersive power of different glasses (⇨ pp. 72–5). He tried to measure the length of the spectra produced, but found it impossible because the edges of the spectra were not sharp enough. Then he considered using light of a single colour, but at first could not fix the position of the colour in the spectrum with sufficient accuracy. This led him to observe the characteristic sharp yellow line in the spectrum of many salts and oils and then to use this as a means of standardizing the needed colour.

Fraunhofer's interest in spectral lines was stimulated by these investigations, and he began to examine the spectrum of the Sun. He discovered dark lines, which had first been seen by the

The Sun's spectrum shows dark absorption lines. These are the result of photons of specific energy being absorbed by elements in the Sun's atmosphere, so that they do not reach Earth. It was by analysis of the solar spectrum that the presence of helium in the Sun was first discovered. (Imperial College, SPL)

English metallurgist William Wollaston (1766–1828) twelve years previously. Wollaston had seen seven lines, but Fraunhofer, by refining his own apparatus, found 574 of them. He then observed the same lines in the light from Venus and many stars and was able to measure the wavelengths of the lines with great precision. Fraunhofer also showed that these lines could be seen in the spectrum formed by a grating, proving that they were properties of the light and not of the glass of prisms.

His reports of this work were ignored, largely because the scientific establishment regarded him as academically inferior. But fifty years later when the work was taken up again by Kirchhoff, scientists realized that Fraunhofer, working in isolation, had turned the spectroscope, then a mere curiosity, into a precision instrument of fundamental scientific importance and enormous practical value. By then, unhappily, Fraunhofer was long dead – at the age of 39, from tuberculosis.

Spectroscopy and new elements

The German physicist Gustav Robert Kirchhoff (1824–87), Professor of Physics at Heidelberg University, was a friend of Robert Wilhelm Bunsen (1811–99), who was Professor of Chemistry there. Bunsen was interested in chemical reactions that produced or absorbed light and was trying to analyse this light. Kirchhoff suggested that he should pass the light through a prism by using coloured filters, so as to see its spectrum. This proved promising and together the two men worked to develop the idea. When they passed the light through a narrow slit before sending it through the prism, they found that multiple images of the slit were formed in different positions by the refraction of the different wavelengths. Bunsen's now famous gas burner proved particularly useful for heating substances, as it could be adjusted to produce very little light on

SPECTROSCOPY AND ASTRONOMY

In 1835 the French philosopher Auguste Comte, defining the kind of knowledge that science could never obtain, cited the chemical constitution of the stars. Yet just a few years after his death in 1857 this very feat was achieved.

Detailed spectroscopy of the stars had to wait for the development of sufficiently powerful reflecting telescopes. By about 1856, however, scientists knew how to make large glass parabolic mirrors, and how to deposit a uniform layer of silver on them to form telescope mirrors. In 1862 the Swedish physicist Anders Jonas Ångström made a detailed analysis of the chemical composition of the Sun. Many others took up the work and progress was rapid.

In 1863, the English physicist Sir William Huggins (1824–1910), a pioneer of astrophysics, published the results of his analysis of star spectra, listing numerous emission lines. In 1864 he discovered two green lines in the spectrum of the Great Nebula in Orion and thought he had discovered a new element, which he called 'Nebulium'; unfortunately, he was mistaken. Nevertheless, between 1866 and 1868, Huggins proceeded to record the spectra of planets, comets and meteors and to show that the bands were identical to those from a hydrocarbon flame. From 1875 onwards he began to use the new dry-plate method of photography and was able to prove that the nebula Orion was gaseous, while Andromeda was composed of stars and was, in fact, a galaxy.

Later developments in spectroscopy have been remarkable. For instance, it was spectroscopy that enabled the American astronomer Vesto Slipher (1875–1969) to establish the existence of the Doppler 'red shift' (⇨ p. 130) for distant nebulae, which Edwin Hubble (1889–1953) used to establish the concept of the expanding universe.

its own, whereas other sources of light caused confusion. The result was the first practical spectroscope.

Kirchhoff realized that for each chemical element made incandescent, there was an invariable and characteristic pattern of coloured lines. He mapped the spectra of all the known elements, and it was at once apparent that here was a valuable method of determining the chemical constituents of any material. The idea was soon put to the test when, in the course of their experiments, he and Bunsen found a mineral giving spectral lines different from those for any known element. In May 1860 they announced that they had discovered a new element, the silvery-white alkali metal caesium. Soon they had discovered another – rubidium. These names

were derived from the Latin words for 'sky blue' and 'red' respectively, since these colours were the most prominent line in each spectrum.

Kirchhoff was familiar with the Fraunhofer lines (⇨ above), which had been named after the letters of the alphabet. He was intrigued by the fact that the prominent double line of sodium coincided exactly with the dark line in the Sun's spectrum that Fraunhofer had labelled D. When he tried to get rid of the dark line by projecting sunlight and sodium light simultaneously through the spectroscope, he was astonished to find that the line became even darker. This led him to propose that the identical wavelengths produced by an element when it was incandescent could also be *absorbed* by that element in gaseous form, and that Fraunhofer's D line must be due to sodium in the Sun's atmosphere. Kirchhoff was right, and this new idea increased even further the usefulness of spectroscopy. The absorption lines of six other elements were quickly found in the Sun's spectrum, and soon it became possible to determine the chemical constitution even of the stars.

The hydrogen lines and the Bohr atom

If light from incandescent hydrogen is analysed by spectroscopy it is found to consist of a series of very sharp lines – always of the same precise wavelengths. These lines are more and more closely spaced with decreasing wavelength. In 1885 the Swiss mathematician Johann Jakob Balmer (1825–98) announced that he had worked out a formula to predict the wavelengths of the whole series of lines. This was of comparatively little interest at the time as there was no explanation for the lines. But it became of crucial importance in 1913, when the Danish physicist Niels Bohr (1922–) proposed a structure for the hydrogen atom that could explain the spectral lines and derive the Balmer formula. Bohr's success in doing this added great weight to his hypothesis (⇨ p. 108). It also prompted others to predict, and then find, additional hydrogen lines in the ultraviolet and infrared spectra.

Spectroscopy today

Optical spectroscopy has proved an indispensable tool for scientists. Each kind of atom produces its unique line spectrum, and modern spectroscopic methods are sensitive enough to detect the most minute quantity of any element. In fact, spectroscopy has now largely displaced other analytic techniques for determining the chemical composition of unknown materials.

Optical spectroscopy has largely been replaced by infrared and other forms of spectroscopy. Visible light spectra correspond to the transition of electrons in atoms from one energy level to another (⇨ p. 108). Infrared spectra are related to the mutual vibration of pairs of atoms

bonded together (⇨ p. 162). The frequency of the vibration depends on the masses of the atoms and the strength of the bond, and is characteristic of the bond pair. For instance, the infrared spectrum of an organic compound will immediately reveal the presence of particular groups, such as a carbonyl group.

Infrared spectroscopy is now being supplemented by nuclear magnetic-resonance spectroscopy, which is considered the best method of analysing complex organic compounds. Atom nuclei behave like tiny magnets, and, in a powerful magnetic field, these align themselves in a typical way. But the application of radio waves in the range 40–360 MHz can cause the nuclear magnets to change their orientation. On resuming the previous alignment they give off characteristic signals that can be detected and the atoms identified.

Instruments are also in use today for spectroscopic analysis of the microwave spectra, largely for research purposes; ultraviolet spectra, especially for determining the concentration of solutions; and X-ray and gamma-ray spectra.

Modern spectral analysis is invaluable for chemical examination (particularly of unknown compounds), investigating molecular structures and energy levels, and for assessing the structure of stars and other celestial bodies. *(Zefa)*

Coherent Light — Masers and Lasers

The *laser*, a highly energetic concentration of light waves, has a place in millions of households and applications in industry, communications, science, warfare and medicine. It is a striking example of the technological application of pure science.

The laser's name is an acronym – Light Amplification by Stimulated Emission of Radiation. Thousands of scientists were involved in its development, but all this work stemmed from the seminal concept of one man and its eventual realization in a practical device. This man was the American physicist Charles Hard Townes

(1915–). After graduating, Townes was appointed as a trainee scientist to the technical staff of Bell Telephone Laboratories where, because of the war in Europe, intensive research was in progress into the development of radar. Operational requirements dictated that the frequencies used should be pushed ever higher. Because frequency and wavelength are reciprocal (⇨ p. 64), equipment such as antennae on aircraft could be reduced to small dimensions only by using very high frequencies.

At Bell Laboratories Townes became an expert on microwaves. In 1948 he went to Columbia University in New York and two years later became a full professor of physics there. By then he was a world authority on microwave spectroscopy (⇨ p. 80) and was invited to join an Office of Naval Research committee of scientists investigating the generation of microwaves of millimetre and submillimetre length. With the equipment available at the time this proved almost impossible. But in 1951 Townes had the idea that was to change the face of scientific technology. It occurred to him that ammonia molecules were the right size to vibrate at the frequency needed to generate such waves using an oscillator. In his own words: 'In a few minutes I had calculated, on the back of an envelope, the critical condition for oscillation in terms of the number of excited molecules which must be supplied and the maximum losses allowable in the cavity.'

CD-DRIVE LASER MECHANISM

Compact disc

Collimator lens (makes parallel rays diverge/ converge, or vice versa)

Objective lens

Plane-parallel plate

Laser source   Grating

Photodiode

In a standard CD drive (music CD or computer CD-ROM), the laser beam, used to 'read' the compact disc, is emitted perpendicular to the surface of the disc. It is rotated through 90°, strikes the compact disc, and then reflects back to the *photodiode* (light-sensitive semiconductor). The laser beam is very finely focused so that it reads no more than one track-width on the CD at a time. It measures only 1μm (micrometre) across at the point of focus.

Oscillating ammonia

When ammonia molecules are excited by energy such as heat or microwaves they absorb energy and flip into a mirror-image form (the excited state). When they revert to their normal form they give off energy. The difference between the two energy levels is equal to the energy content of a photon – a discrete 'packet' of energy – equivalent to an electromagnetic wave with a frequency of 24,000 million cycles per second (MHz) and a wavelength of 1.25 cm (½ in). Usually, when a closed volume of the gas is irradiated by heat or microwaves, the number of excited molecules that revert to normal is the same as the number that become excited, and so the gas is in a state of equilibrium. A substance in equilibrium radiates just like an ordinary hot body. What Townes had in mind was to produce a region of excited ammonia molecules in which the excited number exceeded the nonexcited number (known as *population inversion*). He hoped that these molecules, all oscillating at the same frequency, would radiate an intense beam of microwaves.

As early as 1917, Einstein (⇨ pp. 38–41) had pointed out that if a photon of exactly the right energy struck an already excited molecule, the molecule would revert to its *ground state* (⇨ box), and, in so doing, would emit a photon that had exactly the same energy and was moving in exactly the same direction as the entering photon. Townes realized

A laser beam being used to measure the length of an underground tunnel. Lasers are capable of travelling very long distances without dispersing, and can yield highly accurate results when used as 'tape measures'. The length of time the beam takes to bounce back is recorded, and, because the speed of light is a constant, the distance it has travelled can be calculated. (Zefa)

that if a predominance of ammonia molecules could be placed at the higher energy level, an incoming beam of microwaves at the right frequency would lead to a majority of molecules emitting identical photons and that these would have a chain-reaction effect. One entering photon would quickly lead to an avalanche of photons all of the same size and moving in the same direction. Microwave amplification at a frequency of 24,000 MHz would be achieved. That was the idea; the realization, however, was to prove more difficult.

The Maser

Townes assembled a group of researchers and students and explained his concept. It was decided to use a strong electrostatic field, like that used in a television

THE LASER PRINCIPLE

- The orbiting electrons of atoms may exist in levels at different distances from the nucleus. Those nearer have lower energy; those further out have higher energy.

- To move outwards to a higher energy level an electron must gain energy by absorbing a photon; if it moves inwards it will give off a photon.

- Any photon of electromagnetic radiation (heat, light, microwaves, for instance) of a particular wavelength has a particular energy.

- If a photon with an energy equal to the energy difference between two levels in an atom strikes the atom, the photon will be absorbed. An electron will move outwards to the higher energy level and the atom will be said to be *excited*.

- After a short time the electron will drop down to the lower level, and, in so doing, will give off a photon of light. The atom has now returned to the *ground state*.

- In any normal light source, the many excited atoms and molecules emit photons of different energy levels (*wavelength*) and thus of different colours.

- If, during the brief period of its excitation, an atom is struck by a photon of a particular wavelength, it will give off a photon *identical in energy and direction* to the photon that struck it.

- If the material being irradiated is suitably arranged, these emitted photons will chain react to form a beam of light of a fixed wavelength in which all the waves are in phase with each other (*coherent light*). This is the laser beam (Light Amplification by Stimulated Emission of Radiation).

- Many materials in any phase – solid, liquid or gas – can be used in a laser. Common materials used include ruby, various liquid solutions and dyes, and various gases.

tube, to form excited ammonia molecules into a beam, which would then be focused into a cavity tuned to resonate at exactly 24,000 MHz. For two years they built model after model, tried them, failed, and started again. Costs rose, colleagues urged him to give up and stop wasting government money. Then, one day late in 1953, the latest version of their device began to oscillate. After much discussion the group settled on the name MASER – an acronym for Microwave Amplification by Stimulated Emission of Radiation. Soon it was apparent that the frequency of oscillation was stable to a degree not previously attained. It could not be tuned, but resolutely insisted on oscillating at exactly 24,000 MHz. This precise and invariable oscillation rate made it the basis for a clock – which depends on such precise timing – of unprecedented accuracy: it would have an accumulated error of only one second in 10,000 years.

Almost at once the principle behind the maser became the common property of the scientific world. Every development in the field was seized upon and discussed, research and development rapidly rose in volume. Soon the maser principle was applied to materials other than ammonia. Solid-state, fixed-frequency maser oscillators were succeeded by tunable oscillators and amplifiers. Important applications of these in radar and communications were quickly found and are still in use today.

The optical maser

The frequencies at which masers operate are much lower than those of infrared or visible light – and there was an apparently unbridgeable gap between the two. Because of the dimensions involved there seemed to be no way to make a resonating cavity small enough to raise the frequency of oscillation into the infrared region, so Townes decided that it might be more fruitful to start with visible light and move downwards. In conjunction with his brother-in-law, Arthur L. Schawlow, he began to consider how an optical maser might be made. One idea they considered was to use two parallel mirrors between which light energy might be reflected backwards and forwards through a collection of atoms, most of which were in the excited state. Photons moving perpendicular to the mirrors would stimulate further identical photons in accordance with Einstein's principle; those moving in other directions would escape. In a paper published in 1958, Townes and Schawlow pointed out that light emitted by such a device would be of a single pure frequency with all the waves exactly in phase. This is called coherent light (⇨ pp. 72–5).

This paper aroused great excitement and at once scientists in physics laboratories all over the world started to try to build such a device. The race was won by Theodore H. Maiman, head of the quantum electronics section of the Hughes

USES OF THE LASER

Coherent light is of a fixed wavelength and colour. It will form a beam with barely any divergence, and can be focused to a very fine point of intense brightness and very high temperature. These qualities have made the laser a vital tool in many fields of technology.

It is widely used in the computer and entertainment industries – perhaps most familiarly in light displays at rock and pop concerts, but also in the manufacture of microelectronic chips and holograms, and in printers, compact-disc players and CD-ROM drives. In medicine, for instance in eye surgery, it is sometimes used as a fine cutting tool, with the added advantage that it can cauterize the wound as it cuts. In industrial and medical research, it is used as a driller, cutter, welder or surface etcher, and as a rangefinder or precise, long-distance straight-edge; in the arms industry, as a weapon-sighting device; in laboratories to produce the heat necessary for nuclear fusion research. It is a means of communication in space – and even a possible weapon of war.

As well as having many applications in industry, medicine and science, laser beams make elaborate light displays because of their colourful and unusually piercing nature. (Paul Chave, Horizon)

Research Laboratories in Malibu. There, in July 1960, a ruby crystal with polished, parallel, mirrored ends, irradiated by a xenon electronic flash, produced a thin, dead-straight beam of pure deep-red monochromatic light. The laser had been born.

Townes became Professor of Physics at the Massachusetts Institute of Technology in Boston, Massachusetts, USA, in 1961 and remained there until 1967. He then became Professor-at-large at California University. In 1964, in conjunction with Nikolai Gennadiyevich Basov and Alexander Mikhaylovich Prokhorov (who had independently suggested the maser principle in 1952), he was awarded the Nobel Prize for physics.

The Electromagnetic Spectrum and its Properties

The electromagnetic spectrum is the wide span of all known waves that consist of an electric field and a magnetic field vibrating at right angles to each other. This spectrum covers, in order of decreasing wavelength: radio, television, radar, microwaves, infrared radiation, visible light, ultraviolet radiation, X-rays and gamma rays. The only difference in the nature of all these seemingly different forms of radiation is in their wavelength – and, hence, their frequency.

SEE ALSO

● WHAT IS ENERGY? pp. 46–9
● SOURCES OF ENERGY pp. 58–61
● WHAT ARE WAVES? pp. 64–7
● LIGHT pp. 72–5
● SPECTRA AND SPECTROSCOPY p. 80
● COHERENT LIGHT – MASERS AND LASERS p. 82

A wave of constant wavelength that travels at a constant speed must pass through a fixed number of cycles in a fixed time. It is for this reason that there is a constant reciprocal relationship between wavelength and frequency. Because all electromagnetic radiation is propagated through empty space at the same fixed speed – about 299,792 km/s (185,282 mi/s) – the same rule applies to all. The shorter the wavelength, the higher the frequency – and vice versa. At the long-wavelength end of the spectrum are radio waves with wavelengths hundreds of metres long and frequencies as low as 10,000 Hz (cycles per second). Radar and microwave radiation have wavelengths down to a centimetre or less and frequencies of more than a 1,000 million Hz. At the short-wavelength end of the spectrum are the gamma rays of wavelength equal to billionths of a millimetre and frequencies that are as high as 10,000,000,000,000,000,000,000 Hz.

The origin of electromagnetic radiation

Electromagnetic radiation occurs when electrical charges are made to move, or, in other words, are accelerated. Whenever a charge is in fact accelerated, whether in a regular oscillation, such as a constant or uniform sine wave (p. 64), or not, it loses energy in the form of electromagnetic waves. In radio transmitters this is achieved by electronic oscillators that cause alternating electrical currents to flow in and out of transmitting antennae. These moving charges consist of countless millions of electrons, rapidly moving and changing direction. This results in a radiated electric field, which induces a magnetic field at right angles to itself. A changing electric field cannot exist on its own, but will always be associated with a changing magnetic field. Any acceleration of electrons produces electromagnetic radiation, and, since all matter contains moving electrons, all matter must, therefore, be emitting waves at all times.

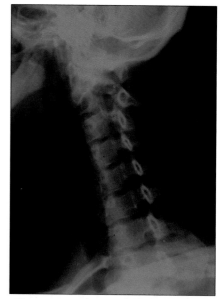

X-rays occupy the part of the electromagnetic spectrum between gamma rays and ultraviolet rays. Their short wavelength and penetrating power facilitate their use as a diagnostic tool, as in this X-ray of a neck. (Zefa)

Temperature and wavelength

Every object in the universe has a finite temperature – that is, a temperature above absolute zero (⇨ p. 50) – and each emits electromagnetic radiation. Such radiation has a mixture of wavelengths. Bodies at 'room' temperature – around 20°C (68°F) – emit radiation almost entirely in the infrared part of the spectrum, with wavelengths longer than those of visible light. As the temperature rises, the average wavelength shortens and comes closer to that of visible light. At around 800°C (1,472°F) most of the electromagnetic radiation from an object is still in the infrared region, but enough shorter-wavelength radiation is emitted for the body to become visible, especially in the dark, and it is said to be 'red hot'. With further increase in temperature the visible emission increases and the colour changes from red to white. A body at about 3,000°C (5,432°F) emits considerable white light and is said to be 'white hot'. This is the temperature of the tungsten filament of an electric light bulb. But even at this temperature, only about 10 per cent of the energy is in the form of light, the remainder being heat, or infrared radiation.

The relationship between temperature and the rate of energy radiation is not linear – that is, the rate at which energy is radiated does not increase uniformly with rise in temperature. In fact the rate of release rises very rapidly with increase in temperature and is proportional to the *fourth power* of the absolute (Kelvin) temperature (⇨ p. 50). Rate of energy radiation can be expressed in watts per square centimetre of surface. A body at 100°C (373 K; 212°F) radiates about 0.03 watts/cm². The same body at 1,000°C (1,273 K; 1,832°F), three and a half times the absolute temperature,

---

ELECTROMAGNETIC RADIATION AND THE HUMAN BODY

Overexposure to ultraviolet light can have harmful effects on the skin. Possible problems range from sunburn through to malignant melanomas. Light-skinned people, especially children, are most at risk. Sun block applied to the most sensitive areas, such as lips and noses, helps prevent damage. (Spectrum)

The effect of electromagnetic radiation on the body is in some cases a matter of serious concern. Visible light of normal intensities is probably harmless but very high-intensity visible light can be damaging to the eyes, and can easily destroy parts of the retinas, especially the central parts most essential for vision.

The ultraviolet part of the spectrum can make its presence felt within minutes or hours by causing sunburn or severe eye irritation. X-rays and gamma rays are not immediately perceived but can, within hours or days, cause severe and readily perceptible effects on the body by ionization (⇨ main text). Whole-body irradiation above a certain level is usually fatal, and a less-than-fatal dosage greatly increases the risk of cancer cells developing. Microwaves can cause internal bodily heating, with effects such as cataracts and brain damage, if the source is close enough and the waves sufficiently intense (however, there is no danger from microwave ovens as these are securely sealed). People working within a metre (or yard) or so of high-power operating radar antennae, for instance, can suffer such effects. Debate continues as to whether the part of the spectrum concerned with radio and television, and the electromagnetic fields from power cables, offer any significant hazard to humans.

radiates 4 watts/cm² – over one hundred and thirty times the energy.

Origin of the different forms

Radio, television and microwaves result from the mass movement of large numbers of electrons or by charged particles forced to circle in strong magnetic fields. The movement of molecules involves the movement of electrons and molecular vibration or rotation is a function of temperature. This movement gives rise to infrared radiation.

Visible and ultraviolet radiation occurs when the outermost electrons of the atoms move from higher to lower energy levels (⇨ p. 108) under the influence of temperature. X-radiation occurs when atoms, usually those of heavy metals, are deliberately bombarded by streams of high-energy electrons. These high-speed electrons can drive off strongly attracted electrons in orbits near the nucleus of atoms, leaving a gap into which an outer electron immediately passes. This movement from a high- to a low-energy band results in the emission of a quantum of high energy of very short wavelength and very high frequency, the X-ray.

Gamma rays are produced from the nuclei of atoms, and their high energy is derived from the powerful forces that hold the nuclear particles (protons and neutrons) together (⇨ p. 112). They occur in the course of the nuclear fission of naturally radioactive elements, and also when elements are bombarded by high-energy particles, either naturally, as by cosmic rays, or by artificial means in a machine (⇨ p. 114).

Properties of electro-magnetic radiation

All electromagnetic waves travel at the same speed through empty space, but are slowed (and may be absorbed partly or wholly) when they pass through a material. This is because the electric and magnetic fields interact with any charged particles in the material causing them to oscillate at the same frequency as the wave. The energy used in causing such oscillation is lost from the electromagnetic wave, which is said to experience a degree of absorption. The lost energy is dissipated in the form of heat. In this way radiation from the Sun heats the Earth after passing unchanged through 92,955,900 mi (149,598,020 km) of empty space.

Such oscillating charges, in turn, have an effect on the incident wave, causing it to slow down by an amount that varies with the material and is characterized by a figure called the index of refraction (⇨ p. 80). One of the consequences is that a beam of radiation passing obliquely through a material is bent. Such refraction is most familiar to us with light passing through transparent material, but is a feature of all electromagnetic radiation traversing matter.

JAMES CLERK MAXWELL AND ELECTROMAGNETIC THEORY

The Scottish physicist James Clerk Maxwell (1831–79) is considered by some to be second in importance only to Newton. As a schoolboy he was known to his peers as 'daftie', but at the age of 14, while still at school, he published his first mathematical paper in the *Proceedings of the Royal Society of Edinburgh*. After an illustrious academic career at Edinburgh University and Cambridge, he was appointed Professor of Natural Philosophy (physics) at Aberdeen in 1856, at the age of 25, and then at King's College, London, in 1860. In 1871 he became the first Cavendish Professor of Experimental Physics at Cambridge.

Maxwell was a close friend of Michael Faraday (⇨ p. 92), who was thirty years his senior, and Faraday's brilliant experiments in electricity and magnetism formed the basis for Maxwell's mathematical understanding of these subjects. Faraday was no mathematician but had an instinct for the expression of empirical truth and could explain his ideas on the theory behind his findings in electricity and magnetism in a manner that immediately inspired Maxwell to mathematical generalizations. Faraday had shown that a moving electric current could produce magnetism and that a moving magnet could produce a current. Maxwell started by expressing these two facts in precise quantitative terms.

Maxwell's great work, *Electricity and Magnetism*, was published in 1873, and is widely regarded as the high point of 19th-century physics. It contains his celebrated partial differential equations, which fully describe how the electromagnetic field is produced by moving electric charges and how it is propagated in space. They show that both the electric and the magnetic components are perpendicular to the direction of propagation and to each other, and that the two components are in phase – that is, that they reach maximum and minimum intensity simultaneously. These equations had, and continue to have, an enormous influence on the subsequent development of science.

Maxwell predicted that it would one day be possible to generate electromagnetic waves in the laboratory. In 1887, just eight years after his death, this was achieved by the German physicist Heinrich Hertz (⇨ p. 10).

Some parts of the spectrum are said to be capable of causing ionization. This means that radiation can displace electrons from atoms or molecules, so that they become positively charged. Molecules that are ionized are usually changed and may be broken by loss of a linking electron. Most of the seriously damaging biological effects of radiation are due to ionization.

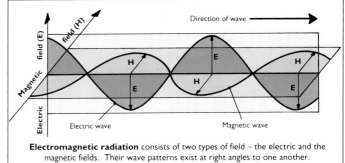

Electromagnetic radiation consists of two types of field – the electric and the magnetic fields. Their wave patterns exist at right angles to one another.

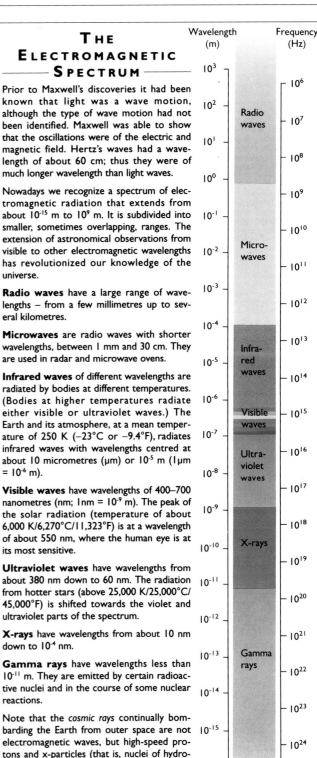

THE ELECTROMAGNETIC SPECTRUM

Prior to Maxwell's discoveries it had been known that light was a wave motion, although the type of wave motion had not been identified. Maxwell was able to show that the oscillations were of the electric and magnetic field. Hertz's waves had a wavelength of about 60 cm; thus they were of much longer wavelength than light waves.

Nowadays we recognize a spectrum of electromagnetic radiation that extends from about 10^{-15} m to 10^9 m. It is subdivided into smaller, sometimes overlapping, ranges. The extension of astronomical observations from visible to other electromagnetic wavelengths has revolutionized our knowledge of the universe.

Radio waves have a large range of wavelengths – from a few millimetres up to several kilometres.

Microwaves are radio waves with shorter wavelengths, between 1 mm and 30 cm. They are used in radar and microwave ovens.

Infrared waves of different wavelengths are radiated by bodies at different temperatures. (Bodies at higher temperatures radiate either visible or ultraviolet waves.) The Earth and its atmosphere, at a mean temperature of 250 K (–23°C or –9.4°F), radiates infrared waves with wavelengths centred at about 10 micrometres (μm) or 10^{-5} m (1μm = 10^{-6} m).

Visible waves have wavelengths of 400–700 nanometres (nm; 1nm = 10^{-9} m). The peak of the solar radiation (temperature of about 6,000 K/6,270°C/11,323°F) is at a wavelength of about 550 nm, where the human eye is at its most sensitive.

Ultraviolet waves have wavelengths from about 380 nm down to 60 nm. The radiation from hotter stars (above 25,000 K/25,000°C/45,000°F) is shifted towards the violet and ultraviolet parts of the spectrum.

X-rays have wavelengths from about 10 nm down to 10^{-4} nm.

Gamma rays have wavelengths less than 10^{-11} m. They are emitted by certain radioactive nuclei and in the course of some nuclear reactions.

Note that the *cosmic rays* continually bombarding the Earth from outer space are not electromagnetic waves, but high-speed protons and x-particles (that is, nuclei of hydrogen and helium atoms), together with some heavier nuclei.

ELECTRICITY
AND
MAGNETISM

Poles, Fields and Charges

The idea of polarity is usually related to the poles of the Earth, which roughly correspond to the two ends of the axis around which the Earth rotates. Even the designations of these poles – North and South – have been applied to other polar concepts, such as those of a permanent magnet.

Superconducting magnet keeping another magnet levitating by means of the repellent forces between them. Maglev (*magnetic levitation*) trains, such as those in use in Japan, make use of this fact to travel suspended above a track. (Zefa)

Static electricity is induced in this comb, to which the boy's hair is attracted, because of the rubbing action between it and the hair. (Zefa)

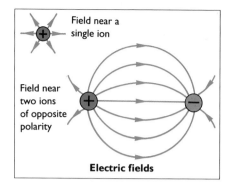

Field near a single ion

Field near two ions of opposite polarity

Electric fields

We can see from simple experiments with magnets that, in the case of magnetic polarity, there is an important difference between the two poles. We also find that surrounding a magnet is a zone of influence – a magnetic *field* – within which iron objects can be attracted or oriented. Poles and fields become readily apparent to the observer when the properties of permanent magnets are investigated. Similarly, but perhaps less obviously, charges, fields and poles can be demonstrated when *electrostatics*, or 'static electricity' is studied. These seemingly diverse phenomena have more in common than is generally appreciated.

The idea of polarity

When the north pole of one bar magnet is brought near the south pole of another there is an attraction between them that is stronger than the attraction either one would have to an unmagnetized piece of iron. The rule is that unlike poles attract. When, however, the north pole of one magnet is brought near the north pole of another, there is a mutual repulsion and it may even be difficult to hold the magnets together. The same thing happens if we bring together two south poles. Like poles repel.

If, instead of magnetic poles, we consider electric charges (⇨ below), we have an exactly analogous situation. Electrons have negative charges and all electrons repel one another. Atoms that have temporarily lost an electron are necessarily positively charged because of the positive charge on the protons in the nucleus (⇨ p. 108). Such a positively charged *ion* (charged atom or group of atoms) will strongly attract electrons or other negatively charged bodies, and will repel other positive ions or posi-‑ tively charged bodies.

This idea of the repulsion of like entities and the attraction of opposites is fundamental to the whole subject of electricity and magnetism. It is, for instance, the basis of the electrical neutrality of the atom, and of the operation of all electric motors (⇨ p. 92). It is also the foundation of voltage, whether considered as a force driving electric current (*electromotive force*) or as a difference in force between two points (*potential difference*). It has wide implications even outside the range of physics and, as the basis for the linking of atoms into molecules, is also fundamental to chemistry (⇨ p. 156).

The electron

For a general understanding of electricity it is sufficient to think of the electron as a tiny body of very low mass, carrying a charge arbitrarily described as negative. This terminology was the result of an early misunderstanding of the nature of electricity by the American scientist and statesman Benjamin Franklin (1706–90), who thought that electricity flowed the opposite way to the way it does. Subsequent clarification showed that it would have been more logical to designate the charge positive, as 'negative ' implies the absence of something, but the usage is now so thoroughly established and has so many wider applications that change is inconceivable. Electrons are always associated with atoms because atoms have positively charged cores (*nuclei*) that attract them. But in the case of many atoms, electrons are loosely attached and can readily be displaced from them. This is especially the case with metals. Some other atoms, however, have their electrons much more firmly attached. The electron can be thought of as the basic particle of electricity; and an electric current can be seen as no more than the movement of electrons (⇨ p. 90).

Electrons in captivity (electrostatic phenomena)

Static electricity exists only on good insulators like amber, vinyl records, polythene, perspex and rubber balloons. If any of these is thoroughly rubbed with a suitable material, some billions of electrons will be rubbed off or on, leaving the atoms of the material positively or negatively charged. And because the rubbed material is a good insulator, electrons cannot move along its surface to be attracted so as to neutralize positively charged atoms, nor are surplus electrons able to get off. Anything brought near to such a charged insulator will either have its electrons concentrated together in the area near the charged body, or will have them repelled away from that area. If the object is light enough it may thus be drawn to it by the attraction between the positively charged atoms of the insulator and its own electrons or repelled from it by the surplus of electrons. While perspex rubbed with wool loses electrons and becomes positively charged, polythene, on the other hand, acquires extra electrons when rubbed with wool, and becomes negatively charged.

The essential difference between insulators and conductors now becomes clear. In insulators, the electrons are firmly bound to their atoms. Any charge caused by local removal of electrons (positive charge), or by the local addition of electrons (negative charge), remains in that place and does not spread over the surface of the insulator. In conductors, however, electrons are free to move about, so any local charge quickly distributes itself over the whole surface. Static

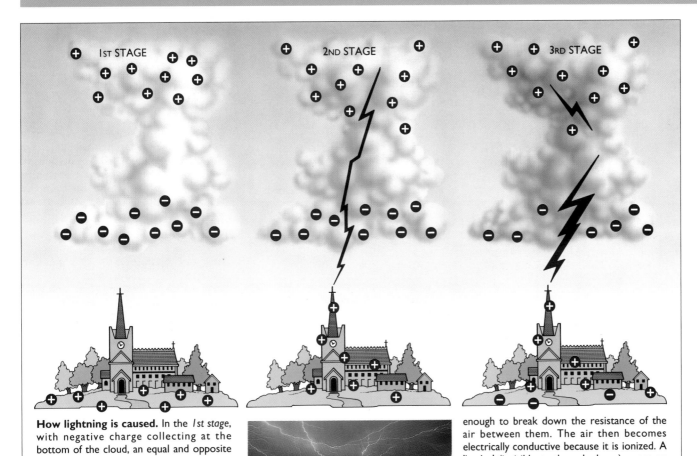

1ST STAGE

2ND STAGE

3RD STAGE

SEE ALSO

- ELECTRONS AND
  CONDUCTANCE p. 90
- SOURCES OF ELECTRICITY
  pp. 92–5
- RESISTANCE p. 96
- CAPACITANCE p. 98
- INDUCTANCE p. 100
- ELECTRONICS pp. 102–5
- THE CLASSICAL THEORY OF
  THE ATOM p. 108
- THE QUARK THEORY p. 110
- FUNDAMENTAL FORCES p. 112
- THE ROTATION AND ORBIT
  OF THE EARTH p. 144
- ATOMS AND MOLECULES
  p. 156
- COMPUTING AND ARTIFICIAL
  INTELLIGENCE pp. 212–25

How lightning is caused. In the *1st stage*, with negative charge collecting at the bottom of the cloud, an equal and opposite charge is induced on the ground because unlike charges attract one another. In the *2nd stage*, if the cloud has become very large, discharges start to take place – that is, the forces between the charges are strong enough to break down the resistance of the air between them. The air then becomes electrically conductive because it is ionized. A 'leader' (invisible to the naked eye) opens an ionized channel through the air – which will allow electricity (flow of negative charge) to follow. In the *3rd stage*, the lightning strikes, following along the path made by the leader.

electricity is the same in nature as current electricity; both consist of electrons. In static electricity, however, the electrons are barely able to move. In current electricity they move easily. Movement of electrons is very important because of the effects such movement causes. Differences in charges in insulators can readily build up to very high levels; charges in conductors do not do so because of the ease with which the electrons can move away. Static electricity charges, although usually small, can have a *potential difference* (difference in total electric charge between two points) relative to an uncharged body (such as the Earth) of thousands of volts. This is why sparks are readily caused. But because the actual amount of charge (number of electrons) is relatively very small, the current that can flow is usually trivial. Current electricity, on the other hand, usually involves the movement of very large charges under the influence of comparatively small potential differences.

Magnetic fields and electric fields

If the filings from a piece of iron are scattered on a sheet of card and a bar magnet is placed under that card, the iron particles will align themselves into a particular pattern that is a representation of the shape of the magnetic field in that plane (⇨ illustration). In exactly the same way, if particles of an insulating material (such as grass seed) are suspended in oil in a glass dish and a strong electric field is applied by means of high-voltage electrodes dipped into the oil, the particles will form a characteristic pattern that outlines the electric field. The shape of the electric field varies with the shape of the electrodes and their relationship to each other.

Magnetic fields and magnetic force are the result of moving charges. In the case of a permanent magnet, the magnetic field is due to the uniform orientation with which electrons in the metal are moving in orbit around the nuclei of their aligned atoms. The repulsion between the north poles of two magnets is due to the fact that the magnetic field caused by the electrons orbiting in one magnet exert a repelling force on the field caused by the electrons orbiting in the other magnet. At the south pole of each magnet, the electrons are orbiting in the opposite direction, and will exert an attracting force. Moving charges will always induce a magnetic field, and a moving magnet will cause charges to move. This, as Michael Faraday discovered (⇨ p. 92) and James Clerk Maxwell explained (⇨ p. 84), is one of the best ways to generate electricity.

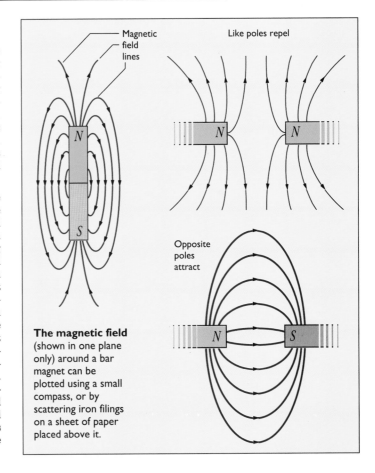

Magnetic field lines

Like poles repel

Opposite poles attract

The magnetic field (shown in one plane only) around a bar magnet can be plotted using a small compass, or by scattering iron filings on a sheet of paper placed above it.

Electrons and Conductance

Electrons are so small, and the charge on them (⇨ p. 88) so seemingly insignificant, that it is hard to credit the power this charge can display. The implications of the simple statement 'like charges repel' are often surprising. A crowded commuter train, for instance, is pushed out of its station solely by the summation of forces produced by this charge.

Because all electrons carry a negative charge, and like charges repel each other, the free electrons in a conductor will always separate from one another so far as the limits of the conductor will allow. These electrons are all exerting a force on each other, and the more electrons present, the greater will be this repelling force. Mutual repulsion of this kind is very similar to the repulsion of gas molecules in a confined space (⇨ p. 50); and in both cases a pressure results. In the case of negative electric charges, this pressure is called *voltage*.

Electrons in motion

If a conductor with a surplus of electrons is touched by another conductor, many of those on the first will be pushed onto the second and, quickly, a new equilibrium will be set up in which the charges are evenly distributed over both. Thus, the pressure, or voltage, is lowered. Whenever a surplus of electrons exists on a body – that is, a number of electrons greater than the number of (positively charged) protons in the material concerned – that body is said to be at a negative voltage, relative to neutrality. A body with a deficiency of free electrons is said to be at a positive voltage. If a body at a particular voltage is connected by a conductor to a body at a different voltage, electrons will flow from the body with the higher concentration of electrons to that with the lower. This flow of electrons is called an *electric current*. So, voltage causes current to flow.

The term 'voltage' derives from the unit of electrical pressure or difference of electrical potential (the sum of the charges at a point), the *volt*, and it was coined in recognition of one of the pioneers of electricity, the Italian Count Alessandro Volta (1745–1827) who made the first electric battery. Volta had noted that different metals, when in contact, produced electricity. In 1799, using discs of metal (alternately copper and zinc) separated by discs of cloth soaked in weak acid, he produced a ready source of electric current. This 'voltaic pile', as it was called, was to make possible a remarkable succession of advances, and within about thirty years most of the basic facts of electricity had been established.

Voltage can be considered in two ways: first it can be thought of as the difference in pressure between two points (one of which is often, but not necessarily, neutral); or, second, as the pressure that causes electrons to move, causing an electric current to flow. When considered in this way, voltage is called the *electromotive* force (EMF). To recap: an electric current is a flow of electrons, and a voltage is the pressure of accumulated electrons that makes it flow – two quite different things. The amount of current that flows under the influence of a given voltage depends on another factor, electrical *resistance* (the degree of opposition to the flow of current presented by the conductor; ⇨ p. 96).

Conductors and insulators

All the pure metals are *elements* – substances with only one kind of atom in them. They are differentiated by virtue of the fact that each has a different number of electrons in the atom. Aluminium, being a light metal, has 13; chromium has 24; iron 26; nickel 28; copper 29; zinc 30; platinum 78; gold 79; and lead 82. Metals are important in electricity because some of their electrons are free to move away from the parent atoms to form a 'sea' of electrons in the metal. These free electrons can readily be caused to move to form an electric current if repelled by a surplus. For this reason metals are good conductors of electricity.

Other materials, such as polythene, most other plastics, glass, porcelain, dry wood, candle wax, resin or rubber do not give rise to free electrons and therefore act as insulators. Wet wood is not a good insulator because water, unless very pure, will conduct electricity quite well. Water with a little salt or acid in it is a good conductor because these materials readily break up into charged particles (*ions*). The best conductors, such as copper or silver, conduct electricity many billions of times better than the best insulators (or worst conductors) such as polythene.

There is a third class of materials with properties somewhere between conductors and insulators. These are called *semiconductors*, and they have proved to be of enormous theoretical and practical importance (⇨ p. 104).

The electric circuit

Electricity can flow momentarily between two connected conductors until the charges are uniformly spread out. This happens very quickly and, once it has, the flow ceases. For an electric current to flow continuously, however, two things are required – an electromotive force (voltage) and a continuous circular pathway provided by a conductor. An electric battery separates charges by chemical means, thereby providing an electromotive force. The amount of this force is determined by the construction of the battery and can be increased by connecting two or more batteries one after the other (*in series*). Such a battery, by producing a sustained EMF, can cause a current to flow through an external conductor, as long as that conductor returns to the battery. This system is called a *circuit*, and may contain useful devices such as a light bulb, an electric motor or a heater. If the circuit is broken, as by means of a switch, the current immediately ceases to flow. When the circuit is intact, however, current flows from the negative pole of the battery, round the circuit and back to the positive pole.

Alessandro Volta (1745–1827) demonstrating his voltaic pile to Napoleon. This invention, a prototype battery, was to open the way to the artificial production of electricity, and led to the understanding of the nature and operation of it. From *Le Petit Journal supplément illustré*, Paris (1901). (AR)

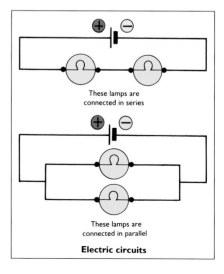

These lamps are connected in series

These lamps are connected in parallel

Electric circuits

DIRECT AND ALTERNATING CURRENTS

Current flowing in one direction only is known as *direct current* (DC). This is the mode of flow produced, for instance, by a battery. For many purposes, however, a different mode of flow offers substantial advantages. This is known as *alternating current* (AC). In this mode, the current first flows in one direction for a short time. It then smoothly reverses direction and flows in the other one, constantly repeating the reversal of direction (⇨ illustration). The principal difference between AC and DC is that, in AC, the voltage can easily be changed using a transformer (⇨ p. 92). It can thus be transmitted at very high voltage/low current, thereby minimizing losses from heating. Transformers of all sizes are so useful both industrially and domestically, that a domestic DC supply is now unthinkable.

Because voltage drives current, voltage levels are represented here at a succession of points of time, reading from left to right. Direct voltage simply causes a current to rise to a maximum and to stay there as long as the voltage continues. Most alternating voltages and currents follow a smooth curve known as a sine wave (⇨ p. 64), as shown here.

For the alternating current, the horizontal line represents zero voltage; the peaks above the line on the voltage curve are peak positive voltage; and the peaks below the line are peak negative voltage. It has been assumed that the circuit concerned contains resistance only and no capacitance (⇨ p. 98) or inductance (⇨ p. 100). Starting from the baseline, the voltage rises to a positive peak so that current flows increasingly towards the source (unlike charges attract). At the peak, the voltage is momentarily stationary then begins to become less positive. This causes the current to slow in its movement towards the source. At the base line the positive voltage has been neutralized and is now zero, so, for a moment there is no flow of current. The voltage now continues to go increasingly negative and as it does so the current reverses its direction, and so begins to flow away from the source (like charges repel). At the negative peak, the rate of movement away from the source is at a maximum. And, as the voltage rises again to the baseline, the movement away slows until, at the baseline, current movement stops again.

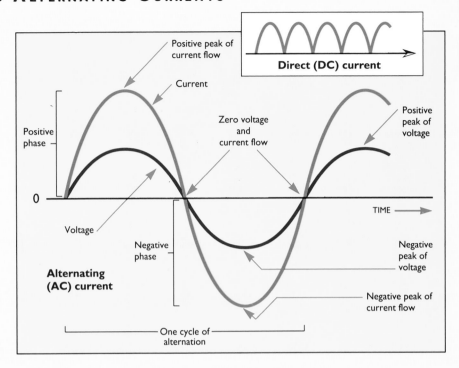

This describes one complete cycle of alternation, and, in most cases of alternating current, this cycle takes a fraction of a second. In Britain, domestic electricity is provided at a carefully controlled mains frequency of 50 cycles per second (Hertz, or Hz). In the USA, however, the domestic frequency is 60 Hz. By controlling and regulating the frequency to an accurate level, it can be used as a standard for many purposes, such as electric clocks and television receivers.

What is an electric current?

An electric current is a mass movement of electrons all in the same direction. Contrary to popular belief, these electrons drift along the conductor quite slowly – at a rate that depends on the current. In a current of 1 amp (⇨ below), for instance, electrons will take about half an hour to travel 1 m. This rate of drift should not be confused with the speed at which the initiation of the movement is propagated along the conductor, since the latter occurs at almost the speed of light. This is the speed at which the electric field that causes the movement travels along the conductor. So, for practical purposes, it can be said that the electrons start moving simultaneously at all points around the circuit.

Although current is a movement of electrons, it can also be considered to be the movement of negative charge. Under the influence of an electromotive force – provided by a battery or other generator – negative charges move in one direction, and positive charges move in the other. Diagrams of electrical systems, by convention, commonly show current as flowing from positive to negative. Since electrons are the charge carriers, however, the real direction of flow is from negative to positive. This anomaly, which arose because the first researchers assumed that it was a positive charge that was circulating (⇨ p. 88), makes no real difference in practice.

Quantity of electricity

The unit of current flow is the *ampere*, named after the French physicist and mathematician André Marie Ampère (1775–1836), whose theoretical and experimental work laid the foundations of *electrodynamics* (the study of the interactions between electrical and mechanical forces). The ampere (usually abbreviated to 'amp') is defined in terms of the current that must flow along two parallel conductors in order to produce a particular strength of force between them, tending to push them apart. This force is caused by the *repulsion of like charges*. Amperage is not, however, a quantity of charge. If a current of 1 amp flows for a particular length of time past a particular point, then a particular quantity of electricity will have passed that point. The unit of quantity of charge is the *coulomb*, and this is the quantity that passes a point when a current of 1 amp flows for 1 second. Therefore, a coulomb is equivalent to an amp-second.

It is helpful to draw the analogy between flow of electricity in a conductor and flow of water in a pipe. A head of water in an elevated tank can be considered as providing voltage in the sense of electromotive force, and the resulting flow can be compared to electrical current. The rate of flow in, for instance, gallons per second or litres per hour is analogous to the amperage, and the volume of water passing is equivalent to the quantity of

electricity in coulombs. When the matter of electrical *resistance* is considered (⇨ p. 96) the water-pipe analogy becomes even more useful since the diameter of the cross section of the pipe (which determines the ease with which the water can pass) corresponds to the degree of resistance in the electrical system.

André Marie Ampère (1775–1836), after whom the unit of current flow, the ampere, is named. From Amédée Guillemin, *The Forces of Nature*, London (1891). (AR)

SEE ALSO

- THE ELECTROMAGNETIC SPECTRUM AND ITS PROPERTIES p. 84
- POLES, FIELDS AND CHARGES p. 88
- SOURCES OF ELECTRICITY pp. 92–5
- RESISTANCE p. 96
- CAPACITANCE p. 98
- INDUCTANCE p. 100
- ELECTRONICS pp. 102–5
- THE CLASSICAL THEORY OF THE ATOM p. 108
- COMPUTING AND ARTIFICIAL INTELLIGENCE pp. 212–25

Sources of Electricity 1

Generation of electricity simply involves forcing electrons (⇨ p. 90) to move. This can be done on a variety of scales, from inside an enormous megawatt power station to inside a tiny mercury cell. Each method has its own advantages – economy in the former, portability in the latter – but the principles remain the same.

The essential problem in generating electricity is to persuade electrons to accumulate in sufficient numbers. If this can be done, their mutual repulsion creates forces that cause them to move in bulk as electric currents. The pressure that is built up by accumulation of electrons is called *voltage* (⇨ p. 88) or *electromotive force* (EMF).

Chemical sources of current

If two different metals are immersed in a solution that can conduct electricity (an *electrolyte* solution) – such as a salt solution or a weak solution of an acid – they give up particles (*ions*) to the solution. In so doing, different metals gain or lose electrons to a certain extent, thus becoming charged to different degrees. Metals that lose electrons become positively charged; those that gain them become negatively charged. If two metals are chosen for the maximum difference in this respect, a considerable voltage (potential difference) can occur between them, and if the two plates are joined

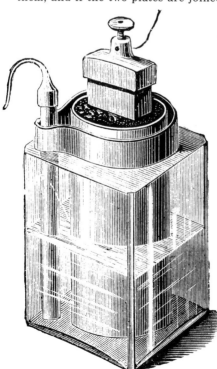

The Leclanché cell, invented in 1866 by French engineer Georges Leclanché (1839–82), is the precursor of the modern dry battery. Whereas this used ammonium chloride as its electrolyte, recent versions use potassium hydroxide. (AR)

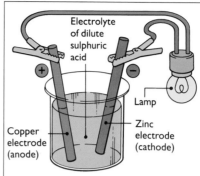

A primary cell. The lamp lights but soon goes out because bubbles of hydrogen cling to the copper electrode, thus decreasing the output of the cell. This is known as polarizing. The zinc electrode is eventually eaten away.

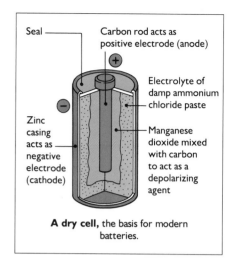

A dry cell, the basis for modern batteries.

externally by means of a conductor (⇨ p. 90), such as a length of wire, a current of electrons will flow through the wire. At the same time a current of ions flows through the solution between the plates, thus completing the circuit. The metal plate that pushes electrons into the external circuit and pulls positive ions from the solution is called the *anode*, or positive pole; the plate that accepts electrons is called the *cathode*, or negative pole.

A simple battery of this kind – a primary cell – cannot continue to supply significant current for long because the flow of ions results in coating of the electrodes, which then quickly cease to give up ions to the solution. This can be countered, though, by surrounding the electrodes with materials that act to prevent this happening.

In the standard Leclanché cell, developed by the French chemist and engineer Georges Leclanché (1839–82), the anode is a carbon rod, packed around with manganese dioxide and crushed carbon, and soaked in the electrolyte solution of ammonium chloride. The cathode is made of zinc, and forms the container for the contents. More recent developments of this cell use an alkali, potassium hydroxide, as the electrolyte. In some, mercuric oxide replaces manganese dioxide at the cathode, since this can provide larger currents.

Secondary or storage batteries, such as the lead–acid batteries used in cars, function by means of a reversible chemical reaction. Immersed in sulphuric acid, the lead plates in these batteries become covered with a layer of lead sulphate. When the battery is charged by rectified current from the car's *alternator* (device for generating an alternating current), the lead sulphate on one plate combines with the water in the sulphuric acid to form lead dioxide. In so doing, each atom of lead takes up two electrons from the current passing into the battery. The other plate is thus reduced to grey lead. On discharge, the electrons flow out in enormous numbers via the external circuit, and the lead dioxide returns to lead sulphate. The chemical equation:

Pb (lead) + PbO$_2$ (lead dioxide) + 2H$_2$SO$_4$ (sulphuric acid) = 2PbSO$_4$ (lead sulphate) + 2H$_2$O (water)

can go in either direction depending on whether energy is added or taken away.

Electricity from moving magnetic fields

Every atom has moving electrons and thus moving charges (⇨ p. 90). Moving charges produce fields of force. As long as atoms are randomly oriented, however, the millions of discrete fields simply cancel each other out. But in certain metals, such as iron, nickel and cobalt, the atoms occupy particular regions, called *domains*, which can actually be seen with an electron microscope. Normally the domains point in every direction, but if a magnetic field is applied to the metal the domains will line up so that they all point the same way. If the external field is then removed,

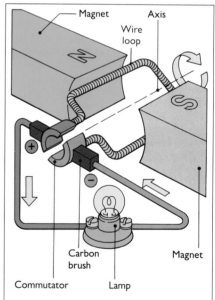

A simple generator. As the loop of wire rotates within the magnetic field, an electrical current is induced within the circuit, illuminating the lamp. This simple device shows the basic principle by which all electricity is generated.

MICHAEL FARADAY AND THE DEVELOPMENT OF ELECTROMAGNETIC INDUCTION

The English physicist and chemist Michael Faraday (1791–1867) had little formal education, but he was good with his hands, and in 1805 was apprenticed to a bookbinder. Faraday voraciously read the books he was binding, especially those on science. One of his customers was so impressed by his knowledge that he arranged for Faraday to attend a course of lectures by the chemist Humphry Davy (1778–1829) at the Royal Institution (a society founded in 1799 for the promotion of knowledge).

Faraday took detailed notes and sent them to Davy, and, as a result, at the age of 21, he was offered a job. From the start, he worked furiously, putting in long hours. Soon he had become indispensable to Davy. But it was not long before the young man's brilliance began to overshadow that of his master.

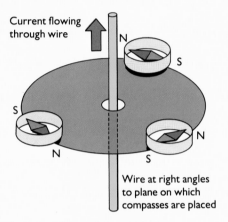

Oersted's discovery. When a current flows through a wire, magnetic compasses on a plane at right angles to the wire will be deflected until they are tangential to a circle drawn round the wire.

Faraday had read a paper by the Danish physicist H. C. Oersted (1777–1851), who had discovered that a magnetic compass needle was deflected by an electric current flowing in a nearby wire. This prompted Faraday to construct a device that could produce a continuous rotary movement of a wire in a pool of mercury. This was the first demonstration of the conversion of electricity into continuous movement and the first electric motor.

In 1831, Faraday carried out a remarkable experiment that was to have profound consequences. He took a soft iron ring, approximately six inches (about fifteen centimetres) in diameter, and wound two coils of wire round it, these being entirely separate from each other and insulated from the iron ring. He labelled one side 'A' and the other 'B'. He took the ends of the B coil to a wire passing closely over a magnetic needle, and connected the ends of the separate A coil to his battery. As soon as he made the contact, the magnet needle swung to one side and then slowly back to its original position. When he broke the contact, the needle swung once again. Faraday was fascinated but puzzled. He had, in fact, invented the *transformer* (a device for transferring electrical current from one AC circuit to another) and had proved the existence of *electromagnetic induction* (the production of an electromotive force in a conductor), but he could not understand why the needle did not show a constant deflection as long as the current was flowing in the first coil. The needle always moved on making or breaking the contact in the A coil, so it was clear that a current was being induced into the B coil at these times. But it seemed that no current flowed in coil B when a steady current flowed in coil A.

Still puzzled, Faraday then pushed a magnet into a coil of wire connected to a meter. The meter showed a deflection when the magnet was moving, but not when it was still. Clearly movement was essential. Now that he knew the principle, its application was straightforward. He saw that electricity could be produced by moving a magnet near a conductor, or a conductor near a magnet. It was now merely a matter of developing machines to do this more efficiently. Faraday arranged for a conductor to move between the poles of a strong magnet, achieving this by setting up a disc of copper on a spindle with a handle, so that it could be turned by hand. One wire to the coil round the compass needle was connected to the spindle and the other rubbed the edge of the disc. The magnet was placed so that the disc rotated between the poles. Thus, when he rotated the handle, a continuous current was generated. Faraday had made the world's first dynamo – probably the most important contribution ever made to the science of electricity.

In a transformer, if two insulated coils of wire are wound on the same soft iron core and an alternating current is passed through one of the coils, a current will be induced in the other coil. The ratio of the numbers of turns on the input coil (N_1) and the output coil (N_2) will determine the ratio of the output voltage (V_2) to the input voltage (V_1).
The relationship is:

$$\frac{V_2}{V_1} = \frac{N_2}{N_1}$$

In this way transformers can either step voltage up or step it down. Note that they have the reverse effect on current. This principle is used for efficient long-distance power transmission.

---

many of the domains remain aligned. This happens more readily with, for example, steel (an alloy of iron and carbon) than with soft iron, and especially well with certain alloys of steel with other metals. These alloys retain excellent domain alignment. Aligned domains allow the orbital electrons to add together their charges, producing a relatively strong current and inducing permanent magnetism, magnetism being the power to attract iron, nickel or cobalt bodies.

When a permanent magnet is moved inside a coil of wire, the lines of force from the orbital electrons interact with the charges on the electrons in the wire, repelling or attracting them depending on which end of the magnet is used. When the magnet is stationary, the electrons will be pushed a little out of their usual position, but will then be held in place by the repulsion of other electrons and there will be no net movement in any particular direction, that is, no current will flow. But whenever the magnet is moving, billions of electrons will be pushed or pulled in the same direction – this is the flow of an electric current.

The magnetic lines of force that are the cause of the electron movement are, in fact, an electromotive force, and this happens whenever any electrical conductor cuts through these lines of force. This principle, discovered by Michael Faraday (⇔ box), is the basis of the generators that produce the great bulk of electricity today.

Practical electric generators are rotary devices driven by turbines (⇔ p. 56) or other engines. Large generators do not use permanent magnets (made by placing suitable alloys within a coil of wire and passing a large electric current through this), but produce strong magnetic fields by means of electromagnets, energized by the currents they produce, or from an external current source. These fields cut through conductors – large windings of heavy-gauge wire – in which very large currents are induced. In one type of generator, the conductors are rotated within a stationary magnetic field, while, in another, a rotating magnetic field cuts through stationary conductors. Generators may give alternating current (AC) or direct current (DC; ⇔ p. 90) depending on their design. Today

almost all commercial generators produce alternating current. These produce megawatts of power (*mega* meaning 'million', and one watt being one volt multiplied by one amp). They can be driven by a variety of methods, including, commonly, steam turbines.

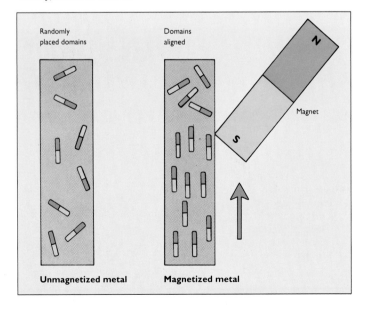

Sources of Electricity 2

Humankind still depends largely on crude and roundabout methods for the generation of the vast amounts of electricity it needs. The process begins with the burning of fossil fuels, such as natural gas, coal and oil (⇨ p. 58), to heat water to produce steam. This is used to drive turbines, and these, in turn, drive generators.

At every stage in the generation of electricity there are energy losses, but, even so, the fossil-fuel method is still currently the cheapest. It is, however, far from the most ecologically acceptable, and, for many years, there has been a quest for better ways of producing electricity. Dynamos (electric generators), for instance, can be driven by a variety of sources of energy, and some of these have been seriously exploited for power generation. Hydroelectric power is another long-established method, but, since falling water powers the turbine, it is applicable only where a suitable head of water is available. And tidal movement, which utilizes the gravitational attraction of the Moon, is attractive in theory but difficult to apply efficiently in practice. Wind power is another renewable resource that is being increasingly exploited. Other possible sources of electricity include solar power (⇨ below), nuclear power and geothermal energy.

Fuel cells

Batteries contain all the chemicals needed to promote the reactions that cause electrons (and hence, an electric current; ⇨ p. 58) to flow, and require no further chemical input. They do, however, become exhausted as the reagents

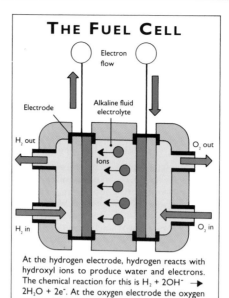

THE FUEL CELL

At the hydrogen electrode, hydrogen reacts with hydroxyl ions to produce water and electrons. The chemical reaction for this is $H_2 + 2OH^- \rightarrow 2H_2O + 2e^-$. At the oxygen electrode the oxygen reacts with water, taking up electrons to produce hydroxyl ions: $O_2 + 2H_2O + 4e^- \rightarrow 4OH^-$.

are used up. But if further quantities of these reagents can be supplied continuously from an outside source, electricity can continue to be generated indefinitely. A device that does this is called a *fuel cell*, and such a cell might, for instance, be supplied with a continuous flow of hydrogen gas. When this gas combines with hydroxyl (negatively charged oxygen and hydrogen) ions from a potassium hydroxide electrolyte in the cell, water is formed and electrons are released. This water must be removed continuously from the cell.

One practical (that is, more efficient) cell uses hydrogen and oxygen fuels, a hot, alkaline electrolyte, and porous, sintered (heated and compressed) nickel electrodes. The cell is divided by the porous electrodes into three compartments, the central one of which contains the alkaline fluid electrolyte, while the outer two contain the gases. One electrode is in contact with oxygen, the other with hydrogen (⇨ illustration). At the oxygen electrode, electrons are removed from water to produce hydroxyl ions, making the electrode positive. And at the hydrogen electrode, hydrogen and hydroxyl ions combine to form water, and, in the process, release electrons, making the electrode negative. The sintered nickel acts as a catalyst (⇨ p. 168) to speed up the reaction. Finely divided (very well powdered) platinum can also be used as a catalyst. While this is expensive, it is not consumed in the reaction, and is, therefore, recoverable. Each such cell produces only 1.1 volts and many may have to be connected in series to produce the required voltage for a particular purpose.

Apart from hydrogen, other fuels, such as hydrocarbons (for example, natural gas), carbon monoxide and alcohols, can be used, and the search for ever more efficient cells, containing suitable ingredients and catalysts to accelerate the reactions, continues. The optimum working temperature differs in different cells. Some work satisfactorily at temperatures

as low as 60–70°C (140–58°F); others operate within a range of 300–1,000°C (572–1,832°F). High gas pressures are also required for reasonable efficiency.

Fuel cells are efficient, silent and highly reliable. They contain no moving parts, need little maintenance, and their waste products are usually environmentally friendly. Were it not for their high capital cost, the cost of purifying their fuels, and for the relatively rare materials from which they are made, they would be an almost ideal source of electricity. At present their cost is justified only for special applications such as their use in crewed space craft, or in remote or inaccessible locations, such as radioactive environments. Even so, experimental plants have been set up, such as the 4.8 megawatt fuel-cell power plant that has been operating in Tokyo since 1984. Larger American plants are projected, and advances in fuel-cell technology may lead in the future to their widespread use in electrically powered vehicles.

Electricity from light

In 1902 the little-known Hungarian physicist Philipp Lenard began to study the way in which incident light (light falling on a surface) caused electrons to be emitted from a metal. Lenard was working before science had advanced enough to explain what was really happening, but, expressed in modern terms, he effectively showed that, when electromagnetic radiation of short enough wavelength (high enough frequency; ⇨ p. 64) falls upon metallic surfaces, it will displace electrons from the metal (the photoelectric effect; ⇨ p. 40). Later research has shown that, for instance, zinc gives off electrons when exposed to ultraviolet light and X-rays; the metal sodium does so when exposed to visible light other than red and yellow (which have long wavelengths), as well as to ultraviolet light and X-rays; and caesium will give off electrons even when exposed to infrared radiation (which has a very long wavelength), as well as to visible light and radiation of higher frequencies.

Different metals emit electrons at different radiation-frequency thresholds. Below that frequency, no electron emission occurs. Above it, the number of electrons emitted in a given time is proportional to the intensity of the radiation. The energy of the emitted electrons varies from almost zero to a maximum, and this maximum depends only on the frequency of the incident radiation, not its intensity. These facts remained unexplained until 1905, when Einstein used Planck's quantum theory to account for them (⇨ p. 40). And we now know that the surface energy barrier holding free electrons onto the surface of metals can be overcome if electron velocity is increased sufficiently, and that this can be done if *photons* (particles of light) of sufficient energy strike the surface. Direct conversion of solar radiation into electricity can be done even more efficiently if *semiconducting materials* (materials with

Skylab space station, launched in May 1973 to carry out experiments in weightlessness, was powered by solar energy, harnessed in its prominent black solar panels. These panels are much more efficient in space than they would be on Earth, since the Sun's rays are not affected by the Earth's atmosphere. (IS)

A THERMOCOUPLE

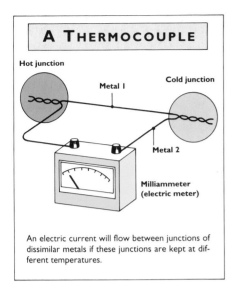

Hot junction

Cold junction

Metal 1

Metal 2

Milliammeter
(electric meter)

An electric current will flow between junctions of dissimilar metals if these junctions are kept at different temperatures.

electrical conductivity intermediate between that of conductors and insulators; ⇨ p. 90) such as selenium or gallium arsenide are used instead of pure metals.

This principle, as that of the fuel cell, has been widely applied to the generation of electricity in inaccessible areas and in space craft. Indeed, without the means of generating electricity direct from sunlight ('solar power' or *photovoltaic energy*) by means of the photoelectric effect, it is doubtful whether space satellites would ever have been feasible.

Electricity from heat

In 1822 the wealthy German research physicist Thomas Johan Seebeck (1770-1831), working in Berlin, made an important discovery. He found that if he took lengths of two different metals – such as iron and copper – and formed them into a loop with two junctions, a compass needle placed within the loop would be deflected if one junction was kept hot and the other cold. Although he did not

know it, Seebeck had in fact demonstrated the direct conversion of heat into electricity (now known as the *Seebeck effect*). He was unaware, though, that a current was flowing and, reasonably enough, called his effect 'thermomagnetism'. It was, of course, the flow of current in the loop that produced the magnetic field (⇨ p. 88) to deflect the compass needle.

Using iron and copper, Seebeck found that if one junction was at 0°C (32°F) and the other at 100°C (212°F), an electromotive force (EMF; ⇨ p. 90) of only about one thousandth of a volt (1 millivolt, or mV) was produced. The flow of current produced in this way could, however, be fairly substantial if the electrical resistance of the loop was very low (⇨ p. 96). When other pairs of metals were tried, such as silver and platinum, or bismuth and antimony, it was found that a greater effect could be produced. A combination of iron and the copper–nickel alloy constantan produces about 10 times the EMF of the copper–iron combination.

After its discovery the Seebeck effect was soon put to use. As the current produced was, over a certain range of temperature, proportional to the temperature difference, a bimetal junction connected to a sensitive electric meter could be used as a thermometer for high temperatures. Such a device came to be known as a *thermocouple* (⇨ p. 50).

It was found that the Seebeck effect is brought about when a single metal loop is heated at one point, and its free electrons become more active and mobile relative to those in the cold part. These, however, migrate towards the cold area (by virtue of their energy and by analogy with simple thermodynamics, where heat always flows from high to low temperature points), producing a current that opposes any current that can be drawn from the hot and cold points. But when dissimilar metals are used, because the

concentration of free electrons is slightly different in the two metals, this increased activity allows a small net current to flow.

Unfortunately, the Seebeck effect, using dissimilar metals, is far too inefficient to offer us a practical way of generating electricity. When we use semiconductors instead of metals, however, the situation is greatly improved. The material bismuth telluride, for instance, gives 50 times the EMF produced by a metal junction; dissimilar semiconductor junctions do better still. Practical sources of electricity have been developed using semiconductor junctions heated by various means, including radioactive sources. Batteries of almost indefinite life for use in space satellites, for instance, can be made from semiconductor junctions heated by radiation from a nearby strontium-90 source. It seems possible that future developments of semiconductor materials capable of retaining their properties at very high temperatures and heated by atomic reactor cores, may make direct electricity generation by the Seebeck effect a feasible proposition.

Complementary to Seebeck's discovery was that of the French physicist Jean Charles Athanase Peltier (1785–1845), who showed in 1834 that a current flowing through the junction of two dissimilar metals caused a rise in temperature when flowing in one direction and a drop in temperature when flowing in the other.

ENVIRONMENTAL DANGERS

Power generation by the burning of fossil fuels has adverse effects on the environment because of its increasing output of both carbon dioxide and sulphur oxides (⇨ pp. 206–9). The environmental risks from nuclear-power generation, however, are much less easily quantified. Serious accidents are always possible, as was proven by the Chernobyl disaster in 1986, among others. In addition, the risks to humans and the environment from minor leakage of radioactive material are the subject of continuing controversy.

SEE ALSO

● WHAT IS ENERGY? pp. 46–9
● SOURCES OF ENERGY pp. 58–61
● POLES, FIELDS AND CHARGES p. 88
● ELECTRONS AND CONDUCTANCE p. 90
● SOURCES OF ELECTRICITY 1 p. 92
● CAPACITANCE p. 98
● INDUCTANCE p. 100
● ELECTRONICS pp. 102–5

ELECTRICITY GENERATION AND TRANSMISSION

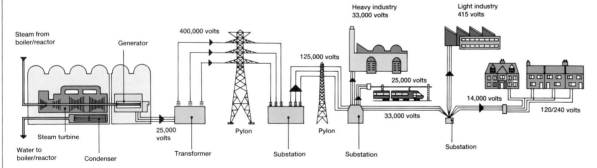

Steam from boiler/reactor

Generator

400,000 volts

Heavy industry 33,000 volts

Light industry 415 volts

125,000 volts

25,000 volts

14,000 volts

33,000 volts

120/240 volts

Steam turbine

25,000 volts

Water to boiler/reactor

Condenser

Transformer

Pylon

Substation

Pylon

Substation

Substation

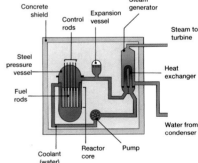

Concrete shield

Control rods

Expansion vessel

Steam generator

Steam to turbine

Steel pressure vessel

Heat exchanger

Fuel rods

Water from condenser

Coolant (water)

Reactor core

Pump

Heat is produced by burning oil or coal in the furnace of a conventional power station, or by nuclear fission in a nuclear reactor. In the case of a coal-fired power station, the fuel is first pulverized to a fine powder, which is then pumped in a stream of air through jets into the furnace. The heat is used to boil water circulating through tubes in the boiler/reactor, so creating steam. The steam is then superheated until it reaches temperatures of up to 600°C (1,112°F).

The superheated steam is channelled to a steam turbine, where it is used to drive the turbine shaft at high

speed. The steam is then passed through a condenser, where it is turned back into water, thus creating a partial vacuum and so improving the flow of steam through the turbine. The condensed water is pumped back to the boiler/reactor under pressure.

The turbine shaft is linked to a generator, where – in the case of the largest modern generators – electricity is generated at around 25,000 volts of alternating current. For efficient transmission, the voltage is stepped up by transformers to very high voltages, typically as high as 400,000 volts – otherwise, significant amounts

of energy would be lost through resistance in the transmission cables.

In many countries, the output is fed into a national-grid system, by means of overhead cables suspended from pylons. A single row of pylons is able to carry the entire output from an average power station. At substations at various points on the grid the supply is stepped down to suitable levels for distribution to consumers, typically at around the voltages shown in the diagram.

The pressurized-water nuclear reactor (PWR). A PWR is essentially a closed loop in which the combined coolant and moderator – ordinary ('light') water – is pressurized to about 150 atmospheres, and pumped through the reactor core. The core, made up of fuel rods containing pellets of enriched uranium dioxide, heats the coolant to around 325°C (617°F), which then passes through a heat exchanger, where it transfers heat to a separate reservoir of water. This water is vaporized to steam, which is then piped off to drive the turbine.

Resistance

The concept of *electrical resistance* explains how voltage – the electromotive force that drives electricity – is related to the amount of current that flows, and how differences in voltage (*potential differences*) occur. The discovery of these relationships by George Ohm was one of the major advances in the understanding of electricity.

Resistance to the flow of electricity is a property of all matter and varies considerably from one substance to another (⇨ p. 90). Solid matter can be divided arbitrarily into *conductors* (which are mostly metals and offer differing but relatively low resistance to the passage of electricity), *insulators* (which offer differing but high resistance) and semiconductors (whose resistance is somewhere in between). Liquids also vary in their resistance. Many, such as pure water, offer a high resistance that drops dramatically when any of various soluble substances are added. This is because many substances dissolved in water will split (*dissociate*) into positively and negatively charged ions whose movement constitutes a flow of electricity. Gases, too, may offer a high resistance that becomes much lower when they are ionized (⇨ p. 88).

Resistivity and resistance

Trials show that the electrical resistance of different metals can be accurately compared only if the samples used are of standard cross section and length. The analogy of the water pipe is helpful here. A wide pipe of a certain length offers low resistance to the flow of water, while a narrow pipe of the same length offers a high resistance. In the same way a block of copper of 1 cm^2 cross section and 1 cm length offers a much lower resistance to the flow of electricity than a 1 cm length of thin copper wire. Resistance varies in this way with cross section simply because the smaller amount of metal offers fewer free electrons. The unit by which electrical resistance is measured is the ohm (⇨ boxes).

Different metals differ in the number of available free electrons and so offer different resistance for the same length and cross section. Some metals offer a much higher resistance than copper (⇨ box). Iron, for instance, has a *resistivity* about seven times that of copper. The differences in the electrical resistance of different solids, such as metals, is known as *specific resistivity*. Other things being equal, the higher the electrical resistance, the lower the electrical current flowing. Electrical devices that consume a lot of power necessarily carry large currents and must, therefore, have a low resistance. A 25-watt electric bulb has a higher resistance than a 100-watt bulb; the 100-watt bulb has a higher resistance than a 1,000-watt electric fire; and the fire has a higher resistance than a 5,000-watt electric kettle. These reducing resistances reflect the increasing currents taken by the respective devices.

The nature of voltage

The term 'voltage' (⇨ pp. 90–3) is used in two closely related ways. It is used for the force that drives current – the electromotive force – and for any potential difference between two or more points within an electrical circuit. This is why voltage is sometimes called EMF and sometimes PD. Voltages must be expressed relative to a standard level and this is usually taken as the zero voltage level (or potential) of the earth. Indeed, those parts of electrical equipment that can be touched – such as the body of an electric fire or kettle – are often, for safety, actually connected by a cable, eventually, to a metal stake buried in the ground, which is at zero potential. If accidental internal connection is made with these parts, the current will flow to ground through the fuses, which will melt and break the circuit.

A potential difference cannot exist between the earth and another point unless there is electrical resistance between these points. If this resistance is very high – as, for instance, when there is nothing but air between the two points – the voltage will be near its maximum possible value. But if there is effectively no electrical resistance – as when the two points are in firm contact – there can be no potential difference and the voltage will be effectively zero. Suppose that a substantial resistance exists between a point x and earth, and the voltage at point x is 100 volts relative to earth. If at another point, point y, in the circuit the resistance between earth and the new point is half of that

---

RESISTANCE IN ELECTRONICS

VALUES	
0	Black
I	Brown
2	Red
3	Orange
4	Yellow
5	Green
6	Blue
7	Purple
8	Grey
9	White

EXAMPLE

First digit of value

Second digit of value

Number of zeros following the two digits

YELLOW — 4
PURPLE — 7
ORANGE — 3   three zeros   0 0 0

In electronic circuits, resistance is used to control voltage and current. This is done by means of *resistors* – small components that have a resistance of anything from a fraction of an ohm to many millions of ohms. Resistors are also rated to carry different levels of current – usually only a few micro- or milliamps. The current-carrying rating is given in watts, or, more commonly, fractions of a watt. The resistance of resistors is shown by an internationally recognized colour code.

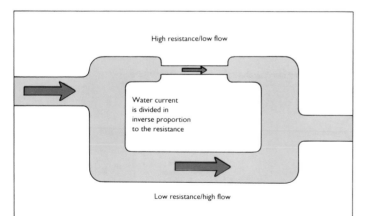

High resistance/low flow

Water current is divided in inverse proportion to the resistance

Low resistance/high flow

The water-pipe analogy of electrical resistance. In the wider section of the pipe the water (like electric current in a circuit) flows more easily than in the narrower section. Electrical resistance occurs when the electron flow is interrupted by collisions with atoms of metal in the circuit conductor. During these collisions electrons give up energy to the atoms, and the current is reduced.

---

between earth and x, the voltage at the new point will be 50 volts. At a point at which the resistance is one tenth, point z, the voltage will be only 10 volts. It follows, therefore, that there is an important relationship in any electrical circuit between voltage and resistance (⇨ graph).

How do voltage and current relate?

There is an equally important relationship between voltage and current. Since voltage is an electromotive force, it follows that, so long as the resistance does not change, the greater the voltage, the greater the current. Current is the rate of flow of electricity (⇨ p. 90), so, if the resistance remains the same, an increase in voltage will cause an increased quantity of electricity to flow in a given time, and a decreased voltage will cause a decreased quantity to flow in the same time.

The third relationship – that between resistance and current – is self-evident. By definition, resistance controls current. So, if the voltage remains fixed, the greater the resistance the lower the current, and the lower the resistance the greater the current.

The relationships between the three variables, resistance, voltage and current, were first appreciated by Georg Ohm (⇨ box) and are known as Ohm's law. This establishes the way in which current varies with voltage and with resistance, and the way voltage varies with resistance. Using the symbols V for voltage, R for resistance and I for current, the law is usually stated:

$$V=IR.$$

This can be read as 'voltage is proportional to current and to resistance' or as 'voltage is equal to current multiplied by resistance'. The equation can easily be rearranged to express current in terms of voltage and resistance, or resistance in terms of voltage and current. As long as the units used are volts, amps and ohms, this simple equation can be used arithmetically to solve problems in direct-current electricity. Ohm's law also holds for alternating current as long as the circuit concerned contains no inductive (⇨ p. 100) or capacitive (⇨ p. 98) elements, but can be generalized for alternating current (AC) as

$$V=IZ,$$

where Z is the *impedance* (AC 'resistance') in the circuit.

In electronic circuits (⇨ p. 90) resistance is extensively used to control current and to realize voltage. Such circuits contain many resistive elements known as *resistors*. These may have a resistance ranging from a few ohms to millions of ohms (*megohms*), and may be rated to carry varying levels of current. Variable resistors, whose resistance changes as a sliding contact moves across a resistive element, are also often used.

SPECIFIC RESISTIVITIES FOR VARIOUS METALS

Using 1 cm³ of the material being measured, resistance is recorded in ohms:

Silver.............. 1.5	Platinum........ 9.0
Copper 1.6	Iron 10.5
Gold 2.0	Nickel 12.4
Aluminium ... 3.0	Tin 13.1
Zinc 5.6	Lead............. 19.5
	Mercury....... 94.8

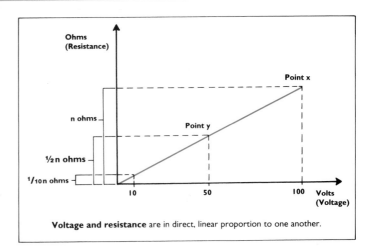

Voltage and resistance are in direct, linear proportion to one another.

GEORG SIMON OHM

The German physicist Georg Simon Ohm (1787–1854) was taught basic science by his father, who was a skilled mechanic. Georg went on to further education in science and became a teacher.

Ambitious to achieve a university appointment, he knew that his only hope was to make an original contribution to science. He had studied the work of the Italian physicist Alessandro Volta (1745–1827; ⇨ p. 58) on the new subject of the flow of electricity, and decided that this would be a good field. Ohm knew that the direction of the flow of heat depended on the difference in temperature between two points, and decided that there was a reasonable chance that the flow of electricity followed the same pattern and probably depended on the difference in electrical potential (voltage).

Eventually, he was able to prove that this was indeed the case, and he showed that the amount of current flowing in a circuit was proportional to the voltage. By using wires of different length and thickness he was also able to show that, if the voltage remained constant, the current became less if the wire was longer, and became greater if the wire was thicker.

Ohm's results, published in 1826, were the first reference to electrical resistance and he knew that he had discovered something important. His claims, and the theory he proposed to back them up, were opposed by the local scientific establishment, and caused so much jealousy and resentment that, far from obtaining the hoped-for university appointment, he found himself dismissed from the school where he taught. Six years of disappointment followed until Ohm learned that his work, while still ignored in Germany, had been accepted by the English Royal Society – this being the most important and prestigious scientific body in the world.

Georg Simon Ohm (1787–1854), discoverer of the relationships between resistance, voltage and current. From Georges Dary, *A travers l'électricité*, Paris (c. 1906). (AR)

SEE ALSO

- WHAT IS ENERGY? pp. 46–9
- SOURCES OF ENERGY pp. 58–61
- POLES, FIELDS AND CHARGES p. 88
- ELECTRONS AND CONDUCTANCE p. 90
- SOURCES OF ELECTRICITY pp. 92–5
- CAPACITANCE p. 98
- INDUCTANCE p. 100
- ELECTRONICS pp. 102–5

Capacitance

Although batteries, are often considered to be devices for storing electricity, they are in fact chemical generators of electricity. Devices that store electrons, however minimally or briefly, are called *capacitors*, and their ability to do so is called *capacitance*.

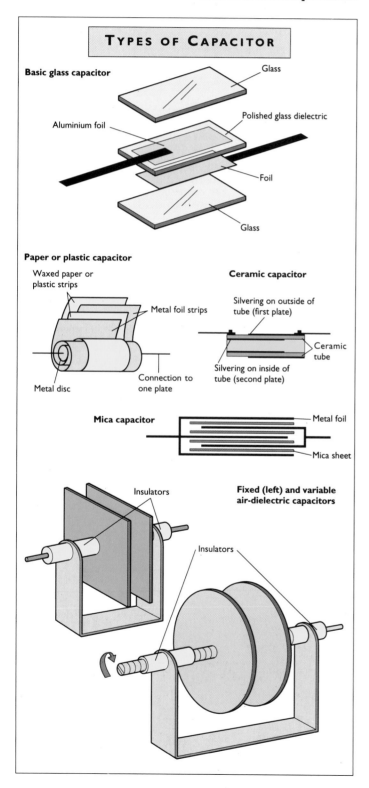

TYPES OF CAPACITOR

Basic glass capacitor

Glass

Aluminium foil

Polished glass dielectric

Foil

Glass

Paper or plastic capacitor

Waxed paper or plastic strips

Metal foil strips

Metal disc

Connection to one plate

Ceramic capacitor

Silvering on outside of tube (first plate)

Ceramic tube

Silvering on inside of tube (second plate)

Mica capacitor

Metal foil

Mica sheet

Insulators

Fixed (left) and variable air-dielectric capacitors

Insulators

Any physical body can acquire an accumulation of electrons – an electric charge (⇨ p. 90). If it is a conductor of electricity the charge can readily flow on or off. The amount of charge (number of electrons) that can be stored on a conductor depends on its size and on the material surrounding it. If this material can conduct electricity, the charge will quickly leak away; if it is a good insulator, the charge will be retained for a long time. Because of its size, the Earth has a very large capacity and any charged body connected to it is quickly discharged ('earthed'). This is why the Earth is usually taken as the zero reference for voltage (⇨ p. 96).

If a conductor has a surplus of electrons it is negatively charged because every electron carries a negative charge. Identical charges repel each other and opposite charges attract each other. In consequence of this, if two conductors are brought close together without touching and one has a negative charge, the adjacent part of the other will immediately acquire a positive charge. Such a pair of separated conductors is called a capacitor. The closer the two conductors are to each other, the more readily the negative charge on one induces a positive charge on the other.

The capacitor

A capacitor is thus any two conductors provided they are separated by an insulator, known as the *dielectric*. This insulator may be air or glass or mica (a rockforming mineral) or a variety of plastic or ceramic materials. To have much electrical capacitance – or, in other words, to be able to store much electricity – a capacitor should have conductors of large area – usually in the form of metal plates – and they should be placed as close together as possible without touching. The larger the area of the plates and the closer the plates are to each other, the higher the capacitance. So capacitance can be increased by increasing the area of the plates, or bringing them closer together, or both. The nature of the insulating material between the plates of a capacitor also affects its capacitance. The amount by which an insulator increases capacitance is measured against the insulating power of a vacuum and is called the *dielectric constant*. The dielectric constant of air is 1.0005; that of polythene is 2.3; perspex 2.6; waxed paper 2.7; mica 7; pure water 80 and barium titanate 1,200. Water is not a suitable practical dielectric as impurities are liable to make it capable of conducting.

Practical capacitors

Practical capacitors may take many forms. Low capacitance, air-dielectric capacitors simply consist of parallel metal plates separated by air. Such a capacitor is connected in a circuit by a wire that is connected to each plate. Foil capacitors, for instance, consist of two long strips of thin metal foil separated by a thin sheet of insulating plastic, and the whole is rolled up to occupy minimum

space. They are often encased in insulating plastic through which protrudes a wire attached to each metal strip. Electrolytic capacitors achieve high capacitance by greatly reducing the separation between the conductors. This is done by making one of metal and the other of a conducting liquid in intimate proximity to the metal, but insulated from it by a very thin film of oxide. The metal electrode is usually etched so as greatly to increase its surface area. Such capacitors must be connected in correct polarity or the oxide layer may be broken and the capacitor destroyed.

The unit of capacitance

The unit of capacitance is the farad, named after Michael Faraday (⇨ p. 88). And the unit for quantity of electricity is the coulomb, named after the French physicist Charles Augustin de Coulomb (1736–1806). A coulomb is the amount of charge passing along a wire when 1 amp is flowing for 1 second, and 1 farad is the capacity that will hold 1 coulomb when an electromotive force (EMF) of 1 volt is driving the current. This is a very large capacitance and most practical capacitors are calibrated in millionths of a farad – the microfarad.

Charging of a capacitor

When a capacitor is connected to a small battery, electrons flow onto one of the plates causing it to acquire a negative charge. This charge simultaneously repels electrons from the other plate, making it positive. The flow of current

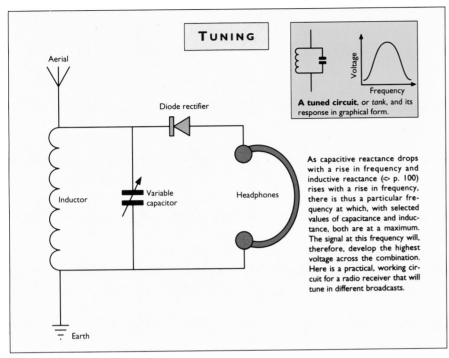

TUNING

A tuned circuit, or *tank*, and its response in graphical form.

As capacitive reactance drops with a rise in frequency and inductive reactance (⇨ p. 100) rises with a rise in frequency, there is thus a particular frequency at which, with selected values of capacitance and inductance, both are at a maximum. The signal at this frequency will, therefore, develop the highest voltage across the combination. Here is a practical, working circuit for a radio receiver that will tune in different broadcasts.

onto the one plate is the same as the flow of current off the other plate, so, for a short time a current flows around the whole circuit, as if there were no physical break between the plates of the capacitor. Soon, however, the charges on the plates oppose any further movement of electrons and the current flow virtually ceases (⇨ below).

The time constant

Charging and discharging capacitors takes a certain length of time, depending on the rate of flow of charge – the current. Since this is limited by resistance (⇨ p. 96), the time taken for a capacitor to charge will depend on its own capacitance and the resistance in the circuit. Many important matters, especially in electronics, depend on the time a capacitor takes to charge. When a fully discharged capacitor begins to charge, it does so very quickly at first; then, as the electrons accumulate and the pressure from their mutual repulsion increases (⇨ p. 90), it does so more and more slowly. This is called an 'exponential' rate, and, in fact, capacitors never charge fully to the level of the applied voltage, because the rate of charge continues to decrease with time. If the time taken for a capacitor to charge to about 99 per cent of the full applied voltage is noted and divided by 6, a figure called the *time constant* is obtained. This is the time taken for a capacitor to charge to 63 per cent of the applied voltage. Time constant is proportional both to capacitance and to the resistance in the charging circuit. In numerical terms, time constant (in seconds) equals capacitance (in farads) multiplied by resistance (in ohms). Thus:

$$T=CR.$$

Since high resistances are more common than high capacitances is it often more useful to take the time constant to be equal to capacitance (in microfarads) multiplied by resistance (in megohms), which amounts to the same thing. Time constants are extensively used in electronics to determine such things as the frequency of oscillation of oscillators and the operation of timing devices.

Capacitors can, of course, be charged more quickly if the resistance in the charging circuit is low. But in every case the current is always at a maximum at the moment of beginning to charge, and becomes less as time passes. They can also be discharged very quickly if the electrodes are connected through a low resistance. In this way energy can be taken from a capacitor very quickly. If a wire is joined to one electrode of a charged 1 microfarad capacitor, and the other end touched to the other electrode, a noisy, colourful spark will be produced. A charged capacitor can, in fact, give a painful electric shock. A photographic flash gun consists of a large capacitor, an electronic converter to produce a high voltage from a small battery, and a switch to discharge the capacitor through the flash tube. The energy is rated in joules. A joule is 1 watt operating for 1 second. The formula for the energy stored in a capacitor is $\frac{1}{2}CV^2$ joules, that is, the capacitance in farads, multiplied by the voltage multiplied by itself.

Capacitors and alternating current

Because there is no electrical connection between the plates of a capacitor, it acts as an 'open circuit' if included in series in a direct-current circuit. At the moment of switching on, the capacitor will begin to charge, and, during charging, current will flow in the circuit. But as the capacitor charges, the current will drop to a very low level, and will then effectively cease to flow. In an alternating-current circuit, however (⇨ p. 90), the effect of a capacitor is very different. As the voltage rises and the capacitor charges, the current is at first large and then falls. The current is at a maximum when the voltage is at a minimum, and, as the voltage rises, the current falls. When the voltage is at a maximum, the current is at a minimum. As the voltage falls, the electrons are able to move off the negative plate and the capacitor begins to discharge. In effect, the current continues to flow in the circuit, reversing its direction in each cycle almost as if the capacitor were not present. However, the changes in the current flowing in the circuit are not in phase with the changes in the voltage, as they are in the case of a DC circuit.

The reactance of capacitors

The resistance offered to alternating current by a capacitor or an inductor (⇨ p. 90) is called the *reactance*. If a voltage is applied to a circuit, the opposition to the flow of the resulting current is called the resistance (⇨ p. 96), and if an alternating voltage is applied to a circuit, the opposition to the flow of the resulting current is called the *impedance*. This is partly, but not all, due to resistance. The part of the impedance not due to pure resistance is the reactance.

Reactance varies with the frequency of the alternating voltage. The higher the frequency the lower the reactance, and vice versa. Electrons can flow on and off plates on a capacitor very easily. Even if a capacitor has a small capacitance, a fairly large current can be made to flow by moving the electrons on and off very quickly – this is what happens with high-frequency AC. A million electrons at 50 Hz is the same current as 50 electrons at 1,000,000 Hz. Clearly then the AC resistance of a capacitor drops as the frequency rises.

SEE ALSO
● POLES, FIELDS AND CHARGES p. 88
● ELECTRONS AND CONDUCTANCE p. 90
● SOURCES OF ELECTRICITY pp. 92–5
● RESISTANCE p. 96
● INDUCTANCE p. 100
● ELECTRONICS pp. 102–5

Michael Faraday (1791–1867), English physicist and chemist after whom the unit of electric capacitance, the farad, is named. (AR)

Inductance

The discovery that an electrical circuit would form a magnetic field or store energy when a current passes through it, the process of *induction*, was vital in learning how to generate electricity in sufficient quantity to be commercially and industrially useful.

In 1831 the English physicist Michael Faraday (1791–1867; ⇨ p. 92) achieved an advance in electrical science that was to revolutionize electrical technology. He noticed that when a magnet was moved through a closed coil of wire it caused an electric current to flow in it (⇨ p. 88). This was the first demonstration of the principle that was later applied to dynamos and other electricity generators. The same discovery was made, independently and almost at the same time, by the American mathematician and physicist Joseph Henry (1797–1878). Henry, to his lifelong regret, failed to publish his findings and priority was given to Faraday. His contribution has not been forgotten, however, and the SI unit of measurement of inductance, the *henry*, is named after him.

Electromagnetic induction

Faraday, however, was not content to leave matters at this stage. He knew that a current flowing in a wire

Joseph Henry (1797–1878), American mathematician and physicist after whom the unit of electrical inductance, the henry, is named. From *The Science Record*, New York (1873). (AR)

produced a magnetic field, and his next advance was to use such an electromagnet to induce a current in another conductor. He did this by tightly winding two independent and unconnected coils of wire round an iron ring. When he passed a current briefly through one of these coils, a current was simultaneously induced in the other. This was the first transformer (⇨ box), the forerunner of the countless millions of such devices in use all over the world today, and one of the chief reasons for preferring alternating current to direct current for industrial and domestic purposes (tranformers will work only with AC). Faraday noticed that the current flowed in one direction at the moment of making the circuit in the other coil, and in the reverse direction at the moment of breaking the circuit. No current flowed in the second coil when a steady current was flowing in the first; it was only at the 'make' and 'break' that current was induced. This fact he correctly interpreted as showing that it was the *change* in the magnetic field that caused the current to be induced in the second coil.

Any flow of electric current is accompanied by a magnetic field around the conductor in which the current is flowing (⇨ p. 88). This effect is readily demonstrable simply by winding insulated wire round a large nail and connecting the ends to a small battery. The nail then becomes magnetized. Any change in a magnetic field surrounding a conductor induces an electric field (*voltage*) and a resulting flow of current in the conductor. This can equally easily be demonstrated by moving a bar magnet inside a coil of wire, the ends of which are connected to milliammeter (the meter needle moves). The creation of an

THE UNIT OF INDUCTANCE

There is a loose analogy between Ohm's law (⇨ p. 96) and the law applying to inductance. In a DC circuit, by Ohm's law, a resistance of 3 ohms results in a current of 3 amps if the EMF is 3 volts. In an AC circuit, an inductance of 3 henries produces an EMF of 3 volts if the current changes uniformly at a rate of 3 amp/s.

If an inductor has an inductance of L henries and if the current in it increases at a steady rate from I_1 to I_2 in t seconds, then the average rate of increase of current, in amp/s, is

$$\frac{I_2 - I_1}{t}$$

And the average back EMF is equal to -L multiplied by this figure.

electric field by a varying magnetic field in this way is called *electromagnetic induction*; and inductance, as we have seen, is the property of an electric circuit to be affected in this way. No current is generated when a stationary magnetic field intersects with a conductor. If this were so, a permanent magnet placed in a coil would cause a current to flow permanently in the coil, thus contravening the law of conservation of energy (⇨ p. 28). Currents are induced only when moving lines of magnetic force cut through a conductor (or a moving conductor cuts through a stationery magnetic field; ⇨ p. 92).

Inductors

The inductance of a conductor, such as a length of wire, is greatly increased if the conductor is wound into a coil. This effect can be even further enhanced if a readily magnetizable metal core – commonly of soft iron – is placed within the coil, as in a transformer (⇨ box and p. 92). Such coils, whether or not provided with a core, are usually described as *inductors*. When a changing magnetic field induces a voltage and a current flow in a conductor, such as a coil of wire, the direction of flow of this current is such as to produce a magnetic field that opposes the field of the magnet. Similarly, when a changing current is made to flow in a coil, the magnetic field that is produced induces a current that opposes the applied current, which comes, for example, from the battery. As a result the current in the winding does not immediately reach its full value, as it would if it were passing through a pure resistance, but builds up comparatively slowly. After it has become steady, no change occurs in the magnetic field. When the applied current is switched off, however, the magnetic field collapses and, in so doing undergoes a very rapid change, which induces a voltage in the coil. The more suddenly the break is made, the more suddenly the magnetic field collapses and the greater the induced voltage. If there are many turns of wire, this voltage can be very large. This is how, for instance, a car's ignition operates.

The voltage induced in a coil by the collapse of a magnetic field depends on how quickly the lines of force (⇨ p. 88) change. Breaking a contact in a circuit containing an inductor (such as a winding in a transformer) causes a very sudden collapse in the magnetic field. In industrial equipment special switches are used that connect a resistance across the switch before making the break. Otherwise, sparks (*arcing*) occur, which can be very dangerous as well as damaging to the equipment.

Back EMF

The opposing voltage (*electromotive force*) that occurs when a changing current flows through an inductor is called back EMF, and the more rapidly the current changes, the higher will be the back EMF and the greater the resistance to the current flow.

Rapid changes in current are a feature of alternating current (⇨ p. 90), so an inductor will always offer greater resistance to the flow of alternating current than direct current. The back EMF is also affected by the inductance of the inductor – mainly by the number of turns on the coil and the nature of the core. The resistance to the flow of alternating current thus depends on the frequency of alternation and on the number of turns cut by the changing lines of magnetic force. With 50-Hz electricity supply, the current is changing fairly slowly, but, even so, it is changing fast enough for the back EMF to make a considerable difference to the effective resistance of an inductor. The total impedance (⇨ p. 98) to the flow of current in an inductor is thus made up of the DC resistance and the effect of the back EMF.

The reactance of an inductor

The faster the magnetic lines of force change, the greater is the opposing voltage induced in the conductor they cut through. It follows that a rise in frequency of AC will cause a greater resistance. This resistance to the passage of AC is called *reactance*. At zero Hz (DC) the reactance is zero and only the resistance matters. At very high frequencies, such as those encountered in television transmission, small inductors can have high reactances. Even a short length of wire may have a significant reactance at

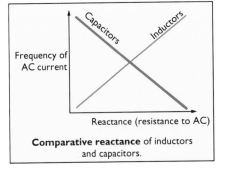

Comparative reactance of inductors and capacitors.

THE TRANSFORMER

Faraday's iron ring with its two coils of wire (⇨ main text) contained all the essentials of the modern electrical transformer. Essentially, the transformer is a converter of alternating voltages. The flow of a direct current does not cause electromagnetic induction. Neglecting losses, the voltage induced in the secondary coil of a transformer is equal to that in the primary coil multiplied by the ratio of the turns of wire in the coils. If the secondary has twice as many turns as the primary, the voltage in the secondary coil will be twice that in the primary coil. If it has ten times the number of turns, the voltage will be ten times larger. These are examples of 'step-up' transformers. If the secondary coil were to have one tenth as many turns, however, the voltage would be one tenth. This would be a 'step-down' transformer (⇨ pp. 92–3).

The law of conservation of energy demands that as the voltage is stepped up, the current must be stepped down in the same proportion, and this is what actually happens. In DC circuits current is proportional to voltage, but the transformer is an AC device and the higher inductance of a secondary winding with more turns causes a proportionate drop in the current.

Transformers are indispensable devices and come in all sizes. They are extensively used in the distribution of electricity supplies over long distances because this can be done with much lower losses if the current is conveyed

at very high voltage and correspondingly lower amperage, which can be carried on smaller-gauge cables. Doubling the voltage reduces the losses to a quarter.

Electricity is generated at about 25,000 volts. At the power stations this is stepped up to 275,000 or 400,000 volts, and fed into the national electricity grid system. Substations contain step-down transformers to reduce the voltage to 33,000 for heavy industry, 415 volts for light industry and 240 volts (120 volts in the USA) for domestic consumption. With each reduction in voltage the current rises and heavier duty cables are required.

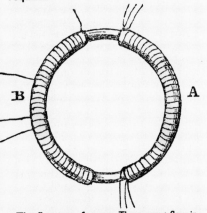

The first transformer. The current flow in wire coil A comes from a battery, and this induces a current in B. Engraving from Faraday's notebook, from Bence Jones, *The Life and Letters of Faraday*, London, (1870). (AR)

---

very high frequencies. What happens with capacitors (⇨ p. 98) is a useful comparison. Very low frequencies, close to DC, make capacitors seem like open circuits where the current flow is broken; very high frequencies, on the other hand, make them seem like short circuits (point of relatively low resistance so that current flows through it, bypassing the rest of the circuit) because of their low reactance. With inductors, very low frequencies result in little or no reactance, so a low-resistance inductor may seem like a short circuit; very high frequencies, though, produce high reactances and an inductor may seem like an open circuit.

Losses in transformers

Transformers without iron cores are very inefficient. But if solid iron cores are used, circulating electric currents are induced in the cores, and much energy is wasted in producing heat. For this reason, transformers use cores made from very thin sheets of iron (laminations), insulated from one another and clamped together to make up the bulk needed. This arrangement greatly limits induced-core currents. But even so, transformer cores commonly run very hot.

SEE ALSO

● POLES, FIELDS AND CHARGES p. 88
● ELECTRONS AND CONDUCTANCE p. 90
● SOURCES OF ELECTRICITY pp. 92–5
● RESISTANCE p. 96
● CAPACITANCE p. 98
● ELECTRONICS pp. 102–5

The ignition coil (black cylinder with silver band, bottom right) in a car's engine is a high-value inductor. It steps up the 12 volts provided by the battery to produce a spark strong enough to ignite the petrol-and-air mixture. (Quadrant)

Electronics 1

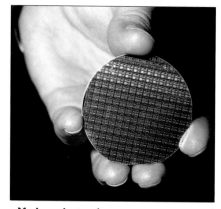

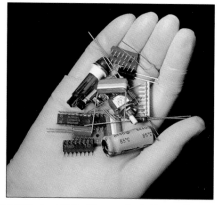

Modern electronics components are now highly miniaturized. This silicon wafer (left) contains a grid of silicon chips, each one of which holds many thousands of transistors. Compared with a handful of old-fashioned components from the 1970s, in which a transistor can be seen (metallic, pronged object, right-hand picture centre left), the degree of miniaturization is stunning. (Images/Adam Hart-Davis, SPL)

Today we live in an electronic age and have become almost wholly dependent on electronic technology. Electronics is both a science and a technology, and it is concerned with the ways in which the movement of electrons through space or solids (⇨ p. 90) is controlled and manipulated. It deals usually with very small currents, in contrast to the science of electricity, which deals with the generation and use of large currents.

Electronics depends on the existence of a small number of devices, of which the transistor is currently the most important. The transistor and its successors were not, however, the beginning of electronics, the bases of which were worked out long before the transistor was ever invented. Prior to the introduction of the transistor, electronic devices were large and clumsy and could not be used in very large numbers because of their considerable power requirements.

The electronic diode

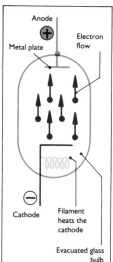

A diode. Electrons emitted by the heated cathode flow through the vacuum to the strongly positively charged anode. A diode allows passage of electricity in one direction only.

The whole science of electronics started in 1904 when the English electrical engineer John Ambrose Fleming (1849–1945), following up a suggestion by the American inventor Thomas Alva Edison (1847–1931), inserted a metal plate into an electric light bulb (⇨ illustration). The lighted bulb filament, being very hot, 'boiled' off electrons; the metal plate, being cold, did not. Electrons could get across the gap from the filament to the plate but not from the plate to the filament. If a battery was used to make the plate positive with respect to the filament, the negatively charged electrons were attracted to it (following the law 'unlike charges attract'), and a strong flow of electrons occurred from filament to plate. In this way, the first measure of control of electrons – a movement in one direction only – was effected. Fleming rapidly realized that he had developed a kind of valve for electricity. As this valve depended on a heated filament or *cathode* (from the Greek *kathodos*, meaning 'a way down'), it was called a *thermionic valve* (the Greek *thermos* means 'hot'). And because the device had two electrodes, it was called a *diode*. The positively charged plate was called the *anode* (from the Greek *anodos*, meaning 'the way up').

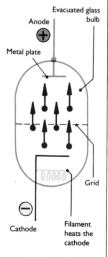

A triode. The potential on the grid controls the flow of electrons between cathode and anode. It can act as a switch or an amplifier.

The ability to limit the flow of electrons to one direction meant that alternating current (AC; ⇨ p. 90) could be 'rectified' – turned to direct current (DC). (If AC is applied across a diode, it will conduct when the anode is positive, but not when it is negative. So the AC is rectified (converted) into a series of pulses of electricity, all going in the same direction.) It also meant that the primitive radio signals of the time – which were carried by an alternating current wave – could be more efficiently detected.

The thermionic triode

In 1906, the American inventor Lee De Forest (1873–1961) took the matter an important step further by inserting a third element, the grid, between the filament (cathode) and the plate (anode; ⇨ illustration). Electrons could pass from the cathode, through the meshes of this grid, to the anode and, as long as it was not charged, the valve simply acted as a rectifying diode. The important fact was, however, that very small changes in negative charge on the grid would impose identical changes on the large current passing from the cathode to the anode. As long as the grid was kept negative, even the tiniest electrical signals on it would result in an identical, but much larger, signal passing between the cathode and the anode. Thus the *amplifier* had been invented. This valve, known as a *triode*, was able to magnify very weak radio signals, and signals from microphones, gramophone pickups, and electrocardiograms – indeed it could magnify fluctuating electrical signals from any source. By 1910, De Forest was using his triodes to broadcast the singing voice of the great Italian tenor Enrico Caruso.

Improvements in valve design quickly followed, and amplification factors and power-handling capacity increased. Quite small triodes commonly worked with a positive voltage of several hundred on the anode and consumed 10 watts or more of filament power. This made them run very hot, and good ventilation was needed. Nevertheless, these devices did what was expected of them, and made possible the rapid development of radio transmission and reception, sound recording (on film, disc, wire and tape) and television. One little-recognized development at the time was to prove of great importance later. This was that the thermionic valve was not only a rectifier and amplifier, but was also a switch that could change from 'on' (passing current), to 'off' (not passing current) very rapidly indeed. Such switching could be effected by an electric current rather than by a physical movement to break a circuit, and was to prove the basis of the computer (⇨ chapter 10).

The development of the transistor

The thermionic diode was by no means the only known rectifier. Early radio receivers were known as 'crystal sets' because the rectification (in this sense, the 'detection') of the radio signal was performed by the junction between a piece of springy copper wire and one of a number of kinds of crystalline mineral, such as lead sulphide (*galena*). Later research showed that an even better crystal rectifier was provided by contact with a crystal of the element germanium, as long as certain impurities were present. Germanium is a semiconductor – an element whose electrical conductance lies about halfway between that of conductors and that of insulators (⇨ p. 90).

In 1947, the American physicist William Shockley (1910–89) was working on semiconductors in the Bell Telephone Laboratories in the USA in conjunction with John Bardeen (1908–91) and Walter Houser Brattain (1902–87). Knowing that semiconductors could do the work of thermionic diodes, their aim was to try to develop the semiconductor equivalent of the thermionic triode. Their first success came with a point-contact germanium device equivalent to a standard crystal rectifier with an additional electrode. This first crude device, the *point-contact transistor* (from 'transfer' and 'resistor'), actually achieved amplification. Encouraged by this, Shockley quickly developed the first junction transistor, using another semiconductor element, silicon (⇨ below).

Transistors are very small, do not require a heated element and, unlike thermionic valves, work at very low voltages. Only a single power supply is needed (whereas valves need two), and they can perform all the functions of the thermionic valve with greatly increased efficiency. For a time, the germanium transistor was dominant, but, at an early stage, silicon was found to have a number of major advantages (cheaper,

HOW THE TRANSISTOR WORKS

The first successful and widely used transistors were nearly all of the junction type, and consisted of a piece of n-type material (⇨ main text) sandwiched between two pieces of p-type material (a *pnp transistor*) or a piece of p-type material sandwiched between two pieces of n-type material (an *npn transistor*). Such transistors can be thought of as two diodes connected back to back. In the case of an npn transistor, a few electrons can migrate from the n-type sides to the central p-type zone, but hardly any can pass right across.

If a voltage is now applied across the whole transistor so that one n-side is made positive and the other negative, electrons will be able to flow easily from the more negative side (the *emitter*) to the more positive side (the *collector*), but not in the opposite direction. Small changes in the charge on the narrow p-type zone between them (the *base*) can then modulate this current, just as small changes on the grid of the thermionic valve modulates the large cathode–anode current (⇨ main text).

Most modern transistors work in a different way and are called *field-effect transistors* (FETs; ⇨ illustration). These are made by forming a narrow channel of n-type material in a body of p-type material, or vice versa. This channel has a contact at each end, one called the *source* and the other the *drain*, to which the power supply voltage is connected. The channel is constructed in such a way that a controlling voltage can be applied to the body material close to the channel (the *gate*). In a typical FET, electrons flow in the channel from the negative source to the positive drain under the influence of the applied power-supply voltage. If the gate is now made negative, the effective width of the channel is reduced by a peripheral depletion zone, and, if the gate voltage is sufficient, the current can be choked off altogether. In this way a small signal on the gate can modulate a much larger current flowing from the source to the drain. FETs use very little current and are highly efficient. Many are of the type known as metal-oxide semiconductor field-effect transistors (MOSFETs). These are 'insulated-gate' FETs, the insulator between the gate electrodes and the channel being silicon dioxide.

more plentiful, able to work at higher temperatures, etc.), and germanium soon became of secondary importance. At first, transistors were made as discrete devices, each in its own metal or plastic 'can' with its three wire contacts protruding. These were then soldered into 'printed-circuit boards' along with other electronic components. Millions of discrete transistors are still made and used

in this form, but the great majority of transistors now in existence are formed simultaneously in large numbers on thin wafers of silicon, each silicon chip on the wafer containing thousands or even millions of separate transistors.

Valency and conduction bands

The electrons in the atoms of solid materials can be thought of as being situated in certain layered bands (⇨ p. 108). Two of these bands affect the behaviour of the material. One is the *valency* band, which is the highest energy band that is filled with electrons. This band is concerned with the linking of atoms together to form molecules. The other, just outside the valency band, is the conduction band, concerned with conduction of electricity. Electrons can move freely in and out of this band. The energy gap between these two bands is virtually nonexistent in the case of good electrical conductors such as metals, and only a very small amount of energy is needed to persuade electrons from the valency band to enter the conduction band. The gap is very large in the case of insulators, so a great deal of energy is needed to persuade electrons to move up into the conduction band. Semiconductors have an energy gap between the valency and conduction bands of intermediate size and, in their case, a few electrons are constantly leaking into the conduction band.

Semiconductor doping

To work in transistors, semiconductor elements such as silicon must have tiny quantities of impurities added to them. This is called *doping*. The impurity added may be of atoms that readily give up electrons (called 'donor material'). When this is done the material is called an *n-type* ('n' for negative) semiconductor. This n-type material has free electrons available to move as current. Alternatively, the impurity may be of an element that is short of electrons in the valency band. Doping with such a material, known as an 'acceptor material', produces a *p-type* semiconductor. Such a material has potential positive charges because of the atoms deficient in electrons. These electron 'vacancies' are called 'holes', and these holes can, quite properly, be said to move. Movement of holes simply means that an electron has entered the vacant space in the valency band of the acceptor-material atom, leaving a vacant space in another atom of the material. The holes thus move in the opposite direction to the electrons.

If a piece of n-type material is placed up against a piece of p-type material, a *pn-junction* is produced. This acts as a diode rectifier. When the p-type side is made more positive, and the n-type more negative, electrons can move readily from the n-type to the p-type side, and the holes go in the opposite direction. But if the p-type side is made negative (by reversal in the battery) and the n-type side positive, the electrons of the n-side will move

away from the p-side to the positive pole, and the holes on the p-side will move away from the n-side towards the negative pole. These charges will simply tend to be neutralized and almost no current will flow.

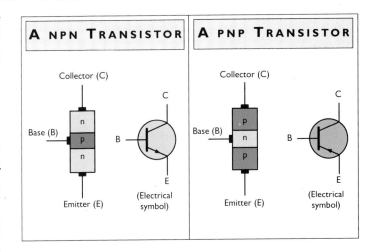

A npn TRANSISTOR   A pnp TRANSISTOR

Collector (C) · Base (B) · Emitter (E) · (Electrical symbol)

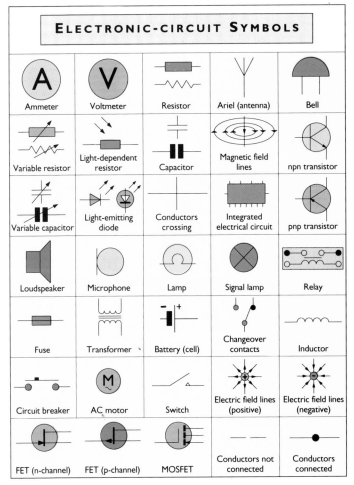

ELECTRONIC-CIRCUIT SYMBOLS

Ammeter	Voltmeter	Resistor	Ariel (antenna)	Bell
Variable resistor	Light-dependent resistor	Capacitor	Magnetic field lines	npn transistor
Variable capacitor	Light-emitting diode	Conductors crossing	Integrated electrical circuit	pnp transistor
Loudspeaker	Microphone	Lamp	Signal lamp	Relay
Fuse	Transformer	Battery (cell)	Changeover contacts	Inductor
Circuit breaker	AC motor	Switch	Electric field lines (positive)	Electric field lines (negative)
FET (n-channel)	FET (p-channel)	MOSFET	Conductors not connected	Conductors connected

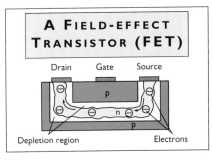

A FIELD-EFFECT TRANSISTOR (FET)

Drain · Gate · Source · Depletion region · Electrons

Electronics 2

The great advance in microelectronics occurred when it was appreciated that many transistors, together with the necessary associated diodes (⇨ p. 102), resistors (⇨ p. 96) and capacitors (⇨ p. 98), can readily be formed on a single, thin slice cut from a crystal of pure silicon, an *integrated circuit* (IC).

The integrated circuit was predicted by the British engineer G. W. A. Dummer in 1952, and first realized by the American Jack Kilby in 1959. Refinement rapidly followed and, by 1962, the mass production of integrated circuits started. By 1967 ICs were being produced containing thousands of transistors.

Such 'large-scale integration' brought a new dimension to electronics and made possible a great range of devices such as calculators, watches, control systems for washing machines, electronic typewriters, video games, industrial robots and other industrial control systems, microcomputers, minicomputers and very large 'mainframe' computers. Some of today's 'very large-scale integration' (VLSI) chips contain millions of transistors and it is now commonplace for the electronics of an entire microcomputer to be fabricated on a single silicon chip just a few millimetres square.

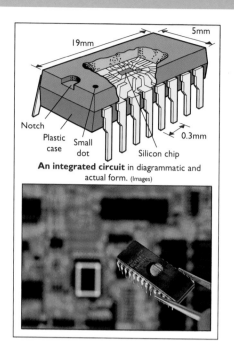

An integrated circuit in diagrammatic and actual form. (Images)

Transistors as amplifiers and oscillators

Soon after they were first developed, transistors (⇨ p. 102) were mostly used as amplifiers, and people were astonished at the small size and lower power requirements of the new radio receivers that flooded the world, mostly from Japan. Such receivers were made on small 'printed-circuit' boards to which half a dozen discrete transistors, together with resistors, tuning coils and capacitors, were soldered. These receivers became so popular that, to many people, the word 'transistor' came to mean such a radio set. The principle of these receivers was exactly the same as that of their bulky predecessors, except that the valves were replaced by transistors. Signals were picked up by a small ferrite (ceramic ferrimagnetic) aerial, tuned by a coil and variable capacitor, amplified, mixed with a fixed signal from a transistor oscillator (⇨ below) to produce a lower 'intermediate frequency' signal, that was again amplified, rectified (converted from AC to DC; ⇨ p. 92), amplified again and fed to a small loudspeaker. In many cases, today, most of these functions are performed by a single integrated circuit.

An *oscillator* is a device that produces an alternating current or a regularly fluctuating (*periodic*) direct current. The output may be a sine wave, a square wave, a sawtooth wave or a more complex waveform (⇨ illustration). Oscillators take various forms depending on what they are used for. If the output of an amplifier, such as a single transistor, or a cascade of transistors, is fed back to the input in phase (⇨ p. 78) with the input signal, the amplifier will oscillate. Alternatively, two transistors can be coupled together in such a way that the ouput of each forms the input of the other. Such an arrangement, called a *multivibrator*, will oscillate readily. The frequency of oscillation of an oscillator can be determined by a tuned circuit consisting of an inductor (⇨ p. 100) in parallel with a capacitor (⇨ p. 98), or it may be fixed by incorporation of a quartz piezoelectric crystal (⇨ p. 70) in the circuit. In the case of multivibrators, the frequency of oscillation is determined by the time constants of the capacitance and resistance in the circuits concerned. Oscillators are used in watches, radio transmitters and receivers, electronic musical instruments, timers, and in a wide range of electronic devices, such as computers, that require a synchronizing clock waveform.

Transistor circuits

To work as an amplifier, a transistor requires a DC power supply, and it must be connected, the right way round, between positive and negative. An npn transistor (⇨ p. 102) has its emitter connected to negative and its collector to positive. For voltage amplification a fairly high resistance must be connected

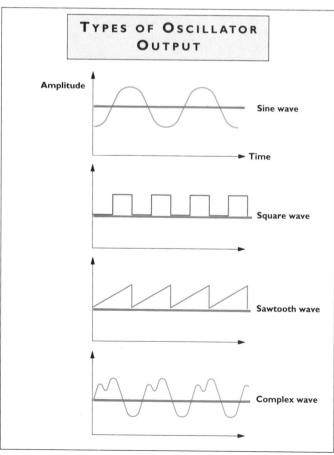

TYPES OF OSCILLATOR OUTPUT

Amplitude

Sine wave

Time

Square wave

Sawtooth wave

Complex wave

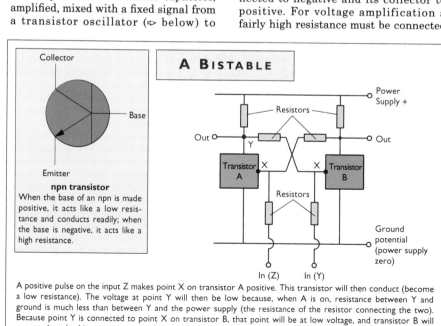

npn transistor
When the base of an npn is made positive, it acts like a low resistance and conducts readily; when the base is negative, it acts like a high resistance.

A BISTABLE

Collector

Base

Emitter

Power Supply +

Resistors

Out

Out

Transistor A   X   X   Transistor B

Resistors

Ground potential (power supply zero)

In (Z)   In (Y)

A positive pulse on the input Z makes point X on transistor A positive. This transistor will then conduct (become a low resistance). The voltage at point Y will then be low because, when A is on, resistance between Y and ground is much less than between Y and the power supply (the resistance of the resistor connecting the two). Because point Y is connected to point X on transistor B, that point will be at low voltage, and transistor B will not conduct. In this state, transistor A is said to be on, and transistor B off. A negative pulse on Z will reverse everything, as will a positive pulse on Y.

HALF- AND FULL-ADDER SYSTEMS

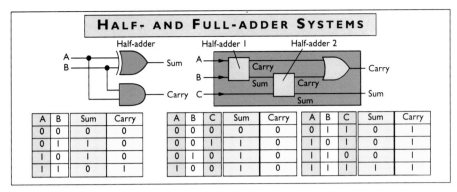

A	B	Sum	Carry
0	0	0	0
0	1	1	0
1	0	1	0
1	1	0	1

A	B	C	Sum	Carry
0	0	0	0	0
0	0	1	1	0
0	1	0	1	0
1	0	0	1	0

A	B	C	Sum	Carry
0	1	1	0	1
1	0	1	0	1
1	1	0	0	1
1	1	1	1	1

Binary code							(Base 2)	Decimal code		(Base 10)
(128)	(64)	(32)	(16)	(8)	(4)	(2)	(1)	(100)	(10)	(1)
							1			1
						1	1			3
					1	0	1			5
				1	1	1	0		1	4
1	1	1	1	1	1	1	1	2	5	5

Binary code uses only the digits 1 and 0. A figure 1 under any heading means 1 times that multiple. So, a 1 under ⑧ means 8. The multiples under each heading are added together to make the decimal total.

between the collector and the power supply. The base is set at a suitable potential (voltage; ⇨ p. 90) by means of a high resistance connected between the power supply line and the base. The signal to be amplified is applied between the base and the negative power line. Changes in the base voltage now cause much larger changes in the current passing through the transistor and the collector resistance. This causes large voltage variations at the collector and these can be tapped off via a capacitor (⇨ p. 98) that blocks DC flow to the output. The output is 180° out of phase with the input (⇨ chapter 4).

Flip-flops, or *bistables*, are circuits consisting of two transistors interconnected in such a way that the combination has two stable states – transistor A 'on' and transistor B 'off', or vice versa. An input pulse can quickly switch the flip-flop from one state to the other. One state can be used to represent a 1 and the other a 0. An input 1 pulse can thus be stored for as long as the power remains on. An array of eight flip-flops can store an eight-bit (eight-digit) number – a *byte*. The bistable is an important circuit because it forms the basis of electronic memory. Such a memory is called 'volatile' because all data is lost as soon as the power is switched off.

Flip-flops can also be used to count pulses by connecting them in sequence. In this arrangement, the second flip-flop changes its state each time the first undergoes a complete cycle of change of state. There is thus one output pulse from the first flip-flop for two input pulses. The third flip-flop changes state each time the second goes through a complete cycle, and so on. In this way the flip-flops act as frequency dividers, each dividing its input frequency by two. Such dividers are widely used: electronic wristwatches, for instance, consist of a tiny quartz oscillator working at a very high frequency, and a succession of stages of frequency division that divides down the oscillator frequency by an integer that gives a final output of one pulse per second. That is, if the oscillator is working at a million hertz (pulses per second), and a succession of stages divides the frequency by a total of exactly one million (for example, by 10, then 10, then 10, then 10, then 10), the final ouput will be one pulse per second. The oscillator and dividers are

in the form of an integrated circuit. The final pulse is used to move the fingers of the watch via an electromagnetic actuator, such as a tiny electromagnet that pulls a wheel around one sixtieth of a revolution each second, or to operate a liquid-crystal display (⇨ p. 74).

Transistors as switches

The great majority of transistors in use today are not, however, used either as amplifiers or as oscillators. Digital electronics, as used in computers and many other devices (⇨ p. 214), depends on transistors being in one of two states – 'on' or 'off'. This can be effected by a very small change in the voltage in the base or gate (⇨ below).

By switching a transistor 'on' or 'off' a definite change occurs in the voltage between the transistor and the power supply. A 'high' voltage, near to that of the supply voltage of the transistor, can be taken to represent a 1, and a low voltage, close to zero, represents a 0. Switching can be performed at a very rapid rate – as high as 50,000,000 times a second – controlled by a 'clock' oscillator.

A numerical system to the base 2 can represent any number using only 1s and 0s. In such a 'binary code', reading from right to left, the 1s represent 1, 2, 4, 8, 16, 32, 64 and 128. Thus, a row of eight transistors, variously switched 'on' or 'off', can represent any number up to 255. Such binary numbers can also be taken to represent alphabetical letters. In the American Standard Code for Information Interchange (*ASCII* code), for instance, numbers 65 to 90 represent the upper-case alphabet and numbers 97 to 122 represent the lower-case alphabet. The number 44 is a comma, 46 a full stop, 58 a colon, 63 a question mark, and so on. Eight bits (one byte) allow a code of 255 characters, so the extended ASCII code can include accented letters, Greek letters, some fractions and various graphical and mathematical symbols.

Logical gates

In computers, transistors are connected together in various ways to produce high-speed logical gates (⇨ p. 216). These have only one of two levels of input and output – high and low – representing, respectively, 1 and 0. All gates have a single output connection and most have two inputs. The output of each gate depends solely on the levels of the inputs

and is best described in the form of a truth table (⇨ illustration).

The simplest gate is a NOT gate. This has only one input and one output. If the input is 1 the output will be 0, and vice versa. Such a gate is sometimes called an 'inverter'. An AND gate has two inputs. If both inputs are 1, the output will be 1. Any other combination of input (0 0, 0 1 or 1 0) gives an output of 0. An OR gate has two inputs. The output is 1 if either or both inputs are 1. So the output is 0 only if both inputs are 0. An exclusive OR gate (XOR) also has two inputs, and has an output of 1 when the inputs are different from each other. The output is 1 for inputs of 1 0 or 0 1. For economy of implementation, logical gates are commonly produced in the form of NAND gates. A NAND gate is simply an AND gate followed by a NOT gate (inverter). The truth table for the NAND gate is the same as that for the AND gate except that, in the output, all 1s become 0s and all 0s become 1s. A NAND gate can be made from a single transistor, and all the other gates can be made using various combinations of NAND gates. For instance, if the two inputs are connected together, the NAND gate becomes a NOT gate.

Such gates are extensively used, both in computers and in various electronic control systems. It is common, for instance, to require an event to occur when two or more other events coincide. One might wish, for instance, to turn on heating when a room is occupied and when the temperature is below a stipulated level. This is done by means of an AND gate together with two sensors that respectively give a 1 output when someone is in the room and when the temperature is below the set value. A 1 output from the gate turns on the heating.

Binary arithmetic

Adding and subtracting binary numbers is readily implemented using various combinations of logical gates. A half-adder that adds two bits, giving the sum and the carry digit, can be made from an exclusive OR gate and an AND gate (⇨ illustration). Two of these, together with an OR gate, form a full-adder that will add three bits at a time, giving the sum and the carry digit (⇨ illustration). Full-adders can be combined to deal with numbers with more bits. Binary arithmetic is of fundamental importance for the field of computing (⇨ chapter 10).

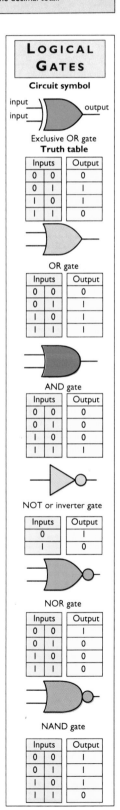

LOGICAL GATES

Circuit symbol

Exclusive OR gate
Truth table

Inputs		Output
0	0	0
0	1	1
1	0	1
1	1	0

OR gate

Inputs		Output
0	0	0
0	1	1
1	0	1
1	1	1

AND gate

Inputs		Output
0	0	0
0	1	0
1	0	0
1	1	1

NOT or inverter gate

Inputs	Output
0	1
1	0

NOR gate

Inputs		Output
0	0	1
0	1	0
1	0	0
1	1	0

NAND gate

Inputs		Output
0	0	1
0	1	1
1	0	1
1	1	0

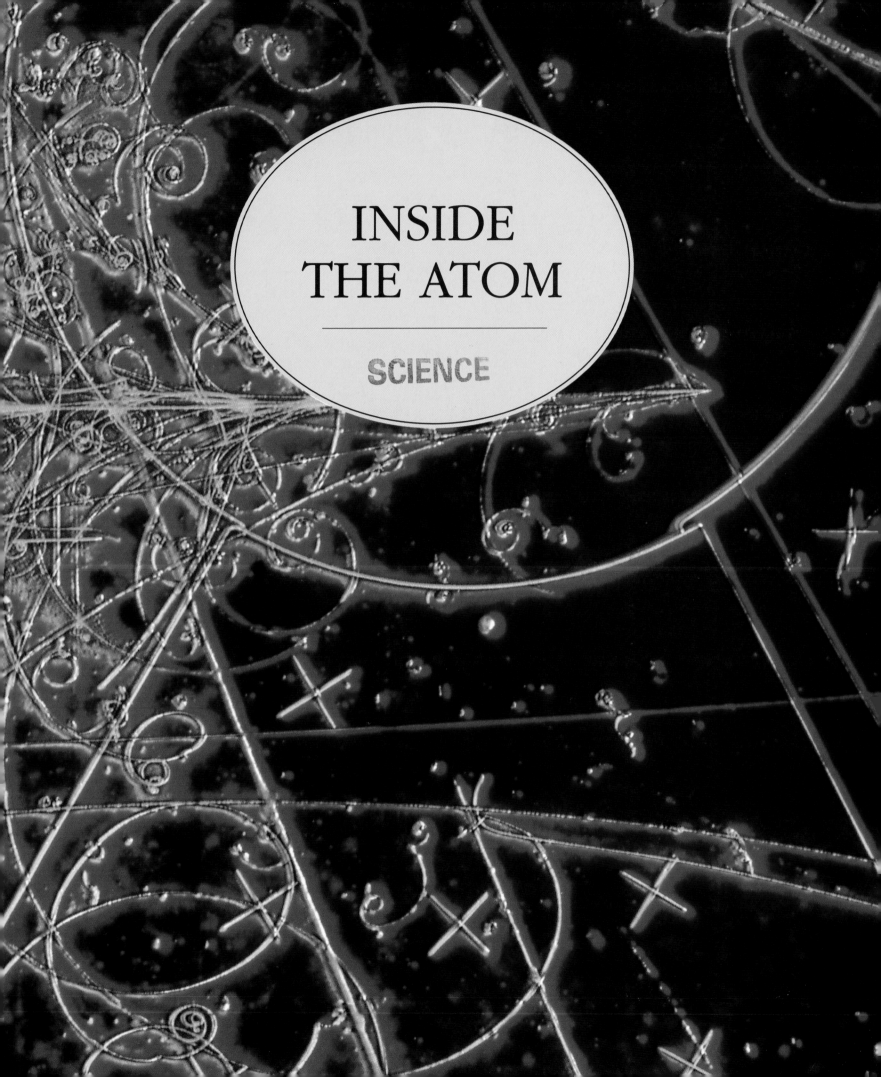

INSIDE
THE ATOM

SCIENCE

The Classical Theory of the Atom

The possibility that there might be a limit to the divisibility of matter has been considered from the earliest times. This led to the concept of the atom – a word derived from the Greek *atomos*, meaning 'not able to be cut'. Although the general notion of very small particles from which all nature is made was recorded nearly 2,500 years ago (▷ box), it was not until the end of the 19th century that any real knowledge of the nature of these particles became available.

At the beginning of the 19th century the idea of atoms became one of practical importance to chemists. The English schoolteacher John Dalton (1766–1844), who was interested in all branches of science, proposed that 'the ultimate particles of all homogeneous bodies are perfectly alike in weight, figure et cetera'. By 'homogeneous bodies' Dalton did not mean only elements, but included compounds such as water. So, in this, he was not distinguishing atoms from molecules. He was, however, aware that the atoms of an element were indivisible and that they remained unchanged while undergoing chemical reactions. He went further. Taking hydrogen as the lightest element he was able to work out the relative weights of the atoms of other elements, such as oxygen, nitrogen and sulphur.

The discovery of the electron

The English physicist J. J. Thomson (1856–1940) knew that the rays in cathode-ray tubes (▷ p. 218), which produced a fine spot on a fluorescent screen on the end of the tube, could be deflected by magnets and by an electric charge on plates within the tube. Changing the polarity of the charge showed that the beam was attracted by a positive charge and repelled by a negative charge. So, because 'like' charges were known to repel each other, the beam itself had to carry a negative charge. Thomson assumed that the beam consisted of a stream of negatively charged 'corpuscles' – in other words, the particles we now call *electrons*. Measuring the deflection of the spot allowed him to quantify the ratio of the charge to the mass of one of these particles. This was shown to be less than one thousandth of the mass of a hydrogen atom. This was the first demonstration of a particle smaller than an atom.

Rutherford's atom

As soon as it became known that the atom contained particles smaller than itself, speculation arose as to its structure. Working briefly under J. J. Thomson at Cambridge was the New Zealand student Ernest Rutherford (1871–1937). Interested in the then new field of radioactivity, he knew that the rays that were given off by radioactive materials were of different kinds. He considered this important and arbitrarily called the positively charged rays *alpha rays* and the negatively charged ones *beta rays*. Later, between 1906 and 1909, assisted by the young Hans Wilhelm Geiger at Manchester University, he was able to prove that alpha rays were streams of helium atoms minus their electrons. These *alpha particles* had a double positive charge.

In 1910, Geiger and another of Rutherford's students fired streams of alpha particles at a very thin sheet of gold foil. Most passed through and were registered on the photographic plate behind. Some, however, about 1 in 20,000, bounced back. This was an astonishing finding. 'It was almost as incredible,' said Rutherford, 'as if you fired a fifteen-inch shell at a sheet of tissue paper and it came back and hit you.'

These observations led Rutherford to two important conclusions: that atoms were mostly empty space, and that they had a positively charged centre, somewhat similar to the alpha particles. Because like charges repel, alpha particles that happened to strike a positively charged atom centre were forced back. Rutherford now felt able to propose a model for the structure of the atom, and he did so in 1911. It consisted, he suggested, of a positively charged central *nucleus*, occupying only a tiny proportion of the whole volume of the atom, surrounded by a large space containing negatively charged electrons. He was able to work out that the mass of the positively charged particle of the nucleus, which he called a *proton*, was more than 1800 times that of an electron. So almost all the mass of the atom resided in the nucleus. Because electrons were of opposite charge to the nucleus and would be attracted to it, they had to have energy of their own in the form of rapid movement around the nucleus. Their angular velocity (▷ p. 30) in their orbits round the nucleus, he suggested, provided just the required degree of force to balance the attraction of the nucleus.

For each proton in the nucleus there was one electron, so the atom remained electrically neutral. Hydrogen had one proton in the nucleus and one electron. Helium had two protons and two electrons. Lithium had three protons and three electrons, chlorine 35 protons and 35 electrons, and so on (▷ periodic table of the elements, p. 158).

Rutherford knew that the helium nucleus had twice the mass it would have if the two protons were all it contained. At first he suggested that it might contain four protons, two of which were neutralized by two electrons. But there were various objections to this explanation and he had reason to believe that an uncharged particle of the same mass as a proton actually existed. It was not until 1934 that Rutherford's former assistant James Chadwick (1891–1974) eventually proved the existence of the *neutron* – the elusive uncharged particle.

Rutherford's concept of the atom immediately provided explanations for many

---

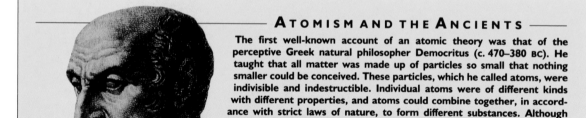

ATOMISM AND THE ANCIENTS

The first well-known account of an atomic theory was that of the perceptive Greek natural philosopher Democritus (c. 470–380 BC). He taught that all matter was made up of particles so small that nothing smaller could be conceived. These particles, which he called atoms, were indivisible and indestructible. Individual atoms were of different kinds with different properties, and atoms could combine together, in accordance with strict laws of nature, to form different substances. Although fanciful in detail, Democritus was remarkably accurate in principle.

The atomism of Democritus was adopted by the Greek philosopher Epicurus (341–270 BC), who took a mechanistic view of the universe. He, in turn, influenced the Roman poet and philosopher Titus Lucretius (c. 99–55 BC). As an illustration of atomism Lucretius described how he stood on a high hill watching an army on a plain so far below him that it resembled a single massive body glittering in the sun. Lucretius' great scientific poem *De Natura Rerum* ('On the Nature of Things') was almost lost and was unknown throughout the Middle Ages. But a single manuscript copy survived and, soon after the invention of printing, the poem was published in full in 1471 and became widely popular. The idea of atomism was thus central to the thinking of many educated people after the Renaissance.

Democritus, the father of atomic theory. He believed that the properties of different substances were determined by the physical features of the atoms – for example, atoms of water were smooth and round, while atoms of fire were thorny. (National Library of Medicine, SPL)

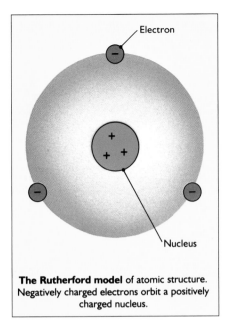

The Rutherford model of atomic structure. Negatively charged electrons orbit a positively charged nucleus.

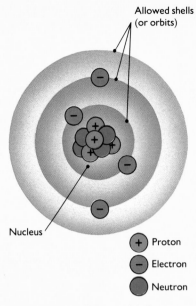

The Rutherford–Bohr model of atomic structure. The number of electrons orbiting the nucleus is equal to the number of positively charged protons within the nucleus. The number of electrons within each orbit or shell is also limited – no more than two in the first shell, eight in the second, 18 in the third, etc.

Proton

Electron

Neutron

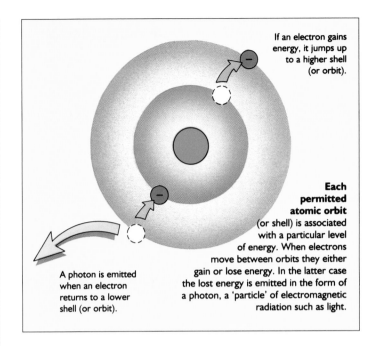

If an electron gains energy, it jumps up to a higher shell (or orbit).

A photon is emitted when an electron returns to a lower shell (or orbit).

Each permitted atomic orbit (or shell) is associated with a particular level of energy. When electrons move between orbits they either gain or lose energy. In the latter case the lost energy is emitted in the form of a photon, a 'particle' of electromagnetic radiation such as light.

well-known chemical and other phenomena and, although far from accurate, was one of the most germinal and fruitful hypotheses in the entire history of science. Both Rutherford and Chadwick were awarded Nobel Prizes for their work.

The classical picture of the atom

Hydrogen is the only atom with no neutron in its nucleus. Helium has two protons and two neutrons, lithium three protons and three neutrons, and so on. The *atomic number* can be taken to be the number of protons and this rises by one with each different heavier element until we reach uranium with 92 protons – the most massive of the naturally occurring elements (▷ p. 158). The number of neutrons, however, is not always the same as the number of protons. Many of the more massive atoms have more neutrons than protons, and many atoms with the same number of protons (that is, of the same element) have different numbers of neutrons. Most samples of uranium, for instance, have a mass equal to 238 protons because the nuclei contain 92 protons and 146 neutrons. Some samples – the kind, for instance, used in the early atom bombs – have a mass of 235, with 92 protons and only 143 neutrons.

The chemical properties of an atom depend on how it links with other atoms by way of its electrons (▷ p. 156). So these properties depend on the number of electrons and, consequently, the number of protons in the nucleus. The chemical properties are quite unaffected by the number of neutrons. Atoms with the same number of protons but different numbers of neutrons are called *isotopes* (literally 'equally placed'). The physical properties, however, depend also on the number of neutrons. Very massive atoms with many neutrons are often unstable and can break down, for example by giving off alpha particles (two protons and two neutrons) from the nucleus. The loss of two protons means a complete change to a

different element with different chemical properties. Elements that undergo spontaneous changes of this kind are said to be *radioactive*. Some isotopes can also be radioactive.

The Bohr atom

Rutherford's model of the atom is not quite satisfactory. This was pointed out by the Danish physicist Niels Bohr (1885–1962), who worked with both J. J. Thomson and Rutherford. Bohr's objection was that an electron moving in a circular orbit is accelerating and must therefore continuously emit radiation (▷ p. 84), lose energy and spiral down to the nucleus. To overcome this difficulty, Bohr proposed that electrons can move only in certain permitted orbits or shells, and that while in these orbits they do not emit radiation. The energy of an electron in a particular orbit is definite and consists of its potential energy by virtue of its height from the nucleus and its kinetic energy from its movement (▷ pp. 46–9). Each permitted orbit, therefore, is associated with a particular level of energy. An electron, he suggested, can move suddenly from an orbit of higher energy to one of lower energy. When it does so the energy difference is emitted as a *quantum*, or 'packet' of electromagnetic radiation of a particular frequency (▷ p. 40).

This model explained certain spectroscopic phenomena, but it also had many shortcomings. It was superseded by a new model, proposed by the Austrian physicist Erwin Schrödinger (1887–1961), based on wave mechanics. Schrödinger's atom incorporates Louis de Broglie's concept of the electron as having wave properties (▷ pp. 38–41). Electrons can be in any orbit around which an exact number of wave-

lengths can occur, setting up what is called a 'standing wave' like the sound waves in an organ pipe. As there was no accelerating charge there was no radiation. 'Permissible' orbits were determined by the need for the exact number of wavelengths to be present. Other potential orbits would involve more or less than a whole number of waves and so would not, therefore, occur.

Schrödinger's model, published in 1926, offered a much more rigorous and mathematically sound account of the atom than that of Bohr.

SEE ALSO

- THE DEVELOPMENT OF SCIENCE pp. 8–11
- BEYOND NEWTON pp. 38–41
- ELECTRONS AND CONDUCTANCE p. 90
- PARTICLE PHYSICS IN ACTION p. 114
- NUCLEAR PHYSICS IN ACTION p. 116
- ATOMS AND MOLECULES p. 156
- RADIOACTIVITY p. 160
- THE NATURE OF THE CHEMICAL BOND p. 162

The discoverer of the electron, Sir Joseph John Thomson. The indivisibility of the atom had been such a firmly entrenched dogma throughout the whole of the 19th century that when, at a meeting at the Royal Institution in 1897, Thomson announced the discovery of the electron, a distinguished physicist told him afterwards that he thought Thomson had been 'pulling their legs'. (AR)

The Quark Theory

For many years, the particles of which the nucleus of the atom is constituted were considered to be ultimately indivisible. Experiments in which protons were bombarded by very-high-speed electrons have shown, however, that the proton is not an indivisible particle and that we must rethink our notions of the fundamental units from which the universe is constructed.

QUARKS AND THEIR CHARGES

Flavour	Charge*
Up	+2/3
Down	-1/3
Strange	-1/3
Charm	+2/3
Bottom	-1/3
Top	+2/3

*Fraction of the charge on an electron

The two-mile-long linear particle accelerator at Stanford in California, USA, allowed particles such as electrons to be accelerated almost to the speed of light. When, in 1972, protons were struck by such high-speed electrons, the pattern of electron scatter produced enabled scientists to determine some details of proton structure. Because the wavelengths of electrons are much smaller than the dimensions of the protons, the electrons were able to strike various points within the protons.

Scientists had previously assumed that the positive charge on a proton was evenly distributed throughout the particle. But these electron-bombardment experiments showed that this was not so. The charge was seen to be localized in smaller constituents of the proton. Even more surprisingly, the strength of the charge on these subproton particles was not the same as that on the proton or on an electron, but was found to be a fraction of that amount – either 1/3 or 2/3, positive or negative. The suggestion that protons and neutrons were made up of smaller particles had long been rejected by most physicists, with good reason. High-energy collisions did not break up these individual nuclear particles to reveal their constituents, as they did in the case of atoms and molecules, and, although such collisions produced showers of mesons (⇨ below), they left the protons and neutrons intact.

One of the two men who, in 1964, put forward the idea of subproton particles, the American particle-physics student George Zweig, was unable to get his paper – now recognized as a classic – published and was, for a time, considered to be a charlatan. Zweig suggested the name 'aces' for these particles, but this never caught on. The other man who, independently, proposed the idea, the well-established American physicist and subsequent Nobel Prizewinner Murray Gell-Mann (1929–), suggested the term 'quark'. This was a nonsense word coined by Gell-Mann and then found by him to exist already in James Joyce's *Finnegans Wake* (a novel that makes experimental use of language) in the phrase, 'three quarks for Muster Mark'. This name has stuck. The Stanford experiments impressively supported the quark theory, and later work at the Conseil Européen pour la Recherce Nucléaire (CERN), the European Laboratory for Particle Physics, virtually confirmed it.

The flavour of quarks

Terminology in particle physics tends to be literary or romantic, almost certainly fanciful. This may, perhaps, be a manifestation of the need for light relief from the very difficult theoretical work in which particular physicists are involved. Words such as 'charm', 'beauty', 'colour', 'strangeness' and 'flavour' come unexpectedly in such a context, but the fact that they may sound whimsical and extravagant does not imply any lack of seriousness on the part of the physicists. Quarks, as far as we know, are the fundamental units of matter, the constituents of protons, neutrons and other elementary particles (⇨ p. 108). Protons and neutrons each have three quarks, and the meson (⇨ illustration) has a quark–antiquark pair. We still refer to protons, neutrons and mesons (known, in common, as *hadrons,* elementary particles capable of being part of a strong nuclear interaction, unlike leptons or photons) as 'elementary' because their constituent quarks cannot be removed from them. This is because quarks are attracted to each other by a force, called the *strong force*, that actually increases with distance. The force between quarks is most easily considered as being like a rubber band that can be stretched easily at first but with greater difficulty as it is elongated. These 'rubber bands' are called *gluons*. Quarks are, of course, very close together; the farthest apart the gluons will allow them to move is about 10^{-15} m.

Quarks move at very high speed, buzzing about inside the hadron so quickly that they seem to be everywhere at once. The effect of this is that such particles seem 'solid'. There are 18 different kinds of quark, and they are differentiated by reason of their properties, known as *flavours* and *colours*. Naturally, in this context, these terms do not carry their normal meaning, but are used arbitrarily for purposes of classification.

SEE ALSO

- FORCE AND MOTION p. 28
- CIRCULAR MOTION AND GRAVITATION p. 30
- BEYOND NEWTON 2: QUANTUM THEORY p. 40
- POLES, FIELDS AND CHARGES p. 88
- ELECTRONS AND CONDUCTANCE p. 90
- THE CLASSICAL THEORY OF THE ATOM p. 108
- FUNDAMENTAL FORCES p. 112
- PARTICLE PHYSICS IN ACTION p. 114
- NUCLEAR PHYSICS IN ACTION p. 116
- ATOMS AND MOLECULES p. 156

The linear accelerator at Stanford Linear Accelerator Center (SLAC) in California, USA, is 3.2 km (2 mi) long. Reaching almost the speed of light, electrons start their journey in the part of the accelerator shown in the foreground. Beyond the freeway they are smashed into their targets, or are used for further acceleration in the electron–positron colliders. (SLAC, SPL)

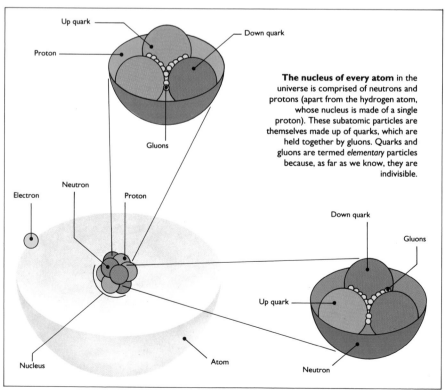

The nucleus of every atom in the universe is comprised of neutrons and protons (apart from the hydrogen atom, whose nucleus is made of a single proton). These subatomic particles are themselves made up of quarks, which are held together by gluons. Quarks and gluons are termed *elementary* particles because, as far as we know, they are indivisible.

THE HIERARCHY OF PARTICLES

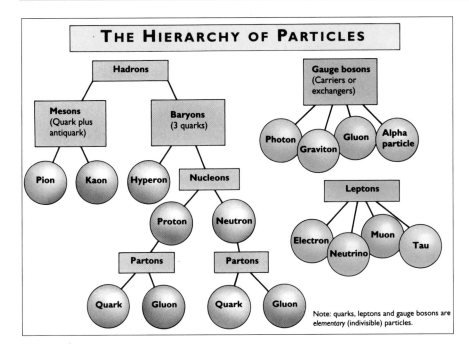

Note: quarks, leptons and gauge bosons are *elementary* (indivisible) particles.

A GLOSSARY OF SUBATOMIC PARTICLES

Alpha particle: a helium nucleus, containing two protons and two neutrons. It is emitted during some radioactive changes.

Antiparticle: a particle with the same mass as a certain other particle, but with opposite properties such as charge or colour.

Antiquark: the corresponding antiparticle of any QUARK.

Baryon: one of the class of particles that includes PROTONS, NEUTRONS and HYPERONS (particles heavier than protons). A particle involved in strong interactions.

Boson: a force-carrying particle that bears one of the four fundamental forces of nature (⇨ p. 112). A particle that does not conform to the Pauli exclusion principle (⇨ p. 128). The bosons are comprised of GRAVITONS (which carry the force of gravity), PHOTONS (which carry electromagnetism), GLUONS (which carry the strong nuclear forces), and WEAK BOSONS (which are responsible for radioactive decay). ALPHA PARTICLES and all atomic nuclei with an even mass number are also bosons.

Electron: a particle of small mass and negative charge (⇨ p. 90).

Gluon: a boson that mediates the strong interaction between quarks and quarks, and between antiquarks and antiquarks.

Graviton: a theoretical quantum (packet) of gravitational energy. A particle of zero charge and rest mass*, and spin** of 2.

Hadron: the class of baryons and mesons. A hadron is an elementary particle that interacts strongly with other particles. All hadrons are colourless, consisting of one red, one blue and one green quark, or one quark and its complementary-coloured quark. PHOTONS and LEPTONS are excluded from the class of hadrons.

Hyperon: a particle of mass equal to or greater than that of the PROTON. Hyperons may have masses as great as 2,584 times that of the ELECTRON.

Kaon: a meson having a positive or negative charge and a rest mass 996 times that of an ELECTRON, or no charge and a rest mass 964 times that of an electron.

Lepton: a fundamental particle that does not interact strongly with other particles. The class of leptons includes the ELECTRON, the negative MUON and the NEUTRINO.

Meson: a HADRON with a mass intermediate between those of ELECTRONS and NUCLEONS. Mesons may have negative, positive or zero charge. They include PIONS and KAONS.

Muon: a fundamental particle with a negative charge, a rest mass equivalent to 106 MeV (million electronvolts), and a very short half-life (about 2 millionths of a second), after which it becomes an ELECTRON.

Neutrino: a LEPTON with zero charge and zero mass. Neutrinos have very weak interactions with matter.

Neutron: one of the two readily recognizable constituents of the atomic nucleus (⇨ p. 108). An uncharged particle with a mass 1,838.6 times that of an ELECTRON.

Nucleon: one of the particles constituting the nucleus of an atom. A PROTON or a NEUTRON.

Parton: a generic term for any particle (QUARK or GLUON) inside a NUCLEON.

Photon: a quantum of electromagnetic radiation (⇨ p. 84).

Pion: a MESON having a positive or negative charge and a rest mass of 273 times that of an ELECTRON, or no charge and a rest mass 264 times that of an electron.

Proton: one of the two recognizable constituents of the atomic nucleus. A particle of mass 1,836.1 times that of the ELECTRON, and of equal but positive charge.

Quark: a fundamental particle that combines with others of its kind to form the constituents of HADRONS. A BARYON consists of three quarks, and a MESON consists of a quark and an ANTIQUARK. Quarks have never been observed in isolation.

* Rest mass is the mass of an object that is still, relative to an observer.

** Spin is the intrinsic *angular momentum* (mass times circular motion about its own axis) of an atomic nucleus or elementary particle (not the angular momentum resulting from its motion about an external axis).

There are six flavours – up, down, strange, charm, bottom (or beauty) and top (or truth). Each flavour can come in one of three colours – red, blue or green. The most obvious properties of a quark are the strength of its electric charge and whether that charge is positive or negative (⇨ box).

The electron has one unit of negative charge; the proton has one unit of positive charge, and the neutron has no charge. A proton consists of two up quarks and one down quark, making a total charge of +1. A neutron consists of one up quark and two down quarks making a total charge of zero. Apart from top, the other flavours of quark can be produced 'artificially' in particle accelerators. Top quark has probably never appeared since the big bang (⇨ p. 126), but the search for it nevertheless continues.

When protons or neutrons are bombarded in high-energy accelerators, new quarks are created. But these never appear as individuals because they are immediately attracted to other quarks by very strong forces, to form new mesons, protons and neutrons.

Quantum chromodynamics and the colour of quarks

Only certain combinations of quarks apparently occur in nature – three for nucleons and a quark–antiquark combination for mesons (⇨ above). No other combinations of quarks have ever been found. Quantum theory (⇨ p. 40) requires that quarks of the same flavour in the same hadron must be different. Three differences are required, and are designated 'colours', red, blue and green.

Hadrons can then be explained as being combinations of quarks that produce no colour. This can occur, by analogy with white light, when all three (primary) colours are present (⇨ p. 76); or it can occur when a hadron consists of a quark whose colour is cancelled by the simultaneous presence of the corresponding antiquark. Quantum chromodynamics (from the Greek *khroma,* meaning 'colour', is the study of the forces between quarks that are determined by their colours. It looks at how quarks combine in such ways that colour is never apparent in the final product. (Quantum chromodynamics is analogous to its sister theory, quantum electrodynamics (⇨ below), which is concerned with the way in which the electromagnetic force between particles results from their electric charge.) The force between coloured quarks is related to the exchange of gluons (⇨ above), which provide the very strong forces that bind quarks together. To make matters more complicated, gluons themselves have colour. Quantum chromodynamics has to explain how the strong forces between gluons increase with distance, so that quarks that are close together can move about freely, but those separated by distances of the order of the diameter of a proton cannot separate. The theory has, so far, been able to explain quark freedom, but not how attractive forces increase with distance.

Quantum electrodynamics views a vacuum not as literal nothingness, but as an ocean of virtual electron–positron pairs. These exist only momentarily and then annihilate one another since they are of opposite charge. They bring about a kind of polarization of the vacuum that has a screening effect on normal electronic charges, diminishing their effect unless they are very close together. In quantum chromodynamics interest is concentrated on the effect on quark colour charges of the analogous ocean of quark–antiquark pairs in the vacuum. The theory shows that this effect is the opposite of that in quantum electrodynamics. The effective strength of the colour charges actually decreases as they come closer together.

Fundamental Forces

Four fundamental forces are currently known to science. Between them, they are believed to determine everything that happens in the universe. They are gravity, electromagnetism, the strong nuclear force and the weak nuclear force.

The history of science has been the history of generalization – the attempt to explain as much as possible with the smallest number of theories. This is the principle known as Ockham's razor (which states that, in explaining a particular thing, one should not unnecessarily amplify assumptions made). Every major fundamental breakthrough in science has been a simplification; indeed particle physicists are, today, contemplating the possibility that a theory may evolve that will explain everything in the universe. The fundamental forces are an important component of such a theory.

The concept of a force (⇨ p. 28) is highly unifying for science. When Isaac Newton formulated his laws of motion and clarified what was meant by mechanical force, a great deal of confusion was at last cleared up. Newton showed that a force is an entity that changes the state of motion of a body. It is not, as Aristotle (⇨ p. 8) had believed, something that keeps a body in motion. He explained the concept of gravitation (⇨ p. 30) but had nothing to say about the other forces with which science has since become familiar. Michael Faraday and James Clerk Maxwell (⇨ pp. 88–91) went on to unify electricity and magnetism, and Maxwell and Heinrich Hertz unified electromagnetism and light (⇨ p. 84). Today, scientists know that the universe is made from only a few different sorts of elementary subatomic particle (⇨ pp. 108–11), and that the interaction between these involves other fundamental forces. The discovery of these fundamental forces of nature has been one of the most powerfully unifying influences in the whole history of science.

Gravity

Gravity (⇨ p. 30) is the weakest of all the forces, but is a property of anything that has mass. It is an attractive force, and exists between all bodies. The greater the mass, the greater the gravitational force. A considerable quantity of mass is needed for the gravitational force to become apparent in practical terms, however. We cannot readily perceive, for instance, the mutual gravitational attraction between two apples, although such attraction does exist. Our experience of gravity is almost exclusively that of the gravitational pull of the Earth. Because the Earth is of such enormous mass compared with any body encountered by it (with the exception of the Sun), the pull of the Earth on such a body is much greater than the pull of the body on the Earth. So, in practice, unsupported bodies always move (fall) towards the centre of the Earth under the force of the Earth's gravitational field.

The force of gravity between two bodies is proportional to the product of their masses, and falls off in proportion to the square of the distance between them – this is the inverse square law. For this reason gravity rapidly lessens with distance, but it extends to the limits of the universe and affects everything in it.

Electromagnetism

Electromagnetism is a much stronger force than gravity (⇨ above) but has one basic difference. Where gravity is an exclusively attractive force, electromagnetism, on the other hand, involves electric charges that can be either attractive or repulsive (⇨ p. 88). Identical, or like, charges (both negative or both positive) repel one other; unlike charges attract each other. Two magnetic north poles repel each other; a north pole will attract a south pole, and vice versa.

Every north pole has a corresponding south pole. However often a bar magnet is cut into pieces, each piece will, in its turn, have a north pole and a south pole. Similarly, every negative charge is associated with a nearby positive charge. The effect of this polarity is to limit, by neutralization, the range of electromagnetic forces. Electromagnetism also conforms to the inverse square law (⇨ above).

The electromagnetic force keeps atomic electrons in place (⇨ p. 108) and thus determines the chemical properties of matter (⇨ pp. 156–9). The nuclei of atoms are positively charged; the peripheral electrons are negatively charged and are retained in position by mutual attraction. Because the number of electrons is the same as the number of positively charged protons in the nucleus, and because the charge on an electron is of the same magnitude, although of opposite sign, as the charge on the proton, atoms are thus electrically neutral.

Individual atoms link together by means of the electromagnetic forces. The way different combinations of atoms form, and the properties of the resulting new materials, are the study of the discipline of chemistry (⇨ chapter 8). All chemistry, therefore, including biochemistry (which is the study of the basis of life), depends on electromagnetism.

The electromagnetic attraction between atoms is very finely balanced. At close range it must be repulsive to avoid matter becoming densely compacted. Further out it must be attractive in order to hold atoms together, but not so strongly attractive that they cannot separate completely at boiling point (as in gases), or in chemical reactions with other sorts of atoms. Although atoms are mainly made up of empty space, matter (which is, of course, composed of atoms) seems solid to us because of the electromagnetic forces at work. When we strike a heavy object, the object 'strikes' back at us (since for every action there is an equal and opposite reaction; ⇨ p. 28) because of the same electromagnetic forces. Even the phenomenon of friction (⇨ p. 32)

James Clerk Maxwell (1831–79), Scottish physicist who made major contributions to the theory of electromagnetism, one of the four fundamental forces. (AR) depends on electromagnetic attraction between atoms to bring about the 'cold welds' between surfaces in contact.

So that they can fully understand how electromagnetic forces operate between subatomic particles, scientists must use mathematical techniques (involving relativity and quantum mechanics) that are not necessary in the everyday world. Because electrons move at very high speeds, approaching that of light, they are not bound by the laws of Newtonian mechanics (⇨ pp. 26–9) and the special theory of relativity (⇨ p. 38) applies. Moreover, the physical laws that govern the behaviour of quantities of matter are statistical and do not apply to the behaviour of individual particles. To deal with the latter it is necessary to use quantum mechanics (⇨ p. 40). Quantum-mechanical methods are indeed applied to electromagnetism in the theory of *quantum electrodynamics*, where the electromagnetic-field force is perceived as being carried by entities called *virtual photons*, which move between the interacting particles. (Unlike photons proper, virtual photons do not exist independently. They also exist only briefly as they move between particles. Electric charges constantly emit and absorb virtual photons.) Repulsion, for instance, occurs when virtual photons from each particle move over to the other and are absorbed.

The strong nuclear force

The only charged particles in the nucleus of the atom are the protons, which carry a positive charge, and are all very close together in the nucleus. If there did not exist some very powerful attractive force, therefore, the nuclei of atoms could not exist as such. The force that prevents the explosive repulsion of the like charges on the protons must be stronger than that repulsive force. It must also operate only over a very short range, because it cannot have an influence outside the nucleus. It is, in fact, about one hundred times as strong as the repulsive force between protons, and is called the *strong nuclear force*. This force does not depend on charge because it binds together the uncharged neutrons in the nucleus as well as the protons. The strong force favours the binding together of pairs of protons and neutrons, and pairs of pairs. (The alpha particle (⇨ p. 110), consisting of a pair of protons and a pair of neutrons, is an exceptionally stable nuclear structure.)

Scientists began to understand the true nature of the strong force when it was proposed, first theoretically, then with backup from high-energy collision experiments, that the nuclear particles – protons and neutrons – were, in fact, made up of even more fundamental particles called quarks. Whereas quantum electrodynamic theory involves the exchange of virtual photons (⇨ above), an analogous process is believed to occur between quarks, the corresponding particles being known as gluons. Photons do not have a charge and do not interact with

each other. Like photons, gluons have no mass. They do, however, in common with quarks, have a kind of charge, known arbitrarily as colour. This charge causes quarks to have a very strong affinity for each other. Colour charges lead to interaction between the eight different kinds of gluon. They also lead to interactions between quarks and gluons. These interactions are described by the theory of *quantum chromodynamics*, and result in effects quite different from electromagnetic interactions. Apparently, quarks can never be pulled out of the proton or other particle because the further they are pulled apart the stronger the attraction between them becomes.

The weak nuclear force

The weak force can change the charge on a nuclear particle, as when a neutron is changed to a proton. Such a change can alter the stability of the nucleus and allow it to manifest radioactivity, a process of spontaneous change (⇨ p. 160).

Radioactivity is a feature of atoms whose nuclei contain more neutrons than protons. During the radioactive process a neutron, which we can think of as a proton and an electron stuck together, might, for instance, 'turn into' a proton and give off a high-speed electron (a *beta

particle). This will change the atom to that of another *element* (substance made of only one sort of atom), and it will have a different atomic number and different chemical properties (⇨ pp. 156–9). Alternatively, the nucleus may eject two protons and two neutrons (which together form a helium nucleus, also called an alpha particle) and, again, change into another element. Radioactivity involves a breakdown of the *weak nuclear force*, which is mediated by the exchange between *nucleons* (particles present in the nucleus, that is, protons or neutrons) of weak-force particles. These have three forms; two are charged, and are known as W^- and W^+. The third is uncharged and is called Z^0. The W and Z particles are massive – some 100 times that of the proton or neutron that ejects them. This seeming paradox is possible because the mass-energy of a particle is subject to quantum uncertainty (that is, the more we can know about the mass, the less we can measure the energy, and vice versa) and, over a very short period of time, this uncertainty as to mass may be considerable, so that estimates of it can be surprising. The exchange of weak-force particles must occur very quickly (before the universe 'notices' the anomaly).

	GRAVITY	ELECTROMAGNETISM	STRONG NUCLEAR FORCE	WEAK NUCLEAR FORCE
Particles affected	All	Charged particles	Quarks	Leptons and quarks
Range of force	0–infinity	0–infinity	10^{-15} m	10^{-17} m
Relative strength	10^{-40}	10^{-2}	1	10^{-5}
Particles exchanged in operation of force	Gravitons	Photons	Gluons	W and Z particles
Force's effect	Mutually attracts all the bodies in the universe	Sets the structure of atoms and molecules	Maintains bonds between quarks	Determines the stability of atomic nuclei

Particle Physics in Action

Particle physics is concerned with the elucidation and simplification of the ultimate laws of nature. Scientists engaged in research in this field think that it is likely to provide truths that will illuminate and may even revolutionize all science.

It is ironic that research into the smallest particles in the universe should involve the use of the largest items of equipment in all science. Particle accelerators – the devices used to probe for the ultimate secrets of nature – are not only large but are also enormously expensive. Indeed, some governments have come seriously to consider whether the costs involved can be justified.

The development of particle accelerators

Nearly all the important experimental advances in particle physics made since about the 1920s have involved the use of particle accelerators. These provide beams of charged particles, such as electrons, protons or ions (⇨ pp. 88–91 and 108–11), which are accelerated to high speed/energy. (In the context of particle physics the terms 'energy' and 'speed' are synonymous.) Electrons carry a negative charge and are attracted towards anything that has a positive charge (because unlike charges attract). The higher the positive voltage with respect to the source of electrons (the cathode), the more powerfully the electrons are accelerated, and the higher their energy. For this reason, the energy of such moving electrons is designated in *electron volts*. An electron volt is the energy developed by an electron accelerated across an electric field that has a potential of 1 volt. If protons, which carry a positive charge, are being accelerated, they must be attracted by a negative potential.

The need for such accelerations for research into the nature of subatomic particles became obvious early in the 20th century. In 1928 the English physicists John Cockcroft (1897–1967) and Ernest Walton (1903–) developed a voltage multiplier that achieved a voltage of 400,000 volts. With this device they succeeded, in 1932, in accelerating protons to a sufficient energy to break up the nuclei of lithium atoms. This famous experiment, which won them the Nobel Prize for physics in 1951, ushered in the nuclear age and initiated the era of the particle accelerator.

Around this time, the American physicist Robert Van de Graaff (1901–67) developed a remarkable electrostatic voltage generator consisting of a hollow metal sphere on top of an insulating column, in which charges accumulated by means of a high-speed moving belt that separated electrons from protons and deposited them at opposite ends of the equipment. Van de Graaff achieved a potential of 8,000,000 volts, and later versions, using chlorofluorocarbons (CFCs) or nitrogen under high pressure, reached 14,000,000 volts. Energies of such orders are designated in million electron volts (MeV). Although the Van de Graaff generator, with its massive, lightning-like flashes, was widely publicized as an 'atom smasher', there are inherent limitations to the voltages that can be achieved by this type of machine. Improved ways of accelerating particles were needed, and, in 1931, the *linear accelerator* was invented. The idea behind this device is that the particles are accelerated in a series of stages, each stage contributing a further push or pull to the moving particles. They pass through a succession of metal tubes on which carefully timed voltages are applied (⇨ illustration). Alternating voltages are

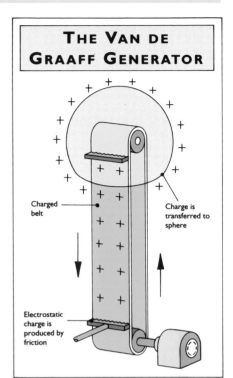

Charged belt

Charge is transferred to sphere

Electrostatic charge is produced by friction

used so that particles approaching a particular electrode are attracted and those just passing it are repelled. (The frequency of the alternating voltage is chosen in relation to the speed of the particles, so that it has gone positive as a negative particle is approaching, and has gone negative as that particle has just passed. The particle thus gets a pull and then a push.)

The cyclotron and after

A major advance during the 1930s was the idea of the cyclotron, proposed by the American physicist Ernest Orlando Lawrence (1901–58). In this design, the path of the particles is bent into a spiral by two powerful D-shaped electromagnets, energized by alternating currents that produce fields alternately pushing and pulling. As the particles speed up, their path swings outwards until they eventually leave the machine in a straight line. The idea of the cyclotron quickly caught on and ever-larger versions were subsequently built.

Lawrence's original model was only about a foot in diameter, but achieved energies of over a million electron volts (1 MeV). But by 1939 a 5-foot-diameter cyclotron had been built at the University of California that reached 20 MeV. This machine was almost too successful. Particles accelerated by it began to show so much mass increase as

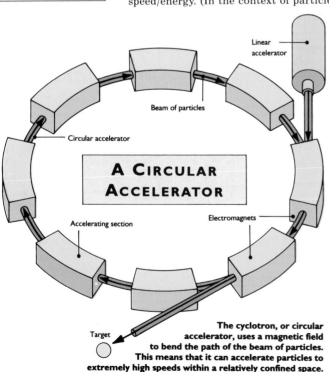

A CIRCULAR ACCELERATOR

Linear accelerator

Beam of particles

Circular accelerator

Accelerating section

Electromagnets

Target

The cyclotron, or circular accelerator, uses a magnetic field to bend the path of the beam of particles. This means that it can accelerate particles to extremely high speeds within a relatively confined space.

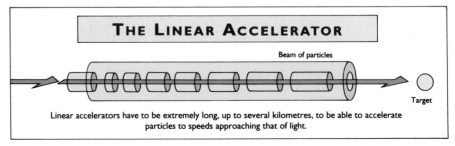

THE LINEAR ACCELERATOR

Beam of particles

Target

Linear accelerators have to be extremely long, up to several kilometres, to be able to accelerate particles to speeds approaching that of light.

a consequence of their speed (more than 90 per cent of the speed of light; ⇨ p. 38) that they lagged behind and fell out of synchronization with the alternating (pushing and pulling) field. This effect was later overcome by a modified cyclotron called the synchrocyclotron, which synchronized the supply frequency with the mass increase. Over the years such machines continued to be built in ever-increasing size, and energies of 200, 400, 700 and 800 MeV were achieved.

To achieve even higher energies, however, a new device was needed. This was the *synchrotron*, and takes the form of an enormous, evacuated, circular pipe, the *accelerating ring*, in which particles move under the influence of electromagnets placed around it. As the particles speed up, the magnetic field is increased and the particles repeatedly follow the same trajectory. A typical synchrotron at the Fermi National Accelerator Laboratory (Fermilab) in Batavia, Illinois, USA, has a ring 2 km (1.2 mi) in diameter and can accelerate protons up to 1,000 giga electronvolts (1,000,000,000,000 eV) energy. Relativistic effects apply a law of diminishing returns: the nearer we get to the speed of light the harder it becomes to get any faster because of the progressive increase in mass. Thus the same amount of energy, when applied, produces less and less effect. Some of the more pessimistic scientists have thought that this is nature's way of concealing her final secrets.

Particle colliders

Despite the limitations of the synchrotron, there was, nevertheless, a way forward. If particles are accelerated in one direction and the respective antiparticles are accelerated in the opposite direction, a collision between the two beams will make all the beam energy available to work its effect on the particles in the beam.

This is the principle of the currently most sophisticated tools available to particle physicists. The storage-ring facility at the Stanford Linear Accelerator Center (SLAC) in California, USA, is such an installation, and was used to prove that protons are made up of constituent parts (⇨ p. 110) and support the quark theory. In 1983 Fermilab completed its Tevatron – a 6.3 km (3.9 mi) circular device that uses superconducting magnets (⇨ pp. 88 and 96), and is cooled by liquid helium, to produce a powerful field to accelerate protons in one direction and antiprotons in the other. The system's massive collider detector, which measures the energy of the particles, weighs about 5,000 tons. The Tevatron can achieve energies of 1.8 tera (million million) electronvolts.

In 1989 CERN (⇨ p. 110) completed its Large Electron–Positron (LEP) Collider, a massive device 26.7 km (16.6 mi) in

circumference, in which four gigantic detectors, Aleph, Delphi, L3 and Opal, record the events associated with the 100 billion electron-volt collisions that take place. CERN is now considering the construction of a facility known as the Large Hadron Collider (LHC), using an existing tunnel under the Jura mountains near Geneva, Switzerland. An even more ambitious project was started in 1989 in America. This was the Superconducting Super Collider, planned to occupy an oval tunnel 85 km (53 mi) long, south of Dallas, Texas. It was planned that, in this tunnel, thousands of superconducting electromagnets would accelerate two beams of protons in opposite directions around the ring to an energy twenty times that of the best existing particle accelerators – up to 20–40 TeV. At collision points, detectors weighing up to tens of thousands of tons were to detect what happens during the collisions. However, in 1993, after $2 billion of the estimated $11 billion budget was spent, and 16 km (10 mi) of tunnel dug, the project was terminated after a decision by the US House of Representatives to reallocate resources. And it is by no means certain that even the cheaper LHC project will go ahead.

The Tevatron particle accelerator at the Fermi National Accelerator Laboratory (Fermilab), Illinois, USA. Two kilometres in diameter, it contains two accelerators, one above the other. The top one uses ordinary magnets and accelerates protons to 150 GeV (giga electronvolts). It then passes them to the lower accelerator, which speeds them up to 1,000 GeV using superconducting magnets. (David Parker, SPL)

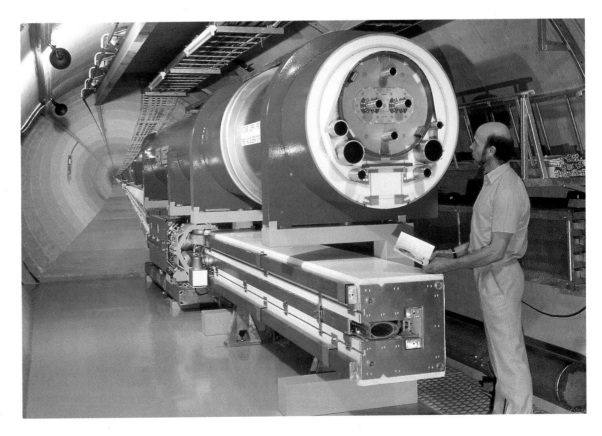

Nuclear Physics in Action

Atoms consist of dense nuclei (which account for almost all the atom's mass) and a 'cloud' of peripheral, orbiting electrons. Nearly all the properties of elements – their chemical reactions, strength, colour and density – depend on these electrons. But nearly all the energy in atoms resides in their nuclei. Since the beginning of the 20th century it has been the dream of scientists to make the energy locked up in the nuclei of atoms safely available for the use of humankind.

Atomic nuclei are unaffected by chemical reactions, however violent. Such reactions – even explosions – merely involve the electrons, and the amount of energy taken up or released is comparatively small. Even so, the energy released by the breakdown of complex chemical substances, such as wood or coal, has, until the early decades of the 20th century, been the only portable source of energy readily available for our use. Atomic nuclei were artificially disrupted for the first time in 1932 when the British nuclear physicist Sir John Douglas Cockcroft (1897–1967) accelerated protons and fired them at a target of

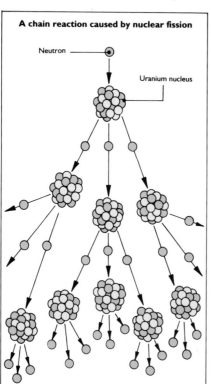

A chain reaction caused by nuclear fission

Neutron

Uranium nucleus

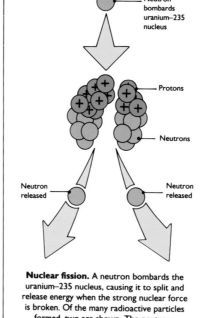

Neutron bombards uranium–235 nucleus

Protons

Neutrons

Neutron released

Neutron released

Nuclear fission. A neutron bombards the uranium–235 nucleus, causing it to split and release energy when the strong nuclear force is broken. Of the many radioactive particles formed, two are shown. The neutrons released may bombard and split other nuclei – further fission can take place. A *chain reaction* will be set up if the mass of uranium–235 is above a certain level – the *critical mass*.

lithium, releasing alpha particles (helium nuclei; ⇨ pp. 112–15). Although he did not know it, Cockcroft had transmuted lithium into helium. Later, he suggested to another famous New Zealand-born British physicist, Ernest Rutherford (1871–1937), that atomic nuclear breakup might prove to be a new source of energy. Rutherford, however, was unimpressed by this and described the idea as 'all moonshine'. Needless to say, he was wrong.

Nuclear fission

Only six years later, in 1938, the German physical chemist Otto Hahn (1879–1968), following up some earlier work by the Italian-born physicist Enrico Fermi (1901–54), discovered that when uranium was bombarded with neutrons the much lighter element barium was produced. Hahn wrote to his former colleague, the Austrian nuclear physicist Lise Meitner (1878–1968), then a refugee from the Nazis in Stockholm. Over Christmas she was visited by her nephew, the Austrian-born British nuclear physicist Otto Frisch (1904–79), and passed on the news to him. Gradually it became clear to them that the uranium nucleus had actually elongated and split into parts – the process called *nuclear fission*. The number of protons in each of these parts would determine what the newly produced element was. At the same time, because heavy elements like uranium had proportionately more neutrons in their nuclei than lighter elements, uranium fission would result in the release of neutrons. This raised the possibility that these neutrons could break up other uranium atoms and that a chain reaction could occur.

Frisch realized that, again, because of the higher proportion of neutrons present, the nuclei of heavy elements like uranium would be much easier to split than those of lighter elements, and worked out that the rare uranium isotope (⇨ box) ^{235}U (which is very good at taking in neutrons) would more readily establish a chain reaction than the more common ^{238}U. He and Lise Meitner also appreciated that the energy released would be enormous, and that some matter would be converted entirely into energy (in accordance with Einstein's famous equation, $E = mc^2$; ⇨ p. 38).

It was also apparent that if enough ^{235}U could be accumulated, an atomic bomb could be made. At the same time, it seemed likely that such a chain reaction could be moderated by absorbing neutrons in various ways. The first atomic reactor – the *atomic pile* – was built in a squash court at the University of Chicago under the direction of Enrico Fermi in December 1942. Blocks of pure uranium and graphite were built up into a pile, along with cadmium rods, which were used to absorb neutrons. When these rods were slowly withdrawn the pile started to heat up. Thus the first self-sustaining nuclear reactor had been achieved.

The subsequent development of atomic fission reactors involved comparatively little additional science but a great deal of new technology. Modern atomic reactors (⇨ p. 94) take many different design forms but all use, as fuel, either natural uranium or uranium enriched by the addition of ^{235}U. Breeder reactors produce more fissionable fuel, particularly the highly dangerous plutonium, than they consume.

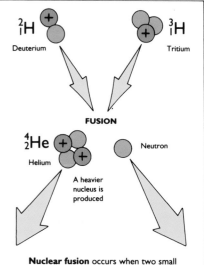

$^{2}_{1}$H   Deuterium

$^{3}_{1}$H   Tritium

FUSION

$^{4}_{2}$He   Helium

Neutron

A heavier nucleus is produced

Nuclear fusion occurs when two small nuclei collide and combine, breaking the weak nuclear force and releasing energy. The reaction shown involves nuclei of deuterium and tritium (isotopes of hydrogen) combining to produce helium (a waste product), a neutron, and released energy. This type of reaction releases considerably more energy than a fission process for a given mass of material. However, the neutrons released have to be contained or controlled in some way.

Nuclear fusion

If the nuclei of light atoms such as hydrogen (one proton) or hydrogen's isotopes deuterium (one proton and one neutron) or tritium (one proton, two neutrons) can be fused together, a heavier element is formed. Before this can happen, the energy bonds holding the neutrons and protons together (⇨ p. 112) must be broken. New bonds are then formed as these particles combine in larger numbers to create the heavier element. The mass of the new nucleus, however, is slightly less than the mass of the nucleons (⇨ p. 110) that have fused, and this mass deficit is converted into energy. Four hydrogen atoms can, for instance, fuse to form a single helium atom. In so doing, two of the protons are converted (by means of the addition of electrons) into neutrons (the helium nucleus consists of two protons and two neutrons). This fusion reaction is what powers the Sun and other stars – which consist largely of hydrogen and helium; indeed the element helium was first detected in the spectrum of the Sun (hence its name, from the Greek *helios*, 'sun'; ⇨ p. 80). In the process of fusion of hydrogen to form helium, nearly 1 per cent of the hydrogen is converted into energy. This represents a huge amount of energy. Since these facts have been known many scientists have dreamt of solving the problem of controlled nuclear fusion. The advantages of nuclear fusion over nuclear fission are overwhelming; fusion is a 'clean' process in which neither the fuel nor the product is dangerous or environmentally damaging. The fuels are cheap, and unlimited quantities are readily available. Deuterium, for instance, is present in water in a ratio with hydrogen of about 1 in 7,000. *Heavy water* (or deuterium oxide – water containing deuterium instead of hydrogen) can be extracted at only a nominal cost. Fusion has already been repeatedly brought about in an uncontrolled manner in hydrogen bombs, in which

deuterium and tritium are fused to produce a helium nucleus. The problems of controlled fusion are, however, enormous. Extremely high temperatures (⇨ box on cold fusion) are needed to provide the energy to overcome the repulsive force (⇨ p. 112) of the like-charged protons. Normal containers cannot tolerate such temperatures, so powerful magnetic fields must be used to confine the ingredients to a certain zone – a kind of magnetic container – in which the reaction can occur. The most promising type of fusion reactor developed so far is the *Tokamak reactor*. This is a doughnut-shaped (*toroidal*) device surrounded by large coils of superconducting material (to produce the magnetic field) and other coils (to heat the contents). At very high temperatures, the molecules in gases lose their electrons and the gas becomes a

plasma. This can conduct heating currents of electricity induced into it by the coils. In some designs the plasma is heated by the injection of high-energy neutral particles or radio waves.

Other possible fusion devices include those that use 10 or more radially-arranged powerful lasers to irradiate and implode a pellet containing deuterium, and those that use pulsed beams of high-energy particles in a similar manner. Critics of experimental fusion devices point out that not all types of proposed reactor are 'clean'. Deuterium–tritium reactors – currently favoured because of their high-power output and easier ignition – would produce large numbers of high-energy neutrons, which would render the machine radioactive. Proponents claim that this difficulty could, however be overcome.

THE TOKAMAK REACTOR

Support structure holding coolant for magnets

Access and maintenance entrances

Central transformer magnet induces an electric current in the plasma

Plasma chamber

Vertical-field magnet keeps plasma centred

Access to plasma chamber

Toroidal-field magnet produces the magnetic 'sleeve' for the plasma

Torus

A large current flows through the plasma, heating it and producing a magnetic field, which confines the plasma to the centre of the torus. Under high pressures and temperatures, fusion takes place within the plasma.

Plasma

The tokamak principle

ISOTOPES

The chemical and many of the physical properties of an element are determined by the number of electrons in the atom. This, in turn is determined by the number of protons in the nucleus. However readily peripheral electrons can be displaced, their number will always tend to return to a number equal to that of the number of nuclear protons. Opposite charges attract each other and each proton has a positive charge equal to the negative charge on an electron.

Most of the lighter elements have neutrons in the nucleus equal to, or slightly greater in number than, the number of protons. The chemical properties of atoms are not affected by the number of neutrons, so apparently identical substances may exist, all with the same number of protons but with varying

numbers of neutrons. These elements are called isotopes, from the Greek *iso* ('equal') and *topos* ('place'). Although they occupy the same place in the periodic table of chemical elements (⇨ p. 158), the physical properties of isotopes do differ, especially with regard to the stability of the nuclei. Some combinations of protons and neutrons are permanently stable; others decay spontaneously, releasing energy in the process, and changing into other elements. Such unstable isotopes are said to be *radioactive* (⇨ p. 160).

Many seemingly pure substances consist of a mixture of isotopes of the same element. Because these isotopes are chemically identical, they are very difficult to separate and physical methods, taking advantage of the slight differences in mass, are needed.

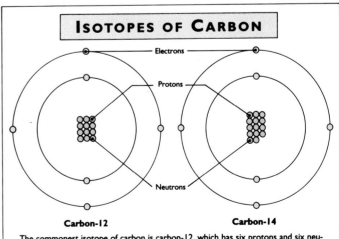

ISOTOPES OF CARBON

Electrons

Protons

Neutrons

Carbon-12

Carbon-14

The commonest isotope of carbon is carbon-12, which has six protons and six neutrons. Carbon-14, however, has two extra neutrons in its nucleus, making it radioactive. Isotopes that are radioactive are called *radioisotopes*.

OUR EARTH,
OUR COSMOS

Cosmology – Understanding the Universe

Cosmology – the study of the universe – is approached in different ways by different people. A philosopher or theologian concentrates mainly on the speculative study of the meaning of the universe; the science historian on the history of the development of cosmological ideas. To the astronomer, cosmology is a study of the ascertainable structure of the universe while, to the astrophysicist, it is centred on the theories concerning the origins and evolution of the universe. A professional cosmologist has to combine a study of mathematics and physics with something taken from each of these different disciplines.

The ideas were, of course, anthropomorphic (based on human experience) and the emotions and motivation attributed to spirits were the same as those attributed to people. The Sun, Moon and stars, like most things on Earth, were thought to be the abode of spirits, and all natural phenomena were considered to be the result of the malignity or goodwill of these spirits.

In *The Golden Bough* (1890), the Scottish anthropologist James Frazer (1854–1941) describes how, as knowledge of the world grew, magic gradually evolved into myth and religion, 'which explains the succession of natural phenomena as regulated by will, passion, or caprice of the spiritual beings like man in kind, though vastly superior to him in power'. Early writings are full of accounts of various creation myths.

Creation myths

Creation myths are common to all cultures but remarkable in the diversity of their detail. The earliest known are those of the Sumerians. Their conception was of a beginning in an 'encircling watery abyss' acted on by the blind force of Tiamat to produce the gods and goddesses that created the universe. The ancient Egyptian myths relate that, living in this watery abyss, was the formless spirit, Nun, which carried within it the source of all existence, Atum. It was Atum who created the gods, goddesses and the universe. The Indian myths, although containing an immensely complicated history of deities, are more sophisticated in acknowledging that the ultimate origin must remain unknown. The *Rig Veda* asks: 'Who can speak of the origins of creation? Did he who controls this world make it? Does he know?' Later documents, commenting on the beginning, state: 'All was darkness, without form, beyond reason and perception, like sleep.' From this arose the all-creating Lord. Chinese ideas were complex and subtle and incorporated the concept that creation was based on earth, air, fire and water – an idea later adopted by the Greeks. They also incorporated the principle of the opposing but complementary qualities of Yin and Yang. The Greeks conceived of four primordial entities – the void (Chaos), the Earth (Gaia), the lower world (Tartarus) and love (Eros). These gave rise to the gods, including Uranus, the sky god. In the Christian tradition, creation, as recounted in the book of Genesis, was the work of a single God.

All early cosmological ideas were anthropocentric; humankind was at the centre of the universe. Aristotle's cosmology of the 4th century BC placed the Earth at the middle of the universe; and this idea, promulgated by Ptolemy, persisted until the beginning of the 16th century – the time of Copernicus.

The Copernican revolution

The first notably scientific attempt at a cosmology was that of the 2nd-century Greek astronomer Claudius Ptolemaeus, known as Ptolemy (AD 90–168). Ptolemy's great compendium of astronomy contained a star map and a treatise on the fixed stars. Most of the astronomy in this book was taken from the prior work of the 2nd-century BC Greek astronomer Hipparchus. Ptolemy assumed that the Earth was the centre of the universe and that the Sun and stars revolved round it. Surrounding the Earth were eight concentric transparent spheres. Each of the first seven spheres carried a single heavenly body – the Moon, Sun and five planets – while the eighth carried all the fixed stars. Beyond were the heavens – the abode of the blessed. Elaborate explanations were given to account for the apparent irregularity of the movement of the planets.

Ptolemy's book was the sole scientific authority on astronomy until his beliefs were challenged by the work of the great Polish astronomer Nicolas Copernik (1473–1543), whose name was Latinized to Copernicus according to the prevailing fashion. Copernicus was the founder of modern astronomy. By careful observation he was able to compile accurate tables of the movement of the planets. These, together with his painstaking calculations, clearly indicated that the planets, including the Earth, rotated around the Sun. This was contrary to the Ptolemaic orthodoxy. Copernicus incorporated his life's work into the book *De revolutionibus orbitum caelestium* ('On the Revolution of the Celestial Spheres'), completed in 1530 and published just before his death in 1543. A printed copy was put into his hands as he lay on his deathbed.

Ptolemy's geocentric (Earth-centred) system of the Sun and planets. From Andreas Cellarius, *Harmonia macrocosmica* (1708). (AR)

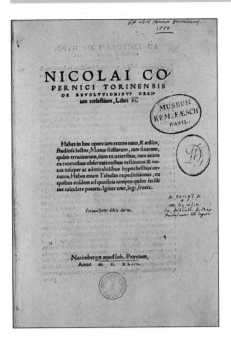

Title page of Copernicus's *De revolutionibus orbitum caelestium* (1543). (AR)

Copernicus's demonstration that the Earth was a planet moving round the Sun seemed to most people of the time at best foolish and perverse, and at worst heretical and damnable. The Earth was manifestly flat and the Sun visibly moved round it. Where, in Copernicus's scheme, was Heaven? Ironically, Copernicus, who was an ecclesiastic, had dedicated the book to the Pope and a cardinal had met the cost of printing it. At the time, few could understand its learned explanations. When its import finally became apparent, the Church hurled anathemas at its author and at any who believed him. Had he lived, he might well have been burned at the stake, as were others who insisted that he was right. The Copernican cosmology was a revolution not only in science but also in human thought and it was not until the 18th century that it was fully assimilated.

Modern theories of cosmology

Modern cosmology is largely concerned with the problem of the origin of the universe. It is only in the 20th century that cosmological theory advanced sufficiently beyond the realm of vague speculation to provide anything approaching a plausible account.

Today, cosmologists are no longer the fanciful dreamers of the past but are hard-headed scientists whose hypotheses are made on the basis of known facts. Their work has become very complex – an amalgam of astronomy, mathematics, physics, particle physics ($\diamond$ p. 114), relativity ($\diamond$ p. 38), quantum theory ($\diamond$ p. 40) and, inevitably, philosophic speculation. At the same time it has become far more plausible because it is based on an increasing volume of established fact. The finding that triggered off modern cosmological thought was the discovery in the 1930s by the

American astronomer Edwin P. Hubble (1889–1953) that the light from all distance galaxies is coming from a receding source. This is the only possible explanation of the fact that the light spectrum is shifted towards the red end – a fact that must be due to the Doppler effect ($\diamond$ p. 68). In 1948 the Russian-born American physicist George Gamow (1904–68), in a theory concerned with the origin of the light elements, interpreted this effect as demonstrating that the universe was expanding. This implied that it had originated in a single point billions of years ago. This idea received wide support but was not widely known outside scientific circles until the British cosmologist Fred Hoyle (1915–), in a highly critical and destructive account, referred to it, satirically, as the 'Big Bang' hypothesis ($\diamond$ p. 126). Ironically, Hoyle's comment had the opposite effect to that which he intended, and the interest of the public was immediately aroused.

Hoyle strenuously opposed the Big Bang idea. He pointed out that the original calculations of the age of the universe, based on Hubble's figures, indicated that it was younger than known geological evidence proved. The theory also failed to account for the formation of elements heavier than helium. Hoyle and two other young Cambridge scientists, Hermann Bondi and Thomas Gold, had already, in 1946, proposed a completely different hypothesis for the origins of the universe – the Steady State theory. This, they claimed could account for the expansion without involving an unrealistic time scale. The Steady State theory suggested that the universe had had no beginning and that matter is being continuously created at a rate exactly that required to compensate for the expansion. Thus the overall density of the universe would remain constant. Critics suggested that this theory contravened the law of conservation of mass and energy ($\diamond$ p. 28). Hoyle replied that so did the Big Bang theory.

The Steady State theory became linked to the idea of *nucleosynthesis* – an explanation of how heavier elements might be made from hydrogen and helium. This theory soon commanded a great deal of support from many who found the Big Bang idea unacceptable. It received a severe setback, however, when observations at Mount Wilson observatory in Pasadena, California, showed that the galaxies were much further away than had previously been supposed. This meant that the calculated age of the universe had to be increased to a minimum of 10 billion years – a figure entirely consistent with geological findings and the Big Bang hypothesis. Unfortunately for the Steady State theory, it predicted a zero temperature for space which was not to be confirmed by later scientific measurement.

The final blow to the Steady State theory came in May 1965. Two scientists working on radio astronomy at the Bell

Laboratories, Arno A. Penzias and Robert W. Wilson, were much troubled by microwave noise in their receiver. Every effort to discover the source of this interference failed, and, eventually, careful tests showed that it was coming from everywhere in the universe. This noise corresponded to the radiation emitted by a black body at a temperature of 2.74 K. This is a very low temperature, a little above the lowest possible temperature, absolute zero (−273.15°C or −549.67°F). Penzias and Wilson were astonished to learn that exactly such radiation had already been predicted.

Bodies in the universe that are at a temperature above absolute zero emit electromagnetic radiation ($\diamond$ p. 84). These 2.74 K signals do not, however, come from cold bodies. They were actually emitted, a very long time ago, by white-hot matter moving rapidly outwards. On their way to us, travelling, like all electromagnetic radiation at the speed of light, they have undergone a profound red shift so to increase their wavelength to that corresponding to a microwave frequency. Calculations based on the parameters of the now standard model of the origins of the universe agree with numerous measurements made during and since the 1970s of the wavelength and uniformity of the 2.74 K radiation.

When the news of the findings at the Bell Laboratories was published, support for the Steady State theory collapsed. Today, no alternative theory to that of the Big Bang is seriously considered by the experts.

SEE ALSO
- THE DEVELOPMENT OF SCIENCE pp. 8–11
- ASTRONOMICAL INSTRUMENTS AND TECHNIQUES pp. 122–5
- THE SUN AND THE SOLAR SYSTEM p. 132
- THE INNER PLANETS p. 134
- THE OUTER PLANETS p. 136
- STARS AND GALAXIES pp. 140–3

Edwin Powell Hubble (1889–1953), American astronomer, seen in front of the 2.5-m (98-in) telescope at Mount Wilson observatory. Hubble's research brought to light the first direct evidence that the universe is expanding. (Hale Observatories, SPL)

Astronomical Instruments and Techniques 1

From earliest times people have observed the heavens and many must have become familiar with the most obvious constellations of stars. Such observations, as well as provoking a sense of wonder and delight, provided an important set of reference points for navigation, especially when sailors were out of sight of land. This fact led to the refinement of methods of sighting, identifying and measuring the position of the celestial bodies long before telescopes were invented.

theNo one knows when the first serious astronomical observations were made. There is much speculation, however, as to the function of the many very ancient stone circles and other megalithic structures found in various places. Stonehenge, for instance, which probably dates from around 3,000 BC, was set up with such precision that many people are convinced that it must have been intended as some kind of astronomical instrument. It is impossible to be sure

Tycho Brahe's contribution consisted less in the advancement of knowledge than in the promotion of method, and in the stimulation of enthusiasm. He subscribed to the view of Ptolemy (⇨ p.120) that the Earth was the centre of the universe. Possibly to appease his many enemies at Court, he claimed to reject the then theologically outrageous heliocentric theory of Copernicus and to insist that the Sun with its train of planets circled around the Earth. This rather weak compromise had no permanent influence on science.

Brahe carried astronomical observation as far as was possible with the unaided eye. His accuracy was remarkable, his readings being correct to about two minutes of an arc (a very small angular measure). His tables of the motions of the planets and the Sun were better than any that had gone before, and he established the length of the year to less than a second. This showed the existing calendar to be causing a cumulative error, and, in 1582, Pope Gregory XIII agreed to a correction. Ten days were cut out – much to the fury of many who believed that their lives were being shortened and who rioted in the streets. Other less major corrections were also ordained, and the Gregorian calendar, as it came to be known, is now in almost universal use.

Tycho Brahe (1546–1601), Danish astonomer who invented and constructed several astronomical instruments, and used them accurately to plot the positions of the planets and stars. (AR)

The respect in which Brahe's name was held by scientists was later revealed when his first name was given to the most prominent crater on the Moon. Aristarchus of Samos (310–230 BC), celebrated as being the first to advance the heliocentric theory of the solar system, Ptolemy and Copernicus all had to make do with lesser craters.

about this, but it may be significant that the axis of symmetry of the structure points roughly to where the Sun rises on the longest day of the year in the northern hemisphere (summer solstice).

Naked-eye observation

A remarkable amount of reliable astronomical information was derived from naked-eye observation, long before the telescope was invented. This observation was not always as careful as it might have been, and, for instance, many tables of planetary motion, relative to the fixed stars, were published with misleading data. People such as Tycho Brahe (1546–1601) spent their lives correcting such tables. Some of the early observations were, however, remarkable, notably those of the great Polish astronomer Nicolas Copernicus (1473–1543; ⇨ p. 120), who, incidentally, also spent many years correcting old tables. Among many other things, Copernicus was actually able, by simple observation and recording, to show that the Earth's axis, if extended into space, described a circle and would eventually generate a cone. This was the explanation of the slow movement of the position (*precession*) of the equinoxes that had been discovered by the 2nd-century BC Greek astronomer Hipparchus, sixteen hundred years before the birth of Copernicus.

The astrolabe, forerunner of the sextant, was used to estimate local time. A sighting rod was pivoted to point at a bright star or at the Sun, the height of which was then measured along a timescale. (Zefa)

The quadrant and the astrolabe

The quadrant is a simple form of protractor with a sighting rule, or *alidade*, used to measure the angle between a star, or the Sun, and the horizontal. A plumb line was used to ensure that the instrument was kept horizontal. When the altitude of the north star was measured and special tables consulted, one could establish the latitude of the point from which the observation was made.

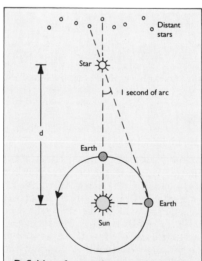

Definition of arcs and parsecs. If the change in angle between the two observations of the star is 1 second of arc, then d = 1 parsec (equivalent to 3.26 light years). In fact, no star is as close to the solar system as 1 parsec. Note that the angle in the diagram has been exaggerated for the sake of clarity.

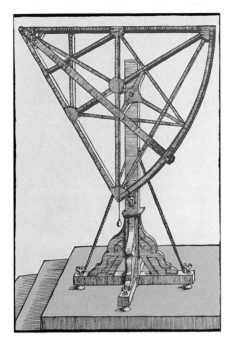

An astronomical sextant. The instrument takes its name from the fact that its arc describes one sixth of a circle. It was used to measure the altitudes of stars (that is, their height above the horizon). From Tycho Brahe's book, *Astronomicae instauratae mechanica* (1598). (Dr Jeremy Burgess, SPL)

ASTRONOMICAL TERMINOLOGY

Aphelion The position of a planet in its orbit when farthest from the Sun.

Apogee The position of the Moon or other Earth satellite in its orbit when farthest from the Earth.

Arc A section of a circle, ellipse or other curve, or of the orbit of a planet or other body.

Asteroid Any minor planet, or planetoid, moving round the Sun, found in greatest number between Mars and Jupiter. Asteroids have diameters of from about 1.5 km (1 mi) to nearly 700 km (435 mi).

Astronomical unit The mean distance between the Earth and the Sun. 1.496×10^8 km (9.3×10^7 mi).

Azimuth The horizontal bearing of a star or other body, reckoned from the north point of the observer's horizon.

Celestial Pertaining to the sky.

Celestial equator The great circle midway between the poles of the celestial sphere.

Celestial sphere An imaginary sphere surrounding the Earth, and with its centre at the Earth's centre, on which it is possible to imagine the position of the stars. The basis for the standard coordinate system in astronomy.

Chromosphere The part of the Sun's atmosphere above the surface and below the corona.

Comet A small body, thought to consist mainly of ice and rock, moving in an elongated elliptical orbit round the Sun.

Corona The outermost region of the Sun's atmosphere, visible as a faint halo during an eclipse.

Declination The angular distance of a celestial body north or south of the celestial equator on the celestial sphere.

Degree 1/360th part of a circle.

Eclipse The visual covering up (occultation) of one heavenly body by another as a result of interposition of one body between the observer and the other body.

Ecliptic The yearly path of the Sun across the celestial sphere.

Equinoxes The points where the Sun crosses the celestial equator when moving north (vernal equinox) or south (autumnal equinox) in the northern hemisphere.

Light year The distance travelled by light in a vacuum in one year. 9.461×10^{12} km (5.879×10^{12} mi).

Meridian The great circle on the celestial sphere that passes through the two poles and the observer's zenith.

Meteor A small particle moving around the Sun that becomes incandescent from friction if it enters the Earth's atmosphere. A 'shooting star'.

Meteorite A meteor large enough to survive passage through the Earth's atmosphere and reach the ground.

Milky Way The luminous band, consisting of millions of stars too small to be seen as individuals with the naked eye, seen when looking along the main plane of our galaxy.

Minute 1/60th degree of arc.

Nebula A diffuse cloud of particles and gases, mainly hydrogen, seen either as a faint patch of light or as a dark patch.

Neutron star A star consisting mainly of neutrons. Neutron stars that rotate rapidly and emit radio waves are called pulsars.

Nova A faint star that explodes and becomes very bright, remaining so for a period of months or years before returning to its former state of brightness.

Occultation The period of disappearance of a celestial body while another is interposed.

Parallax The apparent displacement of the position of a star caused by the movement of the Earth, either on its axis (diurnal parallax) or along its orbit (annual or heliocentric parallax).

Parsec The distance from Earth at which stellar parallax would be 1 second of arc, 3.086×10^{13} km (1.916×10^{13} mi) or 3.262 light years.

Perihelion The point in its orbit at which a planet or other body is nearest to the Sun.

Perturbation The disturbance in the motion of a celestial body caused by another body.

Planet Any of the nine celestial bodies that move round the Sun in elliptical orbits. Mercury, Venus, Earth, Mars, Jupiter, Saturn, Uranus, Neptune or Pluto.

Precession The motion of the axis of a spinning body so that the axis describes a cone. The movement, of this kind, of the poles of the celestial sphere.

Pulsar A neutron star that constantly emits pulses of electromagnetic radiation.

Quasar A star-like object that emits powerful radio waves and may have a high luminosity.

Satellite Any celestial or other body that rotates round a planet or a star.

Second 1/60th minute of arc.

Sidereal time Local time reckoned on the basis of the apparent rotation of the celestial sphere, or time based on the Earth's rotation relative to a particular star.

Solar system The Sun and all its satellites.

Solstices The points in the Sun's path (ecliptic) furthest north and south of the celestial equator.

Star Any celestial body visible in the clear sky as a point of light. A sun.

Supernova A rare, catastrophic and massive stellar explosion caused by instability when nuclear fuel becomes exhausted.

Transit The passage of a celestial body across the meridian of an observer.

Zenith The point in the celestial sphere immediately above the observer's head.

Zodiacal light A faint cone of light visible in the west just after sunset and in the east just before sunrise. Thought to be due to the illumination of dust particles in the plane of the ecliptic.

The altitude of the Sun gave a measure of the time.

The *astrolabe* – literally, a 'star finder' – was a more refined form of quadrant and was made in various models. One popular and portable form consisted of two flat metal discs, 7.5–25 cm (3–10 in) in diameter, capable of being rotated on a common centre. One side of one disc had degrees around its edge and was equipped with an alidade for sighting a star or the Sun. The other side was engraved with a star map and lines to show the horizon, the zenith and the lines of azimuth (⇨ box) and altitude for particular latitudes. The most important treatise on the astrolabe – a book that was studied for centuries by navigators and astronomers – was written by the English poet and humorist Geoffrey Chaucer (1340–1400). In the 18th century, the astrolabe was replaced by the more accurate sextant, invented by Isaac Newton (1642–1727; ⇨ chapter 2).

Plotting the skies

The most notable earliest exponent of the quadrant was the Danish pioneer of astronomy Tycho Brahe (⇨ above), whose work marked the real beginning of astronomical research. Brahe did not have the benefit of a telescope and had to develop new instruments for himself. Among other things, he designed and had constructed an enormous but rather crude astronomical quadrant with a radius of 14 cubits (about 7 m or 23 ft), divided into minutes. This quadrant enabled him to locate the position of hundreds of fixed stars with remarkable accuracy and made him famous. His enthusiasm for science and insistence on exactness paved the way for future advances and inspired his assistant Johannes Kepler (1571–1630) to even greater efforts. In November 1572, Brahe observed a new star in the constellation Cassiopeia where no star was supposed to be. This star was brighter than Venus but faded away in 17 months. Brahe's observations recorded all its changes, and proved not only that it lay beyond the Moon but also was an immeasurable distance away. He published an account of this in the book De nova stella (Concerning the new star) in 1573 and was soon regarded as an astronomer of international renown. Since that time, such exploding stars have been called *novas*.

Astronomical Instruments and Techniques 2

The universe is of unimaginable size but, even so, humankind has been able to examine some of its distant features, and collect information about it from even further away. Scientists are powerfully motivated to probe to the very limits of observation. This has led to the progressive development of instruments that supplement and enhance the power of the human senses, especially that of vision. These instruments take many forms and have enabled us to secure an immense amount of otherwise unobtainable information.

This multiple-mirror telescope (MMT) on Mount Hopkins, Arizona, USA, consists of six separate mirrors, each 1.8 m (72 in) in diameter. Working together, they form what is in effect a single mirror 4.5 m (178 in) across, making this one of the world's largest telescopes. The MMT technique is important since it is not technically possible to make single-mirror telescopes much larger than 8 m (315 in) in diameter. (David Parker, SPL)

Since the time of Galileo (⇨ box) it has been apparent that the telescope is the instrument of central importance in astronomical research. Attempts to make ever larger refracting telescopes, however, met with increasing difficulties resulting from the size, weight and thickness of the object lens needed. Long before this point was reached, however, the solution had been found.

The reflecting telescope

The philosopher and scientist Isaac Newton (1642–1727) was well aware of the damaging effect on the image of colour dispersion (chromatic aberration; ⇨ p. 78) in lenses, and, knowing this to be an inherent property of light,

despaired of ever producing a perfect telescope. Newton's belief led him to consider the use of a concave mirror. Such a mirror can form an image without refraction, so there is no chromatic aberration. Newton then proceeded to construct the first reflecting telescope. This instrument was only 2.5 cm (1 in) in diameter and 15 cm (6 in) long, and had a magnification of 40 times.

It soon became clear that, for large instruments, concave parabolic mirrors were a far better option than large object lenses, which tended to become distorted under their own weight. Improvements in design were made by many later workers, especially the British astronomer William Herschel (1738–1822), who was able, with his reflecting telescope, to discover the planet Uranus in 1781. Later instruments included: a 4-tonne (4-ton), 1.80-m (72-in) telescope, 15 m (50 ft) long, made by the Irish astronomer William Parsons, Lord Rosse (1800–67); the 2.5-m (100-in) Mount Palomar telescope with which the American astronomer Edwin Hubble (1889–1953) established the expansion of the universe; the 5-m (200-in) Hale telescope at Mount Palomar, completed in 1948; and the 6-m (236-in) reflector at Mount Pastukhov in the Caucasus Mountains.

Although no larger instruments have now been produced for many years, the performance of existing ones has been greatly improved. There has, for instance, been a gradual but substantial improvement in the resolution and sensitivity of photographic emulsions. Even more impressive has been the replacement of photographic plates with highly sensitive, high-resolution, electronic detectors capable of improving the sensitivity of telescopes by up to 40 times.

Recent observation methods

Another approach to the problem of improving performance and reducing escalating expense is the multiple-mirror telescope (MMT) idea in which a group of mirrors act together as a single mirror

with a single focus. The 10-m (400-in) Keck telescope on Mauna Kea mountain in Hawaii consists of a mosaic of 36 hexagonal mirrors, each 1.8 m (72 in) across, and each working, under computer control with its neighbours, to produce the effect of a single mirror. This idea is taken further in the concept of multiple telescopes working together, as in the European Southern Observatory's Very Large Telescope (VLT) project. This system uses four separate 7.6-m (300-in) multiple-mirror instruments so arranged that they can work together, on the principle of interferometry (⇨ p. 38), as if they were a single mirror equivalent to one 152 m (6,000 in) in diameter.

Modern large telescopes do far more than simply make visual observations. They are all now fitted with an array of ancillary equipment such as spectrographs, photometers, cameras and ultraviolet-light detectors. Spectroscopy (⇨ p.

THE COSMIC DISTANCE SCALE

Km

10^{24} — Edge of known universe

10^{21} — Most distant visible galaxy

— Diameter of a large cluster of galaxies

10^{18} — One megaparsec (3.26 million light years: the size of the local group of galaxies)

— Diameter of our galaxy

10^{15} — One kiloparsec (3,260 light years)

— Distance of nearest stars

10^{12} — One parsec (3.26 light years)

10^{9} — Radius of Pluto's orbit

— One astronomical unit (AU; mean distance of Earth from Sun)

10^{6} — Radius of the Sun

— Radius of the Earth

10^{3}

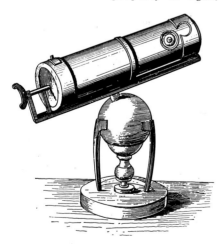

Reflecting telescope designed by the eminent English scientist Sir Isaac Newton (1642–1727). Although most famous for his formulation of the laws of motion and his development of calculus, Newton is also well known for his important contribution to our knowledge of the behaviour of light, as is evident from his book *Opticks* (1704). Illustration from Oliver Lodge, *Pioneers of Science* (1919). (AR)

JOCELYN BELL BURNELL AND THE PULSARS

In July 1967 the 24-year-old Cambridge PhD student Jocelyn Bell Burnell (1943–) noticed an unusual squiggle on a pen-and-paper chart of a radio signal scan of the sky. Later, she saw the same signal again coming from the same part of the sky. The chart was going too slowly to record the details of the squiggle, but, on a later occasion when the effect occurred, she speeded up the recorder and was able to resolve the signal into a series of pulses at intervals of about 1.3 seconds. In her own words: 'I turned on the fast chart recorder, and, as the chart flowed under the pen, it was going "whoop, whoop, whoop" at regular intervals.' Many months of investigation were needed to eliminate an artificial source, and it eventually became clear that these signals were coming from well beyond the solar system but somewhere in our galaxy. The pulsar had been discovered.

We now know that a pulsar is a rapidly spinning neutron star with a strong magnetic field (⇨ p. 88) that emits a narrow rotating beam of radiation that can be detected as a radio signal if it sweeps over the Earth. Several hundred pulsars are now known, with periods varying from 0.0015 seconds to over 4 seconds. Pulsars may also be sources of gamma rays (⇨ p. 130) and visible light pulses. One of the most interesting is NP0532, a light-flashing pulsar in the Crab nebula, which rotates in 1/30th of a second and is thought to be a residuum of the supernova (⇨ p. 130) explosion of the year 1054. The extraordinarily high rate of rotation of the pulsar is due to the smallness of the neutron star, its rate of rotation increasing as it contracts just as spinning skaters will speed up when they pull in their arms (⇨ p. 30).

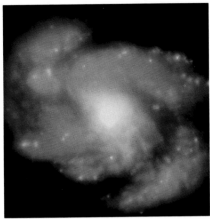

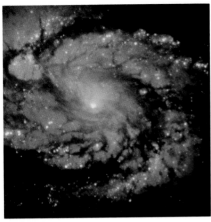

Two images of the spiral galaxy M100 taken by the Hubble Space Telescope (HST) before (left) and after a corrective optics package was installed by astronauts in December 1993. This was necessary because of a late-detected error in the manufacture of its mirror. Since the repair, the HST has been sending back to Earth some of the most impressive and informative astronomical images ever seen.

(Space Telescope Science Institute, NASA, SPL)

— GALILEO AND THE TELESCOPE —

Contrary to popular opinion, the great Italian mathematician and scientist Galileo Galilei (1564–1642), best known by his first name, as is common of many others of that time, did not invent the refracting telescope. This seems to have been the work of a Dutch optician, Hans Lippershey, who flourished at the end of the 16th century, and who had made a novelty device with two spectacle lenses that caused a distant object to seem nearer and upside-down. Galileo, however, understood lenses and knew that it was impossible to magnify a distant object with a single lens. When, in 1609, he heard of the new idea he decided to experiment, and fitted a convex spectacle lens into one end of a section of organ pipe, and a concave lens into the other. In doing this he was forming an inverted image with one lens that could be made upright and magnified with another.

With this telescope Galileo formed an upright image (never seen before) and caused a sensation. He then proceeded to make a bigger and better instrument, grinding the lenses himself. This telescope had a magnification of 30 times, and, with it, he began his great survey of the night sky. He described the craters and other features on the Moon, estimated the heights of some Moon mountains by noting when their tips caught the rising Sun, showed how the Earth reflected sunlight just as the Moon did, showed that the Milky Way was composed of stars, identified as double stars, some that had been thought single, discovered four satellites (moons) of Jupiter and determined their period of revolution, clearly demonstrating the vital importance of the telescope to astronomy.

80) is particularly important as it enables detailed analysis of the composition of celestial bodies to be made.

X-ray telescopes

X-rays cannot be focused by conventional means because they simply penetrate mirrors and lenses with little deflection. Thick lead plates drilled with parallel holes (*collimators*) can give some idea of direction, but do not focus rays from a distance. It has been found, however, that if an X-ray strikes a surface at a very acute angle it will bounce off because of the effective overlap of the atoms of the material. Such surfaces, arranged concentrically, can thus be used as grazing incidence mirrors to bring X-rays to a focus. Instruments based on this principle have been used to provide remarkably high resolutions of beams from distant X-ray sources.

Radio astronomy

In 1930 an engineer at the Bell Telephone laboratory, Karl Guthe Jansky (1905–50), investigating a mysterious interference with radiotelephone communication, managed to localize the source of these signals as the Milky Way. This was the beginning of radio astronomy, which has since become a major discipline, mainly because of the pioneering work of the British radio astronomer Sir Alfred Bernard Lovell (1913–) at the Jodrell Bank radio observatory in Cheshire (now the Nuffield Radio Astronomy Laboratories), which he founded in 1945 using World War II radar equipment. Lovell persuaded the Nuffield Foundation and the British Government to finance the first steerable dish (*paraboloid*) reflector telescope – an instrument 76.2 m (250 ft) in diameter and, in its time, the largest in the world. Arguments about cost were silenced when Lovell used the instrument to track the first Soviet *Sputnik* satellite in 1957. The largest movable dish is now the 100-m (330-ft) diameter Effelsberg reflector in Germany.

Radio astronomy suffers from poor resolution, which can be relieved only by making the receiving antennae very large. To improve the detail, scientists resort to the technique of interferometry, using two or more widely separated radio telescopes working together. This can provide something of the effect of a receiver dish of diameter equal to the separation distance. The United States National Radio Astronomy Observatory in Charlottesville, Virginia, uses 27 radio telescopes, each 25 m (82 ft) in diameter arranged in a Y pattern over 50 km (30 mi) of countryside. A major step forward came when it was realized that such separated instruments need not be connected for synchronization. If data at different telescopes is recorded on tape along with precise timing signals from an atomic clock, this data can later be analysed without problems. This means that stations can be on different continents and an effective telescope nearly the diameter of the Earth can be achieved. This technique is called *very long baseline interferometry*, and current development of the method expects to achieve a resolution 1,000 times that of any existing optical or radio telescope. Artificial satellites can be used in the method, in conjunction with earthbound telescopes.

The Hubble space telescope

One of the main limitations to the use of telescopes is the distorting effect of altering atmospheric density from temperature changes and from pollution. Even the enormous growth in terrestrial illumination (light pollution) has reduced the contrast of images markedly. It is for these reasons that telescopes are sited on high mountains. The ideal situation, however, would be for the telescope to be sited entirely outside the Earth's atmosphere, and it was this motive that prompted the remarkable idea of the Hubble Space Telescope (HST). This is a 10,200-kg (22,500-lb) orbiting instrument, powered by solar power and with a 2.4-m (94-in) mirror. It was placed in an orbit

500 km (300 mi) above the Earth's surface in April 1990 by the space shuttle *Discovery*, having been delayed for four years because of the *Challenger* space shuttle disaster. At a cost of $1.5 billion, this was the most expensive scientific instrument of all time.

It also quickly proved to incorporate what was probably the most embarrassing scientific blunder of all time. HST was to have viewed the universe with ten times the resolution of any previous instrument. A mistake in the testing of the mirror misled the manufacturer into believing that it was correctly shaped when it was not, and the results were disappointingly below expectations. Ingenious correction techniques have, however, been used to compensate for the optical error and the instrument is now providing a great deal of new and valuable data. Trouble was also encountered from juddering of the solar panels as they were expanded by sudden temperature changes. This caused vibration to the whole instrument.

Radio telescopes are often displayed in a group, or *very large array* (VLA), to improve the resolution of information they capture, and to increase the area over which they can operate.

(Gamma)

SEE ALSO

- THE DEVELOPMENT OF SCIENCE pp. 8–11
- SCIENTIFIC INSTRUMENTS pp. 14–17
- REFLECTION AND REFRACTION p. 78
- SPECTRA AND SPECTROSCOPY p. 80
- COSMOLOGY: UNDERSTANDING THE UNIVERSE p. 120
- ASTRONOMICAL INSTRUMENTS AND TECHNIQUES 1 p. 122

Big Bang

Only one scientific theory of the origin of the universe – the Big Bang theory – is seriously held today. The idea that the entire universe had its origin, some 15 billion years ago, in a single minute point, is hard to credit, but no other theory even remotely conforms to the established facts. The Big Bang theory is, however, constantly being refined.

It is common experience that sound from an approaching object rises in pitch and then falls as the object recedes. In 1842 the Austrian physicist Christian Doppler (1803–53; ⇨ p. 68) hit on the explanation. Sound waves emitted by an approaching source reach the observer at shorter intervals than they would if the source were stationary. Effectively, the waves are compressed so that more of them reach the observer in a given time. Thus the pitch gets higher. After passing the observer, the waves are stretched and fewer reach the observer in a given time so the pitch gets lower. The Doppler effect has many important applications in radar, speed measurement and navigation as well as in science generally. Knowing that, like sound, light could also be considered as a wave phenomenon, Doppler predicted that a similar effect should be observable for the colour of light emitted by a moving object such as a star moving relative to the Earth.

The red shift

When light passes through a glass prism its component wavelengths are bent by different amounts. As a result the different colours are spread out in the familiar light spectrum. The spectrum shows many narrow dark regions or lines known as absorption lines (⇨ p. 80). Because of the Doppler effect, if a light source is moving away from an observer (or the observer away from the source) the lines in the spectrum move towards the red end. In 1868, the English astronomer Sir William Huggins (1824–1910) was able to show a small red shift in one of the hydrogen lines in the spectrum from the star Sirius, and was able to calculate the velocity with which Sirius was moving away from the Earth.

Between 1912 and 1926, the American astronomer Vesto Melvin Slipher (1875–1969) painstakingly measured the spectral shifts of light from distant galaxies. Of the 41 checked, 36 had red spectral shifts and five blue shifts. From 1918 until the end of his life, the American astronomer Edwin Powell Hubble (1889–1953) followed up this work using the then largest telescope in the world – the 40-cm (100-in) instrument at the Mount Wilson observatory in Pasadena, California. By 1929, Hubble, using the red shift, had firmly established a law governing the way the receding velocity of the galaxies increased with their distance. This law states that the more distant a galaxy, the more rapidly it is moving away. Doubling the distance doubles the velocity. Hubble calculated that for every million light years' increase in distance, the recession velocity increases by 150 km (93 mi) per second. By the time of his death, he and others had shown that more than eight hundred galaxies had red shifts. Today we know that, apart from a few nearby galaxies, all observable galaxies are receding from each other with velocities proportional to their distances apart. Hubble and others questioned the implication that the red shift implied an expanding universe and tried, in Einstein's words, 'to explain it by means other than the Doppler effect'. *'There is, however,'* he went on, *'no support for such a conception in the known physical facts.'* Einstein's arguments were so cogent that, for most scientists, it has now been established beyond question that the universe is rapidly expanding.

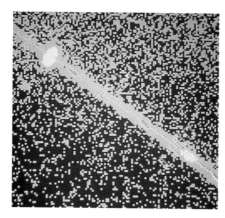

The Doppler effect due to the expansion of the universe, shown in this ultraviolet spectrum of the quasar 3C 273. The red, dotted line represents the centre of the spectrum with wavelengths in angstrom units (1 Å equals 10^{-10} m) superimposed. The white spot next to 1,200 Å is part of hydrogen's spectrum at its usual wavelength, while the spot near 1,400 Å is the same emission as we receive it from the quasar. The gap between these two wavelengths is explained as a Doppler Shift, putting the quasar at 2,100 million light years away from Earth. (Fred Espenak, SPL)

Logical consequences of an expanding universe

At first sight it might seem that if – in whichever direction we look – the universe is seen to be expanding away from us, we must be in the centre. In fact, this does not follow. For instance, from each point on the surface of an expanding balloon that is being blown up, all other points are receding. So we need not imagine that we, on Earth, occupy a uniquely central position in the universe.

Regular uniform expansion implies that the expanding object was smaller in the past. Continued backward extrapolation, therefore, implies a point source. So, however improbable, the inescapable logical consequence of an expanding universe is that, at some time in the past, the universe started as a point. This, the Big Bang theory, is now accepted as the standard model for the origin of the universe. It proposes that the universe began when a single pinhead of infinitely dense and infinitely hot matter suddenly exploded in an unimaginably large release of energy. As it did so, time began, and, from the matter released, all the galaxies, stars and planets were formed. The Big Bang was no ordinary explosion in which matter was driven outwards into existing space. Space itself was created by the explosion. Present estimates of the time elapsed since Big Bang range from 6×10^9 to 1.5×10^{10} years.

Further evidence for the Big Bang theory

In 1956, the Russian-born American physicist George Gamow (1904–68) argued that, if the universe is expanding, then there should be some heat left over from the Big Bang. He was right. In 1964, faint radio signals of a fixed frequency, and *coming from all directions in space,*

COBE

Late in 1989, NASA launched a special satellite known as the *Cosmic Background Explorer* (COBE) specifically to investigate the microwave background cosmic signals first detected in the Bell Telephone laboratories in 1964. COBE was tasked to measure the spectrum of the microwave cosmic radiation. According to the standard model, this radiation should smoothly cover a range of frequencies of the kind known as a black-body spectrum (⇨ p. 84). An ideal black body at a steady temperature radiates at that temperature and the energy distribution depends only on the temperature.

In January 1990 the microwave spectrum from COBE was shown at a meeting of the American Astronomical Society. The chart projected was such a perfect black-body curve that the audience immediately broke out into spontaneous applause. This evidence provides support for the inflation model of the Big Bang theory.

The data from COBE also showed slight temperature variations in the cosmic background, which was just what the Big Bang theorists expected. Such variations are interpreted as coming from small differences in the density of matter and energy occurring early in the life of the universe – differences necessary to explain the condensation of matter under gravity to form the stars and the galaxies.

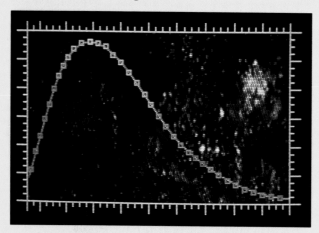

The spectrum of cosmic background radiation (red curve) obtained by COBE confirmed the theory that the universe started with a hot Big Bang. This radiation is the echo of the Big Bang and is now no warmer than a few degrees above absolute zero. (Mehau Kulyk, SPL)

THE END OF BIG BANG

An expanding universe can do one of three things: it can continue to expand for ever; it can slow its expansion until expansion ceases; or it can cease to expand and start to contract. The outcome depends on two factors – the rate of expansion and the density of matter in the universe. All matter attracts all other matter by gravitation, so, if no other factor were operating, the universe would inevitably contract. If the rate of expansion, however, is sufficient to exceed the effect of gravitation, the universe will continue to expand. If it is not, the universe will contract. If it were just great enough to balance gravity, an equilibrium would be established in which the universe would have a fixed size.

The Doppler effect tells us, with remarkable accuracy, the rate at which distant galaxies are moving away. Unfortunately, we do not know very accurately how far away they are so we have only a rough idea of the rate of expansion of the universe. We are even less certain about the present average density of the universe. The sum of all the visible galaxies, together with an estimate of all the others, gives us only about 15 per cent of the amount needed to stop the expansion, even assuming the lowest accepted estimate of the rate of expansion.

were detected (⇨ p. 124). These correspond exactly in wavelength to what would be expected by a red shift of the radiation coming originally from very hot matter.

The proportions of the various atoms in the universe are known. So far as the low-weight atoms such as hydrogen, helium and lithium are concerned, the observed proportions correspond remarkably well with the calculations of what would have been formed during the first few minutes of the life of the universe. Recent advances in fundamental particle physics have also clarified how subatomic particles, such as protons and neutrons (⇨ p. 108), were formed soon after the Big Bang and roughly in what proportions. Measurements of the ratios of photons to protons or neutrons – roughly one billion to one – correspond well with the calculations based on the Big Bang theory.

The inflation model

The standard Big Bang model fails to answer a number of questions, however. Why is the 2.74 K background radiation so uniform? How did the galaxies form? How much matter is there in the universe? Will the universe continue to expand or will it eventually collapse in on itself? Many amendments have been proposed to try to answer some of these questions. Probably the most important current version of Big Bang is the

inflation model, first suggested around 1980 by Prof. Alan H. Guth of the Massachusetts Institute of Technology.

The inflation theory proposes that, to begin with, expansion was not uniform. For a very brief period at the beginning of time, it suggests, the operation of natural forces was altered so that the effect of gravitation was reversed and it became a repulsive rather than attractive force. The gravitational attraction between bodies is proportional to the product of their masses and inversely proportional to the square of their distance apart (⇨ p. 30). Because the primal matter is almost infinitely compact and dense, the reversal of gravity would produce an inconceivably great explosive effect. The region from which the observable universe arose was so tiny and the temperature so high that it was able to reach thermal equilibrium almost immediately. This would account for the uniformity of the background radiation.

In a very tiny fraction of the first second, the universe expanded by about 10^{30} times – a vast expansion – in a positive maelstrom of radiation at a temperature of around a thousand trillion trillion K. Natural laws, as we now know them, then asserted themselves. Cooling was rapid and by the time the universe was one trillionth of a second old, its temperature had dropped to only 10 thousand million million K. With expansion and cooling, particles began to form. After about one millionth of a second, quarks (⇨ p. 110) began to coalesce to form all known particles such as protons, neutrons and electrons.

At this temperature, atomic nuclei cannot form because the thermal energy of the protons and neutrons is higher than the binding energy that holds them together. But after about one second, when the temperature had dropped to about 10 billion K, the light nuclei – those of hydrogen and helium – began to form. It was some 100,000 years, however, before the plasma of these nuclei could stably attract electrons to form atoms. By that time, the temperature had dropped to a mere 10,000 K. Once atoms had formed, normal gravitational forces began to operate. Any variations in local density of matter would quickly be amplified as areas of slightly increased density would be pulled together. This process of gravitational amplification would result in the formation of great

masses from which stars and galaxies would eventually evolve.

Because the early stages of the primal fireball would have put matter and energy into perfect thermal equilibrium, the radiation emitted would have had a uniform black-body spectrum (⇨ p. 84). As received today, billions of years later, it would have just the characteristics of uniformity confirmed by COBE (⇨ see box). So the inflation theory is supported by the fact that the microwave background radiation has almost the same temperature from whatever direction it comes. The COBE findings do not prove the Big Bang inflationary theory but they are highly consistent with it.

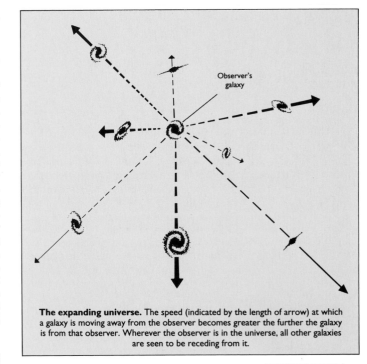

The expanding universe. The speed (indicated by the length of arrow) at which a galaxy is moving away from the observer becomes greater the further the galaxy is from that observer. Wherever the observer is in the universe, all other galaxies are seen to be receding from it.

SEE ALSO

- SCIENTIFIC INSTRUMENTS pp. 14–17
- BEYOND NEWTON I: RELATIVITY p. 38
- SPECTRA AND SPECTROSCOPY p. 80
- THE ELECTROMAGNETIC SPECTRUM AND ITS PROPERTIES p. 84
- FUNDAMENTAL FORCES p. 112
- COSMOLOGY: UNDERSTANDING THE UNIVERSE p. 120
- ASTRONOMICAL INSTRUMENTS AND TECHNIQUES pp. 122–5
- BLACK HOLES p. 128
- SUPERNOVAE p. 130
- STARS AND GALAXIES pp. 140–3

The formation of the universe, based on the theory of the inflationary Big Bang and data from the COBE satellite. A minute fraction of a second after the Big Bang, fluctuations in the energy 'soup' of the universe appear. Rapid inflationary expansion follows, and, 300,000 years later, the fluctuations form 'ripples' in the microwave background (detected by COBE). These energy patterns show that 'dark' matter exists, which provides gravity to form the galaxies (visible now, 15 billion years later). (NASA GSFC, SPL)

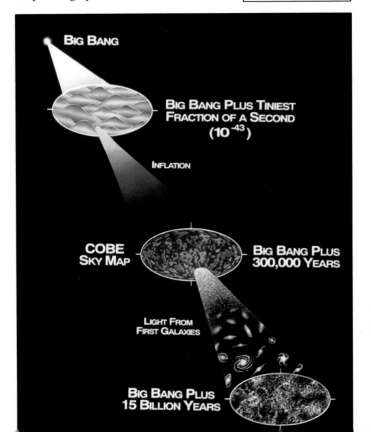

BIG BANG

BIG BANG PLUS TINIEST FRACTION OF A SECOND (10^{-43})

INFLATION

COBE SKY MAP

BIG BANG PLUS 300,000 YEARS

LIGHT FROM FIRST GALAXIES

BIG BANG PLUS 15 BILLION YEARS

Black Holes

Probably the most remarkable, dramatic and near-incredible phenomenon of modern science is the black hole. Baldly stated, the very idea of a region in space from which nothing, not even light, can escape, stretches the imagination to the limit.

A black hole, being of such enormous density, creates a yawning chasm in the fabric of spacetime, 'warping' it for light years around. Objects of smaller mass produce corresponding smaller distortions. A star the size of the Sun (bottom left) makes almost no impression, while a neutron star, although smaller, is more massive, and makes a bigger 'dent'.
(Julian Baum, SPL)

The strangeness of the idea of a black hole is, of course, a reflection of the fact that none of us has ever experienced anything even remotely resembling one. When the phenomenon is accounted for in terms of established principles, however, it becomes, if no less extraordinary, at least comprehensible.

At the end of the 18th century, when light was first believed to consist of a stream of particles, two scientists, the English geologist and seismologist John Mitchell (1724–93) and the French mathematician and astronomer Pierre Simon, Marquis de Laplace (1749–1827), independently suggested that dark bodies – astronomical entities with gravitation so strong that even light could not escape them – might exist. This idea was prompted by Newton's theory of gravitation. When, however, early in the 19th century, light was shown to be a form of

wave motion, Laplace, the survivor of the two, withdrew his suggestion. Ironically, Laplace need not have done so for he and Mitchell had been quite right. After the introduction of Einstein's general theory of relativity (⇨ p. 38) in 1917 it became clear that light *was* affected by gravity. Einstein's theory was triumphantly vindicated in 1919 when, during an eclipse of the Sun, rays of light from a distant star passing close to the Sun's edge were seen to be bent.

The origin of black holes

To understand the theory behind black holes, it is first necessary to bear in mind some basic astronomical ideas about the formation of stars. Gravitation (⇨ p. 30) is a very weak force and requires bodies of great mass – such as those of the mass of the Earth – to make its presence readily felt. And there are many bodies in the universe with masses considerably greater than that of our small planet. Stars begin to be formed when vast quantities of the gas hydrogen are pulled together by gravitation. As the atoms come closer and closer, like air compressed in a bicycle pump, they become more energetic (hotter) and increasingly bounce off each other (⇨ p. 50). The closer they come together, however, the greater is the gravitational attraction.

Eventually the proximity is so great that the atomic nuclei fuse, as in a hydrogen bomb, to form helium (named after the Greek word for the Sun, *helios*). The mass of the helium atom is slightly less

than the combined mass of the hydrogen atoms forming it, and the lost mass is converted into energy, in accordance with Einstein's equation $E=mc^2$ (the energy is equal to the mass multiplied twice by a figure equal to the speed of light; ⇨ p. 38). The fusion reaction (⇨ p. 116) is thus associated with the release of a tremendous amount of heat and other forms of energy, and it is this that makes stars (including our own Sun) luminous and the source of energy for nearby bodies, such as planet Earth. The core of the star now becomes hot and pressurized enough to start other fusion reactions. Helium atoms fuse to form carbon. Carbon forms neon, oxygen, silicon and finally a core of molten iron. Each of these reactions produces energy.

The high-temperature fusional energy is also sufficient to balance the gravitational attraction – just as molecules of boiling water resist gravity – and, as long as there is plenty of nuclear fuel in the form of hydrogen, stability is maintained. When a star begins to run out of fuel, however, gravitation reasserts itself and the star begins to contract. Eventually it will terminate in at least one of four ways, which will be detailed below. The first of these is known as a *white dwarf*. This is a body a few thousand kilometres in diameter and with a density of hundreds of tonnes per cubic centimetre. Many white dwarfs have been identified by astronomers.

Pauli's exclusion principle

The question arises, however, why white dwarfs do not continue to contract. In 1924, the Austrian physicist Wolfgang Pauli (1900–58) had formulated a most important principle, known as the *exclusion principle*. This stated that two similar particles, such as electrons, cannot be in the same energy state, that is, they cannot simultaneously occupy the same position and have the same velocity. If they approach the same position they must have different velocities and so would fly apart. As stars become smaller, their electrons get very close together, and the Pauli exclusion principle ensures that they fly apart. This provides another basis of equilibrium and results in the formation of white dwarfs. Yet another kind of equilibrium can come about when the exclusion principle operates between protons and neutrons. This results in a second kind of termination – that of dead stars of an incredible density of some hundreds of millions of tonnes per cubic centimetre, known as *neutron stars*.

As long as stars are not too large to start with, these mechanisms will operate. But beyond a certain size, the effect of gravitation is so strong that, to escape it, the velocity of avoiding particles would have to reach that of light – the highest possible velocity. This puts a limit to Pauli's exclusion principle. In other words, dead stars larger than a certain size – a size that can be calculated – will go on collapsing under increasing gravity. The

THE EVOLUTION OF A BLACK HOLE

A red supergiant in the last stages of its life.

The star implodes (falls in on itself).

A black hole is created. Light from stars behind the 'hole' is distorted and seen as a halo around it.

together, leading to inconceivable densities, even, possibly, to nonexistence, as the gravitational field becomes so strong that the normal laws of nature no longer apply.

The arguments for the existence of black holes seem irrefutable to most scientists. There can be no doubt that stars collapse under gravitation and that large stars go on collapsing. If there are no black holes, a lot of theory will have to be radically revised and an entirely new theory produced for what happens when a star too massive to become a neutron star collapses when its nuclear fuel is exhausted. One consequence, according to current theory, is the supernova; the other, as we have seen, is the black hole.

Evidence for black holes

If black holes cannot be seen, how can their existence be proved? In fact, although absolute proof is still lacking, there is plenty of highly suggestive evidence. Many pairs of stars – *binary systems* – are known, which, mutually attracted by their gravitational fields, rotate around one another. There are also systems in which an apparently solitary star rotates in orbit around what appears to be an empty point in space. One such is the blue supergiant star HDE 226868 in the constellation of Cygnus the Swan, some 6,000 light years away. Once every five and a half days this star circles around such a point. Calculations show this to be a mere 100 km (62 mi) across but to have a mass of about half that of HDE 226868. Although it cannot be seen, it has been designated Cygnus X-1.

Binary pairs sometimes show another interesting and unexpected property – they emit X-rays (⇨ p. 85). The most satisfactory explanation of this phenomenon is probably that the immensely powerful gravitational field of the black hole drags

A BLACK HOLE AT THE CENTRE OF OUR GALAXY

The centre of our own galaxy – the Milky Way – is about 25,000 light years away. A light year is the distance light travels in a year – 9.461×10^{12} km (5.879×10^{12} mi). This region is obscured to vision by massive clouds of dense gas and dust through which light cannot pass. Shorter-wavelength radiation, such as X-rays and gamma rays, and longer-wavelength radiation, such as infrared and microwaves, can, however, penetrate these clouds. Monitoring of this radiation indicates that the centre of the galaxy is a maelstrom of radiational activity. The infrared energy produced by the inner 10 light years is equal to that of about 6 million of our Sun. Radio astronomy (⇨ p. 124) has also shown that within 5 light years of the centre is a spiral of gas with four arms. There is good reason to suppose that this spiral is orbiting the actual centre of the galaxy.

A black hole cannot radiate energy, but the region surrounding it is in a state of intense activity as it spirals inward, becoming more and more compressed, turbulent and heated. This region is a massive source of electromagnetic energy, which, although deflected by the black hole, can readily escape. Radio-astronomical observations indicate that the source of radio-wavelength radiation is only about 3.2 billion km (2 billion mi) in diameter. The only currently conceivable entity that could emit so much radiation and still be as small in size as this is a massive black hole.

Although many scientists believe that much can be explained about ours and other galaxies on the basis of a central black hole, some remain sceptical. They ask why it is that some galaxies show no radio emission. One possible answer to this may be that our views of different galaxies reveal different orientations. If, as is believed, black holes draw in matter in a flat, disc-like spiral, the radiation may only be emitted in the direction of the axis of rotation. A galactic disc viewed edge-on would seem to be emitting less radiation than one viewed head-on. And this idea does, in fact, make predictions that can be verified by observation.

material off its visible partner and that this material, in spiralling towards the hole, becomes compressed and so hot that it emits radiation of a very short wavelength – namely X-rays. Cygnus X-1 is a well-known X-ray emitter. Two other such X-ray-emitting binary systems have also been discovered.

SEE ALSO

- CIRCULAR MOTION AND GRAVITATION p. 30
- BEYOND NEWTON I: RELATIVITY p. 38
- SPECTRA AND SPECTROSCOPY p. 80
- FUNDAMENTAL FORCES p. 112
- COSMOLOGY: UNDERSTANDING THE UNIVERSE p. 120
- BIG BANG p. 126
- SUPERNOVAE p. 130
- STARS AND GALAXIES pp. 140–3

effects may be one or other of two of the most remarkable phenomena ever described – either the *black hole* or the *supernova*. The latter is so important that it is dealt with separately (⇨ p. 130).

Arguments for the existence of black holes

Ironically, astronomers who, throughout the ages, have been deeply preoccupied with what they can see, are now much concerned, among other things, with entities that can never be seen. Black holes, as postulated, are regions in space occupied by matter of such density that gravitation is strong enough to mean that nothing, not even light, can ever escape from them. The strength of the gravitational field in a black hole increases as the matter comes closer

An artist's impression of a binary-star system consisting of a black hole (foreground) and a blue giant star. The immense gravitational field of the black hole pulls gas away from the atmosphere of its companion. As the gas spirals into the black hole it forms a flat accretion disc, which heats up and emits X-rays (white region at centre). For this reason, systems such as this are termed X-ray binaries. (Julian Baum, SPL)

Supernovae

A *nova* is a star that suddenly brightens by a factor of 10,000 or more. Originally, the term 'nova' was used, in its literal sense ('new'), for a star that suddenly becomes visible to the naked eye. The increase in brightness occurs over the course of a few days and the bright phase lasts for a few weeks before returning to its former magnitude. A *supernova* is an altogether more massive and violent affair. Over the course of a few hours, the brightness flares up until it is greater than that of hundreds of billions of Suns, and may even be visible during the day.

The energy radiated by a supernova beggars the imagination. In the first ten seconds of its life a supernova may generate more energy than the Sun radiates in the whole of its 10-billion-year lifetime – more than the combined energy output of all the other stars and galaxies of the visible universe.

How do supernovae occur?

Every star is subjected to its own gravitational force that tends to pull all the matter in it together so that it contracts. The greater the mass of the star, the greater the force of its own gravity. In the case of massive stars, much greater than our Sun, this force is unthinkably large. The inward pull is, however, opposed by the outward pressure of the nuclear explosion constantly going on. First there is a hydrogen-fusion reaction and this continues until all the hydrogen in about the central one third of the star is converted to helium. In a massive star

THE SIGNIFICANCE OF SUPERNOVAE

Supernovae are far more important than simply cosmic fireworks displays. Hydrogen and helium are believed to have been formed in the first few minutes after the Big Bang (⇨ p. 126). Thereafter, the formation of heavier atoms occurred in the conditions of incredible temperature and pressure at the core of normal stars contracting under gravitation. Elements with atomic weights up to that of iron are constantly being formed in this way but are mainly retained within the stars. Supernovae serve several purposes. Their massive explosion provides the conditions in which elements above the atomic weights of iron can be formed. These are not made in normal stars. The explosion disperses all the elements throughout space in an enormous cloud of gas and dust, and it generates a wave of pressure that concentrates other gas clouds into more compact masses so that gravity can begin to act to form new stars.

Without supernovae, the elements of which our bodies are made would remain trapped in the core of stars like our Sun, and would not be available for use on cool planets, like Earth. For millions of years a continuous process of elemental enrichment, especially of oxygen, has been going on in the universe and these vital elements have been dispersed by the cataclysmic explosions of supernovae.

like Sanduleak -69°202 – about 18 times the mass of our Sun – this takes about 11 million years. When this happens gravity temporarily wins and the core contracts, increasing in density from about 6 g per cc (0.22 lb per cu in) to over 1 kg per cc (36 lb per cu in). This contraction heats up the core from about 40 million K to about 190 million K – a temperature that causes helium nuclei to fuse to form carbon. This rise in energy causes the outer layers of the star to expand to an enormous size – some four times the distance from the Earth to the Sun. At this stage the star is called a *red supergiant*. When the helium in the core is used up – in about a million years – a further contraction occurs and carbon nuclei fuse to form neon, magnesium and sodium at a temperature of 740 million K. The density of the core has now reached about 240 kg per cc (8,660 lb per cu in). Neon fuels a fusion reaction to form silicon at

a temperature of 2 billion degrees and a density of 50,000 kg per cc (800 tons per cu in) and silicon fuses to form iron, nickel, chromium, titanium, cobalt and other elements. At each stage the energy produced is less than that of the previous stage and the contraction is stopped for a shorter period. Carbon fuel halts contraction for only about 1,000 years; neon fuel stops it for only a very few years; silicon is exhausted in about a week. Iron is the most stable of the elements and cannot be used as a nuclear fuel. At this stage, the star is layered like an onion, with an iron core, surrounded by layers mainly of silicon, neon, oxygen, carbon, helium and, on the outside, hydrogen. The figures for temperature and density and for the length of each stage are obtained by computer modelling and are very approximate. Scientists differ as to the details. Now that there is no nuclear fuel

THE BIRTH AND DEATH OF A SUPERNOVA

Star uses up hydrogen fuel

Star begins to burn helium

Core shrinks and star burns heavier fuel

Core is now made of iron and explodes

left, gravity is unopposed and, in a few seconds, the star collapses with a staggering increase in density to about five billion tonnes per cubic centimetre.

At this stage, the temperature and pressure is sufficient to crush electrons and protons together to produce neutrons (⇨ p. 108). This is accompanied by a massive outpouring of *neutrinos*. These are neutral, massless particles that hardly interact with matter and stream out at nearly the speed of light, travelling almost unimpeded to the limits of the universe. In a fraction of a second the iron core of the star collapses into a ball of nuclear material about 100 km (62 mi) in diameter and of inconceivable density – probably around 300 billion kg per cc (5 billion tons per cu in). The reason for what happens next is still a matter of conjecture. Temperature rises critically, and the controlled fusion of the remaining nuclear fuel changes to a massive explosion that blasts the star into a fireball brighter than a billion Suns. This is the supernova. Some scientists hold that there is a limit to the possible density and that, at a certain point, a rebound occurs and the collapse is turned into an explosively rapid expansion causing a massive shock wave. Others suggest that the neutrino flood, which is known to carry an immense amount of energy, causes the shattering of the star. The visible light from a supernova does not leave it at the moment the core explodes. Although the neutrinos pass out almost instantaneously, it takes some time for the shock wave to reach the periphery of the exploding star, where it triggers off the display of visible light. In the case of Supernova 1987A, the ten-second neutrino burst reached Earth and was detected about two hours ahead of the

SUPERNOVA 1987A

On 24 February 1987 a young Canadian astronomer, Ian Shelton, working in Las Campanas Observatory, Chile, developed a routine photograph of the sky in the area of the Large Magellanic Cloud. To his astonishment he found a bright star in an area that, earlier, had shown no visible star. When he told his colleagues about this, he found that another scientist, Oscar Duhalde, had actually seen the new appearance with the naked eye a few hours earlier. Soon, astronomers all over the southern hemisphere were studying this phenomenon, which was below the horizon for most of the observatories in the northern hemisphere. Within hours it was known that the position of the new remarkably bright point was precisely that of a star catalogued as Sanduleak −69°202. This was a very bright star – a blue supergiant with a mass somewhere between 10 and 20 times that of the Sun. Stars of this kind burn up their nuclear fuel very quickly and have a lifetime of only about 20 million years. Within a day astronomers were able to obtain the spectrum (⇨ p. 80) of this phenomenon – to establish the pattern of radiation of different wavelengths given off by it. This proved beyond a doubt that the brightness was caused by the massive explosion of a star and that what was being witnessed was a supernova.

Scientists had previously witnessed hundreds of supernovae – a dozen or so are seen every year – but always from galaxies so distant that very little information could be obtained from them. This one was different. This was the brightest and nearest supernova that had been seen for 380 years. Prior to this, only one supernova – Supernova 1961V – had arisen from a previously identified star. The last supernova seen in our galaxy was described by Johannes Kepler (1571–1630) in 1604, before the telescope was invented. Supernova 1987A had occurred in a galaxy very close to ours – a satellite galaxy – only 160,000 light years away. Only three have been observed in our galaxy in the last 1,000 years. It is natural to think of the supernova as actually occurring at the time of observation, but, of course, Supernova 1987A in fact occurred 160,000 years ago, probably around the time of Neanderthal hominids and light from it has taken that long to reach Earth.

Supernova 1987A provided astronomers with a unique opportunity to investigate this important phenomenon. Its brightness was seen to peak in late May 1987 and then it started to fade.

The creation of supernova 1987A – before and after. The upper photograph was taken in 1969 and the lower one on 26 February 1987, two days after the appearance of the supernova (bright star on the right-hand side). Supernova 1987A lies in the Large Magellanic Cloud, a satellite galaxy of our own Milky Way. (NOAO, SPL)

arrival of the visible light. As it happened, an amateur astronomer in New Zealand was examining the exact point at which the supernova was to appear two hours after the time of the arrival of the neutrino burst and saw nothing. An automatic photograph, taken an hour later, showed, when developed, the first visible sign of the supernova. This interval between the arrival of the neutrinos and the arrival of the light fitted in with the known size of the star Sanduleak −69°202 and confirmed that it was this star that had exploded.

Massively dense neutron star formed out of core

Supernova produced

Expanded gas cloud breaks up

The Sun and the Solar System

The Sun is the only star near enough to us to be observed as more than simply a point of light. Although stars vary greatly in size, the Sun is typical of many, and is identical in size, brightness and energy output to countless others in the universe. It is the source of all our energy and essential to the survival of human and all other life forms. Around it, in various orbits, move the nine planets in our solar system and a huge number of asteroids, meteors and comets – all of them under the Sun's gravitational attraction.

Before the age of scientific sophistication the Sun was supposed to be a kind of spherical bonfire that travelled round the Earth, illuminating it by day and leaving it in darkness by night. This idea left two major questions unanswered: why did the fire not burn up, and where did the Sun go at night? Even when Copernicus (⇨ p. 120) showed that the universe was not

centred upon the Earth but that the Earth and planets were spherical bodies that moved round the Sun, it was still a major puzzle as to how the Sun kept burning (⇨ box). This question became even more pressing when the distance, dimensions, mass and energy output of the Sun became approximately known, and some idea of the length of time it had been burning became apparent. On the basis of these figures, it simply did not make sense to suppose that the Sun was a large coal fire. Such a fire would have burnt itself out well within the span of recorded history.

The Sun's vital statistics

In terms of temperature and brightness, the Sun is a typical star. It is, however, small compared with some stars that are up to 300 times its diameter. It is a mass of high-temperature gas, one quarter helium and three quarters hydrogen, together with a small proportion (about 2 per cent) of other heavier elements. The temperature at the surface is about 5,770 K but the temperature at the centre is much higher – about 15 million K. The Sun's gravity, at its surface, is 27 times that of the Earth and, were it not for the enormous energy of its core, it would collapse inwards under the force of its own gravity. The Sun's energy is derived from a continuous nuclear-fusion reaction (⇨ p. 116) in which hydrogen atoms are fused to form helium. In the course of this, some

matter is converted into energy. This explains how the Sun has been able to continue to radiate at about the same rate for the 4.6 billion years of its estimated life. Since, in that time, only about a quarter of its hydrogen has been converted to helium, there is still fuel for a considerable period. Life as we know it is possible only within a quite narrow temperature band, so we can assume that the Sun's output has not varied very greatly for many millions of years.

The Sun is about 1.4 million km (900,000 mi) in diameter – more than 100 times the diameter of the Earth – and its volume is nearly 1.4 million times that of the Earth. As it is composed mainly of light gases, its average density is, however, much less than that of Earth – only about one quarter. The average distance of the Sun from the Earth is about 150,000,000 km (93,000,000 mi). Most of its energy is given off in the form of ultraviolet, visible light and infrared radiation, but the Sun also radiates all other wavelengths in the electromagnetic spectrum (⇨ p. 84), including the very-short-wavelength gamma rays and X-rays and the longer-wavelength microwaves and radio waves.

The structure of the Sun

The Sun is best considered as consisting of a series of concentric spherical shells. The *core* – the nuclear reactor – is relatively small, being less than one

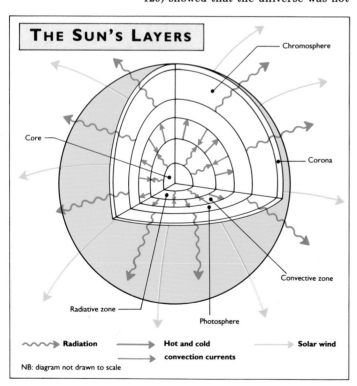

THE SUN'S LAYERS

Chromosphere

Core

Corona

Convective zone

Radiative zone

Photosphere

〰️➡️ Radiation   ➡️ Hot and cold convection currents   ➡️ Solar wind

NB: diagram not drawn to scale

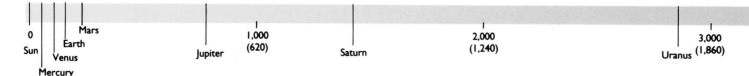

0	Mars	1,000 (620)	2,000 (1,240)	3,000 (1,860)
Sun	Earth	Jupiter	Saturn	Uranus
Mercury Venus				

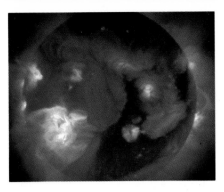

Solar activity. False-colour image of the Sun, made by 'soft' X-rays (250–3,000 electronvolt energy) in which the brightness of the image is proportional to the X-ray intensity. An especially active region is seen towards the bottom left, and a loop-shaped solar flare is visible at centre right. Patches of high X-ray emission are often associated with sunspots (areas of cooler gases on the Sun's surface). (NASA, JISAS, SPL)

thousandth of the total volume. The density of the core is, however, very high, being 160 g per cc (5.8 lb per cu in) – 160 times that of water. Surrounding the core is the *radiative zone* through which energy passes by radiation (⇨ p. 52). Because of the size and density of this zone, radiation is greatly slowed and takes anything up to 10,000,000 years to pass through it. The attenuating effect of the interference of the energetic gas in this zone also has the important consequence that the wavelength of most of the gamma rays and X-rays is lengthened

so that they emerge as visible light and heat (infrared radiation). Around the radiative zone is the *convective zone*. Here, heat is conveyed outwards by convection currents. Hot gases rise to the surface and cooler gases descend to be heated by the radiation passing through the zone below.

Outside the convective zone is the *photosphere*, with a temperature of about 6,000 K from which energy is radiated out into space. This is the source of the Sun's visible light and other radiation. Beyond this is a more rarefied layer known as the *chromosphere*, whose temperature is significantly lower at about 4,300 K. Beyond this is the solar atmosphere, known as the *corona*, which is of very low density but in which the temperature rises again rapidly to between 1,000,000 K and 5,000,000 K. This remarkable rise in temperature is due to the low density of the corona, which allows gas particles to move at much higher speeds than in the denser photosphere and chromosphere. The corona is too rarefied to be visible from Earth under normal conditions, but can be seen briefly during a total eclipse of the Sun. From the corona, a constant stream of particles, mainly protons, neutrons and electrons, flow out into space. This is known as the *solar wind*.

The theory of the formation of the solar system

Our solar system, consisting of the Sun and the nine planets (⇨ pp. 134–7), is the only such system known in detail. Life can exist only on a planetary system so there is considerable scientific interest about the origins of such systems and about whether many other planetary systems exist around other stars.

Many theories have been proposed for the origin of the solar system, which took place some 4,600 million years ago. At the end of the 19th century most astronomers believed that the planets came into existence as a result of a near collision between our Sun and another large celestial body. Today, the general scientific opinion is that our planets arose at the time of the formation of the Sun from gravitational condensation of a diffuse cloud of celestial gas and dust, known as a *nebula*. Nebulae are very common in the universe and many of them are very hot. Some of this matter originates in supernova explosions (⇨ p. 130), and it is possible that such an explosion may have initiated the aggregation of celestial matter to form our solar system. A condensing nebula forms a flat, spinning disc with a dense centre and a less dense periphery. At first, most of the rotational energy (angular momentum; ⇨ p. 30) is in the central

mass, but this can later be transferred to the outer parts. The gravitational attraction of the central mass causes compression and heating, and the star (sun) is thus formed. The cooler outer particles are gravitationally attracted towards each other and gradually coalesce, building up progressively larger bodies orbiting the sun. The larger these become, the greater is their gravitational attraction for other matter. Only small planets can form near the sun, but further out much larger planets can form. As the nuclear reactions in the condensing sun get under way, the solar wind forms to drive away the remaining gas and dust. Many larger debris particles of varying size survive indefinitely and continue to rotate in orbit. This is called the *accretion theory* of the origin of the solar system.

In recent years it has become increasingly evident from advanced methods of investigation that at least some young stars are surrounded by just such discs of gas and dust as the theory postulates. Currently these can be detected by satellite observation around only a few comparatively nearby stars; most stars are too far away for any planetary systems to be seen. The evidence suggests, however, that planetary systems may not be uncommon. It is hoped that the Hubble space telescope (⇨ p. 124) may be able to resolve more of these. If planetary systems prove to be very common, the probability of the existence of extraterrestrial life becomes very high.

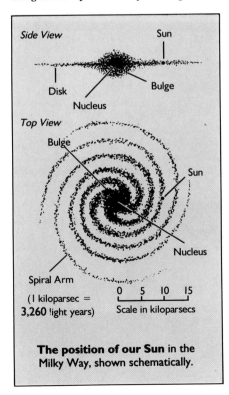

Side View

Sun

Disk

Bulge

Nucleus

Top View

Bulge

Sun

Nucleus

Spiral Arm

(1 kiloparsec = **3,260** light years)

| 0 | 5 | 10 | 15 |

Scale in kiloparsecs

The position of our Sun in the Milky Way, shown schematically.

SEE ALSO

- CIRCULAR MOTION AND GRAVITATION p. 30
- WHAT IS ENERGY? pp. 46–9
- HEAT TRANSFER p. 52
- THERMODYNAMICS p. 54
- SOURCES OF ENERGY pp. 58–61
- LIGHT pp. 72–5
- SPECTRA AND SPECTROSCOPY p. 80
- FUNDAMENTAL FORCES p. 112
- COSMOLOGY: UNDERSTANDING THE UNIVERSE p. 120
- BIG BANG p. 126
- BLACK HOLES p. 128
- SUPERNOVAE p. 130
- THE INNER PLANETS p. 134
- THE OUTER PLANETS p. 136

SUN

Pluto

Mercury

Mars

Venus

Earth

Neptune

Uranus

Saturn

Jupiter

THE SOLAR SYSTEM

The comparative sizes of the planets (above) in order of size, and (left) a scale showing the distances of the planets from the Sun.

4,000
(2,480)

Neptune

5,000
(3,100)

Pluto

Millions of km (mi)

The Inner Planets

Planets are nonluminous celestial bodies that move in orbit around a central star, but the term 'the planets' is usually applied to the nine large satellite bodies of our Sun that form the solar system. Four of the Sun's satellites – Mercury, Venus, Earth and Mars – are known as the *inner planets*, and five – Jupiter, Saturn, Uranus, Neptune and Pluto – are known as the *outer planets*. Separating the inner from the outer planets is the great asteroid belt, between the orbits of Mars and Jupiter. The planetary system of the Sun forms an immense, flat disc, and all the orbits lie roughly in the same plane.

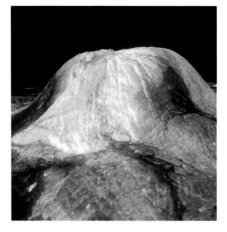

Computer-simulated view of part of the surface of Venus, which is made up vast plains, scattered with mountains and deep impact craters. (IS)

The four terrestrial planets, Earth (top), Mars (lower left), Mercury (centre) and Venus (lower right), drawn to scale against the outer planet Jupiter's Great Red Spot. (Julian Baum, SPL)

The inner planets are comparatively small, relative to the outer planets, but are of higher density, indicating that they are made of solid, rocky material. All have elliptical orbits, that of Mercury being the least circular. All the orbits lie in almost the same plane around the Sun. The orbit of Mercury is inclined at an angle of 7° and its distance from the Sun varies by 24,000,000 km (15,000,000 mi). All the planets move in orbit in the same direction as the rotation of the Sun on its own axis and all, except Venus, also rotate on their own axes in the same direction. Venus, surprisingly, rotates very slowly in the opposite (*retrograde*) direction.

Mercury

Mercury, the planet closest to the Sun, is the smallest of the inner planets. It moves round the Sun taking 88 Earth days to do so, in an elliptical orbit, varying, in distance from the Sun (46–70,000,000 km or 29–43,000,000 mi). It rotates slowly on its axis with a day equal to 58.6 Earth days. Mercury is difficult to see from Earth and appears only about once every two months, always close to the Sun.

Mercury is 4,878 km (3,048 mi) in diameter – about 40 per cent of that of the Earth – and of high density with a large core consisting mainly of iron, probably partly molten. The surface of Mercury is very hot, varying, at midday, according to the distance from the Sun, from 285°C (545°F) to 415°C (779°F). Because of the lack of a blanketing atmosphere the night-time temperature is very low – down to about −175°C (−283°F). There is

very little atmosphere because such daytime temperatures excite any atmospheric particles to a level of energy that allows their escape from the very low gravity of the planet. Mercury has a magnetic field that, although much lower than that of the Earth, is still strong enough to deflect the solar wind (⇨ p. 132) streaming past it.

The American *Mariner* spacecraft passed close to Mercury in 1974 and 1975, and showed that the surface is covered with impact craters very similar to those of our Moon. The largest crater, named the Caloris Basin because it is in one of the hottest areas (from the Latin *calor*, 'heat') of the planet, is about 1,300 km (810 mi) across. The Sun is directly over this crater when Mercury is at its nearest point to the Sun (*perihelion*). The floor of the Caloris Basin is broken up into ridges. Mercury is not so heavily cratered as the Moon and has extensive plains free from cratering. These plains show numerous ridges or scarps, running for hundreds of kilometres, that are thought to be 'wrinkles' thrown up during the contraction of the crust as it cooled and solidified.

Venus

The second minor planet, in order outwards from the Sun, is Venus, sometimes known as the 'morning star' or 'evening star' because it is clearly visible from Earth around sunrise and sunset. Because of its dense, silvery atmosphere, Venus is highly conspicuous as the brightest object in the night sky after the Moon. It is a solid globe 12,104 km (7,565 mi) in diameter and most closely resembles Earth in size, mass and distance from the Sun.

Its orbit around the Sun is almost circular, with a radius of about 108,000,000 km (67,000,000 mi), and one orbit takes 225 Earth days, a Venusian year. Unlike the other planets, Venus rotates on its axis in the opposite direction to that of the Sun's rotation – probably because of the gravitational pull on it of the Earth. This retrograde rotation is, however, very slow, taking 243 Earth days. The Venusian day is thus longer than its year.

The atmosphere is dense and hot, and consists largely of carbon dioxide with swirling vapour clouds of sulphuric acid, hydrochloric acid and hydrofluoric acid. This dense atmosphere prevents loss of

The planet Mercury (right) photographed by *Mariner 10* in 1974. Temperatures on the sunward side reach 400°C (750°F), while the dark side is a chilly −170°C (−274°F). (IS)

The boulder-strewn Martian landscape (far right) as seen by *Viking 2* on Mars's Utopian Plain. (IS)

heat and maintains the surface temperature of the planet at a constant 475°C (887°F) – hot enough to melt lead. It also exerts a pressure at the surface of the planet some 90 times that of the Earth's atmospheric pressure.

Until the latter part of the 20th century, the dense atmosphere prevented astronomers making out any details of the surface, but, as radio waves can penetrate the clouds, radio astronomy (⇔ p. 124) and space probes have been able to plot considerable surface detail. Two uncrewed Soviet spacecraft landed on Venus in 1975 and sent back panoramic photographs of a desert landscape strewn with boulders and rocks. The most extensive information, however, has come from the American NASA spacecraft *Magellan*, fitted with highly sophisticated radar, capable of resolving detail as small as 120 m (394 ft) across. *Magellan* began mapping the surface of Venus in September 1990 and has sent back an immense amount of data.

The surface of Venus appears to be between 100,000,000 and 1,000,000,000 years old and is covered with craters, folded mountain ranges and areas of lava flow and faults, indicating a history of turbulent volcanic activity and impact from large meteors. There are features resembling river beds – probably caused by flowing lava – and mysterious flat circular areas without definite craters.

Earth

Our Earth is the third planet from the Sun. Its structure and properties are dealt with elsewhere (⇔ pp. 144–7).

Mars

Known as the 'red planet' because of the prominence of iron oxide (rust) in its soil and dust, Mars is closer in its characteristics to the Earth than any other planet. Its diameter is about 6,800 km (4,250 mi) – just over half that of Earth – but its mass is only about one tenth that of Earth. The Martian year is equal to 1.88 Earth years, and the day is only 37 minutes longer than the Earth day. Both planets have a tilted axis of rotation so that different amounts of sunlight fall on each hemisphere at different times of the year, causing seasonal weather changes. The difference between the Martian summer and winter is, however, more extreme than on Earth because its orbit round the Sun is more elliptical and the distance from the Sun varies from 206,000,000 km (128,000,000 mi) to 249,000,000 km (155,000,000 mi). This difference of 43,000,000 km (26,000,000 mi) means that the southern hemisphere of Mars receives 40 per cent more solar radiation when nearest to the Sun (perihelion) than when furthest away (*aphelion*), giving a warm summer and a cold winter. The northern hemisphere has a cool summer and a mild winter. Temperatures at the equator can range from 10°C (50°F) to −75°C (−103°F). The distance of Mars from Earth varies from 50,000,000 km (80,000,000 mi) to 100,000,000 km

GIOVANNI SCHIAPARELLI AND THE MARTIAN CANALS

Optical inspection of Mars has always been difficult, even when the planet is at its nearest approach to Earth. In 1877, when Mars was indeed at its nearest point to Earth, the Italian astronomer Giovanni Virginio Schiaparelli (1835–1910), head of the Brera observatory in Milan, published a map of the Martian surface. Schiaparelli's observations were meticulous and close and he assigned names to the bright and dark areas. His map also featured a large number of straight lines that had been noted, the previous year, by the Italian priest Pietro Secchi. Both Secchi and Schiaparelli called these lines *canali* – the Italian for 'channels'. Schiaparelli continued to study Mars and by 1881 he was convinced that the lines were connected to each other.

Unfortunately, when his reports were translated into English, the word *canali* became 'canals' and the view rapidly spread that here was clear evidence of intelligent life on Mars – a system of canals dug to exploit the polar ice caps for purposes of irrigation, agriculture and water supply.

Schiaparelli had never intended to suggest such an interpretation but the idea caught the popular imagination, especially after the publication, in 1895, of a book by the aristocratic American astronomer Percival Lowell (1855–1916). Excited by the supposed Italian findings, the wealthy Lowell set up his own private observatory and, for 15 years, studied Mars, drawing ever more detailed pictures of the 'canals', of the oases at their intersections and of land changes he attributed to the growth of crops. Lowell's findings were never confirmed and were eventually dismissed as artefacts or optical illusions, but his account gave rise to a whole genre of science fiction. Lowell was more successful in another context. Aware of the perturbations in the orbit of the outer planet Uranus, he proposed that these were caused by a new and unknown planet X. His search for this putative planet failed, but in 1930, 14 years after his death, the planet was discovered and named Pluto (⇔ p. 136), after the Greek god of the underworld.

Map of Mars prepared by the 19th-century Italian astronomer Giovanni Schiaparelli, based on his observations between 1877 and 1888. (AR)

(160,000,000 mi), and the closest approach to Earth occurs every 15 or 17 years.

The Martian atmosphere is very thin – about one per cent of that of Earth – and consists mainly of carbon dioxide with some nitrogen and argon along with traces of oxygen and water vapour. The atmospheric pressure is very low. The surface details of Mars have always been difficult to make out because optical observations have to be made through two atmospheres (⇔ box), but thousands of pictures taken by *Mariner* and *Viking* spacecraft have revealed a surface with many features. Two *Viking* spacecraft landed on Mars in 1976 and took many close-up photographs of the rock-strewn surface of dusty, reddish plains. There are many inactive volcanoes, one 24 km (15 mi) high; large numbers of flat-bottomed craters from meteorite impacts, especially in the southern hemisphere; a huge rift valley near the equator running east for 3,000 km (1,875 mi); and many smaller valleys and canyons. These have the appearance of having been caused by water erosion and this is by no means implausible. At each pole is a white cap of snow, ice and frozen carbon dioxide that changes size with the seasons, reaching as far as 45° latitude in

the wintertime. Frosty crater rims protrude upwards through the snow.

Most scientists believe that there is considerable water on Mars in the form of a permafrost. At various periods in the past, floods of water may have occurred. No liquid water can, however, exist today, as, because of the low atmospheric pressure, it would immediately vaporize and circulate to the poles where it would freeze. The darker areas on Mars sometimes appear even darker when the polar ice caps regress. This was once taken to be evidence of the growth of vegetation as the water supply increased, but is now known to be due to the uncovering of dark rock as the fine surface dust is blown away. Dust storms are common on Mars, and these sometimes cover almost the whole planet in a red haze. No conclusive evidence of any life form or of any kind of biological activity or organic chemical compounds, has ever been found on Mars.

Mars has two satellites (moons) – Phobos and Deimos – discovered in 1877 by the American astronomer Asaph Hall (1829–1907) during the same approximation to Earth of Mars in which Giovanni Schiaparelli drew his famous map (⇔ box).

The Outer Planets

Beyond the asteroid belt lie the outer planets, Jupiter, Saturn, Uranus, Neptune and Pluto – four giants and one midget. Much has been discovered about these celestial bodies, especially as a result of the remarkable exploratory journey of *Voyager 2*, between 1978 and 1989.

The distances of the inner planets from the Sun seem a mere step by comparison with the vast and increasing distances between the outer planets. These extend out into the cold vastness of space, so far from the Sun that the most remote can hardly be seen from the Earth even with the best terrestrial telescopes. Even so, with the sole exception of Pluto, we have a remarkable amount of detailed knowledge of all of them.

Jupiter

Jupiter is the largest planet in the solar system and the fifth out from the Sun, which it orbits at a distance of 778,300,000 km (483,700,000 mi) – over five times the distance of the Earth from the Sun. Its composition is very different from that of the Earth. It has an inner solid-rock core surrounded by a liquid zone and a massive atmosphere. Most of Jupiter consists of hydrogen and helium – the two lightest elements. Even so, its total mass is twice that of all the other planets put together, and it is about one thousandth the size and mass of the Sun. Indeed Jupiter more closely resembles the Sun than the other planets. The predominance of hydrogen and helium indicates that these elements were attracted to the massive core by gravitation in the course of the formation of the planet. Jupiter can be considered to represent a

Jupiter's southern hemisphere, photographed by *Voyager 2* in 1979. Io, one of Jupiter's moons, is visible in the foreground. (IS)

The rings of Saturn are made of small chunks of ice and rocks and measure about 275,000 km (170,000 mi) from edge to edge. They are, however only about 100 m (300 ft) thick. Planetary rings, once believed to be a feature only of Saturn, are now known to exist also around Jupiter, Uranus and Neptune. (IS)

'failed star'. If it had been several times larger, its gravitational field would have produced core temperatures and pressures high enough to start off a nuclear-fusion reaction, using the plentiful supply of hydrogen fuel.

Because so much of Jupiter consists of hydrogen and helium, its average density is very low – about 1.3 g per cc (0.05 lb per cu in). Jupiter spins on its axis at a tremendous speed for anything so large, and rotates completely in just under ten Earth hours. This high speed causes it to deviate considerably from a spherical shape and its diameter at the equator – 142,800 km (88,700 mi) – is over 9,000 km (5,600 mi) greater than the distance between the North and South poles. Such a shape, a 'flattened' sphere, is called an *oblate spheroid*.

The Jovian atmosphere consists almost entirely of hydrogen and helium, with traces of water vapour, methane, ammonia, hydrogen sulphide and various other organic compounds. The atmosphere is believed to contain heavy layers of clouds of different colours, forming orange-brown coloured bands, readily visible by telescope from Earth and described as 'belts'. Lightning storms and auroras are common, and these were observed by the *Voyager* spacecraft in 1979. Strong east and west winds sweep round parallel to the equator.

The high internal temperature means that the electrons (⬦ pp. 90 and 156) are stripped off hydrogen atoms making them electrically charged particles (*ions*). The rotation currents of these ions around the core of the planet produces a powerful magnetic field (⬦ p. 88), 4,000 times stronger than that of the Earth. The axis of this field does not quite coincide with the axis of rotation of the planet so the field wobbles rapidly, sending out a strong radio signal.

All the other giant outer planets radiate energy, but Jupiter radiates about twice as much as it receives from the Sun, implying that it has an internal energy source. This is derived from the heat caused by its own gravitational compression during formation 4.6 billion years

ago. The energy from the interior drives mass movement of the atmosphere – visible as changes in the relative position of the darker belts and lighter zones.

Jupiter has four moons, which, remarkably, were detected by Galileo in 1610, using one of the first astronomical telescopes. These moons – Callisto, Ganymede, Europa and Io – move in circular orbits around the planet. Ganymede is the largest planetary moon in the solar system. There are also numerous smaller bodies and dust particles and a tenuous ring system – much less conspicuous than that of Saturn – of microscopic particles of size close to the wavelength of light.

Saturn

Saturn, the sixth planet from the Sun, is the most remarkable in appearance on account of its conspicuous ring system. This can easily be seen with a small telescope. Saturn is somewhat smaller than Jupiter and is the second largest of the planets. Its diameter at the equator is 120,660 km (74,980 mi) and it rotates once in just over ten and a half Earth hours (10 hours 40 minutes). Like Jupiter, it is an oblate spheroid, and is composed mainly of hydrogen and helium with a rocky inner core similar in size to that of Jupiter. Like the other three giant outer planets, Saturn has a dense gaseous atmosphere, and it is this that is seen on optical observation. Its density – 0.69 g per cc (0.025 lb per cu in) – is only about half that of Jupiter, indicating that the core is relatively smaller. The density of water is 1 g per cc.

Saturn orbits the Sun at an average distance of 1.427 billion km (886,000,000 mi), taking nearly thirty Earth years to do so. The orbit is slightly elliptical and is inclined at a small angle to the Earth's orbital plane (the *ecliptic plane*). The Saturnian atmosphere, largely of hydrogen and helium, shows shifting dark belts and light zones similar to those on Jupiter but, about every 30 years or so, a great white spot appears, thought to consist of frozen ammonia. Like Jupiter, Saturn has a powerful magnetic field.

Saturn's rings form a visible disc, observed by Galileo but first identified by the Dutch physicist Christian Huygens (1629–93) in 1655. Later it was noted that the ring disc is in two parts separated by a dark space. At first it was assumed that the ring disc was of solid material, but the British physicist James Clerk Maxwell (1831–79) proved in 1857 that such a system could not survive and that the rings must be particulate in nature. Later investigation, mainly by the *Voyager* spacecraft, showed that most of the ring particles are of ice, of size probably varying from centimetres to metres in diameter, and that the structure of the system is far more complex than had been imagined. It actually consists of an elaboration of hundreds of separate ringlets, some of which are elliptical. In addition to the rings, Saturn has the

Composite image of Uranus and its moons, made from photographs taken by *Voyager 2* in 1986. Uranus is the featureless blue planet at the centre. The moons are (clockwise from bottom) Ariel, Umbriel, Oberon, Titania and Miranda. (NASA, SPL)

largest satellite (moon) system of all the planets. Over 20 orbiting bodies have been identified and six can easily be seen with a telescope. The largest moon is Titan, which is second in size only to the Jovian moon Ganymede (⇨ above), and is the only satellite in the solar system known to have a significant atmosphere. It is largely composed of nitrogen. The atmosphere is determined mainly by the very low temperature of the moon of –180°C (–292°F) at which other gases are either liquid or solid. Some of the other moons are Phoebe, Hyperion, Iapetus, Mimas, Enceladus, Tethys, Dione, Rhea, Epimetheus and Janus.

Uranus

Uranus, the seventh planet and the fourth largest, is not normally visible to the naked eye. It was first identified as a planet by the British astronomer William Herschel (1738–1822) in 1781, who at first thought it was a comet. It had been observed previously, but moved so slowly that it was originally thought to be a star. It is nearly 20 times as far from the Sun as is the Earth – some 2.870 billion km (1.783 billion mi) – and takes over 84 Earth years for each revolution. Remarkably, the axis of rotation of Uranus, instead of being roughly perpendicular to the plane of the orbit, lies almost *in* the plane. This means that in the course of a Uranian year each pole has 42 years of day followed by 42 years of night.

Uranus has a diameter of 51,800 km (32,200 mi) and a density of 1.15 g per cc (0.04 lb per cu in). Relatively more of the

Neptune shown in this *Voyager 2* false-colour image taken in 1989, when the spacecraft passed within 5,000 km (3,100 mi) of Neptune's North pole. The prominent Great Red Spot (centre) is a storm system the size of Earth. (NASA, SPL)

heavier elements, such as carbon, oxygen and nitrogen are present than in Jupiter and Saturn. Its dense atmosphere contains a considerable amount of methane, giving it a bluish colour. Most of this methane is contained in layers of clouds thought to be over 10,000 km (6,220 mi) thick, and this dense cloud covering makes observation difficult. The chief atmospheric gas is hydrogen and, in addition to methane, helium and ammonia are also present.

On 24 January 1986, eight and a half years after its launch, the spacecraft *Voyager 2* sped past Uranus at a distance of only 81,543 km (50,679 mi) and at a speed of 72,405 km (45,000 mi) per hour. Because Uranus is so far from the Sun, the ambient light is only about ¹⁄₄₀₀ that on Earth, so long photographic exposures were needed. This, together with the speed of the craft, made clear photography very difficult. In the event, little was revealed visually, the planet being seen to be blanketed by a pale blue haze. Observations were, however, made of the rate of rotation of the planet and a value of just over 17 Earth hours was obtained. *Voyager 2* also confirmed the existence of a strong magnetic field, at least as strong as that of Saturn.

Uranus has five major moons, Oberon, Titania, Umbriel, Ariel and Miranda. *Voyager 2* obtained remarkable photographs of these moons, especially of Ariel, with detail down to 2.4 km (1½ mi). The spacecraft also discovered 10 new moons ranging in size from about 16 km (10 mi) to 160 km (100 mi) in diameter. The planet also has an inconspicuous system of at least 11 dark rings.

Neptune

The eighth planet from the Sun, Neptune is the most remote and least known of the giants. Its position was predicted before it was seen (⇨ box). It is so far from the Sun – 4.497 billion km (2.794 billion mi) – that it reflects too little light to be seen with the naked eye. One revolution of this enormous orbit takes no less a time than 164.793 Earth years and the planet rotates on its own axis probably in about 18 hours. Neptune is 49,500 km (30,750 mi) in diameter, and its spectrum shows that it is composed of hydrogen, methane and probably ethane. It is a very cold planet with a temperature well below –200°C (–328°F), and it has two moons, Triton and Nereid. The former, 2,720 km (1,690 mi) in diameter, is probably the coldest body in the solar system. It has ice caps of frozen methane, liquid nitrogen and water. In addition there are at least six other smaller satellites ranging in size from 50 to 200 km (31 to 124 mi) in diameter.

Voyager 2 passed Neptune, barely 4,850 km (3,000 mi) above its surface, on 24 August 1989 and sent back thousands of remarkably clear images by radio. These showed a turbulent world beset by massive storms sweeping around its equator at 1,000 km (625 mi) per hour. The planet is covered with banks of silvery cirrus,

JOHN COUCH ADAMS AND THE DISCOVERY OF NEPTUNE

To explain certain known irregularities in the orbit of Uranus, two astronomers, quite independently of each other, calculated, in 1845 and 1846, that a hitherto unknown planet must exist. These scientists were the Englishman John Couch Adams (1819–92) and the Frenchman Urbain Jean Joseph Le Verrier (1811–77). Adams was the first to make the prediction but Le Verrier's, although made nine months later, was, through no fault of Adams, the first to be published. On 23 September 1846, Le Verrier's prediction was confirmed at the Berlin observatory by the German astronomer Johann Gottfried Galle (1812–1910). A new planet was discovered within one degree of the position suggested. Adams's prior prediction was equally good but his repeated attempts to bring it to the attention of the Astronomer Royal failed, and the notes he left with him were ignored until it was too late. This English procrastination led to a bitter dispute over priority and Adams's claim was not recognized for many years, during which the English Royal Society awarded its Copley Medal to Le Verrier alone.

It has recently been hypothesized that a tenth small planet exists beyond the orbit of Pluto.

thin, wispy clouds extending out some 50 km (31 mi) from the watery surface. The atmosphere consists largely of hydrogen, helium and methane, and its core is of molten rock. Neptune has four remarkable, incomplete, thin dust rings. The images of Triton were of astonishing detail, showing great canyons, craters and peaks.

Pluto

Pluto is the ninth planet, the smallest, most remote and the least known. Even the largest of telescopes show it as no more than a featureless blob. Its distance from the Sun averages 5.970 billion km (3.700 billion mi), but its orbit is very eccentric and brings it inside the orbit of Neptune at its closest approach. Fortunately, their paths do not cross. Pluto takes 250 Earth years to move once round the Sun. It has a diameter of about 4,000 km (2,500 mi) and probably consists of a rocky, silicate core surrounded by a blanket of ice of various gases and liquids, including methane frost. When furthest from the Sun, the planet is probably covered with methane snow. And there is methane in the very thin atmosphere. Pluto has one moon, Charon, which was discovered in 1978 and which is about half Pluto's diameter – so large compared with Pluto that they should really be considered a two-planet system.

Artist's impression of Pluto (foreground) and its moon Charon with the Sun in the far distance (top right). Charon orbits Pluto in 6.4 days – exactly the same as Pluto's rotational period. (David Hardy, SPL)

SEE ALSO

- SCIENTIFIC INSTRUMENTS pp. 14–17
- CIRCULAR MOTION AND GRAVITATION p. 30
- COSMOLOGY: UNDERSTANDING THE UNIVERSE p. 120
- ASTRONOMICAL INSTRUMENTS AND TECHNIQUES pp. 122–5
- BIG BANG p. 126
- BLACK HOLES p. 128
- SUPERNOVAE p. 130
- THE SUN AND THE SOLAR SYSTEM p. 132
- THE INNER PLANETS p. 134
- THE MOON p. 138
- THE ROTATION AND ORBIT OF THE EARTH p. 144

The Moon

Often the most conspicuous feature of the night sky, our only natural satellite, the Moon, has always been of special interest. This is because of its apparent size and because it is the only body that appears to the naked eye as more than a point of light.

The Moon is the only extraterrestrial body, other than spacecraft, on which human beings have set foot. In several respects it is unusual in the solar system. Only Charon, Pluto's moon, for instance, which was not discovered until 1978, rivals our Moon in its size relative to its planet. Because of its proximity and accessibility we know more about our Moon than about any other celestial body. The Moon is probably the same age as the Earth – about 4,500 million years – and is made of the same materials as Earth in about the same proportions. These facts were confirmed when samples were brought back after the American NASA *Apollo* Moon landings between 1969 and 1972. On a clear night, one needs only a quite modest telescope, or a good pair of binoculars, to make out a remarkable amount of detail on the Moon's surface. Only one side of the Moon is visible from the Earth because it rotates on its axis in the same time as it revolves around the Earth. This is because the Earth's gravity has had a braking effect on the spin of the Moon, resulting in a *captured rotation*. Other planetary moons suffer the same fate.

Visible features of the Moon

The Moon's surface is highly irregular and consists of dark, flat-looking areas known as the *maria*, or 'seas', numerous craters of greatly varying diameter and

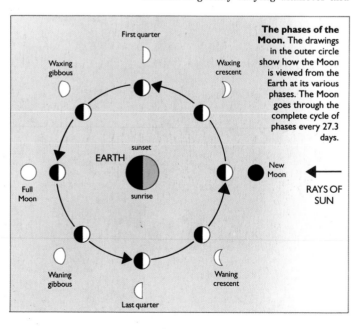

The phases of the Moon. The drawings in the outer circle show how the Moon is viewed from the Earth at its various phases. The Moon goes through the complete cycle of phases every 27.3 days.

First quarter

Waxing gibbous

Waxing crescent

Waning gibbous

Waning crescent

Full Moon

New Moon

Last quarter

EARTH

sunset

sunrise

RAYS OF SUN

THE MOON AND THE TIDES

A body as massive as the Moon must have a significant gravitational effect on the Earth. This is seen most obviously in its effect on the most mobile parts of the Earth's surface – the seas. The Sun also affects the seas but, because the Moon is so much nearer, its effect is more than twice as great as that of the Sun. The rotation of the Earth causes a force that raises a bulge in the oceans, all round. This is balanced by the Earth's inward gravitational pull on the seas. The gravitational pulls of the Moon and the Sun, however, also cause the oceans to bulge outward, but this is greatest in the part of the oceans facing the Moon and the Sun, and least on the other side. The difference between the two causes the tides.

When both Moon and Sun are pulling in the same direction – that is, when the Earth, the Moon and the Sun all lie in roughly a straight line – their effects on the tides are greatest, causing the Spring tides at full Moon and new Moon. When the Moon and the Sun are pulling on the Earth at right angles, at the first quarter and last quarter of the Moon, the tides are less high. These are the *neap tides*. The effect of tidal changes are, of course, greatly modified by coastal features.

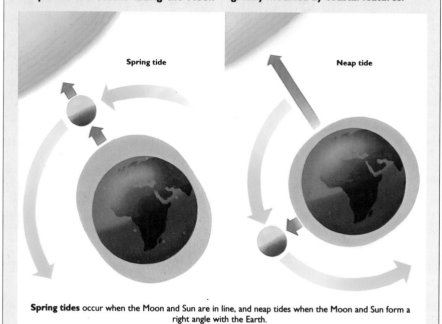

Spring tide

Neap tide

Spring tides occur when the Moon and Sun are in line, and neap tides when the Moon and Sun form a right angle with the Earth.

depth, mountains and mountainous ridges of a brighter appearance and various straight-line features, often radiating from the craters, known as the *rays*. They are not, in fact, seas but plains of solidified lava resulting from earlier volcanic activity, some of them more than 1,000 km (625 mi) across. The mountains are of rocks similar to Earth granite and contain much pure feldspar, which is highly reflective of the Sun's rays.

The craters are irregularly distributed, being densely packed in some areas and relatively sparse in others. They are almost certainly the result of a tremendous bombardment of the Moon by small solid objects or minor planets (*asteroids*) and by masses of frozen grit, dust and other materials (*comets*) that occurred over a period of 200–300 million years during the early development of the solar system (⇨ p. 132). The same bombardment left the surface of the Moon covered with rocky debris and fine dust. The absence of any lunar atmosphere meant that anything striking the Moon would neither be slowed nor weakened before impact. Most would have struck at a speed of several kilometres per second, releasing an enormous amount of energy in so doing. Such impacts would have had the effect

of explosions, causing craters and scattering debris and dust all around. The largest impacts, often with bodies up to 100 km (62 mi) across, would not only have produced massive craters, but would have released so much energy in the form of heat that the inside of the crater would have been layered with molten material that would have set flat. Samples brought back by the Apollo mission confirm that this material consists of grains of preexisting crystalline rock that have been welded together by high temperatures (*breccias*).

Following the period of bombardment, the Moon underwent a period of intense volcanic activity, and an immense amount of molten lava was poured out onto its surface to spread and set. This lava is very similar to volcanic lava on Earth, but with a richer content of iron and titanium. This gives it a darker colour that imparts the dark appearance to the 'seas'.

The most conspicuous feature of the near side of the Moon is the great crater known as Copernicus. This is by no means the largest but it is striking for the thickness of its walls and because of the rays that radiate out from it. Near

Astronaut Edwin E. (Buzz) Aldrin Jr salutes the US flag during the *Apollo* lunar mission in 1969. (IS)

WILHELM BEER AND THE MAPPING OF THE MOON

The German banker and amateur astronomer Wilhelm Beer (1797–1850) was fascinated by the Moon. Wealthy enough to build his own observatory, he spent eight years mapping the visible features of the Moon with great accuracy and measuring the height of many hundreds of lunar mountains. This he did by an ingenious method that had been worked out by Galileo more than two hundred years before. By measuring from the half Moon's edge the distance at which the tips of the mountains caught the rising or setting Sun, the height of the mountain could be calculated by simple geometry and a knowledge of the diameter of the Moon. Many of the mountains were found to be 8 km (5 mi) high or higher.

Previous maps of the Moon had been drawn by various observers, especially by the German astronomer Johannes Hevelius (1611–87) in 1647 and by the Italian astronomer Giovanni Battista Riccioli (1598–1671) in 1651, but Beer's map, which was published in 1836, was far ahead of anything that had ever been done before. It was a metre in diameter and of unprecedented detail and accuracy. Over the course of his entire observation, Beer was able to detect no topographical changes in the Moon and inferred correctly from this that it was a dead satellite.

Copernicus are several other similarly rayed craters. This group is the more obvious because it lies in a large, comparatively smooth 'sea'. About 90° due east of Copernicus is the great smooth *Mare Tranquillitas*, 'Sea of Tranquillity', where the *Apollo 11* astronauts landed. Large areas around the maria are heavily pock-marked with craters of all sizes testifying to the battering the Moon must have taken. The far side of the Moon is somewhat more even in its distribution of craters, and these appear to be of more uniform depth. In addition, this side is almost devoid of maria.

Other features

The Moon has a diameter of 3,476 km (2,160 mi) and is about a quarter the size of the Earth and roughly one eightieth of its mass. It has no atmosphere and its temperature thus varies greatly between the lunar day and night. The surface facing the Sun reaches well above the temperature of boiling water – 100°C (212°F) – and the far side quickly drops to below −200°C (−328°F). This wide and rapid fluctuation of temperature causes expansion and contraction of surface rocks and a slow, crumbling erosion. The Moon's orbit round the Earth is slightly elliptical so that the nearest point to the Earth is 356,000 km (221,000 mi), and the furthest 407,000 km (253,000 mi). The orbit is also tilted about 5° to the plane in which the Earth travels round the Sun. The Moon travels around the Earth and returns to the same position in the sky in just over 27 days, 7 hours and 43 minutes. This is called the *sidereal month* (⇨ p. 144). But because the Earth is travelling round the Sun in the same direction as the Moon, the period between successive

full Moons is longer – just over 29 days, 12 hours and 44 minutes. As the Moon rotates on its own axis once every sidereal month it shows roughly the same face to the Earth at all times. Minor perturbations in its orbit allow about nine per cent more than half of its surface to be seen at various times. The whole of the far side was seen for the first time in 1959 when it was photographed by the Soviet *Luna 3* spacecraft.

Some minor 'moonquakes' occur but the seismographic evidence suggests that the Moon is much less active in this respect than the Earth. There is no metallic core and thus no magnetic field. The Moon's crust is made largely of oxides of silicon (sand), aluminium, calcium, magnesium, iron and titanium. The latter two are present in larger proportions than on Earth. The most abundant element is oxygen, but none of this is free or combined with hydrogen in the form of water.

Theories of origin

Four theories dominate the arguments about the origin of the Moon although none of them has been proved. The consensus opinion, today, seems to be that, early in the course of the evolution of the solar system, the Earth was in collision with a body about the size of Mars, causing a large mass of hot vapour to become detached from the combined and fused masses. This separate segment became established as an autonomous body and then cooled and solidified to form the Moon. Alternatively, the Moon might have been formed quite independently of, but close to, the Earth. Some

The hidden side of the Moon photographed in 1967 by the *Lunar Orbiter III* in its mission to locate potential landing sites. The prominent crater filled with dark material is about 240 km (150 mi) in diameter. (NASA)

theorists hold that, when the Earth was still molten, its rate of rotation might have been high enough (⇨ p. 30) to throw off a large mass of material. Finally, there is the opinion that the Moon may have originated elsewhere in the solar system and happened to approach close enough to the Earth to be captured by mutual gravitational attraction.

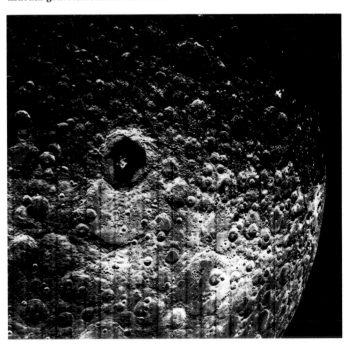

Stars and Galaxies 1

Stars are self-luminous and provide light by which other nonluminous celestial bodies, such as planets or nonradiating nebulae, may be seen. Galaxies are collections of stars, gas and dust and are so called by analogy with our galaxy – the Milky Way. (The Greek word for 'milk' is *gala*.)

Only one star – our own Sun – is near enough to the Earth to be seen, even by the most powerful optical telescopes, as more than a point of light. Some nearby stars can be crudely resolved using the special technique of *speckle interferometry*, a process whereby large numbers of images can be combined to form one.

It was originally thought that the Sun was situated somewhere near the centre of our galaxy – the Milky Way. This was the conclusion, drawn in 1784 by the German-born British astronomer Sir William Herschel (1738–1822), after trying to count the stars visible in all directions. He decided that the galaxy was a flat oval, five times as long as it was broad. Herschel was not influenced by any Ptolemaic-like heliocentric ideas (⇨ p. 120), but he was nevertheless wrong. Later work has shown that our galaxy is much larger than Herschel realized and is

False-colour photograph of the Andromeda galaxy (M31) and its two dwarf elliptical satellite galaxies NGC 205 (top right) and M32 or NGC 221 (bright spot immediately below and on the edge of Andromeda itself). Together with our galaxy, the Milky Way, Andromeda is one of the largest and most important members of what is termed the local group of galaxies.
(Tony Ward, Tetbury, SPL)

THE HERTZSPRUNG-RUSSELL DIAGRAM

It is comparatively easy to measure the brightness of a star and, by measuring its colour, obtain a fairly accurate idea of its temperature. The temperature of any body affects the wavelength of the light given off by it. Our Sun, for instance, with a temperature just under 6,000 K, emits most strongly light from around the middle of the visible spectrum. This makes it appear yellow. A hotter star would appear white or blue or would emit invisible ultraviolet light. A cooler star would appear red or would be an invisible source of infrared radiation.

When the surface temperature of stars is plotted against the amount of light they emit (*luminosity*) or their absolute magnitude (⇨ diagram), with the hottest stars to the left and the most luminous towards the top, it is found that the great majority lie within a fairly narrow band called the *main sequence*. This band slopes down from the high-temperature — high-luminosity upper-left corner of the graph to the low-temperature–low-luminosity lower-right corner. The main sequence contains all the most typical stars, including our Sun. A comparatively small group of stars lies outside the main sequence. Some, of low temperature but high luminosity, must necessarily be very

large, and are known as red giants. They are above the main sequence. White dwarfs are of high temperature (10,000 K or more), but because they are very small, their luminosity is low. They lie below the main sequence. A red giant may be 100 times the diameter of the Sun and a thousand times the luminosity, but may have a temperature of only 3,000 K.

This method of classifying stars is named after the Danish astronomer Ejnar Hertzsprung (1873–1967) and the American astronomer Henry Norris Russell (1877–1957). Their diagram helps us to work out the relative size of stars and to understand star evolution. A star cluster is a large group of stars close together that move together through space at the same speed. Nearly all members of star clusters formed together at about the same time are on the main sequence. These stars remain on the main sequence until the hydrogen-to-helium stage is completed, and then begin to enlarge and leave it. The point at which they leave becomes progressively lower and redder, the longer the time since the birth of the star cluster. This point thus gives an indication of the age of the cluster.

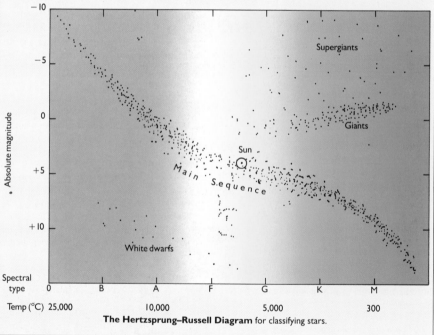

The Hertzsprung–Russell Diagram for classifying stars.

at least 100,000 light years in diameter with the Sun situated about two thirds of the way from the centre to the rim. A light year is the distance that light travels in a year – 9.461×10^{12} km (5.879×10^{12} mi). Current estimates suggest that there are at least 100 billion stars in our galaxy.

The number of the stars

It has always been apparent that there are many, many stars, but it is only comparatively recently that we have had any real idea of how enormous their number really is. As late as the early 1920s it was assumed that the Milky Way was the only galaxy in the universe and that

beyond it was nothing but empty space. Astronomers had, however, observed many distant spiral clouds (*nebulae*) and some, including Herschel, believed them to be distant 'universes'. Everything changed with the building of the 2.5-m (100-in) Mount Wilson telescope and the work done with it by the American astronomer Edwin Powell Hubble (1889–1953; ⇨ p. 124). In 1924 Hubble was at last able to see enough detail in the distant nebulae to show that some of the 'spiral nebulae' were composed of stars. He was able to work out that the nebula in Andromeda, for instance, was at least 800,000 light years away – eight times the distance of the farthest star in the Milky Way. Other nebulae were even more distant – some billions of light years away. Immediately, it was apparent that the universe was enormously larger than we had previously supposed and that our galaxy was only one of many. We now know that there are at least tens of millions of other galaxies, some spiral, some elliptical. Some of these can be viewed edge-on and are seen to have a thickened central hub and a tapering rim. This is how our own galaxy would look if viewed from outside (⇨ p. 132). All this implies that, although the total number of the stars can never be known, it almost certainly exceeds a billion billion.

The origin of stars

A nebula is a diffuse cloud of fine particles and gases, mainly hydrogen. The hydrogen is believed to have been formed at the time of the Big Bang (⇨ p. 126) and the dust and other particles may be the remnants of a supernova explosion (⇨ p. 130). Although of very low mass, hydrogen molecules, dust and other particles exhibit mutual gravitational attraction (⇨ p. 30) and are gradually drawn together. As they aggregate, their mass and gravitational pull increases, and, as they become ever more tightly pressed together, their temperature rises, in accordance with the gas laws (⇨ p. 50). (Anything that is compressed becomes hotter because of increased molecular interactions.) This concept of the first stage in the evolution of stars was first put forward by the British physicist William Thomson, Lord Kelvin (1824–1907), and the German polymath Hermann von Helmholtz (1821–94) and is often known as the Kelvin–Helmholtz contraction.

Neither Kelvin nor Helmholtz could have been aware of the further consequences of continued contraction. Such a contracting mass continues to get hotter until the core temperature reaches about 10 million degrees. At that point a nuclear-fusion reaction (⇨ p. 116) starts in which hydrogen atoms are fused to form helium. This process takes one of two forms, depending on the temperature reached by the core, either the proton–proton reaction, as in our own Sun, or the more complex, six-stage, carbon–nitrogen cycle as in hotter stars. The length of time this goes on for depends on the size of the star, and is less than a million years in the case of the most massive. Our Sun is a 'main-sequence' star on the Hertzsprung–Russell diagram (⇨ box), and is of comparatively small size. Such a star continues in this stage for a period of about ten million years.

Stars with masses of at least 0.4 times that of the Sun can proceed to a further sequence of nuclear-fusion reactions in which helium is converted to carbon and heavier elements.

The evolution and death of stars

Stars with a mass below about 0.06 times of that of the Sun never reach a high enough temperature to start a nuclear reaction. Heavier stars, up to about 1.44 times the mass of the Sun, continue in a stable state, producing energy by nuclear fusion for about 10,000 million years. When a star's core nuclear hydrogen fuel is exhausted and its core no longer has the energy to prevent massive contraction, the density rises to an extraordinary level – as high as 100,000,000 times that of water. This is associated with a temperature rise sufficient to start a further nuclear reaction in the hydrogen around the core, and the whole star expands enormously to form a *red giant*, perhaps a hundred times as large. The interior of a red giant may become hot enough to promote a fusion reaction in which helium is converted, by way of a series of reactions, to carbon. At the end of the red-giant phase, the outer layers are lost to form *planetary nebulae* and the hot, dense core cools to form a *white dwarf* with a core consisting of matter that is so compressed that it is not a gas, liquid nor a solid. Such matter is called *degenerate matter* and the only energy it radiates is its residual heat. A typical white dwarf is about the same size as the Earth but with a mass about equal to that of the Sun. The greatest possible mass for a white dwarf is 1.44 times the mass of the Sun. This is because in a more massive white dwarf the weight of the outer shell could not be supported by the degenerate matter of the core and would either have to lose mass or collapse to form a *neutron star* (⇨ below) or a black hole (⇨ p. 128). This limit of 1.44 solar masses is called the *Chandrasekhar limit* after the Indian-born American astrophysicist Subrahmanian Chandrasekhar (1910–), who made the calculation.

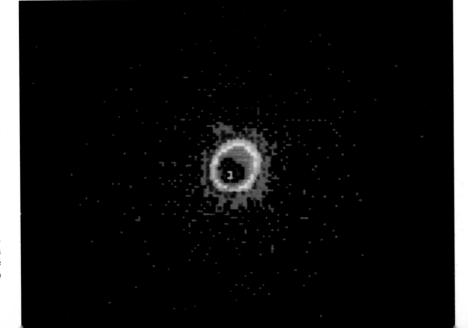

Radio image of Cygnus X-2, a neutron star. Neutron stars are superdense – they may have a mass equal to that of up to three Suns but be only about 20 km (12 mi) in diameter. (IS)

STAR MAGNITUDE

For historical reasons, the term 'magnitude', which is a measure of the brightness of a star, was applied in an inverse manner. The brightest stars are said to have the lowest magnitude and the faintest stars the highest. *Apparent magnitude* is the brightness as seen from Earth; *absolute magnitude* is a measure of the actual brightness. The system arose originally because the brightest stars were described as being of the 'first magnitude', and those that were only just visible were said to be of the sixth magnitude. The modern scale of magnitude is a logarithmic scale in which a first-magnitude star is a hundred times brighter than a sixth-magnitude star. The brightest stars have a magnitude of less than 1 and, as telescopes improved and ever fainter stars were seen, it became necessary to extend the scale to larger numbers. Faint stars of a magnitude of +25 or more can now be seen.

The white dwarf is the commonest terminal stage of a star and there are many in the universe. They radiate hardly any light and so are hard to see, but there are several in the vicinity of our Sun. One forms a companion to the star Sirius. White dwarfs eventually cool down to a nonluminous stage.

A different outcome may occur in the case of very large stars. Those that have developed to the giant-star stage can reach a high stage of evolution in which the core contains elements of increasing atomic weight, up to iron. Stars with masses between the Chandrasekhar limit and about three solar masses evolve more quickly and die younger. Many of these stars are disrupted by a vast supernova explosion (⇨ p. 130) but may retain at their core a very dense structure, perhaps a million times as dense as white-dwarf stars, in which the electrons and protons (⇨ pp. 90, 108 and 156) are crushed together to form neutrons.

The compression of the material is so great that the residual neutron stars may be only 10–20 km (6–12 mi) in diameter, and, although they are very hot, they produce very little light, and so are usually impossible to detect. Rotating neutron stars, however, are detectable as pulsars (⇨ p. 124). Other massive stars well above the Chandrasekhar limit are believed to be able to form black holes (⇨ p. 128).

The relative sizes of different types of stars. Typical red giants are 100 times the size of the Sun, which, in turn, is 100 times the size of a white dwarf. White dwarfs are 1,000 times larger than neutron stars, which typically have a diameter of 10–20 km (6–12 mi). Red supergiants may be 5 times larger than a typical red giant.

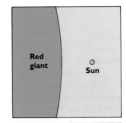

Red giant — Sun

Sun — White dwarf

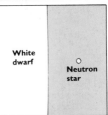

White dwarf — Neutron star

SEE ALSO

- SCIENTIFIC INSTRUMENTS pp. 14–17
- CIRCULAR MOTION AND GRAVITATION p. 30
- BEYOND NEWTON 1: RELATIVITY p. 38
- SPECTRA AND SPECTROSCOPY p. 80
- NUCLEAR PHYSICS IN ACTION p. 116
- COSMOLOGY: UNDERSTANDING THE UNIVERSE p. 120
- ASTRONOMICAL INSTRUMENTS AND TECHNIQUES pp. 122–5
- BIG BANG p. 126
- BLACK HOLES p. 128
- SUPERNOVAE p. 130
- THE SUN AND THE SOLAR SYSTEM p. 132
- STARS AND GALAXIES 2 p. 142

Stars and Galaxies 2

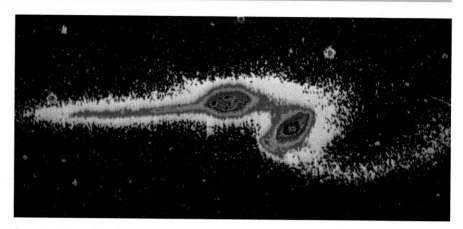

Stars are far too numerous for all of them to be named, and there are enormous numbers that can never be individually designated. All the stars that can be seen with the naked eye are, however, either given a specific name or are numbered in a catalogue. Stars are grouped as clusters, and clusters are grouped into galaxies.

Our own galaxy – the Milky Way – is but one of many millions of galaxies but is considerably larger than any others nearby. It is probably about 15 billion years old. Descriptions of the grosser features of galaxies are necessarily crude and involve an enormous scaling

down in dimension. Much of astronomy, however, is concerned with the scaling of dimensions so vast that they are almost beyond human comprehension. In terms of our galaxy a light year is a very short distance, yet it is the almost inconceivable distance that light travels in one year – 9.461×10^{12} km (5.879×10^{12} mi).

The Milky Way

The galaxy that contains our solar system is called – on a purely descriptive basis – the Milky Way. It contains some 100 billion stars (suns), some, possibly many, of which may have planetary systems. It is roughly disc-shaped with a flattened, central, spherical zone, and is at least 100,000 light years in diameter, probably more (⇨ p. 132). Most of the stars are in the central, thickened bulge, which is about 30,000 light years in diameter. The thinner, outer zone, known as the *halo*, contains fewer stars but much gas and dust. It is here that the stars are being formed from galactic dust, and almost all the young stars are found in the disc. Within the halo of the galaxy are about two hundred dense clusters of stars, fairly evenly distributed, many of them lying above or below the plane of the galaxy. Each of these clusters contains up to some hundreds of thousands of stars in a roughly spherical grouping and are therefore called *globular clusters*.

The older stars are found in the bulge and in the halo. Many stars in the bulge are old red stars and the concentration of these increases towards the centre. The bulge also contains vast quantities of gas arranged in an enormous ring around the centre, heated by younger stars to a temperature of about 10,000 K. Our own Sun lies about 28,000 light years away from the centre of the galaxy and so is well outside the dense, central bulge. Its position, however, means that most of the stars in the galaxy are concealed from us on Earth by interstellar dust and gas.

The exact diameter of the galaxy is impossible to establish and there is reason to believe that beyond its conventional limits may lie a zone, or *corona*, of invisible matter extending for hundreds of thousands of light years. The evidence for this lies in the known speeds of rotation of the galaxy.

Two interacting spiral galaxies NGC 4676a (left) and NGC 4676b (also known as 'the mice'), shown in this false-colour optical image. They are located 270 million light years away in the constellation of Coma Berenices, and form part of the Coma supercluster of galaxies. Their long 'tails' are due to the tidal effects of their interaction as they pass one another in orbit. The long tail appears straight to us but is strongly curved in the horizontal plane. (NOAO, SPL)

Other galaxies

The immediate space surrounding the Milky Way contains over twenty neighbouring galaxies, most of them much smaller than our own. They are called the *local group* and extend out to a distance of about 3,000,000 light years. Their exact number is not known because those close to the plane of our galaxy are obscured. It is only in such nearby galaxies that individual stars can be made out. The problem of the distance of galaxies outside our own was solved by a study of *variable stars* called 'Cepheids' after Delta Cepheid, the first of the type to be found. Cepheids are stars, known since 1784, that show well-defined alterations in brightness and other characteristics with accurate cycles (periods) of approximately one to fifty days.

In 1912 it was discovered that the periods of variable stars were related directly to their apparent magnitudes and, for stars at equal distances, to their absolute magnitude (⇨ p. 140). There are about seven hundred known Cepheids in our own galaxy and a statistical study of these has made it possible to calibrate the relationship between period and true brightness. This known, the absolute magnitude of distant Cepheids can be established. And by comparing the difference between the apparent and the true magnitude, the distance can be found.

The nearest neighbouring galaxies are the Large and Small Magellanic Clouds, named after the great Portuguese navigator Ferdinand Magellan (1480–1521), who was first to observe them whilst attempting to circumnavigate the world. The large cloud is 150,000 light years away and has a diameter of about 31,000 light years. The small cloud is 173,000 light years away and has a diameter of about 24,000 light years. These galaxies can be seen with the naked eye in the

THE CENTRE OF OUR GALAXY

The nature of the centre of our galaxy has long exercised the imagination and skills of scientists, and several important facts are known about it. To account for the high speeds of rotation of gas clouds orbiting near the centre, a mass equal to about 5,000,000 times that of the Sun is necessary. Powerful radio signals come from the centre of the galaxy and most of these signals come from a tiny central area less than ten times the distance from the Sun to the Earth. The centre also emits X-rays. These most commonly come from collapsed stars and the remnants of supernovae (⇨ p. 130). So what is at the centre? There is a growing body of opinion that most of these facts can be explained on the hypothesis that there is a black hole (⇨ p. 128) at the centre.

The Milky Way in the constellations of Scutum and Sagittarius. The galactic centre is towards the lower centre of the photograph, obscured by clouds of gas and dust. (Rev. Ronald Roger, SPL)

False-colour ultraviolet image of the Tarantula nebula in the Large Magellanic Cloud. The intense ultraviolet light, seen as white and yellow patches, comes from a region of hot, young stars. (NASA, SPL)

southern hemisphere. Both float in a single vast cloud of hydrogen with a mass equal to that of 1,000 million Suns. They contain open star clusters and globular clusters, frequent novae (⇨ p. 130), supergiant stars and a pulsar (⇨ p. 124). Because they are so relatively close, the Magellanic clouds are distorted by the gravitational pull of our galaxy and the outer zones of our galaxy are distorted by the Magellanic clouds. The Large Magellanic Cloud contains a huge bright region, 200 light years across, known as the Tarantula nebula. This is lit up by more than one hundred very bright stars, one of which is possibly the largest and most luminous star known.

Further out, and the largest and most striking member of the local group, is the giant Andromeda spiral galaxy,

about 2,200,000 light years away. This galaxy is estimated to be larger than the visible diameter of the Milky Way and to be about 130,000 light years across. Like other neighbouring galaxies, Andromeda was originally thought to be a nebula, but examination with the 2.5-m (100-in) Mount Wilson telescope resolved the individual stars and it was seen to be a galaxy. Like our galaxy, Andromeda has globular clusters and vast nebulae of dust and gas. Indeed all galaxies contain stars, gas and dust, although the proportions vary widely. Many galaxies have a central nucleus that emits enormous amounts of energy.

For the remoter galaxies measurement of distance is less certain. Cepheids can be identified out to about 20,000,000 light years and estimates can be obtained by measuring the magnitudes of globular clusters and novae by highly sensitive photoelectric methods. When it became known in 1929, however, that the amount of the Doppler red shift (⇨ p. 126) was accurately proportional to distance, a method of establishing the distances of very remote objects was obtained.

Beyond the local group lie vast numbers of extragalactic systems. Many occur in pairs or triplets, small groups or clusters, such as the Virgo cluster of galaxies about 50,000,000 light years away. Some actually occur in clusters of clusters of galaxies. There are many types of galaxy, most being spiral, elliptical or irregular in shape. Most of the brightest and conspicuous are spiral, but, as far we know, the greater number in the universe are elliptical.

It should be remembered, however, that the apparent shape depends on the orientation of the galaxy to the observer. Some 3,000 clusters of galaxies have been catalogued, grouped into second-order galaxy clusters each characteristically 300 light years across. These clusters of clusters are the largest known objects in the universe.

Artwork entitled *Bubble Universe,* illustrating the globular structure of the universe. Galaxies tend to group together into clusters, which themselves also clump together to form massive superclusters. Recent surveys of the distribution of these superclusters have found that they are usually organized into enormous 'sheets' separated by large voids. Here the galaxy superclusters form the surfaces of giant bubbles surrounding the empty spaces.

(Sally Bensusen, SPL)

The Rotation and Orbit of the Earth

The familiar sequences of day and night, of the seasons and of the year are all consequences of the rotation of the Earth on its own axis and of its movement in orbit around the Sun.

The Earth's movements are more complex and are affected by more factors than are generally understood. Fortunately, we are wholly unaware of the movement of the Earth and, because it provides us with a frame of reference for the rest of the universe, we experience the illusion that we are stationary and everything else is moving. An *axis of rotation* is an imaginary line around which an object can turn. The spin axis of the Earth is an imaginary line joining the North and South poles around which the Earth can rotate, just as an apple can rotate around a knitting needle pushed through it. The Earth is not spherical but, because of its rapid rotation,

THE SEASONS

SPRING EQUINOX
Spin axis
23.5°
23.5°
SUMMER
SUN
WINTER
Earth's orbit lies in the ecliptic plane
AUTUMN EQUINOX

The diagram shows the order of the seasons in the Northern hemisphere; in the Southern hemisphere the seasons are reversed. The 23.5° tilt of the Earth's axis means that in summer not only is there more daylight, but the Sun's rays reach the Earth's surface more directly through the atmosphere and so lose less of their warmth. In winter, not only is there less daylight, but the Sun's rays strike the Earth more obliquely, so having to pass through more of the atmosphere and losing more of their warmth. Beyond the Arctic and Antarctic Circles (66° 32′ N and S), the Sun does not set in summer or rise in winter; the periods over which this occurs each season increase as one approaches the poles. Conversely, the nearer one approaches the Equator, the less the seasonal variation.

bulges somewhat at the Equator. The diameter at the Equator is 12,756 km (7,928 mi), but the straight-line distance between the poles is only 12,714 km (7,902 mi). This shape – of a sphere flattened at the poles – is called an *oblate spheroid* and, because of the influence of the Sun and Moon's gravitational forces upon it, and of the speed of the Earth's rotation, has an important effect on the way the Earth rotates.

Because the Earth is not a homogeneous (uniform) body, its gravitational field varies from place to place on its surface, depending on the masses of the underlying material. Its oblate shape also affects the local gravitational field, which is less at the Equator than at the poles. Changes in the tides caused by the Moon (⇨ p. 138) also affect the Earth's local gravitational field by effectively altering its shape.

Day and night

The Earth rotates on its spin axis once every day, as judged by its relationship to an object in the sky. Because no celestial objects are actually fixed, the length of the day depends on the object selected as a criterion. If a distant star is selected, the day is known as a *sidereal day* (⇨ p. 138). In practice, we most commonly judge the day by the Sun. But because the Earth is also moving in orbit round the Sun, it will have changed its relationship to the Sun in the course of a single rotation on its axis. The *solar day* is thus longer than the sidereal day – on average about 3 minutes 56 seconds longer.

Solar days are not all of the same length. This is because the Earth's orbit round the Sun is slightly elliptical and its speed in its orbit varies. Successive solar days may vary by as much as 30 seconds. But this is of little practical importance as long as the solar day is not used as a unit of time. In fact, when clocks and watches first became widely used, it was necessary to devise a standard of time based on the average of all the apparent solar days in the year. This was known as *mean time* and, for many years, the standard was set by the Greenwich observatory in London and was known as *Greenwich Mean Time* (GMT). The difference between the apparent and the mean solar times changes as the year progresses and reaches a maximum, about 1 November, of about 16 minutes.

Time is now measured by atomic clocks, which are calibrated by the remarkably accurate period of the spin of caesium atoms. Such clocks are so accurate that they show up irregularities in the rate of the Earth's rotation and thus of the length of the mean solar day.

Daytime, at any point on the Earth's surface, is the period of the rotation of the Earth during which the Sun can – weather permitting – be seen from the Earth's surface. Night-time is the period when the Sun cannot be seen. Because the Earth is our frame of reference we perceive as moving any celestial bodies relative to which the Earth moves. For this

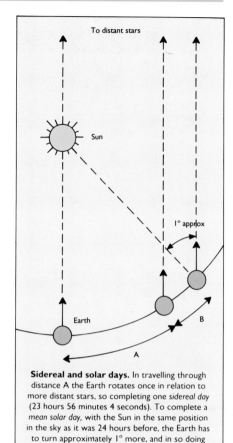

Sidereal and solar days. In travelling through distance A the Earth rotates once in relation to more distant stars, so completing one *sidereal day* (23 hours 56 minutes 4 seconds). To complete a *mean solar day*, with the Sun in the same position in the sky as it was 24 hours before, the Earth has to turn approximately 1° more, and in so doing travels the additional distance B.
(Diagram not to scale.)

reason we perceive the Sun as 'rising' in the east and 'setting' in the west. The Sun appears to rise in the east because the Earth is rotating so that any point on the surface is turning 'down' towards the east.

The orbiting Earth

The Earth revolves around the Sun in a period known as a *year*. This can be defined in various ways, depending on whether the primary interest is astronomical or earthly. The *sidereal year* – the time of orbital rotation with respect to the stars – is equal to 365.2564 mean solar days. The most important astronomical year is called the *tropical year*, and is defined as the time between successive appearances of the *spring equinox* – the point at which the day and night are of exactly equal lengths. The tropical year, at present, is equal to 365.2422 mean solar days, but is becoming very gradually shorter as a result of small changes in the Earth's speed of rotation, which alter the length of the mean solar day and other factors.

For practical reasons, the calendar year must be equal to a whole number of days and is taken as 365 days, three years out of four, and 366 days each fourth (*leap*) year. The average is 365.2425 mean solar days, which corresponds quite well with the tropical year, so the seasons begin at about the same time each year. Because of uncertainties in the uniformity of the Earth's rotation, though, we are unlikely to be able to improve on the present system of adjustment.

THE PRECESSION OF THE EQUINOXES

The bulge at the Earth's Equator affects the mutual gravitational pull of the Sun and the Moon. The effect of this is to cause a *torque* (turning effect; ➪ p. 28) on the Earth, which slowly changes the direction of the spin axis – the effect of gravity commonly seen on a spinning top with an axis that is not quite central. Although the spin axis remains at an angle to the ecliptic, it slowly turns so that each pole describes a truncated cone-shaped figure in space, with each pole describing a small circle. As a result, the angle the spin axis – and hence the Equator – makes with the ecliptic slowly changes. One precessional rotation (the time taken to describe one complete orbit) by the Earth's axis takes about 26,000 years. The change of the angle between the Equator and the ecliptic means that the positions of the equinoxes (the two

points of intersection of the two planes) also slowly change. This change is, somewhat carelessly, called the *precession of the equinoxes*. It is, of course, the spin axis of the Earth that is precessing; the equinoxes are merely changing their time of appearance. As the position of the pole and the Equator changes the equinox moves backwards around the ecliptic at a rate of 50.3 arc seconds each year. There are 1,296,000 arc seconds in a complete circle.

Since precession causes a change in the position of the Equator relative to the stars, and since their positions (*right ascension* and *declination* – two measurements used to locate a celestial object in the sky, similar to latitude and longitude for places on Earth) are described in relation to the Equator and the equinoxes, accurate coordinates require that the date should be given.

Diagram not to scale

Equator

Truncated cone described by the spin axis

Centre of Earth

Ecliptic plane

Precessional circle described by the pole, in a plane parallel to that of the equator

The precession of the spin axis is also affected by the fact that the Moon's orbit around the Earth is inclined at an angle of 5° to the ecliptic, and this also precesses. Because of the equatorial bulge and the inclination of the axis, the Moon's gravitational pull causes smaller 'nodding' irregularities in the Earth's precession called *nutation*. The main nutation pulls each pole about 10 seconds of a degree away from the normal precessional circle. The interaction is thus complex and this accounts for nutation.

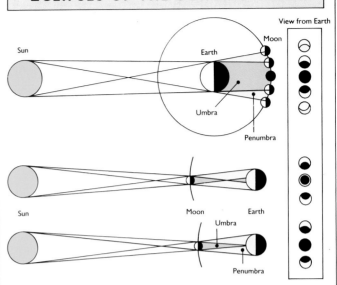

ECLIPSES OF THE SUN AND MOON

View from Earth

Sun · Earth · Moon · Umbra · Penumbra

Sun · Moon · Earth · Umbra

Sun · Umbra · Penumbra

Lunar eclipses (top) occur when the Earth passes directly between the Sun and the Moon. Solar eclipses (bottom) are brought about when the Moon passes between the Sun and the Earth. The distance between the Moon and the Earth has an effect on how much of the Sun is obscured.

tilt of the Earth's axis in relation to the ecliptic. The effect of this tilt is that at the equinoxes the midday Sun is overhead at the Equator. At the longest day of the year in the Northern hemisphere (*summer solstice*) the midday Sun is over the Tropic of Cancer. At the shortest day of the Northern-hemisphere year (*winter solstice*) the Sun is over the Tropic of Capricorn in the Southern hemisphere.

The effect of the Sun's radiation at the Earth's surface is greatly influenced by the angle of incidence. A 'pencil' of radiation falling vertically and striking a surface will affect an area equal to the cross section of the pencil. If the same pencil falls at an oblique angle to the surface it will, however, be distributed over a much larger area, so the radiation received by a given area will be less.

The Earth's orbit round the Sun is almost, but not quite, circular. It is actually an ellipse with the Sun at one focus. The speed of movement of the Earth in this orbit is not uniform, as it would be if the orbit were perfectly circular, but is such that a line from the Sun to the Earth sweeps out equal areas in equal periods of time. This conforms to Kepler's second law after the German astronomer Johannes Kepler (1571–1630) who discovered the laws of planetary motion and founded modern scientific astronomy. The Earth is nearest to the Sun (*perihelion*) early in January and furthest from it early in July (*aphelion*). It speeds up as it approaches perihelion and slows as it approaches aphelion. Its average orbital speed is 30 km (18.6 mi) per second.

In its orbit round the Sun the Earth moves in a plane called the *ecliptic*. The movement of the Earth on the ecliptic causes us to perceive the Sun moving eastward during the day by just under 1° per day, on average, with respect to the

stars. The Earth's spin axis is not perpendicular to the ecliptic; in other words, the plane of the Earth's Equator (90° from the poles) does not coincide with the ecliptic. In fact, the equatorial plane lies at a substantial angle to the ecliptic. This most important fact has a major effect because it determines the seasons of the year. The angle between the equatorial plane and the ecliptic is 23.5° and the two planes intersect at two crucial points in the Earth's orbit. When the Earth is at these points, the day and night are each 12 hours long. This happens twice in the year at times known as the *equinoxes* (from the Latin *equilis*, 'equal', and *nox*, 'night'). In the Northern hemisphere, the spring and autumn equinoxes occur at around 20 March and 23 September; in the Southern hemisphere the dates are reversed.

The seasons

The seasons have nothing to do with changes in the distance of the Earth from the Sun but are determined by the

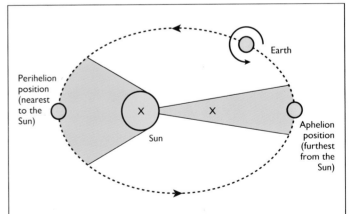

Perihelion position (nearest to the Sun)

Earth

Sun

Aphelion position (furthest from the Sun)

X = focus of ellipse. All ellipses have two foci. The closer they are together, the nearer to a circle the ellipse becomes.

The Earth's elliptical orbit, seen from above. The shaded sectors of the ellipse are equal in area. They represent the areas swept out by an imaginary line connecting the Earth and the Sun in an equal amount of time, with the Earth speeding up as it approaches the perihelion and slowing down on its way to the aphelion. Diagram not to scale.

The Earth and its Structure

The Earth is an almost spherical body, slightly flattened at the poles and about 13,000 km (8,000 mi) in diameter. The outer crust on which we live is relatively very thin and contains only one per cent of the total volume of the planet. Underneath are various layers arranged like the layers of an onion. At least twenty chemical elements are present in considerable quantities, and there are traces of more than seventy others. Most of the Earth is solid, but part of the inner core remains at such a high temperature that it is still liquid.

A surprisingly accurate measure of the size of the Earth was made more than 2,200 years ago by the Greek scientist Eratosthenes (c. 276–195 BC) by checking the angle of the shadow at one location whilst the Sun was directly overhead at another a known distance away. Later, surveying techniques and astronomical observations of the angles of the stars at different locations produced highly accurate figures. The Earth was weighed by the British physicist and chemist Henry Cavendish (1731–1810; ⇨ p. 36) by measuring the gravitational attraction between known very small and heavier bodies, and comparing this with the gravitational pull of the Earth on known bodies. This showed that the mass of the Earth was some 6,600,000,000,000,000, 000,000 tonnes. Once this figure was known it was possible to calculate the density of the Earth, which turned out to be about 5.5 g per cc (0.02 lb per cu in) – 5.5 times the density of water.

A knowledge of the density of the Earth immediately gives some information about its composition and shows that it must consist largely of materials heavier than water.

THE SHAPE OF THE CRUST

Roughly speaking, all radial 'pencils' of equal cross section from the centre of the Earth to the surface contain material of about the same mass. This is a consequence of the necessity for gravitational equilibrium (*isostasy*). Continents are higher than ocean floors because they are made of less dense material; mountain ranges 'float' on regions of greater density than themselves.

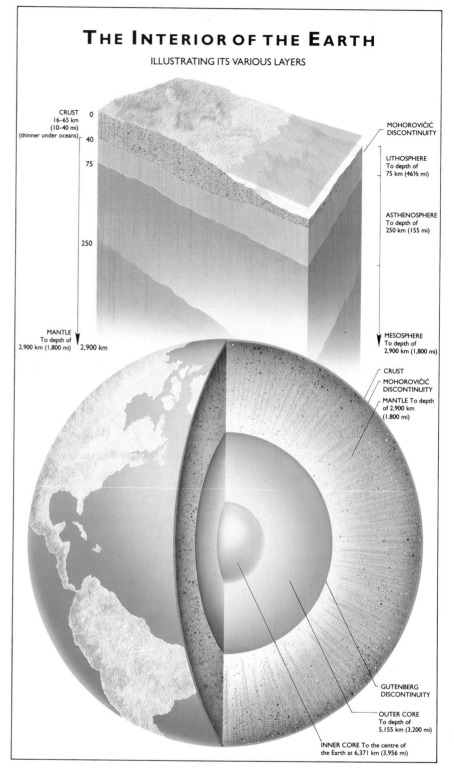

THE INTERIOR OF THE EARTH
ILLUSTRATING ITS VARIOUS LAYERS

CRUST
16–65 km
(10–40 mi)
(thinner under oceans)

0
40
75
250

MANTLE
To depth of
2,900 km (1,800 mi)
2,900 km

MOHOROVIČIĆ DISCONTINUITY

LITHOSPHERE
To depth of
75 km (46½ mi)

ASTHENOSPHERE
To depth of
250 km (155 mi)

MESOSPHERE
To depth of
2,900 km (1,800 mi)

CRUST
MOHOROVIČIĆ DISCONTINUITY
MANTLE To depth of 2,900 km (1,800 mi)

GUTENBERG DISCONTINUITY

OUTER CORE
To depth of
5,155 km (3,200 mi)

INNER CORE To the centre of
the Earth at 6,371 km (3,956 mi)

Structure

One important way of determining what is under the surface of the Earth is to see what happens to the vibrations caused by earthquakes. This was first done in 1909 by the Croatian geologist Andrija Mohorovičić (1857–1936). On studying the seismic charts of a Balkan earthquake, Mohorovičić noticed that shock waves that penetrated deep into the Earth arrived at the seismograph before those travelling near the surface. The only way he could explain this was to suppose that the outer crust of the Earth must rest on a more rigid layer in which vibrations travelled faster. The distinction between the crust and this lower layer must also be sharp, and this separation, somewhere between 16 and 65 km (10 and 40 mi) below sea level, is now known as the *Mohorovičić* ('Moho') *discontinuity*. Under the deepest oceans, the Moho discontinuity is only three or four miles below the ocean bed.

Mohorovičić calculated that the difference in density between the crust and the layer under it – the *mantle* – must be one from 2.9 to 3.3 g per cc (0.011–0.012

lb per cu in). His work aroused interest in the interpretation of seismograph patterns, and later research showed that seismic vibrations passing inwards were striking a liquid region. From such work it was possible to establish that the density at the centre of the Earth was 13.6 g per cc and decreased outwards, in layers, to 13.3, 12.3, 10, 5.5, 3.3 and 2.9 g per cc (0.049, 0.048, 0.044, 0.036, 0.020, 0.012 and 0.011 lb per cu in). Modern research, much of it using artificial shock waves from small explosions, has confirmed that the Earth is actually layered like a giant onion – with an inner core, an outer core, a mantle and a crust. The mantle, in turn, is divided into the semi-solid *mesosphere* (from the Greek *mesos*, 'middle'), the soft, semifluid and weak *asthenosphere* (from the Greek *asthenos*, 'weak') and the brittle, rocky *lithosphere* (from the Greek *lithos*, 'stone').

The core of the Earth is strongly heated by residual temperature from its formation, by pressure and by radioactivity from uranium, thorium and potassium. Core temperature is estimated to be between 3,000°C (5,400°F) and 6,600°C (12,000°F), becoming progressively lower towards the surface. At the Moho discontinuity, the temperature is about 375°C (700°F). Heat passes outwards by conduction and by convection (⇨ p. 52). Although the heat reaching the surface is only a small proportion – some 0.02 per cent – of the heat received from the Sun it is still able to promote much volcanic activity, major geological changes and continental drift (⇨ pp. 148–51).

The solidity of the various layers is affected not only by temperature but also by the enormous pressure of the overlying mass of material. Atmospheric pressure at sea level is 1 atmosphere. At a depth of 35 km (22 mi), at the base of the crust, the pressure is equal to about 10,000 atmospheres. Deeper down, the pressure is proportionally greater. High temperatures liquefy material; pressure has the opposite effect and tends to compact and solidify it. In this way pressure can cause the same materials to adopt different forms – a phenomenon known as a *change of phase*. For instance, carbon crystallizes as graphite at comparatively low pressures; the same material crystallizes as diamond at high pressures. Natural diamonds must exist in large quantities at great depths. They are normally found only in material that has been brought up close to the surface, through fissures in the lithosphere, by internal pressures such as that from steam formed from downward percolating surface water.

Composition

The Earth's crust consists of thousands of different minerals (⇨ p. 150). The commonest rocks are compounds of silicon and aluminium with oxygen, producing granites, quartz, feldspars and micas. And the commonest elements in the whole Earth are oxygen, iron, silicon and magnesium (⇨ box on the elements).

THE ORIGIN OF THE EARTH'S MAGNETIC FIELD

In 1939 the German-born American physicist Walter Maurice Elsasser (1904–) proposed the theory that the rotation of the Earth might set up circulating currents of electricity (*eddy currents*) in the molten iron of the core. Moving currents induce a magnetic field (⇨ p. 88), and this could be the origin of the Earth's magnetism. In this view, which is now generally accepted, the Earth is thought of as a giant dynamo rather than a fixed bar magnet. The fluid layer of the molten core is now believed to allow the mantle and crust to spin with the Earth faster than the solid inner core, which lags behind. Iron contains many free electrons, so there is a movement of electrons in the mantle relative to those in the solid core. This is equivalent to the flow of massive electric currents in a direction concentric with the Equator, that turns the Earth into the equivalent of a huge electromagnet (*solenoid*) and establishes a magnetic field along the direction of the spin axis.

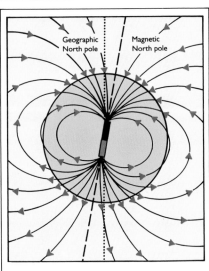

The magnetic field of the Earth (shown here in cross section) is mainly that of a dipole – it has the same shape as that of a giant bar magnet at the centre of the Earth (although the field is actually produced by motions of liquid iron within the Earth's core).

The lines emerging from the magnet are lines of induction; they show the directions in which magnetic compass needles (red arrows) would point if placed in the field.

Most navigational compasses are mounted on a vertical pin, and so can move only on a horizontal plane. However, if a compass needle is suspended on a thread, it will point downwards towards the Earth (in the Northern hemisphere) or upwards (in the Southern hemisphere), as well as towards the magnetic North pole.

Most mineral compounds of silicon have a density of around 3 g per cc (0.011 lb per cu ft), so, to make up the known densities of the Earth, the amount of iron must be considerable. Proportions of the

---

elements in parts other that of the crust have to be estimated. It is thought that the mantle consists mainly of silicon, iron, magnesium and a large amount of oxygen bound up in various oxides of these elements. The peripheral mantle is believed to contain these elements in the form of minerals such as any of the metal silicates in the garnet group, the magnesium–iron silicate – olivine – or the metal silicates of the pyroxene group. In the deeper layers of the mantle, pressure from the overlying material would produce more compact forms of minerals and, in the lower mantle, would reduce them to simple oxides.

The core of the Earth is almost certainly mainly of iron and its compounds such as iron sulphide, with traces of other metals such as platinum, nickel and iridium. It is estimated to be about 90 per cent iron, 9 per cent nickel and 1 per cent sulphur. Around this is the outer core, some 2,285 km (1,420 mi) thick, and consisting of much the same materials molten into liquid form. The mantle is about 2,850 km (1,771 mi) thick.

The Earth's magnetic field

It has been known since ancient times that the Earth is a giant magnet (⇨ pp. 88–91). Naturally magnetic rocks (*lodestones*) suspended by a thread have long been known to turn to point north and south and the mariners' compass consisting of a balanced and pivoted magnetized-steel needle has been an indispensable device for centuries. The cause of the Earth's magnetism was not established, however, until the middle of the 20th century (⇨ box). The magnetic field has some remarkable features: opposite magnetic poles attract and like poles repel (⇨ p. 88), and a suspended bar magnet or compass needle will turn so that its north pole points to the geographic north. So what is commonly described as the north magnetic pole of the Earth is actually a south pole. The magnetic pole is oriented at an angle of about 11° to the rotational axis. It is, however, constantly changing its position, and moves away from or towards true axis north at a rate of several kilometres per year. The two magnetic poles are not exactly opposite each other with respect to the Earth's centre – that is they are not *antipodal*. The strength of the Earth's magnetic field varies considerably from time to time, changing over periods varying from tens to thousands of years perhaps most surprising of all, we now know that the polarity of the Earth's magnetic field has reversed itself at regular intervals in the past, the last time being about 730,000 years ago. During the time of reversal there is almost no field for about 1,000 years. A record of past magnetism is obtained from iron-containing rocks that have solidified with the orientation of their magnetism fixed at that point. This phenomenon is called *palaeomagnetism*.

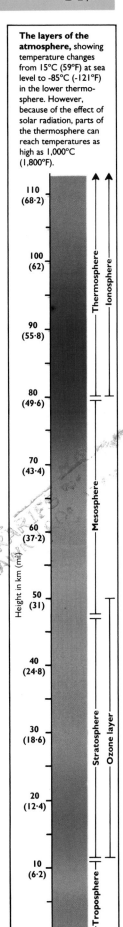

The layers of the atmosphere, showing temperature changes from 15°C (59°F) at sea level to -85°C (-121°F) in the lower thermosphere. However, because of the effect of solar radiation, parts of the thermosphere can reach temperatures as high as 1,000°C (1,800°F).

Plate Tectonics

The term 'tectonics', used in its broadest sense, simply means 'building' or 'construction'. In a narrower sense it is used to refer to the processes by which the surface of the Earth achieves its present particular structure. *Plate tectonics* is an important and major geophysical theory to account for the way in which the land masses of the Earth have acquired their present form.

Until comparatively recently it was assumed that the present position and general shape of the continents and of the oceans had remained unchanged from the time the Earth's crust solidified thousands of millions of years ago. The idea that continents might be 'drifting' was first seriously put forward in 1915 by the German geologist and geophysicist Alfred Lothar Wegener (1880–1930) in his book *Die Entstehung der Kontinente und Ozeane*, published in 1924 in an English translation entitled *Origin of Continents and Oceans*. Although Wegener's ideas of continental drift – the 'Wegener hypothesis' – at first met with considerable hostility, his arguments were so cogent that

EARTHQUAKES

At plate boundaries, plates do not move against each other smoothly but in a series of jerks. These jerks are the cause of earthquakes. The strongest earthquakes occur at collision or at destructive (subduction) boundaries (⇨ main text); those at conservative boundaries are less strong; and those at constructive boundaries are the weakest of all. If, however, a portion of a conservative fault becomes trapped, the pressure caused by continuing movement can build up until a very severe earthquake occurs. This is what happened in the San Francisco area and caused the earthquake of 1906, when the San Andreas fault (California) slipped over a segment 430 km (268 mi) long, and produced shaking that was felt all the way from San Francisco to Coos Bay, Oregon. About seven hundred people were killed.

More than 80 per cent of the 50,000 earthquakes severe enough to be detected without instruments that occur every year do so along the line of plate boundaries that border the Pacific Ocean. Each year about one hundred of these earthquakes cause substantial damage, destroying buildings and disrupting communications, power and water supplies.

many open-minded people were convinced. By about 1960 the theory of plate tectonics had been established as one of the central principles of geophysics.

Arguments for continental drift

Wegener was impressed by the complementary relationship of the east coast of South America and the west coast of Africa. The north African west-coast bulge was also complementary to the hollow in the east coast of North America. It was apparent that the whole west coast of the Old World could be neatly fitted into the whole east coast of the New World. Wegener also had evidence that seemed to suggest that the continents were moving apart. If 19th-century longitude figures were to be believed, Greenland had moved about 1.6 km (1 mi) further away from Europe in the previous one hundred years. Looking for further evidence of continental movement, Wegener found evidence that Paris and Washington were separating at a rate of about 5 m (16 ft) every year. Other indications of continental movement were forthcoming, such as the fact that identical fossil animals had been found on separate continents so far separated by oceans as to make it impossible that animals could have swum so far. These two facts – the jigsaw-puzzle relationship and the movement – were highly suggestive.

Wegener therefore proposed that continents *were* moving. He went further and suggested that, originally, there had been only one land mass – which he called *Pangaea* (from the Greek, 'all Earth') – surrounded by a single large ocean. Pangaea had then broken up into various segments that had slowly drifted apart, allowing the ocean to flow

THE EARTH'S TECTONIC PLATES

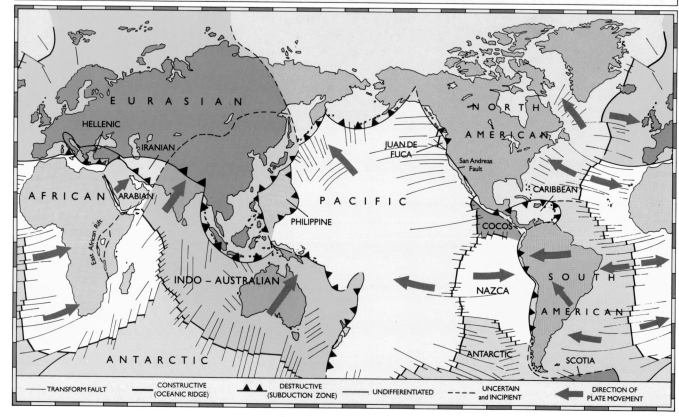

EURASIAN · HELLENIC · IRANIAN · AFRICAN · ARABIAN · East African Rift · INDO – AUSTRALIAN · ANTARCTIC · JUAN DE FUCA · PACIFIC · PHILIPPINE · NORTH AMERICAN · San Andreas Fault · CARIBBEAN · COCOS · NAZCA · SOUTH AMERICAN · ANTARCTIC · SCOTIA

| TRANSFORM FAULT | CONSTRUCTIVE (OCEANIC RIDGE) | DESTRUCTIVE (SUBDUCTION ZONE) | UNDIFFERENTIATED | UNCERTAIN and INCIPIENT | DIRECTION OF PLATE MOVEMENT |

between them and form new seas. Wegener suggested that these continental segments were floating on an underlying liquid layer – a 'basalt ocean' of molten volcanic rock – and, over the course of many millions of years, had moved to the present positions.

Wegener's critics were delighted, however, when it was found that his evidence of continental movement had been based on faulty determinations and that modern and more accurate methods showed no evidence of movement. His ideas, however, explained much that was otherwise inexplicable, and did not depend on evidence of current or recent movement. They accounted, among other things, for changing patterns of glaciation and for the known change in the relationship of the poles to the land masses. Gradually Wegener's ideas gained hold, and, as new and suggestive evidence, such as the structure of the continental shelves and the features of the mid-ocean rift, appeared, his theory became more and more widely accepted.

Critics continued to point out, however, that the continents were not floating on the seas and that the Earth's crust was a continuous single structure, as solid under the ocean floors as elsewhere. It was inconceivable, they suggested, that continents could push their way through the ocean floors.

Modern evidence for Wegener's theory

In the early 1960s new evidence came to light from the study known as *palaeomagnetism* (⬦ p. 146). The Earth's magnetic field is produced by the movement of liquid iron relative to the solid iron core. Other iron-containing rocks become magnetized by induced magnetism (⬦ p. 100), in the same direction as the Earth's field, as they cool below the Curie point (770°C or 1,400°F). When they solidify, their magnetism becomes fixed, thus providing a record of the then orientation of the Earth's magnetic North and South poles. When rocks more than a few million years old are examined for their magnetic orientation, it is found that the position of the Earth's magnetic poles at the time they solidified was different from the present position. The older the rocks, the greater the difference in position. These differences are much too great to be accounted for by the known shifts in the position of the magnetic poles, and the only plausible explanation is that the continents have moved relative to the poles.

The physical basis of plate tectonics

Immediately under the Earth's crust is the shell zone called the lithosphere (⬦ p. 146). Under this lies the partially molten and weaker asthenosphere of the mantle. The plate-tectonic theory proposes that the relatively brittle lithosphere, with its overlying crust, is

---

PLATE BOUNDARIES

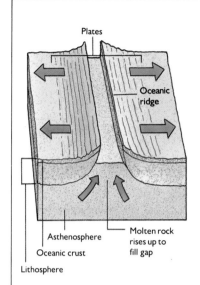

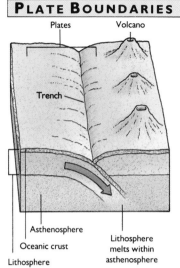

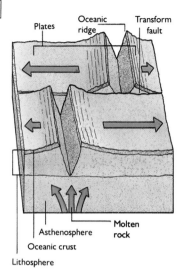

Constructive plate boundary: new lithosphere is formed at oceanic ridges by molten rock rising from the asthenosphere.

Destructive plate boundary: at subduction zones oceanic lithosphere is forced beneath continental lithosphere, descending into the asthenosphere at approximately 45° angle.

Conservative plate boundary: at transform faults, plates slide past each other, with lithosphere being neither created nor destroyed.

---

broken up into slabs or *plates* as a result of the stresses caused by the heat currents (convection; ⬦ p. 52) from the hotter and more fluid underlying layer. When the great oceanic ridges were discovered during the 1950s, an explanation of continental separation became apparent. It is now believed that these ridges are the sites at which the *magma* (hot rock) is forced up through the relatively thin crust, cools and solidifies to create new oceanic lithosphere. The solid lava is then moved sideways as more magma is forced upwards. In this way the asthenosphere is being expanded sideways in this region, carrying the continents with it.

There is, of course, a finite quantity of magma in the asthenosphere and, as some rises to form new lithosphere, there must be a compensatory return of material from the lithosphere to the mantle. This occurs at what are known as *subduction zones*, most of which lie around the edges of the Pacific Ocean. At these zones, expanding lithosphere is forced down into the mantle, where it gradually melts. This is often accompanied by volcanic activity.

Plate movement

Eight major plates and seven minor ones have been identified and these plates can be thought of as floating on the underlying semisolid asthenosphere. Some plates are solely oceanic, but most encompass both ocean and dry land. None of them is exclusively continental.

There are three types of boundary between plates: *constructive plate boundaries,* or spreading margins, where new lithosphere is being formed; *destructive plate boundaries,* or subduction margins, where lithosphere is moving down into the mantle; and *conservative plate boundaries* or *transform faults,* where plate

---

---

edges slide past each other but are neither created nor destroyed. Fortunately, most of the conservative boundaries are on the ocean floor; those that also involve land, such as the San Andreas fault in California, are a dangerous cause of crust movement (on earthquakes; ⬦ box).

Rocks and Minerals

From the surface of the Earth to the centre is about 6,400 km (4,000 mi), all of it inorganic material – rock – in various degrees of solidity, except for comparatively small deposits of gas and oil (⇨ p. 146). The deepest hole yet dug is a mere 12 km (8 mi) deep, only a fraction of the way through the crust. Nature, however, provides us with many samples of material from the interior because there is a constant interchange of material between this interior and the crust.

The science of the classification and description of rocks is called *petrography* and this is a branch of the more general science of rocks – *petrology* – which includes a study of how rocks are formed. There are three broad categories of rock – *igneous, sedimentary* and *metamorphic*. These categories are not primarily a matter of the elements from which the rocks are made but rather a description of *how* they are made. Rocks are compressed collections (*aggregates*) of grains of various minerals or sometimes of glassy material and occasionally organic matter. The study of the various minerals that constitute rocks is called *mineralogy*. The *texture* of rock is a matter of the size, range of sizes, shape, orientation and form of adhesion between the constituent mineral grains. Detailed study of rock is done by microscopic examination of a specimen that has been cut and ground into such a thin slice that it is transparent to light. At the same time, the optical properties of the constituent minerals can be studied and chemical analysis can, if necessary, be performed on single, tiny grains.

Igneous rocks

As the name implies, igneous rocks (from the Latin *ignis*, 'fire') are rocks 'formed in fire', or more precisely, rocks that have crystallized out from the molten state. There is a huge variety of such igneous rock. In the early stages of the evolution of the Earth, even the outer layers were in a molten state and temperatures increased towards the core. In such a 'furnace', a great deal of rapid chemical activity occurred with complex linkages being formed between the atoms of the

eight elements – oxygen, silicon, aluminium, iron, calcium, sodium, magnesium and potassium – that make up 98 per cent of the Earth's crust (⇨ p. 146). Differences in the times of formation of minerals and in the density of the elements led to differentiation of rock types. Less dense elements such as aluminium, silicon and potassium tended to rise to the upper parts of the crust, while denser elements, such as iron, settled lower. The existence of thousands of different varieties of igneous rocks is attributed to physical as well as chemical causes, however. Differential partial melting of the various source materials, and the involvement and assimilation of a range of nonhomogeneous material could account for the variety. The important element – silicon – is present as one of various oxides, especially silicon dioxide (known as 'silica'), quartz, cristobalite, tridymite, glass or sand.

We know that rocks occurring in the output of volcanoes are of igneous origin, but the evidence of the igneous origin of other rocks is derived from similarities in their texture, and mineral and chemical composition to those of volcanic rocks.

The commonest igneous rocks are basalt, andesite and rhyolite. Basalt is by far the most abundant of the volcanic rocks. It is a hard, dark, dense rock with a very fine-grained texture, consisting of silica, aluminium oxide (alumina), iron and smaller quantities of other elements. Basalt minerals are silicates (about 45 per cent silica)

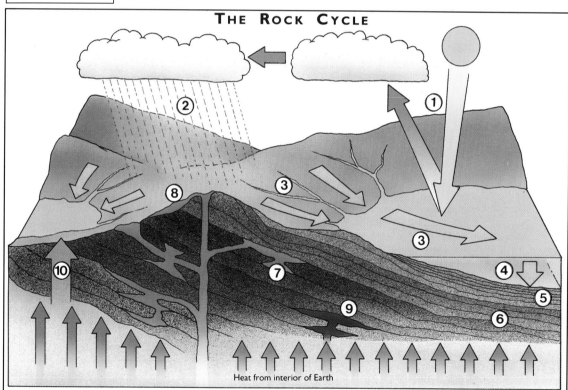

THE ROCK CYCLE

Heat from interior of Earth

1. Heat from the Sun causes evaporation. Water vapour rises and condenses into clouds.

2. Water in cloud precipitates as rain or snow.

3. Water erodes rock, and rivers carry away sediment.

4. Rivers deposit sediment as alluvium on flat ground, or transport it to lakes and seas where it settles on the bottom as clay or sand.

5. As sediment builds up, increasing pressure changes lower layers into sedimentary rock.

6. Deeper sedimentary rock is turned into metamorphic rock by pressure from above and heat from below.

7. Magma – molten rock from deep inside the Earth – rises towards the surface. Some is trapped underground and hardens into intrusive igneous rock.

8. Some magma reaches the Earth's surface via volcanoes and fissures as lava and is classified as extrusive igneous rock.

9. Some intrusive igneous rock is forced deeper by the pressure of sedimentation, and is changed into metamorphic rock. This metamorphosis may be assisted by thermal energy from below.

10. Pressure from colliding continental plates pushes all kinds of rock to the surface, and forces them upwards, where they are eroded. The rock cycle begins again.

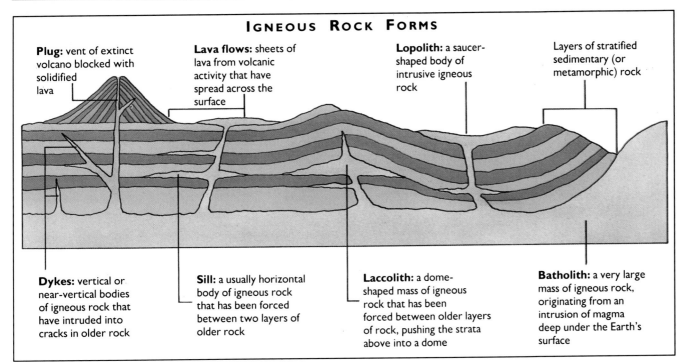

IGNEOUS ROCK FORMS

Plug: vent of extinct volcano blocked with solidified lava

Lava flows: sheets of lava from volcanic activity that have spread across the surface

Lopolith: a saucer-shaped body of intrusive igneous rock

Layers of stratified sedimentary (or metamorphic) rock

Dykes: vertical or near-vertical bodies of igneous rock that have intruded into cracks in older rock

Sill: a usually horizontal body of igneous rock that has been forced between two layers of older rock

Laccolith: a dome-shaped mass of igneous rock that has been forced between older layers of rock, pushing the strata above into a dome

Batholith: a very large mass of igneous rock, originating from an intrusion of magma deep under the Earth's surface

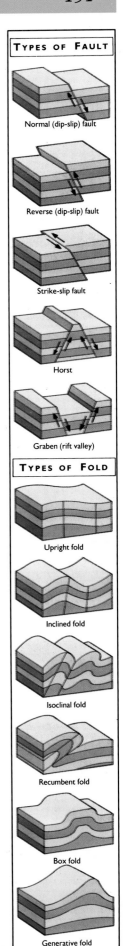

TYPES OF FAULT

Normal (dip-slip) fault

Reverse (dip-slip) fault

Strike-slip fault

Horst

Graben (rift valley)

TYPES OF FOLD

Upright fold

Inclined fold

Isoclinal fold

Recumbent fold

Box fold

Generative fold

such as feldspar and pyroxene mixed up with smaller quantities of other minerals such as magnetite, apatite and olivine. Natural glass is also commonly present.

Andesite is a greyish or black fine-grained rock containing feldspar and other silicate minerals, such as olivine, pyroxene, hornblende or biotite with natural glass. It is similar to basalt but contains a higher proportion of silica (about 50 per cent). Andesite is named after the Andes Mountains along the west coast of South America, where it is common. It is found in lava flows and in regions at the edges of continental plates (⇨ p. 148).

Rhyolite is a fine-grained igneous rock with a very low iron content and a very high silicon content, making it light-coloured. Its silica content is over 70 per cent and it often contains large crystals of quartz or feldspar embedded in a mass of smaller crystals (*phenocrysts*). Molten rhyolite is very viscous because of its high silica content and often occurs in steep-sided dome formations.

Another important class of igneous rocks is granite. This is more coarse-grained than basalt, andesite or rhyolite because it is formed within the Earth's crust from magma that has been forced into the crust but has not reached the surface, thus cooling more slowly and allowing larger crystals to be formed. Such a rock is called an *intrusive* or *plutonic* rock, in contrast to rocks that form on the surface, *extrusive rocks*. Granite is a very hard rock consisting of coarse grains of quartz and potassium and sodium feldspars in varying proportions. Granites vary considerably but may contain 70–80 per cent of silica, 11–13 per cent of alumina and smaller quantities of other materials such as micas (biotite and muscovite), calcium and iron. Of the plutonic rocks, granite is by far the most plentiful constituent of mountain ranges.

Sedimentary rocks

A sedimentary rock is one formed by the settling of particles of material, under the influence of gravity, from a temporary suspension in water. About three quarters of the total surface of the Earth is covered with sedimentary rock, but this layer is relatively thin and the rock accounts for only about one twentieth of the mass of the crust. Most of the Earth's sedimentary rock is derived from the break-up of other pre-existing rocks by gradual erosion into smaller and smaller fragments. This is called *clastic sedimentary rock*. The smaller the fragments, the more readily they are transported by water, wind or glacier. Most of the very small particles end up in the oceans, where they fall as a sediment to the ocean floors. The build-up of sediment leads to increasing pressure on the lower layers, and this results in compaction into rock of varying hardness.

Rock erosion is not the only source of material for sedimentation. Considerable solution of inorganic and organic material occurs in the course of the flow of streams and rivers, and this dissolved material is carried to the seas. When such solutions become saturated they precipitate out as very fine, solid, particulate matter that forms a sediment.

A huge variety of material can go to the formation of sedimentary rocks, but, in view of the preponderance of silica in the crust, the commonest sedimentary rock is sandstone. Carbonate rocks – *limestones* or *dolostones* – are composed of particles of chalky residues of animal skeletons, shells and other sources of chalk (calcium carbonate). Carbonaceous rocks – mostly rock coal – are sedimentary rocks formed by pressure on buried organic material such as tree ferns and peat. The greater the pressure, the harder the coal and the higher the

calorific value (the greater the heat yielded on burning).

Metamorphism and metamorphic rocks

Metamorphism is a change in appearance or structure, or, in the case of rocks, the process that brings about such change. Metamorphic rock is igneous or sedimentary rock, or sometimes organic material that has been altered in structure (and occasionally in mineral composition) by high temperatures and pressures. The degree of metamorphism varies; in some cases it is so extreme that the original component rocks cannot be identified. In other cases, residual effects of the metamorphic process affects the physical properties of the rocks. Some metamorphic rocks show obvious layering or banding and some, as in the case of slate, have obvious planes of cleavage, by which they can easily be split and that reveal the nature of the processes by which they were formed.

The pressures necessary to form metamorphic rocks are to be found at plate boundaries (⇨ p. 148). Metamorphic rock, therefore, occurs in zones up to thousands of kilometres long and up to hundreds of kilometres wide. Common causes of metamorphism are the subduction of a plate edge into an area of high temperature and pressure, or the faulting or folding of areas of sedimentary or igneous rock.

Pure chalk (calcium carbonate) is metamorphosed into marble; sandstone is metamorphosed into a hard mosaic, with the grains welded together, known as quartzite. Since metamorphic rock derives from a wide variety of igneous and sedimentary rock that is then subject to further change, the scope for variety is, therefore, very great.

The Living Planet

A very small proportion of the substance of our planet – perhaps a billionth of it – is of living matter. In spite of its diversity, all living matter, from the simplest lichen to the most complex animal, is constructed from a comparatively small number of elements. About 99 per cent of all living matter consists of carbon, oxygen, hydrogen and nitrogen alone. Much smaller quantities of a few other elements, such as calcium, phosphorus, iron, sodium, potassium and iodine, are also present. All the elements necessary for life exist throughout the universe. This raises the major question – is there life elsewhere?

THE GAIA HYPOTHESIS

Gaia was the 'Earth Mother' goddess of the ancient Greeks. The Gaia hypothesis is the supposition that the Earth is a single, self-regulating, living entity, capable of protecting itself against danger and repairing damage sustained. The proponents of the idea suggest that the Earth employs negative-feedback systems to ensure its own biological stability and safety. As the radiation from the developing Sun has increased, for instance, the Earth has responded by reducing its 'greenhouse' blanket of carbon dioxide so as to allow greater losses of heat. It has done this by means of an increase in the fixation of carbon dioxide by a greater plant mass and an increase in the amount of carbon and oxygen laid down as carbonate rock. Similarly, as living organisms have been destroyed by natural catastrophes, such as meteoric bombardment, there has been less competition for the evolution of new forms of life to take their place.

Many scientists take a sceptical view of this idea and suggest that it belongs more in the realm of speculative philosophy or even theology than in science. Others, however, acknowledge the value of such thinking in promoting new ecological ideas and in drawing attention to the importance of a high level of respect for the welfare of the planet.

Life is possible only on the outer surface of the Earth's crust and a short distance below the surface of the land. The seas are highly suitable for a vast range of life forms. Elsewhere in the Earth, temperatures are unsuitable. Some bacteria survive happily in temperatures approaching that of boiling water, and many can live in the absence of free oxygen, but most life forms require less extreme conditions. When these are present, an amazing diversity of living things exists and multiplies, each striving with the other in a never-ending battle for a share of the means of survival.

The elements

The major molecules of living things consist of a very few chemical elements. The carbohydrates that form the bulk of plant life are made from carbon, hydrogen and oxygen. The 20 amino acids that link to form all the proteins of animal life are made from carbon, oxygen, hydrogen and nitrogen. Fats are made from carbon, oxygen, hydrogen, nitrogen and phosphorus; so is DNA (deoxyribonucleic acid; ⇨ p. 202). These same elements also form large numbers of nonliving inorganic molecules. The distinction between organic and inorganic molecules is that the former are associated with cells (⇨ pp. 186–9) and are incorporated into, or are the products of, self-contained systems known as *organisms* that are capable of reproducing themselves. By extension, because carbon plays such a central role in the formation of organic molecules, the term 'organic' has come to be applied to the whole chemistry of carbon (⇨ pp. 170–3) and its numerous compounds. Even so, virtually all the

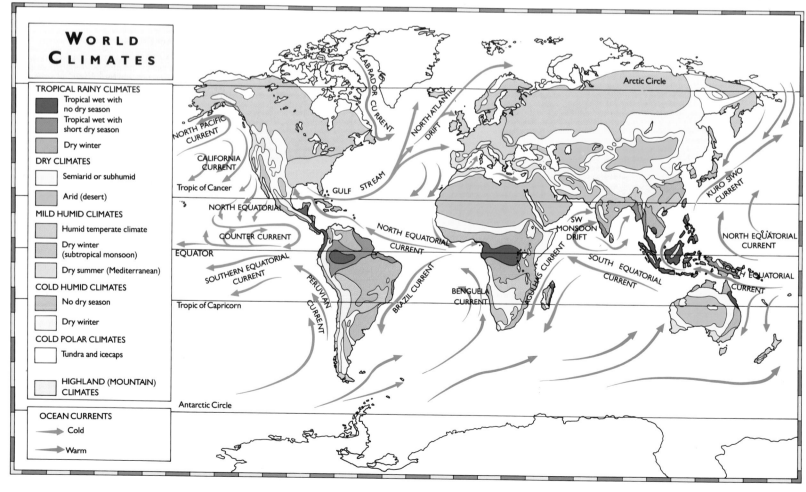

WORLD CLIMATES

TROPICAL RAINY CLIMATES
- Tropical wet with no dry season
- Tropical wet with short dry season
- Dry winter

DRY CLIMATES
- Semiarid or subhumid
- Arid (desert)

MILD HUMID CLIMATES
- Humid temperate climate
- Dry winter (subtropical monsoon)
- Dry summer (Mediterranean)

COLD HUMID CLIMATES
- No dry season
- Dry winter

COLD POLAR CLIMATES
- Tundra and icecaps

- HIGHLAND (MOUNTAIN) CLIMATES

OCEAN CURRENTS
- Cold
- Warm

Arctic Circle

Tropic of Cancer

EQUATOR

Tropic of Capricorn

Antarctic Circle

LABRADOR CURRENT
NORTH PACIFIC CURRENT
CALIFORNIA CURRENT
NORTH ATLANTIC DRIFT
GULF STREAM
NORTH EQUATORIAL
COUNTER CURRENT
NORTH EQUATORIAL CURRENT
SOUTHERN EQUATORIAL CURRENT
PERUVIAN CURRENT
BRAZIL CURRENT
BENGUELA CURRENT
AGULHAS CURRENT
SW MONSOON DRIFT
SOUTH EQUATORIAL CURRENT
KURO SIWO CURRENT
NORTH EQUATORIAL CURRENT
SOUTH EQUATORIAL CURRENT

organic matter in the world is the product of living organisms.

How the Earth provides conditions necessary for life

Chemical reactions are very temperature-sensitive and, within certain limits, roughly double in rate with every 10°C (18°F) rise in temperature. This is because heat is a form of energy, and the energy in atoms available for linkage with other atoms is determined by the temperature. At low temperatures, chemical reactions either do not occur or do so very slowly. At very high temperatures, chemical reactions are so fierce that compounds formed are rapidly destroyed by oxidation (reacting with oxygen; ⇨ p. 168). There are, therefore, strict temperature limits within which the chemical reactions of life can occur.

In addition, the Earth's surface provides a means of ready interchange of chemical elements between the *biotic* (living) and *abiotic* (inanimate) systems. All living things, with the possible exception of laboratory tissue cultures, are mortal. On dying they are, almost always, reduced in chemical complexity, so that the elements of which they are formed are returned to the inorganic domain and become available for recycling. This may occur as a result of enzymatic and free-radical action, usually with digestive enzymes provided by bacteria in the process of putrefaction, or it may occur by more rapid oxidation by

burning. In either event, highly complex molecules are reduced to simpler forms in which the elements become readily accessible. The long chain of building up (*synthesis*), which starts with the production of plant sugars by the action of the Sun and chlorophyll and then passes through further stages of synthesis (of polysaccharides in plants or proteins and fats in animals), is succeeded by a stage of analysis. This endless cycle of growth and decay could occur only in the precise environment provided by our planet's surface.

Environmental limitations

Today's living organisms on the Earth originally evolved in an environment containing a great deal of water and oxygen, and they depend on considerable energy, derived also from the Sun, to power their chemical reactions. In spite of the fact that all the necessary elements are present, life as we know it

could not have arisen in a radically different environment, such as that found on other planets of the solar system. Space research shows that plenty of organic molecules are present, such as the polycyclic hydrocarbons (containing more than one ring of atoms in the molecule), with as many as several hundred carbon atoms; but no evidence of any life form has been found elsewhere in our solar system. Life cannot exist in active stars because of their impossibly high temperatures. But if other stars have planets, there is no inherent reason why life forms could not exist on these – given always that they possess a suitable atmosphere and liquid water, and that their temperature is within the necessary limits. In view of the vast number of the stars and the rules of probability, the question of extraterrestrial life depends on whether other stars have planetary systems (⇨ box above).

IS THERE LIFE ELSEWHERE IN THE UNIVERSE?

The nearest stars to our solar system have been closely scrutinized for indications of the kind of wobble in star movement that would be caused by the gravitational pull of orbiting planets. Such *perturbations* might be detectable as alternating red and blue Doppler shifts (⇨ p. 126). The results of such investigations on nearby stars has been uncertain. If a nearby star happened to have a very large planet, its effect might be observed, but such very large objects are unlikely to be formed from the circumstellar disc.

There is now enormous interest in the question of whether life exists elsewhere, and striking advances are likely in the near future. Much work has also been devoted to listening for 'messages' from intelligent extraterrestrial beings. The space probes *Pioneer 10* and *11* (1972–3) also carried plaques indicating our position in space expressed in units of the wavelength of radiation from the hydrogen atom – 21 cm (6 in). Planets more than sixty light years away will now be receiving our television signals, so we may perhaps get a response after another sixty years or so.

SEE ALSO

- COSMOLOGY: UNDERSTANDING THE UNIVERSE p. 120
- THE ROTATION AND ORBIT OF THE EARTH p. 144
- THE EARTH AND ITS STRUCTURE p. 146
- PLATE TECTONICS p. 148
- ROCKS AND MINERALS p. 150
- ORGANIC CHEMISTRY pp. 170–3
- THE SCIENCE OF LIFE pp. 180–209

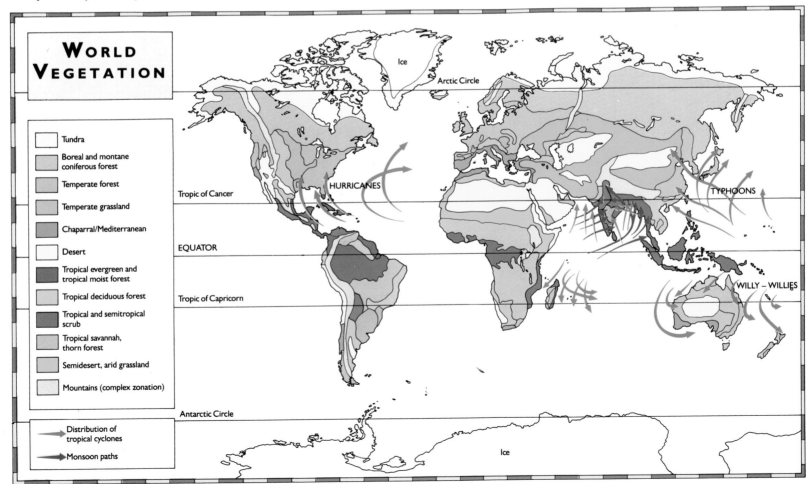

WORLD VEGETATION

- Tundra
- Boreal and montane coniferous forest
- Temperate forest
- Temperate grassland
- Chaparral/Mediterranean
- Desert
- Tropical evergreen and tropical moist forest
- Tropical deciduous forest
- Tropical and semitropical scrub
- Tropical savannah, thorn forest
- Semidesert, arid grassland
- Mountains (complex zonation)

→ Distribution of tropical cyclones
→ Monsoon paths

Ice
Arctic Circle
Tropic of Cancer
HURRICANES
TYPHOONS
EQUATOR
Tropic of Capricorn
WILLY – WILLIES
Antarctic Circle
Ice

THE
CHEMISTRY
OF MATTER

Atoms and Molecules

Chemistry is the study of the composition, properties and interactions of substances. It is concerned with the study of atoms and particularly with the study of the properties conferred on them by the number of electrons (⇨ p. 90) in their outermost shells.

Since atoms (from the Greek *atoma*, 'uncuttable') all have outer electrons that repel each other (⇨ p. 88), this mutual repulsion must be overcome if they are to link together to form molecules. Different atoms differ in the ease with which they are able to do this. Until the atomic theory of matter was taken seriously by the English chemist John Dalton (1766–1844; ⇨ box), chemistry was an empirical study without real scientific

THE STRUCTURE OF SODIUM CHLORIDE (SALT)

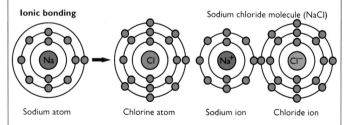

Sodium chloride is an *ionic compound*. It is made up of a three-dimensional lattice of positive sodium *ions* (charged particles) and negative chloride ions. Because of these opposite charges the ions are strongly attracted to one another, and the ionic bond between them makes each atom (sodium or chlorine) within a molecule of sodium chloride very stable, as each has a full complement of electrons.

Ionic bonding

Sodium chloride molecule (NaCl)

Sodium atom   Chlorine atom   Sodium ion   Chloride ion

Highly reactive sodium donates its spare electron to corrosive and poisonous chlorine, leaving the sodium ion positively charged and the chloride ion negatively charged. The ions form an ionic bond and the resulting compound is unreactive, non-corrosive and nonpoisonous.

JOHN DALTON AND THE ATOMIC THEORY

The English chemist and physicist John Dalton (1766–1844), whose work revolutionized scientific thought, was the son of a poor Quaker weaver, who had the good fortune to have as his teacher the skilled instrument-maker and meteorologist Elihu Robinson. Profiting from instruction, he was teaching at the age of 12, and was Principal of a school at 19. In 1793, he became a tutor in physics at Manchester Academy, where he joined the Manchester Literary and Philosophical Society, becoming Secretary and later President. During his membership he presented more than a hundred scientific papers on all

John Dalton (1766–1844), who set out the atomic theory in its modern form. (AR)

sorts of subjects, including the first scientific account of colour blindness (from which he suffered) and which, for many years thereafter, was known as 'Daltonism'.

Dalton's study of gases led him to believe that they must be made up of individual small particles. He went on to formulate the law that, in a mixture of gases, each member exerted the same pressure that it would exert if it alone occupied the whole volume of the mixture. But his most important contribution to science was his idea that all matter was made up of such particles – which, following the example of Democritus (⇨ p. 108), he called atoms – and that the particles (atoms) of different substances could be distinguished by differences in their weights. Atoms combined together to form other substances and they did so in definite proportions. This principle explained many chemical observations and opened up entirely new prospects of experimental research. Dalton produced the first tables of atomic weights, and published his ideas on chemistry in the book *A New System of Chemical Philosophy* (1808). His merits were recognized early and he was widely honoured. He became a Fellow of the Royal Society and a Member of the French Academy of Sciences, was awarded honorary degrees by Oxford and Edinburgh Universities, and a statue of him was erected in Manchester.

basis. The idea that all matter must be made up of small, indivisible particles had been proposed by the 5th-century BC Greek philosopher Leucippus, and developed, popularized and promulgated by his pupil, the Greek philosopher Democritus (c. 460–370 BC; ⇨ p. 108). These ideas were not based on experiment but simply on the general grounds that there must be a limit to the number of times a body can be divided. Democritus suggested that atoms were hard and had shape, mass and motion. The later Greek philosopher Aristotle (384–322 BC), whose influence was powerful and lasted throughout the medieval period, utterly rejected the idea of atoms.

Elements and atoms

In chemistry, an *element* is a substance that cannot be broken down into simpler substances by normal chemical or physical means. Prior to our understanding of nuclear fission (⇨ p. 116), the definition would have ended with the words 'simpler substances'. A pure sample of an element contains atoms of one kind only and nothing else. A *compound*, on the other hand, contains two or more elements combined together in units called *molecules*. The metal sodium is an element and contains only sodium atoms, designated by the chemical shorthand symbol Na (⇨ p. 158). Chlorine is a gaseous element, designated Cl. Sodium chloride (common salt) is a compound, made up of molecules each containing one atom of sodium and one atom of chlorine, and is

designated in chemistry by the molecular formula NaCl.

Ninety-two elements occur in nature, and scientists have artificially created more than a dozen others. The fundamental difference between the atoms of elements is that they have different numbers of positively charged particles – *protons* – in their nuclei (⇨ p. 108). The lightest element, hydrogen, has a single proton; the next, helium, has two; the next, lithium, has three, and so on. Carbon has six protons; uranium, at the other end of the scale, has 92. Thus any atom containing six protons is called carbon; any containing eight protons is called oxygen; any containing 20 protons is called calcium; any containing 26 protons is called iron; and any containing 79 protons is called gold. It is the number of protons that determines both what the element is, and what its chemical properties are. The protons do not, however, directly cause the chemical properties. They do, however, determine the number of *electrons* (negatively charged particles) present in the outer zones of the atom, and it is these that ordain the chemistry.

Atomic number and atomic weight

If the elements are put in ascending order, in accordance with the number of protons in the nucleus of the atoms, we can call the position in the numerical order the *atomic number*. This is a convenient way of identifying elements. The element with the atomic number 50 is tin; that with the atomic number 22 is titanium; and that with the atomic number 7 is nitrogen. It might be thought that this same order of whole numbers would also represent the respective weight of the atoms, but the matter is a little more complicated. In addition to protons, atoms have one other kind of particle in their nuclei – the neutron (⇨ p. 108). This is a particle with no electric charge and with a mass about the same as that of a proton. Most samples of hydrogen consist mainly of atoms, with a proton only, and with no neutrons. All other elements have both protons and neutrons in their nuclei. Hydrogen, however, can exist in three forms – with a single proton only, with a proton and one neutron, and with a proton and two neutrons. As long as there is one proton, the element is hydrogen, regardless of the neutron situation, and will always behave chemically as hydrogen. But, of course, the atoms of these three forms of hydrogen have different weights.

Most elements can have forms in which the number of neutrons differ. There are always at least as many neutrons as protons and, the further up the list of atomic numbers, the greater is the preponderance of neutrons. The place of each element on the list is decided by the number of protons, so each group of atoms with the same number of protons, but different numbers of neutrons, occupies the same place on the list. For this reason they are called *isotopes* (from the Greek *iso*, 'equal', and *topos*, 'place'; ⇨ p. 116). Isotopes are elements with the same atomic number but different atomic weights. Some elements, such as fluorine (atomic number 9), have no isotopes, but most have two or more. Helium has three isotopes; lithium has four; nitrogen has three; oxygen has three; sulphur has five, calcium has nine; and tin has ten.

All the isotopes of a particular element have exactly the same chemical properties because they all have the same number of electrons in the outer shell. For this reason, isotopes are very difficult to separate from one another; none of the normal chemical separation processes is of any use. Isotopes do, however, have slightly different physical properties – notably weight – and this allows various physical means of separation to be used. The scientists involved in the Manhattan Project, who were responsible for developing atomic weapons, had to separate out the fissionable (⇨ p. 116) uranium isotope with 92 protons and 143 neutrons (uranium–235). This isotope is present as only 0.72 per cent in any uranium sample, whereas the much common isotope with 92 protons and 146 neutrons (uranium–238), comprises over 99 per cent. This was why the first atomic bomb was so difficult to make and eventually cost $2,000,000,000.

The atomic weight of an element will thus be an average of the weight of a mixture of isotopes, and will be affected by the proportions of the different isotopes. A standard of atomic weight had to be agreed upon and the carbon isotope

carbon–12 (⇨ p. 116), with six protons and six neutrons, was selected and was given an *atomic mass unit* (amu) of exactly 12. This is the commonest of the three carbon isotopes, and represents 98.9 per cent of all carbon. The weight (mass) of all the other elements is then calculated in terms of the proportion of their weight to that of carbon–12. On this basis the mass of hydrogen is 1.007825 amu; that of helium is 2.014102 amu; that of nitrogen 14.003074 amu; that of iron 55.934939 amu, and so on. The *gram atomic weight* is the quantity of an element, in grams, that has the same numerical value as the mass in atomic mass units. The gram atomic weight of carbon–12 is 12 g; that of iron–56 is 55.934939 g. There are the same number of atoms in 55.934939 g of iron–56 as there are in 12 g of carbon–12, or in the gram atomic weight of any other element. This number is called a *mole*. A mole of any element contains the same number of atoms as are contained in 12 g of carbon 12. This unit, the mole, is the chemist's unit of amount and is about 6×10^{23}.

Molecules and molecular weight

A *molecule* is the smallest unit of a substance that displays the chemical properties of that substance. If a molecule, such as NaCl (sodium chloride), is split into its component atoms, it no longer exhibits the customary properties, such as saltiness and culinary usefulness, but becomes something quite different – in this case a choking, poisonous gas and a dangerously reactive metal. The combination of atoms to form molecules, or the breakdown of molecules and the rearrangement of the atoms in new combinations – different molecules – are called *chemical reactions* (⇨ p. 168).

Most molecules are groups of two or more atoms – sometimes of thousands – held together by forces known as chemical bonds (⇨ p. 162). In some cases, such as helium, neon and iron, the molecule consists of a single atom; in others, as in molecular hydrogen or oxygen, a molecule may consists of two identical atoms bonded together. Rarely, three identical atoms may link to form a molecule, as in the case of ozone (O_3). In organic chemistry (⇨ pp. 170–3) many molecules are large and often consist of long chains of carbon atoms, with other atoms, especially hydrogen and oxygen, bonded to these carbon atoms. In many cases, the carbon atoms link up in rings of six atoms – benzene rings – with other atoms attached, to give what are termed the 'aromatic compounds'. Numerous compounds contain many such carbon rings, and *polycyclic aromatic hydrocarbons* with several hundred carbon atoms have recently even been detected in outer space.

In biochemistry (⇨ pp. 182–5), molecules are often very large; protein molecules, for instance, may contain many thousands of atoms. Even so, every molecule of a particular substance contains

exactly the same number of particular atoms or atom groups, linked together. *Polymers* (from the Greek *poly*, 'many', and *mers*, 'linked') are giant, long-chain molecules consisting of many repetitive units of small chemical groups linked together. The isolated small groups are called *monomers*, and these may link in pairs to form *dimers*. Thus, large numbers of ethene (ethylene) monomers may be linked together to form the polymer polyethylene – commonly called *polythene*. Proteins are polymers made from small monomer chemical groups called amino acids. The celluloses of plants and trees are polymers of a kind called polysaccharides because they are made from many, often identical, sugar monomers, such as glucose, linked together. Silk, wool, cotton and rubber are also polymers, and there is, of course, a very wide range of synthetic polymers, commonly known as *plastics*.

Molecular weight is an important feature of molecules that affects their physical as well as their chemical properties. It is related to the atomic mass unit and is the weight of one molecule of the substance, relative to the weight of the carbon–12 isotope of carbon, which is taken as 12. So since carbon–12 contains six protons and six neutrons, and since protons and neutrons are about the same weight, the molecular weight of a substance is roughly equal to the number of protons and neutrons in the substance. The electrons make little difference to the weight as an electron weighs only about $1/_{1,800}$ of the weight of a proton. Obviously, molecular weights relate to the size of the molecules concerned. Proteins may have molecular weights in the thousands or tens of thousands; other polymers may have molecular weights of from about 50,000 to several million.

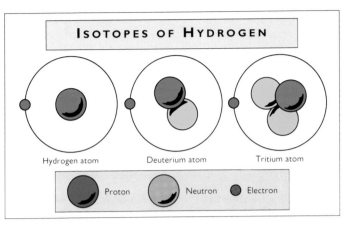

ISOTOPES OF HYDROGEN

Hydrogen atom   Deuterium atom   Tritium atom

Proton   Neutron   Electron

SEE ALSO

● THE DEVELOPMENT OF SCIENCE 2: THE RENAISSANCE AND AFTER p. 10
● GAS LAWS p. 50
● INSIDE THE ATOM pp. 108–17
● THE PERIODIC TABLE p. 158
● RADIOACTIVITY p. 160
● THE NATURE OF THE CHEMICAL BOND p. 162
● TYPES OF MOLECULAR STRUCTURE p. 164
● THE STRUCTURE OF SOLIDS p. 166
● CHEMICAL REACTIONS p. 168
● ORGANIC CHEMISTRY pp. 170–3
● BIOCHEMISTRY pp. 182–5

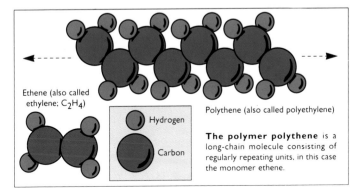

Ethene (also called ethylene: C_2H_4)

Hydrogen

Carbon

Polythene (also called polyethylene)

The polymer polythene is a long-chain molecule consisting of regularly repeating units, in this case the monomer ethene.

The Periodic Table

Once the respective atomic weights of the 92 naturally occurring elements are known, they can be arranged in order of weight. When the ordered sequence of the elements is then split into rows or columns in certain logical ways, some remarkable insights into chemistry emerge. Such an arrangement is called a *periodic table* and the development of the table was one of the most important advances in the history of chemistry.

In the second half of the 19th century, the number of known elements was increasing steadily. Dalton's atomic theory (⇨ p. 156) was almost universally accepted, but there was little or no agreement on some fundamental matters, especially on the question of the atomic weights of the elements. There was also still a good deal of confusion about the difference between atoms and molecules.

DMITRI IVANOVICH MENDELEYEV

The Russian chemist Dmitri Ivanovich Mendeleyev was the youngest of a family of 14 children, but his education was not neglected, and, after a brilliant student career, he took a teaching qualification and a degree in chemistry at St Petersburg. He then did postgraduate study at Paris and Heidelberg, where he worked with the German chemist Robert Bunsen. In 1863 he was appointed Professor of Chemistry at the St Petersburg Technical Institute and later at the University. Unfortunately, Mendeleyev, although acknowledged to be the leading Russian scientist of the time and a brilliant lecturer, was a man of short temper and ready tongue. In 1880 he had a notable quarrel with the Minister of Education, Count Tolstoy. He was also in trouble with the Orthodox Church for marrying within the statutory seven-year period following dissolution of a previous marriage, and was, technically, a bigamist. In 1890, he had a more serious disagreement with Tolstoy's successor, Count Delyanov, on the subject of student reform, was criticized and humiliated, and resigned. Mendeleyev had friends in high places, however, and three years later he was appointed Director of the Bureau of Weights and Measures, where he remained for the rest of his life.

Dmitri Ivanovich Mendeleyev (1834–1907), the Russian chemist who derived the first form of the periodic table of elements. From William A. Tilder, *Chemical Discovery and Invention in the Twentieth Century* (1917).

Mendeleyev's book *Principles of Chemistry* (1870) was the best work that had been published in Russia on the subject. There were eight Russian editions, three in English, and others in French and German. He also had three hundred other publications to his credit, but it was while writing his textbook, and systematically ordering the elements, that the significance of the periodicity of the elements and the organization of the table became apparent. Although his breakthrough was at first greeted with scepticism, its truth became apparent when the elements he had predicted were discovered. Mendeleyev was showered with honours, both at home and abroad.

Atomic weights

In 1860, the great Russian chemist Dmitri Ivanovich Mendeleyev (1834–1907) attended the first ever International Congress of Chemistry, held in Germany, and learned, from a lecture given by the Italian chemist Stanislao Cannizzaro (1826–1910), a method of establishing the atomic weights of elements. This was based on the principle that, at a constant temperature, a given volume of any gas contained the same number of particles (molecules; ⇨ p. 156). This is known as Avogadro's hypothesis after its originator, the Italian physicist Amedeo Avogadro (1776–1856). It was known that, when gases combined to form new compounds, they did so in proportions that were whole numbers. Two parts of hydrogen, for instance, always combined with one part of oxygen to make water (H_2O); one part of nitrogen combined with three parts of hydrogen to form ammonia (NH_3) and so on. Similarly, analysis of solid compounds had shown that all samples contained elements combined in definite, fixed proportions by weight. These facts made it possible to work out the weights of the atoms of elements relative to a standard, such as hydrogen.

Valency

Mendeleyev was aware from the work of other scientists that, when the atoms of elements combined, each one had a characteristic ability to combine with a particular number of those atoms, such as hydrogen, which could combine with only one other atom. Chlorine could combine with only one hydrogen atom; oxygen could combine with two; nitrogen could combine with three; and carbon could combine with four hydrogen atoms. This ability was called *valency*.

By about 1870 at least sixty-three elements were known and Mendeleyev was now able to arrange these in the order of their atomic weights. When he did so and considered the valencies of the atoms, he at once discovered an interesting fact. Lithium had a valency of one; the next element, beryllium, had a valency of two; the next, boron, had a valency of three; and the next, carbon, had a valency of four. After that was nitrogen with a valency of three; oxygen, with a valency of two; and fluorine, with a valency of one. This could have been a coincidence, but Mendeleyev found that the pattern of rise and fall of valencies – a periodic characteristic – held throughout the whole table. Mendeleyev also knew that the elements fell naturally into groups with similar chemical properties – groups like fluorine, chlorine, bromine and iodine (now called the *halogens*) or the metals lithium, sodium and potassium. When he arranged his list – still in order of atomic weight – in vertical columns of identical valencies, he found to his astonishment that all the elements in each column fell into such groups. Chlorine was under fluorine, bromine was under chlorine and iodine was under bromine. The table was thus aptly named the *periodic table*.

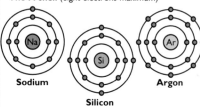

ELEMENTS AND THE BUILD-UP OF ELECTRON SHELLS

The K shell (two electrons maximum)

Hydrogen

Helium

The L shell (eight electrons maximum)

Lithium

Carbon

Neon

The M shell (eight electrons maximum)

Sodium

Silicon

Argon

The number of electrons in an atom's outer shell determines the reactivity of that atom/element. Where the shell is full, the atom will be unreactive and stable. There are four further shells (not shown here), N and O (18 electrons maximum) and P and Q (32 electrons maximum).

The pattern of groups of seven elements with valencies of one, two, three, four, three, two, one held only for the first two periods at the beginning of the table. The next two, he estimated, contained 17 each. Mendeleyev deliberately left gaps in his table so that the elements would fit into the proper columns – a procedure that was widely interpreted as a disingenuous attempt to demonstrate order that did not really exist. But Mendeleyev boldly predicted that elements did exist that would fit into the gaps, but that they had not yet been discovered. He even outlined the chemical properties these elements would have when they were found. These claims were greeted with scepticism and derision. Mendeleyev also stated that, in the case of a number of elements that did not fit into what he deemed to be the proper places in his table, the then assumed atomic weights had been wrongly calculated. When new determinations of the atomic weights of these elements were made, and were found to agree with Mendeleyev's values, other scientists began to take the idea of the periodic table more seriously; and when three elements – gallium, scandium and germanium – which he had predicted, were actually found, and were shown to have the properties he had forecast, his triumph was complete.

Subsequent development of the periodic table

Mendeleyev's table has had to undergo some minor modifications in the light of later discoveries, but its principles are unchanged. At the time, Mendeleyev was unaware of the existence of the group of the rare inert gases, helium, neon, argon, krypton, xenon and radon, which now form a new vertical column at the right-hand side of the table. When argon was discovered, and was found to form no compounds, Mendeleyev pointed out that the new gas had no valency, and so it did not fundamentally change the arrangement. It was immediately obvious that other inert rare gases must exist and, indeed, four more were found before the end of the century.

Today, hydrogen is recognized as a unique element and is placed in a category of its own. The subsequent elements are arranged, as by Mendeleyev, in order of atomic weight, horizontally, until an element occurs that repeats the properties of the first of the previous period. This element forms the first of the new period. The vertical columns now show groups with similar properties.

Mendeleyev's work on the periodic table brought order into what had been a chaotic mass of uncoordinated chemical information, and its effect on the advancement of chemical science was enormous.

The table explained

The definitive periodic table is not ordered by atomic weight – this was the only suitable characteristic available to Mendeleyev – but by the roughly corresponding atomic number (⇨ p. 156). This is the number of protons in the nucleus of the atom. In 1913 the Danish nuclear physicist Niels Bohr (1885–1962) proposed a structure for the atom that went a long way to explaining valency and the periodic table. The outer electrons were arranged, he suggested, in a series of concentric 'shells', designated by letters outwards from the nucleus.

The first shell, the K shell, could contain either only one electron, as in hydrogen, or two, as in helium. With one electron, the shell was incomplete and the atom could link to another atom. With two electrons, the shell was complete and the element was inert with no valency – helium. The next shell, the L shell, could have from one to eight electrons. Lithium has one electron in this shell and is avid for linkages, in which it gives up this electron and so becomes stable; neon has eight electrons in this shell and the shell is full, leaving no valency 'gaps' and causing chemical stability. Carbon has four electrons and can link with up to four other atoms. The M shell is like the L shell and can have from one to eight electrons. Its first element is the highly reactive metal

sodium with one electron and its last the inert gas argon. When there are four electrons in this shell the element is silicon, which, like carbon, is tetravalent and can form many compounds similar to those of carbon.

The next two shells, the N and O shells, can have from one to 18 electrons. The N shell ranges from potassium with one electron to krypton with 18 and the O shell ranges from rubidium with one electron to xenon with 18. The P and Q shells can each have from one to 32 electrons.

We now know that the chemical properties of an element are determined only by the number of electrons in the outer shell. The filled inner shells have no effect. When atoms link together, those with few electrons in the outer shell tend to lose electrons and so become positively charged (electrons are negatively charged) and attract other atoms. Stable compounds achieve a 'fill' of the outer shell. Common salt (sodium chloride; ⇨ p. 156), for example, is a compound formed from sodium, with one electron in the outer shell, and chlorine with seven electrons. When these elements link, the sodium electron fills the single gap in the chlorine outer shell, so completing the shell.

SEE ALSO

● THE DEVELOPMENT OF SCIENCE 2: THE RENAISSANCE AND AFTER p. 10
● INSIDE THE ATOM pp. 108–17
● ATOMS AND MOLECULES p. 156
● RADIOACTIVITY p. 160
● THE NATURE OF THE CHEMICAL BOND p. 162
● TYPES OF MOLECULAR STRUCTURE p. 164
● THE STRUCTURE OF SOLIDS p. 166
● CHEMICAL REACTIONS p. 168
● ORGANIC CHEMISTRY pp. 170–3
● BIOCHEMISTRY pp. 182–5

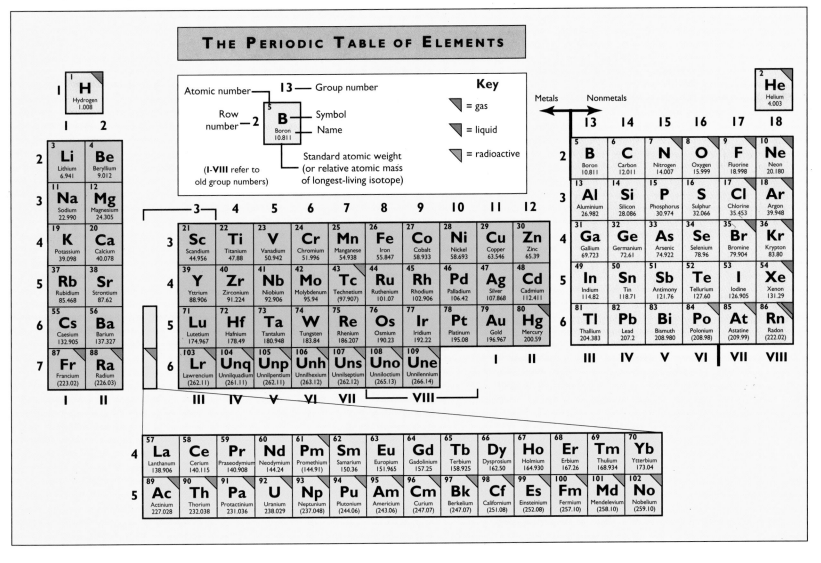

THE PERIODIC TABLE OF ELEMENTS

Radioactivity

At the heavy end of the periodic table (⇨ p. 158) there are some elements that differ in a fundamental way from all the others. These elements spontaneously change into other elements, sometimes moving down the periodic table, sometimes up. In so doing, they emit various kinds of radiation, and are thus said to be *radioactive*.

The discovery of radioactivity (⇨ box) added to scientists' understanding and interpretation of the periodic table (⇨ p. 158) and of the atom, and led, eventually, to the actual creation of new elements – the *transuranic* elements (which have an atomic number of 93 or more). All elements, after the first isotope of hydrogen (⇨ p. 156), have both protons and neutrons in their nuclei. The number of protons determines the nature of the element and its place in the periodic table. The number of neutrons has no effect on the chemical properties of the element and is usually either equal to, or greater than, the number of protons. The heavier

the element, the greater the difference between the number of protons and the number of neutrons. Up to calcium, most elements have isotopes with the same number of neutrons as protons (as well as isotopes with more neutrons). But after calcium, the number of neutrons always exceeds the number of protons. This increase in the ratio of neutrons to protons in the nucleus is the cause of the greater instability of the heavy elements that manifests itself in radioactivity. Nuclei that are unstable for this reason adjust their proton-to-neutron ratio to a more stable one by emitting nuclear particles – *radiation*.

Radiation from naturally radioactive elements is of three kinds: alpha particles, beta particles and gamma rays. Since all matter is essentially a form of radiation, it may seem arbitrary to distinguish between particles and rays in this context, but the alpha and beta particles are, in fact, familiar in other contexts, in which their behaviour is most commonly considered as particulate, while gamma rays are familiar members of the electromagnetic spectrum (⇨ p. 84).

The effect of radiation emission on atoms

The alpha particle consists of an aggregate of two protons and two neutrons, which is also, in fact, the nucleus of a helium atom. Because the two positive charges from the two protons are unbalanced by electrons, as in the neutral helium atom, the alpha particle is positively charged and may be called a helium *ion*. Alpha particles are given off only by elements of high atomic weight. The loss of two protons and two neutrons from an atom's nucleus has a profound effect on the atom. Firstly, the loss of the protons means that the atom has changed to that of a new element two places to the left in the periodic table. The number of electrons in the outer part of the atom is now reduced by two, so all the chemical properties are also changed to those of the new element. Secondly, the atomic weight has been

reduced by four atomic mass units (⇨ p. 156). Depending on the starting point, the new element may be stable or may, itself, be radioactive. In many cases, a series of emissions of radiation occur from each successive new element until a stable element is reached. Uranium, for instance, is changed into a succession of different elements ending with lead.

The beta particle is one of two types. Either it is just an electron, or it is a

ANTOINE HENRI BECQUEREL AND THE DISCOVERY OF RADIOACTIVITY

The French physicist Antoine Henri Becquerel (1852–1908), like his father before him, was especially interested in the phenomenon of fluorescence – the ability of certain substances to emit light of one colour when exposed to light of another colour, or when bombarded by various other forms of radiation. When X-rays were discovered in 1895 by the German physicist Wilhelm Konrad Röntgen (1845–1932), Becquerel, aware that these rays could excite fluorescence (which was how they were discovered), asked himself whether it was possible that fluorescent materials might be emitting X-radiation or cathode radiation (⇨ p. 84). In February 1896, he wrapped up a photographic plate in light-proof black paper, laid some potassium uranyl sulphate (a compound of uranium and a fluorescent material) on top of it, and put it out in the sun so that it would fluoresce. To his satisfaction, he found, when he developed the plate, that it was fogged. This demonstrated that penetrating radiation had passed through the black paper. Becquerel concluded that the sunlight had stimulated the fluorescent material into producing X-rays.

Wishing to repeat the experiment, Becquerel prepared another wrapped photographic plate and put the sulphate on top. A succession of cloudy days followed when nothing could be done. Impatient to make progress, Becquerel, wondering whether the previous exposure to the sun might have left some residual fluorescence in the sulphate, decided to develop the plate. To his astonishment, the plate was strongly fogged. Clearly this material was giving off radiation on its own that had nothing to do with sunlight or with fluorescence. A few more trials confirmed that the potassium uranyl sulphate was spontaneously and continuously emitting rays, similar in property to X-rays. These could penetrate matter and could cause gases to become ionized (electrically charged) so that they would conduct electricity. They could also, however, be deflected by magnets, showing that they contained charged particles. Becquerel was able to show that these particles were high-speed electrons (beta particles; ⇨ main text). For a time, the new radiation was called Becquerel rays. The work on radioactivity was quickly taken up by the husband-and-wife team Pierre and Marie Curie and further advances made, including the discovery of the element radium. In 1903, Becquerel and the Curies were awarded the Nobel Prize for physics.

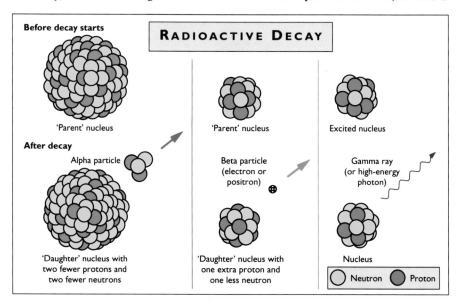

RADIOACTIVE DECAY

Before decay starts

'Parent' nucleus   'Parent' nucleus   Excited nucleus

After decay

Alpha particle   Beta particle (electron or positron) ⊕   Gamma ray (or high-energy photon)

'Daughter' nucleus with two fewer protons and two fewer neutrons   'Daughter' nucleus with one extra proton and one less neutron   Nucleus

○ Neutron   ● Proton

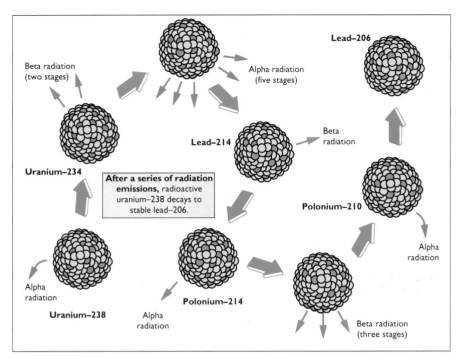

After a series of radiation emissions, radioactive uranium–238 decays to stable lead–206.

Element	Type of radiation emitted	Half-life
Uranium–238	Alpha particles	4,500 million years
Plutonium–239	Alpha particles	24,400 years
Carbon–14	Beta particles	5,730 years
Radium–226	Alpha particles	1,600 years
Strontium–90	Beta particles	28.6 years
Hydrogen–3	Beta particles	12.3 years
Cobalt–60	Gamma rays	5.3 years
Phosphorus–32	Beta particles	14.3 days
Iodine–131	Beta particles	8.1 days
Radon–222	Alpha particles	4 days
Lead–214	Beta particles	27 minutes
Unnilpentium–105	Alpha particles	32 seconds

similar particle but with a positive charge – a *positron*. The effect on an atom of losing an electron from its nucleus is a little more complicated. The simplest way of considering what happens is to suppose that a neutron consists of a proton and an electron stuck together. If such an electron is emitted from a neutron, the neutron will cease to exist and a new proton will exist in its place. Since the electron is of negligible mass compared to the proton or neutron, the atomic weight will not change. But, now that the atom has an extra proton, it moves one place to the right in the periodic table and becomes the next element along. Thus emitting a beta particle causes the element to increase its atomic number but not its atomic weight.

Radioactive isotopes that are unstable because of an excess of protons may become more stable by emitting a positron. When this happens, a proton is converted to a neutron, so the element does not change its atomic weight but moves to the left in the periodic table, and becomes another element of lower atomic number.

The emission of gamma rays does not affect the number of either the protons or the neutrons but, since energy is lost from the nucleus of the atom, it has been reduced from a higher and less stable energy state to one of lower energy and greater stability. This high-energy state most commonly occurs at the time of the loss of a beta particle. The excess energy in the nucleus is dissipated in the form of gamma rays.

The half-life of radioactive elements

The rate at which radioactive elements change (decay) to other elements varies greatly. This rate is expressed in terms of the length of time it takes for half of any quantity of the element to change. So

every element has its characteristic *half-life*. These half-lives vary from a tiny fraction of a second to billions of years. It is never possible to predict when any particular atom will decay. In the case of an element with a long half-life, a particular atom may decay in the next second, or not for a million years. But we can work out, from the half-life, what proportion of all the atoms will decay in any particular time. Uranium–238 has a half-life of 4,500,000,000 years. This is the known age of the Earth, so the present amount of this element is half of the original amount. Uranium decays, after a series of stages, to lead–206, so the amount of lead in the universe is constantly increasing.

Half-lives are of great practical importance. Radioactive elements with long half-lives are likely to do more harm than those with very short half-lives. The Chernobyl nuclear disaster of 1986, for instance, released large quantities of strontium–90 and caesium–137 into the environment. Strontium–90 has a half-life of 28.6 years and caesium–137 has a half-life of 30.2 years. So, the radioactivity of the strontium will not be reduced to half the 1986 level until the year 2000. A knowledge of half-lives is essential for the calibration of dosage when radioactive elements are used in the treatment of cancer. The exposure a patient receives has to be progressively increased, for the same effect, as the element ages.

The isotope carbon–14 (⇨ p. 116) is present in atmospheric carbon dioxide and, in the same proportions, in all living matter. On

the death of an organism, carbon–14 ceases to be taken in, and the isotope continues to decay at a known rate in accordance with its half-life. Atmospheric carbon–14, however, is maintained at a fairly constant level by the action of cosmic rays on atmospheric nitrogen. Carbon–14 has a half-life of about 5,730 years. These facts enable us to determine, to a fair degree of accuracy, the age of most samples of dead organic material that lived within the past million years or so – a facility of major importance in both history and archaeology.

Radiocarbon dating being performed on an ancient sample of reindeer bone. The amounts of the radioisotope carbon–14 and the stable carbon–12 in the sample are measured and their ratio to one another determined. Since the half-life of carbon–14 is known, the ratio of carbon–14 to carbon–12 can be used to fix the sample's date. (James King-Holmes, SPL)

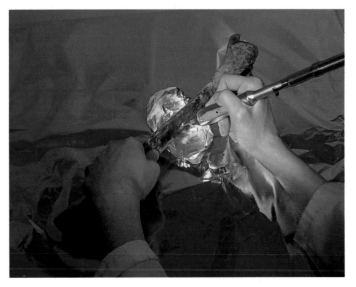

The Nature of the Chemical Bond

The linking together of atoms to form molecules (⇨ p. 156) is the basis of chemistry. Atoms in molecules are held together by electric forces known as *chemical bonds*, which form because the resulting molecule is chemically more stable than the separate atoms constituting it. When atoms link together, they do so by association of the electrons in their outermost shells. The number of these electrons, in relation to the total number the shell can hold, affects the way atoms join together.

In 1852, the English chemist Edward Frankland (1825–99), while making new organic compounds containing metals, noticed that each metal atom appeared to combine with a fixed number of other atoms. This suggested that each kind of atom has a fixed ability to combine with other atoms – a concept known as *valency* (⇨ below). This important idea was a major factor in helping Mendeleyev to develop the periodic table of the elements (⇨ p. 158), which was one of the most fundamental advances in all chemistry. The ease with which atoms join together and, to some extent, even the way in which they do so, is found to depend, to a large extent, on their position in the periodic table. Elements in the vertical column on the right of the table – the rare or *noble* gases, namely, helium, neon, argon, krypton, xenon and radon – simply refuse to combine with any other atoms to form compounds. Those in the next vertical column to the left, and in the column on the extreme left, are highly reactive, and seem avid to link up with other atoms. These facts can be understood by means of an enquiry into the ways in which atoms bond together.

How atoms link together

Atoms consist of positively charged central nuclei surrounded by a cloud of rapidly moving, negatively charged electrons. These electrons occupy shells (⇨ p. 158), or *orbitals,* filling up the inner shells first – those with the lowest energy levels. However many shells there may be in a particular atom, the outermost electron shell is the one that interacts with other atoms and is called the *valency shell.* In the case of hydrogen and helium there is only one shell and this can hold either one electron, as in hydrogen, or two electrons maximum, as in helium. When the shell is filled with two electrons, the atom is

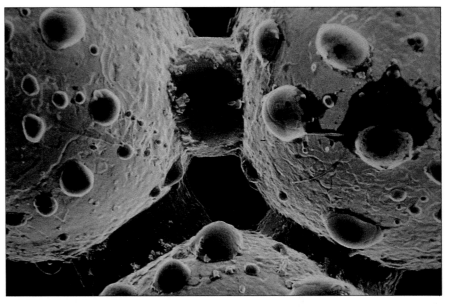

stable and will not form compounds. This is the first of the rare gases. The next two shells can each hold from one to eight electrons. If the shell is filled with eight electrons, the atom concerned – either neon or argon – is stable and does not form compounds. If fewer than eight electrons are present, the atom is able to link up with other atoms to form a molecule. A great many of the atoms involved in common chemical reactions have no more than three shells. When atoms bond together by the interaction of the electrons in the outer shell, they do so in particular ways.

Ionic bonding

If an atom, such as fluorine (F) or chlorine (Cl), has seven electrons in the outer shell, it readily takes up another electron to fill the shell. This extra electron gives it a negative charge and it becomes a *negative ion.* An atom, one such as sodium (Na) or potassium (K), that has only one electron in its outer shell, readily gives up this electron so as to have a filled outer shell. When it does so it has a positive charge because one of the protons (positively charged) in the nucleus is not balanced by an outer electron and the atom becomes a *positive ion.* Unlike charges attract, so the negative chlorine or fluorine ion is attracted to the positive sodium or potassium ion, and they come together to form a molecule of sodium fluoride, potassium fluoride, sodium chloride or potassium chloride. This kind of linkage is called an *ionic bond* (⇨ p. 156). The attraction between the ions results in a speed of approximation high enough to overcome

the mutual repulsion of the like charges of all the electrons in the two atoms. The

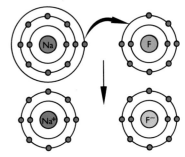

energy of the collision is released as electromagnetic radiation (⇨ p. 84).

Covalent bonding

Atoms may join in a second way, by sharing the same electron. Fluorine atoms, for instance, each have seven outer electrons but require eight to fill the outer shell, as in neon. Two flourine atoms can therefore come together without losing any orbital electrons and in such a way that each atom now appears to have two electrons in its outer shell. Electrons are, of course, in constant energetic movement and the two electrons here can readily pass between the nuclear protons as well as around them. This negative charge between the protons pulls them together by the attraction of opposites and, at a certain distance apart, is able to balance the mutual repulsion of the protons. The fluorine molecule (F_2) is more stable than either of the two isolated fluorine atoms, and fluorine consequently does not normally exist in the atomic form, although it can do so in the presence of strong ionizing radiation. Normally, wherever there is free fluorine, it will be in the form of molecules consisting of pairs of atoms linked together in this way. This kind of linkage is called a *covalent bond.*

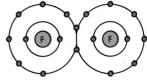

HYDROGEN BONDING

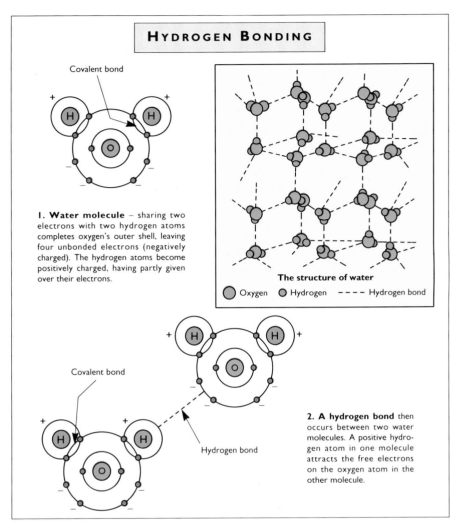

1. **Water molecule** – sharing two electrons with two hydrogen atoms completes oxygen's outer shell, leaving four unbonded electrons (negatively charged). The hydrogen atoms become positively charged, having partly given over their electrons.

The structure of water

○ Oxygen ● Hydrogen - - - - Hydrogen bond

Covalent bond

Hydrogen bond

2. **A hydrogen bond** then occurs between two water molecules. A positive hydrogen atom in one molecule attracts the free electrons on the oxygen atom in the other molecule.

Another kind of covalent bonding occurs in linkage between identical atoms that have six outer electrons and need to share two to fill the shell. Two atoms of oxygen link together in this way. Similarly, two nitrogen atoms, each of which has five orbital electrons, can link together by sharing three electrons. The greater the number of links occurring in this way, the greater is the strength of the attachment. Nitrogen pairs hold together more strongly than oxygen pairs and oxygen pairs link more strongly than hydrogen pairs. This should not be confused with the 'unsaturated' double and triple bonds of carbon atoms, which are actually weaker than single carbon bonds.

Hydrogen bonding

Bonds do not occur only between atoms. Weak linkages also occur between adjacent molecules. Hydrogen atoms, covalently bonded to oxygen or nitrogen in a molecule, are also attracted to the same atoms of a nearby molecule so that a weak link forms between adjacent molecules. This is especially important in the case of water, and the resulting grouping of water molecules determines many of the physical properties of water (⇨ p. 164). Because of the greater separation involved, these hydrogen bonds between separate molecules, or, in the case of very large molecules, between different

parts of the same molecule, are only about one tenth as strong as normal covalent bonds – and are more easily broken. Even so, they have very important functions in determining molecular structure and properties.

Hydrogen bonds, for instance, are involved in maintaining the three-dimensional structure of large molecules, such as those of proteins and DNA. In biochemistry (⇨ pp. 182–5), the ease with which hydrogen bonds can be broken and formed is, literally, of vital importance. In the DNA double helix, for instance, the pairs of nucleotide bases (⇨ p. 202) – the 'rungs of the ladder' – are held together by hydrogen bonds. This allows the two halves of the double helix to be readily 'unzipped' and separated so that new bases can attach themselves and DNA replication can occur.

Metallic bonding

Metallic bonding, which holds the atoms of metal elements together in a metal lattice, is of a different kind. In this case, the bonding is similar to that of covalent bonding except that, because of the way the atoms are arranged in the lattice – six to 12 atoms may surround a central atom – there may not be enough electrons for each pair to link together covalently. As a result, there are many free electrons spread throughout the whole

structure of the lattice. These free electrons make up what is known as the *conduction band* and account for many of the properties of metals, such as their ability to conduct electricity and heat, reflect light and be drawn into wires.

SEE ALSO

● THE CLASSICAL THEORY OF THE ATOM p. 108
● THE QUARK THEORY p. 110
● FUNDAMENTAL FORCES p. 112
● ATOMS AND MOLECULES p. 156
● THE PERIODIC TABLE p. 158
● TYPES OF MOLECULAR STRUCTURE p. 164
● THE STRUCTURE OF SOLIDS p. 166
● CHEMICAL REACTIONS p. 168
● ORGANIC CHEMISTRY pp. 170–3
● BIOCHEMISTRY pp. 182–5

THE IDEA OF VALENCY

A great deal of practical experimentation has shown that Edward Frankland's idea (⇨ main text) of the combining power of atoms was correct. It has also enabled chemists to discover the valency of all the elements. This is basic to all chemistry. When sodium (Na) combines with chlorine (Cl) it always does so in the ratio of one atom of sodium to one atom of chlorine, making NaCl. When hydrogen (H) combines with chlorine (Cl) it also does so in a one-to-one ratio to make a molecule of hydrogen chloride – commonly called hydrochloric acid (HCl). So any atom that links with one atom of hydrogen (or of chlorine) is said to be *monovalent*. All the elements in the vertical column of the periodic table (⇨ p. 158) that contains sodium, and all those in the vertical column that contains fluorine, are monovalent.

When an atom of oxygen links with an atom of hydrogen, it does not do so in a one-to-one ratio. One atom of oxygen (O) links with two atoms of hydrogen (H_2) to form one molecule of water (H_2O). When calcium (Ca) links with chlorine (Cl) one atom of calcium bonds to two atoms of chlorine to make calcium chloride ($CaCl_2$). Oxygen and calcium are therefore said to be *divalent*. So are all the elements in the vertical columns of the table that contains oxygen and calcium. When nitrogen links with hydrogen to form ammonia, one nitrogen atom bonds with three hydrogen atoms. Nitrogen and its fellows in the same vertical column are *trivalent*. Carbon forms the basis of the whole of organic chemistry because it can combine with four *monovalent* atoms, carbon itself being *tetravalent*. The cleaning fluid, carbon tetrachloride, consists of one carbon atom linked to four chlorine atoms (CCl_4). The hydrocarbon, methane (CH_4), consists of one carbon atom linked to four hydrogen atoms, and occurs as natural gas.

The number of electrons that an atom, with four or more electrons in its outer shell (⇨ p. 158), must gain to produce a full outer shell determines the valency of that element. Similarly, the number of electrons that an atom, with fewer than four outer shell electrons, must lose to empty the shell and reveal the full shell below, also establishes the valency.

Today the idea of valency has been largely replaced by the concept of *oxidation states* and *oxidation numbers*. The oxidation number of an element is the number of electrons the atom of the element gains, loses or shares, when it bonds to another atom. Elements in the first column of the periodic table (⇨ p. 158) give up one electron on bonding and so are in an oxidation state of +1, and have oxidation numbers of +1. Those in the second column from the right of the table gain an electron and so have oxidation numbers of −1. Some elements can bond in different ways and so have more than one oxidation number. Nitrogen, for instance, can form five different oxides with oxygen and has oxidation numbers of +1, +2, +3, +4 and +5. Manganese can occur in oxidation states of +2, +3, +4, +6 and +7.

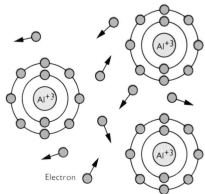

Electron

Aluminium ion

Types of Molecular Structure

A molecule is the smallest particle of a substance that shows the chemical properties of that substance. In chemical terms, isolated atoms are simple structures with a limited range of properties. Molecules, on the other hand, which are aggregations of atoms, may be highly complex, both in the number and variety of the atoms from which they are made and in their three-dimensional structure.

It is a mistake to assume that the chemical properties of a molecule are determined solely by the number and kinds of atoms of which they are constituted. In fact, the way the atoms are put together also affects the nature of the compound formed. Even in the case of some of the simplest molecules, the three-dimensional arrangement of the component atoms is of major importance. This arrangement can profoundly affect the way in which molecules react, not only as chemical substances, but also on each other, and affect the physical properties of the compound concerned. This is especially well shown and important in the case of water (⇨ below and p. 162).

Isomers

Compounds with the same molecular formulae, that is, made from the same kind and number of atoms, but in which the atoms are arranged in different ways, are called *isomers* (from the Greek *iso*, 'equal', and *meros*, 'a part'). In spite of having the same constituent atoms, isomers have different chemical or physical properties. When the atoms in the two molecules are linked together in a different order from one another, the term *structural isomers* is used. An example is ethyl alcohol – present in varying amounts in alcoholic drinks – and the colourless volatile liquid dimethyl ether. Both have the same empirical formula (C_2H_5OH), but have quite different characteristics because of the difference in their structures.

When the molecules differ only in their three-dimensional shape, they are called *stereoisomers* (from the Greek *stereos*, 'solid'). Stereoisomer molecules may have quite different shapes from each other (*geometric isomers*) or may differ only in that one is a mirror image of the other. Such pairs are called *optical isomers*. Solutions of optical isomers can be distinguished by the fact that one will rotate a beam of plane-polarized light (⇨ pp. 72–5) clockwise, while the other will rotate it anticlockwise. Mirror-image molecules are known as *enantiomers* and are said to exhibit *chirality* (from the Greek *cheiro*, 'hand'), as hands, because of their asymmetry, cannot be correctly superimposed one on the other. The effect of chirality is often surprising. The enantiomers of the substance limonene differ in that one smells of lemons, the other of oranges.

Van der Waals forces

The three-dimensional shapes of molecules, and many of their properties, are controlled by weak forces operating between parts of the same molecule or between neighbouring molecules. These weak intermolecular forces are called van der Waals forces, after the Nobel Prize-winning Dutch physicist Johannes van der Waals (1837–1923), who worked out an equation for the relationships among the temperature, pressure and volume of gases. This equation corrected the gas laws of Robert Boyle and Jacques Charles (⇨ p. 50) and made it clear that attractive forces existed between gas molecules. Van der Waals forces are due to dipole-to-dipole attractions (⇨ below) and hydrogen bonding (⇨ p. 162), and they exist between all simple molecules. When solids are melted and liquids boiled, energy is needed to break down the van der Waals forces of attraction. These forces also hold together the layers in solid substances, such as graphite, cadmium iodide, and molybdenum disulphide. These substances, which have a slippery or greasy feel, make good lubricants (⇨ p. 32), because the forces are weak enough to allow the layers to slip over each other.

Hydrogen bonding and physical properties

Water is a simple molecule, consisting of two atoms of hydrogen linked to one atom of oxygen, but it is a molecule with unique properties. These properties are the result, not of its constituent atoms, but of its three-dimensional structure. Other simple hydrogen compounds, like ammonia (NH_3), methane (CH_4), and hydrogen sulphide (H_2S) are all gases at room temperature, yet water must be heated to 100°C (212°F) before it becomes a gas. The geometry of the water molecule – a central oxygen atom with the two hydrogen atoms attached at an angle of 105° to each other – causes what is called a large *dipole moment*. A dipole is a sustained separation of a positive and a negative charge, and a moment is a tendency to produce movement, especially a rotary movement. The molecules of water and other compounds are permanent dipoles, and their dipole moment is large because, although the molecules are electrically neutral, the constituent electrons are unequally shared between the oxygen and hydrogen atoms (⇨ p. 162). Like charges repel and opposite charges attract, so a large dipole moment causes ready association with other polar molecules, and is the reason that water is such a good solvent of many molecules that separate into charged polar groups. Water can surround both positively and negatively charged ions.

When water molecules approach one another they interact strongly. The hydrogen atoms, although bonded to oxygen atoms, are still attracted to the nonbonding pairs of electrons on the oxygen atom

---

WATER AS A SOLVENT

Dipole moment (separation of positive and negative charge plus tendency to movement)

105°

H
H O

Water molecule

(a)

H O H

Chloride ion

(b)

H O H

Na+

Sodium ion

The spatial arrangement of the hydrogen and oxygen atoms in a molecule of water makes water an extremely good solvent because it is attracted to, and can surround, both negatively (a) and positively (b) charged ions.

Molecule		Hydrogen	Water	Oxygen	Ozone	Carbon dioxide	Carbon monoxide
Formula		H_2	H_2O	O_2	O_3	CO_2	CO
Structure							

Single bond —   Intermediate between single and double bond ===

Double bond =

Triple bond ≡   Intermediate between double and triple bond - - -

of another water molecule. This is called *hydrogen intermolecular bonding* (⇨ p. 162). As a result, the water molecules form into relatively strong clusters throughout the bulk of the fluid and on its surface, and considerable energy is needed – in the form of heat – to cause the molecules to separate and disperse as a gas. Other properties, such as *surface tension* and *viscosity*, depend on this clustering phenomenon. When water freezes, the orientation of the hydrogen bonds causes the molecules to adopt a rigid pattern of relationship that occupies more space

than in the liquid phase, when molecules can intersect more readily. This is why water expands on freezing, why ice forms on the surface of water, and why pressure can liquefy ice, so that skating is possible.

Hydrogen bonding can also occur within large molecules. Such intramolecular bonding causes proteins (⇨ p. 182) to be folded into particular three-dimensional shapes necessary for their biological function. Intramolecular hydrogen bonding also occurs between the pairs of bases in the DNA double helix (⇨ p. 202).

Phase and intermolecular attraction

The term *phase* is used in chemistry to distinguish the states of matter, whether solid, liquid or gas. Phase is determined by the energy state of the substance and no one phase can be considered 'normal'. From the liquid phase of matter, a decrease in energy tends in the direction of the solid phase, and an increase in energy tends in the direction of the gaseous phase. We are inclined to think of the 'normal' state of water as being liquid, but, in much of the universe, most of the water is solid. We think this way simply because the range of temperatures to which we are most accustomed lies between the melting point of ice and the boiling point of water.

The phase of a material is a matter of the attractive forces between molecules. In gases, the attractive forces between molecules are very weak; in solids and liquids the intermolecular attractive forces are progressively stronger. In neither case, however, are the attractions between molecules nearly as strong as the bonding forces between atoms to form molecules. The energy that determines phase causes molecules to vibrate and to rotate. Infrared energy (heat) causes vibration; far infrared and microwave energy causes molecular rotation. Increased vibratory movement of molecules tends to increase their separation and this may be sufficient to change the phase of the material from solid to liquid or from liquid to gas. The intermolecular forces differ in different compounds and different amounts of energy are needed to move from one phase to another. At room temperature, some compounds are solid, some liquid and others gaseous. As temperatures increase, some liquids become gaseous and some solids become liquid. And, at even higher temperatures, all compounds are gaseous. With a further rise in temperature, the bonds between the atoms break down so that atoms are freed.

Progressively increased temperatures cause electrons to be stripped off the nuclei of atoms, and an extreme state of matter known as a *plasma* occurs. Alternatively, at very low temperatures, all compounds, and even most elements, are solid.

Alanine

Natural enantiomer | Mirror plane | Unnatural enantiomer

Many organic compounds, such as alanine and limonene, are built up asymmetrically around a central carbon atom and can exist in two mirror-image forms, known as *enantiomers* (⇨ text). In the case of amino acids such as alanine, one enantiomer predominates greatly over the other, the latter having a small role in nature. This apparently superficial difference in form can have a startling effect on the properties of the compound concerned. A trivial but striking example of this is provided by the enantiomers of limonene: one smells strongly of lemons, the other of oranges.

Limonene

Mirror plane

Structural formulae. Chiral carbon atoms are conventionally indicated by an asterisk (*). Covalent bonds located in the plane of the paper are represented by lines (—), while bonds orientated (tetrahedrally) above and below this plane are displayed as wedges (◢) and dashes (۱۱۱) respectively.

In simplified structural formulae (such as those given for limonene, left), the junctions and termini of lines, wedges and dashes represent carbon atoms. It is understood that hydrogen atoms complete the tetracovalency requirement around each carbon atom.

SEE ALSO

● ATOMS AND MOLECULES p. 156
● THE NATURE OF THE CHEMICAL BOND p. 162
● THE STRUCTURE OF SOLIDS p. 166

Methane	Nitrogen	Nitric oxide	Nitrous oxide	Nitrogen dioxide	Ammonia	Sulphur dioxide	Sulphur trioxide
CH_4	N_2	NO	N_2O	NO_2	NH_3	SO_2	SO_3

The Structure of Solids

The idea of solidity, with which we are all familiar, is, in one sense, real but, in another, an illusion. Since atoms consist of very small particles, with a relatively very large amount of empty space between them, and since all matter is composed of atoms, solid bodies consist almost entirely of empty space.

The atoms that make up solids are not simply moving about in a random and disorganized manner, as in the case of a gas, but are arranged in definite patterns. This orderly arrangement of atoms and molecules is called a *crystalline*

NICOLAUS STENO AND THE ORIGINS OF CRYSTALLOGRAPHY

The Danish scientist Niels Stensen (1638–86), who took the name Nicolaus Steno, was the personal physician to the Duke of Tuscany, a royal anatomist, a neurologist and a distinguished geologist. Among many other interests, Steno investigated the nature of crystals. In his book, written in 1669, *De solido intra solidum naturalites contento dissertionis prodromus* ('Of Solids Enclosed Within Solids') he stated that all crystals of the same substance had the same angles between the faces – an observation known as *Steno's Law*. He also came to the conclusion that crystals growing in a solution do so by attaching particles of material to the existing external faces.

After converting from Lutheranism in 1667, Steno became a Roman Catholic priest in 1675. He was as successful in the Church as in science and, two years later, after becoming a bishop and vicar-apostolic to North Germany and Scandinavia, he abandoned his scientific career.

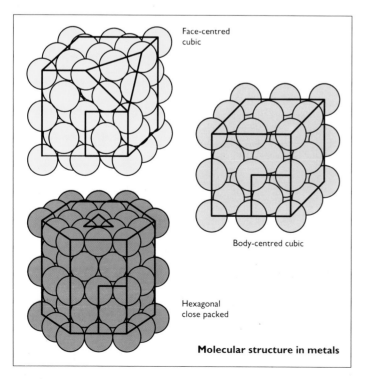

Face-centred cubic

Body-centred cubic

Hexagonal close packed

Molecular structure in metals

structure. We are inclined to think of crystals as objects with flat surfaces (plane faces) intersecting at particular angles and presenting an almost jewel-like appearance. To do so is quite correct since the external appearance of a perfect crystal reflects the orderliness and the relationships of the constituent atoms. But many solids that are never seen as 'crystals' are, nevertheless, crystalline in nature. It is in the nature of solid materials, especially when pure, to have their atoms arranged in a particular, repeating pattern, and the majority are so constituted. Such substances are said to be *crystalline,* as distinct from noncrystalline, or *amorphous* (from the Greek *a*, 'not', and *morphe*, 'form' or 'shape') substances. When single, perfect, large crystals of hard and insoluble materials – especially of carbon – occur, the result is a much valued gemstone. Such crystals are, however, rare. Most solids are *polycrystalline* – made up of small regions of perfect crystalline arrangement called *crystallites* – lying somewhat at random in relation to each other.

Crystal lattices

If powdered table salt (sodium chloride) is examined under a microscope, most of the grains will be seen to be of irregular shape, because they have been damaged in the manufacturing process. Some, however, will be seen to be perfect cubes with their faces set at exactly 90° to one another. If one of these tiny cubes is suspended in a strong solution of sodium chloride in water, it can be made to grow to quite a large cube. Similarly, if a tiny crystal of salt is ground up and the fragments examined at higher magnification, they, too, will be seen to be cubic. The ultimate structural arrangements of the atoms of sodium and chlorine is known as a *crystal lattice*, consisting of charged atoms (*ions*) of the two elements arranged, alternately, at the adjacent corners of the square faces of imaginary cubes (⇨ p. 156). Sodium, with only one electron in its outer shell, readily loses this negatively charged particle to become a positive ion; chlorine, with seven electrons in its outer shell, acquires another to become a negative ion. Ions at the diagonally opposite corners of the squares are of the same type. Because this pattern is continuous throughout the whole crystallite, each ion is common to eight imaginary cubes whose corners meet at that point. Sodium chloride presents a simple crystal lattice in which all the angles are right angles; other crystals show a more complex structure. In all cases, however, the atomic or molecular lattice structure is a miniature version of the microscopic appearance of small crystals and of visibly large (macroscopic) crystals of the material.

X-ray crystallography

The crystal-lattice structure, being an arrangement of atoms, is too fine to be seen by visible light, the wavelength of which is thousands of times longer than the separation distances between the

Sir William Lawrence Bragg (1890–1971), British physicist who developed the law relating to X-ray diffraction by crystal lattices, later refining the technique as an analytical tool with his father. (SPL)

atoms. There is, however, an ingenious method by which this structure can be 'seen' – a method first proposed by the German physicist Max Theodor Felix von Laue (1879–1960). Laue was studying the nature of X-rays and was anxious to resolve the controversy as to whether they were particles or electromagnetic waves (⇨ p. 40). This puzzle had been

Crystals of sulphur shown in this polarized-light micrograph. Sulphur is a yellow, nonmetallic element, belonging to group 16 in the periodic table. (Bruce Iverson, SPL)

investigated for light itself by passing light beams through gratings of very fine, closely spaced parallel lines – diffraction gratings (⇨ p. 72). Because X-rays passed through solid material, it seemed clear that, if they were waves, their wavelength must be very much shorter than that of visible light. It occurred to Laue that a crystal could be used as a diffraction grating, with just the kind of separation needed to check for diffraction of X-rays, and thus prove, or disprove, their wave nature. In 1912 Laue tried out the idea using a crystal of zinc sulphide and, taking into account the physical differences between a simple line grating and the more complex structure of a crystal, the experiment yielded exactly the predicted result. Since then all kinds of crystalline structures have been investigated by the method of X-ray diffraction, most notably by the two William Braggs – father and son (⇨ box) – who used it to determine the structure of many compounds, both inorganic and organic, and of minerals and metals.

X-ray crystallography shows, for instance, that many crystals do not consist of a lattice of discrete molecules of the substance but rather collections of ionized atoms formed into molecular groups known as *unit cells*. This idea is fundamental to modern crystallography. Unit cells may be of several different 'systems', with varying symmetry giving many lattice types. For example, they may have three mutually perpendicular axes of equal length (*isometric system*), as in the case of common salt, diamond, gold, copper and garnet; they may be six-sided with three axes at 60° to each other (*hexagonal*); they may be shaped like a quadrilateral with only two mutually perpendicular sides that are equal in length (*tetragonal*); they may have three mutually

perpendicular axes of unequal length (*orthorhombic*); or they may contain 20-sided (*icosahedral*) structures that repeat in a random manner.

Molecular crystals are lattices of molecules held in place in relation to each other by weak van der Waals forces (⇨ p. 164). An example is ice, which is a lattice of water molecules held together by hydrogen bonds. Other examples are naphthalene; iodine, with a lattice of pairs of iodine atoms linked as molecules; and solid carbon dioxide, with a lattice formed from its molecules. A diamond is a very large crystalline molecule, consisting of carbon atoms, each of which is bonded to four other carbon atoms in a three-dimensional tetrahedral arrangement. A similar structure, in which silicon atoms are bonded to four oxygen atoms, is found in crystals of silicon oxide (quartz or silica). Other substances with very large molecules, such as the chain-structured polymers (⇨ p. 156), also form molecular lattices.

Metal crystals

Most metals are, of course, elements, so only one type of atom is involved in the structure. In metallic crystals the atoms are packed closely together. The tightest packing for a layer of atoms is hexagonal packing, in which each atom is surrounded by six others, the centres of any three adjacent atoms forming a triangle. Alternatively, atoms may be packed less tightly, with the centres of four atoms forming a square (body-centred cubic). These layers are then stacked in various ways. Hexagonally packed layers, for instance, may be stacked as hexagonal close-packing, with each atom in the second layer in relation to three atoms of the first layer.

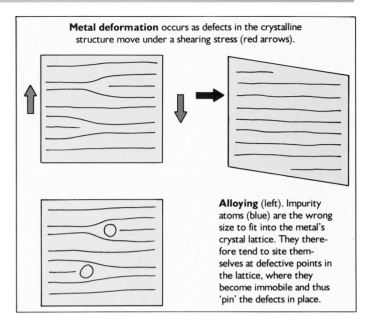

Metal deformation occurs as defects in the crystalline structure move under a shearing stress (red arrows).

Alloying (left). Impurity atoms (blue) are the wrong size to fit into the metal's crystal lattice. They therefore tend to site themselves at defective points in the lattice, where they become immobile and thus 'pin' the defects in place.

Elements in different forms

About half of all the elements can exist either in a crystalline or in a noncrystalline (amorphous) form. Some, such as sulphur, can exist in more than one crystalline form. The different forms of the elements are called *allotropes*. Sulphur, depending on the temperature, can form two kinds of crystals with different lattices and also an unstable plastic (malleable) form. Carbon can exist as the homogeneous lattice, diamond (⇨ above and illustration), or as the layered form, graphite. Phosphorus may exist as molecular crystals (white phosphorus); as a giant molecule with each atom bonded to three other phosphorus atoms (red phosphorus); or, under conditions of very high pressure, as a large-molecule layered structure (black phosphorus).

SEE ALSO

● ATOMS AND MOLECULES p. 156
● THE PERIODIC TABLE p. 158
● RADIOACTIVITY p. 160
● THE NATURE OF THE CHEMICAL BOND p. 162
● TYPES OF MOLECULAR STRUCTURE p. 164
● CHEMICAL REACTIONS p. 168
● ORGANIC CHEMISTRY pp. 170-3

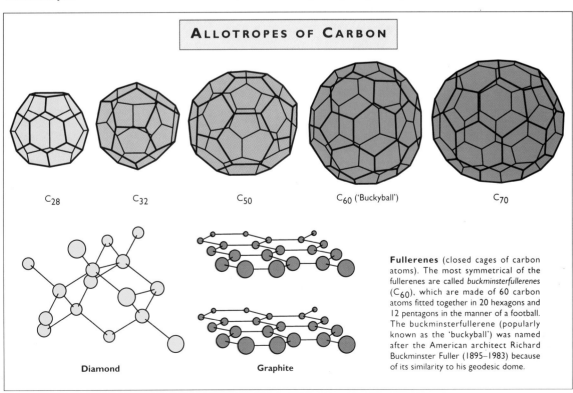

ALLOTROPES OF CARBON

C_{28} C_{32} C_{50} C_{60} ('Buckyball') C_{70}

Diamond

Graphite

Fullerenes (closed cages of carbon atoms). The most symmetrical of the fullerenes are called *buckminsterfullerenes* (C_{60}), which are made of 60 carbon atoms fitted together in 20 hexagons and 12 pentagons in the manner of a football. The buckminsterfullerene (popularly known as the 'buckyball') was named after the American architect Richard Buckminster Fuller (1895-1983) because of its similarity to his geodesic dome.

Chemical Reactions

Chemical reactions do not just occur in scientific laboratories; they go on, almost everywhere, all the time – in the natural world, in our bodies, in cooking ovens, in fires, in washing machines, in car engines, in our rubbish dumps, in the atmosphere and deep in the earth. Some reactions increase the chemical complexity of their products, others break them down into simpler parts.

Chemical reactions concern the fate of more than one hundred different kinds of atom, when they combine with each other to form molecules, or when molecules are broken down to form other molecules, or to release their constituent atoms. Many of these reactions are very simple, even when highly complex molecules are involved. Many chemical reactions involve the interaction of charged atoms (*ions*). Atoms have positive nuclei and are surrounded by a cloud of negative electrons ($\Leftrightarrow$ p. 156). If one (or more) electron is lost from an atom, the positive charge on the nucleus is no longer balanced by the negative electrons, and the atom becomes a positive ion. This commonly occurs with the elements in the left-hand column of the periodic table ($\Leftrightarrow$ p. 158) such as lithium, sodium and potassium. If an atom gains one or more electrons, there is again an imbalance of charges and the atom becomes a negative ion. This commonly occurs to atoms in the second column from the right of the table. Some chemical reactions involve the interaction of neutral atoms rather than ions.

Chemical equations

An equation is a statement that two things are equal. In the case of a chemical equation, the implication is that there is the same number of atoms of each kind on each side of the equation – that is before and after the reaction. A simple chemical reaction expressed as an equation is: $Na + Cl \Leftrightarrow NaCl$. This means that one atom of the metal sodium (Na) added to one atom of the gas chlorine (Cl) yields the salt sodium chloride (NaCl). The equation is balanced because, on either side of the arrow, there are the same number of atoms of each type. This equation is also reversible. If sodium chloride is dissolved in water, it dissociates into separate atoms of sodium and chloride: $NaCl \Leftrightarrow Na + Cl$. A more complex example might be the oxidation of glucose to form water and carbon dioxide: $C_6H_{12}O_6 + 6O_2 \Leftrightarrow 6H_2O + 6CO_2$.

The subscript number after a symbol refers to the number of *atoms* of that element; the full-height number in front of a chemical symbol refers to the number of molecules. In this equation, there are the same number of carbon atoms on each side of the arrow, the same number of hydrogen atoms, and the same number of oxygen atoms, on each side. One molecule of glucose ($C_6H_{12}O_6$) plus six molecules of oxygen (O_2) yields six molecules of water (H_2O) and six molecules of carbon dioxide (CO_2). Considerable energy is released in the process, either rapidly, by burning, or slowly, as at body temperature in cell metabolism ($\Leftrightarrow$ p. 186).

This equation goes from left to right very easily but it is harder to arrange for it to go from right to left. This normally occurs in the process of photosynthesis ($\Leftrightarrow$ p. 48), which requires the input of considerable energy from sunlight.

It may sometimes seem hard to believe that chemical reactions involve exact equations. The burning of a candle at a dinner party is a chemical reaction. Paraffin (candle) wax is a hydrocarbon, a petroleum product containing atoms of hydrogen, oxygen and carbon, bound together to form a solid substance. When the candle burns, some of the hydrogen and some of the oxygen atoms split off from the paraffin molecules and, together with oxygen atoms from the air, join together to form water (H_2O). This is vaporized by the heat of the flame and escapes. Most of the carbon and more oxygen atoms join up to form carbon dioxide (CO_2). This, like water vapour, is a gas that also escapes into the atmosphere. The total weight of water and carbon dioxide and the total number of hydrogen, oxygen and carbon atoms that are lost, are, however, exactly equal to the losses from the candle plus the oxygen taken from the air.

The rate of chemical reactions

Chemical reactions may occur very slowly, as in rusting, or very rapidly, as in a dynamite explosion. The rate at which reactions occur is influenced by many factors. Temperature has a marked effect on chemical reactions. Within a reasonable range, and for most reactions, every rise of 10°C (18°F) will roughly double

The valencies shown are those most commonly exhibited. Many elements can bond in a number of different ways and so exhibit different valencies. There are, for instance, five different oxides of nitrogen and five oxides of manganese. Carbon commonly bonds as if it had a valency of 2.

the rate. This means that a rise of 50°C (90°F) will increase the rate by over thirty times in most cases. The concentration of the reactants, and the surface area over which they can come in contact, are also important in determining the rate of the reaction.

Catalysts are substances that accelerate the rate of chemical reactions without themselves being chemically changed in the process. Catalysts may, however, undergo a physical change. Only very small quantities of catalysts are needed to catalyse a change in large quantities of reactants. Most catalysts are specific to particular reactions, and do not have any catalytic action on other reactions. They can be *poisoned* by certain substances that inhibit their action. Catalysts include finely powdered platinum and nickel, colloidal platinum, kaolin, silica, alumina, and various acids and alkalis. In biochemistry ($\Leftrightarrow$ pp. 182–5), a special class of catalytic agents is of central importance. These are the enzymes by which almost all biochemical reactions are promoted.

Acid–base reactions

Among the most important chemical reactions are those between *acids* (proton donors) and *bases* (proton acceptors). Acids, bases and salts dissociate into electrically charged ions when dissolved in water giving solutions that readily conduct electricity. For this reason, the substances that produce them are often called *electrolytes*. Acids in water produce large quantities of hydrogen ions. These are hydrogen atoms

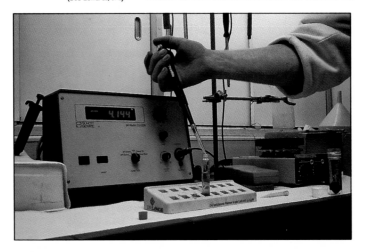

Environmental scientist testing a water sample for pollution in the laboratory of the Greenpeace ship *Beluga*. The pH meter seen here is being used to give an accurate measure of the sample's acidity. (Bob Edwards, SPL)

without the electron and thus positively charged (H⁺). Bases, when added to water, produce ions, each consisting of a combined hydrogen atom and an oxygen atom – a hydroxyl ion, which is negatively charged (OH⁻). When an acid combines with a base it produces a salt and water only.

The hydrogen ions and the hydroxyl ions, being of opposite charge, are attracted together and combine to form water, as in this equation: $HCl + NaOH \leftrightarrow NaCl + H_2O$. Hydrochloric acid plus sodium hydroxide yields sodium chloride (common salt) plus water. The ions have completely neutralized one another and the solution is neither acidic nor basic. The salt is neutral. If the water is evaporated, nothing but salt remains. Large numbers of different salts can be formed

THE pH SCALE

Acid

1	
2	Battery acid
3	Lemon juice
4	
5	Acid rain
	Human skin
6	
7	Distilled water
8	Soap
9	
10	
11	Milk of magnesia
12	
13	Caustic soda
14	

Neutral (at 7)
Alkaline

A piece of litmus paper, when brought into contact with a sample of the substance whose pH is being measured, will turn the colour shown on the scale.

in this way by the reaction of various acids with various bases.

Acids differ greatly in strength and this is primarily due to the extent to which they dissociate in water to release hydrogen ions. Acidity is thus measured in terms of the number of hydrogen ions in a given volume of water – the *hydrogen-ion concentration*. This is designated by the symbol pH. The pH scale is logarithmic, so that an increase or decrease of one unit implies a tenfold increase or decrease in the hydrogen-ion concentration. The scale is also reciprocal; the lower the number, the higher the hydrogen-ion concentration. On the scale, pH 7 indicates neutral; numbers below 7 indicate acidity; numbers above 7 indicate alkalinity.

Inorganic acids and bases are formed from elements such as nitrogen, sulphur and phosphorus. The molecule of the very important industrial acid, sulphuric acid, which has wide application, for instance, is H_2SO_4 – two atoms of hydrogen, one atom of sulphur and four atoms of oxygen. Nitric acid is HNO_3 and can be produced by the action of sulphuric acid on sodium nitrate ($NaNO_3$): $NaNO_3 + H_2SO_4 \leftrightarrow NaHSO_4 + HNO_3$.

A typical strong base is sodium hydroxide (NaOH), consisting of one atom of sodium, one atom of oxygen and one atom of hydrogen. In water, this dissociates into positively charged sodium ions and negatively charged hydroxyl ions (chemical symbol OH⁻).

Oxidation–reduction reactions

The term *oxidation* was first used to describe the formation of an oxide when a metal combined with oxygen. For example, in the formation of iron oxide (rust): $2Fe + O_2 \leftrightarrow 2FeO$; or as when chalk (calcium carbonate) is strongly heated in air to form quicklime (calcium oxide) and carbon dioxide: $CaCO_3 \leftrightarrow CaO + CO_2$. The removal of oxygen, to reverse the process, was called *reduction*, as in the process of heating iron ore with carbon to reduce it to the metal and form the gas carbon monoxide (CO): $FeO + C \leftrightarrow Fe + CO$.

Oxidation and reduction are complementary reactions that occur at the same time and to equivalent extents. When one reactant is oxidized, the other is reduced. The terms are now, however, used to refer to a much more general process in which oxygen need not be involved. The process of oxidation is now defined as the loss of electrons from atoms; and reduction defined as a gain of electrons. Whenever electrons are exchanged between atoms, the oxidation state of the atoms is changed. The substance that acquires electrons in the course of the reaction (and thus is reduced) is known as the oxidizing agent. The most effective oxidizing agents are the electronegative elements, because these readily form negative ions

by acquiring electrons. In the periodic table (⇨ p. 158) the second column from the right contains the elements – the halogens – that require only one electron to fill the outer shell. These are the most active oxidizing agents. Oxygen, which requires two electrons to fill its outer shell, is also a strong oxidizing agent. Some compounds readily give up oxygen to other reactants, becoming reduced as they do so. These substances include hydrogen peroxide (H_2O_2), ozone (O_3), potassium permanganate ($KMnO_4$), nitric acid (HNO_3), sulphuric acid (H_2SO_4) and potassium nitrate (KNO_3).

Those elements that readily form positive ions, by losing one or more electrons, are effective reducing agents. They lie in the left-hand columns of the periodic table (⇨ p. 158) and include such elements as lithium – the strongest reducing agent – sodium, potassium, magnesium and calcium.

Ion-exchange reactions

Ions in solution can be replaced by other ions of like charge in various ways. This process, called *ion exchange*, is very important in industry and is widely used to purify solutions, extract valuable metals, soften hard water, desalinate sea water and perform chemical analysis. The method uses an insoluble solid with an open, net-like molecular structure, often a synthetic organic polymer (⇨ p. 170), known as an *ion-exchange resin*, to carry chemical groups that perform the exchange. Such resins can be prepared specifically for different purposes, or, alternatively, zeolite minerals – natural alumino-silicate clay mixtures – can be used. In either case, as the solution passes through the resin or zeolite, the ion in solution is captured, and its place taken by another ion, commonly sodium. Ion-exchange reactions are reversible, so the reagents can be recharged. Sodium ions, for instance, can be replaced by flushing the zeolite with a strong solution of sodium chloride.

SEE ALSO

- POLES, FIELDS AND CHARGES p. 88
- ATOMS AND MOLECULES p. 156
- THE PERIODIC TABLE p. 158
- RADIOACTIVITY p. 160
- THE NATURE OF THE CHEMICAL BOND p. 162
- TYPES OF MOLECULAR STRUCTURE p. 164
- THE STRUCTURE OF SOLIDS p. 166
- ORGANIC CHEMISTRY pp. 170–3
- CHEMISTRY IN ACTION p. 174
- MATERIALS SCIENCE p. 176
- BIOCHEMISTRY pp. 182–5

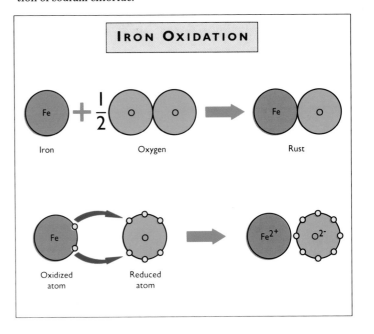

IRON OXIDATION

Iron + ½ Oxygen → Rust

Oxidized atom · Reduced atom → Fe^{2+} · O^{2-}

Organic Chemistry 1

When the term 'organic chemistry' was originally coined it was believed that there was a fundamental difference between substances found in, or derived from, living things and those from nonliving sources. The former group of substances were called *organic* and the latter *inorganic*.

In the latter part of the 18th century, the self-taught Swedish chemist Carl Wilhelm Scheele (1742–86) isolated from living organisms, and categorized, a large number of chemical substances. Later, it was shown that all these organic compounds contained carbon and hydrogen, and that many also contained oxygen and nitrogen. Such compounds came to be known as organic substances and, in spite of chemical advances that have shown that many other compounds share the same kind of structure as those derived from living systems, the name has remained. The term 'organic' has, unfortunately, become even more confused because of a public demand for 'organic' cultivation. Manure and compost are, indeed, organic, but they are of no real value as nutrients to plants until they are broken down by bacterial action into simpler, unequivocally 'inorganic', substances.

Today, organic chemistry is no longer limited to the study of the substances derived from plants and animals. It is

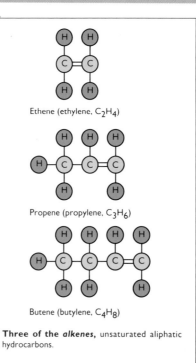

Ethene (ethylene, C_2H_4)

Propene (propylene, C_3H_6)

Butene (butylene, C_4H_8)

Three of the *alkenes*, unsaturated aliphatic hydrocarbons.

more usefully defined as being the chemistry of carbon compounds, in particular of those compounds in which carbon atoms link together in chains or rings. There are many inorganic compounds containing carbon – calcium carbonate, carbon dioxide, carbon monoxide, carbon disulphide, and so on – but these form a tiny group, compared to the millions of different compounds that can be formed by the linking up of carbon atoms with each other and with atoms of a few other elements.

The chemistry of carbon

It is no accident that such an important branch of chemistry should be based on the element carbon. Carbon atoms are able to form strong covalent bonds (⇨ p. 162) with other carbon atoms and with hydrogen, oxygen and nitrogen – and many other elements. The elements carbon, hydrogen, oxygen and nitrogen are by far the most plentiful elements in all living organisms and the permutations of their connections with carbon are virtually unlimited. A single carbon atom can bond to four other monovalent atoms because it is tetravalent (has four electrons in the outer shell; ⇨ p. 158). But it can also bond to one, two, three or four other carbon atoms by single, double or triple bonds as appropriate. Double and triple bonds are more easily broken than single bonds and it is fairly easy to cause compounds with double or triple bonds to split at the bond and react with other substances. Compounds with only single bonds between each carbon atom are called *saturated* compounds; those with double or triple bonds are called *unsaturated* compounds.

The paraffin series

Perhaps the simplest illustration of the way in which organic molecules are formed is the paraffin series. This is one of many series in organic chemistry in

---

The structure of benzene, the simplest of the aromatic compounds, so called because of their characteristic sweet smells.

Single bond   Double Bond

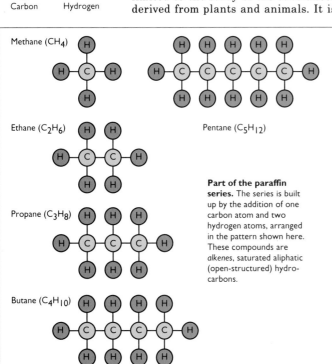

Carbon   Hydrogen

Methane (CH_4)

Ethane (C_2H_6)

Propane (C_3H_8)

Butane (C_4H_{10})

Pentane (C_5H_{12})

Part of the paraffin series. The series is built up by the addition of one carbon atom and two hydrogen atoms, arranged in the pattern shown here. These compounds are *alkenes*, saturated aliphatic (open-structured) hydrocarbons.

A selection of important functional groups. An 'R' indicates a site where another functional group or an atom may be attached.

Alkenes are hydrocarbons that contain one or more carbon double bonds. Alkenes with just one double bond form a series including ethene, propene and butene.

Alcohols. Examples include methanol (CH_3OH) and ethanol (C_2H_5OH).

Ketones. Examples include propanone (acetone; CH_3COCH_3) and MVK (methylvinyl-ketone).

Aldehydes. An important example is methanal (formaldehyde; $HCOH$), used in the production of formalin (a disinfectant) and of synthetic resins.

Carboxylic acids. As well as occurring in organic acids, such as acetic (ethanoic) acid (CH_3CO_2H; vinegar), this group occurs in all amino acids, including alanine.

R — NH_2

Amines, together with the carboxylic-acid group, occur in all amino acids.

Amides. The most important type of amide bond is that formed in protein synthesis, when the carboxylic-acid group of one amino acid condenses with the amine group of another to give a *peptide bond*.

R — SH

Thiols. This group is characterized by a strong, disagreeable odour. An example is ethanethiol.

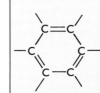

Aromatic compounds. The six-membered ring containing three double bonds is highly stable and is thus a very common characteristic of organic compounds.

---

which each successive member differs, in a systematic and readily perceptible way, from its predecessor in the series. Such a series is called a *homologous* series and the phenomenon, so common in organic chemistry, is called *homology*.

The paraffin series of compounds contains only carbon and hydrogen and the compounds are called *hydrocarbons*. These hydrocarbons should not be confused with *carbohydrates*, which contain oxygen as well as carbon and hydrogen. The first in the paraffin series is the flammable natural gas methane (⇨ pp. 164 and 180), the molecule of which consists of a single carbon atom to which is bonded four hydrogen atoms. Methane thus has the formula CH_4. If a second carbon atom is bonded to the first by a single bond, and each of the carbons has a hydrogen atom attached by each of the remaining three bonds, this gives the compound ethane, also a colourless, flammable gas, with the formula C_2H_6. The next in the series is formed in the same way, by adding another carbon atom and its associated hydrogen atoms, to give the similar gas propane (C_3H_8). Butane (C_4H_{10}) is also a gas. Pentane (C_5H_{12}), so called because it has five carbon atoms, is a flammable liquid used as a solvent. Octane (C_8H_{18}) is a liquid found in petroleum and so on. All these compounds are *alkanes*. An alkane is the generic term for any saturated aliphatic (⇨ below) hydrocarbon having this general formula. A saturated compound is one that contains no multiple bonds and thus has a greater chemical stability than an unsaturated compound, with double or triple bonds, which may readily acquire new linkages so that all four carbon bonds are individually satisfied. An *aliphatic* compound (from the Greek *aleiphat*, 'oil') is simply one with an open carbon-chain structure, as in the paraffin series, as distinct from one in which the carbon atoms are arranged in a ring – an *aromatic* – compound such as benzene.

An *alkene*, on the other hand, is an unsaturated hydrocarbon compound with the general formula C_nH_{2n}. The series builds up by additional carbon linkages to one of the double-bonded carbon atoms and the names of the compounds differ from those of the paraffin series only by one vowel, but are less likely to be confused if the alternative names, ethylene (ethene), propylene (propene), butylene (butene), and so on, are used. These gases are probably more familiar to most people in the form they take when their molecules are linked together in long polymer chains (⇨ p. 156) to form such familiar materials as polyethylene (polythene) and polypropylene (propathene).

Functional groups of organic molecules

Organic molecules are often very large and seem complicated, but can be more readily understood once it is appreciated that most of them consist of particular standardized clusters of atoms, known as *functional groups* or radicals, attached to a hydrocarbon chain known as a *residue*, and designated by the letter R (⇨ illustration). A list of these groups, by which one can recognize molecules as alcohols, aldehydes, sugars, fats, carbohydrates, amino acids, ketones and so on, is given in the table. Such groups confer specific properties on the molecules and also allow them to react readily with the functional groups on other molecules. When functional groups on different molecules interact with each other, they commonly form weak bonds of a type that will form only between certain complementary groups. This ensures a specificity of linkage between molecules that is functionally very important.

Structure of organic molecules

In addition to the functional groups, the position on the molecule at which the functional groups are attached, and even the actual three-dimensional shape of organic molecules (⇨ p. 164), have an important bearing on the properties of molecules and on how they interact with one another. Quite small changes in the position of the groups can radically affect these things. This is one form of *isomerism* – the phenomenon in which identical formulae of atoms are arranged in different spatial configurations – and is an example of positional isomerism. The functional group (⇨ above) may be attached to one of a number of the carbon atoms. It is thus necessary to have some method of designating the exact position of the

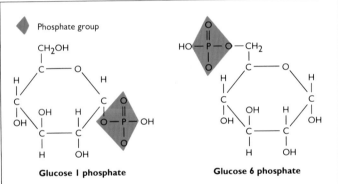

Positional isomers glucose 1 phosphate and glucose 6 phosphate have identical molecular formulae, but differ in the position of the functional group, the phosphate group. This difference in structure means that they have different physicochemical properties.

functional groups. Thus, the central carbons in the molecules are commonly numbered in sequence and the Greek letter alpha (α) is given to denote the carbon atom to which the functional group is attached. Subsequent carbons may then be designated by the sequential Greek letters beta (β), gamma (γ), delta (δ), epsilon (ε), and so on.

Even when identical functional groups are attached at the same place, organic molecules can have markedly different properties if they are of different spatial configurations. A molecule may have an attached group that, without changing its point of attachment, can rotate from one position to another. Another molecule may spring from a roughly chair-like shape to a boat-like shape, altering its properties in so doing. Organic molecules may exist in different forms, one of which is a mirror image of the other, and each would have different properties.

SEE ALSO

- ATOMS AND MOLECULES p. 156
- THE PERIODIC TABLE p. 158
- THE NATURE OF THE CHEMICAL BOND p. 162
- TYPES OF MOLECULAR STRUCTURE p. 164
- THE STRUCTURE OF SOLIDS p. 166
- CHEMICAL REACTIONS p. 168
- ORGANIC CHEMISTRY 2 p. 172
- BIOCHEMISTRY pp. 182–5

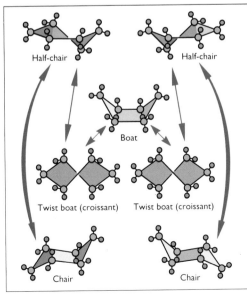

The cyclic saturated hydrocarbon cyclohexane (C_6H_{12}) exists in various shapes (*conformational isomers*). The chair form is the most stable; the half-chair is the least stable. The hydrogen atoms can take up one of two positions – *axial* (more or less perpendicular to the ring molecule's average plane) or *equatorial* (close to the average plane). As the molecule flips from one conformational isomer to its mirror image, equatorial hydrogens become axial and vice versa.

Half-chair | Half-chair

Boat

Twist boat (croissant) | Twist boat (croissant)

Chair | Chair

○ Carbon atom

● Hydrogen atom

Organic Chemistry 2

The number of ways in which carbon atoms and a handful of other atoms can bond together is enormous. This is why organic chemistry is so large a subject and why new compounds can be produced at a rate of many thousands every year. A high proportion of the materials and products on which we now depend are organic – plastics, pharmaceutical drugs, fertilizers, insecticides, cleaning materials, washing powders, dyes, artificial fibres – and there are enormous economic and social pressures to continue the search for new and better products.

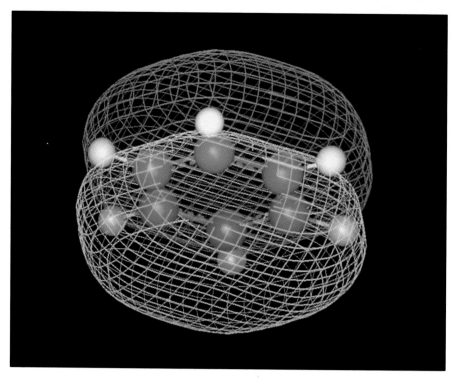

Computer-graphics representation (right) of the structure of benzene (C_6H_6), showing the delocalized, bonding, orbital electrons (yellow and blue cages) that confer greater stability on the molecule than its single- and double-bond structure would lead one to expect. These electrons are termed π orbitals. The benzene ring's carbon atoms are shown in green; hydrogen atoms are white.
(Clive Freeman, The Royal Institution, SPL)

It may seem strange that one element alone – carbon – appears to have this unique property of founding a complete chemistry. Because of the close similarity between carbon and silicon – the element vertically below carbon in the periodic table (⇨ p. 158) – it was once predicted that a whole chemistry, equal in size to that of the chemistry of carbon, but based on silicon, would develop. But this prediction has not, however, been fulfilled. Although silicon, like carbon, is tetravalent, it does not form very strong covalent bonds (⇨ p. 162) with itself, as carbon does. Silicon–oxygen–silicon bonds are strong but this combination does not give rise to the huge diversity of compounds possible with carbon–carbon bonds. Although the chemistry of silicon is expanding rapidly, there is no likelihood that it will ever rival the chemistry of carbon in size.

The number of organic compounds

In 1880 about twelve thousand organic compounds were known, almost all of them of natural origin. By 1980 the number of known organic compounds had risen to over five million, partly because of improved methods of analysis, but largely because of the extraordinary ability of chemists to synthesize new compounds. Today, the number is several times as large and is, theoretically, almost unlimited. A single research chemist, engaged in the synthesis of organic compounds for scientific or industrial reasons, is likely, in a professional lifetime, to produce some hundreds of new compounds – perhaps more than a thousand. As the number of such chemists is now of the order of a million, it is easy to understand the explosive growth in the number of organic compounds, and, inevitably, there is much duplication of effort.

The classes of organic compounds

One way of subdividing organic compounds is to do so in terms of the general shape of their carbon skeleton. All organic compounds with open chains of carbon atoms are called *aliphatic* compounds (⇨ p. 170). The chains may be straight or branched. The links between the carbon atoms may be of single bonds only (*saturated*) or may be double or triple (*unsaturated*). One example of an aliphatic compound is any member of the paraffin series. The class of aliphatic compounds consists of the alkanes, the alkenes and the alkynes (also called acetylenes – hydrocarbons with one or more triple bonds in the molecule).

If the carbon atoms are linked in a closed ring, the compound is said to be *alicyclic* (from the Greek *kuklos*, 'wheel'). Alicyclic compounds retain aliphatic properties in spite of the ring structure and should not be confused with the aromatic compounds (⇨ below and p. 170). An example of an alicyclic compound is cyclohexane (C_6H_{12}).

Aromatic compounds are those that contain a benzene ring in the molecule (⇨ box and p. 170). Although they are unsaturated, they do not easily add to other compounds. In fact, the strength of all the bonds between the carbon atoms is intermediate, between that of a single and that of a double bond. Benzene, itself (C_6H_6) is the archetypal aromatic compound. When a molecule contains a ring of atoms, some of which are carbon and one or more of which are other elements, such as oxygen, nitrogen or sulphur, the compound is said to be *heterocyclic*. The term is derived (from the Greek *heteros*, 'other'). An example of a heterocyclic compound is the solvent liquid pyridine (C_5H_5N) in which a nitrogen atom is substituted for a carbon atom in a benzene ring.

Aromatic compounds

The simple model of the benzene ring (⇨ p. 170) evolved by the German chemist Friedrich Kekulé (⇨ box) consisted of six

The structure of pyridine (C_5H_5N), a heterocyclic aromatic compound.

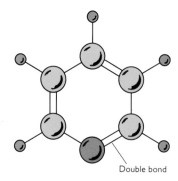

Double bond

◍ Hydrogen   ◍ Carbon   ◍ Nitrogen

The structure of bromobenzene (C_6H_5Br).

Double bond

◍ Hydrogen   ◍ Carbon   ◍ Bromine

KEKULE AND THE BENZENE RING

Much of the credit for developing the idea of the tetravalency of carbon, and the fact that carbon atoms can link on to each other, must go to the German chemist Friedrich August Kekulé von Stradonitz (1829–96). Kekulé was also the originator of the system of representing the atoms of a molecule on paper as specific patterns of the chemical symbols. Another chemist suggested joining the atoms by small dashes and this system quickly caught on. Kekule was greatly exercised, however, over the question of the structure of the important compound benzene, whose formula, C_6H_6, was known. Benzene was being increasingly used in the growing synthetic-dye industry, but progress was impeded by ignorance of the structure.

According to Kekulé's own account, in 1865, he was pondering upon the problem, while half-dozing on a London bus, and visualizing the carbon and hydrogen atoms whirling about in a dance. Suddenly the tail end of one chain of carbon atoms attached itself to the other end to form a ring. With a start, Kekulé woke to the realization that he had solved the problem of how six hydrogen atoms could bond to six carbon atoms (⇨ p. 170). The six carbon atoms were linked by alternating single and double bonds and each carbon was also bonded to a hydrogen atom. This satisfied the tetravalency of each carbon atom. Kekulé recognized that the position of the single and double bonds could be switched, displaying an ambiguity in the structure, and he proposed that the double bonds could move round the ring while still alternating with single bonds.

Although Kekulé's ingenious idea does not, unfortunately, fully stand up to modern analysis of the energies of the molecule (⇨ main text), the benzene ring turned out to be one of the most important structural elements in all organic chemistry. The many compounds that contain such rings are called *aromatic compounds*, because of the strong smell of the parent compound, benzene.

carbon atoms in a hexagonal ring, joined by alternating single and double bonds, and with one hydrogen atom bonded to each carbon atom. This is an unsaturated molecule (⇨ above). It was soon pointed out that the benzene ring did not behave like a typical unsaturated molecule, but was much more stable, and was slower to react with energetic atoms, like bromine, than would be expected. When it does react with bromine, moreover, it does not open at one of the relatively weak double bonds, but simply replaces one of the hydrogen atoms with a bromine atom to yield bromobenzene (C_6H_5Br). Such reactions, in which the three double bonds were preserved, were

surprising and cast doubt on the validity of the Kekulé structure, suggesting that his model had to be expanded in the light of more recent knowledge. As now envisaged, all the bonds between the carbon atoms are the same, and are intermediate in strength between the single and double bonds. Modern theory proposes that the electrons, participating in the carbon–carbon bonds, are 'delocalized' to form a diffuse cloud (a π-electron cloud) around the molecule that confers on it a greater stabilization energy than would be the case with Kekulé's structure.

Polymers

Among the largest molecules of all are the polymers (⇨ p. 156), and some of these substances have become familiar features in the form of the many plastics in everyday use (⇨ p. 176). Polymerization is not, however, confined to synthetic chemistry; many natural substances, such as the polysaccharide starches and celluloses of plants and the polypeptides of proteins, are polymers. A polymer is a giant molecule constructed from large numbers of identical unit parts, called monomers, linked together. Before this can happen, the monomers must have two complementary reactive sites by which they can link to opposite ends of other monomers. Monomers with two such different sites are said to be *difunctional*.

Alkenes (⇨ p. 170) are difunctional and, in the presence of a suitable catalyst (⇨ p. 168), will readily link to form polymers by addition. Ethylene (ethene) molecules are unsaturated – having a double bond – and, under the right chemical conditions, this double bond will open and will link with a similar bond in another ethylene molecule. If this process is repeated, a long paraffin-like chain will form, like a very long saturated-alkane molecule. If only a comparatively small

number of ethylene molecules link up, a material similar to paraffin wax will be formed; but, if a very long chain forms, then polythene (⇨ p. 156) is produced.

Amino acids (⇨ p. 182) are also difunctional, having one carboxyl group and one amino group. The amino group of one will readily join to the carboxyl group of another (a *peptide* linkage) so that long chains, called *polypeptides* are quickly formed. Polypeptides, in turn, link together to form *proteins*, which, because up to 20 different amino acids may be involved, may be among the most complex polymers known.

'Buckyballs'

One of the most interesting developments in late-20th-century chemistry was the discovery, in 1985, that diamond and graphite are not the only molecular forms in which pure carbon can exist. The new form, C_{60} (⇨ p. 166), is a mustard-coloured solid that dissolves in benzene to give a rich magenta-coloured solution. The molecule is of an extraordinary structure, consisting of 60 carbon atoms linked in a geodesic structure rather like that made by the panels on a football. As the structure is reminiscent of the architectural constructions of the American architect Richard Buckminster Fuller (1895–1983), the molecule has been given the somewhat clumsy title of 'buckminsterfullerene'. This is commonly abbreviated to 'buckyball'. The discovery has excited great interest as it is an entirely new concept in molecular structure. Other atoms such as fluorine and some metals can be incorporated into the buckminsterfullerene cage. Buckyball chemistry gives the promise of new materials with lubricant, catalytic, waterproofing and semiconducting properties. Already the scientific literature has assumed huge proportions.

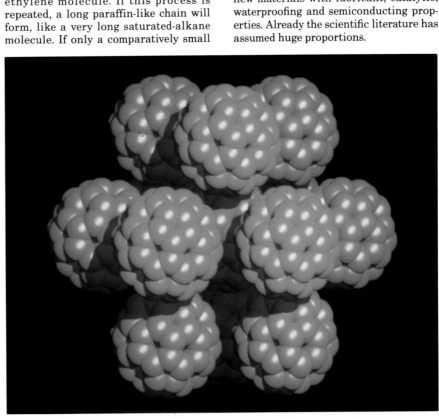

The packing structure of buckminsterfullerene (shown in computer graphics), a new form of carbon. Buckminsterfullerene is set to find applications in molecular-scale packaging or as a lubricant. (Clive Freeman, The Royal Institution, SPL)

Chemistry in Action

Chemical engineering is a major branch of technology, covering a wide range of industrial activity, in which chemical processes, developed in the laboratory, are applied on an industrial scale to produce a wide variety of reagents and materials for use in manufacturing and daily life.

Chemistry is of central importance in our modern society, and the evidence of this is all around us. Every household in most areas of the world contains evidence of the activities of the chemical industries. To take only one category, the wide range of household items made from polythene, polystyrene, polytetrafluoroethylene and other common plastics testifies to the extent to which the chemical industry has provided effective, and often superior, substitutes for natural materials.

In the USA alone, more than fifty substances are being made, or isolated, in quantities of over half a million tonnes every day. Similar or greater quantities are being made in Europe. Among the most important of these substances are sulphuric and nitric acids, ammonia, nitrogen, oxygen, chlorine, calcium oxide (*lime*), ethylene and sodium carbonate. All of these reagents are used by the chemical engineering industry in manufacturing a wide range of other products. Some of them, such as sulphuric acid, can be used in hundreds of different ways. There are considerable links between the different branches of the chemical industry and a great deal of interdependence.

Sulphuric acid

No other single chemical substance is produced in larger quantity than sulphuric acid, H_2SO_4. About half of the total production goes into the manufacture of superphosphate and related fertilizers (⇨ below); the remainder is used for a very wide range of purposes that includes the manufacture of rayon, explosives, high-octane petrol and the white pigment titanium dioxide. Sulphuric acid contains hydrogen, sulphur and oxygen. Large quantities of sulphur are required for its manufacture and this is now mainly derived from underground sources. The acid is produced by one of several processes but, in essence, sulphur is burned in air to produce sulphur dioxide, and this is then combined with more oxygen in a hot reactor, using a platinum or vanadium catalyst (⇨ p. 168), to produce sulphur

trioxide. The latter combines with water to produce sulphuric acid.

Nitrogen

The important element nitrogen is abundant since it comprises 78 per cent by volume of the Earth's atmosphere. Unfortunately, nitrogen compounds, which are in great demand, especially for fertilizers, are difficult to make because nitrogen is an inert element. Because of this there was, at first, considerable exploitation of animal sources of nitrogen compounds, such as the Chilean nitrate deposits from bird droppings. The prospect of the depletion of these sources, and the German requirements for nitrogen compounds for explosives in World War I, led to intensive research. In the end, the problem of nitrogen fixation was finally solved, after years of work, by the German chemist Fritz Haber (1868–1943). Haber demonstrated that, using a suitable catalyst, a pressure of about 200 atmospheres, and a temperature around 500°C (930°F) hydrogen and atmospheric nitrogen could be combined to form ammonia: $N_2 + 3H_2 \rightleftharpoons 2NH_3$.

The gas mixture was pumped continuously through the catalytic converter, from which the ammonia is withdrawn, while the unconverted gases continue to circulate. The hydrogen was obtained by passing superheated steam over red-hot coke. In its essentials, this process is still used today. Haber, whose success averted an agricultural crisis, but also prolonged the war, was awarded the Nobel Prize for chemistry in 1918. Ammonia can be used directly as a fertilizer or, more commonly, as various salts, especially ammonium nitrate, formed by reaction with nitric acid (HNO_3). It has other extensive uses in the chemical industry, especially for the production of nitric acid, and is an important source of hydrogen and nitrogen. It is used as a refrigerant, and, in one process, for the manufacture of the textile fibre rayon.

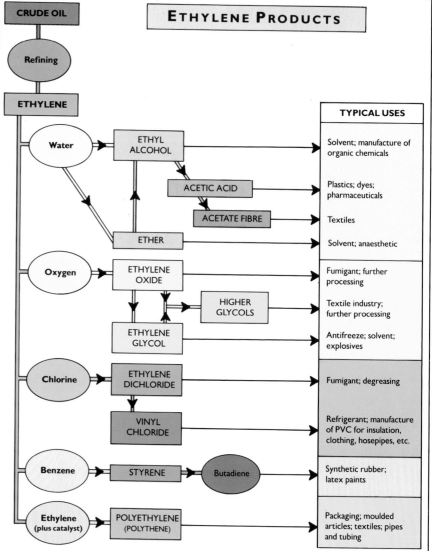

Unlike other manufacturing industries, where several raw materials are typically required to make a single product, the chemical industry derives thousands of useful products from a smaller number of raw materials.

For example, ethylene – a product of the refinement of crude oil – is used to form a few major chemicals, which in turn spawn hundreds of derivative products.

Fertilizers

Although some fertilizers occur naturally, the chemical industry manufactures large quantities of different fertilizers for agricultural use. Growing plants remove elements from the soil, especially nitrogen, potassium and phosphorus. These three elements are abstracted in considerable quantity, and must be replaced if the soil is to remain capable of sustaining plant growth. Other elements, such as calcium, magnesium and sulphur, are taken out in smaller quantity but seldom become deficient. Small traces of other elements are also needed. In the chemical industry, nitrogen is fixed as ammonia (⇨ above) and converted to various salts that can be used as fertilizers. Potassium, enough to last several thousand years, is found in large mineral deposits in many parts of the world, especially in Russia, Germany and Canada. Phosphorus is also found in extensive mineral deposits but, mainly, in an insoluble form. It is, however, converted to a soluble form by the action of sulphuric acid on phosphate rock to form superphosphates. An enormous amount of sulphuric acid is used in this way.

The halogens and their uses

An important group of highly reactive elements is that of the halogens, which consist of fluorine, chlorine, bromine, iodine and astatine (the radioactive-decay product of uranium and thorium). The group forms the vertical column second from the right in the periodic table of the elements (⇨ p. 158).

Although fluorine is abundant, it is, however, found only in small concentrations, in rocks, such as fluorspar – calcium fluoride (CaF_2). It has an important use as a flux (cryolite) in the production of aluminium, by the reduction (⇨ p. 168) of aluminium oxide (Al_2O_3) to the metal, and in the steel industry. Another major use of fluorine has been in the production of the organic chlorofluoromethane compounds, such as the freons, which have been widely used as refrigerants and as propellants in aerosol cans. Chlorofluorocarbon compounds (CFCs) have, however, been found to catalyse the breakdown of high-atmosphere ozone to oxygen, thus damaging the vital protective layer that attenuates solar radiation. Because of this their use is gradually being phased out. Fluorine is also used in the production of the plastic polytetrafluoroethylene (PTFE or 'teflon'), which provides the nonstick coating on pots and pans.

Chlorine is an effective bleaching agent and is widely used to destroy organisms in drinking water and swimming pools. It readily forms compounds with other elements, and its main use is in the manufacture of these compounds. Inorganic chlorine compounds are widely used in the production of organic compounds, such as the solvent carbon tetrachloride, the refrigerant and anaesthetic gases methyl chloride and ethyl chloride, the paint stripper methylene chloride, and the solvents and organic reagents chlorobenzene and dichlorobenzenes. Chlorine is generally derived from common salt (sodium chloride) through decomposition brought about by the passage of an electric current through a solution in water (*electrolysis*). This also breaks down the water, and hydrogen gas and hydroxyl ions are also produced.

Bromine is widely used in the photographic industry for the production of light-sensitive silver-bromide emulsions on films and plates. It is also extensively used as a petrol additive, ethylene dibromide, to scavenge antiknock lead from car cylinders. Methyl bromide is used in fire extinguishers and as a fumigant. Bromides were formerly widely used as sedatives but have long been superseded by barbiturates and the benzodiazepine groups of drugs. Bromine is obtained by processing large volumes of sea water, which contains about seventy parts of bromine per million.

Iodine is also used in photography, as silver iodide, and small quantities are used to iodize table salt in regions where the condition of goitre is endemic because of iodine deficiency. Iodine is relatively opaque to X-rays and is incorporated in various solutions that can be injected into the blood stream. This will then show up soft tissue structures not otherwise easily seen.

Sodium carbonate

Sodium carbonate (Na_2CO_3) – 'washing soda' – is used in huge quantities, especially for the manufacture of soaps and glass, for the production of other sodium salts, for washing textiles and wool, for bleaching linen and cotton, for water softening and for use as a reagent in analytical chemistry. It is produced by treating a strong salt solution (brine) with ammonia and carbon dioxide to give sodium bicarbonate (baking soda) and ammonium chloride. The bicarbonate is then heated to produce the carbonate. The ammonia can be recovered for reuse by treating the ammonium chloride with calcium oxide (lime) to form calcium chloride and release the ammonia. Calcium chloride is of little value except for helping to keep roads free of ice.

Enzyme technology

Enzymes (⇨ p. 184) are powerful protein organic catalysts (⇨ p. 168) with a multitude of valuable functions. Almost the whole of biochemistry (⇨ pp. 182–5) is mediated by enzymes and they have extensive use in science and industry. By the early 1970s, the multibillion-pound detergent industry had become heavily involved in enzyme technology because this offered previously unprecedented cleaning efficiency, even at comparatively low temperatures. Enzymes were then being added to about sixty per cent of all manufactured detergents. Problems arising from allergic contact

False-colour photograph of a Mercedes Unimog machine spraying either a fungicide or an insecticide onto a cereal crop. While modern chemical advances have undoubtedly increased arable yields, they have also brought endangerment and even total destruction to certain species of wildlife, many of these species being not necessarily harmful to the crops being sprayed.
(Dr Jeremy Burgess, SPL)

reactions in workers in the industry and in users led to a decline in the use of enzymes, however, but prompted further research that included the possibility of producing 'designer-protein' enzymes.

In the late 1980s, protein engineering became a major area of research. Its purpose is to change the structure of existing proteins, especially enzymes, so as to modify their function, to make them more suitable for performing existing functions, or make them more suitable for working under adverse conditions. It was obvious that the ability to produce, in quantity, chemical substances with a specified range of functions and activities had enormous economic implications. Enzymes can accelerate almost any chemical reaction, and can perform many tasks almost impossible by other means. They thus have wide applications in the chemical industry generally, as well as in food, fuel, pharmaceutical and other technologies. They can, for instance, rapidly break down toxic industrial waste to safer substances; they can digest and break down blood clots that are clogging either the heart or arteries, so as to free the blood flow and save life; they can divide lengths of DNA (⇨ p. 202) into segments of known function; and they have extensive applications in the preparation and manufacture of a range of foods, textiles, paper, leather and drugs and in the fermentation of wines, beers and ciders. Some enzymes are highly specific in their actions; others have a broad range of activity. They are also very efficient: in some cases one molecule of an enzyme will bring about a reaction in 100,000 molecules of another compound.

Enzymes apart, protein engineering promises to have wide applications, especially in medical and food technology. The production of new proteins by protein engineering is quite distinct from genetic engineering, however, in which existing proteins are formed in quantity by recombinant DNA methods (⇨ p. 202).

SEE ALSO

- ATOMS AND MOLECULES p. 156
- THE PERIODIC TABLE p. 158
- THE NATURE OF THE CHEMICAL BOND p. 162
- TYPES OF MOLECULAR STRUCTURE p. 164
- THE STRUCTURE OF SOLIDS p. 166
- CHEMICAL REACTIONS p. 168
- ORGANIC CHEMISTRY pp. 170–3
- MATERIALS SCIENCE p. 176
- BIOCHEMISTRY pp. 182–5

Materials Science

The mastery of materials has been a central cultural influence throughout human history. Modern materials science lies on the borderlines of several scientific disciplines. It encompasses many different fields of technology, and the materials scientist or engineer may be involved in a very wide range of studies.

Stone Age people made use of such materials as they could find lying about, especially wood, flintstone and clay. These could be modified to serve various purposes. Chemistry began to influence human development when it was discovered that metals with low melting points, such as copper and tin, could be softened by heat and beaten into different shapes. Copper was too soft for many purposes, but the discovery that a small addition of tin would greatly harden it ushered in a new cultural age – the Bronze Age. Later it was found that metals such as iron could be extracted from metallic ore by strong heat, using first charcoal and then coal in forced-draught furnaces, thus bringing about another advance in technology. Metallurgy then progressed, iron was refined and its impurities reduced, making it possible to manufacture all kinds of steel machinery, large ships, bridges and weapons capable of mass killing. The alloying of metals produced a whole new range of useful materials. Cement and concrete technology developed and, with it, the ideas of reinforcement, so that it became possible to build structures of previously unimagined dimensions. Finally, in the 20th century, chemists discovered how to string

small chemical groups together in long chains (polymers; ⇨ pp. 156 and 174) to make plastics (⇨ box), thereby initiating another revolution in materials.

Timber

Wood is a complex cellular structure composed mainly of the polysaccharide *cellulose* – a polymer that is made up of repeated sugar units. Wood is a composite structure consisting of cellulose fibres embedded in a weaker material called *lignin*. It also contains lesser quantities of other polymers, *hemicellulose*, *pectin* and starches and variable quantities of gums, waxes, resins, fats, oils and sugars. Wood is the main strengthening and water-conducting tissue of many large plants, but most timber used as a constructional material is derived from the trunks of forest trees. In addition to traditional uses and applications, wood is used as veneers, veneer plywood and laminboard (blockboard). It is also now extensively used in forms in which it is barely recognizable – as particle board (chipboard) in which wood chips, shavings, flakes or splinters are bonded together with a resin adhesive; as various forms of fibreboard, and as a fine-grained stable material of bonded, homogeneous wood powder.

Metals

Iron is one of the most abundant elements on Earth. Iron from a blast furnace contains about five per cent carbon and is very brittle. Most of this carbon must be removed by oxidation to produce a useful material. Pure iron is little used, however, as its hardness, toughness and rigidity are greatly improved by increasing the carbon content to about two per cent to produce mild steel. This is valuable for a wide variety of purposes, but readily corrodes (⇨ below) and must be painted or otherwise protected, which can be done by depositing a thin layer of zinc (galvanized steel) on the surface or

These glass marbles exploit glass's transparent quality to decorative effect, but glass has numerous other, serious applications. In particular manufacturing processes, for instance, sheets of glass can be laminated or toughened, making them much less brittle, and hence safer to use in doors, windows, car windscreens, etc. (Spectrum)

by plating with nickel and chromium. Stainless steel is iron alloyed with a relatively high proportion of nickel and chromium. Many different steels can be produced by the addition of such alloying elements as aluminium, cobalt, niobium, molybdenum, titanium, vanadium and tungsten. A vast quantity of steel is used in the car industry, in building construction, containers, domestic products, machinery and railways.

Copper – the name is derived from the Island of Cyprus, where it was first found in quantity – was the first metal to be used by humans, probably in about 5000 BC. It is found in an almost pure metallic state, but most is now derived from low-grade ores containing only about two per cent of the metal. The ore is reduced to the metal by heating with carbon in a furnace. Today, copper is little used as a structural material, or for tools, but is extensively required as a conductor of electricity in dynamo and electric-motor windings, and in electronic circuits. It is also widely used as brass and bronze alloys for bearings, tableware, noncorroding springs, chemical-plant and brewery containers, and many other minor uses. More than one thousand different alloys of copper exist. The salt, copper sulphate ($CuSO_4$), which is blue in its hydrated form, has many industrial and agricultural uses.

Aluminium is the third most abundant element in the Earth's crust, after oxygen and silicon, existing mostly as oxides (bauxite) or silicates. It is a silvery-white metal, valued for its lightness and for its ability to form light, but

Wood is the raw material for a wide variety of manufactured products, ranging from building timbers and fine veneers for furniture, through to paper, viscose and rayon, made from wood pulp. (Spectrum)

strong, alloys that are resistant to corrosion. When metallic aluminium is exposed to the air, it immediately forms a thin, hard layer of aluminium oxide (Al_2O_3) that prevents further oxidation by sealing off atmospheric oxygen. Aluminium oxide is tough, nonflaking, very adherent and resists most chemicals. As aluminium is an excellent conductor of electricity, and as it is much lighter than copper, it is extensively used for power-transmission lines. It is also a very good conductor of heat and a highly efficient reflector of radiation.

Aluminium is extracted by an expensive electrolytic process, and is used in the form of one of a number of alloys with elements such as magnesium, silicon, copper, zinc or nickel. The alloy duralumin contains small amounts of copper, magnesium and manganese, and is as strong as mild steel although very much lighter. It is widely used in the construction of aircraft. Aluminium alloys are also widely used in the container industry.

Glass

Glass is a noncrystalline (amorphous; ⇨ p. 166) material made by heating certain substances, especially silicon oxide (sand), sodium carbonate (soda) and calcium carbonate (limestone), until they fuse into a transparent mass at a temperature of about 1,300°C (2,400°F). A typical glass might contain 72 per cent silicon oxide, 15 per cent soda, five per cent lime, with smaller quantities of magnesium oxide (magnesia), aluminium oxide (alumina) and boric oxide. Glass is not a compound but a solution of different substances in each other. It behaves like a solid at room temperature, but it exhibits the properties of a liquid by flowing at higher temperatures. Various additional substances can be added to alter the properties of the glass. The addition of lead produces a heavier glass, with a greater refractive index (⇨ p. 78) and increased transparency, known as *crystal*. Flat glass of high quality is produced by the Pilkington process, in which a continuous strip of molten glass is floated onto the surface of molten metal, usually tin, maintained at a constant temperature.

Composite materials

The properties of many brittle materials such as glass, concrete and certain plastic resins can be greatly enhanced by incorporating within them other materials such as steel mesh, rods or fibres of various kinds. This principle has long been known, and was applied when straw was added to clay to make bricks, and when twigs were incorporated into mud used for building (*wattle and daub*). More recently, steel-reinforced concrete has been extensively used in building and civil engineering. There is now available a wide range of highly useful materials consisting of fibre-reinforced composites, such as fibreglass, in which mats of fine glass fibres are incorporated in a plastic resin, and carbon-fibre-reinforced plastics. The latter use large numbers of very fine carbon fibres, which are stronger and stiffer than glass fibres, and produce a remarkable material stronger than steel, not subject to cracking or fatigue fracture, and very light in weight.

Properties of materials

The mechanical properties of materials vary widely and it is, to a large extent but by no means exclusively, these that determine the choice of materials for various purposes. Mechanical properties are the response to applied forces or stresses. Materials respond to stress by straining or deforming and this is usually acceptable, so long as the deformation remains within the elastic limits of the material so that it reverts to its former shape when the stress is removed (⇨ pp. 26 and 166).

Thermal properties are also often important. The reason that some materials feel 'cold' to the touch while others in the same environment feel 'warm' has less to do with differences in temperature than differences in the rate with which materials conduct heat (⇨ p. 52). If the hand is placed on a block of steel, heat from the blood circulating in the skin is rapidly conducted away into the steel, which feels cold. If the hand is then placed on a block of cork, the rate of conduction is so slow that little heat is lost from the skin and the surface of the cork, warmed by the skin, feels warm. Heat conductance is closely related to electrical conductance and most materials that conduct heat well also conduct electricity well. Most heat insulators are also good electrical insulators. A thermal property, often of greater importance than conductance, is the degree to which a material expands when heated. Some materials are designed, for certain critical purposes, to have as small a coefficient of expansion as possible.

An important property of materials is their tendency spontaneously to undergo the chemical changes known as oxidation (⇨ p. 168). Corrosion of metals is often weakening and destructive of their mechanical properties. This is especially true of iron and steel, which, in the presence of accessible oxygen and water, will inevitably oxidize, and will, eventually, be entirely converted to the oxide.

The optical properties of materials include transparency and opacity to light; the ability to change the speed of transmitted light and hence, if suitably shaped, to bend light beams (refraction; ⇨ p. 78); and the ability to transmit light in one plane and prevent its passage in another (plane polarization ⇨ pp. 72–5). Most of these properties are exploited in various glasses but a number of plastics, such as polymethylmethacrylate ('perspex'), also have valuable optical properties.

Electrical properties include low resistance to the passage of electricity in conductors such as copper and aluminium; high electrical resistance in insulators such as glass and polythene; intermediate but controllable conductivity in semiconductors such as silicon and germanium (⇨ p. 90); and the ability to alter the capacitance of a capacitor – dielectric constant (⇨ p. 98).

PLASTICS AND THEIR USES

Plastic substances are materials of increasing importance and ever-increasing number. Each polymer plastic has a large number of trade names and many more uses than are listed here.

Generic name	A trade name	Uses
Polyethylene	Polythene	Domestic utensils
Polystyrene	Polystyrene	Food packaging, foam
Polyvinyl chloride	PVC	Clothing, upholstery
Polytetrafluoroethylene	Teflon	Frying-pan linings
Polymethylmethacrylate	Perspex	Contact lenses, glasses
Polypropylene	Propathene	Containers, boxes
Polyesters	Terylene	Fibres, clothing
Polyurethane	Lycra	Paints, varnishes, foam
Polyamide	Nylon	Clothing, tooth brushes
Melamine-formaldehyde	Formica	Surface coverings

SEE ALSO

● ATOMS AND MOLECULES p. 156
● THE PERIODIC TABLE p. 158
● THE NATURE OF THE CHEMICAL BOND p. 162
● TYPES OF MOLECULAR STRUCTURE p. 164
● THE STRUCTURE OF SOLIDS p. 166
● CHEMICAL REACTIONS p. 168
● ORGANIC CHEMISTRY pp. 170–3
● CHEMISTRY IN ACTION p. 174

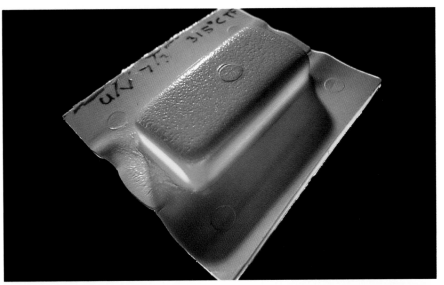

A sample of **polyetherimide resin** into which a depression has been thermoformed. This process involves heating the sample to very high temperatures (315°C/600°F in this case) to make it *ductile* (able to accommodate large deformations beyond the elastic limit without breaking), pressing the desired shape into the polymer, and allowing it to cool. This particular material has a variety of applications in the aerospace industry.

(Bruce Frisch, SPL)

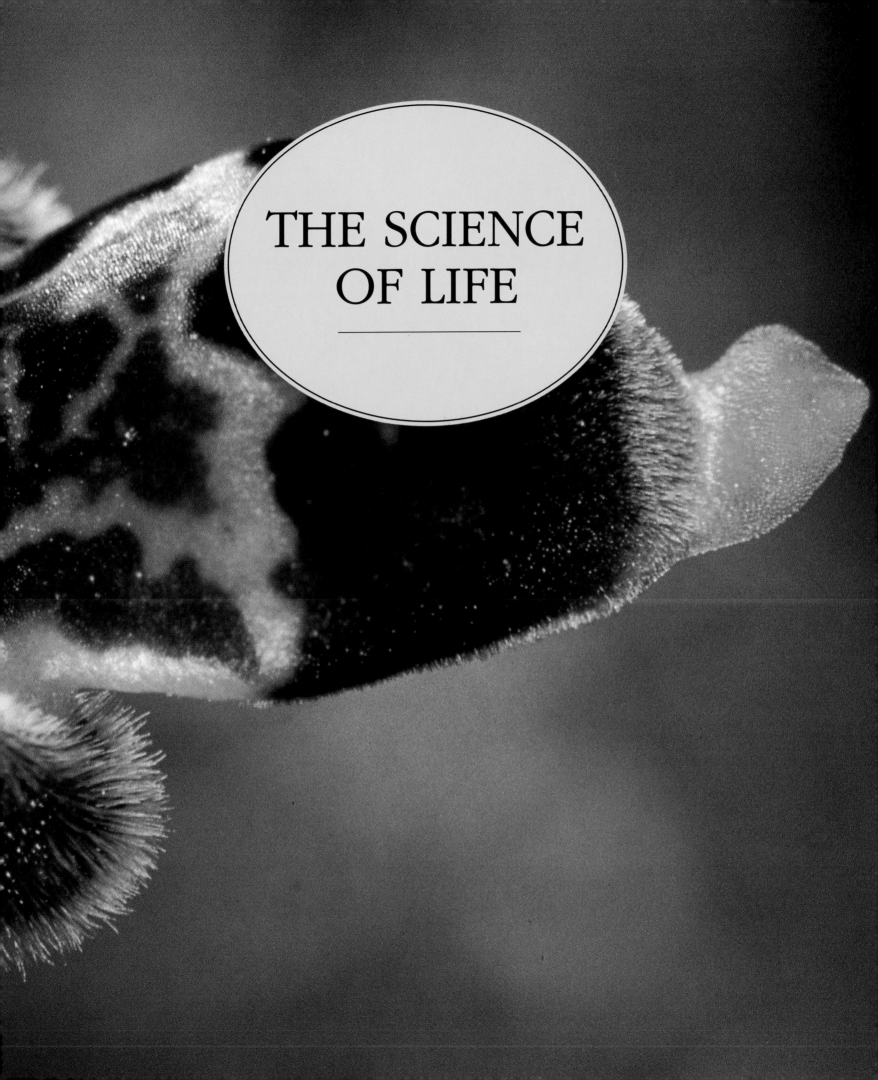

THE SCIENCE OF LIFE

The Nature and Origins of Life

The facts about the origin of life on Earth began to emerge only in the 19th century. Before then, with the exception of a few scientists and free thinkers, people accepted the theological explanations.

Almost until the end of the 19th century, most people accepted the doctrine of *spontaneous generation* (that living things arose, fully formed, from dead organic matter). Indeed, as late as 1864 it was believed that there existed scientific evidence that living things could come into existence without any prior cause. This idea was finally proved wrong, however, by the distinguished French chemist and pioneer of bacteriology Louis Pasteur (1822–95). He demonstrated that if sterilized fermentable fluid was placed in a swan-neck flask (i.e. a flask with a long curved neck that allows air to enter but excludes dust and microorganisms), then the fluid remained clear. However, if the neck of the flask was broken off, allowing dust to enter, contamination swiftly resulted.

Understanding the origins of life became science's next challenge.

The second half of the 19th century was a period of upheaval in biology. No sooner was there general acceptance in scientific circles of the English naturalist Charles Darwin's ideas of evolution (⇨ p. 196) than it became necessary, in consequence of Pasteur's work, to abandon all ideas that life could arise spontaneously. Scientists then saw that, if only some explanation were forthcoming for the origins of the simplest life forms, the whole development of living things, including the most elaborate, could be understood.

Early ideas of spontaneous generation

As late as the middle of the 19th century nearly everyone believed that if meat was allowed to become rancid, maggots would appear spontaneously from it. And insects, worms and other small creatures were believed to be generated in similar ways. The Italian physician Francesco Redi (1626–97) had, however, come across some critical suggestions by the English physician William Harvey (1578–1657), and decided to put the hypothesis of spontaneous generation to the test. Redi took eight flasks containing meat, sealed four of them, and left the other four open to the air. Flies had access to the meat in the four open flasks, and, later, maggots were found to be breeding in them. None of the sealed flasks contained maggots, although the meat within them was found to be just as rotten as that in the open flasks. Redi did the experiment again, but this time he did not seal any of the flasks. He simply covered half of them with gauze so that flies were excluded. Again, maggots

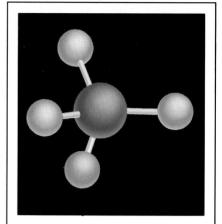

The structure of methane (CH_4) Each molecule consists of an atom of carbon with four hydrogen atoms attached to it.

appeared only in the flasks to which flies had had access.

Redi correctly concluded that the maggots came from eggs laid by the flies, but even this excellently designed experiment failed ultimately to dispel the doctrine of spontaneous generation. At about the same time, the Dutch microscopist Anton van Leeuwenhoek (1632–1723) had shown that stagnant water contained myriad tiny living creatures, and Redi's work did nothing to rule out the possibility that these could arise spontaneously. In 1748 the English naturalist John Turberville Needham (1713–81) carried out an experiment that seemed to prove that spontaneous generation did, indeed, occur. After boiling some mutton broth he sealed it inside glass bottles for several days. Microscopic examination then showed that large numbers of microorganisms were present in the broth. The fallacy in this was, however, soon explained when, in 1768, the Italian biologist Lazzaro Spallanzani (1729–99) carried out the same work much more thoroughly, properly sterilizing the equipment and the contents by boiling them for over half an hour, and sealing everything. When this was done no microorganisms appeared however long the flasks were left. Spallanzani correctly concluded that organisms had been present in their *spore forms* (in which they are very difficult to detect and can withstand extremely high temperatures), and that these had been able to resist boiling for shorter periods.

Those people thoroughly determined to believe in spontaneous generation were not, however, convinced by this experiment, and even came up with a new suggestion for how spontaneous generation occurred. The prolonged boiling, they said, destroyed a 'vital principle' necessary for the breeding of organisms.

Artist's impression of a forest during the Carboniferous period (the 80-million-year-long period in the Palaeozoic era during which coal deposits were laid down). (AR)

This idea seemed plausible to many, and it was another hundred years before the work of Louis Pasteur put the notion of spontaneous generation to rest.

The beginnings of life

One of the simplest organic compounds is methane, a colourless, odourless, flammable gas, each molecule of which consists of a carbon atom with four hydrogen atoms attached to it (CH_4). Early in the evolution of the Earth, carbon and hydrogen atoms reacted together to form atmospheric methane. This gas, known as 'natural gas', is still present in large quantities underground, and forms an important part of the atmosphere of the outer planets (⇨ p. 136). On Earth, the early atmospheric methane was quickly burnt, mainly by lightning flashes, to form carbon dioxide and water, using up much of the available free oxygen that was being produced by the action of light on other molecules (*photolysis*). The remainder was used up in rusting (*oxidizing*) the iron in surface rock, and, as a result, the Earth's atmosphere was virtually free from oxygen for more than a billion years. It was during this period that life began. The first living organisms must have been formed either in the seas or in sea pools (in which immense quantities of various inorganic substances were dissolved), or in an element-rich atmosphere. These ionic substances (⇨ p. 90) would have been in a constant state of mixing and association so that countless trials of various combinations would have occurred. The probability that organic molecules might have been formed in this way increases with the number of trials. If the chances of such an event happening in the course of a single trial are 1 in 1,000, for example, the chances of it happening in 1,000 trials are 1 in 2.7 (37 per cent). In 10,000 trials, the probability becomes almost a certainty. In the course of billions of years and countless trials of chemical combination, organic molecules were thus likely to occur.

Many scientists propose that lightning, acting on the atmosphere or striking the sea, may have provided the energy for the life-forming combination of carbon and other elements. This effect has, in fact, been produced in laboratory experiments. In 1953, Stanley L. Miller, a 23-year-old graduate student at the University of Chicago, fitted a glass container with spark electrodes; filled it with methane, hydrogen, ammonia and water; sealed it; heated the water and then started an 'artificial-lightning' spark discharge. Within a few days the water turned a reddish colour, with a rich mixture of compounds that turned out, on analysis, to be amino acids (⇨ pp. 182) – the 'building blocks' of proteins, which are themselves the fundamental components of cells. Organic compounds formed in this way might have increased in quantity to form a kind of 'primeval soup' in which primitive cellular structures might have developed by chance, probably in a series of stages.

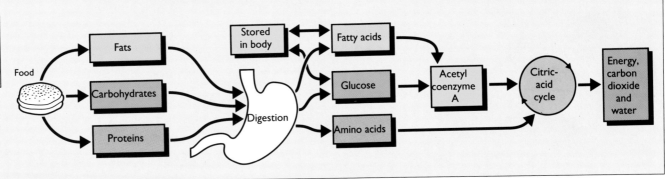

MILLER'S EXPERIMENT

Energy produced by the electrical spark caused the chemicals to react with each other.

Methane, hydrogen, ammonia and water were sealed in a glass container.

In 1953, University of Chicago graduate Stanley Miller sealed a mixture of water, methane, ammonia and hydrogen in a glass container fitted with spark electrodes, to see how the chemicals would react. He found that amino acids were among the new and complex substances formed.

WHAT IS LIFE?

Living matter, however simple, exists in the form of discrete entities known as organisms. The term is used freely to refer to any living thing, from the simplest virus or bacterium through to a human being.

Before self-copying organisms could develop, it was necessary for nucleic acids (the basic genetic material of almost all living cells; ⇨ p. 202) to form. The earliest organisms probably consisted of nothing more than short strands of ribonucleic acid (RNA), and we now know that it is possible for RNA, which most commonly acts as a messenger carrying the code for cell reproduction, to make copies of itself (*replicate*) without the aid of the *enzymes* (complex protein molecules highly specific to particular reactions; ⇨ p. 182) that normally promote this. Double strands of RNA can also join longitudinally to make DNA. The earliest life forms were probably viruslike organisms that developed into bacteria or algae.

The chemical elements needed to form living material – 'nutrient substances' – may exist in the immediate environment. They may be brought to the organism, or the organism can go and find them. To be capable of reproduction, an organism must also be capable of absorbing (*assimilating*) the elements it needs, and so these elements must be present in a soluble form. For example, an organism that needs iron cannot acquire it in the form of carpenters' nails but from a source of a salt of iron, such as ferrous sulphate. An organism must also have the means of bringing about the often complex chemical reactions that are needed to build up the molecules of its body (*anabolism*). This commonly involves the use of enzymes (⇨ p. 182) to promote and accelerate these reactions.

Chemical reactions cannot occur without the exchange of energy; for many of them energy must be supplied from outside the organism itself. To this end, organisms require that some of their nutrient substances are of a kind that can be acted on chemically (in this case, oxidized) so as to provide energy. Often the nutrients used for body building can also be used for fuel. The more complex organisms have developed systems by which they can derive both their anabolic nutrients and their fuels from the same, often chemically complex, foods. This requires means of breaking down these molecules, again using enzymes, to simpler forms, such as sugars, fatty acids and amino acids, that can be used for both purposes. This process is called *digestion*. *Excretion* is the name given to the process by which organisms get rid of the waste products of all their chemical processes (processes collectively known as *metabolism*).

Finally, all organisms, from the simplest to the most complex, require a controlling plan containing details of how elements are put together to form the molecules needed. This programme need only specify the construction of enzymes; once these enzymic proteins are available, all the necessary chemical reactions follow automatically. This programme, which is always passed on from organism to offspring, is called the *genetic code* and is contained in lengths of ribonucleic acid – DNA or RNA.

THE METABOLIC PROCESS

All the processes of metabolism, including digestion and the use of food products to supply energy, are controlled by enzymes.

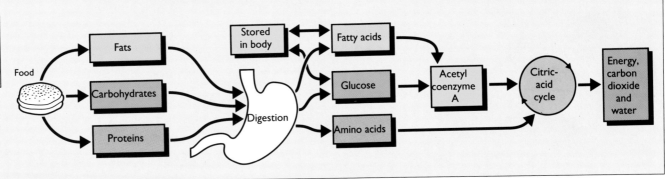

Food → Fats, Carbohydrates, Proteins → Digestion → Stored in body, Fatty acids, Glucose, Amino acids → Acetyl coenzyme A → Citric-acid cycle → Energy, carbon dioxide and water

Biochemistry 1

Organic chemistry is the chemistry of carbon – an element with unique properties that enable its atoms to link together in chains or rings and to form an infinite variety of molecules with a few other elements. *Biochemistry* is the organic chemistry that occurs in living organisms, and is thus deeply concerned with the compounds of carbon.

Nearly all biochemical reactions are brought about, or greatly accelerated, by a certain class of organic compounds, the proteins known as *enzymes* (biological catalysts). After the three major groups of molecules present in most living things – proteins, carbohydrates and fats

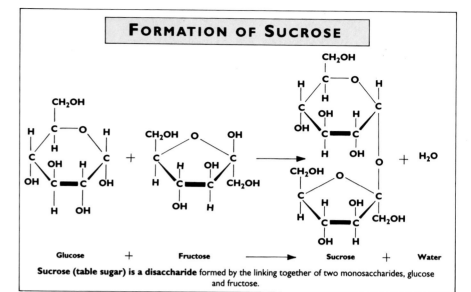

FORMATION OF SUCROSE

Glucose   +   Fructose   ⟶   Sucrose   +   Water

Sucrose (table sugar) is a disaccharide formed by the linking together of two monosaccharides, glucose and fructose.

THE DEMISE OF 'VITALISM'

All life processes conform to the laws of chemistry and physics. The age-old doctrine of 'vitalism' (⇨ p. 180) advocated the idea that living things possess some 'vital principle' not present in nonliving things. This notion was widely held, until it received a serious blow when the German chemist Friedrich Wöhler (1800–82) synthesized the organic compound urea, previously thought to be a product only of living things. Further attacks on this line of thinking followed. In 1847, the German physiologist Karl Friedrich Ludwig (1816–95) showed that no 'vital force', only a simple pumping action by the heart, maintained the circulation of the blood. In 1896, the German chemist Eduard Buchner (1850–1902) struck the final blow when he demonstrated that fermentation, thought to be unique to, and inseparable from, living cells, was the result of specific substances known now as enzymes (⇨ p. 184). Buchner's research showed that yeast enzymes continued to operate normally to ferment sugars, even after all the yeast cells from which they were derived had been killed.

CONFORMATION OF PROTEIN

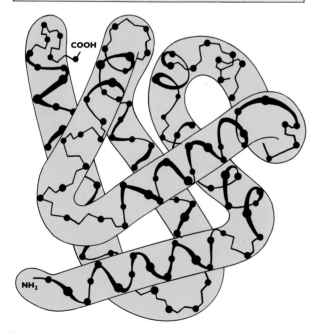

The conformation of a protein molecule (myoglobin). The three-dimensional shape of this molecule significantly affects its properties.

– enzymes and nucleic acids (i.e. DNA and RNA; ⇨ p. 202) are by far the most important of all biochemical molecules.

We tend to think of proteins, fats and carbohydrates in a dietary context, but this is a narrow view determined by the fact that nearly all the foods we eat are the products of living things that have already undergone their own biochemical processes. Humans have many molecules in common with other living things, and the most important of these are grouped into the aforementioned three large classes. Nearly all the members of these classes are more complex than most *inorganic* molecules (i.e. those that are not primarily based on carbon), but they do not possess any inherent features that fundamentally distinguish them from this group. We may call these molecules 'the molecules of life', but, as individuals, they are no more living than any other molecules, either organic or inorganic. No single molecule, even that of DNA (⇨ p. 202), can be said, in any meaningful sense, to be alive. It is only when molecules are associated in large numbers, and organized in an immensely complex cellular structure, that they form systems that show the characteristics of living things (⇨ p. 180).

Carbohydrates and body fuelling

In plants, carbohydrates are predominant, and they are of great importance in humans, in that they provide the body's fuel. However, carbohydrates form only about one per cent of the body weight and three per cent of the total organic matter in humans. All carbohydrates are compounds of carbon, hydrogen and oxygen. In the simpler forms, the hydrogen and oxygen are often present in the same proportions as in water, and the grouping CH_2O is common. Carbohydrates are made of water-linked (*hydrated*) carbon atoms. It is the *hydroxyl* (–OH) group linked to the carbon atom that makes many of them soluble in water.

Carbohydrates include a range of sugars, starches and celluloses. A *saccharide* is any sugar, and a *monosaccharide* is a basic sugar, such as *glucose* (blood sugar), *fructose* (fruit sugar) or *galactose* (milk sugar). Two monosaccharide sugar molecules can link together to form a *disaccharide*. Thus, both glucose and fructose have an –OH group to which they can link, with the elimination of one molecule of water, leaving them joined by a single oxygen atom to form a molecule of sucrose (table sugar).

Monosaccharides are capable of linking together in a long single or branched chain. This process is called *polymerization*, and the large molecules formed in this way are *polysaccharides*. The structural elements in plants – *celluloses* – are polysaccharides, and starch in plants and glycogen in the body are polysaccharides of glucose, differing only in the degree of branching of the chain.

The basic body fuel is glucose, but this is seldom present, as such, in any quantity in food. Therefore the body needs some way of breaking down polysaccharides to form simpler sugars so that they can be absorbed and used. This is done by enzymes provided by the digestive system. Sugars such as sucrose are readily split into monosaccharides, and there are also enzymes for splitting down starch. Unlike cows, human beings have no enzymes capable of breaking up cellulose molecules, and these just pass through the intestine, unaltered, as fibre.

Proteins and body structure

Proteins are made of carbon, hydrogen, oxygen and nitrogen, and sometimes traces of other elements. We are inclined to think of protein in the human body as being contained solely in our muscles. Indeed, much of the protein in the body is in the muscles, but there is also a considerable amount of protein elsewhere; about 17 per cent of body weight and 50 per cent of the body's organic matter consists of protein. The bones and teeth are made of protein (hardened by calcium

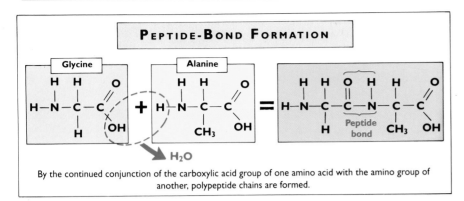

PEPTIDE-BOND FORMATION

By the continued conjunction of the carboxylic acid group of one amino acid with the amino group of another, polypeptide chains are formed.

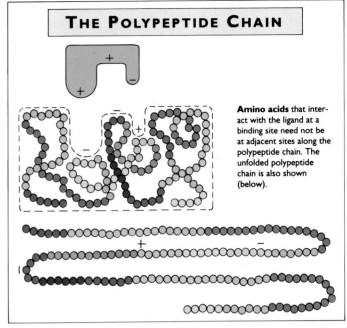

THE POLYPEPTIDE CHAIN

Amino acids that interact with the ligand at a binding site need not be at adjacent sites along the polypeptide chain. The unfolded polypeptide chain is also shown (below).

and phosphates), and much of the skin, hair, nails and most of the structure of the organs are protein. Structural protein exists mainly in the form of the tough, insoluble, triple-helix-stranded form known as *collagen*. This is present in the tendons and ligaments, but is also the main bone protein and occurs widely elsewhere in the form of connective tissue (tissue that participates in the structure of organs or body tissue, or binds them together). Soluble protein is present in the cells and in the blood, the two main forms being albumin and globulin. The former binds and transports fatty acids, and the latter forms antibodies (various proteins produced in the blood in response to the presence of an antigen). Protein that can shorten and lengthen (*contractile* protein) is present in the muscles as *myosin* and in the cells as *actin* and *tubulin*. All of the thousands of different enzymes present in the body are made of protein.

Like most large molecules, protein molecules are composed of smaller 'building units' (*amino acids*), and, like polysaccharides, they are polymers. Proteins are, however, more complex and diverse than polysaccharides.

All amino acids have the same pair of terminations – an amino group (one nitrogen atom linked to two hydrogen atoms – NH_2) and a carboxyl acid (one carbon atom linked to two oxygen atoms and one hydrogen atom – COOH) group. They differ from each other only in the small central portion – the *residue*.

Twenty different amino acids make up the proteins of all living things, and these can be linked together in different orders to form an almost infinite variety of proteins. In so doing, the amino group

of one easily links to the carboxyl group of another in a combination known as a *peptide bond*. Each time a peptide bond is made, the chain keeps an amino group at one end and a carboxyl group at the other. A sequence of amino acids linked in this way is called a *polypeptide*. If the chain contains fewer than an arbitrary 50 amino acids, it is called a *peptide*; if more, it is called a *protein*. However, some proteins contain more than one polypeptide chain, held together by various kinds of bonding between them.

Protein spatial configurations

Proteins can be thought of as chains of different amino acids, like beads strung on a necklace, and the chain can be bent into a number of shapes by hydrogen bonding (the force of attraction between hydrogen and oxygen atoms on neighbouring molecules) and other weak links between different parts of the chain. The resulting three-dimensional shape is known as the *conformation* of the protein, and this largely determines its properties. The regularly occurring peptide bonds along a polypeptide chain can, for instance, lead to hydrogen bonds that force a protein to take up a helical conformation.

Protein-binding sites

Each protein has a particular order of amino acids, as well as a unique shape that determines how it interacts with other molecules. The shape features certain sites, known as *binding sites*, which are complementary in form to that of a molecule, or part of a molecule, that binds to the protein, in the same way that a jigsaw piece is complementary to the piece to which it fits. Anything that binds to the surface of a protein in this way is called a *ligand*. A protein may have one

or several different binding sites, each with a different shape. Because of this, proteins are able to identify particular ligands, and can select those that correspond in shape. The correspondence may be so highly specific that only one ligand can fit; or it may be looser, so that one of a number of ligands will bind on.

Ligands attach themselves to proteins by virtue of electric ionic charges or van der Waals attractions ($\Leftrightarrow$ pp. 88–95). The sites of the zones where these attractions occur need not be adjacent in the polypeptide chains, but are brought close to each other by the folding of the protein. In this way, amino acids offering the required ionic attractions are brought together to form the protein-binding site. The ability of protein-binding sites to be specific in selecting other molecules or ions allows them to carry out a wide variety of functions in the cell. These activities are controlled in various ways. For instance, when a ligand binds to a binding site in a protein, the attraction between the two alters the attractive forces, and the protein changes shape. If there is more than one binding site, the binding of a ligand to one site (the *regulatory site*) can thus change the shape of another site (the *functional site*) and alter its binding characteristics.

The proteins on which binding sites, often called receptor sites, occur lie in cell membranes or inside cells. Their function includes the action of chemical messengers (*hormones*), neurotransmitters, steroids, vitamins, drugs and many other substances that act as ligands.

Those binding sites in cell membranes can affect the ease with which various substances pass into the cell, or the rate at which substances are synthesized in it. In the case of muscle cells, the action of the binding of a ligand can cause the muscle cell to contract or relax. In all cases, the particular effect is brought about by temporary changes in the protein on which the binding site lies.

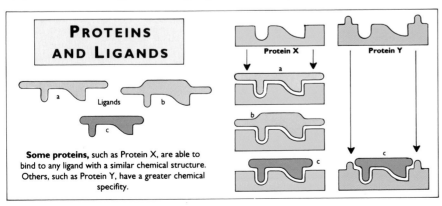

PROTEINS AND LIGANDS

Protein X

Protein Y

Ligands

Some proteins, such as Protein X, are able to bind to any ligand with a similar chemical structure. Others, such as Protein Y, have a greater chemical specificity.

Biochemistry 2

Of the four major body constituents – carbohydrates, fats, proteins (including enzymes) and nucleic acid – most scientific attention has been paid to the latter two. This is because of their complexity and because of the central role they play in body structure, organization and control. Dietary and social interest, on the other hand, tends to concentrate on the carbohydrates and fats. These are not without scientific interest, however, and fats are considerably more intricate than is often realized. Enzymes, the major group of proteins, link the strands of biochemistry together.

SEE ALSO

● THE NATURE AND ORIGINS OF LIFE p. 180
● BIOCHEMISTRY 1 p. 182
● THE CELLULAR BASIS OF LIFE p. 186
● CELLULAR STRUCTURE AND FUNCTION p. 188
● SIMPLE ORGANISMS p. 190
● MULTICELLULAR ORGANISMS pp. 192–5
● DNA AND THE GENETIC CODE p. 202

Fats are only one subgroup of the larger class of *lipids*. These are molecules that consist mainly of carbon and hydrogen, bonded in such a way as to make them insoluble in water. They make up some 40 per cent of the organic matter of the body and about 15 per cent of the total body weight.

Triglycerides

The lipids fall into three distinct groups. The first of these, the substance we commonly call 'fat', is an example of a *triglyceride,* of which there are many different types. A triglyceride is a molecule consisting of a 'backbone' of *glycerol* (glycerine) with three fatty acids attached to it. Whatever the triglyceride, the glycerol component remains the same, but the fatty acids may be of a range of types, and may even differ from each other in the same triglyceride molecule.

Fatty acids consist of chains of carbon atoms with hydrogen atoms attached and a hydroxyl group (⇨ p. 182) at one end. The hydroxyl group attaches the chains to one of the three –OH groups of the

TRIGLYCERIDES AND PHOSPHOLIPIDS

Glycerol and fatty acids are the major subunits that combine to form triglycerides and phospholipids. The shaded areas represent the oxygen bonds between the glycerol 'backbone' and the separate fatty acids.

glycerol molecule, with the loss of a molecule of water.

Fatty acids are formed in the body by the linking of two-carbon fragments, so most of them have an even number of carbon atoms, the most common number being 16 or 18. If all the carbons in the chain of the fatty acid are linked by a single bond, the fatty acid is said to be *saturated*, but if there is a double bond in the chain, the fatty acid is *unsaturated*. If more than one double bond is present, the fatty acid is said to be *polyunsaturated*. Animal fats, such as those present in meat and dairy products, tend to contain a high proportion of saturated fatty acids, while vegetable fats have a preponderance of polyunsaturated fatty acids.

Triglycerides form the main high-calorie energy store of the body and are a very efficient way of storing energy. Fats are laid down under the skin, in the abdomen and elsewhere, and can greatly modify the visible shape of the body. Any food intake surplus to requirement is converted to triglycerides and stored in these 'depots'. When energy is needed and is not available from immediate or recent food intake, the fatty acids are split off from the glycerol residue by a process known as *hydrolysis*, in which there is an interaction with water. The acids released can then be converted in the liver to glucose – the normal energy source – or may be directly used as an 'emergency' energy source.

Phospholipids

The second group of lipids comprises the *phospholipids*. These are very similar to triglycerides, except that one of the fatty acids is replaced by a group containing a phosphorus atom, together with oxygen, carbon and hydrogen atoms. The combination of phosphorus and oxygen is called a *phosphate,* and a small nitrogen-containing end group is usually attached to it. The phosphate and nitrogen groups make this part of the molecule water-attractive, while the rest of the molecule is water-repellent. This has an unusual effect. In water, phospholipids form parallel rows, or layers, and lie with all their

water-attractive ends directed towards the water.

The chief importance of phospholipids is that they are the principal components in cell membranes. These membranes surround entire cells and also enclose most of the internal structures of the cells (the 'little organs' or *organelles*). They have many important functions, but are principally concerned with providing a selective barrier, which allows some molecules to pass through, while others are excluded. Cell membranes are extremely thin and consist of only two layers of phospholipid molecules, with their water-attractive ends directed towards their outer surfaces and their water-repellent ends directed inwards. These molecules are not linked together and can move about freely, giving the membrane a great deal of flexibility. The parallel orientation, however, maintains the general membrane structure. Embedded in the membrane are numerous protein molecules and their binding sites (⇨ p. 182).

The outer cell membrane is not made exclusively of phospholipids – for each phospholipid molecule there is, on average, one cholesterol molecule (⇨ below). Thus, the total amount of cholesterol in the body is considerable.

The steroids

The third group of lipids is the large class of ring-structure molecules – the *steroids* – so called because of their general resemblance to the naturally occurring sterols (a set of mainly unsaturated solid alcohols occurring in the fatty tissues of plants and animals) such as cholesterol and ergosterol. They consist of carbon and hydrogen atoms arranged in four rings, three with six carbon atoms and one with five. These rings are linked together to form a basic structure, common to all the steroids, to which various different chemical groups are attached to form the different types. The steroids include the major bile salt glycocholate, progesterone, cortisone, aldosterone, testosterone, various oestrogens and numerous synthetic steroid drugs based on the four-carbon atom rings.

SATURATED AND UNSATURATED FATS

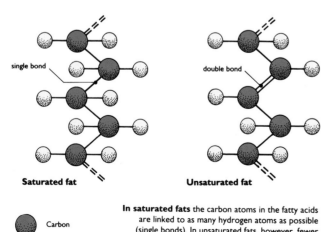

single bond

double bond

Saturated fat

Unsaturated fat

● Carbon

○ Hydrogen

In saturated fats the carbon atoms in the fatty acids are linked to as many hydrogen atoms as possible (single bonds). In unsaturated fats, however, fewer hydrogen atoms are linked to carbon atoms so an extra bond occurs between some of the carbon atoms (double bonds).

STEROID-RING STRUCTURE

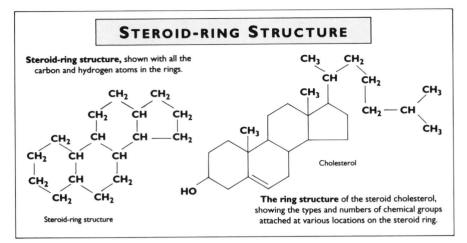

Steroid-ring structure, shown with all the carbon and hydrogen atoms in the rings.

Steroid-ring structure

Cholesterol

The ring structure of the steroid cholesterol, showing the types and numbers of chemical groups attached at various locations on the steroid ring.

Enzymes

From the earliest times it has been known that the bloom on grapes could turn grape juice into wine, and that yeasts could produce a 'ferment' of bubbling activity in a solution of sugar. In 1876, the German physiologist Willy Kuhne (1837–1900) suggested that the active principle causing these effects, previously known as 'ferments', should be given the name 'enzymes', the Greek term for 'in yeast'. The nature of enzymes was unknown, but they were believed to be a part of living things, rather than chemical substances. Early in the 20th century, the German chemist Richard Willstatter (1872–1942) declared, on what seemed good evidence, that enzymes were not proteins. Meanwhile the German chemist Leonor Michaelis (1875–1949) had made some important advances in this area (⇨ box).

In 1926, the American biochemist James Sumner (1877–1955) extracted an enzyme from jack beans that caused urea (the major end product of nitrogen excretion in mammals) to break down to ammonia and carbon dioxide. His extract contained some tiny crystals and, on dissolving these and testing the solution for activity from this enzyme, which he called *urease*, Sumner found that it acted powerfully on urea, and, after repeated attempts, found that he was unable to separate the urease activity from the crystals. In short, he had discovered that the crystals *were* the enzyme. Later, it was proven that all enzymes were proteins. Sumner was awarded the Nobel Prize for chemistry in 1946.

Enzymes act as organic *catalysts* (substances that increase the rate of chemical reactions, often by many hundreds or thousands of times, without themselves being permanently changed). A small quantity of an enzyme can cause a change in a large quantity of another substance; typically, a single molecule of an enzyme may lead to the breakdown of 100,000 molecules of a substance in one second. Enzymes do not bring about reactions that would not occur in their absence, but, in most cases, the reaction would be so slow without the enzyme that it would be of little value..

In order to function, an enzyme must come into contact with the substance to be acted upon (the *substrate*). This contact must be intimate and is, in fact, that of the fixation of a *ligand* (a surface molecule that links cells together in specific ways) to a protein-binding site (⇨ p. 182). The enzyme thus has a specific binding site, known as its *active site*, and the three-dimensional shape of this site is complementary to the shape of the substrate. The combination of the enzyme and the substrate forms an enzyme–substrate complex, and this then breaks down to release the products of the reaction and the unaltered enzyme.

Many enzymes will operate only in the presence of a particular additional substance, known as a *cofactor*. These may operate by binding to regulatory sites on the enzyme molecule, thus altering the shape of the functional site (⇨ p. 182) so that the enzyme and the substrate can bind together. Cofactors operating in this way may be no more than a trace of a metal such as zinc, copper, iron or magnesium. Alternatively, cofactors may be nonprotein, organic molecules, and, in this case, they bind to the functional site and are temporarily changed in such a way that they, in turn, can alter the definitive substrate. In so doing, they are converted back to their original form so that they can be used again. The change in the cofactor involves merely the addition or subtraction of a few atoms. The same change is then effected in the substrate. Cofactors of this kind are known as *coenzymes*, and they are derived from B vitamins such as riboflavin, niacin or folic acid. There are thousands of enzymes in the human body, mediating almost all the body's chemical reactions. A large amount of the genetic coding in DNA (⇨ p. 202) is coding for enzymes, and defects in this lead to the absence or malfunction of important enzymes. Many diseases arise from this.

It is easy to recognize the presence of enzymes in chemical terminology, as their names almost all have the ending -ase. This suffix may be added to the name of the substance they catalyse, as in amylase or lactase; or it may be added to the type of reaction that the enzyme catalyses, as in oxidase or reductase.

LEONOR MICHAELIS AND THE FUNCTION OF ENZYMES

The German chemist Leonor Michaelis (1875–1949) graduated as a doctor in Berlin in 1896, but was deflected from medicine to biochemistry after working with another chemist, Paul Ehrlich (1854–1915), on the development of stains for the microscopic examination of tissue. He rose to become Professor of Biochemistry at Berlin University, but in 1926 moved to the USA.

At the turn of the century, enzymes remained a mystery. No one knew what they were, and there was a general idea that they were inseparably associated with living things (⇨ main text). Michaelis decided to ignore this seemingly fundamental difficulty and see whether he could discover more about the actual function of enzymes. In 1913, he made the important discovery that the speed of a chemical reaction promoted by an enzyme was proportional to the concentration of the substrate (the substance on which the enzyme acts). This variation in rate was subsequently described by an equation, the Michaelis–Menten equation, which he formulated with his assistant. In determining this equation, Michaelis made a suggestion that turned out to be even more crucial – the proposition that enzyme action involved a temporary junction between the enzyme and the substance. Michaelis had no hard evidence for this, but it later proved to be fundamental to the whole theory of enzyme action. The Michaelis–Menten equation made it clear that enzymes should no longer be regarded as mysterious entities connected with the 'life force', but should be treated in the same way as other chemical substances.

ENZYMES AND INHIBITORS

Enzymic action can be blocked in two ways. A competitive inhibitor (a substance very similar to the substrate) will block the possibility of enzyme and substrate combining.

Active site

Substrate

Competitive inhibitor

Enzyme

A non-competitive inhibitor, which may be quite different from the substrate, will distort the active site by acting elsewhere on the enzyme.

Non-competitive inhibitor

Substrate

Active site

Active site distorted

Enzyme

The American biochemist James Sumner (right), shown here with leading geneticist Hermann Muller, received the Nobel Prize for chemistry in 1946 for his discovery that enzymes can be crystallized. (AP)

The Cellular Basis of Life

The most obvious structural difference between living and non-living matter is that the former is always organized into usually tiny circumscribed units known as cells. Life may exist in the form of single independent cells or as small or very large collections of cells joined together, but all life, whether plant or animal, is cellular in nature. Cells vary in size from a thousandth of a millimetre (in the case of a streptococcus) to nearly 20 cm (in the case of an ostrich egg), but all share similar characteristics and properties.

The first indications of the cellular basis of life arose as a result of the observations, in 1665, of the English scientist Robert Hooke (⇨ box). Nearly 200 years were to pass, however, before the matter was taken further.

The cell theory of living things

In 1838, the German botanist Matthias Jakob Schleiden (1804–81), having painstakingly examined hundreds of plant specimens under the microscope, concluded that all plants were of cellular structure.

Schleiden's ideas were generalized, in 1839, by the German biologist Theodor Schwann (1810–82), who is now generally acknowledged as that originator of the cell theory of life. Schwann examined both plant and animal specimens and realized that the units he had observed in animal tissues were the animal equivalent of the well-recognized plant cells. In his book *Researches on the Similarity in the Structure and the Growth of Animals and Plants* (1847) Schwann described the microscopic appearances of a wide range of tissues and came to the correct and important conclusion that the whole of every plant or animal is composed of cells or cell products and that cells are living structures subordinate to the life of the whole organism.

Schwann also recognized that eggs were single cells, greatly expanded by the bulk of the yolk. In 1858 the German physician and pathologist Rudolf Ludwig Virchow (1821–1902) proposed that no living cell could arise except from a pre-existing cell. Schwann's theory was widely taken up and the doctrine of spontaneous generation of living things (⇨ p. 180) was eventually abandoned. His cell theory of life was an advance in biology equal to that of the atomic theory in chemistry, and, like the latter, it promoted a huge extension of research and knowledge. With advances in scientific technology cellular studies have probed ever deeper into the nature of the cell and of life itself. Today, entire disciplines are based on the study, at a molecular level, of what happens in cells.

The gross structure of cells

Cells consist of a very thin outer membrane enclosing a fluid substance called the cytoplasm that contains a number of internal structures, known as organelles (⇨ p. 188). The most obvious feature of the majority of cells, although not all, is the nucleus (from the Latin *nux,* 'a nut'). The cells of most organisms – from amoebae to humans – have nuclei and are called *eukaryotic* cells (simply meaning 'having a good nucleus'). Cells without nuclei, such as the bacteria or the blue-green algae, are called *prokaryotic*. The nucleus of an eukaryotic cell is bounded by a nuclear membrane containing pores, which encloses the mass of DNA genetic chromosomal material (⇨ p. 202). In a prokaryotic cell, there is no defined nucleus and the genetic material is usually a simple ring of DNA lying free in the cell. Prokaryotic cells are much simpler than eukaryotic cells and require less DNA. The chromosomal material in the cell of a multicellular organism is not limited to the DNA required by that particular cell. Every cell contains the entire DNA sequence for the whole organism, but only those parts needed by the cell to perform its own particular functions are 'switched on'.

The cell membrane

Cell membranes, and the membranes that surround the cell nuclei and organelles, are remarkable, consisting of two layers of phospholipid molecules (⇨ p. 184). Each phospholipid molecule has an electrically charged head, which is attracted by water (*hydrophilic*), and two fatty acid tails that are repelled by water (*hydrophobic*). Because both the interior

CELL MEMBRANE

A cell membrane shown in diagramatic cross-section. A membrane is a highly dynamic structure composed of two layers of phospholipids arranged with their hydrophobic (water-hating) 'tails' inwards and their hydrophilic (water-loving) 'heads' facing outwards. Protein molecules are interposed in lipid layers, some being in either the outer or inner lipid layer whilst others traverse the whole membrane. These molecules are mobile and can be moved within the membrane. Carbohydrate molecules are attached to the outer surface of the membrane and are involved with molecular recognition. This total structure is called a unit membrane and is essentially typical in its general form for all membranes in living organisms.

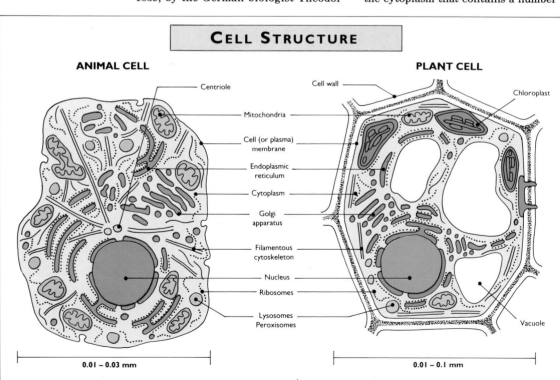

CELL STRUCTURE

These diagrams of thin sections of generalized animal and plant cells show the many similarities of structure between the two basic types of eukaryote cell. Blue links the components of the *endomembrane system* (i.e. the principal linked membrane apart from the outer cell membrane), comprising the nuclear envelope, endoplasmic reticulum, Golgi apparatus, and transport and secretory vesicles.

ROBERT HOOKE

The English scientist Robert Hooke (1635–1703) was without doubt one of the most brilliant and versatile scientific thinkers of his time, and was outshone only by his great contemporary Sir Isaac Newton (⇨ p. 10). He was one of the founders of the Royal Society, and rose to be its Curator and Secretary. His research was extensive and highly successful, but Hooke was also mean-minded, jealous and quarrelsome, and his scientific reputation suffered greatly in his lifetime because of the many controversies in which he became engaged over his claims of priority for discoveries and inventions. He argued with the Dutch physicist Christiaan Huygens (1629–95) over the spring regulator for watches and, in particular, with Newton over various optical questions and over the inverse square law of gravitation (⇨ p. 30). Indeed, there is good reason to believe that Hooke's enmity may have been a major precipitating factor in Newton's psychiatric breakdown.

Hooke was interested in everything scientific and was a genius in the design of scientific instruments. When Dutchman Anton van Leeuwenhoek (1632–1723) reported his invention of the microscope to the Royal Society, Hooke immediately took up microscopy and soon produced a brilliant book, *Micrographia* (1665), containing a series of magnificent drawings of his microscopic observations. Among these were drawings showing the pattern of rows of tiny rectangular spaces in cork. Hooke called these spaces 'cells', although what he was describing was actually the empty residual structure of dead cells. 'These pores, or cells,' he wrote, 'were not very deep, but consisted of a great many little Boxes, separated out of one continuous long pore, by certain Diaphragms.' This was the first ever indication that living matter might be organized on a cellular basis.

of cells and the surrounding environment are watery, the two molecule layers in the cell membrane are aligned with the tails turned towards the interior of the membrane and the heads turned outwards (⇨ illustration). Thus the outside of the membrane attracts water and the inside of the membrane repels water. Between the phospholipids are many cholesterol molecules, similarly aligned. Fat-soluble molecules can dissolve in the fatty – lipid – material of the membrane and pass through. Many of these larger fat-soluble molecules cross the membrane by a process of active transport that involves the consumption of energy.

Membrane ion channels

Certain important ionic substances – electrically-charged atoms – that are needed by the cell cannot pass through the fatty membrane in the same way as fat-soluble molecules. However, the membrane is also penetrated by large protein molecules that create entry and exit pores to allow charged atoms or ions to pass through. These protein molecules have binding sites for specific ionic substances, and when these substances lock on to the binding sites the proteins change into a variety of shapes. Some are capable of forming tube-like structures that can open and close. These protein reactor sites, as they are known, open or close under the influence of hormones or neurotransmitters.

Ionic substances such as sodium, potassium, calcium and chloride are able to pass, in a controlled manner, into or out of the cells through the protein pores and alter the functioning of the cell concerned. Cell membranes have different channels for different ions – such as sodium channels, potassium channels and calcium channels. In the case of nerve cells, for instance, the arrival of an appropriate neurotransmitting substance from another cell can open pores, allow sodium to enter the cell and potassium to leave, and initiate an electrical change that passes along the nerve cell fibre. This is what is known as a nerve impulse, and this can, in turn, provoke the release of neurotransmitter substances at the nerve ending so that the process is repeated in another nerve cell or causes a muscle cell to contract or a gland cell to secrete.

In modern medicine many powerful drugs are designed to mimic the action of the natural substances that bind to the cell membrane through the protein receptor sites, and so affect the function of cells. Membrane proteins on muscle cells have binding sites for acetylcholine, a natural neurotransmitter. The arrival of an acetylcholine molecule causes the protein pores to open, ions to flow in, electrical charges to change and the cells to contract.

The Amazonian arrow poison curare happens to be structurally very close to acetylcholine, and binds to the acetylcholine site even more firmly, preventing the pore from working. When curare enters human cells the natural acetylcholine is unable to open the pores and the affected person is paralysed. Anaesthetists make good use of this reaction to keep semi-conscious patients immobilized during surgery, for half an hour at a time. Calcium-channel blocker drugs such as Verapamil and Nifedipine prevent the movement of calcium ions into the smooth muscle cells in the walls of arteries, thus forcing the muscles to relax completely and the blood vessels to widen. This can be useful in conditions caused by narrowed arteries, such as angina pectoris. Active transport is also mediated by carrier proteins in the cell membrane. These can change shape so as to be open either to the exterior or to the interior of the cell. When open externally, a binding site may be exposed to the exterior so that substances can become attached. The carrier protein can then move a little inwards and open internally to release the substance into the cell.

Semi-permeable membranes and osmotic pressure

Water molecules are small enough to pass through the membranes of cells with ease. However, because water can pass readily through a cell membrane but other, larger, molecules do so with greater difficulty and to varying degrees, important effects occur if the amount of dissolved substances – the concentration – differs in the solutions on the two sides of a membrane.

In a process known as *osmosis,* molecules of water will move from a less concentrated solution to a more concentrated solution through a semi-permeable membrane (⇨ illustration). In this way, there is a tendency for the concentrations of dissolved substances to equalize. The force needed to prevent equalization is called the *osmotic pressure.*

The effect of osmosis can be serious. If, for instance, normal healthy red blood cells are placed in pure water, they will quickly swell up and burst so that they are destroyed. This is because water will flow across the blood cell membrane in the direction of the greater concentration of dissolved substances, in this case into the cell. For this reason, pure water is never used for transfusion to make up fluid loss in the blood. If water is needed, it must have something, such as salt, dissolved in it in order to make it concentrated enough to prevent osmotic flow. A solution with the same concentration of dissolved substance as that of the blood or body fluids is said to be *isotonic.*

SEE ALSO
● CHEMICAL REACTIONS p. 168
● BIOCHEMISTRY pp. 182–5
● CELLULAR STRUCTURE AND FUNCTION p. 188
● SIMPLE ORGANISMS p. 190
● MULTICELLULAR ORGANISMS pp. 192–5

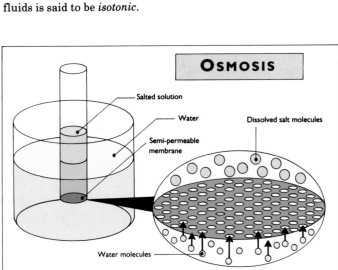

OSMOSIS

Salted solution

Water

Dissolved salt molecules

Semi-permeable membrane

Water molecules

In osmosis water (or another solvent) will move from a solution of low concentration to a solution of high concentration through a semi-permeable membrane. Because the water molecules are so small they can move through the membrane with ease. However, the larger molecules, like dissolved salt, which make a liquid concentrated, cannot move through the membrane. Thus the water will diffuse into the more concentrated solution.

Cellular Structure and Function

Until well into the 20th century, only the larger structures of the interior of the cell – such as the nucleus and the chromosomes – were known to scientists, since the details of the tiny cell organs (*organelles*) were far too small to be visible through ordinary light microscopes. Not until the invention of the electron microscope in 1939 was it possible to see enough of their structure even to begin to guess at what they were for.

The invention of the electron microscope by the Russian-born American physicist Vladimir Kosma Zworykin (1889–1982) marked a turning point in the evolution of the understanding of cell function. Zworykin, who had already developed the first practical television camera and receiver system, based on the cathode-ray tube (▷ p. 162), was aware that cathode rays (streams of electrons) had a wavelength far shorter than that of visible light. Therefore, he reasoned, if electron beams were used instead of light, it would be possible to resolve details that were much smaller than the wavelength of visible light. Working on this principle, and applying his knowledge of the cathode-ray tube, he developed an instrument capable of a magnification 50 times greater than that of the best light microscopes. This immediately opened up a whole new world to biological scientists and helped to found the new discipline of molecular biology. The development of the electron microscope enabled researchers, especially the Romanian-born American physiologist George Emil Palade (1912–), to begin to study the interior of cells in detail. These studies quickly revealed all the most important structures within the cell and, by 1956, most of their functions were known. Modern instruments are capable of a magnification allowing examination of features no more than one or two nanometres (millionths of a millimetre) across, so that large molecules can be made visible. Special recent microscopic techniques have even allowed visualization of arrays of individual atoms.

Cell organelles

The most striking internal feature of a eukaryote cell (▷ p. 21) is the *nucleus*, which is readily visible on light microscopy, especially if stained. Surrounding the nucleus is the fluid medium in which the small organelles are situated. This is called the *cytoplasm*, and is a translucent, colourless, colloidal material, rich in glucose, glycogen, amino acids, proteins, a large number of different enzymes, fatty droplets and other materials.

The nucleus contains the cell's genetic material, and is surrounded by a double membrane. At various points, the two membranes join around a pore that allows communication between the nucleus and the rest of the cell. Molecules pass outwards, through these nuclear pores, to carry genetic information to the cell, and other molecules pass in to regulate the expression of the genes. Within the nucleus is a dense body of tightly coiled material known as the *nucleolus*. This is just visible on light microscopy, and has long been recognized, but its function was unknown until recently. It consists of a mass of DNA, RNA (▷ p. 11) and proteins, and it is busily engaged in synthesizing the subunits from which the *ribosomes* (▷ below) are put together. These subunits pass out through the nuclear pores and settle in the cytoplasm.

The other organelles are the *endoplasmic reticulum* and its associated ribosomes, free ribosomes, the *Golgi apparatus*, the *mitochondria*, and the *lysosomes* and *peroxisomes* (▷ below).

The endoplasmic reticulum and the ribosomes

The most conspicuous of the small organelles is a folded system of thin, flattened sacs or tubules known as the endoplasmic reticulum. The term 'reticulum' simply means 'a network', and, although this is how the membrane often appears in a thin microscope section, the term is not particularly apposite. There are two kinds of reticulum – rough and smooth. The rough, or granular, reticulum is studded with thousands of tiny bodies, the ribosomes. The smooth reticulum, however, is free from ribosomes, and is of a branched, tubular structure, much less flattened and sac-like than the rough reticulum. In addition to the ribosomes attached to the rough reticulum, there are many free in the cytoplasm. These are tiny granules, just over 20 nm (nanometres) in diameter, and are the site of protein synthesis. Each one is made of many proteins and a few molecules of RNA. Proteins formed on free ribosomes are released into the cytoplasm; those formed on reticulum-

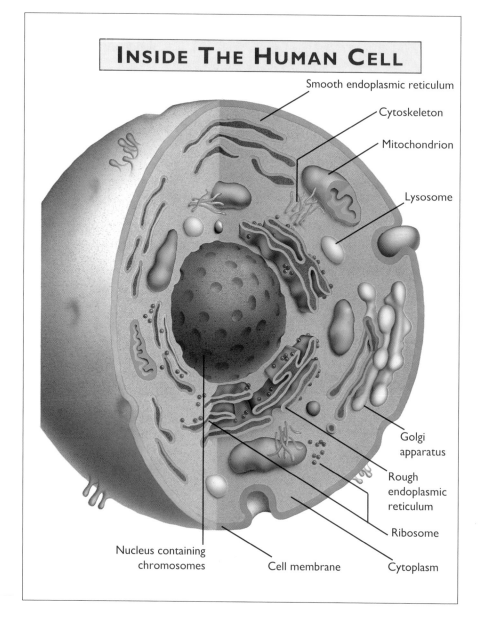

INSIDE THE HUMAN CELL

Smooth endoplasmic reticulum

Cytoskeleton

Mitochondrion

Lysosome

Golgi apparatus

Rough endoplasmic reticulum

Ribosome

Cytoplasm

Cell membrane

Nucleus containing chromosomes

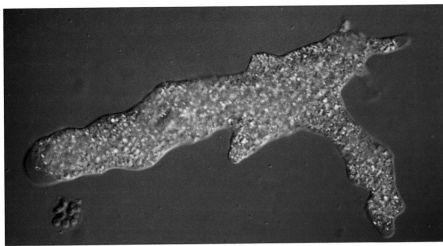

An **amoeba** about to ingest another microscopic organism (green oval, above left). Amoeba are unicellular organisms belonging to the group *Protozoa*. (Michael Abbey, SPL)

SEE ALSO
● THE NATURE AND ORIGINS OF LIFE p. 112
● BIOCHEMISTRY pp. 114–17
● THE CELLULAR BASIS OF LIFE p. 118
● SIMPLE ORGANISMS p. 122
● MULTICELLULAR ORGANISMS pp. 124–7

bound ribosomes are released into the interior of the reticulum sac.

Lengths of messenger RNA are transcribed from DNA in the nucleus and pass out through the nuclear pores to reach the ribosomes. There they activate the ribosomes, and provide them with details of the amino acids needed, and the order in which they must be assembled, in the polypeptide chain (▷ p. 15). The necessary amino acids are always available in the cytoplasm, and these are selected and linked together in the right order by peptide bonds. In this process, the ribosome actually moves along the strand of messenger RNA, which can be reused for the synthesis of a large number of identical protein molecules. These new proteins may be needed either by the cell itself or may be required outside it. The movement of these proteins to the appropriate part of the cell, or to the exterior, is the function of the Golgi apparatus.

The Golgi apparatus

Camillo Golgi (1844–1926), an Italian researcher interested in the microscopic appearance of human tissues, was a pioneer in the investigation of the fine structure of the nervous system. He developed certain important staining methods that revealed an unexpected richness of connection between nerve cells, and, in the course of this work, described, in 1898, a peculiar formation in the cytoplasm of cells, whose function was entirely unknown. This formation was then named the *Golgi apparatus*.

Most cells have only a single Golgi apparatus, but some have several. The apparatus is usually situated close to the nucleus and consists of a series of greatly flattened membranous sacs, invariably slightly curved so as to form a shallow cup-like body. Placed usually in the concavity of the cup is a collection of tiny, roughly spherical, membrane-enclosed sacs known as the *Golgi vesicles*. Within minutes of being formed by the ribosomes on the rough endoplasmic reticulum, proteins are moved to the Golgi apparatus. The way this is done is not yet certain, but it is believed that the proteins are carried in small, spherical vesicles that

bud off the reticulum, move to the Golgi sacs and fuse with them. The Golgi apparatus then sorts out the proteins according to their destinations, forms its own vesicles, which enclose the proteins, and bud these vesicles off into the cytoplasm.

Because of the role they play in sorting and directing proteins, Golgi vesicles are often referred to as the 'traffic police' of the cell. They secrete enzymes that add a chemical 'tag' to proteins so that they will settle only at the proper site in the cell. Some of these enzymes also cut proteins down to their final required form by dividing them into two or three parts. This happens, for instance, in the case of the proinsulin molecule, which is reduced to insulin.

Mitochondria

Mitochondria, rod-shaped or spherical bodies, exist in all cells, but those cells that consume a great deal of energy may contain many hundreds, scattered throughout the cytoplasm. Each mitochondrion has an outer and an inner membrane, the inner of which is heavily folded into sheets or tubules that extend right into its centre.

The function of the mitochondria is to provide energy to the cells, a task they perform by means of a complex chemical process known as the *Krebs cycle*, which runs on enzymes present in the mitochondria. This cycle forms a molecule known as *adenosine triphosphate* (ATP) from which energy can readily be derived, and is fuelled by small molecule fragments, each consisting of two carbon atoms, an oxygen atom and three hydrogen atoms ($CH_3CO–$), known as an acetyl group. These fragments are derived from the breakdown of carbohydrates, fats or proteins. ATP is readily broken down by water (*hydrolysis*) to *adenosine diphosphate* (ADP), and, in so doing, releases a large amount of energy where it is needed for the production of force or movement, as in muscle-cell contraction, for active transport of material across cell membranes, or for the synthesis of organic molecules. The ADP is then reconverted to ATP by the Krebs cycle.

Lysosomes and peroxisomes

The average cell contains several hundred tiny spherical or oval bodies, the lysosomes, surrounded by a single membrane. These are the cell scavengers whose function is to clean up any cell debris, such as damaged or malfunctioning cell organelles, and to take up and try to destroy any bacteria that may have found their way into the cell. To perform this function, lysosomes are provided with powerful digestive enzymes that can break down protein and other molecules. Lysosomes are especially prevalent in those cells of the immune system – the *phagocytes* – responsible for cleaning-up operations throughout the body.

Peroxisomes are very similar in structure to lysosomes but their function is different. They are responsible for the destruction of the damaging products of the action of oxygen free radicals. These radicals, produced in various disease processes and by poisons, radiation and smoking, are very damaging to body cells as they can promote destructive chain reactions.

The cytoskeleton

The cytoplasm of the cell is traversed by numerous delicate microfilamentous fibres and tubules. These form a kind of scaffolding known as the *cytoskeleton*, which helps to maintain the shape of the cell. Since they are made of contractile protein, as in muscle fibres, and are attached to the cell membrane, these structures also allow cells to change shape or even, in the case of some amoeboid free cells, to move about. Cytoskeleton fibres and microtubules also allow movement of some of the internal parts of the cell, such as the movement of organelles or of chromosomes in the process of cell division (▷ p. 18). Some cells have a surface covered with fine hair-like structures that can move, like wind-blown corn, so as to propel external material. These structures are called *cilia*, and each has a core of microtubules that confer the power of movement.

Lichens are composite organisms formed by the symbiosis of a fungus and an alga. The body of the lichen is made up of algal cells distributed among a greater of lesser number of fungal cells, according to type. For mutual benefit, algal cells form carbohydates and vitamins, while fungi absorb water vapour and provide shade for the light-sensitive algae.
(Dr Jeremy Burgess, SPL)

Simple Organisms

Many of the properties and functions of cells are well illustrated by the simplest of living organisms – for example those consisting of a single cell. By far the most numerous of all organisms, single-celled creatures display a remarkable range of properties and characteristics. They play an essential role in the ecology of nature, and have a direct effect on human beings.

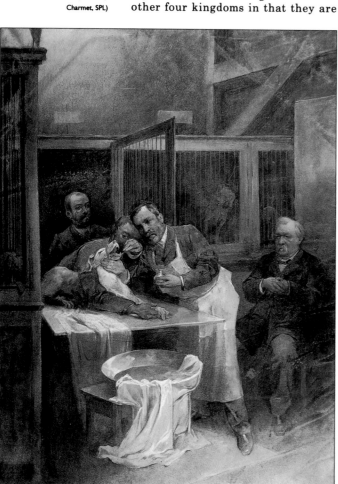

Louis Pasteur (1822–95) carrying out an immunology experiment. He demonstrated that diseases such as rabies and tuberculosis are caused by microorganisms. He, and others, showed that certain diseases were caused by certain bacteria, and between 1875 and 1906 over twenty fatal diseases were understood and made preventable through immunization. (Jean-Loup Charmet, SPL)

The group of simple – single-celled – organisms include bacteria and viruses. A study of fossils suggests that the earliest organisms – dating back some 3 billion years – were bacteria and blue-green algae. From these evolved organisms of ever-greater complexity, which are divided into the five kingdoms of living things – the Monera, Protoctista, Plantae, Fungi and Animalia. The organisms of the Monera kingdom, which include the great range of bacteria and the chlorophyll-containing blue-green algae, differ from the organisms of the other four kingdoms in that they are

VIRUS REPRODUCTION

① Virus

Cell

1 2 3

4 5

1   Virus approaches cell

2   Virus attaches to cell and injects its DNA into it

3   Cell is made to replicate virus's DNA

4   New viruses are formed inside cell

5   The cell bursts and the new viruses are spread out

Viruses, the most basic forms of life, simply consist of a protein coat protecting a strand of DNA. They can reproduce only reproduce inside the living cells of other organisms, and the cells may be destroyed in the process. This is why viruses may cause diseases.

made up from prokaryote cells that do not have nuclei. Such cells are distinguished from the *eukaryote* cells of higher organisms that do have nuclei.

Viruses

It is hard to know where to place viruses in the scheme of classification of living organisms as they are very much in the grey area of living and non-living things. Outside living cells viruses remain wholly inert. They cease being living organisms as they are incapable of any internal function (*metabolism*). Viruses are parasites and prey on every kind of organism, whether mammal, bird, reptile, fish, amphibian, insect, plant, alga, fungus, or even bacterium.

Viruses vary in size, from approximately half the diameter of the smallest bacterium (less than one thousandth of a millimetre) down to about the size of a very large molecule. They also vary considerably in shape. They consist of a core of DNA or RNA (⇨ pp. 202–3) surrounded by a protective coat of protein. In DNA viruses, the genetic material is carried in the usual double helix, but in RNA viruses the genetic material occurs in a single strand of nucleic acid. Before reproduction can occur, a complementary strand must be formed, and this is done by means of an enzyme called *transcriptase*, which is carried by the virus.

The protein *capsid* – the coat of a virus – may be in the form of a simple single layer, but this layer may be surrounded by one or two outer shells, the molecules of which are arranged symmetrically, either as a 20-sided solid or as a spiral tube. Most RNA viruses affecting humans have a spiral capsid. When viruses enter a cell, the protein coat is

partially removed so that the genome – set of genetic information – is exposed and replication can occur (⇨ illustration). Some of the genes of the virus are changed into messenger RNA (⇨ p. 202) which then uses ingredients in the cell to synthesize enzymes required for the replication of a new viral genome. Finally, before leaving the cell, each new virus acquires a capsid.

Special attention has been paid in recent years to the family of *retroviruses*, which includes the HIV (human immunodeficiency virus) that causes AIDS. Retroviruses are RNA viruses with genomes consisting of two copies of the single-strand RNA and containing an enzyme called *reverse transcriptase*. The enzyme helps to produce a complementary copy of the RNA so that replication can occur. This enzyme has been the subject of intense research, in the hope of finding a way to combat HIV.

Viruses can damage the body in various ways. They may shut down the normal biochemical processes of the cells they are parasitizing; damage the cell chromosomes so that their survival is impossible; or they may even convert normal cells to cancer cells. In some cases the massive replication of a virus within cells simply causes the cells to burst. However, the most serious way viruses can cause disease is by interfering with the immune system of the body, which is how the HIV acts. It interferes specifically with the body's helper T-lymphocyte cells that help to protect against viral infections. Without the helper cells the normal immune response to a wide range of infections is lost, leading to the AIDS-related complex, or the full acquired immune deficiency syndrome.

Bacteria

Bacteria are single-celled organisms of microscopic size that commonly grow in colonies containing so many millions of individuals that they are readily visible. They take a variety of shapes – spherical cocci, rod-shaped bacilli, spiral spirochaetes and spirilla and curved vibrios. The average coccus is about one thousandth of a millimetre in diameter, while bacilli may be as large as one hundredth of a millimetre long. A very small minority of bacteria contain chlorophyll, the green pigment that enables plants to synthesize sugar from atmospheric carbon dioxide and water (photosynthesis; ⇨ p. 192). But most bacteria must obtain their nourishment from the environment and are quite selective in their nutritional needs. Most have strong cell walls to protect them from drying up, and many can form thick-walled cysts which can survive for years in adverse conditions.

The great majority of bacteria are harmless to humans and thrive in soil at a much lower temperature than body temperature. Many of these soil bacteria are essential as sources of enzymes for the breakdown of organic matter – dead animals and plants – so that the elements of which they are made can be recycled. Without this action, life on Earth would be impossible. Bacteria that are *pathogenic,* harmful to humans, function and reproduce most efficiently at human body temperature. They damage by means of powerful poisons (*toxins*), which in some cases can be released and diffused into the body (*exotoxins*). In other cases, the toxins are fixed in the bacterial body and must come into direct contact with tissues to cause harm. Some bacterial toxins are amongst the most powerful poisons known. As little as $^1/_{100}$ mg of Botulinum toxin will kill an adult human. Pathogenic bacteria can cause a wide range of different infectious diseases, and, in the days before antibiotics, were by far the most common cause of death.

The Protoctista

The members of the Protoctista kingdom (formerly the Protista) are nearly all single-celled, only a few Protoctista being, to a rudimentary degree, multicellular. All the Protoctista have a well-defined nucleus surrounded by a membrane, and may come together to form colonies. The Protoctista that contain chlorophyll, and are capable of photosynthesis, are described as the 'plant-like' Protoctista and include the yellow-green algae, golden-brown algae, diatoms, euglenoids and dinoflagellates.

Some of the Protoctista without chlorophyll are similar in nature to fungi (⇨ p. 192), but others are free-swimming or actively moving single cells, some highly mobile. These were formerly considered to be simple animals. A major subdivision of the Protoctista kingdom is the group of phyla formerly called the *protozoa*. This group includes a number of free-swimming organisms such as the actively darting *Paramecium, Vorticella* and *Colpoda* species.

Many protozoa are responsible for diseases. Trypanosomes cause African sleeping sickness (trypanosomiasis); a range of Plasmodia cause the various forms of malaria; the actively burrowing amoeba *Entamoeba histolytica* causes amoebic dysentery; *Giardia lamblia*

gives rise to persistent diarrhoea; and *vaginalis* produces persistent vaginal inflammation and discharge. The parasite *Pneumocystis carinii* has come into prominence in recent years because it causes severe pneumonia in people with AIDS. The crescent-shaped protozoan *Toxoplasma gondii* produces toxoplasmosis, which may damage the eyes, the brain and other parts of the body. Similarly several Leishmania species cause kala azar and other forms of leishmaniasis.

Characteristics of single-celled organisms

Many single-celled organisms live a life of free mobility. Movement is achieved in one of several ways. Some organisms are equipped externally with large numbers of fine, hairlike structures, known as *cilia,* which act as oars or propellers when moved in an orderly way. These structures allow some protozoa to achieve rapid movement. The cilia contain protein microtubules capable of contracting, which cause the cilia to bend. The movement of the cilia is coordinated by a network of fine fibrils, like a primitive nervous system that connects them all. Alternatively, many single-celled organisms use a long, whiplike organ called a *flagellum* in a lashing action to provide propulsion. Organisms that move in this way are called *flagellates.*

Another common mode of movement is that known as *amoeboid movement.* Under the action of contractile protein microfilaments, cells can change shape in such a way as to appear to put out long protrusions, known as *pseudopodia,* literally 'false feet'. To achieve directional movement the amoeboid cell will put out a long pseudopodium in the desired direction, and the cytoplasm of the cell, with all its contents, will then simply flow into the pseudopodium. Amoeboid organisms commonly use pseudopodia to engulf material outside the cell. In this case, a kind of funnel pseudopodium is sent out to surround the material until it is entirely enclosed within the cell. This process, known as *endocytosis,* is a common way for amoeboid

organisms to acquire food. It is also the mechanism by which certain specialized cells of the immune system, the *phagocytes,* operate to clean up debris and microorganisms in large multicellular organisms such as human beings. When the material to be engulfed is liquid or in the form of very small particles, the process is called *pinocytosis.* After the material is engulfed it is first absorbed onto the cell membrane at particular binding sites (⇨ p. 186), where the membrane is then pulled into deep, narrow channels so that the material is drawn into the cell. The reverse process, by which unwanted material is ejected from the organism, is called *exocytosis.* This is mediated by the cell lysosomes (⇨ p. 188), which contain digesting enzymes.

Reproduction in single-celled organisms, such as the protozoa, may be sexual or asexual (⇨ p. 192). Like the Monera, many protozoa are capable of forming thick, resistant outer cases and becoming cysts, when conditions for survival are unfavourable.

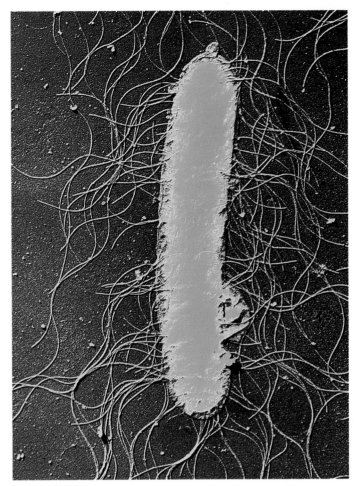

The bacterium *Proteus mirabilis* through a false-colour transmission electron micrograph. Normally harmless in the human intestine, the bacterium does have the potential to cause infections in the urinary tract. The hairlike structures – the flagella – on its surface are used to propel the organism. (A. B. Dowsett, SPL)

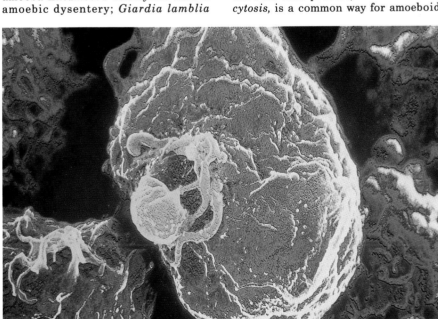

The Human Immunodeficiency virus (HIV) through a false-colour scanning electron micrograph. The AIDS-causing virus is the yellow material budding from the blue plasma membrane of an infected T-lymphocyte (T-cell), an important cell in the human immune system. The virus replicates itself many times over inside the T-cell and then buds away from its host, which is ultimately destroyed. The destruction of the immune system in this way leaves AIDS sufferers open to a number of potentially fatal secondary infections. (Bill Longcore, SPL)

SEE ALSO

● THE NATURE AND ORIGINS OF LIFE p. 180
● BIOCHEMISTRY pp. 182–5
● THE CELLULAR BASIS OF LIFE p. 186
● CELLULAR STRUCTURE AND FUNCTION p. 188
● MULTICELLULAR ORGANISMS pp. 192–5
● THE BIOSPHERE p. 206
● THE PLANET IN DANGER p. 208

Multicellular Organisms 1

In spite of their enormous diversity of appearance, the complex multicellular organisms have a great deal in common. This applies as much to all plants as to all animals. Both the plant and the animal kingdoms have their own particular patterns and common features.

In addition to the common features within their particular kingdoms, plants and animals also have much in common with each other. Both are chemical structures deriving necessary elements from the environment. Both are cellular in nature, and carry within the cell nuclei a DNA genetic code by which they are programmed ($\diamond$ p. 202). The same basic cellular functions are carried out by plants and animals in much the same way, and both are capable of reproduction. Both plants and animals are highly responsive to their environment, although green plants have certain features that distinguish them fundamentally from animals.

Plants

A number of characteristics are unique to plants. They are relatively fixed in one location, although they are able to grow rapidly and spread over wide areas. Their structure is based largely on carbohydrates – especially the polysaccharide cellulose ($\diamond$ p. 182) – with a lower content of protein; while that of animals is based largely on protein with a lower content of carbohydrate. Plant cells are, in essence, the same as animal cells and contain all the same organelles (cell organs; $\diamond$ p.

188), but plant cells have thick cellulose walls, whereas animal cells have exceptionally thin cell membranes, only two molecules thick. Plants synthesize their own nutritional substances and thus provide for themselves everything that is needed for their own growth. In contrast animals depend on plants for the first stages of production in the food chain and could not survive without them.

Photosynthesis

The green colouring material of plants is a pigment called *chlorophyll* contained in plant cell organelles known as *chloroplasts*. Most plant chlorophyll is in the leaves and is thus exposed to light. Chlorophyll reflects green light but powerfully absorbs the rest of the light spectrum – especially the reds and the blues. In this way, a great deal of energy is obtained and is used to break down water molecules into hydrogen and oxygen. Plant leaves are covered with microscopic pores called *stomata* (literally 'mouths'). Through these, the atmospheric gas carbon dioxide passes into the plants and oxygen passes out. The stomata also allow excess water to escape as water vapour and, when the plant is short of water, they close to conserve it. In general, the stomata are open in the light and closed in the dark.

All these structures of a plant are vital for *photosynthesis*. In this process energy derived from sunlight is used to power a series of chemical reactions in which very simple compounds – carbon dioxide from the air and water from the soil – are turned into sugars. These sugar molecules, in turn, are linked together in large numbers to form the polysaccharide starches ($\diamond$ p. 182) and cellulose, which makes up cell walls. All these are carbohydrates, containing only carbon, hydrogen and oxygen.

Some of the complicated chemistry of photosynthesis occurs in the light, some in the dark. In the course of the dark reactions carbon, oxygen and hydrogen are converted into the simple sugar glucose, and oxygen is released. The reactions can be simplified to the form:

$$6CO_2 + 6H_2O \rightarrow C_6H_{12}O_6 + 6O_2$$
Carbon + water $\rightarrow$ glucose + oxygen
dioxide

Nitrogen fixation

About 80 per cent of the atmosphere is nitrogen, but as an inert gas it does not readily participate in chemical reactions. Plants need nitrogen, which combines with the simple sugars (produced by photosynthesis) to make proteins. However plants are unable to 'fix' nitrogen (convert it into a usable form) in the way that they can fix carbon in photosynthesis. However, certain microorganisms such as the *Rhizobium* bacteria, found in the roots of leguminous plants including the groundnut and soyabean, *Azotobacter* species and the cyanobacteria (formerly known as the 'blue-green algae') are capable of combining nitrogen with

hydrogen to produce ammonia (NH_4). This, in turn, is oxidized by soil bacteria – in a process known as *nitrification* – to form compounds containing the nitrate group (NO_3). Nitrates are soluble and are readily taken up by plant roots. In this roundabout way, atmospheric nitrogen is made available to plants ($\diamond$ p. 206 for illustration).

In most higher plants, nitrates are converted to ammonia (NH_4) in the leaves, which then reacts with the carbon-containing glucose to form amino acids. These are the 'building-blocks' of proteins and must be present in the cells so that the genetic code in the DNA ($\diamond$ p. 202) – which specifies the sequence of amino acids – can be executed.

Plant distribution systems

In addition to nitrogen, plants require smaller quantities of various minerals and elements, such as sulphates (containing sulphur), iron compounds and magnesium. These, together with nitrates and water, are taken up into the plants, via the roots. Water, drawn up by the process of osmosis ($\diamond$ p. 186), carries with it the necessary soluble substances. It is distributed, as sap, by a transport system, known as the *xylem*, that extends to every part of the plant. In larger plants and trees, the xylem is reinforced by a strong polymer material ($\diamond$ p. 172) called *lignin,* which is the main constituent of wood.

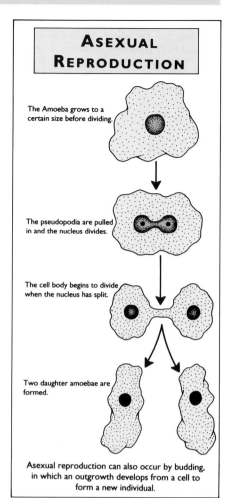

ASEXUAL REPRODUCTION

The Amoeba grows to a certain size before dividing.

The pseudopodia are pulled in and the nucleus divides.

The cell body begins to divide when the nucleus has split.

Two daughter amoebae are formed.

Asexual reproduction can also occur by budding, in which an outgrowth develops from a cell to form a new individual.

A closed stoma, or breathing pore, of a flower leaf through a false-colour scanning electron micrograph. The stoma (plural stomata) of a plant opens and closes to allow the exchange of gases between the atmosphere and the plant. Each stoma consists of two guard cells, which control the movement of the pore, which needs to close in darkness and to conserve water. When the guard cells are full of water the pore will open, when they are dry the pore closes. (Dr Jeremy Burgess, SPL)

The sugar and amino acids synthesized in plants are not carried by the xylem but by a secondary transport system, known as the *phloem*. In woody plants, the phloem lies under the bark. Sugar, mainly *sucrose* (cane sugar), and amino acids are transported, when necessary, to the growing zones of the plant so that they can be used to supply the needs of reproducing cells both for growth and for energy.

Fungi

The fungi are not plants but occupy a kingdom of their own. Because they do not have chlorophyll (and so are incapable of photosynthesis) they must derive their nourishment from their immediate environment. Many of them are parasites, growing on other living organisms – including animals as well as plants. Others are saprophytes, growing on the dead remains of organisms by secreting digestive enzymes (⊳ p. 184) into them and then absorbing the products of digestion through their roots. Some are both parasitic and saprophytic, living on the dead body of a former host. Not surprisingly many fungi have an important role in the decomposition of dead organic material.

Some fungi, such as the yeasts, consist of single cells, each with a single nucleus, but most consist of many nuclei arranged along a series of branched filaments, known as *hyphae*. These aggregate into a mass called a *mycelium*. In the hyphae, there are often no complete partitions between regions containing a nucleus, or there may be partitioned lengths containing several nuclei. Fungi reproduce asexually by simple division and by producing spores that can be widely dispersed. They also reproduce sexually by producing gametes (⊳ p. 194) that fuse to form zygotes (⊳ p. 194) that can germinate to form spores.

The head of a beef tapeworm through a false-colour scanning electron micrograph. The most common tapeworm parasite in humans, it can vary from 4 to 10 metres (13 to 33 feet) in length. Its larvae develop in the muscles of cattle, and humans are infected when they eat undercooked beef. (CNRI, SPL)

A chloroplast seen through a coloured transmission electron micrograph. It is the site of photosynthesis where carbohydrates are produced from a chemical reaction of sunlight, water and carbon dioxide. (Dr Jeremy Burgess, SPL)

While many fungi (such as rusts) are destructive or even dangerous, causing a number of diseases of animals and humans, many are beneficial. Apart from their role in helping the bacteria to prevent the accumulation of dead organic material, they have many important social and industrial applications. Many fungi are edible and are widely used in the food industry, especially in the manufacture of cheese. Yeasts are used to produce carbon dioxide to make bread rise before baking, and to provide the enzymes needed for the fermentation of carbohydrates to make alcoholic drinks. But perhaps most importantly fungi are vital to the production of antibiotics.

Metazoa

The *metazoa* is a sub-kingdom of the animal kingdom consisting of multicellular animals, other than the sponges, with two or more tissue layers and usually some form of nervous system and a gut cavity. The cells of the metazoa are differentiated into tissues with different functions – nervous, digestive, excretory and sexual. There is always considerable coordination and cooperative action between the different cells.

Many biologists have speculated on, and argued over, the origins of the metazoa. They are generally believed, however, to have arisen from a single-celled ancestor, probably ciliated (⊳ p. 190), that somehow formed a flattened, two-layered organism capable of creeping along surfaces and absorbing nutrients through the cells in contact with the surface. Such a creature, *Trichoplax adhaerens*, does, in fact, exist. Interestingly, *Trichoplax* often elevates and hollows out the central part of its body to form a kind of temporary digestive chamber. From this it is possible to guess how more complex animals may have evolved, among these, the flukes.

Flukes

The trematodes, or flukes, belong to the group of parasitic flatworms (characterized by a single opening to the gut). Most flukes are leaf-like but they all have digestive tracts. Some have complicated life cycles with alternating sexual and asexual development in different hosts. They have a non-cellular outer coat raised into spines or ridges over three layers of muscle, which change their shape and assist in locomotion. They have two suckers, one at the fore end, into which the digestive tract opens, and another further back, which the fluke uses to attach itself to its host. They have a simple excretory system ending in an excretory pore at the rear end. Most are *hermaphrodites* – possessing both male and female organs. Many species of flukes prey on humans and can live in

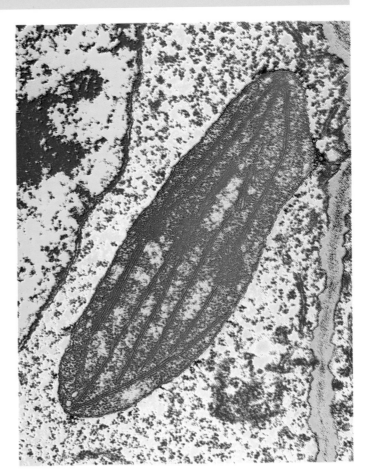

various parts of the human body, such as the liver, the digestive tract, and the excretory and biliary systems for 30 years or more. *Schistosoma* causes the serious disease of schistomiasis, and, unlike other flukes, has both male and female forms, the female being accommodated in a longitudinal fold in the male.

Tapeworms

Tapeworms are really colonies of up to 2,000 individual flatworms linked end to end. Each segment is called a *proglottid* and these bud out progressively from the tiny head, growing in size as they are pushed along by new proglottides. The head carries suckers – and sometimes hooks – by which it attaches itself firmly to the lining of the intestine of the host.

Each proglottid is essentially a reproductive body and contains a vagina, a uterus, an ovary, many testes and a sperm duct. Sperms from one proglottid enter and fertilize another, and the more mature proglottides become packed with over 100,000 fertilized eggs. There is no exit for the eggs, but the segments packed with fertilized eggs break off and are passed out with the stools. If an animal such as a pig, an ox or a dog eats the eggs the embryos hatch and settle as cysts in the muscle, making the animal an intermediate host in the life cycle of the tapeworm. If the animal meat is then eaten by a human, undercooked, the cysts hatch out in the intestine and the cycle continues. Tapeworms can live for up to 25 years and grow to a length of over 20 m (66 ft) inside the host's intestines.

SEE ALSO

- THE CELLULAR BASIS OF LIFE p. 186
- CELLULAR STRUCTURE AND FUNCTION p. 188
- SIMPLE ORGANISMS p. 190
- MULTICELLULAR ORGANISMS 2 p. 194
- EVOLUTION p. 196
- ADAPTATION: EVOLUTION IN ACTION p. 198
- HEREDITY p. 200
- DNA AND THE GENETIC CODE p. 202
- THE BIOSPHERE p. 206

Multicellular Organisms 2

The vast reach of the animal kingdom encompasses a bewildering variety of species, and as we move up the evolutionary scale these become ever more complex. Even the most superficial study of a range of animals shows the similarity of structure and the progressive increase in complexity. However, the more detailed our knowledge of the living world, the more apparent it becomes that there is an underlying order in nature.

The giraffe is the tallest land animal, mature males growing to a height of around 5.5 m (18 ft). Its long neck possesses no more than the usual seven vertebrae found in most mammals, but each is greatly elongated and articulates with a ball-and-socket joint, so allowing great flexibility.
(Planet Earth)

This order has been illustrated by the scientific classification of species into groups according to common characteristics – an activity known as *taxonomy*. There are many systems of classification, the best known being that of Carolus Linnaeus (⇨ box) in which living things are divided into successively smaller groups – kingdom, phylum, division, class, order, family, genus and species. The formal classification of organisms serves a wider purpose than convenience of identification; the clear pattern of similarity in the structure and function of

all multicellular animals testifies to a common origin and to an evolutionary pattern of development.

Worms

The Aschelminthes is a very large phylum of wormlike animals with no definite head. The phylum is divided into five classes, of which the most important is that of the nematodes (roundworms). The nematode population of the world enormously outnumbers the human population. There are many different species of nematodes, many of them parasitic on certain animals, including humans, and plants. They have a long cylindrical body and the majority taper to a point at both ends. Nematodes have a well-formed intestine running almost the full length of the body, with a mouth at one end and an anus at the other, unlike the blind-ended gut of the more simple organisms, the flukes (⇨ p. 192). There is an excretory canal and a primitive nervous system. There is no formal circulatory system, but the body cavity contains fluid. Just under the outer cuticle are layers of longitudinally-placed muscle cells, which contract to make locomotion possible. Female worms have a vagina, seminal receptacle, uterus and ovary. Daily egg production varies in number from 20 to 200,000. Male worms have a single coiled tube differentiated into testes, vas deferens, seminal vesicle and ejaculatory duct, that opens into the anus. The sperms are immature when passed into the female.

The nematodes of medical importance include intestinal roundworm parasites, such as *Ascaris lumbricoides*; hookworms; threadworms (pinworms); the muscle worm *Trichinella spiralis*; *Toxocara canis*; and a range of worms from the *Filariidae* family that cause such conditions as onchocerciasis (river blindness) and elephantiasis.

Molluscs

The molluscs – snails, slugs, clams, oysters, squid and octopus – run to some 50,000 living species and constitute the second largest phylum in the animal kingdom. Although molluscs may differ greatly in external appearance, their internal structure is basically similar. All of them have a soft body consisting of a well-developed muscular foot capable of differential movement to provide locomotion; an overlying mantle that, in many species, contains glands that secrete a shell; and a visceral mass that contains the internal organs, which are more developed than those of the worms. The digestive system shows early differentiation into a stomach and intestine. There is no closed circulation, but there is a heart which circulates blood between the aerating gills (respiratory organs) and the large open sinuses that bathe the tissues. The nervous system is also more advanced, and antennae and primitive eyes are common. The molluscs include various classes, such as the exclusively marine Amphineura, the

snails (Gastropoda), the bivalves (Pelycopoda), and the squid and octopus (Cephalopoda).

Arthropods

The term arthropod literally means 'jointed foot' and the phylum of arthropods is by far the largest of all the phyla. It is estimated that about 80 per cent of all animals belong to the arthropod phylum, which includes the huge class of insects (Insecta), the crustaceans (Crustacea), the centipedes (Chilopoda), and various subphyla containing such organisms as the horseshoe crab, spiders, ticks, mites, and scorpions. Classification of the arthropod is highly complex and is by no means settled.

Arthropods have a skeleton on the outside – an *exoskeleton* – made of a hard non-cellular substance called *chitin*. This is a polysaccharide (⇨ p. 82) secreted by the cells of the outer layer of the soft body (the *epidermis),* and protrusions from it extend well into the body of the animal. The exoskeleton serves both as a protective layer and as an anchorage for muscles. A striking developmental difference between the arthropoda and the molluscs is their muscular systems. In the arthropods, this is divided into separate muscles, with separate functions, running in various directions and capable of operating the limbs. There is no completely closed circulatory system, but the heart and the blood vessels are more fully developed, with arteries carrying blood to and from the open blood sinuses. The nervous system is also much more advanced than that of molluscs and many have elaborate sensory systems with highly developed compound eyes. A number of arthropods have well-developed hormonal (*endocrine*) systems of control to supplement the actions of the nervous system. The sexes are usually separate and the reproductive systems well differentiated to allow internal fertilization by copulation.

Insecta

The mandibulata is a subphylum within the arthropoda. These animals have antennae and a definite lower jaw in their mouthparts. This subphylum has six classes, of which one is the class of the Insecta. The insects include a large number of orders, many of which are designated by the characteristics of the insects' wings (the Greek root *-ptera* means 'a wing'). The most familiar of these, with examples and in some cases wing characteristics, are: Thysanura (silverfish, bristletails); Ephemerida (short-lived mayflies); Odonata (toothed; dragonflies); Orthoptera (straight-winged; crickets, grasshoppers, cockroaches, mantids); Isoptera (equal-winged; termites); Dermaptera (skin-winged; earwigs); Corrodentia (chewing book lice); Anoplura (sucking lice); Mallophaga (chewing lice); Hemiptera (half-winged; bugs); Homoptera (uniform-textured winged; cicadas, aphids, scale insects, leafhoppers); Coleoptera (sheath winged;

CAROLUS LINNAEUS AND THE CLASSIFICATION OF LIVING THINGS

The Swedish botanist Carolus Linnaeus (1707–78) was born Carl von Linné but is nearly always known by the Latin form of his name. His intense interest in plants began in childhood and continued even after he began to train as a doctor. Following his father's financial ruin, he moved to the University of Uppsala, where he began lecturing on botany. His lectures proved very popular and a class of 80 students was soon expanded to 400. In 1733, now renowned as a botanist and plant classifier, he was asked to investigate the flora of Lapland. Linnaeus agreed and recorded his findings on plant and animal life while he covered 7,402 km (4,600 miles). In the course of this journey Linnaeus discovered about 100 new species and, his appetite whetted, he extended his journeys of investigation to England and Western Europe.

However, financial constraints forced him to earn a living, and in 1735 he went to Holland to complete his medical education. While there he published the book *Systema Naturae*, in which he proposed a classification of plants on the basis of their sexual organs. In 1738 he returned to Sweden, where his medical practice flourished, and in 1741 he was appointed Professor of Medicine and Botany at Uppsala. There, his passion for biological classification was given full rein and in 1749 he produced the binomial (two-part) system of classification which is still in use today. In this system the first name refers to the genus – a group comprising all these species that showed obvious similarities with one another – and the second, an adjective, to the species. Thus, in the case of the 'deadly nightshade', *Atropa belladonna*, *Atropa* is the generic name and *belladonna* the specific name (always spelt with a lower-case initial). Those who followed Linnaeus extended and improved his binomial classification system so that the relationship between species, and the inevitability of an evolutionary basis, became evident. Ironically, Linnaeus emphatically rejected all ideas of evolution and insisted that no new species had ever arisen since the Creation.

Carl Linnaeus (SPL).

---

beetles, weevils); Hymenoptera (membrane winged; bees, wasps, ants, sawflies); Siphonaptera (sucking and wingless; fleas); Diptera (two-winged; flies, mosquitoes); Trichoptera (hairy-winged; caddis flies); and Lepidoptera (soft-winged; butterflies, moths).

Vertebrates

The phylum Chordata is the group characterized by a *notochord* – a longitudinal rod, lying along the back above the intestine. Present in embryos, it develops into the vertebral column in many species. A subphylum of the Chordata is that of the vertebrates (Vertebrata) – the animals with backbones. The subphylum includes the classes of bony and cartilaginous fishes, the amphibia, the reptiles, the birds, and the mammals. Vertebrates have an internal skeleton (*endoskeleton*) consisting essentially of a segmented backbone comprising of a series of vertebrae. Associated with the backbone is a long nerve trunk, often with a prominent swelling at the front end – the brain. All vertebrate brains have features in common although they vary greatly in their degree of development from one species to another. However, the vertebrate brain is almost always in three discernible parts – the forebrain, midbrain and hindbrain. Protruding forward from the brain is a prominent olfactory bulb, subserving smell, and optic nerves connecting to the eyes.

Ribs are commonly attached to the vertebrae to form a protective cage for the respiratory system and heart. In the higher vertebrates, bony girdles are also attached to allow the movement of limb bones. All vertebrates have a closed circulatory system with a heart, arteries, veins and capillaries. The digestive system is well differentiated into mouth (equipped with teeth), gullet (oesophagus), stomach and intestines. Associated with the intestines is a liver capable of storing food material and of performing many important biochemical processes. Vertebrates have well-developed kidneys that abstract waste products from the blood and excrete them in solution in urine. The reproductive systems are separate in the two sexes.

Mammals

The class Mammalia, of the subphylum Vertebrata, comprises warm-blooded, hair-bearing animals characterized by much larger brains than those of reptiles. Mammals are able to learn from experience and modify their behaviour in a manner that improves their chances of survival. They have four-chambered hearts, with a circulation that carries blood alternately to the lungs and to the body tissues, and a diaphragm to assist respiration.

The lower jaw (*mandible*) consists of a single bone, and the teeth are shaped so as to serve different purposes, such as cutting, tearing and grinding. A unique feature of mammals is the possession of three sound-conducting bones in the middle ear. With two minor exceptions (the duck-billed platypus and the spiny anteater) mammals do not lay eggs and, after internal fertilization, the embryo develops to a stage of comparative independence within the mother's womb. After birth the offspring are fed initially with milk secreted by the mother's mammary glands. The mammals include dogs, cats, hyenas, raccoons, seals, walruses, bears, sheep, goats, pigs, cattle, antelope, camels, horses, zebras, rhinoceroses, tapirs, elephants, whales, dolphins, porpoises, rats, lions, mice, squirrels, rabbits, bats, moles, shrews, lemurs, monkeys, apes and humans.

Primates

The comparatively small mammalian order of primates includes the lower primates such as lemurs, lorises, pottos, galagos, tarsiers, marmosets, tamarins, and the higher primates such as Old and New World monkeys, apes and humans. Primates are distinguished from other mammals in a number of crucial ways. They have thumbs that can be bent across the palm so as to touch each of the other fingers, which provides a better grasp and ability to manipulate objects. They have fingernails rather than claws, and four central biting teeth (incisors) in both upper and lower jaws. They have well-developed eyes that are directed forward, and large brains, which gives them a great capacity for learning and adaptable behaviour. The large brain also allows complex social interactions to develop. Most primates live mainly in trees, and all produce a small number of young which are nurtured for a long time after birth. In terms of strict classification, man is also an ape.

SEXUAL REPRODUCTION

Most complex animals reproduce by the process of sexual reproduction. New individuals are not formed by simple division from a single parent, as in asexual reproduction (⇨ p. 192), but as a result of the fusion of two sex cells (*gametes*), each of which is derived from a different parent. The parents are usually sexually differentiated, with two different forms (male and female) each producing a particular type of gamete. The internal ducts that store and deliver the gametes differ between the sexes, and the areas surrounding the external openings of the tracts (the external *genitalia*) are often specialized to meet the needs of mating and fertilization.

The two sex cells that fuse to form the new individual are highly specialized. Eggs (*ova*) are produced by the female parent and sperm (*spermatozoa*) by the male. In multicellular animals, the gametes are produced by the gonads – the ovary of the female and the testes of the male. Within these organs, a special group of 'germ cells' divide (by meiosis; ⇨ p. 200) to produce the gametes; both eggs and sperm carry equal amounts of genetic information and are *haploid* – each has half the genetic complement of the parent. Fusion between the two gametes at fertilization produces a new, single-celled individual (the zygote), which is *diploid* (has a full genetic constitution).

Evolution

The doctrine of 'spontaneous generation' (⇨ p. 180), which held that each new species was produced, fully developed, by a separate act of creation, remained largely unquestioned so long as there were no awkward facts to challenge it. The Church had what seemed to be adequate answers to all questions on Creation. The Earth was made in the year 4004 BC and Adam and Eve were created along with a full complement of animal and plant life. Everything else followed satisfactorily. The emergence of irreconcilable facts, however, made this version of events doubtful.

By the middle of the 19th century the scientific community was faced with new evidence for the creation of the world and its animals. Carolus Linnaeus's classification of a variety of animals (⇨ p. 194) had emphasized the close similarities between species, but the similarities remained unexplained. Moreover, the expansion of knowledge of the history and structure of the Earth brought to light a number of facts that contradicted the church's view of Creation and cried out for an explanation.

The evidence of geology

As interest in the structure of the Earth developed and became formalized in the science of geology, three important facts emerged: the time-scale of geology was enormously greater than had previously been supposed and extended back for millions of years; stratified layers of rocks had been formed at different periods in the past; and the fossils found in these different layers were the remains, or the impressions, of organisms that had been living during these periods.

Fossils had, of course, been recognized for thousands of years. Aristotle thought they were failed or abortive attempts at spontaneous generation from mud. Leonardo da Vinci and other Renaissance thinkers, however, recognized them for what they were – the remains of once-living organisms. It was not always safe in those days to make too much of this obvious fact, which contradicted Church thinking. The most impressive fossil find was the record of definite sequences of organisms, living at successive periods, but showing general resemblances to their predecessors. The older the rocks in which they were found, the simpler and more primitive were the life forms. This suggested the probability that modern living things came from earlier life forms by a gradual process of change – by evolution.

Comparative anatomy

Anatomy is the study of body structure, and comparative anatomy is the study of the relationship between the body structure of different animals. Even an ele-

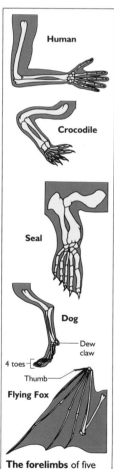

The forelimbs of five different animals, showing that the pentadactyl (five-digit) limb is common to them all. Such basically similar structures are described as *homologous*, and the existence of homologous structures in different organisms suggests they have all evolved from a common ancestor.

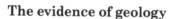

Charles Darwin spent over twenty years after his return from the Galapagos Islands putting together evidence for his theory of evolution. He was prompted to publicize his work in 1858 after he was unexpectedly sent a synopsis on evolution from Alfred Russel Wallace, who had reached the same conclusion. As a retiring man Darwin refused to defend his work publicly despite the considerable criticism and protest. It was Darwin's friend and great debator, T. H. Huxley, who became evolution's public champion. (AR)

mentary knowledge of comparative anatomy immediately illustrates the remarkable similarities between man and the other animals. People had been interested in this matter for centuries, but the first major attempt at a systematized comparative anatomy was that of the French aristocrat Georges Buffon (1707–88). Buffon spent 53 years compiling a monumental 44-volume work, *Natural History, General and Particular* (1749–1804), in which he presented to an appreciative public a great deal of information about the relationships between animal and other species.

A central element in comparative anatomy is the concept of *homology* – the relationship of body organs of different species that have the same evolutionary origin. In closely related species, corresponding structures are so similar as to leave no doubt as to their identity. But scientists such as Richard Owen (1804–92) showed clearly how even less obviously related structures in remote species such as the wings of a bird and the arms of a man, or the flipper of a seal and the hand of a man, also had common developmental and evolutionary origins (⇨ illustration). By the middle of the 19th century the idea of homology was becoming widely appreciated.

The evidence of fossils and homologous studies were pointing to one conclusion. Living things had not initially come into existence in their present form but had, somehow, developed from each other.

Charles Darwin and natural selection

Most scientists believe that the real breakthrough in the understanding of evolution was made by Charles Darwin (1809–82) and Alfred Russel Wallace (1823–1913). Both had essentially the same idea, but Darwin was the first to publicize his work. While on a voyage of scientific exploration in HMS *Beagle,* from 1831 to 1836, Darwin had visited the Galapagos Islands. There he had observed 14 species of finches, each occupying its own island. None of these species, which differed mainly in the shape and size of the bill, were known to exist anywhere else in the world.

Some of the finches were seed-eating, some insectivorous, and the beaks differed accordingly. Darwin knew that there was a single similar species of finch, a seed-eating bird, on the nearby mainland, and it occurred to him that this species might somehow have colonized the islands a very long time before and that its isolated descendants might have evolved into different forms in a series of environments in which they were not in competition with other birds.

Darwin returned to his theory on the finches in 1838 after he read *An Essay on the Principle of Population* by the English clergyman Thomas Robert Malthus (1766–1834). In his book, Malthus suggested that human populations invariably grew faster than the available food supply and that environmental factors such as starvation, disease or war were necessary to limit them. It occurred to Darwin that the first birds to occupy the Galapagos Islands would have multiplied unchecked until they outstripped the available seed supply. Many would have died, but those who happened to be able to adapt to a different diet such as insects – perhaps by a naturally occurring variation such as a differently shaped beak – could then flourish and multiply until, they, in turn, outstripped their food supply. Purely by chance, some variations might prove to be well adapted to the current environment and thus survive to breed, while others might prove poorly adaptive, and disappear. Over the course of millions of years this process, operating very slowly, could be seen, inevitably, to give rise to radical alterations in the characteristics of organisms that shared common ancestors in the past.

New species could evolve by the splitting of one species into two or more different species largely as a result of geographical isolation of populations. Such isolated populations would undergo different environmental pressures, experience different spontaneous changes (mutations; ⇨ p. 198) and could therefore evolve along different lines. If isolation were to prevent interbreeding with other stock derived from the same ancestors, these differences might become great enough to establish a new species that could not successfully interbreed except with its own kind.

This was the great idea of how changes in species occurred by 'natural selection' and Darwin saw that this principle alone was sufficient to explain the process of evolution. Darwin never understood how

inheritable changes occurred or how the necessary spontaneous variations in species (mutations) occurred, but this did not in the least detract from the power or persuasiveness of his theory. To most unbiased scientists of the time Darwin's idea was at once seen to be so persuasive as to be almost self-evident.

Darwin published his findings, *On the Origin of Species by Means of Natural Selection*, or the *Preservation of Favoured Races in the Struggle for Life*, in November 1859. The book brought him fame and, at the time, notoriety. The Church considered his work as a heretical doctrine, intended to limit God's place in Creation.

Criticisms of Darwinism

Darwin's theory, however, was not without scientific problems. Even those who supported his theory could not fathom the problem of sterility between different species. It is one of the definitions of a species that its members are incapable of breeding successfully with members of other species. If species occurred by the selection of small chance changes, why should not close species be able to interbreed? Today, our knowledge of advantages in genetics allows us to understand that different species have incompatible genes and often even different numbers of chromosomes. As a result, the accurate matching up of chromosomes (⬦ p. 202) from the father with those from the mother cannot occur. However, this was unknown at the time and posed difficulties for Darwin's theory.

Today, the main criticism of Darwin's theory is that evolution is not necessarily a steady, gradual process of change from one species to another as Darwin and his contemporaries believed. There is evidence that evolution occurs in sudden jumps. The fossil record suggests that new species appear to enter the record suddenly and to change little during their term of existence. Darwin believed this to be a false impression

Fossils of the extinct ammonites. Abundant around 225–65 million years ago, they died out around 65 million years ago, when the dinosaurs also disappeared. The fossil record consistently supports the theory of evolution by natural selection, and suggests that change might not necessarily have been gradual. The fossils suggest that some developments were in sudden leaps. (Martin Dohrn, SPL)

arising from insufficient data, but the difficulty is still far from being resolved.

In the Precambrian era (4,600 million years ago) only algae-like creatures and the simplest invertebrates are found. Suddenly, about 570 million years ago, in the Cambrian period, a profusion of groups of invertebrates are found. For a long time it has been supposed that the fossil record of such extreme antiquity was incomplete and that we were seeing only a small part of what occurred. Recently, however, it has been suggested that there may be a better explanation. Initially the atmosphere was almost devoid of oxygen and it was not until photosynthesizing organisms became widespread that oxygen was able to accumulate. Photosynthesis (⬦ p. 192) originated in single-celled organisms and these evolved into plants. It may be that this fundamental change occurred around the late Precambrian era, thereby allowing the explosive proliferation of oxygen-breathing animals.

1. Geospiza magnirostris
2. Geospiza fortis.
3. Geospiza parvula.
4. Certhidea olivacea.

Charles Darwin's drawing of the beaks of four species of finches found in the Galapagos Islands. Darwin realized that the finches probably came from a common ancestor, but had evolved to adapt to the food supply on the different islands. (Dr Jeremy Burgess, SPL)

Adaptation: Evolution in Action

Adaptation is the process of change to suit new conditions or needs. Most organisms are capable, as individuals, of a considerable degree of physical or mental adaptation to changing environments, but, because it does not affect the germ cell chromosomes (⇨ p. 200), such adaptation dies with the individual and has no effect on the long-term characteristics of the species. Acquired characteristics are not passed on to the next generation.

A male peacock displaying his plumage to attract a mate. His display, however, could also attract a predator. Although a less noticeable tailless peacock may live much longer, he would have no chance of mating and so the gene for taillessness would die out. The gene for magnificent plumage, on the other hand, would be continued as its carrier would usually find a mate. (Images)

Biological adaptation is a process in which there is a change in the inheritable characteristics of an organism that increases its chances of survival and that of its descendants. Modern thought suggests that the processes of evolution operate for the preservation of genes rather than individual organisms.

Mutations and the gene pool

Each of the physical characteristics of an organism is dictated by a gene (a section of DNA; ⇨ p. 202) or a collection of genes. During sexual reproduction DNA replicates itself, and during this process random errors can arise, which are known as *mutations*. Most of them have little obvious effect, while others are damaging and may be lethal to offspring. But occasionally the mutations bring about a physical change that enables the organism to make a better adaptation to its environment and thus survive to pass on the new characteristic. Gene mutations that make the organism less able to survive will be destroyed as the organism carrying the gene is less likely to live long enough to breed.

We can regard an interbreeding population of plants or animals as a *gene pool*, 'an environment' in which different genes compete for survival. Genes that make organisms that are better at surviving and reproducing will perpetuate themselves and will become more common in the gene pool, while genes that are not so good in this respect will become rarer. As the make-up of the gene pool changes, so will the characteristics of the individuals of the species. Darwin called this process *natural selection*.

However, most mutations are in fact neither harmful nor beneficial. In a process called *genetic drift* they are probably perpetuated during the random shuffling of parental genes that occurs during sexual reproduction (⇨ p. 194). We cannot be certain whether genetic drift is important in determining evolution as natural selection. If initially identical species inhabit markedly different environments, genetic drift and natural selection may, in the end, lead to such obvious differences in the gene pool of the two populations that they would no longer, if brought together, be able to breed successfully with each other. One species would, in this way, have become two.

Adaptive radiation

In adaptive radiation a single species can evolve into many different species, each best suited to a different habitat. This may occur slowly or comparatively rapidly, as when a species occupies a new, geographically isolated, environment. In these cases the organism may be faced with considerable opportunity for increase in population and consequently many divergences may occur, as in the case of Darwin's finches (⇨ p. 196). Adaptive radiation may occur as a result of an unusual mutation that happens to provide an exceptional survival advantage over other contemporaries of the same species so that the mutated line can take advantage of a particular ecological situation. Alternatively, adaptive radiation may occur when new ecological situations arise which happen to suit individuals with particular genetically-determined characteristics.

The selfish gene

It has been customary to think of evolution as the survival and modification of species of organisms, but recent thought has indicated that a more fruitful approach may be to consider that natural selection operates for the preservation of individual genes rather than of organisms. Indeed, genes whose expression favours their own propagation survive, whatever the cost to the organism that carries them. This view was well expressed in the book *The Selfish Gene* (1976) by the English zoologist and evolutionist Richard Dawkins (1941–). In the preface to his book, Dawkins wrote: 'We are survival machines – robots blindly programmed to preserve the selfish molecules known as genes.'

On the basis that it is the gene's survival, rather than that of the individual, that matters, much apparently altruistic behaviour by animals can be understood. For instance, there would, on the face of it, seem to be little survival value in the conspicuous warning white tail flashed by deer, rabbits and pronghorn antelopes while fleeing from a predator, as these flashes draw attention to the animal.

However, it has been observed that in all such circumstances the altruistic individual is fairly closely related to – and thus has a relatively high probability of sharing its genes with – the other members of the group on whose behalf it is acting. The result may be the passing on to succeeding generations of an increased number of identical copies of the genes concerned, even if the altruistic individual dies. In this way it is possible for an animal actually to increase the number of copies of its genes occurring in succeeding generations, by means other than its own reproduction.

The concept of the selfish gene also helps to explain the reason for much animal behaviour and display in the context of sexual selection. Elaborate, colourful and conspicuous plumage may be a positive disadvantage from the point

A rabbit often flashes its white tail when fleeing from a predator, which warns the other rabbits in the group but draws attention to itself. In most cases the altruistic individual is closely related to – and thus probably shares many genes with – the other members of the group that have been warned. The sacrificed rabbit will therefore have its genes passed on to succeeding generations by its relatives in the group rather than its own reproduction. (Eric and David Hosking, FLPA)

THE PEPPERED MOTH

Although Darwin's theory of evolution (⇨ p. 196) quickly commanded widespread acceptance, this was because of its inherent logic. Darwin was unable to cite a single instance of natural selection actually occurring in his own time in England. Since his day, a classic case of evolution in action has been observed. The peppered moth, *Biston betularia*, occurs in two forms – a pale grey speckled form and a mutant black form. Before the Industrial Revolution in England the speckled pattern was the more prevalent and the dark moths almost unknown. During the industrialization of England the tree trunks in many urban areas were blackened by soot, while those in the country remained unaffected. Soon, the dark mutant form of the moth was found to be much more prevalent in the towns than the light form; while the light form was much more prevalent in the country areas where trees were unaffected.

This change was explained by the fact that a dark moth on a dark background – such as a sooty tree – or a light moth on a light background were both less likely to be seen – and eaten – by birds. In the non-polluted areas the dark moths suffered heavy predation but thrived in the dirty cities. Similarly the speckled lighter moths remained in large numbers in the country areas. These observations were reinforced after 1956, when the Clean Air Act came into force and soot pollution rapidly declined. The change in the colour of urban trees was quickly followed by a significant decline in the relative numbers of the dark forms of the moths.

of view of the safety of the individual animal, but, by attracting many mates, will ensure the perpetuation of the individual's genes. The same argument applies in the case of male deer who spend much time and energy fighting rivals so as to secure as many breeding mates as possible, despite the danger to themselves.

Phrases such as 'the selfish gene' are, of course, fanciful and do not imply any volition on the part of the gene. But then, the idea that the organism consciously wishes to perpetuate its genes is equally fanciful. In the broader context, too, it is inaccurate to suppose that evolution is purposeful and is directed to some goal of perfection. So long as life survives, neither the gene pool nor the environment will ever be static.

Types of adaptation

Evolutionary adaptation is not necessarily slow. Trials have shown that in as little as three years, an area of mixed grasses and legumes heavily grazed by cattle will show marked differences in its growth patterns compared with an identical area fenced off and left to grow freely. In the grazed area, tall plants are quickly destroyed and only those small enough to escape the attention of the cattle survive to propagate.

The term *coevolution* is given to the processes of adaptation that occur when different species are dependent on each other for survival. Such pairings, whether cooperative (symbiotic) or parasitic (where one benefits at the expense of the other), commonly provide striking examples of adaptation. Many species of aphids, for instance, have gained efficient protection from ants by acquiring the

power of secreting a sugary honeydew that the ants eat. In return, the ants 'farm' the aphids and promote the exudation of honeydew by caressing the aphids' abdomens. Similarly the algae embedded in lichens provide their host (a fungus) with the nutritional advantages of photosynthesis (⇨ p. 192). This adaptation to a symbiotic state has resulted in an extraordinarily successful relationship capable of surviving the most extreme and inhospitable conditions. Ascomycete fungi and algae or cyanobacteria are entirely remote species and must originally have been separate. Those which, by chance, fell into this close relationship would have immediately gained a considerable survival advantage compared with those which developed separately. This advantage would have been even greater in areas of extremes of temperature.

Perhaps the most striking example of coevolution is illustrated in the way

flowering plants depend on insects for pollination and thus fertilization. Some flowers have adapted to the extent of resembling certain species of female fly, bee or wasp. Male insects are attracted, alight on them, attempt to copulate, become dusted with pollen and carry it to other flowers of the same species. Flowers pollinated by bees are predominantly coloured yellow or blue as bees are red-blind, and usually open only during the day, when bees are active. They also emit aromatic fragrances especially attractive to bees, and commonly provide a convenient protruding lip on which the bee can alight.

SEE ALSO

● EVOLUTION p. 196
● HEREDITY p. 200
● DNA AND THE GENETIC CODE p. 202
● GENES IN ACTION p. 204
● THE BIOSPHERE p. 206

AQUATIC CONVERGENCE

| Early birds | ← | Bird-like reptiles | ← | Ancestral reptiles | → | Mammal-like reptiles | → | Early mammals |

DIVERGENCE **DIVERGENCE**

CONVERGENCE **CONVERGENCE**

Penguin   Ichthyosaur   Dolphin

Convergent evolution is where different organisms have evolved similar solutions to similar problems, even though they have evolved from very different ancestors. Such solutions are usually anatomical modifications, which are known as analogous structures. An example of convergent evolution is provided by the way species of very different ancestry have evolved to exploit opportunities in the marine habitat. In adapting to this habitat, such diverse animals as penguins, dolphins and the long-extinct ichthyosaur have independently developed body forms similar to each other and to that of their remote fish ancestors: all have streamlined, cigar-shaped bodies and fin-like limbs.

Heredity

Heredity is the transmission from parent to offspring of the genetic factors that determine the characteristics of the individual. The fact that characteristics could be inherited has always been self-evident. For centuries, humans have successfully bred domestic animals and plants by selecting for breeding those with the desired features. It was not until the 20th century, however, that there was any real understanding of the way in which these features are passed on.

The transmission of inheritable characteristics is intimately linked with cell division and cell reproduction. The division and reproduction of a body cell in an animal or a plant results in two daughter cells that are genetically identical to the cell from which they come. This means that the new cells will contain exactly the same genetic code as the mother cell.

Chromosomes are the coiled-up strands of DNA that contain the genetic code (⇨ p. 202). The process by which body cell duplication occurs is known as *mitosis*. Division and reproduction of the sex cells to produce sperms and eggs, however, is different and does not result in exact duplication of the chromosomes. In this case the process is called *meiosis* (⇨ illustration).

Sex chromosomes

Chromosomes occur in pairs, of which one is from the father and the other from the mother. One particular pair of chromosomes determine sex, and are known as sex chromosomes. In sexual reproduction of some species, including humans, eggs from the female contain an X chromosome while the sperms from the male contain either an X or a Y. A combination of XX produces a female offspring while a combination of XY produces a male. Thus the sex of an offspring is determined by the type of chromosome passed on by the father. All the chromosomes other than the X and Y are called autosomes, of which there are 44 in humans.

Dominant and recessive inheritance

Genes occur in pairs or pairs of autosomes. Such paired genes are called *alleles*. When alleles are identical – having the same sequence of DNA nucleotide bases – the individual is said to be *homozygous* for that gene. However, if the paired genes consist of different alleles, the individual is said to be *heterozygous*. One allele may be *dominant* in that the gene product it codes for is used by the cell in preference to that of the other allele, which is called *recessive*. The outcome of such interactions between the

A SINGLE-FACTOR INHERITANCE

The simplicity of Mendel's laws is illustrated by a single-factor inheritance, in which an inheritable characteristic is determined by the action of a pair of dominant and recessive alleles of a single gene.

The coloration of rats is an example of such a characteristic, with the allele for black being dominant over the allele for white. If a homozygous black rat (i.e. with two identical alleles) mates with a homozygous white rat, all the offspring will be heterozygous black – each similar in appearance to the black parent, but with a recessive (and unexpressed)

white allele. However, mating between these offspring will result (potentially) in a mixture of black and white rats. The ratio of black rats to white will be on average 3 to 1, any white rat having inherited one recessive white allele from each of its parents.

The same pattern is found in the inheritance of certain human characteristics, including recessive genetic diseases such as cystic fibrosis. The inheritance of characteristics dependent on a number of different genes is more complex, but the underlying principle is the same in all genetic interactions.

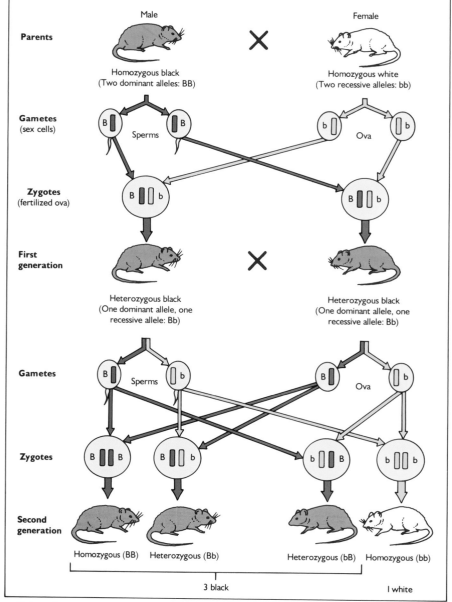

alleles of all the different genes produces the characteristics of an individual (⇨ illustration).

The Austrian monk Gregor Mendel (1822–84) carried out research on the features of generations of the pea plant. By concentrating on just a few features and determining what proportion of each generation received them, he was able to

demonstrate specific patterns of inheritance. He showed that a dominant characteristic could be present even if the species was not true-bred. A recessive characteristic showed itself only in the absence of the dominant characteristic – that is, only if the individual had received the recessive feature from both its parents.

HOW CELLS REPRODUCE

MITOSIS

In mitosis the chromosomes first uncoil to form long threads of DNA. These then split and replicate longitudinally so that the DNA threads are now duplicated (⇨ illustration). The old and new threads now coil up to form pairs of new chromosomes, and these are, at first, stuck together near their centres to produce characteristic X-shaped double or replicated chromosomes (chromatids). These double chromosomes now form up in a rough circle around the equator of the cell, and a delicate structure of fine strands or fibres, radiating to the equator from each end of the cell, appears. This structure is made of contractile protein and it soon pulls the pairs of chromosomes apart, dragging one of each pair to the opposite ends of the cell. The cell now elongates, narrows in the middle, and separates into two, each containing the full complement of 46 chromosomes (in 23 pairs). Cell duplication by mitosis is carried out in all our bodies continually.

MEIOSIS

Body cells in ovaries and testes that become sperms in males and eggs in females, undergo a different, and quite extraordinary, kind of division, known as meiosis. They must do this for two reasons – first, to ensure that they contain half the normal number of chromosomes so that when the sperm fuses with the egg the normal number is made up, and second, to ensure that the mix of characteristics passed on will differ from that of the parents.

The first stages of meiosis are similar to those of mitosis, up to the point at which the chromosomes stick together to form X-shaped double chromosomes. These double chromosomes now congregate in pairs of Xs, but not with any arbitrary partner. Chromosomes can be identified and are numbered. The duplicated number 1 chromosome that came originally from the individual father aligns itself with the duplicated number 1 that came from the individual's mother, number 2 with number 2, and so on for all 23 pairs. The partners in each pair of Xs now twist intimately together and become closely aligned along their entire length. While entwined they exchange several short corresponding segments with each other in a process known as crossing-over. This occurs in a random manner so that the genetic material from the father and the mother becomes thoroughly mixed and new chromosomes are formed, each with a unique blend of the genes from both parents.

The cell now divides, but in this division the doubled chromosomes do not have their arms pulled apart as in mitosis. Instead, one of each of the pairs of the double chromosomes goes intact to each daughter cell. It is a matter of pure chance which of the pairs goes to which daughter cell. As a result, the random redistribution of genes already effected by crossing-over is further increased.

Each daughter cell now has 23 chromosomes. A second division then occurs, but this time the halves are pulled apart by a spindle, as in mitosis, and each daughter cell receives a single chromatid from each pair, a total of 23. So the sperms and eggs now have half the normal number of chromosomes, as the chromatids can now be called.

MITOSIS

1 Chromosomes within the nucleus become shorter and fatter.

2 The nuclear membrane opens.

3 Chromosomes replicate and attach themselves to the spindle fibre.

4 and 5 Separated halves are drawn to opposite ends of the cell.

6 The cytoplasm divides and the nuclear membranes are reformed.

7 Two daughter cells are formed.

MEIOSIS

1 Chromosomes are situated in the nucleus of the cell.

2 They begin to duplicate.

3 and 4 Like chromosomes link together and exchange sections of their length before separating.

5 The chromosomes are pulled across to opposite sides of the cell.

6 Two cells are then formed, each containing one of each pair from the original cell.

7 A second division begins.

8 This time around one half of each chromosome (a chromatid) moves to opposite ends.

9 Four cells are formed. Each chromatid will replicate in due course to form a chromosome.

Most people with a disorder caused by an autosomal dominant allele will have an affected parent. If not, the condition is probably due to a new mutation that has altered one of the gene pairs in a sperm or ovum cell of one of the parents. If a person with a heterozygous autosomal dominant condition mates with a normal person, there is a fifty-fifty chance with each new child that the condition will be inherited. This is because only one gene is needed to produce the disorder and, on average, half the sperms, or ova, of the affected person, will contain the gene. If a person is homozygous for an autosomal dominant gene, all the offspring will, of course, suffer from the condition. Autosomal recessive traits appear only if the mutant gene concerned is present in both parents. A single recessive mutant gene coupled with a normal gene – the heterozygous state – produces no effect, or, occasionally, a very minor effect.

Recessive conditions are rare because they can only be inherited if the affected individual mates with a person who either has the condition or who is heterozygous for it. If two people with the condition mate, all the children will have the condition because all four genes concerned are affected and any combination will involve two affected genes. If a person homozygous for a recessive condition mates with a heterozygous person, there will be a fifty-fifty chance, with each child, that the condition will appear. If two heterozygous people mate there will be a fifty-fifty chance, both for the sperm and the egg, that it will carry the gene. As Mendel appreciated, on average, a quarter of the children will inherit two normal genes and will be normal, a half will inherit one defective gene and will be normal, and a quarter will inherit two defective genes and will be affected.

Because recessive conditions are rare, the parents of children with such conditions are often related and have inherited the same defective gene from a common ancestor. First cousins have a one in eight chance of being heterozygous for the same recessive gene. So if there is a family history of a recessive condition, marrying a cousin greatly increases the risk of offspring developing the disease.

Sex-linked inheritance

Sex-linked disorders are caused by genes situated in one of the sex chromosomes, the X or the Y chromosome. Genes on the X chromosome produce X-linked characteristics or disorders, those on the Y chromosome produce Y-linked features. Since only males have Y chromosomes, Y-linked features occur only in males and all the sons of a man with a Y-linked disorder would inherit it. The Y chromosome is, however, very small and there are no positively proved single gene Y-linked disorders in man. Since all known sex-linked conditions arise from genes on the X chromosome, the terms sex-linked and X-linked, in practice, mean the same thing.

SEE ALSO

● EVOLUTION p. 196
● ADAPTATION: EVOLUTION IN ACTION p. 198
● DNA AND THE GENETIC CODE p. 202
● GENES IN ACTION p. 204

DNA and the Genetic Code

The determination of the structure of DNA in 1953 was one of the greatest scientific advances of all time, and had an explosive influence on the development of biology. The scientists who took the final step in establishing the chemistry of DNA – James Watson and Francis Crick – had based their work on a body of knowledge that went back for almost a century but which had been largely ignored as unimportant. The final crystallization of truth, however, immediately opened up an enormous area of fruitful research.

On 25 April 1953 a short paper from the Cavendish Laboratory, Cambridge, appeared in the scientific journal *Nature*. Written by James Watson (1928–) and Francis Crick (1916–   ), it started with the words 'We wish to suggest a structure for the salt of deoxyribose nucleic acid (D.N.A.). This structure has novel features which are of considerable biological interest.' Near the end of the article the authors modestly stated: 'It has not escaped our notice that the specific pairing we have postulated immediately suggests a possible copying mechanism for the genetic material.'

Throughout the decade that followed, many biology laboratories were engaged in an intense experimental study of the Watson–Crick model, and as the evidence in favour of it mounted and nothing was found to disprove it, the now-celebrated

Identical twins come from the same fertilized egg and have identical DNA. (Gamma)

double-helix structure of the molecule gradually became accepted as beyond dispute. This structure could reproduce itself, could provide a code for the formation of proteins, and contained sufficient information for the estimated requirements of the whole human genetic pool.

The physical basis of heredity

Like other scientists working on the structure of the DNA molecule, Watson and Crick were essentially engaged in solving a jigsaw puzzle. They were trying to fit known pieces together in a way that accounted for a number of known facts and that would, somehow, produce a structure that could reproduce itself automatically. They knew that DNA contained four nitrogenous bases – adenine, guanine, cytosine and thymine. They also knew that the number of adenine bases was the same as the number of thymine bases, and that the number of guanines was the same as the number of cytosines. There was no fixed ratio, however, between adenine and guanine or thymine and cytosine. They had long accepted, from the evidence of X-ray crystallography (⇨ p. 84), that the backbone of the molecule was a helically shaped strip of sugar and phosphate molecules and that the bases were attached to this. But the question was, how?

One major problem was that all four bases were of different size, and it was hard to see how they could be attached to each other and to the backbone without producing unacceptable irregularity. Watson persisted in trying various arrangements of bases between two backbones and suddenly realized that an adenine base linked to a thymine base had the same shape and size as a guanine base linked to a cytosine base. This was chemically impeccable and also explained the riddle of why the number of adenines and thymines was the same and the number of guanines and cytosines was the same. The pairs could be accommodated between two helices running the same way, and the way in which the complementary pairs bonded together meant that adenine could only pair with thymine and guanine could only pair with cytosine (⇨ illustration).

Watson at once realized that given one longitudinal half of the molecule and a nearby supply of the necessary bases, the other half would automatically be constructed. Crick immediately saw the importance of this idea and for the next few days the two men worked frantically to build a model of the new molecule. It was a double helix with the sugar-phosphate backbones on the outside and the base pairs joining them like the steps on a spiral staircase.

When it was completed they checked every detail to ensure that it satisfied both the X-ray data and the laws of chemistry. Everything fitted. None of the rules of stereochemistry was broken. In 1962 Crick, Watson and Maurice Wilkins (1916–   ), whose work on X-ray crystallography they

had used, were jointly awarded the Nobel Prize for Physiology or Medicine.

The genetic code

The double helix backbone is simply a support for the pairs of bases that contain the real information in coded form. Once the structure of DNA was known, the problem was to work out how to read the code. By the early 1960s Francis Crick and other scientists had largely solved this problem. The secret lay in the sequence of bases in the DNA molecule. It was necessary to have a code that could specify 20 different amino acids – the 'building bricks' of proteins. The order of these acids could, obviously, be represented by the order in which the code for each amino acid occurred along the DNA molecule, and the simplest code would be one in which a short sequence of bases would stand for an amino acid. A code consisting of two out of the four bases would not be enough as this gives only 16 possible combinations and 20 are needed. A permutation of three bases out of the four gives 64 combinations, so a triplet of bases is sufficient for the purpose. In the end it was found that a single triplet (*codon*) of bases did indeed specify a single amino acid.

How DNA works

Genes are lengths of DNA. Information is stored in the DNA as a sequence of three bases, taken from a possible four, which are read consecutively. Of all the possible unique triplets of the four bases, 20 stand for the 20 amino acids. The sequence of triplets of bases in the DNA determines the order in which the amino acids occur in the protein that is to be formed. The order of the bases along the DNA molecule is unique for any gene, and each gene forms a single kind of protein.

DNA replication

The copying of DNA is a largely automatic process in which the base adenine always links with thymine and the base guanine always links with cytosine. The effect of this is that if the double helix is split longitudinally so that the base-pairs that form the rungs of the ladder are separated, the single strands so formed will attract to themselves appropriate bases, that are floating about in the cell fluid, so that perfect replicas, running in the opposite direction, are formed. Each single strand acts as a template for the second strand. At the same time a second sugar-phosphate backbone becomes attached to the other side of each of the newly attached bases.

Replication can only occur after chromosomes (⇨ illustration) have unwound to form extended lengths of helical DNA. They do this as a result of the action of an enzyme (⇨ p. 184) called helicase, which unwinds about 100 revolutions each second. Separation of the strand does not start at one end and proceed along to the other. Because of the length of the strand, this would take far too long. The double helix actually separates locally at many points to form loops in which replication occurs. When this occurs in the course of cell reproduction (⇨ p. 200), each of these loops then extends in both directions until the separation is continuous. In this way, a double helix becomes two identical double helices, one of which goes to each of the new cells that are forming. As they do so, the chromatin (⇨ p. 200) coils up into the compact form we recognize as chromosomes. Replication also occurs constantly within non-dividing cells so that DNA can fulfil its function of coding for proteins.

The role of RNA

Proteins are not made directly on the DNA molecule itself but in cell organelles known as *ribosomes*. These lie within the cell fluid, in the part of the cell outside the nucleus. First, a short length of double helix separates longitudinally to form a loop, exposing the sequence of single bases that constitute the gene. A new, short, complementary strand is now made on the exposed bases. This strand is called RNA (*ribonucleic acid*) and it forms at a rate of about 50 bases per second. Base triplets that are different from those coding for amino acids indicate where the gene starts and where it ends.

RNA production is rather slapdash and the accuracy of copying is poor, about one mistake occurring every 100,000 bases. But many copies are made and the occasional wrong one does not matter. RNA uses three of the same bases as DNA, but thymine is not used. Another base called uracil is substituted for thymine, and this links with the DNA adenine.

The RNA chains formed in this way are called *messenger RNA* (mRNA) because they carry the code of the gene out, through pores in the nuclear membrane, to the ribosomes in the cell fluid – cytoplasm. Before the codes are used to sort the amino acids, each mRNA length is 'edited' to get rid of unnecessary sections and the remaining coding sequences are spliced together. It is this edited version of the mRNA that is read by the ribosomes.

The cell fluid contains millions of amino acids, most of which are derived from our food but some of which are synthesized in the body. Before the ribosomes can join these together in the right order to form new protein molecules they have to be brought to the ribosomes in the right sequence. This is done by yet another kind of RNA, *transfer RNA* (tRNA), which is replicated off from the edited mRNA. Transfer RNA moves around in the cell fluid picking up the 20 different amino acids and carrying them to the ribosome site. There, the mRNA, the tRNA and the ribosome all work together to form the chain of protein. The ribosome, a tiny protein body, moves along the strand of mRNA checking the sequence of bases, selecting amino acids from the tRNA in the right order, and linking them together to form proteins.

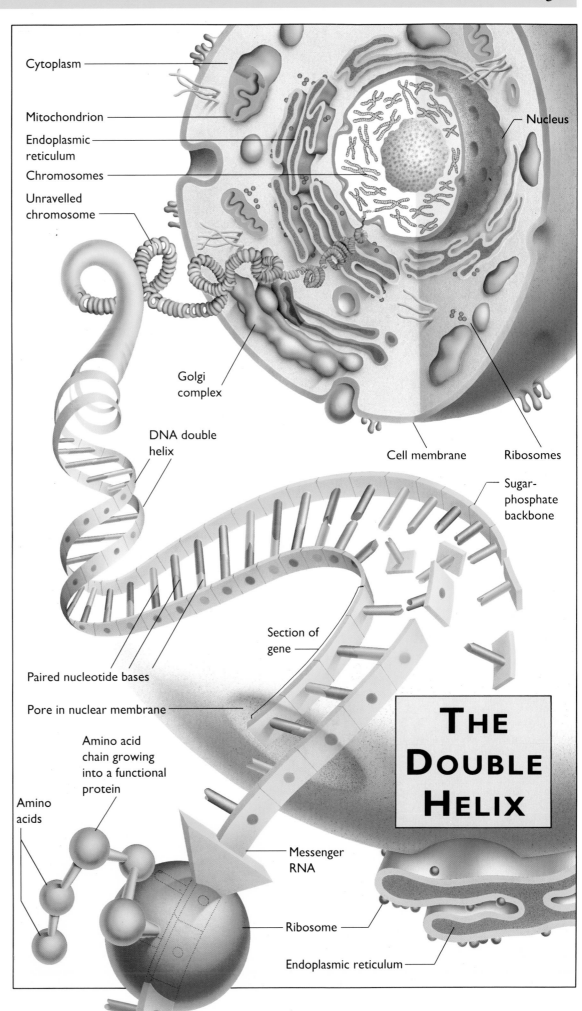

Cytoplasm

Mitochondrion

Endoplasmic reticulum

Chromosomes

Unravelled chromosome

Nucleus

Golgi complex

DNA double helix

Cell membrane

Ribosomes

Sugar-phosphate backbone

Section of gene

Paired nucleotide bases

Pore in nuclear membrane

Amino acid chain growing into a functional protein

Amino acids

Messenger RNA

Ribosome

Endoplasmic reticulum

THE DOUBLE HELIX

Genes in Action

Genetic engineering, in its widest sense, is not new. Effective gene manipulation has been practised for many centuries by cattle breeders and arable farmers to improve their stock and grain, and livestock breeders have long used artificial insemination, which involves the selective combination of DNA (⬦ p. 202). The real revolution in the subject, however, began in the early 1970s, when genetic recombination was performed in the laboratory for the first time. We are now well into the biological revolution, which most scientists agree will have a greater impact on all our lives than any scientific development since atomic energy.

Genetic engineering arouses strong feelings. The experts, aware of its potential, are enthusiastic but the public is uneasy, concerned about the dangers and of the ethical problems involved. One of the pioneers of genetic engineering was so carried away with the fascination of his work that he actually planned to transfer a cancer-causing DNA, from the SV40 virus, to some *Escherichia coli* bacteria – which normally inhabit the human bowel. All the countless billions of identical offspring of these altered organisms would, of course, contain the DNA of the cancer-producing virus, and if they got out of the laboratory could very easily infect humans. It was only when a student happened to mention this intention at a workshop course that other research workers protested in horror and the proposal was abandoned. This case and others led to strong pressure for strict guidelines in genetic engineering research. However, considerable doubts still exist and the ethical dilemma has not been resolved.

Recombinant DNA technology

Genetic engineering depends on the existence of two classes of enzymes – restriction enzymes and DNA ligases. Restriction enzymes are biological catalysts (⬦ p. 182) that split DNA strands (⬦ p. 202) at certain specific points where particular sequences of bases occur. Hundreds of these restriction enzymes have been identified and isolated, mostly from bacterial cells. Each of them is able to cut DNA at a particular site. When DNA is exposed to these enzymes certain fragments are released from the molecule. DNA ligases are much less specific than restriction enzymes. The term ligase comes from the same Greek root as ligature, meaning 'to bind together'. They are enzymes that join any two DNA fragments together by forming new sugar-phosphate linkages (⬦ p. 202). In cutting and joining strands of DNA restriction enzymes are the scissors, ligases are the glue.

These enzymes make it comparatively easy for lengths of DNA from diverse sources to be linked together. Such new combinations of DNA can then be re-introduced into a cell, such as a bacterium, where it will operate to generate the proteins for which it codes (⬦ p. 202). The process is known as *recombinant DNA technique*. More importantly, the living organism into which the new DNA has been inserted will, under conditions suitable for reproduction, continue to divide normally and will produce a large number of identical offspring (clones), each of which contains the new DNA. All of these will be able to generate the coded proteins.

Recombinant DNA techniques were quickly taken up as powerful tools for the study of the molecular structure of genes. Such methods have shown, for instance, that nearly all animal genes are split into separate segments, each coding for a part of a protein, but kept apart by non-coding lengths. After DNA is transcribed to mRNA (⬦ p. 202) these non-coding segments are edited out.

Scientists are now able to identify the segments of mRNA that code for particular proteins in species – such as humans. This is done by elaborate methods involving a knowledge of the sequence of the first 20 or 30 amino acids in the protein molecule. Because the base sequences that code for all the amino acids are known, the scientists can easily work out the base sequences for the complementary DNA lengths. These can now be synthesized and the resulting DNA 'probes' used to identify the full mRNA segments needed. Plasmids are small circles of bacterial DNA that are independent of the main genome (set of genetic information). These have been found especially suitable as vehicles for introducing the spliced-in DNA segment into the bacterial cell, which will harvest large quantities of the protein.

Practical applications

Most applications of genetic engineering, to date, have been in food and medicine. Considerable advances in several areas of food production and agriculture are already well under way. These include the production of improved strains of existing foodstuffs, ingenious methods of biological pest control, and the production of new protein foods by large-scale synthesis through the use of cloned organisms. Bovine growth hormone has been used to produce a 40 per cent increase in milk production by cows. Genetic engineering offers remarkable promise in this context and could help provide a solution to the world's food problems. However, the release of genetically manipulated microbes, often through yeast, and even lighter organisms into the natural environment poses the threat of 'genetic pollution'. Without careful experimentation the balance of natural ecosystems could become upset in unpredictable ways.

The advances in the application of genetic engineering to medicine have been impressive. In 1978, scientists from Genentech, Inc., of San Francisco successfully used recombinant DNA methods to produce human insulin and in 1982 this was approved for medical use by the American Food and Drugs Administration (FDA). By 1988 the price

Genetically modified rice crop being assessed for disease levels. Scientists can now genetically engineer rice grains that are more resilient to disease and so produce a better and bigger crop.
(Nigel Cattlin, Holt)

Genetic fingerprinting, like skin fingerprinting, can accurately distinguish one human being from another as each person's DNA is effectively unique. The DNA pattern can be determined from a sample of skin, hair or semen. Here the results of a genetic fingerprints test will be used as evidence in a court of law. (Wilson/Liai, Gamma)

of this insulin had dropped to about the same as that of insulin derived from pigs and oxen, previously the only other source. A high proportion of people suffering from diabetes are now kept healthy by injections of human insulin.

In the past, human growth hormone – used to treat growth failure in children – has been scarce and very expensive because it was obtained from human cadaver pituitary glands. The glands are buried deep and almost inaccessibly under the brain and about 50 are needed to provide enough hormone to meet the needs of a single patient. All this changed in 1985 when the FDA approved the use of genetically engineered human growth hormone from cloned bacteria into which the gene had been inserted. The hormone is now so freely available that it is being tried out for a variety of purposes other than failure of growth.

Cells infected with viruses produce protein substances called interferons that pass to other cells and provide a measure of protection against the same and other viruses. Interferons also assist the immune system to eliminate cells infected with viruses and have a considerable potential for the treatment of a wide range of diseases. They have, for instance, been shown to be effective against the common cold. In 1980, a human interferon was first produced when the gene for an interferon had been inserted into bacteria.

Further trials, using yeast cells, were also successful. These interferons are now undergoing trials of their effectiveness against such diseases as hepatitis, influenza, rheumatoid arthritis,

multiple myeloma, venereal warts, certain forms of leukaemia and some kinds of cancer, including malignant melanoma, lymphoma, and Kaposi's sarcoma in AIDS.

Many protein substances that are synthesized in the body have been produced by genetic engineering to help people suffering poor health. These include hormones; antibodies against infection; cancer-combating interleukins and tumour-necrosis factor; atrial natriuretic factor for high blood pressure; Factor VIII for haemophilia; the natural enzyme superoxide dismutase that mops up damaging free radicals ($\diamond$ p. 156); and the tissue plasminogen activator (TPA) which, given soon after a coronary thrombosis, can selectively dissolve the clot and restore heart function. These and others have a high potential for medical treatment if they can be produced cheaply in sufficient quantity. Successful research leading to the economical production of such substances is likely to change the face of medicine and may help to counter the steeply-rising cost of medical treatment.

Vaccine production is another growth area with great promise. In this, the methods are simpler. Restriction enzymes are used to delete genes from normally dangerous viruses or bacteria and so make them non-virulent. Clones from these safe organisms make excellent vaccines as they stimulate antibodies as effectively as the natural virulent organisms, but without the danger.

Alternatively, recombinant methods can be used to replicate the surface protein in viruses ($\diamond$ p. 190) that stimulate natural antibody formation. Vaccines using this protein contain no viruses and are thus entirely safe. In 1983 hepatitis surface protein was used to produce immunity against the disease in animals, and in 1985 trials began on the first genetically engineered vaccine against hepatitis B. This proved highly successful and was approved for general use in 1986.

Gene therapy

The very contentious possibility of gene therapy is arousing much scientific interest, but even more moral debate. Although there is no practical way of introducing a new gene into the millions of body cells, a gene inserted into a very young embryo will appear in all the body cells. Similarly, if a gene is added to a stem cell – a cell from which a complete cell line arises – that gene will be propagated in the mature cells of that line. For example, if a gene is added to the stem cell in the bone marrow all the subsequent cells of the blood and immune system will have that gene. Retroviruses, such as the HIV that causes AIDS ($\diamond$ p. 190), insert their own genes into the chromosomes in the cells they infect. It would be possible in theory to use a retrovirus as a means of introducing selected genes into a developed human.

While a general prohibition exists against genetic alteration of human embryos, approval has been given for the use of less hazardous methods of gene therapy in cases that will otherwise be fatal. It has been used, for instance, to treat children suffering from such severe, genetically induced immune deficiency diseases that they have to live in sealed plastic bubbles. These children can have certain of their white blood cells, the T-cells, corrected by the insertion of normal human genetic material, cultured and re-transfused to grow and reproduce normally in the body. Many of the 2,000 or so diseases caused by a single gene defect may, in future, be treated by such methods.

The risks

Whether the risks inherent in genetic engineering can be contained remains uncertain. Some critics, claiming to take a realistic view of human nature, think probably not. For over 20 years, codes of practice and guidelines for the conduct of research have been in existence, and, in large part, so far as can be known, are adhered to. But scientists have seldom been deterred from investigating obvious possibilities just because risk was involved. During World War II German scientists carried out experiments on prisoners in concentration camps and inflicted terrible suffering, all in the name of science. And today, when to the traditional rewards of fame and academic advance is added the incentive of huge financial profits, it seems inevitable that some will succumb to the temptation to take chances. Scientists fully recognize that genetic engineering raises formidable ethical, legal and social problems, and much careful thought continues to be given to control.

SEE ALSO
- SIMPLE ORGANISMS p. 190
- EVOLUTION p. 196
- ADAPTATION: EVOLUTION IN ACTION p. 198
- HEREDITY p. 200
- DNA AND THE GENETIC CODE p. 202

The ugli fruit, a genetically engineered hybrid of a tangerine, grapefruit and orange, has become a commercial commodity. It was named after its unattractive wrinkled skin. (Nigel Cattlin, Holt)

The Biosphere

The biosphere consists of that part of the Earth and its atmosphere that is capable of sustaining or supporting life. It extends to the beds of the oceans and a little way below the surface of the ground as well as several kilometres above the Earth's surface. The energy for the maintenance of life in the biosphere is derived from the Sun (⇨ p. 132), but this energy takes several different forms and becomes widely distributed among the multitude of living things before it is finally dissipated into space.

Many of the chemical elements that form the biosphere are essential to life. Most prominent in organic matter are carbon, hydrogen, oxygen, nitrogen, phosphorus and sulphur, and these elements move constantly between the organic and the inorganic phases of nature. This movement occurs in cycles, in which the elements are built up into complex molecules, using energy in the process, and then broken down, thus releasing energy.

These interactive cycles between communities of living organisms, including humans, and their physical environment constitute an ecosystem; and the biosphere can be considered as the totality of all the Earth's ecosystems.

The carbon cycle

Although carbon makes up less than 1 per cent of the mass of the Earth it is by far the most important element in the living world. Because of the way it combines with itself and with other atoms, it is the key to the chemical structure of all living things. In addition to its structural importance, carbon in the atmosphere – in the form of carbon dioxide – maintains the surface temperatures within a range that makes life possible (⇨ p. 208). Most of our energy needs continue to be derived from carbonaceous fossil fuels – coal and oil – and from recently grown carbon-based vegetable matter.

Most of the carbon present in living things is derived, directly or indirectly, from the carbon in the atmosphere. At any one time the atmosphere contains some 600 billion tonnes of carbon, so the drain from it must be replenished in what is known as the carbon cycle (⇨ illustration). The carbon taken up from the atmosphere by living things is held temporarily in a second pool – the biomass – which is the plants and animals of any ecosystem. Only about 2 billion tonnes of this carbon is held in animal life, the great majority is held in

plants. During photosynthesis (⇨ p. 192) and respiration carbon dioxide is released by plants back into the atmosphere, and the plant tissues that are consumed by animals or pass to the decomposer microbes also eventually become degraded in the same way. So, much of the carbon cycle takes place between the living biomass and the atmosphere.

Much of the carbon ends up in the ground as a long-lasting geochemical carbon pool in the form of coal, oil and limestone rocks. Limestones are compounds of calcium, carbon and other elements, and are mainly chalk (calcium carbonate). There is also a great pool of carbon in the deep ocean layers. When coal and oil are retrieved and burned, large quantities of carbon are returned to the atmosphere.

Another pool of carbon is found in the surface layers of the oceans, and there is also a constant interchange of carbon by solution and diffusion between these layers and the atmosphere. Oceanic carbon is also incorporated into the shells and skeletons of marine life and these eventually sink to the bottom of the seas to become sedimentary limestone rocks. In this way much of the carbon acquired by the oceans by photosynthesis, river drainage and solution ends up as rocks. Eventually, some of this carbon becomes exposed by mountain formation, erosion and weathering and is returned to the atmosphere.

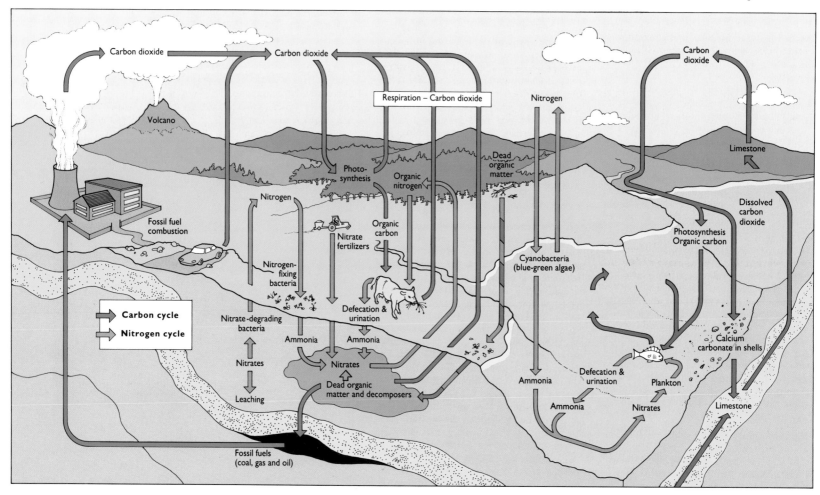

The surface layers of the soil also contain a great deal of carbon – estimated to be about 1,500 billion tonnes. This is a fairly stable pool, but a proportion of it is leached out by rainwater to reach the rivers and oceans by erosion and washing.

The food chain

Carbon fixed by photosynthesis in plants is incorporated into carbohydrates, initially simple sugars. These, in turn, are built up into more complex polysaccharides such as starches and cellulose, and then into proteins and fats (⇨ pp. 182–5). These are eaten by herbivorous or omnivorous animals, which are themselves eaten by carnivorous animals. At each stage after the first, eating is followed by digestion and breakdown of the complex molecules synthesized in the previous stage and then a resynthesis into the body structures of the current organism in the chain. Most of the energy stored in the consumed plant or animal, however, is wasted.

Much more energy is consumed in producing a kilogram of prime steak in an ox than in producing a kilogram of glucose in a plant. This is because energy cannot be released by oxidation and then re-fixed in building up new molecules without substantial losses. It requires the consumption of some 50 kg of grain to produce about 10 kg of weight gain in cattle, but the consumption of 10 kg of meat will produce only about 1 kg of weight gain in a human being. Humans subsisting primarily on grain can gain 1 kg of weight from consuming 5 kg of grain. Because of this expanding energy requirement the food chain seldom, if ever, has more than four or five links. Commonly, however, it forms a complex 'web' involving large numbers of different but interdependent species.

The hydrological cycle

Water is also an essential component for life, and the biosphere also involves a major water cycle. Water covers more than 70 per cent of the Earth's surface and is by far the commonest compound. Most of the incoming energy from the Sun is consumed in driving the hydrological cycle, by which billions of tonnes of water are constantly moved around a

Rainforest in the Northern Range of Trinidad. The vast array of vegetation in rainforests helps take up carbon dioxide and supply oxygen, which is vital in balancing the world's climate. They also include the most diverse collection of species on the Earth. By destroying the forests and its inhabitants we risk inflicting irreparable damage on the biosphere. (Dr Morley Read, SPL)

system that, to date, has remained constantly in equilibrium (⇨ illustration).

The equilibrium of this cycle depends on the maintenance of surface temperatures within a fairly narrow range. Even a small average change in temperatures could have a major effect on the relative amounts of water in the oceans or in the atmosphere. Since the carbon dioxide levels in the atmosphere largely determine the surface temperatures (⇨ p. 208), changes in these levels could greatly alter the sea levels and the climates.

Rainforests

Ecosystems are never in fact entirely independent of one another, but they do provide a useful unit for the ecologist to study. The two most diverse ecosystems are the tropical rainforests and the deserts.

Tropical rainforests are the richest and most complex ecosystems in the world and contain a higher proportion of different species of living things than anywhere else. They occur in regions of heavy rainfall – usually more than about 180 cm (70 in) per year – and most of them are found in the tropics. Average temperatures range between a daytime 30°C (86°F) maximum and a night-time minimum of 20°C (68°F). Relative humidity remains constantly high and the water surplus means that soils remain constantly moist. Rates of evaporation and vegetable transpiration (loss of water through the stomata of the leaves; ⇨ p. 192) from rainforests are high, but, during most if not all of the year, the rate of rainfall is higher.

Because of the high temperatures, decomposition of dead organic material by bacterial and fungal enzyme action is rapid. The elements released in this process are almost immediately reabsorbed by the tree roots and taken up again and there is very little net loss of minerals. Rainforest ecosystems are therefore able to perpetuate themselves indefinitely and can be considered closed. Significantly, the amounts of mineral substances in the large rivers that drain tropical rainforests are barely higher than in rainwater. When forests are cut down and burned, however, the minerals are released in soluble form and are quickly lost in the drainage water. In the absence of artificial fertilization, harvests grown in such areas are seldom good after the first year. The destruction of forests by burning also means the loss of many species and the release of large quantities of carbon dioxide into the atmosphere, adding to the greenhouse effect and global warming (⇨ p. 208).

Deserts

About one third of the total land area of the Earth is desert, which is characterized

by a deficiency of water. The rate of water loss from evaporation exceeds the water gain from precipitation. Deserts occur in areas of consistently high atmospheric pressure or in areas in which mountain ranges prevent moist air from sweeping inland from an ocean. Most deserts lie within the 25° zone on either side of the equator, but can be cold as well as hot. Because they result from permanent geographic features, deserts tend to be permanent, and most of today's deserts have existed for about 15 million years. Deserts do, however, alter somewhat in extent with variations in climate. The areas surrounding deserts are dependent on the correct balance of water and vegetation. Trees that are chopped down to serve as fuel or to make way for agriculture result in soil erosion and the incapacity of the soil to retain such water as is available. This causes desert conditions to spread – a process known as desertification. Attempts to increase the productivity of desert areas by irrigation have often failed because adding water to the soils only serves to enhance the movement of salts to the surface, resulting in salinization. United Nation experts have estimated that 207,200 sq km (80,000 sq mi) of land are rendered useless each year by manmade *desertification*. Attempts to change deserts to productive land are very expensive and require enormous expenditure of energy. This has been achieved on a small scale in some areas by applying sophisticated technology.

SEE ALSO
● ROCKS AND MINERALS p. 150
● THE LIVING PLANET p. 152
● THE NATURE AND ORIGINS OF LIFE p. 180
● MULTICELLULAR ORGANISMS 1 p. 192
● THE PLANET IN DANGER p. 208

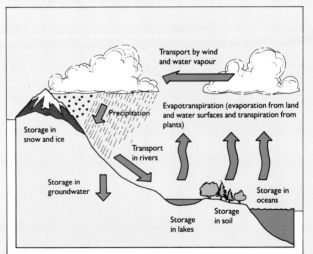

THE HYDROLOGICAL CYCLE

Water exists in three states: liquid, gaseous (water vapour or steam) and solid (snow and ice). It can also pass from one state to another by freezing, melting, condensing and evaporating. New water is not created on the Earth's surface or in its atmosphere; nor is 'old' water lost. Rather, there is a finite amount, and this circulates in what is known as the *hydrological cycle*. Water moves around the cycle both by physically moving and by changing its state, as the diagram shows.

Today, 97 per cent of the water in the hydrological cycle is contained in the world's seas, oceans and saline lakes. The remaining 3 per cent is fresh water. About 75 per cent of all fresh water is contained in glaciers and ice sheets, and just over 24 per cent is groundwater (i.e. underground). The rivers, lakes, soil and atmosphere therefore contain a very small amount (less than 0.5 per cent) of the world's fresh water at any one time.

The Planet in Danger

A hundred years ago it would have seemed impossible that human beings – apparently so small a feature in the mass of the Earth – could, by their actions, endanger all life on the planet. However, the forces of politics and economics have caused pollution and destruction on such a scale that the Earth is now under threat. Today, the depletion of the ozone layer of the atmosphere and the greenhouse effect are major dangers to the future of this planet as a habitat for life as we now know it.

Our planet faces many hazards, among them overpopulation and deforestation (⇨ p. 206), but some dangers are even more fundamental, affecting the very factors that make life on this planet possible. One of the essential ingredients for life on Earth is the possession of an atmosphere of oxygen that is being constantly replenished. Life cannot exist without oxygen and one of our chief sources of oxygen – plant life – is being depleted. Fears have been expressed that the atmosphere would soon be too low in oxygen to sustain life. Another essential factor is the maintenance of surface temperatures within a comparatively narrow range.

The ozone layer

The energy from the Sun that heats the Earth is largely ultraviolet radiation (⇨ p. 132), which, if allowed to reach the Earth's surface, would be of lethal intensity. The atmospheric layer that filters out most of the harmful radiation from the Sun is the ozone layer. Ozone is a gas made up of three oxygen atoms linked together (O_3 or trioxygen). It is a colourless gas with a smell rather like chlorine. It is chemically highly active and powerfully poisonous, and can be used as a bleach or disinfectant.

Normal atmospheric oxygen is in the form of molecules consisting of two linked oxygen atoms (O_2 or dioxygen). When normal atmospheric oxygen is bombarded with the energetic ultraviolet radiation from the Sun below about 240 nanometres wavelength (⇨ p. 84), the two oxygen atoms are split apart, making two highly active free radicals (⇨ p. 156) that can at once attach themselves to other molecules. Some of them attach to normal dioxygen molecules to make ozone. In so doing, considerable energy derived from the ultraviolet light (UVL) is given up to other nearby molecules, especially nitrogen, causing them to vibrate more rapidly and produce heat. The net effect of this is a heated layer in the atmosphere containing a small quantity of ozone – about three parts per million.

The resulting ozone layer reduces the amount of short-wavelength ultraviolet radiation from the Sun reaching the ground. The spectrum of solar radiation, however, also contains a large quantity of longer-wavelength ultraviolet light. This splits the ozone into dioxygen (O_2) molecules and single oxygen atom radicals. The latter then link up with O_2 molecules to form ozone, so that the amount of ozone in the layer remains constant. In splitting ozone, however, much of the energy is removed from the ultraviolet light so that the UVL reaching the ground is greatly attenuated and made relatively safe. Although the ozone layer is very thin, it is able to screen out more than 99 per cent of the UVL from the Sun that would otherwise reach the ground. This mechanism provides a kind of shield all round the Earth, protecting the surface from the dangerous heating and many other effects of solar ultraviolet radiation.

Ozone layer depletion

The balance between ozone production and destruction is delicate and is easily upset. The presence of any atom that can combine readily with oxygen will tend to react with ozone. The main problem is chlorofluorocarbons (CFCs), which degrade to release chlorine atoms, which in turn react with ozone, breaking it down to oxygen. Chlorofluorocarbons are inert, non-poisonous, non-flammable, readily liquefied and light-weight gases. These properties make them of great industrial value and they have seemed ideal agents for aerosol-can propellants, refrigerants in fridges and air conditioners, blowing agents in the manufacture of foam plastics, and for many other purposes. Released into the atmosphere, however, CFCs slowly diffuse in every direction, including upwards, taking an average of about 30 years to reach the ozone layer, where they remain. An estimate made in 1974 suggested that continued use of CFCs would lead to destruction of 30 per cent of the ozone layer by the middle of the 21st century.

Ozone layer depletion is no longer a theoretical concern. From 1976 the concentration of ozone over the Antarctic began to drop sharply and in 1985 it was found to be so low that it was described as a 'hole' in the layer. There are signs that similar holes are appearing over the heavily populated northern latitudes, which include Europe, North America and Russia. There is also evidence of a hole developing over the Arctic.

An excess of ultraviolet radiation reaching the Earth is damaging to all forms of life. Most of the biological harm to humans occurs when UVL reaches the unprotected skin and the eyes. UVL is the cause of three types of skin cancer – basal cell carcinoma (rodent ulcer), squamous carcinoma and malignant melanoma. It is also the cause of the eye conditions solar conjunctivitis, solar keratopathy, pterygium and tropical pinguecula, and many ophthalmologists believe it is an important factor in the cause of cataracts. For every 1 per cent reduction in the ozone layer, 2 per cent more UVL reaches the Earth. It is estimated, for instance, that a 1 per cent increase in UVL would cause a 1 per cent increase in malignant melanoma.

Ultraviolet light increases could also have a serious effect on many plant species, and could kill plankton and interfere with the marine food chain. It would damage the yield of crops and could have quite unpredictable effects on weather patterns.

Most governments have paid lip-service recognition to the problem, but few have taken effective action. In spite of stern warnings of the dangers, CFCs continued to be released and their use rose 25 per cent between 1982 and 1986. The development of safe substitution for aerosols, plastic-foam materials and for refrigeration and air-conditioning systems is lagging behind the need for a rapid phasing-out of CFCs. Even if all production of CFCs was banned immediately, the chemicals would take centuries to fall to the levels of the mid-1970s, and until 2050 even to drop to the level of 1985.

The oilfields of Kuwait set alight by retreating Iraqi forces at the end of the Gulf War (1991). It took nearly a year to extinguish the fires, which caused considerable damage to the environment of the region. (Gamma)

OTHER THREATS TO THE ENVIRONMENT

AIR POLLUTANTS

The internal combustion engine that powers the motor car produces carbon monoxide, an odourless, highly poisonous gas. Car engines also emit hydrocarbons and nitrogen oxides, which, under the influence of sunlight, form *low-atmosphere ozone*, a major irritant and air pollutant. It is the main ingredient in the photochemical smog that afflicts Los Angeles, Tokyo and Athens. Lead, which is added to petrol to improve performance, is also a threat. Excess lead levels in the atmosphere can damage the brain and nervous system, especially in children. Lead-free petrol is becoming more popular, but the switch to unleaded fuel has brought its own problems. In America, the aromatic hydrocarbon content of petrol – benzine, toluene and xylene – has been doubled to help performance. These compounds are known carcinogens (causes of cancer).

But the major form of air pollution comes from another source. Coal-fired power stations and other industrial processes emit sulphur dioxide and nitrogen oxides, which, when combined with atmospheric moisture, create *acid rain* (dilute sulphuric or nitric acid). Acid rain (or snow) is the main atmospheric fallout of industrial pollutants, although these may also occur as dry deposits (such as ash). Acid rain damages forests, plants and agriculture, raises the acid level in lakes and ground water, killing fish, and contaminating drinking water. It upsets the fine chemical balance in lakes that are home to numerous species of fish. Even a slight increase in acidity causes heavy metals such as aluminium and mercury to become more concentrated, decreasing the amount of oxygen available to the fish and eventually causing their death. The absence of large fish destabilizes the ecosystem and the effects are felt throughout the food chain.

Acid rain also causes damage to the soil. High levels of acid rain in the soil cause lead and other heavy metals to become concentrated and interrupt the life-cycles of microorganisms. The bacteria and fungi that help break down organic matter into nutrients are disturbed (⇨ the nitrogen cycle; p. 206), and soils can lose their ability to support forests or agriculture.

WATER POLLUTION

Rivers and seas are also used as dumping grounds for waste products. Excessive amounts of domestic sewage, fertilizers and other toxic chemicals thus disposed of can destroy the life forms that live in water. Water itself is also used to cool industrial factories, but when returned to rivers can cause an increase in the temperature, so destabilizing the natural habitat. Industrial waste products can also contaminate drinking water.

PESTICIDES

Increasingly high levels of pesticides are present in the bodies of most creatures. More than 2,300,000 tonnes (tons) of pesticides were produced in the world in 1986, and their use is increasing worldwide by nearly 13 per cent per year. They become concentrated in the bodies of animals at the top of the food chain (including humans).

NUCLEAR POWER

The nuclear industry produces waste, much of which will remain highly toxic and radioactive for tens of thousands of years. In the USA, high-level waste is stored in stainless steel tanks, which are cooled and buried. But in Britain high-level waste undergoes vitrification, which involves solidifying the radioactive material in glass to facilitate handling. Lower-level waste is usually buried in shallow sites, or in abandoned mines. The problem of nuclear waste has not been solved, only delayed. Most methods involve moving the waste to safer places where future problems may arise.

The greenhouse effect

The surface of the Earth is warmed by solar radiation, much of it in short wavelength form (visible light), which passes easily through the atmosphere to the Earth's surface. There it is absorbed and re-radiated in a longer wavelength form (heat), which is more efficiently trapped by the carbon dioxide (CO_2) in the atmosphere. Thus the light energy is effectively converted to heat and held in by a thermal blanket in precisely the same way as happens in a greenhouse (⇨ p. 52). This process – the greenhouse effect – keeps the temperature of the Earth's surface within quite narrow limits.

So long as the amounts of carbon dioxide in the lower atmosphere remain constant, this temperature equilibrium will be maintained. Unfortunately, the amount of carbon dioxide in the atmosphere has increased. For about 150 years – since the start of the Industrial Revolution – we have been seriously interfering with the balance of the carbon cycle (⇨ p. 206). Carbon dioxide has been passed into the atmosphere at an unprecedented rate from the burning of coal, oil, natural gas and biomass fuel. The burning of these fuels adds some 5 billion tonnes of carbon to the atmosphere each year. Different fossil fuels, weight for weight, add different proportions of carbon when they are burned. Coal contains a high ratio of carbon to hydrogen and releases the greatest amount of carbon. Oil has a higher proportion of hydrogen and releases rather less carbon. Natural gas, methane, has the highest proportion of hydrogen – four atoms for every carbon atom – and releases the lowest amount of carbon into the atmosphere per unit weight. The net effect of all this burning of fossil fuel is a marked increase in atmospheric carbon dioxide.

The atmospheric balance has been further upset by the reduction in the rate at which carbon dioxide is taken from the atmosphere. When forests are destroyed, the rate of carbon uptake by vegetation drops (⇨ p. 206).

It is not yet conclusive that the increase in carbon dioxide has produced significant global warming, but research has shown that over the past 160,000 years there has been a strong correlation between atmospheric carbon dioxide levels and average temperature. The Ice Ages, for instance, were associated with substantial drops in atmospheric carbon dioxide concentrations – a decrease in the greenhouse effect, and the return to normal temperatures were associated with a return to normal carbon dioxide levels. It is possible that we are already seeing some of the consequences of the greenhouse effect. The sea level has risen about 15 cm (6 in) in the course of the 20th century. However, it is unlikely that the rise has been caused by melting icecaps, as has been suggested, because polar ice melting would require a much higher rise in average temperature than has as yet been reached. Some estimates suggest that a rise of 4°C (7.2°F) could lead to a slow collapse of the West Antarctic ice sheet, raising sea levels by 5 metres or more. The present rise in sea levels can be explained solely on the basis of simple thermal expansion of water, as matter expands when heated. If average temperatures rise by 2°C (3.6°F), sea levels will rise by a further 30 cm (12 in).

It is difficult to predict the consequences of global warming. The increased atmospheric CO_2 could be taken up by the oceans, in which the gas is soluble, and also by the world's vegetation, during photosynthesis (⇨ p. 192). However, the latter solution is looking less feasible with the increase in global deforestation. The destruction of the world's forests – usually by burning – will itself release more CO_2 into the atmosphere and also reduce the potential of vegetation to act as a carbon sink.

However, if estimates of rising sea levels from global warming are correct then some areas of the world are in danger of being submerged. The highest estimated rise that has been projected – 0.8–1.8 m (2½–6 ft) – could result in the disappearance of small, low-lying islands such as the Maldives in the Indian Ocean, while a rise of 1.8 m (6 ft) would seriously threaten cities such as London, New York and Venice.

SEE ALSO
● HEAT TRANSFER p. 52
● MULTICELLULAR ORGANISMS I p. 192
● THE BIOSPHERE p. 206

Aerosol sprays, which contain chlorofluorocarbons (CFCs), are thought to be one of the main contributors to the depletion of the ozone layer. Many western nations have agreed to a gradual phasing out of the use of CFCs, but many environmentalists believe that the reductions are not soon enough.
(Sinclair Stammers, SPL)

Acid rain has seriously depleted the temperate forests of the world. The acidity of the rain strips the leaves of their protective covering of wax, which not only causes direct damage to their cells but means that the leaves that are left are unprotected from desiccation and from fungal and bacterial infections. (IS)

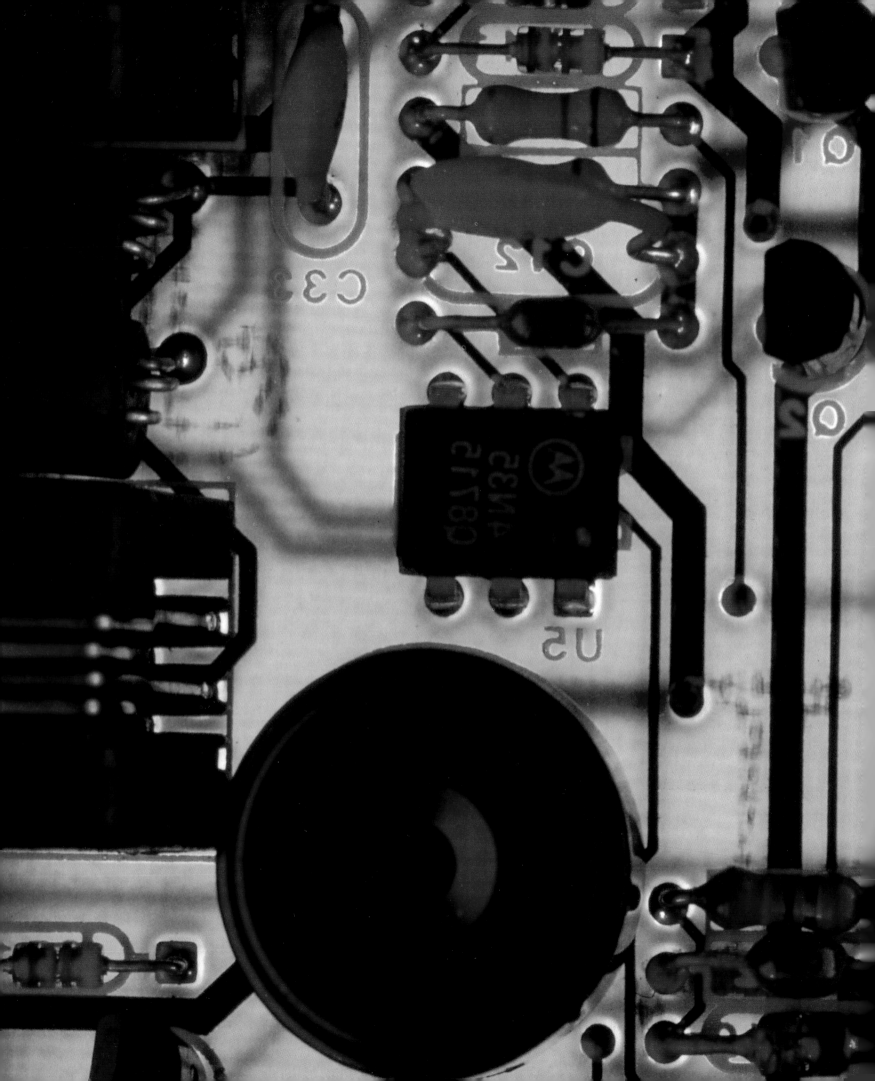

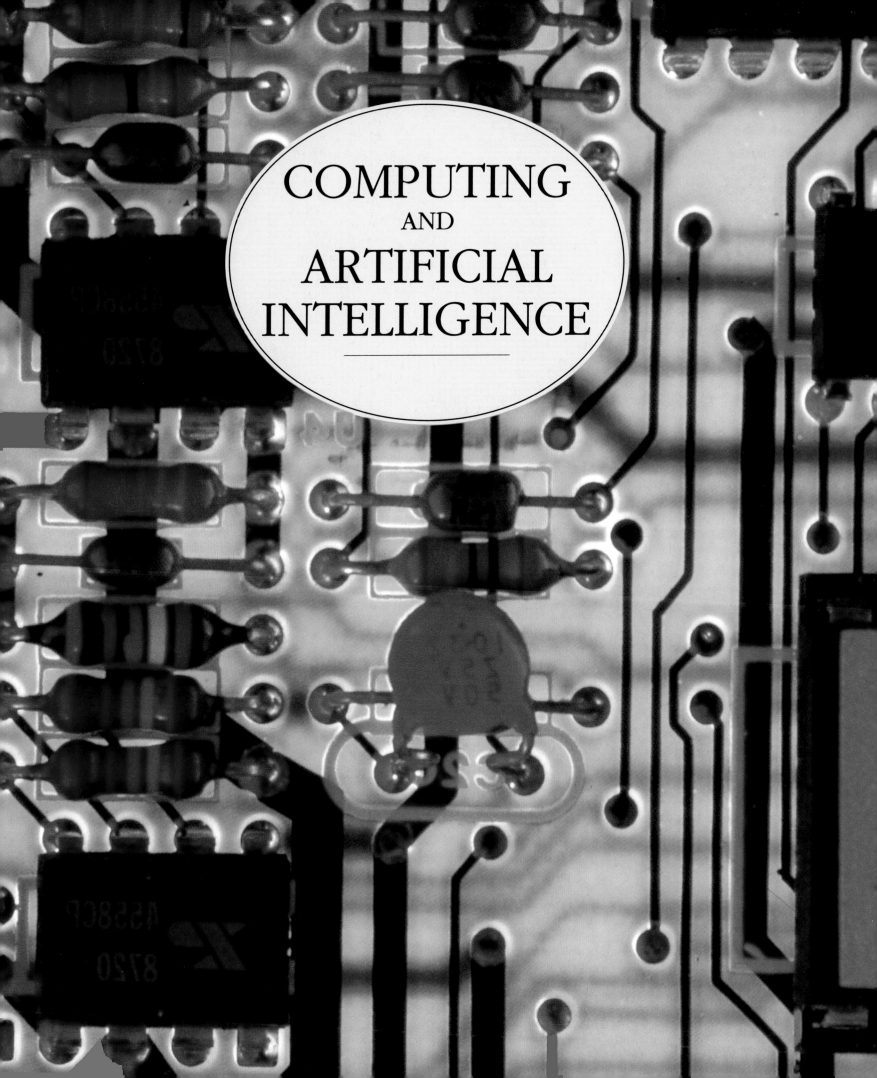

COMPUTING
AND
ARTIFICIAL
INTELLIGENCE

The Development of the Computer

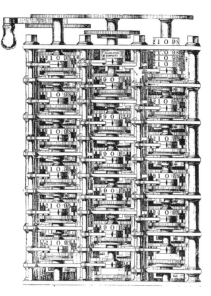

Twenty years ago the standard image of a computer was a large, enormously expensive mainframe machine, often occupying a building of its own, and served by a staff of experts. Of course such machines are still widely used, but today it is the compact desktop microcomputer that has become more familiar. Many of today's smaller machines can outperform, both in capacity and speed, earlier generations of mainframe machines. In terms of computing power the modern microcomputer is also amazingly cheap.

The Difference Engine (above right), designed by Charles Babbage, was an analogue decimal machine in which numbers were represented by the rotation of various wheels. It was designed originally to produce reliable life expectancy tables. Although designed in the early 19th century, the Difference Engine was not built until 1992, when scientists from the Science Museum in London used Babbage's designs to build a fully working analogue computer. (AR)

Countess of Lovelace (Ada Augusta King; 1815–52), daughter of Lord Byron, was the personal assistant of Charles Babbage and wrote the first computer programme (for the analytical engine). The ADA software was named after her. (Crown copyright – The National Physical Laboratory)

Any computer has four essential elements: a *storage* device to record data; a *processor* to manipulate data; an *input/output* device to get data into and out of the machine; and a *program* to control the process. There are many different types of computer program (collectively known as *software*), all of which tell the hardware (the machinery of the computer) precisely what to do at some point in the process of communication or data handling. But computers should not be thought of as simply superior arithmetical calculating devices, as they are also devices for the mass storage, sorting and immediate retrieval of information – whether numerical or textual. It is the computer's ability to perform these operations that gives it its real power and potential. As such it can be thought of as multiplying human ability.

Information access

The information concerned may be no more than the contents of all letters written since the computer was installed, the full details of the accounts of a small business or of the customers' names and addresses. On the other hand, the information may, in theory, extend to almost the whole range of human knowledge. For, today, such has been the effect of the computer revolution, that almost all human knowledge is now accessible in a form which a computer can read. This information can be tapped by way of an ordinary telephone line, or partially stored on a small magnetic or optical disk. A library of the entire text of 1,000 of the world's greatest books can be obtained on a single compact disc and can be read in plain text on a computer screen.

Early analogue computers

In the early days of computing, nearly all computers were *analogue* devices, which are fundamentally different in principle from the modern *digital* computer. In analogue computers, different quantities are represented in various physical ways such as by the position of a rotating wheel, the distances between points on a surface, or by different voltages. Analogue computers were the first widely used practical computers and had many applications.

An early general-purpose analogue computing device was the slide rule invented by John Napier in 1617. In essence, this consisted of two identical logarithmic scales (⇨ p. 18) in which, for instance, the distance from 0 to 1 was the same as from 1 to 10 and from 10 to 100. If such scales are placed together and then one slid along the other so that the zero of scale A lies opposite a number on scale B, all the multiples of that number can be read off on scale B opposite whichever numbers are selected on scale A. Slide rules were widely used by engineers and scientists, but mistakes were liable to be made in reading the scales.

Although the analogue computers of the 19th century were mechanically complicated, they were essentially simple devices. Mechanical calculators worked on decimal decade systems using rows of 10-position wheels each of which rotated one position for each complete revolution of the wheel to the right, on the mileometer (odometer) principle. Wheels could be reversed for subtraction, and mechanical linkages allowed multiplication and division. Lord Kelvin (William Thompson) built a computer in 1876 that made tide calculations. In the 20th century many analogue computers were designed to carry out a particular purpose, such as predicting anti-aircraft gun target positions. Attempts to produce general-purpose electrical analogue computers in which quantities were represented by varying positive or negative voltages that could be summed, resulted in large, cumbersome, crude machines of limited accuracy. Some, however, were able to solve differential equations and were of practical value.

Punched card information storage

A notable stage in the evolution of the modern computer was the fundamentally new idea of storing instructions in physical form for the operation of a machine. This was the idea of the French inventor Joseph-Marie Jacquard (1752–1834), who, in 1805, introduced a weaving loom that used a series of cards punched with holes in different positions that automatically controlled intricate patterns of weaving and produced any desired tapestry or brocade. Jacquard's system was highly successful and rapidly spread throughout the world. Jacquard, although attacked by silk weavers fearful for their livelihood, was awarded the cross of the Legion of Honour, a pension and a royalty on each machine. But Jacquard's remarkable idea was to bear further fruit.

Charles Babbage and the difference engine

Once the idea of the physical storage of information was abroad, others took up the principle. One of these was the British mathematician Charles Babbage (1792–1871), who also adopted Jacquard's idea of using punched cards to input data. Babbage was keenly aware of the inaccuracies of the existing mathematical tables but was equally aware of the tedium of the calculations involved. He therefore resolved to see whether such calculations could be performed mechanically, and proceeded to work on the design of a machine, the *difference engine*, that would do exactly that. After ten years of toil, great expense and dispute with his chief engineer, Babbage's

financial support for the project was withdrawn by the government, and most of the 12,000 parts (about half of the total) that had been made were melted down for scrap. But Babbage's ideas were sound. The Difference Engine No. 2 was finally built in 1990. In November 1991 it performed its first full-scale calculation on the 200th anniversary of Babbage's birth. It has worked perfectly ever since.

Punched card developments

In the late 19th century the punched card idea was further developed by the American inventor Herman Hollerith (1860–1929), who designed machines that could rapidly read data from standard punched cards. In 1890 Hollerith's punched cards and machine were used successfully to tackle the mammoth task of calculating the US Census. Hollerith's idea was then taken up by the International Business Machines (IBM) company and others, whose machines could read large blocks of cards fed in at a rate of up to 250 per minute. For over 50 years – until the 1970s – punched card machines handled most large-scale business information storage and processing. This development was not, however, in any real sense computing.

The electronic digital computer

In the 1930s various attempts were made to develop digital computers using electromechanical relays. These relays, now largely superseded, were once very widely used primarily to switch large electric current with small currents. Relay switches can be off or on. As the American mathematician Claude Shannon (1916–) suggested in his Master's degree thesis in 1937, an 'off' can be considered as a zero and an 'on' as a 1. Using Boolean logic (⇨ p. 22) and the binary system of numbers to the base 2, instead of the conventional decimal system of numbers to the base 10, electrical switches can perform arithmetic and logic (⇨ pp. 102–5 and 214). However,

computers using relays were never practical as they were large, slow, inefficient, noisy and consumed huge currents.

What was needed was an electrically-operated switch that was small and speedy and operated on a small current. At once the thermionic valve suggested itself, and in 1942 the American physicist John V. Atanasoff (1903–) produced one of the first calculating devices using thermionic valves. It was, however, the requirements of the military that really motivated early electronic computer research. Early in World War II physicists of the University of Pennsylvania approached the American government with the suggestion that a computer could be produced that would rapidly calculate gunnery coordinates. Government support was forthcoming and in 1946 physicists J. Presper Eckert (1919–) and John William Mauchly (1907–80) demonstrated the general-purpose computer *Electronic Numerical Integrator And Calculator* (ENIAC). This weighed several tonnes, used 18,000 valves and consumed 100 kilowatts of power. When working, it could perform 5,000 calculations a second. With so many valves and the production of so much heat there was a constant tendency for valve filaments to burn out and stop the operation. There was no programming system and new calculations required a change in the wiring and the setting of a large number of switches.

This latter problem was overcome when the Hungarian-born American mathematician John von Neumann (1903–57) pointed out that there was no reason why the program of instructions for the machine's procedures should not be entered into the machine in the same way as the numerical data. This idea has proved fundamental and led to the modern concept of software. The first commercial electronic digital computer capable of using stored programs was called the *Universal Automatic Calculator*

(UNIVAC). This, too, was designed by Eckert and Mauchly in the 1950s.

Although widely used, thermionic valves continued to prove less than optimum as computing switches and it was not until the invention of the transistor (⇨ pp. 96–101) in 1947 that computers entered a second generation and really became practicable. Transistors were tiny, ran cool, had very small power requirements, and were much more reliable than valves. Some transistor computers used magnetic core memories for data processing and magnetic disks and tape for inputting data and for secondary data storage.

Integrated circuits, in which many transistors were combined, with resistors and capacitors (⇨ pp. 96 and 98) and their associated connections, on a single silicon chip, ushered in the third generation of computers. The most successful of these was the IBM System 360 computers, introduced in 1964, which soon made IBM the world leader in computers. Integrated circuits made it possible to scale down computers to the 'mini' size. These appeared first in 1965 at a fraction of the cost of the large mainframes. Integrated-circuit design continued to progress and ever larger numbers of transistors and associated components were incorporated into a single chip. Medium-scale integration with up to 1,000 components was followed by large-scale integration (LSI) with up to 10,000 components, very-large-scale integration (VLSI) and ultra-large-scale integration (ULSI; over 100,000 components). VLSI and ULSI brought in the fourth generation of computers including, in the mid-1970s, the microcomputer based on the single chip microprocessor (⇨ p. 214).

Microcomputers developed rapidly in the 1980s and 1990s increasing in power and dropping in price at an unprecedented rate. As such the real computing revolution has been in personal access, by ordinary people of limited means, to almost unlimited computing power.

A British computer (left) from 1950. Described as the 'Thinking Machine', it was one of the first electronic computers with a memory. It was capable of dealing with any computation problems, carrying out the arithmetic by an elaborate series of shunting operations. (Popperfoto)

SEE ALSO

- MATHEMATICS 3 p. 22
- ELECTRONICS pp. 102–5
- INSIDE A DIGITAL COMPUTER p. 214
- INFORMATION p. 216
- PROGRAMMING, SOFTWARE AND APPLICATIONS p. 218
- DIGITAL COMMUNICATIONS p. 220
- MICROELECTRONICS AND CONTROL SYSTEMS p. 222
- ARTIFICIAL INTELLIGENCE p. 224
- THE BRAIN–COMPUTER ANALOGY p. 226

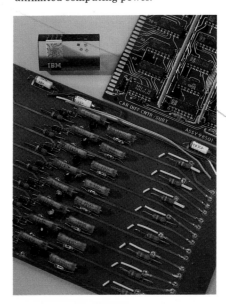

Computer circuit boards from the 1960s and 1970s. The large brown board on the left is part of a Ferranti Atlas I machine of 1963 and features transistors (the black circular components in a row) among other electronic components. The smaller blue board is from the arithmetic logic unit (ALU; ⇨ p. 214) of a UNIVAC 1108 computer of the late 1960s. Further miniaturization in computing is illustrated by the individual integrated circuit in perspex (top) of an IBM 370 machine from the 1970s along with the millimetre-wide silicon chips. Miniature integrated circuits have allowed the growth of even smaller personal computers. (Sheila Terry, SPL)

Inside a Digital Computer

All electronic digital computers, however large or small, contain the same basic components. Differences consist only in the size of the various memories, in the size of the numbers which they can handle at one time, and in the capacity, and sometimes the type, of devices that input and output the data and the programs.

All data is stored and manipulated in a digital computer in *binary* (⇨ p. 22) – a number system that is limited to 1s and 0s. These are called *binary digits*, usually abbreviated to *bits*. In the decimal system of numbers, the value of the numbers in each column is ten times that of those in the column to the right. In the binary system the value is twice that of those in the column to the right. Thus in the binary system, 10 is not ten, but is 2+0 and is equal to decimal 2, 11 is equal to decimal 3 and 111 is equal to decimal 7 (4+2+1). Numbers are commonly represented as eight-digit units called *bytes*. So 10101010 is equal to 170

(128+0+32+0+8+0+2+0) and 11111111 is equal to 255. Eight-bit computers, the most common type, handle numbers eight bits wide and convey data along eight parallel channels simultaneously. Sixteen-bit computers handle 16-bit numbers (2 bytes), and faster and more powerful machines may handle 32- (4 bytes) or even 64-bit (8 byte) numbers.

Memory

Computers spend a great deal of time moving numbers to and from various memories or storage systems. Central to every computer is the *random access memory* (RAM), which is a read or write device in which the basic element, or cell, is a tiny electronic circuit capable of storing or of giving up one bit of information. RAMs are formed from two-dimensional arrays of such elements, organized with *addresses* so that the computer can interrogate any particular group of 8, 16 or 32 cells and read out the number contained in it. RAMs require electric current to operate and if the current is switched off all the information contained in the RAM is lost. For this reason they are known as *volatile* memories. If the information put into the RAM during a work session must be kept, a copy must be made from the RAM to some form of permanent storage, such as a magnetic disk, before the machine is switched off. Beginners commonly lose data by forgetting this. Some systems copy RAM data to disk automatically at designated intervals. Copying material onto disk is known as 'saving'.

Application programs (⇨ p. 218) that determine the operation of the computer must also be temporarily stored in RAM before they can be used. RAMs must be large enough to hold extensive application programs and handle considerable quantities of data. Quite small machines may have RAMs that can hold 4, 8 or 16 million bytes, which can amount to 128 million separate 1-bit cells.

Read-only memories (ROMs) are different. They contain data that is not lost when the power is switched off, and which can be copied whenever required. Every computer has a ROM containing a small essential program and data needed for the immediate starting up of the machine. ROMs are also sometimes used to store other programs that will be constantly needed. Apart from computers, they are commonly used in a wide range of other electronically controlled devices, such as washing machines, other domestic appliances, cars and toys.

The central processing unit

In modern computers the *central processing unit* (CPU) is a complex single chip called a microprocessor (⇨ p. 104). This contains an *arithmetic and logic unit* (ALU) and an *operational control unit* (OCU). The ALU does all the sums and carries out logical operations such as deciding if two numbers are equal or if one number is larger or smaller than another. The OCU receives instructions from the RAM and splits these into small steps so that they can be dealt with in proper order and sequence by the ALU. The *central processing unit* needs to be able to hold several lots of data and instructions temporarily while other material is being processed by the ALU, so it also has small high-speed memories, called *registers* or *buffers,* in which to hold these groups of data as well as the intermediate arithmetical results of the

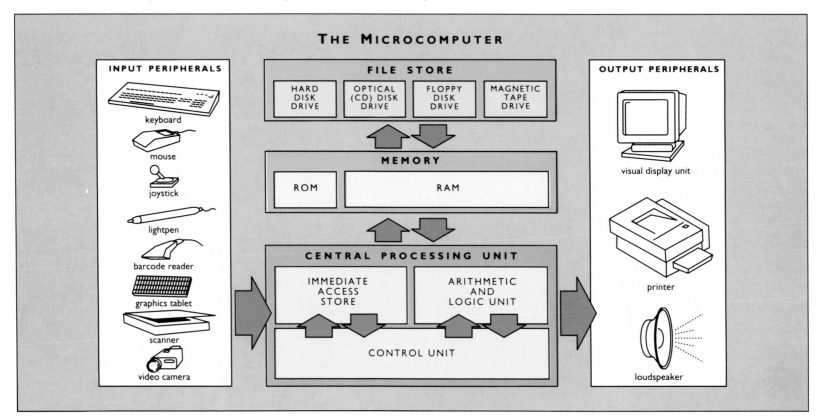

THE MICROCOMPUTER

INPUT PERIPHERALS
- keyboard
- mouse
- joystick
- lightpen
- barcode reader
- graphics tablet
- scanner
- video camera

FILE STORE
| HARD DISK DRIVE | OPTICAL (CD) DISK DRIVE | FLOPPY DISK DRIVE | MAGNETIC TAPE DRIVE |

MEMORY
| ROM | RAM |

CENTRAL PROCESSING UNIT
| IMMEDIATE ACCESS STORE | ARITHMETIC AND LOGIC UNIT |

CONTROL UNIT

OUTPUT PERIPHERALS
- visual display unit
- printer
- loudspeaker

ALU operations. Computers operate under the control of a 'clock' that provides timing pulses to keep all the operations in strict synchronization. Without a clock the computer would become hopelessly muddled, tending to perform operations in the wrong order. The clock is actually a quartz crystal oscillator (⇨ p. 70) producing a stream of square electrical pulses. With each pulse, everything moves forward one step.

The power of a central processing unit depends, among other things, on the amount of RAM it can address. Until around 1985 few computer CPUs could interact with more than one million bytes of memory (1 megabyte). Today, many 32-bit machines can address 16 megabytes of memory and 64-bit machines could, in theory, address a RAM of 4,000 megabytes (4 gigabytes). For simple purposes, such as word processing, text retrieval, communications, running spreadsheets or doing accounts, a RAM of 1 megabyte is ample. But when the computer becomes involved in complex graphics or computer-aided design (CAD) work (⇨ p. 218), much larger quantities of data must be handled and a much larger RAM and more powerful CPU are needed.

Personal computing gained in popularity with the introduction of the Intel 8080, 8-bit microprocessor (CPU) in 1974. This was succeeded by the 8086 and 8088 processors, both 16-bit but commonly used as 8-bit processors. The 8088 was used in the first IBM personal computer. Today these early processors or chips, although still widely used, are obsolete. They have been replaced, successively, by the 80286, 80386, 80486 and the Intel Pentium, introduced in March 1993. Computers have progressed in speed and power and it is common to describe a machine in terms of the number of millions of operations per second (mips) it can perform. Early IBM personal computers could perform about 0.25 mips (250,000 operations per second), while powerful desktop 'workstations' can perform over 100 mips.

The 64-bit Pentium chip can operate at over 100 mips. Tens of millions of computers using these CPUs are currently in use.

The early 8088 microprocessor ran comfortably at a clock speed of 4.77 million pulses a second (4.77 megahertz; Mhz). Although considered fast at the time, the clock speeds of today have increased considerably to over 100 megahertz. Most current machines run at about 30–60 Mhz. Computer speed is not simply a matter of competition between brands, since increased speed becomes essential as computing tasks increase in complexity and size.

Supercomputers have been designed to operate at very high speed. They are capable of performing simple operations in picoseconds (thousand-billionths of a second). In order to reach such speeds, supercomputers employ several processes to work simultaneously (parallel

computing; ⇨ p. 226), and cool processors down to almost absolute zero temperature. Supercomputers perform tasks for the military, weather forecasting and make fluid and aerodynamics calculations. They are also used to design aircraft, cars and ships, and to model crash tests of vehicles. They can save manufacturers months of work and a great deal of money.

Operating systems

The class of personal computers known as MS-DOS (Microsoft disk operating system) machines use the 80286, 80386, 80486 and Pentium chips. But the 8080 series of microprocessors are not the only class of CPUs used in computers. Their rivals, the Motorola 68000 family of chips, are used in the Apple Macintosh computers. In essence, Apple and MS-DOS machines are the same but they are run by different programs known as *operating systems* that present different faces to the user. The operating system in use is loaded into RAM after a computer is switched on, and then proceeds to organize how the machine functions. The Apple operating system is very 'user-friendly' and is based primarily on the use of pictorial images, depicting various functions, which can be selected and activated by the use of a 'mouse'. This is a simple device, the movement of which causes the pointer on the screen to move. When the pointer is advanced to the required 'icon' and a button on the mouse 'clicked', the appropriate function is performed.

The MS-DOS operating system, sold by Microsoft, simply presents a letter indicating which disk drive is currently operative. MS-DOS is less user-friendly but is a powerful operating system, providing many facilities, entirely under the control of the user, and is preferred by those who enjoy the flexibility and satisfaction of directly controlling the machine. The 6th version of MS-DOS was introduced in 1993. Microsoft have succeeded in getting the best of both worlds by introducing an operating system called *Windows* that runs under MS-DOS. This provides a mouse-operated *graphical user interface* (GUI) similar to that of the Apple system. Such systems are evolving very rapidly. The general trend, powered by commercial considerations, is towards ever more user-friendly operating systems. Already a *multimedia* approach allows the user access to textual, voice

and visual communication with other computer operators and with interactive compact discs (CD-I) that are inserted into the machine. Many other operating systems have been written for different purposes and for different classes of machine. Scientists and many general programmers, for instance, often prefer to use the more detailed and intricate operating system known as *Unix*, which has long been established and which exists in various forms.

Storage, input and output devices

Computer programs and data are stored on magnetic disks. These may be sealed devices, known as *hard disks*, usually situated within the machine and with a capacity of from 20 megabytes to about 2,000 megabytes (2 gigabytes). Hard disks allow rapid access to programs and data and are very reliable. The breakdown of a hard disk may, however, result in the loss of invaluable data. Responsible users will always make regular backup copies on removable 'floppy' disks or on tape. All personal computers have at least one, often two, floppy disk drives into which the disks are slotted. New programs are supplied on floppy disks or compact discs and are copied to hard disks via the floppy disk drive. Various other forms of storage device are used, such as optical systems which use lasers to write data in the form of microscopic pits or lands representing 0s and 1s of the binary number system. Compact disc read-only memories (CD-ROMs), capable of holding over 600 megabytes, are now commonly used.

Data can be input to computers in a number of ways. These include standard keyboards, magnetic-ink character readers, bar code readers, *optical character recognition* (OCR) systems that can read normal printed text, educable voice recognition systems and even educable handwriting character readers. Sophisticated OCR systems are now being used to convert the world's printed text to ASCII code (⇨ p. 216). The punched card and tape of earlier machines are now obsolete.

Output of data from computers may also take various forms, the commonest being the visual display unit (VDU). Most VDUs are still cathode-ray tubes (⇨ p. 102) operating in a manner similar to that of television displays, but flat, liquid-crystal displays are used in portable computers. Information shown on the VDU may also be directed to one of several types of printer or phototypesetter. Other output devices include speech synthesizers, graph plotters and computer output on microfilm or microfiche.

Information

Any item of human knowledge, or anything that can add to the sum of human knowledge or experience, is information. It may be conveyed, or recorded, in a multitude of different ways or forms. We live in an information age in which many people are increasingly concerned with the generation, transmission, storage, dissemination, retrieval, assimilation and use of information.

The smallest quantity of computer information is the binary digit or bit. This may be a 1 or a 0, and by using various forms of coding, all information, of whatever form, may be represented using only these two entities (⇨ pp. 21 and 214). It may be in the form of a succession of millions of microscopic pits on the surface of a compact disc (⇨ box) or in a series of electromagnetic pulses transmitted from an Earth satellite. A unique performance of Beethoven's Ninth Symphony can be written down in a book simply as a series of binary numbers. It would be a large book, however, because for each second of music about 30,000 numbers would be needed, making over 100 million numbers in all.

The digital age

Today's technology demands that much of the information we use should be converted into digital form. Human beings can only use information directly if it is in analogue form. The movement of our

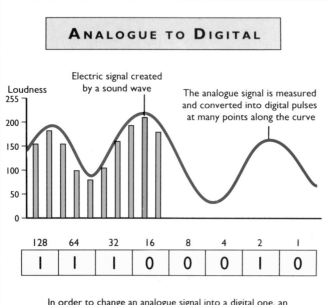

ANALOGUE TO DIGITAL

Loudness
255

Electric signal created by a sound wave

The analogue signal is measured and converted into digital pulses at many points along the curve

200

150

100

50

0

128	64	32	16	8	4	2	1
1	1	1	0	0	0	1	0

In order to change an analogue signal into a digital one, an integrated circuit measures the strength of the analogue signal thousands of times each second. It then changes the measurements into the correct sequence of digital signals. A digital signal is in binary form (⇨ p. 216), which means that it is a sequence of on (1) or off (0). Here the value of 226 is converted into the digital number 11100010, which represents 128 + 64 + 32 + 2.

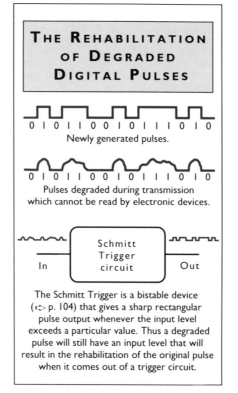

THE REHABILITATION OF DEGRADED DIGITAL PULSES

0 1 0 1 1 0 0 1 0 1 0 1 1 0 1 0
Newly generated pulses.

0 1 0 1 1 0 0 1 0 1 0 1 1 0 1 0
Pulses degraded during transmission which cannot be read by electronic devices.

In → Schmitt Trigger circuit → Out

The Schmitt Trigger is a bistable device (⇨ p. 104) that gives a sharp rectangular pulse output whenever the input level exceeds a particular value. Thus a degraded pulse will still have an input level that will result in the rehabilitation of the original pulse when it comes out of a trigger circuit.

eardrums, for instance, is an analogue of the pressure changes occurring in the surrounding atmosphere as we hear sounds. The images on our retinas are analogues of the objects at which we are looking. Analogue information is, however, very susceptible to corruption and distortion, especially when transmitted. In the days of analogue telephones the information being conveyed was often interfered with by crackles or distortion, largely because such interference was, itself, analogue in nature and was simply added to the desired signal. Engineers use the term 'noise' to describe *any* unwanted addition to the information, whatever its form (⇨ illustration). A flash of light that momentarily disrupts a TV image is noise.

The digital revolution has changed all that. When information is transmitted in digital form, analogue noise or distortion has little or no effect. So long as the digital signal – a series of pulses, each representing a 1, and a series of absences of pulses, each representing a 0 – is able to get through, the original analogue information can be perfectly re-created. Analogue to digital conversion is best understood in an electrical context. Suppose that a piece of symphonic music is picked up by an ideal microphone and converted to a complexly varying voltage. If the voltage is plotted against time as a graph the result will be a single complex waveform (⇨ illustration). Consider a one-second period of this waveform and imagine it sliced vertically into a large number of immediately consecutive slices. Each of these narrow slices will have a particular height that can be represented by a number, and these numbers can be expressed in binary form (⇨ p. 214).

Pulses can easily be sent along a communication medium, such as a wire, a glass fibre or a microwave radio link, at a rate of several million per second. So the numbers can be sent consecutively in 'real time', even if the second is divided into as many as 40,000 slices and each of these requires several bytes (⇨ p. 22). It is not of any particular importance if some or even all of the pulses are somewhat distorted; all the electronic circuits have to do is to distinguish between the presence and absence of a pulse, and this they can easily do. Quite severely reduced or distorted pulses can immediately be reconstituted by trigger circuits (⇨ illustration).

It is natural to think that analogue information, such as music, must somehow be degraded by being sliced up and then reconstituted, but information theory indicates that if the number of slices is sufficient – if the 'sampling rate' is high enough – *all* the information in the original, however complex and subtle, is retained and can be recovered. This is the principle behind music compact discs, where the sampling rate must be at least twice as high as the highest frequency in the original signal to obtain high fidelity.

Digital to analogue and analogue to digital conversion are important technological facilities to which many people have devoted years of research. The result is that we can purchase silicon chip integrated circuits (⇨ p. 104) that perform the conversion, in one direction or the other, with brilliant efficiency. 'A to D' and 'D to A' conversion is now commonplace in electronics.

Digital logic

Once information is coded in terms of binary 1s and 0s and represented as electrical voltages – for example 5 volts for a 1 and less than 1 volt for a 0 – it is a simple matter to organize electronic circuits that can process these voltage levels. These circuits are called *logic*

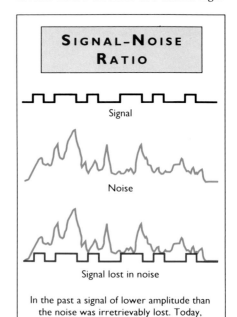

SIGNAL–NOISE RATIO

Signal

Noise

Signal lost in noise

In the past a signal of lower amplitude than the noise was irretrievably lost. Today, various techniques have been developed to retrieve such signals.

gates (⇨ p. 104) and they are based on the work of the English mathematician George Boole (1815–64; ⇨ p. 22), whose 1854 paper *The Laws of Thought* investigated logical problems using binary arithmetic. This work seemed a little academic and pointless at the time but its importance was appreciated by the American Claude Shannon (1916–), who suggested that it was capable of physical realization using switches.

All computers are based on Boolean logical gates which are input with electrical pulses representing 1s and 0s. Gates are designed so that their output depends on particular combinations of input (usually two). An AND gate gives a 1 (true) output only if both inputs are 1; otherwise it gives a 0 (false) output. An OR gate gives a 1 (true) output if *either* or both inputs is a 1. It gives a 0 (false) output if both inputs are 0. A NOT gate has only one input and one output. It gives a 1 (true) output if the input is 0 (false), or a 0 (false) output if the input is 1 (true). NOT gates are also called 'inverters'. In a NOR gate – an OR gate plus a NOT gate (inverter) – the output will be 1 (true) only if both inputs are 0 (false). There is also an exclusive OR gate (XOR). Here an output will be 1 (true) only for inputs of 1 (true) and 0 (false) or 0 (false) and 1 (true). All logical problems can be solved using various combinations of these gates, and the gates can be connected together to form various arithmetical units. To slim down the operation, logical gates are often produced in the form of NAND gates. A NAND gate is an AND gate followed by a NOT gate (inverter). It works in the same way as the AND gate except that, in the output, all 1s become 0s and all 0s become 1s. Any Boolean expression can be realized using only NAND gates as all the other gates can be made using various combinations of NAND gates.

Information coding

The binary system, in which numbers are written to the base two (⇨ p. 214), is not the only way in which decimal numbers can be represented as 1 or 0 bits. In the binary-coded decimal system, for instance, the four-bit binary number corresponding to each of the numbers from 0 to 9 is used to represent each decimal number as it is placed in its particular column in the decimal system. So, in this system, decimal 936 is 1001 (9) 0011 (3) 0110 (6). Various other methods of coding decimal numbers are used. In the octal system, for instance, numbers are written to the base 8. The columns, from the right, represent 1s, 8s, 64s, 512s, and so on. Only the numbers 0 to 7 are used. The conversion from octal to binary is easy as each octal digit can be converted in turn. Thus, the number 7652 in the octal code is 111, 110, 101, 010 in binary. Only three bits are needed to represent in binary each of the numbers from 0 to 7.

The ASCII code

Because eight bits can represent 255 different entities, they can also be used arbitrarily to represent letters and punctuation marks as well as numbers. In the commonly used ASCII code (American Standard Code for Information Interchange), for instance, each upper and lower case letter of the alphabet, each of the numbers 0 to 9, each of the punctuation marks, blank space, and a number of other symbols is given a unique digital number. This is how a computer stores verbal (alphanumeric) information. Each letter or number is stored as the corresponding ASCII code binary number. The extended ASCII code for IBM-compatible personal computers takes the matter further and uses all the numbers up to 254 to represent a wide range of typographical characters and symbols, including accented letters such as é, è, à, ë and ê and some Greek letters such as α, ß, Γ, π, ∑ σ and μ.

Information access and retrieval

Much of the world's information is still stored in printed form and the mass of this information is so great that it is often very difficult to find particular items. This is especially so when it is necessary to find out whether, and if so what, information exists on a particular subject. For many years, the classification and ordering of information has been a preoccupation of librarians and others. Indexing of books and of scientific and other journals has been one important means. But today, in many subjects, the mass of information and the number of publications is so great that consulting indexes has become impracticable. Another constraint is the sheer physical bulk, and the resulting storage problems, of printed information.

Computers are helping greatly to solve both of these problems. Already they are widely used to search digitalized indexes of article titles and summaries, using recognized 'keywords'. Eventually, all the information now printed will be available in digital form, and already, nearly all the new information is recorded in this way. Because of their speed, computers can very quickly find and retrieve any designated 'string' of characters from within any mass of digital information. This in itself is not sufficient, however, because many of the strings that are found will be irrelevant. It would, for instance, be pointless to ask a computer to retrieve every instance of the string 'cancer' in a year's issue of a medical journal, as this would throw up thousands of entries. Computer searches are, therefore, systematized and use Boolean logic. Computers are asked, for instance, to find all entries of a particular word or phrase AND/OR another particular word or phrase, but NOT another word or phrase. In instructing the computer to search the user can insert the symbol ? for any unknown letter and the symbol * for any word or part of a word. Thus, for carcin* the computer will find carcinoma, carcinomatosis, carcinogenic, carcinogenesis, carcinoid, and so on.

COMPACT DISCS

The compact disc (CD) has become the most popular form of audio entertainment, storing music in digital form. The disc, made of aluminium, is etched with a series of pits between which are the reflecting lands. The disc is covered in a transparent plastic coating. It is the pits and lands, which represent numbers in digital code, that store the music. When a CD is played a laser scans the pits and lands and the reflected light forms a sequence of digital numbers representing the sound recorded. A photocell converts the optical signal into electrical form, which is converted to analogue form and sent to amplifiers and loudspeakers.

Audio compact discs. (Damien Lovegrove, SPL)

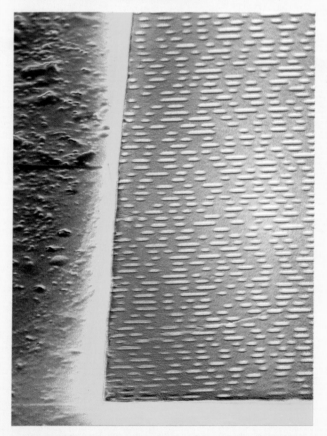

A compact disc through a false-colour scanning electron. It has been cracked to reveal the etched pits and lands that store the musical information. (Dr Jeremy Burgess, SPL)

Programming, Software and Applications

Although computers have much in common with biological brains and perform certain limited functions better than even the best human brains, they are still almost entirely incapable of learning by experience. As a result they need to be programmed – given detailed instructions every time they are asked to do something.

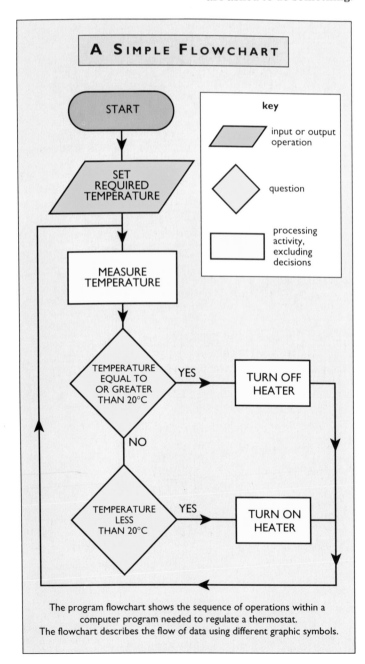

A SIMPLE FLOWCHART

START

SET REQUIRED TEMPERATURE

MEASURE TEMPERATURE

TEMPERATURE EQUAL TO OR GREATER THAN 20°C — YES → TURN OFF HEATER

NO

TEMPERATURE LESS THAN 20°C — YES → TURN ON HEATER

key

input or output operation

question

processing activity, excluding decisions

The program flowchart shows the sequence of operations within a computer program needed to regulate a thermostat.
The flowchart describes the flow of data using different graphic symbols.

The physical aspects of a computer are known, collectively, as the hardware, but, by itself, the hardware can do nothing. If we were to ask a child to look up the word 'software' in a dictionary, it would probably be sufficient to say 'Please look up the word "software" in the dictionary.' The corresponding request to a computer would have to be much more complicated and lengthy. The basic hardware of a computer cannot understand words, only numbers, but even if this request were translated into binary numbers (⋄ pp. 21 and 214) there would be no response from the machine. If one is to put together an instruction that would successfully make a computer perform such an action, that instruction must be broken down into tiny steps. First we would have to look carefully, and in detail, at what actually happens when one consults a dictionary. We might conclude that we hold the word 'software' in our memory while looking through the dictionary for a word that exactly resembles it. To do this with any sort of efficiency, we, as humans, need to know the accepted alphabetical order of letters, and we need to apply this knowledge at least five times in performing this task.

As far as the computer is concerned, the word 'software' is simply a sequence of eight consecutive numbers, known as a '*string*'. In ASCII code (⋄ p. 217) this string would contain 64 bits. The computer's dictionary is contained in a '*file*' consisting of an enormous sequence of numbers, some of them identified as standing for headwords and others as standing for definitions. After loading the dictionary file into RAM (⋄ p. 214), the computer's task is to scan through the headword series of numbers, comparing each with the string for 'software' until it finds an identical string. The computer can do this so quickly that it is indifferent to alphabetization and just starts at the beginning of the file and runs through it. When an identical string is found the computer is instructed to stop and to print out to the screen the headword and the associated definition. This is a trivial task for a computer, but the instructions needed to get the machine to do this can be quite complicated.

Programming

There are several main steps in producing a computer program:

- Analysing the task

- Breaking the task down into logical steps

- Producing a flowchart after deciding on the best sequence of actions

- Converting the flowchart into a sequence of instructions in a form the machine can understand and to which it can respond

- Writing the program manual (documentation)

- Testing in-house (alpha testing)

- Correcting errors (debugging)

- Distributing many copies to outside users to try out and criticize (beta testing)

The first three of these steps are included in the process known as *systems analysis*. This is the most important part of programming and the most difficult. If the analysis is defective, the program will never be able to do what is required of it. Before an adequate analysis can be made it is usually necessary to establish in detail the requirements of the ultimate users of the program and the practical limits to what can be expected of it. Feasibility studies may have to be done to establish whether the expectations of the future users are realistic.

A *flowchart* is a diagram, using standard symbols, of the way information is processed (⋄ illustration). The main sequence of events runs from the top of the chart to the bottom, but arrows may show temporary deviations to perform subsidiary tasks. The symbols, which stand for activities such as start, decision, store, output and stop, are connected by flow lines. These flowcharts are in the form of *algorithms* – logical procedures that determine the solution to a problem. The nodes of the algorithm are arranged so that the 'yes' or 'no' answer to a question determines the subsequent direction of action. Algorithms enable problems to be implemented and must take into account all possibilities. At this stage, the analysis may be shown to be inadequate and it may be necessary to look at it again.

Machine code and programming languages

The first computer programs were very simple, primarily because they had to be introduced into the machines, in the form of binary numbers (⋄ pp. 21 and 214), by closing (1) or opening (0) long sequences of switches. The instructions that today's machines actually use are still sequences of 1s and 0s, known as *machine code*. This code can go straight into the central processing unit or into its buffers (⋄ p. 214) to be operated on and is considered a *low-level* language. To make the programmer's task a little easier, each of the basic instructions or directions to the machine (each of which corresponds to a particular stream of machine code) can be expressed in symbolic form, known as an assembly language.

Assembly language

In *assembly language*, which is the next higher level of language, each instruction that the central processing unit (CPU) can execute is entered by using a precise name. Obviously, the programmer must be thoroughly familiar with the CPU for which he or she is programming and must know its instruction set. The programmer must also be familiar with the operating system (⋄ p. 214) which the computer uses. Computers cannot use assembly language directly,

VIRTUAL REALITY

Virtual Reality is an advanced form of computer simulation that gives the participant the illusion of being part of an artificial environment. Through the use of a headset with two tiny television screens (one for each eye), the participant experiences the artificial environment in 3-D and in stereo sound. Sensors in the headset detect movements of the participant's head or body and cause the view of the environment to change. Participants can also wear gloves fitted with sensors, known as datagloves, which transmit their hand movements to the artificial environment where they can seemingly pick up and move objects. Virtual reality is still in its infancy but is already being used in architecture design and computer video games.

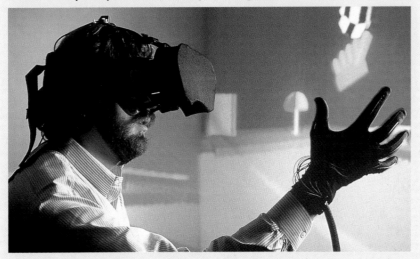

A man playing Cyberspace, a sophisticated videogame using virtual reality. The background display is generated by advanced computer graphics which can be projected through the headset.
(Peter Menzel, SPL)

but after the instructions are entered in assembly language an assembler program automatically converts these into machine code. In computing it is very common for particular sequences of instructions to be needed repeatedly. Programmers and operators constantly find themselves using these identical sequences, and writing them out or keying them in, over and over again, can become very boring. In such cases it is easy to arrange for the computer to translate a short, unique word or sequence of keystrokes into the complete sequence of instructions – a procedure known as a *macro*. A single, brief instruction that initiates a much more lengthy and complex sequence of instructions is clearly a great aid to economy, and macros are extensively used, both by programmers and by the more enterprising of ordinary personal computer users. Assembly languages, although low-level, commonly offer macro facilities.

High-level languages

Programs written in assembly language can be used only on the computer for which they were written, and they need an enormous number of instructions to accomplish quite simple tasks. For this reason, the macro principle has been extended to produce what are known as *high-level languages*. Apart from the enormous saving in time and drudgery, a great advantage of these is that the programmer can devote his or her attention primarily to the problem for which the program is being written, rather than to the characteristics of the machine. In essence, high-level languages allow the programmer to use everyday English or agreed symbols in writing the program.

In a high-level language, each statement used by the programmer has to be translated into a very large number of machine-code instructions. The programmer is, however, spared this task which, in most cases, is performed automatically by a program called a *compiler* which converts the written source program into machine code or *object code*. After the program is written, a copy of it is passed through the compiler and the resulting object code run in the machine. It is very rare for a program to run perfectly the first time and considerable correction is usually needed to eliminate errors in writing the actual code. The incorrect codes are known as *syntax errors*, often spelling mistakes, and the compiler will usually stop when it encounters such an error. A run-time error occurs as the program is running, and cannot be spotted by the computer during compilation, for example trying to divide a number by zero. Programmers also encounter errors in logic. The process of eliminating all these is called *debugging,* which often takes longer than writing the program.

A very large number of high-level languages have been written, the majority of which are used to write programs for special purposes. COBOL, for instance, was written to write programs for business purposes, FORTRAN and ALGOL were written primarily for scientific and mathematical purposes, and BASIC was developed as a language suitable for beginners. Today, most programmers are using general languages such as C or C++. These are programming languages developed for use with the Unix operating system, which combines the convenience and control of high-level language with the useful facility of being able to address the hardware at an assembly language level. C compilers generate very efficient object code. Modern high-level languages of this kind are highly structured and make extensive use of ready-made blocks of code. The current trend is to adopt an *object-oriented* philosophy in programming, which replaces the traditional concepts of procedure and data with *objects* and *messages*. Objects are packets of information of any kind, and messages are specifications of what the programmer wishes to be done to the object.

Applications software

All over the world, many thousands of programmers are continuously at work writing codes for numerous new programs or for updates of existing programs. Most of the software being written is user software to allow people with little knowledge of the details of computers to perform useful tasks with the least trouble. This is called applications software and the production and retailing of successful programs of this kind are among the most profitable of all commercial ventures.

Applications software written to meet unique individual requirements is very expensive, but software that can be used by many different people can be sold cheaply. Computers are very good at copying software and once a program has been written, debugged and proved, millions of copies can be made in a very short time for almost nothing more than the costs of the disks. Such programs include software for accounting, point-of-sale systems, stock control, production control, word processing, spreadsheet programs, statistical packages, computer-aided design (CAD), graphics production, desk-top publishing, personal information managers and many more. Because of the ease and accuracy of copying, software is now proliferating in an almost biological manner.

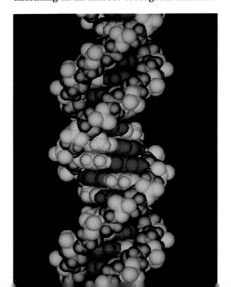

A computer graphics representation of a DNA molecule (⇔ p. 202). The use of computers to generate detailed graphics has become a major feature of biochemical research and a useful tool for learning. (Division of Computer Research and Technology, National Institute of Health, SPL)

Digital Communications

For centuries, people have communicated by speech and writing and, for many decades, by telephone and radio. Digital electronic communication is a new method of spreading information, which has expanded with unprecedented rapidity. It has led to a revolution in communication, which is no longer simply a transmission of data between people. Today, an immense amount of information passes, virtually without human intervention, between machines.

Digital communication is not essentially different from earlier modes, such as telephone and radio, but it has important new features that make it much more reliable. The obvious improvement in the sound quality of our telephones and the greatly reduced frequency of 'bad lines' is due to this. Most telephone messages are now transmitted digitally rather than by the previous analogue system (⇨ p. 216), which was highly susceptible to distortion, fading, crackles and other interference. Formerly, the greater the distance of the caller, the greater the likelihood of trouble, but as a result of digital technology distance is no longer of consequence.

Parallel and serial transmission

If data is to be sent in binary form in eight-bit bytes (⇨ p. 214), there is an obvious advantage in speed if each byte can be sent as a whole. The only way this can be done, however, is to send the eight bits simultaneously along eight parallel wires. This is called parallel transmission of data. For short distances, parallel transmission is satisfactory and is widely used. Length is important because it is essential that the eight bits remain in parallel and do not get out of step with each other. All eight bits must arrive at the other end of the cable at exactly the same time, and this would not occur if the eight wires were of slightly different length. The connections between a personal computer and its printer, for instance, are usually parallel. In this case the eight-way cable is seldom more than about two metres long. The cost of cabling also becomes important when great distances are involved.

Long-distance digital transfer of data is done in a different way, known as serial transmission. This requires only one wire or other conductor (with a ground connection or return wire to complete the circuit). In serial transfer of eight-bit data, the sending computer transmits each of the bits of each byte in turn. The receiving machine then reconstitutes each set of eight bits into a single byte.

Handshaking

Before successful serial transmission can occur, however, it is necessary that the machines at each end of the link should agree on a system of transmission. They must, for instance, agree on how fast the bits should be sent, the *baud rate*, and on whether data is to be sent only in one direction at a time, *half duplex*, as in a walkie-talkie, or in both directions simultaneously, *full duplex*, as in a telephone conversation. They must also agree on whether the communication is to be governed by a clock, *synchronous transmission* (⇨ p. 214), as occurs within all computers, or independently of a synchronizing clock, *asynchronous transmission*. Most communications that take place outside computers are asynchronous.

Computers will also usually have to agree on the use of various techniques for detecting errors and for correcting them, such as parity-bit checking (⇨ below), and they may also have to agree on how data is to be coded and decoded. These various agreements are all included in a set of rules known as a *communications protocol*. Before transmission can occur, the two machines must pass messages to each other confirming the communications protocol. This preliminary process of agreement over the mode of the subsequent data transmission is called *handshaking*.

Parity-bit checking

Serial transmission occurs at very high rates and it is imperative that some system of checking should be adopted to ensure that every bit sent is transferred correctly. This is done by an ingenious method known as *parity checking*. In *even* parity checking (the commonest form), each byte is made to have an even number of 1s. This is achieved by using only seven of the bits for data and adding an extra bit – the parity bit. As each byte is sent, the sending machine counts the number of 1s in the seven data bits. If this is an even number, the computer adds a 0 parity bit; if the total of 1s is odd, the computer adds a 1 parity bit. So every byte sent has an even number of 1s, and this is checked by the receiving machine. If the receiving machine finds any byte that does not have an even number of 1s, it knows that an error has occurred in the course of transmission and it immediately asks for that byte to be repeated.

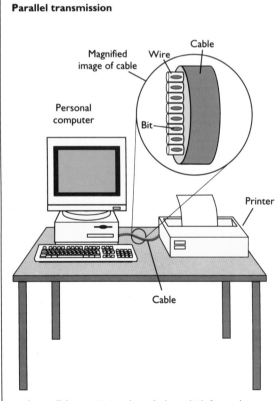

PARALLEL AND SERIAL TRANSMISSION

Parallel transmission

Magnified image of cable
Wire
Cable
Personal computer
Bit
Printer
Cable

In parallel transmission the eight bits which form a byte travel simultaneously along eight parallel wires. They must reach their destination at the same time to transmit the data. Consequently parallel transmission can be carried out only over shorter distances.

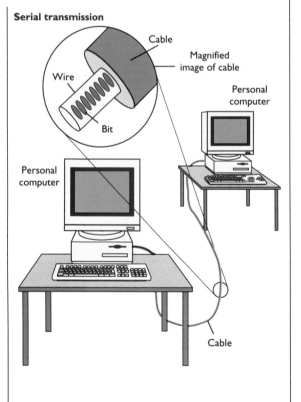

Serial transmission

Cable
Magnified image of cable
Wire
Personal computer
Bit
Personal computer
Cable
Cable

Serial transmission is often used to send information over long distances. The computer sending information transmits each of the eight bits of a byte in turn. The receiving machine then re-constitutes each set of eight bits into a single byte.

A modem at work (left) during the 1990 World Cup. The small grey box by the computer terminal allowed text and pictures from the football event held in Italy to be sent across Europe at any time of the day. (Allsport)

Parity-bit checking is not confined to communications use. Accuracy of data movement and recording is so vital to effective computer function that parity checking is constantly used within computers and every time a personal computer is switched on, the internal memories are tested by a parity-bit check.

Parity-bit checking is highly effective but is not able to detect the unlikely coincidence of either two or four bits being changed in transmission. When 100 per cent accuracy is essential more sophisticated protocols are used. Some of these are laid down by the body that sets standards for international communications – the *Comité Consultatif International Téléphonique et Télégraphique* (CCITT). The CCITT standard protocols are set and universally agreed for half- and full-duplex transmission along telephone lines and computer networks, for facsimile (FAX) communication and for high-speed error detecting.

Modems

Although much of the telephone system has been digitized, a large part of it remains an analogue system in which voice information is transmitted as varying electrical signals. Computers, however, work on a purely digital basis, so if computers are to communicate with each other via telephone lines the digital data must be converted temporarily into audible tones that can be transmitted over any voice-grade telephone line. The device that performs this conversion in both directions is called a *modem* – an abbreviation of MODulator–DEModulator. Modulation means superimposing a signal onto a carrier channel – in this case the telephone voice channel.

In general, modems are simple devices that, at the transmitting end, convert the 1s and the 0s of the digital signal into distinguishable tones, such as can be heard at the beginning of a fax transmission. At the receiving end, the modem converts the tones back into the original digital bits. All personal computers have at least one serial output port through which parallel data is converted to a string of

successive bits. These serial ports conform to an international interface standard and can be connected to an external modem into which the telephone line is plugged. Alternatively computers can be fitted with an internal modem card with a telephone socket accessible at the back of the machine. Modems can use various protocols for transmission and many can switch from one to another. These must be agreed by handshaking before communication occurs.

Modems are, of necessity, very much slower than normal digital transmission; the fastest modems run at about 9,600 bits per second, but most run at about 1,200 bits per second, which is around 25 text words per second. When digital communications advances to the stage at which information is digitized at the telephone receiver, modems will become obsolete.

Optical fibre communications

One of the most important advances in communications has been in the use of fine glass or plastic fibres, up to 0.5 mm in diameter, for the transmission of information. Fibre optic channels are expanding rapidly. They are being used to replace existing long-distance telephone lines and now run across the Atlantic and Pacific Oceans. So far, the cost has precluded the widespread use of fibre-optic connections in domestic locations, but the advantages are so great that such connections are inevitable.

A light beam passed along a fine optical fibre does not escape unless the fibre is sharply bent, but remains in the cable by *total internal reflection*. Optical fibres are given a cladding which prevents the light losses that occur when the fibre touches anything, and they are then protected by a plastic sheath to form part of a cable. It is very easy to convert electrical signals to light signals using devices such as semiconductor lasers (⇨ p. 82). The current through the device determines its light output. Light signals may be analogue (⇨ p. 216) or may first be converted to the preferred digital form.

Light has a very short wavelength and thus a very large number of waves per

second (a very high frequency; ⇨ p. 72). This means that the device that converts electrical signals into light pulses can do so at a very fast rate. Some fibres can carry as many as 2,400 million bits per second (2.4 gigabits per second). In engineering terms, the *bandwidth* – the range of frequencies – in optical fibres is very much higher than normal radio or TV channels. By a method known as *multiplexing*, a large number of different signal channels can be accommodated simultaneously along a single optical fibre. In multiplexing a number of channels, the first bit from each channel is sent, then the second from each, then the third, and so on. In this way, many channels form a single stream of data. At the other end, the successive bits are separated and each sent to its appropriate channel. A fairly normal digital rate of 2,400 megabits per second allows the simultaneous transmission of 14,700 separate telephone voice channels.

Networks and packet switching

Communication networks are various forms of connected computers that allow many individuals or machines to correspond with each other. Local area networks (LANs) might connect all the personal computers in an office or organization, so that all can share centrally-held data and use electronic mail (E-mail). To connect computers further apart fibre-optic networks, carrying all kinds of multiplexed information, have been established worldwide, covering the whole globe with a fine web of glass. However, the organization and control of such large networks with many terminals has become a major problem and protocol and other requirements waste valuable communications time. One solution is *packet switching* in which each item of data has a unique code attached to it that identifies its source and destination. It also includes information on the communications protocol. Packets from many different computers can thus safely use the same network links without delays or confusion.

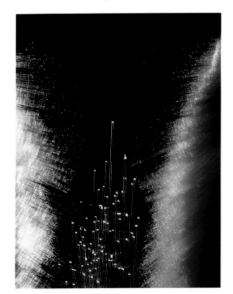

A spray of fibre optic filaments. Each 1-mm-thick filament is made from a special flexible glass that has a high refractive index (⇨ p. 72). They are coated in a protective layer with a low refractive index. A light beam entering the end of the fibre is completely internally reflected and allows the light to travel along the entire cable with little or no absorption. Light signals may be analogue or converted into preferred digital form. (Adam Hart-Davis, SPL)

Microelectronics and Control Systems

Microelectronics allows a large amount of computing power to be packed into a very small space, so that a high degree of control of mechanical systems has become possible. The qualities of today's microprocessor – its compactness, resistance to shock and the ability to provide complex programs, stored permanently in ROMs (⬦ p. 214) – has greatly extended the range of its applications. Control microprocessors are now commonplace in numerous industrial systems as well as in all kinds of domestic appliances, cars and toys.

Effective and reliable control systems regulating mechanical processes always involve *feedback*. This means that information about the effect of the control is passed back to the controlling part of the system so as to adjust it appropriately. Such feedback is called *negative feedback* because the information passing back has the effect of opposing the direction or force of the controlling influence. In driving a car, if the wheel is turned too far clockwise the information fed back is that the vehicle is veering too far to the right. If negative feedback is applied, the wheel will be turned anticlockwise and the deviation corrected. Positive feedback would imply an increased clockwise control movement of the wheel, which would be disastrous. Negative feedback exerts a dampening and regulating effect and nearly always improves performance. For example, when negative feedback is applied to

SERVOMECHANISM AT WORK

Signal from circuit control to lift glass

control circuit with servomechanism

Robotic arm

Signal from sensor

A signal from the sensor at the end of the robotic arm transmits information on the position of the grip of the robotic arm back to the control circuit. The control circuit can then send further information to the arm to correct it s position if necessary.

electronic sound amplifiers, distortion is reduced and tolerance to changes in the components increased.

Negative feedback control systems

Simple negative feedback control systems have been in use for about two hundred years since James Watt (1736–1819) developed a governor for his steam engine. When this centrifugal device increased its speed, it fed back a movement to close the throttle. Such mechanical devices are called *servomechanisms* and the idea has been extended in power, scope and precision by the use of microelectronics. A typical application is the control of a house temperature by a thermostat which

opens an electric switch (breaking the circuit) to the central heating system when the temperature exceeds a set level and closes it (completes the circuit) when the temperature drops below a certain point. By using microelectronics, however, such a system can be greatly improved to allow automatic recognition of other variables, such as the outside temperature, whether the house is occupied, whether the fuel level is getting low, and so on. Computers can readily take account of many such parameters, handling them in accordance with previously designated logic. Such a scheme might, for instance, be: if X and Y apply, but not P or Q, then perform Z.

Cybernetics

Cybernetics is the study of control and communication in all systems whether mechanical, biological or social. It is also concerned with how systems evolve and learn. The term comes from the Greek *kubernetes,* meaning 'a helmsman' or 'governor', and the main lines of the discipline were well established in the first half of the 20th century. Cybernetics attempts to use feedback in control systems. In a cybernetic model, a monitor – whether human, electronic or mechanical – compares what is happening at a particular time with the known standard of what should be happening. The difference, or error, is then fed to a controller so that it can take action. Some physical cybernetic models of biological systems have been amazingly life-like in their functions and are able, for instance, to learn to run mazes and to recognize certain patterns. The ability of cybernetic systems to recognize patterns has made artificial intelligence (⬦ p. 224) a major feature of cybernetics. But the mathematical theory of cybernetics has been most influential in the subsequent development of automation and robotic systems.

Industrial robotics

The term 'robot' comes from the story *Rossum's Universal Robots* by the Czech writer Karel Capek (1890–1938). 'Robot' in Czech simply means 'worker', but the word was retained in the English translation. Although the age of the robot is now very much with us, the robot of today is a far cry from the humanoid robot of science fiction. According to the widely accepted definition formulated by the Robotics Industries Association: 'An industrial robot is a reprogrammable, multi-functional manipulator designed to move materials, parts, tools of specialized devices through various programmed motions for the performance of a variety of tasks.' As the definition suggests, the essence of the robot is its flexibility, its ability to do many different jobs.

The essential features of an industrial robot are that it should have a means of acquiring information (a *sensor*), a means of analysing and comparing that information with the task required of it (a computer), and a means of effecting an action (a manipulator). Sensors are many and

Robots glazing a car windscreen. The high-pressure hoses, either hydraulic or pneumatic, transmit movement to the robotic arms. Because of their suitability for carrying out repetitive tasks, with speed and accuracy, robots are widely used to assemble cars. (Images)

varied but all of them simulate or duplicate the functions of the human senses. Miniature television cameras provide visual data; microphones provide sound information; touch sensors indicate contact and can distinguish different surfaces; movement and position sensors indicate acceleration and a change of location; chemical 'smell' receptors respond to volatile agents in the atmosphere; even taste sensation can be simulated. Devices that perform the latter two functions are called *chemoreceptors*.

Robot senses

The possible range of sensory input to a robot is far greater than that which a human can appreciate. Human eyes respond only to a very narrow band of frequencies between the infrared and the ultraviolet; robotic eyes can be made to respond well into both of these bands, as well as to light visible to humans. Robots can be equipped with sensors for various other parts of the electromagnetic spectrum (⇨ p. 84) and can detect magnetic fields. Robotic ear microphones can respond into the high ultrasound range, well beyond the range of human hearing.

In a robot, sensory input information must be converted into the digital form that a computer can use. Devices, such as TV cameras, microphones and other sensors, that convert energy from one form to another are called *transducers* (⇨ pp. 102–5). Those in robotics convert light, sound, touch, and position change into varying electrical signals. But such transducers are analogue devices (⇨ p. 212) that give an output in the form of a fluctuating electrical voltage, and this must be converted into digital form. Analogue to digital converters (⇨ p. 216) are therefore commonly found in robotic systems, often in the form of one-chip devices.

The robot effector

Robot manipulators are modelled on the human arm. This model has evolved to a high state of perfection and has been well tried out and tested. As a general-purpose activator it is unlikely to be improved upon by the engineers. To be able to work in three dimensions a robotic arm must be capable of moving in a minimum of three directions or as engineers express it, it must have three degrees of freedom. This can be achieved in various ways, the least flexible, but the easiest to control, being the ability for the whole arm to slide in one plane and two parts of it to slide in two other planes. The most flexible type of arm has three degrees of rotational freedom but the computer has to perform complex mathematics to calculate movements and avoid collisions. The latter type is called an *anthropomorphic arm*, but even this is incapable of such a function as turning a screwdriver. For this reason a 'wrist' is commonly fitted to the end of the arm, which may have three degrees of freedom itself. Almost any kind of tool can then be fitted to the part beyond the wrist.

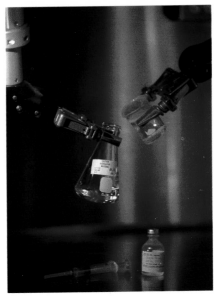

Robots are particularly useful in handling dangerous materials. Here the robot grip, complete with sensors (⇨ text), is able to carry out precise tasks without risk to humans. (Will and Deni McIntyre, SPL)

Movement of the robotic arm can be effected in various ways, none of which are, to date, as smooth or as precisely controlled as biological muscle. Stepper motors, simple electromagnetic devices, create movement in small steps that can easily be counted. Solenoids are electromagnets containing iron cores that are drawn in when the coil is energized. Normal electric motors are used, often geared down to produce a suitably slow rate of movement. Also many arms are driven by hydraulic or pneumatic pressure, which can be recognized by the high-pressure hoses attached to them.

Command and control

For some simple purposes it may be sufficient to issue the robot with the command to move to position X, Y, Z, and then perform a task, such as drill a hole. This may be satisfactory so long as everything else is in order and nothing unexpected happens. Such a robot can, however, be dangerous if it tries to perform the action whatever the circumstances, which may not be favourable. Most robots, therefore, are controlled by a servomechanism with constant feedback of information. Such a mechanism may commonly drive the manipulator to move rapidly when its tool is far from its intended position, and more slowly the nearer it comes to it. Negative feedback ensures accurate control and precision of location.

Many robots are now capable of being taught to perform a particular function. A human machine operator, using a control panel, guides the arm through each step of the new function in turn. Each time the arm performs one step properly it is instructed to store the program it has just executed. This is done until the whole sequence is satisfactorily programmed. Unlike a human operator, the arm does

not need to practise; it merely has to perform each step perfectly on one occasion.

Robotic applications

Industrial robots can carry out any repetitive task that has previously been performed manually by human workers. They are extensively used in factory assembly lines and elsewhere for such purposes as injection moulding, die casting, assembly of sub-components into larger structures, electrical spot-welding, spray painting, soldering, machine tool operation and many others. They can carry out these functions continuously, day and night, with down time only for maintenance. Robots can also perform many tasks that would be too dangerous for human workers. Mobile robots are being used, for instance, in the investigation and controlled destruction of terrorist bombs. Similarly robotic manipulators are widely used in environments of high radioactivity.

Most robots are fixed in position so that the mechanical manipulator arm can be used with precision. Artificial intelligence research (⇨ p. 224), however, is being directed towards allowing robots to acquire so much information about their environment that they will be able to move about safely and thus widen their scope of action. The potential of robots for the creation of wealth is enormous, and their exploitation has only just begun. At the same time, the increasing use of robots to replace human labour is likely to pose major socio-economic problems.

SEE ALSO

- ELECTRONICS pp. 102–5
- THE DEVELOPMENT OF THE COMPUTER p. 212
- INSIDE A DIGITAL COMPUTER p. 214
- INFORMATION p. 216
- PROGRAMMING, SOFTWARE AND APPLICATIONS p. 218
- DIGITAL COMMUNICATIONS p. 220
- ARTIFICIAL INTELLIGENCE p. 224
- THE BRAIN–COMPUTER ANALOGY p. 226

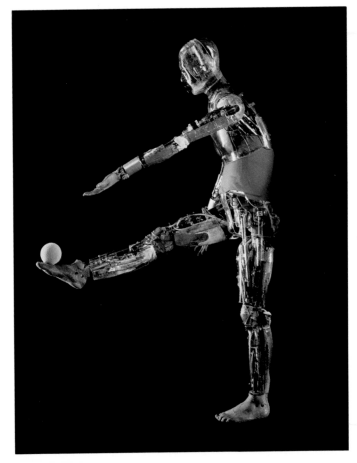

A robotic mannequin has been designed by the US Department of Energy. The robot is fully articulated and can simulate sweating and breathing as it is used to test the suitability of clothing such as space suits, fire-fighting protection and hazardous environment suits. (US Department of Energy, SPL)

Artificial Intelligence

Psychologists have never finally agreed on a definition of intelligence, or even on what is meant by thinking. As a result, a great debate has arisen as to whether machines can exhibit intelligence or can be said to think. Computers have shown at least human levels of ability in intellectual tasks such as playing chess or solving difficult mathematical problems. Their memories are far more reliable than human memories and there is no practical limit to the amount of information they can store and quickly retrieve. But, so far, there is no indication that they will ever be able to exercise imagination or originality, or relate to the real world in any kind of cognitive way.

The artificial intelligence debate is really a modern version of the old argument between those who believe that the mind is an entity in its own right and those who believe it to be a manifestation of the action of the brain (⟺ p. 226). If the brain is a machine, then a machine can think and that is the end of the argument. But if the mind has some kind of existence independent of the brain and is only mediated *through* the brain, then a machine can never be said to think. The problem resolves to a matter of definition, and polarization of opinion on the matter is, in the end, not amenable to logic. Brain–mind arguments, even between scientists, are not always free from emotion.

Differing definitions

A further difficulty in the debate is that artificial intelligence is a large discipline covering a range of activities. It includes cognitive psychological research into the nature of human intelligence, the development of expert systems (⟺ below) – a purely engineering discipline concerned with making computers simulate intelligent behaviour, and enterprises dedicated to the application of artificial intelligence techniques to commercial products. The fact that the phrase 'artificial intelligence' can mean such different things to different people causes confusion and makes it difficult to judge the overall significance or even the validity of the subject. What is common to all of these activities is the expectation that machines can be made to perform more like human beings.

The Turing Test

In the psychological journal *Mind* in 1950 the English mathematician and philosopher Alan Turing (1912–54) suggested the following test, known as the Turing Test: allow a human to conduct a

The mathematician **Alan Turing** became involved with computers after working as a code-breaker in World War II. He firmly believed that one day computers would be able to think, and challenged his critics by devising a way of testing computer intelligence, the Turing Test. His influential career in computing, however, was cut short by his suicide following the disclosure of his homosexuality. (SPL)

dialogue – by means of a computer terminal – with both a machine and another human, hidden behind a screen. Both respondents must answer every question put to them. Turing argued that if the questioner could not decide which of the two was the machine, then the machine would have demonstrated intelligence. It is argued that if we cannot tell the difference between the intelligent responses of a computer and a human we cannot logically attribute intelligence to the human without ascribing it to the machine.

For many years now there have existed programs that enable a computer to engage in a fairly convincing conversation with a person. One of the best known of these is the *Eliza* program, which provides the kind of interaction strongly reminiscent of the kind of psychotherapeutic situation in which the therapist makes no positive contribution to the conversation but merely keeps the subject talking. These programs are becoming more and more sophisticated and the interaction is especially interesting when two programs talk to each other with no human intervention.

Programs of this kind are, however, essentially trivial and are based on a mixture of random responses and responses triggered by certain key words. Their writers would not claim that they display intelligence or that the meaning of any of the words and phrases used is understood by the machine. There have been many impressive performances in a recent competition that offered $100,000 for the first program to pass the Turing Test. The competition required that the winning program should succeed with no restriction on topics. This has, so far, proved beyond the resources of any program but is not inherently impossible.

One of the more serious criticisms of the rules of the competition was that the judge's contributions had to be limited to questions and statements that did not require awareness of the context to be understood. Therefore the winning program would be completely thrown by the sentence, 'Yew are knot righting with a quay bored.' It would respond with comments or questions about wood or about being apathetic about a wharf. No current machine is capable of discerning the context of any arbitrary sequence of questions, and adapting its understanding of the words accordingly. A human being, on the other hand, has no difficulty in perceiving that the sentence really means 'You are not writing with a keyboard.'

Context sensitivity on the part of the computer has, however, been realized to a limited degree in the development known as natural language interfacing. A natural language interface allows a computer user to address the machine in ordinary language. The machine first assigns the role that each word plays in the sentence (parsing), then, if necessary, interrogates the user on the contextual meaning of particular words. Following the request: 'Give me a list of good prospects for endowment life insurance', for instance, the machine would probably be able to interpret the word 'good' as meaning 'likely to buy' rather than as meaning 'of high moral rectitude'.

Speech recognition

Natural language interfacing is not the same as speech recognition. This involves analysing the electrical output from a microphone, distinguishing individual words, converting them into a code the computer can recognize, and matching them to a library of words stored in the machine. The difficulties are considerable. Because human voices and accents vary so much and because the same word may even be pronounced differently by the same person at different times, the system must be able to be trained to recognize the input speech patterns of a particular user. Again, the problem of context sensitivity arises. The words 'one', 'won' and 'wan', for instance, may sound exactly the same but have quite different meanings. A speech recognition system that can effectively replace a keyboard must be able to determine from the context which word is required. This is a large and difficult task.

Expert systems

Expert systems are computer programs, based on large databases of knowledge on specialized subjects, which are able not only to give helpful advice in response to any question, but are also able to update their own knowledge and procedures on the basis of their previous experience. Such systems are based on the application of large numbers of rules, of the IF . . . THEN . . . variety, which enable the program to make decisions. These rules are organized as complex algorithms or flowcharts (⇨ p. 218). In many typical systems, the program will make an initial guess on the basis of the information provided and will then compare this guess with other known information on the subject to see how well the response fits. A medical expert system, for instance, might produce a tentative diagnosis on the basis of a number of symptoms and signs. This diagnosis will then prompt it to ask for supplementary information to see how well this further input fits with the known facts about the disease stored inside the computer. Once a firm diagnosis is established, the program will then suggest the best form of treatment. Such a system can, if requested, outline the logic used to arrive at a diagnosis and can also refer to appropriate papers in the medical literature to back its 'opinion'.

One of the greatest difficulties in designing expert systems is to formulate the rules and to decide whether to stick to unequivocal true–false rules or allow rules that deal in probabilities. The former makes for simplicity and accuracy but greatly limits scope. The latter allows the use of incomplete or imprecise input data and greatly increases versatility, but only at the cost of enormously increased complexity.

Neural networks

The growing field of neural-network theory and practice is a more direct attempt to duplicate the logical function of biological systems, particularly the brain. The human brain is essentially a complex network of interlinking neurons (nerve cells; ⇨ pp. 226–7) and it is this interlinking that is the key to solving problems quickly. Whether realized in electronic terms as hardware or as a software computer program, neural networks are built up from very simple units called neurons. The network consists of a large number of neurons interconnected

together, usually in three layers. The basic neuron has one or more input and output connections. If it is appropriately adjusted (weighted) and the input is as required, the neuron will provide a meaningful output. The weighting, however, is not fixed or built in by the designer, but is determined by the degree to which the input corresponds to the desired output. If this correspondence is good, the weighting adjusts automatically so that the output is large; if it is not good, the neuron will be blocked. This adjustment to the weighting occurs as part of a trial and error learning process.

The larger the number of neurons, the greater the resolution and usefulness. Each input neuron will be connected to a sensor of some kind, often a light-sensitive cell. The network is 'trained' by being given a series of the correct responses to given inputs and thus learns by example. It uses the concept of feedback, where part of the output of a neuron is returned as input for another process, for self-correction. Such trained networks exhibit more intelligence than was built into them by the programmer. Neural networks thus do not operate by rules but by the ease or otherwise of conduction of the neurons, which is determined by *past experience*. This fact has aroused great scientific and philosophic interest because of the analogy with biological systems. One of the most promising features of neural networks is that they can respond to 'fuzzy' inputs and do not require a precise correspondence between the input and the target they have been trained to recognize.

Neural networks are essentially pattern-recognizing devices. They can, for instance, learn to recognize individual faces out of a range of different faces, which they can do even if the face is turned at a slight angle or is partly obscured. They have been applied to a wide

variety of purposes including robotics (⇨ p. 222), speech recognition, handwriting recognition, astronomical research, intensive-care monitoring, atomic fusion research, karaoke music and harmony, economic forecasting, stockmarket predictions, sales forecasts, oil prospecting, and artificial life research. Some very powerful systems can be produced by combining neural networks and expert systems. One way to do this is to arrange for the expert system to provide the training data for the network. Alternatively, the expert system can be used to monitor the responses of a neural network and create new and better training patterns so as to improve the overall performance.

SEE ALSO

● INFORMATION p. 216
● PROGRAMMING, SOFTWARE AND APPLICATIONS p. 218
● DIGITAL COMMUNICATIONS p. 220
● MICROELECTRONICS AND CONTROL SYSTEMS p. 222
● THE BRAIN–COMPUTER ANALOGY p. 226

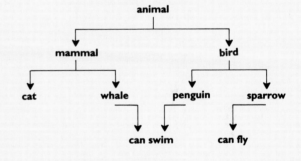
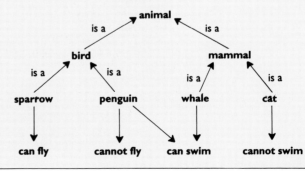

STORING INFORMATION

There are many ways of storing information. Some commonly used approaches include:
Trees: here the relationship between chunks of knowledge is expressed as rules (or branches).
Frames: similar to a series of boxes, where related facts can be stored or pigeon-holed.
Semantic nets: these show the relationships between different chunks of knowledge.
Shown here are different ways of organizing the knowledge that birds and mammals are animals; sparrows and penguins are birds; sparrows can fly but penguins cannot; whales and cats are mammals; whales can swim. The various ways of storing information may be used in compiling expert systems.

TREE STRUCTURE

animal

mammal — bird

cat — whale — penguin — sparrow

can swim — can fly

FRAME

Animal

bird	mammal
instance – penguin	instance – whale
can fly – no	can fly – no
can swim – yes	can swim – yes

SEMANTIC NET

animal

is a — is a

bird — mammal

is a — is a — is a — is a

sparrow — penguin — whale — cat

can fly — cannot fly — can swim — cannot swim

A **10-year-old chess-playing prodigy** pits his wits against a computer. Chess computers can often beat the most gifted players as they can work out all the possible moves ahead. However, scientists are not agreed on whether this is intelligence. *(Gamma)*

The Brain–Computer Analogy

From the time of the earliest electronic computers many people have felt impelled to draw an analogy between the computer and the brain. Greater familiarity with the features of computer function soon dispelled the idea that the computers of the time could seriously rival the human brain. However, subsequent developments in computing, in the miniaturization of computers and in the understanding of brain function have again raised the question.

A comparison between the brain and a computer must start with the obvious fact that a brain is a living entity, while the computer is not. The complex network of nerve cells (neurons) we call the brain is not a fixed structure like a computer. In fact, the brain is both functionally, and structurally, changed by past experience. Experience causes the brain's branching pattern of nerve connections to acquire greater complexity. The number of supporting cells increases and the connections between nerve cells are made more easily. The ability of the brain to change with experience is called *plasticity*, and although plasticity in some areas, such as those concerned with vision, is lost by about the age of seven, plasticity in other parts remains throughout life. Brain neuron connections which have not been challenged by experience retain simpler patterns and lower functional ability. A well-educated person has a wealth of organic change in brain neuron connections. Computers can be improved by plugging in new circuit boards but do not improve by being used.

The brain as a machine
The brain, like a computer, is an assembly of interconnected parts that perform a function. It is a far more complex and compact machine than any that has ever been made by human beings, but there is no logical reason why a machine of equal complexity should not, eventually, be made. Already, the basic structural unit of the brain, the neuron, has been duplicated electronically and can be reproduced in large numbers on a silicon chip. The question that then arises is whether such a machine would have all the characteristics, functions and by-products of the human brain, including consciousness, self-awareness, emotion

and psychological aberration. In short, is the mind a function of complexity?

Similarities and differences
Both the brain and the computer are electrically operated devices, but they use electricity in very different ways. The computer uses electric currents in pulse form (⇨ p. 216) that travel along wires at the speed of light. The brain's electrical conductors are microscopic tubes charged positively on the outside and negatively on the inside. If this charge relationship is locally reversed by the movement of sodium or potassium ions (⇨ p. 186) through the wall, the charge reversal moves along the nerve fibre in both directions. This movement is slow – a few metres per second – much slower than the rate of propagation of electricity, but the brain compensates for this by using a large number of conducting pathways at the same time.

Computers contain a few million active units (transistors) and their connections. The brain is composed of some 100,000 million nerve cells each comprising a cell body, a long, often branched, fibre called the *axon*, and anything from one to several thousand short fibres called *dendrites* (⇨ illustration). Connections between adjacent or widely separated neurons are numerous and complex, and single neurons commonly receive several hundreds to a hundred thousand inputs from other nerves. In general, the cell body and the dendrites receive incoming signals, which are averaged (integrated) in the cell body, and the output signal leaves by way of the axon. The connections between neurons in the brain occur at specialized sites known as *synapses*. They can excite a nerve impulse in the next neuron or inhibit the passage of an impulse. Every neuron may be interconnected, via synapses, to thousands of other neurons.

The complexity of neuron interconnection could hardly be more different from the inherent simplicity of the structure of the ordinary digital computer. Computers work with binary (⇨ p. 216), and recognize only the presence or absence of a pulse (1 or 0, true or false). The brain differentiates between a wide range of signals of different strength. The computer operates with logical gates (⇨ p. 104) each with a very small number of inputs and with usually a single output of 1 or 0. In the brain, the arrangement of stimulatory and inhibitory connections, although not binary, closely mimics the logical gates that are the basis of digital computing. The biological system is capable of realizing all the logical elements found in the central processing unit (⇨ p. 214) of a digital computer, but it is clear from the number of connections in the brain that some kind of (statistical) gating system is normally involved. In such a system, if the number of stimulatory impulses from neurons exceeds the number of inhibitory

impulses then the stimulatory impulses would prevail, and vice versa.

The great majority of present-day computers are single-stream (linear) devices, operating on a single stream of pulses controlled and synchronized by a high-speed clock (⇨ p. 214). Computers do things very quickly, but they do them one at a time. The brain is a parallel computer in which many thousands of different operations are going on at the same time, some independently of each other, some cooperatively.

Another major difference between the brain and modern computers is that whereas computers are general-purpose machines performing different functions in accordance with instructions provided in the software, the brain appears to be 'hard-wired', permanently instructed, to carry out many of its functions. Computers are useless without detailed programs of instructions for their operation; the brain, with its

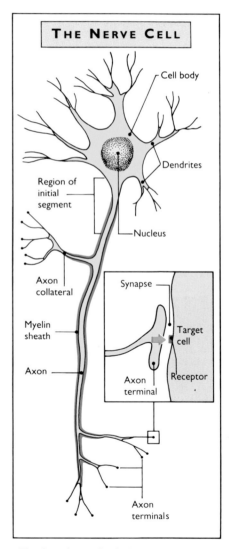

THE NERVE CELL

Cell body

Dendrites

Region of initial segment

Nucleus

Axon collateral

Myelin sheath

Axon

Synapse

Target cell

Axon terminal

Receptor

Axon terminals

The function unit of the nervous tissue in humans is the nerve cell or neuron, of which there are billions in the central nervous system. They vary greatly in shape and size, but all communicate electrochemically with their neighbours, forming an intricate network that far outstrips in complexity the circuitry of the most advanced electronic computer.

range of activities, does not perform different functions, in accordance with different programs. Major subdivisions of brain function – movement, sensation, speech, vision, hearing, and so on – are subserved by particular known parts of the brain, and these are connected by bundles of nerve fibre to the effector or sense organ concerned, as well as to other parts of the brain. Computers are driven into operation by running a program; the brain is activated largely by stimuli entering it by way of the sense organs.

The analogy improves

In recent years there has been enormous interest in, and progress towards, parallel computing, in which more than one computation is carried out at the same time, much as the brain does. New kinds of central processing units have been developed that lend themselves especially to parallel processing. They incorporate reduced instruction sets (RISC) that operate very quickly. Computers are being designed to use hundreds or even thousands of these RISC units. There are many technical problems in organizing parallel computing, especially in writing the operating software (⇨ p. 218), but if these problems are overcome, the future of computing seems likely to lie in parallel processing. In this event, the analogy between the brain and the computer will become much closer.

The remaining major difference between the two systems lies in the enormous perceptive capacity of the brain, with its associated sense organs, compared with that of the computer. But this difference, too, is gradually narrowing. Many present-day machines are equipped with scanners that can accurately read text (*optical character recognition*) and convert it into a form the machine can use. This is a much simpler task than that of attributing any sort of meaning to words, but computers can already, on request, offer definitions of any known word, together with a wide range of synonyms, simply by consulting a stored dictionary and thesaurus. Some programs have even begun, in a limited way, to detect the context of a word and so to select the appropriate meaning from several definitions.

Neural networks

Advances in artificial intelligence, especially in the field of neural networks (⇨ pp. 224–5), are beginning to provide the computer with powers of pattern recognition. As these fields develop, we will all become quite accustomed to computers that can see, hear, taste and smell. An interesting sidelight on this is that neural networks can work satisfactorily on imprecise ('fuzzy') data just as humans can. Other computer inputs have to be precise or they will be rejected or ignored. As neural networks develop in size, and improvements are made in the miniaturization of the various sensory devices (to which each of the input neurons of the neural network is connected), the

Francis Crick turned to neuroscience after his biological research into DNA. In his attempt to explain visual perception, he concluded that the information provided to our brains by our eyes is supplemented by 'fill in' information, which is stored previous experience. Computer scientists are now trying to create computers that can build up their own bank of experience.
(A. Barrington Brown, SPL)

resemblance between the performance of computer systems and that of humans will become closer still.

The problem of consciousness

With few exceptions, scientists who study the workings of the brain now believe that consciousness, if it is to be explained at all, is to be explained in terms of the working of large numbers of neurons. Many of these scientists, however, believe that consciousness, or self-awareness, is either a philosophical concept or is too intangible and ambiguous to be the subject of experimental research. The English scientist Francis Crick (1916–), who shared with James Watson the fame for resolving the structure of the DNA molecule (⇨ p. 202), later turned to neuroscience. For some years Crick and others have been engaged in the experimental study of consciousness, as they are convinced that the problem of self-awareness will yield to research. Consciousness, of course, involves many aspects – the awareness of all the perceptions (visual, auditory, olfactory, gustatory and tactile), thoughts, imaginings, emotions, dreams, and so on. To try to narrow down the

The human brain through a computed tomography scan. Scientists have made great leaps forward in the understanding of how the brain works, and many have agreed that it has similarities with the most advanced computers. However, a number of scientists believe that a computer will never display the characteristics of the human brain such as self-awareness, emotion and psychological problems. (Scott Camazine, SPL)

problem, Crick has been concentrating on visual consciousness.

He points out that the information provided to our brains by our eyes is not, in itself, sufficient to account for our visual awareness of the outside world. The eyes provides a two-dimensional and very incomplete image of the world to which the brain adds a great deal of 'fill-in' information derived from stored previous experience and from 'hard-wired' brain circuits. Many different parts of the brain become active during visual consciousness. Some of the active neurons are engaged in retrieving from the memory store the data needed to manifest the full visual conscious experience. Others are engaged in associating what is currently being seen with the retrieved data.

The more the subject is studied, the more clear it becomes that consciousness is intimately associated with considerable neurological activity in the brain. For many neuroscientists this is sufficient evidence that consciousness is a necessary by-product of such activity. But this is no more than an opinion. Some would claim that it is equally possible that the long-held Cartesian idea of a mind–body duality, in which the brain and mind are two equally irreducible aspects of a person, is correct, and that all this neurological processing is merely an indication of busy interaction between the two. Those who believe in the brain–mind duality are, however, still sceptical of brain–computer analogy as they believe that the computer is a mechanical device while the brain has a metaphysical aspect.

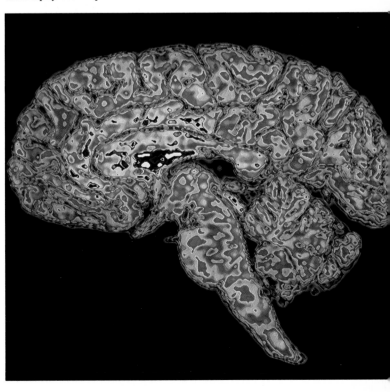

abdomen, the lower or hind part of the trunk of animals. In the higher vertebrates, the abdomen is separated from the chest (*thorax*) by a domed sheet of muscle (the *diaphragm*) that is one of the main muscles of respiration. The abdominal cavity contains the liver, most of the digestive system, the kidneys, the spleen, the pancreas, and some large and important blood vessels. The lower part, the pelvic cavity, contains the bladder, and, in females, the womb (*uterus*), the uterine tubes and the ovaries.

aberration, a defect in the image formed by a lens or a mirror. Chromatic lens aberration is the coloured fringes that occur because light of different wavelengths is bent to different degrees. Spherical aberration results from the fact that rays striking a lens or a mirror at different distances from the centre do not necessarily come to a focus at the same point. Spherical aberration can be reduced by the use of an iris diaphragm to 'stop down' the system (⇨ p.78 and ASTIGMATISM).

abiogenesis, the discredited notion that life commonly arises from nonliving sources, as in the belief that maggots are generated by putrefying meat.

abscissa, the horizontal, or X, coordinate of a point in a two-dimensional system of CARTESIAN COORDINATES. The distance from the Y axis measured parallel to the X axis; ⇨ p. 20.

abscission, the natural separation of fruit, leaves or other parts from the rest of a plant. Separation is effected by the breakdown of a layer of cells in the abscission zone brought about by the growth substance abscisic acid.

absolute code, computer-program code in a form that can be used directly by the central processing unit (⇨ p. 214). Machine code.

absolute zero, theoretically, the lowest possible temperature, at which bodies have minimum energy. The French physicist Jacques Charles (1746–1823) discovered in 1787 that when gases were cooled, they contracted by $1/_{273}$ of their volume at 0°C for each degree of cooling; ⇨ p. 50. This suggested that there might be a limit to cooling. Charles was right. Absolute zero is –273°C (–460°F) or zero Kelvin. The Kelvin scale thus has no negative values. Temperature is molecular motion. The higher the temperature, the higher the speed of vibration of molecules and the greater the volume; the lower the temperature, the lower the speed and the smaller the volume. For this reason, all matter is gaseous at very high temperatures, and, with few exceptions, solid at very low temperatures. Absolute zero is unattainable, but temperatures within one millionth of a degree of it have been reached. At temperatures approaching absolute zero matter exhibits some unexpected properties. Electrical conductors become superconducting (⇨ p. 90) and some fluids lose their viscosity (*superfluidity*).

absorption, in physics, the assimilation of radiation into a body with its partial or complete conversion into another form of energy (such as heat, light, sound, etc). In physiology, the movement of digested food through the wall of the small intestine into the bloodstream.

abyssal zone, the seas at depths of about 2,000 m (6,500 ft) or more to which virtually no light penetrates. Organisms living in the abyssal zone have adapted to conditions of darkness, near-zero temperatures and great pressure.

acceleration, a change of velocity, usually expressed as a change of velocity with time. In SI units, acceleration is expressed in metres per second per second. It can be calculated by subtracting the final velocity from the initial velocity and dividing the result by the time. Acceleration is a vector quantity (⇨ p. 26). If velocity is plotted against time on a graph, the acceleration at any moment is given by the slope of the graph at that moment.

access time, the time taken to retrieve a small item of data from any form of storage in, or connected to, a computer. Access time from RAM may be a very small fraction of a second; from a large magnetic-tape store it may be several minutes. Floppy-disk drives have longer access times than hard disks, and most CD-ROM drives also have long access times.

accommodation, the adjustment of the focus of the eye so that, whatever the range of gaze, a sharp image will be formed on the retina. Accommodation is effected by the internal crystalline lens whose natural elasticity would tend to approximate it to a sphere but for the pull all round its equator of the delicate ligament that suspends it from the circular ciliary muscle. When this muscle contracts, the circle becomes smaller and the pull on the lens is less, thus making it a more powerful converger of light, allowing focusing of the image from near objects. When the ciliary muscle relaxes, more distant objects can be focused. The stimulus for accommodation is the degree of convergence of the rays of light, which can be detected by the variations in depth to which the rays penetrate the light-sensitive cells – the rods and cones – of the retina (⇨ pp. 72–5 and 78).

accumulator, an electric battery (⇨ p. 68) in which the passage of an electric current from an external source brings about a reversible chemical change by which energy is stored. When the electrodes are joined, a current flows and the previous chemical state is restored. In computing, an accumulator is a small memory or BUFFER in which is held the result of successive operations by the arithmetic and logic unit of the central processing unit (⇨ p. 214).

acetabulum, the socket in the side of the bony pelvis into which the spherical head of the thigh bone (*femur*) fits.

acetylcholine, a powerful chemical substance, known as a *neurotransmitter* that is released at SYNAPSES in the autonomic nervous system and some of the central-nervous-system nerves. Acetylcholine diffuses across the synaptic gap, reverses the polarization of the receiving membrane, and propagates the nerve impulse or promotes muscle-fibre contraction or gland secretion. Acetylcholine is the acetic-acid ESTER of choline and is broken down by the enzyme cholinesterase to acetic acid and choline. The choline is then transported back to the axon terminal to be used again. Cholinergic nerve cells cease to function normally in the degenerative brain condition Alzheimer's disease.

Achilles' tendon, the prominent tendon just above the heel, in humans and other primates, by means of which the powerful muscles of the calf are attached to the large heel bone. Contraction of these muscles extends the ankle in walking, running and standing on tiptoe.

achromatic lens, a lens that is free from chromatic aberration. This is achieved by a combination of two or more different kinds of glass with different degrees of light dispersion of the different colours, selected so that the dispersions cancel each other (⇨ p. 78).

acid, a substance that releases hydrogen ions when added to water. A hydrogen ion is the positively charged particle produced when a hydrogen atom loses its electron. It is, therefore, no more than the nucleus of a hydrogen atom, and is thus a proton. Such a particle is powerfully reactive. Acid solutions have a pH of less than 7.0, and acids may be strong or weak. Some strong acids, such as sulphuric acid (H_2SO_2), hydrochloric acid (HCl) or nitric acid (HNO_4) are corrosive and dangerous. Acids neutralize alkalis, react with some metals to release hydrogen, release carbon dioxide from carbonates, and turn blue litmus red; ⇨ p. 168 .

acid–base balance, the maintenance of the acidity (pH) of animal and human blood and tissue fluids within the narrow limits required if health and life are to be preserved. This balance is achieved by a BUFFER mechanism, involving bicarbonates, carbonic acid and haemoglobin, which takes up excess acids and bases, and by the selective excretion in the urine of appropriate ions and adjustment of the rate of carbon-dioxide loss in the expired air. Failure of the mechanism can result from excessive intake or loss of either acid or alkali, resulting in potentially fatal acidosis or alkalosis; ⇨ p. 168.

acidimetry, the use of standard acid solutions to neutralize, and thus determine, the amount of base present in a liquid.

acid rain, rain that has become contaminated with atmospheric acids derived mainly from the sulphur dioxide and nitrogen oxides that are produced by burning coal and fuel oils. These gases readily dissolve in atmospheric water, which becomes acidic and may reach an acidity (pH) of 3.0 or lower. Pure, distilled water has a neutral pH of 7.0. Acid rain causes considerable environmental damage, both by its direct effect on vegetation and by acidification of surface water and soil. The latter can result in the death of fish and other forms of aquatic life, and soil acidification results in the formation of metal salts that are harmful to plants and animals. Acid gases from burning coal and other fuels can be greatly reduced by flue-desulphurization units, which are being fitted to coal-fired power stations (which are among the chief offenders; ⇨ p. 208).

acoustic coupler, a crude form of modem (⇨ p. 220) that can be temporarily attached to a normal telephone. The digital signal to be transmitted is converted into a two-tone sound that is emitted by a small loudspeaker pressed to the telephone microphone. The received signal is picked up by a microphone held close to the telephone earpiece. The system allows modem communication from any location where there is a telephone, but the speed of transmission is low.

acoustic nerve, the short, eighth, cranial nerve that connects the inner ear to the brain, and carries information subserving hearing and balance.

acrylic plastics, synthetic polymers (⇨ p. 164) of ESTERS or other derivatives of acrylic acid (propenoic acid). Among the best known are polymethyl methacrylate (PMMA), sold under the trade names 'perspex', 'diakon', 'lucite' and 'plexiglas'; and polypropenonitrile, sold as 'acrilan' and 'orlon', mainly for the production of artificial fibres.

ACTH, adrenocorticotrophic hormone, or corticotrophin, a hormone produced by the pituitary gland that promotes the secretion of corticosteroids from the adrenal glands. The pituitary releases ACTH as a result of painful or stressful stimuli reaching it from the brain via the hypothalamus; and it reduces its output in response to higher-than-usual blood levels of the natural steroid cortisol.

actinic radiation, radiation, especially light and ultraviolet radiation, that can cause a chemical change, such as the production of the latent image on photographic emulsion or the breakdown of biological or other molecules. The Sun is a major source of actinic electromagnetic radiation.

actinium series, a series of radioactive elements each of which derives from the radioactive decay of its predecessor, ending in a stable atom. The actinium series starts with uranium–235 and ends in an isotope of lead. Two other such series occur naturally, starting respectively with uranium–238 (uranium series), and thorium–232 (thorium series), and also ending with an isotope of lead; ⇨ p. 160.

actinoids, a series of elements in the periodic table (⇨ p. 158) ranging upwards in weight from actinium to lawrencium. The first four members, actinium, thorium, protactinium and uranium, occur naturally; the others, neptunium, plutonium, americium, curium, californium, einsteinium, fermium, mendelevium, nobelium and lawrencium, are artificial. All are radioactive and most are dangerous; the investigation of their chemistry is thus difficult.

action potential, the electrical changes produced in a cell membrane, especially a nerve cell, under the influence of certain stimuli. Essentially, the action potential is a voltage pulse caused by the local reversal of the difference of charge between the inside and the outside of the membrane. In the resting state this is about 40-75 millivolts (thousandths of a volt), positive on the outside and negative on the inside. Local reversal, under the influence of ACETYLCHOLINE or other agent, causes an automatic spread of the repolarization in all directions away from the site of origin. Action potentials can follow one another at a rate of several hundred per second. This is the basis of the nerve impulse upon which all neurological activity, and human thought and action, depend.

activation energy, the minimum energy needed for a chemical reaction to occur. During a chemical reaction in which bonds between atoms are broken and new bonds formed, the energy involved rises to a maximum. At the end of the reaction it declines to that of the energy of the resultant substances. Activation energy is the difference between the energy of the substances taking part in the reaction and the maximum energy. The extent to which a chemical reaction is affected by changes in temperature is determined by the activation energy; ⇨ p. 168.

active device, a component in an electronic circuit that consumes power to effect a change such as amplification or current switching. Transistors (⇨ pp. 102–5) are active devices; resistors, capacitors and inductors (⇨ p. 100) are passive devices.

active site, the area on the surface of an enzyme (⇨ pp. 96–101) or CATALYST at which bio-chemical or chemical activity occurs.

active transport, the movement of dissolved substances through biological membranes in the direction of increased concentration, i.e. against the normal direction of flow under the influence of osmotic pressure. Movement occurs through protein channels embedded in the membrane. Active transport necessarily requires the expenditure of energy; ⇨ pp. 192–5.

adaptation, the adjustment of an organism in part or in whole, to changes in its environment or to external stress. Thus, the pupil of the eye adapts to darkness by enlarging, and to brightness by constricting; the amount of oxygen-carrying haemoglobin in the blood increases at high altitudes where oxygen concentration is lower; the muscles increase in bulk if persistently required to perform more work; and bacteria adapt to an environment containing antibiotics, so that such drugs become less effective. Adaptation is an essential feature of all living things, and the likelihood of survival often depends on how effectively it operates. Acquired abilities to adapt may enhance the chances of survival but die with the individual. Inherent differences in the ability to adapt is the result of chance genetic redistribution or mutation in the parents. If such differences result in effective adaptation and thus increase the probability that an organism will survive to pass on its characteristics to offspring, the result will be a species change; ⇨ pp. 196–9.

addition reaction, a chemical reaction occurring between molecules containing unsaturated bonds (⇨ pp. 162–5) in which breaks occurs at one or more unsaturated bonds and molecules link together. Sometimes this linkage is associated with the elimination of another molecule (*condensation reaction*).

address, a known location in a computer memory at which any item of data can be found. The address is simply a number that identifies the location. A computer instruction might be to take the number held in a particular address, multiply it by the number in another address and put the answer in a third address. An address bus is a set of wires along which signals travel to reach addresses. Data can then be taken from these addresses by way of a data bus.

adduct, to move towards the centre line of the body. Muscles that adduct are called *adductors*.

adenoids, twin masses of gland-like tissue on the back wall of the nose, above the tonsils, which shrivel and disappear in adolescence or early adult life. The adenoids contain lymphocytes (white cells concerned with combating infection) and are part of the body's defence system.

adiabatic process, a process that occurs without any interchange of heat with its surroundings. An adiabatic change involves a change in the temperature within the system but no heat loss or gain. When a volume of air expands and rises adiabatically in the atmosphere, its temperature falls. The adiabatic lapse rate is the rate of decrease of temperature when such a volume of air rises.

adipocere, a wax-like substance, consisting mainly of fatty acids, into which the soft tissues of a dead body, buried in moist earth, are converted. Adipocere delays the normal processes of decomposition so that the body is unnaturally preserved. It is sometimes of medicolegal importance.

adipose tissue, animal fat, which is liquid at body temperature and is contained in thin-walled cells, held together, in large masses, by delicate connective tissue. Adipose tissue forms a layer under the skin where it acts both as an insulant and as a long-term fuel store. Food in excess of requirements is converted to fat and deposited.

admittance, the reciprocal of impedance (⇨ pp. 96–101).

adrenaline, epinephrine, the secretion of the inner part of the adrenal glands and of certain nerve endings. Adrenaline is an important hormone that is produced when the body is required to make unusual efforts. It speeds up the heart, increases the rate and ease of breathing, raises the blood pressure, deflects the blood circulation from the digestive system to the muscles, mobilizes the fuel glucose, and causes a sense of alertness and excitement. All these changes allow more effective physical action, as may be needed in a situation of danger. It has been described as the hormone of 'fright, fight or flight'. The actions of adrenaline are, in general, the same as those of the sympathetic division of the AUTONOMIC NERVOUS SYSTEM.

adsorption, a phenomenon similar to, but essentially different from, absorption, in which a substance, commonly a gas but also a finely divided solid or liquid, adheres to a surface to form a very thin layer, often only one molecule thick. Adsorption involves interaction between molecules at a surface. Powdered, activated charcoal is a highly effective adsorbent and will remove colour from liquids, poisons from liquids in the intestines, and poisonous gases from air passed through it. In *absorption*, the absorbed substance is taken up by the absorbing substance and distributed throughout it, in the manner of blotting paper drawing up water by capillary action.

aerial, a radio antenna, an electrical conductor taking a variety of forms, from which radio signals are transmitted or by which they are received. Aerials may consist of long wires suspended high above the ground, dipoles with twin arms insulated from each other, or short ferrite rods incorporated into a pocket transistor receiver. Often their dimensions are carefully calculated to resonate with the principal wavelength or waveband of interest. They may have reflectors behind them, directors in front of them and may have to be accurately aligned. Aerials for very short wavelengths often consist of a parabolic reflector with the actual aerial set at the focus of the parabola. The *gain* of an aerial is simply the degree to which the performance of an aerial matches that of an approved standard; a passive device such as an aerial cannot, by itself, increase the strength of the signal received. Transmitting aerials correspond dimensionally to effective receiving aerials but have to handle power and may have thicker conductors; ⇨ pp. 102–5.

aerosol, a suspension or dispersion of very small droplets of a liquid or particles of a solid, in a gas. Aerosols may be produced by causing a pressurized gas to blow across the nozzle of a tube dipping into the solution to be dispersed. Alternatively, the gas itself may be pressurized to form a liquid in which the material to be sprayed is dissolved. Chlorofluorocarbon (CFC) gases released from aerosol dispensers are believed to offer a threat to the environment by acting as catalysts to break down the protective ozone layer in the stratosphere. It has been suggested that this effect is leading to an increase in the number of cases of skin cancer; ⇨ pp. 52, 152 and 208.

aflatoxin, a poison produced by the fungus *Aspergillus flavus,* which grows on peanuts and grains stored in damp conditions. Aflatoxin binds to DNA preventing replication and transcription, and has been proved to cause cancer in animals. In association with hepatitis B, it is thought to be one of the reasons for the high incidence of primary liver cancer in certain areas of the world where the fungus is a common contaminant. Primary liver cancer is rare in other areas, such as Europe.

after-image, a visual impression of a bright object or light, which persists for a few seconds after the gaze is shifted or the eyes closed. A negative, or reversed after-image is common, as is one in which colours, complementary to those of the object, are seen. These are normal phenomena, due to transient photochemical changes in the retinas. The actual persistence of a fully formed image of what is seen, for a brief period after a shift of gaze, is an entirely different matter. This is *perseveration* and may be a sign of disease of the brain.

agenesis, absence of an organ or part as a result of failure of development in the early stages. The drug thalidomide caused agenesis of the limbs.

aggression, intimidating or injurious animal behaviour. Aggression need not involve violence and is often symbolic, consisting of various rituals or displays, which are often sufficient to achieve the desired effect – the withdrawal of the opponent or the cessation by the opponent of some unwanted activity or threat. Human aggression has many causes and takes various forms. It is, however, usually the result of a perceived threat or of the desire for some personal advantage. Sometimes it is a manifestation of the need for self-assertion in the context of a sense of personal inferiority.

agnatha, a class of fish-like, vertebrate animals without jaws, but with sucking mouthparts and teeth. Lampreys and hagfishes are the only living examples.

AIDS, acquired immune deficiency syndrome, a disease in which the operation of the human immune system is seriously prejudiced as a result of the action of the human immunodeficiency virus (HIV) on a certain class of small white cells, the helper-T lymphocytes. The result is that the body loses much of its protection against infection and falls prey, not only to common infections such as tuberculosis, but also to organisms that are not normally able to attack humans. The immune system's surveillance against cancer is also damaged, and certain cancers, especially Kaposi's sarcoma, commonly occur. HIV is spread in contaminated blood and body fluids and is most readily acquired during sexual intercourse with an infected person. To date, no effective treatment for established HIV infection has been achieved.

air, a mixture of gases forming the Earth's atmosphere. Its composition varies slightly at different locations and altitudes, but is roughly 79.1 per cent nitrogen, 20.9 per cent oxygen, 0.9 per cent argon, 0.03 per cent carbon dioxide and smaller quantities of various pollutants such as nitrogen oxides, sulphur dioxide, ozone and suspended soot particles. Nitrogen is a relatively inert gas with an important role in the cycle of nature (⇨ p. 206); oxygen is essential for life; argon is an almost wholly inert gas; and carbon dioxide is an essential fuel from which plants synthesize the sugars that form the start of the food chain. The proportions of these gases in the air are maintained relatively constant by a complex cycle involving oxygen production and carbon-dioxide consumption by plants, and oxygen consumption and carbon-dioxide production by animals and fires.

air mass, a large, horizontally disposed volume of atmosphere of fairly uniform temperature and humidity, and (usually) high pressure, that occurs over surface regions of marked uniformity. The interface between different air masses is called a *front.*

albumin, one of a number of globular and soluble proteins found in blood, in the white of an egg (albumen), in milk and in plants. Albumin amounts to about half of the protein in blood and is important in maintaining its osmotic pressure (⇨ p. 192–5). When heated, albumin is greatly altered and becomes insoluble in water.

alcohol, an organic compound that may be regarded as a hydrocarbon in which one or more hydrogen atoms linked to the carbon atom are replaced by a hydroxyl (–OH) group. In *primary alcohols* two hydrogen atoms linked to carbon are joined to the –OH group (CH_2OH). *Secondary alcohols* have one hydrogen atom linked to the carbon (CH.OH), and *tertiary alcohols* have no hydrogen atom on the carbon (C.OH). Alcohols with one –OH group are called *monohydric alcohols*; those with two are called *dihydric alcohols*; and those with three are called *trihydric alcohols.* Monohydric alcohols form a homologous series with ascending density (specific gravity) and boiling point. The lower members are colourless, light liquids; the higher members become more viscous and oil-like; and the highest are solid. Many occur in nature as oils, fats and waxes. Some of the lower members of the alcohol series are methyl alcohol, ethyl alcohol, propyl alcohol, butyl alcohol, amyl alcohol, hexyl alcohol, heptyl, octyl, lauryl, cetyl, melissyl, allyl, benzyl, benzhydrol, triphenyl carbinol, glycol, propylene glycol, and glycerol.

aldehyde, an organic compound containing the aldehyde group –CHO, i.e. a carbonyl group (C=O) with a hydrogen atom linked to the carbon atom. Aldehydes are formed by oxidation of primary ALCOHOLS. Methanal (formaldehyde), for instance, is formed by oxidation of methyl alcohol; ethanal (acetaldehyde) is formed by oxidation of ethyl alcohol; and benzaldehyde is formed by oxidation of benzyl alcohol. Aldehydes can be reconverted to their corresponding alcohol by reduction (⇨ p. 168) with hydrogen. The lower aldehydes, apart from the gas formaldehyde, are neutral volatile liquids. Some aldehydes readily form polymer chains (⇨ p. 164).

algebra, the generalization of arithmetic and its representation in symbolic form. Algebra is not concerned, in the first instance, with numerical data but with the processes by which data can be usefully manipulated, and with the strict rules that govern these processes. Algebraic statements are usually in the form of equations that can be converted into various useful or convenient forms without altering their truth. The equation $(4 + 1)(4 - 1) = 4^2 - 1^2$ is an arithmetical statement and is an example of the more general algebraic statement $(x + y)(x - y) = x^2 - y^2$, which would apply to any two numbers.

algebraic sum, an addition that takes into account the fact that some numbers are negative, some positive. The algebraic sum of +3, +7, +9 and –21 is –2.

algol, a high-level computer-programming language designed primarily for producing problem-solving programs for mathematical and scientific use. The name is an abbreviation of the phrase 'algorithmic language'. Algol passed though several generations, introduced a number of important new concepts, and was highly influential in the development of programming languages.

algorithm, a sequence of instructions to be followed with the intention of finding a solution to a problem. Each step must specify precisely what action is to be taken, and, although there may be many alternative routes through the algorithm, there is only one start point and one end point. Various nodes occur at which decisions must be made by means of questions that can be answered 'yes' or 'no'. The direction taken at these nodes is determined by the answer. A computer program is an algorithm expressed in a particular set of symbols. A flow chart is often used as a preliminary to writing a computer program and this also is an algorithm.

alimentary canal, the digestive tract of most animals or a human being, consisting of the mouth, throat, gullet (*oesophagus*), stomach, small intestine (*duodenum, jejunum* and *ileum*), large intestine (*caecum, colon, sigmoid colon* and *rectum*) and the short anal canal and anus.

alkali, a BASE that is soluble in water and that when dissolved gives hydroxide (–OH) ions (⇨ pp. 156 and 62). A base is a substance that reacts with an acid to form a salt and water only. Most bases are oxides or hydroxides of metals such as sodium, calcium, potassium or magnesium. Alkalis, such as sodium hydroxide (caustic soda) or ammonia solution, are often corrosive and dangerous. Alkalis have a pH of more than 7.0; they can neutralize acids; and they turn red litmus blue; ⇨ p. 168.

alkali metals, the elements in the first group of the periodic table (⇨ p. 158), specifically, lithium, sodium, potassium, rubidium, caesium and francium. All are highly reactive metals that, with the exception of lithium, react violently with water to form hydroxides. (Lithium reacts slowly with water.) In consequence, they are seldom found in the pure state. All readily form stable compounds. The alkali metals have only one electron in the outer shell, which accounts for their reactivity (⇨ pp. 156–9).

alkaline earth metals, the elements in the second group of the periodic table (⇨ p. 158), beryllium, magnesium, calcium, strontium and barium. The designation 'earth' refers to their oxides. All are strongly reactive and form stable compounds, but are less reactive than the group I alkali metals. All react with water to form hydroxides, and, on heating, these form the oxide and water.

alkaloids, a group of mostly poisonous organic compounds derived from plants. They include atropine, cocaine, morphine, quinine, strychnine, coniine, colchicine and caffeine. Several of the alkaloids have useful actions as medicinal drugs and several, or their derivatives, are commonly abused.

allele, one of a series of possible forms of a gene, situated at one of the two corresponding positions on pairs of corresponding chromosomes, and responsible for an inherited characteristic. When alleles are identical, the individual is *homozygous,* when they are different, the individual is *heterozygous.* In heterozygous individuals only one of the alleles may express its effect. This gene is said to be *dominant* and the other, whose effect is masked, is said to be *recessive.* Sometimes both have effect. This is called incomplete dominance. Recessive genes alone will exert their effect if both alleles are the same (homozygous). The term 'allele' is an abbreviation of allelomorph; ⇨ pp. 202–5.

allergy, hypersensitivity to a particular substance (the *allergen*) so that the body reacts abnormally (rash, sneezing, wheezing, etc.) to contact with even a very small amount of the substance. Allergy is a malfunction of the immune system, and some forms of allergic sensitivity, such as eczema and asthma, may be genetically induced. Common allergens are tree and grass pollens, animal dandruff, house mites, some foodstuffs, drugs, and metals such as nickel. Contact with the allergen leads to an abnormal reaction with the antibodies that normally destroy the antigen. In this case the reaction stimulates the release of powerful substances, such as histamine, from granular cells known as *mast cells.* These substances cause the undesirable effects.

allogamy, cross-fertilization in plants.

all-or-none response, a very common feature of various physiological phenomena, in which, if the response to a stimulus occurs, it is the maximal response of which the system is capable. Thus, a muscle fibre cannot contract to varying degrees, but can contract only fully. Variation in muscle power is achieved by varying the number of fibres that contract. A nerve fibre cannot transmit impulses of varying strength; if an impulse occurs, it is a full impulse. Again, variation in strength implies varying numbers of impulses.

allotropy, the existence of two or more different forms of a chemical element. These differences can arise because of different numbers of atoms in the molecule of the element, as in the case of oxygen (O_2) and ozone (O^3); or because of different crystalline structures, as in the case of carbon appearing as graphite, diamond or BUCKMINSTERFULLERENES 'buckyballs'. Sulphur, phosphorus and other elements in groups IV, V and VI of the periodic table (⇨ p. 158) may also take various allotropic forms.

alloy, a mixture of metals melted together, or of metals and nonmetals. There is an infinite number of possible alloys as metals and other materials can be mixed in any proportions. Alloys provide a wide range of valuable properties and are commonly much more useful than the pure metal. Alloys are often harder and more durable than the basic pure metal. Nonmetals commonly used in alloys include carbon, silicon, arsenic and antimony. Among the commonest of alloys are steel (iron and carbon), brass (copper and zinc), bronze (copper and tin), soft solder (lead and tin), duralumin (aluminium and copper), gun metal (copper, zinc and tin), and pewter (lead, tin and antimony). *Alnico* is a trade name for a range of useful alloys of iron, aluminium, nickel, cobalt and copper, from which strong permanent magnets may be made. Alloys of mercury with powdered metal, such as silver, can be mixed cold and are called *amalgam.*

alpha Centauri, a binary star, the second nearest to the Sun after Proxima Centauri, and only 4.3 light years away. A binary star is a pair of stars orbiting around a common centre of mass. Alpha Centauri appears as the third brightest star in the sky. The name indicates that it is the brightest star (alpha) in its constellation (Centaurus).

alphanumeric characters, the 26 letters of the alphabet and the decimal digits 0 to 9. Each of these (and many other characters) is represented in computers by a code such as the ASCII code (⇨ p. 216).

alpha particle, one of the three forms of radioactivity. The alpha particle consists of two protons and two neutrons, and is identical to the nucleus of the helium atom. Alpha particles react readily with matter, causing ionization (⇨ pp. 88 and 156), but are soon slowed by such interactions. Their range in air is only a few centimetres and shielding against them is easy. The other forms of radioactivity are BETA PARTICLES (high-speed electrons) and gamma rays; ⇨ GAMMA-RAY ASTRONOMY.

altruism, animal behaviour that promotes the interests and survival chances of another member of the species, at the possible expense of the altruist. Such behaviour is often adopted to attract a predator away from young. In humans, altruism implies conscious generosity or goodwill. Such motives are not necessarily implied in the case of other animals.

alveolus, one of the many millions of tiny, thin-walled, air sacs in the lungs of mammals and reptiles, whose combined surface area, for exchange of gases between the atmosphere and the bloodstream, approximates, in the case of humans, to that of a tennis court. The term is also applied to the tooth socket.

amber, fossilized resin that was exuded from trees or plants and is found in rocks, especially of the Cetaceous and Tertiary periods.

ambidexterity, the ability to use either hand with the same facility. Literally, 'both right'. True ambidexterity, with no bias to one side, is rare and runs in families. Surgeons, pianists and others often acquire, by long training, a degree of practical ambidexterity.

amethyst, a purple or violet form of quartz, coloured with a small quantity of iron. Popular as a gemstone. The name derives from the Greek roots *a-*, 'not' and *methystos*, 'intoxicated', it being believed, at one time, that the jewel would prevent drunkenness.

amines, organic compounds produced by the decomposition of organic matter when one or more of the hydrogen atoms in ammonia (NH_3) is replaced by an organic group. In primary amines only one hydrogen atom is replaced; in secondary amines, two hydrogen atoms are replaced; and in tertiary amines, all three are replaced. Examples of primary amines are methylamine, ethylamine, propylamine, butylamine and amylamine. These have progressively higher densities and boiling points, but the relationship does not hold for all.

amino acid, a basic constituent, or 'building brick' of protein. Body protein breaks down into 20 different amino acids – alanine, arginine, asparagine, aspartic acid, cysteine, glutamine, glutamic acid, glycine, histidine, isoleucine, leucine, lysine, methionine, phenylalanine, proline, serine, threonine, tryptophan, tyrosine and valine. Some of these can be synthesized by the body but others cannot, and are known as 'essential amino acids'. These must be obtained from protein in the diet. Amino acids group together to form *peptides*. Dipeptides have two amino acids, polypeptides have many. Polypeptides join to form proteins.

ammonia, a pungent, soluble, colourless gas that dissolves readily in water to make a strongly alkaline solution. Its formula is NH_3.

ammonite, an extinct, aquatic, shelled mollusc, whose fossil remains are commonly found in rocks of the Mesozoic era (224 to 65 million years ago).

amnesia, loss of memory as a result of physical or mental disease or injury. Head injury often causes amnesia both for events following the injury and for a period *prior* to the injury. The latter is *retrograde amnesia,* and its length is, in general, a measure of the severity of the injury.

amniocentesis, a method for obtaining a sample of the fluid that surrounds the growing fetus in the womb. A fine needle is passed through the front wall of the abdomen into the womb, under ultrasound imaging, and a small quantity of amniotic fluid is sucked out. This fluid contains cells and other material cast off from, or excreted by, the fetus, and analysis can provide important genetic and other information about it. Sex determination and chromosome analysis for hereditary disease are possible at an early stage.

amnion, one layer of the fluid-filled double membrane surrounding the fetus before birth. The membrane normally ruptures and releases the amniotic fluid ('breaking of the waters') before the baby is born.

amoebocyte, any cell that moves through the tissues of an animal by forming protrusions (*pseudopodia*) into which the cell-body substance flows. Many of the white blood cells

and immune- system cells (*phagocytes*) are amoebocytes; ⇨ p. 188.

amphibians, organisms, such as frogs, toads, newts and salamanders, capable of living both on land and in water. Amphibians can breathe either through the mouth or the nose but have no diaphragm, and air is pumped in and out by the muscles of the mouth and throat. Reproduction is mainly by external fertilization, usually in water. The juvenile forms have gills and develop into adults by metamorphosis. Amphibians evolved about 370 million years ago in the Devonian period and were the first vertebrates to live on land.

amplifier, an electronic device for increasing the strength of a varying electrical signal, ideally with minimal alteration to its characteristics (*minimal distortion*). Amplifiers use low-power transistors to amplify voltage and power transistors to amplify current (⇨ p. 90). Many amplifiers now consist of integrated circuits (⇨ pp. 102–5) except for the power output stages. NEGATIVE FEEDBACK is used to reduce distortion and increase the frequency range over which the amplifier will work well.

amylase, one of a group of enzymes that break down starch, glycogen and other polysaccharides to the simpler sugars glucose and maltose.

analogue, in physical science, a continuous representation, of any kind, of a varying quantity. Thus, the movement of the needle of an electric meter over the scale as the current varies, is an analogue of the current; or the movement of the hands of a clock is an analogue of time. Compare *digital*, in which the representation is noncontinuous, the varying quantity being represented by discrete numbers that change from time to time. An analogue computer performs calculations by the manipulation of analogue quantities such as varying distances or voltages.

analogue-to-digital converter, an electronic device that converts a varying signal, especially a voltage, to a series of numbers. This is done by sampling the signal at short intervals, usually many times a second, and expressing each momentary magnitude as a number.

analysis, in chemistry, the breaking down of a compound into its constituent elements so as to establish its composition. Compare *synthesis*, in which compounds are formed from separate elements. Quantitative analysis implies a determination of the proportions of the constituents. In mathematics, the branch concerned with the strict proofs of propositions and the properties of functions in calculus (⇨ p. 20).

anaplasia, a change in cells, so that the features that distinguish one type from another are lost. Anaplastic cells become smaller and simpler in structure and no longer combine to form recognizable tissues characteristic of particular organs. It is a feature of cancer; in general, the more anaplastic the cells, the more malignant

and dangerous the tumour (⇨ pp. 186–9).

anatomy, the structure of the body, or the study of the structure. Anatomy is subdivided into the study of bones (*osteology*); muscles (*myology*); the brain, spinal cord and peripheral nerves (*neurology*); the digestive, endocrine, respiratory and genito-urinary systems (*splanchnology*); the heart and blood vessels (*cardio-vascular medicine*); the eyes, ears, nose, tongue (*organs of special sense*); the microscopic structure (*histology*); and the development of the body before birth (*embryology*).

androgen, a male sex hormone. The androgens are STEROIDS and include the hormone testosterone and androsterone.

Andromeda galaxy, an enormous mass of stars kept together by gravity. Andromeda is the nearest galaxy to our Milky Way and is 2.2 million light years distant; ⇨ pp. 140–3.

anechoic chamber, an irregularly shaped room in which the walls are covered with small cones or wedges of sound-absorbent material so as to avoid echoes and resonances. Anechoic chambers are acoustically 'dead' and are used to test various instruments such as microphones and to conduct research into noise and other acoustic phenomena.

anemometer, an instrument, consisting of several cups on the end of arms connected to a rotating boss, used to measure wind speed. A hot-wire anemometer contains an electrically heated wire whose electrical resistance is related to its temperature. As the wire is cooled by passing air its electrical resistance decreases and the current through it consequently increases. A meter registering the current can thus be calibrated for wind speed.

angiography, a special form of X-ray examination that renders the blood visible in arteries and veins into which a solution opaque to X-rays (a *contrast medium*) has been injected. Angiography outlines the shape of the blood column and reveals narrowing, irregularity and obliteration of blood vessels as well as ballooning of the vessel itself (*aneurysm*). Angiography can also detect the development of clumps of new vessels and other abnormal patterns that suggest tumours or injury to organs. It is especially important in investigating the state of the arteries supplying the brain and the heart (the *coronary arteries*). The solutions used are oily liquids containing iodine; ⇨ p. 84.

angstrom, a very small unit of length equal to one tenth of a nanometre or one hundred millionth of a centimetre. The angstrom is used to represent the wavelength of radiation at the short-wavelength (high-frequency) end of the electromagnetic spectrum (⇨ p. 84). It was named after the Swedish physicist Anders Ångström (1814–74).

angular magnification, the ratio of the angle formed at the eye by the final image to that formed at the eye by the object. This is also known as the magnifying power of the system.

Linear magnification, on the other hand, is the ratio of the height of the image to that of the object.

angular momentum, the ANGULAR VELOCITY of an object multiplied by its moment of inertia, i.e., in the case of a simple rotating wheel, the velocity of rotation multiplied by its mass multiplied by the square of the distance from its axis of rotation; ⇨ p. 30.

angular velocity, speed of motion in a circle, or, more precisely, the rate of change of angular displacement with time. *Angular acceleration* is the rate of change of angular velocity; ⇨ p. 30.

anhydrous, free of water. The term is used especially of chemical salts that contain no water of crystallization, or of nonwatery liquids that are entirely free of water contamination.

animalia, one of the five taxonomic kingdoms of living things, the others being *fungi, monera, protista* and *plantae*. By definition, an animal is unable to generate its own food and must therefore depend on plants or other animals for its nutrition. This imposes the need, not imposed on plants, for mobility, sensory equipment capable of detecting food and coordinated directing and locomotory systems capable of pursuing and capturing it. Animal cell walls are made of phospholipids, cholesterol and protein, and contain no cellulose; plant cell walls contain much cellulose; ⇨ pp. 186–95.

annihilation, the simultaneous destruction of a colliding particle and its antiparticle with the production of energy equal to the rest-mass energy of both plus their kinetic energies at the moment of collision. An electron striking a positron, for instance, produces two photons of gamma radiation each with an energy of 0.511 million electronvolts. These energies are in accordance with Einstein's equation e = mc²; ⇨ pp. 40 and 110.

anode, a positive electrode towards which negative particles, such as electrons or negative ions, are attracted. Negative ions are called *anions*. In an electric cell or battery, the anode is the electrode that attracts electrons to itself from the external circuit; ⇨ p. 88.

ANSI, the American National Standards Institute, a body that lays down various standards for computers, computer connections, connecting-pin positions, disk and tape drives, software and so on. Many ANSI standards are observed worldwide, and most personal computers have in their operating system directory an ANSI.SYS file that can be read by the machine at the time of switching on.

anterior, an anatomical term meaning at or towards the front of the body. Compare *posterior*, meaning 'at the back'.

antibiotics, drugs capable, in low concentration, of killing or inactivating harmful bacteria without undue damage to the host organism. The first antibiotic was penicillin, which was originally derived from the fungus *Penicillium chrysogenum*. Hundreds of others have been discovered or synthesized. Because of their very short generation time and natural variation, bacteria readily acquire resistance to antibiotics, especially if these are used indiscriminately and in inadequate dosage. Antibiotics have no effect on viruses.

antibodies, proteins, known as *immunoglobulins* capable of reacting with substances foreign to the internal milieu of the human or animal body (*antigens*) so as to render them less dangerous. Such foreign substances include bacteria, viruses, fungi, toxins, venoms and foreign proteins. Antibodies are produced by B lymphocytes (B cells), from a large repertoire of which the most appropriate is selected according to the type of the currently presenting antigen. Antibodies previously produced can, on a later occasion, be produced more quickly and more readily. Active immunity is produced by giving injections of safe forms of anticipated antigens; passive immunity is produced by giving antibodies such as gamma globulin (one of the five classes of immunoglobulins).

anticoagulants, drugs that interfere with the normal clotting properties of the blood. The natural anticoagulant is *heparin*, produced in the liver.

anticyclone, a volume of atmospheric air that is at a higher pressure than the surrounding air. Anticyclones generally move slowly and are surrounded by light, circulating winds, moving clockwise in the Northern hemisphere and anticlockwise in the Southern hemisphere. They are associated with good weather; ⇨ CYCLONE.

antigen, any substance not recognized by the body as 'self' and thus attacked by the immune system. Such substances include bacteria, viruses and other infecting organisms, and tissue grafted from another individual. To prevent graft rejection, some of the functions of the immune system must be artificially suppressed, usually by drugs.

antimatter, the postulated matter made of a family of particles each being the antiparticle to an existing particle and having the opposite charge. When an antiparticle meets its corresponding particle, both are annihilated and the corresponding energy is released as radiant energy (⇨ ANNIHILATION). Some antiparticles have been produced by particle-accelerator/ collider experiments and some are put to practical use, as in the positron-emission tomography (PET) scanner. The theoretical grounds for the existence of antimatter were presented by the English physicist Paul Dirac (1902–84) in 1928 as a prediction of relativistic quantum mechanics (⇨ p. 40). The antiparticle of the electron is the positron, a particle of identical mass and of opposite but equal charge; the antiparticle of the proton is the antiproton, which is identical except that it carries a negative charge; the antiparticle of the neutron is the antineutron, which is identical except that their magnetic moments are of opposite sign relative to their spins. The reason for the general lack of evidence for the existence of an antimatter universe remains unclear; ⇨ also p. 110.

antrum, a hollow cavity or sinus in a bone. Behind both cheekbones are the maxillary antrums. The mastoid bones, below and behind the ears, contain the mastoid antrums, which connect with the middle ears.

aorta, the main, and largest, artery of the body. The aorta arises directly from the left side of the heart, passes vertically upwards in the chest, curves through 180° and runs down through the chest and ABDOMEN then divides into two arteries, one for each leg. In its course, it supplies major branches that run up the neck to the head and brain, a branch for each arm, and numerous smaller branches in the chest and abdomen to supply all the organs.

aperture, the useful or effective diameter of a lens or curved mirror. In practical usage, especially in photography, the term is taken to mean the ratio of the focal length of the lens or mirror to its effective diameter. The numerical value of this ratio is known as the f-number of the lens or mirror. Thus a camera's zoom lens, set at a focal length of 50 mm and an effective diameter (aperture) of 25 mm would have an f-number of two. Set at 100 mm the same aperture would give an f-number of four and only half the exposure for a given shutter speed.

aponeurosis, a thin, flat sheet of tendinous tissue by which broad, flat muscles are connected to bone.

appendix, a worm-like, blind-ended, vestigial structure attached to the beginning of the large intestine in humans and serving no useful function.

application software, programs that carry out specific functions such as word processing, spread- sheet operations, database access, computer-assisted design, accountancy, and so on. Application software is distinguished from computer-operating systems; ⇨ p. 218.

aqua regia, a mixture of three parts of concentrated hydrochloric acid and one part of concentrated nitric acid. Aqua regia will dissolve all but one of the metals, the exception being silver, which forms an insoluble chloride.

aqueous humour, the water that fills the space in the vertebrate eye between the back of the cornea and the front of the iris and internal lens. Continuous secretion of aqueous humour and its emergence into the bloodstream by way of a narrow filter, maintains the shape of the eyeball. Internal eye damage from raised pressure in the aqueous humour, due to interference with its outflow, is called *glaucoma*.

Arachnida, the class of arthropods containing 65,000 different species that includes spiders, ticks, mites and scorpions. Most arachnids are carnivorous and feed on the bodies or body fluids of prey.

arachnoid mater, the intermediate of the three meningeal membranes that surround the brain and the spinal cord. The innermost meninx is the soft pia mater that dips into the grooves in the brain (*sulci*), and the outer is the tough dura mater that lines the bone of the skull and spine. The arachnoid tents over the brain sulci leaving an underlying subarachnoid space that contains the watery cerebrospinal fluid and many blood vessels. Bleeding from one of these vessels (*subarachnoid haemorrhage*) is always serious and often fatal.

architectural acoustics, the study of the features of buildings and auditoria that allow music and speech to be heard clearly and comfortably. Good hall acoustics imply the absence of undue echoes or of the emphasis of any particular pitches by resonances. Large, plane, unbroken surfaces reflect sound and simple dimensions promote resonances. Good acoustics also imply that the reverberation time (the time taken for audible re-echoing to drop to an acceptable level) should be appropriate for the main purpose of the hall. Long reverberation times cause indistinct speech and blurred music; unduly short reverberation times produce a 'dead' effect. Bare rooms with hard surfaces increase reverberation times; carpets, soft furnishing and the presence of an audience reduce reverberation; ⇨ p. 68.

archiving, the movement of a computer file from a position of immediate access, as on a hard disk, to one of less immediate access, as on a remote tape drive or on a remotely stored disk. Archiving may be performed deliberately by the operator or may occur automatically, after a designated period, as part of a programmed process; ⇨ p. 214.

areola, the pink or brown area surrounding the nipple of the human female breast. It contains tiny tubercles (bumps) under which are the glands that lubricate the skin to protect it during suckling.

artery, an elastic, muscular-walled tube that carries blood at high pressure from the heart to any part of the body. By contrast, the veins are thin-walled, inelastic and collapsible and carry blood at low pressure back to the heart.

artificial insemination, a method of achieving pregnancy without sexual intercourse, which is extensively employed in the breeding of cattle and domestic animals. In humans it can be used when sexual intercourse is impossible, or when the male is sterile. A quantity of fresh seminal fluid is taken up in a narrow syringe or pipette and injected high into the female's vagina or even into the opening of the womb (*uterus*). The procedure is timed to coincide with the period in the menstrual cycle when egg production by the woman (*ovulation*) is most likely to occur. Assuming no other reasons for infertility, the success rate is high.

asbestos, one of a range of fibrous minerals that includes crocidolite, amosite, tremolite, and actinolyte, found mainly in Canada and the former USSR. These minerals, which can be spun to make threads and woven into cloth or moulded into blocks, have been extensively used because of their heat-, chemical- and electricity-resistant properties. Inhalation of

asbestos dust is dangerous to the lungs and this has made the use of asbestos less desirable.

ascorbic acid, vitamin C, the vitamin necessary for the production of healthy collagen, the body's main structural protein. Deficiency causes the bleeding disorder *scurvy*. Ascorbic acid is a powerful antioxidant and is now being recommended, in doses several times that of the minimum requirement, as a means of 'mopping up' the oxygen free radicals that cause tissue damage in many disease processes.

asepsis, the absence of all bacteria or other microorganisms capable of causing infection. Modern surgery is performed in an environment in which the nearest possible approach to full asepsis is obtained by sterilizing all instruments, dressings and towels; by providing a sterile barrier between the patient and those working in theatre, in the form of sterile gowns, caps, gloves and masks; and by draping the whole of the patient, except the operation area, in sterile sheets.

asexual reproduction, the formation of a new individual from a single parent cell or organism without the intervention of another individual or the involvement of a sperm or ovum (*gamete*). All animal body cells, even those producing sperms and ova, reproduce asexually, but the whole organism reproduces sexually. A number of simple organisms, especially micro-organisms, plants and lower animals, reproduce asexually.

asphalt lake, a pool of bitumen (a mixture of solid or semisolid hydrocarbons) occurring mainly in the southern states of the US and in South America.

assimilation, the physiological process by which food material that has been digested and absorbed is incorporated into the cells and used to form body materials. Thus, GLUCOSE not immediately required for fuel is converted to the polysaccharide glycogen; fats are stored in fat cells; and AMINO ACIDS are linked to form proteins.

astable, an electronic circuit, usually consisting of two interconnected transistors each of which alternately oscillates between the on and off state. An astable circuit produces a square wave or pulse output, and, if synchronized to an accurate frequency by a quartz crystal or other means, can operate as a timing clock for computers or other devices. Quartz watches and clocks use crystal-controlled astables to generate a high-frequency square wave that is then repeatedly frequency-divided by BISTABLES until a one-second square wave is reached; ⇨ pp. 102–5.

astigmatism, a property of a lens or mirror system in which a surface is not that of a perfect sphere or parabola, but has a greater degree of curvature in one meridian than in the meridian at right angles to that one. Such a *toric* surface produces two foci – one for rays in the plane parallel to that of greatest curvature and one for rays in the plane at right angles. Only one of these sets of rays can be focused at one time. The cornea of the eye is commonly

astigmatic, usually being most steeply curved from top to bottom and least steeply curved from side to side. Ocular astigmatism is corrected by spectacles having *cylindrical* lenses set at the appropriate axis so that the steeper corneal curve is matched by the less steep spectacle lens curve.

astronomical unit, a unit of distance in space equal to the average distance from the Earth to the Sun. One astronomical unit is about 149 million km (92.81 million miles).

astrophysics, the study of the physics and chemistry of the stars, including their origin, evolution and structure, and the generation and movement of energy in and around them. Astrophysics is also concerned with the relationships and dynamics of star clusters and galaxies, and with the study of interstellar dust and molecules, comets, asteroids and any other extraterrestrial matter; ⇨ pp. 140–3.

asymptote, a line approached progressively by a curve that touches it only at infinity.

atlas, the uppermost vertebra of the spine upon which the skull can nod but cannot rotate. Rotation occurs between the atlas and the next vertebra, the *axis*.

atmolysis, separation of gases from a mixture by making use of their different rates of diffusion through porous partitions of membranes.

atmosphere, the mixture of gases that extends for hundreds of kilometres above the Earth's surface, gradually merging into outer space with no sharp division. The atmosphere is divided into four layers on the basis of temperature: the *troposphere*, extending up to 10 km (6.2 mi); the *stratosphere*, extending to about 50 km (31 mi); the *mesosphere*, extending to 80 km (49.6 mi) and the *thermosphere*, extending to about 110 km (38.2 mi). The *ozone layer* occupies the stratosphere and this causes a considerable temperature rise in the upper stratosphere because of absorption of ultraviolet radiation from the Sun (⇨ pp. 52, 146 and 152).

atmospheric pressure, the weight of a column of air vertically above a unit area. One atmosphere is the pressure exerted by this column at sea level, and is equal to 101,325 pascals or 760 mm of mercury. A *pascal* is a newton per square metre, and a *newton* is the force that exerts an acceleration of 1 metre per second per second to a mass of 1 kg. A common practical unit of atmospheric pressure is the *millibar*, equal to the force exerted by 1,000 dynes acting on 1 square cm. A *dyne* is the force that will accelerate 1 gram by 1 cm per second per second. Atmospheric pressure varies with altitude. At the surface, pressure varies with temperature and these variations lead to air motion (*winds*). In general, winds flow out from areas of high pressure and into areas of low pressure. This is complicated, however, by many other factors including the rotation of the Earth.

atomic clock, a means of producing electrical impulses at highly accurate intervals by synchronizing them to one of the exceptionally constant periodic phenomena occurring within an atom or molecule. In the caesium clock, the energy difference between two states of the caesium–133 nucleus when in a magnetic field is used. Atoms excited by radio waves at a frequency corresponding to the energy difference between the two states can be deflected by a magnetic field to hit a detector. The signal from this can be used to lock an oscillator to the exact frequency of the transition. The ammonia clock makes use of the fact that the ammonia molecule, which forms a pyramid of three hydrogen atoms at the base and one nitrogen atom at the apex, inverts and then returns to the original state every 41.8 microseconds. This cycle, with a frequency of 23,870 Hz, can be used to lock an oscillator on to exactly this frequency; ⇨ pp. 108–11.

ATP, adenosine triphosphate, one of the most important substances in all living organisms. ATP has three phosphate groups in its molecule and is the carrier of chemical energy. It readily loses one or two of these groups to become adenosine diphosphate (ADP) or adenosine monophosphate (AMP) and in either reaction it releases a large amount of energy that thus becomes available for any chemical purpose that requires it. Such purposes include the synthesis of new body molecules, the active transport of materials or the contraction of muscles. ADP and AMP then reacquire the lost phosphate groups by making use of the energy derived from oxidation of food, to reconstitute ATP.

atrium, one of the two upper chambers of the vertebrate heart (except in the case of fishes, which have only one).

atrophy, wasting and loss of substance due to cell degeneration and death. This may be a natural ageing process or it may be due to simple disuse. The opposite of atrophy is *hypertrophy* and these two processes are well demonstrated by the muscles, which will soon lose bulk if unused, but may, especially in youth, be built up by regular hard work.

audiometry, measurement of the sensitivity of a person's hearing at different pitches (*frequencies*). Hearing loss is never uniform over the whole range of sounds, from low to high pitch, so it is necessary to test the hearing with sounds of different pitches. Pure tone audiometry is most commonly used, but speech audiometry is often more revealing. In this, two-syllable recorded words are played at gradually increasing volume and a note is made of the intensity at which 50 per cent of the words are repeated correctly. This is the *speech-reception threshold*. The operator also notes what percentage of words are correctly identified at a level much higher than the speech-reception threshold. This is normally 90–100 hundred per cent in outer- and middle-ear (*conductive*) deafness, but is reduced in inner-ear (*sensorineural*) hearing loss; ⇨ p. 68.

aurora, a remarkable phenomenon of rapidly changing coloured rays, arcs, curtains or bands, seen in the sky most frequently near the poles. Often called the *aurora borealis* or

'northern lights' in the Northern hemisphere, or the *aurora australis* or 'southern lights' in the Southern hemisphere, this brilliant show is caused by interaction between atmospheric oxygen and nitrogen and streams of charged particles from the Sun attracted by the Earth's magnetic field; ⇨ p. 146. The interaction occurs at an altitude of about 100 km (62 miles) and causes the oxygen to be energized in much the same way as gas in a neon tube.

autonomic nervous system, the part of the nervous system that controls functions – such as the heartbeat, the secretion of glands and the contraction of blood vessels – that are not normally under conscious volition. Many automatic and unconscious processes are essential for health and even life, and these are controlled by the autonomic nervous system. It is subdivided into two parts, the SYMPATHETIC NERVOUS SYSTEM and the PARASYMPATHETIC NERVOUS SYSTEM, and these are, in general, antagonistic and in balance.

autosome, any ordinary paired chromosome other than one of the sex chromosomes. In humans, there are 22 pairs of autosomes and one pair of sex chromosomes. The great majority of genes are thus autosomal. Those on a sex chromosome are said to be *sex-linked*; ⇨ pp. 202–5.

autotomy, the deliberate casting off by an animal of a part of its body, so as to distract an attacker and facilitate escape from danger. Many small lizards will separate and sacrifice their tails when necessary.

average, the mean of a group of numbers, i.e. the sum of them all divided by the number in the group.

axiom, a proposition generally agreed to be so obviously true as not to require proof. Or a proposition that appears incapable of proof but that is stipulated to be true for purposes of logical argument; ⇨ p. 12.

axon, the long fibre coming from a nerve cell and forming, in bundles with many thousands of other axons, the anatomical structure known as a NERVE. Although cell bodies are microscopic, axons may be very long – sometimes many centimetres. They convey nerve impulses from the cell body to a remote point, connecting with other cells or with muscle fibres or glands.

bacillus, any of the rod-shaped BACTERIA.

backcross, a method of determining whether an organism with a dominant characteristic has two dominant ALLELES or only one and a recessive allele. The organism is allowed to breed with a mate showing the recessive characteristic. If all the offspring have the dominant feature then both alleles are dominant in the parent. If not, one of the parental alleles is recessive.

background radiation, the low-intensity radiation from natural and artificial sources that is constantly present in the environment. This radiation comes from radioactive

substances in rocks and soil, and from cosmic radiation from outer space. Some of the soil and atmospheric radiation comes from long-lasting fallout from nuclear weapons and from waste gases from nuclear power stations, but the total effect of artificial radiation is very small compared to the natural levels. In most areas, background radiation produces a count of about one per second in a Geiger counter and this must be taken into account when measuring radiation from a particular source. Microwave background radiation at 2.7 K is the residual radiation from the big bang (⇨ p. 126).

backup, a copy of important software, especially of data that cannot readily be replaced, made for use in the event of the loss or corruption of the primary source. Some systems automatically make backup copies at intervals that can be specified. It is sound practice to keep backup material in a different building from the primary material; ⇨ p. 216.

bacteria, a large group of single-celled organisms without a membrane around the nucleus (*prokaryotic*) and with a thick cell wall. Bacteria are found everywhere. Most of them are from 0.5 μ (thousandths of a mm) to about 5 μ in size. They may be spherical (*cocci*), rod-shaped (*bacilli*), comma-shaped (*vibrios*) or spiral (*spirilla* or *spirochaetes*). Many can move freely by means of lashing appendages. Some can survive in the absence of free oxygen (*anaerobic*), and many can form resistant spores so as to survive long periods of dryness. Bacteria are essential sources of enzymes for the breakdown of dead organic matter; without them, life would soon be impossible. A small proportion of the total are parasites of animals and some of these cause disease by producing powerful poisons (*toxins*) that damage cells and tissues.

bacteriophage, a class of viruses that invade and parasitize bacteria. Each bacteriophage is specific to the type of bacterium it attacks. Most bacteriophages multiply rapidly within bacteria and destroy them, but in some cases the bacterium survives to produce infected offspring. Bacteriophages are widely used in genetic engineering because they can readily alter the genome (*genetic complement*) of the invaded bacterium.

balance, a weighing device involving a pivoted beam from which are suspended two pans. The substance to be weighed is placed in one pan and accurate standard weights are placed in the other until the pans are level. At this point, the weight of the substance is equal to the weight of the standard weights. By good designs and the use of pivots with minimal friction, laboratory balances can be made to weigh accurately to a hundredth of a milligram or better. Electronic balances do not use weights; the movement of the pan is opposed by an electric force and the amount of movement is a function of the weight on it. Such balances can weigh to a millionth of a milligram.

ballistics, the study of the flight dynamics and path taken by projectiles, the propulsive forces and their effect, and the effect of air resistance and gravity; ⇨ pp. 30 and 36.

balloon angioplasty, a method of widening blood vessels, especially those supplying blood to the vital heart muscle (the *coronary arteries*), that have been narrowed by the disease atherosclerosis. A fine, soft tube with a cylindrical, inflatable section at the end is passed along the vessel until the tip lies just beyond the point of the narrowing. The inflatable section is then ballooned out with air or fluid so that the fatty atherosclerotic plaque is crushed into the wall, thus allowing freer passage of blood. The results are usually excellent.

bandpass filter, an electronic or passive device that greatly reduces the amplitude of (*attenuates*) signals of wavelength outside a prescribed range; ⇨ pp. 64–7.

bandwidth, the range of frequencies (or wavelengths) over which a system is capable of operating within defined limits of efficiency, the range of frequencies (wavelengths) that a communication channel can accommodate, or the frequency spread of a radio signal of a given nominal frequency (wavelength; ⇨ pp. 64–7).

bark, the outer layer of woody plants, trees and their roots. Bark is protective in function and is the partly dead and partly living tissue external to the water-conducting system (the *xylem*). Bark is produced by a layer called the *cork cambium,* whose cells divide to form an outer corky layer and an inner smoother layer. As the stem increases in diameter, the outer corky layer splits, but the layers below it remain impermeable and protective.

barometer, an instrument for measuring atmospheric pressure. There are two main forms. The mercury barometer is a straight glass tube, closed at one end, which is filled with mercury and then inverted with its open end under the surface of an open reservoir of mercury. The column drops, causing a partial vacuum above it, until the weight of the mercury in the column is balanced by the atmospheric pressure on the surface of the reservoir. As this varies, the column rises or falls, and the reading is taken from the upper level, on a scale placed parallel to the tube. The aneroid barometer consists of a corrugated, partially evacuated, thin metal chamber whose dimension changes with the external pressure on it. This change can be magnified by levers to provide a convenient movement against a scale.

baroreceptor, a pressure receptor in the body capable of monitoring blood pressure so that this can be regulated.

Barr body, a small chromosomal structure found only in the cells of females and used as a (controversial) test of sex in athletes and others.

basal metabolic rate, the rate of energy expenditure of an animal or human at rest, measured as the heat production in a given time. Basal metabolic rate (BMR) is the energy consumed in performing the resting basic vital functions such as breathing, heartbeat, nerve-cell conduction, gland secretion, active transport of materials, and so on. The BMR is significantly raised when the thyroid gland is overactive.

base, in chemistry, a substance that will combine with an ACID (accept protons) to produce a salt plus water. Bases are soluble metal oxides, hydroxides or amines, or compounds such as ammonia that give hydroxide (–OH) ions in watery solution (⇨ p. 168). Bases that dissolve in water to give hydroxyl ions are called ALKALIS. In mathematics, a base is a number equal to the number of symbols used in a number system. Thus in the decimal system the base is 10 (10 symbols, 0 to 9 inclusive); in the binary system, the base is 2 (1 and 0).

base analogue, any chemical substance of similar structure to one of the four bases of DNA (⇨ p. 202) that can become incorporated into DNA in place of the normal bases and cause gene mutations.

base deletion, the removal of a nucleotide base from the DNA structure (⇨ p. 202). This completely changes the reading of the local DNA code, which is shifted one place along by the deletion. As each triplet of bases codes for a particular AMINO ACID, the resulting protein, if formed at all, will be seriously modified.

base metal, any of the common metals, as distinct from the precious metals such as platinum, gold and silver.

base pairing, the exclusive linking of guanine with cytosine and adenine with thymine that occurs in DNA (⇨ p. 202).

base unit, a unit of measurement that is defined in terms of physical entities rather being derived from other units.

BASIC, an acronym for Beginner's All-purpose Symbolic Instruction Code, a high-level and very simple programming language developed in the USA in 1964. BASIC became, and remains, very popular for amateur programming and for very short programs, but, in spite of numerous improvements has been superseded for serious professional work; ⇨ p. 218.

battery, two or more electric cells joined either in series or in parallel; ⇨ pp. 88–91.

baud rate, the number of binary digits (*bits*) transmitted per second along a line. More generally, the number of times per second that a data-transmission channel changes its state. The term was derived from the name of the French communications engineer J. M. E. Baudot (1845–1903) who invented an efficient code that replaced the morse code for telegraphic signalling.

bauxite, a reddish-brown substance, the commonest of the aluminium ores, consisting of aluminium oxides and aluminous laterite. The main deposits are in Russia, Australia, Guinea, Jamaica and Brazil; ⇨ p. 150.

B cells, one of the two great classes of lymphocytes – white cells found in the blood, lymph nodes and tissue – which, with other cells, form the immune system of the body. When infection occurs, certain B lymphocytes, selected with the assistance of T lymphocytes, form colonies of identical cells (*clones*) to generate large numbers of identical antibody-manufacturing *plasma cells*. From these, the appropriate antibodies emerge at the rate of about 2,000 per second to attach to and bring about the destruction of the invading organisms.

beats, the effect produced by the interaction of two waveforms of almost, but not quite, identical frequency. Such waves pass in and out of phase with each other and they thus alternately potentiate and cancel each other, giving rise to an additional wave of much lower frequency than either (⇨ p. 64).

Beaufort wind scale, a wind-speed scale proposed by the British naval officer and hydrographer Admiral Sir Francis Beaufort (1774–1857). The modern version ranges through calm, light air, light breeze, gentle breeze, moderate breeze, fresh breeze, strong breeze, near gale, gale, strong gale, storm, violent storm and hurricane. A gentle breeze is a speed of 3.4–5.4 m per second; a violent storm is a speed of 28.5–32.6 m per second; and a hurricane is a wind speed greater than this.

behavioural genetics, the branch of genetics concerned with the attempt to determine how far animal behaviour is the result of genetic rather than environmental factors; ⇨ pp. 202–5.

benignity, not malignant. Not usually tending to cause death. The term derives from the Latin *bene natus,* meaning 'well born'. Although usually safe, a benign tumour may enlarge to a considerable size, and may cause damage by local pressure or by displacing other tissue, especially in a confined space such as the inside of the skull. Apart from such cases, benign tumours seldom cause death. In contrast to malignant tumours, they do not seed off (*metastasize*) and so spread to other parts of the body.

beryl, a semi-precious or precious gemstone consisting of beryllium aluminium silicate, the main ore of the element beryllium. Beryls are most commonly blue, yellow or white. The green variety, the emerald, is rare and greatly valued.

beta particle, a high-speed electron emitted from an atomic nucleus when a neutron is converted into a proton (⇨ p. 160).

beta testing, evaluation and trial of a new or modified software package in normal working conditions, often by large numbers of experienced users, so that faults can be detected. Beta testing is done prior to the commercial release of the package; ⇨ p. 218.

betatron, a particle accelerator that produces high-speed electrons for research purposes. The negative particles are accelerated by powerful electromagnetic fields.

biceps muscle, the prominent and powerful muscle on the front of the upper arm that bends the elbow and rotates the forearm outwards, as in using a large screwdriver. These actions are independent of each other. Screws are made to go in by clockwise rotation because the action of the biceps in turning the forearm in this direction is much stronger than that of the muscles which turn it anticlockwise. The elbow-bending action of the biceps is balanced and opposed by the straightening action of the triceps on the back of the upper arm.

biennial, a plant that completes its life cycle in two consecutive annual growing seasons.

bifurcation, forked, or two-pronged. Bifurcations are very common in the animal body, especially in blood vessels and in the bronchial 'tree' of the lungs. At a bifurcation the sum of the cross-sectional area of the two branches usually exceeds that of the parent branch. Since this happens many times, there is a progressive increase in the volume of the system. This may have important physiological consequences, as, for instance, in the progressive drop in blood pressure in the arterial tree.

bile, a thick, greenish-brown liquid secreted by the liver and concentrated in the gall bladder. The entry of fatty food material into the intestine prompts the production by the duodenum, of a hormone, cholecystokinin, which causes the gall bladder to empty its contents down the bile duct into the duodenum. Bile salts act to emulsify fats so that they can readily be absorbed through the wall of the intestine. The bile pigments, derived from haemoglobin breakdown, colour the faeces. Bile contains much cholesterol but most of this is reabsorbed into the blood. Fibre in the diet can bind with cholesterol and prevent its reabsorption.

binding energy, the energy equivalent to the loss of mass when protons and/or neutrons bind together to form the nucleus of an atom. This energy can be released both by splitting (*fission*) of heavy elements and *fusion* of light elements; ⇨ p. 160.

binocular vision, the ability to see a single image while using the two eyes simultaneously. Binocular vision presupposes a high degree of accuracy in the alignment of the two eyes and this is maintained, for most directions of gaze, by a feedback servomechanism involving the brain and the twelve small eye-moving muscles. Because the eyes are separated laterally, the images formed in each, from fairly near objects, are not identical. The right eye sees further round to the right side of objects than the left and vice versa. The fusion of these dissimilar images provides a sense of solidity (*stereognosis*) and assists in judging distance.

biodegradability, the capability of being decomposed and broken down to simpler substances or elements by enzymes provided by bacteria. All organic matter is ultimately biodegradable, but many artificial materials are not and can thus cause environmental damage; ⇨ p. 208.

bioenergetics, the study of the movement of energy in living organisms and of the balance of energy production and energy consumption.

biofeedback, a method of providing a person with information about the levels of activity of normally unconscious bodily processes in the hope that some control or adjustment may be exercised. Biofeedback methods have been claimed to be effective in the control of many disorders such as excessive muscle tension, headache, anxiety, panic attacks, high blood pressure, and heart rate and rhythm abnormalities. Almost any of the bodily states can be monitored and changes displayed by one of various means such as electric meters, flashing light arrays, musical sounds heard in headphones, and so on. At least in a limited range of conditions, such as abnormal muscle tension, biofeedback can be valuable. The usefulness of its more general application is less certain.

biological clock, one of a number of intrinsic timing devices present in the animal and human body, and probably in plants, by which various biological rhythms, manifested by behavioural or physiological changes, are regulated. Such periodic changes include sleep, ovulation and menstruation, sexual receptivity in most mammals (*heat* or *oestrus*), hibernation in animals, nest building and so on. The circadian rhythm, although probably synchronized by light changes, does not appear to be naturally of a 24-hour periodicity. Human subjects insulated from information about day and night gradually drift into a different cycle. The mechanisms underlying biological clocks have not been established, but there is nothing inherently implausible in the idea of biological oscillators capable of producing such cycles. Various periodic functions exist in the brain-wave patterns of the electroencephalogram.

biology, the study of living things.

bioluminescence, the production of light by living organisms. Bioluminescent systems produce light without heat by the oxidation of a range of substances known as *luciferins* under the influence of an enzyme luciferase.

biomass, the totality of all living things in a particular area. Biomass is an index of the amount of living matter an area can support and of the environmental health of the area; ⇨ p. 206.

bionics, the study of the relationship between brain function and electronics (⇨ pp. 102–5), or the engineering discipline concerned with the design and production of artificial and functional body parts, organs, limbs, walking devices, and so on.

biophysics, the study of those aspects of physics that apply to biological processes and structures, and to living things generally.

biopsy, taking a specimen of tissue from the body for the purpose of microscopic examination so as to determine what is wrong. The term is also applied to the specimen itself.

bioremediation, the deliberate use of bacteria as scavengers and biodegrading agents to help to clean up environmental pollution, especially by oil and oil products. Some strains of bacteria have a remarkable capacity for breaking down hydrocarbons, and can rapidly dispose of oil spills, especially in the sea.

BIOS, an acronym for Basic Input–Output System, the permanent small program that is built into every personal computer and that carries out the operations concerned with the input and output of data, such as the control of the keyboard, the screen display, the disk drives, and the serial and parallel communication connections. The BIOS is usually held on a ROM chip fitted in the machine so that it is always available and BOOTING is possible. BIOS is usually copied from the ROM to the faster RAM soon after switching on.

bird, a vertebrate of the class Aves, featuring feathers, modified forelimbs used as wings, a beak or bill, no teeth, controlled body temperature, internal fertilization and the production of a shelled egg that is incubated externally.

bistable, an electronic circuit element, usually consisting of two linked transistors, one being turned on and the other off, which is capable of being in either of two states. One state can represent a 1, the other a 0. Bistables form the basis of most computer RANDOM-ACCESS MEMORIES, but are volatile. If the supply current is turned off, all data held in a collection of bistable memories is lost. Bistables are often called *flip-flops*; ⇨ pp. 102–5.

bit, a binary digit (⇨ chapter 10).

bit mapping, an arrangement by which an image for display on a computer screen can be stored. The image is represented in the store by a succession of small-dot picture elements (*pixels*) arranged in rows and columns. Each pixel is stored as one or more bits of data – a single bit for the presence or absence of light in a simple monochrome system, or several if shades of grey or colours are required. The number of dots per row or column determines the detail (*resolution*) of the image, and this is usually expressed in terms of the number of rows and columns. Text can be represented as a bit-mapped image, differing fundamentally from text represented as ASCII (⇨ p. 216) or other alphanumeric code. Bit-mapped text, obtained by using a scanner, can be converted to code by means of optical-character-recognition (OCR) software.

Bitter pattern, the microscopic appearance of the magnetic domains in a ferromagnetic material revealed by spreading on its surface a colloidal suspension of very fine iron particles.

biuret test, a test for the presence of proteins in a solution.

black body, a theoretical body that absorbs all the radiation, of whatever kind, that falls on it; ⇨ pp. 38 and 84.

black-body radiation, the electromagnetic radiation emitted by a BLACK BODY. This extends over the whole range of wavelengths and has a characteristic energy distribution, with a maximum at a certain wavelength (⇨ p. 38). The peak of this energy varies with the temperature. The higher the temperature, the further the peak moves towards the shorter wavelengths; the lower the temperature, the further it moves towards the long wavelengths.

black box, a useful scientific concept or technique in which the units of any system are considered simply as boxes that effect particular functions, or have particular properties, without taking any account of how these functions or properties are achieved.

bladder, any bag-shaped structure such as is common in animals and plants. In humans and many other vertebrates the term refers to the urinary bladder in which the continuously secreted urine is temporarily stored until it can conveniently be disposed of.

blastula, the hollow ball or disc of cells formed as the first stage in the development of the animal and human embryo after the fertilization of the egg (*ovum*). In vertebrates, the blastula forms as a disc on the surface of the egg yolk. In mammals the blastula is called a *blastocyst*.

blind spot, the projection into space of the head of the optic nerve (the *optic disc*), which consists solely of nerve fibres and has no receptor elements (*rods* and *cones*). The blind spot occurs, in the field of vision of each eye, about fifteen degrees to the outer side of whatever point we are looking at. If an eye is turned outwards to align itself on the point that was previously the projection of the optic disc, the blind spot will simply move fifteen degrees further out. It is mainly because of this that we are unaware of it. The blind spot can, however, easily be demonstrated by closing the left eye, looking at a small black spot on a sheet of paper and then moving the eye slowly along, horizontally, to the left. When the image of the spot falls on the optic nerve head it will no longer be seen. Acquired blind spots are due to damage to the retina or to the fibres passing back from it to the brain. Such spots (*scotomas*) can easily be plotted and their progress checked.

blood, a red fluid in vertebrates, vital to life, that is circulated through the blood vessels by the pumping action of the heart. The average adult human has about 5 litres (10 pt) of blood. Blood has several major functions. It is a transport medium, especially for oxygen, which it carries in the red blood cells, linked to the haemoglobin with which they are filled. It also transports dissolved sugars, dissolved proteins such as albumin and globulin, protein constituents (AMINO ACIDS), fat–protein combinations (*lipoproteins*), emulsified fats (*triglycerides*), vitamins, minerals, waste products such as carbon dioxide, urea, lactic acid, and innumerable other substances. In addition to the millions of red cells (about 5,000,000 per ml in humans) the blood carries enormous numbers of uncoloured cells most of which are concerned in the defence of the individual against infection and cancer. These cells constitute the main part of the immune system. The blood also carries hormones – chemicals produced by the endocrine glands (the pituitary, thyroid, parathyroids, adrenals, pancreas and sex glands) and carried throughout the body to exercise a constant, balanced control of many important functions. Blood is continually being replenished with new cells manufactured in the marrow of the flat bones such as the shoulder blades (*scapulas*) or breastbone (*sternum*). Red cells have a life of about 120 days, after which they break down and release their haemoglobin. This is used by the liver and converted to a useful byproduct bilirubin. Conservation of blood is so important that the circulation has an automatic self-sealing mechanism – the blood coagulation system – which operates when a blood vessel is damaged.

blood–brain barrier, the impediment to the passage of certain substances, including some drugs, from the blood to the tissue fluid surrounding the brain cells. CAPILLARIES in the brain differ from those elsewhere in the body in that the edges of the cells of which they are made abut against each other leaving no gaps. Substances from the blood must therefore pass *through* the cells. The drug heroin is fat soluble and can pass through the blood–brain barrier, but morphine is fat-insoluble and cannot. As soon as heroin is through, however, enzymes remove its acetyl groups converting it to morphine, which is unable to escape, and remains to exert its effect on the brain.

blood clotting, an essential property of the BLOOD to prevent dangerous loss in the event of injury to a blood vessel. In clotting (*coagulation*), the blood at the site of the injury comes into contact with damaged tissue or some foreign substance. This contact triggers off the complex sequence of biochemical events by which the soluble blood protein, fibrinogen, is converted to the soluble protein fibrin and forms a solid mass to seal the leaking point. Many different factors, present in the blood and tissues, are essential for coagulation. These include Factor VIII, the absence of which causes haemophilia A, and Factor IX, or Christmas factor, which is absent in haemophilia B. The blood of people with a hereditary deficiency of these factors does not clot normally, and injury is followed by profuse and prolonged bleeding.

blood enzymes, enzymes that are released into the blood when cells are damaged. The identification of the type and quantity of these enzymes can provide information about the site and degree of damage. Blood-enzyme measurement is especially valuable after a heart attack (*coronary thrombosis*) in which there has been damage to, or death of, part of the heart muscle. The larger the area of damage, the higher will be the levels of these enzymes in the blood. Blood-enzyme levels are also important in the investigation of other forms of tissue damage, especially in liver disease. Large quantities of enzymes are released when the body is infected with hepatitis.

blood groups, four main categories of blood that determine which type of blood may safely be mixed with which. Human red blood cells fall into four groups, A, B, AB and O. The serum of the blood – the fluid part, without cells – contains *antibodies* to the groups not present in the red cells. The red cells are antigenic and clump together if brought into contact with serum containing antibodies to them. The red-cell *antigens* are hereditarily determined, both A and B being dominant over O. Normally, antibodies develop as a result of exposure to foreign antigens, such as bacteria, viruses, foreign protein, and so on. This case is unique in that the serum antibodies are 'natural antibodies' produced by the body without such exposure. They are present in high concentration from early in life, and their cause is unknown. Group A blood with A antigens in the red cells has antibodies, in its serum, against B red cells. Group B blood has serum antibodies against A cells. Group O blood is not antigenic so its serum can, and does, safely contain both anti-A and anti-B antibodies. And group AB is antigenic to both, so has no antibodies in its serum. Group A blood, with A antigens, can safely be given to Group A and Group AB people; Group B blood, with B antigens, is safe for Group B and Group AB recipients; Group AB blood, with both A and B antigens, can be given safely only to Group AB people; and Group O blood, with no antigens, can be given to anyone. Group AB people can safely receive blood from anyone; they are called *universal recipients*. Group O people can accept neither A nor B blood and must have O blood, but they are *universal donors* and their blood can be given safely to anyone. Before transfusion, blood is always cross-matched, by mixing some of the donor cells with the patient's serum, just to be sure.

blood plasma, BLOOD from which the cells have been removed. Plasma can still clot.

blood serum, BLOOD from which the cells and the fibrin and other clotting substances have been removed. Serum does not clot and still contains the protein antibodies.

blood vessels, the ARTERIES, small arteries (*arterioles*), CAPILLARIES, small veins (*venules*) and VEINS, forming the blood circulation, or blood vascular system, through which blood is driven by the heart.

boiling point, the temperature, at any particular atmospheric pressure, at which the saturated vapour pressure of a liquid is equal to the atmospheric pressure. This equation allows bubbles to form in the liquid and particles to escape from it, without a change of temperature until all the liquid has evaporated. Boiling points are given at the standard atmospheric pressure of 760 mm of mercury; ⇨ pp. 50–5.

bomb calorimeter, a thick-walled, insulated container in which organic material, such as foodstuff, is electrically ignited and completely burned. The heat produced is accurately measured so that the energy content of the food in calories or joules can be determined. References to the calorific value of food determined in this way presuppose that all the food can actually be digested and assimilated – which is not necessarily the case.

bonding, the especially close and persistent relationship developing between individuals, especially those who come into close contact soon after the birth of one of them. Bonding is common also between male and female birds. The concept is now applied widely and used to indicate the formation of a strong relationship, particularly that between a mother and her newborn child. Bonding is important for the future psychological wellbeing of the infant.

bone, the structural tissues that form the skeleton of most complex animals. Bone consists of cells and a structural framework of fibres of the protein collagen. Bone differs from other CONNECTIVE TISSUE in that the structural frame contains a heavy deposit of calcium salts, mainly complex phosphates, with small amounts of carbonates. This calcification, which accounts for over 60 per cent of the weight of the bone, greatly adds to its strength and rigidity. The collagen framework is laid down in strands in a manner conforming to sound engineering principles, the struts and girders being disposed so as best to withstand all the normal stresses. Bone is a dynamic tissue with an excellent blood supply, by way of which a constant interchange of calcium occurs. Bones contain cells called *osteoblasts* that lay down the collagen structure during growth and after fracture. The deposition of calcium is controlled by various factors, one of the most important being the loads applied and the demands made. Another factor controlling calcification is the effect of male and female sex hormones, which promote osteoblast activity and calcification throughout life. In this respect women are at a disadvantage and the large drop in oestrogen levels that occurs after the menopause contributes to the common thinning and weakening of bone (*osteoporosis*) that is a feature of age.

bone marrow, the soft material occupying the hollow interior of BONES. There are two kinds of bone marrow – red marrow in the flat bones and the vertebrae, and yellow marrow in adult long bones. The latter is mainly fat. Children also have red marrow in the long bones. Red marrow in healthy young adults totals about one and a half litres, but the quantity becomes less in old age, the active red marrow being replaced by yellow fat cells. Red marrow is the site of blood-cell and immune-system cell formation. The parent cell of the blood-cell series in the marrow is called the *stem cell*. This differentiates into five distinguishable daughters and these, in turn, give rise to the haemoglobin-carrying red cells, the scavenging (*phagocyte*) and other white cells, the immunologically competent lymphocytes, and the platelets that are essential for blood clotting.

booting, the process of bringing a personal computer to the state in which it can accept an applications program such as a word processor or a spreadsheet. A computer cannot function without a program and cannot even begin to operate without first running a short program to tell it how to prepare itself. Such a program is usually held in a nonvolatile read-only memory (ROM) and runs automatically when the machine is switched on. Among other things, this program loads the basic operating system of the machine so that it can then accept other programs. Booting may be done by inserting a floppy disk with the command program (the *boot disk*) before switching on, or by arranging for the machine to look automatically for the boot program on the hard disk. The term derives from the tales of the fantastic adventures of Baron Münchhausen by the English writer R. E. Raspe (1737–94). The Baron, finding himself sinking in a swamp, lifted himself out by his bootstraps; ⇨ pp. 212–5.

botany, the study of all aspects of plant life.

botulism, poisoning with the toxin of the organism *Clostridium botulinum*, one of the most powerful poisons known. This organism lives in the absence of free oxygen and forms resistant spores that may contaminate preserved food such as meat pastes that have been inadequately sterilized. Botulinum toxin causes selective paralysis of muscles so that the eyelids droop, swallowing becomes impossible and the muscles of respiration fail so that the victim is unable to breathe and dies of asphyxia.

boundary layer, the very thin layer of fluid molecules surrounding a body immersed in a liquid. These molecules are linked to the molecules of the body and do not move when it moves relative to the fluid; ⇨ p. 34.

bronchus, a branch of the windpipe (*trachea*). The trachea divides into two main bronchi, one for each lung. These, in turn, divide into further, smaller bronchi, known as *bronchioles*. Bronchi have muscular walls with supporting rings of cartilage to keep them open and are lined with a layer of cells covered with fine hair-like processes (*cilia*) and containing many mucus-secreting *goblet cells*.

brown dwarf, a celestial body with insufficient mass to become strongly heated by the compressive effect of gravitational attraction. The nuclear- fusion reaction common to visible stars thus does not start and the body does not become self-luminous. Brown dwarfs are thus very hard to detect and only a few have been identified; ⇨ pp. 140–3 .

brown fat, animal fat stored as a multitude of tiny droplets held in supporting tissue, rather than in fat cells, as is generally the case with normal yellow fat. Brown fat is better supplied with blood vessels and is more readily available for rapid conversion to heat than is yellow fat. It also has a higher proportion of unsaturated fatty acids than yellow fat. It is believed that hibernating animals use their brown fat in the recovery from the winter state. Small human babies have deposits of brown fat around the spine.

Brownian motion, the constant random movement observed under the microscope in tiny solid particles immersed in liquid. This is due to the random bombardment of the particles by the moving molecules of the liquid. Brownian movement also occurs in smoke particles suspended in still air. In 1905, the physicist Albert Einstein (1879–1955) produced an equation that described how unbalanced forces caused by molecular motion would produce the effect, and this work later enabled the size of water molecules to be determined. Brownian movement was first observed by the Scottish botanist Robert Brown (1773–1858) while examining pollen grains. He was unable to account for the phenomenon; ⇨ p. 50.

bubble chamber, a method of demonstrating the movement of the sub-atomic particles of ionizing radiation. The chamber contains liquid hydrogen kept at a very low temperature, just above its boiling point, but under high pressure so as to prevent vaporization. Immediately before the radiation is to be observed, the pressure in the chamber is suddenly reduced so that the liquid boils. The moving particles then leave a wake of tiny bubbles that can easily be photographed. The device was invented in 1952 by the American physicist Donald Glaser (1926–).

buccal, relating to the cheek. The buccal mucosa, for instance, is the mucous membrane lining the inside of the cheek.

buckminsterfullerene, a recently discovered material, the molecule of which consists of 60 carbon atoms arranged in a geodesic pattern to form a ball, popularly known as a 'buckyball'; ⇨ pp. 164–7.

buffer, in chemistry, a solution that is able, within limits, to resist a change of acidity or alkalinity (pH) when ACIDS or ALKALIS are added to it. Acidic buffers are weak acids together with a salt of the acid, which provides a negative ion. When acid is added most of the additional hydrogen ions (positive) are combined with the negative ion from the salt. When alkali is added most of the extra hydroxide ions (–OH) are removed by combining with the acid to produce salt plus water. In this way the pH changes very little. Buffers are very important in animal and human physiology in maintaining the pH of the blood and tissue fluids within narrow limits; ⇨ p. 168. When they fail, the conditions of acidosis or alkalosis occur and these may be fatal. In computing, a buffer is a temporary memory used to hold data while it awaits further processing; ⇨ p. 216.

bug, in entomology an order of insects known as the *Hemiptera*. Bugs have flattened bodies, two pairs of wings and mouthparts suitable for piercing and sucking. Many bugs, such as the aphids, feed destructively on plants; others are blood-sucking, and a few can transmit disease. In computing, a bug is an error accidentally introduced into a program so that it either fails to implement the intention of the programmer or fails to operate at all. Debugging often takes longer than writing the program, but software exists to facilitate the process of detecting and eliminating bugs. The term arose from an incident in the early days of electromechanical relay computers when a fault was traced to an insect in an electrical contact.

bulb, a modified underground plant shoot in which nutrients formed in the previous growing season are stored, so as to enable the plant to survive from one season to the next.

burette, a glass tube calibrated with a scale and ending in a controllable tap and a narrowed outlet tube. The burette is often held vertically, clamped in a stand, and allows accurate volumes of a liquid to be released into a container, especially for the process of adding to another solution until a particular reaction is shown by a colour change to be complete (*titration*).

bus, a system of electrical connections or wires that carry data or instructions between the various parts of a computer. Ideally, the number of lines in a bus is equal to the number of bits (⇨ p. 216) in the word size the machine is capable of managing. Thus an 8-bit bus would, most efficiently, have 8 lines. Computers now commonly use 16, 32 or even 64-bit words and as multichannel buses are expensive and difficult to miniaturize, various expedients such as multiplexing are adopted.

byte, a collection of binary digits (⇨ pp. 102–5 and chapter 10), usually numbering eight on modern systems, but sometimes seven, and usually coding for a number or a character. A kilobyte is not 1,000 bytes, but 1,024, and a megabyte is not 1,000,000 bytes, but 1,048,576. These are the decimal representations of the binary numbers nearest to the nominal number. A gigabyte is something over 1,000,000,000 bytes; ⇨ p. 216.

C, a widely used, high-level, and compact programming language developed in the mid-1970s and popular with programmers, especially for use in personal computers. C can be used for a variety of purposes, and, because it is close to machine language, produces highly efficient code. A development of C, C++, provides programmers with the ability to define the type of a data structure and also the kind of operations or functions that can be applied to the data structure. The data structure is thus regarded as an *object* that includes both data *and* functions. This is a highly modular and efficient method of working known as *object-oriented programming* (OOP).

cache memory, a high-speed computer memory, common in high-performance systems, and independent of both the main RANDOM-ACCESS MEMORY (RAM) and the hard disk, but sometimes a part of the RAM set aside. Cache memory may be situated between the hard-disk memory and the central processing unit. Because access to it is much faster than access to the hard-disk, it can, if used to hold material to which reference is repeatedly made, greatly speed up the operation of the machine.

CAD, computer-aided design. CAD programs allow designers to implement designs in graphic form without having to make actual physical models. These designs can be viewed from various directions, zoomed in and out of dimensionally altered, rendered, coloured, modified in many ways and printed out in full colour. When one design value is changed, the computer will automatically change other dependent values. Many design decisions can thus be made very much more cheaply and quickly than formerly.

CAD/CAM, an acronym for Computer-aided Design/Computer-aided Manufacture. This is a system in which the software, after assisting with the design, can be used to control the manufacturing processes.

calcitonin, a hormone concerned with the control of calcium levels in the blood. Calcitonin is secreted by cells in the thyroid gland and is released into the blood. But, like the four parathyroid glands embedded in the thyroid, has nothing to do with the thyroid hormones. Its action is on bone, where it interferes with release of calcium. The specialized cells in the thyroid gland that produce calcitonin also monitor the blood-calcium level continuously. If the level falls, less calcitonin is produced and there is less interference with calcium release by the bones. If the blood calcium rises, more calcitonin is secreted and calcium release inhibited. This kind of negative-feedback control mechanism is very common in the body. Calcitonin control of calcium-blood levels acts in opposition to the parathyroid hormone system. It is less important in calcium balance than the parathyroids.

calorie, the amount of heat needed to raise one gram of water one degree centigrade, specifically from 15° to 16°C. For nutritional purposes, the calorie is inconveniently small and the Calorie (capital C) is used. This is equal to 1,000 calories and is sometimes called the *kilocalorie*. The *calorific value* of a fuel (including food) is the number of heat units obtained by burning it completely in a closed container such as a BOMB CALORIMETER. This value can be expressed in calories per gram or in joules per gram. Thus, the calorific value of protein and carbohydrate is about 4 Calories per gram, that of fat about 9 Calories per gram and that of alcohol about 7 Calories per gram. In the now widely used SI system of units, the calorie is replaced by the joule. One calorie is equal to 4.184 joules. The same relationship applies to Calories and kilojoules; ⇨ p. 52.

cambium, the actively reproducing parts of a plant responsible for increasing girth (secondary growth). The vascular cambium is found in the stem and root and the cork cambium occurs under the bark.

Cambrian, the first part of the Palaeozoic era that began some 570 million years ago and lasted for about 100 million years. Cambrian rocks contain large numbers of fossils of shelled marine animals including trilobites, echinoderms and molluscs.

capillarity, one of the consequences of surface tension, the tendency for the surface of a liquid in contact with a solid to be raised or depressed above or below the level it would reach if unconfined. The surface of water in a narrow tube becomes domed upwards. Capillarity is of fundamental importance in nature because it allows the transport of water in plants against the force of gravity. Surface tension is very strong in water because of the hydrogen bonding between molecules (⇨ p. 162) and this tends to maintain the integrity of the surface. But the attraction between the water molecules and the walls of the tube may be even greater and these commonly exceed the combined effects of gravity and the attractive forces within the liquid.

capillary, any tube of small diameter. In anatomy, the smallest BLOOD VESSEL in the circulatory system. BLOOD capillaries consist of a single layer of cells, with gaps between their edges, through which oxygen and nutrients can readily pass outwards, and carbon dioxide and other waste products can readily pass in. Blood achieves its function only in capillary beds, which occur in every part of the body, lying between the high-pressure ARTERIES and arterioles and the low-pressure VEINS. If all body structures except the capillaries were removed, the body's shape would be readily recognizable.

carapace, the hard back part of the exoskeleton of some crustaceans that forms a shield over several segments of the head and thorax.

carat, a measure of the purity of gold, expressed as a proportion of 24. Twenty-four-carat gold is pure; 16-carat gold contains 16 parts gold to 8 parts of a base metal, such as copper. In gemology, a carat is a unit of weight equal to one fifth of a gram. A 5-carat diamond weighs 1 g.

carbohydrates, sugars (*saccharides*) or more complex polymers, such as starches, glycogen or cellulose, made up of many sugars linked together (*polysaccharides*). Carbohydrates form the greater part of the diet of many animals, including humans; ⇨ pp. 182–5.

carbonate, any salt of carbonic acid containing the carbonate radical CO_3.

carbon dioxide, a simple compound in which an atom of carbon is linked to two atoms of oxygen (CO_2). Carbon dioxide is a colourless, odourless gas at normal temperatures. It is one of the chief waste products of tissue metabolism, and an increase in metabolic activity, as during exercise, results in increased oxygen usage and increased CO_2 production. Carbon dioxide is soluble in water, forming a pleasant-tasting solution that is more readily absorbed by mucous membranes than plain water. Almost any blandly flavoured water can be turned into a tempting one by this simple expedient. The same applies to even the most indifferent of white wines, which can be made palatable in this way. Champagne bubbles are CO_2 gas, derived from continuing fermentation, in the bottle, of grape sugar. The process necessitates strong bottles and wired-down corks. Carbon dioxide is easily formed into a semi-solid at a temperature of –80°C, by allowing the gas to escape into a suitable container from a high-pressure cylinder. This is called *carbon-dioxide* *snow*. Carbon dioxide is denser than air and tends to sink downwards. Danger arises if the concentration becomes too high. In an atmosphere above about 7 per cent CO_2 there will be rapid breathing, headache, confusion, dizziness and palpitations. At a concentration of 10 per cent or more, unconsciousness and death will occur.

carbon monoxide, an odourless, colourless, inflammable and very poisonous gas with the formula CO. It is produced when hydrocarbons such as natural gas or petrol are burned in an atmosphere of insufficient oxygen so that the combustion of the carbon is incomplete. Much of the CO in the urban environment comes from motor vehicle exhausts. CO burns in air to give CARBON DIOXIDE . Carbon monoxide binds readily with metals to form stable compounds. This accounts for its toxicity. If breathed, it combines strongly with the iron in haemoglobin forming carboxyhaemoglobin, which is much more stable than the normal oxyhaemoglobin, thus preventing the blood from carrying oxygen and causing death from oxygen lack (*anoxia*).

carcinogen, anything that can cause cancer. Carcinogens include various forms of radiation such as ultraviolet light, X-rays and gamma rays, many industrial and other chemicals, certain drugs, and cigarette smoke.

carcinoma, a cancer of a surface layer of part of the body (an *epithelium*). Cancers of solid tissues, such as bone, muscle, fat, etc., are called *sarcomas*. Carcinomas thus start only on body linings or coverings, such as those of the skin, the inside of the intestines, the air tubes in the lungs, the milk ducts of the breast and the ducts of the pancreas and prostate gland. Glandular tissue is common in many parts of the body and all such tissue is epithelial in nature. Cancers of glandular tissue are called *adenocarcinomas*.

Carnivora, an order of flesh-eating mammals. Carnivores may be predators or may eat only carrion. They have a keen sense of smell, good eyesight and hearing and powerful biting muscles. The teeth are modified for piercing and tearing (canines), and the jawbone articulation with the skull prevents sideways motion as in herbivores. The order includes cats, dogs, wolves, bears, hyenas, raccoons, weasels, and possibly seals.

carnivorous plants, plants that derive a supply of nitrates from small animals, especially insects, which they trap and digest to release the required nutrient substances. The group includes the remarkable Venus fly trap with spiky-edged hinged leaves that spring shut around entering insects, sundews that catch insects on a sticky secretion, and various pitcher plants in which insects drown.

carotenoids, a group of yellow, orange or red plant pigments responsible for the colour of carrots and tomatoes and autumn leaf tints. Some of the carotenoids are broken down during digestion to yield vitamin A.

carpal bone, one of the bones of the wrist, which vary in number in different species. The human wrist has eight carpal bones.

carrier wave, a radiated (electromagnetic) waveform on which information is superimposed by altering either its magnitude (*amplitude*) or the number of its cycles per second (*frequency*). This superimposition on the plain wave is called *modulation*. All radio communication is mediated by carrier waves that may be amplitude modulated (AM), frequency modulated (FM) or pulse code modulated (PCM). The latter two are much less susceptible to interference than the former. FM is preferred for public broadcasting and PCM for data transfer; ⇨ pp. 68–71.

Cartesian coordinates, any system of locating a point on a plane by specifying the distance along two axes (usually a horizontal X axis and a vertical Y axis), or a point in space by specifying the distance along three axes (X, Y and Z). The axes intersect at the *origin*. Below the origin the values on the Y axis are negative, and to the left of the origin those on the X axis are negative; ⇨ pp. 18–21. The system is named after its originator, the French philosopher and mathematician René Descartes (1596–1650).

Cartesian dualism, the long-held idea, first formalized by René Descartes, that the brain and the mind are two entirely separate but somehow associated entities. With advances in neuroscience, this idea is gradually giving way to the theory that the mind is a product of neurological activity, with no separate existence apart from the brain; ⇨ p. 12.

cartilage, a smooth, firm, flexible connective tissue widely distributed in the animal kingdom. Cartilage or gristle consists mainly of a compound of protein and carbohydrate known as a *mucopolysaccharide*, which is secreted by cells called *chondrocytes*. It forms the skeleton of cartilaginous fish such as sharks and the skeleton of the embryos of other vertebrates, but is replaced by bone in the course of development. Cartilage persists in many parts of adult vertebrates, especially as bearing surfaces on joints and as flexible linkages for the ribs.

catalyst, a substance that accelerates a chemical reaction without itself being changed; ⇨ p. 168. An ENZYME is an organic catalyst. A catalyst provides an alternative pathway, for a chemical reaction, that involves a lower ACTIVATION ENERGY.

catenary, the curve formed by a heavy but flexible rope when suspended at both ends and allowed to droop. The graph of y = cosh x is a catenary. Cosh x is the hyperbolic (⇨ p. 20) cosine of x.

cathode, an electrode from which electrons (negatively charged particles) emerge and, because unlike charges mutually attract, travel to the positively charged ANODE. A *cation* is an ion that is attracted to the cathode and is thus positively charged. An *anion* is negatively charged; ⇨ p. 88.

cathode-ray tube, a widely used electronic-display device consisting of an evacuated glass tube with an expanded and flattened end, the screen, coated on the inside with phosphors that emit visible light when struck by a beam of electrons. The electron beam is produced by a heated filament at the narrow end of the tube and the negatively charged electrons are accelerated towards the screen by a strong positive voltage applied to it. The electron beam, being charged, can easily be focused and deflected by an electric or a magnetic field. Two electronic oscillators, the *time bases*, provide fluctuating voltages that cause the electron beam to scan rapidly horizontally and more slowly vertically, thus covering the whole screen in a fraction of a second. While so doing, the beam is repeatedly interrupted so that no light is produced. The image on the screen, whether textual or graphic, is built up by the uninterrupted beam. Cathode-ray tubes are used in televisions, personal computers, oscilloscopes, radar displays and various communication systems. They are gradually being displaced by more compact and flat display systems such as liquid-crystal screens.

caudal vertebrae, the vertebral bones in animals that form the skeleton of the tail.

cellulose, a polysaccharide consisting of a long, unbranched chain of linked GLUCOSE molecules that is the main structural element in plant cell walls. Cellulose is a CARBOHYDRATE, but its constituent sugars are not available when it is included in the human diet, as the digestive system does not contain ENZYMES capable of freeing the glucose molecules. It is, however, an important constituent of dietary fibre.

Celsius temperature scale, a scale in which the zero is set as the temperature at which ice melts and 100° is set as the temperature at which water turns to steam at standard pressure. The degree is the same size as the kelvin in the absolute temperature scale (⇨ ABSOLUTE ZERO). This scale is identical to the formerly named centigrade scale, but the name was changed in 1948 to avoid confusion with the grade (one hundredth part of a right angle) and to honour the Swedish astronomer Anders Celsius (1701–44) who invented a similar, but inverted, scale in 1742 and whose surname conveniently began with a C.

CD-ROM, a standard compact disk used as a large-capacity data store for textual or graphic information. CD-ROMs are identical to music compact disks in which the information is stored in digital form as microscopic pits representing 0s and the intervening reflecting surface representing 1s. A CD-ROM can store about 600 megabytes of information – about 100 million words of text – and this can be substantially increased by various compression techniques. It thus represents a very efficient and compact form of information storage that is being widely exploited by archivists and librarians. CD- ROMs can be read by standard personal computers fitted with a suitable drive, that is addressed in exactly the same way as a standard floppy-disk drive. With suitable search and retrieval software, information access is much quicker than from printed books.

Cenozoic, the geological era from about 65 million years ago to the present. During this period the Himalayas and the Alps were formed and mammals became the dominant animals.

centre of mass, the point at which the whole of the mass of a body can be considered to be concentrated and to act for gravitational or other purposes. The centre of mass is the same as the centre of gravity; ⇨ p. 30.

centrifugal force, an imaginary entity, conveniently deemed to act outwards as a balance for the centripetal force – the force acting inwards that causes a body to move in a circular path (⇨ p. 20). It is not centrifugal force that causes a stone swung on a string to move off at a tangent when the string breaks; it is the sudden loss of the centripetal force that allows the stone to continue to conform to Newton's first law of motion (⇨ p. 28) and to proceed in a straight line.

cephalization, the tendency in animals for the mouth, the brain and the special sense organs (of sight, smell and hearing) to be situated at the front, head (*cephalic*), end of the organism.

cerebrum, the larger and principal part of the vertebrate brain, divided into two cerebral hemispheres joined by a large, multi-way, nerve trunk called the *corpus callosum*.

Cerenkov radiation, the electromagnetic radiation effect, analogous to the sonic boom in acoustics, in which a bluish light is emitted when a beam of high-energy particles pass though a transparent medium at a speed greater than the speed of light in that medium. Light travels more slowly through transparent media than in a vacuum; ⇨ p. 78.

CERN, Conseil Europeén pour la Recherche Nucléaire, the European organization for atomic research in Geneva. This is one of the major high-energy physics research centres in the world (⇨ p. 114).

Cetacea, the order of marine mammals known as the whales, that contains the largest known animal – the blue whale.

c.g.s. units, a system of units based on the centimetre, the gram and the second, that never proved comfortably consistent with the equivalent units for heat and electricity and which, for many scientific purposes, have been superseded by the Système International (SI) system of units.

chalk, an extensively deposited, white, fine-grained rock consisting of the fossilized remains of marine plankton (*coccoliths*). Chalk is mainly calcium carbonate ($CaCO_3$).

character-based system, a program that uses, and is capable of displaying, only ASCII-code (⇨ p. 216) characters and the characters of the extended ASCII code set. Many word processors are character-based. Typically, the screen display in such a system is divided into 25 rows and 80 vertical columns, and characters can occur only at the 2,000 intersections of these rows and columns. The extended ASCII set contains element that can be joined to form boxes and simple pictures of straight lines, but cannot display the graphics that are possible on a BIT-MAPPING system such as *Windows* or the Apple Mackintosh system.

charcoal, a form of carbon produced by heating organic matter in an atmosphere of diminished oxygen so that most of the constituents, except the carbon, are distilled away. As a result, all forms of charcoal are porous and present a large surface area. This gives charcoal exceptional powers of ADSORPTION. Activated charcoal is charcoal that has been treated with steam or heated in a vacuum so as to improve its adsorptive power. Charcoals differ according to the organic matter used. Common sources include wood, coconut shells and animal bones.

chemical dating, a method of estimating the age of a substance that undergoes a characteristic chemical change at a known rate. For instance, AMINO ACIDS incorporated into proteins in living organisms are *laevo-optical isomers* (i.e. they rotate a beam of plane-polarized light to the left). After death these amino acids gradually racemize (i.e. the proportions of laevo-rotary and dextro-rotary forms equalize so that they lose their optical rotary properties). The time since death can thus be assessed by determining the proportions of laevo-rotary and dextro-rotary amino acids present; ⇨ p. 174.

chemotaxis, the movement of a microorganism in a particular direction in response to a chemical stimulus. Some of the actively participant cells of the body's immune system, such as the phagocytes, are attracted to areas of high bacterial concentration by such means and proceed to these areas where many of them are killed in the defence of the body.

chemotropism, the growth or movement of a plant in a particular direction under the influence of a chemical stimulus.

chimera, an organism whose cells contain more than one genetic constitution. This can be brought about artificially or can occur if a mutation occurs in a cell in an early embryo. All the cells and tissues derived from this cell will carry the mutation, while those from the other cells will not. If, as in this case, both cell lines derive from the same fertilized ovum (*zygote*), the individual is more correctly described as a *mosaic*; ⇨ MOSAICISM.

Chiroptera, the order of flying mammals consisting of bats.

chlorophylls, the two pigments that confer the green colour on plants and that absorb light, thereby securing the energy needed for the conversion of carbon dioxide and water to sugar and starch (*photosynthesis*). Chlorophylls consist of two substances, chlorophyll a and chlorophyll b. These are porphyrins, chemically related to the haem of HAEMOGLOBIN but containing an atom of magnesium rather than one of iron. The molecules contain networks of alternating single and double bonds (⇨ p. 162), which give them very strong absorption in the visible part of the electromagnetic spectrum – an absorption among the highest observed for any organic compound. The two chlorophylls have slightly different absorption spectra and complement each other. Every day, some 300 million tons of carbon from the atmosphere is assimilated into new-formed carbohydrates by chlorophyll-driven photosynthesis.

Chlorophyta, green algae that contain CHLOROPHYLLS and closely resemble plants.

chloroplasts, lens-shaped, chlorophyll-containing cell organs (*organelles*) present in large numbers in the cells of plants undertaking photosynthesis.

choke, an electronic circuit element consisting of an inductor (⇨ p. 100) with a high inductance but a low electrical resistance, that offers a high impedance to alternating or fluctuating current but a low impedance to direct current. Chokes are useful in smoothing power supplies after rectification of alternating current.

chorionic villus sampling, a method of obtaining genetic information about an early EMBRYO. The *chorionic villi* are the finger-like processes of the developing placenta that run into the wall of the womb (*uterus*) and link up with the mother's BLOOD VESSELS. Since both placenta and developing fetus arise from the same two original cells, they have the same chromosomes, and any genetic abnormality in one will also be present in the other. A small sample of chorionic villi can be sucked out with a syringe through a fine, flexible tube passed through the vagina and the neck of the womb (*cervix*) and guided to the site of the placenta under ultrasound-scanning control. Sometimes the sample is taken by passing a needle through the abdominal wall. Cells obtained in this way can be cultured, and chromosome analysis or DNA studies can be done. The main advantage of this method over AMNIOCENTESIS is that it is done between eight and ten weeks of pregnancy – about two months earlier.

choroid, the densely pigmented layer of blood vessels that lies just under the retina of the eye and that contributes importantly to its fuel and oxygen supply. Disorders of the choroid almost always adversely affect the overlying retina leading to visual loss, but this is often patchy and peripheral, and may not be noticed by the sufferer.

chromaticity, an objective description of the quality of a colour, made by reference to its peak wavelength, or defined in terms of the amounts of three reference colours whose mixture would exactly match the colour; ⇨ p. 76.

chromosome analysis, a method of chromosomal study in which the chromosomes, in cell culture, are stimulated by a drug to enter a stage at which they are most widely separated and most easily visualized. They may then be stained, photographed and set out in an orderly arrangement known as a *karyotype*. The matching in pairs and the inspection of the banding pattern revealed by the staining allows each one to be individually identified by its number. It is thus possible to discover whether, in any particular person, the karyotype is normal or abnormal. This process allows ready diagnosis of a range of conditions known to be the result of gross chromosome, rather than gene, abnormalities. Chromosome analysis is useful in the investigation of small infants who fail to make normal progress, in those suspected of learning difficulties, in those of ambiguous sex, and in those with organic disorder of a type characteristic of chromosomal abnormality. It is also useful in investigating infertile adults, women who abort repeatedly, and men who wish to become sperm donors; ⇨ pp. 202–5.

circle, a closed curve of which every point is at the same distance (the *radius*) from one point (the *centre*) within it.

circuit board, a thin, rigid board of insulating material on which a very thin layer of copper is deposited, usually on both sides, and that is chemically cut into thin interconnecting strips by which microchips, resistors, capacitors, quartz crystals and other electronic components (⇨ pp. 102–5) are interconnected. The circuit board nearly always has a multiway edge connector or connectors by which it can be plugged into other circuits or to which power supply connectors can be attached. System failure can thus rapidly be remedied by removing and replacing the board with a faulty component.

circular measure, a way of measuring an angle by considering it to be the angle formed at the centre of a circle by the lines running to the centre from the ends of an arc of the circumference. The unit of circular measure is the *radian*, the angle subtended at the centre of a circle by an arc equal to the radius of the circle. The circumference of a circle is 2π times the radius, so the whole circumference will subtend an angle of $2\pi r$ divided by r radians, which is 2π radians. Thus 360° is equal to 2π radians and 1 radian is equal to 57.296°.

citric-acid cycle, another name for the Krebs cycle by which energy is transferred from the oxidation of food materials to ATP.

classical physics, the state of theoretical physics before the advent of the quantum theory and relativity in 1900 and 1905 respectively. Classical physics was based primarily on Newtonian ideas and on Clerk Maxwell's equations for electromagnetism. It is still entirely valid for most observable phenomena involving bodies containing large numbers of atoms and speeds well below that of light; ⇨ pp. 26–37.

clavicle, the collar bone, a comparatively delicate bone that is readily fractured either by direct violence or by a force applied indirectly, as in a fall on the outstretched arm.

clay, a deposit of fine particles mainly of silicates of aluminium or occasionally silicates of iron or magnesium. Clay minerals include vermiculite, illite, halloysite and kaolinite. Wet clay is highly plastic and can be formed into detailed shapes. It is almost impermeable to water.

clipboard, a small segment of memory or a file, in which data, copied, or cut, from one place, is stored temporarily until it can be *pasted* into another place. Most word processors, for instance, allow cutting of a block of text from one document on the screen, storing it in a clipboard, and then pasting it into another document, or another part of the same document.

clitoris, the principal erectile sexual organ in women and the main erogenic centre. It is liberally supplied with sensory nerves. The clitoris varies in size, from one woman to another, and its most sensitive part, the glans, or tip, is partly hooded by a fold of connective tissue and skin called the *prepuce*. This fold is connected to the labia minora.

clone, the set of organisms or single cells that have arisen from a single individual by asexual reproduction and that are thus genetically identical to that organism and to each other; ⇨ p. 202.

coaxial cable, an electric cable consisting of a central conductor separated by insulation from a second, cylindrical, conductor that surrounds it on the same axis. Coaxial cable is used to carry high- frequency electrical signals as it is relatively immune to external interference and carries signals with minimal losses. TV aerials (antennae) are usually connected to their receivers by coaxial cable.

COBE, the cosmic background explorer spacecraft; ⇨ p. 124.

coccyx, the residual tail bone in humans, consisting of four small vertebrae fused together and joined to the curved sacrum.

cochlea, the part of the inner ear of mammals, birds and some reptiles that converts sound vibrations into frequency-modulated nerve impulses. The cochlea contains the basilar membrane, different parts of which have different resonant frequencies that vibrate selectively according to the pitch of the sound. These vibrations are transferred to hair-cell transducers that convert them into nerve impulses. The maximum frequency of nerve-impulse transmission in the human acoustic nerve is only about 400 Hz (cycles per second), but precise information is, nevertheless, transferred to the brain for the range of frequencies up to as high as 20,000 Hz. This is done in terms of the location of the peripheral connections of the nerve fibres at the basilar membrane; impulses on fibres coming from the various parts of the membrane denote the different frequencies. A resolution of perception of less than a semitone is possible over the whole audible spectrum from about 16 Hz to the upper limit of audibility.

coefficient, in algebra, the numerical part of a term. In the expression $17p^2q^2$, the coefficient of p^2q^2 is 17. The term is also widely used to refer to a numerical constant specific to a particular entity, as in the case of the coefficient of friction of a surface, or the coefficient of expansion of a metal; ⇨ p. 20.

collagen, an important protein structural element in the body. Collagen fibres are very strong and make up much of the connective tissue. When formed into bundles, as in tendons, they provide remarkable tensile strength. The collagen fibres, themselves, are composed of bundles of fibrils which, in turn, are assembled from collagen molecules. Each of these consists of a triple helix of three polypeptide chains coiled together. The stability and strength of the helix depends on cross-linkages between certain of the AMINO ACIDS, of which the polypeptide chains are made, and the linkages depend on vitamin C. Scurvy is a disorder of weakened collagen caused by a deficiency of vitamin C.

colon, the *large* intestine, so called because of its diameter rather than its length. It is about 1.5 m (5 ft) long and forms a kind of festoon in the ABDOMEN, starting on the lower right side at the pouch-like *caecum* with the appendix hanging from it, rising on the right side (*ascending colon*), crossing, with a droop, to a point opposite on the left side (*transverse colon*), descending on the left (*descending colon*), and curving back and down towards the midline (*sigmoid colon*) to run into the rectum. The main function of the colon is to conserve water by abstracting it from the bowel contents. The process of water withdrawal is very efficient and, if given long enough to act, will turn the faeces into hard, dried pellets. The colon contains millions of bacteria and these are useful, producing, among other materials, valuable vitamins that are readily absorbed. These bacteria also have the ability to ferment some forms of carbohydrate – such as those found in peas and beans – that are not digested by the enzymes of the small intestine. This fermentation and other bacterial action produces large quantities of a gas that is a mixture of nitrogen, carbon dioxide, hydrogen, methane and hydrogen sulphide.

colonoscopy, examination of the inside of the large intestine (⇨ COLON) by means of a viewing device inserted through the anus and passed carefully upwards. Many endoscopes are 'steerable' by means of rotating knobs at the control ends and contain separate fibre-optic viewing and illuminating channels. In addition, endoscopes allow the passage of various fine instruments, by which sample (⇨ BIOPSY) material can be taken, and a channel through which water or air can be passed to facilitate viewing.

colposcopy, microscopic examination of the surface of the neck of the womb (the *cervix*). The microscope has a long focus so that it can be used well outside the vulva, and the vagina is held open by an instrument called a *speculum*. Colposcopy makes it possible to detect suspicious areas from which samples can be taken. It is the routine next step after a cervical smear has shown some abnormality. In addition to accurate diagnosis, colposcopy allows local treatment under direct visual control. Lasers or other instruments can be used.

COM FILE, an MS-DOS command file with a

name ending in .COM. COM files can be directly executed and will perform some function. They are limited to 64 kilobytes, however, and most major DOS programs have the extension .EXE.

command.com, the file that contains all the internal commands for the standard Microsoft disk operating system (MS-DOS) on which the majority of personal computers operate. This file must be present and must be automatically read by the machine before a personal computer can BOOT and be used.

conditioned reflex, the phenomenon, first demonstrated by the Russian physiologist Ivan Pavlov (1849–1936), that a stimulus that does not normally evoke a particular effect, can be made to do so by associating it with another stimulus that normally does produce the effect. Pavlov showed that if, on a sufficient number of occasions, a bell was rung when food was presented to a hungry dog, then, eventually, ringing the bell alone, without producing the food, would cause the dog to salivate and secrete stomach juices. This is but one example of many such processes. The conditioned reflex is an important feature of the functioning of the brain, and examples of its operation abound in all human activity. Pavlov believed that all learning could be explained by conditioning, and that complex behavioural patterns could be built up from a series of simpler conditioned responses. This view was enthusiastically endorsed by the behaviourist school who suggested that all human behaviour can be determined in this way. The idea has not been universally popular and opposition to the suggestion that undesirable behaviour can be corrected by human conditioning has been reinforced by reports of 'brainwashing'.

config.sys, the file that organizes (configures) the way a personal computer using the MS-DOS or other similar operating systems is set up, so that it can proceed to run various application programs. On booting up the computer automatically reads the config.sys file and carries out any commands contained in it. On installing new programs it is often necessary for the config.sys file to be modified, but this is usually done by the installation program.

connective tissue, one of the four classes of tissue of which the animal body is made, the others being muscular, nervous and lining tissue (*epithelia*). Connective tissue includes loose or dense collections of collagen and elastic fibres, which aid in the structure of, and form the packing or filling material within and between, the components of organs. Connective tissue also includes specialized tissues, such as cartilage, bone, tooth dentine, blood and lymphoid tissue.

cornea, the outer, and principal, lens of the eye. Through the transparent cornea can be seen the coloured iris with its central hole (the *pupil*) appearing as a black disc. The cornea is transparent because of the uniform gauge of the collagen fibrils from which it is formed. Collagen is naturally transparent, but elsewhere in the body, as in the white of the eye (*sclera*), the fibrils are of variable diameter and

scatter the light in a random manner. In the cornea, all light rays passing through are uniformly treated. Nearly all the bending of the light, to focus the image, occurs at the interface between the air and the cornea. The internal crystalline lens of the eye is immersed in water, so its optical power is much reduced. It is responsible only for the fine adjustment of focusing (accommodation).

coronary artery, the two arteries that arise from the main artery of the body, the AORTA, immediately above the heart, and spread, branching, over its upper surface like a crown, supplying the highly active heart muscle with blood. The left coronary artery divides immediately into two large trunks, giving the impression that there are three coronary arteries.

cortex, the outer distinguishable zone of any solid organ. The cerebral cortex, for instance, is the outer layer of grey matter of the brain consisting of nerve-cell bodies. The adrenal cortex is quite different in function from the inner part, the medulla. The cortex secretes cortisol and the adrenal medulla secretes adrenaline.

corticosteroid hormones, natural steroid hormones secreted by the outer zone (*cortex*) of the adrenal glands. They include cortisol, corticosterone, aldosterone and andro-sterone. Cortisol and corticosterone are called *glucocorticoids* because they are concerned with the body's usage of GLUCOSE and other nutrients. Aldosterone is called a *mineral-corticoid* because it is responsible for the control of blood levels of minerals such as sodium and potassium. Androsterone is an androgen, a male sex hormone similar to testosterone produced in the testicles.

critical mass, the amount of fissionable material needed to sustain a chain reaction and produce an atomic explosion or a controlled fission reaction; ⇨ p. 160.

critical-path analysis, a method of achieving maximum efficiency in the organization of a large and complex project by determining the best allocation of resources, the accurate timing of the start of each part of the work and of the supply of necessary materials. Critical-path analysis is usually performed by a computer program that must be supplied with all necessary data.

cross section, the plane shape that results when a body is cut, actually or in the imagination, at right angles to a central line running through it (*its axis of symmetry*). Compare the *longitudinal section*, which is cut along, or parallel to, the axis of symmetry.

cryopreservation, the prevention of destructive bacterial action and biochemical change by maintaining material, such as tissue for grafting, human embryos, seminal fluid, etc., at a low temperature. Cryopreservation can be considered a kind of 'suspended animation'. Semen, deep frozen at −196°C with liquid nitrogen, can be kept indefinitely without loss of fertility.

CT scanning, computerized-tomography scanning. This is a form of X-ray examination in which, instead of using a wide beam of radiation, the scanner sends out a succession of short-duration, very narrow, fan-shaped beams of radiation, each passing through the body at a slightly different angle from the previous one. These beams are produced by a small X-ray source that rotates around the subject on a circular arm, and the radiation is picked up by a number of separate detectors arranged in an arc on the other side. With each pulse of radiation these detectors produce electrical outputs that are stored in a computer. When the beam has been right round, the process may be repeated for other 'slices' and all the information obtained is stored. The computer is then able, by solving thousands of differential equations, to reconstruct, from all these data, detailed images of the body in any plane. A *tomogram* is an X-ray taken in 'slices'; computerized tomography (CT) combines many tomograms. CT scans can detect many hundreds of levels of contrast, bringing out detail impossible with conventional X-rays. In addition, the method eliminates the confusing shadows of overlying structures such as BONES. CT scanning is especially valuable for investigating the inside of the head for possible brain tumours, bleeding, swellings on arteries (*aneurysms*) or injuries. It is also useful for studying the structures in the central, solid part of the chest that show up poorly on conventional X-rays, and to detect abnormalities anywhere in the abdomen, including tumours, abscesses and injuries to organs.

cyclic-AMP, a variety of adenosine monophosphate (⇨ ATP) in which the phosphate group is attached to the adenosine part of the molecule in two places so that this part of the molecule forms a closed ring. Cyclic-AMP occurs in most animal tissues where it affects the activity of many enzymes and hormones. Cell membranes carry receptor sites for HORMONES. The combination of the hormone with the receptor leads to increased levels of cyclic-AMP in the cell. This then results in a change in the cell's activities. In this context, cyclic-AMP is known as a *second messenger*.

cyclone, opposite of ANTICYCLCONE.

cystoscopy, examination of the inside of the urinary bladder by means of a straight, narrow, self-illuminating optical instrument that is passed in through the urinary exit channel (the *urethra*). In the male, a general anaesthetic is usually needed, but in the female, the urethra is very short and cystoscopy can be performed with a local anaesthetic. Cystoscopy allows diagnosis of conditions such as infections, polyps, cancers and stones in the bladder, and enables the surgeon to take BIOPSY specimens and perform local treatment by means of an electric hot wire (*cautery*) or laser.

daisychaining, in computing a method of connecting a series of devices to a single controlling circuit, using a single cable interrupted by each device.

damping, the reducing effect on the amplitude

of oscillation of any oscillating system that results from loss of energy for any reason. Damping can be important in electronic circuits and in electro- mechanical measuring instruments in which excessive oscillation of a needle can make accurate reading impossible.

dance of bees, a method of communication in bees in which a pattern of movement conveys information to others on the direction and distance of food sources (also known as the *waggle dance*).

dark matter, matter in the universe whose presence can be only deduced. Calculations of the mass of the universe exceed by several times the total estimated mass of the visible stars. The difference might be accounted for by black holes (⇨ p. 128), by nonluminous dwarf stars or by other unidentified matter.

databank, a central depository of computer-accessible data that may be accessed by many users, usually on payment of a fee. A databank is normally organized as a DATABASE; ⇨ p. 216.

database, an electronic filing system, a collection of computer-accessible information (⇨ p. 216) on any subject, coded and stored on magnetic, optical or other medium, and so arranged that any item can be quickly retrieved for use. Minimal items of information are called *fields*; groups of these are called *records*; and collections of records are called *files*. A database-management system is a collection of programs that allow storage, organization, amendment and retrieval of database information. Database organization can be simple but rigid (*flatfile*), hierarchical, or complex but versatile (*relational*).

data communications, the process of transferring information from one point to another. In practice, the phrase tends to be used in a narrower sense and to imply the interchange of digitally coded information, whether alphanumeric or graphic. The world is now a felted network of data communications and these are becoming ever more complex and sophisticated. An important development in recent years is packet switching.

data compression, one of several methods of treating coded data so that, without any loss of information, the material can be stored using a reduced number of binary digits. Textual material contains a great deal of redundancy and can be reduced by a factor of four. Other forms of data, such as graphics, cannot be so efficiently compressed. The capacity of data-storage systems, such as hard disks in personal computers, can readily be doubled by purely software-compression methods.

day, the time taken for the Earth to rotate once on its axis (⇨ p. 144). The length of the day varies with the external reference point chosen. A *sidereal day* is a rotation relative to the fixed stars and this is about four minutes shorter than the *solar day*, which is the time between two returns of the Sun to the same meridian. The *mean solar day* is the average of all the solar days in one year; ⇨ p. 144.

DDT, dichloro-diphenyl-trichloroethane, the first of the widely used and highly effective insecticides. It is a nerve poison, especially effective against flies, mosquitos, and lice. Mites and ticks are barely affected. DDT has saved millions of lives since it was first used as an insecticide in 1939. By destroying the insect carriers of many diseases, it has prevented countless cases of malaria (carried by mosquitos), yellow fever (mosquitos), typhus (lice), plague (lice), river blindness or onchocerciasis (biting black flies), dysentery (house flies), sleeping sickness (tsetse flies) and filariasis (mosquitos). Many areas that were almost uninhabitable because of insect vectors of disease have been made safe for human habitation, and malaria has been eradicated from more than twenty countries, largely by the use of DDT. In India, the use of DDT reduced the annual death rate from malaria from one million to fewer than five thousand and the average life span was increased from 32 years to 47 years. These advantages were not achieved without cost, however, and in the 1960s it began to be apparent that bird life was suffering heavily from the effects of DDT, which, because of its chemical stability, was increasing in concentration in the animal food chain. Infertile, or otherwise abnormal, eggs were being produced. In 1972 DDT was banned in the USA, being replaced by other insecticides. Since then the bird population has again increased. DDT has not been shown to be a serious toxic threat to humans, which cannot be said for its replacements, the organo-phosphorous insecticides such as malathion, parathion and paraquat, but these do break down rapidly in the soil to harmless compounds.

deamination, the removal of an amino group ($-NH_2$) from a molecule. This process, performed by enzymes in the liver, is an important part of amino acid metabolism, in which the amino group is removed as ammonia and converted to urea.

death, the cessation of the processes of living, whether in cells, organs or in the entire organism. Local tissue death is called *gangrene* and is usually due to a major deprivation of blood supply, almost always from disease of the supplying arteries. Death of the whole organism (*somatic death*) results from a general failure of the supply of essential nutrition to the tissues, especially oxygen and sugar, or from the inability of the tissues to use them, because of poisoning or other damage. Oxygen and sugar are supplied via the BLOOD and this is circulated by the heart and kept oxygenated by the lungs. So common causes of somatic death are stoppage of the heart or failure of the lungs to supply oxygen to the blood. The brain maintains the muscle action of breathing, so brain damage can cause somatic death if the result is a stoppage of the nerve impulses to the muscles of respiration. When the vital supplies are cut off for more than about ten minutes, widespread cell death begins, starting with the brain and at a certain point this becomes irreversible. In this case, certain changes occur in the body as a whole. The temperature begins to drop, the muscles stiffen (*rigor mortis*), the blood begins to clot in the vessels, and bacterial enzymes in the body begin to cause chemical breakdown of the cells and connective tissue (*putrefaction*). These processes can be slowed by cooling the tissues.

de Broglie wavelength, the wavelength of the wave associated with a moving particle, such as an electron (⇨ p. 90). The wavelength is equal to Planck's constant divided by the product of the mass of the particle and its velocity (the momentum of the body); ⇨ pp. 26–9 and 40.

Decapoda, the order of crustaceans that includes shrimps, prawns, crayfish, lobsters and crabs. They have five pairs of walking legs of which the first pair form powerful pincers, and the back shield (*carapace*) is fused with the thorax and head. The term is also used for the order of cephalopods that includes the squids and cuttlefishes.

decay, the spontaneous change of a radioactive element into another element with the emission of particles or photons. In the process, the atomic number may rise or fall (⇨ p. 160). The *half-life* of the element is the time taken for half of the element to decay. If the original amount of the element is x, then the time taken for x to reach x/2 is the same as for x/2 to reach x/4, and so on.

decibel, a unit of comparison between an arbitrary standard power level and any other level. It is not, as is often thought, a unit of sound intensity. The decibel is commonly used to compare sound intensities or electrical signals. In sound levels, 1 decibel is about the smallest difference perceptible. The decibel is a logarithmic unit, equal to one tenth of a bel. The latter is seldom if ever used.

deciduous, pertaining to plants that shed their leaves each growing season. By limiting transpiration, this helps to retain water. Most woody plants in temperate climates are deciduous. Some of these change to an evergreen habit if grown in a warm climate.

decimal number system, the numbering system in wide use in arithmetic, in which the base is equal to the number of fingers on the two hands. Numbers are represented in terms of the powers of 10. Those in the furthest column to the right are equal to the number written multiplied by 10 to the power 0 (1). Those in the next column to the left are equal to the number multiplied by 10 to the power 1. Those in the next, 10 to the power 2, and so on.

decision gate, an electronic logic circuit that discriminates between true and false logical relationships, giving an appropriate output, such as a 1 for true and a 0 for false. Discrimination might be as to whether it is true or false that one number is equal to another, or greater or less than another; ⇨ pp. 102–5.

declination, the angle between the geographic meridian and the magnetic meridian at any point on the Earth's surface. In astronomy, the angular distance of a star north or south of the celestial equator (⇨ pp. 140–5). Angles north of the celestial equator are shown as positive and those south as negative.

decoder/demultiplexer, an electronic switching circuit that separates and directs to their appropriate outputs the sequential packets of data in a multiplexed signal.

decomposition, a chemical reaction in which molecules are split into smaller molecules or elements.

deep inelastic collisions, the brief interaction between two colliding atomic nuclei while their surfaces are overlapping. Energy and mass flow from one to the other and neutrons and protons (⇨ p. 108) are exchanged.

deficiency disease, one of a large range of conditions resulting from the lack of any of the essential nutritional elements, such as vitamins or minerals, or from the body's inability to digest, absorb or utilize these. In some cases, deficiency diseases may be due to an abnormal output of needed substances, or from an abnormal demand.

degaussing, the process of removing the magnetization of an object that has become magnetized. This is commonly done by applying a rapidly diminishing alternating current to a coil so as to produce an alternating and diminishing magnetic field.

degenerative disease, disease caused by usually gradual structural alteration of body tissue or organs, either from ageing or misuse, which leads to functional impairment, usually progressive. Degenerative diseases are characterized by a gradual wearing away of a tissue, as in osteoarthritis; a gradual deterioration in the functional efficiency, as in atherosclerosis; or the gradual loss of structural bulk, as in osteoporosis. In general, degeneration causes tissues to lose their healthy, specialized properties. Structural materials, such as COLLAGEN, are chemically altered, with resultant loss of tissue elasticity; muscle cells are damaged, muscle bulk declines, specialized cells are replaced by non-functioning fibrous tissue, and many cells die. By their nature, degenerative diseases are difficult to treat. Established degeneration is irremediable, except by organ transplant or the use of artificial (*prosthetic*) parts, such as hip-joints. But as the nature and causes of the degenerative diseases gradually become clearer, more can be done to delay or arrest the processes of degeneration.

deglutition, swallowing.

degrees of freedom, the number of different mutually perpendicular planes in which a system can move, or, more generally, the number of independent parameters required to specify the configuration of a system. In chemistry, the phrase is used for the number of variables (such as, in the case of a gas, temperature and pressure) needed to define the state of a system.

dehiscence, the spontaneous splitting open of a fruit, seed pod or anther so as to disperse the pollen or seeds. In surgery, the spontaneous opening of a surgically closed wound.

dehydration, a body state in which the normal water content is reduced. Dehydration is usually due to excessive fluid loss which is not balanced by an appropriate increase in intake, but may be due to intake deficiency alone. It commonly results from prolonged diarrhoea and vomiting and excessive sweating, as in long fevers. Cholera is a classic example, in which death results solely from the extreme dehydration resulting from gross fluid loss from the bowel. Dehydration leads to an alteration in the vital balance of chemical substances dissolved in the blood and tissue fluids, especially sodium and potassium. The function of many cells is critically dependent on the maintenance of correct levels of these substances, and serious and often fatal effects result from any change. The risk is especially great in babies and infants whose high mortality, from conditions such as gastro-enteritis, is largely attributable to dehydration.

dehydrogenase, any enzyme that catalyses the removal of hydrogen atoms from organic molecules.

déjà vu, the sudden mistaken conviction that the current new experience has happened before. Literally, 'already seen'. There is a compelling sense of familiarity, usually lasting for only a few seconds, and a persuasion, almost always disappointed, that one knows what is round the next corner. One possible explanation is that the phenomenon results from a brief neurological short-circuit, with data from the current observation reaching the memory store before it reaches consciousness. The conscious experience of such a memory would be very strong, as it is so recent. This suggestion gains support from the fact that déjà vu is a very common symptom of disorders resulting from brain damage, such as temporal-lobe epilepsy. Some experts suggest that memory is not a matter of recall of a fixed, established event, but a process of reconstruction, from stored components, that involves elaborations, distortions and omissions. Each successive recall of the event is merely the recall of the last reconstruction. The sense of recognition, they suggest, involves achieving a good 'match' between the present experience and our stored data. It may be that this sense of recognition can be experienced although the match may have a fatal flaw so that we 'know' we have never experienced the event before.

delayed neutron emission, the spontaneous emission of a neutron (⇨ p. 108) from the nucleus of an atom of a radioactive element as a result of energy derived from prior radioactive decay. In a nuclear reactor using uranium–235, 0.7 per cent of emitted neutrons are delayed. This is fortunate, as prompt neutrons take only about one thousandth of a second to be absorbed, produce fission and generate further neutron emission. Were it not for the delayed neutrons, there would be very little time to move in the control rods in the event of a threatened runaway chain reaction. The delayed neutrons increase the safe response time from milliseconds to a few seconds.

delay line, a component that produces a lag in the time of arrival of a signal in an electronic circuit compared with the signal in a conductor that by-passes the delay line.

deliquescence, absorption of water by a solid from the atmosphere to such an extent that the solid eventually dissolves in it.

delirium, a mental disturbance resulting from organic disorder of brain function, featuring confusion of thought, disorientation, restlessness, trembling, fearfulness and often fantasies, unwarranted conviction (DELUSION) and disorder of sensation (HALLUCINATION). Sometimes there is maniacal excitement. Delirium may be caused by high fever, head injury, drug intoxication, drug overdosage and drug withdrawal. The commonest form is probably delirium tremens from alcohol withdrawal, but the same state may be induced by cocaine, especially 'crack', marijuana, LSD, mescaline and other abused substances.

delta, the triangular deposit of silt at the mouth of a river. Deposition of sediment occurs there because, as a result of the widening and the interaction with the sea, the speed of flow of the river decreases sharply.

deltoid, triangular. Literally, 'like the letter D', which, in Greek, is shaped like a triangle Δ. The deltoid muscle is the large, triangular 'shoulder-pad' muscle that elevates the arm sideways. The deltoid ligament is the strong triangular ligament on the inner side of the ankle, that helps to bind the foot to the leg and that is readily torn if the foot is forcibly turned inwards.

delusion, a fixed belief, unassailable by reason, in something manifestly absurd or untrue. Delusions cannot always be easily distinguished from rigidly held, but generally rejected, opinions, especially if these are shared by a group. But most are so intrinsically improbable or so obviously based on defective perceptions or reasoning as to indicate serious mental disturbance. Psychotic delusions fall into several categories, the commonest being delusions of persecution (*paranoid delusions*). Others are: delusions of grandeur; hypochondriacal delusions; delusions of abnormality of body shape; delusions of unreality or depersonalization; delusions of being influenced by others or by malignant forces; and self-deprecatory delusions of unworthiness, which are a feature of severe depression. Delusions sometimes serve useful purposes by providing an acceptable explanation for what would otherwise be too unpleasant to be borne. Systematized delusions often have an inherent logic that, the defective premises on which they are based being accepted, cannot be faulted.

dementia, a syndrome of failing memory and progressive loss of intellectual power due to continuing degenerative disease of the brain. About 50 per cent of cases are due to the brain shrinkage (*atrophy*) of Alzheimer's disease; about 10 per cent are due to small repeated strokes with progressive destruction of brain tissue by blood supply deprivation; 5–10 per cent are due to alcoholic damage from long-term over-indulgence; about 5 per cent are caused by brain tumours and 5 per cent by 'water on the brain' (*hydrocephalus*); 3 per cent are due to long-term drug intoxication and 3 per cent to the hereditary disease Huntington's chorea; most of the remainder are not dementias, but are psychiatric conditions that mimic dementia.

demodulation, the retrieval of the information content of a modulated carrier wave. Demodulation occurs in every radio receiver; ⇨ pp. 102–5.

demyelination, loss of the insulating fatty (myelin) sheath of nerve fibres. These carry electrical impulses in the body. Local areas of demyelination, in the form of 'plaques' that extend across large numbers of nerve-fibre bundles, are the hallmark of multiple sclerosis. It also occurs, much less commonly, in the condition of acute disseminated encephalomyelitis, which occasionally follows measles, chicken-pox or mumps or may follow rabies vaccination. The effect of demyelination is to block the passage of nerve impulses along the affected nerve fibres. Thus, depending on the fibres involved, this may cause disturbance of any function involving muscle contraction (*motor function*), partial loss of sensation, or partial loss of the special senses such as vision. There may be partial paralysis, disturbance of bladder or bowel control, interference with the balancing mechanisms, indeed disturbance of any of the important faculties subserved by nerve conduction.

denature, to alter the structure of a protein or nucleic acid so that its biological or physical properties are changed. When an egg is boiled the albumen is denatured.

dendrochronology, a method of dating using unique alterations in the annual growth rings of trees. Wide rings occur in rainy seasons when growth is rapid, narrow rings occur in dry seasons. Each ring in a living tree can, in this way, be dated, and corresponding rings in wood specimens or fossil trees can provide accurate dating. Dendrochronology has been used to correct and verify carbon dating and to amplify the history of climate.

dendrology, the botany of trees, with special reference to their identification, description, naming and the recognition of their characteristic habitat.

denitrification, the release of gaseous nitrogen from soil nitrates into the atmosphere, under the influence of bacteria. This is the opposite process from nitrogen fixation.

densitometry, the process of measuring the optical density of a semitransparent medium such as a photographic film. Light is shone through the medium and its intensity is then measured by a photoelectric cell and meter.

density, mass per unit volume. Density is not quite the same as SPECIFIC GRAVITY. This is actually the ratio of the density of a material to that of a standard such as water at a standard temperature, which is taken as 1. Because

nearly all materials change volume with changes in temperature, density is a FUNCTION of temperature. In the case of gases, it is also a function of pressure. Density of a uniform material is found by determining the volume of a sample and then weighing it. Volume can be determined by immersing the body in a liquid in a graduated container and noting the rise in the level. A better way of determining volume is to weigh the body in air and then to weigh it immersed in a liquid of known density. The volume is equal to the reduction in weight in the liquid divided by the density of the liquid; ⇨ pp. 26–35.

dentine, the hard tissue that makes up the bulk of the tooth. Dentine is harder than BONE, but softer than the outer enamel coating and contains tubules of cells that connect the inner pulp of the tooth to the surface. These cells, the *odontoblasts*, are responsible for producing dentine and act to repair areas where the enamel has been worn or damaged. They also transmit temperature and pain-producing stimuli, such as tapping or pressure, to the nerves in the pulp.

dentition, the number, type and arrangement of the teeth of a species.

deodorants, substances such as activated charcoal, Fuller's earth (aluminium silicate) or silica gel that have powerful adsorptive properties and that will remove odour particles from air. Air can also be deodorized by passing it through water or other solutions to remove the particles. Body deodorants contain aluminium or zinc salts and act mainly by reducing the production of sweat secretion from the glands in the armpits and groins (apocrine sweat). Apocrine sweat is broken down by skin bacteria to produce unpleasant-smelling compounds. Destruction of the bacteria themselves can help, but antiseptics are not approved of. The effective germicide hexachlorophene, once widely used in deodorants, has been restricted because of the danger of nerve toxicity. Daily washing and changing of clothes is usually effective.

deoxyribonucleic acid, DNA. The vehicle of hereditary information for almost all living things apart from certain viruses. Deoxyribonucleic acid is a very long polymer (⇨ p. 164) made up of a double helical 'backbone' of alternating 2-deoxyribose sugars and phosphate groups. Attached to the sugars, and joining the two helices, like the rungs of a ladder, are pairs of purine or pyrimidine bases linked by weak hydrogen bonds. A purine always links to a pyrimidine; adenine always links to thymine (and vice versa) and guanine always links to cytosine (and vice versa). The sequence of these bases along the molecule is unique for each individual except for identical (*monozygotic*) twins or other multiples derived from the same genome. The rules of base bonding and the relative ease of separation of the two longitudinal halves of the DNA molecule at the hydrogen bonds between the purine and pyrimidine bases provides a mechanism for automatic replication of the molecule as long as bases, sugars and phosphates are present in the cell fluid – which

is invariably the case. This replication occurs prior to the reproduction of cells. The base sequence, taken in threes (*codons*), provides a code for the selection of AMINO ACIDS from the cell fluid. There are codon triplets for each of the 20 amino acids. Before actually functioning, the genetic code is transferred from DNA to a single-strand ribonucleic acid (RNA) of complementary bases. The order and identity of the amino acids selected determines the nature of the proteins formed. Most of these are enzymes. Any length of DNA coding for a single protein is called a *gene* (⇨ pp. 202–5). DNA, when inactive, coils up into chromosomes. A separate genome of DNA also occurs in the mitochondria (⇨ p. 188). This DNA is derived from the ovum and hence only from the mother. Bacteria carry DNA in bodies known as *plasmids*.

depersonalization, a loss of the sense of one's own reality, often with a dream-like feeling of being detached from one's own body or with a sense that one's body is unreal or strange. Depersonalization is common, as an occasional, brief, isolated episode, and has been experienced by many healthy people. It often occurs in children as they develop self-awareness and is commoner in young people than in the elderly. The out-of-the-body experience often features a conviction that the identity is located some feet above the physical body, which can be observed below. Depersonalization may involve size or shape distortion of parts of the body. The fingers may, for instance, feel enormously long and fat or much smaller than normal. The sense of distortion is powerful and is not dispelled by visual evidence of normality.

depilatory, a preparation or procedure for removing hair or destroying the hair-forming skin tubes (*follicles*). Depilatories may be chemical, thermal or mechanical. Various chemicals, such as barium sulphide or thioglycollic acid salts, can soften and dissolve hairs, so that they can be wiped off, but those that are safe do not affect the follicles, and the hair grows again. Wax depilatories merely provide a convenient way of gripping many hairs at once so that they can quickly be ripped out of the follicles. *Electrolysis* is a method applied to one follicle at a time. The electric current of a few milliamps that flows through the follicle, does not destroy it by electrolysis, but merely by heat.

depletion layer, a zone in a semiconductor with fewer than the usual number of mobile charge carriers (electrons and holes). Depletion layers form at the interface between p-type and n-type material, and semiconductor function depends on this fact (⇨ pp. 102–5).

depolarization, the use of a material to prevent the poles of a primary electric cell (⇨ p. 92) from becoming polarized and thus offering a high resistance (⇨ p. 96) to the flow of current. In physiology, the local area of reversal of electric charge on a cell membrane that is the basis of the nerve impulse or ACTION POTENTIAL.

depolymerization, the breaking down of a polymer (⇨ p. 164) to release its constituent monomers.

deposition, the process by which sedimentary rocks are formed from eroded material carried to the oceans by rivers, glaciers or winds.

depression, in meteorology, an area of low atmospheric pressure surrounded by closed isobars. Depressions usually move northeast in the Northern hemisphere and southeast in the Southern hemisphere. The low pressure leads to winds and rain precipitation. In psychiatry, a mood of sustained sadness or unhappiness. Normal reactive unhappiness is experienced at times by all, but genuine depressive illness, or clinical depression, involves a degree of hopeless despondency, dejection, fear and irritability out of all proportion to any external cause. Often there is no apparent cause. It is associated with a general slowing down of body and mind, slow speech, poor concentration, confusion, self-reproach, self- accusation and loss of self-esteem. There may be restlessness and agitation. Insomnia, with early morning waking, is common. Sexual interest may be lost and suicide is an ever-present threat.

depth of field, the distance on either side of the point of best focus of an optical instrument within which objects are acceptably well focused.

depth of focus, the range of distance between a lens and a focal plane in which the image remains acceptably sharp.

Dermaptera, the order of insects that comprises the earwigs.

dermatitis, a general term meaning inflammation of the skin from any cause. Dermatitis is not a specific disease, but any one of a considerable range of disorders of an inflammatory nature. The appearance of many of these conditions is similar, with redness, blister formation, swelling, weeping and crusting. There is itching and burning and a strong impulse to scratch, which often makes the condition worse and may perpetuate it. Different kinds of dermatitis may have a similar appearance, but the causes may be very diverse.

dermatographia, skin writing. A form of skin sensitivity in which a raised swollen line, surrounded by a red flare, results when the skin is scratched or firmly stroked with a blunt object. The effect is strikingly shown if the form of a word is stroked on the skin. Dermatographia permanently affects some people for no known reason, but in most cases is associated with the form of allergy known as urticaria.

dermatome, the area of skin from which the sensory nerves enter a single pair of nerve roots of the spinal cord. The anatomical dermatomes are paired and correspond to the segments into which the body was divided at an early embryonic stage. The body surface can be mapped out in strips corresponding to the dermatomes.

dermatophytosis, fungus infection of the skin, often called 'ringworm'. These fungi, mainly *Trichophyton*, *Microsporum* and *Epidermophyton*, affect only the surface (*epidermal*) layers of the skin, which are already dead and are in the process of being cast off. The common medical name for these infections is *tinea*, and this is qualified by reference to the site – head, usually scalp, involvement is *tinea capitis*; body, *tinea corporis*; crutch, *tinea cruris*; feet, *tinea pedis* or 'athlete's foot'; nails, *tinea unguium*; beard area, *tinea barbae*. The term 'ringworm' is simply a description of the tendency of these fungi to involve new skin while disappearing from previously affected parts. Because of this, any small patch will form a ring which expands outwards while clearing centrally.

dermis, the inner, wholly living layer of the skin of vertebrates, distinguished from the EPIDERMIS, which is stratified and of which the outer cells are cornified and dead.

desalination, removal of salt from sea water so that it can be used for agricultural and drinking purposes. All the desalination processes, unfortunately, require considerable energy. They include DISTILLATION, flash evaporation under reduced pressure, freezing, ion-exchange methods and the electrolytic movement of ions (⇨ pp. 90 and 156) through arrays of semipermeable membranes (*electrodialysis*).

desmids, single-celled algae in the form of two mirror-image halves joined by a narrow neck. Desmids are a major group in plankton.

desorption, the opposite of ADSORPTION.

destructive distillation, heating material in the absence of air and condensing the volatile products that come off at different temperatures. The destructive DISTILLATION of coal was formerly one of the most important of all industrial chemical processes and was a principal means of obtaining industrial raw materials.

detergent, a material that furnishes water with the power to dissolve fats and oils and that can act as a wetting agent, emulsifier or foam stabilizer. In *ionic detergents* the active part is a positive or negative ion, respectively *cationic* and *anionic* detergents. Non-ionic detergents have polar groups that form hydrogen bonds (⇨ p. 162) with the water.

deuterium, the isotope of hydrogen that has a neutron as well as a proton in the nucleus. Heavy hydrogen or hydrogen–2, with a mass number of 2. It occurs as deuterium oxide (heavy water) from which it can be obtained by fractional DISTILLATION or electrolysis. Deuterium, having the same single electron as hydrogen, behaves chemically in a very similar way, but its physical properties are slightly different; ⇨ p. 164.

deuteron, the nucleus of a deuterium atom.

device driver, a software program that controls a device such as a printer, a disk drive, a keyboard, a mouse or a modem. Devices will operate correctly only if the commands they understand are issued. Device drivers translate computer instructions into these correct commands. The CONFIG.SYS file in DOS and OS/2 computers contains instructions for the loading of the software device drivers.

Devonian, a geological period in the Palaeozoic era that extended from about 395–345 million years ago. The Devonian saw the formation of the Old Red Sandstone and its fossils include corals, brachiopods, fishes and the earliest land plants.

dew point, the temperature at which the atmospheric air becomes saturated with its water vapour and this begins to condense as droplets.

dextrocardia, a major, but usually harmless congenital anomaly in which the apex of the heart points to the right instead of the left. Dextrocardia is often associated with a similar mirror-image reversal of the abdominal organs, so that the liver is on the left, the stomach and spleen on the right and the appendix on the left. This is called *situs inversus*. The condition is harmless.

dextrorotatory, the property of rotating the plane of polarization of plane-polarized light in a clockwise direction from the point of view of an observer facing the source of the light. This property is shared by many chemical compounds when placed in solution. Compare laevorotatory, in which the rotation is in the opposite direction.

dextrose, DEXTROROTATORY glucose (the usual form).

dialysis, the removal of substances from a solution by using membranes through which molecules of the substance can pass. Membranes, such as cellophane, have pore sizes that allow small molecules to pass while retaining larger molecules. These are called *semipermeable membranes*. If such a membrane is used to separate two liquids, one containing the small molecules in solution and the other being plain water, the molecules will pass through into the water until the concentration is the same on both sides of the membrane. The principle is used in medicine to produce an *artificial kidney*. This consists of a long, narrow tube of membrane, coiled around a drum and immersed in water. The patient's blood is directed through the tube and unwanted small molecules, such as urea and salt, pass out into the water. Large molecules, such as proteins, or large particles, such as red blood cells, are retained. The water surrounding the tube is changed constantly, so that the concentration of small molecules in it is never allowed to rise to the equilibrium level. Patients on permanent dialysis have an external connection (*shunt*) made surgically between an artery and a vein in the arm. This takes the form of a short plastic tube, from the artery, connected to a tube that enters the vein. Before dialysis, the tube from the artery is connected to the machine and the vein tube is connected to the return flow of blood from the machine. A period of about six hours, twice a week, is usually sufficient to keep the level of waste substances in the blood at a low enough level for health.

diamond, an allotropic form (⇨ p. 164) of pure carbon crystallized as cubes or octahedra. Diamond is the hardest known mineral and has wide industrial uses for cutting and grinding. Most industrial diamonds are now made synthetically.

diaphragm, any thin, dividing membrane. In photography and optics, a membrane with a central hole of variable or adjustable size used to reduce the amount of light passing through. In anatomy, the upwardly domed sheet of muscle and tendon that separates the chest from the abdomen, and, on contracting, flattens so as to increase the volume of the chest and draw air into the lungs.

diastole, the period between contraction of the heart muscle (beats). Compare *systole,* the period during the contraction.

diathermy, a method of bloodless surgical cutting in which high frequency alternating electric current is used to produce a sharply localized burning effect. Diathermy may also be used to seal off bleeding vessels that have already been cut, or to destroy unwanted tissue, such as a tumour. Two electrodes are necessary to complete the electrical circuit. One is wide and is bandaged to the patient's leg. The other takes the form of a fine metal point, or a pair of tweezer-type forceps, at which the current is concentrated. Alternatively, both electrical connections may be made to the forceps, one to each blade (the blades being insulated from each other) so that the high-frequency current passes between the tips of the blades and anything held in the forceps is coagulated. Diathermy can also be used to produce more diffuse heating as a form of physiotherapy.

diazo compounds, compounds in which two molecules are linked by a nitrogen-to-nitrogen double bond. Compounds of the general form R.N=N.R. Diazo compounds are extensively used in the manufacture of dyes.

dichogamy, the maturing of the male and female organs of a flower at different times so that self-fertilization cannot occur.

dichroism, the power of absorbing light vibrations in one plane while allowing those in the perpendicular plane to pass through. This property is possessed by crystals of tourmaline and by synthetic materials such as that used in *Polaroid.*

dicotyledonous, having two seed leaves within the seed. Dicotyledonous plants are one of the two subclasses of plants within the angiosperms, and include many food plants, ornamental plants, herbaceous plants, shrubs and hardwood trees.

Dictyoptera, an order of insects comprising cockroaches and mantids.

dielectric, an electrically insulating substance in which the application of an electric field

causes a displacement of electrons relative to the atomic nuclei, but not a flow of electrons. The result is a DIPOLE with an electric moment in the direction of the field. Dielectrics situated between the plates of a capacitor (⇨ p. 98) increase the capacitance by a factor known as the *dielectric constant* or *relative permittivity.* The *dielectric strength* is the volts per mm that can be applied to the material without causing it to break down.

dielectric heating, a method of heating a dielectric material by placing it between metal plates and applying a high-frequency alternating current to them so that an oscillating electric field is formed through the dielectric, causing rapid movement of the electrons relative to the atomic nuclei.

differential equation, an equation that contains a derivative of any quantity y with respect to another quantity x as well as the variables x and y. There are many different kinds of differential equation, each solved in its own way. Differential equations usually have to be solved using numerical methods because they cannot be solved using exact (analytical) methods.

diffraction, the interference effects produced when an obstacle or aperture is placed in the path of a travelling wave. The diffraction pattern formed at a large distance from the obstacle or aperture is known as a Fraunhofer diffraction pattern; close to, it forms a Fresnel pattern.

digital, pertaining to the method of representing information of any kind as a sequence of discrete numbers, rather than by a continuous varying quantity (⇨ ANALOGUE). Any system based on discontinuous events. A digital clock changes its figures at intervals such as those of a second or a minute; an analogue clock has continuously moving hands. Digital representations are only approximations of analogue events, but the approximation can be made ever closer by increasing the number of samples taken in a given time, until the difference is imperceptible. The information on a music compact disk is purely digital but because the music was sampled some 40,000 times a second, the loss of detail is negligible. After digital-to-analogue conversion the original sound is recreated with remarkable fidelity and the discontinuity of such short intervals cannot be appreciated. Digital computers handle only digital information, and that in BINARY form. Digitized information is inherently much less prone to interference and distortion than analogue information; ⇨ pp. 214–19.

dihedral, the angle formed when two planes, such as those on the surface of a crystal, intersect. In aeronautics, the slight upward tilt of the wings of an aircraft that reduces the tendency to roll.

dimer, two molecules, identical (*homo-dimer*) or otherwise (*hetero-dimer*), linked together. When many such linkages occur the result is a *polymer* (⇨ p. 164).

dimorphism, the occurrence of two physically different types within a species, as in the case of the often obvious differences in size and plumage between the two sexes (*sexual dimorphism*).

dinosaur, one of many extinct reptiles of the orders Saurischia and Ornithischia that flourished during the Mesozoic era. Many were of enormous size. The Saurischia mainly ran on two legs and were carnivorous. The Ornithischia and some of the Saurischia were quadruped herbivores. Many dinosaurs were amphibious. The extinction of the dinosaurs occurred about 65 million years ago and various theories have been put forward to account for it (⇨ K-T BOUNDARY).

diode, an electronic circuit component that allows flow of current in only one direction. Most diodes are semiconductors and are used for signal DEMODULATION, rectification of AC, voltage regulation (zener diodes) and other purposes; ⇨ pp. 102–5.

dioptre, a measure of lens power. Lens power can also be expressed as the focal length – the distance from the lens to the point at which parallel rays are brought to a focus. But the focal length becomes inconvenient as a measure of lens power when lenses are combined. Two lenses of focal length ten centimetres have a combined focal length of five centimetres. A lens of twenty centimetres in combination with a lens of ten centimetres produces a focal length of just below seven centimetres. To calculate the focal length of the combination it is necessary to take the reciprocal of each focal length (1 divided by the length), add them, and then take the reciprocal of the result. To get round this difficulty, thin lenses, such as are used in spectacles, are graded, not by focal length, but by the reciprocal of the focal length. This is called the *dioptre.* A lens of one metre focal length has a power of one dioptre. A lens of fifty centimetre focal length has a power of two dioptres, and one of twenty centimetre focal length has a power of five dioptres. The dioptric power is simply obtained by dividing 100 by the focal length in centimetres. The ability to add, to a given lens, other lenses, of plus or minus power, is indispensable to opticians when testing eyes for spectacles. Most spectacles contain lenses of between one half and five dioptres. Reading glasses, for those with normal distance vision, will start at one dioptre of plus power at the age of about forty-five, and rise to about two and a half dioptres, at the age of sixty.

dioxins, highly toxic contaminant byproducts of the manufacture of chlorinated phenols, such as the polychlorinated biphenyls (PCB), used as insecticides, herbicides and fungicides. Dioxins can cause severe skin disorders, cancer and fetal malformations.

dipole, a pair of opposite, separated but associated electric charges. In radio transmission and reception, a dipole is a form of aerial routinely used for high frequencies made to particular dimensions to correspond to the desired wavelength. It consists of two short rods arranged in a straight line with the inner ends close together but insulated from each other. The connections are made to these inner ends.

dipole moment, the product of the positive charge of a DIPOLE and the distance between its two charges. Dipole moments are important in chemistry as they determine the polar nature of the bonds between atoms.

diptera, a large order of insects containing all the two-winged flies, including house flies, horse flies, gadflies, biting black flies, sandflies, mosquitos and midges.

directory, a collection of files, usually having some feature in common, in a computer data store. Computer operating systems allow for the organization of files in directories and subdirectories that may be highly structured so that information can be stored in a systematic and logical way and needed files quickly found.

disassembler, a program that attempts to convert MACHINE CODE to assembly language.

disorientation, a state of extreme bewilderment or confusion about the current state of the real world and of the affected person's relationship to it. A disoriented person may be unable to give the date, or the year, or be able to state where, or even who, he or she is. Awareness of time, place and person are usually lost in that order and, on recovery, return in the reverse order. Disorientation may be caused by drug intoxication, DEMENTIA, delusional disorders, severe DEPRESSION and other psychiatric disorders.

dispersion, the phenomenon in which waves of different frequency travelling in a dispersing medium are separated because they travel at different speeds. A common example is the splitting of white light into its component colours that occurs when light passes through a prism of transparent material. Rays travelling at different speeds are deviated to different degrees; ⇨ pp. 64–7 and 78.

displacement activity, inappropriate behaviour that occurs when an animal or human is faced with strongly conflicting stimuli. In humans it is one of the psychological defence mechanisms. The emotion engendered by a person, idea or object is perceived as unacceptable and is transferred to another, more tolerable, person, idea or object. A young employee with a strong desire to punch a tyrannical boss, will go out at lunch time and hit a squash ball with pent-up fury and force.

dissociative disorders, a group of mental conditions characterized by sudden and usually temporary loss of a major faculty such as memory, orientation, or some aspect of self-awareness. The dissociative disorders include loss of memory for important personal details (AMNESIA); a wandering away, far from home, and the assuming of a new identity and occupation, with an apparent inability to remember the past life (*fugue*); a splitting of the personality into two (usually mutually) amnesiac personalities with different characteristics (*multiple-personality disorder*);

an alteration in the perception of self, so that the sense of one's own reality is lost (*depersonalization disorder*); and the entering into trance-like states with severely reduced response to external stimuli. These disorders are a response to some powerfully traumatic or stressful event with which the personality of the sufferer is unable to cope. They may result from the inability to face some event in the personal life and may particularly affect military personnel exposed to extreme risk or to prolonged periods of great danger.

distal, an anatomical term meaning situated at a point beyond, or away from, any reference point. The usual reference point is the centre of the body, so the hand is said to be distal to the forearm or to the elbow. The opposite of distal is *proximal*. The knee is distal to the hip, but proximal to the foot.

distillation, a method of removing one or more components of a liquid mixture by heating, vaporizing the desired material and directing the vapour to a cooler area where it condenses and can be collected. Distillation depends on the fact that different liquids have different boiling points.

distortion, a change, other than in amplitude and power, between the input and the output of a system, especially of an electronic amplifier. Distortion may be one of differences in amplitude at different frequencies (*frequency distortion*), one of a change in the levels of various harmonics (*harmonic distortion*), one of the effects of beating between different frequencies (*intermodulation distortion*), one of change of phase (*phase distortion*), and so on; ⇨ pp. 102–5.

dizygotic twins, twins derived simultaneously from different ova fertilized by different sperms. Nonidentical twins.

DNA ⇨ DEOXYRIBONUCLEIC ACID.

DNA fingerprinting, a method of recording on transparent film a pattern of bands that correspond to a sequence of regions in the DNA of the individual. These *core sequences* are repeated a different number of times in different people and are unique to each unrelated individuals. They contain common features in closely related people. To prepare a DNA 'fingerprint', a sample of DNA is obtained. Only a tiny quantity of blood, semen or of any body tissue is needed to provide the DNA. The sample is cut into fragments with restriction enzymes, and these are then separated on a sheet of gel by ELECTROPHORESIS. The double-helix fragments are then separated into single strands and blotted onto a sheet of nylon or nitrocellulose that fixes them in place. Radioactive gene probes that bind to any fragment containing the core sequence are now added. In this way, the core sequences become radioactive and this can be shown up by putting a photographic film in contact with the membrane. Bands are produced on the photographic film by the action of the radiation. Banding patterns from different individuals, or from different samples from the same individual, can now be compared. DNA

fingerprinting can be used as a means of positive identification or of paternity testing and has enormous forensic significance. Since no two people, apart from identical twins, have identical DNA, the test is, in theory, infallible. Questions have been raised in court, however, as to the validity of the methods used to conduct and interpret the method.

DNAase, an enzyme that promotes the splitting of the DNA molecule (⇨ p. 202) into shorter fragments.

dominance, the power of a gene (⇨ p. 204) to express itself regardless of the nature of its ALLELE.

dopamine, a precursor of adrenaline that also acts as a NEUROTRANSMITTER.

dorsal, relating to the back.

double-blind trial, a trial, usually of a new medical treatment, in which neither the patients nor the persons conducting the trial know which of two identical-seeming treatments is genuine and which is a dummy. In the case of a trial of a new drug, a pharmacist makes up two sets of tablets or capsules that cannot be distinguished by appearance, taste, etc. One set contains the active ingredient and the other an inert substance. Only the pharmacist knows which is which. The medication is allocated randomly and the key as to who gets what is locked away until the end of the trial. After the results are known, the key is checked to see whether those who had the active drug did significantly better than those who took the dummy. The purpose of the double-blind arrangement is to balance out the *placebo effect* that is so psychologically powerful that a single trial of a (useless) drug will usually suggest that it is of medical value.

downloading, the receipt of data by a remote computer from a central or controlling machine, by way of a local connecting network, modem or other communication channel.

drag coefficient, a measure of the resistance to the movement of a body through a fluid medium, such as air. Air resistance to movement varies with the *square* of the speed of the body. In a motor vehicle, the power needed to overcome drag increases with the *cube* of the speed. Drag increases with the frontal area of the vehicle and with its shape. Streamlining and reduction of the frontal area can reduce drag coefficient considerably.

dreaming, the subjective experience of partial consciousness during sleep. Dreaming occurs during periods of apparently light sleep, when the electroencephalogram (EEG) shows rapid waves, of a frequency almost equal to that of the awake brain, and the eyes move rapidly beneath the lids. This is called rapid-eye-movement (REM) sleep and in this stage, which occurs several times a night, the breathing and heart rate become irregular and, in males, the penis becomes erect. Dream thought is often irrational, confused, mixed and repetitive. It appears to be an attempt on the part of the higher centres of the brain to make some kind of sense of a random mass of disparate collections of information arriving from the lower centres, such as the sensory nuclei and the cerebellum. Dream content relating to recent experience and preoccupations is probably used merely in an attempt to structure the random signals.

drop-out, the loss of data due to local defects on the surface of a magnetic recording medium such as a floppy or hard disk.

drowning, death from suffocation as a result of exclusion of air from the lungs by fluid, usually water. The breathing reflexes are so powerful that when the nose and mouth are immersed in a fluid, that fluid will, eventually, in spite of the efforts of the person concerned, be inhaled into the lungs. Drowning may also occur in fluid produced within the lungs themselves (*pulmonary oedema*) as a result of the inhalation of irritants or from lung or other disease. The exclusion of air from the lungs, and, consequently, of oxygen from the blood, soon leads to brain dysfunction and loss of consciousness. Within four or five minutes, in most cases, irrecoverable damage is caused to the higher centres of the brain. Notable exceptions to this rule have often occurred, especially in very cold conditions in which the body metabolism is slowed and the oxygen requirement is reduced. Children have been rescued and restored to apparent normality after immersion in water, under ice, for half an hour.

drug addiction, a physical and psychological dependence on repeated doses of a drug for comfort of body and mind. Addiction has three main features: long duration of usage, difficulty in stopping and withdrawal symptoms. These features are well recognized by habitual cigarette smokers, who are currently the commonest drug addicts. Dependent people will go to great lengths to maintain access to their drug, often resorting to crime and neglecting family and other duties. The strength of the dependence can be assessed by noting the lengths to which people will go to maintain the supply. Nicotine addicts may beg cigarettes from friends, but will seldom steal or engage in prostitution to obtain the drug, as might heroin addicts. The intensity of the withdrawal syndrome also varies with the drug, being greater with heroin than with nicotine or caffeine.

dry ice, solid carbon dioxide. CARBON DIOXIDE (CO_2) is a gas at normal temperatures, having a boiling point of $-78°C$, but solidifying at $-80°C$. Dry ice can be produced by releasing the gas under pressure from a cylinder of liquid CO_2 fitted with an internal tube. The evaporation of the liquid causes further cooling, by abstracting the latent heat of vaporization, and CO_2 snow is formed. The jet may be directed into a cylinder and a candle of solid CO_2 will form. Dry ice is widely used as a refrigerant and also has various medical applications. It is used, for instance, to destroy diseased tissue.

ductility, the ability of a metal to retain its strength even when substantially deformed or drawn into wires.

dumping, copying of data from a memory to a peripheral device such as a printer or a FLOPPY-DISK drive for backing up; ⇨ p. 216.

duodenum, the first part of the small intestine. The duodenum is the widest, shortest and most immobile part of the small bowel and forms an almost circular curve from the outlet of the STOMACH to the beginning of the JEJUNUM. It ends just below and to the left side of its starting point. The passage of stomach contents into the duodenum is controlled by a muscular ring at the outlet of the stomach, called the pylorus or pyloric SPHINCTER. About the middle of the descending curve, the duodenum is entered by the ducts from the pancreas and the gall bladder, thereby receiving a plentiful supply of digestive juices (*pancreatic enzymes*) and a quantity of a detergent-like emulsifying agent (bile salts), which break up ingested fats into a milky emulsion that is easily absorbed.

duplex operation, the transmission of data in both directions at the same time, as in an ordinary telephone conversation. Half-duplex allows transmission in only one direction at a time, as in 'walky-talky' operation.

dwarfism, abnormal shortness of stature. This may be the result of having very short parents, but more commonly results from one of a considerable number of disorders, inherited or acquired. These include Down's syndrome, glandular defects such as pituitary-growth-hormone deficiency or defective response to pituitary growth hormone, primary thyroid deficiency (*cretinism*) or secondary thyroid underaction, premature sex-hormone production with precocious puberty and early closure of the growing ends of the bones, diabetes, or adrenal-gland insufficiency. Dwarfism also results from various inborn errors of metabolism, such as Hurler's syndrome, Tay-Sach's disease, Niemann-Pick disease and Gaucher's disease. Achondroplasia is an inherited disorder of the growth zones of the long bones. This is the common form of dwarfism. Dwarfism also occurs as a result of growth retardation in the womb from placental insufficiency or infection; from social and economic disadvantage during childhood; or from neglect, rejection or simply inadequate physical contact.

dyes, substances used to change the colour of materials by virtue of a chemical group called a chromophore. Many are organic compounds containing pairs of double bonds separated by a single bond (*conjugated double bonds*). In acid dyes, the chromophore is part of a negative ion, and in basic dyes the chromophore is part of a positive ion. There are many other classes of dyes.

dynamic random-access memory (DRAM), a semiconductor memory in which bits are stored as charges on the small capacitance in the gate of a metal-oxide silicon transistor (⇨ pp. 102–5). These charges quickly leak away and must be refreshed at short intervals. DRAMs can store millions of binary digits (*bits*).

dynamometer, an instrument, such as a spring balance, used to measure a force.

dyslexia, an inability to achieve an average performance in reading or in comprehension of what is read, in a person of usual or high intelligence and of standard educational and sociocultural opportunity and emotional stability. Dyslexia is independent of visual or speech defect, and may vary from a very minor disadvantage to an almost total inability to read. It is more common in males, tends to run in families, and persists into adult life. There are clear indications of cognitive disability, with much greater than usual difficulty in the use, meaning, spelling and pronunciation of words.

dysplasia, an abnormal alteration in a tissue, excluding cancerous change, due to abnormality in the function of the component cells. Dysplasias include the absence of growth, an abnormal degree of growth, and abnormalities in cell structure. Some dysplasias are regarded as a stage in the development of cancer, but many are not. Dysplasia may affect any cell type in the body and is commonly described in the neck of the womb (cervix), in the lungs of infants, in the teeth, in the bones and in the thymus.

echo, the reflection of a wave of any kind by a surface.

eclipse, the obscuring of the light from a celestial body when another body is interposed. An eclipse of the Moon occurs when the Earth's shadow falls on it. An eclipse of the Sun occurs when the Moon is interposed between the Sun and the Earth; ⇨ p. 144.

ecology, the study of the relationship between living things and their environment.

ectoparasite, a parasite that lives on the outside of the body of its host. Compare *endoparasite* in which the parasite is internal.

ectopic, situated in a place remote from the usual location. Ectopic foci of thymus tissue, situated away from the site of the thymus gland in the upper chest, are thought to maintain thymus immunological function after the normal atrophy of the gland in adolescence. An ectopic pregnancy is one occurring outside the womb.

eddy current, the electric current that is induced in a conductor cut by a changing magnetic field. If the resistance of the conductor is low, as in the case of a block of metal, the eddy currents can be very large and can cause heating and considerable energy loss. For this reason transformer cores are made of stacks of thin sheets of metal, each sheet being insulated; ⇨ pp. 90 and 96.

efficiency, the ratio of the energy output of a machine to the energy input. Efficiency usually varies with the load and is a measure of the extent to which avoidable losses have in fact been avoided. *Thermal efficiency* is the ratio of the work done to the heat supplied by the fuel; ⇨ pp. 46–57.

egg, the ovum. The female reproductive cell (*gamete*), produced by the ovary. In humans this occurs about half-way between two menstrual periods. Human ovaries usually produce one egg per month, but often produce more than one. The egg contains half the chromosomes required by the new individual, and the other half are supplied by the sperm at the moment of fertilization. The egg is a very large cell, much larger than a sperm, and is about one tenth of a millimetre in diameter. Its size is determined by the need to contain nutritive material (*yolk*) to supply the embryo in its earliest stages before it can establish a supply from the mother via the placenta. If more than one egg is produced and fertilized, a multiple pregnancy results, but the offspring are not identical since half the chromosomes in each come from different sperms, with different genetic material. If a fertilized ovum divides and each of the two halves forms a new individual, these will be identical twins, with identical chromosomes. In egg-laying animals, the egg is the fertilized ovum or *zygote* and is covered by protective membranes that may include a shell; ⇨ pp. 186–9 and 200–5.

EISA, extended industry standard architecture, a microcomputer BUS structure for machines using Intel 32-bit processors such as the MS-DOS personal computers.

ejaculation, the emission of semen from the penis in spasmodic spurts. This is the usual accompaniment of the male orgasm and, once started, becomes involuntary. During sexual intercourse, ejaculation is forceful enough to ensure that, unless prevented by some barrier, semen is deposited in or about the cervix of the uterus.

elastic collision, a collision is which no loss of kinetic energy (⇨ pp. 46–9) occurs. Elastic collisions do not occur between particles or bodies larger than atoms; ⇨ pp. 108–11 and 156.

elasticity, the ability of a body to return to its original dimensions after a deforming stress has been removed. The deformity is called the *strain* and, beyond a certain point (the *elastic limit*), the body remains permanently deformed; ⇨ p. 28.

electret, a body with a permanent electric charge, analogous to the permanent magnetic field of a permanent magnet. Electrets can be used in microphones; ⇨ p. 88.

electric field, an area in which forces are exerted on electric charges.

electricity-cable-field dangers, the alleged medical risk to people living near electricity cables. Magnetic fields are measured in gauss units. One gauss is the field strength 1 cm from a wire carrying a current of 5 amps. At 10 cm the field strength has fallen to 0.01 gauss and at 1 m to 0.0001 gauss. This is the order of the alternating-field strength experienced by all of us in a domestic environment. The highest field recorded, immediately under the largest British power lines, is less than half a gauss. The Earth's magnetic field (⇨ p. 146) varies with position, but averages about half a gauss. This is, however, a static field and power lines carry alternating current, varying at a frequency of 50 or 60 cycles per second. Any iron within the field will vibrate slightly at that frequency. BLOOD contains iron in the HAEMOGLOBIN of the red cells. Animal studies done to test the effects of alternating fields have shown no detectable blood changes. Vibration is not, in itself, harmful; heat, light and sound are all mediated by vibration. Studies in Denver, Colorado, of the incidence of childhood cancers, especially leukaemia, seem to show that those most highly exposed to power lines had a slightly higher than average incidence of cancer. Various other studies showed no clear association between power lines and cancer.

electric organ, a collection of modified muscle cells in certain eels and rays, that can give an electric shock if touched. The cells produce a voltage (⇨ p. 88–91) when stimulated and are connected in series so that a high voltage is built up.

electrocardiogram, a machine for recording the electrical changes associated with contraction of the heart muscle. These changes can be detected as varying voltage differences between different points on the surface of the body. Five connections are made to the ECG machine in the standard lead system – one from each limb and one (lead V) from various positions on the front and side of the chest. The voltages provide a highly detailed record of much of what is happening in the heart. The method is useful in diagnosing a wide range of abnormalities. An ECG may be taken during exercise and this will often bring to light latent abnormalities that do not show on the resting tracing.

electroencephalogram, a multiple tracing, made by voltmeter-operated pens, of the electrical activity of the brain, picked up between pairs of points on the scalp of the subject, by electrodes of silver wire glued to the scalp. The normal EEG is dominated by the alpha rhythm, a steady alternation at 8–13 cycles per second. The beta rhythm is faster (of higher frequency) and of lower amplitude than the alpha rhythm. Theta and delta rhythms are very slow and, if prominent, suggest abnormal brain function. An individual's EEG remains remarkably constant throughout most of adult life and major alterations are highly significant. The EEG is affected, characteristically, by sleep and the standard sleep pattern is strikingly disturbed during the periods of rapid-eye-movement (REM) sleep. It is affected by hyperventilation, drugs, concussion, brain injury and tumours, bleeding within the brain (*cerebral haemorrhage*), brain inflammation (*encephalitis*) and various psychiatric conditions. In particular, the EEG is affected by epilepsy, and is an important means of distinguishing the various forms of the condition. The EEG also assists in the determination of legal death and is important as an aid to making decisions about taking organs for transplantation.

electrolysis, the decomposition of a solution by the passage of an electric current, as, for instance, in the breakdown of slightly salty water into hydrogen and oxygen, by the action of an electric current. Positive ions (⇨ p. 88) are attracted to the negative electrode (*cathode*) and negative ions to the positive electrode (*anode*). The term is also used to refer to the process by which hair follicles are destroyed by the passage of a few milliamps of current through a needle inserted in the hair pore (DEPILATORY). In fact, although some electrolysis does occur, and bubbles of gas can be seen emerging from the pore, the main destructive effect is one of heating.

electrolyte, a solution that conducts electricity by virtue of the presence of positive or negative ions (⇨ p. 88). The term is also applied to substances that readily ionize in solution.

electromagnet, a magnet produced by the effect of a current flowing in a coil surrounding a soft iron core; ⇨ pp. 88–91.

electromagnetic radiation, the energy that results from the acceleration of electric charges. This energy is radiated through space (a vacuum) at the speed of light, in the form of oscillating electric and magnetic fields at right angles to each other and to the direction of propagation. Through various media the speed is slower. Electromagnetic radiation can also be regarded as a stream of photons travelling at the speed of light, each with an energy equal to Planck's constant multiplied by the speed of light, divided by the wavelength of the associated wave; ⇨ pp. 72–5, 84.

electron ⇨ pp. 90, 108–9 and 156–61.

electron-beam lithography, a method of etching very fine lines using a powerful beam of focused electrons (⇨ p. 90), used to prepare the masks for the production of electronic microchips.

electronic mail, the multi-way transmission of personal and business correspondence via digital communication channels (⇨ p. 220). One correspondent writes a letter, using a word processor, checks and corrects it, and then, using communications software, directs it to one or many other correspondents, situated in the same office or halfway round the world, on whose screen or screens it immediately appears. Printing and mailing are unnecessary, and copies can be kept on disk for later perusal by the sender and by all recipients.

electron microscope, a device that magnifies very small objects using an electron beam instead of visible light. The magnification of light microscopes is limited by the wavelength of light to about two thousand times because an object smaller than this cannot be resolved. To overcome this limitation a medium of shorter wavelength that can be deflected by lenses is required. A beam of accelerated electrons meets this requirement. The greater the momentum, the shorter the effective wavelength. Modern instruments enable objects smaller than one nanometre (one millionth of a millimetre) to be seen. This is almost down to atomic level. The transmission electron microscope is analogous in optical design to the light microscope. The source of electrons is a filament, similar to that in a television tube. Because electrons are negatively charged they are easily accelerated by high positive voltages (20,000 to well over

1,000,000 volts), and are easily deflected by electric or magnetic fields obtained from charged plates or current-carrying coils, respectively. The shape of these fields is determined by the physical shape of the plates or coils, and they can be arranged to have an effect on the electron beam, identical to that of optical lenses on light. The final image is produced on a fluorescent screen, as in a CATHODE-RAY TUBE or on photographic film or plate. Specimens for electron microscopy must be extremely thin and must be able to withstand the effects of the vacuum and the electron bombardment. Evaporated metal, such as platinum, may be deposited on the surface of the specimen to reveal topographical features. The scanning electron microscope operates in a manner similar to the way the electron beam in a television tube builds up the picture by moving rapidly over the inner surface of the tube. Specimens are metal coated and a very narrow electron beam scans the surface. Reflected or transmitted electrons are picked up by a device that produces a varying current. This is applied, as a video signal, to a television monitor synchronized with the microscope-beam deflection. Electron microscopes are tools of the highest importance in science, especially in biology. They have enormously extended our knowledge of the structure of cells and cell components. The science of virology has been revolutionised by electron microscopy.

electronvolt, a unit of energy equal to the work done in moving an electron (⇨ pp. 90, 108–17 and 156–61) through a potential difference (⇨ pp. 88–91) of one volt. The electronvolt is used as a measure of the energy of particles.

electrophoresis, the process by which charged particles in a solution (*ions*) are separated by the application of an electric current. Many substances ionize naturally when dissolved to give positive and negative particles. A molecule of common salt (NaCl), for instance, separates into two ions, a positively charged sodium ion (Na^+) and a negatively charged chlorine ion (Cl^-). If an electric current is applied to the solution, the positive ions are attracted to the negative electrode and the negative ions to the positive electrode. In electrophoresis the solution of the ions is spread out on a surface, such as filter paper or a gel, and the electric current is applied across it. The movement of the ions occurs on the surface and the extent of the movement is dependent on the molecular weight and the charge of the ions. Ions of low weight move more quickly than those of high weight, so separation occurs. After a time, the surface can be stained so that the characteristic patterns of separation can be recognized. In this way mixtures of substances can be separated. Electrophoresis is used, for instance, to separate mixtures of proteins. The technique is widely used in medicine to identify and measure the albumin, globulin, and fibrinogen (three kinds of plasma proteins) present in the blood and to separate the various globulin fractions constituting the different antibodies (immunoglobulins). It is used to identify the various abnormal haemoglobins causing sickle-cell anaemia and other similar conditions, and is a convenient way of separating and identifying the various kinds of low- and high-

density lipoproteins in people with abnormal blood-fat (*lipid*) levels.

electrostriction, the change in the dimensions of a body when placed in an electric field.

ELISA test, the enzyme-linked immunosorbent assay test. This is one of the most important tests used to identify antibodies in the blood, and is a commonly used screening test for AIDS. The test requires a sample of the organism (the *antigen*) whose antibody is being looked for. This sample is allowed to adhere to a hollow in a plastic plate, and the blood specimen that may possibly contain the antibody is added. If the specific antibody to the organism is present, it will attach itself to the antigen. The plate is now washed to remove any other antibodies. A substance called a ligand (⇨ pp. 182–5), chemically linked to the enzyme peroxidase, which can cause a colourless solution to become coloured, is now added. This substance will detect any antibody and will adhere to it. When the colourless solution is added, the colour appears and the test is positive for that antibody. If the antibody is not present, no colour will appear. The ELISA test can detect antibodies to anything from specific viruses to parasitic-worm proteins. Kits, for pathology laboratories, are produced to identify a very wide range of antibodies. The ELISA test for AIDS quickly attracted very large sums of money in the USA, and, since the AIDS virus was the antigen needed for the test, a dispute over the right to use it became a matter of contention between the Pasteur Institute in Paris and the National Cancer Institute, Bethesda, Maryland, both of whom claimed to have discovered the virus.

embalming, a method of temporarily preserving a dead body by removing the blood and replacing it with disinfectant and preservative fluids, such as formalin (formaldehyde), which discourage the growth of organisms responsible for putrefaction. It is of value if, for any reason, cremation or burial must be delayed. Embalming is often associated with cosmetic treatment intended to preserve, for a time, a life-like appearance.

embolism, the sudden blocking of an artery by solid, semi-solid or gaseous material brought to the site of the obstruction in the bloodstream. The object, or material, causing the embolism is called an *embolus*. It is always abnormal for any nonfluid material to be present in the circulation, and because blood proceeding through arteries encounters ever smaller branches, such material will inevitably impact and cause blockage, thereby depriving a part of the body of its essential blood supply. Several different forms of emboli occur. Embolism is commonly caused by blood-clot emboli, often arising in the veins and passing through the right side of the heart to enter the arteries carrying blood to the lungs. It may also be caused by crystals of cholesterol from plaques of atheroma in larger arteries, by clumps of infected material in severe injuries, by air or nitrogen in diving accidents, by bone marrow and fat in fractures of large bones, and by tumour cells and other substances.

embryo, a mammalian organism in the early stages of development following implantation into the wall of the womb. In humans, the embryo becomes a fetus at the end of the seventh or eighth week of life. During the embryonic stage, growth is rapid, the main organ systems become differentiated and the external features of the body become recognizably human.

emotion, a state of physiological arousal involving a mixed mental and bodily reaction to important events, or to memories of such events, that affect, or threaten to affect, our personal advantage. There are many different emotions – fear, anger, hate, disgust, disappointment, love, joy, jealousy, dread, grief, pride, shame, lust, cowardice – and all can involve strong feelings that may be pleasant or unpleasant. All are associated, to a greater or lesser degree, with physiological changes, such as a rapid heart beat, dry mouth, sweating palms, tense stomach, pallor, flushing or trembling. Although emotions are very varied, the physiological hormonal responses are few and amount to little more than the secretion of adrenaline and cortisol. An injection of adrenaline will produce either fear or pleasurable excitement depending on the external circumstances and the state of mind of the subject. Many of the emotions are common to a wide range of animals. Smiling, frowning, sneering, and so on, are not learned activities, but are an inherent result of our genetic make-up. Blind babies, who have never seen facial expression in others, still smile, laugh, cry and show fear and distress appropriately. The limbic system and the hypothalamus of the brain are the mediators of emotional expression and feeling. The hypothalamus lies immediately above the stalk of the pituitary gland and is intimately connected with it both by many nerve fibres and by hormonal means. The pituitary is the central controlling organ of the whole hormonal system. Mental activity and interpretation of events determine the kind of emotional response, in any given situation, and it is here, at the interface between neurological and hormonal action, that thought gives rise to the hormonal bodily response (*visceral arousal*), which is the necessary condition for emotional experience. The hormonal effect is diffuse and general; the specific type of emotion depends on the perception of the circumstances.

empirical, derived from observation or 'trial and error' rather than from logical theory or deduction. Based on practical experience rather than scientific proof.

emulator, an item of hardware or, more often, software by the use of which a computer of one kind can be made to behave as if it were of another kind so that programs intended for the latter can be run; ⇨ p. 218.

emulsion, a colloid in which, under the influence of an emulsifying agent, small particles of one liquid are evenly dispersed in another liquid. Most emulsions are of an oil in water or water in an oil. Emulsifying agents include soaps, DETERGENTS and bile salts.

endorphins,   morphine-like   substances

occurring in the animal and human for which specific receptor sites occur naturally. Endorphins consist of a sequence of five amino acids (an opioid core peptide). Endorphins are neurotransmitters and have a wide range of functions. They help to regulate heart action, general hormone function, the mechanisms of shock from blood loss and the perception of pain, and are believed to be involved, in some way, in controlling mood, emotion and motivation. They act on the centres of the brain concerned with the heart beat and the control of blood pressure and on the pituitary gland. Endorphins are also believed to be involved in the mechanisms that link stress with a reduction in pain perception, and this suggestion has given rise to the half-humorous suggestion that marathon runners get hooked on their own endorphins. There is also some interesting evidence that an increase in the levels of circulating endorphins occurs after one has been given a tablet that one believes to contain a pain-killing drug, even if it is an inactive placebo. Endorphins are also known as encephalins.

endoscopy, direct visual examination of any part of the interior of the body by means of an optical viewing instrument. The instrument may be introduced through a natural orifice – the nose, mouth, urethra or anus – or through a small surgical incision made for the purpose. Endoscopes are steerable, flexible, cylindrical instruments usually containing multiple channels and equipped with fibre optics for illumination and viewing. Other channels allow washing of the area under view, suction, gas inflation to ease viewing, the use of snares, cauteries, forceps and other small operating instruments, the use of lasers and the means of taking biopsy specimens. Much use is made of endoscopes by gastroenterologists for stomach and colon examination, by gynaecologists, especially for sterilization of women by tying off the fallopian tubes (*tubal ligation*), and by obstetricians for examining the fetus in the womb (*fetoscopy*).

endothelium, the single layer of cells lining the inside of BLOOD and lymphatic vessels, the inside of the heart and other cavities. The inner layer of the cornea is an endothelium. Most other surfaces in the body are covered with an EPITHELIUM.

energy, a measure of the ability to do work. Energy is expressed in the same units as work; ⇨ pp. 46–9.

energy bands, bands of allowed energies, each representing many quantum states that electrons can exist in in a crystalline solid. Between the energy bands are forbidden bands. The *valence band*, that with the highest energy, is formed from the outer electrons of the atoms – those participating in chemical bonds. The electrical properties of solids are determined by their band structure. Electrical conduction can occur only if there is an unfilled band – the *conduction band* – and this must be close to, or overlap, the valence band. In insulators these bands are separated by a wide forbidden band, which electrons do not have enough energy to cross. Semiconductors depend on energy bands

for their function.

enzyme, a biochemical catalyst that accelerates, or promotes, a chemical reaction (⇨ pp. 182–5).

ephemeral, a plant with a very short life cycle so that more than one generation can occur in a growing season. Many ephemerals are weeds. The term is also applied to animals, such as the mayfly, with a very short life.

epidemiology, the study of the occurrence of diseases in populations. Although epidemics commonly involve infectious diseases, epidemiology is concerned with the whole range of conditions that affect health, such as heart disease and cancer. It includes the study of the attack rate of the various diseases and the number of people suffering from each condition at any one time. Industrial and environmental health problems are an important aspect of epidemiology which is an essential factor in health administration and has contributed notably to medical research and knowledge. The relationship between cigarette smoking and both lung and circulatory disorders, for instance, was elicited largely from epidemiological studies.

epidermis, the outermost layer of the skin. The epidermis is structurally simple with no NERVES, BLOOD VESSELS, or hair FOLLICLES, and acts as a rapidly replaceable surface capable of tolerating much abrasion and trauma. The deepest layer of the epidermis is called the basal-cell layer, which contains the pigment melanin in a concentration that varies from person to person, thereby occasioning skin colour. Above the basal layer is the prickle-cell layer, where cells grow abnormally in common warts. The outermost cells of the epidermis are dead and are continuously shed.

epiglottis, a leaf-like cartilaginous structure, below and behind the back of the tongue, which acts as a 'lid' to cover the entrance to the voicebox (*larynx*) and prevent food or liquid entering it during the act of swallowing.

epiphysis, the growing sector at the end of a long bone. During the period of growth, the epiphysis is separated by a plate of cartilage from the shaft of the bone. The edge of this plate nearest the shaft becomes progressively converted into bone, while the other edge develops new cartilage. In this way, the bone lengthens. This process occurs under the control of the pituitary growth hormone. When body growth is complete, the epiphysis turns to bone, fusing the ends to the shaft. No further growth can occur.

epitaxy, a way of forming a thin layer of a material, such as gallium arsenide, on a base of another material so that semiconductors can be formed. Gallium arsenide, for instance, can be deposited by firing ions of the compound onto the base; ⇨ pp. 90–5.

epithelium, the coating tissue for all surfaces of the animal and body except the insides of blood and lymph vessels. Epithelium is a 'nonstick' surface which, in health, prevents layers from healing together. It may consist of a single

layer of cells, or it may be in several layers, with the cells becoming flatter and more scaly towards the surface, as in the skin (*stratified epithelium*). It may be covered with fine wafting hair-like structures of microscopic size (*cilia*) as in the respiratory tract and it may contain mucus-secreting cells.

epoxy resins, synthetic substances formed by polymerizing (⇨ p. 164) epoxide compounds and phenols. Epoxides are compounds containing an oxygen atom joined to two different groups that are themselves joined to other groups. They are usually thick liquids that can be hardened by the addition of substances that cause cross-linkages and are used as adhesives, insulators and structural materials, often reinforced by glass or other fibres.

EPROM, erasable programmable read-only memory, a non-volatile ROM whose stored material can be changed by the user.

equator, the diameter of any sphere that is equidistant from its poles; ⇨ the Earth's equator p. 144.

equilibrium, a state of balance or a stable condition in which forces cancel one another. A body in stable equilibrium will, after a slight displacement, return to its former position. Thermal equilibrium is the state of a body in which no net heat flow occurs between it and its surroundings.

equivalent weight, the weight of a substance that will combine with or displace 1 gram of hydrogen (or 8 grams of oxygen).

erase, to delete a computer file from the storage mechanism – usually a magnetic tape or disk – on which it has previously been saved. In the MS-DOS system the delete command ('del') is more commonly used. Deletion does not remove the magnetic record but merely frees the part of the disk so that it can be overwritten by subsequent data. At any time before this is done the erased file can be retrieved by a program in the disk-operating system. If another file is saved to the same area, however, the data is irretrievably lost; ⇨ pp. 216–19.

erection, a temporary state of enlargement and relative rigidity of the penis (*tumescence*), due to engorgement with blood under pressure, which makes insertion of the penis into the vagina possible. The penis contains three columns of spongy tissue, to which arteries are connected. When these are emptied of blood, the penis is small and flaccid; when full, the organ is erect.

escape velocity, the speed that a body must attain in order to escape from the gravitational attraction of another body. The escape velocity from Earth is 11,200 m/s; ⇨ p. 30.

ester, one of a class of compounds produced by a reaction between acids and alcohols with the elimination of water. Esters with low molecular weights are usually volatile liquids with a fragrant smell. Fats are solid molecules with three ester groups; ⇨ pp. 168 and 182–5.

ethyl group, the group C_2H_5; ⇨ p. 164.

etoilation, the pale, small leaves, abnormally long shoots and reduced root systems of plants grown in darkness.

eugenics, the control of human breeding by selective mating so as to 'improve' the stock. The term was coined in 1883 by the English scientist Francis Galton (1822–1911), when, influenced by his cousin Charles Darwin's theory of natural selection, he decided that the improvement of species, especially the human one, need not be left to the vicissitudes of chance. Eugenics raises so many questions of human rights and the dangers inherent in the exercise of such power, that, with a few exceptions, it has never been more than a theoretical consideration.

eunuch, a castrated man. The loss, prior to puberty, of the male sex hormones secreted in the testicles results in the failure of development of the secondary sexual characteristics – the beard, the enlarged voice box (*larynx*), the growth of the penis, and the characteristically male body shape and muscular development. After puberty, the physical effects of castration are barely discernible.

eustachian tube, a short passage leading backwards from the back of the nose, just above the soft palate, on either side, to the cavity of the middle ear. Air is able to pass to or from the middle ear cavity, depending on whether the pressure in the middle ear is higher or lower than atmospheric pressure. This balances the pressure on either side of the ear drum so that it can move freely in response to air vibrations.

eutheria, the subclass of mammals in which the embryos grow in the womb and the fetuses are nourished by a placenta.

evaporation, loss of some of the more energetic molecules of a liquid as a gas, at a temperature below the boiling point of the liquid. The loss of energetic molecules reduces the temperature of the liquid; ⇨ pp. 46–51.

excitation, the acquisition by a particle, atom, ion or molecule of energy that raises it to a quantum state higher than that of its lowest stable energy state (*ground state*); ⇨ p. 160.

executable file, a file that a computer can run as a functioning program and that has been compiled or assembled from the original source code; ⇨ p. 216.

exon, a base sequence in a gene that codes for the gene product, or part of it, or for a control operator. Exons are separated by non-coding lengths called *introns*; ⇨ p. 202.

exothermic reaction, one that releases heat into the surroundings; ⇨ p. 168.

exotoxin, a powerful poison, formed by certain types of bacteria, that is released by them and that may cause severe damage either locally or, if carried away by the blood, at a remote distance. The diphtheria organism, for instance, secretes an exotoxin that can destroy tissue lining the throat, where the organism settles, but that can also travel to damage the heart and the kidneys. Bacterial exotoxins are among the most poisonous substances known.

expansion card, a circuit-board card that can be plugged into a personal computer to increase its capabilities in one of many directions. Expansion cards may confer additional memory, extra disk controllers, modems, fax facilities, CD-ROM facilities and so on; ⇨ p. 218.

exponential, a function (⇨ p. 20) that varies as the power of another quantity. In the equation $y = ax$, y varies exponentially with x. In exponential growth of a group, the rate of growth is related to the number of individuals in the group, and is slow when the number is small and increasingly rapid as the number increases.

extrasensory perception, the claimed ability to convey information from one person to another without the use of any of the normal channels of communication. There are said to be four categories of extrasensory perception (ESP) – thought transfer (*telepathy*), seeing things not present to the senses (*clairvoyance*), foretelling the future (*precognition*) and knowing of past events without normal sources of evidence (*retrocognition*). Many people have had experiences that convince them that they have had some sort of preknowledge of a significant event. But coincidence makes such a strong impression that such events are remembered while the numerous occasions on which nothing of the kind happened are forgotten. Experiments purporting to prove ESP cannot, on demand, be replicated and it is fundamental to scientific acceptance that claims should be capable of independent verification anywhere. This requirement is particularly important when the basic laws of science are being challenged, for it is more reasonable to reject propositions of this kind, which cannot be verified, than to reject or modify laws that are eminently verifiable and that hold true in all other circumstances. Precognition, for instance, involves a reversal of the principle of causation, implying that an effect can precede a cause.

extrovert, the personality type of the individual whose concerns are directed outward rather than inward. The extrovert is active, optimistic, gregarious, talkative, impulsive, fond of jokes and of excitement, aggressive and sometimes unreliable. The concept was invented by the Swiss psychologist Carl Jung (1875–1961) who also described the opposite personality type, the *introvert*. No one is wholly extroverted or introverted, but many people show a fairly obvious trend in one or other of these directions. Also known as *extravert*.

facsimile (fax) transmission, electronic transmission of documents of any kind, including photographs, by a scanning system that converts the image into an analogue or digital (⇨ p. 202) signal that is passed to the receiving end where the image is reconstituted on paper. Telephone lines are commonly used for fax transmission.

factor VIII, one of the substances involved in the cascade of reactions that ends in the clotting of blood. Factor VIII is a soluble protein, a deficiency of which causes the condition of haemophilia. It can be made from genetically engineered cells in culture, thus obviating the former need for concentration from large quantities of donated blood.

faeces, intestinal waste material consisting mainly of bacteria, many of them dead, cast off cells from the lining of the intestine, various secretions from the cells of the intestinal wall and from the major glands opening into the intestine, bile secretions from the liver, and a small amount of food residue, mostly cellulose.

Fahrenheit scale, the temperature scale that, widely used for many years, has now long been replaced by the Celsius scale. In the Fahrenheit scale, the melting point of ice is 32°, and the boiling point of water is 212°. To convert Fahrenheit to Celsius, subtract 32 and multiply by 0.555 or $^5/_9$.

fallopian tube, the open-ended tube that conducts ova from the ovaries to the womb (*uterus*). The open end of each fallopian tube bears many tiny, muscular, finger-like processes, poised above the ovary. The inner surface of the fingers is lined with a membrane bearing millions of fine hairs (*cilia*), which move so as to waft small bodies into the tube. At the time the EGG is released (ovulation), these fingers sweep over the surface of the ovary, covering about two thirds of the upper surface. There is also a suction effect tending to draw material in. Ova must be fertilized in the tube if the timing of the subsequent development is to be correct for implantation. Therefore, the sperms must have made their way into the tube either just before or during the transit of the egg.

fallout, the deposition of radioactive particles produced by a nuclear explosion and carried by prevailing winds in the atmosphere often a long distance from the site of origin. The yield from high explosions may fall anywhere on the surface of the Earth and may continue for years. Fallout of isotopes with a long half-life, such as strontium–90 and iodine–131, is the most significant, as both will enter the food chain and have effects for many years.

family, a classification group in biology consisting of a number of closely related genera.

fascia, thin sheets or layers of tendon-like connective tissue that lies under the skin, between the muscles and around the organs, the BLOOD VESSELS and the NERVES, forming sheaths and compartments throughout the body. Some fascia is dense, some delicate, and much of it is bulked out by fat cells. The *superficial fascia* just under the skin is one of the main fat stores of the body.

fatigue, tiredness, which may be physical or mental. Physical fatigue is due to the accumulation, in the muscles, of the breakdown products of fuel consumption and energy production. A short period of rest will allow time for the normal blood flow through the muscles to 'wash out' these *metabolites*. In most cases, physical fatigue has a mental component, and sometimes purely mental fatigue masquerades as physical fatigue. Mental fatigue has nothing to do with overuse of the mental faculties. It is the result of over-long concentration on a single task, boredom, anxiety, frustration, fear or disinclination to perform particular work.

fault, a linear break in the Earth's crust with movement of the rock on one side of it relative to the rock on the other side. Movement may be horizontal, vertical or oblique.

femur, the thighbone of vertebrates and the third segment of the leg of insects.

Fermat's principle, the important proposition by the French mathematician Pierre de Fermat (1601–65) that the path taken by light between two points is always that which requires the least time. The laws of optics are based on this principle.

fermentation, a enzymatic respiratory process in yeasts and other microorganisms in which glucose is broken down to pyruvate (*glycolysis*) and, in the relative absence of oxygen, pyruvate is converted to ethyl alcohol (ethanol) and carbon dioxide. It is the evolution of the latter gas that suggested the term 'ferment'. Alcoholic drinks are produced by fermentation. Anaerobic glycolysis produces alcohol; aerobic glycolysis is the basis of energy production from food in humans and other animals.

fermions, subatomic particles whose spin can be expressed in half integers and obey Fermi-Dirac statistics. Protons, neutrons and electrons are fermions. Particles whose spins can be expressed as whole numbers are called *bosons*; ⇨ pp. 108–13.

ferrites, a group of magnetic ceramic compounds of the oxides of metals such as cobalt, manganese or zinc linked to iron oxides. Ferrites are not electrical conductors (⇨ p. 90) and avoid large EDDY CURRENTS. They are useful as magnetic cores in high- frequency circuits providing high inductance (⇨ p. 100) with low resistance (⇨ p. 96) and low losses.

fetus, a mammal in the developmental stages beyond that of the embryo, with features recognizable as those of the species. In humans, the individual from about eight weeks after conception until birth.

fever, elevation of body temperature above the normal range, which, in humans, is 37–37.5°C (98.4–99°F). Body temperature is kept within the normal range by a 'thermostat' mechanism in the hypothalamus region of the brain. This monitors the blood temperature and, if it is too high, causes the skin BLOOD VESSELS to widen and sweating to increase, so that heat is lost. If the temperature is too low, the muscles are induced to shiver so as to produce heat. In fever, however, the thermostat is reset at a

higher level and the normal blood temperature is read as being too low. Heat production is thus automatically increased.This resetting is done by a substance known as interleukin–1, which is released by certain white cells (known as *macrophages* and *monocytes*) under the influence of a range of substances called *exogenous pyrogens*. Interleukin–1, acting in the hypothalamus, causes the release of prostaglandins, which stimulate heat production in the muscles. Infecting organisms reproduce best at normal body temperature and are discouraged by fever, so it is not always desirable to bring down the temperature. But temperatures above about 44.5°C (112°F) usually cause fatal brain damage and urgent cooling of the body is vital.

Feynman diagram, a graphical representation in terms of quantum mechanics (⇨ p. 40) of the space-time events – the exchange of photons – involved in the interaction of subatomic particles such as the collision of a moving electron with a proton (⇨ pp. 108–17).

fibre, a long plant cell with its wall thickened with lignin. In zoology, any elongated cell, such as a muscle cell or a nerve cell, of an elongated collagen molecule. In human dietetics, fibre is the food residue for which digestive enzymes are not available. It consists of cellulose, hemicelluloses, lignins, pectins, gums and mucilages, and may be soluble or insoluble. Soluble fibre such as pectins and gums can bind the cholesterol in bile so that it is not reabsorbed by the gut.

fibre optics, a branch of optics concerned with the transmission of light along optical fibres – fine, flexible rods of glass or other transparent materials. Fibre optics have become increasingly important in communications and in situations requiring direct visual inspection of inaccessible cavities as in medicine and surgery. Optical fibres are used to guide light – for both illumination and viewing – around complex bends or sharp corners by making use of the principle of total internal reflection (⇨ pp. 72–5 and 78). Fibres with a diameter of as little as 0.02 mm are arranged in tight bundles and, as long as the fibres remain in registration at both ends of the bundle, they can be bent and manoeuvred into otherwise inaccessible places. 'Steerable' endoscopes are extensively used in medicine.

fibrin, the insoluble protein that binds together the edges of a wound and forms the basis of blood clots.

fibrosis, scarring and thickening of an organ or surface by the laying down of fibrous (*scar*) tissue, usually following injury or inflammation. Fibrosis is the body's main healing process, and the scar tissue formed is usually very strong.

fibula, the slender splint bone on the outer side of the main bone (the *tibia*) of the lower leg. The fibula is fixed to the tibia by ligaments and helps to form the ankle joint, but plays little part in weight bearing.

field, the region in which a body experiences a

force occasioned by another body. Fields may be gravitational, magnetic or electric and the force may be attractive or repulsive; ⇨ p. 28.

fifth-generation computers, intelligent machines using parallel computing (⇨ p. 226) and applying knowledge-based systems and human interfaces allowing speech recognition and synthesized-speech output.

film badge, a method of monitoring the risks of excessive radiation dosage in people working in environments in which exposure to radiation (⇨ p. 160) is possible. The film badge is a small light-tight container for a piece of photographic film, which would be fogged if exposed to radiation. All personnel at risk carry film badges, usually pinned to the clothing, and the films are regularly developed and replaced. A fogged film indicates that an accident has occurred and this can be investigated.

filtration, the process of separation of solid particles from a liquid in which they are suspended by passing the liquid through a medium having interstices smaller than the particles. The use of any device that changes the relative amplitude of different wavelengths, as in the use of photographic or electronic filters.

fixed stars, stars that do not appear to change their position on the celestial sphere (⇨ p. 144). The fixity is not absolute, but is relative to the comparatively rapid motion of the planets of our solar system.

flagellum, a whip-like, usually propulsive, structure on many single-celled organisms, such as some bacteria and protozoa, and on spermatozoa. Some organisms use the flagellum to move surrounding water; ⇨ pp. 186–91.

flame, the luminous effect of high-temperature combustion of gases caused by the excitation of molecules or incandescent carbon and other particles. Chemical reactions in a flame are mainly FREE- RADICAL chain reactions.

flash point, the temperature at which an evaporating inflammable liquid forms a mixture with air that can briefly ignite.

fleas, small wingless, bloodsucking insects of the order *Siphonaptera*, that feed on warm-blooded animals, including humans. Fleas have enormously well-developed muscular hindlegs that are adapted for jumping and that confer a remarkable performance. The Oriental rat flea, *Xenopsylla cheopis,* is the transmitter of bubonic plague from rats to humans. Rat fleas also transmit mouse typhus to humans.

Fleming's right-hand rule, a mnemonic for the directions of the magnetic FIELD, current and force in an electrical generator. The forefinger points forwards, the thumb upwards and the second finger to the left, all three being at right angles to each other. If the second finger shows the direction of the current, the forefinger will show the direction of the magnetic field, and the thumb will show the direction of the force. The rule was proposed by the English electrical engineer Sir John Ambrose Fleming

(1849–1945). The analogous left-hand rule applies to electric motors.

flies, insects with one pair of wings, of the Order *Diptera*. Flies include mosquitoes, biting midges, biting blackflies, sandflies, gadflies, blowflies, botflies, Tsetse flies and the common house fly *Musca domestica*. Sandflies cause irritating bites and transmit sandfly fever, and Leishmaniasis. Mosquitos also cause persistently irritating bites and transmit malaria, yellow fever, filariasis, and dengue. Midges often attack in swarms, causing multiple skin bumps and sometimes fever and general upset. Blackflies transmit the form of filariasis known as river blindness (*onchocerciasis*). The common housefly is a notorious vector of typhoid, bacillary dysentery (*shigellosis*) and amoebic dysentery. Almost any organism that can contaminate food can be spread by the housefly. In endemic areas of the world, the blinding disease trachoma is spread from eye to eye by this vector.

floppy disk, a thin disk of flexible plastic, coated with a magnetic material that can rotate within a suitably protective container. The whole is slotted into a personal-computer disk drive with an electromagnetic read-write head that bears on the surface of the disk to 'play-back' previously recorded binary data, or to save a copy of data produced in, and temporarily or permanently stored in, the machine; ⇨ p. 216.

fluorescence, light emission not associated with a rise in temperature. Fluorescence occurs when atoms that have been excited by ambient photons (⇨ p. 108) or by chemical reaction (⇨ p. 168) return to the ground state, emitting photons as they do so. Also known as *luminescence*.

fluoridation, the deliberate addition of compounds of fluorine to drinking-water supplies in areas deficient in fluoride. The practice is based on the knowledge that an appropriate level of fluoride in water – about one part per million – promotes stronger and healthier teeth, with reduced tendency to caries.

fluorocarbons, compounds formed when the hydrogen atoms of hydrocarbons are replaced by fluorine atoms. Such compounds are very stable and inert, and have many uses.

focus, a point in an optical or other radiational system towards which, or at which, rays converge. In optical systems, the *focal length* of a lens is the distance from the centre of the lens to the point of principal focus; ⇨ p. 78.

folic acid, a vitamin of the B group necessary for the synthesis of DNA and red blood cells. Folic acid is plentiful in leafy vegetables and in liver but is also produced by bacteria in the bowel and then absorbed into the circulation. Because of this, a deficiency may occur when people are treated with powerful antibiotics, which kill the bacteria, or with sulphonamides, which interfere with the synthesis, by the bacteria, of the vitamin.

follicle, a depression or cavity, of a sac-like, glandular or cystic nature. Examples are hair follicles, which generate hairs, and the Graafian follicles of the ovaries, which contain the ova prior to ovulation.

fontanelle, a bony deficit in the skull of a young baby. The vault of the growing skull of the baby and young infant is made of separate plates of bone, which are close together except at the points where more than two meet. Towards the front of the vertex of the head, the meeting of four large plates – the two forehead (*frontal*) bones and the two side (*parietal*) bones – leaves a central gap known as the *anterior fontanelle*. The rear (*posterior*) fontanelle also lies centrally between the two parietal bones and the single rear occipital bone. The fontanelles are covered by scalp and skin and can easily be felt, as soft depressions, by gentle pressure with the fingers. They allow moulding of the skull during birth and allow for growth of the bone. The anterior fontanelle normally closes between 10 and 14 months of age, but the limits are wide and may extend from three to 18 months. The posterior fontanelle usually closes after two months.

food irradiation, the treatment of food by strong ionizing radiation, such as gamma rays (⇨ p. 160), so as to kill bacteria and insect pests and to delay natural changes in fruit and vegetables. Irradiation does not eliminate existing toxins or viruses. If the food is tightly sealed in a container, such as a polythene bag, before irradiation, contained organisms are destroyed and further contamination does not occur. Food irradiation by gamma rays does not induce radioactivity; the effects are chemical only. The main effect is the production of highly reactive, short-lived substances (*free radicals*), which can cause cell death in living organisms. Food molecules are also affected and there may be changes in flavour and some loss of vitamins. A committee of the World Health Organization has expressed the view that irradiation of any food commodity, up to a dose of one million rads, would present no nutritional or bacteriological hazard to the consumer. WHO experts point out the benefits of irradiation – the destruction of disease germs, such as salmonella in poultry, and the prolongation of shelf-life, increasing the food supply. Food irradiation is employed in at least forty countries.

foramen, a natural hole in a bone, for the passage of some other structure such as a NERVE, ARTERY or a VEIN.

force, any influence that causes a resting body to move, or that changes the momentum of a moving body. The magnitude of the force is equal to the product of the mass of the body and its acceleration. Any influence that produces an elastic strain in a body or system or that sustains weight; ⇨ pp. 26–33.

forensic medicine, the application of science in the investigation of criminal cases. Forensic scientists must be experts in the science of disease processes (*pathology*), in the action of poisons (*toxicology*), in the actions and effects of firearms and other offensive weapons, in the sign of assault, in some aspects of dentistry, and in the principles of determining the time of death. They are concerned with establishing the cause of death, and will usually perform a postmortem examination (*autopsy*) on the victim to determine signs of injury or disease that may have contributed to the death. They must be familiar with the detection of the presence of poisons or drugs found in a victim's body. Forensic anthropology is a speciality concerned with the study of human bones and skeletal remains and, if possible, the reconstruction from these of an identifiable image of the deceased. Forensic dentistry applies dental evidence to the identification of human remains, and is concerned mainly with bite-mark impressions. Forensic chemists and biologists are concerned with the evidential significance of materials such as dust, soil, skin scrapings, hair, seminal fluid, blood, natural and synthetic fibres, paint chips, fingerprints and many others. Genetic fingerprinting has become an important means of identification or elimination of suspects.

formatting, the initialization of a computer disk by erasing the addresses of all prior material, recording on it a standard pattern of magnetic sectors to receive data, the checking of these sectors and the noting of those that are unreliable so that they will not be used. Files cannot be saved to floppy disks until they have been formatted. This is done by putting the disk in the drive and issuing the format command; ⇨ p. 218.

formula, in chemistry (⇨ chapter 8), a representation of a compound using agreed symbols for the atoms. Molecular formulae give the types and numbers of the atoms present, as in H_2SO_4. A structural formula indicates something of the ways the atoms are related in space and linked. In mathematics, a formula is a proposition or physical law expressed in algebraic symbols, often as an equation; ⇨ p. 20.

fourth dimension, in the context of the space–time continuum, time; ⇨ p. 38.

fractal, a curve or area produced by repetitive reproduction of the same polygonal or polyhedral shape in fixed subdivided dimensions.

free fall, movement under the influence of gravitation that is not impeded by frictional resistance. Free fall acceleration is constant; ⇨ pp. 28–33.

free radical, an atom or group of atoms with an unpaired valence electron (⇨ p. 156), formed when a chemical bond is broken but an ion is not formed. Free radicals are highly reactive and destructive and commonly form chain reactions (⇨ p. 160). They can be formed by the action of a wide spectrum of radiation, by heat and by various chemical agencies. Oxygen free radicals are responsible for much of the cellular and tissue damage occurring in various disease processes, and are implicated in the damage caused to the body by smoking cigarettes.

free space, an imaginary region containing no matter and no gravitational or electromagnetic fields, a temperature of *absolute zero* and a refractive index of one. If light were to pass through free space, its speed would be maximal (*c*); ⇨ p. 38.

frequency, the number of repetitions of a regularly-occurring event in a given time. The term is most commonly applied to a wave oscillation and expressed in cycles per second (Hertz or Hz). Because electromagnetic waves (⇨ p. 84) have a constant speed in a vacuum, there is a fixed reciprocal relationship between frequency and wavelength (frequency = velocity divided by wavelength; ⇨ pp. 64–7).

front, the interface between air masses of different temperatures and humidity. Warm fronts usually occur at the front of DEPRESSIONS; cold fronts at the rear of them. The latter are associated with heavy rain.

fructose, a simple sugar (monosaccharide) found in most fruits, in sugarcane and sugar beets. In domestic 'sugar', fructose is linked to another monosaccharide, glucose, to form the disaccharide sucrose. Fructose is sweeter than glucose, but provides the same energy value; ⇨ pp. 182–5.

fruit, the structure formed from the ovary of a plant with ovules (the small bodies that develop into seeds) enclosed in an ovary (angiosperm), usually after fertilization of the ovules.

function, a relationship between variables such that a change in one will result in a corresponding change in the other. If a change in *a* results in a change in *b*, then *b* is the *dependent variable* and *a* is the *independent variable*; ⇨ p. 20.

fuzzy logic, computer logical processes that do not require precision or certainty in their data but can operate on degrees of truth or falsity. This approximates more closely to human logical processes, and is of major interest to those dealing with artificial intelligence and neural networks (⇨ p. 226).

gain, the increase in voltage (⇨ p. 90) or power produced by an amplifier.

galaxy cluster, galaxies, mainly in groups of hundreds to thousands, but sometimes containing fewer than a hundred; ⇨ pp. 140–3.

Galileo spacecraft, an exploratory NASA spacecraft launched in 1989 and scheduled to reach Jupiter in 1995 and to remain permanently in orbit around that planet. The craft uses a plutonium generator.

gall bladder, a small, pear-shaped sac, lying just under the LIVER, which stores and concentrates the bile secreted by the liver. The gall bladder empties, by way of the bile duct, into the DUODENUM, at the start of the small intestine. When a fatty meal is eaten, the presence of fat in the intestine releases a hormone, cholecystokinin, which enters the BLOOD, circulates to the biliary system and causes the muscle fibres in the wall of the gall bladder to contract.

galliformes, the order of birds that contains, among others, grouse, turkeys, pheasants, partridges and quails.

gallium arsenide, a semiconductor compound used in the manufacture of high-speed, low-power-consumption, microelectronic, integrated circuits. Gallium arsenide chips are more expensive to make than silicon chips. Ion beam EPITAXY is usually employed; ⇨ p. 90.

galvanometer, a sensitive instrument for measuring small electric currents. Most galvanometers are of the moving-coil type, in which a coil of fine insulated wire can rotate between the poles of a strong permanent magnet (⇨ p. 88). The current to be measured is passed through the coil and produces a magnetic field that interacts with the field of the permanent magnet to cause the coil to turn against the resistance (⇨ p. 96) of a light hairspring. The coil carries a light pointer, or a small mirror to deflect a beam of light across a scale ('weightless pointer'). The stronger the current, the greater the deflection of the pointer or beam; ⇨ p. 90.

gamete, a sperm or an egg. Male and female gametes fuse in the act of fertilization to form a *zygote* from which a new individual can develop.

game theory, a method of mathematical analysis applied to models of various kinds of competition, such as wars and economic rivalry, designed to establish the best strategies for solving complex problems.

gametophyte, the stage or generation in the life cycle of a plant in which the GAMETES are produced.

gamma globulin, the most prevalent of the five classes of immunoglobulins in humans. Gamma globulin provides the body's main defence against bacteria, viruses and toxins. Gamma globulin is so widely effective that it is produced commercially, from pooled human plasma, and used as a means of passive protection against many infections including hepatitis A and B, chickenpox, measles and poliomyelitis. It is also very useful for people who have an inherent or acquired immune deficiency, such as the condition of *agammaglobulinaemia*.

gamma-ray astronomy, the study of any information that can be derived from gamma rays of astronomical origin. This includes the formation of matter within and between the stars and the origin of cosmic rays. Celestial gamma rays were first detected by an American satellite in 1972 and it was soon found that the gamma-radiation intensity was highest from those regions of the galaxy where matter is most dense. Two pulsars (⇨ pp. 140–3) were found to be emitting gamma rays in pulses, and gamma rays were found to be coming from quasars and radio stars. Gamma rays are detected by batteries of scintillators using substances that emit visible light when struck by gamma rays. Some high-energy gamma rays even produce flashes of light in the atmosphere.

ganglion, a collection of nerve-cell bodies outside the central nervous system, with nerve fibre interconnections. Collections of nerve cells inside the central nervous system are called *nuclei*; ⇨ p. 188.

gangrene, tissue death, usually from an inadequacy of the blood supply to the affected part. The commonest cause of this is the arterial disease *atherosclerosis*. Other important causes include EMBOLISM, THROMBOSIS, severe arterial injury and the obstructive arterial condition affecting smokers, Buerger's disease (*thromboangiitis obliterans*). Mechanical obstruction to the arterial-blood supply can cause gangrene, as occurs in the bowel with a strangulated hernia or a gangrenous appendix. If infection is avoided, the affected part becomes dry and turns brown or black. At the interface between dead and living tissue is a zone of inflammation; sometimes this marks the plane of cleavage at which the dead part drops off. This form of 'dry' gangrene is commonest in the smaller extremities, such as the fingers and toes. When infection takes place, putrefaction occurs, producing the 'wet' type of gangrene.

garbage in–garbage out (GIGO), a slang expression of the fact that a computer supplied with defective data or programs will respond with rubbish, if it responds at all; ⇨ pp. 216–19.

garnet, a dense crystalline silicate material containing iron, manganese, magnesium, calcium, aluminium and chromium. Garnets are hard enough to be useful abrasives (6–7 on the Mohs scale compared with 10 for diamond), and are valued as semi-precious gemstones.

gas, a phase of matter featuring relatively wide separation of molecules, high fluidity, low density and a tendency to fill any container; ⇨ p. 50.

gastrin, a hormone, stimulated by the presence of food in the stomach, that promotes the secretion of hydrochloric acid and the digestive enzyme (⇨ pp. 182–5) pepsin.

gastrolith, a pebble swallowed by an animal and retained in the stomach to help in grinding up food.

Gastropoda, the snails, the largest class in the Mollusca phylum, numbering some 74,000.

gaussmeter, an instrument for measuring the strength of a magnetic field; ⇨ p. 88.

Geiger counter, an instrument used to detect and measure radiation capable of causing ionization (ionizing radiation). The Geiger counter consists of a sealed tube containing gas, such as neon or argon, and a two electrodes with a potential difference of about 1,000 volts between them. If a quantum of radiation causes an ion to form in the gas, this ion, being a charged particle, is strongly attracted to one of the electrodes. Its velocity causes an avalanche of collisions and further ionizations and a spike of current passes between the electrodes causing an electrical pulse that can be heard as a sound in a loudspeaker or shown as a sudden brief deflection of the needle on an electric meter. Heavy ambient radiation causes a sustained sound or a persistent deflection of the meter. This can be calibrated in units of received radiation. The counter was invented in 1908 by the German physicist Hans Geiger (1882–1945).

Geissler tube, a tube that shows the lighting effect of the passage of an electric current between electrodes through ionized, low-pressure gas, and that can be used as a light source for spectroscopy (⇨ p. 80). The tube was developed by the German mechanic Heinrich Geissler (1814–79).

gel, a substance containing dispersed fine particles of another substance, that has condensed into a solid, semi-solid or jelly-like state by developing a loose network of linked molecules of the dispersed material; ⇨ p. 164.

gelatine, a protein obtained from animal collagen by boiling it with water and filtering and evaporating the solution to form clear or slightly yellow 'pearls', slabs or sheets. Gelatine swells in cold water but does not dissolve. It is soluble in hot water and a 1 per cent or stronger solution forms a GEL on cooling. It has extensive uses as an adhesive, a clarifying agent, in cooking and confectionery, in photographic emulsions, capsules for medication, bacteriological culture plates and surgical foam to control bleeding.

gene cloning, a method of obtaining large numbers of copies of a gene. The required gene sequences are removed from DNA (⇨ p. 202) using restriction enzymes and are inserted into the DNA of an organism such as a bacterium. This is then cultured under ideal conditions for reproduction, so that millions of identical offspring, each containing a copy of the gene, are produced.

gene pool, all the genes of a population of organisms; ⇨ pp. 202–5.

genome, the total of the genes of one each of the pairs of all the chromosomes of an organism; ⇨ pp. 202–5.

genome mapping, the determination of the entire base sequence of the DNA (⇨ p. 202) of an organism and hence the sequence of proteins that it programs. The human genome is currently being mapped in an enormous project that was started in 1988. This genome contains about 3,000 million (6 billion) base pairs in about 100,000 genes. It is the sequence of these bases, along the length of each chromosome, that has to be determined. This is thus a scientific task of greater size than anything previously attempted. Using manual methods, a research worker could decode up to 100,000 bases a year. So it would take one worker 30,000 years to do the job. Fortunately, automatic sequencing machines have been developed that make the task feasible.

genotype, the genetic composition of an organism. Compare *phenotype,* which is the totality of the characteristics determined by the genotype; ⇨ p. 202.

genus, in biology a group of closely related species.

geochemistry, the study of the chemical composition of the Earth's crust; ⇨ p. 146.

geodesic, a straight line joining two points on any surface including curved surfaces.

geological time scale, the period from the formation of the Earth to the present. The timescale is divided into four eras – the Precambrian (4.5 billion years to 570 million years ago), Palaeozoic (570 million years to 230 million years ago), Mesozoic (230 million years to 65 million years ago) and Cenozoic (65 million years ago to the present). The Cambrian is the first 70 million years of the Palaeozoic era and the Precambrian is the whole period before that. The root *-zoic* means 'pertaining to life'. *Palaeo* means 'ancient'; *meso* means 'middle'; and *ceno* means 'modern'. In the Palaeozoic era, the Cambrian period is followed by the Ordovician (500–435 million years ago), Silurian (435–400), Devonian (400–345), Carboniferous (345–280) and the Permian (280–230). The periods in the Mesozoic era are the Triassic (230–195), the Jurassic (195–140) and the Cretaceous (140–65). And in the Cenozoic era the periods are the Tertiary (65–2 million years ago) and the Quaternary (2 million years ago to the present).

geology, the study of the Earth, its origins, structure, GEOCHEMISTRY, GEOPHYSICS, mineralogy, fossil content (palaeontology), rock formation (stratigraphy) and age; ⇨ pp. 146–51.

geomagnetism, the study of the Earth's magnetic field; ⇨ p. 146.

geometrical optics, the geometry of light rays passing through optical systems and forming images.

geometric series, a series of numbers with a constant ratio between successive terms, as in 1, 3, 9, 27, 81, 243. Compare *arithmetic series* in which there is a constant difference between successive terms, as in 1, 4, 7, 10, 13.

geomorphology, the study of the origin and evolution of the shape and structure of the land masses of the earth.

geophysics, the study of the physical properties of the Earth. Geophysics includes such subjects as geothermometry, seismology, glaciology, oceanography, geomagnetism and geochronology; ⇨ pp. 146–9.

geostationary orbit, the orbit of a satellite that makes exactly one rotation of the Earth in the time taken for the Earth to rotate on its axis. If it is in the equatorial plane (⇨ p. 144), the satellite will remain permanently above the same point on the Earth's surface and will appear to be stationary. Such a satellite will be at an altitude of 35,900 km (22,307 mi).

germanium, the semiconductor element from which the earliest transistors were made.

Germanium has been largely replaced by silicon.

gerontology, the study of the changes that occur with age in the cells and tissues of the body. These changes, both of structure and of function, tend gradually to limit the body's ability to respond to and adapt to changing stimuli, until, eventually, the cells cease to reproduce themselves and die. It seems to be an inherent characteristic of normal human cells that they are able to undergo a limited number of divisions. This imposes a finite maximum life span, in the human species, of about one hundred and ten years. At about this age, regardless of how healthy they may have been, people may be expected to die. Increasing longevity merely means that people are approaching ever nearer to the maximum. Ageing is an intrinsic property of all normal living organisms, but there are certain tissues that do seem to be immortal. Normal human tissue cultures in the laboratory undergo between fifty and one hundred generations, thereafter gradually losing their power of reproduction. Some cancer cells, on the other hand, go on dividing indefinitely, as long as they are kept in suitable conditions and provided with nourishment. Studies of human tissue cultures are being closely pursued and are an important aspect of gerontology. Other concerns of gerontology include the relationship of the biological to the temporal age, the reasons for cell death and for the loss of structural bulk in organs with age, the biochemical changes in ageing individuals, the age structures of different populations, the effects of lifestyle and physical activity on longevity, and the changing age patterns in a given population.

gestation period, the time from fertilization to birth in mammals. This varies widely in different species, covering a range of a very few weeks to over a year. The human gestation period averages 40 weeks (270–95 days).

gigantism, the state of any organism that has grown to a size beyond the upper limit of the normal range. Gigantism is usually caused by the excessive production of pituitary-gland growth hormone early in life, before the growing ends of the bones (the EPIPHYSES) have fused. Human gigantism is rare and is almost always due to a nonmalignant (benign) tumour of the gland – a *pituitary adenoma.* The result of the excessive production of hormone is that the rate of growth of all parts – both bones and soft tissue – is uniformly increased. Height may exceed 2.4 m (94 in). There is often delayed puberty and underproduction of the sex hormones.

gills, structures, especially in fish, through which materials in solution, such as ammonia and urea, and gases, such as oxygen and carbon dioxide, may be exchanged between water and the blood.

gland, a cell or organ that synthesizes or selects substances from the BLOOD and secretes them into or onto other bodily structures. The simplest glands are the mucus-secreting goblet cells of the intestine. The most complex are major organs such as the PANCREAS, which is a gland both of internal (*endocrine*) secretion in its production of insulin, and of external secretion in its production of the intestinal juice, rich in digestive enzymes, which it passes into the small intestine. Most of the glands of the endocrine system are pure glands of internal secretion and produce several different hormones. They include the PITUITARY GLAND, the thyroid, the parathyroids, the adrenal glands and those parts of the testes and ovaries not concerned with sperm and egg production. The glands of external secretion (*exocrine glands*) discharge their products onto a surface, either directly or through ducts. They include the millions of glands in the inner lining of the intestines, the sweat glands, the tear glands, the salivary glands, the milk (mammary) glands, and the mucus glands of the genitalia that lubricate sexual intercourse. The popularly described 'glands' of the neck, groin and elsewhere, which become swollen and sometimes tender during infections, are not glands, but lymph nodes.

glass, a material made by melting together certain material, such as silicates, sodium carbonate (soda) and calcium oxide (lime), and then cooling the melt in such a way that the materials do not crystallize but remain in an amorphous state as a highly viscous liquid.

globular protein, one of the two classes of protein, the other being the fibrous proteins. The class of globular proteins includes albumin, globulin, haemoglobin and casein. Globular protein molecules are roughly spherical; fibrous protein molecules are elongated; ⇨ pp. 182–5.

globulins, one of the main groups of soluble protein substances found in the BLOOD, the others being the albumins and fibrinogen. The animal globulins form the family of *immunoglobulins*, or ANTIBODIES, and are divided into five classes, each of which contains thousands of different individual and unique antibodies. The term 'immunoglobulin' is usually abbreviated to 'Ig', and the five classes are IgG (GAMMA GLOBULIN) and IgM, which, between them, combat most bacteria and viruses; IgE, connected with allergy; IgA, which operates mainly in the intestine, lungs and urinary system and which is the main group of antibodies in milk; and IgD, whose function is still uncertain. The globulins are produced by plasma cells, which arise from selected B cells (B lymphocytes) of the immune system, following an infection or invasion of foreign matter.

glottis, a term applied both to the narrow, slit-like opening between the vocal cords and to the whole vocal apparatus, consisting of the true and false vocal cords and the spaces between them. The glottis is the narrowest, and thus the most vulnerable part of the airway. Any swelling here can be rapidly fatal by cutting off the supply of air to the lungs. Oedema of the glottis may occur from acute allergic conditions or from local irritation or injury. In such a case, an artificial opening into the windpipe (*tracheostomy*) may be the only hope of saving life.

glucagon, a protein hormone produced by the Islet cells of the pancreas, that has an effect opposite to that of insulin. By causing GLYCOGEN, stored in the liver, to break down to glucose, a process known as *gluconeogenesis*, it increases the amount of sugar in the bloodstream. Glucagon is also involved in the mobilization of fatty acids for energy purposes. It is used as an emergency measure if the blood sugar levels are dangerously low and must be rapidly raised. In this case a glucagon injection can save brain damage or even life.

glucose, a simple sugar (monosaccharide carbohydrate) of central importance in the animal body. It is also known as dextrose, grape sugar or corn sugar and is present in the diet in natural form, or derived from the breakdown in the intestine of more complex sugars, disaccharides and polysaccharides, such as sucrose, fructose, galactose and starch. Glucose is the basic fuel of the body; ⇨ pp. 182–5.

gluten, the insoluble protein constituent of wheat, consisting of the proteins gliadin and glutenin. As the name suggests, gluten is an adhesive. It is insoluble, but can be washed out of flour and gives dough and uncooked pasta its characteristic elastic quality.

gluteus maximus, the largest of the three flat muscles that form each buttock. The others are gluteus medius and gluteus minimus.

glycogen, the primary fuel store of the body. Glycogen is a polysaccharide formed from many molecules of the monosaccharide glucose and is stored in the liver and in the muscles. It is sometimes called 'animal starch'. It is a white powder that dissolves readily in cold water, forming an opalescent, colloidal solution. Its chemical structure resembles that of starch and it is readily broken down by enzymes to release many glucose molecules for use as fuel.

Gödel's theorem, a proposition by the American mathematician Kurt Gödel (1906–78) to the effect that in a formal axiomatic system, such as logic or mathematics, it is impossible to prove everything within the system without using methods from outside the system. All such logical systems must contain more statements than can be proved using their own set of rules. Some have taken Gödel's theorem to indicate that a computing system can never exceed human intelligence because its knowledge is restricted to the fixed set of axioms built in by the programmers, while humans can discover new concepts; ⇨ p. 226.

gonads, the sex glands, consisting of the OVARIES in the female and the testicles (testes) in the male. In addition to producing the ova and sperms the gonads secrete sex hormones, respectively oestrogen and testosterone, which bring about the growth of the sex organs and the development of the secondary sexual characteristics at puberty. The production of sex hormones by the gonads is under the control of the gonadotrophic hormones produced by the front (anterior) lobe of the PITUITARY GLAND.

grand unified theories, theories attempting to find a single combined explanation for electromagnetic, strong nuclear and weak nuclear forces. A fully unified theory would also include gravitational force; ⇨ p. 112.

graphical user interface (GUI), a program interposed between the user and the operating system of a computer to provide a more 'friendly' system of operation, usually involving screen symbols and a MOUSE. Commands are issued by moving the cursor to the desired symbol and 'clicking' the mouse button.

gravitons, hypothetical particles that convey gravitational force in the way that photons convey electromagnetism; ⇨ p. 110.

great attractor, a hypothetical mass of great magnitude that is causing the Milky Way and associated galaxies to move towards it; ⇨ pp. 140–3.

great circle, the circle 'cut' on the Earth's surface by a plane that passes through the centre of the globe. Segments of great circles offer the shortest route between two points on the surface and such routes are usually taken by long-distance aircraft and ships. Radio waves also travel along great-circle paths.

grey matter, those areas of the central nervous system that consist largely of nerve-cell bodies. In the brain, the grey matter consists of the convoluted outer layer (the *cortex*) and a number of internal cell masses called *nuclei*. In the cord, the white fibres run up and down in the outer layers while the grey matter occupies a central column.

groin, the area of the sloping crease where the thigh joins the ABDOMEN. The main feature of the groin is a strong ligament running outward and upward from the pubic bone to the bony prominence on the front of the hip, immediately under the crease. In males, the spermatic cord runs over this ligament and some of the muscles of the abdominal wall are attached to it. The main BLOOD VESSELS to the leg run under the groin ligament (*inguinal* ligament) and it is surrounded by a number of prominent lymph nodes. These become enlarged, and sometimes tender to pressure, in the presence of any significant infection anywhere in the leg or the genitalia. Both femoral and inguinal hernias appear in the groin region. The groin should not be confused with the loin, which is the area of the back, just under the ribs.

ground state, the natural state of lowest energy of a particle, atom or molecule that is in its least excited condition; ⇨ p. 160.

growth, increase of any quantity. Animal growth is a feature of the first period of life and the attainable size and height of an individual is genetically determined, but also influenced by many environmental factors, such as malnutrition, that can limit it. Malnutrition is most influential very early in life. In humans, there are two periods of maximal growth rate. The first, up to the age of two, is really an extension of the extraordinarily rapid period of fetal growth. The second period starts at puberty and progresses until the early twenties. All body growth is normally complete by the age of twenty-five. Body growth occurs under the influence of GROWTH HORMONE and other hormones including thyroid hormone, which controls the rate of tissue buildup and breakdown (metabolism; ⇨ pp. 182–5); insulin, which controls the levels of fuel (glucose) in the blood and its rate of utilization; and sex hormones (androgens and oestrogens), which control the development of the male and female sexual characteristics, including body shape and bulk.

growth hormone, the hormone produced by the PITUITARY GLAND that promotes the growth of many animals and of humans. Increase in body length occurs at the growing ends of the long bones of the skeleton. These have growth zones called EPIPHYSES, which remain active until the end of adolescence and then fuse with the rest of the bone. The pituitary growth hormone somatotrophin controls this process. Normal growth in bulk, as distinct from height, is essentially a matter of protein production. Growth hormone, in addition to causing elongation of the body, also promotes the synthesis of protein in many tissues other than bone. It does this by increasing the transport of AMINO ACIDS into cells and by boosting the activity of RNA and ribosomes within the cells. It also causes a major increase in the rate of cell division, and hence reproduction, which is another central element in growth. Deficiency of growth hormone in children causes dwarfism. Growth hormone is not produced continuously, but is secreted in bursts. During the day, if the individual remains sedentary, there is little growth-hormone production. Exercise and stress, however, cause a burst of secretion large enough for the hormone to exert its effects. A similar outpouring of the hormone occurs an hour or two after falling asleep.

habit, a sequence of learned behaviour occurring in a particular context or as a response to particular events. Much animal and human behaviour consists in the manifestation of habits, which organize life, sometimes in minute detail. Habits are often conditioned, performed automatically and unconsciously, and eliminate much decision making. They begin as an observation of the effect produced by behaviour. If the effect seems desirable, the behaviour is repeated. The strength and stability of a habit depends on repetition of rewards, or repeated avoidance of unpleasantness, such as punishment. These lead to reinforcement and eventual strong establishment of the habit. Once a habit is well established, it may be maintained, even if the factors that began it no longer operate.

haemoglobin, the iron-containing complex protein that fills the red BLOOD cells and that has the unique property of being able to combine loosely with oxygen when it is in an environment of high-oxygen concentration, and to release it when it enters an environment low in oxygen. This means that when blood passes through the lungs, the red cells automatically take up oxygen. And when they are circulated to the tissues, where oxygen consumption is high, they automatically give it up to the surrounding cells. Haemoglobin linked to oxygen is called *oxyhaemoglobin,* and is of a bright red colour. This is the characteristic of arterial blood, having just returned from the lungs. When free of oxygen, haemoglobin is a dark purplish colour, as in the veins returning blood from the tissues.

Hall effect, the production of a transverse voltage difference in a conductor (⇨ p. 90) caused by the disturbance of the lines of electrical current flow occuring on the application of a magnetic field perpendicular to the direction of current flow. The Hall effect can be usefully applied in semiconductors.

hallucination, a sense perception not caused by an external stimulus. It is thus a hallucination to see something that is not present or to hear voices that do not come from any present source of sound. Hallucinations should be distinguished from *delusions* – which are mistaken ideas. Hallucinations are very common, both in health and disease, and are a feature of many psychiatric disorders. They may be visual, auditory – sometimes musical – tactile, or may relate to taste or smell (*gustatory* or *olfactory*), or to the size of things (*lilliputian*). They commonly occur in normal people as they are falling asleep or while waking from sleep. They also occur in alcoholic delirium (*delirium tremens*), from cocaine abuse and from the use of hallucinogenic drugs. They are a common feature of schizophrenia, temporal-lobe epilepsy, depression and organic brain disease.

hamstring muscles, the three long, cylindrical muscles at the back of the thigh, whose prominent tendons can be felt at the back of the knee on either side. These muscles are the 'hams' and the name 'hamstrings' refers to the tendons rather than to the muscles. All three muscles arise from bony bumps on the under side of the pelvis and their tendons are inserted into the back of the upper end of the bone of the lower leg – the *tibia.* The hamstring muscles, on contracting, thus bend the knee and straighten the hip joint.

handedness, the preferential use of one hand, rather than the other, in voluntary actions. Ambidexterity – the ability to use either hand with equal skill – is very rare. About 90 per cent of people are right-handed and this correlates with the half of the brain that is dominant for speech. Some 97 per cent of right-handed people have left-hemisphere dominance for speech, and only 60 per cent of left-handed people are right-hemisphere dominant for speech.

hands on, computer control by an operator, usually at a keyboard. Some computer programs run without operator intervention. This is known as 'hands off' operation.

hanging, a state in which a computer ceases to operate and may have to be deliberately restarted. A computer will hang for various reasons, sometimes due to a BUG in the program, sometimes because of operator error such as failing to insert a disk, or asking the computer to look for a file in the wrong directory.

hard disk, a computer recording device consisting of one, or usually more, firm metal disks coated with magnetic material. The disks rotate at high speed on the same spindle and each is provided with a radially moving read/write electromagnetic head that can thus cover the active area of its disk. The heads do not actually touch the magnetic surface but come very close to it, and their radial position can be set very quickly with high accuracy under the control of the disk controller circuit and the program. Before use hard disks must be formatted – laid out, magnetically, into tracks and sectors that can, thereafter, readily be found. When material is 'written' to a disk, a note of its name and location is kept in a file on the disk known as the *file-allocation table* (FAT); when a file is deleted (erased) its name is removed from the FAT. Hard disks are nonvolatile memories from which data and programs can rapidly and repeatedly be retrieved. Currently, typical capacities of hard-disk drives in personal computers are 100– 200 million BYTES (megabytes), i.e. 800–1,600 million bits (megabits). Drives of 1,000 megabytes (1 gigabyte) are common. The capacity of a hard disk can be at least doubled by the use of data-compression methods. Current versions of the MS-DOS operating system provide software for this purpose; ⇨ pp. 216–19.

hardness scale, a measure of the resistance of a material to indentation, cutting, drilling, abrasion or wearing. Resistance to scratching is defined by the Mohs scale, in which comparisons are made with 10 minerals, of increasing hardness, each being given an integral number. These are 1, talc; 2, gypsum; 3, calcite; 4, fluorite; 5, apatite; 6, orthoclase; 7, quartz; 8, topaz; 9, corundum; 10, diamond.

hardware, the physical machinery of a computer which is incapable, by itself, of doing anything. Compare *software,* the programs that instruct the hardware and prompt it into action. When a computer is switched on, it immediately reads some of its software and carries out certain initial instructions. It then waits for further instructions from the keyboard or other input device; ⇨ p. 214.

hardwired, pertaining to electronic or computer circuits, or, by analogy, neurological circuits, that are permanently wired up to perform particular functions, as compared with general-purpose circuits that operate under SOFTWARE control.

healing, the reparative processes that commonly follow injury or disease in an organism. It is a property and function of the organism and occurs automatically unless prevented by some agency such as infection, persistent injury, cancer, foreign material, radiation or great age. Healing is a passive process that will occur if the influences preventing it are removed. To do so is the function of the physician.

heapsort, a computer sorting algorithm that uses the information gained in one stage to save on subsequent comparisons (tree selection; ⇨ p. 216).

heart–lung machine, a device that can, for

short periods, carry out the functions of the heart and the lungs, so as to allow surgery on the heart. Once the heart–lung machine has taken over the maintenance of the circulation and the oxygenation of the blood, the patient's heart can be cooled and stopped so that the operation may proceed. At the point at which blood would normally be returned to the heart, it is carried from the body to the machine in sterile plastic tubes. There, it is artificially oxygenated, and the waste carbon dioxide removed. It is then pumped back into the body, being re-introduced at the point at which blood from the lungs would normally leave the heart. The pumps are of the tube-compression, roller kind to minimize damage to red blood cells. The blood passing through the machine is often cooled so as to lower the patient's body temperature (*hypothermia*) and decrease the nutritional and oxygen needs of the tissues. Anticoagulant drugs are used to prevent the blood from clotting.

heat capacity, the quantity of heat required to raise the temperature of a given weight of a substance or body by one degree, provided that no chemical change occurs; ⇨ p. 52.

heat insulation, materials that retard the flow of heat in a particular direction, either by reflection or by slowing transmission. Materials that achieve the latter do so by breaking up the heat-flow path (⇨ p. 52) into a large number of air spaces and by interposing barriers to radiation of heat. They include, wool and vegetable fibres, asbestos, calcium silicates, expanded materials, foam plastics and diatomite.

heavy water, the oxide of deuterium (D_2O). Deuterium (hydrogen–2) is the isotope of hydrogen that differs from hydrogen–1 in having a neutron in the nucleus; ⇨ pp. 160–5.

Hemiptera, an order of insects that comprises the true bugs. The forewings have a thickened basal area and are membranous towards the tips. They include the bedbugs, plant bugs, stink bugs, assassin bugs, kissing bugs, squash bugs, lace bugs and back swimmers. There are about 25,000 different species.

herbicides, chemicals used to kill vegetation, either selectively or indifferently. Many of them are halogenated hydrocarbons such as the chlorinated biphenyls.

hermaphroditism, the possession of both male and female sex organs. Hermaphroditism is common among simpler forms of animal life such as annelids and molluscs, but is rare in higher animals, in whom it is usually considered abnormal. Humans, however, sometimes show PSEUDOHERMAPHRODITISM.

heterocyclic compounds, ring compounds (⇨ p. 164) in which a ring, or one or more of several rings, include at least one atom different from the others.

heterodyne principle, a design feature of almost all radio and television receivers in which the incoming signal is mixed with a signal from a local oscillator that is tuned along with the incoming signal so that there is a constant difference between the two frequencies. The resulting difference frequency is amplified by the *intermediate-frequency amplifier* before being demodulated. The advantage is that the bulk of the amplification takes place at a fixed, low frequency – the intermediate frequency – rather than at a wide range of frequencies, which would require all the stages to be tuned simultaneously. Highly sensitive communications receivers may have several stages of IF amplification, giving high selectivity and high gain without the complication of having to keep several variably tuned circuits in step with each other; ⇨ pp. 102–5.

heuristics, a nonalgorithmic set of rules for solving problems in which educated guesses and a 'trial-and-error' approach replace the application of established knowledge. Heuristics is of great interest to workers in the field of artificial intelligence (⇨ p. 224).

hibernation, a period of torpor and dormancy occurring, when the ambient temperature is low, in cold-blooded animals, in those without internal temperature regulation (*pokilotherms*), and in some normally hot-blooded vertebrates. During hibernation, the animal's body temperature varies accurately with the environmental temperature. *Estivation* is a similar phenomenon occurring in conditions of prolonged drought or oppressively hot conditions. Cold-blooded hibernators and estivators include reptiles, amphibians, fishes, insects and molluscs. Warm-blooded hibernators include bats, rodents, marsupials and some primates. Many other vertebrates remain drowsy for long periods in the winter. Hibernating animals can wake at any time and do so at intervals of a few days in order to feed, often on stores accumulated for the purpose. Those who do not store food rely on body-fat stores for nutrition.

hierarchical database, a DATABASE arranged on the concept of 'ownership', with the restriction that each item of basic information (the *record*) is 'owned' by one other record only (the *owner*), and each type of owned record is owned by only one owner-record type. In a network-database system, each record type may be owned by a number of owner-record types. Hierarchical and network databases are inferior in flexibility and usefulness to fully *relational* databases; ⇨ p. 216.

high-density lipoproteins, the microscopic bodies in the BLOOD that carry cholesterol from the body tissues back to the liver. Compare LOW-DENSITY LIPOPROTEINS that carry cholesterol from the liver and the intestines to the tissues, including the arteries.

high-pass filter, an electronic device that discriminates between different frequencies of current (⇨ p. 90), allowing those above a given frequency to pass with little hindrance (low impedance), while offering a high impedance to those below the particular frequency.

high-temperature materials, materials, such as certain metals, alloys and ceramics capable of retaining their physical properties at temperatures above about 540°C (1,000°F). Such materials are needed for use in furnaces, gas turbines, aircraft jet engines, and nuclear reactors. They must be inherently strong and resistant to oxidation.

hirudinea, the class of annelid worms known as leeches. They are blood-sucking aquatic parasites provided with suckers for attachment to their prey and saw-like jaws, just inside the mouth, for cutting the skin.

histamine, a powerful chemical substance manufactured in certain white blood and tissue cells called *mast cells* and stored in them. Histamine is released from the mast cells when antibodies attached to them come into contact with substances such as pollens. Free histamine acts on small BLOOD VESSELS causing them to dilate and to become more permeable to protein. This causes the local effects we call an *allergic reaction.*

histocompatibility antigens, groups of proteins situated on the outer membrane of all the cells of the animal body, which provide an identifying code unique for each individual. These groups are genetically determined and are called antigens because they act to stimulate antibodies if placed in a foreign environment such as another body. The only two individuals with identical histocompatibility antigens are identical twins. It is the histocompatibility antigens that, unless prevented, cause rejection of grafted organs and tissues. They play a central part in immunology. The histocompatibility antigens were first discovered on white blood cells (leukocytes) and are often called *human leukocyte-associated antigens*, usually abbreviated to HLA antigens. HLA types can be classified, with individuals falling into a finite number of HLA groups. Some of these groups are known to confer a special susceptibility to certain diseases. The HLA B27 group, for instance, is prone to the spinal disease ankylosing spondylitis and the inflammatory eye disease uveitis.

HIV ⇨ AIDS.

histogram, a chart of vertical rectangles of varying height and width whose areas are proportional to the number of occurrences of the phenomenon being described in a given sample or time (frequency) and whose widths are proportional to the class intervals.

holes, vacant ELECTRON energy states near the top of energy bands in solids. The absence of the negative electron is equivalent to a positive charge, and holes behave exactly as if they were positive charges. They can move through solids in the opposite direction to the movement of electrons. Hole conduction is an essential feature of semiconductor action and can be promoted by 'doping' semiconductors with a very small proportion of donor atoms with a lower vacancy than the main material; ⇨ p. 90.

holographic memory, a computer-memory store in the form of a hologram (⇨ p. 82) that is read by a low-power laser. Such memories can securely store large amounts of data in a small physical space.

homeostasis, the maintenance of constant conditions in a biological or electronic system by automatic feed-back mechanisms that counter trends away from the fixed limits of normality. This fundamental principle of biology and CYBERNETICS is recognized as essential to the continuation of health and life. Self-regulating mechanisms operate at all levels of organization in the animal and human body. These involve constant monitoring and correction of many variables, including the concentrations of a wide range of substances in the blood, the acidity (pH) of the BLOOD, the levels of OXYGEN and CARBON DIOXIDE in the blood and tissues, the levels of many HORMONES, the body temperature, the heart rate and the blood pressure. At the cellular level, a homeostatic mechanism called *contact inhibition* controls the rate of reproduction of cells in contact with each other so that cell populations do not grow larger than they should. This control mechanism is lost in cancer. Many hormones participate in the process of homeostasis. For example, an undue rise in the blood sugar is monitored by cells in the pancreas, and extra insulin is secreted into the blood to increase the rate of removal of sugar. Trends towards alteration of many bodily states lead to nerve inputs to the brain. These are reflected in changes in the output of hormones from the PITUITARY GLAND, whose actions on other endocrine glands correct the deviation.

Homoptera, an order of sucking insects, allied to the HEMIPTERA, that includes aphids, leaf hoppers, lantern flies, harvest flies, spittle bugs and cicadas.

homosexuality, a sexual preference for the same anatomical sex. Homosexuality is not confined to humans and homosexual behaviour has been observed in most animal species. Human sexual preference probably lies somewhere on a spectrum between exclusively heterosexual and exclusively homosexual. Many people experience some homosexual interest or engage in homosexual activity at some point in their lives. A reliable figure for established homosexuality remains uncertain, but is probably in the region of 2 per cent for any human population. A distinction must be made between homosexual *preference* and homosexual *behaviour*. The latter is common in conditions where heterosexual contacts are limited or absent, such as prisons, boarding schools, convents and so on, but such behaviour is often a substitute for heterosexual activity and is also often accompanied by heterosexual fantasies. There is no reason to believe that homosexuality is caused in this way, but a pre-existing homosexual identity can be reinforced and established by homosexual experience. In spite of the discovery in mid-1993 that the Xq28 region of the X chromosome is strongly linked with male homosexuality, the actual causation of homosexuality remains obscure. The Xq28 region is large enough to accommodate several hundred genes.

hormones, chemical substances produced by the various endocrine glands and released into the bloodstream to effect actions, by way of specific receptor sites, in other parts of the body. These substances control and coordinate body growth and the build up and break down of body tissues (*metabolism*; ⇨ pp. 182–5), nutrition, body temperature, the circulation of the blood, salt and water balance, the development of the secondary sexual characteristics and reproduction. The hormonal system of the animal and human body is under the overall combined control of psychic stimuli, external stimuli and HOMEOSTASIS mechanisms, which interact and operate on the hypothalamus of the brain. This controls the PITUITARY GLAND, which releases a range of hormones that stimulate the action of the other endocrine glands. These are adrenocorticotropin, to prompt cortisone release from the adrenal cortex; follicle-stimulating and luteinizing hormones, to produce sperm and egg maturation in the testis and ovary; prolactin for milk secretion in the breast; thyroid-stimulating hormone for the thyroid; growth hormone for the bones and muscles; melanotropin for the pigment cells (*melanocytes*); and antidiuretic hormone for water reabsorption in the kidneys. The endocrine glands, in turn, produce their own hormones, such as adrenaline from the inner part of the adrenal glands, cortisol (corticosteroid) from the outer part of the adrenals, thyroxine from the thyroid gland, insulin and GLUCAGON from the pancreas, parathyroid hormone and calcitonin from the parathyroid glands, oestrogen and progesterone from the ovaries, and testosterone from the testicles. All have specific functions. The levels of these hormones in the blood is monitored by the hypothalamus so that HOMEOSTASIS is achieved.

housekeeping, software activity directed to improving the internal tidiness or orderliness of a program or to its efficient distribution in a storage medium; ⇨ p. 218.

Hubble's constant, a figure based on the assumption that there is a direct relationship between the distance of a celestial object and its recessional velocity. The velocity divided by the distance should always give the same number, known as *Hubble's constant* after the American astronomer Edwin Powell Hubble (1889–1953), whose work on the recession of the galaxies led to the concept of the expanding universe. Hubble's constant is not universally agreed, but widely accepted values are 15 and 29 km per second per million light years. If Hubble's figure *is* a constant then the age of the universe is its reciprocal. Other estimates, from geological evidence, especially of the amounts of radioactive elements (⇨ p. 160), generally agree with these figures, which are 10,000 million to 19,000 million years. The most commonly held age for the universe is about 15,000 million years; ⇨ pp. 140–3.

humerus, the long upper-arm bone, which, at its upper end, forms a joint with a shallow cup on a side process of the shoulder blade and, at its lower end, articulates, at the elbow, with the radius and ulna of the lower arm.

humidity, the amount of water vapour in the atmosphere, usually expressed as the relative humidity. This is the amount held relative to the maximum amount that can be held when the air is saturated.

hydrate, the form of a solid compound to which water molecules are attached or related by hydrogen bonding (⇨ p. 162) or merely present in the crystal lattice. Hydration is the process of incorporating water molecules into a solid compound in this way.

hydride, any compound containing hydrogen and one other element.

hydrogen bomb, an atomic weapon in which a fusion reaction (⇨ p. 160) occurs in heavy hydrogen (DEUTERIUM) as a result of a triggering fission reaction in uranium or plutonium. For fusion to be self-sustaining a temperature of about 350 million K is necessary. The only practicable way to achieve this in a weapon is to explode a conventional fission atomic bomb. At this temperature the energy released by the initial fission is sufficient to maintain the temperature in the heavy hydrogen and initiate a fusion chain reaction. The ultimate destructive power of such a weapon, used aggressively, beggars the imagination.

Hydroida, an order of coelenterates that includes many of the smaller jellyfish and the freshwater hydras.

hydrolysis, the breaking down or alteration of a chemical compound by water, as in the formation of an ACID and a BASE from a salt by interaction with water. Hydrolysis is also a common reaction with organic compounds, as when the polysaccharide starch, boiled with dilute acids, yields the simpler sugars, the disaccharide maltose and the monosaccharide glucose; ⇨ pp. 182–5.

hydrometer, an instrument for measuring the density of liquids. The hydrometer is a weighted narrow glass tube with an internal scale that is floated in the liquid. The depth to which it sinks depends on the density of the liquid. The scale is read at the liquid level. Hydrometers are commonly used to measure the percentage of alcohol in water, as the specific gravity (the density relative to water) varies with the percentage.

hydroxide, one of the types of -OH (hydroxyl)-containing compound that is capable of neutralizing acid, which turns red litmus blue, and is slippery to the touch. Hydroxides are BASES; ⇨ p. 168.

hygrometer, an instrument for measuring the amount of water vapour in the air, usually in terms of relative HUMIDITY. In simple hygrometers a small bundle of human hairs are held under slight tension by a spring. The extension and contraction that occur with changes in humidity are magnified by a lever system and move a pointer over a scale. Changes in the electrical resistance (⇨ p. 96) of hygroscopic materials with changes in humidity can also be used as the basis for a hygrometer.

Hymenoptera, the large order of insects that contains bees, wasps, ants and sawflies. There are probably over 100,000 species. Many of the Hymenoptera are parasitic on other insects or on spiders, laying their eggs in or on them.

hyoid bone, the tiny, U-shaped bone that is suspended in the midline of the front of the neck just above the Adam's apple (*larynx*). The hyoid may be felt between the finger and thumb just where the floor of the chin meets the neck, and may easily be moved from side to side. It provides attachment to no fewer than 18 muscles, nine on each side, and provides a base for the movements of the tongue. The hyoid is of medicolegal importance as it is often fractured when the neck is gripped violently, as in manual strangulation.

hyperbaric oxygen, a method of medical treatment in which the patient is placed in an airtight chamber and exposed to oxygen at pressures up to three times that of the atmosphere. Because of the high pressure, considerable quantities of oxygen dissolve in the blood serum so the oxygen-carrying capacity of the blood is greatly enhanced and the tissues of the whole body receive an excellent supply, independently of the HAEMOGLOBIN-transport mechanism. Hyperbaric oxygen is useful in decompression sickness (the 'bends'), severe respiratory and circulatory disorders, recent carbon monoxide and cyanide poisoning, gas gangrene and bone damage from radiation. Unfortunately, excessive oxygen is toxic to the nervous system and a limit of about three hours' treatment is therefore imposed.

hyperkeratosis, thickening of the outer layer of the skin so as to produce a 'horn-like' layer. Hyperkeratosis is a normal response to local pressure and produces corns or callosities, which are essentially protective. The condition may, however, occur as an inherited disorder affecting the palms and the soles, or as a general disorder, called *ichthyosis*, affecting most or all of the body.

hyperplasia, an increase in the number of cells in a tissue or organ so that there is an increase in its size. Hyperplasia is not a cancerous change and may be a normal response to increased demand. It is not the same as HYPERTROPHY.

hypertrophy, an increase in the size of a tissue or organ caused by the enlargement of the individual cells rather than by an increase in their number. Hypertrophy is in no sense tumorous or malignant, but is usually a normal response to an increased demand. The increase in muscle bulk that results if increased physical work is performed is a hypertrophy. Some conditions, such as certain types of muscle dystrophy, cause *pseudo-hypertrophy* in which the appearance of increased bulk is actually due to the deposition, in the tissue, of abnormal substances.

hypnosis, a state of high suggestibility and responsiveness in which, as directed by a hypnotist, instructions are closely followed, opinions and even memories are apparently modified, and hallucinatory sensations experienced. These effects can be extended to apply to a period after the period of hypnosis (*post-hypnotic suggestion*). The hypnotic state is induced by asking the subject to relax and focus the attention fixedly on some object. The hypnotist then indicates, in an authoritative, but calm, manner, that concentration on the object will increase, but that the eyes will become heavy and tired, the lids will droop, and the eyes will soon close. This occurs, and the subject appears to be asleep. The hypnotized subject may appear to be asleep, but is not so, and the electroencephalographic patterns are those of a person fully awake. The suggestion is now made that the eyes are so heavy that they cannot be opened. Often, this is found to be the case, and the operator may then proceed, with confidence, to make other suggestions. It may, for instance, be suggested that the subject is growing younger. In this case, the subject may begin to behave and talk as a child, relating events and experiences purporting to be those of his or her childhood.

hypochondrium, the region of the ABDOMEN immediately below the lower ribs on either side. The lower ribs are joined to the breastbone by cartilages and the term, literally, means 'below the cartilages'.

hypoplasia, underdevelopment of a tissue or organ as a result of a failure of a sufficient number of cells to be reproduced.

hypoxia, a deficiency of OXYGEN in the tissues. If local, this can lead to tissue death (*gangrene*); if general, to the death of the individual. Hypoxia is the principal immediate cause of death in the Western world, mainly as a result of occlusive diseases of the arteries (*atherosclerosis*). It also occurs as a result of suffocation, respiratory disease (which prevents access of oxygen to the blood) and *anaemia*, in which the oxygen-carrying capacity of the blood is reduced. Some poisons, such as carbon monoxide, cause hypoxia in the same way.

hysteresis, the phenomenon in which the effect lags behind the cause of the effect. Hysteresis is common in science, but the best-known example is when the magnetism induced into a ferromagnetic material lags behind the changes in the external field causing the magnetism. In general, if the effect Y is plotted against the cause X, a closed curve, known as the *hysteresis loop*, is formed. The term is derived from Greek *husteros*, meaning 'coming after'.

ice ages, the 17 known periods during the past 600 million years in which great sheets of ice extended from the poles to cover about one-third of the land area of the world. The last ice age persisted from about 40,000 years ago until about 10,000 years ago, and the three ice ages before that each lasted for about 100,000 years. An ice age can occur if a winter's snow persists through the subsequent summer. This allows a buildup to occur by positive feedback and glaciers to form. The precipitating cause remains obscure, but is probably related to changes in solar radiation reaching the Earth (⇨ also LITTLE ICE AGE).

igneous rock, rock that has congealed from molten material called *magma* formed deep in the Earth's interior; ⇨ p. 146.

ileum, the third, and lowest, part of the small intestine, the other two being the DUODENUM and the JEJUNUM. The ileum joins the large intestine (the colon) at the wide, sac-like caecum.

illusion, a false sense perception resulting from a misinterpretation of the incoming stimulus. Many illusions are normal and are experienced by all of us. Optical illusions are particularly well known, but similar illusions can be produced in the acoustic sphere. Much has been learned about modes of brain function from studying illusions. Illusions of a more serious nature are common in many psychiatric conditions, especially depression. They include a tendency to misinterpret the sound or meaning of actual words spoken by others so that they are taken to be critical or conspiratorial. Note that such an illusion may contain the *delusion* (persistent belief in the face of contrary evidence) that one is being persecuted. HALLUCINATIONS are quite different from illusions.

immunity, the body's ability to resist infection by means of antibodies and a complex cellular defence mechanism. Absolute immunity to infection does not, of course, exist. To many organisms, human immunity is almost absolute, but to many others it is relative only. It is, essentially, a question of the relative strength of the opposing forces. A minor assault, by a small dose of organisms of fairly low virulence, is easily repulsed. But a large dose of highly virulent organisms might be overwhelming. Organisms mutate and vary in the severity of their effects. The immune system also varies, both in its overall efficiency, and in its specific ability to deal quickly with a new invader. Active immunity is the responsive process by which antibodies are produced by the body to deal with infections or are deliberately stimulated into production by medical immunization. Such active immunization may last for a lifetime or may need booster doses from time to time. *Passive immunity* is that conferred when antibodies from another person or animal are injected or when antibodies pass across the placenta into the bloodstream of the unborn child or are received in the breast milk after birth. Passive immunity is short-lived, but can be life-saving.

immunoassay, one of a number of methods of determining the amount of ANTIBODY or ANTIGEN present in a sample.

immunofluorescence, a method of detecting the presence of particular ANTIBODIES. The appropriate ANTIGEN is linked to a small quantity of the material fluorescein, which fluoresces brightly in ultraviolet light. If the antibody is present, the antigen will attach itself to the antibody. The specimen, illuminated by ultraviolet light, may then be examined under the microscope and the site of the antibody seen by the bright yellowish-green glow.

impedance match, the condition that ensures the maximum transmission of power when a source of alternating current is connected to a load. Impedance matching is especially important when the impedance of the source is high and a low load impedance would result in heavy losses. Maximal power transfer occurs at any frequency when the two impedances are equal. Maximum voltage transfer occurs when the impedance of the load is very high compared to that of the source ⇨ pp. 96–107.

impulse generator, a device that delivers a short surge of electrical power, usually for testing insulators or the effect of such surges on electrical equipment, or for other purposes such as the magnetization of permanent magnets. It consists of a high value capacitor (⇨ p. 98) that can be charged slowly and discharged quickly through a low-resistance (⇨ p. 96) circuit.

incandescence, the emission of visible light by a hot body. For a dark-adapted eye this occurs at a temperature of about 390°C (730°F) as a colourless glow. Dull red incandescence occurs at a temperature of about 500°C (930°F).

incandescent lamp, an electric LIGHT BULB that produces light by heating a filament, usually of tungsten, to a temperature at which yellow or white light (⇨ pp. 72–5) is produced. Infrared and ultraviolet light are also produced, thus reducing the efficiency of the device as a visible-light source. The filament is enclosed in an evacuated bulb so as to avoid oxidation, and is usually in the form of a coil or a coiled coil. The electrical resistance (⇨ p. 96) of the filament varies with the supply voltage (⇨ p. 88) and the light output.

incest, sexual intercourse between close blood relatives, especially between brothers and sisters, fathers and daughters, and mothers and sons. The 'degrees of prohibition' are arbitrary and variable, and there is no instinctive revulsion against incest. In some cases, the prohibition has applied to any member of the father's family; in others, to any member of the mother's.

incidence, the frequency with which an event, such as a disease, occurs in a particular population over a given period of time. Incidence should be distinguished from *prevalence*, which is the number of existing instances of an event in a particular population, either at a particular point in time, or during a given period. So a statement about the number of cases of a disease occurring in a particular country every year is a statement of incidence, while a statement about the number of people suffering from the disease in 1990 is a statement of prevalence.

incubation period, the time interval between the entry of the infecting organisms and the first appearance of symptoms of the resulting disease. In spite of considerable variation in the size of the dose acquired and in the resistance of the host, the incubation period is a characteristic of the organism rather than of these other factors. It reflects the organism's rate of reproduction, its mode of infection and the route taken by it to reach its objective. Incubation periods vary widely. Cholera may strike a person down within an hour or two of drinking contaminated water; rabies may start months after a bite on the foot. In the former, the organisms reach the point of attack – the bowel – almost at once; in the latter, the viruses have to make their way slowly up the immensely long journey, by nerve fibre, to reach the brain. The incubation period of rabies depends on the proximity of the bite to the brain.

incubator, a piece of equipment providing a closed, insulated and controllable environment so as to achieve optimum conditions for the maintenance and growth of an organism, whether bacterial, animal or human. A central item of equipment in the bacteriological laboratory is the incubator in which cultures of organisms are grown, usually at body temperature. This is the temperature at which organisms pathogenic to humans grow best. In the premature-baby incubator, other environmental factors, besides temperature, may also be important. These include relative absence of infecting organisms, higher-than-normal oxygen concentration and controlled humidity of the air.

index fossil, remains of a plant or animal used to date the rock – almost exclusively sedimentary rock – in which they are found.

induction coil, a form of electrical transformer used to produce a high-voltage, low-current, alternating current from a low-voltage source of direct current. The source current is regularly interrupted by a switch of some kind, usually mechanical, and flows in the primary winding, which consists of a relatively small number of turns of thick insulated wire wrapped around a soft-iron core. The secondary winding consists of a large number of turns of thin, insulated wire, wrapped around the primary winding. The spark plugs of car petrol engines are supplied by an induction coil by way of the distributor; ⇨ p. 100.

induction heating, the use of induced EDDY CURRENTS to heat a material that can conduct electricity. A coil, through which a large alternating current flows, is placed closely around the material to be heated. Induction heating is extensively used in the metalworking industry to melt metals and produce ALLOYS; ⇨ pp. 100 and 166.

induction motor, an alternating-current electric motor in which the current in the secondary winding (rotor or stator) is caused to flow by induction (⇨ p. 100) from the magnetic field caused by the current flowing in the primary winding.

infant mortality, the number of infants under the age of one year who die, for every thousand live births. This is a sensitive index of the level of social and medical advance in a society and of the standards of public health.

infarction, the deprivation of a part of a tissue of its blood supply so that an area of dead tissue (an *infarct*) forms. Any tissue can develop an infarct if its supplying BLOOD VESSELS become blocked or too narrowed to pass sufficient blood to maintain its vital processes. The type and bulk of the tissue involved determines the gravity of the event. A *myocardial* infarction is what happens when a coronary-artery thrombosis occurs, and this is the real cause of death or disability. An infarction of the brain causes death or a stroke, depending on the area and the size. Infarction of the lung results from a pulmonary EMBOLISM.

infection, the entry into the body of, and the establishment within the body of colonies of, any organism capable of causing disease. Many organisms gain access to the body, but only a small proportion are able to overcome the basic defence mechanisms and cause infection. Most swallowed organisms are destroyed by the acid in the stomach, but some, such as the SALMONELLA group, are able to resist even this and establish themselves in the bowel. The intact skin provides a good barrier to infection, but cuts and abrasions allow access to areas where the second line of defence – the immune system – must operate. Organisms may exist in certain parts of the body without causing any harm but may become harmful if they gain access to other parts. Perforation of the bowel allows organisms access to the sterile region around the outside of the organs (the *peritoneal cavity*), and the serious condition of *peritonitis* then occurs. Infection may be acquired before or during birth. When organisms gain access to normally sterile areas, the outcome depends on the balance between the number and virulence of the organisms, on the one hand, and the effectiveness of the defences, on the other. Good hygienic principles – regular washing, sanitary habits, fastidiousness about food, avoidance of obvious sources of infection, and a realistic cynicism about the personal habits of others – help to reduce the strength of the attack. The pursuit of good health helps to maintain good defences.

inferior, an anatomical term meaning 'below' any point in the upright body. No value judgement is implied when the word is used in this context.

infestation, the condition of being attacked by parasites. In medicine, the term is usually restricted to animal parasites, such as lice, mites or ticks, on, in or just under the skin, and to worms in the intestine or the body tissues.

inflammation, the response of living tissue to injury of any kind, and hence the most common manifestation of disease or disorder. The signs of inflammation are redness, heat, pain, swelling and loss of function. The frequency with which inflammation occurs is testified to by the number of conditions whose names end in '-itis', the medical suffix for inflammation. When a tissue suffers inflammation, its BLOOD VESSELS widen and the blood flow through it increases markedly. At the same time the cells in the walls of the smallest vessels, the CAPILLARIES, separate sufficiently to allow protein molecules in the blood, including ANTIBODIES, to pass out. This leads to a protein-rich *exudate* (exuded substance) in the inflamed area. White cells also emigrate from the blood vessels by squeezing through these tiny openings and proceed to try to deal with the cause of the inflammation. Pus is mainly dead white blood cells. These effects account for the redness, heat and swelling. The pain is caused by the release, from damaged cells, of substances called *prostaglandins*, which strongly stimulate pain nerve endings. Inflammation can be caused by many factors, of which the commonest are the toxins released by bacteria and other organisms in the course of infection. But it may result from any kind of injury (such as a blow or a cut), damage from chemical, radiational or heat energy, or even from the body's own immunological processes as in hypersensitivity reactions (*allergy*) or autoimmune disease. Inflammation is, in general, protective and leads to a return to normality. But it may become persistent (*chronic*), lasting for weeks or months leading, to the formation of scar tissue, which may have undesirable effects.

information processing, the derivation of information from other information or the reorganization or reallocation to different sites of information. All human and animal activity involves information processing both in the sense of neurological activity and in the sense of the result of such activity. Information processing is the chief function of the computer and the chief occupation of the employed.

innominate bone, the bone forming the front and side parts of the pelvis and bearing the ACETABULUM – the deep hollow for the head of the thighbone. This bone so little resembles any other shape that early anatomists are said to have adopted the term *innominate,* which means 'nameless'.

input device, anything by which data can be transferred to a computer, such as a keyboard, bar-code reader, data tablet, document reader, magnetic- card reader, speech-recognition device, or scanner; ⇨ p. 214.

Insecta, one of the classes in the phylum Arthropoda, and the largest of all the classes of animals. Approaching a million species have been described, but the total is known to be much larger. The insecta are divided into many different orders.

insight, self-awareness or self-understanding. People suffering from neurotic illnesses usually have considerable insight about their condition, although this seldom enables them to do anything about it. People suffering from psychotic illnesses are thought not to have such insight.

instinct, fixed action pattern or stereotyped complex behaviour shown by all members of a species, independently of the experience of the individual. The physical basis for instincts is 'hard-wired' into the brain, and the instincts themselves might be thought of as simply the way the nervous system operates. Instincts are all triggered off by sensory input of one kind or another, and, because the neurological organization is basically the same in all members of a species, the effects are, broadly, the same in all. Instinctive responses can, of course, be inhibited by later programming, and much of social activity consists in the complex interplay of instinctive responses modified by education.

instruction set, the list of computer-program machine-code instructions that a microprocessor can recognize and act on; ⇨ pp. 214 and 218.

integrated circuit, a complete electronic circuit on a silicon or other chip, containing often many thousands, or even millions, of active units (*transistors*) and the associated resistors and capacitors (⇨ pp. 96–9). Integrated circuits may range from a very simple circuit such as a voltage amplifier or a digital gate to almost the complete electronics of a computer; ⇨ pp. 102–5.

intelligence, an entity about whose definition no consensus has been reached. It is not even generally agreed that intelligence is what intelligence tests measure. Most psychologists agree that intelligence consists of a group of separate, but correlated, abilities, each of which can be present to a varying degree. These abilities include memory, the speed with which relationships can be perceived, verbal skills, numerical skills and visuo-spatial perception. Few now believe in the existence of raw, undifferentiated intelligence. Bright children, appropriately motivated, do well at school and score highly on intelligence tests. The intelligence quotient (IQ), in general, equates well with scholastic performance and with subsequent success in business or professional life. Many pedigree studies of families noted for high intelligence, and of those noted for low, have suggested that intelligence is largely inherited. Critics of this view have pointed out that intelligence is judged by such criteria as verbal facility and that this is environmentally available to one group and not the other. But studies have shown that identical twins (who have identical genetics) brought up in different families are more alike than non-identical twins (with different genetics) reared in the same family. Various estimates of the relative importance of inheritance over post-natal programming have been made, and some are as high as four-to-one in favour of inheritance. The Swiss developmental psychologist Jean Piaget (1896–1980) postulated that intelligence matures in discrete, age-related stages, progressing from the earliest perception of sense input and movement, through stages in which a sense of the permanence of objects and of how they fit into groups is established, to the levels of conceptualization and then, finally, abstract thought. Although these stages are not universally agreed, Piaget's view has been very influential. In particular, most psychologists now agree with his view that the development of intelligence is the result of a dynamic and never-ceasing interaction between the child's very general and unrefined information-processing capacity, and its environment. There is no discrete part of the brain that can be said to be the site of intelligence, and it is clear from the study of neurological disease that intelligence is a function of the brain as a whole. Local damage to brain matter in certain areas results in loss of specific functions, such as speech or speech comprehension, but does not, in itself, diminish intelligence. But if the loss of brain substance exceeds about 50 ml, there is a reduction in the speed of mental functions and impairment of reasoning power. Abstract reasoning power is affected adversely if the nerve connections between the frontal lobes and other parts of the brain are damaged.

interactive computing, the use of programs whose responses vary as a result of the users' response to questions posed by the program (⇨ p. 218). This does not imply artificial intelligence, however (⇨ p. 224). Many educational programs are interactive, each movement to the next stage being determined by the user inputting a correct answer to a question on the screen.

intercostal, between the ribs.

interferons, natural products of the body, produced by cells that have been invaded and destroyed by viruses. The reproduction of viruses inside a cell commonly leads to its rupture, accompanied by the release of tiny quantities of these powerful chemical substances. Interferons pass to other cells, causing them to arm themselves against invasion, not only by the original virus, but also by any other infecting organism. They also modify various cell-regulating mechanisms, and slow down the growth of cancers. Interferons have proved successful in the treatment of various conditions, including Kaposi's sarcoma, the common cold, herpes simplex infections, genital warts, and an uncommon form of leukaemia – hairy-cell leukaemia. When injected, interferons cause influenza-like symptoms, possibly because the symptoms of natural 'flu are caused by interferon release. Genetic engineering techniques are used to produce interferons for medical purposes.

interplanetary matter, small, solid particles and gas present in space between the planets. Most interplanetary gas derives from the Sun. The solid material comes from asteroids and comets; ⇨ pp. 140–3 .

interrupt I/O, a method of controlling the central processing unit (CPU) of a computer when data must be moved in or out. A signal is sent to the CPU that sets a program interrupt, which, at an appropriate time, determined by various priorities, causes the CPU to interrupt the program so that data can be moved in or out; ⇨ pp. 214–17.

interstellar matter, small, solid particles and gas present between the stars. Interstellar matter makes up a small but significant proportion of the total mass of the universe. It is the raw material from which new stars are formed as a result of aggregation by gravitational attraction (⇨ pp. 30, 126, 130, 140–3).

intestine, the long tube that starts at the lower part of the throat and ends, some 9 m (26 ft) further down, at the anus. It consists, sequentially, of the *oesophagus*, the *stomach*, the DUODENUM, the second part of the small intestine (the JEJUNUM), the third part of the small intestine (the ILEUM), the wide, pouch-like *caecum*, which carries the *appendix*, the large intestine, or *colon*, which ascends on the right side, crosses to the left upper corner of the abdomen, and descends on the left side, to run down into the pelvis as the S-shaped (*sigmoid*) colon to the rectum and anus. The intestine is suspended from a complex, folded 'curtain', called the *mesentery*, which, at its attachment to the back inner wall of the abdomen, is less than a foot long, and at its attachment to the bowel is more than 20 ft long. The mesentery also carries the arteries taking blood to the intestine and the veins carrying the nutrient-rich blood back from the intestine to the liver.

intoxication, any kind of poisoning, especially that by alcohol. The term comes from the Latin *intoxicare*, meaning 'to smear with poison'. This, in turn, comes from the Greek *toxon*, meaning 'a bow'. The root *toxon* occurs in *toxocara* – a bow-shaped worm and *toxoplasma* – a bow-shaped parasite, but here, the reference is to the tipping of arrows with poison.

intron, a part of a split gene that does not code for protein and that is removed during RNA processing.

introvert ⇨ EXTROVERT.

in vitro, literally, 'in glass'. In-vitro processes or reactions are those, normally occurring in the body that, for various reasons, are deliberately conducted in a glass disk or test-tube or other laboratory receptacle. The same process in the body is said to occur *in vivo* ('in life').

I/O, input/output to or from a computer system; ⇨ p. 214.

I/O bus, a signal route to which various input or output devices can be connected in parallel.

ion implantation, a method of adding materials to the surface region of other materials by bombarding them with a high-energy beam of ions (⇨ p. 90). This can be done with great precision as to location, area and depth, and is an important procedure in the manufacture of semiconductor devices.

ion propulsion, a form of vehicular propulsion for artificial satellites and space ships in which ions (⇨ p. 90) of various substances are accelerated to a high speed by an electric field, and are driven out of the rear of the vehicle so as to produce forward motion by reaction. Power for the purpose can be obtained from the Sun using solar-electric generators, or from a nuclear reactor. The method is very economical on materials, which is an important consideration in space.

ischaemia, an inadequate flow of blood to any part of the body, usually because of narrowing, from disease, of the supplying arteries. Ischaemia is the cause of much disease, disability and deaths and accounts for a high proportion of the morbidity of humankind in the Western world. Angina pectoris is caused by ischaemia, and, when this reaches a

sufficiently severe degree, a heart attack (*coronary thrombosis*) may follow. Stroke is caused by ischaemia, as is intermittent claudication. Ischaemia commonly causes INFARCTION.

isobars, lines drawn on a map that join points of equal atmospheric pressure and demonstrate the presence of areas of high and low pressure. Isobar patterns are useful in showing the probable movements of large masses of air and hence in predicting weather.

isomers, compounds having the same molecular formula but a different arrangement of atoms within the molecule. Isomerization is the process of rearranging the atoms in a molecule, especially a hydrocarbon molecule; ⇨ p. 164.

Isoptera, the order of insects containing termites.

jasper, an impure form of quartz, variously coloured and banded and of variable hardness, used as a semiprecious gemstone.

jaundice, yellowing of the skin and of the whites of the eyes by the natural colouring substance bilirubin, released from the HAEMOGLOBIN in red BLOOD cells at the end of their working lives. Excess bilirubin is normally disposed of by the liver into the intestine, but any obstruction to the outflow through the bile ducts or any liver disease that interferes with the excretion of bile leads to its accumulation in the blood and deposition in the skin and elsewhere. The causes of jaundice in humans include hepatitis, gallstone obstruction of the bile duct, cancer of the pancreas with obstruction of the lower end of the bile duct, and an abnormally high rate of breakdown of red blood cells (*haemolytic anaemia*).

jejunum, the part of the small intestine that lies between the DUODENUM and the ILEUM. The name *jejunum* means 'empty', and in this part of the bowel the contents are very fluid and pass quickly along under the influence of PERISTALSIS. The jejunum is wider and thicker-walled than the ileum and occupies the middle part of the ABDOMEN.

jet, a hard, black mineral, a form of lignite coal that takes a high polish and can be carved and turned to make beads and other decorative items.

jet lag, the syndrome caused by loss of synchronization between the body's biological clocks and resulting physiological rhythms and local time. Jet lag results from rapid transit, by air, across time zones. The most obvious effect is on sleeping, which is commonly disturbed for several days, but other activities, such as digestion, bowel habit and mental functioning, are also affected. There is wakefulness during the night, the desire to sleep during the day, a sense of fatigue, inefficiency, lapses of memory and poor physical and mental efficiency. Recovery takes about one day for each time zone crossed. The problem is worst on an eastward journey, when the need is to shorten the day, and less troublesome when going west. This is partly because the body's innate

circadian rhythm has a period of somewhat more than twenty-four hours. The pineal gland in the brain secretes a hormone called melatonin during darkness, and suppresses it in the light. This hormone is believed to control some of the biorhythms and has been used experimentally in attempts to prevent jet lag. Although some subjects claim benefit from treatment with this hormone, the evidence is dubious. Not enough is known of the other effects of melatonin to justify its use for purposes such as this.

joints, junctions between bones, whether or not obvious movement is possible. There are three types of joints – *fibrous, cartilaginous,* and *synovial*. In fibrous joints, such as those between the spines of the vertebral column, the bones of the pelvis or the bones making up the skull, little or no movement is possible because the bones are held firmly together by LIGAMENTS. Cartilaginous joints, such as those between the ribs and the breastbone (*sternum*), have flexible cartilage fusing the bones together, allowing some limited movement. Synovial joints, such as the shoulder, elbow, hip and knee joints, are freely movable. Although the bearing surfaces of synovial joints are covered with cartilage, there is a space between these surfaces that is well lubricated with synovial fluid. The whole joint is enclosed in a capsule of tough, fibrous tissue, lined with a fluid-secreting membrane, the *synovial membrane*. Synovial joints include ball-and-socket joints, as in the shoulder and hip, which allow movement in any direction; hinge joints, such as those in the fingers and at the knees, allowing movement in one direction only; rotating joints, as in the head of the radius at the elbow, and between the upper two vertebrae of the spine; and sliding joints, as at the wrists and in the feet. Some sliding also occurs at the knee joints. In all cases, the range of possible movement is restricted by ligaments, which may be external to the joint, internal, or both.

Josephson junction, a superconducting device consisting of a junction between two metals that exhibits controllable electron tunnelling. The Josephson junction can be used as a very fast electronic switch, changing from 'on' to 'off' in less than 1 nanosecond, and requiring minimal power. Computer hardware based on this principle must be immersed in liquid nitrogen or liquid helium, but the speed of operation will often justify this inconvenience.

joule, in electrical terms, the joule is the watt-second. One hundred joules are needed to run a 100-watt bulb for one second. The joule is the unit of work, energy and heat. Although defined in terms of work, the joule is a unit of heat energy and is being used increasingly to replace the CALORIE in nutritional contexts. The calorie is the amount of heat required to raise 1 g of water by 1°C, but in nutrition, the calorie is taken to be one thousand times this figure and is called a *kilocalorie*. A (kilo)calorie is equal to 4.2 (kilo)joules; ⇨ pp. 26–9.

Joule's law, the relationship between the electric current flowing in a conductor (⇨ p. 90) and the heat produced as a result. Joule's law in its modern form states that the rate of heat produced (in watts) is proportional to the resistance of the conductor (in ohms), multiplied by the square of the current (in amps). The law was first stated by the English physicist James Prescott Joule (1818–89).

jugular veins, the four main veins, running down the front and side of the neck that return the BLOOD from the head to the heart. The jugulars are the right and left internal and external veins. They are of variable structure and heavily branched. The internal jugulars are large vein trunks but the pressure in them is so low that the greatest risk, from major injury to them, is not loss of blood but the risk that air will be sucked into them, and then directly into the heart.

junction detector, a detector of ionizing radiation using a reverse-biased semiconductor junction ($\Leftrightarrow$ p. 102–5). Reverse bias normally prevents current flow, but the ionizing effect of radiation allows a current to pass that is directly proportional to the strength of the radiation. The junction detector is one of the most important quantitative methods of radiation detection and measurement, and has wide applications in space science, astronomy, electron microscopy and medicine.

Jurassic period, the second of the three periods of the Mesozoic era ($\Leftrightarrow$ GEOLOGICAL TIME SCALE) during which the dinosaurs were the dominant form of animal life, and primitive mammals and birds first appeared. The name derived from the Jura mountains in France where fossils of this period were first found.

Karnaugh map, a pictorial representation of Boolean truth tables done as an aid to simplification or minimalization; $\Leftrightarrow$ pp. 18–21.

Kb $\Leftrightarrow$ KILOBYTE.

keratin, a hard protein and a major structural component of skin, hair and nails. Hair and nails are almost entirely made of keratin. The keratin molecule is a rigid, cylinder-shaped helix and confers great strength. In the skin, the outer layer contains keratin and is, thereby, waterproof.

ketosis, the presence of abnormally high levels of ketones in the BLOOD. Ketones are produced when there is insufficient available GLUCOSE fuel and fats have to be used. Fats are *triglycerides* and consist of molecules of glycerol to each of which three fatty acids are attached. When fats are used excessively as fuels, these fatty acids are released into the blood where they are converted to the ketones acetoacetic acid, hydroxybutyric acid and acetone. Normally the blood ketone levels are low but in starvation, untreated diabetes, and when the diet is very high in fats and low in carbohydrates, the levels rise. Ketones are volatile substances and confer on the breath the sickly, fruity odour of nail-varnish remover. The danger, however, is that ketones are acidic and high levels make the blood abnormally acid. This leads to loss of water, sodium and potassium, and a major biochemical upset in the body. There is nausea, vomiting, abdominal

pain, confusion, and, if the condition is not rapidly treated, coma and death. Mild ketosis may be a feature of excessive morning sickness in pregnancy.

keyboard, an array of electrical switches, operated by depressing buttons, by which a succession of coded signals is sent to a computer or other electronic device. The key switches on the keyboards of personal computers are continuously interrogated; the depression of a key is detected and a code, unique to that key, is generated. Keyboard buffers allow a variable number of key codes to be accumulated until they can be 'entered' with the 'enter' (or 'return') key, and until they can be handled by the program. In addition to the designated keys, combinations of keys with the 'control' and, in MS-DOS machines, the 'alt' key allow various nonstandard characters and other codes to be sent. The *function keys* can be programmed to perform various program functions that usually differ in different programs. Cursor keys allow the flashing screen indicator to be positioned as required; $\Leftrightarrow$ p. 214.

kidneys, the organs that filter waste material from the BLOOD and adjust the levels of various essential chemical substances, so as to keep them within necessary limits. In humans, the kidneys are paired, reddish brown, bean-shaped structures, each about 11 cm (4.5 in) long, lying in pads of fat on the inside of the back wall of the ABDOMEN, one on each side of the spine. Large arteries run into them directly from the largest artery in the body (the AORTA), and large veins run from them, back to the main collecting vein of the body (the *inferior vena cava*). The output from each kidney– urine – is collected in a conical drain called the pelvis of the kidney and passes into a hollow tube, the *ureter*, which is 40–5 cm (16–18 in) long and runs down to end in the urinary bladder. A shorter single tube, the *urethra*, carries urine from the bladder to the exterior. Urine contains water, urea, uric acids and various inorganic salts in varying concentrations. The kidneys are also largely responsible for ensuring that the body contains the right amount of water and that the blood is of the correct degree of acidity. Most drugs or their breakdown products are eliminated through the kidneys. The kidneys produce a substance, erythropoietin, that stimulates the rate of formation of blood cells in the bone marrow. Each kidney contains at least a million microscopic structures called *nephrons*, and each of these is the basic filtering unit of the kidney. Each nephron consists of a filtering capsule and a long, looped *tubule* that ends in a urine-collecting tubule. All the collecting tubules run into the pelvis of the kidney. Each nephron capsule contains a roughly spherical tuft of tiny blood vessels and through the walls of these escape all the components of the blood, except the cells and the larger molecules. Proteins, fats and all the cells of the blood remain in the circulation. About 170 litres of filtrate are produced each day but the kidney tubules have a remarkable power of selectively passing back into the blood vessels surrounding them all the constituents which are required by the body, including much of the water, sodium, potassium, calcium,

chloride, bicarbonate, phosphate, GLUCOSE, AMINO ACIDS, VITAMINS and many other substances. When the blood pressure falls below normal, or there is excessive loss of fluid from the body, the kidneys release the enzyme renin into the blood. This results in the formation of a further hormone, angiotensin, which rapidly causes blood vessels throughout the body to constrict. This at once raises the blood pressure. Angiotensin also stimulates the secretion of the hormone aldosterone from the adrenal glands. This hormone acts on the tubules of the kidneys to increase the active reabsorption of sodium into the blood and, as a result, increase water retention in the body.

kilobyte, a widely used unit of size or capacity for computer files or memories. In a decimal system *kilo* means 1,000. But in a binary system a kilo is 2 to the 10th power, which is 1,024. A kilobyte is thus 1,024 bytes and a megabyte is 1,024,000 bytes; $\Leftrightarrow$ p. 214.

kilocalorie, the amount of heat needed to raise the temperature of a kilogram of water from 15° to 16°C. The joule is now becoming more commonly used as a unit of energy, and the kilojoule is equal to one thousand joules; 1 kilocalorie is equal to 4.2 kilojoules.

kinetic theory of matter, the theory that the particles of all matter, gas, liquid and solid, are in a state of constant, vigorous, temperature-related motion. The theory is most readily appreciated in the case of gases, where it explains the observable facts about gases and the gas laws ($\Leftrightarrow$ p. 50). In solids, particle movement is known as LATTICE VIBRATION.

Kirchhoff's laws, two general laws concerning the relationship of voltage and current in networks of electrical conductors ($\Leftrightarrow$ p. 90). Kirchhoff's current law states that at any moment in time the sum of all the currents flowing towards a point junction in a circuit is equal to the sum of all the currents flowing away from it. That is, that the ALGEBRAIC SUM of all the electric currents meeting at any point in a circuit is zero. The voltage law states that in a closed loop of conductors the algebraic sum of all the voltage rises is equal to the algebraic sum of all the voltage drops, these being reckoned in the same direction around the loop. These laws facilitate calculations of currents and voltages in complex circuits. They were first enunciated by the German physicist Gustav Robert Kirchhoff (1824–87).

K-mesons, subatomic particles ($\Leftrightarrow$ p. 110) believed to be responsible for holding together the protons in the atomic nucleus in spite of the mutual repulsion of their like charges. Like charges repel one another; unlike charges attract. A powerful force is, therefore, needed to prevent such closely aggregated like charges from flying apart.

knee, the hinge joint between the thighbone (*femur*) and the main lower-leg bone (*tibia*). So that the lower bearing surfaces of the femur can better fit the upper surface of the tibia. Two crescentic cartilage plates, the *menisci* or *semi-lunar cartilages*, are fitted between them. Powerful internal ligaments hold the two bones in apposition and limit the possible amount of movement. On either side are other strong supporting ligaments that merge into a surrounding fibrous tissue capsule. This is lined with a membrane that secretes a lubricant fluid into the joint, allowing smooth and free movement of one surface on the other.

knot theory, a study of the classification of knots, as in string, usually as two-dimensional projections with designated loops, directions and over or under crossings. Thousands of uniquely different knots have been identified, and the theory has applications to understanding the unravelling of DNA and to certain aspects of theoretical physics.

knuckle, the common name for a finger joint.

Krebs cycle, a complicated sequence of enzymatic reactions by which many organisms produce and utilize energy. The reactions of the Krebs cycle also produce a number of essential substances needed for biosynthesis. The cycle, which is also known as the citric-acid cycle or the tricarboxylic-acid-cycle, was elucidated by the German-born British biochemist Sir Hans Adolf Krebs (1900–81).

krypton standard, a definition of the length of a metre as equal to 1,650,763.73 wavelengths of radiation from the element krypton–86.

K-T boundary, the short geological period at the junction between the Cretaceous and the Tertiary periods about 65 million years ago. K is the symbol for Cretaceous ($\Leftrightarrow$ GEOLOGICAL TIME SCALE). The K-T boundary saw the extinction of the dinosaurs together with a major proportion of the living things on Earth. The cause of this has been endlessly argued, and hypotheses range from climatic change or volcanic activity to a collision between a giant asteroid and the Earth (throwing up enough dust to block out sunlight, causing the death of plants, the dinosaurs' main food source). The latter theory has had considerable support and it has been suggested that the impact occurred in the Caribbean sea where considerable quantities of shocked quartz grains have been found and where evidence suggestive of a huge wave has been found.

labia, the four elongated lips of the female genitalia that surround the entrance to the VAGINA and the external opening of the urine tube (*urethra*). The inner of the two pairs, the *labia minora*, are narrow, wrinkled and of varying depth. Each one forks, at the front, to form a hood over the front of the head of the clitoris. The outer pair, the LABIA MAJORA, are long, well-padded folds, containing muscle and fibro-fatty tissue, and covered with hair. At the front, they join in the lower part of the pubic mound (*mons veneris*). As they run back between the thighs, they become more prominent. Behind, they join together about an inch in front of the anus.

labile, unstable, liable to change unexpectedly, whether of a chemical reaction, of the action of the heart, the blood pressure, the state of the emotions or of any other phenomenon.

lacrimal system, the tear-production and drainage system of the eyes. Tears are produced by the lacrimal glands, which lie in the upper and outer parts of the bony eye socket, behind the upper lids. They are also produced by large numbers of microscopic 'accessory' lacrimal glands in the membrane covering the whites of the eyes (the *conjunctiva*). Excessive tears are disposed of into the nose by way of tiny ducts with openings at the inner corners of the four eyelids. These run into the lacrimal sacs, just inwards of the corners of the eyes, and from there down into the nose.

lactase, an enzyme ($\Leftrightarrow$ pp. 182–5) found in the intestinal secretions of mammals that breaks down milk sugar (*lactose*) to GLUCOSE and galactose.

lactate, a salt or ESTER of lactic acid, in which hydrogen of the carboxyl group (-COOH) has been replaced by a metal, such as calcium, sodium, aluminium or iron.

lactation, milk production in mammals. Milk is synthesized in the mammary glands from fats, proteins, sugars and other substances taken from the BLOOD. This occurs under hormonal control only after the end of a pregnancy, but can usually be perpetuated indefinitely under the stimulus of a baby's suckling.

Lagomorpha, the order of mammals that includes rabbits, hares and American coneys.

laminar flow, streamline flow in a fluid medium in which the fluid moves in layers without turbulence. Laminar flow occurs in lubricating oil between bearing surfaces and sometimes in air passing over aircraft at very high altitudes; $\Leftrightarrow$ pp. 34–7.

lanugo, the normal short, soft, downy, colourless hair that covers the fetus from about the fourth month of life in the womb (*uterus*) up to shortly before the time of birth.

large-scale integration, microchip technology in which at least 10,000 transistors and associated components are fabricated on to a single silicon chip; $\Leftrightarrow$ pp. 102–5 and 214.

larynx, the 'Adam's apple' or voice box. The larynx is situated at the upper end of the windpipe (*trachea*), and contains the vocal cords, which, in humans, provide the basic pitched sounds from which speech and song are produced. It also has, at its inlet, a sensitive and rapidly acting flap mechanism, the EPIGLOTTIS, which directs swallowed food into the gullet (*oesophagus*), preventing it from entering the air passages. The larynx extends from the throat (*pharynx*) to the top of the trachea. It has walls of cartilage and is lined with a moist mucous membrane. The vocal cords, situated in its upper region, are two folds of the mucous membrane extending from the wall. Tiny muscles, in the cords and in the adjoining larynx, control the tension and rate of vibration of the cords as air passes through them. In normal breathing the vocal muscles remain loose, so that air can pass easily in and out. The tighter the vocal cords, the higher the pitch of the sound produced. The gap between

the folds is called the GLOTTIS.

laser Doppler velocimeter, an instrument that uses a laser ($\Leftrightarrow$ p. 82) and the Doppler effect ($\Leftrightarrow$ p. 68) to measure the velocity of particles in a fluid.

laser photochemistry, the use of lasers ($\Leftrightarrow$ p. 82) to induce or affect chemical reactions.

laser spectroscopy, spectroscopy ($\Leftrightarrow$ p. 80) using laser light rather than noncoherent light. This has improved the resolution and extended the value of a wide range of spectroscopic techniques.

latch, an electronic circuit that can store a single binary digit (bit) until the next clock pulse arrives; $\Leftrightarrow$ pp. 102–5 and 216.

latent image, the undiscernible image on a photographic emulsion before development.

lateral, of, at, or towards the side. The term comes from the Latin military word *latus*, meaning a 'flank' or 'wing'. *Unilateral* means occurring only on one side; *bilateral* means relating to two sides.

lattice vibration, periodic, heat-related, oscillations of the atoms in a crystal lattice about their mean positions. The excursion of the vibration increases with temperature until, at the melting point of the solid, the atoms leave their lattice sites. Atomic movement decreases with lowering temperature but never completely ceases, even at ABSOLUTE ZERO. The residual vibration at absolute zero is called *zero-point vibration* and is a consequence of the uncertainty principle of quantum mechanics ($\Leftrightarrow$ p. 40). Lattice vibration is the means by which heat is conducted through a solid ($\Leftrightarrow$ p. 52). The scattering of conduction electrons in metals ($\Leftrightarrow$ p. 166) by lattice vibration results in the increase in the electrical resistance ($\Leftrightarrow$ p. 96) observed with a rise in temperature and the decrease in resistance with a fall in temperature.

lava, molten rock from the Earth's interior that reaches the surface through volcanic vents and other openings. The term is also applied to the igneous rock formed when molten lava cools and solidifies. Lava varies widely in composition; $\Leftrightarrow$ pp. 146–51.

LCD $\Leftrightarrow$ LIQUID-CRYSTAL DISPLAY.

leaching, the removal of a soluble substance from an associated insoluble solid by dissolving it in a suitable solvent.

leap second, a correction to the calendar necessary to keep the accepted atomic-time standard in synchronization with Earth time. The leap second is needed because of slight slowing of the Earth's rotation ($\Leftrightarrow$ p. 144). A second has been added annually to all but a few years since 1972.

LED $\Leftrightarrow$ LIGHT-EMITTING DIODE.

Lenz's law, the principle that when an electromotive force ($\Leftrightarrow$ p. 90) is induced in a conductor it is always in such a direction that the current it produces will oppose the change that caused the electromagnetic force. This change is commonly the movement of a conductor through a magnetic field (⇨ p. 88), so the current will produce a force that opposes the movement. Alternatively, the change may be the movement of a magnetic field in relation to a conductor. In this case the current will produce an opposing magnetic field. The law was first stated by the German physicist H. F. E. Lenz (1804–65).

Lepidoptera, the order of scaly-winged insects that includes the 100,000 or so species of butterflies, moths and skippers (Hesperiidae).

lesion, any injury, wound, infection, or any structural or other form of abnormality anywhere in the body. The term is derived from the Latin *laesio,* meaning 'an attack or injury'.

lethal gene, a gene (⇨ pp. 202–5) that causes the death of the organism that inherits it. Lethal genes are common mutations and are usually recessive manifest themselves only if present in both ALLELES. Dominant lethal genes are quickly eliminated.

leukocidins, substances produced by bacteria that kill white blood cells of the immune system.

leukocyte, any kind of white blood cell. The leukocytes include, among others, the phagocytes, the macrophages and the T and B lymphocytes of the immune system (⇨ IMMUNITY).

leukotrienes, powerful chemical agents released by white blood cells known as *mast cells* are involved in many immunological processes including allergic reactions. In asthma they cause the narrowing of the air passages and the secretion of mucus. They can be inhibited by corticosteroid drugs.

lice, common parasites of humans and other animals. Lice are small, wingless insects, of which three varieties (two species and two subspecies) inhabit humans. These are head lice, body lice and pubic lice. The head louse, *Pediculus humanus capitis,* lives on the scalp and feeds by sucking blood, causing intense itching. The females lay eggs (popularly known as 'nits'), which they glue to the shaft of hairs near the scalp. These hatch in about a week. Spread is by direct contact. The body louse, *Pediculus humanus corporis,* lives in the seams of clothing close to the skin, and move on to the body only to feed. The eggs are laid in the clothing. Body lice have been responsible for great epidemics of typhus in times of war and other civil disturbance. They also transmit relapsing fever. The crab louse, *Phthirius pubis,* so called because of its squat, crab-like appearance, infests the pubic hair and, occasionally, the chest hair, armpit hair or even the eyebrows. *Phthirius pubis* is usually transmitted by sexual contact, and once established, likes to remain in one place, causing constant irritation. Crab lice soon become surrounded by louse faeces. The scratching of the infested person inoculates both these and the lice bodies into the skin,

leading to a severe dermatitis. Unlike body lice, crab lice do not transmit any significant disease.

lie detector, a popular term for the *polygraph,* a collection of devices that simultaneously monitor, and record, in graphic form, several changeable features of the human body, such as the pulse rate, the blood pressure, the evenness and rate of breathing and the moistness – and hence the electrical resistance – of the skin. While this monitoring is in progress, the subject is asked a series of questions to some of which an emotional response is likely. Such a response cannot be concealed by any action on the part of the subject and will be apparent on the tracings. Emotional responses to certain questions do not, however, necessarily indicate that the subject is lying or concealing the truth, and such results must be interpreted with great care and imagination.

life span (human), the maximum time a human being may expect to live in the absence of disease or injury. This is about 110 years. To some extent this is determined by genetic factors and people with long-lived parents may, in general, expect to live longer than those whose parents died younger. There is no evidence to suggest that life span is increasing, although the time people *do* live (*life expectancy*) certainly is. As a result of a higher standard of nutrition and hygiene, and because of medical advances, more and more people are tending to reach the natural life span. There is reason to believe that the natural life span may be determined by the number of times body cells are capable of dividing. If cells from a young person are artificially cultured, they undergo a certain number of population doublings by division and then cease to divide further and die. Cells from an older person divide less often before dying and cells from a very old person may not divide at all. The number of population doublings varies with the type of cell cultured. For the common collagen-producing fibroblasts it is about 50. Ironically, certain cancer cell cultures appear to be immortal.

ligament, a tough, band-like tissue of collagen fibres that binds BONES together. Ligaments may be white and inelastic or yellow and slightly compliant.

light amplifier, an image intensifier that produces an image of more intense brightness than that seen by the unaided and dark-adapted eye.

light bulbs, the commonest source of electric light. The power or wattage of a bulb is the product of the voltage and the current flowing through it (⇨ p. 90) and is inversely proportional to the resistance (⇨ p. 96) of the filament. The higher the wattage, the lower the resistance. Wattage in a light bulb is not a measure of light intensity although the two are roughly proportional. Light output is measured in *lumens;* the number of lumens per watt is an indication of the efficiency of the bulb. A 60-watt bulb might provide 870 lumens, while a 100-watt bulb will provide 1,759 lumens, equal to that of two 60-watt bulbs. In general, higher

wattage bulbs will provide more light output per watt than lower wattage bulbs.

light-emitting diode, a small electronic device (⇨ pp. 102–5) consisting of a semiconductor junction that produces a cold light, usually red, when a small electric current passes through it, i.e. when it is forward biased. LEDs are widely used as 'on' indicators and, because they can produce a very small point of light, can be combined to form displays of alphanumeric characters or more complex image displays. They are cheap, long-lived and have very small current and voltage requirements, although greater than those of LIQUID-CRYSTAL DISPLAYS.

lightning, the luminous effect of a large electrical discharge through air containing suspended water droplets. This results from the separation of electrical negative and positive charges that occurs within cumulonimbus clouds in association with the strong upward air currents that are a feature of these clouds. Charge separation results in the higher parts of the clouds becoming positively charged and the lower parts negatively charged. When the voltage difference reaches about 100,000 volts per metre, flashover occurs. The resulting heat causes rapid expansion of air, which is heard as a thunderclap.

light year, a measure of distance – the distance light travels in a year. The light year is about 9,461,000,000,000 km (5,879,000,000,000 mi). The nearest star to our Sun, proxima Centauri is about 4.5 light years away.

limbic system, developmentally a relatively early part of the brain, centrally situated and arranged in a ring. It consists of a number of interconnected nerve-cell nuclei and constitutes much of the brain in the less-developed mammals. The limbic system is concerned with the coordination and regulation of unconscious and automatic body function (*autonomic nervous-system function*), but also involves associated emotional reactions, especially rage, fright and sexual interest, common to humans and other animals. The limbic system is also concerned with the regulation of respiration, body temperature, hunger, thirst, wakefulness, sexual activity and the link between neurological and hormonal function, mediated by the hypothalamus and the PITUITARY GLAND. Disorders of the limbic system cause emotional disturbances, forced or spasmodic laughing and crying, aggression, anger, violence, placidity, apathy, anxiety, fear, depression and diminished sexual interest.

limestone, a sedimentary rock (⇨ p. 150) consisting mainly of calcium carbonate (chalk) and magnesium carbonate.

linear relationship, the relationship of two quantities when a change in one causes a directly proportional arithmetical change in the other. The term *linearity* is often applied to electronic amplifiers to describe the uniformity of the degree of amplification over the working frequency range. The term describes the fact that if the two quantities are plotted on a graph the result will be a straight line.

linkage, the association of two or more genes near each other on the same chromosome (⇨ p. 202), which persists even after the exchange and redistribution of chromosome segments that occur in the cell divisions in which the sperm cells and ova are formed (*meiosis*; ⇨ p. 188). Linkage can be inferred from associations in the inheritance of characteristics and, from this, the proximity or otherwise of genes or chromosomes can be deduced.

lipids, long-chain organic hydrocarbons and their derivatives including fats and oils (TRIGLYCERIDES), waxes (fatty acid esters of long-chain alcohols), STEROIDS and other more complex compounds; ⇨ pp. 182–5.

liquid, the state or phase of matter between solid and gas. The shape of a given mass of a liquid depends on the container. Unlike a gas, a liquid does not expand indefinitely to fill a container. Also unlike gases, liquids are virtually incompressible. Although they do not have the crystalline lattice structure of solids, they do have more structural regularity than gases, whose molecules are randomly arranged. Liquids readily conduct heat and some conduct electricity. They can efficiently transmit force. Liquids diffuse readily to form homogeneous mixtures with other miscible liquids; ⇨ p. 34.

liquid-crystal display (LCD), a type of display used in clocks, watches, portable computers, panel meters, etc., using a combination of polarizing filters and crystals capable of changing state under the influence of an electric field. The crystals are sandwiched between two transparent electrodes. Liquid crystals are *nematic* substances – substances that exist in an intermediate state between liquid and solid (*mesomorphic*) in which a linear orientation of the molecules changes their physical properties. The application of an electric field causes crystals to realign so as to prevent light passing through the area concerned. In this way individual areas are darkened. In most applications, bar-shaped segments that can form alphanumeric characters are used. Computer LCD screens use an array of small dots to form picture elements (*pixels*). Displays may be monochrome or colour, and are often backlit so as to make them more legible in bright conditions. Colour displays may be of the double-supertwist nematic type or of the thin-film transistor type. The former is cheap but reacts slowly and does not give particularly sharp colours. The latter produces an excellent display but is expensive; ⇨ pp. 72–5.

Lissajous figures, patterns formed on an oscilloscope (CATHODE-RAY TUBE) screen when the electron beam is moved simultaneously by the electric fields of two sinusoidal voltages at right angles to each other. If the frequencies are equal, a single closed figure, such as a circle, is formed on the screen. If one is twice that of the other, a figure-of-eight is formed. Three loops are formed if one frequency is three times that of the other, and so on. So long as one frequency is an integral multiple of the other, a close figure with multiple loops is formed. Lissajous figures are a useful way of comparing the frequencies of two sinusoidal voltages applied to the plates of an oscilloscope. If a source of sinusoidal voltage of accurately known frequencies (a *signal generator*) is connected to one set of plates, the instrument can act as a frequency meter. The shape of the curves also provides information about the relative phase of the two voltages. The idea was proposed by the French physicist Jules A. Lissajous (1822–80), who used vibrating mirrors.

lithotripsy, a method of fragmenting stones in the urinary system and in the gall bladder, by focused and concentrated ultrasonic shock waves, without the necessity for a surgical incision. Ultrasound waves can be focused to a point by parabolic reflectors and aimed so that the point of focus, and maximum energy, coincides with the stone. The patient is anaesthetized and the position of the stone accurately determined by an X-ray-image intensifier. Shock waves are generated by a high-voltage spark discharge and focused on the stone. When the shock is fired, a great deal of energy is liberated; the stone shatters and is reduced to particles small enough to be passed naturally in the urine or into the bile duct and bowel. Up to 90 per cent of stones that previously could have been removed only by open surgery, can now be dealt with by this method; ⇨ p. 70.

little ice age, a period during which the average temperature of the Earth declines by a few degrees. The last little ice age persisted from about AD 1500 to 1900 when the temperature was was about 3° below average, glaciers advanced and agriculture was, in places, seriously affected. Little ice ages are said to occur every 2,500 years.

liver, a spongy, reddish-brown organ occurring in all vertebrates. In humans it occupies the upper-right corner of the ABDOMEN and extends across the mid-line to the left side. The liver is the largest organ in the abdomen. BLOOD from the intestine, the spleen and the stomach passes to the liver by way of a short, wide vein called the *portal vein,* which enters on the underside. At about the same point, a large and important artery from the general circulation, the *hepatic artery,* also enters the liver. Within the liver, these two vessels divide into tree-like structures the smallest branches of which end in millions of tiny liver lobules where the blood from them comes into intimate contact with the liver cells. These lobules are the functional units of the liver; in them many complex biochemical processes go on. In parallel with the blood system of the liver is a network of fine, branching, drainage tubules – the *biliary system.* These end up in the bile duct, which runs into the small intestine at the DUODENUM and which has a short side branch to the gall bladder, under the liver, where the bile is stored and concentrated. The liver is the major chemical processing organ of the body and has a wide range of activities. The raw materials, such as GLUCOSE, AMINO ACIDS, fats, minerals, VITAMINS, enter in the nutrient-rich blood from the intestine. From this blood, the liver takes up glucose and synthesizes from it a highly concentrated storage form of carbohydrate called GLYCOGEN. On demand, glucose can immediately be released from this material. The liver also deals with fats and proteins, converting them into forms required by the body. It can even convert one into the other. Amino acids are built up into the complex proteins required by the blood and the immune system, or broken down and converted to carbohydrate or fat, as the need dictates. The liver takes up the products of old red blood cells, largely from the spleen, and converts these into a pigment, bilirubin, that (together with other substances) forms the bile. The liver has remarkable powers of breaking down toxic substances into safer forms. Ammonia produced from protein breakdown is converted into urea, which is excreted in the urine. Alcohol and other drugs are altered to safer forms. To a remarkable degree, the liver is able to regenerate itself after disease, toxic damage or injury.

lobe, a well-defined subdivision of an organ. The brain, the LUNG, the LIVER, the PITUITARY, the thyroid gland and the prostate gland are divided into lobes.

local-area network (LAN), a way of connecting personal computers within a building or small area so that they can communicate with each other and with a central *file server* computer with large storage capacity, from which they can derive data. Networking involves special problems and requires sophisticated software; ⇨ p. 218.

logic circuits, electronic circuits that process information coded in terms of voltage levels, usually representing 1s and 0s or 'true' or 'false'. The logic is implemented by three basic *gates,* the AND, OR and NOT gates, or the derivatives of these, the NAND and NOR gates; ⇨ pp. 102–5.

logic state, the state of truth or falsity of a binary signal. Only these two states are allowed in Boolean logic (⇨ p. 18) and nearly all computers still operate on this basis, using LOGIC CIRCUITS. 'Fuzzy' logic, allowing a range of values between true and false, corresponds more closely to how biological systems operate and is used in neural networks (⇨ p. 224) and other attempts to implement artificial intelligence.

log in, the act by which a computer user identifies himself or herself to the machine and is thus authorized to have access. Log in usually involves a form of authentication, often by typing in a recognized password. Log in implies that at the end of the session, the user will log out.

loins, the soft tissue of the back, on either side of the spine, between the lowest ribs and the pelvis.

loudness, the subjective experience of the intensity of sound or the amplitude of sound waves. Because the human ear varies in sensitivity at different frequencies, loudness is not the same for different frequencies at the same sound amplitude. Sensitivity is highest between 1,000 and 4,000 Hz and is lower above and below this range. Loudnesses are compared using a logarithmic scale that is adjusted to take into account these differences in sensitivity.

low-density lipoproteins, the microscopic bodies, consisting of proteins and fats, especially cholesterol, that transport these substances from the intestines and the LIVER to all parts of the body, including the arteries. LDLs do not directly deposit cholesterol in the walls of the arteries but do so after they have been oxidized by oxygen FREE RADICALS – a process that makes them biochemically more active. The result is *atherosclerosis*, an arterial disease that restricts blood flow and causes more deaths (mainly from heart attacks and strokes) than any other single cause. Antioxidants such as vitamins E and C can 'mop up' free radicals. Compare HIGH-DENSITY LIPOPROTEINS.

luminescence, light emission (⇨ pp. 72–5) other than that caused by purely thermal energy. Light may be produced by part of the energy release by slow chemical reactions (*chemoluminescence*), it may be produced by the exciting effect of various forms of radiation (*radioluminescence* or *photoluminescence*). Alternatively it may be produced by the presence of an electric field (*electroluminescence*).

luminous energy, energy radiated in the visible part of the electromagnetic spectrum, specifically at a wavelength of 380–760 nanometres; ⇨ pp. 72–5 and 84.

lungs, the organs of gas exchange between the BLOOD and the atmosphere. The whole blood volume is constantly circulated by the right side of the heart, which acts as a pump to drive the blood to the lungs before returning to the left side of the heart and, from there, to the rest of the body. In humans, the air tubes begin with the central wind-pipe (*trachea*) just below the voicebox (*larynx*). This passes downwards behind the large BLOOD VESSELS at the upper border of the heart, and, at the level of the upper part of the breastbone (*sternum*), the trachea branches into the two main bronchi. The right bronchus is shorter than the left and more directly in line with the trachea. Soon after the division of the trachea, the bronchi enter the lungs and immediately branch into three smaller bronchi on the right side and two on the left. These continue to branch, leading to three lung lobes on the right and two on the left, which are, in turn, subdivided into a total of nineteen separate lung segments. The smallest air passages end in grape-like clusters of air sacs, the alveoli (⇨ ALVEOLUS), and the walls of these are very thin and contain the terminal branches of the blood vessels. Thus the air comes into intimate contact with the blood so that the interchange of gases can easily occur.

lymph, the fluid in the lymph vessels, which they drain from the tissue spaces and from the intestine. Lymph varies in constitution in different parts of the body. Lymph from the tissues is largely fluid that has leaked out of the smallest BLOOD VESSELS (the capillaries). It

contains large numbers of white cells, mainly LYMPHOCYTES, and is usually clear. Lymph from the intestines is milky, especially after a meal, because of the large number of tiny fat globules that it contains. Fat-laden lymph is called *chyle*.

lymph gland, a common, but incorrect, name for a LYMPH NODE. These are not organs of secretion and cannot accurately be called glands.

lymph nodes, small oval bodies, up to 2 cm (0.75 in) in length, situated in groups along the course of the lymph-drainage vessels. Each node has a fibrous capsule and contains large masses of LYMPHOCYTES. In humans, the main groups of lymph nodes are situated in the groin, the armpits, in the neck, deep in the ABDOMEN around the main BLOOD VESSELS, in the suspensory curtain of the bowels (the *mesentery*) and in the central partition of the chest (the *mediastinum*). The lymph nodes are an important defence against the spread of infection from the surface tissues to the deeper parts of the body, and from the internal organs to the bloodstream. Their lymphocytes produce large quantities of ANTIBODIES (immunoglobulins) to combat infection, and the nodes are often the site of a major conflict with invading organisms. In this event the nodes often become swollen and tender.

lymphocytes, specialized white blood cells concerned in the body's immune system (⇨ IMMUNITY). They are of two general types – B cells and T cells. B cells produce ANTIBODIES and T cells, which are of several kinds, attack infecting organisms and cancer cells directly or participate in the attack on organisms.

lyophilization, freeze-drying. Removal of a solvent from a material by freezing it below the freezing point of all components of the mixture (the *eutectic point*) and then providing enough heat to effect SUBLIMATION of the frozen solid (latent heat of sublimation). The process is usually done under conditions of reduced pressure.

lysis, the destruction of a living cell by disruption of its limiting membrane. *Haemolysis* is lysis of red blood cells. This occurs if they are placed in pure water, which will flow into them by OSMOSIS, stretching them until they burst.

machine code, the software that provides immediate instructions to a computer's central processing unit (CPU) in a form that can immediately be 'understood' by it. Machine code is the lowest-level programming language and consists simply of a string of numbers. It is thus an almost impossible language in which to write a computer program in it, so higher-level languages are used that contain actual instructions expressed in words. High-level languages are translated into machine code by a *compiler* program. An assembly language is a low-level language that contains the same instructions as machine code, but expressed in names rather than numbers. Assembly language is translated into machine code by an *assembler* program; ⇨ p. 218.

Mach number, the ratio of the speed of a body

to the speed of sound at sea level (740 mph). A body travelling at a speed in excess of Mach 1 is moving at supersonic speed (⇨ p. 68). Mach 2 is 1,480 mph, and so on. The term honours the Austrian physicist and philosopher Ernst Mach (1838–1916) who proposed the system. Mach also founded the philosophical system of logical positivism, which holds that nothing should be believed until its truth has been demonstrated by empirical testing.

macro, a macroinstruction, a sequence of commonly used computer instructions contained in a short program that can be called up and put into operation with a single command. The use of macros can save a great deal of time in programming at all levels.

Magellanic clouds, the most readily visible galaxies outside the Milky Way. Both the Small and the Large Magellanic clouds (⇨ pp. 140–3) can be seen with the naked eye. The large cloud is probably a barred spiral.

magma, the molten material, largely of silicon but also of sulphur, phosphates, carbonates, etc., from which igneous rocks (⇨ p. 150) are made.

magnet, an iron-containing body with domains (⇨ p. 88) sufficiently well aligned to produce an external magnetic field and to experience a turning force (*torque*; ⇨ p. 28) when placed in another magnetic field.

magnetic-bubble memory, a form of nonvolatile computer memory using thin films of a material, such as garnet, that can readily be magnetized in one direction but not in the other. Integrated-circuit manufacturing techniques are used to fabricate a surface to which tiny magnetic fields can be applied so as to modify the magnetic state locally to form a microscopic domain change called a *bubble*. Each bubble, or absence of a bubble, corresponds to a binary digit. This is retained even when the current is switched off but can be read and changed by purely electronic means. Bubble memories are more expensive than semiconductor memories and have not fulfilled their early promise.

magnetic disk, a computer storage system providing rapid access to data files or programs. Magnetic disks may be HARD or FLOPPY DISKS; ⇨ p. 214.

magnetic field, a space surrounding a permanent magnet or an electric conductor carrying a current, in which a magnetic force can be detected by its effect on iron-containing bodies or on charged particles. Magnetism can be induced into a suitable body by bringing it into a magnetic field, and an electric current will be induced into any electrical conductor that is moved in a magnetic field (⇨ pp. 88–91).

magnetic moment, the relationship between a MAGNETIC FIELD and the turning force (*torque*; ⇨ p. 28) it exerts on an iron-containing body, a charged body or electric current; ⇨ pp. 88–91.

magnetic permeability, the readiness to which a material can be magnetized by a given

MAGNETIC FIELD. Permeability is proportional to the strength of the induced magnetism (*flux density*) divided by the intensity of the field.

magnetic resonance, a phenomenon based on the fact that the inner core (*nuclei*) of atoms spin constantly. Protons carry a positive charge so atomic nuclei, in spinning, create a tiny magnetic field. Hydrogen atoms behave in this way. When such atoms are placed in a strong magnetic field, the two magnetic fields interact and all the atoms are forced into alignment in a particular direction. The spin frequency of these atomic nuclei is known, and when another set of radio signals (an electromagnetic field), oscillating at this frequency, is briefly applied at an angle to the main field, the axes of these spinning nuclei are turned through an angle. The return movement to their former position, after the applied pulse ceases, causes these atomic magnets to generate tiny electro-magnetic signals (radio waves), and these can easily be detected and the position of their origin accurately calculated and recorded.

magnetic-resonance imaging, a method of obtaining detailed visual information about the internal structure of an object such as the human body. The principle of MAGNETIC RESONANCE has been applied to a valuable method of scanning capable of a degree of resolution of detail greater than that possible with CT scanning. As in the CT scanner, the very large number of separate readings obtained can be stored in a computer that can then rapidly perform thousands of differential equations to recover the strength of the signals coming from all the different points in the field under examination, and reconstitute from them a cross-sectional image of the part. Every molecule of water contains an atom of hydrogen so the presence of water causes a strong signal to be emitted. Less strong signals are sent out by other materials with proportionally less hydrogen in them. In this way the MRI scanner is capable of resolving subtle abnormalities in soft tissue such as brain and nerves. Differences in tissue composition are easily seen. Thus, for instance, the characteristic plaques of multiple sclerosis are clearly revealed. An area of brain deprived of its blood supply, as in a stroke, is easily visible, and in some cases it is even possible not only to show the presence of a tumour, but to differentiate between benign and malignant types. MRI is safer than other forms of scanning. The radio waves used are of the same wavelengths as normal short-wave broadcasts and these have been passing through our bodies since birth. The main magnetic field, within which the patient lies, is, however, very strong indeed and all metal objects must be kept well away. To produce such a field requires superconducting electromagnets and these are, at present, very bulky and expensive, requiring liquid helium to reach the necessary low temperature. New and more efficient superconducting materials are, however, being developed, operating at higher temperatures.

magnetism, a class of phenomena in which a field of force is caused by the alignment of the magnetic moments of atoms in the same direction (*ferromagnetism*) or by a moving electric charge (*electromagnetism*). *Diamagnetism* is the phenomenon caused by the orbital motion of electrons in the atoms of any material. *Paramagnetism* is due to the alignment of unpaired spins of electrons in atoms of a material. All materials thus respond to some extent to a MAGNETIC FIELD, but only ferromagnetic materials show a readily apparent response; ⇨ p. 88.

magnetoencephalography, a way of inves-tigating brain function by detecting the increase in the very small MAGNETIC FIELDS generated by the sum of the nerve impulses in a particularly active part of the brain.

magnetohydrodynamics, a propulsion system for sea vehicles in which an electric current between immersed electrodes generates a MAGNETIC FIELD that is repulsed by the powerful field of superconducting magnets. The conducting salt water is driven out of the open back of the vehicle creating a forward thrust.

magnetostriction, the change in the dimensions of an iron-containing body when it is subjected to a MAGNETIC FIELD. The direction of the change depends on the direction of the applied magnetic field. Magnetostriction is applied in various TRANSDUCERS especially those producing high-frequency sound (*ultrasound*). Such a device consists simply of a coil of wire wrapped round a rod of the ferromagnetic material.

magnification, a measure of the degree of optical enlargement or reduction. Magni-fication may be linear or angular. Linear magnification is the ratio of the size of the image to that of the object. Angular magnification is the ratio of the angles formed at the eye by the image and the object.

malabsorption, a failure of the normal movement of some of the elements of the diet from the small intestine into the bloodstream. This may be because of the absence of the chemical substances, enzymes, necessary for the breakup of the food into absorbable form, or to some structural change in the lining of the intestine. Malabsorption may lead to MALNUTRITION, even if an adequate diet is taken.

malar, relating to the cheekbone. The Latin word *mala* means the 'cheek or cheekbone', and the term may also relate to the Latin *malum*, meaning 'an apple'.

malignancy, a term derived from the Latin *malignus* meaning 'evil' and usually applied to cancerous tumours that spread remotely in the body. The term 'malignant' is opposite in meaning to the term 'benign'. It is also used to qualify unusually serious forms of various diseases. In general, a malignant disorder is one tending to cause death in the absence of effective medical intervention.

malnutrition, insufficient food or, more generally, a diet inappropriate in quantity or quality for the promotion of health and development. Infant malnutrition is widespread in many parts of the world and especially in those areas of the developing world affected by war and natural calamity. Malnutrition leads to the population stunted in body becoming stunted, often accompanied by a restriction in mental capacity.

malt, cereal grains that have been dried after being allowed to germinate by soaking in water.

maltase, an enzyme (⇨ pp. 182–5) that breaks down a molecule of malt sugar (maltose) into two molecules of GLUCOSE. It occurs widely in nature and is present in the digestive juices of vertebrates.

mammary gland, the breast. Milk production by the mammary gland is called LACTATION.

mammography, a form of X-ray examination used in cases of suspected breast cancer and as a screening procedure on groups of women.

manometer, an instrument for measuring pressure, especially in gases. A manometer consists of a U-shaped glass tube containing a liquid such as water or mercury, and a scale placed behind the upper level of the liquid in one arm. If a single pressure is to be measured the source of pressure is connected to the top of one arm so that a rise of pressure forces the liquid down in that arm and up in the other. If two pressures are to be compared, connections are made to both arms; ⇨ pp. 34 and 50.

marble, any limestone or calcium magnesium carbonate (dolomite) hard enough to take a polish; ⇨ p. 150.

marsupials, an order of animals in which the females have a skin pocket or pouch on the abdomen, covering teats. After birth, the young, crawl into the pouch where they remain to feed until mature enough to emerge. The marsupials include kangaroos, opossums, bandicoots and wallabies.

mass, the measure of a body's resistance (⇨ p. 96) to acceleration (⇨ p. 28). Mass, unlike WEIGHT, does not change when subjected to different gravitational forces; ⇨ p. 30.

mass number, the total of the protons and neutrons in the nucleus of an element; ⇨ pp. 156–61.

mast cell, the central cell type in the allergic reaction. Mast cells, when stained for microscopy, are seen to contain numerous large granules. These are collections of powerful chemical substances such as histamine. In people with allergies, a particular form of antibody, IgE, remains attached to the mast cells. When the substance causing the allergy (the *allergen*) contacts the IgE, the mast cell is triggered to release these powerful substances and the result is the range of allergic symptoms and signs.

mastoid, shaped like a breast or nipple. The mastoid process of the temporal bone of the skull is the bony lump behind the ear. This process is honeycombed with spaces that communicate with the middle ear. Infection can spread from the ear to the mastoid process and from there to the membranes covering the brain (the *meninges*) to cause *meningitis*, or even to the brain itself to cause a brain abscess. Fortunately, antibiotics are so effective in controlling middle-ear infection, that mastoiditis is now rare.

matrix, a rectangular array of addresses consisting of horizontal rows and vertical columns. The rows are numbered from top to bottom and the columns form left to right. Any ADDRESS can thus be identified by referring to the appropriate row and column. In this elementary sense matrices are used in computer memories, spreadsheets, etc. In mathematics, statistics, engineering, economics, psychology and many other disciplines, matrices are used as computational techniques to solve a wide variety of problems.

maxilla, the upper jaw.

mechanical advantage, a measure of the effectiveness of simple machines such as the lever. *Mechanical advantage* is the ratio of the force exerted by the machine to the force applied to it. In general, an increase in the output force will be associated with a decrease in the distance through which it operates compared with the distance through which the input force operates; ⇨ p. 28.

medial, situated towards the midline of a structure, such as the human body. Compare LATERAL.

mega-, a multiple of 1 million. The symbol is M. One megabyte (1 Mbyte) is a million bytes. 1 megahertz (1 Mhz) is a million cycles per second.

meiosis, the form of cell division (⇨ p. 188) performed in the sex organs of all sexually reproducing plants and animals to convert normal body cells, with their full complement of chromosomes (*diploid number*), to sperms and ova, with half the number of chromosomes (*haploid number*). Meiosis also involves two processes that result in a radical 'shuffling' of the genetic material – *crossing over* and exchange of segments of chromosomes between similar (*homologous*) pairs, and the redistribution to different cells of different members of the homologous pairs, i.e. those derived originally from the father and those from the mother. Crossing over occurs after homologous pairs of chromosomes have entwined intimately together. Meiosis involves three or four stages of division and a radical redistribution of the genes between pairs. Thus, in animals with many chromosomes it is unlikely that any two particular sperms or ova will be genetically identical to one set of the chromosomes of either parent. The full number of chromosomes is restored at conception when the sperm fuses with the egg.

melting point, the temperature at which a solid changes to a liquid at normal atmospheric pressure (⇨ p. 52). At the melting point heat is absorbed and most substances, but not water, expand. Water contracts when changing phase from solid to liquid.

memory, in biology, the capacity to recall information. In computing, a device or medium capable of retaining information in such a way that it can be recalled as often as required (⇨ p. 216). A volatile memory is a semiconductor memory whose contents are retained only for as long as the power supply is maintained. A random-access memory (RAM) is a volatile MATRIX memory in which data is stored (written into) known ADDRESSES from which they can be retrieved and left, or over-written as required. A read-only memory (ROM) is a nonvolatile memory that cannot, in normal practice, be written to, but can be read from whenever needed.

meninges, the three layers of membrane that surround the brain and the spinal cord. The innermost, the *pia mater*, follows the surface closely, remaining in contact even in the depths of the brain furrows (*sulci*). The spider-web-like *arachnoid mater* bridges over the furrows, leaving the subarachnoid space, which contains cerebro-spinal fluid. The outer later, the *dura mater*, is a tough, fibrous covering offering excellent protection.

menopause, the cessation of ovulation and of the menstrual periods in human females. This is associated with a reduction in the production of oestrogen hormones by the ovaries. In most cases the menopause occurs between the ages of 48 and 54, but an earlier onset is common. After the menopause reproduction by conventional means can no longer occur.

meridian, one of the infinite number of imaginary lines joining the poles of the Earth and crossing the EQUATOR at right angles (⇨ p. 144). The intersection at the surface of a sphere with the plane that passes through the centre and an arbitrary pole (the GREAT CIRCLE). In physiological optics, the term is used less rigorously to refer to any curve on the surface of a lens or the cornea of the eye that passes through the optical centre. In this sense, meridia can have different radii of curvature, as in the case of an astigmatic cornea, and thus need not refer to a sphere.

metastasis, the spread of any disease, but especially cancer, from its original site to a remote point in the body where the disease process starts up anew. The word is also used to describe the new focus of disease. Malignant tumours have a strong tendency to metastasize. This they do by 'seeding off' small clumps of tumour cells from the primary tumour. These are then carried elsewhere to start up a new, secondary, tumour. Cancers commonly metastasize to the LUNGS, the LIVER, the brain and the BONES, but secondaries can occur literally anywhere in the body. Metastasis may occur by way of the bloodstream, by spreading along the lymphatic vessels, or, in the case of lung cancer, by coughing and re-inhalation of affected particles to other parts of the lung.

micro-, a submultiple of one millionth of any particular unit. The symbol is μ. A microgram (μg) is a millionth of a gram. A microsecond (μs is a millionth of a second.

microlithography, the use of a very fine beam of laser light (⇨ p. 82), electrons (⇨ p. 90) or X-rays (⇨ p. 84) to cut the microscopic circuit detail in the masks from which electronic microchips are made. Shadow-masking using these masks and light or X-rays on silicon wafers coated with a light-sensitive resist allows the pattern of the circuit to be transferred to the wafer in terms of unaltered resist, which can then be removed with a solvent.

microprocessor, a computer-central-processor unit in a single integrated-circuit chip (⇨ pp. 102–5 and 218). A microprocessor forms the heart of a microcomputer but is used in many other applications such as process controllers in domestic and industrial equipment, interactive toys, machine-tool controllers, point-of- sale and other terminals, and car-fuel and engine-control systems. Microprocessors vary considerably (⇨ PERSONAL COMPUTER) but all contain an arithmetic and logic unit (ALU), a control unit, a control memory, a BUS control, an internal memory and a working register. The whole operation of the microprocessor is kept in SYNCHRONIZATION by a clock that produces a SQUARE-WAVE output. The microprocessor also has its own software in the form of an instruction set for carrying out input and output operations, logic, arithmetic, data transfer, and so on.

microsurgery, operative surgery carried out at magnifications of two to about twenty times, using an operating microscope and appropriately miniaturized operating instruments. Microsurgery allows a degree of precision in the cutting, manipulation and approximation of small parts that is unobtainable by other means. It makes possible procedures that would almost certainly fail if attempted using conventional techniques, and has, in certain limited fields, allowed major advances. The operating microscope is a binocular instrument, often providing binocular facilities for both surgeon and assistant. The surgeon is able to control focus, movement and zoom magnification by means of a panel of controls operated by his or her feet. The operating field is brightly illuminated by a beam of light from the microscope itself, often following the same path (*co-axial illumination*) as the viewing optics. Microsurgery is universally used in almost all eye (*ophthalmic*) operations and has revolutionized the results. In addition delicate operations are performed on the middle and inner ears, often to cure conductive deafness, and the joining up of small arteries (*vascular microsurgery*) often makes it possible successfully to re-attach severed arms or legs. To a lesser extent, microsurgery is being employed in gynaecology and urology.

microwaves, radiation lying between radio waves and the infrared in the electromagnetic spectrum (⇨ p. 84). Microwaves have wave-lengths of a few centimetres to a few millimetres, and frequencies of hundreds of millions of cycles per second (hundreds of Megahertz) to tens of thousands of Megahertz. They are produced by OSCILLATORS such as klystrons and magnetrons, and are conducted along waveguides or COAXIAL CABLES. They can be transmitted in the same way as other radio waves and have the advantage that aerials are appropriately small. They are usually transmitted in beams using small dipole aerials at the focus of parabolic-dish reflectors. Because of their high frequency, microwave bands provide a wide range of usable channels. They are used in telecommunications, radar, heating and cooking.

milk, the secretion from the mammary gland (breast) of any mammal. Because of its similarity to human milk, cow's milk is a useful food for humans, providing an excellent balance of CARBOHYDRATE, fat, protein, minerals and VITAMINS. As a result, it has been commercially exploited on an enormous scale. Although close in composition, cow's milk is not identical to human milk, the chief difference being in the composition of the milk fats. Human-milk fats contain a higher proportion of long-chain and unsaturated fatty acids, which provide greater resistance to organisms commonly affecting the bowel, such as those causing dysentery, than do fatty acids from cow's milk. Even more important, human milk contains protective ANTIBODIES produced by the mother's immune system, which provide her baby with protection against many organisms, until such time as the baby can produce its own. The main carbohydrate in milk is lactose. Some people do not have the enzyme that breaks this down to simpler sugars and, since the unaltered lactose cannot be absorbed, it remains in the bowel and ferments, causing bloating, distention, pain and diarrhoea. This is called *lactose intolerance.*

milli-, a submultiple of 1 thousandth of any unit. The symbol is m. One milligram (1 mg) is a thousandth of a gram. One millisecond (1 ms) is a thousandth of a second.

minicomputer, a class of computer lying nominally between a microcomputer (PERSONAL COMPUTER) and a mainframe in size and power. Originally the minicomputer was a machine accommodated in a single large cabinet. Many present-day personal computers, especially WORKSTATIONS, are as powerful as previous minicomputers. The term is now seldom used.

mips, millions of instructions per second. This is a measure of the speed and power of a computer (⇨ chapter 10).

mitosis, the major form of cell division employed by cells other than those forming sperms or eggs. In mitosis there is exact duplication of chromosomes so that daughter cells have exactly the same genetic content as the parent cells. In mitosis, each chromosome unwinds to form a long thread of chromatin. This is precisely replicated and the new chromosomes then separate to opposite ends of the cell, which then elongates and splits into two cells; ⇨ p. 188. Compare MEIOSIS.

modem, a device that allows computers to communicate with each other along ordinary telephone lines; ⇨ pp. 218–23.

modular programming, in computing the

normal method of proceeding, in which programs are written in sections (*modules*), each of reasonable and manageable size, and each performing a particular, well-defined, function. Modules, once written and tested, can be exported to other programs; ⇨ p. 218.

modulation, the process of superimposing a signal carrying information on to another wave (the *carrier wave*) or on to an electron beam. The superimposition may involve changing the amplitude, the frequency, the phase or the continuity of the carrier wave (⇨ pp. 64–7). The carrier wave will usually have a much higher frequency than the information signal, as in the case of amplitude-modulation (AM) radio in which the carrier wave may be of a frequency of many Megahertz, while the information is of audio frequencies (about 20–20,000 Hz). In frequency modulation, the amplitude remains constant while the frequency is changed at a rate corresponding to the changes in the information. In phase modulation, periodic alterations occur in the timing of the start of each cycle of the carrier wave (*phase*) in accordance with the information frequencies. In pulse modulation the carrier is switched on and off in pulses to form a binary code conveying the information; ⇨ p. 216.

Mohs scale, HARDNESS SCALE for minerals introduced by the German mineralogist Friedrich Mohs (1773–1839), with talc as hardness 1 and diamond as hardness 10.

Moiré pattern, the changing pattern of curved lines seen when two families of curves are superimposed at an angle of less than about 45°. A Moiré pattern can be seen even when the separation of the curves of the individual systems are below the resolution of the eye. Moiré patterns, named after watered silk, can be used to measure very small angles, down to about 1 second or arc, and to investigate stresses in metals and aberrations in lenses.

molecular weight, the total of the atomic weights of all the atoms in a MOLECULE; ⇨ p. 156.

molecule, the smallest unit of a chemical compound. In the case of a number of elements, the molecule consisting of two identical atoms linked together by chemical bonds. More often, the molecule consists of two or more different atoms bonded together; ⇨ pp. 162–5.

Mollusca, a large phylum of the animal kingdom containing many similarly formed, soft-bodied, often shelled creatures including snails, slugs, oysters, clams, squids and octopuses. There are believed to be over 110,000 different species of molluscs.

Monera, one of the five taxonomic kingdoms of living things. The Monera include blue-green algae and bacteria.

monoclonal antibodies, ANTIBODIES of a particular, unique type that have become available in large quantity following a major advance in immunological science. Antibodies are produced by B cells (*B lymphocytes*). There is a type of cancer, called *myelomatosis,* in

which a single B cell develops into a tumour (a *myeloma*) of antibody-secreting cells. This results in enormous quantities of a single immunoglobulin – a *monoclonal antibody.* Mice readily develop myelomas and these have provided scientists with unprecedented quantities of monoclonal antibodies. These, however, were specific to a particular, unknown, antigen and could not be used for other antigens. In 1975, however, the German immunologist George Köhler (1946–) and his colleague, the Argentine-born immunologist César Milstein (1927–), found a way of taking normal mouse B cells and fusing them to cultured myeloma cells to form immortal lines of cells that continue indefinitely to generate the particular antibody produced by the B cell concerned. So it became possible to produce hybrid cell tumours, called *hybridomas,* that grow like myelomas but produce large quantities of a chosen and identifiable monoclonal antibody. This was one of the most important biotechnological advances of the 20th century. It is now possible to obtain monoclonal antibodies that can recognize individual antigenic sites on any organism, indeed on almost any molecule, and the research and treatment implications have been enormous. Monoclonal-antibody production has made possible tests for the presence of an almost unlimited range of organisms and for different types of cells, including cancer cells. Since monoclonal antibodies can be made to seek out and recognize cancers, wherever they might be in the body, much research has been done into the possibility of using this method to carry a toxic agent to the tumour cells and destroy them.

monosodium glutamate, the sodium salt of glutamic acid, commonly produced by the action of acids or enzymes on vegetable protein such as wheat gluten or soya bean. It is also known as 'Ajinomoto', 'Vetsin', 'Chinese seasoning', 'Accent' and 'Zest'. It is a white crystalline powder, with a meat-like taste, that imparts a meat flavour to blander foods if used with a little salt. It has also been used to improve the flavour of tobacco. Monosodium glutamate has been suspected of being the cause of an acute reaction featuring a burning on the face, head and chest, nausea, headache and dizziness (the *Chinese-restaurant syndrome*).

morbidity, the state of being diseased. The morbidity rate is the number of cases of a disease occurring in a given number (usually 100,000) of the population. The annual morbidity figures for a disease, in a particular population, are the incidence figures – the number of new cases reported – in the year.

mortality rate, the ratio of the total number of deaths from one or any cause, in a year, to the number of people in the population. 'Crude mortality' is the number of deaths in a year per thousand total population. The age-specified mortality rate is the number of deaths occurring in a year in people of a particular age or in a particular age-group. Mortality rates are a useful way of checking the state of health of a population and of assessing any changes in disease trends. Rates for the whole population may be compared with rates within certain socioeconomic groups or in certain occupations, thus highlighting possible causes of disease or death; ⇨ also INFANT MORTALITY.

mosaicism, the existence of two or more genetically different types of cell in the same individual. Normal human body cells contain 23 pairs of chromosomes. In mosaicism, the cells do not all possess the same number of chromosomes although they are all derived from the same fertilized egg. In some cases of mosaicism some cells have an additional chromosome while the other cells are normal. Mosaicism may, for instance, occur in *Down's syndrome*. This is caused by an additional chromosome 21 (*trisomy 21*). But in about 1 per cent of cases there are two different cell lines, one normal and the other having the additional chromosome 21. Mosaicism may considerably modify the effect of the chromosome abnormality, sometimes reducing its effect almost to insignificance.

MOSFET, an acronym for metal oxide semiconductor field effect transistor (⇨ pp. 102–5). A type of transistor fabrication suited for large-scale chip integration, with a low power consumption and high switching speed compared to earlier transistors. A high proportion of computer chips are currently of MOSFET construction.

motion, a change of position with the elapse of time relative to an observer (⇨ p. 28). Absolute motion has no meaning (⇨ p. 38).

motor, anything that causes movement. In physiology, a motor nerve is one that stimulates muscles into contraction. The motor pathways in the nervous system are the large pyramidal tracts of nerve fibres sweeping down from the part of the surface of the brain subserving movement (the motor cortex) to the spinal cord to link with the motor nerves running out of the cord to the muscles.

mouse, any of the many species of small, long-tailed rodents of the families *Muridae* and *Cricetidae* that are similar to, but smaller than, rats. They include fieldmice, harvest mice and the domestic house mouse. In personal computing this is a simple device, attached to a computer, that can be moved about on a flat surface. The movement is sensed electro-magnetically, usually by the rotation of a small ball on the underside of the mouse, and the resulting signal is sent to the machine. This is applied in such a way that movement is accompanied by a corresponding movement on the screen of the *cursor*, the flashing indicator of the position at which keyboard usage will affect the screen – the point, for instance, at which typed letters will appear. The mouse is equipped with one or more microswitches activated by a small downward movement of a finger (a 'click'). In many application programs (⇨ p. 218) the appearance of the cursor changes as it is moved to different parts of the screen. It might, for instance, change to an arrow or some other symbol as it moves beyond a border on the screen, or as different parts of the program are used. Clicking will then have different effects, depending on the appearance of the cursor. It might cause a menu to appear, from which a selection of actions can be made by moving the cursor to the desired item and clicking. Some functions are activated by clicking twice in rapid succession ('double-clicking').

mucous membrane, the inner lining of many of the cavities and hollow internal organs of the body. Mucous membrane lines the mouth, the nose, the eyelids, the intestine, the gall bladder, the urinary bladder, the URETHRA, the VAGINA, the UTERUS and many other structures. It contains large numbers of goblet-shaped cells, which secrete MUCUS, keeping them moist and lubricated.

mucus, a clear, slimy, jelly-like material, chemically a *mucopolysaccharide* or *glyco-protein*, which is produced by the goblet cells of MUCOUS MEMBRANES. It has essential lubricating and protective properties and, without it, life would be unpleasant, and perhaps impossible. Mucus prevents acid from destroying the stomach wall, and enzymes from digesting the intestine. It assists in the conditioning of inhaled air and in the clearance of smoke and other foreign particles from the lungs. It eases swallowing and the movement of the bowel contents by PERISTALSIS and facilitates sexual intercourse.

multiplexing, the combining of a number of different signals in a common channel of communication so that they can be transmitted together and later separated. This can be done in a variety of different ways. In time-division multiplexing, for instance, a sequence of consecutive, very short, time slots is used and these are allocated, one after the other, to the different signals. Thus signals A, B, C and D might each be allocated one thousandth of a second in which to transmit. After four thousandths of a second, the cycle is repeated, and so on. When the signals are separated the gaps are inappreciable.

muon, a subatomic particle (⇨ pp. 108–11) with a negative charge, a mass 207 times that of the ELECTRON and a very brief life.

muscle, a protein tissue consisting of numerous elongated cells called muscle *fibres*, capable, on receipt of a stimulus, of rapidly shortening. Between 40 and 50 per cent of the weight of the human body consists of muscle. Muscles fibres cannot contract to a variable degree. Either they contract fully or not at all. Body muscles are made up of considerable bundles of fibres and the number that contract at any time depends on the force required. Under maximum effort, almost all the fibres in the muscle will contract. Muscle fibres convert chemical energy into mechanical energy and their main function is to produce movement in the body. For this reason, most muscles are connected to bones and lie across a joint with one end attached on either side. Contraction of the muscle thus causes the joint to flex. Muscle action of this kind is never unopposed and there is always another muscle, or group of muscles, on the other side of the joint, exerting an opposite effect on the joint. Muscles that bend a joint are called *flexors*; those that straighten it are called *extensors*. There are three kinds of muscle – striated or voluntary muscle, which is attached to bone; smooth or involuntary muscle, which occurs in such places as the walls of blood vessels, the intestine and the urinary tract; and heart muscle (*myocardium*), which is a network of muscle fibres with the special property of automatic regular contraction.

mutagen, any agent capable of causing genetic change in a cell (MUTATION) and hence, should the cell survive and continue to reproduce, in all that cell's descendants. Mutations in body cells may cause cancers; those in the cells producing ova or spermatozoa may cause inherited abnormalities or diseases. Mutagens include X-rays, gamma rays from radioactive material, other forms of ionizing radiation and a wide range of chemical substances. Among the commonest mutagens in humans are the tars and other substances derived from burning tobacco.

mutation, any change in the genetic material (DNA) of a cell. This most commonly involves a single gene on a chromosome, but may involve the whole, or a major part of, a chromosome, even causing reduplication so that the number of chromosomes is increased. Mutations occurring in the sex cells are inherited if the affected cell happens to take part in fertilization. This is more likely to happen if the mutation occurs in a precursor cell of sperms or ova. The presence of MUTAGENS in the environment increases the likelihood of mutation. Mutations are rare and most are unfavourable, often leading to the death of the cell or interfering with its power to reproduce. Mutation provides the basis for the variations necessary for evolution by natural selection (⇨ p. 198).

myelin, the fatty, whitish, insulating material surrounding most nerve fibres. Accumulations of nerve-cell bodies have a grey appearance but bundles of myelinated fibres look white. De-myelination is the loss of the myelin sheath and is a feature of nerve degeneration and certain nerve diseases. The most significant of the demyelinating diseases is *multiple sclerosis* in which plaques of demyelination occur, affecting many adjacent nerve fibres.

myoglobin, the muscle equivalent of the HAEMOGLOBIN of the BLOOD.

nails, fastening devices, usually of metal, that can be hammered into wood or other material. In biology, nails are protective covers for the vulnerable finger and toe ends, and provide useful tools for many manipulative purposes. The nail consists of a curved plate of a tough protein called *keratin*, resting on the nail bed and growing outwards from the nail matrix. The base of each nail shows a variable-sized 'half moon'. The inturned skin edge around the nail is called the *nail fold*. In humans, fingernails take four to five months to grow from matrix to finger-tip, growing at a rate of about one centimetre in three months. Toenails take about three times as long.

nano-, a submultiple of one billionth (1 thousand

millionth) of any unit. The symbol is n. One nanosecond (1 ns) is one billionth of a second.

nanotechnology, the physical manipulation of matter at molecular level by effecting actual movement using the tip of a SCANNING TUNNEL MICROSCOPE.

narcosis, a sleep-like or stuporous state, caused by a drug, from which the affected person cannot immediately be fully aroused. The word derives from the Greek *narke,* meaning 'numbness'.

nasopharynx, the space at the back of the nose, above and behind the soft palate, and the space at the back of the mouth running down to the top of the throat. The back wall of the nasopharynx bears the ADENOIDS in childhood, and, on either side, the openings of the *eustachian tubes* along which air passes to the middle ear to equalize air pressure inside and outside the eardrum.

native elements, elements that are found in a pure state in nature. They are gold, silver, platinum, copper, lead, tin, zinc, mercury, tantalum, bismuth, antimony, arsenic, selenium, tellurium, sulphur and carbon (as diamond or graphite). Occasionally, iron is found in a relatively pure state.

natriuretic factor, a protein-like substance present in higher than normal levels in people with persistent heart failure. This substance, which was discovered in 1981 and has been intensively studied ever since, causes BLOOD VESSELS to widen and increases the output of URINE. It appears to have a selective action on the KIDNEYS, which is beneficial to those with heart failure, and shows promise of being useful in treatment.

natural gas, an important nonrenewable energy source (⇨ p. 92) consisting of about 85 per cent methane and up to about 10 per cent of ethane. Smaller proportions of butane, pentane and other hydrocarbons in the paraffin series (⇨ p. 164) may be present. For domestic use, natural gas is much safer than the former coal gas, which contained a significant proportion of the poisonous CARBON MONOXIDE.

nebula, an astronomical entity, either an extragalactic star system – an external galaxy – or a diffuse cloud of dust particles and gas, mainly hydrogen, which, if excited by external energy, may be seen as a hazy patch of light, an *emission nebula,* or which may appear as an irregular dark region – a *dark nebula.* Gaseous nebulae are components in the Milky Way galaxy; ⇨ pp. 140–3.

neck, the conduit between the brain and its locomotory and nutritional maintenance systems, and the route of transmission for much of the bodily information required by the brain, and of the brain output data required by the body. The neck thus contains some structures of vital importance, notably the carotid and vertebral ARTERIES carrying BLOOD, with OXYGEN, fuel and hormones up to the head, the windpipe (*trachea*) carrying vital oxygen to the LUNGS, and the cervical spinal cord, conveying

nerve-impulse information to and from the brain. Centrally, at the front of the neck, just above the trachea, is the LARYNX, containing the vocal cords and straddled by the THYROID GLAND, in which are embedded the parathyroid glands. Running down, just behind the trachea is the gullet (*oesophagus*) through which food is conveyed to the STOMACH, and, on either side, at the front, the four large JUGULAR VEINS, carrying blood back to the heart from the head. The skeleton of the neck consists of the upper seven vertebrae of the spine, and connected to these, and to the base of the skull, to the jawbone (*mandible*), the collar bones (*clavicles*) and the upper ribs, is a complex structure of muscles supporting, and allowing carefully controlled movement of, the head.

necrosis, death of a body tissue. Gangrene. The commonest cause of necrosis is inadequacy or loss of blood supply (ISCHAEMIA), but tissue death can result from overwhelming local infection; physical injury from heat, cold or trauma; chemical injury, as from corrosive substances; or radiational injury from X-rays (⇨ p. 84), gamma rays or other forms of radiation.

negative feedback, an arrangement by which a small portion of the output of an amplifying system is fed back to the input in opposite phase to the ingoing signal. The effect of this is to correct distortion occurring within the system and greatly to improve its stability. Negative feedback is an important element in many mechanical, electronic and biological systems.

negative logic, computer logic (⇨ p. 216) in which a high voltage is taken to represent 0 (false) and a low voltage to represent 1 (true). This is merely an arbitrary convention and does not affect in any way the working of the system.

nematodes, a phylum of unsegmented worms containing many classes.

neoplasm, literally, a 'new growth'. A neoplasm is the result of an abnormal local increase in the numbers of body cells so that a mass of cells, called a tumour or neoplasm, develops. A neoplasm may be malignant (a *cancer*) and spread both locally and distantly; or it may be benign and form a local, usually encapsulated, mass.

nerve, a collection of nerve fibres running together in a bundle outside the brain or spinal cord. Individual fibres are usually insulated with a layer of white, fatty material called MYELIN, which imparts a shiny, white appearance to the nerve. The fibres are held together by connective tissue. Most nerves contain fibres running from the central nervous system to the periphery, and fibres running from the periphery to the central nervous system. The former run mainly to supply muscles and cause them to contract; the latter are mainly sensory nerves carrying information to the brain. Such a nerve is called a *mixed nerve.* Within the central nervous system bundles of nerve fibres running together form a *neural tract.* The white matter of the brain consists of many such tracts. Coming directly from the brain are 12 pairs of *cranial nerves,*

and coming directly from the spinal cord are 31 pairs of *spinal nerves.* These 86 nerves connect to all the muscles in the body and receive information from the whole area of the skin and from all internal organs.

nervous breakdown, a popular term of uncertain definition, used to describe a range of emotional crises varying from a brief attack of 'hysterical' behaviour to a major psycho-neurotic illness with severe, long-term effects on the life of the victim. The term is also sometimes used as a euphemism for a psychiatric illness such as schizophrenia.

network, a communication system involving more than two terminals, such as a LOCAL AREA NETWORK or a wide area network; ⇨ chapter 10.

neuron, the functional unit of the nervous system. A neuron is a single nerve cell consisting of a cell body, a long nerve fibre or *axon,* running out of it, and usually one or more shorter nerve processes, known as *dendrites,* running into the nerve body. The cell body contains the nucleus. Neurons interconnect with each other at specialized junctions called *synapses;* at most of these, the electrical nerve impulse ACTION-POTENTIAL activity is trans-mitted by release of chemical messengers called NEUROTRANSMITTERS. Synapses occur mainly between the end of the axon of one neuron and the cell body or the dendrites of another, but may occur between dendrites and axons. Many neurons receive up to 15,000 synapses (some more than 100,000) and the great majority are *interneurons* connecting with other nerve cells, rather than with muscles of glands. This arrangement allows for a system of transmission of nerve impulses, some excitatory, some inhibitory, which can operate similarly to electronic gates in computers (⇨ pp. 102–5 and 216–21) and by which all logical functions may be performed. The same arrangement, assuming a constant flow of nerve impulses, provides a physical basis for memory. This network of neurons is functionally and structurally affected by past experience, which causes the brain to acquire greater complexity of the branching pattern of dendrites, an increase in the number of supporting cells, and changes in the structure and ease of firing of synapses.

neurosis, any persisting mental disorder causing distress to the person concerned and recognized by the sufferer as abnormal, but in which contact with reality is retained. There is no obvious causal factor and the behaviour of the sufferer does not grossly violate social norms. Earlier classification included anxiety neurosis, phobic neurosis, obsessive–com-pulsive neurosis, hysteria, depressive neurosis, narcissistic neurosis, depersonalization and others, but experience showed that, in practice, it was often impossible accurately to apply these labels. The tendency, today, is to recognize that most neurotic people suffer from anxiety that is either experienced directly or expressed through defence mechanisms, and appears as one or more of a variety of symptoms, such as a phobia, an obsession, a compulsion or as sexual dysfunction. The disorders formerly classified as neurotic are now described as *anxiety disorders, somatoform* or *conversion* disorders (formerly 'hysteria'), *dissociative disorders* (amnesia, fugue, multiple personality, depersonalization), *sexual disorders* and *dysthymic disorders* (neurotic depression). These various conditions are probably best regarded as being the result of a form of conditioning or programming inappropriate to the mores of society. The most hopeful form of treatment would seem to be some form of behaviour therapy.

neurotransmitter, a chemical substance selectively released from a NERVE ending by the arrival of a nerve impulse. The neurotransmitter then interacts with a receptor on an adjacent structure to trigger off some kind of response. The adjacent structure may be another nerve, a muscle fibre or a GLAND. Nerve action, mediated by neurotransmitters, is a precise process that can be increased or decreased as needed, and, because the chemical structure of many of the neurotransmitters is known, they can be used as drugs to modulate some of the most important actions of the nervous system. In addition, many highly effective drugs act by simulating the action of neurotransmitters, by modifying their action or by blocking the receptor sites at which they normally act. The main neurotransmitters are acetylcholine, dopamine, norepinephrine, serotonin, GABA (gamma-amino- butyric acid), the endorphins, the enkephalins, glycine, glutamate, aspartine, adrenaline, histamine, vasopressin and bradykinin. Growing knowledge of neurotransmitters and their action is throwing light on many of the aspects of brain function and neurological disorder. An increasing number of diseases of the nervous system are being shown to be due to disorders of neurotransmitter production or action.

neutron, one of the two major components of the atomic nucleus ($\Rightarrow$ pp. 108–11 and 156–61), the other being the PROTON. Only hydrogen–1 has no neutron in the nucleus. The neutron has a mass very close to that of the proton but has no electric charge. Protons are positively charged and since like charges repel each other, two or more protons could not exist together within the dimensions of atom nuclei were it not for the presence of neutrons. Neutrons weaken the electrostatic repulsion without weakening the forces that bind nuclear particles together ($\Rightarrow$ p. 112). In the lighter elements the number of neutrons and protons is about equal; in the heavier element the number of neutrons predominates. *Isotopes* are different varieties of the same element having the same number of protons but different numbers of neutrons. Free neutrons emitted from nuclei are needed to sustain nuclear-fission chain reactions ($\Rightarrow$ p. 160).

nicotine, a powerful alkaloid drug derived from the leaves of the tobacco plants *Nicotiana tabacum* and *Nicotiana rustica*. It is a colourless to amber oil with a strong smell of tobacco and an intensely bitter taste. Nicotine is highly toxic and is sometimes used as an insecticide. Nicotine poisoning causes severe nausea and vomiting, spontaneous emptying of the bladder and bowels, mental confusion and convulsions. Like many other poisons, nicotine, taken in

very small dosage, is valued for its stimulant properties. In smoking, the drug passes rapidly into the bloodstream and gives a quick 'lift' by its NEUROTRANSMITTER-like action on the brain until broken down in the liver and excreted in the urine. In those who are habituated, it increases the heart rate and raises the blood pressure by narrowing small arteries. This effect can be dangerous in certain arterial diseases. The dangers of nicotine are, however, trivial compared to the dangers of the other constituents of tobacco smoke.

nitrate, a salt derived from nitric acid (HNO_3) containing the negative NO_3- ion. Most of the metallic nitrates are readily soluble in water. Nitrates contain NITROGEN in its highest oxidation state and are thus important in compounds, such as explosives, in which rapid access to plentiful supplies of oxygen is needed. Nitrates are useful oxidizing agents. They are widely used as fertilizers.

nitrogen, a chemically inert, colourless and odourless gas making up about 80 per cent of the Earth's atmosphere. Nitrogen is a constituent of animal and other proteins, and it appears in URINE in the form of UREA, the main nitrogenous waste product of the body. The nitrogen cycle ($\Rightarrow$ p. 206) is essential for life. Nitrogen oxides are among the most important and dangerous of the atmospheric pollutants. They derive mainly from motor-vehicle exhausts acted on by sunlight, and can cause severe respiratory disorders.

nitrosamines, a class of neutral, yellow, oily compounds containing the divalent group N-N=O. NITRATES and nitrites are used to preserve certain foods, such as bacon, ham, corned beef and some fish. There is some evidence that nitrosamines can be formed from such foods. They are also acquired from cigarette smoke and other atmospheric pollutants. Nitrosamines can cause cancer in animals.

noise, any unwanted signal or information added to a communication channel in the course of its use. Noise need not be, indeed, seldom is, acoustic in nature, although it may be audible if the information leaves the communication channel in audible form. It is usually electrical in nature. Noise may, for instance, be visible on a VDU as light flashes. Noise can degrade the quality of an information channel by producing spurious signals and by rendering voltage logic levels ambiguous. A television screen displays considerable noise after television transmission has ceased. Frequency MODULATION (FM) transmission is inherently less sensitive to noise than amplitude modulation (AM) transmission.

nonbinary logic, multivalue logic.

normal, in mathematics and physics, a term meaning perpendicular to, or perpendicular to the tangent to a curve at a particular point; $\Rightarrow$ p. 20.

nuclear binding energy, the difference between the mass of an atom and the sum of the masses of the protons, neutrons and electrons of which

it is constituted. This mass difference, expressed in energetic terms is the nuclear binding energy that holds the atom together; $\Rightarrow$ p. 112.

nuclear energy, also known as atomic energy, the energy released, principally in the form of heat, light, and radiation, as a result of changes in the nuclei of atoms. Nuclear energy is released in certain natural processes, such as the spontaneous decay of naturally occurring radioactive substances ($\Rightarrow$ p. 160), and the nuclear reactions that power the Sun and other stars. It is also released in devices such as nuclear reactors and nuclear weapons. Nuclear radiations are the radiation and particles emitted from the cores (*nuclei*) of radioactive atoms during radioactive decay and nuclear reactions. They are the nuclei of helium atoms (*alpha particles*), electrons (*beta particles*), and electromagnetic radiation of wavelength shorter than visible light, or X-rays and gamma rays ($\Rightarrow$ p. 84). These radiations have different powers of penetration, the beta particles being least penetrative and the gamma rays most. Ionizing radiations such as these are capable of dislodging linking electrons from molecules and thus breaking them into smaller molecules. The effect of this on the body is to produce biological changes in structures such as the chromosomes, in which mutations may occur, or to form active or toxic products in the cells. In general, radiations are most destructive to those cells most rapidly dividing. They thus tend to have their greatest effect on the reproductive organs, on the lining of the digestive tract and on the skin.

nucleus, the central core of an atom ($\Rightarrow$ pp. 108–11 and 156–61) or of a cell ($\Rightarrow$ pp. 186–9). The atomic nucleus is the core of PROTONS and NEUTRONS, and is surrounded by a rapidly moving cloud of ELECTRONS, widely separated from it. Almost all the mass of the atom is in the nucleus. The forces that bind together the particles of which the nucleus is composed are immensely powerful. It is these forces that are released in an atomic explosion. The *nucleus* of a body cell is the central structure consisting of the tightly bundled chromosomes surrounded by a nuclear membrane. *Nucleus* is the Latin word for a little 'nut' or 'kernel' – something right at the centre of something else.

object-oriented programming, a type of computer programming in which the formerly conventional ideas of the distinction between data and procedures are set aside. They are replaced by ideas of *objects* and *messages*. Objects are collections of information each with a description of its particular manipulation; messages are specifications of what is to be done with objects. OOP languages include Smalltalk, C and C++, and these are rapidly replacing the previously more widely used languages; $\Rightarrow$ pp. 216–19.

occiput, the back of the head.

occultation, the disappearance of a star or planet behind the Moon, or of any planetary satellite behind the parent body. Occultation by the Moon can be used to determine longitude.

octahedron, in mathematics, a solid with eight faces. A regular octahedron has faces that are equal-sided (*equilateral*) triangles, identical in all respects (*congruent*).

Octopoda, the order of cephalopods that contains the octopus and about 150 other similar species. Octopoda have eight arms each equipped with suckers.

Odonata, the order of insects that contains dragonflies, of which there are some 3,000 species.

oedema, excessive accumulation of fluid, mainly water, in the body. The accumulation may be general, or in a particular location. In generalized oedema, fluid accumulates in any of the tissues, but especially in the air spaces of the LUNGS and in the spaces in the ABDOMEN surrounding the bowels and other organs (peritoneal cavity). This cannot occur in a healthy person, however much fluid is drunk, because the KIDNEYS dispose of the surplus fluid in the URINE. Generalized oedema occurs if loss of dissolved substances from the BLOOD, such as protein and salt, reduces the power of the blood to withdraw fluid from the surrounding tissues by the process known as OSMOSIS. This may result from kidney disease, liver disease or from starvation, in which the intake of protein is inadequate. Oedema also occurs in heart failure, in which the heart is unable to pump blood round fast enough to clear fluid from the tissues. There is a rise in back pressure in the veins and fluid accumulation. Stagnating blood always results in a net outflow of water to the tissues. Oedema of the legs occurs in varicose veins for this reason. Local oedema is the result of injury to a part and results from an increase in the water permeability of the injured blood vessels, which is a normal feature of INFLAMMATION. In most cases local oedema settles as the inflammation resolves.

oesophagus, the gullet or swallowing tube that extends downwards from the throat to pass through the DIAPHRAGM and enter the STOMACH. In humans the oesophagus is about 24 cm (9.5 in) long, and is a muscular tube lying just in front of the spine and behind the windpipe. Food is carried down by controlled contraction of the muscular walls (PERISTALSIS) and at the bottom, immediately above the stomach, is an important muscle ring, the *cardiac sphincter*, that normally closes after swallowing, to prevent the stomach contents from returning.

olfactory nerve, one of the paired nerves of smell. The two nerves run forward, close together, on either side of the mid-line, on the floor of the cranial cavity and send tiny, hair-like filaments down through perforated bony plates into the upper part of the nose. Odorous materials can be detected at very low concentrations by chemical interaction with the olfactory nerve endings. The sense of smell is very much more sensitive and discriminating than the sense of taste.

omenta, two double folds of membrane, the greater and lesser omenta, that hang down within the ABDOMEN from the LIVER and STOMACH to cover to a variable degree the coils of small intestine. The omenta contain fat globules and BLOOD VESSELS and have a useful function in sealing down any local areas of inflammation (peritonitis) and preventing this from becoming general.

oncogenes, genes that encode proteins that contribute to malignant tendencies in cells. They are mutations of normal-cell genes and must work together to cause cancer. A single oncogene cannot do so. When it was shown that certain retroviruses could cause cancer, an intensive study of these was undertaken. It was found that they had only three genes – *gag*, *pol* and *env* – and that these code for all the proteins needed for the replication of the viruses. Replacement of one of these by an oncogene made the virus capable of causing cancer. Cancer cells have lost the normal control over dividing (reproduction) caused by contact with other cells (contact inhibition). In one experiment, done in 1981, it was shown that DNA extracted from human cancer cells and inserted into normal cells in culture could cause them to become cancerous. DNA from normal cells did not. The difference was traced to an oncogene, *ras*, first described in a retrovirus that causes cancer in rats. The proteins coded by oncogenes show similarities to certain known growth factors, to growth-factor receptors on cells and to the enzymes associated with the receptors. The fact that different oncogenes must work in association with each other to produce cancer suggests that some kind of cascade action is necessary, with the various stages being produced by different oncogenes.

onyx, banded quartz, of which the variety known as sardonyx is regarded as a gemstone. Sardonyx has reddish-brown and white or black straight and parallel bands.

oogenesis, the process by which egg cells are produced in the ovaries and are prepared for release and fertilization. Oogenesis includes the process by which the number of chromosomes is reduced to half the normal, so that, on fertilization the full complement will be restored by a half-number contribution from the sperm.

opal, a hydrated form of silicon dioxide (silica) valued as a gemstone for its opalescence. Opal may be of many colours and has a hardness of 5–6 on the MOHS SCALE.

operand, a number, quantity or function on which a mathematical or logical operation is performed; ⇨ pp. 22 and 218.

operating system, the software that controls the basic running of a computer; ⇨ p. 218.

operational amplifier, a very-high-voltage gain, directly coupled, usually integrated-circuit amplifier with a large amount of NEGATIVE FEEDBACK from output to input, a very-high-input impedance and a low-output impedance. Gain is stabilized by the negative feedback, and the absence of capacitors (⇨ p. 98) in the coupling between the stages allows amplification at frequencies down to DC.

Operational amplifiers have been used extensively in analogue computing (⇨ p. 220) and in instrumentation, and are still widely used as conveniently-packaged, general-purpose voltage amplifiers.

operon, a row of contiguous genes (⇨ pp. 202–5) on a chromosome that operates as a unit. Genes in an operon are preceded by two regulatory sites in the chromosome containing two regulatory genes, the *promoter* and the *operator*. These are essential for the expression of the operon. Genes in an operon have related and sequential functions, so that successive steps in the synthesis of a protein or in the promotion of some biochemical event occur as they should. All the genes in the operon are turned on and off together. For genes to be expressed, they must first be transcribed into a piece of complementary RNA (ribonucleic acid) called *messenger RNA*. All the genes in an operon are transcribed into one large segment of messenger RNA.

optical activity, the ability of different forms of the same compound, in solution, to rotate the plane of a beam of plane-polarized light (⇨ pp. 72–5), either clockwise or anticlockwise. The effect is due to the fact that some molecules exist in two forms that are mirror images of each other, but have an asymmetry, like that of the right and left hands, that prevents them from being superimposed on each other. These forms are called *optical isomers* or *enantiomers*. Dextrorotary (right) forms may have subtly different properties from laevorotary (left) forms in that they may interact differently with other asymmetric molecules. Some drugs, for instance, are more active in one form than in the other.

optical character recognition (OCR), a method of rapidly converting large amounts of printed text to digital code (⇨ p. 220) so that it can be stored, rapidly accessed and used by computers. Text must first be scanned by a machine that produces a computer-storable image of the page, resolved into millions of tiny dots (*bit-mapped*). The position of the picture elements (pixels) of the first letter is then compared with those of a stored vocabulary of letters of the same typeface until a match is found. The event is used to generate the ASCII code (⇨ p. 216) for the letter concerned. This process is then repeated with each letter in turn. Spaces generate the code for a space. OCR software varies in its sophistication. Some programs can be 'taught' to recognize unusual type-faces, hand-printed letters or even normal handwriting. OCR is likely to be used to convert all printed material worth preserving to machine-usable code.

optic nerve, one of the paired nerves that connect the eyes to the brain. In humans each optic nerve contains about a million nerve fibres. These originate in nerve cells on the surface of the retina and come together at the *optic disc* to pass through a hole in the white of the eye (the *sclera*) to form a tight bundle and acquire a fibrous coat. Because there are no light receptors in the optic disc, the projection of this into space is known as the *blind spot*. The optic nerve has an 'S' bend, to provide slack so as to allow free eye movement, and at the back of the bony socket (*orbit*) it passes through a channel in the bone to reach the inside of the skull. There it meets its fellow from the other side, and the fibres from the inner half of each retina cross over to join those from the outer half of the retina on the other side. The two optic *tracts* so formed run into the brain. This arrangement ensures that the signals from the right field of vision pass to the left half of the brain, and vice versa.

optoelectronics, the interface between electronics and associated light signals conveying information. Optoelectronics is concerned, for instance, with the conversion of information ($\Leftrightarrow$ p. 216) in the form of electrical signals into a form that can be transmitted in a laser beam ($\Leftrightarrow$ p. 82) along a glass fibre-optic channel, and the re-conversion, at the other end, into electronic form. It is also concerned with the possibilities of implementing logic by means of lasers and ultra-rapid light switches. LIQUID-CRYSTAL DISPLAYS ($\Leftrightarrow$ pp. 72–5) are another aspect of optoelectronics.

organism, any living animal or plant. The most elaborate known example is the human being (*Homo sapiens*). Microorganisms include the single-celled protozoa, fungi, bacteria and viruses. Between microorganisms and humans is an almost infinite variety of organisms of all degrees of complexity.

orgasm, a sequence of bodily processes, occurring at the climax of sexual intercourse, and involving the pleasurable release of heightened muscle tension. In men, orgasm features a succession of spasmodic muscle contractions that cause the ejaculation of seminal fluid. Orgasm in women has no such reproductive function and is less well defined. It is rare for men, even those who are impotent (can achieve only a soft erection, insufficient for penetration), to fail to achieve orgasm. Women may fail to experience orgasm through failure of sexual arousal, but absence of orgasm is common even if arousal is high. In most cases, the female orgasm consists of a relatively low peak of sexual excitement centred in the CLITORIS. This may be single or multiple with one peak running into another. Rarely, the male-type experience occurs – an intense peak, that precludes the desire for further stimulation.

Ornithischia, one of the two orders of DINOSAURS. The Ornithischia had bird-like pelves and are believed to have been herbivores. The other order of dinosaurs was the Saurischia.

orthogonal, consisting of, or containing, right angles.

Orthoptera, a large order of insects containing grasshoppers, crickets, katydids, locusts, stick insects, mantids, cockroaches and others.

oscillator, a simple electronic circuit that converts direct current electricity into an alternating current ($\Leftrightarrow$ p. 90) at a relatively fixed or variable frequency. There are many different kinds of oscillators, some inherently stable, some less so. They are extensively used in electronics. In general, oscillators can be considered as amplifiers with considerable feedback from output to input. Any small amount of NOISE in the input signal is amplified, and the amplified signal then becomes the input signal to the amplifier. This builds up rapidly, giving an ever-increasing output. Feedback of this kind in which the input signal is in PHASE with feedback signal is called *positive feedback*. Various elements, especially inductance ($\Leftrightarrow$ p. 100) and capacitance ($\Leftrightarrow$ p. 98) in the amplifier, will determine that the circuit has a natural resonant frequency, and the output signal will rise and fall at that frequency. Many oscillators employ a *tuned circuit* consisting of a capacitance in parallel with an inductance in the feedback loop. These are inherently stable. Even more stable are quartz crystal oscillators ($\Leftrightarrow$ QUARTZ CLOCK). Relaxation oscillators contain a capacitor that charges at a certain rate until the voltage across it reaches the level at which a device, such as a neon lamp, connected in parallel with the capacitor, begins to conduct. As it does, the capacitor is short-circuited and the voltage across it drops well below the striking voltage of the lamp, which goes out. The cycle is then repeated.

oscilloscope, a widely used scientific instrument consisting of a CATHODE-RAY TUBE and associated electronic circuitry that allows rapidly varying voltages to be accurately represented in graphical form with virtually no distortion from the inertia of the system. The oscilloscope can display the details of the waveform of periodic voltages of all frequencies, can measure frequencies ($\Leftrightarrow$ LISSAJOUS FIGURES), and can compare the simultaneously displayed waveforms of a signal before and after its passage through an electronic circuit or filter network.

osmosis, the passage of water or other solvents through a semipermeable membrane from a solution of high concentration to one of lower concentration, so as to tend to equalize the concentrations on each side. A semipermeable membrane is one that allows liquid, such as water, to pass through but not certain substances dissolved in the liquid. Most of the membranes in the body are semipermeable, and osmosis is occurring constantly everywhere in the body. If such a membrane, placed vertically, separates a pure liquid from one in which substances are dissolved, the pure liquid will pass through the membrane to dilute the solution on the other side. This will cause the level to rise on the side of the solution, and the level will continue to rise until the extra weight of liquid on that side just balances the tendency of the liquid to pass through. The pressure exerted by the extra liquid is said to be equal to the *osmotic pressure* of the solution. Osmotic pressure is determined by the *number* of molecules dissolved in a particular quantity of the solution. Since every cell in the animal body is surrounded by a semipermeable membrane, the effect of osmosis is universal. Biological membranes are, in general, more or less permeable to water, but do not allow passage of substances of molecular weight of more than a few thousands. Thus, in general, inorganic molecules pass easily but organic molecules do not. Membranes can, however, by consuming energy, transmit various substances actively, against the direction of osmotic pressure. Osmosis is readily shown by placing living cells in solutions of various osmotic pressures. If cells are placed in solutions of low pressure, such as distilled water, water flows into them and they swell up and may burst. If placed in solutions of high pressure, they shrink and collapse. For most cells, a 0.9 per cent solution of salt will cause no net movement of fluid either way, and this is called an *isotonic* solution. Such a solution, used for infusion, is called *normal saline*.

ossicle, a small bone. The auditory ossicles are the three tiny bones forming a chain, in the middle ear, which links the eardrum to the inner ear.

ossification, the process of the formation of BONE. This is a dynamic process, continuously occurring throughout life, but is more active during the period of body growth and following a fracture. Ossification sometimes occurs in tissues not normally associated with bone, and may follow long- term INFLAMMATION.

ovary, one of the paired female GONADS. In humans the ovaries are situated in the pelvis one on each side of the womb (UTERUS), just under, and inward of, the open ends of the FALLOPIAN TUBES. They are almond-shaped and about 3 cm (1 in) long, with prominent BLOOD VESSELS. Once a month, one (or sometimes more than one) egg site (*Graafian follicle*) matures and releases an egg (*ovum*). This is called *ovulation*. Each ruptured follicle is replaced by a yellow body known as a *corpus luteum*. In addition to the production of ova, the ovary synthesizes three types of steroid hormone – oestrogens, progesterones and androgens (male sex hormone).

oxide, a compound of OXYGEN and another element. Because most elements, apart from all but one of the inert gases, will combine with oxygen, oxides are the most common compounds found in nature. Much of the Earth's crust is formed from various oxides, such as those of silicon, iron and aluminium. Many elements will form several different oxides. Oxygen in combined form is the most abundant element in the Earth's crust.

oxidizing agents, substances that absorb ELECTRONS from other substances, thereby facilitating their linkage with OXYGEN atoms, which are immediately provided. They include oxygen, fluorine, nitric acid (HNO_3), ozone (O_3) and permanganate (MNO_4).

oxygen, an invisible, odourless gas constituting about one-fifth of the Earth's atmosphere. Oxygen is the most vital necessity for life, and deprivation for more than a few minutes is fatal. It is taken into the body in inspiration and conveyed to all parts by the BLOOD, in the form of oxyhaemoglobin – a loose combination with the HAEMOGLOBIN in the red blood cells. Oxygen is needed for the fundamental process of oxidation of fuel to release energy. This is a highly complex biochemical process known as *oxidative phosphorylation*, involving the synthesis of the universal energy carrier ATP (adenosine triphosphate) in the inner membranes of the mitochondria of cells. In energetic terms, however, it is similar to the release of energy, as heat, that occurs when hydrogen is burned in oxygen to form hydrogen oxide, more commonly known as water (H_2O). Much of medicine is concerned with circumstances and factors that, actually or potentially, prejudice the supply of oxygen to the tissues. These include lung disorders, blood diseases, disorders of the heart and the blood vessels, many poisons, and injuries involving loss of blood and interference with air access to the lungs.

ozone, a powerfully toxic and unstable gas produced by the action of ultraviolet radiation or electrical discharge on OXYGEN in air. The molecule consists of a ring of three oxygen atoms (O_3), and only a small quantity is normally present in atmospheric air. There is a layer of ozone in the stratosphere produced continuously by the action of ultraviolet radiation from the Sun. This layer forms a protective barrier, cutting down the intensity of the ultraviolet component in sunlight. The ozone shield lies in the region 10–50 km above the Earth's surface, and is most concentrated at an altitude of 20–25 km. This shield maximally absorbs ultraviolet light of wavelength about 250 nanometres, which is biologically very damaging. Without the ozone layer human beings would suffer serious biological effects from solar radiation, including a large increase in the incidence of skin cancer and irritating eye disorders. Under normal circumstances, the rate of production of ozone is balanced by the rate of its natural breakdown, so the layer remains unchanged. Chlorofluorocarbons (CFCs), such as freon, released from aerosol sprays, plastic-foam blowers and refrigerators, drift slowly upwards and are capable of forming FREE RADICALS – chemical groups with an unpaired ELECTRON. These chlorine radicals act as catalysts, breaking down ozone to oxygen and then being released unchanged to go on acting. Although the million tonnes or so of CFCs released annually is a very small quantity in the context of the volume of the atmosphere, catalysts can have powerful effects even in very low concentration. The free-radical effect may persist for more than a hundred years. Released CFCs take decades to reach the ozone layer. Much concern has been felt over observations of 'holes' in the stratospheric layer over the antarctic. Under the auspices of the UN, the major industrial countries of the world have agreed, in principle, to limit CFC production, but there is little agreement on action.

pacemaker, a device used in certain heart disorders to ensure that the heart continues to beat at a suitable rate. Permanent, implanted, pacemakers are small, battery-driven electronic OSCILLATORS that deliver short pulses of electricity, at 3–4 volts, to cause the heart muscle to contract. They are used in people with a defect of the conducting system of the heart (*heart block*). The pulse generator is buried under the skin of the chest and often forms one contact. The electrode, which is well insulated except for the tip, runs into a large vein, and from there into the heart, usually the upper-right chamber. Pacemakers may run at a fixed rate, but these limit physical activity, and most, nowadays, are triggered by the demands of the heart or are programmable from the outside by means of radio signals. The battery, in the generator, lasts for about ten years. External pacemakers are widely used in the emergency treatment of heart block to maintain heart action until the block recovers spontaneously or more permanent arrangements can be made. External pacemakers are connected to the heart by a double-insulated electrode, which is inserted into a vein and moved, under X-ray control, into the heart.

packet switching, a widely used method of digital communication (⇨ p. 220) between multiple points. Messages are divided into segments of fixed size, each carrying a code identifying the addressee. Packets are sent serially, without regard to the addressees, so as to fill up the communication time and space available, and avoid wastage. The identifying code ensures that addressees receive only the appropriate packets. These are then reassembled in order into complete messages.

palate, the partition forming the roof of the mouth and separating it from the nose. The hard palate consists of a plate of bone, part of the upper jawbone (*maxilla*), covered with MUCOUS MEMBRANE. Attached to the back of the hard palate is the SOFT PALATE.

pancreas, a dual-function GLAND that secretes digestive enzymes (⇨ pp. 182–5) into the small intestine and the sugar-controlling HORMONES insulin and GLUCAGON into the BLOOD. The pancreas contains groups of specialized cells, in areas known as the 'Islets of Langerhans', which monitor the concentration of GLUCOSE in the blood and secrete appropriate amounts of these hormones to lower or raise the amounts of sugar, as necessary.

Pangaea, the single land mass that formed as the molten Earth cooled and before the land began to break up into continents, 200 million years ago.

parabola, one of the class of curves formed when a plane intersects with a cone. A conic section (⇨ p. 20). The trajectory taken by a bullet fired from a gun is a parabola.

paradigm, a concept of the general nature of things that influences attitudes and behaviour. A conception of the nature of scientific activity that governs the way science is undertaken. A *paradigm shift* becomes necessary when new scientific discoveries demonstrate deficiencies in the prior paradigm. Some people are unable to adapt to new paradigms; ⇨ p. 12.

paraffins, the group of hydrocarbons now known as the *alkanes*; ⇨ pp. 162–5.

parallax, the difference in the direction of a remote object, such as a star, when observed from two separated points (the ends of the *baseline*). The diameter of the Earth provides a convenient baseline for parallax in observations of bodies in the solar system (⇨ p. 132), and the limits of the Earth's orbit provide a baseline for parallax in observing the nearer stars. Parallax allows comparatively accurate measurements to be made of the distance of stars – a calculation complicated, however, by the movement of stars during the year interval between observations.

parallel computing, computing in which more than one central processor is in action at the same time in the same machine, and the work is divided between processors. Parallel computing generally uses reduced-instruction-set (RISC) microprocessors; ⇨ pp. 218–23.

paramagnetism, the property of materials that, when placed in a MAGNETIC FIELD, become magnetized parallel to the field and to a degree that is proportional to the strength of the field. All metals are paramagnetic, as are atoms and molecules with an odd number of ELECTRONS.

parameter, an arbitrary quantity in a mathematical FUNCTION whose value is selected as required. Also, a variable in terms of which other interrelated variables can be expressed and can be regarded as being dependent on the parameter. An auxiliary variable whose functions give the coordinates (⇨ p. 20) of a curve or a surface.

parametric amplifier, an amplifier for very high frequencies or microwave frequencies, consisting of a variable inductor (⇨ p. 100) or capacitor (⇨ p. 98) whose reactance is altered at an even higher frequency by another pump signal. *Varactor diodes* can behave in this way and are commonly used. The resultant mixing of frequencies produces additional signals at beat frequencies. These can be at a higher power than the input frequency, gaining energy from the pump signal, thus effecting amplification. Parametric amplifiers contribute a very low NOISE level to the signal and are often used as the input stages of microwave receivers.

parametric equations, equations used to represent the coordinates (⇨ p. 20) of points on curves on a plane or in three-dimensional space, in terms of other variables – PARAMETERS.

parasite, an organism living on or in the body of another living organism. *Ecto*parasites live on the surface, *endo*parasites live inside. Parasites derive their nourishment from the host but do not contribute anything to the host's welfare. They are often harmful. Almost every organism is parasitized by other organisms and the human being is not exempt. Hundreds of human diseases are caused by parasites, including many different viruses, a wide variety of bacteria, some fungi, various protozoa, a range of worms, a few types of flukes, some ticks, four types of lice, some bugs, a few burrowing flies and a variety of leeches. Protozoal parasites include: amoebae, which cause dysentery; flagellata, which cause vaginal discharge and irritation; ciliata, which are often harmless; and sporozoa, which cause malaria. Worms include tapeworms, roundworms, hookworms and threadworms.

parasympathetic nervous system, one of the two divisions of the autonomic nervous system, which effects automatic and largely unconscious control of bodily functions. The parasympathetic is mainly concerned with those functions operating while the body is at rest, such as stimulating digestion, slowing the heart, constricting the air passages, and so on. Compare the *sympathetic* division of the autonomic, which copes with the emergency demands of danger, fright, flight and distress.

parathyroid glands, four small, bean-shaped organs, each about half a centimetre long, which lie in the substance of the vertebrate thyroid gland. The parathyroids secrete a hormone, *parathormone*, that regulates the fate of calcium and phosphorus in the body. This hormone is automatically produced if the level of calcium in the blood drops, and its presence causes the blood-calcium levels to rise again by the release of calcium from the BONES, a reduction in calcium loss by the KIDNEYS and increased absorption from the bowel. Excess phosphorus is excreted in URINE so that the correct balance between the two is maintained.

parenchyma, in plants, a soft round tissue consisting of simple thin-walled cells and air spaces, concerned with the synthesis and storage of food. The greater part of fruits, stems and roots consists of parenchyma. In animals it is the specialized or functional part of an organ as distinct from the connective tissue and BLOOD VESSELS.

parity bit, a binary digit added to a byte as a means of checking that the byte has not been changed in transmission; ⇨ p. 216.

parotid gland, the largest of the three pairs of salivary glands. Each parotid lies over the angle of the jaw, below and in front of the lower half of the ear, and has a duct that runs forward and then passes through the cheek to open on the inside of the mouth at about the level of the upper molar teeth. Like the other GLANDS on each side (the *submandibular* and the *sublingual*), the parotids produce a slow continuous secretion of saliva, which contains water, mucus, various salts, and the enzyme amylase. This enzyme is capable of breaking down starch to simpler sugars. The stimulus of food in the mouth, or even the contemplation of a meal, leads to a considerable increase in the rate of salivary secretion.

parsec, a unit of astronomical distance equal to 3.26 LIGHT YEARS. It is the distance away a star must be to produce a parallax shift of one second of arc. A parallax shift is the change in the apparent position of a star when it is viewed from the two extremes of the Earth's annual orbit round the Sun.

parthenogenesis, the development of an unfertilized egg into an adult organism. A normal ovum, having half the usual number of chromosomes (*haploid*), cannot produce an organism, so some change is necessary in the early cell divisions (*meiosis*) to produce the full number. If such a cell continues to divide as does a fertilized cell, the result will be parthenogenesis. The resultant organism will be a clone of the mother identical to her in all respects. Only females can be produced by parthenogenesis, as no male (Y) chromosome is present. Parthenogenesis is common in bees and ants (and sometimes chickens and turkeys) and has been produced experimentally in frogs, mice and rabbits. Ova can sometimes be induced to begin to divide by pricking them with a fine, glass fibre. Human parthenogenesis is a theoretical possibility and, if achieved, would make men biologically redundant.

particle, in classical physics, a body of small but finite mass but of no appreciable size. As a result, although a particle has inertia and is susceptible to gravitation, any force acting on it can cause only displacement and cannot cause rotational acceleration. The term also implies *elementary particle* (⇨ p. 108). In the grosser world, a particle is a solid or a liquid in a finely divided state; each particle consists of a large number of molecules. A collection of dry solid particles is called a *powder*. Particles suspended in a fluid produce a *dispersoid* or *hydrosol*. A suspension of particles, either solid or liquid, in a gas is called an *aerosol*.

Pascal, a structured programming language, once widely used but now being superseded by OBJECT-ORIENTED PROGRAMMING languages (⇨ p. 218). Pascal has been much used for teaching computer science.

passive star network, a computer communications network arrangement in which peripheral terminals are connected by radiating links to a central node that simply connects them to each other without any processing of the information; ⇨ p. 220.

pasteurization, a method of destroying bacteria and other microorganisms in milk and other liquid foods. The method most commonly used today is the high-temperature, short-time process. Milk is passed, in one direction, between thin, stainless steel plates separated by gaskets, while hot water is pumped in the other direction, on the other side of the plates. In this way, the milk is rapidly heated to about 78°C and maintained at that temperature for fifteen seconds. It is then rapidly cooled to below 10°C. Standards of pasteurization in milk are tested by checking for the presence of a milk enzyme that is destroyed at the correct temperature, and for the presence of the bacterium *Coxiella burnetti*. Pasteurized liquid eggs are tested for the presence of two species of salmonella bacteria. Other food products can be pasteurized by blowing in high-temperature steam. The process is named after the French chemist and bacteriologist Louis Pasteur (1822–95).

patella, the kneecap. This is a flat, roughly circular BONE that is entirely enclosed in the large common tendon of the front muscles of the thigh as it crosses in front of the knee joint to be inserted into the front of the top of the main lower leg bone (the *tibia*).

pearl, an opalescent chalky (calcareous) concretion formed by a saltwater pearl oyster or by one of several freshwater clams. Pearls form when an irritating material of any kind occurs in the mantle of the bivalve mollusc – a flat tissue lying between the muscular body and the valves. This results in the secretion of 'mother-of-pearl' (*nacre*) around the irritant material. The nacre does not, however, apparently, relieve the irritation, and the growing body maintains the stimulus to further nacre secretion. In this way the pearl continues to grow in size. Beads, inserted into the mantle of oysters, produce 'cultured pearls'.

peat, a fibrous, black or dark brown, slowly inflammable material, the partially disintegrated products of marsh plants and trees. Peat can be considered as the earliest stage in coal formation, but coal is produced only if peat is deeply buried by geological changes, and subjected to pressure and raised temperatures.

pectin, one of a number of polysaccharides (⇨ pp. 182–5) occurring in and between the cell walls of plants. Pectins are soluble 'fibre' and are widely used in the preparation of food gels and for other culinary purposes.

peek, to use a high-level language, to examine the contents of an ADDRESS in a computer memory. Compare *poke*, which is to use such a language to insert a datum into a memory address or to modify its contents.

pegmatites, coarse-grained, crystalline rock inclusions in ordinary igneous rocks (⇨ p. 150). Pegmatites contain quartz, feldspar, micas, many different elements, often large crystals, and sometimes gemstones.

Peltier effect, the rise or fall in temperature that occurs at the junction of dissimilar metals when an electric current (⇨ p. 90) flows through it. The direction of temperature change depends on the direction of current flow. The phenomenon can be put to practical use if semiconductor junctions are employed. The effect was first noted in 1834 by the French physicist J. C. A. Peltier (1785–1845).

pelvis, the bony girdle formed in invertebrates by the junction of the two hipbones (INNOMINATE BONES), on either side, with the triangular, curved sacrum, behind. The innominate bones are held together in front by a mid-line joint called the *symphysis pubis*. Each innominate bone contains a deep, spherical cup, called the ACETABULUM, into which the head of the thighbone (*femur*) fits. The pelvis provides attachment for many muscles, including those of the abdominal wall and the loin and those of the thighs, buttocks and hams. It contains the urinary bladder and the rectum in both sexes; the VAGINA, UTERUS, FALLOPIAN TUBES and OVARIES in women; and the PROSTATE GLAND, seminal vesicles and semen tubes (*vasa deferentes*) in men.

pendulum, an elongated body, free to swing on a pivot under the influence of gravity about a horizontal axis. The lower end of the pendulum describes *simple harmonic* or *periodic* motion. The time for one complete excursion of the swing (the *period*) is independent of the MASS or weight of the pendulum and is affected only by its length and by the local value of the gravitational constant *g* (⇨ p. 30). The period is also almost independent of the amplitude of the swing. The time for a complete swing both ways is equal to 2π multiplied by the square root of the length of the pendulum.

penis, the erectile male organ of copulation and urination in most higher vertebrates. The penis is a triple structure, consisting of two main longitudinal, cylindrical bodies of sponge-like tissue, the *corpora cavernosa*, lying side by side. Beneath them lies a single, central, smaller column, the *corpus spongiosum*, through which runs the tube for URINE and semen (the URETHRA). The corpora cavernosa are connected by a wall of fibrous tissue that is incomplete in places, to allow BLOOD to pass from one to the other and thus equalize the pressure. In some mammals this wall contains a bone, the *os penis*. The corpus spongiosum, also of spongy tissue, expands near the tip of the penis into a conical, cap-shaped swelling called the glans (*glans penis*). At the root of the penis, the two corpora cavernosa separate and the corpus spongiosum expands to form the bulb of the penis, where the urethra enters it from above. Into each of these three bodies runs an ARTERY capable of supplying blood under pressure. These arteries open directly into the spaces of the corpora without intervening capillaries and are able, during sexual excitement, to distend these rapidly, compressing the draining veins, so that the normally small and flaccid penis becomes enlarged, erect and rigid enough to allow coitus. In detumescence, the compression on the veins is released and they are able to carry the surplus blood away, so that the penis rapidly shrinks.

peptide, a subdivision of a protein; ⇨ pp. 180–5.

period, the time taken for a single cycle of a PERIODIC FUNCTION.

periodic function, a FUNCTION that regularly repeats itself. For instance, the sine wave graph of y = sin x repeats itself every 360° and is a periodic function; ⇨ p. 20.

periodic motion, any movement that precisely repeats itself, taking equal intervals of time to do so. The swing of a PENDULUM is an example of periodic motion, as are the mass movements of ELECTRONS in mains supply alternating current (⇨ p. 90). A graph of the voltage changes in an AC supply is a representation of periodic motion.

periodic table, an arrangement of the elements placed in the order of the number of PROTONS in the nucleus of each and divided into rows and columns so as to bring out the similarities in chemical properties; ⇨ p. 158.

peristalsis, the automatic and coordinated contraction and relaxation of the circularly placed muscles in the wall of the bowel, which ensures that the contents are moved along and do not cause obstruction. Repetitive waves of contraction occur at points progressively along the bowel in the direction of its lower end. Peristalsis occurs in the gullet (*oesophagus*) during swallowing, allowing this to occur even when the body is upside-down. Stomach peristalsis aids in the mixing of food with gastric juices and, in conjunction with a strong muscle ring (*sphincter*) at the outlet, controls the movement of altered food into the DUODENUM. After a meal, peristalsis in the small intestine changes to a slow, churning movement, with little forward progress, to allow more time for absorption. Once this is well advanced, normal peristalsis is resumed. Peristalsis in the colon (large intestine) is much slower than in the rest of the bowel and contraction may occur only once in 30 minutes. Three or four times a day, usually following a meal, a strong, sustained wave of peristalsis passes over the colon, forcing the contents into the rectum and prompting the desire for evacuation.

permutation, one of all the possible arrangements of a set of numbers. There are n! (*factorial n*) permutations of n numbers, taken all at a time. Factorial n means the product of all the integers up to and including n. Thus factorial 6 is $1 \times 2 \times 3 \times 4 \times 5 \times 6$, i.e. 720. Therefore, there are 720 permutations of all of any 6 numbers.

personal computer, a microcomputer intended primarily for use by a single individual for a variety of business and other applications, but readily connectable to a LOCAL-AREA NETWORK. The term was originally used as a trade name by IBM for the basic model of their microcomputer range. This model, although very limited by today's standards, set a precedent for a range of mutually compatible machines using the MS-DOS operating system. The PC has long been superseded by more powerful machines and the term has acquired a wider significance. As new and improved microprocessors were developed, the de facto standard for the IBM-compatible personal computer rapidly passed through a series of models that superseded the original PC. These were the XT, the AT ('advanced technology') also known as the 80286 because of the Intel 80286 chip used, the 80386, 80486 and the Pentium. In parallel with the MS-DOS machines, the Apple company produced a hierarchy of personal computers that were soon concentrating on graphical displays using icons selected by a MOUSE.

perturbation, the deviation or digression of a celestial body from the path it would take if subject only to a single influencing force. Perturbation may be caused by gravitational forces (⇨ p. 30) or by variation in centripetal force occasioned by the nonsphericality of an attracting mass. The Earth, for instance, is an oblate (pole-flattened) spheroid (⇨ pp. 144–7) and exerts a varying centripetal force with changes in the position of any body influenced by its gravitation.

pesticide, any poison used in the attempt to eradicate pests of any kind, including unwanted birds, rodents, insects, plants, fungi, and microorganisms. Modern agriculture is dependent on pesticides for its efficiency, as are public-health authorities for the control of the many insect-borne diseases, but much concern has arisen because of the scale of usage, especially of insecticides, herbicides, and fungicides, and because of the potential or actual dangers of residual poisons to human and wildlife. Pesticide residues in food, dangers to agricultural workers, ecological damage and many other concerns relating to pesticides are an increasing preoccupation of governments throughout the world.

petrifaction, the turning to stone of an organic body. Petrifaction is the process by which fossils are preserved. The organic material becomes impregnated with mineral salts that are deposited from solution. Being finely divided, these can reflect every detail of the original. The deposited material is insoluble, resists further solution and is thus preserved. Sometimes whole forests have become petrified.

pharynx, the passage running down from the back of the nose, by way of the back of the mouth, to the beginning of the gullet (*oesophagus*). The part above and behind the soft palate is called the *nasopharynx*; the part at the back of the mouth is the *oropharynx*; and the lowest part, which communicates with the oesophagus and the larynx, is called the *laryngopharynx*.

phase, the point in a cycle of any PERIODIC FUNCTION or periodic quantity reached at a specific time. Since a periodic function can be said to repeat itself in 360°, phase can be expressed as an angle. Two or more periodic quantities can be said to be 'in phase' or 'out of phase' (⇨ pp. 64–7) with each other and this difference can be quantified in degrees. Equal-amplitude waves 180° out of phase with each other will cancel each other.

phase-locked loop, an electronic circuit containing a variably alternating-current generator (voltage-controlled OSCILLATOR) that is locked into PHASE with an incoming signal. The output is passed through a low-pass filter that removes all the alternating current, leaving the direct current signal. The effect of this is to remove NOISE from the signal and effectively regenerate an almost perfect replica of the signal. Should the signal vary in frequency, the phase-locked loop circuit will follow it and maintain the signal, which might otherwise be lost. The phase-locked loop principle is widely used in TV and radio receivers and the circuit is commonly fabricated on a single silicon chip as an integrated circuit.

phloem, the tissue in higher plants that conducts photosynthesized food substances to all parts of the plant.

phosphate, a negative ion (⇨ p. 90) PO_4 derived from phosphoric acid (H_3PO_4). Phosphates occur in BONES and teeth, in the BLOOD and in the double-helix 'backbone' of DNA (⇨ p. 202).

photoconductive cell, a passive, crystalline semiconductor device that changes its electrical resistance in proportion to the intensity of light falling on it. If the cell is included in a series circuit with a source of electricity and a sensitive electric meter, it can be used to measure light intensity. If the meter is replaced by a semiconductor or other relay, large currents can be switched on by a small change in light intensity.

photoelectric cell, a device that generates a voltage when irradiated with light ($\Leftrightarrow$ pp. 72–5). Such devices can be connected in series and parallel to produce practical amounts of electric power. A photoemissive cell consists of a CATHODE that emits ELECTRONS when irradiated, and a positively charged nearby ANODE to attract the electrons and thus cause a current to flow.

photometry, the measurement of light intensity, colour, rate of flow of light energy (*flux*), point brightness (*luminance*), reflectance and transmittance; $\Leftrightarrow$ pp. 72–5.

photomultiplier, a highly sensitive instrument capable of detecting and measuring very low levels of light intensity. The photomultiplier consists of a cascaded series of photoemissive stages ($\Leftrightarrow$ PHOTOELECTRIC CELL) in which the output of one stage forms the input of the next so that the gain rapidly rises.

phototransistor, a light-sensitive semi-conductor device whose characteristics change with ambient-light intensity. Phototransistors act as amplifying PHOTOELECTRIC CELLS.

phylogeny, the sequence of events involved in the evolution of a species. The history and lineage of organisms and the timescale of their evolution; $\Leftrightarrow$ pp. 196–9.

phylum, a major taxonomic division of animals and plants that contains one or more classes. In taxonomy, the phylum lies below Kingdom (or subkingdom) and above Class (or super-class). The basic classification divisions are Kingdom, Phylum, Class, Order, Family, Genus and Species.

pico-, a submultiple of a millionth of a millionth of any unit. The symbol is p. Thus, a picosecond is 10^{-12} s.

piezoelectricity, voltages generated by certain dielectric crystals when subject to mechanical pressure or strain. Also the deformation that occurs in the same materials when subject to an electric field. This double effect allows many practical applications as TRANSDUCERS. Piezoelectric crystals can resonate at a very precise frequency and are commonly incorporated into OSCILLATORS on this account. Every PERSONAL COMPUTER and every digital clock and wristwatch relies on piezoelectricity to stabilize its clock oscillator. Piezoelectricity ($\Leftrightarrow$ pp. 102–5) is a feature of crystals of quartz, barium titanate, Rochelle salt, zincblende (ZnS), ethylene diamine tartrate and other materials.

pinch effect, the effect of the magnetic self-attraction occurring when an electric current flows ($\Leftrightarrow$ p. 90). The inward pressure effect on metallic conductors can usually be neglected unless very large currents are flowing. The effect is used in one method of attempting to achieve a nuclear-fusion reaction. A very large current flowing through a *plasma* (high-

temperature gas with its electrons stripped off; $\Leftrightarrow$ pp. 114–17) will, by virtue of the pinch effect, raise the temperature and pressure even higher and will help to keep the area concerned clear of the walls of the containing equipment. The pinch is, however, unstable.

pinna, the external, visible, part of the ear.

pipette, a uniform tube of glass of plastic, sometimes graduated with a volume scale, used to deliver accurate quantities of a fluid. Pipettes may be equipped with a small, thick-walled rubber or plastic balloon at the upper end by means of which fluid can be sucked up and discharged.

pitch, the subjective sense of the height or depth of a musical sound ($\Leftrightarrow$ p. 68), corresponding to the objective variable, *frequency*. Doubling of the frequency produces the subjective sense of the same tone sounded higher. These two pitches are said to be *octave-related*. The standard diatonic musical scale consists of seven rising pitches and the octave. In the major scale these are said to form *intervals* of a tone or halftone. Each tone interval consists of two halftones. The octave thus contains 12 approximately equal intervals known as *semitones*. The smallest difference in pitch appreciated by most people is about a quarter of a tone.

pituitary gland, the major endocrine GLAND of vertebrates. The pituitary is a small, pea-sized organ connected to the middle of the underside of the brain by a short stalk, lying in a hollow in the central bone of the base of the skull (*sphenoid bone*), just behind the cavity of the nose. It connects to the hypothalamus area of the brain and is the central HORMONE-producing gland and the controller of all the other glands that secrete hormones into the bloodstream (glands of internal secretion). It is the nodal point of the whole endocrine system and, in conjunction with the hypothalamus, forms the link between the nervous system (movement, sensation, mental activity) and the chemical control system (all metabolic, growth and regulatory processes) of the body. The pituitary gland secretes a variety of different hormones. They are the growth hormone; prolactin, which promotes milk production at the end of pregnancy; thyroid-stimulating hormone, which controls the output of thyroid hormone; follicle-stimulating hormone and luteinizing hormone, which control the production of eggs (*ova*) from the ovary and the maintenance of pregnancy after fertilization; adrenocorticotrophic hormone (ACTH), which controls the output of cortisol from the adrenal grands; oxytocin, which releases milk from the breast and causes the womb (*uterus*) to contract; vasopressin, also called the *antidiuretic* hormone, which increases the reabsorption of water in the kidneys and controls water loss; and the melanocyte-stimulating hormone, which stimulates the growth of pigment cells in the skin.

pixel, a picture element. One of the very large number of points of light or darkness, coloured or monochrome, that makes up a computer-graphic image. Alternatively, a pixel is an

element in a MATRIX that holds the information specifying the brightness and colour for such a point in an image. The position in the matrix automatically specifies the position of the pixel in the image.

plant cell, the structural unit of plants. Plant cells have a rigidity absent in animal cells. This is because of the polysaccharide cellulose that is a major feature of the plant-cell wall and is secreted outside the soft cell membrane. Wood contains 40–50 per cent cellulose. In other respects plant cells are similar to animal cells and contain all the same organelles ($\Leftrightarrow$ p. 188). Plant cells also contain green bodies known as *chloroplasts*. These contain chlorophyll, the pigment that absorbs the light energy needed for photosynthesis ($\Leftrightarrow$ pp. 46–9).

plant hormones, chemical messengers that bring about physiological changes and exercise controlling effects in plants. Plants have nothing corresponding to the nervous system in animals but exercise internal regulation and growth control by means of HORMONES.

plant physiology, the internal functioning of plants, including their respiration, nutrition, metabolism, growth, movement, uptake of materials, biochemistry, photosynthesis, reproduction and energetics; $\Leftrightarrow$ pp. 190–5.

plaque, the material that forms around the necks of the teeth when food particles, dried saliva, bacteria and other substances are allowed to accumulate. Plaque, which consists largely of bacteria, has the ability to form and concentrate acid. This leads to dental caries and the formation of holes in the enamel and dentine, so that bacteria can gain access to the pulp and cause damaging infection there.

plasma, in physics, a gas consisting of roughly equal numbers of unassociated free positive ions ($\Leftrightarrow$ p. 90) and ELECTRONS. Plasmas readily conduct electricity and are influenced by electric and magnetic fields ($\Leftrightarrow$ pp. 88 and 114–17). In physiology, BLOOD from which the red cells (*erythrocytes*) have been removed but that still contains proteins and retains the ability to clot.

plasma display, a flat-screen computer display in which the PIXELS are formed by electrical discharge through an ionized gas. A high-resolution screen made on this principle is very expensive and gives only a reddish or orange monochrome display.

plasticity, the property of being able to undergo a permanent change of shape as the result of the application of a STRESS greater than that needed to overcome its elastic limits; $\Leftrightarrow$ p. 28.

plastics, substances formed by polymerizing ($\Leftrightarrow$ pp. 162–5) smaller units known as *monomers*.

Platyhelminthes, the phylum of invertebrates known as flatworms. They include many flukes and tapeworms that are parasitic on, and disease-producing in, other animals, including humans.

pleura, a double-layered membrane, one layer of which is firmly attached to the inside of the wall of the chest, the other being firmly attached to the outsides of the two LUNGS. The two layers are normally in close contact, separated only by a thin layer of lubricating fluid, and are able to slide freely on each other as the chest wall rises and falls, and the lungs expand and relax.

plotter, a printing device that produces a pictorial representation of computer-held information by a drawing process using moving pens on stationary or moving paper. Plotters are widely used to produce plans and architectural drawings from CAD programs; ⇨ pp. 216–19 .

plutonium, an artificial element with atomic number 94 and a number of isotopes (⇨ pp. 160 and 164), the most important being 239-Pu. This isotope, which is formed in 'breeder' nuclear reactors, has a half-life of 24,131 years, and is usable in reactors and as a fissile material for atomic weapons. Plutonium forms many compounds and is one of the most toxic and dangerous substances known.

point-of-sale system, a computer system used in retailing in which all the information on each transaction is immediately passed to a central computer to keep accounts, facilitate stock-taking and replenishment, and so on. Bar codes and laser readers are used to note and record the retail price of all items purchased, and to make totals, calculate sales tax and print lists.

polarization, of a radiated wave, being oriented in a predictable direction perpendicular to the direction of propagation. In plane-polarized radiation, such as light (⇨ pp. 72–5), the waves are all confined to a particular plane.

pollen, the powder consisting of large numbers of the tiny male reproductive bodies (*gametes*) produced by the anthers of the stamens of seed plants. Pollen grains have double walls with apertures and/or spines, and are often coated with sticky oils. They contain half the number (the *haploid* number) of chromosomes of the normal plant cell. Pollen grains germinate on the stigma of the pistil of a flower of the same species. A tube from the pollen grain penetrates the ovule of the ovary of the pistil and releases two sperms. One forms a food-accumulating tissue, the *endosperm*; the other unites with the egg to form a ZYGOTE, which develops into an embryo.

pollutants, substances, produced by human activity, which are in any way dangerous or damaging to people, animals or plants. The most serious are those that are difficult or impossible to remove. Many thousands of substances can pollute the environment, but the major pollutants fall into a comparatively small number of groups. These include metal poisons such as lead, cadmium and mercury; organic solvents like carbon tetrachloride, trichloroethylene, toluene, benzene and xylene; and, especially, the halogenated organic compounds. These are chemicals in which chlorine, bromine, iodine or fluorine are incorporated in organic molecules. They are used as PESTICIDES, herbicides, solvents and fire retardants and in the manufacture of plastics. Many of those most widely used are very toxic to the nervous system. Widespread pollution of water has occurred, for instance, from the dumping of polychlorinated biphenyls (PCBs), used in electrical-appliance manufacture. The fire-retardant polybrominated biphenyl (PBB) has contaminated animal feed, leading to the need for the destruction of thousands of affected farm animals. Residents in the affected areas retain this substance in their bodies. The most dangerous of the organo-halogen compounds is probably dioxin. This substance was present in the herbicide Agent Orange, which was used by the US Army during the Vietnam war to defoliate large areas in South Vietnam. Much suffering was caused to the local population from the dioxin, which killed many animals and is believed to have been responsible for a high abortion rate and an increase in the incidence of congenital defects in Vietnamese babies. Another dioxin disaster resulted from a factory explosion in Italy. Aromatic hydrocarbons, such as benzene, are known to cause cancer, leukaemia and brain damage. These compounds are released when petrol and various waste materials are burned. Other pollutants include radioactive fallout from nuclear accidents, asbestos, arsenic and sulphites.

polymerization, the linking together of small molecules known, in this context, as *monomers* to form long-chain molecules known as *polymers* (⇨ p. 164). Polymers are common in nature and many are made synthetically. They are the basis of the plastics industry.

posterior ⇨ ANTERIOR.

pour point, the lowest temperature at which an oil will pour.

precious stones, minerals and other substances valued for such properties as beauty, rarity, permanence and for the ways in which they can be embellished by being cut into certain shapes. They include fossilized gum or amber, beryl (emerald, aquamarine), corundum (ruby and sapphire), diamond, feldspar (moonstone), garnet, jade, jet, lapis lazuli, malachite, opal, quartz (amethyst, citrine, agate), topaz, tourmaline, turquoise and zircon.

pressure, force per unit area; ⇨ p. 28.

printed circuit, an electronic or electrical circuit made by depositing a thin layer of copper on an insulating board and then etching away unwanted metal to leave the needed connections. Boards are often double-sided, and connections may be made through holes from one side to the other. Components, such as chips, resistors, capacitors, inductors, transistors, diodes and quartz crystals, are usually mounted on one side only, but may be on both sides. These components are connected in circuit by soldering. Printed-circuit boards are the standard electronic subunits in computers and may have various pronged plugs or sockets by means of which connections are made to power supplies and other parts of the machine. Alternatively, they may have multi-way edge connectors that can be pushed into long multi-way sockets. The main printed-circuit board in a personal computer is called the *mother board*. Boards that can be plugged into this are called *daughter boards*; ⇨ pp. 220–3.

progeria, a condition of accelerated ageing in which the usual processes of bodily decline and deterioration take place over the course of only a few years. Progeria is very rare and occurs in two forms. In the Hutchinson-Gilford syndrome, the condition appears in children before the age of four and by 10 or 12 the affected individual has all the physical characteristics of old age – lax, wrinkled skin, loss of hair, and all the other common degenerative changes including widespread atherosclerosis. Death usually occurs about the age of 13, from coronary thrombosis or stroke. Adult progeria, or Werner's syndrome, starts in early adult life and follows, over the course of about a decade, the same rapid progression to senility, with balding or grey hair, deafness, arthritis, cataract, loss of teeth, and atherosclerosis. In both forms there is severe resistance to administered insulin. Werner's syndrome also features increased levels in the tissues of hyaluronic acid – a substance that interferes with the development of small BLOOD VESSELS, especially during development. Little is known of the cause of progeria. Both the Hutchinson-Gilford syndrome and Werner's syndrome can be transmitted by autosomal (non-sex-linked) recessive inheritance (⇨ p. 200) but many occur as a fresh dominant mutation. Cultures of cells, such as the normally rapidly reproducing skin fibroblasts, taken from people with progeria, undergo only a few cell divisions and then cease. Cell cultures from normal children produce fifty or more generations before reproduction stops.

program, a set of instructions or statements that can be represented in a form capable of being read by a computer and that cause the machine to perform specified actions. A program may be only a few bytes or many megabytes long; ⇨ p. 218.

programmable ROM, a read-only memory the contents of which are entered after manufacture and may or may not, thereafter, be possible to change.

programming, all the activities, analytical, creative and evaluative, involved in the procedure of producing a computer PROGRAM (⇨ p. 218). The final stages of programming involve the coding and testing of the program, and the detection and elimination of faults and defects.

PROLOG, a computer-programming language based on formal logic and used to write artificial- intelligence programs; ⇨ pp. 218 and 224.

PROM ⇨ PROGRAMMABLE ROM.

pronation, turning the whole body, or any part of it, into the face down (*prone*) position. Applied to the hand and arm, the term means rotating the forearm so that the palm of the hand faces downward. The opposite of pronation is *supination*.

proprioception, the neurological process of continuous monitoring of the position and movement of the limbs and the state of muscle tension, so that information is constantly supplied to the brain about the relative orientation of the parts of the body and their position in space. Proprioceptive information comes from sensory nerve endings and special receptors in the joints, tendons and muscles. This information is integrated with other data coming from the balancing, gravitational and acceleration receptors in the inner ears and visual information from the eyes. Proprioception is largely unconscious and the corrective action taken, in response to it, automatic. Functions such as walking, or even standing, would be impossible without an efficient proprioceptive system providing feedback and controlling information. Many of the disabling effects of disease or damage to the nervous system are due to interference with normal proprioceptive function.

prostate gland, a gland present in most male mammals, which, in humans, is comparable in size, shape, colour and consistency to a chestnut, and surrounds the first inch or so of the urine tube (URETHRA). The prostate lies immediately under the bladder and close in front of the wall of the rectum. It secretes a thin, milky, slightly alkaline fluid that keeps the spermatozoa active.

proton, a positively charged particle occurring in the nucleus of all atoms (pp. 108–11 and 156). The charge is equal in magnitude but opposite in sign to that on the ELECTRON. Protons are believed to have an infinite lifespan, but this is still a debatable point in theoretical physics.

pseudohermaphroditism, a congenital abnormality of the genitalia so that they resemble those of both sexes. A true *hermaphrodite* is an individual with both male and female genitalia. Thus, in humans, a woman with pseudohermaphroditism may appear to be a hermaphrodite because of an enlarged clitoris that looks like a penis and enlarged LABIA that resemble a scrotum. A man with a very small penis and a divided scrotum, simulating labia majora, may also appear, wrongly, to be a hermaphrodite.

pseudoscience, a collection of assertions that are claimed to be based on scientific principles and derived from scientific observation and experimental verification, but that are, in fact, not derived in this way.

pulmonary, relating to the LUNGS.

pulsar, a remote radio source that produces repeated short bursts of intense radio emission (⊳ pp. 84 and 140–3).

pulse, in medicine, the thrusting impulse felt over an ARTERY shortly after each contraction of the lower chambers (*ventricles*) of the heart. In electronics and computing, a brief and quickly reversed change in voltage or current,

usually such as to produce a waveform that is roughly rectangular; ⊳ pp. 72–5.

pulse code modulation, ANALOGUE-to-DIGITAL conversion of an electrical signal (⊳ p. 220). The analogue signal is sampled many times a second, and the amplitude of each sample is measured and represented as a number that is then sent as a digital code.

pulse generator, an electronic circuit with an electrical output the waveform of which is a very short duration SQUARE WAVE or rectangular wave; ⊳ pp. 72–5.

pupil, the black disc in the centre of the iris of the eye. This is actually a circular hole in the iris to admit light to the inner parts of the eye. It changes size automatically with variations in external brightness and constricts on focusing (*accommodation*), and when the eyes simultaneously turn inwards (*converge*). The iris contains muscle fibres arranged in a circle around the pupil. When these contract the pupil becomes small. It also contains radially arranged muscles, contraction of which enlarges the pupil. Constriction of the pupil in bright light improves the optical performance of the eye and may permit reading impossible in dimmer conditions.

pylorus, a muscular ring at the outlet of the STOMACH that controls the passage of stomach contents into the DUODENUM. Also known as the *pyloric sphincter.*

pyrogen, any substance causing fever. The immediately acting pyrogen is the substance interleukin–1, which is released by macrophage cells following infection with BACTERIA, VIRUSES, yeasts, or spirochaetes, or in the presence of progesterone, certain drugs and other substances. All these substances are also called pyrogens (*exogenous pyrogens*). Interleukin–1 acts on the temperature-regulating centres in the hypothalamus of the brain, resetting the thermostat at a higher level, so that the blood temperature is interpreted as being too low. Heat-production action, by shivering, then rapidly raises the body temperature.

pyrometer, an instrument for measuring very high temperatures, or an instrument that measures any thermal radiation.

Q, a term standing for 'quality', the ratio of reactance to resistance (⊳ p. 96). A high reactance and a low resistance in a resonant circuit means that such a circuit will resonate at a more precise frequency rather than over a wider frequency range. In other words, the greater the Q, the sharper the tuning of the circuit. A high Q inductance (⊳ p. 100) can be achieved by surrounding a low-resistance coil with a ferrite material that greatly increases the inductance without affecting the resistance.

quadriceps muscle, the massive muscle group forming the front of the thigh in primates. The quadriceps consists of four muscles that take origin from the thighbone (*femur*) and from the front of the PELVIS. All four muscles end, below, in a stout tendon, the quadriceps tendon, which is large enough to accommodate the kneecap

(*patella*), and which is firmly attached to a bump on the upper end of the front of the main bone of the lower leg (*tibia*). In contracting, the quadriceps muscles therefore exert a powerful straightening action on the knee, lifting almost the whole weight of the body and allowing walking.

quartz, silicon dioxide, the most abundant compound in the world. Quartz occurs in all kinds of rocks – igneous, sedimentary and metamorphic (⊳ p. 150). Crystalline quartz has a hardness of 7 on the MOHS SCALE and some forms are regarded as gemstones. They may be colourless or may be of almost any pale or deep spectral colour, or brownish-black. Bluish-violet quartz is known as AMETHYST. It is PIEZOELECTRIC and is widely used in electronic clocks, watches and in computer-clock OSCILLATORS. It is more transparent to ultraviolet light than most glasses.

quartz clock, an accurate timepiece based on the PIEZOELECTRIC properties of a QUARTZ crystal. If such a crystal, cut as a thin slice, is clamped between two metal plates, or has metal deposited on opposite faces and is then connected into an electronic OSCILLATOR, the electric field applied to the crystal will cause it to deform. This will immediately apply a small voltage to the circuit. The natural resonant frequency (⊳ pp. 64–7) of the crystal will then determine the frequency of the oscillator, which will oscillate at this frequency with a precision and stability determined only by the physical properties of the quartz crystal. These are inherently stable and can be made more so by keeping the crystal in a temperature-controlled environment (a *crystal oven*). The output of the oscillator is then formed into a SQUARE-WAVE train and electronically divided. Each tenth pulse, for instance, might be directed to another similar divider, and so on. When a suitably low frequency has been reached the alternating current is applied to a synchronous motor with a gear train and clock-face hands. Alternatively, one-second pulses can be used to activate a digital display and can also be divided twice by 60 to give minutes and hours. The term 'quartz clock' is also applied to the quartz oscillator used in computers and other devices to synchronize the electronic activity.

quasar, a term derived from the phrase 'quasistellar object'. A quasar is a very compact astronomical entity that appears on a photographic plate as a star and may be millions of times brighter than normal galaxies. Many quasars are coloured more blue than most stars; most blue quasars emit strong X-radiation (⊳ p. 84). Others emit powerful radio waves. But quasars have a red shift (⊳ pp. 140–3) of such magnitude as to preclude their being stars. This red shift implies that they are travelling away at speeds approaching those of light, and are billions of light years away and correspondingly old. They are thought possibly to have been new-forming galaxies at the time light left them, and that observing a quasar is tantamount to observing the origins of the universe. They were first discovered in 1963.

rad, radiation absorbed dose, a unit of dosage of absorbed ionizing radiation. The rad is the energy absorption of 0.01 JOULE per kilogram of the material being irradiated. Most people would be killed by an instantaneous radiation dose over 500 rads.

radar, RAdio Detection And Ranging, a method of locating objects, such as ships or aircraft, at a distance and determining their position. Radar works by projecting a pulsed beam of high-frequency radio waves of a wavelength that is short compared to the object to be detected. Such waves are reflected from the object, and their returned echoes detected. Because the speed of propagation of radio waves is known, the distance can readily be computed from the time that elapses between emission and the arrival of the echo. The transmitted pulse and the returning pulse can be displayed as blips on a CATHODE-RAY TUBE with a radially moving spot and a rotating radius whose position exactly mirrors that of the rotating aerial. The distance from the centre of the display is a FUNCTION of the distance of the object, and its bearing is a function of the position of the rotating transmitting/receiving aerial at the time.

radian, the angle at the centre of a circle formed by two radii running to the ends of an arc of the circle equal in length to the radius.

radiance, the objective physical property corresponding to the subjective sensation of the brightness of a surface.

radiation, the emission and dissemination of energy. Also, the radiated energy itself; ⇨ pp. 46–9, 58–61, 116 and 160. Radiation covers a wide spectrum of wavelengths, from those of radio waves, which may be thousands of metres long, to those of X-rays and gamma rays, which have wavelengths of the order of millionths of millionths of millimetres. Radiation is a form of physical energy and it interacts with any matter it encounters. Radiation of relatively long wavelength, such as that from radio transmitters, microwave ovens, ultrasound machines, electric light bulbs, the Sun and ultraviolet-light sources, is described as *nonionizing radiation*. This means that such radiation, although it may cause atoms and molecules of the body to vibrate strongly, does not actually break up molecules. Short-wavelength radiation, such as X-rays, gamma rays, neutrons or charged particles (alpha and beta particles), can displace linking ELECTRONS from molecules and cause them to break up into smaller charged bodies or chemical groups called *ions* or FREE RADICALS. For this reason it is called *ionizing radiation*. The sources of ionizing radiation include outer space and the Sun (cosmic rays); medical X-ray machines; radioactive elements, such as uranium and radium; radioactive isotopes, many of which are artificial (i.e. not found in nature); radioactive fallout from atomic explosions and industrial accidents; and leakage from atomic power stations. Ionizing radiation can damage any molecules in the body, including the large DNA molecules that make up the chromosomes of human body cells. Radiation that kills cells causes dozens of breaks in, and other damage to, the DNA. Lesser damage can, up to a point, be repaired by the cells, but the risk of a permanent and inheritable change (a *genetic*

mutation) is always there. Cells that are dividing rapidly, such as those in the BLOOD-forming tissue of the bone marrow, the testicles, intestine and skin, are more susceptible to radiation damage than cells that are dividing infrequently, or not at all. On the other hand, when cells are killed by radiation, those that divide most rapidly can more easily make up the losses and resume normal function. Others may be replaced by scar tissue or sustain permanent damage, as in the greying of hair, the formation of cataracts, or the production of cancers under the influence of high-radiation dosage. The higher the radiation, the higher the percentage of cells killed, and, if the dose is high enough, death of the individual occurs. A burst of high-level radiation, lasting for a few minutes and covering the whole body, might be fatal. But if the same whole-body dose were spread over a month, immediate death would not result, although life might be shortened. The size of the area of the body exposed to radiation is also very important. An intensity of radiation that, if applied to the whole body, would certainly cause death, can be safely applied, for purposes of treatment, to a small area.

radiation pressure, the very small pressure exerted on an irradiated object by the RADIATION. This pressure occurs because all radiation has momentum and energy.

radio, the communication of information between remote points using electromagnetic RADIATION (⇨ p. 84) as the medium of transmission. Radio waves are of the same nature as other electromagnetic radiation but occupy that part of the electromagnetic spectrum between about 500,000 cycles per second (500 KHz) and 100 million cycles per second (100 MHz). Radio uses an alternating-current *carrier wave*. Such a wave is propagated through space in much the same way as is light, and can be received direct or reflected from the part of the atmosphere above about 60 km (37 mi) where there is a high concentration of free electrons (the *ionosphere*). Imposed on the carrier wave is a MODULATION of various kinds, such as *amplitude modulation* (AM), *frequency modulation* (FM), *pulse-code modulation,* and so on. When the modulated wave strikes an aerial it induces a small alternating electric current in it, which is greatly amplified by the radio receiver. The carrier wave is then removed in a process known as *demodulation,* and the information retrieved. In addition to amplifying the tiny induced currents, radio receivers can select, from all the carrier waves picked up by the aerial, that which is required. This is done by means of *tuned circuits* that resonate at the required frequency. Most radio receivers use the SUPERHETERODYNE principle.

radiometry, the detection and measurement of electromagnetic (⇨ p. 84) radiant energy, especially that in the infrared part of the spectrum.

radius, one of the two long bones of the forearm, the other being the *ulna*. With the palm facing forward, the radius is the outer bone, on the thumb side, and runs parallel to the ulna. When the palm is turned downward, the radius

rotates at its upper end and its lower end crosses over the ulna. So that it can do this, the upper end of the radius is a small, slightly hollow disc which can turn easily on the surface of the outer boss at the lower end of the upper arm bone (the humerus). The lower end of the radius is broad and articulates with two of the small wrist bones and with the side of the lower end of the ulna.

rainbow, the familiar coloured arc seen in the sky or when sunlight passes through a fine mist of water from a hose. The rainbow is caused by the dispersion of parallel beams of light (⇨ pp. 72–5) by millions of small water droplets. Most rays are bent through a large angle, are reduced in intensity, and are not seen; some, however, are bent through a small angle and appear at maximum intensity. The extent of the bending of these rays depends on the wavelength of the light and since different wavelengths correspond to different colours, the colours are separated. Because the rays enter the drops exactly parallel, all those producing each colour emerge exactly parallel to form a band of colour, with red on top and blue on the bottom. A secondary rainbow is sometimes perceived with the order of the colours reversed.

RAM ⇨ RANDOM-ACCESS MEMORY (RAM).

random-access memory (RAM), a high-speed semiconductor computer memory used as the main functional memory store into which programs and data in use are copied and which is constantly modified in a manner reflected by what has been visible on the screen. RAMs are organized as two-dimensional arrays (⇨ MATRIX) in which each cell can be independently addressed in a fixed access time and the contents read or over-written. RAM may be *static* or *dynamic*. Static RAM maintains its information so long as the power supply is maintained; dynamic RAM must be automatically refreshed at regular intervals, otherwise the data would be lost. RAM is volatile, i.e. everything in it will be lost as soon as the power supply is switched off. Anything that must be preserved has to be copied to a permanent medium, such as a floppy disk or hard disk, before the machine is turned off. As software develops, programs make increasing demand on RAM and the recognized standard size is increasing steadily. For non-graphical purposes in microcomputers, 8 or 16 million bytes (megabytes) of RAM are currently considered adequate; but for high-resolution images, greater RAM capacity is required.

reactance, the impedance that a capacitor (⇨ p. 98) or an inductor (⇨ p. 100) offer to alternating current (⇨ p. 90). For a pure inductor or capacitor, the ratio of the voltage across the device to the current through it at any moment in time. Reactance is measured in ohms.

read-only memory (ROM), a computer memory the contents of which are permanently retained and are not lost when the machine's power supplies are switched off. Most ROMs are smaller than most RAMS and contain operating programs required to get the machine started as well as frequently used software. Although the contents of the ROM are readily accessible they cannot be changed by the user of the machine.

real-time systems, computer systems that operate quickly enough for the result to be available for use in concurrent events in the real world without appreciable or unacceptable delay. The time from input to response in real-time systems is often of the order of thousandths of a second. For many purposes a longer delay is acceptable; for some, the response must be more rapid.

rectifier, a device that allows electric current to flow freely in one direction but offers high resistance (⇨ p. 96) to flow in the reverse direction. Rectifiers, such as semiconductor junctions, are widely used to convert alternating current (⇨ p. 90) to unidirectional direct current. Rectified AC consists of a series of pulses, but these can easily be smoothed by capacitors (⇨ p. 98) into a direct current of uniform amplitude.

rectum, the short, but distensible, length of bowel immediately above the anal canal.

red dwarf, a small star of low luminosity occurring in very large numbers throughout the universe. Red dwarfs are the most numerous class of stars but are often so faint as to be inapparent to direct observation.

red shift, a Doppler effect (⇨ p. 68) on light indicating that an object is receding (⇨ pp. 140–3).

redundancy, in computing and biological systems, the provisions of physical components extra to the minimum needed for proper functioning. The purpose of redundancy is to ensure continued operation even in the event of component failure. Organs like the KIDNEYS have so much redundancy that the body can operate satisfactorily on one. Redundancy is also used in software, especially in communications (⇨ p. 220), to ensure that essential information is transmitted correctly.

reflex, an automatic and predictable response to a stimulus impinging on the body or arising within it. Standing and walking would be impossible without the spinal reflexes that automatically tense muscles when their opponent muscle groups contract and put them on the stretch. Spinal reflex arcs involve the spinal cord only; the integrity of the input and output channels of these arcs, to and from the cord, can be tested by tapping muscle tendons anywhere in the body. Sneezing and coughing are reflexes, as are movements to preserve balance, the response of the pupils to light and dark, and the blink or screwing up of the eyelids in response to immediate threat to the eyes. Much of the internal control of biochemical stability (HOMEOSTASIS) is reflexive in nature. CONDITIONED REFLEXES are those that are built up, over a period, as a result of experience. Much animal and human behaviour is reflexive and predictable; indeed some thinkers believe that *all* human functioning is reflex.

relational database, a DATABASE in which items of information (⇨ p. 216) are treated as subsets of other information and can be retrieved in accordance with a logical formula (⇨ LOGIC CIRCUITS). Such a database, for instance, could find all instances that fulfil certain criteria AND/OR certain others but NOT stated others. Instances sought might also be equal to, less than, or more than stated values.

REM sleep, rapid-eye-movement sleep. REM sleep periods are those in which the eyeballs of a sleeping person can be seen to be moving constantly behind the closed lids. The muscles twitch, dreaming occurs and, in men, the penis becomes erect. REM sleep occurs in periods totalling about twenty per cent of the sleeping time, and is necessary for health. Sleepers are hardest to wake during these periods, and if awakened will agree that they have been dreaming.

renin, an enzyme (⇨ pp. 182–5) produced by the KIDNEY if the BLOOD pressure becomes too low. Renin acts on a protein globulin, *angiotensinogen*, in the blood to split off the substance angiotensin I. This, in turn, is converted to angiotensin II by a *converting enzyme* found in the blood vessels in the LUNGS. Angiotensin II acts strongly on the adrenal GLANDS, causing the secretion of the hormone aldosterone, which acts on the kidneys to reduce the loss of sodium in the URINE. The increased sodium retention raises the blood pressure. One way to treat high blood pressure is to use drugs that block the action of the angiotensin-converting enzyme.

resonance, the state of a body capable of vibration or oscillation when it is subjected to a periodic disturbance at a frequency close to or equal to the frequency at which it naturally tends to vibrate or oscillate. At this frequency the body displays increased amplitude of oscillation or vibration. The natural resonant frequency depends on material, dimensions and shape. Resonance within the audible range produces sustained audible sounds. A body may, however, resonate at a very much higher frequency than the highest-audible frequencies. The QUARTZ crystal in a watch, for instance, may resonate at many millions of cycles per second (Megahertz). Resonance is also exhibited by electrical circuits. A coil (*inductor*; ⇨ p. 100) in parallel with a capacitor (⇨ p. 98) will resonate, as the charge on the capacitor causes a current to flow in the inductor, and vice versa. This occurs at a frequency determined by the capacitance and the inductance, and is the basis of RADIO tuning and many OSCILLATORS. Resonance occurs in MOLECULES, atoms and elementary particles.

respiration, the acquisition of OXYGEN from the atmosphere and the release of CARBON DIOXIDE (CO_2) into it. This exchange of gases is vital to life and is a two-stage process. In the LUNGS, oxygen enters the BLOOD and CO_2 leaves it to be removed in the expired air. In the tissues, oxygen leaves the blood and enters the cells, and CO_2 leaves the tissue and enters the blood.

respirator, a mechanical device used to maintain the breathing movements or the regular supply of oxygen to the LUNGS, in those incapable of breathing spontaneously, by reason of temporary or permanent paralysis. Almost all respirators are of the intermittent positive-pressure type. In these, air or oxygen is blown into the lungs through a tube fitted tightly into the windpipe (*trachea*) through the nose, mouth or through a tracheostomy opening in the neck. The pressure is applied, intermittently, at the normal rate of breathing and, during release periods, the air is expelled from the lungs by the collapse caused by their normal elasticity. Respirators of the iron-lung or cuirass type are now obsolete.

rest mass, the property of a body that determines its inertia and its internal energy; ⇨ pp. 26–9.

retina, the membrane lining the inside of the back of the eye and corresponding to a film in a camera or, more accurately, to the image orthicon or vidicon in a TV camera. The retina is a direct extension of the brain and the optic nerve, which connects the eye to the brain is really a tract of the brain, corresponding to other, internal, tracts. Images cast on the retina by the cornea and crystalline lens are converted to nerve impulses by specialized nerve cells, the rods and cones. These impulses are processed by a network of connecting and integrating cells. The resulting signals are conveyed to the brain by the long fibres of some of these cells – about 1,000,000 from each eye, and these fibres make up the optic nerves. The rods are colour-blind but are exceptionally sensitive, responding to very dim light. The cones are less sensitive, but produce impulses that vary in strength with the colour of the light striking them, each cone giving a maximal output at one of three points in the light spectrum. Towards the centre of the retina cones predominate, but at the peripheries the light receptors are almost all rods. In the centre of the retina is a spot called the *macula lutea*. There are no retinal blood vessels in this area and the light-sensitive cells are tightly packed together so that the visual resolution is highest here. Only the macular area is capable of the degree of discrimination necessary for reading, telling time or recognizing faces.

reverberation, the effect of repeated reflection of sound (⇨ p. 68) by the walls of a large enclosed space after the sound that caused the original reflection has ceased. Moderate reverberation improves the acoustics of a room or building; excessive reverberation seriously interferes with discrimination of speech or music.

rheology, the study of the flow properties of matter, especially viscous liquids; ⇨ p. 34.

rhesus factor, a blood group in humans additional to the A, B, AB and O blood groups. The gene that makes a person rhesus positive is called D and is present in 85 per cent of the population. The gene is dominant, so a person is rhesus positive even if only one of the gene pair (ALLELES) is D. All the offspring of a rhesus-positive father with two D genes (*homozygous*) will be rhesus positive. If the father has only one D allele (*heterozygous*), each pregnancy will have a 50 per cent chance of producing a rhesus-positive baby. When a rhesus-positive father produces a rhesus-positive baby in a rhesus-negative mother, the baby's red BLOOD cells will act as ANTIGENS capable of causing the mother to produce ANTIBODIES against them. These antigens do not normally reach the mother's blood until labour so they are unlikely to cause serious harm in the first pregnancy. But in subsequent pregnancies, the levels of these antibodies in the mother's blood rise rapidly and soon reach a point at which they are able to destroy the red cells of the fetus. In the most severe cases, the fetus dies in the womb, usually after the 28th week. If born alive, the child is deeply jaundiced with an enlarged LIVER and SPLEEN and a low HAEMOGLOBIN level in the blood. Excess haemoglobin in the blood leads to excess bile-pigment (*bilirubin*) production. This has a much more serious effect than merely to stain the skin and cause jaundice. Bilirubin is very toxic to the brain, which becomes bile-stained and this leads to paralysis, spasticity, mental disability and defects of sight and hearing. A badly affected baby can have an exchange transfusion, via the umbilical cord, as soon as it is born, or even while still in the womb. This corrects the anaemia and gets rid of the bilirubin. Exposure to intense blue light soon after birth assists in converting the bilirubin in the skin to a form that is harmless to the brain. Rhesus-negative women can be prevented from developing antibodies by being given an injection of anti-D GAMMA GLOBULIN within 60 hours of the birth of a rhesus-positive baby. In order to protect future babies, this is done in all such cases.

ribose, a water-soluble monosaccharide sugar with five carbon atoms in the molecule (a *pentose*) that, in conjunction with 2-deoxy-D-ribose, forms the carbohydrate part of DNA (⇨ p. 202).

ribosomes, the minute cell organs (*organelles*) that synthesize protein in cells (⇨ pp. 186–9) on the basis of the DNA genetic code.

ribs, the flat, curved bones that form a strong, protective, flexible cage for the LUNGS, the heart and the great BLOOD VESSELS leaving and entering it.

rigor mortis, the stiffening of muscles that occurs after death. When the supply of BLOOD stops, the GLUCOSE in the muscles is reduced to lactic acid, which causes the muscle plasma to coagulate and the muscles to lose their elasticity. Strenuous exercise before death causes an increase in muscle lactic acid and hastens the onset of rigor mortis. On average, rigor starts three to four hours after death and reaches a maximum within 24 hours, usually after about 12 hours. But during this time, enzymes are starting to work to break down and soften the muscles, and the stiffness gradually lessens over the next two to three days. A number of factors, especially the effect of environmental temperature on the temperature of the body, affects the timing of these biochemical changes. These factors must be taken into account if the state of rigor mortis is being used to help in establishing the time of death for medicolegal purposes.

RISC, reduced-instruction-set computer. A machine using a microprocessor with a minimal set of instructions so that it can operate very quickly. The necessary complexity is transferred to software; ⇨ p. 218.

rocket, a propulsive system suitable for space vehicles. Rockets operate excellently in near-vacuum conditions and do not operate by pushing against the atmosphere. In a rocket engine of whatever type, gases are formed very rapidly from solid or liquid fuel. These expand within a container and exert powerful pressure against all the walls of the container. One end of the container is, however, open and the gases emerge from this open end at high speed. The result is that the force exerted at this point is very much less than the forces exerted on all other parts of the inside of the container. The force exerted on the side opposite the open end is unbalanced and drives the vehicle forward. The forces exerted at right angles to the direction of travel are balanced and produce no net movement. The nozzle of a rocket is exposed to very high temperatures and must not erode unevenly. If it does so the direction of rocket movement will change.

ROM ⇨ READ-ONLY MEMORY.

root, the anchoring and absorbing structure of a plant. Root tips and hairs take up water and dissolved minerals from the soil by CAPILLARY action.

routine, a discrete part of a computer program that achieves a particular task. Other parts of a program may repeatedly call on routines; ⇨ p. 218.

ruby, aluminium oxide (*corundum*) in its rare deep-red-coloured form. Pure corundum is colourless, but it also occurs in grey, blue or purple (*sapphire*), green, yellow and brown forms. Rubies have been made synthetically.

Salmonella, a genus of rod-shaped bacteria, of which over 1,500 species have been identified. There are over 700 different species known to cause food poisoning, and these may infect the intestines of poultry (especially chickens and turkeys), pigs, cattle, dogs, tortoises, terrapins and other animals. Salmonella organisms are responsible for a variety of human and animal diseases, including typhoid and paratyphoid fevers, gastroenteritis and food poisoning. After an attack of salmonella gastroenteritis, the affected individual usually excretes the organisms in the faeces for six weeks or longer and may transmit the infection to others. Food handlers are especially dangerous. Salmonella gastroenteritis has become very common in modern industrial societies, largely because of developments in the food industries, especially in relation to mass production and poultry-feeding methods. Salmonella are frequently present in poultry, meat, sausages and eggs. Inadequate kitchen hygiene, inadequate thawing of frozen food before cooking, and inadequate cooking all contribute to outbreaks of gastroenteritis.

salt, a compound that results when one or more of the hydrogen atoms of an ACID are replaced by cations from a base, as when the H of HCl (hydrochloric acid) is replaced by the Na (sodium ion) of NaOH (sodium hydroxide), giving NaCl (sodium chloride) and leaving the H to combine with the OH to form H_2O (water). Acids react with BASES to give salts plus water. Because there are many acids and many bases there is a great variety of salts. In neutral salts, such as NaCl, all the hydrogen ions of the acids and all the hydroxyl ions of the bases are replaced. In acid salts, such as $NaHSO_4$, one or more of the hydrogen atoms of the acid remains. In basic salts, such as Pb(OH)Cl, one or more of the hydroxyl groups of the base remain. Salts formed from a strong acid and a strong base will give a neutral solution in water; those from a strong acid and a weak base will give an acidic solution in water; those of a weak acid and a strong base will give an alkaline solution; ⇨ p. 168.

sand, a powdery or particulate material consisting of small pieces of minerals of many kinds produced by WEATHERING. These include silicon oxides (silicates), carbonates (limestones), metal oxides, compounds of calcium, phosphorus and sulphur (cinder or slag) and other substances. The nature of sand is commonly modified by the selective effect of running water and winds.

sapphire, the mineral *corundum* in sufficiently attractive form to be regarded as a gemstone. Sapphire may be clear, yellow, blue, pink, orange, green, purple, or even black. It has a hardness of 9 on the MOHS SCALE. Star sapphires incorporate needle-like rays of the impurity rutile and are cut in such a way as to enhance the effect.

Saurischia, one of the two orders of DINOSAURS.

sawtooth waveform, a periodic electrical wave (⇨ pp. 64–7), each cycle of which rises steadily from zero to a particular maximum over the course of almost the whole cycle and then suddenly drops to zero at the end of the cycle. Also known as a *ramp* waveform. If a sawtooth-voltage waveform is applied to the plates in a CATHODE-RAY TUBE that move the beam horizontally the result will be a horizontal line on the screen caused by the steady transverse movement of the spot and then its sudden return to the start of the line. If, at the same time, a lower-frequency sawtooth voltage is applied to the plates that move the beam vertically, the returning spot will start each line a little below the previous, and will soon cover the whole screen with (almost horizontal) lines. Frequencies can easily be chosen so that each horizontal line lies immediately below the one above and the screen is filled with light. On–off and brightness modulation of the electron beam will result in a pattern being formed on the screen. The trace formed by the two sawtooth waveforms, respectively *line* and *frame*, is called a *raster*. This idea is the basis of television and computer displays and is used in television cameras (⇨ also SYNCHRONIZATION).

scanning tunnel microscope, an instrument for examining surfaces at a molecular and even atomic level. A very fine metal tip is positioned within a distance from a surface equal to the diameter of a few atoms. At such distances ELECTRONS can jump (*tunnel*) across the gap. A movement of electrons is an electric current ($\Leftrightarrow$ p. 90), which varies with the distance from the surface. The changing current is amplified and used to adjust the tip's distance from the surface so as to keep the current constant. The up-and-down movement of the tip thus reflects the contours of the surface, and can do so to a resolution equal to individual atoms. If the tip is kept close to the surface, individual atoms can be moved to a new position.

scapula, the shoulder blade. The scapula is a flat, triangular bone, lying over the upper RIBS of the back and bearing, at its upper and outer angle, a shallow hollow in which the rounded head of the upper arm bone (the *humerus*) fits. On the back of the scapula, near the top, is a prominent spine, sloping upwards and outwards and ending in a bony process that connects with the outer end of the collar bone (*clavicle*). Together, the outer parts of these two bones form the skeleton for the prominence of the shoulder.

Schmidt camera, a camera using a spherical mirror and a correcting plate to compensate for the spherical aberration ($\Leftrightarrow$ p. 78) of the mirror instead of a lens. Such a system allows large apertures, freedom from chromatic and spherical aberration and long focal length. The camera is used for astronomical and general purposes; $\Leftrightarrow$ pp. 14 and 124.

Schmitt trigger, an electronic circuit whose output can be one or other of two voltages – high or low, corresponding to the 1 or 0 in binary electronic systems. If the input is above a certain level, the output will be high; if below that level, low. A sinusoidal voltage applied to a Schmitt trigger thus gives a sharp square-wave output ($\Leftrightarrow$ pp. 64–7). All digital electronic systems work on square waves. The Schmitt trigger is an essential element for restoring sharpness when square waves have been degraded or corrupted by interference or other causes.

Schottky diode, a metal-semiconductor, two-electrode circuit element with a low forwards-bias- voltage drop – about half that of other semiconductor diodes – and a higher switching speed. Integrated-circuit transistors can be made incorporating Schottky diodes.

Schuler pendulum, anything that swings under the influence of gravity ($\Leftrightarrow$ p. 30) with a period of 84.4 minutes. This is the period of a pendulum equal in length to the radius of the Earth, and it has been shown that such a pendulum will remain vertical however the pivot may move. Gyroscopes can slow a natural pendulum of practical length so that its period is increased to 84.4 minutes, and these are used for navigation. Inertial navigation is based on the principle of the Schuler pendulum.

sciatic nerves, the large, paired nerve trunks in vertebrates formed from several of the lower spinal nerves that activate the muscles of, and provide sensation to, the rear limbs or, in humans, the legs.

scintillation counter, a detector of radiation in which the receipt of a quantum of radiation is signalled by a flash of light that is usually detected and amplified by a photomultiplier tube. The basis is a material, usually crystalline, that emits a flash of luminescence when struck by X-rays, gamma rays ($\Leftrightarrow$ p. 84) or high-speed particles ($\Leftrightarrow$ p. 110). Scintillation counters also quantify the scintillation and so are able to measure the energy of the radiation.

sclerosis, the hardening of normally soft biological tissue.

Scorpionida, the order of Arachnida that have a sting at the tip of the tail, a carapace over the unsegmented head and thorax, and a segmented abdomen. There are about 1,000 species of scorpions but only a minority are capable of a dangerous sting.

scratchpad memory, a semiconductor memory of small capacity but very short access time, used to store intermediate results in the course of computation; $\Leftrightarrow$ p. 216.

scrolling, the movement, off the top, bottom or side of a screen, of a display of data with the simultaneous appearance of more data at the opposite edge. On a PERSONAL COMPUTER scrolling is usually effected vertically by using the cursor arrow keys to run the cursor to the top or bottom of the screen, or by means of the 'page up' or 'page down' keys.

scrotum, the hanging skin-and-muscle receptacle in mammals for the testicles and the beginning of the tubes (*vasa deferentes*) that carry the sperm up to the seminal vesicles. The thin layer of muscle under the skin is called the *dartos muscle*. When this contracts, the scrotum tightens and becomes smaller.

searching, a computer facility in which the machine is directed to interrogate a file or files until an exact match is found with a given sequence of characters (a *string*). When the match is found the search is stopped and the environment of the found string displayed. *Search and replace* is an additional facility in which the string, once found, is replaced by another given string. Search and replace can be used to amend, in a few seconds or minutes, every instance of the string in a large file. It is especially useful in word processing.

secondary emission, the emission of ELECTRONS from the surface of a solid when it is bombarded by high-speed particles, especially electrons. Under certain circumstances the number of electrons emitted may exceed the bombarding number, and this fact can be used to make photomultipliers and other instruments of scientific value. Secondary emission occurs most readily with insulators ($\Leftrightarrow$ p. 90) or semiconductors such as caesium antimonide, potassium chloride, beryllium oxide and magnesium oxide.

sedimentary rocks, rocks formed by the gradual deposition from water of suspended particles produced by WEATHERING; $\Leftrightarrow$ p. 150.

Seebeck effect, the flow of electric current in a circuit consisting of two wires of different metals twisted together to form a ring when the two junctions are at different temperatures. The direction of current flow depends on which is the hotter junction. The effect was discovered in 1821 by the Russian-born German physicist Thomas Johann Seebeck (1770–1831). Compare the Peltier effect in which a current caused to flow through such a circuit by a battery produces a raised temperature at one junction and a lowered temperature at the other (named after the French physicist Jean Peltier, 1785–1845).

seed, a fertilized plant egg cell (*ovule*) containing an embryo from which a new plant can form on sprouting (*germination*). In flowering plants (*angiosperms*) the seeds develop within a fruit. In conifers and similar plants, the seeds occur on the open surface of a structure. The embryo consists of a central cellular structure with attached seed leaves (*cotyledons*). The seed is covered by one or two envelopes of tissue known as the *integuments*.

selectivity, the ability of a radio receiver to abstract a signal with a comparatively narrow frequency bandwidth, from the spectrum of transmitted frequencies, and to reject the others, especially those of similar frequencies. Selectivity is achieved by the use of several cascaded, sharply tuned circuits that offer a high ratio of reactance to resistance (i.e. a high Q; $\Leftrightarrow$ p. 96). The HETERODYNE PRINCIPLE facilitates the practical duplication of successive tuned circuits.

semiconductor diode, a two-connection circuit element consisting either of a junction between a conductor and a semiconductor, or a junction between p-type and n-type semiconductor materials ($\Leftrightarrow$ pp. 102–5). Such a diode allows current to flow in one direction only. Semiconductor diodes with p-n junctions can be arranged to function as light sources (LIGHT-EMITTING DIODES or LEDs), as switches, as VOLTAGE REGULATORS ($\Leftrightarrow$ ZENER DIODE) or as variable capacitors (*varicaps*; $\Leftrightarrow$ p. 98).

semiconductor laser, a device in which laser action ($\Leftrightarrow$ p. 82) occurs through the stimulated recombination of free electrons and HOLES in the valency band in a semiconductor crystal such as gallium arsenide. In so doing energy is released and radiated as a quantum of light. A current passed through a p-n junction ($\Leftrightarrow$ pp. 102–5) in such a material results in large numbers of electrons and holes being brought together. The flat ends of the crystals act as mirrors to promote lasing.

semiconductor rectifier, a semiconductor device for converting an alternating current ($\Leftrightarrow$ p. 90) into a direct current by allowing current to flow in one direction only. Silicon p-n junctions ($\Leftrightarrow$ pp. 102–5) are used, and these can pass currents of from less than 1 amp to as much as 5,000 amps. Diodes can be connected in parallel to carry greater current, or in series to resist higher voltages. A third electrode can be introduced to exert a controlling effect on the current passing. These are called *silicon-controlled rectifiers* (SCRs) or *thyristors,* and are extensively used as power-control components, such as light dimmers.

seminal fluid, the creamy, greyish or yellowish, sticky, gell-like material ejaculated from the penis during the sexual orgasm. Seminal fluid is secreted by the prostate gland, the storage seminal vesicles, the lining of the sperm tubes (*epididymis* and *vas deferens*) and some small associated GLANDS. In humans, the volume of the ejaculate varies considerably, especially with age, and ranges from 2–6 ml in youth to almost nothing in elderly men. The volume rises after ten days or so of continence and drops if ejaculation occurs more than twice a day. Each millilitre contains from 50 million to 150 million sperms (*spermatozoa*). After ejaculation semen remains gell-like for about twenty minutes, but then liquifies. Until it does the sperms hardly move. It contains the sugar fructose, which provides the spermatozoa with energy.

sensory deprivation, the state in which there is a major reduction in incoming sensory information. Prolonged sensory deprivation is very damaging as the body, being an essentially reactive entity, depends for its health and normal function on constant stimulation. The main input sensory channels are the eyes, the ears, the skin and the nose. If input from all of these is blocked, there is loss of the sense of reality, distortion of time and imagined space, hallucinations, bizarre thought patterns and other indications of neurological dysfunction. Even minimal sensory deprivation in early childhood can have a serious long-term effect. An eye covered for a few months in infancy remains effectively blind for life. Early deprivation of normal hearing can produce severe intellectual and educational damage. Deprivation of the normal contact and stimulation provided to the baby by the parent can cause personality disturbance in later life.

serial and parallel transfer, alternative ways of sending binary information. In serial transmission the bits are sent one after the other. This can be done using a single line and a return line. In parallel transmission, an eight-bit byte (or longer word) is sent along eight (or more) parallel channels, the bits moving together. Parallel connection is commonly used to send data to a printer, but, for economic and other reasons, is rarely used for long-distance transmission.

serial interface, a connection at a computer at which digital information (⇨ p. 220) passes out or in one bit at a time. Serial interfaces can convert parallel data to serial and vice versa. A common standard for serial interfaces is the RS232 standard.

serum, the fluid that separates from clotted BLOOD when it is allowed to stand. It consists of blood less the red cells and proteins, including fibrin, that form the clot. Serum is 93 per cent water and contains a very large number of substances in solution. These include: many electrolytes, such as sodium, potassium, calcium, magnesium, chloride, bicarbonate and phosphate; proteins, such as albumin and the range of immunoglobulins (ANTIBODIES); nutrients such as AMINO ACIDS, CARBOHYDRATES, fats, cholesterol and VITAMINS; HORMONES; trace minerals; and waste products, such as UREA, creatinine, uric acid and bilirubin.

server, a point in a computer network, such as a LOCAL-AREA NETWORK at which a particular service is provided to the network. A *file server* is a substantial storage facility, usually consisting of a large-capacity hard disk, to which individuals on the network have access. Other such services include printing and remote communication facilities; ⇨ pp. 214–21.

seven-segment display, a squared-off figure-of-eight composed of seven bars, each of which can be displayed or not displayed. By selecting bars, any letter of the alphabet or any of the numbers can be displayed. Seven-segment displays are widely used in clocks, LIQUID-CRYSTAL DISPLAYS and other electronically operated machine/human interfaces.

sex selection, the deliberate attempt to achieve gender choice before birth. If an ovum is fertilized by a sperm carrying an X chromosome, the baby will be a girl; if by a sperm carrying a Y, the baby will be a boy. 'Female' sperms contain about three per cent more DNA than 'males' and are heavier and slower moving, but can travel further. Attempts to make use of these facts to select the sex of the future child – by depositing semen further away from the site of fertilisation in the Fallopian tube if a girl was desired – have not been universally successful. The separation of sperms into X-bearing and Y-bearing types can be done in the laboratory by various methods, and this can increase the percentage of Y-bearing sperms from fifty to about eighty. Artificial insemination, with the Y-enriched semen, can then be used. X-enrichment is also possible. Women can be 'immunized' against proteins present only in the Y-bearing sperms, but this is not thought to have been a successful method of sex-determination for their offspring. The overall success rate in sex determination, by the most effective current methods, is less than eighty per cent. Although effective sex selection would not necessarily change the balance between males and females in a population, these facts raise major ethical problems.

sexual 'deviation', a term of uncertain and insecure meaning, sometimes applied to any form of physical sexual activity outside the convention of heterosexual, penile/vaginal intercourse. Widely regarded as deviant are sexual activity with children (*paedophilia*) or animals (*bestiality*), exhibitionism, sadism, masochism, sexual fetishism and transvestism. Other activities often regarded as deviations include watching the sexual activity of others (*voyeurism*), making obscene telephone calls (*telephone scatologia*), rubbing the penis against women in crowded places (*frotteurism*), and taking sexual pleasure in defecating on a partner or in being defecated upon (*coprophilia*).

shift register, a small computer memory consisting of a ladder-like array of places, each of which can accommodate a whole eight bit or larger word. With the arrival of each clock pulse, the whole word is shifted along one place, the end word being ejected into a BUS and a place being left, at the other end, for a new word to enter. Shift registers are widely used in computing and may be implemented either as actual HARDWARE or as SOFTWARE; ⇨ pp. 216–19.

shivering, an important means of heat production in the body. Shivering is a rapid succession of contractions and relaxations of muscles. This occurs automatically when extra heat is required to maintain body temperature, and is thus a feature of exposure to cold. The power of the contraction depends on the rate of heat production needed, and may be considerable, leading to a *rigor* (violent shivering). The correct response to shivering from cold is to improve the body's insulation by suitable clothing and so reduce heat loss. The body contains a 'thermostat', in the form of certain temperature-sensitive NERVE cells in the hypothalamus of the brain, and a drop in the temperature of the BLOOD is sensed by these nerves, and the shivering reflex initiated. In fever, the BACTERIA, TOXINS, etc., release from some of the white cells of the blood a substance called INTERLEUKIN-1, which resets the thermostat at a higher point. The nervous system then responds as if the blood were too cold and shivering results. In this case, the extra heat production may or may not be beneficial, depending on the cause, but, in general, heat loss from the body should be encouraged.

shock, a dangerous and often critical medical condition caused by a reduction in the volume of the circulating BLOOD. This may be due to: severe blood loss after an injury; loss of fluid as a result of major burns or damage to the blood vessels from severe infection (*septic shock*); the presence of bacterial poisons (TOXINS) in the blood (*toxic shock*); failure of the heart to function properly, as after a heart attack; abnormal loss of tension in the blood vessels; or obstruction in major ARTERIES, as in blockage of a pulmonary artery by a blood clot in the LUNGS. In shock there is a drop in blood pressure, the heart beats rapidly to try to maintain the circulation, but the pulse is weak and thready. The SKIN is pale, but moist, and the production of URINE drops. Unless rapidly reversed by fluid transfusion, shock is likely to be fatal. The term is commonly confused, outside medical circles, with the acute emotional disturbance experienced by anyone exposed to a distressing event, also commonly called shock.

short circuit, an electrical connection of negligible resistance (⇨ p. 96) that bypasses a part of an electrical circuit (⇨ p. 90). Because the resistance is so low a maximal current will flow though a short circuit and this may have a dangerous heating effect.

shunt, anything that bypasses a usual route. Sensitive electric-current meters in series with a conductor carrying a heavy current (⇨ p. 90) are always by-passed by a very-low-resistance

(⇨ p. 96) parallel conductor so that only a small, but fixed, proportion of the current passes through the meter. In surgery, the term is applied to a bypass that allows BLOOD or other fluid to be diverted from its normal direction of flow. An arterio-venous shunt allows blood to go directly from an ARTERY to a VEIN without passing through the CAPILLARIES, in the usual way. Such a shunt may be made artificially in the arm in those who have to be repeatedly connected to a DIALYSIS machine, or may occur as a result of penetrating injury, such as a gunshot wound, involving both vessels. A shunt commonly occurs in congenital heart disorders when an abnormal opening, such as a defect in the wall between the two sides – a 'hole in the heart' – allows blood to pass from the left side of the heart to the right. Sometime shunting occurs in the opposite direction so that the LUNGS are bypassed. Shunts are successfully used in treating 'water on the brain' (*hydrocephalus*), to allow free drainage of cerebrospinal fluid, by way of a plastic tube containing a pressure-operated valve, from the brain spaces to the heart or the abdominal cavity. A shunt may also be used between the portal vein of the LIVER and the main vein of the body (*portacaval shunt*) in order to prevent the development, in cirrhosis of the liver, of dangerous varicose veins at the lower end of the gullet.

Siamese twins, twins joined together at birth. The junction is usually along the trunk or between the two heads, at the front, back or sides. In some cases, organs are shared and this makes separation of the twins difficult or impossible. The name derives from the male twins Chang and Eng, born in Siam in 1811, who survived until they were 63. Although Chang and Eng were joined face to face from breastbone to navel they both married nevertheless, and each contrived to father several children. Siamese twins are derived from a single fertilized ovum and are uniovular, identical twins. In the normal case, at the time of the first division of the ovum, the two resulting daughter cells either remain joined to produce one individual, or separate completely to produce two identical individuals, which then develop separately. In the case of Siamese twins, this separation is incomplete.

sign, the quality of positivity or negativity of a quantity or a number. In computers, sign is indicated by a *sign bit*, often the leftmost bit in a word. Since most quantities are positive, the sign bit is usually a 1 for minus and a 0 for plus; ⇨ p. 220.

sign bit ⇨ SIGN.

silica, silicon oxide (SiO_2), which occurs in a variety of forms (*polymorphs*) including quartz, cristobalite, coesite, tridymite and stishovite.

silicates, compounds based on an atom of silicon linked to four atoms of oxygen (SiO_4). Silicate minerals constitute the greater part of the Earth's crust (⇨ p. 146), and include many mineral groups such as andalusite, chlorite, feldspar, garnet, humite, mica, olivine, scapolite, serpentine and zeolite. Inorganic polymers of silicates include asbestos, sheet mica and borosilicate glasses including 'pyrex'.

sine wave, the projection on a plane surface of the path of a point moving around a circle at uniform speed; and the graph of the function $y = \sin x$ or $y = \cos x$. It is also the projection onto a uniformly moving plane of a point on a pendulum swinging above it (⇨ p. 28). Sine waves of different frequencies and amplitudes are the waves into which any other periodic waveform, however complex, can be analysed by the process of Fourier analysis (⇨ pp. 18–23). A sine wave has no harmonics and an acoustic sine wave sounds pure and rather dull, like a low note on a flute played softly. Domestic alternating current is sinusoidal.

singularity, a hypothetical point in space at which the general theory of relativity (⇨ p. 38) does not apply because matter is infinitely compressed to a single infinitesimal point. This was the situation immediately before big bang (⇨ p. 126) and is the situation in a black hole (⇨ p. 128).

sinus, an air cavity in a BONE. The *paranasal sinuses* are mucous-membrane-lined spaces in the skull bones surrounding the nose. In humans, they are: the two frontal sinuses, in the bones of the forehead (*frontal bones*), behind and above the eyebrows; the two maxillary sinuses, or antrums, in the cheekbones (*maxillae*); the two multicelled *ethmoidal sinuses* in the bones between the cavity of the nose and the eye sockets; and the *sphenoidal sinuses* in the central part of the large, winged bird-shaped bone (the *sphenoid*) that forms the central part of the base of the skull, at the back of the nose. All the paranasal sinuses drain through openings into the nose, but, in the upright posture, these openings do not all drain as well in humans as they do in quadrupeds.

Siphonaptera, the order of bloodsucking insects known as fleas.

skeleton, a bony, cartilaginous or hornlike framework or support for an animal body that may be internal (*endoskeleton*) or external (*exoskeleton*). Vertebrates have an endoskeleton; skeletal invertebrates (*arthropods*) have an exoskeleton of a polysaccharide material called *chitin*.

skin, a waterproof cover for the body, and a major organ in humans, 1.5–2 m² (14–18 ft²) in area. Self-renewing and self-repairing, it provides heat regulation for the body and protection from the outside world. The skin is exquisitely sensitive to touch, pressure, pain, irritation, heat and cold, and is an important sensory interface between the body and the outer world, endlessly sending environmental information to the brain. It screens against light damage by absorbing light energy into the pigment melanin. Bacterial attack is resisted by the healthy skin, and the constant shedding of the outer hornlike layer of the outer layer of the skin (the EPIDERMIS) also actively dislodges microorganisms. The skin also synthesizes vitamin D. The epidermis is the outermost layer of the skin, lying outside the true skin, or DERMIS. The epidermis is structurally simple with none of the NERVES, BLOOD VESSELS, or hair FOLLICLES of the dermis, and acts as a rapidly replaceable surface capable of tolerating much abrasion and trauma. The deepest layer of the epidermis is called the basal-cell layer; this layer contains the pigment melanin in concentration that varies from person to person, thereby occasioning the characteristic skin colour.

skull, the vertebrate braincase. The interior of the skull is fashioned to fit precisely to the shape of the brain and contains 'shelves' to support the brain's lobes. In the centre of the base of the skull is a large opening, the *foramen magnum*, through which the downward continuation of the brain, the spinal cord, passes. In the front of the upper and outer parts are the two bony sockets (the orbits) that accommodate and protect the eyes. At the back of the orbits are holes in the bone to allow the optic nerves to pass back to the brain, and the nerves that move the eye muscles to run forward from the brain. Between these is the opening for the air passages of the nose. The floor of the nose is formed by the bony palate that also forms the roof of the mouth. Under the orbits are the paired *maxillae* – the bones of the upper jaw. These bear the upper teeth. The hinged lower jaw (*mandible*) carries a corresponding set of lower teeth. The vault of the skull consists of the wide forehead bone (*frontal* bone), the paired, upper and rear side bones (*parietal* bones), the paired lower-front *temporal* bones, and the single lower-rear *occipital* bone. The prominence of the cheeks and part of the outer walls and floors of the orbits are formed by the *zygomatic* bones.

sleep, the regular, daily period of unconsciousness, that occupies one quarter to one third of the duration of each person's life. Sleep requirements vary considerably, the limits, in health, being about 4–10 hours in each 24-hour period. On falling asleep, the level of consciousness declines gradually, through a half-awake stage to a stage of loss of awareness of external events, and then a stage in which the brain's electrical activity is markedly diminished. This level is interrupted several times each night by periods in which much neurological activity occurs, showing itself by an increase in the BLOOD flow through the brain, rapid changes in the heart and respiration rate, quick, roving movements of the eyes and erection of the penis in males. These periods are called rapid-eye-movement (REM) sleep, and it is during these that dreaming occurs. The state of the brain during REM sleep is similar to that during emotional arousal. The purpose of sleep is unknown but prolonged deprivation of non-REM sleep is harmful, causing lethargy, depression, seizures and severe mental disturbances, including hallucinations. Less severe deprivation causes fatigue, irritability, loss of concentration and skills, and deterioration of work performance. Repeated short periods of 'dropping off' then occur.

smoke, fine particles of solid or liquid suspended in air. Smokes characteristically arise from the incomplete combustion of organic materials such as wood, coal, oil and tobacco, and consist of soots, metal oxides, oil vapours and mists of various chemicals. Many smokes are highly complex mixtures of many substances. Tobacco smoke, for instance, contains at least 3,000 different substances, both solid and liquid, some of them highly toxic. Some of the components of inhaled smoke remain in the air passage; others are absorbed into the bloodstream and are carried to all parts of the body.

sneezing, a barely controllable reflex caused by irritation, from any cause, within the nose. The effect of sneezing is to tend to remove the cause of the irritation. Sneezing is important in young children, who have not yet learned to blow their noses, as it is the means of removing excess mucus, dried secretions, or other irritating material. The reflex response begins with a deep indrawing of breath followed by tight closure of the vocal cords. The air in the chest is then compressed by elevation of the diaphragm and lowering of the ribs, the tongue is pressed against the roof of the mouth, and the vocal cords are suddenly separated. The resulting blast of air through the nose is the sneeze.

soft keyboard, a computer KEYBOARD in which the effect of a given keystroke (key press) can be arbitrarily changed by software control from a program (⇨ p. 218). Personal computers have soft keyboards.

soft palate, a small flap of muscle and fibrous tissue, enclosed in a fold of mucous membrane and attached to the back of the hard palate. The soft palate extends the palate backwards, separating the back of the mouth from the nasopharynx. It is able to press firmly against the back wall of the pharynx, sealing off the opening to the nose during swallowing and blowing out through the mouth. Without this action, some of the food being swallowed would pass up into the nose. In humans, the soft-palate action is necessary for normal speech.

software, the programs of instructions or the collections of data used by computers (⇨ p. 218). Software, whatever its usable content, consists of sequences of binary numbers representing instructions and data, and is thus intangible. These numbers are usually preserved in the form of tiny magnetic points on a magnetizable medium or, more permanently, as microscopic pits on the surface of a compact disc. These discs or other media are not software; the software is constituted by the information on them. By association, however, the discs are sometimes referred to as software. Software can easily and quickly be copied from one disc to another, and, in spite of the fact that millions of binary digits (*bits*) are involved and that one mistake might render a program inoperative, this copying is achieved with an accuracy comparable to that of the replication in living organisms of DNA (⇨ p. 202). Because of the ease of copying and of electronic distribution, software tends to proliferate in an almost 'biological manner'. Useful software quickly spreads all over the world. The same, however, applies to maliciously destructive software (*computer viruses*).

soil, a mixture of finely divided inorganic particles from weathered rocks and organic material derived from the breakdown of living organisms, both plant and animal. Soils vary considerably in their composition depending on their location and history. They contain very large numbers of micro-organisms with a vital function in fixing nitrogen and decomposing complex organic matter.

solar wind, the stream of charged particles constantly given off by the Sun that contributes to the AURORA and to the tails of comets; ⇨ pp. 132 and 140–3.

solution, a uniformly distributed mixture of two or more solids, liquids or gases in which the molecules or atoms of the substances are completely dispersed.

sound absorption, the process in which sound energy is diminished by its conversion into heat in the course of its interaction with matter. Soft and easily deformed material is a more efficient absorber of sound than hard, reflective material; ⇨ p. 68.

somatotype, a particular body configuration. The description of somatotypes was originally an attempt to find a correlation between body shape and personality type and the tendency to develop certain patterns of mental illness. Ernst Kretschmer, in the 1920s, described the tall, thin (*asthenic*), round-bodied (*pyknic*) and burly (*athletic*) types. In addition W. H. Sheldon, in the 1940s, selected the roughly corresponding *ectomorph*, *endomorph* and *mesomorph*. Although there seems to be some correlation between an asthenic build and a tendency to schizophrenia, and a pyknic build and a tendency to *cyclothymia* (a mood disorder featuring swings from elation to depression), the somatotypes do not offer any useful guidance in diagnosis, and interest in the matter has dropped off.

space, the property associated with extension in three directions each perpendicular to the others. In theoretical considerations, space is independent of matter but may contain it. In the real universe, space always contains matter. Space is part of the space–time continuum (⇨ p. 38) by which all events are uniquely located. It cannot be perceived, only conceived, but its presence is inferred by the perception of matter and events within it. In terms of extraterrestrial transportation, space is the region in which a vehicle cannot rely on an atmosphere for any purpose and cannot obtain exogenous oxygen to support life; ⇨ pp. 38 and 126–43.

space probe, a vehicle carrying scientific instruments (⇨ pp. 122–5) and designed to perform exploratory missions to the Moon, the planets and beyond, for the purpose of gathering new information. The instruments carried may include telescopes, television cameras, spectroscopes (⇨ p. 80), cosmic-ray detectors and telescopes, gamma-ray detectors and telescopes, magnetometers, plasma detectors, meteoroid detectors and various kinds of surface scanner.

space shuttle, a reusable vehicle capable of going into low orbits around the Earth to carry out tasks of scientific, commercial and military importance, such as placing, repairing or retrieving artificial satellites, carrying out scientific experiments, building space stations, and so on. The shuttle consists of an orbiter, three main engines, an external tank and two solid-fuel rocket boosters. The external tank is abandoned on each flight, but the other components can be used again. The shuttle has a crew of from four to seven and a considerable payload. It can remain in orbit for a week and could, if necessary, have a turn-round time between trips of 14 days. At launch, all three engines and boosters burn in parallel, and the latter separate after about two minutes. The main engine ceases to fire about eight minutes after lift-off, and at this point the external tank separates. The orbit is initially elliptical but is corrected to circular at an altitude of about 280 km (175 mi). Once in orbit the orbiter is turned into a tail-first attitude so that the engines can be used for slowing when de-orbiting is required. It is then turned nose-first for re-entry. Heat-resistant, low-conductivity tiles prevent the heat produced by friction (⇨ p. 32) with the atmosphere from being transmitted into the interior of the orbiter.

space station, a permanent or semipermanent orbiting vehicle capable of sustaining humans in conditions of virtually zero gravity and freedom from the Earth's atmosphere for prolonged periods, so as to allow a variety of space activities of scientific, technological and commercial importance. Space stations have been in use since the early 1970s.

speciation, the process of evolution of new species of living things from previous species by spontaneous genetic change (*mutation*) and natural selection (⇨ pp. 196–9). When separated and usually isolated populations change so much that they are no longer able, for genetic reasons, successfully to interbreed, speciation is said to have occurred.

specific gravity, the ratio of the density of a material to the density of some standard material, often water at a temperature of 15°C (60°F). Density is mass per unit volume.

specific heat, the ratio of the amount of heat required to raise the temperature of a given weight of a material by one degree to the heat required to raise the same weight of an accepted standard material, usually water, by the same temperature and starting at the same temperature; ⇨ p. 52.

speckle, the patterns of random-intensity light sparkles produced when a laser beam is reflected from a rough surface. This pattern is caused by many coherent wavelets that interfere (⇨ pp. 64–7) with each other to form a granular pattern on the surface of most objects viewed by coherent light (⇨ p. 82). Speckle has been applied scientifically in measurement (metrology) and in speckle interferometry in astronomy.

spectacles, frames fitted with simple, thin lenses used for the correction of short sight (*myopia*), long sight (*hypermetropia*), ASTIGMATISM and presbyopia (⇨ below). Myopic eyes focus too strongly and need concave, weakening lenses (minus lenses); hypermetropic eyes may not be able to focus strongly enough either for reading or even for distance viewing, and require convex, strengthening lenses (plus lenses). In astigmatism, the eye has a maximal focus for lines oriented at a particular orientation and a minimal focus for lines at right angles to this orientation. Correction is required for one, and sometimes both, orientations. So astigmatism needs lenses more steeply curved in one meridian than in the other (*cylindrical*, or *toric*, lenses). In presbyopia the eye is unable to make sufficient adjustment to increase its power for near viewing, so the lenses needed are of the same type as in hypermetropia. As an addition to the distance correction – which may be zero – presbyopes aged about 45, need, on average, one DIOPTRE, those of 50, 1.5 D; those of 55, 2 D; and those of 60, 2.5 D. A lens of 2.5 D focuses at 40 cm, which is a convenient reading distance, so the near addition should seldom exceed this power. Bifocal spectacles are capable of focusing at two distances and are prescribed for presbyopes who also need a distant correction. They are essentially glasses for distance but with a small reading segment, placed below, of stronger power, that brings near objects into focus. It is natural to look down, and a little inwards, when reading, so the lower segment is set on the inner side of each lens and should, ideally, be as small as possible.

speech recognition, computer analysis of an acoustic (⇨ p. 68) speech signal, received by a microphone, so that linguistic and sometimes semantic information can be extracted from it. The simpler systems are limited to a fairly short vocabulary of unequivocal key words, each of which results in a rigidly standardized response, usually the performance of a routine computer task, such as the basic word-processing commands. The computer may have to be 'taught' to recognize the user's pronunciation. More complex systems may be able to distinguish, from the context, the different meanings of phonetically identical words. Such systems necessarily involve artificial intelligence; ⇨ p. 224.

spermatogenesis, the process of forming SPERMS from body cells by a special method of division (meiosis; ⇨ pp. 186–9) involving a reduction by half in the number of chromosomes (⇨ p. 202).

sperms, spermatozoa or male gametes, which carry all the genetic contribution from the father and bear either an X chromosome to produce a female, or a Y chromosome to produce a male offspring. Sperms are produced in the testicles, pass up the vas deferens on each side, and are stored in these tubes until ejected during EJACULATION. Only one sperm in hundreds of millions succeeds in fertilizing an ovum. All the others are wasted. Sperms are microscopic, about 0.05 mm long, and are present in millions in the seminal fluid. They have thrashing tails by which they achieve motility and move actively towards the ovum in the FALLOPIAN TUBE, taking from a few minutes to about three hours to do so. They then try to penetrate. Only the most active and healthy of the sperms reach the ovum. As soon as one sperm enters, a protective barrier forms in the ovum membrane, preventing any other sperm from penetrating.

Sphenisciformes, the order of penguins containing the 16 species found around certain coasts in the Southern hemisphere, some as far north as the equator. No penguins occur naturally in the Northern hemisphere.

sphenoid bone, the central bone of the base of the skull.

sphere, the solid body generated when a line of fixed length (a radius) is fixed at one end and the other end is moved into all possible positions. A sphere is the locus of all points in three-dimensional space at a fixed distance from a certain point, the centre of the sphere.

spherical aberration, the defect in the quality of an image formed by a lens or concave mirror due to the fact that all parallel rays are not brought to a common focus. Also known as *aperture aberration*; ⇨ p. 78.

sphincter, a muscle ring, surrounding a tubular passage or opening, which, on tightening, narrows or closes off the passageway. The anal sphincter, for instance, is a highly efficient means of retaining accumulated faeces in the rectum. The body contains many sphincters including: those controlling the entrance to, and exit from, the STOMACH; the outflow from the BLADDER; and the outflow from the PANCREAS and GALL BLADDER. The iris of the eye is a sphincter that automatically controls the amount of light entering the eye, in response to changes in brightness.

spin, in quantum mechanics, the inherent *angular momentum* (circular motion round an axis of rotation) of a particle when it is at rest, distinguished from the *orbital* angular momentum of the particle. A particle in a particular energy level has a definite spin, and this is one of its intrinsic characteristics; ⇨ pp. 108–11.

spinal nerves, the set of pairs of nerves that arise directly from the spinal cord, emerging between adjacent bones of the spine (*vertebrae*). Each spinal nerve contains a large motor and sensory component.

spine, a curved column of individual bones (*vertebrae*), all of the same general shape but varying progressively in size and proportion from the top of the column to the bottom. Each vertebra consists of a stout, roughly circular body, in front, behind which is an arch enclosing an opening to accommodate the spinal cord. Three bony processes, one pointing back and one to each side, arise from the vertebral arch. The bones fit neatly together, the bodies being separated by the intervertebral disc and the arches making contact by four smooth surfaces, two above and two below. The vertebrae in the neck are the smallest but have the largest cord opening. Those at the bottom of the column are massive. In humans there are seven vertebrae for the neck, 12 for the back and five for the lumbar

region. The fifth lumbar vertebra sits on top of the sacrum, which is formed from the fusion of five vertebrae into one bone and which forms the centre of the back of the PELVIS. The COCCYX, hanging from the lower tip of the sacrum, is the fused remnant of the tail.

spirochaete, a class of bacteria notable for their spiral form. Spirochaetes are highly motile by means of a lashing tail. The three most important groups are the Treponema genus, which includes the causal agent of syphilis *Treponema pallidum*; the Leptospira, which include *Leptospira icterohaemorrhagiae*, the cause of leptospirosis; and the Borrelia, which include the cause of relapsing fever, *B. recurrentis*, and of Lyme disease, *B. burgdorferi*.

spleen, a solid, dark purplish organ in vertebrates, situated high up on the left side of the ABDOMEN, close to the outer wall and immediately under the DIAPHRAGM. It lies immediately under the lower RIBS between the STOMACH and the left KIDNEY. A large ARTERY, arising from a branch of the AORTA, runs along behind the stomach, to supply it with BLOOD. The spleen has an elastic, fibrous capsule with many fibrous bands running inwards to form a 'sponge'. In the spaces between these bands is the largest collection of lymph tissue in the body – a mass of pulpy material consisting mostly of LYMPHOCYTES, phagocytes and red blood cells. The spleen is the main filter of the blood, clearing from it the products of the constant breakdown of red blood cells, and other foreign and unwanted semi-solid material. It is also a source of new lymphocytes and a major site of antibody formation.

sponges, the members of the phylum *Porifera*, most of which are marine animals, but a few of which live in fresh water.

Squamata, the main order of reptiles containing the snakes and the lizards. Approaching 5,000 species have been described, about half of them snakes. Squamata are distinguished from other reptiles by the characteristic shape of the skull and by enlarged and movable upper jawbones (*quadrate*) that articulate with the lower jaw.

square wave, an electrical waveform that alternates between a high and a low voltage (⇨ p. 90), changing very suddenly from one to the other. The high voltage is taken to correspond to a binary 1 and the low voltage to a 0. In computers a square wave is produced by a quartz-crystal-controlled oscillator, and is maintained by a wave-shaping circuit such as a SCHMITT TRIGGER. The train of square waves forms the synchronizing *clock* signal by which the whole machine is kept in step. Transistors are operated in a switching, on-off, mode which essentially produces square waves; and the switching itself is effected by square-wave voltages applied to the transistors.

staining, in microscopic anatomy (*histology*) and microbiology, a method of producing differences in optical density and colour in normally transparent parts of cells and tissues so as to enable them to be distinguished on microscopy. Also a method of differentiating two large classes of bacteria (Gram positive and

Gram negative) in accordance with their staining characteristics.

stalactites and stalagmites, respectively pendant and rising columns of limestone occurring in limestone caves, through the roofs of which water carrying calcium carbonate percolates. Stalactites lengthen progressively as evaporation leads to deposition of suspended or dissolved material. Stalagmites usually form on the floor below stalactites and grow upwards, sometimes until the two meet and fuse.

statics, the branch of mechanics (⇨ p. 26) concerned with bodies acted on by balanced forces (⇨ p. 28) so that they remain at rest or in uniform motion.

statistics, the discipline concerned with the collection, analysis and presentation of data and with the critical study of the reliability of information and conclusions derived from them. Statistics is concerned, among other things, with: the selection and assessment of the validity of samples, and with the appropriateness of their size; with whether results are likely to be due to factors under investigation rather than pure chance; with the distribution of natural variations in populations; and with the degree of confidence that can be placed on conclusions derived from the analysis of data. Much use is made of such basic concepts as the *mean* (the average, or sum of a set of numbers divided by the number of numbers), the *median* (the value of the middle number of a set of numbers), the *mode* (the number that occurs most often in a set of numbers), and the *standard deviation* (a measure of the spread, or dispersion, of individual items from the mean of the set). The latter is calculated by noting the differences from the mean as positive or negative numbers, squaring all these, taking the mean of these squares (the *variance*) and then finding the square root of the variance. This, the *root mean square*, is the standard deviation. A percentile is one of 99 parts into which the range of a frequency distribution of a characteristic is divided with equal frequencies. 70 per cent of the data lie below the 70th percentile, 40 per cent lie below the 40th percentile, and so on. A quartile, in contrast, is one of three such parts. Various tests of statistical significance are applied to data and the confidence interval expressed. This is an interval of values, bounded by confidence limits, within which the true value of a population variable is stated to lie with a degree of probability that is specifically stated.

stereochemistry, the study of the atomic structure of molecules in three dimensions, of the rules that determine the three-dimensional relationship of atoms and groups, and of the chemical and physical properties that result from such arrangements. Molecules with the same atoms but different spacial arrangements are called *stereoisomers*. These may be mirror images and superimposable (*diastereomers*), or they may not have reflection symmetry (and be like the backs of a right and a left hand) in which case they are called *enantiomers*; ⇨ p. 164.

stereoscopy, simultaneous visual perception with both eyes and fusion of the two images, with a subjective sense of solidity. This is derived from the fact that the eyes are separated so that the right eye sees further round the right side of a solid object than does the left eye, and the left eye sees further round the left side than does the right eye. The fusion of the two slightly dissimilar images produces a kind of rivalry between the images presented to the brain that can be resolved psychologically only on the basis that the perceived object is solid.

sterilization, the act of making sterile, either in the sense of being unable to procreate or of being unable to infect. Human sterilization is done by occluding or cutting tubes along which the SPERMS or the *ova* (eggs) pass. The procedures are, respectively, *vasectomy* and clipping or tying of the FALLOPIAN TUBES. Bacterial, viral and fungal sterilization may be achieved by dry heat, boiling, autoclaving in a steam-pressure vessel, immersion in one of many different antiseptic chemical solutions, exposure to toxic vapours or gases, irradiation with gamma rays or short-wavelength ultraviolet light (⇨ p. 84), or exposure to intense ultrasound waves (⇨ p. 70). Liquids can be sterilized by forcing them through filters of such small pore size that even viruses cannot pass. Some organisms form resistant spores that are able to survive some of the methods of sterilization. Some are also capable of surviving temperatures many degrees below freezing.

sternum, the breastbone. The sternum is the protective, flat, vertical plate of bone forming the central part of the front of the chest. In humans it has three parts, an upper, roughly diamond-shaped portion called the *manubrium*, a long, narrow body, and a small, lower, flexible, leaf-like part called the *xiphoid process*. This is made of cartilage in youth but turns partly to bone in later life. The sternum provides an anchorage, at its upper end, for the inner ends of the two collar bones (*clavicles*) and, on either side, for the seven pairs of cartilages, the *costal* cartilages, which join it to the RIBS. These provide flexible jointage with the ribs so that the sternum may rise and fall, relatively unimpeded, in breathing.

steroids, organic compounds based on a series of four rings of carbon atoms. A large group of fat-soluble molecules that include many HORMONES, such as the male and female sex hormones, steroid alcohols such as cholesterol and ergosterol (sterols), bile acids and the D VITAMINS. Steroids have many important physiological actions.

stochastic process, any process controlled by the rules of probability. The hardness of a table top, for instance, is determined by the probability that atomic movement will continue to result in a net homogeneity and will not result in a local deficit.

stomach, the bag-like organ in vertebrates into which swallowed food passes, by way of the OESOPHAGUS. The stomach empties into the first part of the small intestine. Upward movement of stomach contents is controlled by a SPHINCTER at the lower end of the oesophagus; and the onward passage of partially digested food is controlled by the *pyloric sphincter* at the lower outlet of the stomach. Unduly large lumps of food tend to cause the pyloric sphincter to close so that they are retained longer in the stomach for further chemical action (*digestion*). The average human stomach can hold about three pints. The stomach acid, hydrochloric acid, and its digestive juices (*enzymes*) work together to process food. These chemicals also protect against infection, many organisms being destroyed by the acid.

strain, deformation of a material caused by STRESS; ⇨ p. 28.

strain gauge, any device that measures STRAIN. Strain gauges are attached in such a way to objects likely to experience strain that the gauge itself suffers strain. By various means, such as change in electrical resistance (⇨ p. 96), capacitance (⇨ p. 98) or inductance (⇨ p. 100) this deformation is converted into an electrical change that can conveniently be measured.

stratification, the way in which rocks form into layers by sedimentation and other means (⇨ p. 150). In general, the lower strata are the older rocks and the details of the stratification can be used to assess relative ages. The fossil record also provides important evidence of age as particular fossils are always associated with particular strata, even if these have been displaced from their original position relative to other strata as a result of geological activity.

streamline flow, nonturbulent flow of a fluid, such as air or water, over an object or through a pipe; ⇨ p. 36.

streamlining, the contouring of an object so as to lead to STREAMLINE FLOW and minimize the resistance of its motion through a fluid; ⇨ pp. 34–7.

stress, in physics an external force applied to an object so as to tend to deform it (⇨ p. 28). A measure of the tendency of the molecules or atoms of a body to resist mutual sliding, compaction or separation, respectively by shearing, compressive or tensile stresses. In psychology, a term applied to any of a range of unpleasant experiences that affect the body by increased production of cortisol and adrenaline, with raised heart rate and blood pressure, muscle tension and raised blood sugar. Many people are able to sustain high levels of stress for long periods with apparent impunity; others succumb. It is claimed that prolonged stress can lead to organic disease such as peptic ulcers, high blood pressure, asthma, atherosclerosis, rheumatoid arthritis, thyroid-gland overactivity and ulcerative colitis, but there is little evidence that these disorders are actually caused in this way. People burdened by overwhelming troubles do develop severe symptoms and disabilities (the *post-traumatic stress disorder*), but this remains the only condition unequivocally known to be caused by a significantly stressful event.

Strigiformes, the order of birds containing owls (true owls and barn owls).

string, in computing, any sequence of characters. Strings may be searched for, compared, matched, replaced, joined (*concatenated*), stored, retrieved, or manipulated in other ways; ⇨ p. 216.

stroboscope, an instrument, usually taking the form of a lamp, capable of producing bright flashes of light at a controllable frequency. Such a lamp can be synchronized with the periodic movement or rotation of an object so as to illuminate it only when it returns to the same position, thus producing the illusion that the object is stationary. This allows inspection or photography of machinery, etc., while actually in use. Since the instrument is calibrated in terms of the number of flashes per second, it can be used to measure the rate of rotation or frequency of vibration of an object.

subconscious, the very large human 'database' of information, of which only a small part is in consciousness at any time, but which may be drawn upon, with varying degrees of success, at will. The term is also used as an adjective applied to data that can be made conscious. The Austrian psychoanalyst Sigmund Freud (1856–1939) is popularly acclaimed as being the 'discoverer' of the subconscious, but the existence of a large memory store has, of course, always been obvious. Freud's writings on the subject were preceded by hundreds of publications, spanning about 2,000 years, postulating the existence of a subconscious mind. In psychoanalytic theory, the subconscious is considered to be a 'level' of the mind through which information passes on its way 'up' to full consciousness from the unconscious mind.

sublimation, in chemistry the transformation of a solid directly to the gaseous state without passing through the liquid phase. All solids exhibit sublimation at temperatures below their melting point, but in most cases the vapour pressure of the solid phase is very low and the net loss of material is negligible. A few solids, such as iodine, have a high vapour pressure in the solid phase. In psychology, any socially acceptable redirection of normally unacceptable impulses or energy.

sucrose, cane, beet or maple sugar, found widely in plants and in honey. Sucrose is a disaccharide that is readily broken down by enzyme action to GLUCOSE and FRUCTOSE.

sulphate, the negative ion SO$_4$, derived from sulphuric acid H$_2$SO$_4$. Sulphates are salts of sulphuric acid formed when the acid reacts with certain metals, metallic oxides, hydroxides and carbonates. Because the acid has two hydrogen atoms it can form two kinds of sulphates, normal and acid (bisulphates).

sulphide, the negative ion S, derived from hydrogen sulphide (H$_2$S). Many sulphides are formed by direct combination of sulphur with a metal.

sulphites, salts of sulphurous acid, a solution of

sulphur dioxide in water (SO$_2$). Sulphurous acid is the hypothetical acid H$_2$SO$_3$. The corresponding salts, the sulphites, are quite common.

sunspot, a dark area observable on the Sun caused by a local lowering in surface temperature. Sunspots show a marked periodicity, occurring every 11 years. They are associated with strong magnetic fields and sometimes magnetic storms on Earth; ⇨ p. 132.

superacid, an ACID with an exceptional power of donating protons, i.e. equal to or greater than that of pure sulphuric acid.

supercomputer, an arbitrary term referring to the currently most powerful form of computer in terms of MIPS, memory size, number of central processors, capacity for parallel processing, and so on.

superconducting devices, devices that are able to carry out functions, by virtue of being superconducting at very low temperatures, that would not be possible or economical with normal conductivity. They include: high-speed semiconductor switches with a switching time of less than a nanosecond; microwave-radiation detectors; magnetic flux-change detectors (superconducting quantum-interference devices or SQUIDs); large and powerful magnets for magnetic-resonance imaging machines (MRI scanners), high-energy particle accelerators, controlled-fusion reactors and other purposes; highly efficient electric generators, and superconducting electric motors.

supercooled, cooled below the normal boiling or freezing point without becoming liquid or solid, respectively (i.e. without change of phase).

superfetation, fertilization of an ovum in an already-pregnant woman so that fetuses at two different stages of development occur.

superfluidity, the frictionless (⇨ p. 32) flow of liquid helium, which remains liquid at temperatures at which all other elements are solid.

superheterodyne radio receiver, a receiver that uses the HETERODYNE PRINCIPLE.

supersaturation, the state in which more solute is dissolved in a solvent than is normally possible without the solute crystallizing out. This can be achieved only if great care is taken to avoid the presence of any solid matter in the solution, which will immediately precipitate crystallization. Supersaturation can often be achieved by heating the solution, adding carefully gauged amounts of solvent, and then cooling very slowly.

supertransuranics, a group of hypothetical elements with atomic numbers in the region of 114 that might conceivably be made in the future. It is predicted that such elements would have half-lives of a year or more; ⇨ pp. 158–61.

switching circuits, electronic circuits (⇨ pp. 102–5) capable of rapidly moving from the 'on' to the 'off' condition of a small electric current.

All digital electronics, including all digital computing (⇨ pp. 214 and 220), is based on switching of currents whose presence denotes a 1 and whose absence denotes a 0. It is thus of central concern that switching should be as rapid as possible; and enormous research effort has been devoted to the production of ever more rapidly acting electronic switching devices, such as transistors. Today specialized switches can change state in less than a nanosecond (less than one thousand millionth of a second; ⇨ also SCHMITT TRIGGER, SQUARE WAVE.

sympathetic nervous system, one of the two divisions of the autonomic nervous system in vertebrates, the other one being the PARASYMPATHETIC NERVOUS SYSTEM. The sympathetic system arises from the spinal cord in the back and lumbar region, and is concerned with the automatic responses of the body to sudden stressful situations. The sympathetic system is involved in the 'fight-or-flight' situation and its operation causes constriction of BLOOD VESSELS in the SKIN and INTESTINES and widening (*dilatation*) of blood vessels in the MUSCLES. There is an increase in the heart rate, dilatation of the pupils, widening of the bronchial air tubes, contraction of the muscles that cause the hair to rise, possible ejaculation of semen in men, relaxation of the bladder and a reduction in the activity of the bowel. The adrenal gland is stimulated to produce adrenaline and this hormone, in turn, causes widespread similar effects.

synapse, the area of association between two NERVES, or between a nerve and the effector organ – a MUSCLE fibre or a GLAND – across which nerve impulses are transmitted by means of a chemical NEUROTRANSMITTER, such as acetylcholine or noradrenaline. A synapse is not an area of direct contact and there is invariably a narrow gap across which the neurotransmitter diffuses to pass on the stimulus. Synapses are polarized so that the impulse can pass in one direction only. Many synapses occur between large numbers of nerve endings and the body of a single nerve cell. Some brain cells have more than 100,000 synapses with other cells; it is this complexity that, partly or wholly, underlies the complexity of brain function. Much of the computational and storage functions of the brain can be understood, at least in principle, in terms of synaptic arrangement and the resulting biological equivalents of LOGIC CIRCUITS (gates).

synchronization, maintaining two regularly repetitively moving (*periodic*) systems in step with each other, either on a one-step-to-one-step basis or on the basis of some other ratio of steps. Synchronization is an essential feature of many electronic devices. Sync signals are transmitted with the video television signal, for instance, so that the line and frame oscillators that move the electron beam horizontally and vertically respectively are kept running at just the right speed to ensure that the spots on the screen correspond exactly to those on the television-camera tube. Electronic frequency dividers may use a 10-to-1 synchronization so that accurate frequencies from a crystal oscillator are divided by exactly 10. Digital watches may incorporate a cascade of such dividers. Mechanical synchronization can occur by inapparent coupling so that two systems running at approximately the same frequency may, apparently spontaneously, fall into synchronization. A small amount of energy applied to a periodic system at a synchronized frequency can result in the buildup of considerable energy in the system. An example is a small push given repeatedly to a child's swing in sync with the period of the swing.

synchronous motor, an electric motor that runs at a fixed speed by rotating a number of times per second that bears a whole-number ratio to the frequency of the alternating-current electricity supply. Prior to the introduction of quartz oscillator-controlled digital clocks, the most accurate domestic clocks were those operating on this principle. Their accuracy was the same as that of the electricity mains frequency, which is usually kept within narrow limits.

syndrome, in medicine a unique combination of sometimes apparently unrelated symptoms or signs, forming a distinct medical entity. In most cases the elements of a syndrome arise from a common cause and are merely separate effects of that cause. Sometimes the relationship is purely one of observed association and the causal link is not yet understood.

tachometer, an instrument that measures rotational speed, such as that of a wheel or shaft, in revolutions per minute or per some other interval of time.

tachycardia, a rapid heart rate, whether as a normal reaction to exertion or emotion, or whether caused by heart disorder.

tachyon, a theoretical particle that can travel faster than light by virtue of being massless.

tangent, the relationship between a line or a plane that touches a curve or a curved surface at one point only. In trigonometry, the tangent of an angle in a right-angled triangle is the length of the side opposite the angle divided by the length of the side other than that opposite the right angle (the *hypotenuse*). It is also the sine of the angle divided by the cosine of the angle; ⇨ p. 20.

tank circuit, a tuned electrical circuit consisting of an inductor and a capacitor (⇨ pp. 98–101) in parallel. Such a circuit will resonate at a particular frequency.

tardyon, any particle that moves at a speed less than that of light.

tartrate, a salt or ester of tartaric acid. There are many tartrates. They include potassium monotartrate (cream of tartar) and sodium-potassium tartrate (Rochelle salt). Calcium tartrate is used in dyeing.

taste, the gustatory sense by which the basic flavours of substances are perceived. Taste operates by the chemical stimulation, by dissolved substances, of some of the 10,000 or so specialized nerve endings (*taste buds*) on the tongue and surrounding areas of the mouth in humans and mammals. The experience is traditionally said to be limited to sweet, salty, sour and bitter, but individual receptors can respond in varying degrees to many different chemical substances, and to those in more than one of these categories. Appreciation of flavours involves smell as well as taste and the number of permutations of these two modalities is very great.

taxis, movement of an animal or plant in a direction determined by a source of stimulation, usually either towards (*positive taxis*) or away from (*negative taxis*) the stimulus. Many different stimuli may cause taxis. These include light, physical contact, sound, chemical substances, gravity and air and water currents.

taxon, any group of organisms (⇨ pp. 190–5), such as the contents of a genus, species or phylum, to which a taxonomic rank or category is applied. Taxa at any level in the taxonomic hierarchy consist of one or more taxa of the next lower level.

taxonomy, the science of classification of living and previously living organisms.

telemetry, the obtaining, over a period of time, of data at a remote or inaccessible site and its transmission to a convenient location, usually by radio. Telemetry has many applications. It may, for instance, be used to: monitor internal conditions and changes from within the human or animal body; determine conditions on the surface of a distant planet or within a space satellite; or obtain continuous information about changes in various atmospheric parameters from a geographically remote site or a research balloon.

television camera, an optical camera containing a light-sensitive device on which the image is focused and that converts images into a serial video electrical signal. This device is quite small but has a very-fine-grained structure of discrete, sensitive elements, each of whose electrical state (*charge*; ⇨ p. 88) is related to the brightness of the light falling on it and forming that particular part of the image. When the image area is scanned by a moving electron beam or other means, a rapid succession of changes of electric current is given off, each quantum being proportional to the light on each element. The first successful TV-camera tubes were called *image orthicons*. Later tubes had photoconductors as the light-sensitive element and were called *vidicons*. They used materials such as porous antimony trisulphide and cadmium selenide. Modern TV-camera tubes use integrated-circuit silicon solid-state devices that combine the functions of charge formation and scanning read-out, and contain hundreds of thousands of separate points, each corresponding to a picture element (*pixel*) in the image. The charges from each of these points is transferred out sequentially to be amplified, and to form the video signal for transmission.

temperature inversion, a rise in air temperature with an increase in height so that an upper layer is warmer than a layer below it. Such inversion exists normally in the upper atmosphere but is abnormal in the lower levels. It can occur when a lower layer loses heat by radiation, by heating of an upper layer on descending, or by lateral movement of warm air over cold air or cold air under warm air. Temperature inversion prevents vertical movement of air so that atmospheric contaminants, such as smoke and nitrogen oxides, cannot rise and are trapped near the ground. This can present a serious hazard to health.

tendon, a band or string of tough, white fibres of the protein COLLAGEN that connect MUSCLES to BONE and transmit the force of muscle contraction so as to effect movement. Tendons are extremely strong, flexible, and inelastic. Most are cylindrical in shape, but a few, such as those attached to the flat muscles of the abdominal wall, consist of wide sheets of fibres known as *aponeuroses*.

territoriality, animal behaviour patterns motivated by the need to identify and defend areas over which rights are assumed. Such behaviour is widespread in the animal kingdom.

tetrahedron, a six-edged, solid figure bounded by four triangular planes. Many of the properties of a tetrahedron are extensions of those of the triangle.

theorem, a proposition derived by logical deduction from a set of premises or axioms. A theorem, however correct, cannot be said to be true unless it receives independent corroboration by experiment of observation; ⇨ p. 12.

thermionic emission, the ejection of ELECTRONS into an evacuated space by a heated electrical conductor (⇨ p. 90). Prior to the development of the transistor, thermionic emission was the basis of electronics (⇨ pp. 102–5). Thermionic valves are now obsolete, but the principle continues to be used in other devices, especially in CATHODE-RAY TUBES.

thermistor, a small semiconductor device whose electrical resistance (⇨ p. 96) decreases as its temperature increases. This useful property allows it to be used as a thermometer and a means of compensating for the rise of resistance with temperature (positive temperature coefficient) of normal resistors.

thiocyanate, a salt or ESTER of cyanic acid.

thiosulphate, a salt of the unstable thiosulphuric acid.

thirst, a strong desire to drink water or other liquid, arising from a degree of *dehydration* (water shortage) in the body, or from an increase in the concentration of substances dissolved in the BLOOD, or a drop in blood volume. Thirst may thus result from inadequate intake or excessive loss of water, as in profuse sweating or severe and prolonged diarrhoea. It may also result from excessive intake of salt or other materials readily absorbed into the bloodstream. When concentrated blood passes through certain areas in each side of the hypothalamus in the brain, nerve receptors, sensitive to changes in the osmotic pressure of the blood, are stimulated and thirst is induced by a nerve reflex. From the same area of the brain, and prompted by the same stimulus, a hormone *vasopressin* is released and is carried to the KIDNEYS where it controls water loss. Although thirst normally causes dryness of the mouth, dryness will cause thirst, even in the absence of dehydration, and may be relieved merely by moistening the mouth.

thorax, the front or upper region of the body of animals, which, in vertebrates, contains the heart and LUNGS. In mammals it is separated from the ABDOMEN by the DIAPHRAGM. In insects the thorax is segmented into three parts, each of which carries a pair of legs, and the rear two of which each carry a pair of wings. In crustaceans and arachnids, the head and thorax are fused to form the *cephalothorax.*

thought disorders, derangement of mental functioning of various kinds that occur in various psychotic conditions. Thought disorders are classified into disorders of content, form and process. Disorders of content include false beliefs and ideas (*delusions*), and a loss of the sense of the limits of one's power and influence. Disorders of form are manifested by the use of meaningless or invented words (*neologisms*), incoherent language, abnormal verbal associations, word repetition, and by mutism. Disorders of process include loss of memory, poverty of thought content, thought blocking, sudden flight of ideas from one to another, loss of the power of attention, loss of abstracting ability and the relating of words by their phonetic resemblance (*clang associations*) rather than by logical association .

thrombosis, clotting of BLOOD within an ARTERY or VEIN. Thrombosis, which is common in humans, is always abnormal and often very dangerous as it may restrict, or even totally cut off, the flow of blood. Thrombosis, when it affects vital arteries, such as the coronary arteries (*coronary thrombosis* – heart attack) or the arteries supplying the brain with blood, is a major cause of death and serious illness, such as stroke.

thymus, a flat organ in vertebrates lying in the upper part of the THORAX, near the front, in early life and regressing after sexual maturity. Its function is concerned with the maturation and activation of certain cells (T *lymphocytes*) of the immune system.

thyristor, a semiconductor silicon rectifier (silicon- controlled rectifier) whose current flow is regulated by signals applied to a third electrode. Thyristors are widely used as convenient means of accurately controlling current flow in circuits (⇨ p. 90).

thyroid gland, one of the glands of internal secretion of the *endocrine system.* In humans, the thyroid lies in the neck just below the larynx. Its hormones, thyroxine (T4) and triiodothyronine (T3), exert a powerful stimulating effect on the activity of almost every cell in the body and so have a marked effect on general body metabolism. The secretion of these hormones is controlled by a negative-feedback mechanism involving the PITUITARY GLAND, the production of whose *thyroid-stimulating* hormone is determined by the levels of thyroid hormones in the blood.

tibia, the shin bone, the main bone of the lower leg. The upper end forms part of the knee joint and the lower end, in association with the delicate accompanying long bone, the *fibula*, forms part of the ankle joint.

tincture, a solution of a substance in alcohol.

tissue, a connected group of similar animal or plant cells, which together perform a particular function. Different tissues aggregate to form organs.

tissue culture, a collection of living animal or plant cells grown on a nutrient medium outside the body for scientific or other purposes. Cultures of normal body cells have a comparatively short life; those of certain cancerous cells appear to be immortal. Plant-tissue cultures have allowed regeneration of complete plants.

tissue typing, the identification of the cell types of individuals. All human body cells carry on their surfaces certain chemical groups by which they can be identified as belonging to that person. These groups are called the *histocompatibility antigens.* Of these, the most useful for typing are the human-leukocyte antigens (HLAs). HLAs are short chains of linked AMINO ACIDS, present on the outer surface membranes of all cells and unique to all individuals, except identical twins whose HLAs are identical. Tissue typing is most important when a question of organ donation for grafting arises. If tissue from one person is introduced into the body of another, the HLAs immediately provoke the production, by the immune system (⇨ IMMUNITY) of the recipient, of ANTIBODIES dedicated to the destruction of the donated tissue. The HLAs are determined by cell genes and fall into definite groups. It is thus possible to select, from a panel of donors, those whose broad HLA grouping is the same as that of the recipient. In general, it will be easiest to find such donors among close relatives, such as siblings. In addition to the major histocompatibility antigens, minor antigens, such as those responsible for the blood groups, must also be properly matched. By tissue matching, the success rate of organ transplantation can be greatly improved.

topaz, an aluminium silicate mineral valued as a gemstone. It has a hardness of 8 on the MOHS SCALE and occurs as clear, pale yellow and (when heated) rose-pink stones.

topology, the branch of mathematics concerned with those surface properties of objects that are not affected by deformation such as stretching or twisting.

toxicity, the property or degree of poisonousness. Toxicity refers to any poisonous substance whether it be a toxin of bacterial origin, a plant poison, or any other poisonous chemical substance. The unit of toxicity is the LD50 (50 per cent lethal dose) – the dose of the poison that kills half of those exposed to it. Toxicity is almost always a matter of the dosage. A very large range of substances not normally considered toxic are poisonous if taken in sufficient amount. Highly toxic substances are those that are dangerous if taken in very tiny amounts.

toxin, a poison produced by any living organism. BACTERIA that produce disease do so largely as a result of the poisonous effect on the human body of the toxins that they produce. Some bacteria produce, and release, exotoxins that may be carried to remote parts of the body by the BLOOD; others produce only endotoxins, which have effect only in the immediate environs of the organisms. Bacterial toxins are among the most poisonous substances known. In many cases only a few micrograms (millionths of a gram) are sufficient to kill. Some toxins can, however, be neutralized by antitoxins. Some can be converted, by treatment with heat or formalin, to 'toxoids', which can safely be used to immunize people against the effects of the corresponding organism. Tetanus toxin is highly dangerous; tetanus toxoid is routinely used as a highly effective and safe immunization agent.

trachea, the windpipe, a cylindrical air tube that, in adult humans, extends downwards from the voicebox (*larynx*) for about 11 cm (4.4 in) to a point behind the upper part of the breastbone, where it divides into the two main *bronchi*, one for each lung. The trachea is made of a tube of MUCOUS MEMBRANE reinforced and held open by rings of cartilage. The inner surface bears millions of microscopic hairlike processes that beat rapidly, like wind-blown corn, to carry foreign particles trapped in MUCUS upwards and out of the respiratory system.

transamination, an enzyme-mediated biochemical reaction in which an amine group is transferred from an AMINO ACID to a keto acid to form a new amino acid. A keto acid is an acid related to acetoacetic acid, a ketone body formed when fatty acids are oxidized at the expense of carbohydrates.

transducer, any device that converts energy in one form, such as sound or pressure variations, light, heat, etc., into a corresponding electrical signal, or any device that can convert an electrical signal into corresponding changes in another form of energy. Examples of transducers are microphones, loudspeakers, photoelectric cells, piezoelectric pickups, ultrasound generators, and so on.

transplantation, the introduction of donated organs or tissues into the body in the hope that they may survive and continue to function or maintain structure. Two main advances have made successful transplantation possible – developments in microsurgical techniques, especially in the joining up of ARTERIES, and developments in the understanding of immunology (⇨ IMMUNITY) and the mechanisms of rejection of 'foreign' tissue. Transplants between identical twins do not lead to rejection problems because the tissues are immunologically identical. The discovery of the tissue types based on the HISTOCOMPATIBILITY ANTIGENS soon led to the finding that transplants between tissue-matched siblings do almost as well as those between identical twins. *Immunosuppression* is the deliberate and artificial blocking of the reactions that lead to rejection, and drugs now exist that effectively achieve this. Such drugs are universally used in transplantation, but are clearly not without disadvantage. KIDNEY grafting has been the most successful type of organ transplantation, and the results have been excellent, especially since the introduction of the selective immunosuppressive drug *cyclosporin*.

transsexualism, a persistent conviction that one's true gender does not correspond to one's anatomical sex. Transsexuals often seek sex-reassignment surgery so that they can live fully as members of the opposite sex.

trephination, the surgical use of a tubular, cylindrical cutting instrument with the edge at one end sharpened or saw-toothed. The cutting end of the trephine is pressed hard against the tissue to be cut and the instrument rotated. Trephines are used to cut a circular hole in bone, cornea or other tissue. In corneal grafting, the same trephine is used to cut the opening in the cornea and the disc from the donated eye so that the graft fits perfectly. Trephines have been widely used to make holes in the skull that can then be joined with saw cuts so that a flap of bone may be removed. Trephination, or trepanning, of the skull to release evil spirits has been performed throughout the ages and many very old skulls with trephine holes have been found by archaeologists.

triglycerides, ESTERS of glycerol (glycerine) in which each of the three hydroxyl (-OH) groups is esterified with a fatty acid. The triglyceride molecule can be considered as a 'backbone' of glycerol with three fatty acids attached to it. The three fatty acids may be identical to one another or different and may be saturated or unsaturated. Triglycerides are the main constituents of fats and oils. Saturated fats, such as lard, tend to be solid at room temperatures; unsaturated fats, such as sunflower oil, tend to remain liquid.

triple point, the temperature and pressure at which the three phases of a substance (solid, liquid and vapour) are in equilibrium. The triple point for water is at 273.16 K.

trisomy, the condition in which there are three, instead of two, of a particular chromosome. This is always serious and has effects varying from death of the fetus in the womb to a range of structural abnormalities affecting parts such as the heart, the face, the skeleton or the brain. Down's syndrome is caused by trisomy of chromosome number 21.

tropism, the directional growth of a plant or part of a plant under the influence of an external stimulus. Tropism may be towards (*positive tropism*) or away from (*negative tropism*) the stimulus. Stimuli are commonly light, physical contact or gravity. Compare TAXIS.

tunnel vision, an informal term for severe contraction of the peripheral fields of vision. These normally extend out to about 90° on either side when we look straight ahead. Perception in the peripheral visual fields is vague and the power of resolving detail is very low, but the fields of vision are important in providing us with information and warnings about what is happening around us. In tunnel vision the central vision may be normal. Visual-field loss may be caused by disorders of the peripheral parts of the retinas, or any disorder that restricts the function of the optic nerves or their connections with the brain (visual pathways). The commonest cause of tunnel vision is persistently raised pressure within the eye with resulting damage to optic-nerve fibres (*glaucoma*). Other possible causes of tunnel vision include retinitis pigmentosa, brain tumour, stroke, severe head injury or multiple sclerosis.

twin paradox, a seeming anomalous consequence of time dilation as described by the special theory of relativity (⇨ p. 38). When a body moves, its time, as measured by a stationary observer, slows. At normal speeds the effect is negligible, but at speeds approaching that of light the effect becomes ever greater until at the speed of light time would stand still. Twin A remains on Earth; twin B goes on a space journey in a rocket travelling at speeds approaching the speed of light. Because of time dilation, twin B's time slows, relative to that on Earth and with it all his or her bodily processes. When twin B returns it is to find that the other twin has apparently lived longer than the perceived time of the journey and is now much older than the traveller. The German-born US physicist Albert Einstein (1879–1955), of course, did not acknowledge that this was a paradox. And, in fact, it is not. The apparent symmetry of the problem (that either twin could be regarded as the 'traveller' and the other as 'stationary') is denied by the fact that the twin in the rocket has to undergo acceleration and deceleration.

twins, two offspring from a single pregnancy. In humans, the incidence of twins is about one in 90 pregnancies. Twins may be identical, if they both arise from one fertilized egg (*ovum*), or nonidentical, if two separate ova are separately fertilized by separate spermatozoa (⇨ SPERMS). Twins developing from a single ovum are called *monozygotic* or *monovular* twins, and have identical genetic material. They occur if the fertilized ovum separates completely, at an early stage of development, into two embryos, each of which then proceeds to develop normally. Very rarely, this division occurs too late so that separation is incomplete, resulting in SIAMESE TWINS. Monozygotic twins are both nourished by the same single placenta. They may differ in size at birth, but are always of the same sex and appearance. *Dizygotic* or *binovular* twins imply the release of more than one ovum from one or both ovaries. Apart from age, they have no more in common than any other pair of siblings and may be of the same or of different sexes. Each dizygotic twin has its own placenta. Some families have a history of dizygotic twins.

ulcer, any bodily surface that has lost its immediate covering layer as a result of local destruction of tissue. Once the protection of the surface layer has gone, INFECTION occurs and makes the ulcer worse. Ulcers may be caused by mechanical, chemical or biochemical damage, by loss of BLOOD supply and by bacterial or other infection. Ulcers of the STOMACH or INTESTINE are called *peptic ulcers*. Sustained pressure over bony points, as occurs when a debilitated person lies unmoving for long periods, interferes with the local blood supply and causes bed sores (*decubitus ulcers*). Arterial disease can so reduce blood supply to a limb, that the SKIN breaks down to form ulcers. Skin ulcers are commonly caused by bacterial TOXINS, as in anthrax, tuberculosis, diphtheria or syphilis (*chancre*). Leg ulcers are common in cases of severe varicose veins, as a result of blood stagnation. Varicose ulcers are often very persistent and slow to heal.

ulna, one of the two long bones of the forearm, lying on the little finger side. The upper end of the ulna has a hook-like process that curls round behind a boss on the lower end of the upper arm bone (the *humerus*) to form the elbow joint and prevent over-extension at the elbow.

ultrasound scanning, a method of obtaining visual information about the interior of any structure that contains interfaces of different density, from which sound can be reflected. Unlike electromagnetic radiations such as X-rays and gamma rays (⇨ p. 84), which pass easily through a vacuum, sound is a vibration of the molecules of a gas, liquid or solid (⇨ p. 68). Vibrations between about 16 cycles per second (Hz) and 20,000 cycles per second are perceptible as sound. Audible sound waves have long wavelengths – often several metres long – and can be reflected only by very large surfaces, such as the sides of mountains, to cause echoes. The higher the frequency of the vibration, the shorter the wavelength and the smaller the area needed for reflection. In ultrasound scanning, a beam of 'sound', of a frequency of about 3–10 *million* cycles per second, with correspondingly short wave-lengths, is projected into the object to be examined. Whenever it meets a surface between tissues of different density, echoes are created and these return to the source. The time taken to do so depends on the distance. The ultrasound waves are produced by feeding short pulses of alternating current, at the desired frequency, to a piezoelectric crystal in the scanner head. The electrical variations cause the crystal to vibrate at the same frequency. Piezoelectric materials have the property of working in both directions – they change shape when electricity is applied to them, but they also generate electricity if their shape is distorted. So the returning echoes cause the crystal to act as a microphone and this, in turn, generates a tiny electric current. The length of time between the emitted pulse and the returning echo is a measure of the distance to the interface. The simplest form of scanner uses a simple CATHODE-RAY TUBE display, which merely shows a series of 'blips' on a horizontal line, corresponding to returning echoes (A scan). This is capable of highly accurate measurements, but does not produce a pictorial representation. In the B scan system, the ultrasound is focused into a narrow, parallel beam that is scanned from side to side in one plane. The returning echoes are correlated in a computer with the corresponding angle of the beam, which enables a two-dimensional picture to be built up. The quality of the display is much less good than CT or MRI scanning. So far as is known, ultrasound, of the intensity and frequency used in body scanning, is completely harmless.

ultraviolet light, electromagnetic radiation (⇨ p. 84) of shorter wavelengths than visible light, but longer wavelength than X-rays. Ultraviolet light (UVL) is invisible to the human eye and is sometimes called 'black light'. The spectrum of UVL is arbitrarily divided into three zones. That nearest to visible light (UVA) covers wavelengths from 380 down to 320 nanometres (billionth of a metre); UVB extends from 320 down to 290; and UVC from 290 down to one tenth of a nanometre. UVC is especially penetrating and harmful to human tissue but is strongly absorbed by the ozone layer in the Earth's stratosphere. Most of the UVB content is also filtered out by this layer. Ultraviolet light causes sunburning and, in excessive dosage, can damage the elastic protein, COLLAGEN, in the skin, leading to its excessive wrinkling and premature ageing. UVL is also a major factor in the development of the skin condition, solar keratosis, and the skin cancers rodent ulcer, malignant melanoma and squamous-cell carcinoma. Fluorescent and mercury-vapour lamps can produce large amounts of UVL, but there is no biological danger from ordinary domestic fluorescent lighting. Artificially produced UVC can be used to sterilize air and the surface of materials.

umbilical cord, the temporary blood vascular channel that connects the fetus to the placenta during intrauterine life and provides the whole of the fetal nourishment. After birth the cord is tied and cut and the stump shrivels and forms a scar known as the umbilicus or navel.

ungulates, herbivorous animals with hooves.

unicellular, consisting of a single cell.

UNIX, an important computer operating system widely used by minicomputers and by the more powerful PERSONAL COMPUTERS especially WORKSTATIONS. UNIX was introduced in 1971 for the DEC PDP 11 series of minicomputers and has become widely popular among scientists and others. It is a true multitasking, multiuser system, but was initially intended to be used by programmers and was less 'friendly' than some other operating systems. Various versions of UNIX have appeared and there has been considerable lack of standardization. One version, popular with serious users of personal computers, is called Xenix. MS-DOS programs can be made to run under UNIX but to do so is severely to limit the power of the operating system; ⇨ p. 218.

urea, an organic molecule containing a large quantity of NITROGEN. Urea is the body's principal means of disposing of the excess nitrogen derived from the breakdown of AMINO ACIDS. It is formed in the LIVER by combining nitrogen with carbon and OXYGEN from CARBON DIOXIDE and excreted by the KIDNEYS in solution in the URINE.

ureter, the narrow tube that runs downward from each KIDNEY to enter the rear lower part of the urinary bladder, to convey URINE formed in the kidneys to the BLADDER for temporary storage.

urethra, a tube leading from the urinary bladder to the exterior, through which URINE passes, and through which, in most mammalian male, the seminal fluid is ejaculated during coitus. At the outlet of the bladder are two SPHINCTERS that control the loss of urine until it can conveniently be passed.

urine, a watery solution of UREA and other organic and inorganic substances, most of which are bodily waste products. Urine normally has a pale yellow colour due to a pigment called urochrome, but the colour varies greatly with the degree of bodily dehydration.

urography, any X-ray or scanning investigation of any part of the urinary system. Urography usually involves the use of a solution partially opaque to X-rays that is introduced into the URINE by way of the BLOOD or via the URETHRA and URETERS.

uterus, the womb. The muscular female organ in mammals in which the embryo implants, the placenta forms and the fetus grows. The lining of the womb (*endometrium*) is specially adapted to form a suitable bed for the early nourishment of the embryo and has an excellent BLOOD supply. As the fetus grows, the womb expands.

vacuole, a membrane-bound cavity within a cell containing fluid, solid material or gas and often digestive enzymes. Vacuoles may be nutritional, scavenging, transportative, excretory or digestive, and commonly expand or collapse.

vacuum, a gas pressure less than that of the atmosphere, usually containing relatively few molecules or atoms. A perfect vacuum is an unattainable ideal as a vacuum must be contained by material and all materials have some vapour pressure.

vacuum distillation, DISTILLATION under reduced pressure so that the boiling point of the liquids concerned are depressed and possible heat damage may be avoided.

vacuum tubes, electronic devices consisting of an evacuated, usually glass, container, with a heated CATHODE, an ANODE, held at a high positive voltage, and various interposed grids and other electrodes capable of exerting a controlling effect on the passage of the current between the cathode and the anode. Vacuum-tube diodes, triodes, tetrodes, pentodes, etc., were made in hundreds of different varieties and powers and, prior to the invention of the transistor, were the basis of all electronics and all radio and television transmission and reception. Almost all are now obsolete for such purposes, but vacuum tubes persist in the form of CATHODE-RAY TUBES, X-ray tubes and a few other devices.

vagina, the short passage in females running from the outlet of the womb to the exterior in which the PENIS is accommodated during copulation and through which the baby is born. In some animals the vagina is closed except when the animal is sexually receptive. The term derives from the Latin *vagina* meaning a 'sheath'.

vagus nerve, the paired, tenth cranial nerve in humans. The nerve supplies autonomic fibres to many organs including the heart, LUNGS and INTESTINES.

valence, the combining power of the atoms of an element for those of other elements. Thus, one atom of hydrogen will commonly combine with one other atom of hydrogen, while one atom of OXYGEN will commonly combine with two atoms of hydrogen. One atom of hydrogen will commonly combine with one atom of chlorine, and one atom of carbon will commonly combine with four atoms of chlorine. Atoms tend to combine in such a way as to form closed outer ELECTRON shells, equivalent to those of the inert, or noble, gases in the last column of the periodic table (⇨ p. 158).

valve, any device that regulates, cuts off or allows the passage of a fluid or an electric current (⇨ p. 90), or that allows movement of fluid or current in one direction only. Thermionic valves, which allow movement of ELECTRONS from CATHODE to ANODE, but not vice versa, have largely been replaced by semiconductor devices with similar properties. Fluid-controlling valves may take many forms and are important in industry and technology, especially in the water industry and in chemical engineering. The animal body contains many valves. They occur in the heart, where they convert the squeezing force of the heart muscle on the BLOOD into a continuous circulation. They are also found in the veins, the lymphatics, in the nasolacrimal duct, and occasionally in the ureters or urethra. The muscular rings – SPHINCTERS – at the junction of the STOMACH and DUODENUM and of the small INTESTINE and large intestine, are controlling valves.

Van Allen belts, two zones of high-energy charged particles lying at distances of 1,000–5,000 km (620–3,100 mi) and 15,000–25,000 km (9,300–16,000 mi) from the surface of the Earth. The Van Allen belts, named after their discoverer the American physicist James Van Allen (1914–), are trapped in the Earth's magnetic field (⇨ p. 144) and are sources of intense radiation. The outer belt consists mainly of ELECTRONS; the inner contains protons also. They were first detected by satellite studies in 1958.

vapour lamps, light sources in which ionization of a gas forms a conducting path (⇨ p. 90) between two electrodes so that a current can pass, exciting the gas to emit either mainly visible or ultraviolet light (⇨ pp. 72–5 and 84). The gaseous element varies and can be neon, argon, mercury vapour, xenon, sodium metal-halide vapour or others. Also known as *gas-discharge lamps.*

vapour pressure, the pressure exerted by the free molecules or atoms given off by all solids and liquids. If this evaporation occurs in an enclosed space, an equilibrium between the vapour pressure and the material will be reached that depends on the volatility of the material and the temperature.

variable, any quantity having a range of possible values. In computing, a string of characters denoting some value stored in the machine, that can be changed in the course of execution of a program; ⇨ pp. 216–19.

vascular, pertaining to vessels or tubes in a living system through which fluids (⇨ p. 34) can pass. In all but the simplest animals the BLOOD circulates through the blood-vascular system; in plants, fluids pass through VASCULAR BUNDLES.

vascular bundle, a continuous tubular strand in plants that extends from the roots, through the stem, into the leaves. It consists of the PHLOEM and the XYLEM, and these structures are always in close association.

vasoconstriction, narrowing of BLOOD VESSELS by contraction of circular muscles in the vessel walls. The effect is to reduce the rate of blood flow and increase the blood pressure. Compare *vasodilatation,* in which the vessels widen.

VDU ⇨ VISUAL DISPLAY UNIT.

vein ⇨ ARTERY.

vegetative reproduction, a form of propagation in plants in which new individuals develop from specialized structures, such as bulbs, tubers, runners and corms, that have detached from the parent plant, or from cuttings or artificial grafting.

vegetative state, the condition of living without consciousness or the ability to initiate voluntary action, as a result of brain damage. People in the vegetative state may sometimes give the appearance of being awake and conscious, with open eyes. They may make random movements of the limbs or head, and may pick or rub with the fingers, but there is no response to any form of communication and no reason to suppose that there is any awareness of the environment. Voluntary movement, all forms of sensation, vision and hearing, and the higher functions, such as thought and memory, all depend on the normal functioning of the outer layer of the brain (the *cortex*). The vegetative state results when this part of the brain is extensively damaged while the deeper structures, which maintain the more primitive functions – breathing, heartbeat, maintenance of body temperature, and crude response to stimuli – continue to operate normally. The vegetative state must be distinguished from apparently similar conditions such as the rare psychiatric condition of *catatonia,* in which consciousness is retained and from which full recovery is possible, and the locked-in syndrome from damage to the brain stem, in which the patient is conscious but unable to speak or make any movement of any part of the body, except for blinking and upward eye movements, which allow signalling.

venation, the arrangements of veins in a leaf or in the wings of an insect.

Venn diagram, a graphic representation of one or more mathematical sets and their relationships. A universal set is shown as a simple rectangle and a subset of that as a circle wholly within the rectangle. Subsets may lie wholly within subsets or may overlap each other. A subset may also lie wholly or partially within the overlap of two other subsets.

venom, a poison produced by a few snakes, spiders, insects and scorpions. Venoms may affect the nervous system to cause paralysis or may affect the BLOOD, causing either extensive clotting or bleeding (*haemorrhage*). Venoms are seldom fatal unless the victim is very young or debilitated, or the dose very large, as in multiple bee, wasp or hornet stings.

ventilator, a mechanical device consisting essentially of an electric motor driving an air pump or bellows, providing an intermittent flow of air or oxygen under pressure. Ventilators are commonly used to maintain the respiration of patients who are paralysed by anaesthetic agents, or in people who have, through brain damage or other causes, lost the power of spontaneous breathing and who would, without artificial respiration, quickly die. The outlet of the ventilator is attached to a tube that has been inserted into the person's windpipe (TRACHEA), and the pressure is sufficient to expand and fill the person's lungs. The tracheal tube may have been inserted through the mouth or nose or through an artificial opening in the neck (*tracheostomy*). At the end of each input cycle, which can be adjusted in volume and time, the pressure is suddenly released and the elastic collapse of the LUNGS drives out the air, which can leave easily through a light valve.

ventral, relating to the front of the body. The term comes from the Latin word *venter* meaning 'the belly'.

ventricle, one of the main pumping chambers of the heart that receives BLOOD from the VEINS by way of a thinner-walled chamber (*atrium*) and passes it on to an arterial system, either to the LUNGS (right ventricle in humans) or to the general circulation (left ventricle in humans). The term is also used for one of the four fluid-filled spaces in the vertebrate brain – the two lateral ventricles and the two midline ventricles.

vertebra, one of the bones of the spine that, together, form the vertebral column (spine) and, in many animals, the tail. Vertebrae have LATERAL processes by which they fit together and by which they are held in association by short, linking LIGAMENTS. Each vertebra has a large central hole; in the vertebral column these line up to form the spinal canal in which the spinal cord and the parts of the spinal nerves lie. One pair of spinal nerves emerges for each vertebra. One of the major subdivisions of the animal kingdom is the subphylum VERTEBRATA containing all the animals with backbones, from fish to mammals.

Vertebrata, a subphylum of the phylum Chordata of the animal kingdom containing all animals possessing a backbone (*vertebral column*). The vertebrates include fish, amphibia, reptiles, birds and mammals. The *Gnathostomata* are the vertebrates with jaws and the *Agnatha* are those without.

very high frequency (VHF), radio or television frequencies in the range 30 million cycles per second (30 MHz) to 300 million cycles per second (300 Mhz), and a corresponding wavelength of 1–10 m (3–30 ft). The term is a victim of technological progress since such frequencies are no longer considered to be very high.

video amplifier, an electronic high-frequency amplifier capable of amplifying, with minimal DISTORTION, alternating voltages of frequencies of about 2–100 million cycles per second (Megahertz or Mhz). They are used in TV receivers, VDUs and other devices.

videotext, a form of data communication, using telephone lines, in which each terminal has a keyboard, microprocessor and VDU, allowing correspondence to be transmitted in both directions. The term is also used for database systems, such as *Prestel*, that can be accessed using commercial TV receivers.

villus, one of millions of finger-like projections on the inside of the small intestine through which nutrient material digested from the food is absorbed into the bloodstream and the lymphatic vessels. Each villus contains a tiny ARTERY and VEIN, with a CAPILLARY network between them, and a small lymph vessel called a *lacteal*. Because of the villi and the folds in the lining of the INTESTINE, the area available for absorption is increased by several hundred times. The total surface area is hundreds of square metres.

virilism, the state of masculinization in the female caused by an excess of certain male sex hormones (*androgens*). There is: increased growth of body hair, in the male distribution pattern, with balding at the temples; reduction or cessation of the menstrual periods; loss of the characteristic fat deposits around the hips; enlargement of the clitoris; an increase in the development of the arm and shoulder muscles; acne; and deepening of the voice due to enlargement of the voicebox (*larynx*). Virilization occurs in certain diseases in which the adrenal glands and, to a lesser extent, the OVARIES, secrete excess of the normal male HORMONES.

virion, a rudimentary VIRUS particle in its

infective form, consisting of no more than the genetic material (DNA or RNA) and a protein coat.

virtual memory, a computer arrangement in which the workspace required is larger than the available RAM and some of the material in use is temporarily transferred to an alternative memory space such as a HARD DISK. When the program refers to a memory location, the machine checks whether this is in RAM. If it is not, the system temporarily retrieves the needed data from the backing store, making room for it, if necessary, by moving other data to the hard disk or elsewhere; ⇨ pp. 216–19.

virulence, the capacity of a particular infective microorganism to injure or kill a susceptible host. Virulence cannot be considered except in the context of the ability of the infected person (the *host*) to resist. So any particular organism may have a high virulence to one person – who may be immunocompromised – and a low virulence to a person with high immune competence. Virulence also depends on other factors such as the numbers of the organism present, the site at which the organisms present themselves (*portal of entry*) and whether local defensive factors are operating well. Thus, certain organisms may be harmless if confined to the inside of the bowel, but may exert a highly virulent effect if an opening in the wall of the bowel allows them access to the peritoneal cavity of the ABDOMEN. Human SKIN, at most times, carries potentially virulent organisms, but these may remain harmless unless access occurs through a cut or an abrasion.

viruses, infectious agents of very small size and structural simplicity, the largest being only a few hundred millionths of a metre (microns) in diameter. Viruses cannot maintain a life cycle unless they gain access to the interior of a living cell, where they take over part of the cell function in order to reproduce. They consist of a core of nucleic acid (genetic material), either deoxyribonucleic acid (DNA) or ribonucleic acid (RNA) encased in a protein shell. So far as is known, all living cells, whether of plant or animal, are susceptible to virus infection. Some are roughly spherical, some bullet-shaped, some loaf-shaped and some polyhedral. Many have a strict geometrical and symmetrical shape. Each virus has a definite composition, the larger viruses being more complex than the smaller and containing, in addition to the nucleic-acid core, outer capsules consisting of variable amounts of protein, fat (*lipid*) and CARBOHYDRATE. The protein components of viruses are mainly responsible for their powers of stimulating ANTIBODY production within the body, and consist of repeating AMINO-ACID subunits forming 'peptide' chains with which the RNA or DNA is more or less closely associated. A single virus particle can start the process of virus multiplication, but this does not occur by growth and division, as in the case of BACTERIA, but by the replication of the DNA or RNA genetic material and its subsequent coating with the other components. This can be done only if the virus can inject its genetic material into a cell or if it can penetrate the cell intact and then shed its coatings. Inside the

cell, the viral nucleic acid takes over cell function, using the normal cell processes for its own purposes – the replication of new viral nucleic acid and its subsequent coating. Some viruses even succeed in destroying the DNA of the host cell. In other cases the host DNA is preserved and viral replication is assisted by the host's nucleic acid. Usually, these activities within the cell lead to its death, but this is not necessarily so.

virus interference, the protection of host cells against VIRUS infection, as a result of prior virus infections. Interference occurs between viruses both of the same and of different types, and can even be induced by inactivated viruses. Interference is caused by the production of specific proteins, called INTERFERONS, by the body cells in response to viral infections and other stimuli. These attach to the membranes of other cells and prompt them to produce enzymes that interfere with the replication of subsequent viral invaders. Interferons also stimulate killer LYMPHOCYTES to attack and destroy cells that have been invaded with viruses.

viscera, the organs within the body cavity of an organism.

viscosity, the resistance to flow offered by a liquid or gas by virtue of its internal friction; ⇨ p. 32. .

visual display unit, a computer output device that displays information. This information is either in alphanumeric or graphical form, and either currently held in a volatile memory or in files on a disk drive. Most VDUs employ a monochrome or colour CATHODE-RAY TUBE, but flat, LIQUID-CRYSTAL DISPLAYS are becoming more common.

vital signs, indications of life. Vital signs include breathing, the presence of a pulse, and constriction of the pupils in response to bright light. Any response to a strong, painful stimulus, such as a vibratory pressure of the knuckles on the breast-bone (sternum), is also a vital sign, as is the indication of electrical activity in the brain on the ELECTRO-ENCEPHALOGRAM.

vital statistics, figures of birth, marriage and death rates for a population. Vital statistics are concerned with the rate of natural increase in a population, the number of births per childbearing woman (*fertility rate*), the marriage and divorce rates, the life expectancy at birth, and the major causes of death.

vitamins, chemical compounds necessary for normal functioning of the animal and human body. Vitamins take part in many of the enzyme systems of the body, operating within the cells (⇨ pp. 186–9), and are necessary for the synthesis of tissue building material, HORMONES and chemical regulators, for energy production, and for the breakdown of waste products and toxic substances. The B group of vitamins function as *co-enzymes* – substances without which the vital enzyme-accelerated chemical processes of the body cannot occur, or do so abnormally. The result of a co-enzyme

deficiency is always serious. Vitamins are largely derived from the diet and are present in food in small but usually adequate quantities. They have been analysed and can be made synthetically with exactly the same chemical structure, and, consequently, biochemical function, as the natural substances. With the exceptions of vitamins C and E, if vitamins are taken in excess of the minimum requirement, no advantage is gained. In some cases, notably those of vitamins A and D, there may be danger with excessive intake. Vitamin deficiency is uncommon in well-nourished populations but is very common in underdeveloped areas. It can, however, occur: in people who cultivate fad diets or extreme forms of vegetarianism; in those with malabsorption disorders; in alcoholics who derive sufficient calories from alcohol to fulfil their energy requirements and who feel no need to eat; in people taking certain drugs, such as hydralazine, penicillamine and oestrogens; and in those whose diet is poor. Vitamins are conventionally divided into the fat-soluble group A, D, E and K, and the water-soluble group, vitamin C (ascorbic acid) and the B vitamins – B1 (thiamine), B2 (riboflavine), nicotinic acid, B6 (pyridoxine), pantothenic acid, biotin, folic acid and B12. Because of their metabolic function, they are found in highest concentration in the most metabolically active parts of animal and plant tissues – the LIVER and seed germs.

vitreous humour, a transparent, watery gel that fills the rear compartment of the eye between the back of the crystalline lens and the retina. Although the vitreous humour consists almost entirely of water, it is capable of local condensation to form bands that may pull on the retina and cause tears and retinal detachment. In humans there is a strong tendency for the vitreous humour to shrink with age and in most people over 65 it has separated from the retina. This separation is usually harmless, but often causes numerous annoying 'floaters' to be seen in the fields of vision. These usually disperse with time.

vocal cords, a pair of sharp-edged folds of MUCOUS MEMBRANE in the LARYNX, between which all inspired and expired air passes. For most of the time, the vocal cords are well separated so that air can pass freely, but when tensed, they press together so that the passage of air between them causes them to vibrate. The sound produced varies in pitch with changes in the tension, and the resulting tones are modulated by complex movements of the tongue and lips to produce speech or singing.

volatile memory, a computer memory whose contents are irretrievably lost if the power supply is switched off. Some volatile memories have a battery-power-supply backup. In most cases, however, the user will copy the contents to a magnetic disk (backup) before switching off the power.

voltage multiplier, a rectifier circuit so arranged that the DC output voltage is equal to two or more times the peak AC input voltage. This is achieved by an arrangement of rectifier diodes and capacitors allowing voltages to be 'stacked' one on top of the other. No transformer is necessary, and the system is useful when high-voltage, low-current supplies are needed.

voltage regulation, the maintenance of the voltage (⇨ p. 90) of a power supply within certain limits, in spite of large changes in the load. Regulator circuits necessarily involve greater power losses than non-regulated power supplies. A reference voltage is provided by a constant voltage diode (ZENER DIODE), which is used to maintain the voltage output of a power transistor that acts as a variable-resistance device, operating across the output of the power supply compensating for the effect of changes in the load resistance. For low-power circuits, the Zener diode alone may be sufficient.

vomiting, involuntary expulsion of the STOMACH contents via the OESOPHAGUS and the mouth. Vomiting is usually, although not always, preceded by severe nausea and indications of overactivity of the parasympathetic nervous system – sweating, excessive salivation, pallor and slowing of the heart rate. The brain mechanism for vomiting consists of a vomiting centre, which receives information from the digestive tract and other parts of the body, and a chemoreceptor trigger zone, which responds to vomit-stimulating substances in the BLOOD and then prompts the vomiting centre to initiate the act. The stomach plays an almost passive role in vomiting, the ejection of the contents being brought about by sudden pressure on it from the surrounding structures, as a result of forceful simultaneous downward movement of the DIAPHRAGM and inward movement of the wall of the ABDOMEN. At the same time, the upper part of the stomach, and the SPHINCTER between the stomach and the oesophagus, relax, while the sphincter at the lower outlet of the stomach closes tightly. To prevent the dangerous entry of stomach contents into the lungs, the VOCAL CORDS are pressed tightly together during vomiting and breathing is temporarily impossible. The process of retching, which often precedes vomiting, is, in part, an attempt to overcome this reflex and to take breath.

vulva, the external genitalia in women.

water, one of the two oxides of hydrogen, H_2O. Water is a liquid or a gas at temperatures at 0–100°C (32–212°F). Above that temperature it is always an invisible gas, and at 0°C it becomes a solid. The other oxide, hydrogen peroxide (H_2O_2), readily decomposes to water with the release of oxygen. The molecules in liquid water are held together by hydrogen bonds (⇨ p. 162). Water heated from 0°C contracts until it reaches 4°C (39°F). After that it expands. It is a good conductor of electricity (⇨ p. 90), especially if traces of dissolved substances are present. Water is one of the commonest chemical compounds in the world and is essential for life; 99 per cent of the molecules in the body are water, but water represents a smaller proportion of the body weight. The body of an average man (70 kg) contains just over 40 litres of water. A little over half the total body water is within the cells and the remainder outside, partly in the BLOOD, but

mainly in the tissue spaces surrounding the cells. Water molecules are so small that they move freely across all cell membranes, and redistribution constantly occurs. Water is actually produced within the body, by the oxidation of nutrients and almost as much is acquired by eating solid food as by drinking. Water is lost by four routes, the proportion leaving the body by each of these varying with the circumstances. Most water is lost in the urine, but a considerable volume leaves in the form of vapour in the breath and 'insensible' evaporation from the skin. Loss in sweat varies with the environmental conditions and a small amount is lost in the faeces. The maintenance of the normal body-water volume is largely achieved by automatic alteration in the quantity of urine passed, and by thirst, which prompts additional intake when body water is depleted. A persistent state of excess water in the tissues is called OEDEMA. The presence of less than the normal amount is called DEHYDRATION.

water pollution, the contamination of WATER with harmful or poisonous substances. Population and industrial growth have greatly increased the risk and actuality of adding undesirable substances to natural water. These substances alter the biological safety of this vital element, both to humans and to water life, and may, in consequence, endanger health and even human life. Natural water contains considerable OXYGEN in solution. This is essential for the respiration of fish and other aquatic life forms, and is depleted by raised temperatures and by the presence of many pollutant substances. Many waste materials deposited in water are broken down by BACTERIA, which, in the presence of such nutrients, multiply enormously, using dissolved oxygen for respiration. If the oxygen is entirely consumed, all larger living forms are destroyed and the water becomes septic and offensive. Inadequately separated domestic waste contributes faeces and URINE, kitchen waste, household cleaning agents and detergents, and may promote the risk of water-borne disease, especially typhoid and dysentery. Industrial waste water may contain a very wide range of toxic and water-degrading material.

water table, the upper surface of the Earth's crust below which pores and fissures in the rock strata (⇨ p. 150) are saturated with WATER and are not confined by impermeable rock. The water table conforms roughly to the contours of the ground.

wavelength, the distance between two corresponding points on a wave – two peaks or two troughs. If the velocity of a wave transmission through a given medium is constant, as is commonly the case, the wavelength will be a reciprocal of the frequency, and vice versa; ⇨ pp. 64–7.

wave mechanics, the theory of matter, first postulated by the French physicist Prince Louis de Broglie (1892–1987), that elementary particles, such as ELECTRONS, PROTONS and NEUTRONS, can behave as waves. In 1924 de Broglie suggested that they showed the same wave–particle duality then known to be the

case with light. This was subsequently proved and became the basis for quantum mechanics; ⇨ p. 40.

wavemeter, a device for determining the frequency, i.e. the number of cycles per second (Hz), of an electromagnetic wave (⇨ p. 84). Wavemeters work by applying the wave to a system that can resonate at the wave frequency; they then detect the energy produced. A variable, tuned circuit consisting of an inductance (⇨ p. 100) in parallel with a capacitance (⇨ p. 98) can be used up to about 100 million Hz. Resonance is indicated by a peak in the current flowing in the circuit. Above such frequencies, short wires or wave-guides, adjusted in physical size to match the wavelength being measured, are used.

wave optics, a branch of optics that recognizes the wave nature of light and is concerned with such phenomena as diffraction, interference and polarization (⇨ pp. 64–7, 72–5 and 78). Compare GEOMETRIC OPTICS.

wave shaping, the modification of time-varying electrical current or voltages by passive filters (high-pass, low-pass or band-pass) or current limiters, or by active electronic means such as sine-wave, square-wave or sawtooth oscillators or by various gating circuits.

waxes, substances containing mixtures of ESTERS of higher fatty ACIDS and long-chain monohydric ALCOHOLS. An ester is produced by reaction between an acid and alcohol with the elimination of WATER. A monohydric alcohol is one containing a single hydroxyl group (-OH) per molecule.

weather, short-term changes in the local condition of the Earth's atmosphere with particular reference to temperature, humidity, wind, rain and pressure. Snow, hail, frost, dew, cloud density, and the effect of fog and other influences on visibility are also of interest.

weathering, the alteration of rocks by mechanical, chemical and biological processes operating on or near the Earth's surface. The effect is a continuing reduction in the size of the particles or fragments of the rocks. Factors in weathering are the expansion of water on freezing, expansion and contraction of rocks on changes of temperature, the action of wind, the action of plant roots while growing, chemical oxidation, HYDROLYSIS, carbonation by CARBON DIOXIDE, and solution in WATER. Weathering results in the production of soil and an increase in the capacity for plant growth on which the whole of the animal kingdom is dependent.

weight, the force exerted on a body by the Earth's gravitational pull (⇨ p. 30). This force is proportional to the mass of the body and is affected by its distance from the centre of the Earth, being greater at the poles than at the equator by a factor of about 0.3 per cent, because the poles are nearer to the centre than the equator (⇨ pp. 144–7). The gravitational attraction between two bodies is inversely proportional to the square of the distance between their centres. The mass of a body is not affected by its relationship to other bodies.

weightlessness, a relative term used to describe the state of a body situated so far from another massive body (such as the Earth) that the effect of gravitation is negligible. Weightlessness is also appreciated when the effect of gravitation is opposed by an equal and opposite inertial force.

white noise, sustained NOISE of even amplitude containing the whole range of audible frequencies at substantially equal energies for all frequencies. The hiss of escaping steam resembles white noise. When certain bands of frequency predominate the noise may be described as 'pink noise', 'blue noise' and so on.

wind, air motion relative to the surface of the Earth. Cyclonic and anticyclonic air movement implies curved rotation about a central point. Cyclonic movement is movement in the same direction as the movement of the surface of the Earth (anticlockwise in the Northern hemisphere, clockwise in the Southern); anticyclonic movement is movement in the opposite direction to the direction of the Earth's movement. When the airstream lines completely surround a point, the pattern is called a CYCLONE or an ANTICYCLONE, as the case may be. The centre of a cyclone tends to be a point of minimum atmospheric pressure.

Windows, a popular microcomputer program, working under the MS-DOS operating system and developed and sold by the Microsoft company, that provides the user with a graphical interface so that a MOUSE can be used to 'point and click' and largely replace the keys normally used to move the cursor. The chief feature of Windows is that a number of bordered areas can be opened up on the screen, simultaneously or sequentially, within each of which a separate program can be run. Windows can be expanded to fill the screen, moved about, changed in size or reduced to a small symbol (*icon*). In the latter event the program 'in the window' need not be lost and can be retrieved and taken up where it was left off. Data can be taken from one window and 'pasted' into another.

work, the transfer of energy occurring when a force is applied to a body to cause it to move. The work done is the product of the force and the distance moved by its point of application along the line of action of the force. Work can be considered as one manifestation of energy; ⇨ pp. 26–7 and 46–9.

workstation, a powerful PERSONAL COMPUTER with a large RAM, usually a reduced-instruction-set (RISC) high-speed microprocessor, a UNIX multi- tasking operating system, a 32-or 64-bit architecture and a substantial disk-storage system. Workstations are capable of carrying out work that, two or three decades ago, would have required a mainframe or MINICOMPUTER.

WYSIWYG, 'what you see is what you get'. Computerese for the facility of being able to see on the screen an exact replica, in terms of typeface, illustrations, layout, etc., of what will be printed. Pronounced 'wizzywig'.

X-linked disorders, genetically caused disorders in which the gene is located on the X (sex) chromosome. Examples are agammaglobulinaemia, albinism, Alport syndrome, Charcot-Marie-Tooth peroneal muscular atrophy, colour blindness, diabetes insipidus, ectodermal dysplasia, glucose–6- phosphate dehydrogenase deficiency, Fabry disease, glycogens storage disease VIII, gonadal dysgenesis, haemophilia A, one form of hydrocephalus, hypophosphataemia, ichthyosis, Turner's syndrome, one form of mental retardation, Becker and Duchesse muscular dystrophy, one form of retinitis pigmentosa and the testicular feminization syndrome.

X-ray astronomy, the study of the X-rays produced by sources outside the solar system (⇨ GAMMA-RAY ASTRONOMY).

X-rays, the electromagnetic radiation (⇨ p. 84) produced when a high-speed beam of ELECTRONS, accelerated by a high voltage, strikes a metal, such as copper or tungsten. This radiation, which comes from the tightly bound inner shell electrons of atoms, is of a frequency between that of ultraviolet light and that of gamma rays, and has the power to penetrate matter to varying degrees, depending on the shortness of its wavelength and the density of the matter. X-rays act on photographic film in much the same way as does visible light. These properties make X-radiation extremely valuable in scientific research, industry and medicine, and X-rays have been in use for diagnostic purposes, especially medical, for almost a century. Many millions of X-ray photographs are taken each year, mainly for medical reasons. X-radiation, however, is damaging to living cells because of its ionizing power and because of the production of large numbers of damaging free radicals, which can start destructive chain reactions in tissues. For this reason X-rays are avoided if any alternative form of imaging is available and suitable. X-rays are particularly avoided in early pregnancy as they are known to increase the risk, to the fetus, of later cancer, especially leukaemia. CT SCANNING is a form of X-ray examination.

xylem, the main water-conducting and supporting system of plants. In association with the PHLOEM, the xylem forms the vascular system of higher plants. In conifer trees, the xylem forms the timber known as softwood; in angiosperms, it forms hardwood.

xylose, a pentose sugar present in many woody materials. Polymerized (⇨ p. 164) xylose forms the polysaccharide xylan.

yawning, a normally involuntary act of slow, deep breathing associated with a strong desire to open the mouth widely. Yawning is associated with sleepiness, but its purpose remains a matter of speculation. It has been suggested that it may serve to stretch, open out and ventilate the air sacs of the LUNGS, which, in the somnolent state, are apt to collapse. Yawning helps to improve the return of BLOOD to the heart by way of the large VEINS. This reduces stagnation and improves the level of oxygen in the blood. Yawning also has an odd unexplained psychological effect in that it is undeniably 'infectious'.

yeasts, single-celled plants classified with fungi. Yeasts contain powerful enzymes that, in the process known as *fermentation*, break down CARBOHYDRATES to form ALCOHOL and CARBON DIOXIDE – the source of the 'ferment'. They grow easily and quickly and are also cultivated as a source of food rich in B vitamins. The chief medical interest in yeasts arises from the strong tendency for those such as the Candida and Monilia species to cause skin infections commonly known as *thrush* (candidiasis).

Young's modulus, the ratio of any stress (force; ⇨ p. 28) applied to an elastic body to the resulting strain (*deformation*) as long as the elastic limits are not exceeded. The modulus applies to a tensile or compressive stress applied to such things as a thin rod or to a beam to cause it to bend. It is a measure of the stiffness of a material. The modulus is named after the English physicist Thomas Young (1773–1829).

Zener diode, a simple semiconductor device (p-n junction diode) that, when a voltage (⇨ p. 90) higher than a stated value is applied to it through a resistance (⇨ p. 96), will immediately pass enough reverse current to reduce the voltage across it to the stated value (the Zener voltage). This diode voltage is maintained over a wide range of applied voltages and can be used as a reference voltage in VOLTAGE REGULATION. The diode was developed by the American physicist C. M. Zener (1905–).

zenith, the point directly overhead in the sky. Compare *nadir*, the diametrically opposite point.

zircon, a mineral containing the elements zirconium, silicon and OXYGEN with various impurities. It often occurs as comparatively large crystals ranging in colour from clear or pale yellow to green or blue and with a hardness of 7 on the MOHS SCALE. The pale stones are popular as semiprecious gemstones resembling DIAMONDS.

zodiac, an imaginary zone of the sky about 18° wide and centred on the path of the Sun, the Moon and the planets. The *ecliptic*. The constellation of stars in the zodiac have the names mostly of animals and are divided arbitrarily into 12 equal sections, named after the corresponding constellations. These are Aries, Taurus, Gemini, Cancer, Leo, Virgo, Libra, Scorpio, Sagittarius, Capricorn, Aquarius and Pisces. When so named, some 200 years ago, the vernal equinox (⇨ p. 144) was at Aries. The precession of the equinoxes has since then, however, caused a 30° westward shift of the signs along the ecliptic, so each sign is now displaced into its former neighbour's place.

zone refining, a method of producing metallic, semiconductor and other material of a high degree of purity. The procedure is to shape the material into an elongated form and, by INDUCTION HEATING or other means, to cause a narrow molten zone to pass slowly along the specimen. Impurities either raise or lower the melting point and are thus segregated, usually in the same direction as the movement of the zone (because most impurities lower the melting point). The process is repeated until the desired degree of purity is achieved.

zoonoses, infectious diseases of animals that can, in some conditions, also affect people. The zoonoses do not include those diseases that are primarily human and that are transmitted from person to person by animals.

zygote, an egg (*ovum*) that has been penetrated by a SPERM so that fusion of the nuclear material has occurred. The zygote thus contains all the genetic code for a new individual. In this context, the ovum and sperm are called GAMETES. The chromosomes in the gametes are unpaired so gametes contain half the normal (*haploid*) number of chromosomes of a body cell. The fusion of the two gametes to form the zygote restores this number to the normal (*diploid*). Each chromosome from the male gamete is paired with a chromosome from the female gamete, so the inherited characteristics are a mix of those of both parents. The term 'zygote' is applied only to the fertilized ovum before it begins on its massive programme of division to form a new individual. After cell division starts, it is called an EMBRYO.

PICTURE ACKNOWLEDGEMENTS

The publishers would like to thank the following for permission to reproduce the pictures in this book,
which are individually credited by the abbreviations listed below:

AKG	Archiv für Kunst und Geschichte	IB	Image Bank	Spectrum	Spectrum
Allsport	Allsport-Vandystadt	Images	Images	SPL	Science Photo Library
AP	Associated Press	IS	Image Select	TCL	Telegraph Colour Library
AR	Ann Ronan	Kobal	Kobal	Topham	Topham Picture Source
FLPA	Frank Lane Picture Agency	ME	Mary Evans	TSM/S&SPL	The Science Museum/Science &
Gamma	Gamma	Planet Earth	Planet Earth Pictures		Society Picture Library
Holt	Holt Studios International	Popper	Popperfoto	Zefa	Zefa
Horizon	Horizon	Quadrant	Quadrant Picture Library		
Hulton	Hulton-Deutsch Collection	RC	Ronald Chapman for Guinness Publishing